South Africa,
Lesotho & Swaziland
a Lonely Planet travel survival kit

Jon Murray
Richard Everist
Jeff Williams

South Africa, Lesotho & Swaziland

2nd edition

Published by
  Lonely Planet Publications
  Head Office: PO Box 617, Hawthorn, Vic 3122, Australia
  Branches: 155 Filbert St, Suite 251, Oakland, CA 94607, USA
                 10 Barley Mow Passage, Chiswick, London W4 4PH, UK
                 71 bis rue du Cardinal Lemoine, 75005 Paris, France

Printed by
  Colorcraft Ltd, Hong Kong

Photographs by
  Glenn Beanland   Big Game Parks of Swaziland   Richard Everist   Di Jones (Malealea Lodge)
  Jon Murray   Micky Reilly   Deanna Swaney   Luba Vangelova
  Jeff Williams   Jeanette Woolerton
  Title pages: Richard Everist, Giraffe, Kruger National Park; Jon Murray, Coast Road to Hermanus,
                 Western Cape Province; Di Jones, Chief Mafa, Headman of a village near Malealea,
                 Lesotho; Lex Hes, Black Rhino, Mkhaya Game Reserve
  Front cover: Ponch Hawkes (Community Aid Abroad)

Safari Guide illustrations by
  Matt King

First Published
  January 1993

This Edition
  January 1996

**Although the authors and publisher have tried to make the information
as accurate as possible, they accept no responsibility for any loss, injury or
inconvenience sustained by any person using this book.**

National Library of Australia Cataloguing in Publication Data

Murray, Jon
  South Africa, Lesotho & Swaziland

  2nd ed.
  Includes index.
  ISBN 0 86442 323 3.

  1. South Africa – Guidebooks. 2. Lesotho – Guidebooks.
  3. Swaziland – Guidebooks. I. Everist, Richard. South
  Africa, Lesotho & Swaziland. II. Williams, Jeff, 1954 Dec.
  15 – III. Title. IV. Title. South Africa, Lesotho &
  Swaziland. (Series: Lonely Planet travel survival kit).

916.80464

Jon Murray

Jon Murray spent time alternating between travelling and working with various publishing companies in Melbourne (Australia) before joining Lonely Planet as an editor. He was soon travelling again, this time researching Lonely Planet's guidebooks. He has co-authored both editions of this book, written Lonely Planet's *New South Wales & the ACT* and updated several other Lonely Planet books, including *Papua New Guinea* and sections of *Australia*. He lives in Melbourne but spends a lot of time battling blackberries on his bush block which is near Daylesford.

Richard Everist

Richard grew up in Geelong, Australia, has travelled a bit and had a wide variety of jobs. He worked full time at Lonely Planet's head office in Melbourne before jumping the fence to become a writer. In late 1994 he was lured back into the home paddock to be Co-General Manager.

He has co-written LP's travel survival kits *Nepal*, *South Africa* and *Britain*, updated *Papua New Guinea*, and contributed to the shoestring guides for *West Asia*, *Africa*, *Western Europe* and *Mediterranean Europe*.

Jeff Williams

Jeff is a Kiwi from Greymouth on the West Coast of New Zealand's South Island. He lives in Melbourne with his wife, Alison, and son, Callum, and his computer (recently connected to the Internet).

Jeff is a co-author of *New Zealand*, *Australia*, *Outback Australia* and *Tramping in New Zealand* and author of *Western Australia*.

He dreams of returning to South Africa to see a homogeneous blend of Afrikaners and Blacks in Soweto and in Sandton; and of walking through Hillbrow in Jo'burg knowing that his son will be safe.

From the Authors

Jon Murray Thanks to all the travellers I met while researching this book, especially Marie-Helene Ellenboudt, Larry Mah and Jurgen Dorrenboom (thanks for the article,

Jurgen). Several hostel owners in Cape Town helped to make my stay there very enjoyable – thanks to Lee & Tony Backpack, Darryl

Zebra, Fred St Johns and Dietlof Oak. Rob, Roo and Amelia Rockey helped me to enjoy Johannesburg.

Jeff Williams Thanks to Jon Murray for entrusting an exciting half of the country to me, and for breaking me into Jo'burg. Thanks also to Nelson Mandela for making the 'march to freedom' possible; to the beautiful people of Dobsonville, Soweto, for sharing music, dance, and hope; to Patrick Moroney in Durban; Hercille Stuart of Durban Unlimited; the staff of Khoka Moya in Manyeleti Game Reserve; the staff of Kolobe Lodge in the Lapalala Wilderness; Kirk in Port St John; Rob and Marks in Yeoville; the staff of the Central Free State Tourist office in Kroonstad (surprised! – you were the best organised in the OFS); Frik and the eclectic mix at Rustler's Valley; Jeunesse Serle of Trees for Africa; the Kaiser Chiefs; the staff of various Satour and information offices from Pietersburg to Barbeton to East London; Darron and Tracy of the Royal Swazi National Parks, Swaziland; Pasqualina N'Chaga Luthy (The Voice of Lesotho) in Maseru, Lesotho; and the friendly folk (Jones's) at Malealea Lodge, Lesotho.

This Book
The first edition of this book was researched and written by Richard Everist and Jon Murray. This edition was updated by Jon Murray and Jeff Williams.

From the Publisher
Frith Pike and Susan Noonan edited and proofed this second edition of *South Africa, Lesotho & Swaziland* with assistance from David Meagher, Helen Castle, Diana Saad, Christine Niven, Samantha Carew and Carolyn Hubbard. Mapping and design were coordinated by Richard Stewart and layout was done by Sally Woodward. Ralph Roob, Andrew Smith and Sandra Smythe assisted with the mapping. Illustrations were drawn by Trudi Canavan, Greg Herriman, Margie Jung, Reita Wilson and Peter Morris. The index was compiled by Kerrie Williams.

The Safari Guide was originally written by Geoff Crowther and Deanna Swaney; additional material was provided by Jon Murray. The Safari Guide was edited by David Meagher, proofed by Diana Saad and Christine Niven and designed by Vicki Beale and Greg Herriman. Special thanks to Matt King for the Safari Guide illustrations.

Thanks also to our readers' letters team: Marina Bonnamy, Bethune Carmichael, Gayle Ellis, Greg Mills, Richard Nebesky, Shelley Preston, Julie Young and Vicky Wayland; and to Rafiki in Fitzroy for allowing us to photograph their African arts and crafts. Finally, thanks to Jane Marks for researching the scientific names of flora.

Thanks
Last but not least, a special thanks to those readers who found the time and energy to write to us from all over the world with suggestions and comments. Their names appear at the end of the book.

Warning & Request
Things change – prices go up, schedules change, good places go bad and bad places go bankrupt – nothing stays the same. So if you find things better or worse, recently opened or long since closed, please write and tell us and help make the next edition better.

Your letters will be used to help update future editions and, where possible, important changes will also be included in a Stop Press section in reprints.

We greatly appreciate all information that is sent to us by travellers. Back at Lonely Planet we employ a hard-working readers' letters team to sort through the many letters we receive. The best ones will be rewarded with a free copy of the next edition or another Lonely Planet guide if you prefer. We give away lots of books, but, unfortunately, not every letter/postcard receives one.

Contents

KWAZULU/NATAL **305**

WESTERN CAPE PROVINCE **389**

Map Legend

BOUNDARIES

⋯⋯⋯⋯⋯ International Boundary
⋯⋯⋯⋯⋯ Regional Boundary

ROUTES

⋯⋯⋯⋯⋯ Freeway
⋯⋯⋯⋯⋯ Highway
⋯⋯⋯⋯⋯ Major Road
⋯⋯⋯⋯⋯ Unsealed Road or Track
⋯⋯⋯⋯⋯ Four Wheel Drive Track
⋯⋯⋯⋯⋯ City Road
⋯⋯⋯⋯⋯ City Street
⋯⋯⋯⋯⋯ Railway
⋯⋯⋯⋯⋯ Tram
⋯⋯⋯⋯⋯ Bridge
⋯⋯⋯⋯⋯ Walking Track
⋯⋯⋯⋯⋯ Bicycle Track
⋯⋯⋯⋯⋯ Cable Car or Chairlift

AREA FEATURES

⋯⋯⋯⋯⋯ Parks
⋯⋯⋯⋯⋯ Built-Up Area
⋯⋯⋯⋯⋯ Pedestrian Mall
⋯⋯⋯⋯⋯ Market
⋯⋯⋯⋯⋯ Cemetery
⋯⋯⋯⋯⋯ Reef
⋯⋯⋯⋯⋯ Beach or Desert
⋯⋯⋯⋯⋯ Rocks

HYDROGRAPHIC FEATURES

⋯⋯⋯⋯⋯ Coastline
⋯⋯⋯⋯⋯ River, Creek
⋯⋯⋯⋯⋯ Intermittent River or Creek
⋯⋯⋯⋯⋯ Rapids, Waterfalls
⋯⋯⋯⋯⋯ Lake, Intermittent Lake
⋯⋯⋯⋯⋯ Canal
⋯⋯⋯⋯⋯ Swamp

SYMBOLS

✪ CAPITAL		National Capital
◉ Capital		Regional Capital
◯ CITY		Major City
● City		City
● Town		Town
● Village		Village
■ ▼		Place to Stay, Place to Eat
✖ �		Cafe, Pub or Bar
✉ ☎		Post Office, Telephone
❶ ❸		Tourist Information, Bank
⬤ ℗		Transport, Parking
🏛 ⛺		Museum, Youth Hostel
⚏ ⚊		Caravan Park, Camping Ground
✝ ✚		Church, Cathedral
☾ ☸		Mosque, Hindu Temple
☷ ☗		Buddhist Temple, Other Temple
✛ ★		Hospital, Police Station

◔ ⓟ		Embassy, Petrol Station
✈ ✝		Airport, Airfield
▭ ✿		Swimming Pool, Gardens
❖ 🐘		Shopping Centre, Zoo
⚲ ⌂		Winery or Vineyard, Picnic Site
← A25		One Way Street, Route Number
⌂ ⚐		Stately Home, Monument
♖ ▣		Castle, Tomb
⌒ ⌂		Cave, Hut or Chalet
▲ ☀		Mountain or Hill, Lookout
🗼 ✗		Lighthouse, Shipwreck
)(⌐		Pass, Golf Course
⚑ ⚐		Beach, Surf Beach
∴		Archaeological Site or Ruins
		Ancient or City Wall
		Cliff or Escarpment, Tunnel
		Railway Station

Note: not all symbols displayed above appear in this book

Introduction

The countries of South Africa, Lesotho and Swaziland make up a beautiful region of Africa that is just beginning to realise its enormous potential.

The national parks are among the greatest in the world and there are few better places to see Africa's wildlife. The thrill of seeing animals like elephants and lions in the wild cannot be overestimated.

The beaches are amongst the best and least crowded in the world, and the surf and fishing are as good as you can get. The countryside and particularly the mountains, are spectacular, and the walking and touring possibilities are endless.

The climate is kind, and there is the added advantage that it is summer in southern Africa while the northern hemisphere is in the depths of winter.

The region's infrastructure, by African standards, is extremely good – the transport and communications systems all work. With some notable exceptions, the hotels and the restaurants are not particularly sophisticated, but wherever you are, you can find somewhere clean and comfortable to stay, and somewhere with decent food.

The mixture of cultures is tremendously interesting and, since South Africa's peaceful transition to democracy in 1994, that country seems ready to meld a new society of great energy and significance. Political violence is a thing of the past and among the vast majority of the people there is a desire to get on with building a new nation. It's an exciting time to visit.

Swaziland, in contrast to South Africa's new democracy, retains its beloved monarchy and the tiny country is proof that a pre-industrial culture can thrive in a modern nation. Lesotho, 'the kingdom in the sky', also offers travellers contact with traditional village life, whether pony trekking or hiking through the highland wilderness.

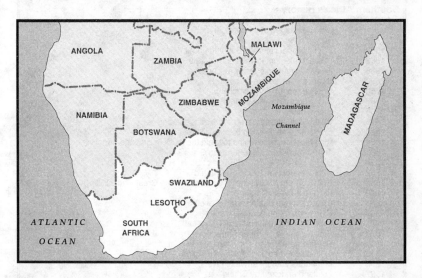

Facts about the Region

The current national boundaries in southern Africa are, in large part, creations of the 19th and 20th centuries. The modern nation states owe their form to the competitive ambitions of European imperialist powers, colonists and invaders – not, to a large degree, to intrinsic geographical, cultural or historical logic. The Republic of South Africa, Lesotho and Swaziland are, therefore, more usefully seen as a whole, at least until the late 19th century in terms of their history, and even today in terms of language, culture, and flora & fauna.

HISTORY
Pre-History

Southern Africa's pre-history before the coming of the Iron Age peoples is uncertain. Sites in Eastern Transvaal and other places have produced evidence of various 'missing links', dating back about three million years, and human bones 100,000 years old have been found in Swaziland.

San & Khoikhoi

The San (known to Europeans as Bushmen) were nomadic hunters and gatherers, and the Khoikhoi (known as Hottentot) were semi-nomadic hunters and pastoralists. Both groups were closely related, however, so the distinction was by no means hard and fast. Because of this, the term Khoisan is now widely used.

It is probable that the San have lived in southern Africa for 40,000 years – the earliest dated painting attributed to them is about 28,000 years old. Culturally and physically, they developed differently to the negroid peoples of Africa.

The San are generally shorter (averaging

Southern Africa's History

c.40,000 BC	San people settle southern Africa
c.300 AD	Bantu people arrive in KwaZulu area
1487	Bartholomeu Dias sails around the Cape
c.1500	Sotho people settle in (Basutholand) Lesotho
1652	Dutch settlement in Table Bay (Cape Town)
1688	French Huguenots arrive at Cape
c.1690	Boers move into the hinterland
c.1750	Nguni people settle Swaziland
1780	Dutch fight Xhosa at Great Fish River
1795	British capture Cape Town
1815	Shaka Zulu seizes power – the difaqane begins
1820	British settlers arrive in Eastern Cape
1824	King Moshoeshoe begins to meld the modern Basutho people
1830s	The Voortrekkers undertake the Great Trek
1838	Boers defeat the Zulu at Battle of Blood River
1852	Boer Republic of Transvaal created
1858	British defeat Xhosa after the disaster of the Great Cattle Killing
1860	Indians arrive in Natal
1868	British annexe Basutholand (Lesotho)
1869	Diamonds found near Kimberley
1871	Gold discovered in Eastern Transvaal
1877	British annexe the Boer Republic of Transvaal
1881	Boers defeat British and Transvaal becomes the South African Republic
1886	Gold discovered on the Witwatersrand
1893	Mohandas Gandhi arrives in Natal
1897	Zululand annexed by Britain

around 140 cm in height) than the Khoikhoi, perhaps because the Khoikhoi diet was richer, but there are a number of similarities. Both groups are characterised by fairly light, almost honey-coloured skin; well developed buttocks, which can store reserves of fat; high cheekbones, with an almost Asiatic cast to their faces; and hair that forms tight curls. There is also a close relationship between the San and Khoikhoi languages, which are the origin of the unique 'clicks' common in southern African languages.

It is now believed the Khoikhoi developed from San groups in present day Botswana. Perhaps they came in contact with pastoralist Bantu tribes, as in addition to hunting and gathering food, they became pastoralists, with cattle, oxen and sheep. They migrated south reaching the Cape of Good Hope about 2000 years ago. For centuries, perhaps even millennia, the San and the Khoikhoi inter-married and coexisted. It was not uncommon for impoverished Khoikhoi to revert to a hunter-gatherer existence, or for San to acquire domestic animals (perhaps by working as servants for wealthy Khoikhoi).

The first threat to the Khoisan was posed by Bantu-speaking tribes. These tribes not only had domestic animals, but farmed crops (particularly maize), were metal workers and potters, and lived in settled villages. They migrated down the eastern coastal belt reaching today's KwaZulu/Natal before the 3rd century.

It seems that the first settlements were limited to areas with more than about 600 mm of rain, but between the 12th and 15th centuries they expanded onto the highveld of today's Northern Transvaal, Gauteng and Orange Free State. Once again rainfall, or the lack of it, seems to have provided a natural barrier between the Bantu and Khoisan. There are no known Bantu settlements west of the Great Fish River or into the territory that receives less than 200 mm of rain. The Bantu crops could not survive with less rain.

Although this migration must have made an impact on the eastern Khoisan it seems the two groups either integrated, or found a way

1899-1902	Anglo-Boer War
1905	Government commission recommends separate development for blacks, with inferior education
1910	Union of South Africa created, federating the British colonies and the old Boer republics. Blacks denied the vote. Lesotho and Swaziland become British protectorates.
1912	South African Native National Council established, the forerunner of the ANC
1913	Natives Land Act restricts black ownership of land to 7½% of the country
1928	Communist Party begins agitation for full democracy
1948	National Party wins government. The party retains control until 1994. Apartheid laws, such as the one making inter-racial sex illegal, begin to be passed.
1955	ANC adopts Freedom Charter
1960	Sharpeville massacre. ANC banned.
1961	South Africa leaves the Commonwealth and becomes a republic
1963	Nelson Mandela jailed for life
1966	Lesotho gains independence from Britain
1968	Swaziland gains independence from Britain
1975	South Africa invades Angola
1976	Soweto uprisings begin
1977	Steve Biko murdered
1982	Swazi King Sobhuza II, then the world's longest-reigning monarch, dies
1985	State of Emergency declared – official murder and torture become rife, black resistance strengthens
1990	ANC ban lifted; Nelson Mandela freed
1991	Talks on a new constitution begin; political violence escalates
1992	Whites-only referendum agrees to reform
1994	Democratic elections held and Nelson Mandela elected president

to coexist. There was intermarriage and the Xhosa and Zulu languages adopted Khoisan 'clicks'. Khoisan artefacts are commonly found at the sites of Bantu settlements. Curiously, only one Bantu tribe adopted the use of bows and arrows, the most important Khoisan weapons. West of the 200-mm rain zone, and even in the Drakensberg, the Khoisan remained undisturbed until white colonists arrived in the 18th and 19th centuries.

Bantu

Just when the Bantu-speaking peoples moved into southern Africa is uncertain but by the 3rd century AD they had settled the east coast as far south as modern KwaZulu/ Natal. By the 15th century they had moved inland to settle most of the eastern half of southern Africa – that is, most of the land suitable for growing staple crops and grazing cattle. These tribes were primarily pastoral, held land in common and undertook some form of agriculture. There were extensive trade links throughout the region. They were Iron Age peoples and the smelting techniques of some tribes were not surpassed in Europe until the Industrial Revolution. Gold, copper and tin were also mined, and shafts 25 metres deep have been discovered. These were people who, in Zimbabwe, found *every* known gold deposit except one.

The newcomers and the San appear to have lived in relative harmony, trading not only goods but language and culture as well.

Most southern African peoples are classified as being either Nguni (Zulu, Swazi, Xhosa) or Sotho-Tswana (Tswana, Pedi, Basotho). This classification is based on 19th-century linguistic theories and is suspect, but there is some evidence for two broad immigration patterns. The Nguni are grouped around the south and east coasts, and the Sotho-Tswana mainly live on the highveld. The origin of the Venda peoples is uncertain, with some historians arguing that they are relatively late arrivals.

Little is known about the history of these tribes and peoples before the twin disasters of European invasion and the *difaqane* (forced migration), when several of the most

important modern peoples – the Basotho, the Swazi and the Zulu – became prominent.

European Exploration

The Muslim expansion across North Africa and Turkey threw Christian Europe's trade routes into chaos, prompting the Portuguese and Spanish to search for a sea route to India. They sought to guarantee and hopefully monopolise the supply of one of the most precious medieval commodities – spice.

At the end of 1487 Bartholomeu Dias and his expedition (two tiny caravels and a store ship) rounded a cape, which Dias named Cabo da Boa Esperanca (Cape of Good Hope). Ten years later Vasco da Gama rounded the Cape and finally reached India in 1498.

Portuguese eyes were fixed on the east coast of Africa and India. It was as if they didn't see southern Africa, let alone its potential. To them, the region offered little more than fresh water; attempts to trade with the Khoikhoi often ended in violence and the coast and its fierce weather posed a terrible threat to their caravels.

By the end of the 16th century the English and Dutch were beginning to challenge the Portuguese traders, and the Cape became a regular stopover for their scurvy-ridden crews. In 1647 a Dutch East Indiaman was wrecked in Table Bay and the crew built a fort and stayed for a year before they were rescued.

This crystallised the value of a permanent settlement in the minds of the directors of the Dutch East India Company (Vereenigde Oost-Indische Compagnie or VOC). They had no intention of colonising the country, but simply of establishing a secure base where ships could shelter and stock up on fresh supplies of meat, fruit and vegetables. To this end, a small expedition of VOC employees, under the command of Jan van Riebeeck, reached Table Bay on 6 April 1652.

Company Rule

Although the settlement traded with the neighbouring Khoikhoi there was a deliberate attempt to restrict contact. Partly as a consequence of this, the small number of

VOC employees found themselves faced with a labour shortage. Van Riebeeck made two moves to deal with this problem, both with far-reaching consequences. Slaves were imported and a handful of burghers were allowed to establish their own farms.

The burghers were still theoretically subject to VOC control, however, and were forced to sell their produce at prices determined by the company. The colony was soon producing fruit, vegetables, wheat and wine so successfully that there was a problem with oversupply. As a result, many farmers turned away from intensive farming to raising livestock.

The number of burghers grew slowly, but steadily. The majority were of Dutch descent, but there were also significant numbers of Germans. Their church was the Calvinist Reformed Church of the Netherlands. In 1688 they were joined by a group of about 150 French Huguenots who were also Calvinists, and had fled religious persecution under King Louis XIV. This small group was more significant than might be imagined; in crude numerical terms it increased the white population by over 15%.

Some trace the Afrikaner idea of a chosen people (and racial superiority) to Calvin's doctrine of predestination, which says that an individual's salvation or damnation is preordained. Surrounded by primitive heathens, the whites had no doubts which race was superior and who had been chosen.

...(the Khoikhoi) yet show so little humanity that truly they more resemble the unreasonable beasts than reasonable man...having no knowledge of God ...
**Quoted in *The Mind of South Africa*
by Allister Sparkes**

The Boers
The population of whites did not reach 1000 until 1745, but small numbers of free burghers had begun to drift away from the close grip of the company, and into Africa. They had crossed the Oliphants River to the north and were pushing east towards the Great Fish River. These were the first of the trekboers – completely independent of all official control, extraordinarily self-sufficient and isolated.

Many pursued a semi-nomadic pastoralist lifestyle, in some ways not far removed from that of the Khoikhoi. In addition to its herds a family might have had a wagon, a tent, a Bible and a couple of guns. As they became more settled a mud-walled cottage would have been built, but it would – often by choice – have been days of hard travel away from the nearest European.

This isolation and lifestyle produced courageous individualists, but also a backward people whose only source of knowledge was the Bible. The trekboers were completely cut off from the great intellectual developments that occurred in Europe in the 18th century – the French Revolution and all the associated ideas of liberalism and democracy.

They possessed guns and a religious faith that established both a physical and an imagined superiority that set them apart absolutely. What evolved was a semiliterate peasantry with the social status of a landed gentry.
**Quoted in *The Mind of South Africa*
by Allister Sparkes**

The Impact on the Khoisan
The inevitable confrontations between whites and the Khoisan were disastrous. The Khoisan were driven from their traditional lands, decimated by introduced diseases, and destroyed by superior weapons when they fought back – which they did in a number of major 'wars' and with guerrilla resistance that continued into the 19th century.

Most survivors were left with no option but to work for Europeans in a form of bondage little different to slavery. They were exploited both for labour and for sex and in time also inter-mixed with the slaves who had been imported (mostly from the Indonesian archipelago, Madagascar, and Mozambique). The offspring of these unions formed the basis for today's coloured population.

One Khoikhoi group, the Grigriqua, who had originally lived on the west coast between St Helena Bay and the Cederberg, managed to acquire guns and horses. Around 1770, in a pattern to be followed 60 years later by the Boers, they trekked east and north. The Grigriqua were joined by other groups of Khoisan, coloureds and even white adventurers, and proved to be a formidable military force. They reached the highveld around modern-day Kimberley and carved out territory that came to be known as Griqualand. This was forcibly annexed by the British in 1871.

Although small numbers of whites came into tenuous contact with the Sotho-Tswana on the northern frontier in about 1700, the Xhosa to the west of the Great Fish River first encountered the trekboers in the 1770s. The first of nine frontier wars broke out in 1779.

The British Arrive

Dutch power was fading as the century closed, and in 1795, the British invaded to prevent the Cape falling into French hands. They found a colony with 25,000 slaves, 20,000 white colonists, 15,000 Khoisan and 1000 free blacks (freed slaves).

Power was restricted to a white elite in Cape Town, and differentiation on the basis of colour was deeply entrenched. In large part it was a society that had been hermetically sealed from the rest of the world. With the exception of Cape Town and the immediate hinterland, the country was populated by isolated black and white pastoralists whose lifestyles and beliefs were almost medieval.

The initial British occupation had little impact on society and, in 1803, the colony was handed over to the Batavian Republic. Not long after, however, in response to the Napoleonic wars, the British once again decided to secure the Cape against French occupation. In 1806, at Bloubergstrand 25 km north of Cape Town, the British again defeated the Dutch. The colony was permanently ceded to the British on 13 August 1814.

This time the British did start to meddle in local affairs. The British Empire was reaching its height in power and confidence and at the vanguard of the new capitalist world. Missionaries were its shock troops and teachers were its foot soldiers. Religion aside, the most important motive was profit, and the empire had a new and seemingly insatiable appetite for labour, raw materials and manufactured goods. Industrialisation and urbanisation were changing the shape of the world.

The Settlers

In 1820, 5000 middle-class British immigrants arrived to settle near the eastern frontier of the colony. The peaceful land of plenty that had been promoted to them was, in reality, a heavily contested border region. The Boers were on the west side of the Great Fish River, the Xhosa were on the east, and both battled interminably over the coastal plain known as the Suurveld.

The immigrants were intended to create a buffer of market gardeners between the cattle-farming Boers and Xhosa, but the Suurveld was completely unsuitable for intensive cultivation. It was not long before the immigrant families found farming untenable. By 1823 almost half of the settlers had retreated to the towns to pursue the trades and businesses they had followed in Britain.

As a result, Grahamstown developed into a trading and manufacturing centre, quickly becoming the second largest city in the country. And the relative unity of white South Africa was over – there were now two language groups and two very different cultures. A pattern had also been established – English speakers were highly urbanised and dominated politics, trade, finance, mining and manufacturing.

Despite their power, however, and despite the fact that they did make some positive changes to institutionalised racism, the settlers' middle class conservatism and sense of racial superiority prevented them from making any radical reforms. Apart from anything else, the system served them too well. Slavery was abolished in 1833, but a Masters and Servants Ordinance perpetuating white control was passed in 1841.

British numbers increased rapidly in Cape Town, the east of the Cape Colony, Natal, and the Transvaal (but not until the discovery of gold and diamonds). Thanks to the British, the border wars with the Xhosa reached new depths of depravity. Traditionally the Xhosa had always spared women and children; the British had no such compunctions and pursued scorched earth policies.

RICHARD EVERIST

DI JONES

LUBA VANGELOVA

RICHARD EVERIST

RICHARD EVERIST

A: *Pananomus* species, a member of the *Proteaceae* family
B: *Leucadendron* (fruiting)
C: Spiral aloe *(Aloe polyphylla)*
D: King protea (*Protea cynaroides*)
E: Pig-face, a member of the *Aizoaceae* family

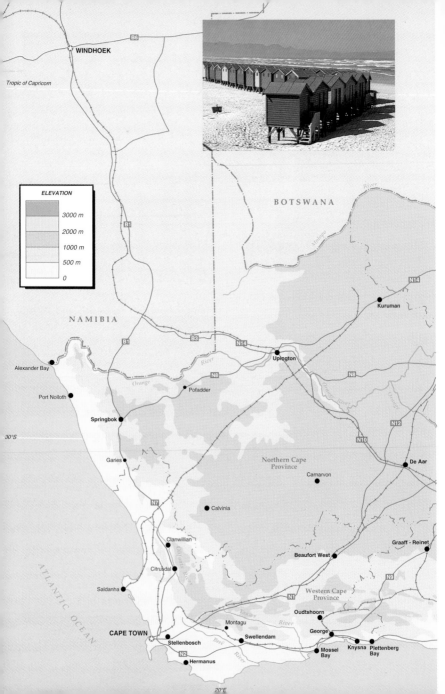

ELEVATION

3000 m

2000 m

1000 m

500 m

0

WINDHOEK

Tropic of Capricorn

BOTSWANA

NAMIBIA

Kuruman

N14

Alexander Bay

Port Nolloth

Springbok

Garies

Upington

Pofadder

Orange

River

N6

B1

B3

N14

N8

Orange River

N12

N10

De Aar

30°S

Northern Cape
Province

Camarvon

Calvinia

Clanwilliam

Citrusdal

Saldanha

Beaufort West

Graaff - Reinet

N9

Western Cape
Province

N1

Montagu

Swellendam

Oudtshoorn

George

Mossel
Bay

Knysna

Plettenberg
Bay

N7

Olifants River

ATLANTIC

OCEAN

CAPE TOWN

Stellenbosch

N2

Hermanus

Breede River

Bree

River

20°E

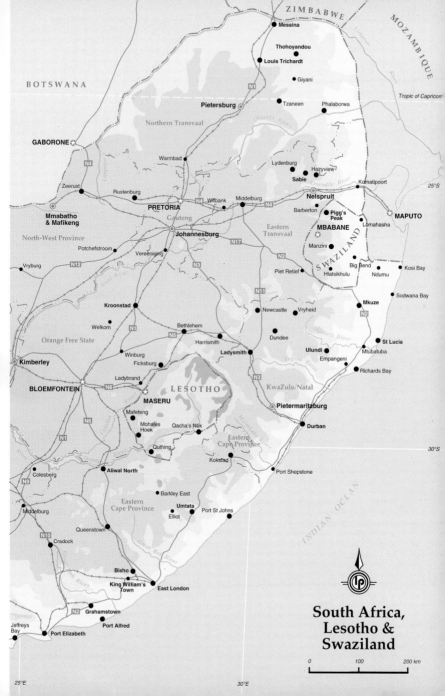

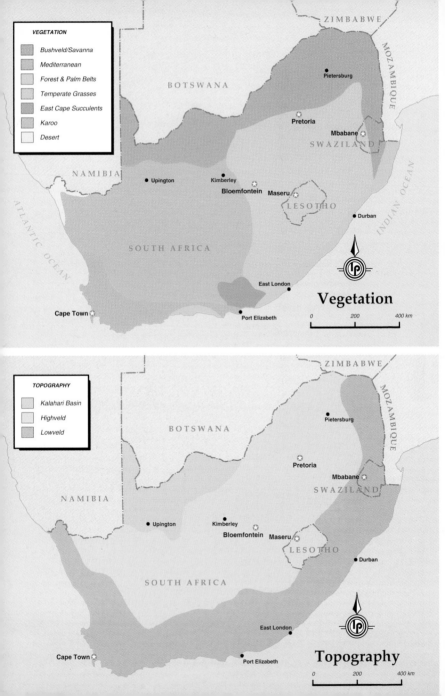

VEGETATION

- Bushveld/Savanna
- Mediterranean
- Forest & Palm Belts
- Temperate Grasses
- East Cape Succulents
- Karoo
- Desert

ZIMBABWE

BOTSWANA

MOZAMBIQUE

Pietersburg

Pretoria

Mbabane

SWAZILAND

NAMIBIA

Upington

Kimberley

Bloemfontein

Maseru

LESOTHO

Durban

INDIAN OCEAN

ATLANTIC OCEAN

SOUTH AFRICA

East London

Cape Town

Port Elizabeth

Vegetation

0   200   400 km

TOPOGRAPHY

- Kalahari Basin
- Highveld
- Lowveld

ZIMBABWE

BOTSWANA

MOZAMBIQUE

Pietersburg

Pretoria

Mbabane

SWAZILAND

NAMIBIA

Upington

Kimberley

Bloemfontein

Maseru

LESOTHO

Durban

SOUTH AFRICA

East London

Cape Town

Port Elizabeth

Topography

0   200   400 km

The Grand Tour

In such a large and diverse region it is very tempting to plan a long trip. Where to go and what to do depends, as anywhere, on your available time and money. It's often the case that the people who have the most money have the least time, and vice versa. You could easily spend a few months meandering around on minibus taxis; you could just as easily spend a week in a luxury private game reserve – and pay not much less.

The following Grand Tour of about 10 weeks takes in most of the major attractions, but it could be extended almost indefinitely by taking side-trips to areas it bypasses. The best way to decide where to go is to read through this book and also contact Satour for brochures before you leave home.

All of the places mentioned here are accessible by public transport of one sort or another, although in a few areas, such as the Transkei region and Zululand, you won't find many luxury buses and will have to rely on local bus services and minibus taxis. In the national parks you do need your own vehicle.

Possible Itinerary The following represents just one of many possibilities for a grand tour of the region:

- Johannesburg – Jo'burg is still the main air gateway into the region, so chances are you'll have to begin here. Although it has a bad crime problem, it's an interesting city (two or three days)
- Pretoria (one or two days)
- Sun City (one day)
- Northern Transvaal (two days transit, a week or so if visiting parks and reserves)
- Venda area (two days)
- Kruger National Park (minimum three days)
- Swaziland via Nelspruit & Barberton (three days)
- Northern KwaZulu/Natal coast (two days transit, two weeks if visiting the superb national parks and beaches)
- Durban (minimum three days)
- Drakensberg – You can either travel north parallel to the escarpment or concentrate on the southern Drakensberg, from where there is road entry to Lesotho. It will require a good vehicle or a relaxed timetable to penetrate further into 'the Kingdom in the Sky' from here, however, most people enter from the north side of the country near Maseru (one week)
- Transkei Region – Visit Port St Johns (one or two days) or undertake one of the walks along the unspoilt sub-tropical coast (from five days)
- Ciskei Region (one day transit, a week or so visiting the parks and beaches)
- The Karoo – You can head north into this vast, empty area from anywhere along the south coast, but the lovely old town of Graaff Reinet is a highlight and is most easily accessible from the port Elizabeth area (minimum three days)
- Garden Route (minimum three days)
- Little Karoo (two days)
- Breede River Valley (two days)
- Cape Winelands (four days)
- Cape Town and the Cape Peninsula (minimum one week)
- Cederberg Wilderness (minimum two days)
- Namaqualand (two days transit)
- Kalahari Gemsbok National Park (two days plus travel time)
- Orange Free State (one day transit, four days sightseeing)
- Lesotho (minimum three days)
- To Jo'burg via eastern Orange Free State (two days)

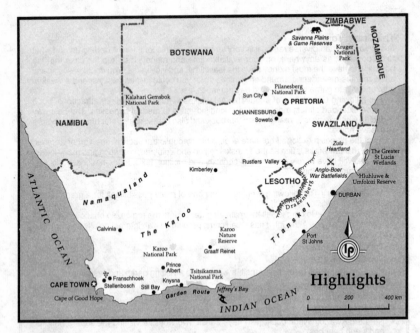

Highlights

Cape Town is one of the world's most beautiful cities, and probably the most relaxed in Africa. It's a manageable size and as well as the best food and nightlife in South Africa, it offers superb natural attractions. There are plenty of beaches (some deserted, some extremely fashionable) and **Table Mountain** is right in the middle of the city. On the city's doorstep is the **Cape of Good Hope**, part of a national park, and the **winelands** which make an easy day excursion.

Although you can easily visit the winelands from Cape Town, it makes sense to *stay* in the winelands, at least overnight. Many of the vineyards welcome visitors for sampling and cellar door sales, and some offer good food. **Stellenbosch** is a delightful old town and **Franschhoek** is a village set in one of the most beautiful valleys in the country.

The **Garden Route** is one of South Africa's most well-known attractions (it gets crowded in summer), and with its warm-water beaches, resort towns and forests, it isn't difficult to see why. **Knysna**, set on a beautiful lagoon system and surrounded by forest, is probably the best town to start from, although there is much more to the Garden Route than holiday towns. For example, **Tsitsikamma National Park** is stunningly beautiful and has famous hiking trails.

Jeffrey's Bay has perhaps the best surfing in the world, and it's a relaxed little town that welcomes surfies. For the non-surfer, there are great beaches in this area that don't get as crowded as those on the Garden Route.

The **Karoo** might not be everybody's cup of tea, but the wide, empty spaces can be fascinating. There are also some very nice old Karoo towns, such as **Calvinia** and **Graaff Reinet**, which are welcome oases. For a taste of the Karoo and also the rugged mountains that border it, visit the village of **Prince Albert**, not far from Oudtshoorn.

The **Transkei region**, once the 'independent homeland' of the Xhosa people, remains largely undeveloped, and this is its major attraction. A hiking trail runs the length of the region's long subtropical coastline, and on it is the small, idyllic and backpacker-friendly town of **Port St Johns**.

Durban is the beach resort city for southern Africa, and in summer it is a lively place. It has a subtropical climate and excellent surf beaches in the heart of the city. With a large population of Indian-descended people the atmosphere is very different from other South African cities.

The spectacular **Drakensberg escarpment** forms the border between South Africa and Lesotho and is a chain of rugged national parks and nature reserves. The area is a magnet for hikers and climbers.

The **Zulu heartland** has some outstanding national parks, such as **Hluhluwe/Umfolozi** and the **St Lucia area**, and offers glimpses of Zulu culture. For Anglo-Boer War buffs, this area is littered with important battlefields.

Lesotho, the Kingdom in the Sky (its lowest point is the highest of any country in the world), is still largely undiscovered by visitors. It offers unlimited hiking and pony trekking, with the possibility of staying in friendly traditional villages.

Swaziland is a very friendly monarchy where the traditional way of life remains strong. There are some good game reserves with hiking and rafting facilities.

Kruger National Park is perhaps the best in the world. You would be unlucky not to see many of the 'big five', and the accommodation in the various rest camps is superb and reasonably priced. But avoid Kruger during school holidays!

Johannesburg has earned itself a bad reputation for crime, but as the richest and arguably most important city in Africa it's worth a visit. This is where change, good and bad, is happening first in South Africa. You can safely visit **Soweto**, the powerhouse of the new South Africa, on tours run by locals. If Johannesburg sounds too scary, sedate **Pretoria** is just up the road and is a good place to relax.

Perhaps the world's largest piece of kitsch, **Sun City** is definitely worth visiting, even if you can't afford R10,000 for a suite at The Palace. You can take a day trip from Johannesburg or Pretoria. Nearby is **Pilanesberg National Park**, not as spectacular as some of South Africa's parks, but offering inexpensive accommodation and a good chance to see animals.

The **Kalahari Basin** verges on desert but it's a remote region with its own magic. **Kalahari Gemsbok National Park**, home to the unique Kalahari lion, is a complete contrast to the crowds at Kruger and other more accessible parks.

South Africa's astounding **wildflowers** are at their best in the **Namaqualand region**, but the dramatic landscapes and bleakly atmospheric coast are worth visiting at any time.

Kimberley, the diamond city, is a welcome oasis in the harsh Karoo, and also has some worthwhile attractions, such as the excellent Mine Museum and, of course, the Big Hole, from where most of the boom-time diamonds were extracted. ■

The Difaqane

The difaqane ('forced migration' in Sotho) or *mfeqane* ('the crushing' in Zulu) was a time of immense upheaval and suffering among the tribes of southern Africa.

In the early 19th century the Nguni tribes around the Mkuzi and Tugela rivers (in modern KwaZulu/Natal) underwent a dramatic change from loosely organised collections of chiefdoms into a centralised, militarist state. The process began under Dingiswayo, chief of the Mthethwa, and reached its peak under the chief Shaka, born into a small clan called Zulu.

Dingiswayo (died 1818) was a powerful leader, who developed disciplined *impis* (regiments) of soldiers armed with stabbing spears and protected by large ox-hide shields. His initial expansion produced local chaos, during which he was succeeded by one of his commanders, Shaka.

Shaka increased the size of the armies and placed them under the control of his officers rather than hereditary chiefs. He began a massive programme of conquest in which his main weapon was terror. Previous inter-tribal conflict had often been settled by battles between champions, but now there

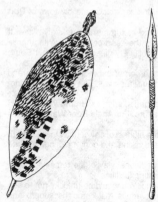

Shield & stabbing stick

Not surprisingly, tribes in the path of Shaka's increasingly powerful armies fled, and they in turn became aggressors upon their neighbours. This wave of disruption and terror spread throughout southern Africa, with refugees reaching, and conquering, as far as Lake Tanganyika. Two notable successes among the destruction were the Swazi and Basotho peoples, both of whom used the tide of refugees to their advantage and forged powerful nations.

The Boers, whose Great Trek coincided with the difaqane, mistakenly believed that what they found – deserted pasture lands, disorganised bands of refugees and tales of brutality – was the normal state of affairs. The Afrikaner myths, now dying hard, that the Great Trek was into unoccupied territory or that the blacks and the Boers both arrived at much the same time, stem from this. It also added emphasis to their belief that European occupation meant the coming of civilisation to a savage land.

Shaka was killed in 1828 by Dingaan, his half-brother, who became king. Dingaan

was total war. The best a conquered people could hope for was slavery, but often whole tribes were wiped out and their crops razed. Shaka's soldiers were subject to similar rigours – failure in battle meant death.

Shaka: Genius or Madman?

Historians have advanced many explanations for the difaqane. Some say that the centralisation of power which enabled the creation of a powerful Zulu state resulted from the ivory trade with the Portuguese at Delagoa Bay (modern Maputo in Mozambique). Inter-tribal cooperation was necessary to keep the trade routes open and standover tactics could win control of the whole lucrative system. It has also been suggested that contact with Europeans taught the tribes the value of large standing armies, impossible to maintain in a loosely organised, decentralised state. Population pressure has also been blamed as it not only produced the likelihood of conflict but in so doing gave the means of relieving it: Shaka's impis were forbidden to marry, and many thousands of people were killed or fled the area during his reign.

Other researchers have concentrated on Shaka's personality, with opinion divided between those who think he was mad and those who maintain that he was a superb tactician. Shaka's disturbed childhood offers scope for Freudians and the scale of his violence is exceptional – on the death of his mother he had thousands of his people killed for displaying insufficient grief – and there have been questions about his asexual nature. His insistence that his soldiers did not marry has often been cited as an example of his perversity, but it is interesting that one of the British demands to Chief Cetshwayo in the 1878 ultimatum was that the Zulu impis be allowed to marry: bachelor soldiers were seen as a greater threat than married ones. ∎

PHOTOGRAPH BY LUBA VANGELOVA

relaxed military discipline and attempted to establish friendly relations with the British traders setting up on the Natal coast, but events were unfolding which were to see the demise of Zulu independence.

The Great Trek

From the 1820s groups of Boers dissatisfied with the British rule in the Cape colony had trekked off into the interior in search of freedom. From the mid-1830s increasing numbers of frontier communities were abandoning their farms and crossing the Orange River in a decade of migration known as the Great Trek.

Tensions between the Boers and the government had been building for some time, but the reason given by many trekkers for leaving was the 1833 act banning slavery. Most Boers grudgingly accepted that slavery might be wrong, but the British seemed to go a step further and proclaim the equality of races. This resulted in, for example, servants bringing actions against their masters for non-payment of wages or for assault. For an illiterate farmer who rarely saw a government official, much less ventured to Cape Town, to be summoned to a distant court which used a language he could not speak, all on the complaint of a coloured servant, was an extreme insult. It seemed to go against nature. If the law would not distinguish between races, how could a people maintain their culture, their purity?

Reports from early treks told of vast, uninhabited – or at least poorly defended – grazing lands, and from 1836 increasing numbers of *Voortrekkers* ('fore-trekkers', pioneers) crossed the Orange River. The trekkers had entered their promised land, with space enough for their cattle to graze and for their culture of anti-urban independence to flourish.

The trek leaders, who were the heads of large families or district leaders, now occupy high places in the Afrikaner pantheon. Names such as Retief, Trichardt, van Rensburg, Maritz and Uys are synonymous with daring and enterprise.

The peoples of the plains which were occupied by the trekkers were disorganised by the difaqane; they lacked both horses and firearms so their resistance was easily overcome. The mountains where Moshoeshoe's Basotho nation was being melded and the wooded valleys of Zululand were a more difficult proposition, and there began the skirmishes, squabbles and flimsy treaties which were to litter the next 50 years of increasing white domination.

The Voortrekkers Meet the Zulu The Great Trek's first halt was at Thaba 'Nchu, near modern Bloemfontein, where a republic was established. After a disagreement, Maritz, Retief and Uys moved on to Natal, and Potgieter headed north to establish the republics of Winburg (in the Orange Free State) and Potchefstroom, later the Republic of Transvaal.

By 1837 Retief's party had crossed the Drakensberg and wanted to establish a republic. Zulu king Dingaan (Shaka's successor) agreed to this and, in February 1838, Retief and some others visited his capital Mgungundlovu (near modern Ulundi) to sign the title deed. It was a trap. The deed assigning all Natal to the Boers was signed but immediately afterwards Dingaan's men massacred the entire party. There was a further massacre at Weenen and other Boer settlements were attacked.

In December 1838 Andries Pretorius arrived in Natal and organised a revenge attack on the Zulus. Sarel Celliers climbed onto a gun carriage to lead the party in a vow that if they won the battle the Boers would ever after celebrate the day as one of deliverance.

Pretorius' party reached the Ncome River and on 16 December the Zulus attacked. After three hours of carnage the river ran red and was named Blood River by the Boers. Three Boers had slight injuries; 3000 Zulus had been killed.

After such a 'miraculous' victory (the result of good tactics and vastly superior weapons) it seemed that Boer expansion really did have that long-suspected stamp of divine approval, and 16 December was

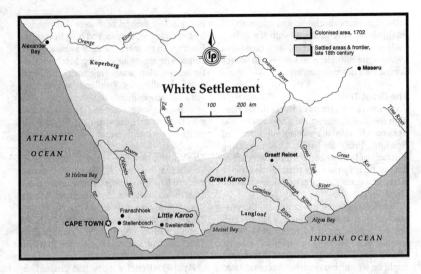

celebrated as the Day of the Vow until 1994, when it was renamed the Day of Reconciliation.

Perhaps more miraculously, when the Boers pushed on to Mgungundlovu they found the remains of Piet Retief and his party and the deed granting them Natal. With both military success and a title deed, it isn't surprising that they considered Natal to be well and truly theirs. That was not to be. The British annexed the republic in 1843 and most of the Boers moved north into the Transvaal, with yet another grievance against the British.

The Boer Republics

Several short-lived Boer republics sprang up but soon the only serious contenders were the Orange Free State and the Transvaal. The Transvaal Boers were too far away for the British to do much about, but the Orange Free State was more accessible and promised to be a headache because of the Boers' constant encroachment on Basotho land around the Caledon River.

The years between the Battle of Blood River (1838), and the conventions of Sand River (1852) and Bloemfontein (1854),

which gave independence to the Transvaal and the Orange Free State, are full of confusion and conflict. The Boers knew what they wanted: land and freedom. The aims of the black tribes were similar, but the British government, which commanded the strongest forces in the area, wasn't at all sure of what it wanted.

There were two differing viewpoints in successive British governments. One held that the boundaries of the colony should be expanded to take in the areas settled by the Boers, both to enlarge the colony and to prevent other Europeans having a stake in southern Africa.

The other view considered that colonies were expensive things. Even India, with its fabulous wealth, was run by a private company rather than the government until after the 1857 Mutiny, and southern Africa promised much less in the way of trade and taxes. From this viewpoint the Boers shouldn't have been allowed to trek in the first place, and their republics were to be discouraged.

Besides, Britain had non-aggression treaties with many of the peoples with whom the Boers were coming into conflict. When the

Boers, as de facto British subjects, broke those treaties, the British were obliged to send in the army to enforce the peace. This was not just out of a desire to see justice prevail. The British knew that any large-scale disturbance had a domino effect and they did not want to upset their precarious relations with tribes bordering the Cape colony. However, because of changing policies their armies and officials often had no idea of whether they should be restraining Boers, protecting blacks, enforcing British treaties, revenging Boer losses or carving out new British colonies. Nobody knew what orders would arrive on the next mail boat from England.

The Orange Free State was intermittently at war with the powerful Basotho, sometimes with British assistance, sometimes without. At various times the British placed Residents in Bloemfontein and Moshoeshoe's court, annexed the Free State, gave it independence, wrote treaties, tore the treaties up, revised borders, supervised a few ceasefires and finally, in 1871, they annexed Basutholand.

That solved the problem of land for the Free State. The settlement terms of the 1865 Basutho-Free State War had been generous and now there was no chance of Moshoeshoe reclaiming his land.

The Transvaal Republic's problems were mostly internal, with several leaders and breakaway republics threatening civil war until Paul Kruger settled the issue with a short, sharp campaign in 1864.

The financial position of the republics was always precarious. With small populations, no industry and precious little agriculture, they depended entirely on cattle. Most trade was by barter. There were few towns and the infrastructure of a nation was almost entirely lacking. Their contact with the outside world was minimal and that was the way they wanted it.

Just when it seemed that the republics, with their thinly spread population of fiercely independent Boers, were beginning to settle into stable states, diamonds were discovered near Kimberley in 1869. They were discovered on land belonging to the Griqua people but to which both Transvaal and the Free State laid claim. Britain stepped in quickly and annexed the area.

The diamond mines resulted in a rush of European immigrants and a migration of black labour. Towns sprang up in which the 'proper separation' of white and black was ignored. The Boers were disturbed by the foreigners, both black and white, and angry that their impoverished republics were missing out on the economic benefits of the mines.

Meanwhile, Britain became nervous about the existence of independent republics in southern Africa, especially as gold had been found in the Transvaal. The solution, as usual, was annexation and in 1877 the Transvaal lost its independence.

Anglo-Boer Wars

After the annexation, the Transvaal drifted into rebellion and the First Anglo-Boer War, known by Afrikaners as the War of Independence, broke out. It was over almost as soon as it began, with a crushing Boer victory at the Battle of Majuba in early 1881 and the republic regained its independence as the Zuid-Afrikaansche Republiek (ZAR, South African Republic).

Paul Kruger, who had been one of the leaders of the uprising and had earlier lead a delegation to London to argue for an end to the annexation, became president of the ZAR in 1883.

Kruger was born in Cape Province but his family had joined Potgieter's party on the trek into the Transvaal. He received little education and at 16 he left home to run his own farm – an apparently inauspicious background for a man who was to take on the British Empire at its most ravenous.

The British desire to federate the southern African colonies and republics was growing, but not just because federation would solve local difficulties. Victoria was now Queen Empress and her empire builders had visions of a British Africa stretching from Cairo to the Cape. Almost the only obstacles in the path of that imperial dream were the Boer republics.

Paul Kruger became the first president of the Zuid-Afrikaansche Republiek.

With the discovery of a huge reef of gold in the Witwatersrand (the area around Johannesburg) in 1886 and the explosive growth of Johannesburg, the ZAR was suddenly host to thousands of *uitlanders* (foreigners), black and white. By 1887 Johannesburg had a stock exchange and a racecourse. Within five years it was a city, complete with wealthy magnates and financiers, none of whom were Afrikaners. The influx of black labour to the area was also disturbing for the Boers, many of whom were going through hard times and bitterly resented the black wage earners.

With little experience of towns, none of cities, no access to the international finance which poured into the mining companies, and a deep suspicion of foreign ways, Kruger's government did its best to isolate the republic from the gold rush. The foreigners were paying taxes but they were not allowed to vote.

The enormous wealth of the Witwatersrand was an irresistible target for the British imperialists. In 1895 a raiding party lead by Dr Jameson entered the ZAR with the intention of sparking an uprising on the Witwatersrand and installing a British administration. This was a fiasco, but it was obvious to Kruger that the raid had at least the tacit approval of the British government and that his republic was in danger. He formed an alliance with the Orange Free State.

In 1899 the British demanded that voting rights be given to the 60,000 foreign whites on the Witwatersrand. Kruger refused, demanding that British troops massing on the ZAR borders be withdrawn by 11 October or he would consider the republic to be at war.

The British, confident that their vastly superior numbers of experienced troops would win swiftly, took him on. They were shocked to find that the Boers were no pushover, and the British were for a time in disarray. The Boers first invaded Natal, where they won important battles. They besieged Ladysmith but this, like the siege of Mafeking, was a mistake as it gave British time to bring in more troops and new commanders, Lords Roberts and Kitchener.

The abilities of the Boer commandos were no longer underestimated and an army of 450,000 men was brought to bear on them. The 80,000 Boers from the ZAR, the Free State and the Cape gave way rapidly and by 5 June 1900 Pretoria, the last of the major towns, had surrendered.

It seemed as though the war was over but instead it entered a second, bitter phase. Commando raiders, freed from the now-broken central command, denied the enemy control of the countryside. There was no possibility that the British could be defeated but maintaining an occupying army would be a very expensive proposition.

The British had no enemy army to face, just commandos who could instantly become innocuous farmers, and they decided to exact reprisals. If a railway line was blown up, the nearest farmhouse was destroyed; if a shot was fired from a farm, the house was burnt down, the crops destroyed and the animals killed. The women and children from the farms were collected and taken to concentration camps – a British invention. As the guerrilla war dragged on the burnings and detentions became more systematic. By the end of the war 26,000 people, mainly children, had died of disease and neglect in the camps.

The Boer leaders were in a dilemma. Their growing hatred of the British deepened their resolve to fight until the end, but the horror stories from the concentration camps compelled them to finish the war quickly. Public feeling in Britain and Europe was swinging against the British government, (largely due to the efforts of Emily Hobhouse, an Englishwoman who worked in the camps), but it was too late to influence the outcome of the war. On 31 May 1902 the Peace of Vereeniging was signed and the Boer republics became British colonies. Paul Kruger fled to Europe, where he died in 1904.

The terms of the peace were generous. The British extracted no payments and in 1906 a new government in Britain granted limited self-government. This was small solace for the Afrikaners, who found themselves again ruled by Britain and in the ignominious position of poor farmers in a country where big mining ventures and foreign capital made them irrelevant.

British Rule

The British response after their victory was a curious mixture of appeasement and insensitive imperialism. It was essential for the Boers and British to work together. The nonwhites were scarcely considered, other than as potential labour, despite the fact that they constituted nearly 80% of the combined population of the provinces. The Treaty of Vereeniging did nothing to ensure that blacks or coloureds would be given political rights, despite British propaganda during the war that blacks would be freed from 'Boer slavery' – a failure that was regarded as a betrayal by the tens of thousands who had fought on Britain's side.

After the war, the Cape Province was the only state where political rights were shared between races, but even there only 15% of the registered voters were non-white. Political awareness was growing however. Mohandas (later Mahatma) Gandhi was working with the Indian populations of the Natal and Transvaal and men like John Jabavu, Walter Rubusana and Abdullah Abdurahman laid the foundations for new non-tribal black political groups. There was a considerable amount of black unrest, which in Natal developed into the Bambatha Rebellion. Bambatha, a Zulu chief, began a guerrilla war of independence, but it was crushed at the cost of 4000 black lives.

The colonial government, under Lord Milner, spent millions of pounds on reconstructing the country after the devastation of the war, although a primary focus was to get the mines functioning again. By 1907 the mines of the Witwatersrand were producing almost one-third of the world's output of gold.

Resettlement was less successful and poor Boers, ill-equipped for urban life, flooded into the cities. There they found a world dominated by the English and their language and they were at the mercy of English oppressors. Worst of all, they were forced to compete for jobs with blacks on an equal footing. Partly as a backlash to this, Afrikaans came to be seen as the *volkstaal*

After the Anglo-Boer War, Walter Rubusana began developing non-tribal black political groups.

Abdullah Abdurahman was another key figure in developing black political groups.

(people's language) and a symbol of Afrikaner nationhood, and a number of nationalistic organisations sprang up.

The former republics were given representative government in 1906/7, and moves towards union began almost immediately. The pressures were largely economic – the smaller provinces were unsustainable in a world that required integrated economies and infrastructures, proper tax bases and centralised bureaucracies.

The most contentious issue was the question of voter franchise, which varied from colony to colony. Despite a major campaign by non-whites the eventual compromise agreement allowed each colony to retain its existing arrangements, but only whites could be elected to Parliament. English and Dutch were made the official languages.

The Union of South Africa was established on 31 May 1910. Cape Town was to be the legislative capital, Pretoria the administrative capital, Bloemfontein the seat of the Supreme Court, while Pietermaritzburg was given financial compensation. The three British High Commission Territories of Basutholand (now Lesotho), Bechuanaland (now Botswana), Swaziland, and Rhodesia (now Zimbabwe) were excluded from the Union.

For more information about the history of South Africa from the Union to present day see the South African Facts about the Country chapter.

FLORA

In some eyes, southern Africa's most impressive endowment is its flora. There are more than 22,000 species, accounting for 10% of the world's total – that's more than in the USA, which is seven times larger. It is not just impressive numerically, it is both fascinating and spectacularly beautiful.

South Africa is the only country with one of the world's six floral kingdoms within its borders. This is the Cape kingdom, in Western Cape, with its characteristic *fynbos* (fine bush), primarily proteas, heaths and ericas. There are over 8500 species, and the Cape Peninsula alone has more native plants than the entire British Isles.

In the drier regions there are weird succulents, dominated by euphorbias and aloes, and annuals, which flower brilliantly after spring rainfall – see the Namaqualand section in the Northern Cape Province chapter. An extraordinary number of domesticated flowers grow wild in South Africa – daisies, pelargoniums, gladioli, ixias, arum lilies, strelitzia, irises, freesias, proteas, watsonias, agapanthus and red hot pokers amongst them.

In contrast to this wealth southern Africa is very poor in natural forests. Although they were more widespread in the past, they were never particularly extensive. Today only a few protected remnants remain. Temperate forests occur on the coastal strip between George and Humansdorp (Western Cape), in the Drakensberg and in Eastern Transvaal. There is some subtropical forest north-east of Port Elizabeth through the Transkei area and KwaZulu/Natal.

Large areas in the north are covered by a savannah-type vegetation, which is characterised by acacias and thorn trees, like the umbrella thorn and sweet thorn.

FAUNA

The region is rich in wildlife though most of the large game is now concentrated in South Africa's national parks, particularly the huge Kruger and Kalahari Gemsbok national parks.

South Africa has the world's largest land mammal (the African elephant), the second biggest (the white rhinoceros), the third biggest (the hippopotamus), the tallest (the giraffe), the fastest (the cheetah) and the smallest (the pygmy shrew).

Conservation of the native fauna is an active concern and although one can only dimly imagine the extent of the loss since the arrival of Europeans a significant amount remains. The country is home to the last substantial populations of black and white rhinos – with horns intact – and the problem with elephant numbers is not that they are declining, but that they are increasing too rapidly.

You probably have a better chance of seeing the 'big five' in South Africa – buffalo, lion, leopard, elephant and black rhino – than in any other African country. There is also a lesser known 'little five' – the buffalo weaver, rhinoceros beetle, elephant shrew, leopard tortoise and ant lion – if you are looking for a challenge.

There is a spectacular variety of birds, with 900 species, 113 of which are endemic. They range from the largest in the world (ostrich), the largest flying bird (the Kori bustard), to spectacularly coloured sunbirds, flamingoes, and the extraordinary sociable weaver birds whose huge colonies live in 'cities' of woven grass.

CULTURE

Superficially, urbanised European culture doesn't seem to differ much from that found in other Western countries. There are shopping malls, freeways and all the trappings of Western consumer culture. However, the unique experience of the white people of Africa has given them a self awareness that has raised culture to an issue of central importance, far beyond the arts pages of a weekend newspaper. Those of Afrikaner and British descent form distinct subgroups.

Despite the strength of traditional black culture in the countryside, the mingling of peoples in South Africa's urban areas means that old cultures are fading and others are emerging. There is nothing new in this: culture is never static and always responds to external events. Even during the short recorded history of the black peoples of southern Africa there have been several huge changes to cultures, caused by the difaqane and white invasion. The idea that a people can have an intrinsic and unchangeable cultural identity is one of the racist myths promulgated by the apartheid regime to justify its Homelands policy.

In Swaziland traditional culture is one of the most powerful forces in the society, whereas in Lesotho it persists mainly in rural areas.

Although there are several major and many minor groupings in the traditional black cultures, there are broad similarities. All the traditional cultures are based on beliefs in a masculine deity, ancestral spirits and various supernatural forces. Marriage customs and taboos differ (but are always important) but polygamy (ie men can have more than one wife but not vice versa) is permitted and a dowry *(lobolo)* is usually paid. First-born males have inheritance rights. Cattle play an important part in many cultures, as symbols of wealth and as sacrificial animals.

Most black peoples belong to the Nguni (Ndebele, Swazi, Xhosa, Zulu) or the Sotho (Tswana, Batswana, Pedi, Basotho) linguistic and cultural groupings. The Nguni tended to live in scattered, semi-independent settlements, while the Sotho had larger communities. The Nguni feared incest and marriage to a relative was prohibited; the Sotho encouraged the marriage of cousins, perhaps because it meant that the dowry remained in the family.

San

The San (or Bushmen) culture did not survive the impact of white settlement.

The San, known to the Europeans as
'Bushmen', were nomadic hunters & gatherers.

South Africa were their canvas, and the whole country is littered with examples. For natural detail, purity of line and an almost eerie sense of movement, the paintings, some of which date back 26,000 years, cannot be surpassed.

There are quite a number of accessible sites in the KwaZulu/Natal Drakensberg, particularly in Giant's Castle Game Reserve. *The Drakensberg Bushmen & Their Art* by AR Willcox (Drakensberg Publications, R17) has detailed information on a number of the sites.

In the Cape provinces relatively few sites are easily accessible and those that are have often been destroyed by deliberate vandalism, or by people who have thoughtlessly sprayed the paintings with water to temporarily brighten the colours. Most are on private land and the owners of the land are rarely forthcoming about their existence, both to protect them from vandals and to prevent any government interference.

Introduced diseases and deliberate genocide on the part of whites meant that they have virtually disappeared as a separate race. Many survivors inter-bred with other racial groups and their descendants are now considered a part of the coloured population.

There are small numbers of San at Twee Rivieren (Northern Cape Province), Kagga Kamma (Western Cape Province), and at Lake Chrissie (Eastern Transvaal). Larger groups survive in Botswana. Their traditional nomadic hunting lifestyle has completely disappeared, except for the semi-artificial lifestyle of the Kagga Kamma project and a few small bands living in Botswana.

Although their technology was simple, they adapted very successfully to the African environment. Their main hunting weapon was the bow and poisoned arrows and their tracking and hunting abilities were exceptional. Their principle cultural legacy is their extraordinary art. The rocks and caves of

Elaborate rock paintings, found throughout southern Africa, are the only tangible reminders of the San people.

Khoikhoi

Like the San, the Khoikhoi (Hottentot) and their culture have been submerged in the Christianised and Westernised coloured population of the Cape. Originally sheep and cattle herders closely related to the San, they have, at least according to official sources, disappeared as a people.

The Khoikhoi were semi-nomadic and like the San, hunted with bows and arrows. They lived in easily transportable beehive huts, made with saplings covered with woven mats and followed pasturage on a seasonal basis.

The Nama, one of the main tribes, still build the characteristic huts (these days using hessian) around Steinkopf on the north-west coast and are still small-scale pastoralists. Another group, the Griqua, settled around Kimberley.

Dotted around the Cape provinces are small mission stations where the Khoikhoi sought some kind of refuge, and many of these places are still functioning today, including Mamre, Goederwacht, Wittewater, Keimoes, Genadendal, Onseekpans, Elim, Pella, Wuppertal. The people speak a form of Afrikaans, and hymns and choirs are a feature of their communal life.

Nguni

Zulu The Zulu traditionally believe that the creator of the world is Unkulunkulu (the old, old man), but his daughter uNomkubulwana is more important to day-to-day life as she controls the rain. Still more important are ancestors who can make most things go well or badly depending on how assiduously a person has carried out the required sacrifices and observances.

Zulu Beadwork

Zulu beadwork is worth looking out for. It takes many forms, from the small, square *umgexo*, which is widely available and makes a good gift, to the more elaborate *umbelenja*, a short skirt or tasselled belt worn by women at puberty, but before marriage. Bead anklets *(amadavathi)* are worn by men and women. Today beadwork is still common but, with the exception of traditional ceremonies, it is used mainly for decoration of people or objects, such as a beaded match-box cover.

As in other societies, beads were used for decoration and as symbols of status, but the Zulu people have also traditionally used them as a means of communication, especially as love letters. The colours and arrangement of the beads give the message.

Some of the colours and their meanings are: red, passion or anger; black, difficulties or night; blue, yearning; deep blue, elopement (refers to the flight of the ibis); white or pale blue, pure love; brown, disgust or despondency; and green, peace or bliss. The more subtle meanings of the beads have been largely forgotten and there were always ambiguities. For example, a 'letter' predominantly red and black could be promising a night of passion or it could mean that the sender was annoyed.

Some bead-sculptors make social and political comment in their work, often weaving elaborate tableaux; the most famous exponent was the late Sizakale Mchunu. The Durban Art Gallery has monthly classes in beadwork in an effort to preserve this ancient art. A good place to buy beadwork is at the Dalton Road Hostel market in Durban. One of the best collections on display is in the KwaZulu Cultural Museum, Ulundi. ∎

Zulu beadwork

In common with other peoples, the important stages of life – birth, puberty, marriage, death – are marked by ceremonies. The clothes people wear reflect their status and their age. For example, girls may not wear long skirts until they become engaged. Animal skins are worn to reflect status, with a leopard-skin cloak signifying a chief.

Since Shaka's time, when the Zulu became a large and dominant tribe, the king (inoksa) has been the leader of all the people. Before Shaka there was a looser organisation of local chiefs and almost self-sufficient family groups.

The Zulu kraal (village) is usually circular, often with a defensive wall of dead saplings and branches. The huts are hemispherical and made of tightly woven grasses. Inside the hut the right-hand side is for the men and the left-hand for the women, with ancestral spirits allocated a space at the rear. The floor is hard-packed dung, so well made that at Ondini, some floors remain in the kraal that was burnt by British troops in 1879.

Dancing and singing are important and if you see an IFP (Inkatha Freedom Party) demonstration you'll feel something of the power of massed Zulu singing.

Xhosa The Xhosa who maintain a traditional lifestyle are known as red people because of the red-dyed clothing worn by most adults. Different subgroups wear different costumes, colours and arrangements of beads. The Tembu and Bomvana favour red and orange ochres in the dyeing of their clothing and the Pondo and Mpondomise use a very light-blue ochre (although chemical dyes are now much in use).

The Xhosa deity is known variously as uDali, Tixo and Qwamata. This deity also figured in the San religion and it's probable that the invading Xhosa adopted it from them. There are numerous minor spirits and a rich folklore which persists in rural areas. A belief in witches (male or female) is strong and witch-burning is not unknown. Most witchcraft is evil, and the main fear is that people will be possessed by depraved spirits.

The main source of evil is the tokoloshe which lives in water but is also kept by witches. However, water is not always evil. If someone drowns and their body is not recovered, it is assumed, joyously, that they have gone to join the People of the Sea. Often the drowned are reincarnated as people with special knowledge and understanding.

The igqirha (spiritual healer) holds an important place in traditional society because he/she can deal with the forces of nature and the trouble caused by witches. Amagqirha wear white. The ixhwele (herbalist) performs some magic but is more concerned with health. Mbongi are the holders and performers of a group's oral history and are something like a cross between a bard and a court jester.

While there is a hierarchy of chiefs the structure of Xhosa society is much looser than that of the Zulus.

Many people have the top of their left-hand little finger removed during childhood to prevent misfortune. Puberty rituals figure heavily. Boys must not be seen by women during the three-month initiation period following circumcision and disguise themselves with white clay or in intricate costumes made of dried palm leaves. In another puberty ritual, a girl is confined in a darkened hut while her friends tour the area singing for gifts.

Marriage customs and rituals are also important. Unmarried girls wear short skirts which are worn longer as marriage approaches. Married women wear long skirts and cover their breasts. They often put white clay on their faces and wear large, turban-like cloth hats. Smoking long-stemmed pipes is also popular among married women.

Beadwork and jewellery are important. The danga is a long turquoise necklace which identifies the wearer to his/her ancestors. The ngxowa yebokwe is a goatskin bag carried over the left shoulder on important occasions.

Ndebele The Ndebele are a Nguni group, surrounded by Sotho groups in the Northern Transvaal, but their strikingly painted houses and the women's elaborate costume and decoration make them stand out. Their beadwork is dazzling and women can reach outstanding proportions as they load on 25 kg of beads and jewellery. Some of the costume is so elaborate that it cannot be removed without destroying it, and the masses of copper rings on the ankles and neck are there for life.

You can visit a Ndebele village in Botshabolo National Park, west of Johannesburg.

Swazi Mkhulumnchanti is the Swazi deity. Respect for both the aged and ancestors plays a large part in the complex structure of Swazi traditional society. It is a conservative monarchist society and in many ways it is illiberal, but it works and is popular.

Unlike in many other post-colonial countries, the wearing of traditional clothing is as common among people in the Westernised middle classes as it is among rural labourers. It's not unusual to see a man on his way to work wearing an *amahiya* robe, with a spear in one hand and a briefcase in the other.

The self-identity of the Swazi nation is maintained by a system of age-related royal regiments which boys join. They graduate to others as they grow older. These regiments provided the military clout to hold off invaders during the difaqane and have helped to minimise the potentially divisive differences between clans while emphasising loyalty to the king and nation. Annual rituals like the important *Incwala* and the *Umhlanga* ceremonies (see the Swaziland chapter for details) have the same effect.

The rich and vigorous culture of the Swazi people is vested in the monarchy, both the king (*Ngwenyama* – the lion) and his mother (*Ndlovukazi* – the she-elephant). The Swazi people's forebears were a clan living on the coast in modern Mozambique, and even today their most important ritual involves the waters of the Indian Ocean.

Most Swazis rely at least partly on traditional medicine. There are two types of practitioners, the *inyanga* (usually a man) and the *sangoma* (usually a woman). The inyanga analyses problems and predicts the future by studying the patterns of thrown bones. The sangoma is more of a counsellor, although like the inyanga she is also a herbalist. Sangomas in South Africa are pressing to be recognised as part of the health care system.

Singing is important to Swazis and there are many songs to mark occasions or just to pass the time. Some may not be sung except at specified times.

Sotho

Northern Sotho This is a broad classification which covers many unconnected groups. Traditional villages (*kgoros*) were large – the Tswana had towns of 15,000 people – and had a sophisticated political structure.

The various groups each have totem animals, which they must not kill.

The Lobedu people are unique in that they have a Rain Queen, the *Modjadji*, who brings rain to the lush Lebowa area. The *Modjadji* is supposedly immortal, as she does not marry and thus theoretically has no children. In fact, the queen dies by ritual suicide and is succeeded by a daughter. She is regarded with awe by her people and her reputation is widespread: even Shaka avoided attacking the Lobedu. Henry Rider Haggard's novel *She* is based on the story of the original Modjadji, a 16th-century refugee princess.

Southern Sotho The Southern Sotho group comprises mainly the Basotho people of Lesotho. See the Lesotho chapter for information on Basotho culture.

VhaVenda

The VhaVenda people are something of an enigma. No one is certain of their origin and there are signs that the Lemba subgroup is of Semitic origin. They do not eat pork or animals which have not been bled. That their traditional economy was based on manufacture and trade rather than agriculture also sets them apart.

Traditional society is matriarchal, with female priests who supervise the worship of female ancestors. The *domba* (python dance) is a puberty rite performed by girls but the boys are included in the ceremony. Very few societies allow both sexes to attend puberty rituals.

The VhaVenda, especially the Lemba, mined, smelted and worked iron, copper and gold for centuries. They travelled throughout southern Africa to trade their metal. Most of the lore was lost when cheaper European metal became available but the quality of Venda iron is astonishingly high. Pottery is an important craft and the skills have survived.

Because of the tsetse fly, cattle have not figured highly in Venda culture.

Before the Venda area acquired 'independent Homeland' status (and a South-African supported dictator) there were about 30 independent chiefdoms, with no overall leader.

Afrikaner

The Boers' remarkable history, and their geographical isolation combined with often deliberate cultural isolation has created a unique people – often called the white tribe of Africa.

The ethnic composition of the Afrikaners is difficult to quantify, but the white government estimates 40% Dutch, 40% German, 7.5% French, 7.5% British, and 5% other. Some historians have argued that the '5% other' figure includes a significant proportion of blacks and coloureds – a claim that would still be regarded as highly offensive by most Afrikaners.

The Afrikaners speak Afrikaans, the only Germanic language to have evolved outside Europe. Spoken as a mother tongue by a mere 5½ million people it is central to the Afrikaner identity, but it has also served to reinforce their isolation from the outside world. The Afrikaners are a religious people and their brand of Christian fundamentalism based on 17th-century Calvinism is still a powerful influence.

Determination and courage were required by the first trekboers who launched themselves into Africa, and again by the Boers in their long and bitter struggle against the British Empire. This history has been heavily mythologised and the concepts of culture and race are tightly fused. Folk songs are sung like hymns at political rallies.

All this has created a proud and resourceful people, quick to violence, with a volatile streak of arrogance and bitterness. In 1948, the new prime minister and Afrikaner patriot DF Malan exclaimed:

The last hundred years have witnessed a miracle behind which must lie a divine plan. Indeed, the history of the Afrikaner reveals a will and a determination which makes one feel that Afrikanerdom is not the work of men but the creation of God.
**Quoted in *The Mind of South Africa*
by Allister Sparkes**

The South African countryside, with the exception of Eastern Cape and KwaZulu/Natal and the ex-Homelands, is still dominated by Afrikaners, and outsiders are often regarded with a degree of suspicion. Women are still expected to be wives and mothers.

Life in the country towns revolve around the Dutch Reformed churches which include the Nederduitse Gereformeerde Kerk (the NG Kerk), the Gereformeerde Kerk and the Gereformeerde Hervormde Kerk. The NG Kerk, sometimes called the National Party at prayer, is the largest and most influential church; after years of support it explicitly rejected apartheid in 1990.

There are a number of influential Afrikaner cultural organisations, including the secret Afrikaner Broederbond, which has dominated National Party politics, the Federasie van Afrikaanse Kultuurvereniginge (FAK), which coordinates cultural events and movements, and the Voortrekkers, an Afrikaner youth organisation based on the scouting movement.

Significant numbers of Afrikaners still dream of an independent, racially pure Boer state *(Volkstaat)* where the only citizens would be direct descendants of the Voortrekkers or those who fought in the Anglo-Boer wars. Of course, there would be lots of non-citizens with black skins to do the manual work.

The urbanised middle class tends to be considerably more moderate in its chauvinism, but historical events still find echoes in icons like wagon-wheel fences, and people are proud of old Boer names. Regular *braaisvleis* (barbecues) are compulsory. Afrikaaner rednecks (no, that isn't quite a tautology) tend to belong to the 'one-two-three' crowd – one litre of brandy, two litres of Coke and a three-litre Cortina.

European

Aside from the Afrikaners, the majority (around 1.9 million) of European South Africans are of British extraction. There is also a large and influential Jewish population (130,000); significant minorities of Portuguese (36,000), many of whom are refugees from Angola and Mozambique; Germans (34,000); Dutch (28,000); Italians (16,000) and Greeks (10,000).

The British have always had a slightly equivocal position in South African society, exemplified by a not so friendly Afrikaans term of abuse: *soutpiel*, literally meaning salt dick and referring to a man with one foot in South Africa and one in Britain. The Afrikaners' have often felt (rightly in many cases) that the English-speakers' commitment to Africa was at a completely different level to their own. Apart from anything else, many of the British who arrived in the 20th century can return 'home' if things get really tough.

The British are much more highly urbanised than the Afrikaners and, particularly up until the 1960s, completely dominated the mining, manufacturing, financial and retail sectors, much to the resentment of the Boers. Although they have traditionally been regarded as a more liberal force politically, a significant number have supported the post-war National Party governments.

Their numerical inferiority meant that they were doomed to political impotence, but with some noble exceptions their opposition to apartheid was at best muted. It is hard not to come to the cynical conclusion that they were happy to let the Afrikaners do the dirty work, while they, in their dominant economic position, reaped many of the ben-

efits. They even had the luxury of tut-tutting from the corner.

Most lead a suburban existence that, except for the ubiquitous servants, could be transplanted unchanged from Australia or North America. Their culture is the culture of the West.

The English-speaking community does not burn with a sense of grievance or mission. It has no positive, purposeful creed. It lacks cohesion: it is an amorphous community with little sense of any collective identity. They do not even have a proper name: 'English-speaking South Africans' is an appellation so vague as to make them almost anonymous.
The Mind of South Africa by Allister Sparks

RELIGION
South Africa

Most of the country is Christian, but among the Christians there is an enormous diversity, from the 4000 African Indigenous churches to the racist sub-sects which have split from the Dutch Reformed churches. The Indigenous churches are run by and for blacks, independent of the mainstream churches. They broadly follow either the Ethiopian line, which split from the early Methodist missions, or the later Zionist line, which developed as a result of the activities of American Pentecostal missions early this century. The largest church in the country is the Zion Christian Church, whose members wear a silver star on a green background. At Easter millions of people congregate at the church's headquarters near Tzaneen in Northern Transvaal.

The Dutch Reformed churches cover at least three major groups of Afrikaner churches, all conservative. The Church of England is also represented; it has a high profile because of Archbishop Desmond Tutu.

Hindus make up about 70% of the Indian population and about 20% are Muslims.

A minority of blacks follow traditional religions. Amongst different peoples, beliefs and practices vary but there is usually a belief in a supreme deity, but with more emphasis on ancestor worship. Magic plays a large part in beliefs and ceremonies. The distinction between religion and what would be considered folklore in Western societies is blurred on a day-to-day level. So much so that many more blacks have no problem in combining Christianity with traditional beliefs, in much the same way that Christianity adopted 'pagan' rituals in its spread through Europe.

Johan Heyns

The conservative churches, long a bulwark of apartheid, finally agreed to its abolition, thanks in part to Johan Heyns, moderator of the Dutch Reformed Church. Although he became convinced that Christians could not support apartheid, he was not a liberal – a fact that proved crucial in persuading church members to change their views. Heyns was assassinated in 1994, some believe by white racists. ■

Lesotho

Lesotho is a largely Roman Catholic country, thanks to the French missionaries who helped Moshoeshoe. Traditional beliefs still play their part in daily life.

Swaziland

Nearly half the population belong to the Zion Apostolic Church. While traditional religion is not widely practised, Swazi traditional culture continues strongly and many ceremonies have religious significance.

Language

In all three countries English is one of the official languages and in most places you'll find English speakers, although outside the main towns in Lesotho and Swaziland you might have to search for one.

In Lesotho the other official language is seSotho and in Swaziland it's siSwati.

South Africa's official languages were once English and Afrikaans but nine others have been added: isiNdebele, seSotho

sa Lebowa, seSotho, siSwati, Xitsonga, Setswana, Tshivenda, isiXhosa and isiZulu. The most widely spoken are Afrikaans, English, seSotho, isiXhosa and isiZulu. The relegation of Afrikaans from one of two official languages to one of 11 has caused some anguish among Afrikaners, who fear for the language's survival. Still, the proportion of TV and radio programmes, road signs and forms etc in Afrikaans is still way above the 9.1% allowed.

In South Africa, forms, brochures and timetables are usually printed in both English and Afrikaans; road signs alternate between the two languages. Most Afrikaans speakers also speak good English, but this is not always the case in small rural towns and amongst the older generations. However, it's not uncommon for blacks in cities to speak at least six languages – whites can usually speak two.

With so many languages, compromises are inevitable, and in the black townships where all the languages come it contact with against each other, pure forms are disappearing. The common tongue used in most townships is either a hybrid form of Zulu and Xhosa or some Sotho variation. Although language purists find this development unfortunate these hybrids are fast becoming the most important communication links. It is quite possible that one will be officially developed and recognised as a lingua franca.

Fanakalo, a pidgin language based on Afrikaans, English and Zulu, was developed for use by black workers. This was once hailed as a future lingua franca, but for many blacks it represents oppression and it is rarely used outside the workplace.

The TALK (Transfer of African Language Knowledge) project aims to teach African languages by teaming up each student with a mother-tongue speaker. This method of language-learning has proved highly successful, and of course it's also a good way to get to know another culture. TALK courses run for at least six weeks and cost from R250 (most of which goes to the mother-tongue speaker). For more information contact TALK (☎ (011) 487 1798), 155 Hunter St,

Bellevue East, Johannesburg, 2198. TALK also operates in Cape Town.

If you're completely lost for words, remember that the thumbs-up gesture is a universal gesture of goodwill, and can have an amazingly positive effect.

SOUTH AFRICAN ENGLISH

English has undergone some changes during its time in Africa. Quite a few words have changed meaning, new words have been appropriated, and a distinctive accent, thanks to the influence of Afrikaans, has developed. British rather than US practice is followed in grammar and spelling. In some cases British words are preferred to their US equivalent, (eg, lift not elevator, petrol not gas) but colloquial US terms are becoming increasingly common. See the glossary at the back of this book for some examples.

AFRIKAANS

Although Afrikaans has been closely associated with the tribal identity of the Boers, it is also spoken as a first language by many coloureds. Ironically, it was probably first used as a common language by the polyglot coloured community of the Cape, and passed back to whites by nannies and servants. Around 5½ million people speak the language, roughly half of whom are Afrikaner and half of whom are coloured.

Afrikaans developed from the High Dutch of the 17th century. It has abandoned the complicated grammar and incorporated vocabulary from French, English, indigenous African languages and even Asian languages (thanks to East-Asian slaves). It's inventive, powerful and expressive, but it was not recognised as one of the country's official languages until 1925; before then it was officially regarded as a dialect of Dutch.

Afrikaans is a phonetic language and words are generally pronounced as they are spelled, with the characteristic guttural emphasis and rolled 'r' of germanic languages. The following pronunciation guide is not exhaustive, but it includes the more difficult sounds that differ from English.

a	like 'u' in pup
e	like 'e' in hen
i	like 'e' in angel
o	like 'o' in fort, or 'oy' in boy
u	like 'e' in angel, but with lips pouted
r	should be rolled
aai	like 'y' in why
ae	like 'ah'
ee	like 'ee' in deer
ei	like 'ay' in play
oe	like 'oo' in loot
oë	like 'oe' in doer
ooi	like 'oi' in oil, preceded by w
oei	like 'ooey' in phooey, preceded by w
tj	like 'ch' in chunk

Greetings & Civilities

Hello.	Hallo.
Good morning, sir.	Goeiemôre, meneer pronounced 'geemorreh'.
Good afternoon, madam.	Goeiemiddag, mevrou.
Good evening, miss.	Goeienaand, juffrou.
Good night.	Goeienag.
please	asseblief
thank you	dankie
How are you?	Hoegaand?
Good thank you.	Goed dankie.
pardon	ekskuus

Profanity & Abuse

Although these words are not attractive they are in reasonably common use in South Africa. It's not a wise idea to use them yourself but, in certain situations, it may be necessary to know what they mean.

black person	kaffir (derogatory, dangerous to use!)
nigger lover	kaffirboetie
Afrikaner	Dutchman

English South African	*soutpiel* (literally salt dick – a person with one foot in South Africa and one in England)
	rooinek (literally red-neck)
dero/bum	*bergie*
red-neck conservative	*gom*
narrow-minded	*verkrampt*
black threat	*swart gevaar*

Useful Words & Phrases

yes	*ja*
no	*nee*
What?	*Wat?*
How?	*Hoe?*
How many/ how much?	*Hoeveel?*
When?	*Wanneer?*
Where?	*Waar?*
emergency	*nood*
Do you speak English/Afrikaans?	*Praat u Engels/u Afrikaans?*
I only understand a little Afrikaans.	*Ek verstaan maar slegs 'n bietjie Afrikaans.*
Where are you from?	*Waarvandaan kom u?*
from...	*van...*
Where do you live?	*Waar woon u?*
overseas	*oorsee*
What is your occupation?	*Wat is jou beroep?*
yes, no, maybe, sure	*ja-nee*
soon	*nou-nou*
Isn't that so?	*Né?*
sons	*seuns*
daughters	*dogters*
wife	*vrou/eggenote*
husband	*man/eggenoot*
mother	*ma*
father	*pa*
sister	*suster*
brother	*broer*
nice/good/pleasant	*lekker*
bad	*sleg*
cheap	*goedkoop*
expensive	*duur*

Numbers

1	*een*
2	*twee*
3	*drie*
4	*vier*
5	*vyf*
6	*ses*
7	*sewe*
8	*agt*
9	*nege*
10	*tien*
11	*elf*
12	*twaalf*
13	*dertien*
14	*veertien*
15	*vyftien*
16	*sestien*
17	*sewentien*
18	*agtien*
19	*negentien*
20	*twintig*
21	*een en twintig*
30	*dertig*
40	*veertig*
50	*vyftig*
60	*sestig*
70	*sewentig*
80	*tagtig*
90	*negentig*
100	*honderd*
1000	*duisend*

Days of the Week

Monday	*Maandag*, abbreviated to *Ma*
Tuesday	*Dinsdag, Di*
Wednesday	*Woensdag, Wo*
Thursday	*Donderdag, Do*
Friday	*Vrydag, Vr*
Saturday	*Saterdag, Sa*
Sunday	*Sondag, So*

Travel Terms

travel	*reis*
arrival	*aankoms*
departure	*vertrek*
to	*na*
from	*van*

today	*vandag*
tomorrow	*môre*
yesterday	*gister*
public holiday	*algemene vakansiedag*
daily	*daagliks*
single	*enkel*
return	*retoer*
ticket	*kaartjie*
am	*vm*
pm	*nm*

Getting Around – town

left	*links*
right	*regs*
exit	*uitgang*
at the corner	*op die hoek*
city	*stad*
city centre	*middestad*
town	*dorp*
avenue	*laan*
street	*straat*
road	*pad verkeerslig*
traffic light	*robot*
tourist bureau	*toeristeburo*
information	*inligting*
enquiries	*navrae*
rooms	*kamers*
office	*kantoor*
building	*gebou*
art gallery	*kunsgalery*
pharmacy/chemist	*apteek*
station	*stasie*
church	*kerk*
priest	*dominee*

Getting Around – country

utility/pick-up	*bakkie*
river	*rivier*
mountain	*berg*
bay	*baai*
ford	*drif*
road	*pad*
point	*punt*
beach	*strand*
field, or plain	*veld*
marsh	*vlei*
caravan park	*woonwapark*
game reserve	*wildtuin*
hiking trail	*wandelpad*

Food & Drinks

vegetables	*groente*
fruit	*vrugte*
meat	*vleis*
farm sausage	*boerewors*
dried and salted meat	*biltong*
fish	*vis*
cheese	*kaas*
bread	*brood*
cup of coffee	*koppie koffie*
glass of milk	*glas melk*
wine	*wyn*
beer	*bier*
hotel bar	*kroeg*
barbecue	*braaivleis* or *braai*

SISWATI

SiSwati is the language of the Swazi people. It is very similar to Zulu, and the two speakers can understand one another. Tonality (rising and falling 'notes' in the words) plays a part in siSwati, and there are some clicks to contend with.

Useful Words & Phrases

Hello. (to one person)	*Sawubona.* (I see you)
Hello. (to more than one)	*Sanibona.*
How are you?	*Kunjani?*
I'm fine.	*Kulungile.*
Goodbye. (if you are leaving)	*Sala kahle.*(stay well)
Goodbye. (if you are staying)	*Hamba kahle.* (go well)
please	*tsine*
I thank you.	*Ngiyabonga.*
We thank you.	*Siyabonga.*
yes	*yebo* (an all purpose greeting)
no	*(click) ha*
sorry!	*lucolo*
Do you have...?	*Une...yini?*
How much?	*malini?*
today	*lamuhla*
tomorrow	*kusasa*
yesterday	*itolo*

Is there a bus to...?	*Kukhona ibhasi yini leya...?*
When does it leave?	*Isuka nini?*
morning	*ekuseni*
afternoon	*entsambaba*
evening	*kusihlwa*
night	*ebusuku*

Yebo is often said as a casual greeting. It is the custom to greet everyone you meet. Often you will be asked *u ya phi?* (Where are you going?).

SESOTHO

There are two forms of seSotho, the language of the Sotho peoples. Southern Sotho is spoken in Lesotho and by Basotho people in South Africa. It's useful to know some words and phrases if you're planning to visit Lesotho, especially if you want to trek in remote areas.

Greetings

Greetings father.	*Lumela ntate.* (du-may-lah n-tah-tee)
Peace father.	*Khotso ntate.* (ko-tso n-tah-tee)
Greetings mother.	*Lumela 'me.*
Peace mother.	*Khotso 'me.*
Greetings brother.	*Lumela abuti.*
Peace brother.	*Khotso abuti.*
Greetings sister.	*Lumela ausi.*
Peace sister.	*Khotso ausi.*

There are three possible ways to say 'How are you?' They are:

How are you?	*O kae? (singular)* *le kae? (plural)*
How do you live?	*O phela joang? (s)* *le phela joang? (p)*
How did you get up?	*O tsohele joang? (s)* *Le tsohele joang? (p)*

The answers to these questions are:

I am here.	*Ke teng. (singular)* *Re teng. (plural)*
I live well.	*Ke phela hantle. (s)* *Re phela hantle. (p)*
I got up well.	*Ke tsohile hantle. (s)* *Re tsohile hantle. (p)*

These questions and answers are quite interchangeable. Someone could ask you *o phela joang?* and you could answer *ke teng*.

When trekking, people always ask *lea kae?* (Where are you going?) and *o tsoa kae?* or the plural *le tsoa kae?* (Where have you come from?). When parting, use the following expressions:

Stay well.	*sala hantle. (singular)* *salang hantle. (plural)*
Go well.	*tsamaea hantle. (s)* *tsamaeang hantle. (p)*

You must always add *ntate* or *'me* (or *bo*) for the plural.

'Thank you' is *kea leboha* (pronounced 'keya lebowah'). The herd boys often ask for money (*chelete*) or sweets (*lipompong*) (pronounced dee-pom-pong). If you want to say 'I don't have any', the answer is *ha dio* (pronounced 'ha dee-oh').

ISIXHOSA

The language of the Xhosa people is isiXhosa, the dominant indigenous language in Eastern Cape Province, although you'll meet isiXhosa speakers everywhere.

Good morning.	*Molo.*
Goodnight.	*Rhonanai*
Do you speak English?	*Uyakwazi ukuthetha siNgesi?*

father (term of respect for older man)	*bawo*
Are you well?	*Uphilile na namhlanje?*
Yes, I am well.	*Ewe, ndiphilile kanye.*
Where do you come from?	*Uvela phi na okanye ngaphi na?*
I come from...	*ndivela...*
When do we arrive?	*Siya kufika nini na?*
The road is good.	*Indlela ilungile.*
The road is bad.	*Indlela imbi.*
I am lost.	*Ndilahlekile*
Is this the road to...?	*Yindlela eya...yini le?*
Would you show me the way to...?	*Ungandibonisa na indlela eye...?*
Is it possible to cross the river?	*Kunokwenzeka ukuwela umlambo?*
How much does it cost?	*Idla ntoni na?*
day	*usuku*
week	*iveki*
month (moon)	*inyanga*
east	*empumalanga*
west	*entshonalanga*
It is all one.	*Yint' enye.*

ISIZULU

Zulu people speak isiZulu. As with several other Nguni languages, isiZulu uses a variety of 'clicks', very hard to reproduce without practice. Many people don't try (the 'Kwa' in KwaZulu is a click, but you rarely hear it from whites) but it's worth the effort, if just to provide amusement for your listeners. To ask a question, add *na?* to the end of a sentence.

please	*jabulisa*
thank you	*ngiyabonga*
Where does this road go?	*Iqondaphi lendlela na?*
Which is the road to...?	*Iphi indlela yokuya ku...?*
Is it far?	*Kukude yini?*
yes	*yebo*
no	*cha*
north	*inyakatho*
south	*iningizumi*
east	*impumalanga*
west	*intshonalanga*
water	*amanzi*
food	*ukudla*
lion	*ibhubesi*
rhino (black)	*ubhejane*
rhino (white)	*umkhombe*
snake	*inyoka*

Facts for the Visitor

VISAS

Visas were once the bane of travel to this part of the world but the situation has improved considerably. For many visitors, Lesotho is the only country for which you need to arrange a visa before arrival (and you can do it in South Africa). See the Facts for the Visitor chapters for each of the three countries for detailed information.

WHEN TO GO
South Africa

In many places, especially the lowveld, summer can be uncomfortably hot. In KwaZulu/Natal and Eastern Transvaal, humidity can also be annoying. The warm waters of the east coast make swimming a year-round proposition. Spring is the best time for wild flowers in the Northern and Western Cape provinces and they are at their peak in Namaqualand (Northern Cape) from mid-August to mid-September. Winters are mild everywhere except in the highest country, where there are frosts and occasional snowfalls. There is skiing in Lesotho and in the Eastern Cape. Summer brings warmer weather but also rain and mist to the mountains.

Many South Africans take their annual holidays in summer, with several overlapping waves of holiday-makers streaming out of the cities from mid-December to late January. Then, as well as during the other school holidays, resorts and national parks are heavily booked and prices on the coast can more than double. The KwaZulu/Natal coast, especially south of Durban, is packed. The different South African provinces have differing dates for school holidays and they all change annually. Roughly, there are two-week holidays in April, a month around July, a month around September, and about two months from early December to late January. The peak time is mid-December to early January. Contact Satour for the exact dates.

Lesotho

Lesotho is worth visiting year-round, but the weather can determine what you do. In winter be prepared for cold conditions and snow. In summer, it's rain and mist which have to be taken into account. In remote areas (which make up a large proportion of the country) roads are often cut by flooding rivers in summer.

Swaziland

Swaziland's climate is much the same as that of Eastern Transvaal, with the hot summers alleviated by rain on the high country, and mild winters with little rain. The two most important Swazi cultural ceremonies, the Umhlanga (Reed) Dance and the Incwala ceremony are held in August or September and late December or early January, respectively.

WHAT TO BRING

With such a variety of things to do in the region, it's hard to generalise about what to bring. With so much dramatic scenery and so many good nature reserves, a pair of binoculars will come in handy.

A sleeping bag is vital for budget travellers, useful in backpackers' hostels and in rondavels (circular huts) and cabins in the caravan parks. Camping is definitely a viable option.

You can buy just about anything you need in the major cities in South Africa, and clothes are often cheaper here than in other Western countries. Lightweight camping equipment and other specialised items are of good quality but there isn't much choice and prices tend to be high. Swaziland and Lesotho have a very limited range of consumer goods available.

TIME

All three countries use South African Standard Time (SAST), which is two hours ahead of GMT/UTC, seven hours ahead of US

Eastern Standard Time, and eight hours behind Australian Eastern Standard Time. There is no daylight saving.

ELECTRICITY
Most power systems are 220/230 V AC at 50 cycles per second. The Pretoria system is 250 V and the Port Elizabeth system is 220/250 V. Plugs have three round pins, but are not the same as the UK system. You can buy adaptors in hardware stores and some travel agencies.

WEIGHTS & MEASURES
All three countries use the metric system. See the inside back cover of this book for conversion from other units.

BOOKS
Most books are published in different editions by different publishers in different countries. As a result, a book might be a hardcover rarity in one country while it's readily available in paperback in another. Fortunately, bookshops and libraries search by title or author, so your local bookshop or library is best placed to advise you on the availability of the following recommendations.

There are a number of excellent writers who can help unlock something of the region's soul, not least Nadine Gordimer, the 1991 Nobel Prize winner. The South African publishing industry churns out high-quality coffee table books (my favourite is *The Ndebele* by Margaret Courtney Clarke, R253) and there is an increasing number of guidebooks for most activities.

Guidebooks
Satour, the national tourism organisation, used to publish very comprehensive guides covering every caravan park and hotel in the country, and you might still find outdated editions of these – they can be useful. After considerable reorganisation following the 1994 elections, Satour is again producing guides but only to hotels and guesthouses (paperback, about R28) and to B&Bs (paperback, about R28). While the new guides are

glossier they seem to be less comprehensive. Each establishment is graded, which is useful up to a point.

The Automobile Association (AA) publishes some handy paperback guides to caravan parks and hotels. They have reasonably descriptive entries but don't venture into giving opinions. Nonetheless, they're useful: the *Guide to Caravan Parks in Southern Africa* and *Guide to Hotels in Southern Africa* cost around R25 each.

The *Info Colour pages* (paperback, R39) is a glossy production, and while the accommodation and restaurants listed have paid to be in it, it does contain some useful information and transport timetables. Many more locally published guides have started to appear, but most concentrate firmly on attractions that appeal to the tastes and the pockets of white middle-class South Africans.

The paperback *Swaziland Jumbo Tourist Guide* by Hazel Hussey has some useful information hidden among the glossy ads. It's geared towards South Africans going away for weekends.

The owner of Sani Lodge, a backpacker hostel on Sani Pass, produces a handy little guide to Lesotho (about R15).

Politics & History
There are no longer any 'standard' histories of South Africa; most of the old ones have been discredited and the new ones have yet to be written. For a brief introduction, Kevin Shillington's *History of Southern Africa* (paperback, about R60) is good, although it is intended as a school text. For a more partisan, but nonetheless accurate view, *Foundations of the New South Africa* by John Pampallis (paperback, R35) was originally written as a history textbook for exiled South African students in Tanzania and gives South African history from the ANC's point of view.

A History of the African People of South Africa by Paul Maylam (paperback, about R40) is a detailed and fascinating book.

The best introduction to white South African history is *The Mind of South Africa* by Allister Sparks, (paperback, R40). It's opinionated, and some will find it controversial, but it's readable and insightful – highly recommended. Also good is *The Afrikaners – Their Last Great Trek* by Graham Leach (paperback, R40). It gives a detailed analysis of the Afrikaner people and their political development. Allister Sparks' latest book, *Tomorrow is Another Country* (paperback, R61), is the inside story of the CODESA negotiations.

For a history of the ANC, read *South Africa Belongs to Us* by Francis Meli (paperback, R68).

The 'They Fought for Freedom' series of paperbacks, published by Maskew Miller Longman, cost around R21 each and feature important figures from recent South African history, including Steve Biko, Yusef Dadoo, Ruth First, Chris Hani and Oliver Tambo. For the story (so far) of a turbulent life, read *The Lady – the Life & Times of Winnie Mandela* by Emma Gilbey (paperback R51).

If you're at all interested in the political process, buy *Election '94 South Africa*, edited by Andrew Reynolds (paperback, R40), which gives a fascinating and detailed account of the parties and the election. *Political Organisations in South Africa A-Z* by Hennie Kotze at Anneke Greyling (paperback, about R70) covers every significant political group, which can be handy if you become baffled by the acronyms. It's updated annually.

For detailed insights into the Boer side of the Anglo-Boer wars, read *Jan Smuts: Memoirs of the Boer War*, edited by Spies & Nattras (hardback, R90).

Culture

Indaba My Children (paperback, R68) is an interesting book of folk tales, history, legends, customs and beliefs, collected and told by Vusamazulu Credo Mutwa.

Religion in Africa (paperback R122), published by the David M Kennedy Centre at Princeton University, is thick and scholarly but is one of the few books that gives an overview of this subject.

In Lesotho you occasionally see booklets on various aspects of Basutho culture, often produced under the auspices of the various missions. These are worth reading because they tend to be straight descriptions or oral history, without the ideological and intellectual baggage of more scholarly texts. Two titles which are available with a bit of searching in Maseru are *Customs & Superstitions in Basutholand* by Justinus Sechefo (M10.60) and *Basutho Music & Dancing* by A G Mokhali (M5.70).

Personal Accounts

There are some books that seem to have such a powerful sense of place they become compulsory reading for foreign visitors to a country. There can be no more obvious or important example than Nelson Mandela's autobiography, *Long Road to Freedom* (hardback, R100; R500 for an autographed copy) – despite the fact that the man was behind bars for nearly three decades.

If you want to read more of Mandela's words, look for the collections of his writings and speeches in *The Struggle is My Life* and *Nelson Mandela Speaks* (paperback, about R50 each). They can be pretty dry but do offer an insight into the steadfastness of this amazing man – and also how his message was refocussed depending on the audience he addressed. He might be a hero of the people but he is also a consummate politician.

For a white perspective on the apartheid years read the excellent *My Traitor's Heart* by Rian Malan (paperback, R46). It is an outstanding autobiography of an Afrikaner attempting to come to grips with his heritage and his future. Breyten Breytenbach, a political prisoner and exile under the apartheid regime, writes of his return to South Africa in *Return to Paradise* (paperback, R45). It's a very personal and rather poetic account.

The Lost World of the Kalahari and *The Heart of the Hunter* by Laurens van der Post (paperbacks, about R45) both chronicle the author's exploration of the Kalahari and give a sympathetic interpretation of San culture. It's a poetic and thought-provoking analysis, giving an insight into the mystical relationship between nomadic hunters and their world.

Jock of the Bushveld by Sir James Percy Fitzpatrick was written in 1907 and is a vivid portrayal of the time when the country was still dependent on ox-wagons for its transport, and of the relationship between a man and his dog. It's a classic. In the same class is John Buchan's *Prester John*. It's a typical Buchan 'ripping yarn', with some interesting descriptions of people and landscape amongst the racist jingoism.

Literature

Nadine Gordimer was awarded the Nobel Prize for Literature in 1991. Her first novel, *The Lying Days*, was published in 1953. In her subsequent novels she has explored with a merciless eye South Africa, its people and their interaction. *The Conservationist* was the joint winner of the 1974 Booker Prize. Her more recent work explores the interracial dynamics of the country. Look for *July's People* and *A Sport of Nature*.

J M Coetzee is another contemporary writer who has received international acclaim; *The Life & Times of Michael K* won the 1983 Booker Prize.

Being There, edited by Robin Malan (paperback, R35), is a good introductory collection of short stories from southern African authors, including Doris Lessing and Nadine Gordimer.

The most famous exponent of the short story in South Africa is Herman Charles Bosman. He is an accessible writer and is . widely popular for stories that blend humour and pathos, and capture the essence of rural South Africa. The most popular collection is *Makeking Road*, but there are a number of compilations available. He wrote mainly in the 1930s and '40s and is reminiscent of Australia's Henry Lawson.

Alan Paton was responsible for one of the most famous South African novels, *Cry the Beloved Country* (paperback, R38), an epic that follows a black man's sufferings in a white and urban society. This was written in 1948. Paton returned to the theme of apartheid in *Ah, but Your Land is Beautiful*. André

Brink is another noted South African author worth reading.

Circles in a Forest by Dalene Mathee, translated from the Afrikaans, is a historical novel about the area around Knysna and written from the Afrikaner point of view. It's melodramatic, moving and entertaining – the story of the woodcutters and elephants who lived in the forests – a must if you spend time on the Garden Route.

As you travel around the Karoo you'll notice many old houses with plaques proclaiming them an 'Olive Schreiner house'. This writer seems to have moved house very frequently. Olive Schreiner (1855-1920) wrote *The Story of an African Farm* (published 1883) which was immediately popular and established her enduring reputation as one of South Africa's seminal novelists. Despite the novel's being adopted as part of the folk heritage of white South Africa, Olive Schreiner was a feminist, an anti-racist (to an extent) and held left-wing political views.

Literature by non-white authors is in short supply but that situation will change.

Special Interest Books

Animals *Mammals of Southern Africa* by Chris & Tilde Stuart (paperback, R70) includes a great deal of information and many excellent photos. *Whale Watching in South Africa* by Peter Best (paperback, R17) contains handy information about the leviathans you have a good chance of seeing.

Birds *Newman's Birds of Southern Africa* by Kenneth Newman (paperback, R81) is an excellent, comprehensive field guide with full-colour paintings.

Ian Sinclair's pocket-sized *Southern African Birds* (paperback, R46) is an excellent guide with colour photos, particularly suitable for a short-term visitor as it does not cover obscure birds. Sinclair's larger *Field Guide to Southern African Birds* (paperback, R76) is more comprehensive.

Flora *Southern African Trees* by Piet van Wyk (paperback, R43) is a handy little guide full of information and photos.

Namaqualand in Flower by Sima Eliovson (paperback, R60) is a detailed book on the flora of Namaqualand. It has excellent colour plates.

Reserves *Guide to Southern African Game & Nature Reserves* by Chris & Tilde Stuart (paperback, R70) gives comprehensive coverage of every game and nature reserve, with lots of maps, photos and basic information.

Surfing *Surfing in South Africa* by Mark Jury (paperback, R30) is one of the best surfing guides around, with good tips and maps. This book is out of print but you might find a secondhand copy.

Astronomy If you're from the northern hemisphere, you might want a guide to all those unfamiliar stars. There's the *Struik Pocket Guide to the Night Skies of South Africa* (paperback, R28).

Walking *Exploring Southern Africa on Foot; Guide to Hiking Trails* by Willie & Sandra Olivier (R80) doesn't cover all the trails (there are so many!) but otherwise this book is simply outstanding. Highly recommended.

The Complete Guide to Walks & Trails in Southern Africa by Jaynee Levy (hardback, R110) *does* cover all trails and contains an extraordinary amount of information. It's not a trail guide but gives you a good idea of what a walk entails in advance. It's far too big and heavy to carry.

There are lots of small books detailing walks in various areas of the country. Look for *Western Cape Walks* by David Bristow (paperback, R50) which details 70 walks of varying length and standard.

Wine *John Platter's South African Wine Guide* (paperback, R34) is updated annually and is incredibly detailed, covering all available wines. It's worth reading the introduction to the 1995 edition to feel some of the euphoria which swept the country after the elections. More down-to-earth is *The South African Plonk Buyer's Guide* by David Briggs (paperback, R17).

MAPS
South Africa
Good maps are widely available. The Map Studio series is recommended and, as always, Michelin maps are excellent.

The Map Office (☎ (011) 339 4951), 3rd Floor, Standard Bank Building, De Korte St, Braamfontein (Johannesburg), sells government topographic maps for R9 a sheet. You probably have a better chance of quick service if you deal with this shop rather than battle with the bureaucracy. The Map Office's postal address is Box 207, Wits 2050, Gauteng.

The 1:50,000 scale maps of the KwaZulu/Natal Drakensberg drawn by Peter Slingsby for the Forestry Branch of the Department of Environmental Affairs are a must for hikers. Trails are shown with detailed information for hikers, such as dangerous river crossings, distances and difficult sections. They are usually available at the various trailheads, or write to the department c/o Private Bag X447, Pretoria 0001.

Lesotho
The Department of Land Surveys & Physical Planning in Maseru sells some excellent maps of Lesotho. Best for driving is the 1:250,000 map which covers the whole country (yes, it's that small) and costs M18. For trekking or driving in very rugged areas you might want the 1:50,000 series, at about M10 each. The problem with these maps is that Lesotho's rapid programme of road building and upgrading has left them behind. Ask the friendly staff at the department for the latest information.

The maps are produced in conjunction with the British government and you can buy them in the UK from the Ordnance Survey, Romsey Rd, Southampton, SO9 4DH, UK. To order maps from Lesotho write to the Department of Land Surveys & Physical Planning, Ministry of the Interior, PO Box 876, Maseru 100, Lesotho.

Swaziland
The free maps available in various brochures and at the tourist office in Mbabane are good

enough to get around this tiny country, although if you're driving you might have to ask directions if you get off the main roads. There's a good 1:250,000 scale map available from the Surveyor-General's office at the Ministry of Works in Mbabane (PO Box 58), and if you're serious about hiking there are also 1:50,000 maps.

FILM & PHOTOGRAPHY

Films, cameras and accessories are readily available in larger towns. Processing is generally of a high standard. The approximate prices for 36-exposure films is R26 for transparencies (not including processing), R20 for colour negatives. Printing a roll of film costs about R50.

In Swaziland and Lesotho be careful about taking photos of soldiers, police, airports and government buildings. This also applies to police and defence installations in South Africa.

HEALTH

Apart from malaria and bilharzia in some areas, and the possibility of hikers drinking contaminated water, there are few health problems in these countries. Good medical care is never too far away except in the remote areas, where air evacuation of emergency cases is routine. Make sure you have enough insurance.

Travel health depends on your pre-departure preparations, your day-to-day health care while travelling and how you handle any medical problem or emergency that does develop. If you're planning to venture into less developed areas of Africa you might want to read *Staying Healthy in Asia, Africa & Latin America*, Moon Publications. This is probably the best all-round guide to carry as it's compact but very detailed and well organised. There's also *Travellers' Health* by Dr Richard Dawood (Oxford University Press). It's comprehensive, easy to read, authoritative and also highly recommended, although rather large to lug around.

Travel with Children by Maureen Wheeler is a Lonely Planet guide which includes basic advice on travel health for young children.

Problem Areas

Malaria is mainly confined to the eastern half of the region (Northern and Eastern Transvaal, northern KwaZulu/Natal and Swaziland), especially on the lowveld. Kalahari Gemsbok National Park and parts of the North-West Province might also be malarial. Bilharzia is also found mainly in the east but outbreaks do occur in other places so you should always check with knowledgeable local people before drinking water or swimming in it.

While hiking in the ex-Homelands, Lesotho or Swaziland, or wherever you find yourself drinking from streams, make sure that there isn't an upstream village, even if there is no bilharzia. Typhoid is rare but it does occur. Industrial pollution is common in more settled areas.

Medical Problems & Treatment

The number one rule in a medical emergency or serious illness is to get qualified help as soon as possible.

Sunburn Both on the lowveld and in the mountains you can get sunburnt surprisingly quickly, even through cloud. The hole in the ozone layer affects southern Africa and you risk skin cancer later in life if you are exposed to too much UV radiation. Use a sunscreen and take extra care to cover areas which don't normally see sun – eg, your feet. A hat provides added protection, and you should also use zinc cream or some other barrier cream for your nose, lips and ears. Calamine lotion is good for easing mild sunburn.

Heat Exhaustion Dehydration or salt deficiency can cause heat exhaustion. Take time to acclimatise to high temperatures and make sure you get sufficient liquids. In hot weather make sure you drink enough – don't rely on feeling thirsty to indicate when you should drink. Not needing to urinate or very dark yellow urine is a danger sign. Remember to always carry a water bottle with you on long trips. Excessive sweating can lead to loss of electrolytes (eg, salt) and therefore muscle cramping.

Salt deficiency is characterised by fatigue, lethargy, headaches, giddiness and muscle cramps and in this case salt tablets may help – much better, however, are rehydration mixes which are available from chemists. Sports drinks are fine for mild cases. Vomiting or diarrhoea can deplete your liquid and salt levels. Anhydrotic heat exhaustion, caused by an inability to sweat, is quite rare. Unlike other forms of heat exhaustion it is likely to strike people who'e been in a hot climate for some time.

Heat Stroke This serious, potentially fatal, condition can occur if the body's heat-regulating mechanism breaks down and the body temperature rises to dangerous levels. Long, continuous periods of exposure to high temperatures can leave you vulnerable to heat stroke.

Avoid excessive alcohol or strenuous activity when you first arrive in a hot climate.

The symptoms are feeling unwell, not sweating very much or at all and a high body temperature (39°C to 41°C). Where sweating has ceased the skin becomes flushed and red. Severe, throbbing headaches and lack of coordination will also occur, and the sufferer

---

Predeparture Preparations

If you wear glasses take a spare pair and your prescription. Losing your glasses is a major hassle but there are plenty of optometrists in South Africa where you can get new spectacles.

If you use a particular medication regularly, take the prescription or, better still, part of the packaging showing the generic rather than the brand name (which may not be locally available), as it will make getting replacements easier. South Africa tends to sell drugs over-the-counter which would require a prescription in some other countries, but it's still a wise idea to have a legible prescription with you to show that you legally use the medication.

Vaccinations Assuming that you are up to date with your boosters for the standard childhood vaccinations such as TB, polio and tetanus, no additional vaccinations are essential. Off the beaten track typhoid is a possibility (as it is almost everywhere) so make sure your vaccination is current. If you're planning to spend time in remote villages a hepatitis shot might not be a bad idea.

People who have travelled through the yellow-fever zone in Africa (or South America) must have an International Certificate of Vaccination against yellow fever before entering South Africa.

Health Insurance A travel-insurance policy to cover theft, loss and medical problems is a wise idea. Although there are excellent private hospitals in South Africa, the public health system is underfunded and overcrowded and is not free. Services such as ambulances are often run by private enterprise and are expensive. If you suffer a major illness or injury in the ex-Homelands, Swaziland or Lesotho you might want to use your air-evacuation cover. There is a wide variety of policies and your travel agent will have recommendations. The international student travel policies handled by STA or other student travel organisations are usually good value. Check the small print:

- some policies specifically exclude 'dangerous activities' which can include scuba diving, motorcycling, even trekking. If such activities are on your agenda you don't want that sort of policy.

- You may prefer a policy which pays doctors or hospitals directly rather than you having to pay on the spot and claim later. If you have to claim later make sure you keep all documentation. Some policies ask you to call back (reversing the charges) to a centre in your home country where an immediate assessment of your problem is made.

- Check if the policy covers ambulances or an emergency flight home. If you have to stretch out you will need two seats and somebody has to pay for them! ∎

may be confused or aggressive. Eventually the victim will become delirious or convulse. Hospitalisation is essential, but meanwhile get patients out of the sun, remove their clothing, cover them with a wet sheet or towel and then fan them continually.

Cold Too much cold is just as dangerous as too much heat, particularly if it leads to hypothermia.

Hypothermia occurs when the body loses heat faster than it can produce it and the core temperature of the body falls. It is surprisingly easy to progress from very cold to dangerously cold due to a combination of wind, wet clothing, fatigue and hunger, even if the air temperature is above freezing. It is best to dress in layers; silk, wool and some of the new artificial fibres are all good insulating materials. A hat is important, as a lot of heat is lost through the head. A strong, waterproof outer layer is essential, as keeping dry is vital. Carry basic supplies, including food containing simple sugars to generate heat quickly, and lots of fluid to drink.

Symptoms of hypothermia are exhaustion, numb skin (particularly toes and fingers), shivering, slurred speech, irrational or violent behaviour, lethargy, stumbling, dizzy spells, muscle cramps and violent bursts of energy. Irrationality may take the form of sufferers claiming they are warm and trying to take off their clothes.

To treat hypothermia, first get the patient out of the wind and/or rain, remove any wet clothing and replace it with dry, warm clothing. Give them hot liquids – not alcohol – and some high-kilojoule, easily digestible food. This should be enough for the early stages of hypothermia, but if it has gone further it may be necessary to place the victim in a warm sleeping bag and get in with them. Do not rub patients, place them near a fire or remove their wet clothes in the wind. If possible, place a sufferer in a warm (not hot) bath.

Malaria This serious disease is spread by mosquito bites. If you are travelling in endemic areas it is extremely important to take malarial prophylactics. Symptoms include headaches, fever, chills and sweating which may subside and recur. Without treatment malaria can develop more serious, potentially fatal effects. Antimalarial drugs do not actually prevent the disease but suppress its symptoms. Consult your doctor for advice on the prophylactic most suitable for southern Africa.

A considerable part of the South African population live in malarial areas and many more people travel to them, so South African doctors and chemists have good information and advice. You don't need a prescription to buy some prophylactics. The most usual is Dramal (chloroquin), sold in packets of 20 for about R22.

When travelling in malarial areas the main messages are:

1. Avoid being bitten! Mosquitoes that transmit malaria bite from dusk to dawn and during this period travellers are advised to:
   - wear light-coloured clothing
   - wear long pants and long-sleeved shirts
   - use mosquito repellents containing the compound DEET on exposed areas avoid highly scented perfumes or aftershave
   - use a mosquito net – it may be worth taking your own

2. While no antimalarial is 100% effective, taking the most appropriate drug significantly reduces the risk of contracting the disease.

3. No one should ever die from malaria. It can be diagnosed by a simple blood test. Symptoms range from fever, chills and sweating, headache and abdominal pains to a vague feeling of ill-health, so seek examination immediately if there is any suggestion of malaria.

Contrary to popular belief, once a traveller contracts malaria he/she does not have it for life. One of the parasites may lie dormant in the liver but this can also be eradicated using a specific medication. Malaria is curable, as long as the traveller seeks medical help when symptoms occur.

Bilharzia Bilharzia is carried in water by minute worms. The larvae infect certain varieties of freshwater snails found in rivers, streams, lakes and, particularly, dams. The worms multiply and are eventually discharged into the water surrounding the snails.

The worm enters through the skin, and the first symptom may be a tingling and sometimes a light rash around the area where it entered. The worm eventually attaches itself to your intestines or bladder, where it produces large numbers of eggs. Weeks later, when the worm is busy producing eggs, a high fever may develop. A general feeling of being unwell may be the first symptom; once the disease is established, abdominal pain and blood in the urine are other signs.

Avoiding swimming or bathing in fresh water where bilharzia is present is the main method of preventing the disease. If you do get wet dry off quickly and dry your clothes as well. Seek medical attention if you have been exposed to the disease and tell the doctor your suspicions, as bilharzia in the early stages can be confused with malaria or typhoid.

Sexually Transmitted Diseases Sexual contact with an infected sexual partner spreads these diseases. While abstinence is the only 100% preventive, using condoms is also effective. Gonorrhoea and syphilis are the most common of these diseases; sores, blisters or rashes around the genitals, discharges or pain when urinating are common symptoms. Symptoms may be less marked or not observed at all in women. Syphilis symptoms eventually disappear completely but the disease continues and can cause severe problems in later years. The treatment of gonorrhoea and syphilis is by antibiotics.

There are numerous other sexually transmitted diseases, for most of which effective treatment is available. However, there is no cure for herpes or AIDS.

HIV/AIDS HIV (Human Immunodeficiency Virus) may develop into AIDS (Acquired Immune Deficiency Syndrome). Any exposure to blood, blood products or bodily fluids may put the individual at risk. In many developing countries transmission is predominantly through heterosexual sexual activity. Apart from abstinence, the most effective preventive is always to practise safe sex using condoms. It is impossible to detect the HIV-positive status of an otherwise healthy-looking person without a blood test.

South Africa, Lesotho and Swaziland are probably not as badly affected by AIDS as some areas of Africa and a belated public awareness campaign has begun. However, AIDS is certainly present and possibly widespread in the heterosexual community.

Water Purification
Practically everywhere in this region high-quality water is available and you need not fear drinking from taps. Hikers drinking from streams might be at risk of water-borne diseases (eg, gastroenteritis or, rarely, typhoid) especially if they take water downstream of unsewered villages.

The simplest way of purifying water is to boil it thoroughly for 10 minutes. At high altitude water boils at a lower temperature, so germs are less likely to be killed.

Simple filtering doesn't remove all dangerous organisms, so if you cannot boil water it should be treated chemically. Chlorine tablets (Puritabs, Steritabs or other brand names) will kill many but not all nasties, including giardia and amoebic cysts. Iodine is very effective in purifying water and is available in tablet form (such as Potable Aqua), but follow the directions carefully and remember that too much iodine can be harmful.

If you can't find tablets, use tincture of iodine (2%). Four drops of tincture of iodine per litre or quart of clear water is the recommended dosage; the treated water should be left to stand for 20 to 30 minutes before drinking. Iodine crystals (dangerous things to have around) can also be used to purify water but this is a more complicated process, as you have to first prepare a saturated iodine solution. ■

Snakes To minimise your chances of being bitten by snakes always wear boots, socks and long trousers when walking through undergrowth where snakes may be present. Don't put your hands into holes and crevices, and be careful when collecting firewood.

Snake bites do not cause instantaneous death and antivenins are usually available. Keep the victim calm and still, wrap the bitten limb very tightly, as you would for a sprained ankle, and attach a splint to immobilise it. Then seek medical help, if possible with the dead snake for identification. Don't attempt to catch the snake if there is even a remote possibility of being bitten; the victim must not blunder around trying to catch the snake. Tourniquets and sucking out the poison are now comprehensively discredited.

Although reaching medical assistance is of paramount importance, weigh up the dangers of moving the victim. The tightly wrapped bandage means that the poison enters his/her system slowly and, hopefully, at a rate their body can cope with. If the victim is moved their blood circulation will speed up, delivering large doses of poison.

Leeches & Ticks Leeches may be present in damp forests; they attach themselves to your skin to suck your blood. Trekkers often get them on their legs or in their boots. Salt or a lighted cigarette end will make them fall off. Do not pull them off, as the bite is then more likely to become infected. An insect repellent may keep them away. Vaseline, alcohol or oil will persuade a tick to let go. You should always check your body if you have been walking through a tick-infested area (practically any scrubland, even in city limits – such as Table Mountain in Cape Town), as they can spread typhus. Apparently ticks like to congregate under camel thorn trees.

Women's Health
Gynaecological Problems Poor diet, lowered resistance due to the use of antibiotics for stomach upsets and even contraceptive pills can lead to vaginal infections when travelling in hot climates. Keeping the genital area clean, and wearing skirts or loose-fitting trousers and cotton underwear will help to prevent infections.

Yeast infections, characterised by a rash, itch and discharge, can be treated with a vinegar or even lemon juice douche or with natural yoghurt. Nystatin suppositories are the usual medical prescription. Trichomonas is a more serious infection; symptoms are a discharge and a burning sensation when urinating, and if a vinegar water douche is not effective, medical attention should be sought. Flagyl is the prescribed drug. Male sexual partners must also be treated.

Pregnancy Most miscarriages occur during the first three months of pregnancy, so this is the most risky time to travel. The last three months should also be spent within reasonable distance of good medical care, as quite serious problems can develop at this time. Pregnant women should avoid all unnecessary medication, but vaccinations and malarial prophylactics should still be taken where possible – ask a doctor. Additional care should be taken to prevent illness and particular attention should be paid to diet and nutrition.

WOMEN TRAVELLERS
Most South African men, whatever their colour, have sexism in common. People who do anything technical or physical (including sport) are inevitably referred to as 'guys', serious newspapers have 'pretty miss' photos and you'll be expected to take a serious interest in beauty contests, of which there are many. Until recently, modelling was one of the few prestigious careers open to most South African women. If you want to find out what life for women was like in Western countries in the '50s, talk to well-off white women in South Africa.

New-fangled ideas such as the equality of the sexes haven't filtered through to many people, especially away from the cities. Although attitudes are more liberal in the cities, the statistics for sexual assault are horrendous, and they are particularly bad in the black townships. Common sense and caution, particularly at night, are essential.

A non-black woman travelling alone is a rarity (not being married sets you apart, for a start). This gives single women a curiosity value that makes them conspicuous, but will also bring forth numerous generous offers of assistance and hospitality. It is always difficult to quantify the risk of assault – and there is one – but plenty of women do travel alone and safely in southern Africa.

Obviously the risk varies depending on where you go and what you do. Hitching alone is extremely foolhardy, for instance. Particularly in the current environment of rapid change, the best advice on what can and can't be undertaken safely will come from local women. Unfortunately, many white women are likely to be appalled at the idea of lone travel and will do their best to discourage you with horrendous stories, often of dubious accuracy.

What risks there are, however, are significantly reduced if two women travel together or, even better, if a woman travels as part of a mixed-sex couple or group. However you travel, especially inland and in the more traditional black communities, it's best to behave conservatively. On the coast, casual dress (and undress) is the norm, but elsewhere dress modestly (full-length clothes that aren't too tight) if you do not wish to draw attention to yourself.

In traditional black cultures, women often have a very tough time, but this is changing to some extent because a surprising number of girls have the opportunity to stay at school while the boys are sent away to work.

In the ex-Homelands, Lesotho and Swaziland, many of the staff in tourist offices, government departments and so on are well-educated black women. It's worth talking to them to get their perspective on the region's problems. In South Africa, affirmative action programmes mean that counter staff in some government offices are black women, whose outlook on life can be much closer to yours than that of the manicured white staff.

DANGERS & ANNOYANCES

Throughout the region keep in mind the natural dangers, from freezing storms in the Drakensberg to crippling heat on the lowveld. Bilharzia isn't the only danger in the water – crocodiles and hippos can be deadly. Be careful near any lowveld stream.

Animals

Crocodiles are now rare but they do occur in lowveld rivers and streams. Hippos can also be very dangerous. If you meet one (most likely on and near the KwaZulu/Natal north coast) do not approach it and be prepared to get away or up a tree very fast. Lions, rhinos and elephants are very unlikely to be encountered when you are walking, but take seriously the warning not to leave your vehicle in wildlife reserves.

Out of the water, venomous snakes are a potential problem (see the earlier Health section), but by far the biggest threat is posed by manic drivers.

South Africa

Crime rates in the cities are soaring and some crime is pretty nasty. Be very careful at night and bear in mind that daylight muggings are not uncommon in parts of Johannesburg.

The large-scale political violence that gave South Africa such a bad reputation in the months and years leading up to the 1994 election has all but vanished. However, it's a moot point whether being attacked in a township is a result of political, antisocial or criminal motives. It would be unwise for an outsider of any race to venture into a township without knowing the current situation and, usually, without a guide.

Incidents such as taxi wars (between rival minibus taxi companies) have lead to massacres. Once again, it's a matter of knowing the current situation and avoiding being in the wrong place at the wrong time. There are very, very few wrong places and times.

Most blacks aren't racist, but in some circumstances it doesn't hurt to make it clear you are not South African.

Survival Tactics

None of these countries is particularly dangerous, especially compared to other African countries – or even North America. However, in the cities you should be cautious. Johannesburg is earning a reputation as the mugging capital of southern Africa and some of the crime is violent. There are some simple rules that should help keep you out of trouble in big cities.

- Never carry anything you can't afford to lose
- Never look like you might be carrying valuables (wearing an extravagant T-shirt makes you look just as rich as wearing jewellery or a suit does)
- Avoid groups of young men; trust older mixed-sex groups
- Always have some money to give if you are mugged
- Don't resist muggers
- Listen to local advice on unsafe areas
- Avoid deserted areas (such as downtown on weekends) even in daylight

Unfortunately, the most effective tactics are the most difficult for newcomers to use:

- Don't look apprehensive or lost
- Don't assume that everyone is out to get you
- Make friends!

Lesotho

The last Friday of the month is when many people are paid, and by mid-afternoon some towns become like street parties. These can be fun but as the day wears on some of the drunks become depressingly familiar to an Australian – over-friendly, boisterous and ultimately aggressive. In Maseru this phenomenon usually expresses itself as a big night in the discos, but be careful.

Outside a few large towns crime is negligible and aggressive racism almost unheard of.

Swaziland

Street crime in Mbabane and Manzini is rising so take common-sense precautions such as being careful at night and not walking home drunk. Elsewhere, courtesy and respect for local customs are all that is required.

The permitted blood-alcohol level for drivers is 0.15%, triple that of many other countries, so watch out for drunk drivers.

DRUGS

Marijuana was an important commodity in the Xhosa's trade with the San. Today *dagga* or *zol* is illegal but widely available. There are heavy penalties for use and possession but it's estimated that the majority of black men smoke the drug. The legal system doesn't distinguish between soft and hard drugs which are increasingly available.

ACTIVITIES
Organised Activities & Tours

With increasing numbers of foreign visitors, many outfits aimed at the 'adventure' or 'eco' market are appearing. They offer a range of activities, such as hiking, canoeing and rafting, and some have trips into other African countries. There are plenty of options, so shop around. We've had many good and a few bad reports from travellers who have tried some of these outfits. The bad reports seem to stem mainly from the operators' inexperience, so hopefully they will have either learnt or gone out of business by the time you arrive. The best way to find out who is currently reliable is to ask other travellers.

In addition to longer trips there are a lot of smaller outfits offering day trips and these can be excellent. Cape Town in particular offers interesting activities, but keep your eyes open everywhere.

Hostels often take bookings for adventure activities and travel, but remember that a particular hostel might have an agreement with a particular company. See what the others are offering. Also, it might be possible to book larger companies through a travel agent in your home country.

Some of the larger companies include African Routes (☎ (031) 83 3348, fax 83 7234) and Drifters (☎ (011) 888 1160). Smaller operators include Bundu Bus (☎ (011) 693 1621), with five-day tours of Eastern Transvaal and Kruger National Park for R450. For something a little different, see what you can arrange with Max Maximum Tours (☎ (011) 933 4177). Max runs Soweto tours (he lives there) but has proved useful to budget travellers wanting to negotiate longer trips.

'Footprints that's all we leave behind Pty Ltd' is the long-winded name of a company that has been operating low-impact hiking, walking and cultural tours in Namibia and Botswana for some years. They have recently expanded in South Africa and

Mozambique. The emphasis is on staying in villages (and some townships in South Africa). It sounds very interesting and well worth checking out. Most of their tours run for one or three weeks, and you can arrange a package that includes flights from Holland (tours are Dutch and English-speaking). Make reservations through their Johannesburg office (☎ (011) 792 2664), PO Box 1522, Ferndale, 2160 or their HQ in Utrecht, Holland (☎ (030) 300038, fax 34 3213).

Hiking
South Africa South Africa has an excellent system of hiking trails, usually with accommodation. They are popular and most must be booked well in advance. Satour's brochure on hiking is useful and if you plan to do a lot of hiking pick up a copy of Jaynee Levy's *Complete Guide to Walks & Trails in Southern Africa* (hardback, R110).

There are also many hiking clubs; contact

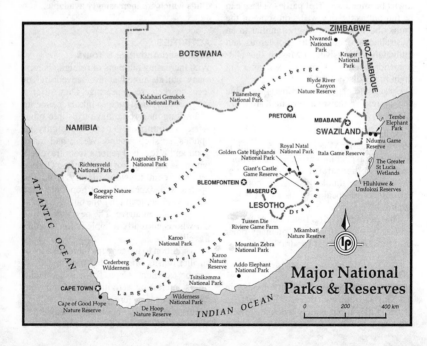

Major National Parks & Reserves

the Hiking Federation of South Africa (☎ (011) 886 6507), 420 Nedbank Centre, Bordeaux, Johannesburg. Several of the adventure travel outfits offer organised hikes. The National Hiking Way Board (☎ (012) 310 3839, 299 9111) is slowly developing a nationwide network of trails.

Most trails are administered by the National Parks Board or the various Forest Regions, although the Natal Parks Board controls most trails in KwaZulu/Natal. Some of the best known trails and addresses for booking are:

KwaZulu/Natal

Giant's Cup – up to five days in the southern Drakensberg. Natal Parks Board, PO Box 662, Pietermaritzburg 3200 (☎ (0331) 47 1981). There are also 'wilderness trails', guided walks, in Umfolozi, Mkuzi and St Lucia National Parks. Natal Parks Board.

Eastern Transvaal

Blyderivierspoort – up to five days in the Blyde River Gorge area. The Officer-in-Charge, Blyde River Canyon Nature Reserve, Private Bag X431, Graskop 1270 (☎ (01315) 81216 or 41058). Kruger National Park – there are 'wilderness trails', guided walks, in this national park. National Parks Board.

Northern Transvaal

Soutpansberg – up to four days in the Soutpansberg range. Forestry Branch, Northern Transvaal office, Private Bag X2431, Louis Trichardt 0920 (☎ (01551) 2201). Mabudashango – four days in ex-Venda. Department of Agriculture & Forestry, Private Bag X2247, Sibasa 0970 (☎ (015581) 31211).

Orange Free State

Rhebok – two days in Golden Gate Highlands National Park. National Parks Board.

Western Cape

Outeniqua – up to eight days in indigenous forest near Knysna. Regional Director, Southern Cape Forest Region, Private Bag X12, Knysna 6570 (☎ (0445) 23037). Otter Trail – five days on the coast in Garden Route. National Parks Board.

Eastern Cape

Wild Coast – three five-day sections along the Transkei coast. Nature Conservation Division, Agriculture & Forestry Department, Private Bag X5002, Umtata, Eastern Cape (☎ (0471) 31 2711). Amatola – up to six days in ex-Ciskei. Contour, PO Box 186, Bisho, Eastern Cape (☎ (0401) 95 2115).

There are many, many other trails. The following wilderness areas offer superb hiking in remote areas with few facilities. Some of them include:

Cederberg Wilderness Area, Western Cape. Contact Chief Nature Conservator, Cederberg State Forest, Private bag X1, Citrusdal 7340 (☎ (022) 921 2289).

Mkhomazi, Mdedlelo & Mzimkulu Wilderness Areas, KwaZulu/Natal Drakensberg. Contact Natal Parks Board.

Ntendeka Wilderness Area, KwaZulu/Natal. Contact State Forester, Ngome State Forest, Private Bag X21306 Vryheid 3100 (☎ (0386) 71883).

Lesotho Other than a few suggested walks in Sehlabathebe National Park, Lesotho has no formal hiking trails. However, the whole country is available for trekkers and the rugged mountains offer great wilderness hiking. There are scattered towns and villages where you can often arrange accommodation. See the Lesotho Facts for the Visitor chapter for details.

Swaziland There are good hiking trails in the Malolotja Nature Reserve and others are being developed in the Mlawula Nature Reserve. Phone ☎ 61178 for bookings, or see the National Trust Commission in the National Museum, Lobamba. It's possible to walk through most of the country as long as you respect crops and always ask permission before you camp.

Air Sports

Flying, hang-gliding, ballooning and parachuting are popular activities. Table Mountain in Cape Town must be one of the most beautiful hang-gliding sites, but there are numerous possibilities along the escarpment and particularly in the Drakensberg. Flying lessons are cheap on an international scale, and flying conditions are superb. Learner pilots are attracted from around the world.

Speak to Satour for more details, or contact the Aeroclub of South Africa (☎ (011) 805 0366), PO Box 1993, 1685 Halfway House.

Animal Viewing in National Parks & Reserves

	Addo Elephant National Park	Giant's Castle Game Reserve	Hluhluwe/ Umfolozi Game Reserve	Itala Game Reserve	Kalahari Gemsbok National Park
Antelope (many species)					
Baboon					
Bat-eared fox					
Black rhino	✔		✔	✔	
Black wildebeest		✔			
Black-backed jackal					✔
Blesbok		✔			
Blue wildebeest			✔		✔
Brown hyena				✔	✔
Buffalo	✔		✔		
Bushbuck	✔	✔			
Cape clawless otter					
Cape Mountain zebra					
Cheetah			✔	✔	✔
Duiker	✔			✔	✔
Eland	✔	✔			✔
Elephant	✔		✔		
Gemsbok					✔
Giraffe			✔		
Grysbok	✔				
Hippo					
Hyena					✔
Hyrax		✔			
Impala			✔	✔	
Jackal					
Kalahari lion					✔
Klipspringer		✔			
Kudu	✔		✔	✔	
Leopard			✔	✔	✔
Lion			✔		
Mountain reedbuck					
Mountain zebra					
Nyala			✔	✔	
Oribi		✔			
Red hartebeest	✔	✔			✔
Reedbuck		✔		✔	
Rhebok		✔			
Spotted hyena			✔		✔
Springbok					✔
Steenbok					✔
Vervet monkey					
Waterbuck			✔	✔	
White rhino			✔	✔	
Wild dog					✔
Zebra			✔	✔	

This table is not exhaustive – it lists only the more numerous animals and doesn't cover all parks

Karoo National Park	Kruger National Park	Mkhaya Nature Reserve	Pilanesberg National Park	Tsitsikamma National Park	Tsolwana Game Reserve
	✔				
				✔	
✔	✔				
	✔	✔	✔		
					✔
					✔
		✔			
			✔		
	✔				
				✔	
				✔	
✔					
	✔		✔		
✔	✔	✔	✔		
✔	✔		✔		✔
	✔	✔	✔		
	✔				
			✔		
				✔	
	✔				
✔		✔	✔		
	✔		✔		
	✔				
✔					
✔					✔
✔					
✔		✔			✔
				✔	
		✔			
	✔		✔		✔
	✔	✔	✔		✔

Birdwatching

With 900 species of birds, 113 of which are endemic, South Africa is a paradise for birdwatchers. The regional variation is huge so keen birdwatchers should aim to cover a range of habitats – Kruger National Park is particularly renowned. Even those with a passing interest will find that binoculars and a field guide are worthwhile investments.

There are birdwatching clubs in the major cities.

Canoeing & Rafting

South Africa is a dry country and it has few major rivers by international standards. This limits the canoeing and rafting potential, but there are, nonetheless, some interesting possibilities. The Orange River is the giant among South African rivers, running west across the country for 2340 km. Other major rivers include the Tugela (KwaZulu/Natal), the Komati (Eastern Transvaal and Swaziland) and the Olifants, Berg and Breede (Western Cape).

Rafting and canoeing trips on the Orange River in the far north-west, where it forms the border with Namibia, have become very popular. The main attraction is that you float through a beautiful desert wilderness; the rapids are not demanding. The river passes between lush banks surrounded by desert and the high, dry Richtersveld mountains.

The Tugela offers rather more challenging rafting, although it is highly variable depending on the rainfall. It is at its best from late December to mid-March.

Two rafting operators who have been highly recommended for quality and environmental responsibility are: Felix Unite with offices in Johannesburg (☎ (011) 463 3167, fax 706 6115) and Cape Town (☎ (021) 762 6935, fax 761 9259); and River Runners with offices in Johannesburg (☎ (011) 403 2512, fax 339 1380) and Cape Town (☎ (021) 762 2350). A four-day trip on the Orange River will cost around R700; a six-day trip will cost around R900.

Canoeists should contact the SA Canoe Federation, PO Box 1069, Durban 4000.

Diving

The KwaZulu/Natal north coast, particularly around Sodwana Bay, offers excellent warm-water diving and there are some good reefs. In addition, most resort towns along Western Cape's Garden Route have diving schools.

Fishing & Hunting

Sea fishing is a popular pastime and there is a wide range of species in the warm and cold currents which flow past the east and west coasts. River fishing, especially for introduced trout, is popular in parks and reserves, with some good highland streams in Lesotho. You usually need a licence, generally available for a few rand at the park office. In some places equipment is available for hire.

Hunting is a bit of a misnomer. It is generally conducted as part of the annual cull in private game reserves and as most of these are small, the animals don't stand much of a chance. Still, hunting is tremendously popular and many more people apply to take part in the culls than there are places available. The other version of hunting involves paying enormous fees to shoot just about anything you want in private reserves.

Horse-Riding

Many places, including some national parks, offer horse-riding. There are overnight and longer trails. Pony trekking in Lesotho offers the best chance to go on a long ride.

Rock Climbing

There are some challenging climbs, especially in the KwaZulu/Natal Drakensberg and over the escarpment in Lesotho. Contact the Mountain Club of South Africa, 97 Hatfield St, Cape Town 8001 for addresses of regional clubs. In Johannesburg there's the South African Climbers Club, 71 12th St, Parkhurst 2153.

Surfing

South Africa has some of the best, least crowded surfing in the world. Most surfers will have heard of Jeffreys Bay, but there are myriad alternatives, particularly along the east and south coasts. The best time of the year for surfing in Natal, Transkei and the south-eastern Cape is early winter – April to July.

Boards and surfing gear can be bought in most of the big coastal cities. New boards sell for R700 to R900; good quality second-hand boards for R250 to R600. A Rip Curl steamer sells for about R400. It's now out of print but you might find a secondhand copy of *Surfing in Southern Africa* by Mark Jury, which has excellent practical information on when and where to go. If you plan to surf Jeffreys Bay you'll need a decent-sized board – it's a big, very fast wave.

Vineyards

The valleys to the east of Cape Town have some of the best and most beautiful vineyards in the world. First planted at the end of the 17th century, they have thrived in an ideal climate. The buildings are typical of Cape Dutch architecture and the surrounding mountains are superb. The classic tourist promotional material, showing rows of immaculately tended vines, and a white-washed, thatched homestead overshadowed by blue mountains, is a reality.

The wine itself is cheap and of a high standard. Most vineyards and wineries are open to the public and have free tastings. If you buy at the vineyard, good quality wine can be bought for less than R10, but an average figure would be from R15 to R25. If you have a vague interest, they can absorb a couple of days. If you are really interested you'll need at least a week. Numerous tours are available from Cape Town.

Wildlife Safaris

South Africa can boast very well organised national parks and reserves. Rest camps in game reserves are built within protected enclosures, the roads are of a high standard, and it is easy to tour them in a private car. There are a large number of privately owned

---

The KwaZulu/Natal Surf Scene

Durban and the KwaZulu/Natal coast has a surf culture, quality and history to match anywhere in the world. It is the home of true legends like Shaun Tomson and up-and-comers like (hotdogger deluxe) Frankie Oberholzer.

'Town' itself is a smorgasbord of quality breaks, all best when the sou'wester blows. South Beach and Addington are normally the best beginner spots, but with the right swell they can throw some gaping barrels. Wedge Reef, next to Old West Street Pier can be testy, while Dairy Pier has the best left-hander of the lot. New Pier, North Beach, Bay of Plenty and Snake Park can be long and hollow, often with picture perfect right-handers breaking off the piers.

In July, North Beach is the home of the Gunston 500, the feature event of the Ocean Africa Festival. Ocean Africa is a unique extravaganza encompassing every beach activity possible, including night surfing, beauty contests, fashion shows, beer tents, bands and stands selling everything imaginable. The turnout is usually huge and the action on the beach rivals that in the water. Joe Kool's and the Cattleman, right on North Beach, are the most popular after-surfing 'jols'.

The northern town beaches, Battery and Tekweni, can also have quality waves with less crowds. Further north are breaks too numerous to mention. The pick of these are Westbrook (arguably the hollowest wave around), Ballito Bay and Zinkwazi.

The Bluff, just south of Durban, has some good spots with the infamous Cave Rock being its showpiece. Often compared with Hawaii's Backdoor, The Rock is for experienced surfers only.

The KwaZulu/Natal Coast really comes into its own south from the Bluff. The best time is winter, from April to August, before 10 or 11 am, when you're basically guaranteed a north-west land breeze. The solid groundswells roll in from the south, hitting Greenpoint, Scottsburgh, Happy Wanderers and The Spot (all right-handers) at a perfect angle. Each produces incredibly rideable four to eight-foot-plus grinders over rock and sand bottom, with the occasional couple-of-hundred-metre rides. Plenty of barrels are to be had, but check with locals to be safe. Further south are more right-hand points right along the Transkei coast with plenty of quality waves in between.

Patrick Moroney

game reserves where tours are conducted in open vehicles. For visitors without their own transport, many companies arrange coach tours.

Springbok Atlas (☎ (011) 493 3780) is a large national operator with numerous tours. They're not cheap, but they do have a good reputation. Three days in Kruger National Park will cost around R 1770/2700 for one/two people.

Connex Travel (☎ (011) 884 8110) is another large coach tour operator, with similar rates. Unless you really want to go on a tour it would be much cheaper to visit Kruger in a hire car. Papadi Tours (☎ (011) 958 1373) will organise individual itineraries for small groups.

We haven't had any feedback on Mac Safaris (☎ (011) 315 0921), but their price is right. A tour of Kruger from Johannesburg, including three nights in the park, costs about R500.

Another new outfit with good credentials is the Bundu Bus (☎ (011) 693 1621). Bundu Bus has five-day tours of Eastern Transvaal and Kruger National Park for R450. Several other adventure travel outfits aiming at the backpacker market offer safaris.

Mountain Biking

South Africans have discovered mountain biking and have taken to it in a big way. Some reserves and parks are putting in mountainbike trails.

There are quite a few outfits around that organise trips. One which was recommended to me is Casual Adventures (☎ (011) 650 7090, (012) 998 5963, fax (012) 98 2591, e-mail rowan@ilink.nis.za), PO Box 99856 Garsfontein, Pretoria 0042. Casual Adventures organises some interesting day, overnight and longer bike rides. You'll pay around R200 for day rides and R250 a day for longer rides in most areas of the country, such as the Drakensberg, the Cederberg, the Western Cape winelands, Eastern Transvaal, the Garden Route etc. Some trips involve rafting as well. There's a more expensive but very tempting ride in some of the private game reserves adjoining Kruger National Park. See the Big Five from your saddle!

There's a minimum of five or six people on overnight rides, but there's a regular calendar of rides and individuals can join in. On some trips you need your own bike, but Casual Adventures will rent you one if necessary.

Getting There & Away

This chapter gives general information on the various methods of travelling to southern Africa, and how to go about finding the ticket(s) that will suit you. For specific information on travel to and from South Africa, Lesotho or Swaziland, see those countries' Getting There & Away chapters. Those chapters also cover travel between the three countries.

However you're travelling, it's worth taking out travel insurance. Work out what you need. You may not want to insure that grotty old army surplus backpack – but everyone should be covered for the worst possible case: an accident, for example, that will require hospital treatment and a flight home. It's a good idea to make a copy of your policy, in case the original is lost.

If you are planning to travel for a long time, the insurance may seem very expensive – but if you can't afford it, you certainly won't be able to afford to deal with a medical emergency overseas.

AIR

About 50 airlines now fly to South Africa, a great increase on the handful that flew here during the apartheid days. However, southern Africa still isn't exactly a hub of international travel. Airfares to or from Europe, North America and Australia certainly reflect that. About the only relief you'll get are fares for the low season which fortunately coincides with the nicest weather anyway. The region's main international airport is in Johannesburg but there are an increasing number of flights to Cape Town and a few to Durban.

Low-season fares to southern Africa from Europe and North America are typically applicable in April and May while the high season is between July and September. The rest of the year, with the exception of several weeks around Christmas, which is considered high season, falls into the shoulder season category.

Buying a Plane Ticket

The plane ticket will probably be the single most expensive item in your budget, and buying it can be an intimidating business. There is likely to be a multitude of airlines and travel agents hoping to separate you from your money. It is always worth putting aside a few hours to research the current state of the market.

Start early; some of the cheapest tickets have to be bought months in advance, and some popular flights sell out early. Talk to other recent travellers – they may be able to stop you making some of the same old mistakes. Look at the ads in newspapers and magazines (not forgetting the press of the ethnic group whose country you plan to visit), consult reference books and watch for special offers. Then phone around travel agents for bargains. (Airlines can supply information on routes and timetables; however, except at times of inter-airline war they do not supply the cheapest tickets.) Find out the fare, the route, the duration of the journey and any restrictions on the ticket. (See restrictions in the Air Travel Glossary at the back of this book.) Then sit back and decide which is best for you.

You may discover that those impossibly cheap flights are 'fully booked, but we have another one that costs a bit more...' Or the flight is on an airline notorious for its poor safety standards and leaves you in the world's least favourite airport in mid-journey for 14 hours. Or they claim only to have the last two seats available for that country for the whole of July, which they will hold for you for a maximum of two hours. Don't panic – keep ringing around.

Use the fares quoted in this book as a guide only. They are approximate and based on the rates advertised by travel agents at the time of going to press. Also, quoted airfares do not necessarily constitute a recommendation for the carrier.

If you're travelling from the UK or the

USA, you'll probably find that the cheapest flights are being advertised by obscure bucket shops whose names haven't yet reached the telephone directory. Many such firms are honest and solvent, but there are a few rogues who will take your money and disappear, to reopen elsewhere a month or two later under a new name. If you feel suspicious about a firm, don't give them all the money at once – leave a deposit of 20% or so and pay the balance when you get the ticket. If they insist on cash in advance, go somewhere else. And once you have the ticket, ring the airline to confirm that you are actually booked onto the flight.

You may decide to pay more than the rock-bottom fare by opting for the safety of a better known travel agent. Firms such as STA, which has offices worldwide, Council Travel in the USA or Travel CUTS in Canada are not going to disappear overnight, leaving you clutching a receipt for a nonexistent ticket and they do offer good prices to most destinations.

Once you have your ticket, write the number down, together with the flight number and other details, and keep the information somewhere separate. If the ticket is lost or stolen, this will help you get a replacement.

It's sensible to buy travel insurance as early as possible. If you buy it the week before you fly, you may find, for example, that you're not covered for delays to your flight caused by industrial action.

Air Travellers with Special Needs

If you have special needs of any sort – you've broken a leg, you're vegetarian, travelling in a wheelchair, taking the baby, terrified of flying – you should let the airline know as soon as possible so that they can make arrangements accordingly. You should remind them when you reconfirm your booking (at least 72 hours before departure) and again when you check in at the airport. It may also be worth ringing round the airlines before you make your booking to find out how they can handle your particular needs.

Airports and airlines can be surprisingly helpful, but they do need advance warning.

Most international airports will provide escorts from the check-in desk to the plane where needed, and there should be ramps, lifts, accessible toilets and reachable phones. Aircraft toilets, on the other hand, are likely to present a problem; travellers should discuss this with the airline at an early stage and, if necessary, with their doctor.

Guide dogs for the blind will often have to travel in a specially pressurised baggage compartment with other animals, away from their owner, though smaller guide dogs may be admitted to the cabin. All guide dogs will be subject to the same quarantine laws (six months in isolation etc) as any other animal when entering or returning to countries currently free of rabies such as Britain or Australia.

Deaf travellers can ask for airport and in-flight announcements to be written down for them.

Children under two travel for 10% of the standard fare (or free, on some airlines), as long as they don't occupy a seat. They don't get a baggage allowance either. 'Skycots' should be provided by the airline if requested in advance; these will take a child weighing up to about 10 kg. Children aged between two and 12 years can usually occupy a seat for half to two-thirds of the full fare, and do get a baggage allowance. Push chairs can often be taken as hand luggage.

To/From the USA

The *New York Times*, the *LA Times*, the *Chicago Tribune* and the *San Francisco Examiner* all produce weekly travel sections in which you'll find any number of travel agents' ads. *Travel Unlimited* (PO Box 1058, Allston, MA 02134) publishes details of the cheapest airfares and courier possibilities for destinations all over the world from the USA.

Council Travel and STA Travel have offices in major cities nationwide. You may have to produce proof of student status and in some cases be under 26 years of age to qualify for their discounted fares.

North America is a relative newcomer to the bucket-shop traditions of Europe and

Asia so ticket availability and the restrictions attached to them need to be weighed against what is offered on the standard APEX or full economy tickets.

It may well be cheaper in the long run to fly first to London on Virgin or another inexpensive airline, then buy a bucket-shop ticket from there to Africa. Do some homework before setting off, however. Magazines specialising in bucket-shop advertisements in London (see To/From the UK) will post copies so you can study current prices before you decide on a course of action.

From the US west coast it should be possible to get some good deals via Asia. Malaysian Airline System (MAS) flies from Los Angeles to Kuala Lumpur (Malaysia) and from there to Johannesburg and Cape Town. There are no direct flights, but Malaysia usually has good stopover deals. From Cape Town, Malaysia flies to Buenos Aires, so you could put together a very interesting trip.

There are direct flights between New York and Johannesburg and there was talk of a direct flight starting up between Washington DC and Johannesburg.

To/From Canada
Travel CUTS has offices in all major cities. The *Toronto Globe & Mail* and the *Vancouver Sun* carry travel agents' ads. *Great Expeditions* (PO Box 8000-411, Abbotsford, BC V2S 6H1) is useful.

To/From the UK
Most British travel agents are registered with ABTA (Association of British Travel Agents). If you have paid an ABTA-registered agent who then goes out of business for your flight, ABTA will guarantee a refund or an alternative. Buying from unregistered bucket shops is riskier but sometimes cheaper.

The following companies are reliable:

Africa Travel Centre
4 Medway Crt, Leigh St, London WC1H 9QX, (☎ (0171) 387 1211) – specialising in Africa, with a video lounge and giveaway newspaper

Campus Travel
52 Grosvenor Gardens, London SW1W OAG (☎ (0171) 730 8111) – offices in large YHA Adventure Shops
CTS
44 Goodge St, London W1 (☎ (0171) 637 5601)
STA Travel
86 Old Brompton Rd, SW7 (☎ (0171) 937 9962), tube: South Kensington – the largest, worldwide student/budget agency
Trailfinders
194 Kensington High St, W8 (☎ (0171) 938 3939) – a complete travel service, including a bookshop, information centre, visa service and immunisation centre

It's worth checking the Sunday newspapers for ads. In London, there are also several magazines with lots of info and ads:

Trailfinder A magazine put out quarterly by Trailfinders (see list of agencies). It's free if you pick it up in London but if you want it mailed, it costs UK£8 for four issues in the UK or Ireland and UK£12 or the equivalent for four issues in Europe or elsewhere (airmail).
Time Out This is London's weekly entertainment guide and contains travel information and advertising. It's available everywhere. Subscription enquiries should be addressed to Time Out Subs, Unit 8, Grove Ash, Bletchley, Milton Keynes MK1 1BZ, UK.
TNT Magazine This is a free magazine which can be picked up at most London Underground stations and on street corners around Earls Court and Kensington. It caters to Australians and New Zealanders working in the UK and is therefore full of travel advertising. They're at 14-15 Child's Place, Earls Court, London SW5 9RX, UK (☎ (0171) 373 3377).

In these magazines, you'll find discounted fares to Johannesburg as well as other parts of Africa. Many of them use Aeroflot or Eastern European and Middle Eastern Airlines.

To/From Europe
There are bucket shops by the dozen in Paris, Amsterdam, Brussels, Frankfurt and a few other places. In Amsterdam, NBBS is a popular travel agent.

To/From Australia & New Zealand
STA and Flight Centres International are

major dealers in cheap airfares. The Africa Travel Centre (☎ (02) 267 3048) specialises in African travel and have lots of free information. The best publications for finding good deals are the Saturday editions of the *Sydney Morning Herald* and the Melbourne *Age*. Discuss your options with several travel agents before buying because many have had very little experience with inexpensive routings to Africa.

There are flights from Sydney and Perth to Johannesburg and Cape Town – New Zealanders will have to get to Sydney. Fares are steep so it makes sense for Australasians to think in terms of a RTW ticket or a return ticket to Europe with a stopover in southern Africa. South African Airways (SAA) offers an Australia-UK/Europe (or USA) ticket with a South Africa stopover for A$1330/2150. You might do better than this, so shop around.

To/From Asia

Hong Kong is the discount plane ticket capital of the region. Its bucket shops are at least as unreliable as those of other cities. Bangkok is another possibility. Ask the advice of other travellers before buying a ticket. STA, which is reliable, has branches in Hong Kong, Tokyo, Singapore, Bangkok and Kuala Lumpur.

Air India flies from Bombay to Johannesburg and Durban. There are marginal bucket shops in New Delhi, Bombay and Calcutta. In New Delhi, Tripsout Travel, 72/7 Tolstoy Lane, behind the Government of India Tourist Office, Janpath, is recommended. It's very popular with travellers and has been in business for many years.

To/From Africa

Most regional African airlines now fly to/from South Africa. For example, Air Afrique flies to various West African countries, Air Gabon flies to Libreville (Gabon) with connections to West Africa and Europe, Uganda Airlines flies to Harare (Zimbabwe) and Uganda, Air Namibia flies between Cape Town and Windhoek (and on to Europe), and Air Botswana flies to various southern African cities. There are plenty of other regional airlines and SAA also has inter-Africa flights. Some European airlines stop in various African countries en route to South Africa.

LAND

If you're planning this sort of trip through Africa you really need a copy of Lonely Planet's *Africa on a shoestring*.

With the exception of the Israel-Egypt connection, all overland travel to Africa will have to be done through Europe and even that will involve a ferry crossing at some point.

Whether you're hitching, taking a bus or travelling by train across Europe, you should decide which of the two routes south through Africa you want to take – through the Sahara from Morocco or Algeria to West Africa or up the Nile from Egypt to Uganda and Kenya. It's impossible to travel overland between the two routes in North Africa due to the roadblock imposed by Libya so those wishing to travel between Morocco, Algeria or Tunisia, and Egypt will have to fly. Also bear in mind that even the fortunate travellers who can somehow wangle a Sudanese visa won't be able to travel overland south of Khartoum due to the civil war there, so the Nile route will probably entail a flight between Cairo – or at best from Khartoum – and Kampala or Nairobi.

From Nairobi, there are several options for reaching Zimbabwe, Botswana and Namibia. The most popular route seems to be the TanZam Railway between Dar es Salaam in Tanzania (accessible by bus or plane from Nairobi) and Kapiri Mposhi in Zambia, from where it's possible to pick up another train on to Lusaka and Livingstone (both also in Zambia). It's extremely inexpensive for the distance travelled but be prepared for a slow pace and uncomfortable conditions.

Another option takes you across Tanzania to Kigoma on Lake Tanganyika, then by steamer to Mpulungu (Zambia) and overland to Chitipa, Malawi, or Lusaka (Zambia). It's also possible to enter Zambia at Nakonde or

Malawi between Mbeya and Karonda. There's no public transport along the latter route so it will require hitching.

Other possibilities from Nairobi include travelling through Uganda, Zaïre, Rwanda and Burundi, catching the Lake Tanganyika steamer from Bujumbura, Burundi, and connecting up with the previously outlined route at Mpulungu, Zambia.

The final option – which could require months – is a very long and tedious route through Uganda or Burundi and Zaïre to Zambia. Once you've completed it, you may not feel like travelling any further!

Once you're in Zambia, however, it's fairly straightforward getting to Lusaka or Livingstone and entering Zimbabwe at Chirundu, Kariba or Victoria Falls, or Botswana at Kazungula. There are good straightforward connections from Botswana and Zimbabwe to Johannesburg. See the South Africa Getting There & Away chapter for details of these routes.

Overland Tours
Although the days of travelling from Cairo to the Cape are over for the time being, quite a few overland operators have taken up the trans-Sahara route through Algeria and West Africa, across the Central African Republic, Zaïre and Uganda to Kenya and on to Zimbabwe, Botswana and South Africa. These trips are very popular, but aren't for everyone. They are designed primarily for first-time travellers who feel uncomfortable striking out on their own or for those who prefer guaranteed social interaction to the uncertainties of the road.

If you have the slightest inclination towards independence or would feel confined travelling with the same group of 25 or so people for most of the trip (quite a few normally drop out along the way), think twice before booking something like this. One reader who found her truck hell, had read this warning but says that she was distracted by the colour brochures. So – think twice and close your eyes!

If you'd like more information or a list of agents selling overland packages in your home country, contact one of the following Africa overland operators, all of which are based in the UK (Exodus and Encounter also have offices in Australia, New Zealand, USA and Canada):

Dragoman
  Camp Green, Kenton Rd, Debenham, Suffolk IP14 6LA (☎ (01728) 86 1133, fax 86 1127)
Encounter Overland
  267 Old Brompton Rd, London SW5 9JA (☎ (0171) 370 6845)
Exodus Expeditions
  9 Weir Rd, London SW12 0LT (☎ (0181) 673 7966)
Guerba Expeditions
  101 Eden Vale Rd, Westbury, Wiltshire BA13 3QX (☎ (01373) 82 6689)
Top Deck
  The Adventure Centre, 131/135 Earls Court Rd, London SW5 9RH (☎ (0171) 330 4555, fax 373 6201)

There's a modest boom in overland truck journeys from South Africa to other African countries. Once again, these are mainly for people who haven't the confidence to travel on their own and many of the customers are white South Africans who are just beginning to realise that the rest of the continent isn't full of bloodthirsty savages, but can't quite conceive of actually mixing too much with locals. On the other hand, many backpackers go along and have a good time. Most of these are round trips and few if any run all the way to Europe. Expect to pay at least US$30 a day. Companies include African Routes, Epic, Wayfarers and Which Way Adventures. Many hostels will book you on a truck trip.

Private Vehicles
Drivers of cars and riders of motorbikes will need the vehicle's registration papers, liability insurance and an International Driving Permit in addition to their domestic licence. Beware: there are two kinds of international permit, one of which is needed mostly for former British colonies. In Africa you will also need a *Carnet de passage en douane*, which is effectively a passport for the vehicle, and acts as a temporary waiver of import duty. The carnet may also need to list

any expensive spares that you're planning to carry with you, such as a gearbox. This is designed to prevent car-import rackets. Contact your local automobile association for details about all documentation.

Liability insurance is not available in advance for many out-of-the-way countries, but has to be bought when crossing the border. The cost and quality of such local insurance varies wildly, and you will find in some countries that you are effectively travelling uninsured.

Anyone who is planning to take their own vehicle with them needs to check in advance what spares and petrol are likely to be available. Lead-free petrol is not on sale worldwide, and neither is every little part for your car.

Bicycles

Cycling is a cheap, convenient, healthy, environmentally sound and above all a fun way of travelling. One note of caution: before you leave home, go over your bike with a fine-toothed comb and fill your repair kit with every imaginable spare. As with cars and motorbikes, you won't necessarily be able to buy that crucial gizmo for your machine when it breaks down somewhere in the back of beyond as the sun sets.

Bicycles can travel by air. You *can* take them to pieces and put them in a bike bag or box, but it's much easier simply to wheel your bike to the check-in desk, where it should be treated as a piece of baggage. You may have to remove the pedals and turn the handlebars sideways so that it takes up less space in the aircraft's hold; check all this with the airline well in advance, preferably before you pay for your ticket.

WARNING

The information in this chapter is particularly vulnerable to change: prices for international travel are volatile, routes are introduced and cancelled, schedules change, special deals come and go, and rules and visa requirements are amended. Airlines and governments seem to take a perverse pleasure in making price structures and regulations as complicated as possible. You should check directly with the airline or a travel agent to make sure you understand how a fare (and ticket you may buy) works. In addition, the travel industry is highly competitive and there are many lurks and perks.

The upshot of this is that you should get opinions, quotes and advice from as many airlines and travel agents as possible before you part with your hard-earned cash. The details given in this chapter should be regarded as pointers and are not a substitute for your own careful, up-to-date research.

Safari Guide

PRIMATES

Baboons

Papio ursinus (Chacma Baboon)

The Chacma baboon, just one of at least five species of baboon, is the one most commonly sighted in southern Africa. The dog-like snouts of baboons give them a more aggressive appearance than most other primates, which have much more human-like facial features. Having said that, when you watch them playing or merely sitting around contemplating their surroundings, it's difficult not to make anthropomorphic comparisons.

Baboons live in large troops of up to 150 animals, each of which has its own two to 30 sq km area and is headed by one dominant male. Individuals spend much of their time searching for insects, spiders and birds' eggs.

They've also discovered that lodges, camp sites and picnic areas provide easy pickings, especially those occupied by idiotic tourists who throw food and leave their tents unzipped. Often baboons become such a nuisance that they have to be dealt with harshly by park officials, so please resist the temptation to feed them!

Farmers hunt baboons (which are not protected in South Africa), so you'll see them most often in parks and reserves, or on steep mountain passes. Other than people, baboons' greatest enemies are leopards, for whom they're a favourite meal. Young baboons are also taken by lions and hunting dogs.

DAVID WALL

Chacma Baboon

Bushbabies

Otolemur crassicaudatus (Greater or Giant Bushbaby)
Galago senegalensis (Lesser Bushbaby)

The greater bushbaby, which resembles an Australian possum, is in fact a small pro-simian (lemur-like) creature about the size of a rabbit. It inhabits forest areas in the east of South Africa and in southern Swaziland, but it's nocturnal and is therefore rarely observed. The bushbaby has a small head, large rounded ears, dark brown fur, a thick bushy tail and the enormous eyes that are typical of nocturnal primates. On average, adults weigh under two kg and measure 80 cm in length, but 45 cm of this is tail.

The lesser bushbaby is about half the size of the greater bushbaby. It is a very light grey and has yellowish colouring on the legs. It is present in Kruger National Park and Northern Transvaal.

Greater or Giant Bushbaby

Samango Monkey (White-Throated Guenon)
Cercopithecus mitis

Also known as the white-throated guenon or diademed monkey, the Samango monkey inhabits much of eastern Africa. In South Africa you're most likely to see it in KwaZulu/Natal, especially in the north-east.

The face is grey to black, but most of the back and the flanks and upper limbs have a greenish cast. The rump is yellow and the lower limbs are black. Mature males make coughing sounds; females and young of both sexes make chirping and chattering sounds.

The Samango monkey feeds in the early morning and late afternoon in the higher treetops, descending into shady areas during the day. They normally live in social groups of four to 12 and eat mainly shoots, leaves, young birds, insects, moss, fungi, fruit, berries and eggs. They occasionally even raid plantations, taking chickens. Enemies include leopards, pythons and eagles.

Samango Monkey (White-Throated Guenon)

Vervet Monkey (Savanna Monkey)
Cercopithecus aethiops

The playful vervet monkey is southern Africa's most common monkey. It occurs in much of the east of the country and along the Orange River, as well as the Eastern Cape Coast. It's easily recognisable by its black face fringed with white hair. The hair is yellowish-grey hair elsewhere, except on the underparts, which are whitish. The male has an extraordinary bright blue scrotum.

Vervet monkeys usually live in woodland and savanna, running in groups of up to 30. They're extremely cheeky and inquisitive, as you may well find when camping in the game reserves. Many have become habituated to humans and will stop at nothing to steal food or secure handouts, including making themselves welcome at dining tables or inside tents or cars.

DAVID WALL

Vervet Monkey (Savanna Monkey)

CARNIVORES

In East African parks, carnivores are the animals most seriously affected by tourism, and often find themselves trailing dozens of white minibuses while trying to hunt. In South African parks, however, tourism is better regulated, so natural patterns are little altered by human onlookers.

Just remember to keep as low a profile as possible; if an animal is obviously hunting, try to control your excitement and avoid the temptation to move in too close, lest you distract the predator or spook the intended prey.

Mongooses

Mungos mungo (Banded Mongoose)
*Galerella pulverulenta (*Small Grey Mongoose)

Southern Africa has at least eight species of mongoose, but the most common is the banded (or Zebra) mongoose, which is present in Kruger National Park and Northern Transvaal, and the small grey mongoose which occurs in the Cape provinces.

The banded mongoose is brown or grey, measures about 40 cm in length, weighs 1.3 to 2.3 kg, and is easily identified by the dark bands which stretch from the shoulder to the tail. The small grey is about the same size but has no bands.

Banded mongooses are very sociable animals, living in packs of 30 to 50 individuals. They emit a range of sounds which they use for communication within the pack. When threatened they make growling and spitting noises, much like a domestic cat. Small greys are usually solitary.

Being diurnal animals they enjoy sunning themselves by day, but at night, they retire to warrens in rock crevices, hollow trees and abandoned anthills.

A mongoose's favourite foods are insects, grubs and larvae, but they'll also eat amphibians, reptiles, birds, eggs, fruit and berries. Its main predators are birds of prey, though they are also taken by lions, leopards and wild dogs.

Banded Mongoose

Bat-Eared Fox
Otocyon megalotis

True to its name, the bat-eared fox is basically a long-legged fox with enormous ears. As you'd expect, its sense of hearing is exceptional. Its tail is very bushy and the body is brown with white markings and black-tipped ears. The bat-eared fox eats mainly insects, small animals, fruits and berries, and while foraging for subterranean insects it can hear even faint sounds coming from below ground. By lowering its head towards the soil, ears parallel, it can use a sort of triangulation to get an exact fix on potential food. This is followed by a burst of frantic digging to capture the prey.

The bat-eared fox normally inhabits multi-roomed burrows with several entrances, which it either digs or takes over. It's active at night, especially just after sunset. Its only enemies are large birds of prey and hyenas. They live in much of the western half of South Africa and there's a good chance of seeing some in Kalahari Gemsbok National Park.

The bat-eared fox is often mistaken for the **Cape Fox** *Vulpes chama*, which occurs in much the same area. The cape fox has smaller ears and is lighter in colour – it looks more like a European fox.

Bat-Eared Fox

Black-Backed Jackal
Canis mesomelas

Black-backed jackals occur widely in all three countries, although they are disliked by farmers so they tend to be restricted to parks and reserves.

Their backs, which are actually more grizzled than black, are wide at the neck and taper to the tail. Although jackals are dogs, their bushy tails and large ears cause them to more closely resemble foxes.

Jackals are mostly scavengers, and commonly hang around kills awaiting morsels. If nothing is forthcoming they'll often hunt insects, birds, rodents and even the occasional small antelope. They also hang about outside human settlements and often go for sheep, poultry and young calves or foals.

Each jackal pair looks after a home territory of around 250 hectares. Pups are born in litters of five to seven. Although they don't reach maturity until they're almost a year old, most jackal pups are on their own at the age of just two months, and are especially vulnerable to enemies, such as leopards, cheetahs and eagles.

In Kruger National Park you might also see the **Side-striped Jackal** *Canis adustus*, which is slightly larger and has a more uniform grey appearance.

DAVID WALL
Black-Backed Jackal

Cape Clawless Otter
Aonyx capensis

The Cape clawless otter, a river otter, is found in wet areas of the eastern half of South Africa and in Lesotho and Swaziland. In South Africa's Eastern Cape Province it occurs in the intertidal zone, especially in Tsitsikamma National Park. It has a light greyish brown back; the snout, face and throat are white or cream-coloured and each cheek has a large rectangular spot. Unlike most otters, Cape clawless otters don't have webbed feet, and although some are truly clawless, others have short pointed claws on the third and fourth toes.

The otters are normally active by day, and with a bit of luck may be seen playing, swimming and diving throughout the afternoon. In areas where they're hunted by humans, however, otters have adopted a nocturnal schedule.

Their main foods include fish, crabs, frogs, and both bird and crocodile eggs. Their only known natural enemy is the crocodile.

Cape Clawless Otter

Caracal (African Lynx)
Felis caracal

Once considered to be a true lynx, the caracal is now placed in the small-cat genus *Felis*. The caracal is certainly very cat-like, and despite its sometimes sleepy appearance is the fastest cat of its size.

It occurs widely in all three countries, although you will be lucky to see one.

The caracal is distinguished by its height (about 50 cm at the shoulder), relatively small head, long, narrow ears densely tufted with long hairs at the tips, lack of whiskers on the face, and long, stout legs. The colour of the coat ranges from reddish-brown to yellow-grey, with a white underside and a black line joining the nose and eye.

Caracals are 80 to 120 cm long (including a tail of 20 to 30 cm), and weigh between 13 and 23 kg. They live in porcupine burrows, rocky crevices or dense vegetation. They inhabit many areas, but prefer dry country (woodland, savanna and scrub) and avoid sandy deserts.

Their favourite prey are birds, rodents and other small mammals, including young deer. They stalk their prey until a quick dash or leap can capture it. They are usually active at twilight, but they may hunt by night in hot weather and by day in cold weather. They are generally solitary animals, but might sometimes be seen in pairs with their young. They are believed to be territorial, marking the territory with urine sprays. The calls are typical of cats – miaows, growls, hisses and coughing noises.

Litters of one to four kittens (usually three) can be born at any time of the year. The kittens open their eyes after 10 days, are weaned at 10 to 25 weeks, and can breed from as young as six months.

Caracal (African Lynx)

Cheetah
Acinonyx jubatus

The cheetah is one of nature's most magnificent accomplishments; this sleek, streamlined and graceful creature exists in limited numbers in Kruger and Kalahari Gemsbok national parks, and has been reintroduced to some parks in KwaZulu/Natal.

Although it superficially resembles a leopard, the cheetah is longer and lighter, and has a slightly bowed back and a much smaller and rounder face. It stands around 80 cm at the shoulder, measures around 210 cm in length, including the tail, and weighs from 40 to 60 kg. Occasionally, a beautiful genetic mutation produces what's known as a king cheetah; instead of spots, it has a marbled coat and striped legs. King cheetahs are most common in Kruger National Park.

Normally cheetahs hunt in early morning or late evening. While hunting, a cheetah stalks its prey as closely as possible. When the time is ripe, it launches into an incredible 100-metre sprint in which it can reach a speed of up to 110 km/h. However, this phenomenal speed can only be sustained for a short distance. If it fails to bring down its intended victim, it gives up and tries elsewhere. The prey, often a small antelope, may be brought to the ground with a flick of the paw to trip it up. Other favourite meals include hares, jackals and young warthogs.

The main breeding period is between March and December, when mature females produce litters of two to four cubs. The cubs reach maturity at around one year, but stay with the mother much longer to learn hunting and survival skills. Cheetahs rarely fight, but do suffer from predation by lions, leopards and hyenas; most victims are cubs.

HUGH FINLAY

Cheetah

Civit (African Civet)
Viverra (Civetticus) civetta

The civet is a medium-sized omnivore around 40 cm high at the shoulder and 90 cm long, excluding the tail, with some canine features and short, partially retractile claws. Its long, coarse and mainly grey coat is specked with a varying pattern of black spots, with one set of black bands stretching from the ears to the lower neck and another around the upper hind legs. When the animal is moving, the black tail, which is bushy at the grey-banded base and thinner towards the tip, is held out straight. The head is mostly greyish white and the small, rounded ears are tipped with white hairs. Another conspicuous feature is a set of musk glands in the anal region which produce a foul-smelling oily substance used to mark territory. This musk is used in manufacturing perfumes, though in Western countries it's collected from captive animals.

They occur in Northern and Eastern Transvaal, although they are solitary, nocturnal animals and hard to spot; by day they nestle in thickets, tall grass or abandoned burrows.

Civets have a varied diet consisting of amphibians, birds, rodents, eggs, reptiles, snails, insects (especially ants and termites), berries, young shoots and fruit. Litters consist of up to four cubs, which have a similar but slightly darker colour to the adults.

Civet (African Civet)

Genet
Genetta genetta (felina) (Small-Spotted Genet)
Genetta tigrina (Large-Spotted Genet)

More than the civet, the genet resembles the domestic cat, although the body is considerably longer, the long, coarse coat has a prominent crest along the spine and the tail is longer and bushier. The basic colour varies from grey to fawn, patterned from the neck to the tail with dark brown to black spots. The tail, which has a white tip, is banded with nine or 10 similarly coloured rings.

The small-spotted genet occurs throughout South Africa, except in KwaZulu/Natal, while the large-spotted genet lives mainly in Swaziland, Northern Transvaal, KwaZulu/Natal and along the south coast.

Genets live singly or in pairs in riverine forests and dry scrub savanna and open country. They're agile climbers, but are seldom sighted because they're only active nocturnally. By day they sleep in abandoned burrows, rock crevices or hollow trees, or up on high branches, apparently returning to the same spot each day.

Genets may climb trees to seek out nesting birds and their eggs, but normally hunt on the ground. Like the domestic cat, they stalk prey by crouching flat on the ground. Their diet consists of small rodents, birds, reptiles, insects and fruits. They're well known for being wasteful killers, often eating only small bits of the animals they catch. Like domestic cats, genets spit and growl when angered. Litters typically consist of two or three kittens.

Small-Spotted Genet

Honey Badger (Ratel)
Mellivora ratel

The honey badger is of a similar size and shape to the European badger and is every bit as ferocious. They've even been known to attack creatures as large as Cape buffalo! They're present throughout the region except in the Orange Free State and Lesotho. They are normally active between dusk and dawn.

Honey badgers subsist on fish, frogs, scorpions, spiders, and reptiles, including poisonous snakes; at times they'll even take young antelopes. They also eat a variety of roots, honey, berries and eggs, and are adept at raiding rubbish bins.

Honey Badger (Ratel)

Hunting Dog
Lycaon pictus

The scruffy looking hunting dog (or wild dog) is now rare, and in this region occurs only in Kruger National Park. It's the size of a large domestic dog, but has big, round ears and a blotchy black, brown and white coat, with a white tail.

Hunting dogs rarely scavenge, preferring to kill their own prey. They move in packs of four to 40 and work well together. Once the prey has been selected and the chase is on, two lead dogs will chase hard while the rest pace themselves; once the first two tire another pair steps in, and so on until the quarry is exhausted. Favoured prey include springbok, impala and other mid-sized antelope, but they can kill animals as large as buffalo.

Litters of seven to 15 pups are born in grass-lined burrows; by six months of age they're competent hunters and have abandoned the burrow. The hunting dog has no common predators, although unguarded pups may fall prey to hyenas and eagles.

Hunting Dog

MIKE SCOTT

Hyena

Hyena
Crocuta crocuta (Spotted Hyena)
Hyena brunnea (Brown or African Laughing Hyena)

Hyenas appear distinctly canine, but are generally larger and more powerfully built than your average dog, and have a broad head, large eyes, weak hindquarters and a sloping back that gives them a characteristic loping gait when running. The short coat is dull grey to buff-coloured and patterned with black spots except on the throat. Its powerful jaws and teeth enable it to crush and swallow bones, which give its scat a characteristic calcium whitewash.

Both the spotted and the african laughing hyenas live in Kruger National Park, and may still be found in parts of Northern Transvaal. There's a hyena den under one of the main roads near Kruger's Pretorius-kop restcamp, and the denizens sometimes snooze on the road.

Although they're mainly nocturnal, hyenas are often seen during the day, especially around lion or cheetah kills, impatiently squabbling with the vultures for a turn at the carcass. Otherwise, a hyena's days are spent in long grass, abandoned aardvark holes or large burrows, which they excavate up to a metre below the surface. They're noisy animals; at night you'll frequently hear the hyena's spine-chilling yelp, which rises in a crescendo to a high-pitched scream. On other occasions, particularly when it's successful at finding food or mating, it's also known to 'laugh' with what might only be described as macabre glee.

Hyenas have highly developed senses of smell, sight and hearing, which are all important in locating carrion or live prey and for mutual recognition among pack members and mating pairs. They're also well known as scavengers and often follow lions and hunting dogs – usually at a respectable distance – though they occasionally do force larger animals to abandon a kill. Carrion does form an important part of their diet, but hyenas are also true predators. Running hyenas can reach speeds of up to 60 km/h and a pack of them will often bring down small antelope, wildebeest and zebras. They also stalk pregnant antelope to snatch and kill the newly born calf – and occasionally the mother as well. They also prey on domestic stock.

During the mating season – especially on moonlit nights – hyenas assemble in large numbers for a bit of night-time chorus, which sounds like hell has broken loose. In their den, females produce a litter of up to four pups after a gestation period of about 110 days. The pups are weaned at around six weeks old and are on their own shortly.

Humans are the hyena's main enemies, but wild dogs will occasionally kill or mutilate a hyena that approaches a kill.

Leopard (Panther)
Panthera pardus

Leopards are among the most widespread of African carnivores but in this region farming and hunting has restricted them to Northern Transvaal, parts of Eastern Transvaal and Swaziland, the Drakensberg escarpment in KwaZulu/Natal and Lesotho, and in the mountain ranges of Eastern and Western Cape provinces.

They're mainly nocturnal and are therefore rarely observed. Leopards are agile and climb as well as domestic cats, and normally spend their days resting in trees up to five metres above the ground. They also protect their kills by dragging them up trees, where they're out of reach of scavengers and other would-be freeloaders.

The leopard's short orange coat is densely covered with mostly hollow black spots, although some individuals – often called panthers – are black all over. The underparts are white with fewer spots. Coats of savanna-dwelling leopards are generally lighter than those of forest dwellers. Leopards are heard more often than seen; their cry sounds very much like a hacksaw cutting through metal.

This powerfully built animal uses cunning to catch its prey, which consists mainly of birds, reptiles and mammals including large rodents, dassies, warthogs, small antelope, monkeys and baboons (a particular favourite). Occasionally, they also take domestic animals such as goats, sheep, poultry and dogs, and often enjoy a very poor reputation among the human population.

Leopards are solitary animals, except during the mating season when the male and female cohabit. A litter of up to three cubs is produced after a gestation period of three months.

DAVID WALL

Leopard (Panther)

DAVID WALL

TONY WHEELER

Lions

Lion
Panthera leo

Lions are big attractions in Kruger and Kalahari Gemsbok national parks, where indigenous populations still exist. They are also being reintroduced to other parks. Lions are most active in the late afternoon, but spend much of the day lying under bushes or in other attractive places. They are most easily seen in the dry season when they congregate near waterholes.

Lions are hardly the human-eaters their reputation would have you believe, but older or irritable individuals do occasionally attack people, so take seriously the warnings not to get out of your vehicle in national parks. The most dangerous lions are those which can no longer bring down more fleet-footed animals. More often than not, however, they're off like a shot at the first unusual noise or sudden movement.

Lions are territorial beasts. A pride of up to three males and 15 accompanying females and young will defend an area of anything from 20 to 400 sq km, depending on the type of terrain and the amount of game food available. Lions generally hunt in prides; males drive the prey toward the concealed females, who do the actual killing. Although they cooperate well together, lions aren't the most efficient hunters and as many as four out of five attempts are unsuccessful.

Cubs are born in litters of two or three and become sexually mature by 1½ years. Males are driven from the family group shortly after, but don't reach full maturity until around six years of age. Unguarded cubs are preyed on by hyenas, leopards, pythons and hunting dogs.

Serval
Felis (Lepitailurus) serval

The serval, a type of wild cat, is about the size of a domestic cat but has much longer legs. It inhabits thick bush and tall grass around streams in Northern Transvaal and parts of Swaziland, KwaZulu/Natal and eastern Orange Free State.

Servals stand about 50 cm high and measure 130 cm long, including the tail. Their dirty yellow coat is dotted with large black spots which form lines along the length of the body. Other prominent features include large upright ears, a long neck and a relatively short tail. It's an adept hunter, favouring birds, hares and rodents, and can catch birds in mid-flight by leaping into the air. Owing to its nocturnal nature, the serval is usually observed only in the early morning or late evening.

Kittens are born in litters of up to four. Although they leave their mother after one year, they don't reach sexual maturity until two years of age.

Serval

UNGULATES

Antelope
Bushbuck
Tragelaphus scriptus

Although the bushbuck exists in Northern and Eastern Transvaal and down through KwaZulu/Natal to the south coast, it's a shy and solitary animal and is rarely sighted.

Standing about 80 cm at the shoulder, the bushbuck is chestnut to dark brown in colour. It has a variable number of white vertical stripes on the body between the neck and rump, and usually two horizontal white stripes lower down which give the animal a harnessed appearance, as well as a number of white spots on the upper thigh and a white splash on the neck. Normally only the males grow horns, but females have been known to grow them on rare occasions. The horns are straight with gentle spirals and average about 30 cm long.

Bushbuck are rarely found in groups of more than two, and prefer to stick to areas with heavy brush cover. When startled they bolt and crash loudly through the undergrowth. They're nocturnal browsers, yet rarely move far from their home turf. Though shy and elusive they can be aggressive and dangerous when cornered. Their main predators are leopards and pythons.

MIKE SCOTT

Bushbuck

Common or Grey Duiker
Silvicapra grimmia

As the name would suggest, the common duiker is the most common of the 16 duiker species in Africa and it lives throughout this region. Even so, it's largely nocturnal and is sighted only infrequently. Duikers usually live in pairs, and prefer areas with good scrub cover. Only 60 cm high at the shoulder, the common duiker is greyish light-brown in colour, with a white belly and a dark brown vertical stripe on the face. Only the males have horns, which are straight and pointed, and grow to only 20 cm in length.

Common duikers are almost exclusively browsers and only rarely eat grasses, though they appear to supplement their diet with insects and guinea fowl chicks. They're capable of going without water for long periods but will drink whenever water is available.

The rare **blue duiker** *(Cephalophus monticola)* is sometimes spotted on the south-east coast. It's significantly smaller than the common duiker and its coat is grey or dark brown with a characteristic blue sheen.

Common or Grey Duiker

Eland
Taurotragus oryx

The eland is the largest antelope species, standing about 170 cm at the shoulder; a mature bull can weigh up to 1000 kg. Oddly enough, eland resemble some varieties of cattle native to the Indian subcontinent. Those remaining in this region live in Kruger National Park, with a few to be found in the KwaZulu/Natal Drakensberg.

Eland have light brown coats with up to 15 vertical white stripes on the body, although they're often almost indistinguishable. Both sexes have horns about 65 cm long, which spiral at the base and sweep straight back. The male of the species has a much hairier head than the female, and its horns are stouter and shorter.

Eland prefer savanna scrub to open spaces, but they avoid thick forest. They feed on grass and tree foliage in the early morning and late afternoon, and are also active on moonlit nights. They normally drink daily, but can go for a month or more without water.

Eland usually live in groups of around six to 12, but herds can contain as many as 50 individuals. A small herd normally consists of several females and one male, but in larger herds there may be several males, which is made possible by a strict hierarchy. Females reach sexual maturity at around two years and can bear up to 12 calves in a lifetime. The young are born in October or November.

Eland

Gemsbok (South African Oryx)
Oryx gazella

The gemsbok, a large grey antelope standing around 120 cm at the shoulder, is common in the Kalahari Gemsbok National Park. It is a solid but stately animal, with impressively long, straight horns, an attractive grey-fawn body with black on the flanks and white on the underside, and a black and white pattern on the face. The tail is hairy, like a horse's.

Gemsbok are principally grazers, but will also browse on thorny shrubs. They can survive for long periods without water.

Herds vary from five to 40 individuals, but the bulls normally prefer a solitary existence.

Gemsbok (South African Oryx)

Greater Kudu
Tragelaphus strepsiceros

The beautiful greater kudu, one of the largest antelope, is found in Northern Transvaal, Kruger National Park, parts of Eastern Transvaal and Swaziland, and in some of the wilder areas inland from the south coast. Kudu prefers hilly country with fairly dense bush cover.

Kudu stand around 1.5 metres at the shoulder, with a long neck and broad ears, and weigh up to 250 kg, yet they're very regal in appearance. Their bodies are light grey in colour with six to 10 vertical white stripes along the sides and a white chevron between the eyes. The horns, carried only by males, form large spirals; an old buck can have up to three complete twists.

Kudu live in small herds of up to five females and their young, but during rainy periods, the herds often split. The normally solitary males occasionally band into small herds.

Kudu are mainly browsers and can eat a variety of leaves which would be poisonous to other animals. On occasion, they also eat grasses.

Although they're somewhat clumsy, when on the move kudu can easily clear obstacles of over two metres and are known for their unhealthy habit of leaping in front of oncoming vehicles.

Greater Kudu

Grysboks
Raphiceros sharpei (Sharpe's Grysbok)
Raphicerus melanotis (Cape Grysbok)

Sharpe's grysbok is a small, stocky antelope which is reddish-brown with a pale red underside. The back and sides are speckled with individual white hairs from the nape of the neck to the rump, hence the Afrikaans name grysbok, or 'grey buck'. Sharpe's grysbok stand only about 50 cm high and weigh no more than nine kg. Only the males have horns, which are small, sharp and straight. It is found in the north-east of South Africa, in both bushy and woodland savanna country and rocky koppies, feeding primarily on shoots and leaves. They also like to munch the reeds which grow in wetlands.

The Cape grysbok looks similar to Sharpe's, but it is found only in the extreme south-west of South Africa, where it inhabits the unique *fynbos* vegetation – and sometimes feeds on vines in the Cape Winelands area, making it unpopular.

Grysbok are solitary, and you'll rarely see more than two together. They're most active from morning to late afternoon, spending the night resting in bushy thickets and stony outcrops.

Sharpe's Grysbok

Hartebeest

Hartebeest
Alcelaphus buselaphus (Red Hartebeest)
Sigmoceros lichtensteinii (Lichtenstein's Hartebeest)

The hartebeest is a medium-size antelope. Once found in this region, it has been reintroduced to many parks including Kruger National Park, Kalahari Gemsbok National Park and Addo Elephant National Park.

Hartebeest are easily recognised by their long, narrow face and short horns, which are distinctively angular and heavily ridged. In both sexes, the horns form a heart shape, hence their name (which means 'heart beast' in Afrikaans). The back slopes away from the humped shoulders and is light brown, becoming lighter towards the rear and underside.

Hartebeest prefer grassy plains for grazing but are also found in sparsely forested savanna or hills. They feed exclusively on grass and usually drink twice daily, although they can go for months without water if necessary.

They're social beasts and often mingle with animals such as zebra and wildebeest. Sexual maturity is reached at around two years, and hartebeest can calve at any time of year, although activity peaks in February and August. Predators are mainly the large cats, hyenas and hunting dogs.

Impala
Aepyceros melampus

The graceful impala is found in large numbers in Kruger National Park, as well as in Northern Transvaal, parts of Swaziland and north-eastern Kwa-Zulu/Natal.

Individuals weigh from 50 to 60 kg and stand about 80 cm at the shoulder. The coat is a glossy rufous colour, though more pale on the flanks, and the underparts, rump, throat and chin are white. A narrow black band runs from the middle of the rump to about halfway down the tail and there's also a vertical black stripe on the back of the thighs. Males have long, lyre-shaped horns averaging 75 cm in length.

Impala are both browsers and grazers, and are active day and night. They're very dependent on water but are capable of existing on dew for fairly long periods.

Impala are gregarious animals, and males have harems of up to 100 females, although 15 to 20 are more common. Single males form bachelor groups, and there is fierce competition and fighting between them during the rutting season. The normal gestation period is six to seven months, but that can be prolonged if low rainfall has produced insufficient grass to nourish the young. Males usually leave the herd before they reach breeding age.

Impala are known for their speed and ability to leap; they can spring as much as 10 metres in a single bound or three metres off the ground – and frequently do – even when there's nothing to jump over! And it's lucky they can; impala are the rabbits of Africa, and make a tasty meal for all large predators, including lions, leopards, cheetahs, wild dogs and even hyenas.

HUGH FINLAY

Impala

Klipspringer

Klipspringer
Oreotragus oreotragus

The delicate little klipspringer, which stands about 50 cm at the shoulder, is shy and easily disturbed. It's easily recognised by its curious tip-toe stance – the hooves are adapted for balance and grip on rocky surfaces – and the greenish tinge of its coarse speckled hair. The widely-spaced 10-cm-long horns are present only on the male.

Klipspringers normally inhabit rocky outcrops and are found in many places in this region, from Northern Transvaal to the KwaZulu/Natal Drakensberg, to the coastal ranges in the three Cape provinces. They also venture into adjacent grasslands, but when alarmed they retreat into the rocks for safety. These amazingly agile and sure-footed creatures are capable of bounding up impossibly rough rock faces. They get all the water they need from their diet of greenery and go for long periods without drinking. They're most active around midday, and single males often keep watch from a good vantage point.

Each male has a clearly defined territory and lives with one or two females. They reach sexual maturity at around one year, and females bear one calf twice annually. Calves may stay with their parents for up to a year, but young males normally establish their own territory even sooner.

Main predators are leopards, crowned eagles, jackals and baboons.

Nyala
Tragelaphus angasii (Common Nyala)
Tragelaphus buxtoni (Mountain Nyala)

The medium-size nyala is one of Africa's rarest and most beautiful antelope. Males are grey with a mane and long hair under the throat and hind legs. They also have vertical stripes down the back and long, lyre-shaped horns with white tips. Females are a ruddy colour with vertical white stripes, but have no horns.

Nyalas are found in Kruger National Park and a few remaining habitats in north-eastern KwaZulu/Natal. Their main foods are shoots, buds, bark, fruit and leaves of trees and bushes. During the dry season they're active only in the morning and evening, while during the rains, they more often feed at night.

Female nyala and their young live in small groups, with one older dominant male to guard and defend them from young males, which organise their own social groups. Nyala defend themselves bravely against humans and enemies – mainly leopards and lions. The young may even be taken by baboons and birds of prey.

Nyala

Oribi
Ourebia ourebi

Similar to the duiker in appearance, the small oribi is relatively difficult to see; your best chance of spotting one is in one of the parks in the KwaZulu/Natal Drakensberg.

Oribi are a uniform golden brown with white on the belly and the insides of the legs. The males have short straight horns about 10 cm long. The oribi's most distinguishing mark – although you'll need binoculars to spot it – is a circular patch of naked black skin below the ear, which is actually a scent gland. Another identifying characteristic is the tuft of black hair on the tip of the short tail.

Being quite small, the oribi has many predators, including the larger cats. They usually graze on high grass savanna plains, where they're well sheltered from predators. They can go without water for long periods, but if it's available, they'll drink. When alarmed they bolt, making erratic bounces with all four legs held rigid. It's thought this helps them with orientation in high grasses. After 100 metres or so, they stop to assess the danger.

Oribi are territorial and usually live in pairs. They reach sexual maturity at around one year, and the females bear one calf twice annually.

Oribi

Reedbuck
Redunca arundinum (Common Reedbuck)
Redunca fulvorufula (Mountain Reedbuck)

The dusky brown reedbuck is found on wetlands or riverine areas in parts of Northern Transvaal, Swaziland and KwaZulu/Natal. It never strays more than a few km from a permanent water source. The rarer mountain reedbuck inhabits a wider area, in hill country from Northern Transvaal down through Swaziland, Lesotho, KwaZulu/Natal, Orange Free State and Eastern Cape Province.

These medium-size antelope stand around 80 cm at the shoulder and males have distinctive forward-curving horns. The underbelly, inside of the thighs, throat and underside of the bushy tail are white.

Reedbuck are territorial and live in small groups of up to 10 animals. Groups usually consist of an older male and accompanying females and young. Their diet consists almost exclusively of grass and some foliage.

At mating time, competing males fight with spirit. After sexual maturity at 1½ years, females bear one calf at a time. Predators include big cats, hyenas and hunting dogs.

Reedbuck

Ringed (Common) Waterbuck
Kobus ellipsiprymnus

The ringed waterbuck, so called because of the bulls-eye ring around its rump, has white markings on the face and throat. It's a solid animal with a thick, shaggy, dark brown coat, white inner thighs and proportionally long neck and short legs. It's commonly seen in Kruger National park and sometimes in the north-east corner of KwaZulu/Natal.

Only the males have horns, which curve gradually outward before shooting straight up to a length of about 75 cm. Waterbuck are good swimmers and readily enter the water to escape predators. They never stray far from water, and a male's territory will always include a water source. Herds are small and consist of cows, calves and one mature bull, while younger bulls live in small groups apart from the herd.

The bulk of the waterbuck's diet consists mainly of grass, but it also eats some foliage. Sexual maturity is reached at just over one year, although a male will not become dominant in the herd until around five years of age. Females and younger males are permitted to wander at will through territories of breeding males.

Predators such as lions, leopards and hunting dogs go for the young calves and females, but mature waterbucks are not a favoured prey species because of their tough flesh and the distinct odour of the meat.

Ringed (Common) Waterbuck

Roan Antelope
Hippotragus equinus

The roan is one of southern Africa's rarest antelope species, but still exists in Kruger National Park. As a grazer, it prefers tall grasses and sites with ample shade and fresh water.

The roan is the third largest antelope species, after eland and kudu, reaching up to 150 cm at the shoulder. It bears a striking resemblance to a horse. Bulls can weigh up to 270 kg.

The coat varies from reddish fawn to dark rufous, with white underparts and a conspicuous mane of stiff, black-tipped hairs stretching from the nape to the shoulders. There's another mane of sorts on the underside of the neck, consisting of long dark hairs. The ears are long, narrow and pointed, with a brown tassel at the tip. The face has a distinctive black and white pattern. Both sexes have curving, back-swept horns up to 70 cm long.

It has an extremely aggressive nature and fight from an early age, thus deterring predators. For most of the year roans are arranged in small herds of normally less than 20 individuals, led by a master bull. However, in the mating season, bulls become solitary and take a female from the herd. The pair remain together until the calf is born, after which the females and calves form a separate herd; when the dry season comes, the females and calves rejoin the original herd.

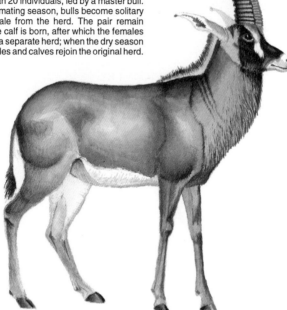

Roan Antelope

Sable Antelope
Hippotragus niger

The sable is present in Kruger National Park and nearby areas of Northern Transvaal. Sable are slightly smaller than roan, but are more solidly built. The colouring is dark brown to black, with a white belly and face markings. Both sexes carry 80-cm sweeping horns, but those of the male are longer and more curved. Sable feed mainly on grass, but foliage accounts for around 10% of their diet.

Sable live in territorial herds of up to 25 – sometimes more in the dry season – and are active mainly in the early morning and late afternoon. Each herd occupies its own area, within which each individual male has his own territory of up to 30 hectares.

Females start bearing calves at around three years of age; most are borne in January and September. Like the roan, the sable is a fierce fighter and has been known to kill lions when attacked. Other predators include leopards, hyenas and hunting dogs.

Sable Antelope

Springbok
Antidorcas marsupialis

The springbok, the only gazelle in southern Africa, is found in the north-western corner of South Africa, including Kalahari Gemsbok National Park.

Springbok are easily recognised by their white head, with a black stripe connecting the nose and eye. The fawn-coloured back and white belly are separated by a ruddy brown stripe along the animal's side. Both male and female springbok have ribbed, lyre-shaped horns of medium length. It's one of several species of antelope known for its pronking (leaping vertically in the air).

They generally move in herds of 20 to 100 animals; sometimes herds of several hundred can be seen. Male springbok are only territorial during the rutting season, when they collect harems of females and defend them against other potential suitors. At other times, herds consist of mixed groups of males and females, although groups made up entirely of bachelors are often observed.

Springbok are active early in the morning and from late afternoon to dusk. They also emerge on nights with strong moonlight. They eat grass and the leaves of low bushes, and occasionally dig out roots and tubers. Females calve from December to January.

They drink often, but can survive for long periods without water. Occasionally, in conditions of severe drought, huge herds migrate in search of water; in the great migration of 1896, the surface area covered by millions of springbok was 220 km long and 25 km wide. In Namibia, great herds, driven mad by thirst or hunger,have in the past flocked to the coast, drank seawater and died, leaving the shoreline littered with carcasses.

DEANNA SWANEY

Springbok herd

Steenbok
Raphiceros campestris

The steenbok, sometimes spelt 'steinbock', bears a resemblance to both the duiker and the grysbok, with a short tail and proportionally long and slender legs. The back and hindquarters range from light reddish brown to dark brown, and on the upper edge of the nose is a black, wedge-shaped spot. Males have small, straight and widely separated horns.

Steenbok live mainly on open plains, but can be found almost anywhere in this region. They're solitary animals, and only have contact with others during the mating season.

Normally, steenbok are active in the morning and evening, but may stay out late when there's a bright moon. At other times, they seek out high grass or bear holes which offer some protection from enemies, which include leopards, eagles, pythons, monitor lizards, jackals and hyenas.

DEANNA SWANEY

Steenbok

Tsessebi (Topi)
Damaliscus lunatus

The tsessebi is like the hartebeest in appearance but is darker – in some cases appearing almost violet – with black patches on the rear thighs, front legs and face. Its horns, carried by both sexes, curve gently up, out and back. The tsessebi is found in Kruger National Park.

A highly gregarious antelope, it lives in herds of at least 15 and frequently mingles with wildebeest, hartebeest and zebras. During the mating season, bulls select a well-defined patch which they defend against all rivals, while females wander from one patch to another. After mating, herds divide into separate male and female groups.

Tsessebi are exclusively grazers. Although they can live on dry grasses spurned by other antelope, they prefer floodplains and moist areas which support lush pasture. When water is available they drink frequently, but they are also capable of surviving long periods without water as long as sufficient grass is available. Lions are their main predators.

Tsessebi (Topi)

Wildebeest (Gnu)
Connochaetes taurinus (Blue Wildebeest or Brindled Gnu)
Connochaetes gnou (Black Wildebeest or White-tailed Gnu)

The wildebeest, also called the gnu after its low and languid grunt, is to the African savanna what the bison once was to the American prairies. Wildebeest are gregarious, to say the least, and sometimes move about in herds up to tens of thousands strong, normally in association with zebras and other herbivores, accompanied by a cacophony of amusing snorts and low grunts. In South Africa, numbers are today much smaller, but you'll see wildebeest in many of the drier national parks, from Kalahari Gemsbok to Kruger.

The wildebeest's ungainly appearance makes it unmistakable; it's heavily built and has a massive head and wild, frayed mane. It has been described as having the forequarters of an ox, the hind parts of an antelope and the tail of a horse. It's also known for its rather eccentric behaviour, which includes snorting, cavorting, frantically shaking the head, bucking, running around in circles and rolling in the dust. This is thought to be a reaction to the botfly larva which finds its way up the nostrils and into the brain.

During the mating season, groups of up to 150 females and their young are gathered by up to three bulls, which defend a defined territory against rivals, even when on the move. There's apparently no hierarchy amongst the bulls and, at the end of the mating season, breeding herds are reabsorbed into the main herds.

Wildebeest are almost exclusively grazers, and move constantly in search of good pasture and water. Because they prefer to drink daily and can survive only five days without water, wildebeest will migrate up to 50 km to find it. During the rainy season they graze haphazardly, without any apparent social organisation, but in the dry season they coalesce around waterholes.

Major predators include lions, cheetahs and wild dogs, and hyenas are also partial to young wildebeest calves.

TONY WHEELER

Wildebeest (Gnu)

TONY WHEELER

Cape Buffalo

Other Ungulates
Cape Buffalo
Syncerus caffer

Cape (or African) buffalo occur in Kruger National Park, with some smaller populations in north-eastern KwaZulu/Natal and elsewhere. Both sexes have the distinctive curving horns which broaden and almost meet over the forehead, but those of the female are usually smaller. Their coloration varies from ruddy brown to black.

Buffalo have a penetrating gaze, and one safari operator has noted that 'buffalo always look at you as if you owe them a lot of money'. Although for the most part they're docile and stay out of humans' way, these 800-kg creatures can be very dangerous and should be treated with caution. Solitary rogue bulls and females protecting young are the most aggressive.

Cape buffalo are territorial, but when food and water are plentiful the herds, which normally consist of 100 or more individuals, may disperse over an area 100 km in diameter. However, they never stray far from water, especially in dry periods.

Giraffe
Giraffa camelopardalis

As well as odd specimens in game reserves and parks around the country, you'll find giraffe in Kruger National Park and nearby.

The name giraffe is derived from the Arabic *zarafah* ('the one who walks quickly'). The main distinguishing feature of the Masai giraffe is its irregular, star-like spots, compared with the more regular pattern of the reticulated giraffe. The reticulated giraffe is a deeper brown and its body has a more intricate tortoise-shell pattern.

The average male is around 5½ metres tall. Females are 4½ metres and are normally lighter in colour and have less well-defined markings. Both sexes have 'horns', actually just short projections of skin-covered bone and probably a remnant of what might once have been antlers. Despite the giraffe's incredibly long neck, it still has only seven cervical vertebrae – the same number as all mammals, including humans.

Giraffes are out and about in the early morning and afternoon, browsing on acacia. You may be surprised to see them chewing bones, a practice known as *pica*, which indicates a shortage of minerals in their diet. When the sun is high and hot, they relax in a cool, shady spot. At night they also rest for several hours.

Giraffes most often drink in the late afternoon or early evening, but they must go through all sorts of contortions to reach water level. They're at their most vulnerable at waterholes and always appear hesitant and visibly nervous when drinking. In fact, if they feel the slightest uncertainty about the safety of the situation, they'll often forgo their drink altogether.

DAVID WALL

Giraffe

Hippopotamus
Hippopotamus amphibius

The hippo is found in many watercourses in north-eastern South Africa, and in Swaziland. The best places to see them are in Kruger National Park and the St Lucia Wetlands reserves in KwaZulu/Natal.

Hippos, as you probably already know, are huge, fat animals with enormous heads and short legs. When fully grown they weigh in at 1350 to 2600 kg. Their ears, eyes and nostrils are so placed that they can remain inconspicuously above water even when the animal is submerged.

Hippos spend most of the day submerged, feeding on bottom vegetation and surfacing only occasionally to grab a breath of air before plunging again. Only at night do they emerge from the water, often wandering up to several km from their aquatic haunts to graze. They're voracious feeders and can consume up to 60 kg of vegetable matter, mostly a variety of grasses, each night. They urinate and defecate in well-defined areas – often in the water – dispersing the excreta with their tails.

They're very gregarious animals and live in schools of 15 to 30 or more. Each school generally contains an equal number of bulls and cows (with their calves) and hippo society operates under an established hierarchy. They may appear placid, but the males do frequently fight among themselves for dominance and some of the resulting wounds can be quite horrific. Virtually every male hippo bears the scars of such conflicts.

To humans, hippos are statistically Africa's most dangerous animal. Most accidents occur when hippos surface beneath boats and canoes or when someone sets up camp on a riverside hippo run or blocks a hippo's retreat route to the water. They may look sluggish but they do manage considerable speeds and don't much care what stands in their way.

Hippos breed year-round. Cows give birth to a single calf after a gestation period of 230 days and suckle it both in the water and on land for four to six months. At this time it begins to graze on its own. Hippos live for about 30 years and sexual maturity is reached at about four years.

The hippo's only natural predators are lions and crocodiles, which prey on the young. Though they occasionally tangle fishing nets, they're considered beneficial because their wallowing stirs up the bottom mud and their excreta is a valuable fertiliser which encourages the growth of aquatic organisms.

GEOFF CROWTHER

Hippopotamus

DAVID WALL

White or Square-lipped Rhinoceros

DAVID WALL

Black or Hook-lipped Rhinoceros

Rhinoceros

Ceratotherium simum (White or Square-lipped Rhinoceros)

Diceros bicornis (Black or Hook-lipped Rhinoceros)

White rhinos are in fact lighter in colour (and much bulkier) than black rhinos, but their name is a corruption of *wide*-lipped rhino, as opposed to the hook-lipped black rhino.

Rhinos are Africa's most endangered large animals, thanks mainly to the Asian belief that rhino horn has medicinal and aphrodisiac properties, and the Yemeni notion that all real men need a dagger made of rhino horn. Poaching has caused dramatic declines in rhino numbers in recent years, and in many countries they've been completely exterminated.

Luckily for visitors to South Africa and Swaziland, poaching is not out of control, and you have a very good chance of getting close to rhino in Kruger National Park, and in several parks in KwaZulu/Natal and in Swaziland.

Black rhinos are browsers, living in scrubby country and eating mainly leaves, shoots and buds, while white rhinos are grazers and prefer open plains. Both species feed in the cooler hours of the morning or late afternoon.

While white rhinos are generally docile, black rhinos are prone to charging when alarmed, but their eyesight is extremely poor and chances are they'll miss their target anyway. They've even been known to charge trains or elephant carcasses! A black rhino's territory can range from two to 50 sq km, depending on the terrain and availability of food, but only white rhino males actively defend these territories.

Rhinos reach sexual maturity by five years but females first breed at around seven years of age. Calves average 40 kg at birth and grow to 140 kg at three months of age. Adult black rhinos weigh from 800 to 1100 kg but the much larger white rhinos tip the scales at 1200 to 1600 kg. Both species are solitary, only socialising during the mating season. Calves stay with the mother for up to three years, although they're weaned after one year.

Warthog
Phacochoerus aethiopicus

Warthogs are found in parts of Northern Transvaal, Kruger National Park, north-eastern KwaZulu/Natal and elsewhere. They take their name from the rather unusual wart-like growths on the face. They usually live in family groups, known as 'sounders', which include a boar, a sow and three or four young. Their most endearing habit is the way they trot away with their thin tufted tail stuck straight up in the air like antennae.

Males are usually larger than females, measuring up to one metre long and weighing around 100 kg. They grow two sets of tusks; the upper ones curve outwards and upwards and grow as long as 60 cm; the lower ones are usually less than 15 cm long.

Warthogs feed mainly on grass, but also eat fruit and bark. In hard times they'll burrow with their snout for roots and bulbs. They also rest and give birth in abandoned burrows, or sometimes excavate cavities in abandoned termite mounds. Piglets are born in litters of two to eight.

TONY WHEELER

Warthog

Zebra
Equus burchelli (Common or Burchell's Zebra
Equus zebra zebra (Cape Mountain Zebra)

Zebras were once widely distributed, but today you'll only see them in parks and reserves such as Kruger National Park (Burchell's zebra) and Mountain Zebra National Park (Cape mountain zebra). Burchell's zebras have shadow lines between the black stripes; mountain zebras don't have shadows but do have a gridiron pattern of black stripes just above the tail.

Zebras are grazers but occasionally browse on leaves and scrub. They need water daily and rarely wander far from a waterhole. They often mingle with other animals, such as wildebeest, elephants and impala.

During the breeding season, stallions engage in fierce battles for control over a herd of mares. A single foal is born after a gestation period of 12 months. Lions are the zebra's worst enemy, but they're also taken by hyenas and wild dogs.

DAVID WALL

Zebra

OTHER ANIMALS

Aardvark (Antbear)
Orycteropus afer

The porcine-looking aardvark has thick and wrinkled pink-grey skin with very sparse and stiff greyish hair. Its has an elongated tubular snout and a round, sticky, pink tongue, which are used to lap up ants and termites dug from nests and rotting wood with the long claws of its front feet.

Aardvarks dig metre-long holes which are also used as burrows by many other species, including hares, hyenas, jackals, warthogs, owls and rodents. They normally emerge only at night, but in the morning after a cold night they may bask in the sun awhile before retiring underground. When aardvark holes are occupied, the entrances are sealed except for small ventilation holes. When confronted by an enemy, aardvarks somersault and bleat loudly or if there's time, quickly excavate a refuge. When cornered, they resist attack with the foreclaws, shoulders and tail.

Aardvarks are normally solitary animals; only mother and offspring live together. They are found all over this region and can co-exist with cattle farms.

Aardvark (Antbear)

African Elephant
Loxodonta africana

African elephants are much larger than their Asian counterparts and their ears are wider and flatter. A fully grown bull can weigh more than 6½ tonnes.

Elephants are present in Kruger National Park, some parks in KwaZulu/Natal, and a few others, including the Addo Elephant Park, where you'd be unlucky not to see elephants. There are also a very few in the forests around Knysna.

Both males and females grow tusks, although the female's are usually smaller. The tusks on an old bull can weigh as much as 50 kg each but 15 kg to 25 kg is more usual.

Elephants are gregarious animals, and usually live in herds of 10 to 20. These herds will consist of one mature bull and a couple of younger bulls, cows and calves, but herds may incorporate up to 50 individuals. Old bulls appear to lose the herding instinct and eventually leave to pursue a solitary existence, rejoining the herd only for mating. Because elephants communicate using a range of sounds, herds often make a great deal of noise: snorting, bellowing, rumbling and belching produced by the trunk or mouth. The best-known elephant call, however, is the high-pitched trumpeting which they produce when they're frightened or want to appear threatening.

Herds are on the move night and day in pursuit of water and fodder, both of which they consume in vast quantities. An adult's average daily food intake is about 250 kg. Elephants are grazers and browsers and feed on a wide variety of vegetable matter, including grasses, leaves, twigs, bark, roots and fruits, and

DAVID WALL
African Elephant

they frequently knock down quite large trees to get at the leaves. Especially in drought years, they're capable of turning dense woodland into open grassland in a relatively short time. Because of this destructive capacity they're often perceived as a serious threat to a fragile environment, but some schools of thought maintain that elephant damage is necessary in the natural cycle of the bushveld.

Mineral salts obtained from 'salt licks' are also essential in an elephant's diet. Salt is dug out of the earth with the tusks and devoured in large quantities.

Elephants breed year-round and have a gestation period of 22 to 24 months. Expectant mothers leave the herd along with one or two other females and select a secluded spot to give birth, then rejoin the herd a few days later. Calves weigh around 130 kg at birth and stand just under a metre high. They're very playful and are guarded carefully and fondly by their mothers until weaned at two years of age. They continue to grow for the next 20 years, reaching puberty at around 10 to 12 years. On average, an elephant's life span is 60 to 70 years, though some individuals reach the ripe old age of 100 or more.

DAVID WALL

African Elephant

Cape Pangolin
Manis temminckii

The Cape pangolin (also called Temminck's Ground Pangolin) is one of four species of African pangolins, but it is the only species in southern Africa. Pangolins are sometimes known as scaly anteaters because they're covered with large rounded scales over the back and tail, with hair only around the eyes, ears, cheeks and belly. Their primary foods include ants and termites dug from termite mounds, rotting wood and dung heaps. They walk on the outside edges of their hands, with claws pointed inward. They rarely excavate their own holes, however, and prefer to live in abandoned aardvark holes.

Despite the name, Cape pangolins are present mainly in Swaziland and the north and north-east of South Africa, including Kruger National Park. They normally keep to dry scrubby country, especially areas with light sandy soil. They're mainly nocturnal but are most active between midnight and dawn and are therefore rarely seen.

Cape Pangolin

Rock Hyraxes

Hyrax
Procavia capensis (Rock Dassie or Cape Hyrax)

Southern Africa's most common hyrax species is the rock dassie, or rock hyrax. This small but robust animal is about the size of a rabbit, with a short and pointed snout, large ears and thick fur. The tail is either absent or reduced to a stump.

Rock dassies occur practically everywhere there are mountains or rocky outcrops.

Hyraxes are sociable animals and live in colonies of up to 60 individuals, usually in rocky, scrub-covered locales, such as rock koppies. They feed in the morning and evening on grass, bulbs, roots, grasshoppers and locusts. During the rest of the day hyraxes sun themselves on rocks or chase each other in play. Where they're habituated to humans (such as on top of Table Mountain in Cape Town) they're often quite tame, but otherwise they dash into rock crevices when alarmed, uttering shrill screams. They have excellent hearing and eyesight.

Hyraxes breed all year and have a gestation of around seven months, which is a remarkably long period for an animal of this size. Up to six young are born at a time, and are cared for by the entire colony. Predators include leopards, wild dogs, eagles, mongooses and pythons.

Despite its small size, the hyrax is thought to be more closely related to the elephant than any other living creature, but the exact relationship is unclear.

DEANNA SWANEY
Short-Tailed Porcupine

Short-Tailed Porcupine
Hystrix africaeaustralis

The prickly porcupine, the largest rodent native to southern Africa, can weigh as much as 24 kg and measure up to a metre in length. It occurs all over this region but is nocturnal and quite difficult to observe. On cooler days, it may emerge during daylight hours.

Porcupines are covered with a spread of long black and white banded quills from the shoulders to the tail. Along the ridge from the head to the shoulders runs a crest of long coarse hair, which stands on end when the animal is alarmed.

For shelter, they either occupy rock caves or excavate their own burrows. Their diet consists mainly of bark, tubers, seeds and a variety of plants and ground-level foliage. The young are born during the hot summer months, normally in litters of one or two.

SOUTH AFRICA

Facts about the Country

HISTORY
Aftermath of War

The second Anglo-Boer War ended in May 1902 with the defeat of the Boer republics (the Zuid-Afrikaansche Republiek, or Transvaal, and the Orange Free State). The British had pursued a scorched earth policy to deny the Boer guerrillas supplies, while Boer women and children had been confined to concentration camps. The country was devastated and there was a legacy of enormous bitterness, particularly on the Boer side; 22,000 British, 34,000 Boer and 15,000 black lives had been lost.

The colonial government, under Lord Milner, spent millions of pounds reconstructing the country. Attempts were made to rebuild the Boers' agricultural base, but tens of thousands of Boers, ill-equipped for urban life, flooded into the cities. There they found a world dominated by the English and their language. Worst of all, they were forced to compete for jobs with blacks on an equal footing. Partly as a backlash to this Afrikaans came to be seen as the *volkstaal* (people's language), a symbol of Afrikaner nationhood. A number of nationalistic organisations sprang up also.

The British realised that reconstruction could only occur in some sort of partnership with the Boers. In 1906-07, the former republics were given representative government, and moves toward union began almost immediately. The pressures were largely economic – the smaller provinces were unsustainable in a world that required integrated economies and infrastructures, proper tax bases and centralised bureaucracies.

The most contentious issue was the question of voter franchise, which varied from colony to colony. Despite a major nationwide campaign by non-whites, the eventual compromise agreement allowed each colony to retain its existing arrangements, but only whites could be elected to parliament. The only province where non-whites did

SOUTH AFRICA	
Area: 1,233,404 sq km	
Population: 38,000,000	
Capital: Johannesburg	
Head of State: Nelson Mandela	
Official Language: 11 official languages *(see Facts about the Region language section)*	
Currency: Rand	
Exchange Rate: US$1 = R3.66	
Per Capita GNP: US$2600	
Time: GMT/UTC + 2	

have political rights to any meaningful degree was the Cape – the franchise was based on a wealth qualification – but even there only 15% of the registered voters were non-white.

Union of South Africa

The Union of South Africa was established on 31 May 1910. Cape Town was the legislative capital, Pretoria the administrative capital, Bloemfontein the seat of the Supreme Court, and Pietermaritzburg was given financial compensation. The three British High Commission Territories of Basutoland (now Lesotho), Bechuanaland (now Botswana), Swaziland and Rhodesia (now Zimbabwe) were excluded from the Union.

English and Dutch were made the official languages – Afrikaans was not recognised as the official language until 1925.

The first election was held in September 1910. The South African National Party (soon known as the South African Party, or SAP), a diverse coalition of conciliatory Boer groups under General Louis Botha and the brilliant General Jan Smuts, won the election and Botha became the first prime minister.

The most divisive issues were raised by General Barry Hertzog who championed Afrikaner interests, advocated separate development for the two white groups and independence from Britain. He and his supporters formed the National Party (NP).

Soon after the union was established, a barrage of repressive legislation was passed. It became illegal for black workers to strike; skilled jobs were reserved for whites; blacks were barred from military service; and pass laws, restricting black freedom of movement, were tightened.

In 1912, Pixley ka Isaka Seme formed a national democratic organisation to represent blacks. It was initially called the South African Native Congress, but from 1923, it was known as the African National Congress (ANC).

In 1913 the Natives Land Act set aside 7.5% of South Africa's land for black occupancy. No black African (and they made up more than 70% of the population) was allowed to buy, rent or have a sharecropper outside this area. Thousands of squatters were evicted from farms and forced into increasingly overcrowded and impoverished reserves, or into the cities. Those that remained were reduced to the status of landless labourers.

Louis Botha, member of the South African Party, became the first prime minister in 1910.

The main players were on the scene and the foundations for modern apartheid were laid. From the first day of union, race relations would be the major problem facing the country.

WW I

In 1914 South Africa, as a part of the British Empire, found itself automatically at war with Germany and saddled with the responsibility of dealing with German South West Africa (now Namibia). South Africa's involvement on the British side prompted the last major violent Afrikaner rebellion – over 300 men were killed. After the war, South West Africa became a part of South Africa under 'mandate' from the League of Nations.

During the war, General Smuts rose to international prominence, actually becoming a member of the British War Cabinet (along with his old enemy, Lord Milner) without ever facing a British election. Smuts made an important contribution to the establishment of the League of Nations and perhaps because he, too, had once been defeated in war, he was one of the few that saw the Treaty of Versailles as 'an impossible and wrong peace'. He became South Africa's second prime minister in 1919.

Fusion

In 1924 the National Party under Hertzog came to power, with an agenda that included promoting Afrikaner interests, independence and racial segregation. In the 1929 election the *swaartgevaar* (black threat) was made the dominant issue for the first time, with Hertzog successfully portraying himself and the NP as the champion of the white man and Smuts and the SAP as advocates of racial equality.

In reality, their respective positions were not so far apart and, in 1933, the two parties formed a coalition, with Hertzog as the prime minister and Smuts as his deputy. The 'Fusion' or 'Pact' government did not collapse until 1939, and then over the question of South Africa's participation in WW II. Hertzog – who argued for neutrality – was forced to resign in favour of Smuts by the governor general.

Fusion had been rejected by Dr D F Malan and his followers. They formed the Purified National Party, which quickly became the dominant force in Afrikaner political life. The Afrikaner Broederbond, a secret ultra-nationalistic Afrikaner brotherhood, became an extraordinarily influential force behind the party and a range of political, cultural and economic organisations designed to promote the *volk* (Afrikaners). From 1948, every prime minister and president was a member of the Broederbond.

Parity with the English, Hertzog's goal, was no longer enough for the resurgent Afrikaners. At the far right, the Ossewa-Brandwag (Sentinels of the Ox-wagon, or OB) grew into a popular militaristic organisation with strong German sympathies, and an obvious affinity with Hitler's doctrine of a master race. Elements within the organisation pursued an active policy of sabotaging the South African war effort.

PHOTOGRAPH BY JON MURRAY

The Group Areas Act required blacks to carry a pass book at all times

Nonetheless, many South Africans volunteered for service, and troops fought with distinction in Africa and Italy.

The economy boomed during the war and the black urban population nearly doubled. Enormous squatter camps grew up on the outskirts of Johannesburg and, to a lesser extent, outside the other major cities. Black labour became increasingly important to the burgeoning mining and manufacturing industries. Conditions in the townships were appalling, but poverty was by no means only the province of blacks; wartime surveys found that 40% of white school children were malnourished.

Apartheid

The National Party fought the 1948 election on the basis of its policy of *apartheid* (literally, the state of being apart). They gained around 40% of the vote and won 70 of the 150 seats. In coalition with the Afrikaner Party, which had won nine seats, they took control. With the help of creative electoral boundaries and an impressive gerrymander they held power right up to the first democratic election in 1994.

Malan lost no time in instituting the necessary legal apparatus. Mixed marriages were prohibited. Interracial sex was made illegal. Every individual was classified by race and a classification board was established to rule in questionable cases. The Group Areas Act enforcing the physical separation of residential areas was promulgated. The Separate Amenities Act created separate public facilities – separate beaches, separate buses, separate toilets, separate schools and separate park benches. The pass laws were further strengthened and blacks were compelled to carry identity documents at all times and were prohibited from remaining in towns, or even visiting them, without specific permission.

Thanks to the Dutch Reformed churches, apartheid was even given a religious justification: the separateness of the races was divinely ordained and the volk had a holy mission to preserve the purity of the white race in its promised land.

Until WW II there was nothing even vaguely unusual about racist attitudes or whites dominating non-white people. White South Africans had been, to a large degree, in step with the attitudes of the time. The English, French, Belgian, Dutch and Portuguese all saw the possession of colonies and domination of their indigenous people as their natural right.

Allister Sparkes, in *The Mind of South Africa,* argues that the Nazis' excesses created a revulsion towards racist attitudes that sparked a revolution in attitudes among whites and blacks. The days of guiltless racial domination were ended with WW II. However, at the very time the rest of the white world was attempting to abandon old prejudices, and to pack up the old empires and go home, white South Africa moved decisively in the opposite direction. Of course, there was no 'home' to which a 10th-generation Afrikaner could return.

Black Action
In 1949 the ANC developed a programme of action that for the first time advocated open resistance in the form of strikes, acts of public disobedience and protest marches. These continued intermittently throughout the 1950s, with occasional violent clashes.

In June 1955, at a congress held at Kliptown near Johannesburg, a number of organisations, including the Indian Congress and the ANC, adopted a Freedom Charter. This articulated a vision of a non-racial democratic state and is still central to the ANC's vision of a new South Africa.

On 21 March 1960 the Pan African Congress (PAC) called for nationwide demonstrations against the hated pass laws. When demonstrators surrounded a police station in Sharpeville (near Vereeniging) police opened fire, killing 69 people and wounding 160. In many domestic and international eyes the struggle had crossed a crucial line – there could no longer be any doubts about the nature of the white regime.

Soon after, the PAC and ANC were banned and the security forces were given the right to detain people indefinitely without trial. Prime Minister Verwoerd announced a referendum on whether the country should become a republic, and a slim majority of white voters gave their approval to the change. Verwoerd withdrew from the (British) Commonwealth, and in May 1961 the Republic of South Africa came into existence.

Nelson Mandela became the leader of the underground ANC and Oliver Tambo went abroad to establish the organisation in exile. As increasing numbers of black activists were arrested, the ANC and PAC began a campaign of sabotage through the armed wings of their organisations, respectively Umkonto We Sizwe (Spear of the Nation; usually known as MK) and Poqo (Pure). In July 1963 Nelson Mandela, along with a number of other ANC and communist leaders, was arrested, charged with fomenting violent revolution and sentenced to life imprisonment.

The time comes in the life of any nation when there remain only two choices: submit or fight. That time has now come to South Africa. We shall not submit and we have no choice but to hit back by all means within our power in defence of our people, our future and our freedom...Refusal to resort to force has been interpreted by the government as an invitation to use armed force against the people without any fear of reprisals.
Umkonto we Sizwe Manifesto, 1961

The Homelands
Verwoerd was assassinated in parliament in 1966 (there was apparently no political motive) and was succeeded by B J Vorster, who was followed in 1978 by P W Botha. Both men continued to pursue the insane dream of separate black Homelands and a white South Africa.

The plan was to restrict blacks to Homelands that were, in terms of the propaganda, to become self-sufficient, self-governing states on the traditional lands of particular tribal groups. In reality, these traditional lands had virtually no infrastructure, no industry and were therefore incapable of producing sufficient food for the burgeoning black population. They were based on the

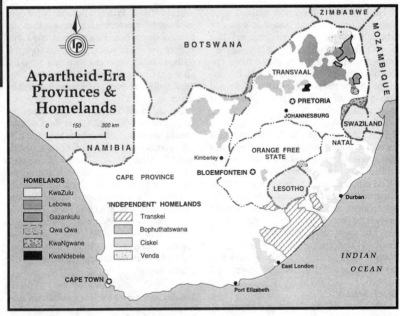

Apartheid-Era Provinces & Homelands

0   150   300 km

HOMELANDS
- KwaZulu
- Lebowa
- Gazankulu
- Qwa Qwa
- KwaNgwane
- KwaNdebele

'INDEPENDENT' HOMELANDS
- Transkei
- Bophuthatswana
- Ciskei
- Venda

ZIMBABWE
BOTSWANA
TRANSVAAL
MOZAMBIQUE
✪ PRETORIA
JOHANNESBURG
SWAZILAND
NATAL
NAMIBIA
Kimberley ●
ORANGE FREE STATE
BLOEMFONTEIN ✪
CAPE PROVINCE
LESOTHO
Durban ●
CAPE TOWN ✪
INDIAN OCEAN
East London ●
Port Elizabeth ●

land that had been set aside for blacks in the 1913 Natives Lands Act. Under the plan, 13% of the country's total land area was to be the home to 75% of the population.

Irrespective of where they had been born, blacks were divided into one of 10 tribal groups and were made citizens of the Homeland that had been established for their group. Blacks were to have no rights in South Africa and could not even be present outside their particular Homeland without a pass and explicit permission.

The Homelands policy ignored the fact that in the 19th century, the tribes had been in a complete state of chaos because of the difaqane, and that the ethnological grounds for distinguishing 10 tribal groups were extremely shaky. In the meantime, there had also been extremely rapid urbanisation and economic integration – blacks had lived and worked on 'white' land and in 'white' cities for several generations.

Millions of people were forcibly dispos-sessed and resettled – in particular, the elderly, the unfit, women and children and the unem-ployed were targeted. First their houses were flattened and then they were dumped in Homelands they had often never seen. They were given rations for a limited period, but were expected to be self-sufficient on over-populated countryside that was rapidly exhausted. There was intense, widespread suffering. In particular, families were frac-tured as the men were forced to return alone to the cities as guest workers without rights.

The crusading government banned the employment of blacks as shop assistants, receptionists, typists and clerks. The con-struction of housing in the black locations (dormitory suburbs for black workers) was halted, and enormous single-sex hostels were built instead. Despite this, however, many families returned to the cities as soon as they could. Life was tough in the squatter camps where they were forced to live, but the Homelands were worse.

The Homelands were first given internal self-government, and were then expected to accept a nominal independence. Chief Mangosuthu Buthelezi, who controlled the KwaZulu legislature with the help of his Inkatha movement, attempted to unite the Homeland leaders in resistance to South Africa's ploy.

However, power proved irresistible to the leaders of Transkei, Bophuthatswana, Venda and Ciskei. Between 1976 and 1981 the collaborators accepted 'independence', and then they proceeded to crush all of the resistance to themselves and to the South African government.

War with Acronyms

In 1966 the United Nations began a series of unsuccessful attempts to take over the administration of South West Africa. South Africa's mandate (dating from the end of WW I) was withdrawn and its presence in the country was declared unlawful. South Africa's response was to deploy a large military force against SWAPO (South West Africa People's Organisation), the liberation movement that began a guerrilla war of independence.

After a coup in 1974, Portugal began to withdraw from its African colonies. By 1975 both Angola and Mozambique had become independent and South Africa was confronted by two Marxist-oriented black states sympathetic to the ANC and PAC. In addition, Botswana and Lesotho were also outspoken in their criticism of apartheid and supported black movements.

In 1975 and '76 the South African Defence Force (SADF) made full-scale invasions of Angola both to attack SWAPO bases and to aid UNITA and the FNLA, organisations fighting the Cuba-backed MPLA regime which had seized power. In Mozambique, South Africa supported the rebel RENAMO guerrillas against the socialist FRELIMO government.

In 1980, after a bitter guerrilla war the leader of ZANU, Robert Mugabe, was elected the prime minister of an independent Zimbabwe (formerly Rhodesia) and South Africa found itself the last white-controlled state in Africa. Increasing numbers of Western countries imposed sanctions of various kinds and the ANC and PAC received direct support from the governments of black Africa (with the exception of Malawi and Swaziland), many of whom were, in turn, receiving support from the countries of the communist bloc.

South Africa increasingly saw itself as a bastion besieged by communism, atheism and black anarchy. From 1978 to 1988 the SADF made a number of major attacks inside Angola, Mozambique, Zimbabwe, Botswana and Lesotho. These ranged from full-scale deployment in Angola and Namibia to more limited attacks on ANC targets in Lesotho.

In 1988 the formidable SADF suffered its first major reverse at the town of Cuito Cuanavale in Angola, largely due to the intervention of the Cubans and particularly their airforce. The war suddenly began to look very expensive in terms of both lives and treasure and serious negotiations commenced.

Thanks in no small part to Gorbachev's new spirit of détente a peace was finally brokered. This opened the way for independence in Namibia. In early 1989 South African troops withdrew from Namibia and

The African National Congress was at the forefront of the political and military struggle for freedom.

Cuban troops withdrew from Angola. An election was held in Namibia under UN auspices and SWAPO won a huge majority. Namibia became independent in 1990.

The SADF was (and still is) the largest and best equipped army in Africa. All white males were liable for national service, and as a result of arms embargoes, and thanks to Armscor (the government armaments producer), it became remarkably self-sufficient in supplies and equipment. Thousands of young white South Africans were forced into exile to avoid conscription. Thousands more were scarred mentally and physically by the vicious struggles in Namibia and Angola, or in the townships of South Africa.

Soweto Uprising

Within the borders of South Africa, large-scale violence finally broke out on 16 June 1976 when the Soweto Students' Representative Council organised protests against the use of Afrikaans (regarded as the language of the oppressor) in black schools. Police opened fire on a student march, beginning a round of nationwide demonstrations, strikes, mass arrests and riots that, over the next 12 months, took over 1000 lives.

Steve Biko, the charismatic leader of the Black Consciousness movement, which stressed the need for psychological liberation and black pride, was killed in September 1977. Unidentified security police bashed him until he lapsed into a fatal coma – he went without medical treatment for three days and finally died in Pretoria. At the subsequent inquest, the magistrate found no one was to blame.

South Africa was never to be the same again – a generation of young blacks committed themselves to a revolutionary struggle against apartheid and the black communities were politicised. World opinion turned decisively against the white regime. The white South Africans, however, were by no means ready to face reality.

P W Botha rewrote the constitution in 1983 and two-thirds of the white population supported the changes. The powers of the state president were increased and three legislative chambers of parliament were created: a House of Assembly for whites, a House of Representatives for coloureds, and a House of Delegates for Indians. Needless to say, the white chamber was larger than the other two put together.

Apart from completely alienating three-quarters of the population (the blacks, who were given no role at all), it was an insanely complicated system. What chamber should control what? Each chamber administered its own education department, the whites controlled black education, and there were education departments within each of the Homelands.

Violent protest built up steadily over the next two years until, in 1985, the government declared a state of emergency which was to stay in force for the next five years. The media was strictly censored and, by 1988, 30,000 people had been detained without trial. Thousands were tortured. The violence was not only between the United Democratic Front (UDF), which had adopted the ANC's Freedom Charter, and the government, but increasingly between Inkatha and the UDF.

Botha repealed the pass laws, but this failed to mollify the black protesters and also created a white backlash. Dr Andries Treurnicht – Dr No – and his Conservative Party developed into a serious force and a number of neo-Nazi paramilitary groups

The logo of the neo-Nazi Afrikaner-Weerstandsbeweging is like the swastika.

emerged, notably the frightening Afrikaner-Weerstandsbeweging (AWB). The AWB is distinctive, both for its swastika look-alike emblems and the demagoguery of its leader Eugène Terre'Blanche – Eugène White Earth.

Botha's reforms also failed to impress the rest of the world, and economic sanctions began to bite. In particular, foreign banks refused to roll over government loans and the value of the rand collapsed. In late 1989, Botha was replaced by F W De Klerk.

Reform

At his opening address to the parliament on 2 February 1990, De Klerk announced that he would repeal discriminatory laws and the ANC, PAC and the Communist Party were legalised. Media restrictions were lifted, and De Klerk undertook to release political prisoners not guilty of common-law crimes. On 11 February he released Nelson Mandela, 27 years after he had first been incarcerated. In March, at an occasion that would have been totally unimaginable three years earlier, both men attended the independence celebrations of Namibia.

During 1990 and '91, virtually all the old apartheid regulations were repealed. The Separate Amenities Act, the Group Areas Act (which reserved racially based residential areas), and the Population Registration Act (classifying people by race) were all swept away.

On 21 December 1991, the Convention for a Democratic South Africa (CODESA) began negotiations on the formation of a multiracial transitional government and a new constitution extending political rights to

FW De Klerk took office in 1990 and immediately began changing the political structure of South Africa.

all groups. The convention was attended by delegates from every major organisation in the country, with the exception of the Conservative Party and other far-right groups like the AWB.

After losing a by-election to the Conservative Party, De Klerk showed his shrewdness and political nerve by calling a referendum seeking a mandate for his policies of change. In a result that exceeded the most optimistic predictions, 68.7% of the white electorate gave that mandate and clearly rejected the Conservative Party and its right-wing allies. In the cities the vote in favour of reform exceeded 80%; it was much closer in the conservative countryside, especially in the Transvaal and northern Cape, but only one

Soweto Uprisings

Try to see the film *A Dry White Season* (1989), a powerful depiction of the 1976 Soweto uprisings and the vicious reaction by the police state, tacitly condoned by the majority of whites. The role of the *Rand Daily Mail* newspaper as a liberal voice is emphasised – but what the film doesn't show in its 'happy' ending is that the paper was soon to be banned by the government. The film is based on a novel by André Brink. This is, for a Hollywood movie, a remarkably straight telling of an horrific story. The only problem is that for the sake of the story the scale of the events is reduced to a few goodies and baddies. In reality, the detentions, torture and murders involved thousands and thousands of innocent people, mainly blacks but including a few whites. ■

of the 12 electoral districts, Pietersburg in the northern Transvaal, recorded a negative vote.

After nearly 350 years of domination, the great majority of whites had accepted that they could no longer deny equal political and human rights to the non-white population. Remarkably, most of the non-white population and its leaders seemed to harbour very little bitterness and the ANC consistently emphasised that whites were not in any way 'the enemy'.

The right-wing response to this crushing loss was muted, but with 30% of the white population behind them, fanatical and heavily armed right-wing groups were still a potential threat to reform.

Township Violence

From the mid-1980s the majority of deaths attributed to political violence were the result of black-on-black violence. The Human Rights Commission estimated that more than 4300 people died in 1993 alone. There were clashes between political rivals, tribal enemies, opportunistic gangsters, and between those who lived in the huge migrant-workers' hostels and their township neighbours.

Chief Buthelezi, leader of the Inkatha Freedom Party.

The violence was often characterised as straightforward tribal war between members of the right-wing Zulu-based Inkatha party and left-wing Xhosa-based ANC. Inkatha's leader, Chief Mangosuthu Buthelezi, is a skilful politician who played an ambiguous role fighting for black (particularly Zulu) rights on one hand, but receiving direct financial and military support from the white regime on the other. Buthelezi's fear that his people would be dominated in a new, unitary state controlled by the ANC came close to precipitating civil war several times on the way to the 1994 election. Nevertheless, this view of the township violence is too simple.

The roots of the violence were clearly buried in the years of apartheid. Firstly, there was (and still is) massive economic and social deprivation in the black communities. In some areas over 90% of the population is unemployed, and living conditions for most people are appalling. The government's migrant-worker policies broke up millions of families, and black education and health policies were completely inadequate. Whole generations were brutalised by political and criminal violence.

The enormous single-sex hostels (sometimes housing more than 10,000 men) were often at the centre of the violence. Again, it is simplistic to characterise this simply as a conflict between the Xhosa/ANC/township dwellers and the Zulu/Inkatha/hostel dwellers.

There is a cultural gulf between the educated, urbanised blacks in the township suburbs and those in the hostels, many of whom are recent arrivals from traditional communities in the countryside (where the cult of the warrior survives). During the years of township violence the hostels became virtually ungovernable armed camps inhabited by men who were unemployed, uneducated, and unused to city life in the centre of township suburbs. Violent clashes were hardly surprising, even without the addition of political, cultural and linguistic differences.

There is also clear evidence that sections of the white-controlled security forces were directly, though covertly, involved in the killing. In addition to sins of commission, including assassinations, there were sins of omission – the forces often appeared unwilling to intervene, especially in cases where Inkatha supporters had been on a rampage.

Towards Democracy

The CODESA negotiations did not proceed smoothly or easily but it was apparent that both the National Party and the ANC were determined that free elections of some sort would take place at some time. However, thrashing out the details was a complex process and the ANC suspected that the government was committed to drawing it out as long as possible. The political violence that was wracking the country could only hurt the ANC's vote at the election.

In June 1992, 42 men, women and children were massacred in Boipatong, a township to the south of Johannesburg, allegedly by members of the nearby Kwa-Madala hostel, controlled by the Inkatha movement. Witnesses in the township and a black police constable consistently alleged that security forces were involved. For the ANC, Boipatong was the final straw, and they withdrew from CODESA.

No longer involved in negotiations, the ANC played its trump card – mass action. Months of strikes and a rekindling of fervour for the struggle among grassroots ANC supporters convinced the government to agree to some of the ANC's demands and the talks resumed. The violence continued to build and non-military white targets were attacked. Chris Hani, the popular secretary general of the Communist Party, was assassinated by right-wingers.

By now the CODESA talks had become a straight negotiation between the National Party and the ANC, excluding the smaller parties. The Zulu-based Inkatha movement (now called the Inkatha Freedom Party – IFP) and some of the Homelands governments left CODESA, demanding a federal structure for the new constitution. Right-wing whites, who wanted a *Volkstaat* (literally, people's state – a Boer homeland), joined them in an unlikely alliance.

Archbishop Desmond Tutu

Now, with white support drifting to the right-wing parties, the National Party needed to hurry negotiations. Also, it needed to demonstrate that it was not simply handing the country over to the ANC. The Nationals demanded an interim government with power-sharing arrangements and a hand in writing the final version of the constitution. The ANC didn't want the old government to retain any real control after the election, but at the same time it could not afford to frighten the whites. The radical right-wing was as much a threat to the ANC as it was to the Nationals, and it was essential for the economy that as few whites as possible fled the country.

A compromise was reached and both sides accepted an interim government of national unity to rule after the election for no more than five years. They also agreed that the final version of the constitution be written within two years by members of the new parliament to be elected on 26 and 27 April 1994.

The right-wing threat was lessened when the right's most respected leader, General Constand Viljoen, hastily formed the Freedom Front party and agreed to participate in the election. Viljoen had learned that the right-wing militants were not the inheritors of Boer ideals but a rabble of thugs. Just days before the election, Chief Buthelezi's IFP also agreed to participate.

Two last-minute amendments to the interim constitution help to explain why these holdouts joined in: one enabled the setting-up of a committee to consider the establishment of a Volkstaat and the other allowed future provincial governments to recognise traditional monarchs – by far the most powerful of whom is the Zulu king.

Free Elections

Across the country at midnight on 26-27 April 1994, *Die Stem* (the old national anthem) was sung and the old flag was lowered. Then the new rainbow flag was raised and the new anthem, *Nkosi Sikelele Afrika* (God Bless Africa) was sung – once, people were jailed for singing this beautiful hymn.

Voting for 'special' voters (mainly the old and disabled) had been held on the 26th, under the eyes of thousands of foreign observers and an equally large foreign press corps. Although there had been a couple of serious bombings by far-right militants, it was clear that the biggest problems when general voting began the next day would be poor organisation and a lack of ballot papers.

This proved to be the case, and the 27th was a day of queues several km long, closed polling stations, and allegations of irregularities. Surprisingly, though, this didn't result in chaos and people generally took the delays in good spirit. That night the army was called in to help print and airlift nine million additional ballot papers and on the 28th voting proceeded more smoothly. The polls were kept open until everyone who wanted to vote had done so, and there was a further day of

---

The Old South Africa

It's useful to have an idea of how the old South Africa operated, if only to understand some of the quirks you'll find in the new South Africa.

South Africa had a Westminster-style system of government, modified several times, from union in 1910 until 1984, when the constitution was rewritten. The constitution promised, in part, 'to uphold Christian values and civilised norms...'

There were three chambers to the parliament, for coloureds, Indians and whites. Blacks could not vote (most blacks were not considered to be citizens of South Africa). The State President had enormous power, including the power to decide whether an issue was an 'own affair' or a 'general affair'. Own affairs were deliberated by the individual houses and general affairs by all three. That was the theory, anyway. Since the white chamber was larger than the others combined, whites retained control when it counted. In addition, there was the President's Council which had the power to resolve deadlocks, and nearly half the members were nominated by the president.

As a result of the compromises made at the time of union there were three capitals: Pretoria, the administrative capital and capital of the Transvaal; Cape Town, the legislative capital and capital of the Cape Province; Bloemfontein, the judicial capital and capital of the Orange Free State. The only provincial capital to miss out on the action was Pietermaritzburg, the capital of Natal.

There were four provinces: Transvaal (most of Gauteng, Northern Transvaal and Eastern Transvaal, and part of North-West Province), Natal (now KwaZulu/Natal), the Orange Free State and Cape Province (most of Northern, Eastern and Western Cape provinces). There were once elected provincial assemblies, but after 1986 the provinces were run by authorities appointed by the president.

In addition there were the Homelands, the cornerstones of apartheid. The six 'self-governing Homelands' – Gazankulu, KwaNdebele, KwaNgwane, KwaZulu, Lebowa and Qwa Qwa – had internal self-government. Transkei, Ciskei, Venda and Bophuthatswana were considered by South Africa (but not by the United Nations) to be independent countries. They had their own puppet presidents, armies, border controls and ludicrous trappings such as 'international airports'.

One of the many fringe benefits for white South Africans was that these 'independent countries' weren't bound by South Africa's puritanical laws. A visit to a Homeland casino, to gamble or see a porn movie, became a popular outing. ■

voting in remote areas in some of the ex-Homelands.

Observers agreed that there had been some problems and probably some cheating, but on the whole the election was free and fair. More importantly, the vast majority of South Africans perceived it to have been so. The biggest problems were in KwaZulu/Natal and during the counting process there was considerable behind-the-scenes work (including the juggling of figures) to compensate for logistical and political hitches.

The ANC won 62.7% of the vote, less than the 66.7% which would have enabled it to overrule the interim constitution. However, as the interim constitution is largely the work of the ANC, that isn't a problem, and the public perception that it cannot ride roughshod over the constitution is good for stability. As well as deciding the national government, the election decided the provincial governments, and the ANC won in all but two of the provinces.

The National Party won 20.4% of the vote, enough to guarantee it representation in cabinet. Given that white voters are only 15% of the electorate this is a good result for the party. De Klerk became the South African Vice President. The Nationals also won the provincial election in Western Cape, thanks to a scaremongering campaign among the coloured population.

The IFP won 10.5% of the national vote and Chief Buthelezi became Minister for Home Affairs. However, in a dispute over concessions granted before the election, he and the IFP have considered boycotting the National Assembly. The IFP had a decisive victory in the KwaZulu/Natal provincial election, but Buthelezi has had a falling-out with the Zulu royal family, so the domestic politics of the province will remain interesting for some time to come. A return to serious violence is not impossible.

The only other parties to win seats in the National Assembly were the white conservative Freedom Front (2.2%), the mainly white liberal Democratic Party (1.7%), the black hard-line PAC (1.3%) and the African Christian Democratic Party (0.5%).

For the full story of the election, read the excellent book *Election '94 South Africa* edited by Andrew Reynolds (paperback, R40).

The New South Africa

Despite the scars of the past and the enormous problems ahead, South Africa today is an immeasurably more optimistic and relaxed country than it was a few years ago. Among whites there is a sort of dazed relief that while their oldest fears (three centuries old) have come true, nothing much has changed. Some are even finding that life without racism is much more enjoyable. Among blacks there is the exhilaration of freedom gained and optimism for the future. New and old arts and cultures, long denigrated, are flowering. There is a lot of catching up to do and the next few years will be very exciting.

The people of South Africa seem to have invented a political structure strong enough to hold together the diverse cultures of the region, although whether it is flexible enough to allow each group to fulfil its legitimate aspirations remains to be seen. Recent events in Europe testify to the difficulties of creating multicultural states and graphically illustrate how such states cannot be successful unless their legitimacy is voluntarily accepted by each group they encompass.

Economic inequality presents an equally thorny problem. Although the apartheid system is dead, economic apartheid lives on, despite affirmative-action programmes. With an economy geared to low wages and a legacy of very poor education for blacks, it will be a generation at least before the majority gain much economic benefit from their freedom. As a traveller you'll notice just how little black involvement there is in the economy. Chances are that the only black-owned business you will deal with is a minibus taxi company.

Housing is the most urgent need and will be the major indicator of how the government is fulfilling its promise of a better life for all. As well as the generally substandard housing endured by blacks, it is estimated that nine million people live in appalling conditions in squatter camps. The government has agreed to give homeless people a serviced plot with a concrete slab. They will build their own houses – contributing 'sweat equity' to the deal.

The most important piece of legislation passed in the first session of the new parliament was the Land Rights Bill. It sets out to reverse (or compensate) the forced removals which began in 1913 with the Natives Lands Act that allowed blacks to own just 13% of the country's total area. This will assist many, many people but of course there were even more substantial removals before 1913. The IFP voted against the legislation because it did not address land appropriation before 1913 (most Zulu land was taken in the 19th century).

Nelson Rolihlahla Mandela

Nelson Mandela, the son of the third wife of a Xhosa chief, was born on 18 July 1918 in the small village of Mveso on the Mbashe River. When he was very young his family moved to Qunu, south of Umtata. He attended school in the Transkei before going to Johannesburg where, after a few false starts, he undertook legal studies and set up a law practice with Oliver Tambo. He shunned the opportunities offered to educated blacks and adopted a more militant stance, aspiring to help in the liberation of his people.

In 1944 he helped form the youth league of the African National Congress (ANC) with Walter Sisulu and Oliver Tambo. Its aim was to end the racist policies of the white South African government. Mandela took up boxing to keep fit. He met Nomzamo Winnifred Madikizela ('Winnie') who he married after receiving a divorce from his first wife, Evelyn.

In 1964, after establishing the ANC's military wing, he was captured and sentenced to life imprisonment at the infamous Robben Island prison near Cape Town. In the early 1970s rules were sufficiently relaxed to allow Mandela to write his now-famous prison notebooks and teach politics.

Mandela was released from prison in 1990 after the ANC was declared a legal organisation. In 1991 he was elected president of the ANC and began the long negotiations which were to end minority rule. He shared the 1993 Nobel Peace Prize with F W De Klerk and, in the first free elections the following year, was elected president of South Africa.

On 2 May 1994, in front of Coretta Scott King, wife of the late Martin Luther King Jr, he said to his people: 'You have shown such a calm, patient determination to reclaim this country as your own and now the joy that we can loudly proclaim from the rooftops – Free at last! Free at last! I stand before you humbled by your courage, with a heart full of love for all of you. I regard it as the highest honour to lead the ANC at this moment in our history. I am your servant...this is the time to heal the old wounds and build a new South Africa.'

President Mandela is walking one of the thinnest tightropes imaginable. Freeing people from 20 generations of repression would, in any other post-colonial country, have resulted in an understandable chaos. Mandela, however, must ensure that as many whites as possible stay in the country and that their businesses remain lucrative. The ANC is a genuinely non-racial organisation and Mandela seems sincere in his desire to create a truly non-racial South Africa. For the many, many thousands who suffered – physically, mentally and economically – under apartheid, this must be a bitter pill. ∎

The crimes of the apartheid era are due to be exposed (but not necessarily punished) by a Truth Commission. Meanwhile, newspapers such as *The Sowetan* regularly print reliable stories about atrocities committed by the apartheid government and its security forces. One of the more bizarre covert operations was the infecting of prostitutes in Johannesburg's largely black Hillbrow area with AIDS, presumably on the insane premise that most clients of these prostitutes were black, and most ANC members were black, so... After successful operations, such as blowing up the World Council of Churches building in Johannesburg (and blaming it on the ANC), senior politicians reportedly visited the covert operations HQ to drink champagne with the officers.

The security forces have a long way to go to rehabilitate their reputation, but the process has begun. Incorporating the ANC's MK soldiers into the army caused some hiccups but on the whole it seems to have gone surprisingly smoothly.

Other perspectives are also altering. A few months after the election *The Sowetan* newspaper, a staunch ally of the socialist ANC during the Struggle, held a competition in which the first prize was a share portfolio!

GEOGRAPHY

South Africa is divided into nine provinces: Gauteng, Northern Transvaal, Eastern Transvaal, Orange Free State, Kwazulu/Natal, North-West, Northern Cape, Eastern Cape and Western Cape.

Most of these provinces were formed during the run-up to the 1994 election and were carved from the old provinces of Cape, Transvaal, Orange Free State and Natal. It's likely that the names of some of the new provinces will change.

The Homelands no longer exist as political entities, but because of their very different histories and economies it will be some time before you don't notice a marked change when you cross one of the old borders. In this guide we sometimes refer to the old Homelands by name. Transkei and Ciskei have been absorbed into Eastern Cape

(a small chunk of Transkei has been claimed by Kwazulu/Natal), Venda into Northern Transvaal, and Bophuthatswana into the North-West (Thaba N'Chu, an isolated chunk of Bop, is in Orange Free State). The smaller Homelands (Gazankulu, Lebowa, KaNgwane, KwaNdebele, KwaZulu and QwaQwa), which were regarded as self-governing rather than independent countries by the apartheid regime, have been more easily reabsorbed into the surrounding provinces.

The country's real, unofficial capital was always Johannesburg and that has now been recognised. The city lies at the centre of an enormous urban conurbation known as the PWV (Pretoria, Witwatersrand, Vereeniging – now Gauteng Province). It is the largest, the richest and the most important city in the country.

Pretoria and Cape Town are locked in a struggle to gain/retain the status of legislative capital. Pretoria points out that it is ridiculous to have the parliament so far from the public servants, and that within 200 km of the city is 27% of the county's population, most of the country's 11 official languages are spoken, there are 14 airports and so on. However, I'd put my money on Cape Town retaining the parliament.

The provincial capitals are: Johannesburg (Gauteng), Pietersburg (Northern Transvaal), Nelspruit (Eastern Transvaal), Mmabatho (North-West), Bloemfontein (Orange Free State), Kimberley (Northern Cape) and Cape Town (Western Cape). The capital of Eastern Cape hasn't yet been settled but it will be either East London or nearby Bisho, once the capital of Ciskei. The capital of KwaZulu/Natal might be Durban (the largest city), Pietermaritzburg (the old capital of Natal) or Ulundi (the old capital of Kwazulu).

South Africa is a big country, nearly 2000 km from the Limpopo River in the north to Cape Agulhas in the south, and nearly 1500 km from Port Nolloth in the west to Durban in the east. It's mostly dry and sunny, lying just to the south of the Tropic of Capricorn – Sydney, Australia, is almost the same latitude as Cape Town, and Brisbane, Australia, is about the same as Johannesburg. The major influence on the climate, however, is not the country's latitude, but its topography and the surrounding oceans.

The country can be divided into three major parts: the vast interior plateau (the highveld), the Great Escarpment at its edge (the Kalahari Basin), and a narrow coastal plain (the lowveld). Although Johannesburg is not far south of the tropics, its altitude, around 1700 metres above sea level, and its distance from the sea moderates its climate. It is 1500 km further north than Cape Town, but its average temperatures are only 1°C higher.

The cold, nutrient-rich Benguela current from the Antarctic runs north up the west coast, lowering temperatures and severely limiting rainfall. The warm Agulhas current from the tropical Indian Ocean runs south down the east coast. Durban is an average of 6°C warmer than Port Nolloth and receives 16 times more rain (1000 mm), although they are both on much the same latitude.

CLIMATE

The eastern plateau region (including Johannesburg) has a dry, sunny climate in winter with maximum temperatures around 20°C and crisp nights with temperatures dropping to around 5°C. Between October and April there are late-afternoon showers often accompanied by spectacular thunder and lightning, but it rarely gets unpleasantly hot. Heavy hailstorms cause quite a lot of damage each year. It can, however, get very hot in the Karoo (the semi-desert heart of all three Cape provinces) and the far north (the Kalahari).

The Western Cape has dry sunny summers with maximum temperatures around 26°C. It is often windy, however, and the south-easterly 'Cape Doctor' can reach gale force. Winters can get cold, with average minimum temperatures of around 5°C, and maximum

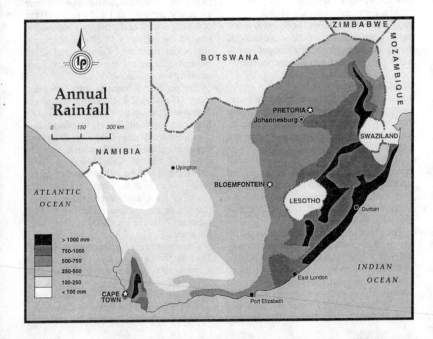

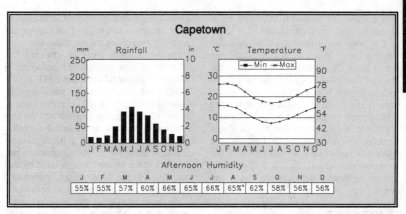

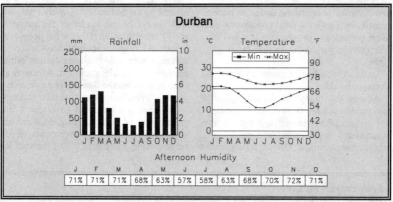

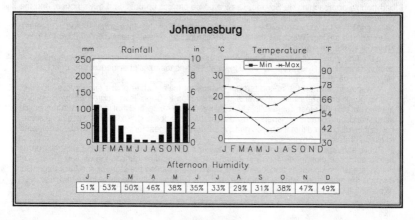

temperatures of around 17°C, with occasional snow on the higher peaks.

The coast north from the Cape becomes progressively drier and hotter. Along the south coast the weather is temperate, but the east coast becomes increasingly tropical the further north you go. The Transkei region and KwaZulu/Natal can be hot and unpleasantly humid in summer, although the highlands are still pleasant; this is also a summer rainfall area. The Eastern and Northern Transvaal lowveld gets very hot in summer, when there are spectacular storms. In winter the days are sunny and warm.

GOVERNMENT

South Africa is operating under an interim constitution, with the final constitution due to be written and passed into law in 1996. The current parliament is due to sit until 1999.

South Africa has rejoined the (British) Commonwealth.

Among the many Fundamental Rights protected under the constitution is the right not to be discriminated against on any grounds and 'in particular: race, gender, sex, ethnic or social origin, colour, sexual orientation, age, disability, religion, conscience, belief, culture or language'. That must cover just about everything except shoe size.

The constitution gives an amnesty for political crimes committed between 8 October 1990 and 6 December 1993.

There are two houses of parliament, a National Assembly of 400 members and a Senate of 90 members. Members of the National Assembly are elected directly (using the proportional representation method – there are no constituencies) but members of the senate are appointed by the provincial legislatures. Each province, regardless of its size, appoints 10 senators.

The head of state is the president, currently Nelson Mandela. The president is elected by the National Assembly (and thus will always be the leader of the majority party) rather than directly by the people. A South African president has more in common with a Westminster system prime minister than a US president, although as head of state he/she does have some executive powers denied most prime ministers.

The current transitional government is a government of national unity, so there are some power-sharing arrangements. Each party winning more than 5% of the vote for

---

Enforcing Law & Order

The police force has been reorganised and for most people a police car is no longer a sign of very bad trouble approaching. In Soweto, I saw a police car pull up outside a guy's house, and the white officer got out, not bothering to put on his cap or remove his cigarette, but making sure his pistol-grip shotgun was handy. The householder walked down his drive, arms spread in greeting, beaming and saying, 'Welcome the South African police'. A wise precaution? Taking the piss? Maybe a little each way.

In the first months of the new South Africa the police had trouble winning prosecutions in the courts. It seems that they were not used to ideas such as the rules of evidence, and 'confessions' were much harder to come by.

Newspapers carried the all-too-familiar pictures of mainly white police firing into a crowd of mainly black protesters the day after a demonstration in Cape Town turned nasty. Someone pointed out that this wasn't compatible with the new South Africa, and that in other countries police used shields and batons to disperse crowds – perhaps the police should look into acquiring some. It was then discovered that the police had owned riot control gear for years but had never bothered to use it, preferring shotguns.

Public attitudes to violence are also a little warped. The morning after striking security guards held a demonstration in the centre of Johannesburg, firing their guns in the air and (maybe) at police, smashing up shops and looting, the newspapers carried the story on the front page. But it wasn't the main story. The big headlines read 'Bus Chaos in City', because there had also been a (peaceful) bus drivers' strike. ■

the National Assembly (the IFP, NP and ANC) is entitled to proportional representation in Cabinet, and Cabinet decisions are supposed to be consensual. However, when it comes to the crunch there is nothing to stop the majority party (the ANC) from getting its way.

There are also provincial legislatures, with memberships varying with population: Northern Cape is the smallest with 30 members, the largest is Gauteng with 86. Each province has a premier. Provincial governments have strictly limited powers and are bound by the national constitution.

In addition to the Western-style democratic system there is a system of traditional leaders. There is a Council of Traditional Leaders, to which all legislation pertaining to indigenous law, traditions or customs must be referred. Although the Council cannot veto or amend legislation it can delay its passage. In each province where there have been recognised traditional authorities (every province except Gauteng, Western Cape and Northern Cape), a House of Tradi-

tional Leaders will be established. The House will have similar powers to the Council, but when the provinces write their constitutions, the powers of traditional leaders may be widened.

An amendment to the constitution passed just two days before the 1994 election will allow provincial legislatures to 'provide for the institution, role, authority and status of a traditional monarch'. This applies mainly to the powerful Zulu king and might be a can of worms waiting to be opened.

Meanwhile, democracy is alive and very well. Members of the new parliament who also served in the old parliament are amazed that ANC members ask ministers tricky questions, and that ANC members of parliamentary committees query legislation and actually refer it back to the people for their input.

ECONOMY

South Africa's economy is a mixture of first and third world with a marked disparity in incomes, standards of living, lifestyles, edu-

---

Legal System

South Africa's legal system is a blend of the Dutch-Roman and British systems. The British influence is seen most strongly in criminal justice procedures. Cases are tried by magistrates or judges without juries, at the instigation of police 'dockets' or private actions. Clients are represented by solicitors *(prokureurs* in Afrikaans) and advocates *(advokates –* the equivalent of barristers).

Magistrates *(landdrost)* in Afrikaans) were first appointed while the colony was under VOC rule, and they were essentially governors of their areas. Drostdys, the homes and offices of the landdrost, are today some of the earliest and most impressive buildings in the country. The Drostdy Museum at Swellendam (Western Cape) and the various Drostdy buildings in Graaff Reinet (Eastern Cape) are among the best examples.

Unlike a British magistrate, whose decisions are partially influenced by the values of the local community, the landdrost was a company and later government official responsible for enforcing policy rather than dispensing an abstract justice. This notion persisted, and until the new constitution came into force in 1994 the judicial system was subservient to the government, in particular the State President, resulting in some politicised decisions.

Now, the highest power in the land is the constitution, which is interpreted and enforced by the new Constitutional Court. Choosing the members of the court was one of the most crucial post-election tasks for the new South Africa. Although women are under-represented (so what's new?), the court is generally accepted as an eminent and impartial body.

The Constitutional Court's independence was demonstrated in 1995 when it decided that capital punishment was unconstitutional and banned it. This was despite a large majority of South Africans being in favour of capital punishment (more than 100 people were hanged each year throughout the 1980s). With one of the world's most enlightened constitutions and a court willing and able to defend it, the legal system will be a major factor in ensuring the success of the new South Africa. ■

cation and work opportunities. On one hand there is a modern industrialised and urban economy; on the other there is a subsistence agricultural economy little changed from the 19th century.

While there is tremendous poverty within the country, on an African scale the economy is not only reasonably successful, but it dwarfs all the other economies on the continent. The success is based, to a large degree, on tremendous natural wealth and an abundance of low-paid black labour.

According to government statistics, South Africa produces 50% of all the electricity produced in Africa, 40% of the continent's industrial output, 45% of mining production, and is the largest agricultural exporter by a wide margin.

Within South Africa, wealth is further concentrated in the Pretoria, Witwatersrand, Vereeniging (PWV) area centred on Johannesburg (now the province of Gauteng), which, it is claimed, accounts for about 65% of the country's gross domestic product (GDP) and no less than 25% of the entire continent's gross product.

South Africa has a well-developed infrastructure with a good road and rail system linking the interior of the country, and the wider region, with a number of modern ports. There is tremendous potential for the economy to facilitate development in the rest of southern Africa. Wars and trade sanctions have seriously hampered the whole region, and both by virtue of its wealth and its infrastructure, South Africa holds the key to its recovery.

Until the discovery of diamonds at Kimberley (1871) and the gold reef on the Witwatersrand (1886) the economy was exclusively agricultural. Since then, mineral wealth has been the key to development. Mining remains central to the economy, and South Africa is the world's leading supplier of gold, chromium, manganese, vanadium and platinum. Mining accounts for over 70% of exports and 13% of GDP.

The manufacturing industry grew rapidly during and after WW II, mostly to meet local demand. The government has been a major participant in its development through its ownership of enormous operations like Eskom (electricity), Iscor (coal, iron and steel), Sasol (coal to oil), and Armscor (armaments).

Previous governments successfully sought, through involvement in the economy, to redirect wealth into Afrikaner hands. The public sector accounts for over 35% of GDP, even though National Party governments since the 1980s favoured privatisation. It seems somewhat ironic there was such concern over the ANC's socialist-oriented policies, which are designed to shift wealth to the black population.

The private sector is highly centralised and is dominated by the enormous, interrelated De Beers and Anglo-American corporations. Their combined market capitalisation is over four times greater than their nearest competition.

Towards the end of white minority rule, international sanctions bit deeper, and black mass action also destabilised the economy. Add to that a general world economic downturn and a serious drought, and the economy was in serious trouble. The country faced an annual inflation rate running at around 15% and unemployment was rising. Things have improved somewhat since the 1994 election but the economy will take time to recover and inflation is still a problem.

However, even if the economy recovers to its boom-time peak, almost the only people to immediately benefit will be whites. Blacks in South Africa have never shared in the fruits of their labour and it will be very difficult for the new government to ensure that they do so in future. The economy is still geared to a limitless pool of black labour paid third-world rates, and restructuring will be a long and slow process.

Some of the proposed changes seem to miss the point. For example, most domestic workers (ie, maids) are paid just R300 a month. It has been suggested that a domestic workers' training course be established, with the graduates commanding wages of R650 to R900 a month. Sure, the wages might triple but they would still be pathetic and a system of gross inequality amounting to servitude would still be in place.

It's still disturbingly common for whites to justify low black wages by saying, 'the black doesn't have the same expenses as the white man'. True, a house in Soweto doesn't cost as much as a house in Sandton, but so what? In many counties similar arguments were once used to justify lower wages for women performing the same jobs as men. On the other hand, some white liberals see themselves as performing a social service by employing maids. Buying a pension plan for a maid is seen as an extremely enlightened thing to do – the idea that the maid might be paid a living wage so that she can make her own decisions is still an alien one. There is a long way to go.

The challenges the whites face are not dissimilar to those facing the rest of the first world. Is it ever possible to justify gross economic inequality that is based on race or nationality? Can, for instance, a Californian defend his/her wealth to a Mexican (who by a stroke of fate was born a km south of an arbitrary border), or for that matter, an Australian defend his/her wealth to an Indonesian?

The difference for South Africa is that these questions must be dealt with and solved within the country itself. The new government has to find a way to both create and redistribute wealth within the economy without alienating the white community, foreign investors or the majority of poverty-stricken people.

Apart from travelling in minibus taxis and maybe taking a township tour, there is practically no situation (except giving to beggars) where your money goes directly to the poorest people. Even your R25 for a hostel bunk contributes only a few cents to the wages of the black staff.

POPULATION & PEOPLE

Of the population of 38 million, some 29 million are black, five million white, three million 'coloured' (ie, mixed race) and one million of Indian descent. Some 60% of the whites are of Afrikaner descent and most of the rest are of British descent.

Most of the 'coloured' population lives in

Northern and Western Cape provinces. Most South Africans of Indian descent live in KwaZulu/Natal.

The Transvaal provinces and the Orange Free State are the Afrikaner heartlands. People of British descent are concentrated in KwaZulu/Natal and Western and Eastern Cape provinces.

Most black people you meet outside the old Homelands areas will be Zulu, Xhosa or Sotho.

The Homelands system was based on the white wishful thinking that the various black groups had areas to which they belonged and where most of them lived – and if they didn't live there they would be 'assisted' to do so.

There are places of historic and traditional importance to the different peoples, but you will find blacks from all groups and tribes throughout South Africa.

Although the Homelands no longer have any political meaning and were never realistic indicators of the area's cultural diversity, it's useful to have some idea of where the Homelands were and who lived (and still live) in them. The Homelands and their peoples were:

Bophuthatswana – Tswana
Ciskei – Xhosa
Gazankulu – Tsonga
KwaNdebele – Ndebele
KwaNgwane – Swazi
KwaZulu – Zulu
Lebowa – Lobedu
QwaQwa – southern Sotho
Transkei – Xhosa
Venda – VhaVenda

Zulus are the largest group in the whole region (seven million), followed by the Xhosa (six million) and the various north Sotho peoples, most of whom are Tswana. The smallest group are the VhaVenda (500,000). These figures are highly suspect as the last census was held in 1985, when many, many thousands of 'illegal immigrants' in South Africa would have avoided being counted. Also, it's hard to imagine that the apartheid regime spent

Dealing with Racism

In its 1986 confession of the sin of apartheid, the General Synod of the Dutch Reformed Church defined racism:

'Whoever in theory or by attitude and deed implies that one race, people, or group of people is inherently superior, or one group of people is inherently inferior, is guilty of racism. Racism is a sin which tends to take on collective and structural forms. As a moral aberration it deprives a human being of his dignity, his obligations and his rights. It must be rejected and opposed in all its manifestations because it leads to oppression and exploitation.'

Not a bad definition (if sexist). In this book we make use of the old apartheid terms: white, black, coloured and Asian. We thought hard before including them, because this does in some ways perpetuate the offensive notion that skin colour alone is a useful or accurate distinguishing characteristic. By using these terms are we not implicitly validating a racist philosophy? Perhaps this is true to an extent, but it is impossible to pretend that these distinctions have disappeared from South Africa overnight. It is also true that many non-racists proudly identify themselves with one or other of these groups.

The bottom line is that we have no problem with someone arguing there are cultural differences (based on language, shared beliefs, ancestry, place of birth, tribe, political belief, or religion) which sometimes correlate to some degree with skin colour. We do have a problem if these generalisations do not allow for the existence of numerous individual exceptions, or if they are used to justify inequality, intolerance or pre-judgement.

We have also decided to include population figures for the different racial groups. For all their inherent inaccuracies, they do paint a stark picture of political and economic inequality. It is an inescapable fact that until 1990, racial categorisation officially determined the rights and opportunities a person had – and the apartheid regime's own numbers illustrate how lopsided, unjust, and plain crazy this was. ◼

much money on getting accurate statistics on blacks, judging by the amount it spent on black health and education. The high black birthrate also adds to the unreliability of these figures.

ARTS & CULTURE

For information on traditional cultures, black and white, see the Facts about the Region chapter. The Books section in the regional Facts for the Visitor chapter suggests some South African literature.

Although South Africa is home to a great diversity of cultures, most were suppressed during the apartheid years. To an extent, the Homelands kept alive some of the traditional cultures but in a static form. The day-to-day realities of traditional and contemporary cultures were ignored, trivialised or destroyed. The most striking example of this was the bulldozing of both District Six, a vibrant multicultural area in Cape Town, and Johannesburg's Sophiatown, where internationally famous musicians learned their craft in an area once described as 'a skeleton with a permanent grin'.

Many artists, black and white, were involved in the anti-apartheid campaign and some were banned. In a society where you could be jailed for owning a politically incorrect painting, serious art was forced underground and blandness ruled in the galleries and theatres. Many people asked themselves whether it was ethically possible to produce art in such circumstances. For an overview of South African art during these bad times, see *Resistance Art in South Africa* by Sue Williamson (paperback, R97).

It will take time for the damage to be undone, but there are hopeful signs. Many galleries are holding retrospectives of black artists, contemporary and traditional, and musicians from around Africa perform in major festivals.

One of the most exciting aspects of the new South Africa is that the country is in the process of reinventing itself and, with such a large proportion of the population marginalised from the economic mainstream, this is occurring without much input from professional image makers. The new South Africa is being created on the streets of the townships and the cities.

NATIONAL PARKS & RESERVES

National parks and reserves are among South Africa's premier attractions. The scenery is spectacular, the fauna and flora are abundant – and the prices are extremely reasonable. Most people, especially those with private transport, will find that the parks are a highlight – generally much more interesting than the towns and cities.

In addition to the South African National Parks Board, which is a country-wide organisation, the provinces also have conservation bodies. In fact, the provinces control wilderness areas that are sometimes larger and more spectacular than the better known national parks. Unless otherwise indicated, however, the following parks all fall under the control of the National Parks Board. Please note, only a small selection is listed here.

A very useful book is Chris & Tilde Stuart's *Guide to Southern African Game & Nature Reserves* published by Struik in South Africa. It covers more than 400 places and is well worth R70.

Many of the Homelands once had their equivalents of the National Parks Board (often very well run), and with several of the old provinces now split into smaller provinces, the jurisdiction of the various bodies is in a state of flux. The National Parks Board wants to take over control of some of the provincial parks but the provinces are resisting. It's probable that some of the contact addresses for parks listed here will change.

In the Kruger (with exceptions) and Kalahari Gemsbok national parks, visitors are confined to vehicles so if you don't have a car, you'll have to take a tour or hitch. Probably the best way both to get to and around the parks is to rent a vehicle (4WD is not necessary). The quality of the infrastructure and information is high so you don't need a guide.

If you do want to do overnight walks in any of the other parks or reserves, it is necessary to get permits from the appropriate authorities in advance, and you are nearly always restricted to official camp sites or huts. In South Africa's national parks, there's no wandering off with a pack on your back whenever you feel like it.

The national parks all have rest camps that offer a variety of good-value accommodation, from cottages to camp sites. Most of the camps have restaurants, shops and petrol pumps. Although it is not usually necessary to book camp sites, it is necessary to book cottages. There are restrictions on visitor numbers to Kruger; see the section on Kruger National Park.

The entrances to parks and reserves generally close around sunset; check if you think you are going to arrive late. Listed here are some of the main booking addresses; for others see the following summary of major parks and the individual park entries later in the book. Note that some of the old provincial offices are still operating, some aren't. You can expect the new provinces to open their own offices, so check with Satour or the National Parks Board for the latest information.

South African National Parks Board
> PO Box 787, Pretoria 0001 (☎ (012) 343 1991, fax 343 0905)
> PO Box 7400, Rogge Bay, Cape Town 8012 (☎ (021) 22 2810, fax (021) 24 6211)

Orange Free State, Dept of Nature Conservation
> PO Box 517, Bloemfontein 9300 (☎ (051) 70511)

Transvaal, Nature Conservation
> Private Bag X209, Pretoria 0001 (☎ (012) 201 4358/2565)

KwaZulu/Natal Parks Board
> PO Box 662, Pietermaritzburg (☎ (0331) 47 1981)

Cape Nature Conservation
> This organisation controlled all nature reserves in the old Cape Province. It will probably retain control of the Western Cape reserves. PO Box X9086, Cape Town (☎ (021) 483 4085)

Contour
> Contour was the Ciskei government's conservation and tourism department and still controls parks in the ex-Homeland. It's possible that

Contour (probably by another name) will take over the running of all other parks in Eastern Cape. PO Box 186, Bisho, Eastern Cape Province (☎ (0401) 95 2115, fax 92 765)

There are many private game reserves and while they generally cost more than public parks and reserves, you can usually get closer to the animals. Before deciding which private reserve to visit, it's worth contacting a specialist travel agent to find out if there are any special deals going. Pathfinders Travel (☎ (011) 453 1113/4, fax 453 1483), 17 Chaucer Ave, Senderwood, Bedfordview, Johannesburg, is very helpful. After hours contact Annemarie Berger (☎ /fax (011) 706 6629).

Western Cape Province

Bontebok National Park Proclaimed to protect the last herds of bontebok, a beautiful antelope unique to the Cape Province, the park is only small. It is just to the south of Swellendam.

Cape of Good Hope Nature Reserve The reserve protects a dramatic coastline and some of the best examples of fynbos, the unique Cape floral kingdom. There are numerous walks, a number of beaches (there's 40 km of coast within the reserve) hard-to-spot eland, bontebok, rhebok, grysbok and abundant birdlife.

Cederberg Wilderness The Cederberg Wilderness, administered by the Cape, is 71,000

hectares of rugged valleys and peaks (up to 2000 metres), characterised by extraordinary sandstone formations. The vegetation is predominantly mountain fynbos, and includes the rare Clanwilliam cedar. Mammals include the baboon, rhebok, klipspringer and predators like the honey badger and caracal. There are some extensive walks, and the nearest major town is Clanwilliam.

De Hoop Nature Reserve De Hoop includes a scenic coastline with lonely stretches of beach, rocky cliffs, large coastal sand dunes, a freshwater lake and the Potberg mountain range. This is one of the best places to see both mountain and lowland fynbos. Fauna includes the Cape mountain zebra, bontebok and a wealth of birdlife. The coast is an important breeding area for the southern right whale. The reserve covers 41,000 hectares to the east of Bredasdorp and is administered by the Cape Province. Hikers can tackle beach walks and trails of various lengths on Potberg mountain.

Karoo National Park The park, near Beaufort West, encloses 32,000 hectares of classic Karoo landscape and a representative selection of its flora and fauna. There's a three-day hiking trail and excellent accommodation.

Tsitsikamma National Park The coastal park encompasses a narrow band of spectacular coast between Plettenberg Bay and Jeffrey's Bay. It is traversed by one of the most famous walks in the country – the Otter

---

Too Many Elephants

Unlike most other African countries, South Africa's problem is that it has too many elephants, and they are increasing in number every year. Elephants in the national parks are culled, despite protests from environmentalists who feel that there should be better ways of controlling the population than killing 'surplus' animals. The culled elephants present another problem: what is to be done with their tusks?

South Africa doesn't sell ivory, but there is pressure to do so. Selling the stockpiles would raise much-needed cash to help conservation projects. However, it can be argued that even legal and responsible ivory sales would encourage poachers who are destroying elephant herds elsewhere in Africa.

How could you be sure that the ivory you bought really came from a culled South African elephant? If your country relaxed its complete ban on importing ivory to allow sales of South African ivory, would its ability to stop the importation of illegal ivory be compromised? ■

Trail, which is an easy five-day 41-km trail along the coast. Unfortunately, it is booked up months in advance and there is virtually no chance of getting a place. It's still worth visiting for some of the shorter day walks – which can include a very good section of the Otter Trail.

Eastern Cape Province
Addo Elephant National Park The park protects the last remnant of the great herds that once roamed the province. It is only small, but the unusual bush (spekboom, sneezewood and guarri) supports a high density of elephants. Nothing in this world is guaranteed, but you would be unlucky not to see one of the 130 elephants living in the park which is north of Port Elizabeth.

Karoo Nature Reserve The reserve, just outside Graaff Reinet, has extraordinary flora, with the weird Karoo succulents well represented. There's also wildlife, interesting birdlife and spectacular rock formations. There are a number of day walks and one overnight hike. The reserve is within walking distance of town and is administered by the Cape Province.

Mountain Zebra National Park The park is only 6500 hectares in extent, and was proclaimed to ensure the survival of the Cape mountain zebra – there are now more than 200 in this park and many more around the province. The park covers the rugged northern slopes of the Bankberg range and there are magnificent views across the mountains and the Karoo plains.

Transkei Area
The Transkei area's coastline is largely untouched, but there are several conservation areas set aside. **Mkambati Nature Reserve** is a coastal reserve with some great scenery, including the Misikaba River Gorge. Other reserves include **Dwesa**, between Coffee Bay and Kei Mouth; **Hluleka**, on the Coffee Bay Trail; and **Silaka**, just south of Port St Johns.

For bookings and more information contact the Department of Agriculture & Forestry (☎ (0471) 31 2711) in Umtata.

Northern Cape Province
Kalahari Gemsbok National Park The Kalahari Gemsbok National Park is not as well known or famous as many other African parks, but it is, nonetheless, one of the greatest. Including the Botswana section (and there are no fences) the park exceeds 36,000 sq km. This allows the unhindered migration of animals who, because of the unpredictable nature of the rainfall, are forced to travel great distances to reach water and food.

Although the countryside is described as semi-desert (with around 200 mm of rain a year) it is richer than it appears and supports large populations of birds, reptiles, small mammals, springbok, gemsbok, blue wildebeest, red hartebeest and eland. These in turn support a large population of predators – there is arguably no better place to see lions, leopards, cheetahs, hyena, jackals and foxes.

Augrabies Falls National Park This park, 120 km west of Upington, features the dramatic Augrabies Falls, where the Orange River drops into a solid granite ravine. Particularly when the river is in flood, the sight is spectacular, but for many the area is most interesting for the rich variety of plant life that survives in almost desert conditions.

Goegap Nature Reserve The reserve, 10 km from Springbok, is famous for its extraordinary display of spring flowers and its nursery of over 200 amazing Karoo and Namaqualand succulents. In addition to the flora, there are springbok, zebras and birds. It is administered by the Cape Province, but there is no accommodation.

Richtersveld National Park The newest park in South Africa, the Richtersveld was declared in July 1991. It protects 162,000 hectares of high-altitude, mountainous desert bordering the Orange River in the north-west corner of the province. The countryside and the flora are spectacular. The park is very rugged and it will be a while before it is easily accessible.

Eastern Transvaal

Blyde River Canyon A spectacular 60-km canyon follows the Blyde River down from the Drakensberg escarpment to the lowveld, and has a huge range of flora and fauna. Book the popular hiking trail through Blyde River Canyon Nature Reserve (☎ 0020, ask for 15), PO Box 281, Hoedspruit 1380.

Northern Transvaal

Lapalala Wilderness This private reserve north in the Warterberg mountains has white rhinos, zebras, blue wildebeests and several antelope species, plus crocodiles in the bilharzia-free rivers. You can canoe or hike. Book on ☎ (011) 53 1814.

Lesheba Wilderness In the Soutpansberg range, this private reserve has dramatic and varied country and there are plenty of animals, including rhinos. To book phone ☎ 015562 and ask for 3004.

Wolkberg Wilderness Area There is good hiking in this wilderness area in the northern tail of the Drakensberg and some strands of indigenous forest. There are also a fair number of animals, including a few shy leopards and hyena. Book hiking trails through The State Forester, Serala State Forest, Private Bag, Haenertsburg 0730.

Nwanedi National Park In the undeveloped Venda area, this park is on the northern side of the Soutpansberg mountains and the country is in the lowveld rather than rainforest. Book through the Department of Agriculture & Forestry, Private Bag X2247, Sibasa, Northern Transvaal or contact the tourist information centre in Thohoyandu (☎ (0159) 41100, 41821).

Kruger National Park Kruger is one of the best parks in Africa, if not the world. With all of the 'big five' animals (lion, elephant, buffalo, leopard, black rhino), inexpensive accommodation and walking trails (book early), it's not to be missed. Book through the National Parks Board.

Private Reserves near Kruger Park The area just west of Kruger Park contains a large number of private reserves, usually sharing a border with Kruger and thus you may be able to see most of the 'big five' animals. Most of the reserves offer bush camps, walking and open-vehicle game drives. They are often extremely expensive.

Timbavati is jointly owned by a large number of people dedicated to conservation and within it there are a number of operations. **Timbavati Wilderness Trails** (☎ (031) 207 1565, fax 207 3960 for bookings) has an all-inclusive four-day/night package for R880 (R440 for children). The minimum group size is eight and the maximum is 10. See the Northern Transvaal chapter for more details.

KwaZulu/Natal

Most major parks and reserves in KwaZulu/Natal are administered by the Parks Board of KwaZulu/Natal. The Board's HQ is in Pietermaritzburg, and it's here you book all accommodation with the exception of camp sites, which are booked through the individual parks and reserves. You can make phone bookings with a credit card on ☎ (0331) 471981. The office is open on weekdays from 8.30 am to 12.45 pm and 2 to 3.30 pm.

In addition to camp sites there are 16 categories of accommodation, ranging from self-contained bungalows to caves, although not all are found in all the parks.

Drakensberg Reserves Along with Golden Gate Highlands National Park in the Orange Free State, there are two main reserves in the dramatic KwaZulu/Natal Drakensberg; **Giant's Castle Game Reserve** and **Royal Natal National Park**. Both have spectacular scenery, walking trails and good accommodation. In addition there are the **Mkhomazi & Mzimkulu** and **Mzimkulwana** wilderness areas, with excellent hiking.

Hluhluwe & Umfolozi Reserves These large, adjoining game reserves have rhinos, lions and elephants. Umfolozi's wilderness trails offer guided hiking.

Itala With facilities rivalling much more expensive private reserves, the Natal Parks Board's flagship reserve is worth visiting.

Lake St Lucia Area This complex of Natal Parks Board reserves centres on Lake St Lucia on the north coast. There are crocodile and hippos as well as good fishing and hiking trails.

Ntendeka Wilderness In the Zulu heartland, this is a beautiful area of grassland and indigenous forest, with some dramatic cliffs. There are hiking trails. For more information phone (0386) 71883.

Ndumu Game Reserve On the Mozambique border, about 100 km north of Mkuze, this remote reserve has black and white rhinos, hippos, crocodiles, antelope and a wide range of birdlife.

Tembe Elephant Park This park on the Mozambique border was established in 1991 to protect South Africa's last free-ranging elephants and there are now about 100 in the area. Currently you can only visit the park on a tour.

Orange Free State
Golden Gate Highlands Park One of the spectacular Drakensberg reserves, this national park is close to the northern border of Lesotho in the Orange Free State. The main attraction is the scenery, around which you can walk or ride horses. Book accommodation through the National Parks Board.

Tussen Die Riviere Game Farm This game farm near Aliwal North has more animals than any other in the Orange Free State, mostly various antelope species but also white rhinos and hippos.

The QwaQwa Conservation Area This reserve is in the foothills of both the Maluti mountains and the Drakensberg. The conservation area was once administered by the QwaQwa Tourism & Nature Conservation Corporation (☎ (058) 713 4444, fax 713 4342) in Phuthaditjhaba; who will administer it in the future is still being decided. Trails must be booked at least two weeks in advance.

Stokstert Hiking Trail This overnight trail is in the Caledon River Conservacy Area, around Smithfield. This huge area (300,000 hectares) is on the land of 65 farmers who have adopted conservation-minded techniques.

North-West Province
Pilanesberg National Park The park surrounds Sun City and covers 500 sq km of extinct volcanic craters. It is well worth visiting. There are black and white rhinos, giraffes, and all sorts of bucks.

Facts for the Visitor

VISAS & EMBASSIES

Since the 1994 elections the visa situation has improved. A South African visa in your passport no longer means hassles in other African countries and the dismantling of South Africa's sham 'Homelands' means that you no longer need visas to enter areas such as Transkei. However, remember that Swaziland and Lesotho are independent countries.

The visa situation has changed several times since 1994, and could change again, so check before you arrive.

Entry permits are issued on arrival to holiday visitors from many (British) Commonwealth countries and other countries including Japan, Republic of Ireland, Switzerland and Germany. You are entitled to 90 days, but they might write the date of your flight home as the date of expiry.

If you need a visa it's worth getting it (free) before you depart for Africa, but allow a couple of weeks for the process. Visas are not issued at the border. There are embassies in Australia, Brazil, Canada, France, Germany, Italy, the Netherlands, Spain, the UK and the USA, among other countries. South Africa has at least consular representation in most countries.

In Africa there are embassies in Lilongwe (Malawi) and St Denis (Réunion) but visas are obtainable from trade missions in many southern African nations including Botswana, Lesotho, Mauritius and Zimbabwe. It's likely that more South African embassies will open throughout Africa in the near future.

Note that if you do need a visa (rather than an entry permit) it must be multiple-entry if you plan to go to travel to a neighbouring country (such as Lesotho) then return to South Africa.

On arrival you must satisfy an immigration officer that you have sufficient funds for your stay in South Africa. Obviously, 'sufficient' is open to interpretation, so it pays to be neat, clean and polite.

. If you arrive by air you must have an onward ticket of some sort. An air ticket is best but overland seems to be OK. However, we've heard from some unlucky travellers who were required to pay a US$2000 bond because they didn't have a return air ticket to their *home country*, not just another African country. If you come by land things are more relaxed, although you'll still need to show sufficient funds.

Apply for visa extensions or a re-entry visa at the Department of Home Affairs at 77 Harrison St, Johannesburg (☎ (011) 836 3228), or at 56 Barrack St, Cape Town (☎ (021) 462 4970).

South African Embassies & Missions

Australia
    Rhodes Place, Yarralumla, Canberra ACT 2600 (☎ (06) 273 2424, fax 273 2669)
Brazil
    Rua Lauro Muller 116/1107 (Torre Rio Sul), Botafogo 22299, Rio de Janeiro (☎ (021) 542 6191, fax 542 6043)
Canada
    15 Sussex Drive, Ottawa K1M 1M8 (☎ (613) 744 0330, fax 744 8287)
    Suite 2515, Exchange Tower, Toronto M5X 1E3 (☎ (416) 364 0314, fax 363 8974)
Denmark
    1st Floor, Montergade 1, Copenhagen DK-1011 (☎ (01) 18 0155)
France
    59 Quai d'Orsay, Paris 75007 (☎ (01) 4555 9237, fax 4551 8812)
Germany
    Auf der Hostert 3, Bonn 5300 (☎ (228) 82010, fax 35 2579)
Israel
    Yakhin House, 2 Kaplan St, Tel Aviv 64734 (☎ (03) 525 2566)
Malawi
    Mpico Building, City Centre, Lilongwe 3 (☎ (09265) 73 3722)
Netherlands
    Wassenaarseweg 40, The Hague (☎ (70) 392 4501, fax 45 8226)

Réunion
Immeuble Cie des Indes, 20 Rue de la Compagnie BP 1117, 97482 Saint Denis Cedex (☎ (09262) 21 5005, fax 41718)
Spain
Edificio Lista, Calle de Claudio Coello 91-6 (☎ (01) 435 6688, fax 593 1384)
Sweden
Linnégatan 76, 11523 Stockholm (☎ (0946) 24 3950, fax 660 7136)
UK
South Africa House, Trafalgar Sq, London WC2N 5DP (☎ (0171) 930 4488, fax 839 1419)
USA
3051 Massachusetts Ave NW, Washington DC 20008 (☎ (202) 232 4400, fax 265 1607)
Suite 300, 50 North La Cienega Blvd, Beverly Hills, CA 90211 (☎ (213) 657 9200, fax 657 9215)
Zimbabwe
Temple Bar House, Baker Ave, Harare (☎ (04) 75 3150)

Foreign Embassies & Missions in South Africa

Most countries have their main embassy in Pretoria, with an office or consulate in Cape Town, which becomes the official embassy during Cape Town's parliamentary sessions. However, most countries also maintain consulates (which can arrange visas and passports) in Johannesburg. Some, like Mozambique and Zimbabwe, only have representation in Johannesburg. See the appropriate cities for listings.

DOCUMENTS

All people who have travelled through the yellow-fever zone in Africa or South America (including Brazil) must have an International Certificate of Vaccination against yellow fever. Vaccination against smallpox and cholera is no longer required.

CUSTOMS

South Africa, Botswana, Swaziland and Lesotho are all part of the South African Customs Union, which means the internal borders are effectively open from a customs point of view. When you enter the union, however, you're restricted in the normal way to personal effects; one litre of spirits, two litres of wine, and 400 cigarettes. Motor vehicles must be covered by a triptyque or carnet. For information contact the Department of Customs & Excise in Pretoria (☎ (012) 28 4308).

MONEY

The unit of currency is the rand (R), which is divided into 100 cents. The import and export of local currency is limited to R500. There is no black market.

South Africa has introduced new coins and notes. The only old note you're likely to see is the R5 (which has been replaced by a coin) but old coins are common, making it damn difficult to establish familiarity. The coins are: 1, 2, 5, 10, 20 and 50 cents; 1, 2 and 5 rand. The notes are: 5 (being withdrawn), 10, 20, 50, 100 and 200 rand. The R200 note looks a lot like the R20 note, so take care.

The Thomas Cook agent is Rennies Travel, a large chain of travel agencies, and there are American Express offices in the big cities. Nedbank is associated with American Express. Most banks change travellers' cheques in major currencies, with various commissions. These can vary between branches of the same bank, but as a rule of thumb here are commissions charged by major banks:

Bank	Commission	Minimum Fee
Trust	1%	R10
Volkskas	1%	R10
Standard	1%	R15
Boland	1%	R20
First National	0.25%	R30

Keep at least some of the receipts you get when changing money as you'll need to show them to reconvert your rands when you leave.

Thomas Cook now has travellers' cheques in rand, useful for the countries covered in this book but probably less so outside southern Africa.

Credit cards, especially Visa and MasterCard, are widely accepted. Some ATMs will give Visa cash advances.

Exchange Rates

Australia	A$1 =	R2.71
United Kingdom	UK£1 =	R5.67
USA	US$1 =	R3.66
Japan	Y100 =	R3.79
Germany	DM1 =	R2.49
Switzerland	Sfr1 =	R3.03
France	FFr1 =	R0.72
New Zealand	NZ$1 =	R2.38

Costs

Although South Africa is certainly not as cheap to travel in as many poorer countries, it is very good value by European, US and Australian standards. This is due, in large part, to the collapse in the value of the rand, which gives those converting from a hard currency a major advantage.

On the negative side, in 1995 inflation was running at close to 15% (with prices of basic foodstuffs rising by 50%), so the prices in this book can be expected to change at a corresponding rate. In such circumstances, however, the rand is also likely to continue to devalue (meaning you'll get more rands when you convert from another currency). Inflation and devaluation may well cancel each other out. Don't expect imported or manufactured goods (including books) to be cheap.

Shoestring travellers will find that camping or staying in hostels, on-site caravans or bungalows where they can self-cater are the cheapest options, often working out to around R25 per person. Sit-down meals in restaurants (without getting into haute cuisine) consistently work out to between R25 and R35 per person, and less in pubs. Steak dishes, in particular, are incredibly cheap. Fresh produce is good value.

The distances in South Africa are large, so transport can be sparse and expensive; hiring or buying a car can be worthwhile both for convenience and economy.

Tipping

Tipping is pretty well mandatory because of the very low wages. Around 10 to 15% is usual.

TOURIST OFFICES

The South African Tourist Corporation (Satour) used to produce some excellent literature – maps, accommodation and transport digests, booklets containing detailed descriptions of just about everything you're likely to want to see. Satour was in a bit of a shambles after the 1994 elections and didn't have much up-to-date material but hopefully the high standards will return.

How Much Is...?
Hostel dorm bed – R25
Hostel double room – about R75
Cottage, sleeping two – from R60
Two-star hotel room – from R90/150 a single/double
Five-star hotel room – around R400/500 a single/double
36-exposure transparency (slide) film – R26
36-exposure print film – R20
36-exposure processing & prints – R50
Hamburger & chips – R10
Steak – from R20
1 litre milk – R2
1 loaf bread – R2
1 stubby beer – R2.50
A one-way economy air ticket from Johannesburg to Cape Town – R670
Deluxe bus from Johannesburg to Cape Town – R290
Minibus taxi from Johannesburg to Cape Town – R150

Value Added Tax

There is a Value Added Tax (VAT) of 14%, but foreign visitors can reclaim some of their VAT expenses on departure. This applies only to goods that you are taking out of the country; you can't claim back the VAT you've paid on food or car rental, for example. Also, the goods have to be bought at a shop participating in the VAT Foreign Tourist Sales scheme.

To make a claim you need the tax invoices (usually the receipt, but make sure that the shop knows that you want a full receipt). They must be originals – no photocopies. You also have to fill in a form or two and show the goods to a customs inspector (so make your VAT claim *before* you check in your luggage). The total value of the goods must exceed R250. After you've gone through immigration you pick up your refund cheque – at some airports you can then cash it immediately at the bank, in any major currency. If your claim comes to more than R3000 your cheque is mailed to your home address.

You can claim only at the international airports in Johannesburg, Cape Town and Durban, at the Beit Bridge and Komatipoort land borders and at some harbours. ∎

Satour brochures are generally free if you get them outside South Africa but there's a charge for many of the brochures in the country. Satour offices abroad include:

Australia
   Level 6, 285 Clarence St, Sydney NSW 2000 (☎ (02) 9261 3424, fax 9261 3414)
France
   61, rue La Boëtie, 75008, Paris (☎ (01) 4561 0197, fax 4561 0196)
Germany
   Alemannia Haus, An der Hauptwache 11, D-60313 Frankfurt/Main 1, Postfach 101940, 60019 Frankfurt (☎ (69) 20658, fax 28 0950)
Japan
   Akasaka Lions Building, 2nd Floor, 1-1-2 Moto Akasaka, Minato-ku, Tokyo 107 (☎ (3) 3 478 7601, fax 3 478 7605)
UK
   5 Alt Grove London SW19 4DZ (☎ (0181) 944 8080, fax 944 6705)
USA
   500 Fifth Ave, 20th Floor, New York, NY 10010 (☎ (212) 730 2929, (800) 822 5368, fax (212) 764 1980)
   9841 Airport Blvd, Suite 1524, Los Angeles, CA 90045 (☎ (310) 641 8444, (800) 782 9772, fax (310) 641 5812)
Zimbabwe
   Offices 9 & 10, Mon Repos Building, Newlands Shopping Centre, Harare (☎ (04) 70 7766, fax 70 7767)

Satour offices will probably reopen in other countries. Check with the South African embassy in your country.

In South Africa there are Satour offices in Bloemfontein, Cape Town, Durban, East London, George, Johannesburg, Kimberley, Nelspruit, Pietersburg, Port Elizabeth, Potchefstroom and Pretoria.

The various provinces are in the process of re-establishing tourism boards (the creation of new provinces and the reincorporation of the Homelands has played havoc with jurisdictions) and most towns have tourist offices; if not, information is usually available at the library or the town hall.

BUSINESS HOURS & HOLIDAYS

Banking hours vary, but are usually from 9 am to 3.30 pm on weekdays. Many branches also open from 8.30 to 11 am on Saturday. Post offices usually open from 8 am to 4.30 pm on weekdays and 8 am to noon on Saturday. Both banks and post offices close for lunch in smaller towns.

Most shops are open between 8.30 am and 5 pm on weekdays and Saturday morning. Bars usually close around 11 pm except in the major cities. Outside the cities it's difficult to get a drink without a meal on Sunday.

Public holidays underwent a dramatic shake-up after the 1994 elections. For example the Day of the Vow, which celebrated the massacre of Zulus, has become the Day of Reconciliation. The officially ignored but widely observed Soweto Day, marking the student uprisings which eventually lead to liberation, is now celebrated as

Youth Day. Public holidays and approximate dates are:

New Year's Day	1	January
Human Rights Day	21	March
Good Friday		(varies)
Family Day	17	April
Constitution Day	27	April
Workers' Day	1	May
Youth Day	16	June
Women's Day	9	August
Heritage Day	24	September
Day of Reconciliation	16	December
Christmas Day	25	December
Day of Goodwill	26	December

School Holidays

It's useful to know the dates of school holidays as accommodation at reserves and resorts is at a premium during these times. The dates for 1995 are given below; dates for following years will be slightly different. Contact Satour for the exact dates.

Gauteng, Eastern Transvaal & Northern Transvaal
    1-18 April, 8-31 July, 30 September-10 October, 1 December-early February.
Orange Free State, North-West & Northern Cape
    1-18 April, 23 June-17 July, 23 September-1 October, 8 December-early February
KwaZulu/Natal & Eastern Cape
    8-18 April, 1-24 July, 30 September-10 October, 8 December-early February

POST & TELECOMMUNICATIONS

South Africa has reasonably good post and telecommunications. Most post offices are open from 8.30 am to 4.30 pm on weekdays and from 8 am to noon on Saturday. Aerograms and standard size postcards cost 90c. Airmail letters start at R1.15 (Europe), R1.40 (North America) and R1.65 (Australia). Internal letters cost 50c. Internal delivery can be very slow and international delivery isn't exactly lightning fast, partly due to the limited number of international flights to some countries.

Local telephone calls are timed and although you get a decent amount of time for each R0.30 unit, if you're calling a government department you might go through a few units.

Long-distance and international telephone calls are expensive. You'll use up a large chunk of an R10 phonecard with a 'Hello, how are you, please ring me back on...' call to Australia. There are international phone call centres in the major cities' GPOs where you pay cash after you call. There are also private operations which are usually more convenient but more expensive. Some of the private mail and fax operations offer reasonable phone rates and excellent comfort.

Except in remote country areas, telephones are fully automatic with direct dialling facilities to most parts of the world. If you are staying in a hotel, beware the hefty surcharge that is usually added to phone calls.

When using a public phone you might find that you have credit left after you've finished a call. If you want to make another call don't hang up or you'll lose the credit. Press the black button under the receiver hook.

All telephone books give full details of service numbers and codes. You'll also notice that phone books carry long lists of numbers that are due to change. The phone system seems to be in a perpetual state of upgrading and there's a good chance that many of the numbers (including some area codes) in this guidebook will have changed by the time you get to South Africa.

Useful Numbers

Enquiries (national & international)	1025
Enquiries (local)	1023
Collect calls (national)	0020
Collect calls (international)	0090

The following numbers are international area codes:

Australia	0961
Botswana	09267
Canada	091
Denmark	0945
France	0933
Germany	0949
Japan	0981
Netherlands	0931
New Zealand	0964
Spain	0946
Sweden	0946
UK	0944
USA	091

Australia Direct	0800 990061
Belgium Direct	0800 990032
Canada Direct	0800 990014
Denmark Direct	0800 990045
Ireland Direct	0800 990353
Japan Direct	0800 990081
Netherlands Direct	0800 990031
New Zealand Direct	0800 99006
UK Direct – BT	0800 990044
UK Direct – Call UK	0800 990544
USA Direct – AT&T	0800 990123
USA Direct – MCI Call USA	0800 990011
USA Direct – Sprint Express	0800 990001

TIME

South African Standard Time is two hours ahead of GMT/UTC (at noon in London it's 2 pm in Johannesburg); seven hours ahead of USA Eastern Standard Time (at noon in New York it's 7 pm in Johannesburg); and eight hours behind Australian Eastern Standard Time (at noon in Sydney it's 4 am in Johannesburg). There is no daylight saving.

MEDIA
Newspapers & Magazines

Major English-language newspapers are published in the cities and sold across the country, although in Afrikaans-speaking areas and the ex-Homelands they may not be available in every little town.

During the years of the emergency (1985 to 1990) all media were heavily censored, and although the papers are now free to print pretty much what they like, the art of political journalism is in its infancy. You see very few pieces analysing government policy.

The Johannesburg *Star* is the best middle-of-the-road daily, although there can't be many other serious broadsheets in the world which have a 'back-page girl' (always clothed but often poolside – her reported aspirations usually involve a career in modelling).

The Sowetan is the biggest selling paper in the country and its background of support for the Struggle makes it interesting reading. Despite catering to a largely poorly educated audience, it has a much more sophisticated political and social outlook than the major white papers. Some of its education supple-

ments are outstanding. *The Nation* and *South* are other black papers which upheld journalistic standards during the apartheid years. *IMVO* (roughly, 'my view') is published weekly in both English and Xhosa editions and is sold mainly in Eastern Cape Province. The paper was founded in 1884 and is essential reading if you want to understand the situation in this volatile area of the country.

The best newspaper/magazine for investigative journalism, sensible overviews and high-quality columnists, not to mention a week's worth of Doonesbury and a good entertainment section, is *The Weekly Mail/ Guardian*. It also includes a shortened version of the British *Guardian*'s international edition, which itself includes features from *Le Monde* and the *Washington Post*.

For an insight into conservative white thinking, buy *The Citizen*. It always seems to carry at least one letter from a reader whining about 'whining, demanding and ungrateful' blacks.

TV

The monolithic and conservative South African Broadcasting Corporation (SABC) was the mouthpiece of the government, and although times have changed decisively you'll still find most of its fare rather timid. There are a few exceptions, though, such as the flamboyant Dali Tambo's innovative talk show *People of the South*. The current affairs programme *Agenda* has its moments too, such as the night a studio interview with a Zulu prince was stopped by Chief Buthelezi and some gun-wielding bodyguards. Soap opera fans are in for a treat, as US daytime soaps are shown in prime time, and Brits and Aussies hooked on *Home & Away* can catch up on some very early episodes. *Melrose Place* dubbed in Afrikaans is a must.

Currently most programmes are in English or Afrikaans, but with 11 official languages to accommodate, that will change. Unfortunately, subtitling is rare.

As well as the SABC there is the pay channel M-Net, which shows some good movies. Some of the Homelands had their own TV stations and some are still in operation.

Radio

The mainstream SABC stations (AM and FM) play dreary music and offer drearier chat about recipes and the like, but the stations geared to a black audience often play good music. Radio Lotus caters to South Africans of Indian descent and plays a lot of weird and wonderful Indian film music. Cigarette ads are still played on radio and there are some gems that sound like they were made in the '50s.

The BBC World Service is available on short-wave, medium wave and, if you're near Lesotho (where the transmitter is), FM. If you're about to travel through Africa the Beeb's nightly *Focus On Africa* programme is essential listening.

WORK

South Africa is experiencing a serious recession. Jobs are hard to find and the demand for skilled labour has dropped considerably. As a result, the authorities are making it more difficult for foreigners to obtain work permits or residence permits. There are stiff penalties for people caught employing illegal foreign workers, although we haven't heard of any waiters or barpeople being busted. The bottom line is that work cannot be guaranteed.

The best time to look for casual work in restaurants and bars on the coast is in October and November, before the holiday season starts and before university students finish term. Don't expect decent pay – something like R3.50 to R5 per hour, plus tips (which can be good), is usual. It's possible to share apartments for between R150 and R300 per month so you can earn enough to live on.

ACCOMMODATION

Other than hostels and self-catering cottages (usually on farms), both of which have become a boom industry, there's a scarcity of budget accommodation. There are very few rock-bottom hotels – poor whites are usually too poor to travel – and almost none catering to the country's poorest people, the blacks. There were once cheap boarding houses for whites but many have closed

because of the recession. However, if you're prepared to camp or pay a little more for a pub or a B&B, accommodation is plentiful and generally good.

Many places, including caravan parks, have seasonal rates. The high season is usually the summer school holidays, especially around Christmas and the New Year, and Easter. Prices can double or triple and there might be a minimum stay of a week. The other school holidays are often high season as well, but some places classify them as mid-season and charge a little less.

There's one annoying thing to watch out for in accommodation advertising. You might see an advertisement for a three-star hotel boasting that rooms cost from R95. It means R95 *per person* in a twin or double room. A single room might cost R170.

Satour used to publish comprehensive guides which star-rated most accommodation in the country. Those guides are no longer published (you might be able to find old copies, which are out of date but useful) but Satour has instituted a new rating system and is gradually producing new guides. Currently they are concentrating on more up-market places and don't have a caravan park guide.

Camping

Camping and caravanning are very popular with whites and most towns have an inexpensive municipal caravan park or resort close to the centre of town. These can be very basic, but are often both pleasant and good value. The National Parks Board and the provincial authorities operate particularly high-quality camping grounds. Depending on the level of facilities, camp sites (without power) range from about R25 to R35 (cheaper in parks and reserves). In summer at beach resorts you might have to pay R60 or more for a site, as they are geared to large tents and family holidays. You might be able to negotiate a lower rate for a two-person tent, but don't count on it. There's a good chance that a popular resort town will have a backpacker hostel where you might be able to pitch your tent for less.

Note that many places, especially the privately owned caravan parks and resorts, don't permit you to use non-porous groundsheets (ie, the floor of most small tents). This rule is designed to stop the grass being killed by big tents pitched for weeks at a time, so if you're only staying a night or two you might convince the manager that your tent won't do any damage. It's probably best just to avoid the subject.

Chains such as Aventura have elaborate resorts, with guards on the gate, swimming pools, restaurants and sometimes on-site supermarkets. A lot of the accommodation is in chalets and cottages (see below). Club Caravelle is another reliable chain and their resorts tend to be less elaborate and have a wider variety of standards and prices.

In some rural backwaters of the ex-Homelands (where there are few official camp sites) you can still free-camp. *Always* ask permission from the nearest village or home before setting up your tent. This is not just good manners; you are at serious risk of robbery or worse if you ignore local sensibilities. Permission given by children doesn't count. Find the most important person you can but don't go stomping into a village demanding to see the chief.

Self-Catering Cottages

The cheapest self-catering accommodation is usually in farm cottages, which can be excellent value. You might find something for about R45 for two people, although most start around R60. They are usually comfortable but in some you'll have to do without electricity and you might even have to pump water. Small town information centres are the best places to find out about inexpensive farm cottages, and in a small community there's a chance that you can get a ride to the cottage if you don't have transport.

Self-catering cottages are often available in caravan parks and resorts. The National Parks Board has excellent-value, fully equipped cottages, but there are also a number of private resort chains such as Aventura that have particularly high standards, and some excellent municipal resorts as well.

To confuse things a little, self-catering cottages are also called chalets, cabins and rondavels (which refer to circular, often thatched, huts). At the top end, a comfortable cottage will be equipped with air-conditioning, bedding and a fully equipped kitchen. At the bottom end, a rondavel might simply have a couple of bunks, with mattresses but no bedding, a table and chairs, and a basin – rudimentary but adequate if you are travelling with a sleeping bag and basic cooking equipment.

At the basic bottom end, a rondavel sleeping from two to four people can cost from around R40 for two people; in the middle, from R60 per person; and at the top end, over R100 a double. In popular resorts, especially at the beach, peak holiday prices can more than double.

House-Sitting

This is one way to beat the cost of accommodation and to get a glimpse of what life is like for white South Africans. For a very small rent you get to look after a house, and although it's preferred that you stay at least a week it's sometimes possible to sit for a couple of days.

As long as you don't look like a liability, about the only qualifications required are that you don't have children and that you like animals. House Sitters used to be a national agency but they now operate only in Johannesburg and Durban. However, it's worth asking the tourist office in other places as there might be local agencies. House Sitters charges about R15 per night for two people, with a minimum stay of 10 days. You might be able to stay for less time but you'll still be charged for 10 days. There are lower rates if you're staying a month or more. Their addresses are:

Durban
    12 Canal Dr, Westville 3630 (☎ (031) 86 1541)
Johannesburg
    17 Sylvan Pl, 96 Hendrick Verwoerd Dr, Ferndale; PO Box 1563, Honeydew 2040 (☎ (011) 789 1250)

Hostels

There has been an explosion in the number of backpacker hostels in the past few years. South Africa has gone from being one of the least to one of the most backpacker-friendly countries in the world. However, the hostels are clustered in the popular areas, such as Cape Town and along the Garden Route, so there are still large areas of the country where camping is the only option for shoestringers. Nearly all hostels are of a high standard and a dorm bed costs in the region of R25 a night. Many hostels also offer private rooms which cost about R50/70 a single/double.

It seems likely that more hostels will open, and to find the latest list of them, look out for the little *BUG* (Backpackers' Up-To-Date Guide) book, available in some hostels.

The international YHA organisation is represented (it's called Hostelling International here) and has a number of hostels. You can contact their head office in Cape Town at 101 Boston House, 46 Strand St (☎ (021) 419 1853, fax 21 6937). There are also fledgeling local organisations which are still in a state of flux. However, nearly all hostels carry information on other hostels regardless of their affiliation.

'Overnight Rooms'

Many small towns on major routes have at least one place offering *kamers* (rooms) to locals travelling on a budget. Try asking at the café (milk bar) or at the petrol station. The standard of accommodation varies but is usually pretty basic and if there's a caravan park in town you'd probably be better-off there. Expect to pay around R40 or R50 a double.

B&Bs & Guesthouses

The distinction between a B&B and a guesthouse is usually pretty vague. Even places offering a number of guest rooms are usually private houses (admittedly fairly large houses) and the service is always very personal.

There is an enormous number of B&Bs, and it's a rare town that doesn't have at least one of these. Some of the cheaper places aren't much better than basic Overnight Rooms but on the whole the standard is extremely high.

If you're travelling on the sort of budget which would allow you to stay in B&Bs in the UK or cheap motels in Australia or the USA, you will be pleasantly surprised by the standards and prices of B&B places here. Unlike a British B&B, many South African establishments offer much more than someone's spare room, and unlike a motel they are individual and often luxurious. Antique furniture, a private verandah, big gardens and a pool are common. Many have separate guest

---

B&B Organisations

Many regions have B&B organisations (ask at local tourist offices). For a nationwide chain, contact Bed 'n Breakfast Pty Ltd (☎ (011) 482 2206, fax 726 6915), PO Box 91309, Auckland Park, 2006 Johannesburg. This company handles bookings for many places, with rates from R90/160 to R120/200 for singles/doubles. There's a booking fee of R15, although that covers more than one place if you want to book several. For the addresses of their many regional offices contact the central office in Johannesburg.

For consistently excellent places to stay covering a wide range of budgets (from about R80/110 to about R250/500 a single/double), travel with the booklets produced by the Portfolio Collection: *The Bed & Breakfast Collection*, *The Retreats Collection* (guesthouses, lodges and country hotels) and *The Country Places Collection* (guesthouses, hotels and game lodges) – highly recommended. Contact them in Johannesburg at Shop 5E, Mutual Square, Oxford Rd, Rosebank, 2196, by mail at PO Box 52350, Saxonwold 2123, by phone on ☎ (011) 880 3414 or by fax on (011) 788 4802.

There's also the South African Farm Holiday Association (☎ (021) 96 8621), 'Farm & Country Holiday', Head Office, PO Box 247, Durbanville, Cape Town 7550. ■

entrances and en-suite bathrooms are common.

Breakfasts are enormous and usually excellent. Many hosts offer regional specialities and traditional dishes which give you an insight into South African food which you don't get in restaurants.

In big towns the houses are usually out in suburbia or in the countryside, which might be an attraction but can make them difficult to get to if you don't have transport.

Hotels

Until the boom in B&B accommodation began, almost every town in the country had at least one hotel offering reasonable accommodation and meals. Now, many of the cheaper places have found that they can't compete and have either lifted standards and prices or have stopped offering accommodation altogether. This is a pity, as some of those old country town pubs were basic but pleasant places with real atmosphere.

The average country town hotel rated one or two stars charges from around R110/150 a single/double, often including breakfast. There might be cheaper rooms with shared bathrooms (maybe R50 per person) but this isn't usual. In areas of tourist interest prices are usually higher. It's rare to find a hotel which is less than clean and comfortable, though, and the bar is always a good place to meet locals. Most rooms have TV and direct-dial phones. Larger towns have more expensive hotels as well.

In the ex-Homelands the hotel situation is a bit different. There is almost always a top-end Sun hotel with an attached casino, but with a few exceptions the smaller pubs are usually just drinking places.

FOOD

Despite the fact that South Africa produces some of the best meat, fresh produce and seafood in the world, the food is often disappointing. The British can take most of the blame. Large steaks (admittedly, usually excellent), overboiled vegetables and fried chips seem to be the staple diet for whites. Vegetarians will find the country a nightmare.

In the cities and in tourist areas such as the Western Cape winelands and along the Garden Route there are a few places serving more interesting (and healthy) food and they show what can be done with some

---

Hotel Chains

The rapidly expanding **Formule 1** chain offers basic but modern, clean and secure accommodation at around R100 for up to three people. They are pretty sterile but reasonable places. (Judging by the couples who leave late at night in separate cars, the anonymity of the self-check-in is appreciated.)

There are several chains of more expensive hotels, such as **Holiday Inn Garden Court** (☎ (011) 482 3500 for central booking) and **Protea** (☎ 0800 11 9000 toll-free for central booking, fax (011) 484 2752). Rooms start around R200/250, but always ask about special deals. The standard at Protea hotels can be a bit inconsistent. **Karos** is another chain in this price range. As well as the cheaper Holiday Inn Garden Court hotels there are also **Holiday Inn** hotels, with higher service levels.

Leading Hotels of Southern Africa (☎ (011) 884 3583 for central bookings, fax 884 0676) has a small list of very interesting hotels and other places to stay, aimed at tourists rather than business people, and at prices that aren't much higher than the other chains'. See the earlier B&B Organisations boxed text for information on the Portfolio Collection, which has some outstanding places to stay.

Sun International (☎ (011) 780 7800, fax 780 7449) is a chain of tourist hotels, almost all of which are in the ex-Homelands – because gambling was legal in the Homelands and Sun hotels invariably have casinos attached. Standards and prices vary a little but are never less than high. A cheaper Sun hotel might cost about R200/240 a single/double; you can pay R10,000 a night for a suite at the Palace in Sun City. ■

imagination. Unfortunately, you're more likely to find restaurants offering international dishes that have been South Africanised. Minestrone is not supposed to be 'a hearty broth'; Thai chicken shouldn't have 'a rich honey sauce'. Basically, if a dish can have spices removed and sugar or animal fat added in large amounts, it will.

Prices are remarkably consistent. In pubs and steakhouses, steak or fish will cost

---

Glossary of Food Terms

biltong
  dried meat made from virtually anything
braaisvleis or *braai*
  a barbecue in any other country, but a religious ritual in South Africa
bredie
  traditional dish; vegetables and lamb braised and stewed
bobotie
  traditional dish; delicately flavoured Malay curry served with stewed fruits and chutney
boerewors
  spicy sausages (often sold like hot dogs by street vendors), essential at any *braai*
bunny chow
  quarter of a loaf of bread hollowed out and filled with curry; a black takeaway speciality
groente
  vegetables
kingklip
  an excellent firm-fleshed fish, usually served fried
kroeg
  hotel bar
line fish
  school fish, usually fresh
mielies
  maize
mieliemeal
  maize porridge; the staple diet for rural blacks, served with stew
monkey gland sauce
  sweet and spicy sauce served with steak
mopane worms
  caterpillars found on mopane trees, dried and served in spicy sauce – a crunchy snack
peri-peri
  a spicy pepper sauce
potjiekos
  traditional stew cooked at *braais* in three-legged pots
samosa
  spicy Indian pastry
snoek
  a firm-fleshed migratory fish that appears off the Cape in June and July, sometimes served smoked, salted or as a curry
steak
  usually plate-sized and served with sauce; see *monkey gland sauce*
SteersSpur
  ubiquitous steakhouse chain
vleis
  meat
waterblommetjie bredie
  traditional dish; mutton stew with water-hyacinth flowers (faintly peppery) and white wine

Kingklip

between R20 and R25. Pizzas are also popular and these cost around R15. It is worth trying to sample some of the traditional Cape cuisine, which is an intriguing mix of Malay and Dutch.

Most restaurants are licensed, but some allow you to bring your own wine, especially in the Cape. This works out cheaply, especially if you've done the rounds of a few vineyards. Ring ahead to check the restaurant's policy.

Most hotels allow nonresidents to use their dining rooms and, even if you're travelling on a tight budget, it's worth buying a breakfast buffet in an expensive hotel. You'll pay around R20 but you will definitely have enough food to last you all day – and enough cholesterol to fill your quota for at least a week. Many whites also eat two other meals this size each day, so it's easy to see why many white men use belts not so much to hold up their trousers but to restrain an avalanche of fat. God knows how white women stay thin.

Boerewors (farmers' sausage) is the traditional sausage and it's sold everywhere. Even committed carnivores can find this unappetising but that's partly because what you're being sold sometimes isn't boerewors but *braaiwors*, an inferior grade. Real boerewors must be 90% meat, of which 30% can be fat and no offal is allowed. You can imagine what goes into unregulated braaiwors!

There is a handful of restaurants serving African dishes, most of which don't originate in South Africa. The staple for most blacks is rice or mielie (maize) meal, served in a variety of forms. Although it isn't especially appetising it's cheap. Servings of rice and stew are sold for about R5 around minibus taxi parks.

DRINKS
Pubs
Surprisingly, there are few bars and pubs in South Africa. Johannesburg, Durban and especially Cape Town have a decent range of drinking places, but in most other towns and cities the situation is dire. Most towns have

at least one hotel, but they are usually not very social places.

In the bad old days most pubs had a bar (or *kroeg*) where the white men would drink, a Ladies Lounge/Bar where white couples would drink, and a hole in the wall where bottles would be sold to the blacks or coloureds. Since the collapse of apartheid, hotels are obliged to serve everyone everywhere, but unofficial segregation is the norm.

In most places, blacks have taken over the bar and the white males have taken over the Ladies. As far as we could discover, women are not served through the wall. You will find the occasional white couple in the Ladies, but unaccompanied females (white or black) are rarely seen in any part of any hotel.

The men in the Ladies are very often embittered travelling salesmen, travel writers and drunks, who study the bottom of their glasses as if they were looking into a crystal ball. In general the bar, with its cheerful and gregarious black clientele, will be far more congenial for travellers, once they have established their bona fides. Be warned that in the bar, beer is usually served in a 750 ml bottle.

Draught beers are unusual. In places where they are sold they'll be served in large (500 ml) or small (250 ml) glasses. Usually you will be sold lager-style beer in cans or stubbies (small bottles) for around R2.50 to R3.50. There are a number of lager brands: Castle is probably the most popular, but Amstel and Carlsberg are also good. In the Cape, look out for Mitchell's Beers which come from a couple of small breweries around the province. Brandy and coke is a popular poison – brandy's popularity dates back to the early days of white settlement.

The alcohol content of beer is around 5%, about the same as Australian beer but much stronger than UK or US beer. Even Castle Lite has 4% alcohol.

Wine
Wine was first made in South Africa in 1659. It is now an enormous industry, employing around 30,000 people in Western

Cape Province. The wine is of a high standard, and it is very reasonably priced. If you buy direct from a vineyard you can get bottles for as little as R6.50, but in a bottle store R12 and up is a more realistic price. Of course, you can pay a lot more and, as always, there is a pretty close correlation between quality and price. Most restaurants have long wine lists and stock a few varieties in 250 ml bottles, which is very handy if you want to try a few wines or are eating alone.

There are over 2500 wines on the market. No wine may use any estate, cultivar, vintage or origin declaration on its label without being certified and carrying a certification sticker to that effect. No South African sparkling wine may be called champagne, although there are a number of producers using Chardonnay and Pinot Noir blends and the méthode champenoise.

There is a range of excellent dry whites made from Sauvignon Blanc, Riesling, Colombar and Chenin Blanc. The most widely available blends are called Blanc de Blanc (mainly Chenin Blanc), and Premier Grand Crû (usually Colombar, Chenin Blanc and Riesling; this is not a quality classification as in France).

The most popular red cultivars are Cabernet Sauvignon, Pinotage (an interesting local cultivar crossed from Pinot and Cinsaut, which was known as Hermitage), Shiraz, Cinsaut and Pinot Noir. There are some excellent fortified wines (sherry, port, hanepoot, jerepigo and muscadel) and very high-quality brandies.

ENTERTAINMENT

The low-class 'jazz halls' of the Coloured people's quarters in Durban, with their night-long orgies of drinking, gambling, indecent dancing and immorality, illustrate the depths of degradation to which the Natives, and in this case Asiatics of both sexes, fall when left to their own devices.

South Africa, A Planned Tour, AW Wells, 1939

The writer would have been pleased that the apartheid governments stamped-out this sort of behaviour. Unfortunately for those of us who think that it sounds pretty good, the stifling effects of the apartheid years have not yet worn off and nightlife remains a scarce commodity.

In Cape Town, Durban and Johannesburg you can find most forms of entertainment associated with big, Westernised cities. The quality is often high but the range is limited. There are good entertainment listings (which include the small but healthy 'alternative' scene) in the *Weekly Mail*.

Visiting a township shebeen (previously illegal bars) is probably the most interesting entertainment, and some have good music and dancing. However, it's potentially very dangerous. You'd be crazy to enter a township at night (or even during the day) without a trustworthy guide. Some hostels and backpacker-oriented activities outfits run tours which visit shebeens.

Outside the three big cities nightlife comes down to bars and cinemas.

Sport

Soccer is the most popular sport among blacks. You come across some great team names, such as:

Dangerous Darkies
Eleven Men in Flight
Highway Never Die
Hot Chillies
Hungry Vultures
Pot o' Gold
Young Cannibals
Inyonikayiphumuli (tricky for fans: 'Give us an *I*...')

Cricket fans tend to be English-speakers but after South Africa's return to international sport in the 1992 World Cup, cricket occupied centre stage. The euphoria following South Africa's surprising success in the competition probably helped the Yes vote in the referendum on constitutional reform.

Rugby (Union, not League) was traditionally the Afrikaners' sport until the 1995 World Cup, which was hosted and won by South Africa. The entire white and coloured population went rugby mad – the black population was officially part of the celebrations but the response was a little muted. Rugby had been seen (and continues to be seen by many whites) as epitomising the Afrikaners' he-man social values. And those social values were extremely closely linked to apartheid.

Still, there are now rugby development programmes in the townships, and Ellis Park echoed to 65,000 mainly white fans chanting 'Nelson' when the president, wearing a Springbok jumper, met the teams at the World Cup final. When the game ended and South Africa had won the World Cup, the Springbok team dropped to their knees in a prayer of thanksgiving, which raised some disturbing images of other famous prayers in Afrikaner history.

It had been agreed that South African international sporting teams would no longer be named Springboks because of the all-white connotations of the name. It had been boasted that no black would ever wear a Springbok jumper. However, there is almost no chance that the new name, the Proteas, will catch on, and even Desmond Tutu now argues that the Springbok name should be retained.

There are traditional Afrikaner games, the most popular of which is *jukskei*. This game is something like horseshoe-tossing but uses items associated with trek-wagons. Kroonstad (in the Orange Free State) is the centre for national competition.

Getting There & Away

This chapter deals with travel to/from South Africa only. For information on alternative routes that involve other African destinations and overland routes north of Zimbabwe, Botswana and Namibia see the introductory Getting There & Away chapter.

Lesotho and Swaziland have air links to a number of African countries, and air and road links with South Africa. See the Lesotho and Swaziland Getting There & Away chapters for details.

Johannesburg is the most important gateway to the region for both land and air transport, although an increasing number of flights use Cape Town and some go to Durban.

See the Johannesburg section for an extensive list of airline addresses and phone numbers. There aren't many discount travel outlets in South Africa, but as always it is worth shopping around. The following companies will give you a good start:

South African Students' Travel Service (SASTS)
  This is a national student travel organisation (you don't have to be a student to use their services). Once, this organisation was mainly concerned with getting South African students to Europe and back, but now it offers some very good deals on one-way tickets as well – definitely worth checking out. There are also offices at universities in Cape Town, Durban, Grahamstown, Pietermaritzburg and Port Elizabeth. Student Union Building, University of Witwatersrand (☎ (011) 716 3045).
Rennies Travel
  This is a comprehensive network of agencies throughout South Africa, and is the agent for Thomas Cook. 124 Main St, Johannesburg (☎ (011) 331 5898).
Pathfinders Travel
  This small agency specialises in eco-tourism and personalised itineraries.17 Chaucer Ave, Senderwood, Bedfordview, Johannesburg (☎ (011) 453 1113/4, ah 706 6629, fax 453 1483).

WITHIN AFRICA

Most regional African airlines now fly to/from South Africa.

To/From Botswana

Air Between them Air Botswana and Comair have daily flights between Johannesburg and Gaborone, for around R450.

Bus Greyhound buses run between Johannesburg and Gaborone three times a week for R85. See the Mafikeng section in the North-West chapter for details of minibus taxis to Gaborone. Mafikeng is accessible from Johannesburg on inexpensive Transtate buses.

Border Crossings Most land border crossings between Botswana and South Africa are all open between 7 or 8 am and 4 pm. The main border crossings are Ramatlabama, north of Mafeking, which is open from 7 am to 4 pm; Pioneer Gate, north-west of Zeerust, which is open from 7 am to 8 pm; and Tlokweng Gate, north of Zeerust, which is open from 7 am to 10 pm.

To/From Lesotho

See the Lesotho section for information on land routes, including hiking and horse trails through the Drakensberg, and border crossings.

Air Lesotho Airways flies at least daily between Moshoeshoe International Airport, 18 km from Maseru, and Johannesburg in South Africa. A one-way/return ticket costs R288/599 (or R432 return if you stay away for more than four days and less than one month). There is also a weekly flight from Lesotho to Swaziland (R461/922).

Departure Tax
There's an airport departure tax of R25 or R38 to neighbouring African countries. This is usually included in your ticket price but check. ■

Bus Transtate buses run from Johannesburg and Durban to Maseru. See the Transtate section in the Getting Around chapter.

To/From Mozambique

Air Metavia flies between Johannesburg and Maputo for about R500. There are also flights connecting Maputo with Swaziland and Lesotho.

Bus Panthera Azul (☎ (011) 337 7409 or 887 0383) runs buses from Johannesburg to Maputo on Monday, Thursday and Saturday, returning on Tuesday, Friday and Sunday. The fare is R150. In Johannesburg the bus departs from Expedition Mozambique, on the corner of Polly and Kerk Sts in the city centre. Protours run from Jo'burg to Maputo on Thursday and Saturday for R145, R275 return. For more information contact the Golden Wheels desk (☎ (011) 852 5420) at the Rotunda bus station.

Train The *Komati* runs between Johannesburg and Komatipoort, on the Mozambique border, and continues on to Maputo. See the Train section in the Getting Around chapter for details.

To/From Namibia

Air Air Namibia connects Windhoek with Johannesburg (about R680 one way) and Cape Town (about R700 one way).

Bus Intercape Mainliner buses run between Cape Town and Windhoek four times a week for R270. See the Cape Town section of the Western Cape chapter for details. You can travel between Windhoek and Johannesburg with Intercape, but you will probably have to stay overnight in Upington. See Upington (Northern Cape chapter) and Johannesburg (Gauteng chapter) for details.

Passenger trains recently stopped running between Windhoek and South Africa, so it's possible that more bus services will run in the future.

Border Crossings It is no longer possible to cross the Namibia-South Africa border to/from the Kalahari Gemsbok National Park. The nearest alternative is to cross at Rietfontein, which is open 24 hours. The main crossing west of Upington is at Ariamsvlei, also open 24 hours. The main crossing on the west coast is at Vioolsdrif and that is also open 24 hours.

To/From Swaziland

See the Swaziland chapter for details on land routes and border crossings.

Air Royal Swazi Airlines flies to Johannesburg daily (about R300).

Bus The best way into Swaziland from Johannesburg is the weekday Transtate bus to Manzini via Mbabane (the capital). The fare is about R50. There are also services from Durban; see the Transtate section in the Getting Around South Africa chapter for details.

To/From Zimbabwe

Air Air Zimbabwe (☎ (011) 331 1541, fax 331 6970 in Johannesburg) flies from Johannesburg to Harare (about R800) daily. There are also flights to Bulawayo and Victoria Falls. Some flights leave from Durban.

Bus Translux runs buses at least daily between Johannesburg and Harare (some services run via Bulawayo) for R200. See the Translux section in the Getting Around chapter for details. There are several other operators, such as Silverbird (☎ (011) 337 7215), charging R330/590 for single/return, and cheaper companies such as Zimbus. Ask around at the Rotunda bus station in Johannesburg for current deals.

See Johannesburg (Gauteng chapter) and Messina (Northern Transvaal chapter) for information on minibus taxis.

Train The *Limpopo* runs weekly between Johannesburg and Harare for R321/220 in 1st/2nd class (no 3rd class on this train). See the Train section in the Getting Around chapter for details.

Border Crossings The only border post between Zimbabwe and South Africa is at Beitbridge on the Limpopo River, which is open from 6 am to 8 pm. Lengthy waits used to be common but apparently things have improved lately. There's a lot of smuggling so searches are thorough. Messina is the closest South African town to the border (15 km) and this is where you can change money.

TO/FROM AUSTRALIA

The return flight between Australia and Johannesburg is expensive, at around A$2400 for a standard mid-season economy fare. You should be able to find a discounted fare for around A$1900. Air Mauritius has a few direct flights from Perth to Mauritius with a stopover, then a direct flight to Johannesburg. They have other flights to South Africa via Mauritius originating in Singapore, Hong Kong and Bombay.

Malaysian Airline System (MAS) often has the cheapest flights from Sydney or Melbourne to Johannesburg and Cape Town. The hassle is that you fly via Kuala Lumpur, a long way out of the way. There are more or less direct connections but you might want to take advantage of MAS' good stopover deals in Kuala Lumpur.

The other alternative is to check out RTW deals or a return ticket to Europe via southern Africa.

From South Africa, South African Students' Travel Service (SASTS) has one-way cheapies to Sydney from as low as R2440.

TO/FROM UK

Flight prices from the UK are quite competitive, and could become even more so now that tourism is taking off. It's worth shopping around, but you should be able to get a return flight to Johannesburg for under £600. Some airlines will allow you to fly into Cape Town and leave from Johannesburg or vice versa.

Although it is a long-haul flight, it's pretty easy to handle (nothing like flying to Asia or Australia). The flight takes about 13½ hours, but it is overnight and South Africa is only two hours ahead of GMT/UTC so the body clock doesn't get too badly out of whack.

There are also interesting tickets available that include other ports in Africa like Cairo, Nairobi and Harare. If you have plenty of time up your sleeve, you may find some good value round-the-world tickets that can build in Johannesburg. Return tickets to Australia via Johannesburg are also worth looking at.

About the cheapest consistently available fare directly to southern Africa from London is the laborious flight on Balkan Bulgarian Airlines, stopping in Sofia (Bulgaria). Given the bare bones service, combined with typically severe overbooking and an obstinate reluctance to change reservations or tickets, it may be worthwhile to pay for something more reliable.

From South Africa to London, SASTS fares can get as low as R1350 (to New York) plus £115.

TO/FROM EUROPE

Most of the major European airlines fly to Johannesburg, with many flights continuing on to Cape Town. An increasing number, including British Airways, fly direct to Cape Town.

TO/FROM ASIA

Air India, Cathay Pacific, MAS, Singapore Airlines, Thai Airways and other Asian airlines now fly to South Africa – most to Johannesburg. At the time of writing, MAS had good deals via Kuala Lumpur.

From South Africa, a one-way fare to India is around R2800, although you can usually find significant discounts. Air India has a twice-weekly service between Bombay and Johannesburg and Durban.

TO/FROM NORTH AMERICA

SAA flies to/from New York and Miami, and by now there should be direct flights to/from Washington. You should be able to find singles/returns from New York for US$1335/1699, and from Los Angeles for US$1926/2179. Particularly if you are coming from the West Coast of the USA, it is worth looking into fares via Asia (eg, Kuala Lumpur) which can be as low as US$1785 return. It is also worth exploring the possibility of flying to

London, and buying a bucket shop ticket there. See the introductory Getting There & Away chapter.

SASTS one-way fares to New York can get down to R1350.

TO/FROM SOUTH AMERICA

SAA and Varig link Johannesburg and Cape Town with Rio de Janeiro and Sao Paulo. Currently, MAS offers the best deal on flights from South Africa to South America, with a one-way/return fares to Buenos Aires at R1900/2800.

Getting Around

South Africa is geared towards travel by private car, with some very good highways but limited and expensive mainstream public transport. If you want to cover a lot of country in a limited time, hiring or buying a car might be necessary. If you don't have much money but have time to spare, you can hitch to most places, and if you don't mind a modicum of discomfort there's the extensive network of minibus taxis, Transtate buses and 3rd-class train seats.

In areas which were once Homelands you can expect roads to be in poorer condition (not much money was spent on areas where no whites lived). Transtate buses are usually the mainstay of long-distance transport in these areas, plus the usual minibus taxis.

AIR

SAA is a domestic as well as an international carrier. To most destinations there are plenty of daily flights. Fares aren't cheap, but if you plan to do a lot of flying in South Africa check with a travel agent before you leave home for special deals on advance purchase tickets. Once you're in South Africa there are a few discount options.

Most SAA flights have a limited number of 15% discount seats, sold on a first-come, first-served basis. If you book and pay two weeks in advance there's a 30% discount and three months in advance earns you 50% off. There might be specials on late-night flights.

The free baggage allowance is 40/30/20 kg in 1st/business/economy class. Excess baggage is charged at a flat rate of R8 per kg.

SAA flights can be booked at travel agents or by ringing any of these numbers:

Bloemfontein	(051)	47 3811
Cape Town	(021)	25 4610
Durban	(031)	305 6491
East London	(0431)	44 5299
George	(0441)	73 8448
Johannesburg	(011)	333 6504
Kimberley	(0531)	51 1231
Port Elizabeth	(041)	34 4444
Pretoria	(012)	315 2929
Upington	(054)	25656

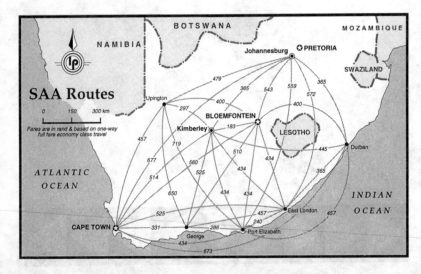

SAA Routes

0   150   300 km

Fares are in rand & based on one-way full fare economy class travel

South African Airways logo

A new airline, Phoenix (☎ (011) 970 1511), has recently commenced business. It flies much the same routes as SAA, at much lower fares. Phoenix is running into problems common to new airlines challenging monopolies. Its flights usually have to land on the runways furthest from the terminals, departure lounges are inconveniently sited, and so on. Let's hope it survives.

Comair (☎ (011) 921 0222) is known for arranging fly-in packages to the private game reserves in Eastern Transvaal, but is now developing into a general airline. There are at least daily flights between Johannesburg and Cape Town (R490 full one-way fare), Durban (R296), Richard's Bay (R365) and Skukuza (Kruger National Park; R422). There are various advance purchase deals which can mean up to 40% discount. Comair also flies to Gaborone in Botswana (R490), Harare in Zimbabwe (R1030) and Manzini in Swaziland (R340).

There are also several regional airlines. Airlink covers the eastern half of the country, with flights between Johannesburg, Durban, East London, Bloemfontein, Nelspruit, Phalaborwa, Port Elizabeth, Umtata, Maseru (Lesotho), Matsapha (Swaziland) and Maputo (Mozambique). Fares are roughly equivalent to SAA's and there are advance purchase discounts of up to 50%. For more information contact central reservations in Johannesburg (☎ (011) 394 2430, fax 394 2649). There are also offices in major centres.

National Airlines (☎ (021) 934 0350 in Cape Town, (011) 659 2506 in Johannesburg) flies to Cape Town, Springbok, Alexander Bay and Johannesburg. Theron Airways (☎ (011) 659 2738) flies from Johannesburg to Thohoyandu and Pietersburg.

Sun Air (☎ (011) 970 1623, fax 970 1906) is the new incarnation of Bop Air, the 'national' carrier of the defunct Bophuthatswana Homeland. Sun Air flies between Pilanesberg (Sun City) and Cape Town, Durban and Johannesburg. There are also flights to/from Mmabatho. See the Sun City section of the North-West Province chapter for more details.

Transkei Airways (☎ (011) 970 2057 in Johannesburg) flies to Johannesburg and Durban from Umtata, and has charter flights within the Transkei region. See the Eastern Cape chapter.

BUS

Translux, part of the semi-privatised government transport service called Autonet, runs most long-distance buses. The other main national operator is Greyhound, which covers quite a lot of the country at fares a little higher than Translux. With the exception of Transtate (a poor relation of Translux) and local services geared towards blacks, bus travel isn't cheap and there are no 'bus pass' deals (although they might be coming). Return fares are double the one-way fares.

Translux

Translux runs express services on the main routes. Tickets must be booked 24 hours in advance. You can get on without a booking if there's a spare seat, but you won't know that until the bus arrives and if there isn't a seat you could have a couple of days' wait for the next bus. You usually can't book a seat to a nearby town, but prices for short sectors are exorbitant anyway – you're better-off looking for a local bus or a minibus taxi. Computicket takes bookings, as do many travel agents and some railway stations. There are also reservations offices around the country, including:

Bloemfontein	(051) 408 3431
Cape Town	(021) 405 3333
Durban	(031) 361 8333
East London	(0431) 44 2333
Johannesburg	(011) 774 3333
Pietermaritzburg	(0331) 958 2012
Port Elizabeth	(041) 507 3333
Pretoria	(012) 315 3333

Translux offices have details of the few remaining City to City services (which are cheaper than Translux) but they won't tell you about them unless you ask. The most useful are the services to Umtata from Cape Town and Johannesburg – see those cities for details.

Translux Routes

Johannesburg/Pretoria – Bloemfontein
Departs daily except Tuesday and Wednesday, and takes seven hours. Stops and fares from Jo'burg/Bloemfontein include Kroonstad, R100/100; Welkom, R120/80; Bloemfontein, R130.

Johannesburg/Pretoria – Cape Town
Departs at least once daily. Stops and fares from Jo'burg/Cape Town/ include Kroonstad, R100/250; Bloemfontein, R130/240; Beaufort West, R200/140; Worcester, R250/85; Cape Town, R280.

Johannesburg/Pretoria – Cape Town via Kimberley
Departs on Sunday and Friday. The trip takes 15 hours to/from Jo'burg. Stops and fares from Jo'burg/Cape Town include Potchefstroom, R100/260; Kimberley, R140/240; Beaufort West, R200/140; Worcester, R250/85; Cape Town, R280.

Johannesburg/Pretoria – Durban
Departs daily and takes 8½ hours to/from Jo'burg. There's also at least one express service daily that takes an hour less. Stops and fares from Johannesburg/Durban include Harrismith, R100/95; Montrose, R100/95; Pietermaritzburg, R110/30; Durban, R120.

Johannesburg/Pretoria – East London
Departs from Pretoria and Johannesburg on Sunday, Monday, Tuesday, Wednesday and Saturday; departs from East London on Sunday, Monday, Tuesday, Thursday and Friday. The trip takes 12 hours to/from Jo'burg. Stops and fares from Jo'burg/East London include Kroonstad, R100/190; Bloemfontein, R130/160; Aliwal North, R130/115; Queenstown, R150/85; King

William's Town, R200/65; East London R200.

Johannesburg – Harare (Zimbabwe)
Departs at least once daily and takes 21 hours via Bulawayo, 17 hours direct. Direct buses depart Johannesburg and Harare on Monday, Wednesday and Friday. Stops and fares from Johannesburg/Harare include Pretoria, R30/205; Pietersburg, R75/160; Louis Trichardt, R85/155; Messina, R100/130; Beitbridge (border), R110/125.

Johannesburg/Pretoria – Knysna
The trip takes 16½ hours to/from Jo'burg. On Sunday and Thursday the southbound buses run via Kimberley and on Wednesday and Friday the northbound buses do. On the other days buses run via Bloemfontein. Stops and fares from Jo'burg/Knysna include Welkom, R120/190; Bloemfontein, R130/190; Kimberley, R140/165; Beaufort West, R200/100; Oudtshoorn, R210/50; Mossel Bay, R210/50; George, R210/40; Knysna R210.

Johannesburg/Pretoria – Port Elizabeth
Departs from Johannesburg and Pretoria on Sunday and Tuesday, departs from Port Elizabeth on Monday and Saturday. The trip takes 14 hours. Stops and fares from Jo'burg/Port Elizabeth include Kroonstad, R100/180; Bloemfontein, R130/165; Cradock, 180/155; Port Elizabeth, R220.

Cape Town – Durban via Bloemfontein
Departs from Cape Town on Tuesday, Thursday, Friday, Saturday and Sunday; departs from Durban on Sunday, Monday, Wednesday, Friday and Saturday. The trip takes 20 hours. Stops and fares from Cape Town/Durban include Paarl, R85/280; Beaufort West, R140/225; Bloemfontein, R240/130; Bethlehem, R260/95; Harrismith, R260/95; Pietermaritzburg, R280/30; Durban, R290.

Cape Town – East London
Departs from Cape Town on Sunday, Tuesday, Thursday and Friday; departs from East London on Sunday, Monday, Wednesday and Friday. The trip takes 14½ hours. Stops and fares

from Cape Town/East London include Paarl, R85/170; Beaufort West, R140/140; Graaff Reinet, R150/140; Cradock, R155/135; Queenstown, R160/85; King William's Town R170/65; East London, R170.

Cape Town – Port Elizabeth via Coast

Departs daily, with a slightly different time-table on weekends. The trip takes 10 hours. Stops and fares from Cape Town/Port Elizabeth include Swellendam, R60/105; Mossel Bay, R75/90; Oudtshoorn, R85/80 (this is a connection); George, R85/80; Knysna, R95/65; Plettenberg Bay, R100/50; Humansdorp, R115/40; Port Elizabeth R115.

This is a daytime service. There's also a night service departing Cape Town on Tuesday, Thursday, Saturday and Sunday; departing Port Elizabeth on Monday, Wednesday, Friday and Saturday. It runs the same route except that it stops in Oudtshoorn and also in Stellenbosch (R40/115). This route takes 11½ hours.

Cape Town – Port Elizabeth via Mountains

Departs from Cape Town on Monday and Wednesday, departs from Port Elizabeth on Tuesday and Thursday. The trip takes 11½ hours. Stops and fares from Cape Town/Port Elizabeth include Stellenbosch, R40/115; Paarl, R85/115; Robertson, R85/100; Montagu, R85/100; Oudtshoorn, R85/80; Humansdorp, R115/40; Port Elizabeth, R115.

Another service, departing Cape Town on Friday and Port Elizabeth on Sunday, runs the same route to Oudtshoorn then runs to Port Elizabeth through George (R85/80), Knysna (R95/65) and Plettenberg Bay (R100/50).

Durban – Port Elizabeth

Departs daily and takes 13½ hours. Stops and fares from Durban/Port Elizabeth include Port Shepstone, R60/165; Kokstad, R75/145; Umtata, R105/115; East London, R135/70; Grahamstown, R160/70; Port Elizabeth R170.

Transtate

Transtate's services are slow and aren't air-conditioned, but on every other count it beats the pants off Translux and Greyhound.

Transtate services were originally intended to carry people from the Homelands, Lesotho and Swaziland to and from the big cities where they were guest workers under the apartheid regime. So Transtate buses are cheap, run very interesting routes and stop just about everywhere. You can't book but that's rarely a problem. In a sense Transtate is third-world transport, but compared with buses in most third-world countries, it is luxurious.

Transtate's stops and few offices can be difficult to find, and little printed information on routes and timetables is available. Transtate often stops at railway stations, so you can try asking there. (A black employee is more likely to be able to help you than a white one.) Even though Translux is related to Transtate (both are part of the semi-government Autonet system), you won't find information on Transtate at Translux counters. In fact many Translux staff have never heard of Transtate – or are appalled at the idea of a Westerner travelling on what was once blacks-only transport. Transtate is beginning to realise that its service appeals to adventurous travellers and is making things easier. Still, information can be difficult to find, so here are a few of the more interesting routes.

Some Transtate Routes

Johannesburg – Acornhoek This service runs via Nelspruit, White River and Hazyview and takes 10½ hours. It departs from Johannesburg at 8 am on weekdays and returns daily except Saturday. Nelspruit, White River and Hazyview are near the south of Kruger Park and the Transvaal Drakensberg. Jo'burg to Acornhoek costs R60. There are also several night services on this route.

Johannesburg – Sibasa This daily service via Pietersburg takes 11 hours and costs R55.

Johannesburg – Manzini (Swaziland)
Departing Jo'burg on weekdays at 7.30 am, this service takes 10½ hours and costs about R50. It runs via Mbabane, the capital of Swaziland, and is the best way into Swaziland from Johannesburg.

Johannesburg – Hlathikulu (Swaziland)
This trip, via Piet Retief and Nhlangano, takes 10 hours and costs R50. It departs from Johannesburg weekdays at 8 am and returns daily except Saturday.

Johannesburg – Queenstown Departs from either end daily at 6 pm, takes 12 hours and costs R80. It runs via Zastron and Aliwal North. There's also a service running via Bloemfontein.

Johannesburg – Mtubatuba This service takes 11 hours, costs R65 and runs via Piet Retief, Pongola, Mkuze and Hluhluwe. It departs from Johannesburg Tuesday (8 am) and Friday (8 pm from Germiston) and returns Wednesday and Sunday (both night).

Johannesburg – Nongoma This service takes 10½ hours, costs R55 and runs via Newcastle and Vryheid. It departs from Johannesburg on Tuesday (8 am) and Friday (8.45 pm) and returns on Monday (4 pm), Wednesday (1 pm) and Sunday (5 pm).

Johannesburg – Umtata This daily service takes 15 hours, costs R85 and runs via Harrismith, Pietermaritzburg, Kokstad and Mt Frere. It departs from Jo'burg at 6 pm and Umtata at midday. There's also a service following a slightly different route departing Jo'burg at 7 pm on Tuesday and Friday.

Johannesburg – Lusikisiki This service takes 14 hours and runs via Harrismith, Pietermaritzburg and Kokstad. It departs from Johannesburg weekdays at 3 pm and returns at midday daily except Saturday.

Johannesburg – Matatiele A good service for getting to the KwaZulu/Natal's southern Drakensberg. It takes 10½ hours, via Harrismith and Underberg. It departs from Johannesburg weekdays at 5 pm and returns daily except Saturday.

Johannesburg – Mafikeng This service takes 5¼ hours, costs R40 and runs via Krugersdorp and Zeerust. It departs from Johannesburg at 7 am daily except Sunday and it returns daily from Mafikeng except Saturday at 12.30 pm.

Welkom – Ficksburg A five-hour service via Virginia and Winburg, departing Welkom at 7 am daily except Sunday (plus other services on most days) and returning daily at 12.30 pm, 1 pm on Sunday (plus other services most days). The fare is R25. Ficksburg is on the Lesotho border. It costs R25. You can connect with a service from Welkom to Jo'burg (R35, via Kroonstad) Monday to Thursday, but the Jo'burg to Welkom service (via Potchefstroom and Klerksdorp) leaves from Carletonville.

Johannesburg – Maseru (Lesotho) – Lady Grey A 10-hour service (six hours to Maseru) via Zastron, departing at 8 am on Monday, Wednesday and Friday, returning at 6 am on Tuesday, Thursday and Sunday.

Johannesburg – Lobatse (Botswana) This service takes six-hours and runs via Zeerust, Mafikeng and the Ramatlabama border post. It departs from Carletonville (a Jo'burg suburb) at 6 am on Wednesday and returns, all the way to Jo'burg station, at 11 am on Tuesday and Thursday.

Johannesburg – Kuruman There's no direct service, but you can catch a bus from Jo'burg to Rustenburg daily at 8 am (R20, three buses), then one to Kuruman (R50, 9½ hours) on Tuesday, Wednesday and Friday at 8.30 am. Running the other way, buses leave Kuruman at 6 am on Monday and Thursday, and Rustenburg at 1 pm daily.

Johannesburg – Pietersburg A daily express run that takes four hours and costs R40. It departs from Jo'burg at 8 am and

Pietersburg at 1 pm. Many buses running north from Pretoria also stop in Pietersburg.

Johannesburg – Giyani A daily 8½-hour service via Pietersburg and Louis Trichardt, departing Jo'burg at 8 am.

Durban – Umtata A daily service taking 10 hours and costing R45. It departs from both Durban and Umtata at 7 am and runs via Pietermaritzburg, Kokstad and Mt Frere.

Durban – Maseru (Lesotho) A 14-hour run via Pietermaritzburg, Bethlehem, Ficksburg and Ladybrand. The fare is R65. It departs from Durban at 7 pm from Friday to Tuesday; Maseru at midday from Wednesday to Sunday.

Durban – Ongeluksnek (Lesotho) This daily 9½-hour trip passes through Port Shepstone, Kokstad and Matatiele. It departs from Durban at 6 am (7 am Sunday), Ongeluksnek at 6 am (8.30 am Sunday).

Durban – Fort Beaufort Running daily except Sunday, this useful service departs from Durban at 4 pm and runs via Butterworth, East London, King William's Town and Alice, taking 14 hours to Fort Beaufort. Return buses departs at 11 am for a daylight run through some interesting country. The fare is about R60.

Durban – eManguse (KwaNgwanase) A useful daily service that takes 10 hours and runs via Stanger, Empangeni, Mtubatuba, Hluhluwe and Mkuze. It departs from Durban at 8 am (11 am Sunday) and returns at 6 am (11 and 11.30 am Sunday).

Durban – Port St Johns Departs daily at 6 am in either direction and takes nine hours, running via Port Shepstone and Lusikisiki.

Durban – Mtubatuba A daily 9½-hour service running via Stanger, Eshowe, Melmoth, Ulundi and Nongoma. A useful service, taking some of Zululand's main towns, passing close to Hluhluwe and Umfolozi game reserves, and ending on the coast near the Lake St Lucia complex of parks – and all in daylight. It departs from Durban at 6 am (8 am Sunday), Mtubatuba at 7.30 am (10 am Sunday). The fare is R25.

Durban – Pongola This daily nine-hour service costs R47 and runs via Stanger, Empangeni, Mtubatuba, Hluhluwe, Mkuze and Golela, on the Swaziland border. It departs from Durban at 6 am (9 am Sunday) and Pongola at 7.30 am (10.30 am Sunday).

Durban – Mbabane (Swaziland) On Monday, Wednesday and Friday express buses depart Durban at 2.30 pm, arriving in Mbabane at 3 am. Return buses depart Mbabane at 4 pm the following days (R55).

Durban – Queenstown Running via Umtata, this service departs from Durban at 3 pm on Tuesday, Thursday and Sunday, returning at 3 pm the following day. The trip takes 10 hours.

Johannesburg – Empangeni A circuitous but interesting route to the KwaZulu/Natal north coast, running via Newcastle, Itala, Melmoth and Eshowe. It departs from Jo'burg at 8.45 pm on Friday, Empangeni at 2 pm on Sunday. The trip takes 15½ hours and costs R65.

Cape Town – Umtata A 20-hour service running via Stellenbosch, Paarl, Worcester, Beaufort West, Graaff Reinet, Cradock, Queenstown and Cofimvaba. It departs from Cape Town at 4 pm on Sunday, Umtata at 9 am on Thursday. The fare is R115 from Cape Town but only R95 from Umtata. It might be possible to continue on to Port St Johns and Lusikisiki on this bus.

Welkom – Nongoma This useful service runs via Bethlehem, Harrismith, Ladysmith, Dundee, Vryheid and Ulundi. It departs from Welkom at 6 pm on Tuesday and 7 pm on Wednesday, returning at 1 pm on Wednesday and Sunday. The whole trip takes 11 hours.

Klerksdorp – Lusikisiki Although not many people will want to use the full length of this service, it does connect some important areas. It stops in Bloemfontein, Zastron, Lady Grey, Barkly East, Maclear and Kokstad. The whole trip takes 16 hours and departs from Klerksdorp at 5 pm on Monday, Tuesday and Wednesday, plus 6 pm on Friday. Return buses depart at midday from Tuesday to Friday.

Other Lines

Greyhound offers services on much the same routes as Translux, at prices that are usually a little higher. The exception is the express run between Johannesburg and Kimberley (R72). There are a few Greyhound routes where you don't have the option of taking Translux. From Johannesburg to Nelspruit there's a daily service for R99; Durban to Upington (R260) via Bloemfontein (R130 from Durban, R120 from Upington) and Kimberley (R165, R95) runs three times a week. There's also a thrice-weekly service between Johannesburg and Gaborone (Botswana) for R85.

Intercape Mainliner (☎ (021) 934 4400) is a major line in the western half of the country and generally charges appreciably less than Translux. Routes include Johannesburg to Upington (R140), Cape Town to Upington (R130), Windhoek (Namibia) to Upington (R200), Cape Town to Windhoek (R270), Cape Town to Port Elizabeth (R105), and Port Elizabeth to East London (R70). See the relevant towns for more information.

There are various regional operators, including Garden Line (☎ (0441) 74 2823) with services between Johannesburg and Mossel Bay via Kimberley or Bloemfontein. Fares are significantly lower than with Translux.

TRAIN

Spoornet, the company which runs South Africa's railway system, has been partially privatised and the result was the closing of passenger services on all but the main lines. The only regular passenger services are on 'name trains'. They are a good way to get between major cities and 3rd class is very cheap.

The Blue Train

Some people come to South Africa just to ride on the famous *Blue Train*, running between Pretoria/Johannesburg and Cape Town. This 25-hour journey is one of the world's most luxurious train trips – dressing for dinner is customary. If you can't afford to take the whole trip, consider a section. It's possible to travel between Johannesburg and Pretoria, for example, and at R65 for the cheapest seat the one-hour trip might be worth it. From Cape Town to Worcester, near the winelands, it's R230, including lunch.

Blue Train bookings can be made in Johannesburg (☎ (011) 774 4469), Cape Town (☎ (021) 218 2672), Pretoria (☎ (012) 315 2436) and Durban (☎ (031) 361 8425). For group bookings (for 10 or more people) phone (011) 773 7631. Some travel agents, both in South Africa and in other countries, take bookings. Departures are on Monday, Wednesday and Friday. The train leaves Pretoria at 10 am, Johannesburg at 11.30 am, and arrives in Cape Town at 11 am the next day. Northbound, it leaves Cape Town at 10.50 am. The train is popular and you should book well in advance.

Name Trains

On overnight trains the fare includes a sleeping berth (more expensive private compartments can also be hired), but there's a charge for bedding hire – R15 if you pay when you book or a little more if you hire it on the train. Meals are à la carte.

First and 2nd class must be booked at least 24 hours in advance; you can't book 3rd class. Most stations accept bookings, or phone one of the major reservation centres:

Johannesburg	(011)	773 2944
Pretoria	(012)	315 2401
Bloemfontein	(051)	408 2941
Cape Town	(021)	405 3871
East London	(0431)	44 2719
Durban	(031)	361 7621
Kimberley	(0531)	88 2631
Nelspruit	(01311)	288 2203
Port Elizabeth	(041)	507 2400)

Name Train Routes & Fares
Return fares are twice one-way fares (given here in 1st/2nd/3rd class).

Algoa Johannesburg/Port Elizabeth, 19 hours. Departs from Johannesburg at 2.30 pm on Tuesday, Thursday and Sunday; departs from Port Elizabeth at 2.45 pm on Monday, Wednesday and Friday. Stops include Kroonstad, R54/38/22 from Johannesburg, R196/133/82 from Port Elizabeth; Bloemfontein, R95/65/39, R156/106/65; Cradock R183/124/77, R68/47/28; and Port Elizabeth, R240/162/101.

Amatola Johannesburg/East London, 20 hours. Departs from Johannesburg 12.45 pm daily except Saturday, departs from East London at midday, daily except Sunday. Stops include Kroonstad, R53/38/23 from Johannesburg, R173/120/77 from East London; Bloemfontein, R92/65/41, R134/93/60; Queenstown, R172/119/77, R53/38/23; and East London, R215/149/96.

Bosvelder Johannesburg/Messina, daily, 14½ hours. Departs from Johannesburg at 6.50 pm, departs from Messina at 2.27 pm. Stops include Pretoria, R25/19/10 from Johannesburg, R124/86/51 from Messina; Pietersburg, R83/58/33, R66/47/27; Louis Trichardt, R112/78/46, R37/27/14; and Messina, R139/95/56.

Diamond Express Pretoria/Bloemfontein via Kimberley, daily except Saturday, 15 hours (10 hours between Johannesburg and Kimberley). Departs from Johannesburg at 8 pm, departs from Bloemfontein at 5 pm. The fare between Johannesburg and Kimberley is R113/77/45, with the luxury Diamondpax class costing R164.

Komati Johannesburg/Komatipoort, daily, 12 hours. This service theoretically connects with a train to Maputo in Mozambique. Departs from Johannesburg at 5.45 pm, departs from Komatipoort at 4 pm. Stops include Pretoria, R25/19/10 from Johannesburg, R106/75/42 from Komatipoort; Middelburg, R56/40/22, R76/54/30; Nelspruit, R99/69/39, R33/25/13; Komatipoort, R121/85/48; and Maputo, R151/108/60. Maputo to Komatipoort costs R30 and Maputo to Nelspruit is R63. Note that the return train terminates in Pretoria.

Limpopo Johannesburg to Harare (Zimbabwe), 25½ hours. Departs Johannesburg on Friday at 8.30 am and Harare on Sunday at 7 am. Stops at Pretoria, R27/21 from Johannesburg, R305/209 from Harare; Pietersburg, R92/65, R241/165; Louis Trichardt, R125/87, R208/143; Messina R154/107, R179/123; Beitbridge, R159/110, R174/120; and Harare, R321/220.

Marula Johannesburg/Louis Trichardt, daily. Stops include Pretoria, R25/19/10 from Johannesburg, R98/68/40 from Louis Trichardt; Pietersburg, R83/58/33, R40/29/16; and Louis Trichardt, R112/78/46.

Southern Cross Cape Town to Port Elizabeth, nearly 24 hours. Departs from Cape Town Friday, departs from Port Elizabeth Sunday. Stops and fares from Cape Town include Swellendam, R52/38/21; George, R86/62/35; Oudtshoorn, R96/69/39; and Port Elizabeth, R159/114/65.

Trans Karoo Johannesburg/Cape Town, daily, 27 hours. Departs from Cape Town at 9.20 am, departs from Johannesburg at 11.19 am. Stops include Kimberley, R113/77/41 from Johannesburg, R224/152/94 from Cape Town; De Aar, R161/110/67, R176/119/74; Beaufort West R214/145/90, R122/84/51; and Cape Town, R326/220/137.

Trans Natal Johannesburg/Durban, daily, 13½ hours. Departs from both Johannesburg and Durban at 6.30 pm. Stops include Newcastle R78/52/31 from Johannesburg, R97/65/39 from Durban; Ladysmith, R104/69/42, R71/48/29; Estcourt, R118/78/48, R57/39/23; Pietermaritzburg, R142/93/58, R33/23/13; and Durban R164/108/67.

Trans Oranje Cape Town/Durban, 30½

hours. Departs from Cape Town on Monday at 6.50 pm, departs from Durban on Thursday at 5.30 pm. Stops include Wellington, R26/19/10 from Cape Town, R410/276/173 from Durban; Beaufort West R122/84/51, R313/211/132/; De Aar R176/119/74, R260/176/109; Kimberley R224/152/94, R213/145/90; Bloemfontein R258/174/108, R178/121/75; Kroonstad R298/201/125, R139/95/58; Bethlehem R325/219/137, R111/76/46; Ladysmith, R366/247/154, R69/48/29; Pietermaritzburg R403/272/170, R32/24/13, and Durban R425/286/179.

Local Trains

There are Metro services in and around several cities. Trains in the Johannesburg area are no longer the death-traps they were before 1994, but you should still get advice before taking one, especially in 3rd class. Robbery is a possibility in 3rd class anywhere.

Steam Trains

There are a few steam train trips to be made, (and longer steam train tours; see the Tours section later in this chapter). They include the *Apple Express* from Port Elizabeth, the *Outeniqua Choo-Tjoe* between Knysna and George, and the *Banana Express* along the KwaZulu/Natal South Coast from Port Shepstone. See the Western Cape, Eastern Cape and KwaZulu/Natal chapters for details.

MINIBUS TAXI

If you don't have a car the only way to get between many – most – places is to hitch or take a minibus taxi.

If you've come overland through Africa you're in for a pleasant surprise. Minibus taxis here are less crowded and in better condition than in other countries, although most don't carry luggage on the roof so stowing packs can be a hassle. They don't have distorted music blaring out of cassettes either. Fares are about R1 per 10 km on long runs, more for shorter distances. From Johannesburg to Cape Town you'll pay

R150, slightly more than 3rd class on the train.

As well as the usual 'leave when full' taxis, there is a small but increasing number of door-to-door services, which you can book. These tend to run on the longer routes and, while they cost a little more, they are convenient.

Minibus taxis tend to run on relatively short routes, generally only to neighbouring towns, although you'll nearly always find a few running to a distant big city. Because many of the taxi services shuttle blacks between the location or township where they live and the town where they work (often a long way apart), and because townships and locations are rarely named on maps, finding out where a taxi is going can be a problem, and there's always a chance that you'll end up stuck on the 'wrong' side of a big town. Which brings us to the question of safety.

Away from the big cities robbery on taxis is not much of a problem, and since the 1994 elections, politically motivated attacks on taxis have ceased. But these have been replaced by commercially motivated attacks in isolated outbreaks of 'taxi wars' between rival companies. Crowded taxis have been machine-gunned. However, given the number of taxis the incidence of attacks is very low if you avoid problem areas. Cape

---

Minibus Taxi Etiquette

- People with lots of luggage (usually women) sit in the first row behind the driver
- Pay the fare with coins, not notes. Pass money forward (your fare and those of people around you) when the taxi is full. Give it to one of the front seat passengers, not the driver. If you're sitting in the front seat you might have to collect the fares and make change.
- If you sit on the folding seat by the door it's your job to open and close the door when other people get out. You'll have to get out of the taxi each time.
- Say 'Thank you!' when you want to get out, not 'Stop!'

Town's taxi war flares regularly and a few other areas have had trouble. Read the newspapers and ask around.

CAR & MOTORBIKE

South Africa is a good country to drive in. Most major roads are excellent and carry relatively little traffic, and off the big roads are some interesting backroads to explore.

The country is crossed by National Routes (N1 etc), and some sections of these are freeways, on some of which a toll is payable. You pay a fee per axle, which usually works out to about R3.60 for a car. There's always an alternative route. Most other roads in the country are numbered (R123, for example). Signposts show these numbers and when you ask directions most people refer to these numbers rather than destinations, so it pays to have a good road map. The Map Studio produces good road atlases, available in most bookshops. The AA's free city and regional guides are very useful, especially their route maps, which can help you through the maze of freeways which surround even small towns.

Petrol stations are often open 24 hours – because of cheap labour. Fuel costs around R1.50 per litre, depending on the octane level you choose. There is no unleaded petrol. Note that few petrol stations accept credit cards.

Road Rules

You can use your driving licence if it carries your photo, otherwise you'll need an International Driving Permit, obtainable from a motoring organisation in your country.

South Africans drive on the left-hand side of the road just like in the UK, Japan, Australia and most other countries in south and east Asia and the Pacific.

There are a few local variations on road rules. The main one is the 'four-way stop', which can occur even on major roads. If you're used to a system where drivers on major roads always have priority over drivers on smaller roads you'll need to stay alert. When you arrive at a four-way stop, you must stop. If there are other vehicles at the intersection, those which arrived before you get to cross before you. Before you proceed, make sure that it *is* a four-way stop – if so, you can safely cross ahead of approaching cars; if you've mistaken an ordinary stop sign for a four-way stop, the approaching cars won't be slowing down...

Speed Limits The speed limit is 100 km/h (roughly 60 miles per hour), 120 km/h on motorways. Some dangerous sections of rural roads have a limit of less than 100 km/h. The usual limit in towns is 60 km/h.

If you stick to the highway speed limit you'll feel lonely – most white traffic travels much faster, most black traffic travels much slower.

Hazards

South Africa has a horrific road fatality rate: almost 10,000 people die on the roads every year. Out of a population of about 40 million – the vast majority of whom don't own cars – that's appalling. Most of the carnage is caused by dangerous driving.

Other Drivers On highways, fast cars coming up behind you will expect you to move over into the emergency lane to let them pass. The problem is that there might be pedestrians or a slow-moving vehicle already in the emergency lane. Don't move over unless it's safe.

It is becoming common for an overtaking car to rely on *oncoming* traffic to move into

---

Highway Etiquette
On freeways, a faster car will expect you to move into the emergency lane to let it pass. If you do, it will probably say, 'Thank you' by flashing its hazard lights; you might (if you want to descend to US depths of politeness) say, 'You're welcome' by flashing your high-beam lights. ■

What's *this* place?
You might still encounter apartheid-era problems of navigation. Most maps didn't (and many still don't) show black townships or 'locations'. That isn't so much of a problem when these areas are on the outskirts of a town, but in many cases, especially in the minor apartheid-era Homelands such as Lebowa or KaNgwane (which themselves didn't make it onto many maps), you can be driving along and come to a large town which just isn't on the map. People naturally give directions involving these major but invisible towns, and if you're using the local transport system you might have a hard time working out just where the bus or minibus taxi is going. ■

---

the emergency lane! This is sheer lunacy and you must remain constantly alert. When two cars travelling in opposite directions decide that they will overtake despite oncoming traffic, things get really hairy, especially if the protagonists are travelling at the usual 160 km/h!

Head-on collisions between fast white-driven cars must account for an awful lot of road deaths, but who do whites blame for the high accident rate? Blacks, of course. They say that if it wasn't for those slow-moving black vehicles, they wouldn't have to drive so dangerously. Sure.

Drivers on little-used rural roads often speed and they often assume that there is no other traffic. Be careful of oncoming cars at blind corners on country roads.

Drink-driving has not been treated as a problem until recently. It is a major hazard – be careful.

Roads In the ex-Homelands beware of dangerous potholes, washouts, unannounced hairpins and the like.

Anywhere in the country you don't have to get very far off the beaten track to find yourself on dirt roads. Most are regularly graded and reasonably smooth and it's often possible to travel at high speed. Don't.

If you're travelling along a dirt road at 100 km/h and you come to a corner, you won't go around that corner, you'll sail off into the veldt. If you put on the brakes to slow down you'll probably spin or roll. If you swerve sharply to avoid a pothole you'll go into an exciting four-wheel drift then find out what happens when your car meets a telegraph pole. Worst of all, if another car approaches

and you have to move to the edge of the road, you'll lose control and collide head-on.

On dirt roads that are dry, flat, straight, traffic-free and wide enough to allow for unexpected slewing as you hit potholes and drifted sand, you could, with practise, drive at about 80 km/h. Otherwise, treat dirt like ice.

Animals & Pedestrians In rural areas slow down and also watch out for people and animals on the roads. Standard white advice is that if you hit an animal in a black area, don't stop – drive to the nearest police station and report it there. This might be paranoia or arrogance, but then again it might not be. If the animal you hit is a cow or a horse, leaving the scene might not be an option.

Weather Thick fog can slow you to a crawl during the rainy season. This is particularly a problem in KwaZulu/Natal, where it can be a clear day on the coast while up in the hills visibility is down to a few metres. Hailstorms on the lowveld can damage your car.

Crime Car-jacking is a problem in Johannesburg and to a lesser extent in the other big cities. People have been killed for their cars. Stay alert and keep windows wound up at night.

Rental
The major international companies, such as Avis (☎ 0800 021 111 toll-free) and Budget (☎ 0800 016 622 toll-free), are represented. They have offices or agents across the country. Their rates are high, but if you book through your local agent at home before you

arrive they will be significantly lower – but still higher than the cheaper companies in South Africa.

Other than the big companies there are local companies. These come and go, but currently the larger companies include Imperial (☎ 0800 118 898 toll-free), Tempest (☎ 0800 031 666 toll-free) and Dolphin (☎ 0800 01 1344 toll-free), which is associated with Europcar. They have agents in the main cities and a few other places.

A step down from these are smaller and cheaper outfits such as Alisa (☎ 0800 21515 toll-free) and Panther (☎ (011) 397 1469, fax 397 2507 in Johannesburg; (021) 511 6196, fax 511 7802 in Cape Town). Still further down the scale are a few outfits in the big cities renting older cars. These can be good value for getting around a local area but usually not for longer trips.

When you're getting quotes make sure that they include VAT, as that 14% slug makes a big difference.

The following table compares rates for a week's rental of a Group B car (such as a manual 1.6-litre Toyota Corolla with aircon). They include insurance, waivers and personal insurance. By the time you get here the rates might be higher but the differentials should be similar.

Company	Free km	Cost	Excess
Budget	200	R1361	from R2000
Imperial	200	R1354.50	from R2000
Panther	400	R1106	R1300

If you have booked the Budget car with the Budget agent in your own country before arriving in South Africa you would pay slightly less (about R1300 in Australia), receive unlimited km and be liable for an insurance excess of only R500.

South Africa is a big country, but unless you are a travel writer on a tight schedule, you probably don't need unlimited km rates. For meandering around, 400 km a day should be more than enough, and if you plan to stop for a day here and there, 200 km a day might be sufficient.

One-way rentals aren't usually a problem with the larger companies, between major cities, anyway. They might be with the smaller companies.

Read the contract carefully before you sign. Some insurance policies don't cover you or the car for 'political unrest', so avoid stone-throwers. Hail damage is a distinct and costly possibility so see if it's covered. Many contracts used to stipulate that you couldn't enter townships – maybe that has changed, but check.

Choose a car powerful enough to do the job. The smallest cars are OK for one person but with any more they'll be straining on the hills, which even on major highways are steep. Steep hills can also make automatics unpleasant to drive.

Insurance Excess One problem with nearly all car rental companies is the excess – the amount that you are liable for before the insurance takes over. Even on a small car you will pay at least R2000 and as much as

---

Giving Lifts

In rural areas you'll see many black hitchhikers. While I was driving in South Africa I made a point of picking up hitchhikers (partly because I knew that I'd be soon hitching myself and needed all the good karma I could get). I met a great many nice people and had conversations I wouldn't have had in most other situations, where the black/white role-playing of South African society stultifies relationships.

Whites warn you not to pick up hitchhikers (no surprise), but so do an increasing number of blacks. That advice might be good near big towns or if the hikers are a group of young men, but if you failed to give a lift to an old man in the middle of nowhere, or a woman with a baby in the rain, I'd say that the apartheid mentality had corrupted your thinking. On the other hand, the only hitchhikers I regretted picking up were a group of poor whites who stubbed out cigarettes on the seats. ■

R4000 for a single-vehicle accident. Visitors with little experience of driving on dirt roads have a high accident rate on South Africa's dirt roads, so this could be an important consideration. Felix Unite (☎ (021) 762 6935/6/7) is a rental broking company (as well as an adventure activities company) which offers a much lower excess than many rental outfits and has unlimited-km deals. Their rates are competitive with the larger local companies.

Camper Vans A way around South Africa's high accommodation and transport costs is to hire a camper van. Note that one-way rentals might not be possible or attract big fees with these vehicles.

One company with a range of deals is Leisure Mobiles (☎ (011) 477 2374) in Johannesburg at 22 Amatola Villas, Montpark Dr (on the corner of John Adamson Dr), Montgomery Park 2195. Landrover campers sleeping four cost from around R3000 a week with unlimited km, and big camper vans sleeping six are from around R3200 a week with 1400 free km. There are also basic two-person 'bakkie' campers – Toyota Hi-Lux pick-ups with a canopy, mattress, sleeping bags, gas stove and cooking utensils. Weekly rates with unlimited km are about R2500.

Another Johannesburg company is Campers Corner (☎ (011) 787 9105, fax 787 6900), 357 Jan Smuts Ave, Craighall Park; PO Box 4891 Rooseveldt Park, Johannesburg 2129.

Purchase

Buying your own car is one way around the high cost of transport – if you can sell it again for a good price. See the Getting There & Away sections in the Johannesburg and Cape Town chapters for details.

Motorbike Rental

Renting a bike isn't cheap but the idea of riding around South Africa is attractive. See the Cape Town Getting There & Away section for more information.

BICYCLE

South Africa is a good country to cycle in, with a wide variety of terrain and climate, plenty of camping places and many good roads, most of which don't carry a lot of traffic. Most of the National Routes are too busy for comfort, although there are quieter sections, in northern KwaZulu/Natal and the Cape provinces.

Keep in mind that parts of South Africa are very hilly and even on main roads gradients are steep.

Much of the country (except for the Western Cape and west coast) gets most of its rain in summer, in the form of violent thunderstorms. When it isn't raining it can be hot, especially on the lowveld where extreme heat and humidity make things pretty unpleasant in summer. See the Climate section in the Facts about the Region chapter for more details.

Distances between major towns can be long but except in isolated areas like the Karoo or Northern Transvaal you're rarely very far from a village or a farmhouse (in Australian terms, that is – you'll sometimes feel very alone if you've come from Europe).

Away from the big cities you might have trouble finding specialised parts, although there are basic bike shops in many towns.

If you decide to give up and take public transport you might have to arrange expensive transport for your bike with a carrier, as train lines are few and far between and buses aren't keen on bikes in their luggage holds. The exception to this is Transtate. Minibus taxis don't carry luggage on the roof.

Theft is a problem – bring a good lock and chain.

Where you go depends on how long you have, how fit you are and what you want to do. There are a few places where meandering between small towns is possible (although these tend to be hilly areas) such as the southern Orange Free State. Cycling through the Transkei area of Eastern Cape (a mountain bike would be best here) would be a good adventure and the Transvaal lowveld offers endless empty plains.

There is a boom in mountain biking

Transporting Your Bicycle Overseas
It's possible to bring your own bike by plane. Some airlines just want you to cover the chain, remove the pedals and turn the handlebars sideways; others require it to be completely dismantled and in a box. Cardboard bike boxes are available for a small charge or free from bike shops. Your bike is probably safer if it's not in a box, as it will probably be stowed upright or on top of the other luggage. My bike has flown 11 times, suffering a few scratches (in India) and one badly buckled wheel (at Heathrow). ■

(usually with support vehicles, braais and beer – see the Activities section of the regional Facts for the Visitor chapter) so mountain bikes are sold everywhere. The bottom end of the top-quality range will cost about R2000. Touring bikes are harder to come by except in the major cities.

HITCHING

Hitching is never entirely safe in any country, and it's not a form of travel we can recommend. People who decide to hitch should understand that they are taking a small but potentially serious risk. They will be safer if they travel in pairs and let someone know they are going.

That said, hitching is sometimes the only way to get to smaller towns, and even if you're travelling between larger ones the choice is sometimes to wait a day or two for a bus or hitch. Although blacks hitch often, it's rare to see whites hitching, and those who do tend to be down-and-out. Make it obvious that you're a clean-cut foreign visitor. You might have to wait a while for a lift, especially on major roads, but when you get one there's a good chance that you'll be offered other hospitality, such as a bed for the night.

It helps to carry a sign stating your destination. Rather than write out the whole word, use the number-plate prefix for the town or area you want. For example, CA is Cape Town, ND is Durban.

If you've waited long enough for a lift and want to flag down a minibus taxi you'll have to exert yourself (maybe wave money) because whites so rarely use them that the driver won't think of stopping for you.

Hitching always involves a degree of risk, but this is particularly so in and around major cities. You are best to catch public transport well beyond the city limits before you start to hitch.

We've only heard of one traveller having police problems while hitching, and they weren't the usual problems:

If you're hitching the Calvinia-Keimoes route and get stuck in Kenhardt, one of the policemen's wives has rooms to rent at R30. The policeman was so keen for us to stay that he knocked the price down to R25 and then (we're sure) diverted the traffic to prevent us getting a lift. He underestimated our stickability and we got a lift in a truck three hours later.

Kate Wall, NZ

LOCAL TRANSPORT

Getting around in towns isn't easy, and many of them sprawl a long way. This is a major pain if you're hitching, especially if the town is bypassed by the freeway. The big cities and some of the larger towns have bus systems. Services often stop running early in the evening. Many towns, even some quite large ones, don't have taxis. If there is a taxi, chances are you'll have to telephone for it. You can sometimes make use of minibus taxis but they tend not to run through the areas where there are hotels. Often, you'll end up walking.

In Durban and a few other places you'll find that mainstay of Asian public transport, the tuk-tuk. Tuk-tuks run mainly in downtown or tourist areas.

TOURS
Air

Comair (☎ (011) 973 2911) has several 'Wings to the Wild' packages, flying to reserves. For example, the Skukuza Costcutter is a three-night package for about R2900 per person for two people, flying from Johannesburg – additional nights are R700.

Bus

The main long-distance coach tour operators is Springbok-Atlas. They have a wide range of fairly expensive tours covering popular routes, as well as day tours. Their clientele tends to be older tourists. Springbok-Atlas has offices in Cape Town (☎ (021) 448 6545), Durban (☎ (031) 304 7938) and Johannesburg (☎ (011) 493 3780).

There is a multitude of other companies, with backpackers (and less formal visitors in general) increasingly well catered for. For information on safari-style tours and adventure holidays see the Activities section in the regional Facts for the Visitor chapter.

Train

Union Ltd Steam Rail Tours (☎ (021) 405 4390, fax 405 4395 in Cape Town; (011) 773 9118 in Johannesburg), a division of Spoornet, runs restored steam trains. The *Union Limited* was the pre-*Blue Train* king of the line in South Africa, running to Cape Town with passengers meeting liners to Europe.

The five-day Golden Thread tour, on the *Union Limited*, runs from Cape Town along the coast to Oudtshoorn and back, a leisurely trip. It costs R1750 per person including meals and bedding – not bad value. There are also various nine and 14-day steam safaris, including one to Victoria Falls, for about R5000 to R7000 per person. The train was in its time luxurious and it has been meticulously restored, without anachronisms such as air-con. Passengers have more room than they once did, though, as two people share four-berth compartments and singles get two-berth compartments.

Another company doing similar things is Rovos Rail (☎ (012) 323 6052) which runs superbly restored old trains within South Africa and elsewhere – for about US$6000 you can go on an 11-night trip from Cape Town to Dar es Salaam.

Gauteng

The province of Gauteng (Sotho for 'place of gold') takes in the mineral-rich area once known as the PWV – Pretoria, Witwatersrand and Vereeniging. The new province was called PWV for a few months but, as Krijan Lemmer wrote in the *Weekly Mail & Guardian*, who wants to live somewhere that sounds like an abbreviation of a livestock disease?

Gauteng is by far the smallest province of South Africa (about 19,000 sq km) but with around 10 million people (including more than 40% of the country's whites) it has by far the largest population. It has been claimed that Gauteng accounts for 65% of the country's gross domestic product and no less than 25% of the gross product of all Africa!

The area is rich in history (see the Johannesburg and Pretoria sections), but for most visitors a quick visit to Johannesburg and perhaps Pretoria will be more than enough. The province's countryside is fairly crowded, and somewhat polluted by power stations.

Orientation

Johannesburg lies at the centre of an enormous conurbation, rapidly developing into a megalopolis. Diminishing green belts separate it from Pretoria to the north, but in all other directions the sprawl rolls on apace.

The Witwatersrand, which is often shortened to 'the Rand', literally means 'ridge of white waters'. The ridge runs from Randfontein through Johannesburg and east beyond Brakpan and Springs. The term is now used to describe most of southern Gauteng, which is heavily developed and urbanised.

Although the ridge is over 1700 metres above sea level at its highest point, it is not particularly impressive. It's more famous for its underground geology than its aboveground form. It was on the ridge that an Australian prospector, George Harrison, dis-

> **GAUTENG PROVINCE**
> **Capital:** Johannesburg
> **Main Languages:** All South African languages are spoken in this densely-populated area
> **Pre-1994:** Gauteng takes in the PWV region of the old Transvaal Province
> **Highlights:**
> - Soweto Tours
> - Nightlife in Jo'burg's Yeoville area
> - Africana Museum in Jo'burg
> - Not being mugged in Jo'burg!

covered a surface outcrop of the world's richest gold reef – the reason for Johannesburg's existence. The rest of the reef tilts underground. At Carletonville, the Western Deep Levels mine extracts ore from 3.5 km below the surface.

The Vaal Triangle lies to the south of the Rand and is another heavily developed area, occupying the triangle formed by Vanderbijlpark, Vereeniging and Sasolburg (the latter is actually just across the border in the Orange Free State).

GAUTENG

Johannesburg

It can be quite a shock arriving in Jo'burg (Jo'burg, Jozi or eGoli, 'the city of gold', never Johannesburg). A mere hundred years old, it's by far the largest city in South Africa and the largest city in Africa south of Cairo. It's a brash, fast-growing and often ugly infant with three redeeming features – wealth, energy and a beautiful climate.

For the poor and the ambitious, Jo'burg is an irresistible lure. In the last official census

in 1985, the population of greater Jo'burg was three million: two million whites and a million blacks, coloureds and Asians. Even then, the figures for non-whites were massively inaccurate, as they made no allowance for squatters (those without official passes allowing them to live legally in the black townships that ring the city).

In 1991, some estimates placed the total population of Soweto, the largest black township, at over two million, which would mean that greater Jo'burg was probably approaching six million. Since the repeal of pass laws, the population has probably increased significantly. Squatters alone amount to 750,000 people.

On first appearances, Jo'burg is just another anonymous, big, Western-style city that could just as easily be in the USA. You can expect fortified middle-class suburbs, a city centre overshadowed by modern glass skyscrapers, air-conditioned shops and shopping malls; some pretty scary crime; black ghettos (townships) and lots of guns.

Johannesburg's sole reason for existence is the reef of gold that lies under the highveld. Greed plays a role in building every city, but it is as naked and unashamed in Jo'burg as it is in Manhattan. The inhabitants – black and white – are single-minded in their pursuit of the rand.

Cities also seem to answer a deep human need for interaction. This need is usually met by restaurants, cafés, pubs, bars, clubs, markets, churches and theatres – none of which are strictly necessary from an economic point of view. In most cities these cultural assets are an integral and prized part of urban life, but not in Jo'burg. In Jo'burg the main idea seems to have been to keep people apart. For a city at the centre of a conurbation approaching 10 million people, the cultural assets are pitifully thin on the ground.

You can count the number of pleasant pubs and bars on one hand. There is no world-class gallery, museum or concert theatre. Not counting the township shebeens, the few inner-city bars seem often to be pick-up joints for prostitutes. The restaurants are generally scattered around the suburbs, accessible only by car, and isolated in shopping centres.

However, with South Africa taking its place in Africa, Jo'burg is attracting tourists and businesspeople from across the continent, and if you stay in one of the middle-level hotels in Hillbrow or Berea you'll meet some interesting people. Culturally too, Jo'burg is opening up to the arts of the continent and there are some good exhibitions and concerts.

Unfortunately, at the time this book went to press the townships were still off-limits to lone wanderers, which means that much of the real life of the city is inaccessible. Although large-scale outbreaks of violence are a thing of the past, violent crime is rampant. However, it is currently safe to visit the townships with a tour or with a contact to guide you in and out, and make introductions.

If your time isn't limited and you can organise some night transport (private car or taxi) you'll find Jo'burg a stimulating and interesting place that *is* definitely worth a couple of days of your time. This is the heart of the new South Africa, and this is where change – good and bad – is happening first.

Why Visit Jo'burg?

If your time and finances are limited, it is best to go through Jo'burg as quickly as possible, or miss it altogether. However, you may not have a choice in the matter as Jo'burg has the major South African international airport and is a major hub for all forms of domestic transport. Most tourists only stay a day or two and few have a kind word to say about the city.

However, if you really do want to see South Africa and try to understand it, Jo'burg has to be on your itinerary. Not even the old regime succeeded in completely crushing the life from the city. Beginning with the reforms of 1990 and accelerating since the elections there have been some radical and positive changes. Hillbrow, Berea and Yeoville remain the only multiracial suburbs of note in South Africa.

It's still difficult to cross the racial divide in South Africa, but you stand a better chance of meeting blacks on relatively equal terms in Jo'burg than almost anywhere else. Unlike many South African cities where there are so few black faces you could forget that you are in Africa, the centre of Jo'burg has been reclaimed and the sidewalks are jammed with black hawkers and stalls of every description. There's also a growing multiracial music and theatre scene. ■

HISTORY

At the beginning of 1886 the undistinguished stretch of the Transvaal highveld that was to become Johannesburg consisted of four sleepy farms: Braamfontein, Doornfontein, Turffontein and Langlaagte. In March of that year, however, an Australian prospector, George Harrison, found traces of gold on Langlaagte. Poor George didn't realise it, but he had stumbled on the only surface outcrop of the richest gold-bearing reef that has ever been discovered. He sold his claim for £10.

Within a matter of months thousands of diggers descended on this site and by December, vacant land between the original farms had been surveyed, subdivided and auctioned. In the beginning, diggers lived in tents and covered ox-wagons, but permanent buildings soon appeared – and kept on appearing.

Because the gold was deep – in reef form, not the more easily accessible alluvial form – mining was quickly concentrated in the hands of men who had the capital to finance large underground mines. Mining magnates who had made their money at the Kimberley diamond field bought up the small claims and soon came to be known as the Randlords – Cecil John Rhodes and Barney Barnato were among them.

By 1889 Jo'burg was the largest town in southern Africa – a rowdy town full of the inevitable bars and brothels. The multicultural fortune seekers – blacks and whites – were regarded with deep distrust by the Boers, by the Transvaal government, and especially by the president, Paul Kruger. Although mining boosted the government coffers the Boers feared their hard won independence would be swamped by the huge influx of English-speaking *uitlanders* (outsiders, mainly from the USA and the British colonies) and blacks. Kruger introduced electoral laws that effectively restricted voting rights to Boers, and laws aimed at controlling the movement of blacks were passed.

The tensions between the Randlords and uitlanders on one side and the Transvaal government on the other were crucial factors in the events that led to the Anglo-Boer War of 1899-1902. Jo'burg, which had a population in excess of 100,000, became a ghost town during the war, but it recovered quickly when the British took control and massive new mines were developed to the east and west. Although the British entrenched the privileged position of white workers, the miners' unions were growing stronger and peace was not to last.

By 1921 the 21,000 white miners earned almost twice as much as the 180,000 black miners – which suggested an obvious possibility to the mining companies. In 1922 the Chamber of Mines attempted to lower costs by employing blacks in skilled jobs that had previously been reserved for whites. The strike called by the white unionists soon became an open revolt – the Imperial Light Horse was ambushed at Ellis Park and artillery and aircraft were used against the strikers. By the time peace was restored, over 200 people, including 129 soldiers and policemen, had died in what has become known as the Rand Revolt.

Although gold mining remained the backbone of the city's economy, manufacturing industries soon began to spring up, gaining fresh impetus during WW II. Under increasing pressure in the countryside, thousands of blacks moved to the city in search of jobs. Racial segregation had become entrenched during the years between the world wars, and from the 1930s onwards, vast squatter camps had sprung up around Jo'burg, particularly around Orlando to the south-west.

Under black leadership – most notably of James Mpanza, who is regarded as the founder of Soweto – these became well-organised cities, despite their gross overcrowding and negligible services. In the late 1940s, many of the camps were destroyed by the authorities and the people were moved to new suburbs known as the South-Western Townships, now shortened to Soweto.

The official development of apartheid during the 1960s did nothing to slow the expansion of the city or the arrival of black squatters. Large-scale violence finally broke out in 1976 when the Soweto Students' Rep-

James Mpanza, the founder of Soweto.

resentative Council organised protests against the use of Afrikaans (regarded as the language of the oppressor) in black schools. On 12 June, police opened fire on a student march, beginning a round of demonstrations, strikes, mass arrests and riots that took over 1000 lives over the next 12 months. Jo'burg and South Africa were never to be the same again – a generation of young blacks committed themselves to a revolutionary struggle against apartheid, and the black communities were politicised.

The regulations of apartheid were finally abandoned in February 1990, and since the 1994 elections the city has in theory been free of discriminatory laws. The black townships are being integrated into the municipal government system; the city centre is vibrant with black hawkers and street stalls; and a number of inner suburbs are quickly becoming multiracial.

Unfortunately, serious problems remain. Crime is rampant and middle-class whites are retreating to the northern suburbs where new shopping malls and satellite business centres are mushrooming. It's another world out there in the northern suburbs, practically a Volkstaat by default.

Gold mining is no longer undertaken in the city area, and the old, pale-yellow mine dumps that created such a surreal landscape on the edge of the city are being carted away and reprocessed. Modern recovery methods allow metallurgists to recover gold from tailings that were regarded as valueless waste. The classic view of Jo'burg with a mine dump in the foreground and skyscrapers in the background will be retained, however, as some dumps are being preserved as historical monuments.

ORIENTATION

Despite its size, it's not difficult to find your way around Jo'burg. Jan Smuts Airport is 25 km north-east of the city centre, accessible by freeway. Regular buses connect the airport with the Rotunda bus terminal which is beside Jo'burg Railway Station on the northern edge of the city centre (see the Getting Around section in this chapter).

Two major communication towers on the ridges to the north of the city centre make good landmarks. The JG Strijdom Tower, just behind Hillbrow, is 269 metres high and used by the post office. There is an observation room at the top, but it has been closed for some time for security reasons. To the north-west of the city, the South African Broadcasting Commission runs the 239-metre-high Brixton Tower.

The city centre, which is laid out on a straightforward grid, is dominated by office blocks, in particular the 50-storey Carlton Centre on Commissioner St. There's an observation deck on the top floor, ideal for orienting yourself.

There's no particular advantage in staying in the city centre. With the exception of the red-light district around the intersection of Bree St and Troye, the centre becomes a ghost town after the shops close – and it becomes extremely unsafe unless you're in a car, and maybe even then.

North of the city centre, a steep ridge runs east-west from Braamfontein across to Hillbrow and Berea, where you can find most of the cheap hotels and numerous bars (mostly seedy) and restaurants. From the

GAUTENG

GAUTENG

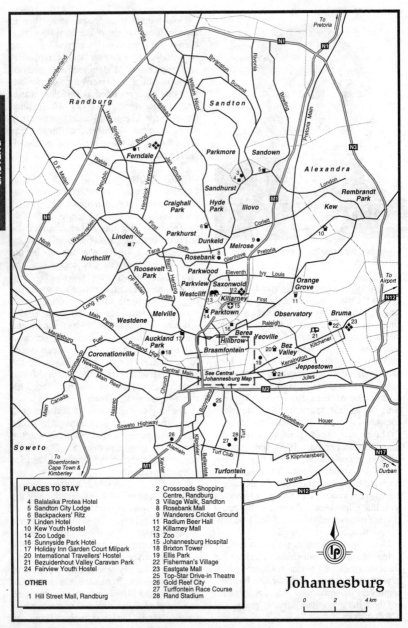

PLACES TO STAY

4 Balalaika Protea Hotel
5 Sandton City Lodge
6 Backpackers' Ritz
7 Linden Hotel
10 Kew Youth Hostel
14 Zoo Lodge
16 Sunnyside Park Hotel
17 Holiday Inn Garden Court Milpark
20 International Travellers' Hostel
21 Bezuidenhout Valley Caravan Park
24 Fairview Youth Hostel

OTHER

1 Hill Street Mall, Randburg

2 Crossroads Shopping
   Centre, Randburg
3 Village Walk, Sandton
8 Rosebank Mall
9 Wanderers Cricket Ground
11 Radium Beer Hall
12 Killarney Mall
13 Zoo
15 Johannesburg Hospital
18 Brixton Tower
19 Ellis Park
22 Fisherman's Village
23 Eastgate Mall
25 Top-Star Drive-in Theatre
26 Gold Reef City
27 Turffontein Race Course
28 Rand Stadium

Johannesburg

0   2   4 km

railway station, Hillbrow is a 15 to 20-minute walk, and a walk to the Carlton Centre takes from 10 to 15 minutes – but before you start walking read the Dangers & Annoyances entry in this section.

The northern suburbs are white middle-class ghettos stretching away to the north within an arc formed by the N1 and N3 freeways. This is where to go if you want to pretend you're not in Africa. White people driving Mercs and BMWs whisk to busy, antiseptic shopping malls and the only blacks are neatly uniformed maids and gardeners waiting for minibus taxis. Sadly, there is little communal life, although, scattered about, you'll find many of the city's best restaurants and shops. Serious shoppers and eaters may well be lured to the shopping centres at Rosebank, or even further out to Randburg and Sandton.

If you've noted the lack of trees in the city centre, you'll find the northern suburbs compensate. The enormous houses and private gardens are dominated by beautiful purple-flowering jacarandas in spring, and the lawns are always green and manicured. Most properties have high walls and large dogs – which go into a frenzy at the sound of pedestrians' footsteps. The really wealthy suburbs include Saxonwold, Westcliff, Parkwood, Parkhurst and Rosebank. New offices are springing up in areas like Parktown (sometimes in old mansions) as the whites' lemming-like rush to abandon the city centre accelerates.

The so-called black townships ring the city and are a grotesque contrast to the northern suburbs. Conditions within them range from basic to appalling. Accessibility and convenience were never factors in the planning process, so they are a considerable distance from the city centre and the white suburbs (out of sight and out of mind). black workers are forced to live away from their families, or to commute, which is both time-consuming and expensive.

The main township is Soweto (to the south-west), but there are also large developments at Tokoza (south of Alberton), Kwa-Thema and Tsakane (south of Brakpan),

Daveyton (east of Benoni), Tembisa (to the north-east) and Alexandra (inside the N3 freeway to the north).

INFORMATION
Tourist Offices
The Johannesburg Publicity Association has offices at Jan Smuts Airport (☎ (011) 970 1220), open from 5 am, at the Rotunda bus terminal (☎ (011) 337 6650/1/2) and in the city centre (☎ (011) 336 4961, fax 336 4965) on the corner of Market and Kruis Sts. They have the excellent (if inconveniently large) *Johannesburg Gateway* booklet and a good selection of information on restaurants and places to stay.

Satour (☎ (011) 333 8082), the national tourism body, is in temporary disarray as it adjusts to the new South Africa, and is sharing the Johannesburg Publicity Association's Kruis St office. It also has an office at the airport (☎ (011) 970 1669). Satour still has some good brochures, but you'll have to pay for them.

Some provinces and neighbouring countries have worthwhile information offices in Jo'burg. They include:

Captour (Western Cape Province)
    123 Rosebank Mall, Rosebank (☎ (011) 442 4707)
Mozambique
    3 Stiemens St, Braamfontein (☎ (011) 339 7281)
Namibia
    Shop 209, Carlton Centre, Commissioner St (☎ (011) 331 7055)
Swaziland
    132 Jan Smuts Ave, Parkwood (☎ (011) 788 0742)
Zimbabwe
    4th Floor, Carlton Centre, Commissioner St (☎ (011) 331 3137)

National Parks Board
Unfortunately, the National Parks Board doesn't have an office in Jo'burg. To make bookings you either have to phone Pretoria (☎ (012) 343 1991, fax (012) 343 0905), which is sometimes difficult because the lines are engaged, or visit their desk at Pretoria's Tourist Rendezvous Centre. Their head office is inconveniently located on the

GAUTENG

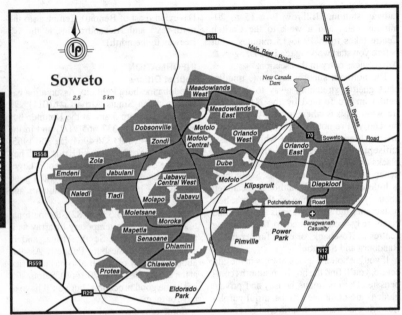

Soweto

southern outskirts of Pretoria at 643 Leyds St, Muckleneuk. In cases of desperation, contact the Cape Town office (☎ (021) 22 2810, fax (021) 24 6212).

Hiking

You can contact the Hiking Federation of South Africa on ☎ (011) 886 6507. The National Hiking Way Board is in Pretoria (☎ (012) 310 3839).

Money

Banks are open Monday to Friday from 9 am to 3.30 pm and on Saturday from 9 to 11 am. There are foreign-exchange counters at Jan Smuts Airport that open two hours before all international departures and two hours after arrivals.

The main American Express office (☎ (011) 331 7201) is on the 21st floor of the Kine Centre, 141 Commissioner St; it is open weekdays from 8.30 am to 4 pm. They also have an office in the lobby of the Carlton

Hotel (☎ (011) 331 2301 – but this number will change). On weekdays the Carlton Hotel branch is open from 8.30 to 1 pm, 2 to 4 pm and 5.30 to 8 pm; on Saturday from 8.30 to 11 am and noon to 6 pm; on Sunday from 10 am to 6 pm. If you're staying in Yeoville or Berea the nearest Amex office is at Travelmore (☎ (011) 487 3420), a travel agency on the corner of Harrow Rd and Raleigh St (which becomes Rockey St). There are other offices in the northern suburbs.

Rennies Travel is the agent for Thomas Cook. They have foreign-exchange outlets at 35 Rissik St (☎ (011) 492 1990), 145 Commissioner St (☎ (011) 331 1552) and 95 Kerk St (☎ (011) 333 0460). They also have a useful combined travel agency/exchange outlet on the corner of Pretoria and Twist St in Hillbrow (☎ (011) 642 7451), open from 8.30 am to 4.30 pm weekdays and until noon on Saturday. The Rennies branch at the big Eastgate shopping centre (☎ (011) 616 1241/51) is open on weekdays from 8.30 am

Soweto

For the majority of Jo'burg's inhabitants, home is in one of the black townships surrounding the city – probably Soweto. Despite this, most white South Africans are completely ignorant of life in the townships and very few have ever been inside one. Their picture is of unmitigated hostility, and a nightmare environment of drugs, superstition, tribal warfare, depravity and violent crime of every kind.

The first impression as one approaches a township is of an enormous, grim, undifferentiated sprawl, punctuated by light towers that would seem more appropriate in a concentration camp. In fact, some suburbs within the townships are quite acceptable, not all that far removed from suburbs anywhere, while others are as bad as any third world slum.

In descending order there's a tiny wealthy elite that live in comfortable bungalows; the privileged who live in monotonous rows of government-built three-roomed houses with an outside tap and toilet; the lucky who have been provided with a block of land, a prefabricated toilet and a tap, and who are allowed to build whatever they can; the fortunate who live in shacks erected in backyards; the squatters who build wherever they can and have virtually no facilities at all; and at the bottom of the pile, the men who live in dormitories in vast dilapidated hostels.

It is striking how neat and clean the houses, shacks and yards are. Unfortunately the streets and open places are buried under a blizzard of plastic bags and rubbish. This is at least partly because each house only gets one rubbish bin that is emptied once a week. This may be adequate when one family lives in a house; it is hopelessly inadequate when three or four additional families live in the backyard, and irrelevant if you are a squatter.

The townships played a crucial role in the struggle against apartheid. This was a struggle against a government that routinely used bullets, tear gas, imprisonment without trial, torture and summary execution of men, women and children. Soweto was in a virtual state of war from 1976, when the first protesting school students were killed, until the 1994 elections. During that time many thousands died. No one is quite sure exactly how many.

Given the townships' recent history, the courtesy and friendliness that is generally shown to white visitors is almost shocking. If you visit on a Sunday, the most militant sight you will see is thousands of Christians dressed in immaculate uniforms (based on those worn by European medieval religious orders) on their way to and from church. The majority of people seem to have entirely middle-class aspirations – they want a job, decent housing, affordable education and a reasonable opportunity for their children to better themselves.

Although outsiders, even including whites, are *not* automatically targeted, the townships are still in a state of acute social trauma, and violent crime is commonplace. Try to get objective advice on the current situation. This isn't easy, however, since most whites would not dream of visiting and have no first-hand experience of doing so. Certainly, unless things change markedly for the better, visiting without a companion who has local knowledge is likely to be disastrous. If a trustworthy black friend is happy to escort you, however, you should have no problems, and tours have been operated safely for over five years.

Visiting a large township is an unforgettable experience. It may seem grotesque treating these places as just another tourist attraction, but to get any kind of appreciation for South African reality you have to visit them. If the only way you can do it safely is with a tour, then a tour it must be.

A number of operators take tourists into Soweto. Most tours are designed to be serious educational experiences, so they can be earnest, and a little dry. If a visit to the huge Baragwanath Hospital is on the itinerary, you might want to ask the guide to drop it – even thick-skinned Westerners can feel a little uncomfortable at turning gunshot wounds into tourist attractions.

Max Maximum Tours (☎ (011) 933 4177 or (082) 533 1587) is recommended. Max is a long-time Soweto resident, a nice bloke and a good guide. He charges about R60. Max might also be available to take you further afield – have a beer and discuss it with him. Soweto Tours is another good operator. Contact Peter or Dorcas (☎ (011) 932 0000, 932 3536) or Mrs Sithole (☎ (011) 930 2184).

The biggest operator is Jimmy's Face to Face Tours (☎ (011) 331 6109, 331 6209). Its popular morning and afternoon tours leave from Rosebank and Sandton (R90), and city hotels (R75). ■

PHOTOGRAPH BY JON MURRAY

to 4.30 pm and 5 to 7 pm, on Saturday from 8.30 am to 2 pm, and on Sunday from 10 am to 12 pm.

Post & Telecommunications

Telephone 1023 for local directory enquiries and 1025 for national enquiries. The main GPO is on Jeppe St, between Von Brandis and Smal St Mall. It's open from 8 am to 4.30 pm weekdays and from 8 am to noon on Saturday. There's a poste-restante service (in theory you need some sort of identification, although they're not very strict about this) and an international telephone exchange. For normal business it's worth using the 19th-century Rissik St Post Office, opposite the city hall – it's a beautiful building, one of the oldest in the city, and it's less hectic than the GPO.

There are plenty of commercial phone services around the city. Check the rates before making a long-distance call. In Hillbrow there is a 24-hour phone service at the taxi rank on Quartz St.

Dialling directory information in Jo'burg often means a wait of at least five minutes. Still, you'll learn useful Afrikaans phrases such as 'We do appreciate your patience...'.

Visa Extensions

See the Department of Home Affairs (☎ (011) 836 3228), 77 Harrison St (near the corner of Plein St).

Foreign Consulates & Trade Missions

Most countries have their main embassy in Pretoria, with an office or consulate in Cape Town which becomes the official embassy during Cape Town's parliamentary sessions. However, many countries also maintain consulates (which can arrange visas and passports) in Jo'burg. Some, like Mozamique and Zimbabwe, only have representation in Jo'burg. Rennies Travel will arrange visas, as will the Visa Service (☎ (011) 333 1717), Essanby House, 175 Jeppe St. Their charges are reasonable.

Where possible, weekday opening hours are given; where they are not given you're best to assume they're open in the mornings only.

Australia
  4th Floor, Norwich Life Tower, Fredman Dr, Sandton (☎ (011) 784 0620)
Belgium
  118 Jorissen St, Braamfontein (☎ (011) 403 2934)
Botswana
  123 De Korte St, Braamfontein (☎ (011) 403 3748); open from 9 am to noon
Denmark
  EAC Graphics Building, 19 Eastern Service Rd, Eastgate Extension 6, Sandton (☎ (011) 804 3374); open from 10 am to noon
France
  Valley Towers, Grayston Dr, Sandown (☎ (011) 884 4003); open from 9 am to 1 pm
Germany
  5th Floor, Community Centre of the German Lutheran Church, 16 Kapteijn St, Hillbrow (☎ (011) 725 1519); open from 8.30 am to noon, also 2 to 4 pm on Wednesday
Ireland
  8-10 London House, Loveday St (☎ (011) 338 3315); open from 10 am to 2 pm
Malawi
  Sable House, 41 De Korte St, Braamfontein (☎ (011) 339 1569); open from 8.30 am to noon, 1.30 to 4.30 pm
Mozambique
  2nd Floor, Glencairn Building, 73 Market St (☎ (011) 23 4907)
Namibia
  Shop 209, Carlton Centre, Commissioner St (☎ (011) 331 7055); open from 8 am to 4 pm
Norway
  2nd Floor, Argent House, 21 Loveday St South, (☎ (011) 838 2655); open from 10 am to noon
Swaziland
  915 Rand Central Building, 165 Jeppe St (☎ (011) 336 9776); open from 9.30 to 1 pm, and 2 to 3 pm
Switzerland
  Cradock Heights, Cradock Ave, Rosebank (☎ (011) 442 7500)
UK
  19th Floor, Sanlam Centre, on the corner of Jeppe and Von Weilligh Sts (☎ (011) 337 8940); open from 9 am to 2 pm
USA
  11th Floor, Kine Centre, on the corner of Commissioner and Kruis Sts (☎ (011) 331 1681); open from 8 am to noon
Zimbabwe
  6th Floor, Bank of Lisbon Building, 37 Sauer St (☎ (011) 838 2156); open from 8.30 am to noon

Climate & When to Go

Jo'burg has an excellent climate, and uncomfortable extremes are rare. Summers are hot, but maximum temperatures rarely exceed 30°C. Most of the rain falls between October and April, usually in late afternoon storms, often accompanied by spectacular thunder, lightning and hail. Winter days are sunny and warm with crisp nights; temperatures range between 6°C and 17°C. There's no right or wrong time to visit, although accommodation can fill in December (which is also the time that a great many whites head for the coast on holidays – at this time the traffic reports on Jo'burg radio stations extend all the way to Durban).

Travel Agencies

The South African Students' Travel Service (SASTS) is a national organisation with a number of offices around the country. You don't have to be a student to use their services. They offer all the regular facilities plus student and youth cards, youth-hostel membership, and special fares and flights. They also know about cheap tours through Africa. They have a branch in the Student Union Building of the University of Witwatersrand (☎ (011) 716 3045), open Monday to Friday from 9 am to 4 pm.

Rennies Travel has a comprehensive network of agencies, with a distinctive red livery, throughout South Africa, including Jo'burg. They're the agent for Thomas Cook travellers' cheques (see the previous money section) and handle international and domestic bookings. They will also arrange visas for a moderate charge. Their offices include those on the 11th Floor of the ISM Building, 124 Main St (☎ (011) 331 5898); and on the corner of Pretoria and Twist St, Hillbrow (☎ (011) 643 8451).

Pathfinders Travel (☎ (011) 453 1113/4, fax 453 1483), 17 Chaucer Ave, Senderwood, Bedfordview, Johannesburg, is a small agency that concentrates on eco-tourism and sending people off the beaten track. If you're looking for information on private game parks, national parks or unusual tours (hiking, rafting, horse-riding etc) they're worth contacting.

Bookshops

Rockey St, Yeoville, is full of secondhand bookshops that can be a bibliophile's delight; you can find some interesting old histories and travel guides, and the odd first edition. Phambili Books sells mainly alternative political and social theory books. There's another Phambili in the city, on Kruise St just south of President St, which stocks more overtly left-wing political titles. They have a good South Africa section.

Sheldon's, in the Eastgate Mall shopping centre, is a good general bookshop with a range of African titles. They have a coffee shop next door where you can relax (as much as is possible in this vast and noisy mall) with your purchases. Take the escalator outside the CNA store.

For road atlases, locally published guidebooks and glossy picture books it's worth visiting the combination stationer, newsagent and bookshop known as CNA. They have a network of branches throughout Jo'burg, including Rockey St in Yeoville, Eastgate Mall, and in the arrivals hall at the airport.

Exclusive Books is probably the best bookshop in town, but they no longer have an easily accessible outlet.

Laundry

There's a generous scattering of launderettes. A service wash (drop your clothes in the morning, pick them up in the afternoon) is only marginally more expensive than doing it yourself. International Laundromat is reliable. They have branches at 296 Bree St, City (on the corner of Delvers), the Nedbank Plaza, Hillbrow (Pretoria, between Edith Cavell and Twist St) and at High-Rise Flats, Primrose Terrace, Berea. An average wash will cost around R15.

There's a laundromat in the Highpoint Centre on Kotze St, Hillbrow.

Luggage Repair

The Three-Minute Heel Bar (☎ (011) 333 5391) on the corner of Jeppe and Joubert Sts will repair backpacks. If you have a disaster

Walking Tour

Jo'burg has shown scant regard for its architectural and historical legacy, and even less regard for pedestrians and quality of life. You get the distinct feeling that buildings more than 30 years old have survived through some oversight – and that the mistake will soon be rectified. The more recent office blocks are insensitive, alienating and ugly – the Carlton Centre, the Johannesburg Holiday Inn (on the corner of Jeppe and Von Weilligh), and No 11 Diagonal St are all memorable examples.

In spite of this, the centre of Jo'burg is an interesting and vibrant place. At street level, it's very much an African city and the pavements are crowded with shoppers and hawkers. It's not really vital to have a set walking tour, but the suggested route gives a pretty comprehensive introduction. It's a circuit so you could start at any point.

Warning Before you set out on this walk, check the newspapers to see if there are any ongoing disturbances in the city centre and divest yourself of all valuables. Wear discreet clothes.

The **Johannesburg Railway Station** serves more than 250,000 people a day – it's the terminal for all country trains. Train buffs should check out the first train to serve the Witwatersrand, which is at the north end of the concourse outside the train information office and the **Railways Museum**. Walk towards the city and the old southern entry on De Villiers. When you leave the building you come out on to a plaza area with a number of stalls selling cheap leather footwear and T-shirts.

Turn left into De Villiers and proceed until you reach Hoek Mall and **St Mary's Anglican Cathedral**, built of dressed sandstone in 1926 and designed by Sir Herbert Baker. Walk down the mall and take the second left into Bree St. Jo'burg's rowdy past lives on in the blatant 'massage parlours' around the intersection of Bree, Klein and Von Weilligh.

Turn right into Von Weilligh and first right into Jeppe past the extraordinary **Johannesburg Holiday Inn Hotel**. Immediately after the hotel and before the GPO, turn left into the **Smal St Mall**, which is full of trendy shops, including a number of art and craft galleries.

Continue down the mall and through the Nedbank Mall (a continuation) to Commissioner St and the **Carlton Centre** with its huge shopping complex and tower (which houses an observation floor and Satour). From the Carlton Centre head down to Fox St; the **Rand Club** is on the right between Loveday and Harrison Sts. It was built in 1904, modelled on the Reform Club in London, and was the favourite haunt for the Randlords.

Commissioner St takes you west to one of the only surviving sections of old Jo'burg – a couple of blocks of interesting Indian shops with shady verandahs and a comfortable lived-in atmosphere. There's a **Hindu Temple** on the corner of Commissioner and Becker. Turn right into Becker and right again into Market. Backtrack until you get to Diagonal St, the only exception to the the city's grid plan. There's a muti shop, **Kwa Dabgulamanzi** on the corner (No 14) which sells African herbal remedies that are prescribed by a sangoma (traditional doctor and spiritual medium).

Diagonal St is home to an extraordinary skyscraper (No 11) that towers incongruously over a section of old Indian shops that have been tarted up and trendified. The **Stock Exchange**, on the corner of Diagonal and Pritchard, has guided tours on weekdays at 11 am and 2.30 pm. From here it's a relatively short walk to the Market Theatre and Oriental Plaza (mentioned later in this section) which are both good places for lunch.

If you choose to continue the circuit, however, from Pritchard turn right into Sauer, which takes you past the offices of the Jo'burg Star newspaper. Then turn left into President which takes you past the Library. President will also take you past the **Johannesburg City Hall**, and the impressive **Rissik St Post Office**, which hasn't changed significantly (inside or out) since 1897. The city hall has public toilets – a rare luxury – on the corner of President and Harrison.

To finish the circuit, turn left into the tree-lined and pleasant Eloff, which will take you back to the railway station past several of the major department stores. ■

at the airport, Airport Baggage Services (☎ (011) 394 9030) stocks straps, locks and soft bags. It's open from 6 am to 10 pm daily.

Medical Services

Medical services are of a high standard, but they are expensive (make sure you're insured). Doctors are listed under Medical in the phone book. They generally arrange for hospitalisation, although in an emergency you can go direct to the casualty department of the Johannesburg Hospital (☎ (011) 488 4911) less than one km north of Hillbrow. Ring the police (☎ 10111) to get directions to the nearest hospital. The Hillbrow Pharmacy (☎ (011) 642 6936) in Pretoria St stays open late (maybe 24 hours) and the Yeoville Medical Centre on Rockey St stays open until 9 pm every night.

Emergency

For an ambulance call ☎ 999, for the police flying squad ☎ 10111, and for the fire brigade ☎ 331 2222 (883 2800 in Sandton).

The 702 Crisis Centre (it's sponsored by a radio station) is on the corner of Tudhope and Honey Sts in Berea and is open from 5 to 11 pm.

The phones at the Rape Crisis Centre (☎ (011) 642 4345) are staffed from 6 am to 8 pm. There's a Lifeline service (☎ (011) 728 1347).

Dangers & Annoyances

Many people don't have any problems walking around Jo'burg, but there are enough true-life horror stories to make caution essential. South Africa has an appalling tradition of violence and there's a huge gulf between rich and poor; as a consequence, Jo'burg has a very high rate of crime.

A combination of common sense and cowardice will always be your best defence. At no time should you advertise your wealth, or your tourist status – moon bags and dangling cameras are a dead giveaway. A shoulder bag, day pack, or plastic shopping bag is less conspicuous. Don't carry anything (even in a money belt) that can't easily be replaced. Use your hotel or hostel safe.

Be aware of what's going on around you. Walk on the road side of the footpath and don't hesitate to cross the street to avoid an alleyway or a threatening individual or group. In general, you're safe so long as there are plenty of people around, or you're in a group.

Avoid the city centre at night and on weekends when the shops close and the crowds drop. With the exception of the busy Yeoville streets, you would be crazy to walk around at night. Daylight muggings in the city centre and other inner suburbs, notably Hillbrow, are not uncommon. If you have a car, make sure your doors are locked, and when you're at stop lights leave a car's length between you and the vehicle in front so you can drive away if necessary. Running a red light is not illegal if you're in reasonable fear of assault.

If you arrive at night and don't have a car, catch a taxi to your final destination; there are always taxis available at the Rotunda for arrivals on the airport bus, or at the train station. If you do get held up, don't try to be a hero. Give your assailants any possessions they want and try not to make any threatening moves. Jo'burg is inundated with guns and knives and their owners don't hesitate to use them.

There are plenty of beggars on the streets – both black and white. Some of them can be very insistent. Consider carrying a rand or two in change in an accessible pocket, so that you can give without flashing your wallet or purse around.

HILLBROW

On the ridge to the north-east of the railway station (a 20-minute walk, if you dare), Hillbrow is the most lively and interesting suburb in Johannesburg. It's the centre of the most densely populated two or three sq km in Africa, dominated by towering apartment buildings and residential and tourist hotels. At last count there were 55,000 people (650 people per hectare), but with thousands of people flocking to the area, many of them destitute illegal immigrants, there are now probably many more.

Hillbrow is still South Africa's answer to Soho (London), Greenwich Village (New York) and King's Cross (Sydney), although it is on the verge of breaking down into outlaw territory. The bourgeoisie steer well clear. There are late night restaurants, cafés, bars, discos, several excellent music shops, and interesting crafts sold by footpath hawkers. It's also pretty seedy – with more than its fair share of prostitutes, drunks, beggars and street kids – so a certain amount of common-sense caution is necessary.

Over the last few years Hillbrow and adjoining Berea have become increasingly dominated by black arrivals and the area has almost become a ghetto. But not quite, and all sorts of races and cultures still coexist in an amiable sort of way – which actually gives some hope for the future. This is one of the very few places in South Africa where mixed-race couples don't create a sensation. It's an enjoyable place just to walk around (if you aren't carrying valuables or look like you might be) and there's a stimulating big-city vibe.

YEOVILLE

Rockey St, Yeoville, was the counter-cultural capital of South Africa, a world leader in the resuscitation of the '70s, or maybe where the '70s never went away. Black clothes (perhaps with an embroidered T-shirt

from Kathmandu), long hair, and earnest conversations over cappuccinos were the rule. That has changed somewhat, and some of the old Hillbrow seediness is creeping in, but despite this (or because of this) the atmosphere is relaxed, congenial and non-racial. There are plenty of good-value restaurants and bars, some of which have live music. There are also some interesting shops, including a clutch of craft shops in the Bizarre Centre Mall. It is practically the only street in Jo'burg and one of the few in South Africa where walking around at night is both safe and stimulating.

Rockey St is an easy 30-minute walk north-east from Hillbrow, although this would not be wise at night. Buses (R2) run to Rockey St via Pretoria St, Hillbrow, from Vanderbijl Square, the main local bus terminus in the city. Look for bus Nos 19a and 20; they are frequent from 6.45 to 8.40 am and from 4 to 7 pm, hourly during the middle of the day, and nonexistent after 7 pm.

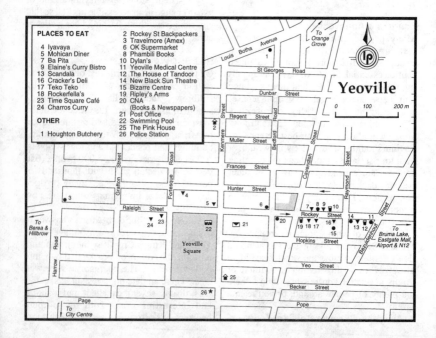

PLACES TO EAT
4 Iyavaya
5 Mohican Diner
7 Ba Pita
9 Elaine's Curry Bistro
13 Scandala
16 Cracker's Deli
17 Teko Teko
18 Rockerfella's
23 Time Square Café
24 Charros Curry

OTHER
1 Houghton Butchery

2 Rockey St Backpackers
3 Travelmore (Amex)
6 OK Supermarket
8 Phambili Books
10 Dylan's
11 Yeoville Medical Centre
12 The House of Tandoor
14 New Black Sun Theatre
15 Bizarre Centre
19 Ripley's Arms
20 CNA
   (Books & Newspapers)
21 Post Office
22 Swimming Pool
25 The Pink House
26 Police Station

Yeoville

MUSEUMS
Museum Africa

Founded in the 1930s, this important museum (☎ (011) 833 5624) has finally been housed in a suitable building and has room to expand. The museum (previously known as the Africana Museum) has taken over the impressive old fruit market on Bree St, next to the Market Theatre complex. As yet the displays are a little scanty – the largest exhibit is a quirky collection of photographic paraphenalia – but there are signs of a brilliant future. The Sophiatown display and the re-creation of a township are outstanding. There's also a large collection of rock art.

The museum is open daily except Monday from 9 am to 5 pm. Admission is R2, free on Sunday. If you're walking here from the city centre, it's reputedly safer to walk along Jeppe St than Bree St.

Jewish Museum

On the corner of Kruis and Main Sts, the Jewish Museum (☎ (011) 331 0331) covers the history of Judaism in South Africa from the 1920s onwards. It's open weekdays from 9 am to 1 pm and 2 to 5 pm. There's a surprisingly large Jewish community in South Africa, particularly in Jo'burg, many of whom arrived in the '20s.

Transport Museum

This museum, in the main railway station, will only appeal to gricers (railway enthusiasts) and fetishists of that ilk. You can see old signalling equipment and an exhibition of model railways. It is open from 7.30 am to 3.45 pm on weekdays.

National Museum of Military History

One might have hoped that this would only appeal to a small number of Rambos, warmongers and fetishists of that ilk. Apparently, however, it's the most popular museum in Jo'burg. You can see artefacts and implements of destruction from the Anglo-Boer War through to the Namibian wars. It's at the east end of the zoo grounds and is open daily from 9 am to 4.30 pm.

MARKETS
Market Theatre

This is held on Saturdays between 9 am and 1 pm in the car park opposite the Market Theatre. There's a lively, cheerful atmosphere, and although most of the stalls sell flea-market rubbish – T-shirts, and useless knick-knacks suitable for Christmas presents to distant relatives – there is also some reasonable craftwork amongst the dross. It makes a pleasant weekend expedition. Now that South Africa is again part of Africa, you'll find increasing numbers of vendors from other countries – at the moment Zaïrians are well represented, for some reason. Slip across to the Yard of Ale opposite the Market Theatre when you get thirsty.

Windybrow People's Market

This is a fairly small-scale market in Hillbrow on Claim St, between Kapteijn and Pietersen. It's a good place to look for cheap shoes, clothing and electrical goods.

Flea Market World

This big, fairly commercial operation is open daily except Monday. It's on Marcia St, not far from Bruma Lake and Eastgate Mall. On the opposite footpath many craft stalls are usually set up. There is a very wide range, although you'll look hard for high quality.

GALLERIES
Johannesburg Art Gallery

This gallery (☎ (011) 725 3180) on the Klein St side of Joubert Park, was once disappointing, despite being housed in a lovely little building. The exhibits were mostly uninspiring European and white South African landscape and figurative paintings. Those are still there but there is an increasing number of exhibitions featuring more adventurous contemporary work and long-overdue retrospectives of black artists.

As well as the art, the gallery makes a quiet escape from the real world, and there's a pleasant coffee shop. Entry is free and it's open daily from 10 am to 5 pm, except Monday.

Standard Bank Centre Gallery

On the corner of Simmonds and Frederick, this gallery (☎ (011) 636 4231) has changing exhibitions, often of a high standard. It's open weekdays from 8 am to 4.30 pm, and Saturday from 9 am to 1 pm.

Gertrude Posel Gallery

This gallery (☎ (011) 716 3632) in Senate House, University of Witwatersrand, houses the Standard Bank Foundation Collection of African tribal art, which includes masks, beadwork and Ndebele fertility dolls. It's open from Tuesday to Friday from 10 am to 4 pm and on Saturday by appointment.

CARLTON CENTRE & PANORAMA

The Carlton Centre – all 50 floors of it – is an unmistakable landmark on Commissioner St. It has a three-tier shopping centre built around the Rondehof, a central display area that is used for all sorts of exhibitions and promotions. A remarkable number seem to feature women in bikinis.

The **Carlton Panorama** (☎ (011) 331 6608) is on the 50th floor and is accessible by lifts from level 100 of the Rondehof (fare R6.50). The view is suitably spectacular and it's a good way to orient yourself. You can still see how the city grew up alongside its mines, although the evidence is fast disappearing as the old mine tailings are reprocessed.

On top of one artificial mountain is the spectacularly sited Top-Star Drive-in Theatre, just to the south of the M2 freeway. The freeway divides the city from the area that was mined – the extensive tunnelling and the resulting instability of the ground means that high-rise buildings cannot be built to the south.

The luxury **Carlton Hotel**, the starting point for many of the local tours, is in the south-west corner of the centre (on the corner of Main and Kruis Sts).

MARKET THEATRE

The Market Theatre complex (☎ (011) 832 1641) on Bree St, at the north-west corner of the city centre makes up one of the highlights

of Jo'burg. There are four live theatre venues, an art gallery, coffee shop, some interesting shops, The Yard of Ale (a pub with a pleasant outdoor area that serves cheap meals) and Kippies Bar (☎ (011) 823 1645), which is an excellent jazz venue.

There is always some interesting theatre, ranging from sharply critical contemporary plays to musicals and stand-up comedians. Check the *Weekly Mail & Guardian* entertainment section for information on current performances. Bookings are often necessary.

Developed in old, recycled market buildings, the complex is an attractive and enjoyable place to hang around. With the Museum Africa next door, this corner of Jo'burg could easily absorb most of a day and a fair part of the night – especially on Saturday when the market sets up across the road.

ORIENTAL PLAZA

A short walk from the Market Theatre complex, further west along Bree St from the city (between Bree and Main Sts, Fordsburg), the Oriental Plaza has over 300 Indian-owned shops. If you have a reasonable idea of prices and don't mind bargaining, you'll make some good buys. At the very least you'll find some cheap and delicious samosas.

JOHANNESBURG FORT

The fort at the end of Kotze St in Hillbrow was built in the 1890s to defend and garrison the military forces who were responsible for keeping the miners under control. It has never seen action and after the Anglo-Boer War it was converted into a prison. Number Four, as it was known, was where pass-law violators were incarcerated, and it is remembered with dread.

JOHANNESBURG ZOOLOGICAL GARDENS

It seems rather bizarre going to a zoo in Africa, but you can combine a visit with the South African Museum of Military History. The zoo (☎ (011) 646 2000) is open daily from 8.30 am to 5.30 pm and admission is

R8. There are also thrice-weekly night tours for R23 (no children); book through Computicket. Take bus Nos 78, 80 or 80B from Eloff St or No 79 from Rissik St.

UNIVERSITY OF WITWATERSRAND

The University of Witwatersrand, in Jan Smuts Ave, Braamfontein, is the largest English-language university in the country with over 16,000 multiracial students. It's an attractive campus; visitors might choose to visit the Gertrude Posel Gallery (see the previous Galleries section), Jan Smuts House to see the great man's study, the Student Union Building for a cheap cafeteria meal, or to call on the Student Travel (SASTS) office. Also on campus is the **Planetarium** (☎ (011) 716 3199), in Yale Rd. It has various programmes that have been recommended by various travellers. They last an hour and cost R11. One traveller reported being mugged walking back from Wits on a weekend.

GOLD REEF CITY

Gold Reef City (☎ (011) 496 1600) is a serious tourist trap that can't quite make up its mind whether it's a Disneyland clone or a serious historical reconstruction of old Jo'burg. It's pretty glitzy and antiseptic, but it's also good fun – just the thing to help fill a Jo'burg weekend. There are not many other options after the shops close on Saturday.

It features scary rides, a Victorian fun fair and various historical reconstructions (including a bank, brewery, pub and newspaper office), and you can go down a shaft to see a gold mine from the inside, watch a gold pour, and see a programme of tribal dancing. The dancers perform twice a day during the week and three times on weekends. Despite being highly commercial, the dancing is quite exhilarating – ring ahead to make sure you're there for a performance.

There are numerous places to eat and drink, and a particularly good craft/souvenir shop (Gold Reef City Arts & Crafts Centre – it's along the street from the more obvious Egoli Village craft shop). There are often special programmes on the weekend, sometimes involving live music in an open-sided

amphitheatre, and fireworks. Keep an eye on the entertainment section in the *Star* for details.

The complex is open from 9 am to 5 pm and admission is R16, or R18 on weekends. All rides and exhibits are free except for the mine tour, which costs R10. Many of the eating and drinking places stay open until 11 pm, and admission after 5 pm is free. The entire complex is closed on Monday except if it is a public holiday.

Gold Reef City is six km south of the city, just off the M1 freeway. Unfortunately, it's a bit tricky to reach by public transport, and a taxi would be expensive. By bus, catch the No 55 (R2) from Vanderbijl Square, the main local bus terminus in the city, two blocks west of the Carlton Centre. From Tuesday to Saturday buses leave every 20 minutes or so; on Sunday the frequency drops to one every two hours, so check the timetable. Get off at stop 14, Althan Rd, Robertsham; walk west along Alamein Rd, go under the freeway and you'll see Gold Reef City on your right. Most day tours include Gold Reef City on their itineraries.

GOLD MINES

The Chamber of Mines (☎ (011) 498 7100) runs excellent tours of working gold mines. However, they're dependent on the hospitality of the mining companies who, apparently, aren't very enthusiastic. There's rarely more than one tour a week (on Tuesday, Wednesday or Thursday) and in December there are none at all. Contact the chamber as far in advance as possible. You have to be pretty committed because the all-day tours cost at least R140 or R180 if you go all the way to the Orange Free State goldfields, and depart as early as 5 am.

Unfortunately, it is no longer possible to visit the displays of traditional dancing that were held on Sunday in the mines' accommodation compounds.

ORGANISED TOURS

Springbok Atlas (☎ (011) 0493 0827), the largest tour operator in the country, has city tours for R85 and longer tours including

Gold Reef City for R115. Abeona Tours (☎ (011) 882 3066) has a three-hour city highlights tour for R70 per person, with a minimum of just two people. They also have tours of nearby lion and rhino parks for R100 per park.

Dumela Africa (☎ (011) 837 9928) charges R125 per person for a half-day tour or R75 if there are more than four of you. Their full day tour (which includes Pretoria) is R260 per person or R160 for more than four people. Historical Walks of Johannesburg (☎ (011) 922 5739) offers two-hour walking tours in the city for a minimum of four people.

See the earlier boxed story on Soweto for Soweto tours. The Publicity Association's *Gateway* booklet lists many other options.

FESTIVALS

The big Arts Alive Festival is held in September and October. Since South Africa's liberation the arts have been going through an exciting time, with an explosion of optimism and the mainstream acceptance of long-suppressed talents. A strong element in the festival is workshops exposing South Africans to their continent's rich cultures, so long denigrated by the Eurocentrism of the apartheid years.

The festival is a particularly good time to hear excellent music, on and off the official programme. Keep an eye on venues such as the House of Tandoor in Yeoville.

PLACES TO STAY – BOTTOM END
Caravan Parks

The *Safari Caravan Park* (☎ (011) 942 1404) is on the M27, the old Jo'burg-Vereeniging highway, 12 km south of the city. They have 50 caravan stands, tents are allowed, and there are nearby shops. A stand costs R20, more or less, depending on whether you need electricity.

The best-placed park is the *Bezuidenhout Valley Caravan Park* (☎ (011) 648 6302) 180 Third Ave, off Observatory Rd, Bezuidenhout Valley, near Bruma Lake four km to the east of Hillbrow. Unfortunately, tents are not accepted. A van site is R20.

Hostels

Jo'burg has a good range of hostels, mostly recent arrivals. Many will pick you up from the airport or the Rotunda and most are excellent sources of travel information. One or two are having trouble making ends meet and take in long-term locals (causing potential security and atmosphere problems), but with South Africa's continuing backpacker boom this should change.

Warning Although some of these hostels are only a few km from the Rotunda (the main bus station and the drop-off point for the airport bus) you'd be very unwise to walk to them, even in daylight, if you are carrying luggage or arriving in Africa for the first time. Phone for a pick-up or take a taxi. You could take a bus to or near many of the hostels, but blundering around downtown Jo'burg with all your possessions on your back trying to find the right bus is asking for trouble.

The *Johannesburg Central Youth Hostel* (☎ (011) 643 1213), 4 Fife Ave, Berea, is fairly large and is central to Hillbrow – and a lot of crime. There is secure parking. A café sells toasties, etc. Dorm beds cost R20 and doubles are about R45.

There are a couple of good choices in Yeoville, which is arguably the best area to stay in Jo'burg. *Rockey St Backpackers* (☎ (011) 648 8786, fax 648 8423) isn't on Rockey St, but it is just a short (and safe) walk away at 34 Regent St. The management is very friendly, the atmosphere is good, the facilities are reasonable (with a plunge pool and a bar) and it's clean. What more could you want? Recommended. Dorms go for R25 and doubles are R70. If there's room you might be able to take a double as a single for about R50. *The Pink House* (☎ (011) 487 1991), 73 Becker St, also receives good reports from travellers. They are stricter about smoking inside than Rockey St, but they don't do airport pick-ups. Dorms are R25 and singles/doubles are R50/70. You can camp if the hostel is full.

One km or so south-east of Hillbrow and

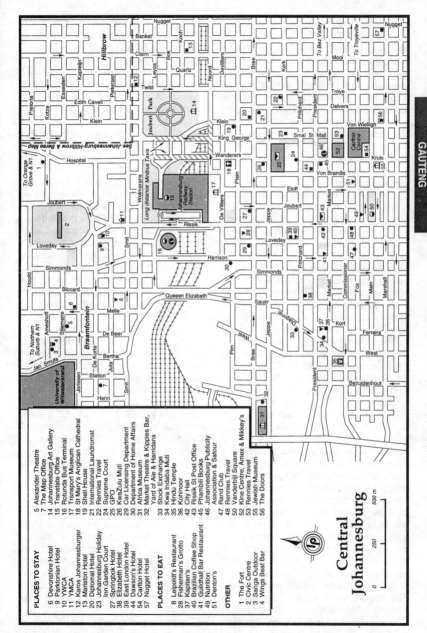

Central Johannesburg

0   250   500 m

PLACES TO STAY

6 Devonshire Hotel
9 Parktonian Hotel
10 YWCA
11 YMCA
12 Karos Johannesburger
13 Mariston Hotel
20 Diplomat Hotel
23 Johannesburg Holiday
   Inn Garden Court
27 Springbok Hotel
38 Elizabeth Hotel
39 East London Hotel
44 Dawson's Hotel
54 Carlton Hotel
57 Nugget Hotel

PLACES TO EAT

8 Leipoldt's Restaurant
28 Fisherman's Grotto
37 Kapitan's
40 Brazilian Coffee Shop
41 Guildhall Bar Restaurant
49 Nutrition
51 Denton's

OTHER

1 The Fort
2 Civic Centre
3 Sanga Outdoor
4 Wings Beat Bar
5 Alexander Theatre
7 The Map Office
14 Johannesburg Art Gallery
15 Transtate Office
16 Rotunda Bus Terminal
17 Transport Museum
18 St Mary's Anglican Cathedral
19 Shell House
21 International Laundromat
22 Rennies Travel
24 Supreme Court
25 GPO
26 KwaZulu Muti
29 Car Licensing Department
30 Department of Home Affairs
31 Africa Museum
32 Market Theatre & Kippies Bar,
   Yard of Ale & Harridans
33 Stock Exchange
34 Kwa Indaba Muti
35 Hindu Temple
36 Kohinoor
42 City Hall
43 Rissik St Post Office
45 Phambili Books
46 Johannesburg Publicity
   Association & Satour
47 Rand Club
48 Rennies Travel
50 Vanderbijl Square
52 Kine Centre, Amex & Mikkey's
53 Rennies Travel
55 Jewish Museum
56 The Doors

Yeoville, in the Bez (Bezuidenhout) Valley, *International Travellers' Hostel* (ITH) (☎ (011) 614 4640, fax 614 2497), 55 First St, is bigger than it looks from the street, and more rooms are being built. The dorms are a reasonable size, but they'd want to be as the bunks are triple-deckers. There's a decent bar and separate lounge and pool rooms. The hostel doesn't have a pool, but it's reasonably close to a free public pool. Dorms cost R25 and singles/doubles start at R50/75. There has been some negative feedback from travellers who have run into problems with one of the owners.

Fairview Youth Hostel (☎ (011) 618 2048), 4 College St (off Commissioner St), is three km east of the city centre in unlovely Troyeville. It's a large old house with sunny rooms and a cheerful atmosphere. Dorm beds are just R20. From Eloff St take bus No 32 to the second stop after the Fairview Fire Station (which has a distinctive tower). The last buses leave around 6.30 pm.

Zoo Lodge (☎ (011) 486 0011), 40 Jan Smuts Ave (corner of Alyth St) in Forest Town, is in a pleasant old house with a large garden, where there's a pool. The hostel is a fair way from everywhere (except the zoo) but buses run past. Take No 75 or 78 from the city centre and get off at stop 14. Currently, many of the guests are traders from around Africa.

Even further out, but within an easy walk of the Hyde Park (Dunkeld) shopping centre and a longer walk to the good Rosebank Mall, is the *Backpackers' Ritz* (☎ (011) 327 0229, fax 792 1376). The Ritz was one of South Africa's original backpacker hostels and it has recently moved to a new and considerably more salubrious address. It's now an impressive operation with two houses, one huge, each in a very large garden with a pool. There's only one tennis court, bar and café. A travel agency is planned. If you want to relax in comfort rather than experience the gritty delights of inner Jo'burg, this is definitely the place to come. The dorms (from R20) are fairly large but you won't feel cramped. Singles are R40 or R50 and doubles are R70. Camping in the

grounds (a pleasant option) costs R15. Bus Nos 73 and 80B from Eloff St and No 80 from the Rotunda run to the Dunkeld shops, a short walk from the Ritz.

Kew Youth Hostel (☎ (011) 887 9072) 5 Johannesburg Rd (the M20), Kew, is inconveniently located in the northern suburbs, ten km from the city centre. It might be worth considering if you have a car. The hostel is a luxury suburban home with a pool, and they allow camping. Dorms are R22 and doubles are R44. Several buses do run past or nearby – ring for information.

The *YMCA* (☎ (011) 403 3426), 104 Rissik St, Braamfontein, is just north of the city centre in a convenient, though rather lifeless, part of town. Hillbrow is a 15-minute walk away. The hostel accepts couples. It's not dirty, but it's definitely scuffed around the edges and very large. There's something depressing about it, although the prices make a pretty good argument for staying there. A single room costs R43, sharing it's R36 per person. Breakfast costs R.9.55, lunch R5.20 and dinner R12.

The *YWCA* (☎ (011) 403 3830), 128 De Korte St, Braamfontein, is much nicer than the YMCA across the road. It's for women only so it's cleaner and better organised – I can't think of any other reasons. Food is supplied and you will probably find a ready-made network of friends. Beds in shared rooms cost R65 (R390 per week). A single room and board is R70 (R420 per week). They try to keep four or five rooms free for travellers. Monthly rates are much cheaper but you have to stay three months to qualify for them.

Hotels

Hillbrow & Berea Hillbrow and Berea are the most interesting and convenient suburbs in which to stay. They're full of life, but they are also pretty seedy and parts are dangerous. Hillbrow is full of restaurants, takeaways, cafés and shops; Berea, the next suburb to the east, is a dormitory suburb full of multi-storey hotels and apartment buildings.

The better-quality budget hotels are often

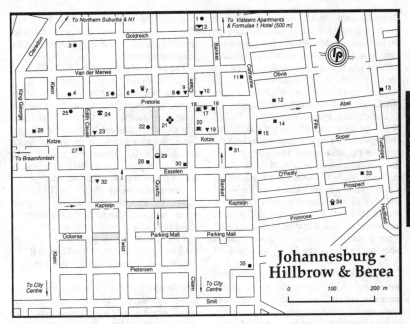

GAUTENG

Johannesburg –
Hillbrow & Berea

0   100   200 m

PLACES TO STAY		PLACES TO EAT		4	Kwa Indaba Muti
				5	Rennies Travel
6	Harrison Reef Hotel	9	Three Sisters' Café	7	Bella Napoli
11	Hotel Park Lane	10	Wimpy	8	Look & Listen
12	Crest Hotel	18	Café Gattopado	17	Hillbrow Pharmacy
13	African Sun	19	Poor Man's Pub	21	Highpoint Centre
14	Protea Ridge Hotel	20	Café Kranzler	22	CNA (Books &
15	Chelsea Hotel	23	Africa Hut		Newspapers)
16	Ambassador Hotel	32	Porterhouse Carvery	24	Use a Phone
26	Hotel Quirinale			25	Nu Metro Cinemas
27	The Pads	**OTHER**		29	Taxi Rank
28	Hilton Plaza Hotel			31	Score Supermarket
30	Moulin Rouge Hotel	1	JG Strijdom Tower	35	Windybrow Theatre
33	Mark Hotel		(Hillbrow Tower)		Complex
34	Johannesburg	2	Post Office (Card		
	Central Youth		Phones)		
	Hostel	3	Hare Krisna Temple		

booked out, particularly on weekends. Most are relatively modern multi-storey buildings that are beginning to get a bit tatty around the edges. Many of them have a high proportion of permanent residents and don't have much room for casuals. It's worth booking ahead if possible, or contacting them around 9 am

in the morning. Ring ahead before you start lugging your gear around.

Some of the cheaper places support blatant prostitution, with prostitutes soliciting in their bars and living in their rooms. There's no reason why this should affect you unless you want it to.

Rock Bottom The cheapest place is by no means the worst. *African Sun*, 28 Tudhope St, Berea is an old house with a garden and very spartan but clean rooms with shared bath for just R35 a single or twin. There are cooking facilities. They don't yet have a phone. This place is probably a flop-house, but it seems to be a reasonable one.

The *Hilton Plaza Hotel* (☎ (011) 725 3640), on the corner of Esselen and Quartz, Hillbrow, has no official connection with the chain of the same name. This place typifies the alarming slide in standards in cheap Hillbrow hotels. It's *totally* run down, the lift doesn't work (a major hassle as it's high-rise) and a lot of guests seem to work from their rooms. However, it is cheap, at R40 a room, and it's lively. When I called in, the desk staff were concerned about a rumour that a sangoma had been interfering with the food in the kitchen!

The *Chelsea Hotel* (☎ (011) 642 4541) on the corner of Catherine and Kotze St has been about to undergo a renovation for some years now. It's in desperate need of one. It's another lively hotel and less depressing than some of Hillbrow's other rock-bottom places. They have some security, but check there's a decent lock on your door. You have to be prepared to put up with a lot of noise; try to put as much distance as possible between you and the disco on the 2nd floor. The hot water supply is dubious. Singles/doubles are R40/50 and four-person rooms are R80.

One of the cheapest options, especially for a couple or a group, is the furnished apartments known as *The Pads* (☎ (011) 725 3570) at 42 Kotze St. The apartments are basic (the bathrooms have baths but not showers) but they do have telephones, and stoves in the kitchens (but not crockery). Try to get a feel for the security situation before moving in, though.

Better The *Crest Hotel* (☎ (011) 642 7641), 7 Abel Rd, is a very comfortable, convenient and well-run hotel. Rooms are large and well-maintained, with radios and telephones, and there is security parking. Singles/doubles

cost only R60/90 – a real bargain. They only have a limited number of rooms available; most are occupied by elderly members of the Jewish community.

The *Mark Hotel* (☎ (011) 643 6731), 24 O'Reilly, Berea, is recommended. It's a modern, comfortable multi-storey hotel, a five-minute walk from the centre of Hillbrow. The rooms have telephones, there's parking, and singles or doubles are R90. There are also some unrenovated rooms let by the month for about R700. These aren't such good value, as they are just smallish hotel rooms with a fridge and a hotplate added.

The *Ambassador Hotel* (☎ (011) 642 5051), 52 Pretoria St, Hillbrow, is good value. Although standards are slipping, it's going to seed in a genteel manner. It's clean and the rooms are a good size. Singles/doubles cost R65/95 with breakfast, or R375/545 per week. There's also a civilised bar.

City Centre Most of the bottom-end places in the city centre are run-down and depressing. There are a few exceptions, but the problem with staying in the city centre is that you can't really go out at night on foot.

Dawson's Hotel (☎ (011) 337 5010), 117 President, on the corner of Von Brandis, is excellent value and is recommended. It's a clean and comfortable old-style hotel with a restaurant (breakfast R11.50) a couple of decent bars and live music. We've listed it in the bottom end section because of its prices, not its standards. Rooms (single or double, go for just R75 Sunday to Thursday and R105 on weekends (additional guests R40 per person). Luxury rooms, which are larger, are R85, or R110 on and weekends. Suites go for R100, or R165 on weekends. Weekly rates start at R470 for standard rooms.

The *Nugget Hotel* (☎ (011) 334 0059), on the corner of Nugget and Marshall Sts, is fairly run-down but it feels like a country hotel gone to seed rather than a dive. It's spartan but clean and the beds are good. Singles with shared bath are R55 and singles/doubles with bath are R70/85. You don't want a room above the 1st-floor disco. (Disco patrons are body-searched for weapons – I'm not sure whether this is reassuring or disconcerting.)

The *Diplomat Hotel* (☎ (011) 29 2161) on the corner of Klein and Bree Sts, is rundown, but it's livelier and less depressing than some of the others. A double rooms costs R80.

Then there are the depressing places. If you're desperate you could try the *Elizabeth Hotel* (☎ (011) 838 7861) on the corner of Pritchard and Sauer Sts, which charges R50/70 for singles/doubles or R60/80 with bath. You don't want a room above the 1st-floor disco. The *East London Hotel* (☎ (011) 834 3425), Loveday St just north of Pritchard St, charges R50/75, or R60/75 with bath. Some rooms are suites.

PLACES TO STAY – MIDDLE
B&Bs
There are surprisingly few independent bed & breakfast operations. One exception is *Joel House* (☎ (011) 643 8714), 61 Joel Rd, Berea, which is an extremely comfortable old house that has been specially restored. There are five bedrooms with en suites which cost R170/260.

Fortunately the excellent Bed & Breakfast organisation (☎ (011) 482 2206/7, fax (011) 726 6915) has a number of members in and around the northern suburbs. The accommodation is exceptionally good value. Most rooms are in large, luxurious suburban houses (often with swimming pools) and all have private bathrooms. The only problem is that Bed & Breakfast prefers advance bookings (preferably at least a week but you'll probably find something on less notice) and most houses are difficult to get to without private transport. Prices range from R92/164 to R125/202.

The Portfolio organisation (☎ (011) 880 3414, fax 788 4802) also lists a number of high-quality B&Bs in the northern suburbs.

Hotels & Apartments
Hillbrow & Berea Some of the more expensive hotels in this area are good value because the escalating crime rate has chased away custom.

On the corner of Esselen and Claim Sts, the *Moulin Rouge Hotel* (☎ (011) 725 4840) is tizzy but clean and in good condition. It's quite a good deal at R90 for doubles, R110 for rooms with TV. The *Harrison Reef Hotel* (☎ (011) 643 4941), 27 Pretoria, Hillbrow, is dowdy but in quite good condition. Singles/doubles are R90/130, triple and quads are R150/160. The restaurant has steaks for R20.

Up in Berea at 12 Mitchell St (near the corner of Louis Botha Ave), *Vistaero Apartments* (☎ (011) 643 4954) are good value and are within easy (and currently safe) walking distance of both Yeoville and Hillbrow. Single/double serviced bed-sit apartments with stove, fridge and phone (TVs can be hired) are R88/100 or R555/630 per week. Monthly rates are available. There's a pool and secure parking. The disadvantages are that the beds aren't comfortable and, as one wall is mainly glass, apartments on lower floors get street noise.

The *Hotel Quirinale* (☎ (011) 720 5250), 27 Kotze St, Hillbrow, is deteriorating and a bit over-priced at R140 for a double. A few blocks north in Berea, the *Safari International* (☎ (011) 642 7625) on the corner of Banket and Yettah Sts is a better deal at R115/145 (ask about specials). The rooms are fairly small but they are in good condition. The service at reception could be better.

The *Protea Ridge Hotel* (☎ (011) 643 4911), 8 Abel Rd, Berea, has an excellent situation on the edge of Hillbrow. This would be a good choice. It's nothing spectacular – a typical large soulless hotel, but it is comfortable, and very convenient. There's off-street parking and singles/doubles are R130/165 with breakfast.

The nearby *Hotel Park Lane* (☎ (011) 642 7425), 54 Van der Merwe, is similar. Singles/doubles are R125/160 with breakfast. Rooms are a little small but they do have balconies. It's in good condition but you get the impression that it could go to seed fairly quickly. The *Protea Gardens* (☎ (011) 643 6610), 35 O'Reilly, Berea, doesn't have quite as good a position as its relative on Abel Rd, but it is a comfortable place to stay. It

GAUTENG

would want to be, with singles/doubles for R170/190.

City Centre See the earlier bottom-end section for Dawson's Hotel, which offers excellent value. Another of the few old-style to maintain standards is the *Springbok Hotel* (☎ (011) 337 8336), on the corner of Joubert and Bree Sts. It offers frilly rooms for R100/130.

The *Mariston Hotel* (☎ (011) 725 4130), on the corner of Claim St and Koch, is an enormous multi-storey hotel halfway between the city centre and Hillbrow. It's too large and there are a lot of permanents, but it's not bad value. You get most facilities, including security parking, and prices have dropped in the past few years because of the deterioration of the neighbourhood. Singles or doubles can go as low as R100.

Nearer Joubert Park, the *Karos Johannesburger* (☎ (011) 725 3753), 60 Twist St, is another large international-style hotel with covered parking. It too has dropped its prices lately, and charges a little more than the Mariston.

Northern Suburbs The *Linden Hotel* (☎ (011) 782 4905) on the corner of 7th St and 4th Ave, Linden, is an attractive and comfortable personalised hotel. Unfortunately it's a long way from the city centre. Singles/doubles start at R165/215 with breakfast.

The City Lodge group offers good-value accommodation at three locations. The *Jan Smuts Airport City Lodge* (☎ (011) 392 1750) is at the Isando exit on the R24 freeway to the airport. Singles/doubles are R205/220; they will arrange transport to/from the airport. Booking is advised. The *Randburg City Lodge* (☎ (011) 706 7800) is a couple of km north of the Randburg centre. Singles/doubles are R205/220. There are plenty of restaurants in the area. The *Sandton City Lodge* (☎ (011) 444 5300) on the corner of Katherine and Grayston Dr, Sandown, is within walking distance of the shops. Singles/doubles are R207/230.

PLACES TO STAY – TOP END
Hotels

City Centre The *Johannesburg Holiday Inn Garden Court* (☎ (011) 336 7011, fax 336 0515), 84 Smal St, is a striking modern tower, bang in the middle of the city. While it's a luxury hotel, the crime rate in the centre of the city has lowered its appeal and room rates can go as low as R180 a double – good value.

The five-star *Carlton Hotel* (☎ (011) 331 8911, fax (011) 331 3555), adjoining the Carlton Centre, has a great position if you are doing business in the city and, although the area is a bit barren at night, there are plenty of restaurants and bars to keep you busy within the building. There are special offers, but expect to pay from around R450/520 a single/double.

The *Parktonian Hotel* (☎ (011) 403 5740), 120 De Korte St, charges R375/440, with weekend specials at R185/250 if you stay two nights. Technically, it is in Braamfontein but it isn't too far from the city centre. Further west and definitely in Braamfontein, the *Devonshire Hotel* (☎ (011) 339 5611) on the corner of Melle and Jorissen St is a comfortable medium-sized hotel. It has all mod-cons, including under-cover parking. Singles/doubles are about R250/350, including breakfast.

Northern Suburbs The four-star *Sunnyside Park Hotel* (☎ (011) 643 7226), 2 York Rd (the entrance is actually off Carse O'Gowrie Rd), Parktown, is recommended. It's an old-style hotel set in attractive gardens and it's a 20-minute walk north of Hillbrow. Singles/doubles go for R350/470, with weekend specials for less than half that. It's not far from the city, Yeoville and Hillbrow, so basing yourself here and getting around by taxi wouldn't be too expensive.

Although you might assume the *Balalaika Protea Hotel* (☎ (011) 884 1400), 20 Maud St, Sandown, is a Greek-style hotel, you'd be wrong. The theme is English, with thatched roofs, a recreation of an English pub, an outdoor area called the Village Green and so on. It's only a short walk from the Sandton shops. Singles/doubles are R397/484.

There are a few *Holiday Inn Garden Courts* scattered around. They're all of a dependable high standard. There's one at Jan Smuts Airport (☎ (011) 975 1121), R214/236 a single/double; one at Milpark (☎ (011) 726 5100) on the corner of Owl and Empire Rds, five km from the centre and set in a pleasant garden, R199 single or double; and one at Sandton (☎ (011) 783 5262) close to excellent shopping and restaurants, R219/248.

Elsewhere Out at Gold Reef City, the *Gold Reef City Hotel* (☎ (011) 496 1626) offers luxurious accommodation in an utterly secure environment. Singles/doubles start at R250/350 and the same people also have cheaper and more expensive accommodation in nearby buildings.

PLACES TO EAT

Johannesburg is stacked with places to eat. There are cuisines of every type catering for almost every budget. Unfortunately for visitors, especially those without cars, most of these places are scattered around the northern suburbs and they be difficult to find. The Publicity Association's *Gateway* brochure lists restaurants by cuisine.

All the major hotels have a variety of high-quality restaurants on their premises, and in just about every shopping centre you'll find at least one franchised steak house such as *Spur*.

City Centre

Snacks There's a marked shortage of cafés and cheap eating places in the city. There's no shortage of takeaways, but they aren't very inspiring. There are a few alternatives in the Smal St Mall and the Carlton Centre – have a wander and see what takes your fancy.

Just finding somewhere to sit down is a major problem. The *Guildhall Bar & Restaurant* on the corner of Harrison and Market Sts has tables on a 1st-floor balcony, offering a rare chance to take a leisurely look at the bustling streets without worrying about being mugged. It's one of the oldest remaining pubs in the city. Another reasonable place

to sit down and have a quiet coffee is the *Brazilian Coffee Shop*, on the corner of Pritchard and Loveday Sts. The coffee shop in the *Art Gallery* in Joubert Park is another possibility.

On New St North, opposite the Vanderbijl Square bus information office, the *Nutrition* snack bar promises 'health food'. Compared with most downtown Jo'burg snackeries the fare is healthy, but there's a lot of meat on the menu. Sandwiches and rolls cost from R5, salads from R4. For a cheap meal of pap and stew, try the many stalls around the long-distance taxi ranks on Wanderers and the nearby streets.

Meals In the Kine Centre is *Mikkey's*, a steakhouse which used to be a member of the Mike's Kitchen chain.

Upstairs at 11A Kort St, one of the few remaining Indian streets, *Kapitan's* (☎ (011) 834 8048) is a cheerful, old-fashioned restaurant with authentic Indian food. Vegetable curry is R15, meat curries are R22, chicken vindaloo or biryani is R28. The owner has one of the largest collection of Cuban cigars in the country and he might just be persuaded to sell you one of his cheaper cigars, say around R100.

Denton's, upstairs on Fox St near the corner of Eloff St is a quality French-influenced restaurant and a nice respite from the downtown stresses. Soups are R9, salads about R12, entrées R15, fish around R30 and steaks from R30 to R35. *Fisherman's Grotto* (☎ (011) 834 6211), 14 Plein St, between Loveday and Rissik Sts, is the place to go for fish.

The *Yard of Ale* in the Market Theatre complex has basic pub-style meals and you can sit outside. It's closed on Sunday and Monday evenings. In a completely different price bracket and style, popular *Harridan's* (☎ (011) 838 6960) is also in the Market Theatre complex. It has a bright and interesting décor, matched by a bright and interesting nouveau-style menu, and specialities are terrines, venison, duck and line fish. It's closed for Saturday lunch, and all Sunday and Monday.

Troyeville

Troyeville is a run-down, lower-middle-class white suburb on the eastern edge of the city centre. At the time of writing there wasn't a lot happening there, but it wouldn't be surprising if gentrification began soon. It's close enough to the city to become another Melville or even Yeoville. Meanwhile, there's the good *Quasimodo Bistro* (☎ (011) 614 5585) on Commissioner St, just before it becomes College St. It's open from noon to 3 pm and 5 pm to midnight on weekdays, with earlier opening on Saturday. Quasimodo is a pleasant coffee shop and restaurant, with folk or blues music some nights. Snacks cost abut R10; most main courses are under R20; and there are always vegetarian dishes, such as stirfry and rice, for R16.

Hillbrow

Travellers on a budget looking for some street life and an informal atmosphere will find it in Hillbrow. Most Hillbrow restaurants are not all that far removed from the takeaway joints that infest the area. They're definitely casual, and the quality of the food is often mediocre. Nonetheless, they're cheap, and the entertainment value is high.

If you're staying in the area and want to prepare your own food, there are several supermarkets, including the inexpensive Score on the corner of Banket and Koetze Sts.

For standard chain-store food there's a *Wimpy* on Pretoria St east of Claim St. For 24-hour African fast food such as stew and rice for R7.50 try the *Africa Hut* on the corner of Edith Cavell and Kotze St. There's an opulent *Hare Krisna temple* on Goldreich St near the corner of Twist St.

The *Three Sisters' Café* on the corner of Pretoria and Claim Sts is the prime spot for people-watching and coffee-drinking. It has a dozen outside tables, and good coffee. The excellent vegetarian platter is R20, curries cost from R16 as does grilled fish, steaks are around R25, and the seafood platter is R30. There's no better place to watch the passing parade of Hillbrow weirdos, beggars, black yuppies, white trash and parking valets.

Café Gattopardo, 48 Pretoria St, is a great place to watch the street (from a safe distance) and consume good, strong coffee – perhaps the best in town. They also serve pasta-based meals but these will either be microwaved or take 45 minutes to prepare. They aren't exactly in vigorous pursuit of customers. *Café Kranzler* on Kotze St, between Banket and Claim Sts, is a good spot to relax with a cup of coffee, and to take the weight off your feet if you've been tramping around Jo'burg. There's a mouthwatering selection of continental cakes.

The *Porterhouse Carvery* (☎ (011) 725 5403) on the corner of Edith Cavell and Esselen St is a classic and very popular South African steakhouse. Steaks range from R22 to R40, mostly around R25. They're excellent and they'll hang over the side of your plate in true South African style. They also have good specials such as 10 prawns, rice and chips for R15.

As a sign of how Hillbrow has gone downmarket, the Mike's Kitchen on Kotze St has closed and the premises have been taken over by the *Poor Man's Pub* with bar meals such as eggs, chips and sausages for R8.

Yeoville

In general, the Yeoville restaurants are unpretentious, informal places. Most are strung along Rockey St between Cavendish and Bezuidenhout Sts, although the strip is expanding and there are now places further east and west. The food may not be outstanding (although it's pretty good), but there's a pleasantly relaxed atmosphere and the prices are reasonable. There are a number of bars, some of which have live music, so you can kick on late.

Cracker's Deli, on Rockey St near Raymond St, is a good place to start an exploration of the street's delights. Although it's more a café than a restaurant, there's a good variety of dishes and the food is both good and cheap. Toasted sandwiches are R3.95, a grilled kebab is R18.95. Vegetarian dishes are around R15, with specials such as vegetable curry and rice for R7.50. They also have a pleasant outdoor area at the rear, surrounded by some of the Bizarre Centre's interesting shops.

Across the road and up the block at No 5, *Ba Pita* was once the place to agonise over your existentialist dilemmas to the accompaniment of good coffee and Pink Floyd tapes. Not much has changed, except the tapes are now more likely to be Nirvana and they're played too loudly to allow much introspection. There's a pleasant atmosphere and the food – I guess you'd call it Mediterranean/Middle Eastern – is simple, cheap and tasty.

Nearby at No 9A, *Elaine's Curry Bistro* (☎ (011) 648 0801) is a curry restaurant with an extensive menu and a good reputation. Vegetarian main courses are under R20, others are around R25, more for seafood. *Scandala* (☎ (011) 648 0109), 24A Rockey St, is a pleasant, casual Greek restaurant with reasonable prices. The usual dips and dolmades are well under R10 and main courses, both Greek dishes and steaks, cost from R20. They also have good pizzas at around R15.

If the weather allows and you don't feel conspicuous among the yuppies, *Rockerfella's* combination café, bar and restaurant has an outside terrace just off the street – just the place for a slow beer on a Saturday afternoon. There's sometimes live music on weekends.

Further east along Rockey St from Cracker's Deli, *The House of Tandoor* (☎ (011) 487 1569) is both a venue and a café. With a combination of good food and live music (usually Wednesday and Saturday) it has everything going for it. As well as the restaurant there's a barn-like space for bands and a roof-top bar. Curries cost from R14 and most other dishes are around R16. Vegetarians are well looked after. There's a cover charge for the music, usually between R5 and R10. If you've seen bunny chow advertised on signs outside black cafés and haven't been game to try it, this is your chance – it's a loaf of bread, hollowed out and filled with curry. A quarter of a loaf filled with curry is R8.

For African food, head to *Iyavaya*, a block from Rockey St on Hunter St, near the corner of Fortesque Rd. It's a pleasant place with a broad menu of delicious food. The prices might seem a little high for backpackers, but the servings are ridiculously large and one main course would do for at least two people. Or just have a couple of entrées (R6 to R10). Try Mother-in-law Stew (spicy beans and spinach, R25) or an entrée of Mopani Worms (crispy sun-dried caterpillars, R6.50 for all you'll ever want to eat). Ostrich goes for R28 and there are fish or chicken dishes for around R20.

On the corner of Fortesque Rd and Raleigh St (the westward continuation of Rockey St), the Time Square complex has several café-style restaurants popular with people-watchers. *Time Square Café* has a good R10 breakfast, a range of salads and other meals costs up to R20. At the back of the courtyard is *Charros Curry*, a good place to eat simple but authentic Indian food. There are outdoor tables and a small menu of delicious food. Curries are around R16 (vegetarian R11), plus papadams, dhal, raita etc. Make sure you try their excellent homemade pickles (R3.50). They also do schwarmas (R12), bunny chow (from R8, or R6 vegetarian) and vegie burgers (R5).

If you just want a feed without atmosphere, interesting menus or entertainment, the *Mohican Diner*, on the corner of Rockey and Kenmere Sts, is a good standby. It's relaxed and has burgers for under R7 and steaks for up to R28. There's always a good special or two. For even more basic refuelling, head down Rockey St to *Teko Teko*, a takeaway place with a few tables. Schwarmas are R10 and kebabs R7. Their hamburgers are OK.

Yeoville locals say that *Houghton Butchery*, a few blocks north of Rockey St near the corner of Louis Botha Ave and Bedford, is the best source of biltong.

Fisherman's Village
It's worth considering an expedition to Fisherman's Village, a kitsch South African version of a Mediterranean village, beside

GAUTENG

Bruma Lake. There are a number of popular restaurants, including *Mar-e-Sol* (☎ (011) 622 6162), which is an interesting Portuguese/Mozambican restaurant, and *Late Nite Al's* (☎ (011) 662 6162) a steakhouse with an attached rock 'n roll venue. Fisherman's Village is about four km east of Yeoville. Continue along Rockey St, which becomes Observatory St, then Marcia St.

Northern Suburbs

In general, the restaurants in the northern suburbs are high quality and, relatively speaking, highly priced. They should only be considered if you don't mind giving your credit card a thrashing.

A number of large companies have their head offices around Braamfontein, and the University of Witwatersrand is close by, so there a number of decent restaurants in the area. Some of them are only open for the lunch trade.

Leipoldt's Restaurant (☎ (011) 339 2765), at 94 Juta St, between Melle and Biccard, has a superb smorgasbord of traditional Cape Dutch cuisine. It's open for lunch and dinner on weekdays and for dinner on Saturday. It is advisable to book, and you may feel rather conspicuous unless you look smart. The entrée and main meal costs R48.50, but you'll almost certainly get sucked into buying a bottle of wine and a coffee or two in addition. It's good value – the food is excellent, and you don't get many opportunities to sample such an extraordinary range of traditional dishes. Plan on spending several hours and don't schedule any strenuous activities after your meal!

The *Sunnyside Park Hotel*, 2 York Rd, Parktown, has a popular terrace bar, shaded by large trees. It makes a pleasant oasis for a long lunch. It's about a 30-minute walk from Yeoville.

Melville, just north-west of Braamfontein, is becoming popular for its restaurants. You'll find a selection on 7th St. *Koala Blu* (☎ (011) 482 2477), near the corner of 4th Ave, is a Thai place (you wouldn't guess it from the name) where all entrées are R15 and main courses cost around R30 to R35. Down

the road between Second and Third Aves, the *Bass Line*, a fine jazz venue, has meals for around R15 or R25 for steaks. When there's music (six nights a week) there's an admission charge of R10. Other nearby places include the *San Francisco Coffee Roastery* at 9 7th St, open daily until late for coffee and snacks. There are more places to eat a few blocks away on Main Rd.

La Margaux (☎ (011) 788 5624), 3 Rivonia Rd, Illovo, is a Jo'burg institution. Much of the food is prepared at the table, but the menu varies from assorted pasta to seafood and steaks. It is a classy place, French with an Italian influence, and much loved by the local elite. They like pseudo-French ambience in the northern suburbs. *Le Chablis* (☎ (011) 884 1000), in the Sandown Centre, on the corner of Maud St and Rivonia Rd, Sandown, is a relaxed bistro with exceptional, imaginative food.

There's a branch of the legendary Cape Town Italian restaurant *San Marco* (☎ (011) 884 7597) on Village Walk, Sandton.

ENTERTAINMENT

The best guide to entertainment is in the *Weekly Mail & Guardian* (R2.50); you can't do without a copy.

For entertainment bookings contact Computicket (☎ (011) 331 9991), a computerised booking agency that has *every* seat for *every* theatre, cinema and sports venue on its system. You can be shown the available seats and get your ticket on the spot. They have branches all over the place, including in the Carlton Centre. You can make bookings over the phone, but you have to pay for your tickets with cash – there are no credit card debiting facilities yet. Since they have everything on their system they can also give advice about what's on. In addition to the entertainment sphere, they also accept classified advertising for major newspapers and bookings for various bus lines.

Bars & Other Hang-Outs

If your best outfit consists of a clean pair of jeans, the best place to wander is Yeoville where there are some late-night bars and music venues, most on Rockey St between Cavendish and Bezuidenhout. It all tends towards the grungy, but it's also the only area of town where you're likely to meet interesting people and hear non-mainstream music in a safe environment. Try the Ripley's Arms or Rockerfella's for more standard watering holes. Dylan's, the House of Tandoor (go upstairs to the roof garden) or the Lizard Lounge are where the less conservative citizens hang out. Other places come and go. On a hot evening the courtyard in the Time Square complex (on the corner of Fortesque Rd and Raleigh/Rockey St) is a good place for a quiet drink.

Hillbrow is a bit too exciting for late-night wandering these days, although with a knowledgeable local and a car or a taxi you should be OK. Just don't take anything you can't afford to lose. There are several relaxed bars in the Ambassador Hotel, 52 Pretoria St. In the slightly bizarre terminology of South Africa, the small ladies bar (upstairs) is the more up-market option, while the bar proper (ground floor, rear to the right) is the better alternative. There's also the Pink Cadillac with live music.

There's a surprising paucity of civilised bars in the city centre, although there are suitably flashy saloons in the big hotels. Some would dispute that 'civilised' was the appropriate word, but the Press Bar in the Elizabeth Hotel, on the corner of Pritchard and Sauer Sts opposite the *Star* newspaper offices, is a good spot to stop for refreshment in the city. Another possibility is Dawson's Hotel on the corner of President and Von Brandis.

The Yard of Ale (☎ (011) 836 6611) near the Market Theatre complex has a pleasant outdoor area, although it's closed on Sunday during the day and on Monday. It's most popular on Saturday afternoons and Sunday evenings. Kippies, in the complex, is a small but very popular jazz venue.

The Terrace at the Sunnyside Park Hotel is a very pleasant spot for a quiet afternoon soak, and it's popular at weekends. It's about a 30-minute walk from Yeoville.

The Radium Beer Hall, 282 Louis Botha Ave in Orange Grove, is one of the few neighbourhood pubs left in Jo'burg. It's the sort of pub that you might imagine would be ubiquitous in South Africa – masculine but civilised and dedicated to the thirst of workers. That isn't the case, though, and the Radium is almost unique. The bar counter dates from 1895, although the Radium is much younger than that, and the ceiling is of pressed metal. Bar meals cost less than R10 and there's plenty of choice. In the adjacent dining area, main courses are R20 to R30.

There are a couple of possibilities in Gold Reef City (☎ (011) 496 1600), including one pub that brews its own beer. After 5 pm it's free to enter the complex (the tourist attractions are closed). There are occasionally special events on weekends – they'll be promoted in the *Star*.

Music & Dancing

Kippies (☎ (011) 832 1641) at the Market Theatre complex is one of the best places to see South African jazz talent, which happens to be exceptional; it's closed on Monday. Another good place to see jazz and township music on weekends is the Get Ahead Shebeen (☎ (011) 442 5964) in Rosebank Mall, an unlikely venture which has successfully brought a shebeen (township bar) to one of the richest white suburbs in the country.

There's more good jazz at Mojo's (☎ (011) 483 1282), 206 Louis Botha Ave, Orange Grove. The nearby Radium Beer Hall (see the earlier Bars section) also sometimes has jazz. The Bass Line (☎ (011) 482 6915), on 7th St in Melville, has jazz nightly except Sunday. On Friday and Saturday the emphasis is on blues. The cover charge is R10. The venue is also a restaurant, with main courses from R15. A few blocks west on Main Rd, Melville, are some clean-cut clubs and bars catering mainly to a clean-cut young crowd. The Roxy Rhythm Bar in the Melville Hotel is the best known.

For a student crowd check out the Wings Beat Bar (☎ (011) 339 4492), 8 Ameshof St, Braamfontein. Entry is just R5 and the music is often live.

One of the best venues for interesting music and a mixed crowd is the House of Tandoor (☎ (011) 487 1569) at the east end of Rockey St, Yeoville. There's usually something on Wednesday and Saturday nights, with a cover charge of around R10 to R20, depending on who is playing. Acts range from local garage bands to big-name musicians from across Africa. Be warned that the venue is just a smoky barn with a concrete floor – pretty depressing unless there's a good crowd. If not, go upstairs to the rooftop bar. Elsewhere on Rockey St there are venues such as Dylan's, Rockerfella's and the Lizard Lounge, where the emphasis is more on drinking (and drinking) and dancing.

In nearby Hillbrow, Bella Napoli, 31 Pretoria St, sounds unlikely and looks unlikely. It is, however, a popular club with alternative music (of a fairly mainstream sort) downstairs and mainstream pop upstairs. Entry is around R10 but free on Thursday, which is students' night and probably the most interesting time to go.

In contrast, the disco in the Chelsea Hotel, Catherine St, Hillbrow, is extremely popular with a mainly black clientele. Entry is free. The Pub with No Name on the Hotel Park Lane, 54 Van der Merwe St, Hillbrow (on the corner of Catherine St), is a hot (as in temperature), crowded (largely black) and friendly bar with loud bands that cheerfully play requests (even *Happy Birthday*). Heed the warnings about Hillbrow-by-night scattered throughout this Jo'burg section.

Downtown there is a constantly changing batch of dance clubs. Weekends are the busiest times. Check the *Weekly Mail & Guardian* for current favourites. A club that has been around for a while is The Doors, 161 Marshall St, which has a young crowd, loud rock and pool tables. Gothic fans can check out Alcatraz at 180 Commissioner St, or Sanctuary on Main St. The Escape Club, on the corner of Claim and De Villiers Sts, is another downtown venue. Dawson's Hotel (☎ (011) 337 5788), 117 President St, on the corner of Von Brandis, has been a venue for years and features everything from jazz to performance poetry, acid house and funk. The Diplomat Hotel, on the corner of Klein and Bree Sts, also has a lively disco.

The Dungeon, on the corner of Marshall St and Goud (which becomes Gold), is a popular gay venue with an occasional cabaret.

Sport

There are some excellent spectator venues. Ellis Park in Doornfontein, just to the east of the city centre, is the headquarters of Transvaal Rugby Union, and the main stadium hosts everything from rugby to rock concerts. Rugby supporters are a fanatical breed, and Ellis Park can hold 100,000 of them – a Saturday afternoon at the football can be quite an experience. Ellis Park is also home to the South African Open Tennis Tournament.

The most important cricket venue is Wanderers, on Corlett Dr, Melrose North, just off the M1 freeway to Pretoria, one of the most beautiful cricket grounds in the world. The uninitiated will find the game fairly obscure, but if you go to a one-day game with someone who can explain the rules you'll certainly get plenty of entertainment. Believe it or not, test matches go for five days. A new first-class cricket ground has opened in Soweto, called Elkah Oval.

Kyalami, off the M1 between Jo'burg and Pretoria, is the venue for motor sports and the home of the South African Grand Prix, which is held in November.

There are a number of racetracks, but the best known is the attractive Turffontein, three km south of the city. There are race meetings virtually every week; buses leave from Vanderbijl Square.

The Rand Stadium, near Turffontein; and Soccer City, further east on Baragwanath Rd, are the major venues for soccer, which is the sport that most black South Africans follow passionately. The enormous new Soccer City holds 130,000 spectators. The most popular teams are the Orlando Pirates (known as Bucs) and the Kaiser Chiefs.

Theatres

The Market Theatre (☎ (011) 832 1641) complex is the most important venue for live theatre. The quality varies, of course, but a visit is highly recommended. There are other venues that are worth keeping your eye on, including the Windybrow Theatre Complex (☎ (011) 720 7009), on Nugget St, north of Smit between Joubert Park and Hillbrow, and the Alexander Theatre (☎ (011) 339 3461), on Stiemens St between Melle and De Beer, Braamfontein. The New Black Sun Theatre (☎ (011) 648 9709), on the corner of Rockey and Raymond Sts in Yeoville (above the Coffee Society café) is a new incarnation of a theatre institution which has been specialising in the alternative for years.

THINGS TO BUY

Jo'burg prides itself on its shops. The big shopping complexes are jammed with Western consumer goodies of every description – you have to pinch yourself to remember you're in Africa.

Shopaholics would do well to start in the Carlton Centre and Smal St Mall, but if you're a serious buyer make an expedition to Rosebank, which has an interlocking series of malls. (There's central parking on the corner of Cradock Ave and Baker.) Sandton and Randburg are large shopping centres, both a half-hour drive north of the city. Another handy shopping centre is the big Eastgate Mall, off the N12 just east of Bruma Lake. Most shops are open daily. Bus No 32 runs here from Eloff St and some minibus taxis running east on Rockey St, Yeoville, go to or near Eastgate.

Look & Listen, on Pretoria St, Hillbrow, just west of the corner of Claim St, has a very wide selection of music, with the emphasis on jazz, blues and African. One of the best sources of ethnic/African music is Kohinoor, with a number of branches including 11 Kort St, downtown (off Market St). Unfortunately they have a lot more vinyl and cassettes than CDs.

The ANC's Movement Trading Store in Shell House, 51 Plein St, has closed, but on the footpath outside you'll find a street stall selling everything from ANC T-shirts to tie pins.

If you wish to remind yourself that you're still in Africa, visit a muti shop. WK Indaba is at 14 Diagonal St, City, and on the corner of Koch and Twist St opposite the Art Gallery. Muti shops sell herbs and potions prescribed by a sangoma. Many problems, from broken hearts to headaches, are treated. Despite being dim, pungent caves of animal parts, muti shops are definitely businesses – the KwaZulu Muti on Kruis St offers a wholesale discount to Inyanyas.

The muti tradition, which has religious overtones, is regarded with great seriousness by most black South Africans. Don't demean the sangomas or yourself by treating it as a joke. Cynicism is fine, but have the decency to show respect. There are some who would argue that there are equally strange Western beliefs – like blind faith in 'science', or certain Christian rituals such as communion.

Crafts

There are a number of good shops where you can buy traditional carvings, beadwork, jewellery and fertility dolls, although prices in Jo'burg are high. Unfortunately, it's quite possible that you won't have a better opportunity to see and buy such a wide range of items.

Start at the Smal St Mall. The craft shop on the corner of President St has some excellent Ndebele beadwork at reasonable prices. They buy from the Operation Hunger craft project, so your purchases indirectly benefit worthwhile projects.

There are a number of street vendors who set up on the footpaths around town and sell crafts. There's some awful rubbish, but there's good stuff as well. Bargaining is expected. There are a couple of good stalls along Pretoria St in Hillbrow. In Yeoville, African Magic at the Bizarre Centre (behind Cracker's deli on Rockey St) has a fascinating, though pricey, collection. Across from Flea Market World, on Marcia St near Bruma Lake, there are plenty of craft sellers with a very wide range but lots of kitsch.

There's an unexpectedly good-value shop

GAUTENG

at Gold Reef City. Gold Reef City Arts & Crafts has a fine collection of interesting crafts and antiques from all over Africa, and they're well priced.

Camping

There are a number of specialist camping stores where you can buy all kinds of up-to-date equipment. The biggest group is the combined ME Stores and Camp & Climb chain. ME Stores have branches at the Kine Centre, 146 Market St, City, (☎ (011) 331 6811) and the Crossroads Shopping Centre, Hill St, Randburg (☎ (011) 789 1604). Camp & Climb (☎ (011) 403 1354) has a shop on the corner of Juta St and De Beer, Braamfontein and in the same area is Sanga Outdoor on Ameshof St (next to the Wings Beat Bar). Another good shop is Camping in Africa (☎ (011) 787 3524) on the Hill St Mall, Oak Ave, Randburg.

If you're looking for less specialised equipment – say aluminium chairs, gas cooking equipment, and cooking and eating utensils – you'll find the large chain-stores like Dion and OK Bazaar are the best value. Dion and OK Bazaar have stores around Jo'burg, including two monsters at Randburg. Check the phone book for the nearest branch.

Maps

The Map Office (☎ (011) 339 4951), on the 3rd floor of the Standard Bank Building on De Korte St, Braamfontein, sells government maps for R9 a sheet. Note that maps of the Drakensberg are available only from the KwaZulu/Natal Parks Board. The Map Office's postal address is Box 207, Wits 2050, Gauteng.

GETTING THERE & AWAY
Air

Jan Smuts Airport (☎ (011) 333 6504; 975 9963 for flight enquiries) is South Africa's major international and domestic airport. There are direct links with most African and European capitals, North America, Asia and Australia – see the previous Getting There & Away chapter. There are also air links with

major towns in Lesotho, Swaziland and throughout South Africa.

Distances in South Africa are large, so if you're in a hurry some domestic flights are definitely worth considering. There are flights to Cape Town, George, Port Elizabeth, East London, Durban, Kimberley and Upington; with smaller airlines reaching most places in the country. See the Getting Around South Africa chapter for fares.

Note that there are significant discounts for advance purchase, so if you're planning a trip to South Africa consult your travel agent early. Make sure that your agent knows about Phoenix, a new and inexpensive domestic airline.

Comair (☎ (011) 921 0222) charges R479 to Cape Town and R262 to Durban, with significant advance purchase discounts.

Sun Air (☎ (011) 970 1623, fax 970 1906) has flights to Sun City, daily except Saturday, for R171. There are also flights to/from Cape Town (R627) and Durban (R388).

Lesotho Airways flies at least daily between Moshoeshoe International Airport, 18 km from Maseru, and Johannesburg; a one-way ticket costs about R280. Royal Swazi Airlines flies between Manzini and Johannesburg daily; a one-way fare is about R290 – there are good deals on advance purchase return fares.

Numerous airlines have offices in the city, including:

Air Afrique
    196 Oxford Rd, Illovo (☎ (011) 880 8537)
Air France
    196 Oxford Rd, Illovo (☎ (011) 880 8040)
Air India
(☎ (011) 442 4421)
Air Mauritius
    701 Carlton Tower, Commissioner St (☎ (011) 331 1918)
Air Namibia
    (☎ (011) 442 4461)
Air Zimbabwe
    Carlton Centre, Commissioner St (☎ (011) 331 1541)
Balkan Bulgaria
    (011) 883 0957
British Airways
    158 Jan Smuts Ave, Rosebank (☎ (011) 331 0011)

Comair
  (☎ (011) 921 0222)
KLM
  1A Stan Rd, Morningside (☎ (011) 881 9600)
Luxavia
  (☎ (011) 331 3034)
Malaysian Airlines System (MAS)
  196 Oxford Rd, Illovo (☎ (011) 880 9614)
Qantas Airways
  3rd Floor, Village Walk, Sandton (☎ (011) 884 5300)
Royal Swazi Airlines
  2nd Floor, Finance House, Ernest Oppenheimer Dr, Bruma (☎ (011) 616 7323)
SAA
  14th Floor, Carlton Centre, Commissioner St (☎ (011) 333 6504)
Sun Air
  302 Administration Building, Jan Smuts Airport (☎ (011) 970 1623)
Thai Airways
  Norwich Life Towers, 13 Fredman Dr, Sandton (☎ (011) 883 9068)
Varig
  (☎ (011) 331 2471)

Bus

A number of international bus services leave Jo'burg for Lesotho, Botswana, Mozambique, Namibia, Swaziland and Zimbabwe. See the Getting There & Away chapter for more details.

The main long-distance bus lines (national and international) depart and arrive from the Rotunda, a short walk west of the Johannesburg railway station. There are booking counters and a Johannesburg Publicity Association information desk in the Rotunda. Transtate, the inexpensive government bus service, leaves from the railway station, not far from the Rotunda – walk through the underpass across the road from the Rotunda and turn right.

You can leave luggage at the Impala office at the Rotunda between 7 am and 7 pm for R2.

Some of the smaller lines that service Lesotho, Swaziland and the Homelands depart/arrive from the enormous minibus-taxi station at Baragwanath on the edge of Soweto. Numerous minibus taxis travel to and from the city (R3). Under normal circumstances this method of transport would

be safe, but we are talking Soweto, so check. If there is a taxi war in the offing its effects are likely to be more severe in Soweto than in the city.

The most comprehensive range of services are with the government-owned lines, Translux (☎ (011) 774 3313) and Transtate (☎ (011) 773 6002 from 7 to 10 am and 5 to 9 pm; otherwise try the head office, 774 7741). In general, Translux is a little cheaper than Greyhound (☎ (011) 333 2130/1/2/3), and Transtate is the cheapest of all. Another company with a wide coverage is Intercape (☎ (011) 333 52312).

The government's mid-price Trancity service has disappeared, replaced by City to City. There is no printed information on City to City and Translux counter staff don't mention it unless you specifically ask.

To Sun City Sun City Buses (bookings through Computicket; ☎ (011) 331 9991) has daily buses from the Rotunda: 9 and 11.45 am and 3 pm Monday to Thursday; 9 and 11 am, and 5 pm on Friday; 9 and 11.45 am and 2 pm on Saturday; and 9 and 11.45 am on Sunday. The return fare is R45, which includes a few freebies, or R65 with entry to the Valley of the Waves.

To Kruger National Park The nearest large town to Kruger is Nelspruit, and Greyhound runs there daily for R99, taking five hours.

Transtate has some slow but cheap services from Jo'burg to Nelspruit (R45, 7 hours) that continue on to the hamlet of Hazyview (R55, 8 hours), which is much closer to Kruger than Nelspruit and has a couple of backpacker hostels. There are daytime services on weekdays, plus a Friday night run that arrives in Hazyview at 3 am.

City to City (a Translux subsidiary) runs north to Phalaborwa on Tuesday, Thursday and Sunday for R85. The trip takes about 7½ hours. LT Tours also runs buses between Jo'burg and Phalaborwa (R107). Fares (from Jo'burg/Phalaborwa) are Pretoria (R11/96), Naboomspruit (R40/64), Potgietersrus (R50/54), Pietersburg (R59/43), Tzaneen (R85/22) and Louis Trichardt (R85/22). Kruger's

Phalaborwa Gate is much further from Jo'burg than some of the others, but you might want to enter the park in the north and work your way down. You can hire cars in Phalaborwa.

To Durban Translux has at least one daily bus to Durban for R120. Greyhound has four buses a day between Jo'burg and Durban for R130. The trip takes seven hours. Several Transtate services stop in Pietermaritzburg, handy for Durban, on the daily run to Umtata. This is cheap but slow.

Several small companies, such as Golden Wheels (☎ (011) 852 1423) and Roadshow Intercity (☎ (082) 449 9037), run to Durban. You'll pay considerably less for these buses.

Routes to Cape Town Translux has at least one bus each day running from Pretoria/Jo'burg to Cape Town via Bloemfontein (16½ hours to Cape Town). Also, two services (Sunday and Friday) run via Kimberley (17½ hours to Cape Town). From Jo'burg the fare on either service is R280. From Jo'burg to Bloemfontein costs R130, to Kimberley it's R140.

Greyhound has buses to Cape Town via Bloemfontein (daily except Monday) or Kimberley (Monday), for R295. From Jo'burg to Bloemfontein or Kimberley costs R145 – but note that Greyhound also has a daily express bus to Kimberley for just R72.

Intercape has four services a week to Cape Town via Upington, for R270. You might have to change buses in Upington but it is usually a direct connection; if so from Jo'burg to Cape Town takes about 19 hours. From Jo'burg to Upington costs R140. From Upington you can also get an Intercape bus to Windhoek (Namibia), but there isn't a direct connection. Still, Upington isn't a bad place to spend the night.

Routes to the South Coast Translux runs a service from Pretoria/Jo'burg to East London, via Bloemfontein daily except Thursday and Friday. The fare is R200 and the trip takes 12 hours.

Translux also has a twice weekly (Sunday and Tuesday) services from Pretoria/Jo'burg to Port Elizabeth via Bloemfontein and Middelburg. The fare is R220 and the trip takes 11 hours. There might also be a service via Graaff Reinet. Greyhound has overnight buses from Jo'burg to Port Elizabeth for R235.

Translux runs to Knysna (R210) via Kimberley (Sunday and Thursday) or Bloemfontein (Monday, Tuesday, Wednesday and Friday) then Oudtshoorn (R210), Mossel Bay (R210) and George (R210). The trip takes 17 hours.

Garden Line Transport (☎ (0441) 74 2823) has buses between Jo'burg and Mossel Bay (R160) via Bloemfontein (R120), Colesberg (R135), Oudtshoorn (R155) and George (R155). The journey takes 15½ hours. They also have a service via Kimberley (R125).

City to City (a Translux subsidiary) runs to Umtata, the closest large town to Port St Johns, on Tuesday and Friday at 7 pm, for R100. Transtate runs to Umtata at least once daily. The fare is R80.

Routes North Several services run north up the N1. For example, Translux has at least one bus each day to Beitbridge (and on to Harare) via Pietersburg (R75), Louis Trichardt (R85) and Messina (R100). Various Transtate services winding north through townships and ex-Homelands also stop in the major towns on the N1. LT Tours has buses running north as far as Louis Trichardt.

Travelling between Jo'burg and Pretoria is much cheaper and easier by train.

Routes West City Link (☎ (011) 333 4412) runs twice daily to Mafikeng/Mmabatho from the Rotunda for R50. Transtate has a variety of useful services, to Rustenburg daily (R20), and another to Mafikeng (R40). Greyhound passes through Rustenburg and Zeerust on its Jo'burg to Gaborone (Botswana) service on Thursday, Friday and Sunday; returning Monday, Friday and Saturday.

Intercape runs to Cape Town and Windhoek

(Namibia) via Upington – see the Upington section in the Northern Cape chapter for details.

Train

Overseas visitors are no longer eligible for a 25% discount, but there has been a long-running special whereby *everyone* is entitled to a 25% discount on train fares, so ask if this is still available. If it is, 1st-class fares are very competitive with Translux and Greyhound buses. If not, 2nd-class fares are less than bus fares. Third class on the train is generally cheaper than Transtate (the cheapest buses). For more information contact Spoornet (☎ (011) 773 5878 for information, 773 2944 for reservations, 773 5879 for 3rd class).

On the main concourse at Jo'burg station there's a Spoornet Information Office, but it doesn't really have any information (god knows why the office is there); go to the Mainline ticket office further along. You can make bookings here between 7.30 am and 5 pm on weekdays and until 1 pm on Saturday.

The station's left-luggage department is open daily from 6 am to 7 pm (7 am to 6 pm on Sunday). There's a R1.55 per day charge for each piece of luggage.

Blue Train to Cape Town The *Blue Train* (☎ (011) 774 4469) is an extremely luxurious train between Cape Town and Jo'burg. It has individual suites and compartments of varying degrees of comfort and expense. There are departures on Monday, Wednesday and Friday, but it is essential to book in advance. The train leaves Pretoria at 8.50 am and Jo'burg at 10.10 am, and arrives in Cape Town at noon the next day. Northbound, it leaves Cape Town at 11 am. Luxury suites are R6300 for one or two people; compartments cost between R1825 and R2530 per person.

It's possible to get a brief taste of this luxury (from R105) on the section between Jo'burg and Pretoria (where it originates/terminates). However, if you plan to be in Cape Town at some stage you'd be better-off taking a longer short journey on the *Blue Train* from there – see the Cape Town section for more information.

Trans Karoo to Cape Town The *Trans Karoo* runs daily to Cape Town via Kimberley, De Aar, Beaufort West, Matjiesfontein, Worcester and Wellington. The southbound train leaves Jo'burg at 12.30 pm and arrives in Cape Town 25¾ hours later at 2.15 pm. The northbound train leaves Cape Town at 9.20 am and arrives in Jo'burg at 10.15 am. First/2nd/3rd-class tickets are R326/R220/137. Although it takes an extra eight hours, it is definitely worth considering taking the train rather than the bus.

Trans Natal to Durban The *Trans Natal* runs every night between Jo'burg and Durban. The train leaves Jo'burg at 6.30 pm and arrives in Durban at 8 am. First/2nd/3rd-class tickets are R164/108/67. The train fares are competitive, but the buses run during the day and only take about seven hours.

Amatola to East London The *Amatola* runs daily except Saturday between Jo'burg and East London via Bloemfontein. The train leaves Jo'burg at 12.45 pm and gets to East London at 8.30 am the next morning. First/2nd/3rd-class tickets are R215/149/96.

Algoa to Port Elizabeth The *Algoa* operates between Jo'burg and Port Elizabeth via Bloemfontein on Sunday, Tuesday and Thursday. The southbound train departs from Jo'burg at 2.30 pm and arrives in PE at 9.25 am the next day. First/2nd/3rd-class tickets are R240/162/101.

Komati to Nelspruit & Komatipoort The *Komati* operates eastwards to Komatipoort, on the border with Mozambique, via Nelspruit, which is a jumping-off point for the Kruger National Park. It's a daily service (on Monday, Wednesday and Friday it continues on to Maputo, capital of Mozambique). The train leaves Jo'burg at 5.45 pm, arrives in Nelspruit at 3.30 am the next day and in Komatipoort at 6 am. First/2nd/

GAUTENG

3rd-class tickets from Jo'burg to Nelspruit are R99/85/48.

Minibus Taxi

The main long-distance taxi ranks are between the railway station and Joubert Park, mainly on Wanderers and King George Sts. There are set areas for taxis to particular destinations, but you'll probably do a lot of walking around to find the one you're looking for. Despite the apparent chaos, the ranks are well-organised. Ask for the queue marshal. You'll find taxis for the Kimberley and Upington direction on Wanderers St near Leyds St.

Because of the risk of mugging it isn't a good idea to go searching for a taxi while carrying your luggage. Go down and collect information then return in a taxi with your luggage.

Some examples of destinations and fares from Jo'burg are Cape Town R150, Kimberley R80, Louis Trichardt R55, Nelspruit R45, Pietersburg R50, Pretoria R10 and Upington R95.

For information about taxis to Beitbridge (the Zimbabwe border) try phoning the Jo'burg Taxi Association (☎ (011) 29 1989).

As well as these taxis, which leave when they are full, there are a few door-to-door services which you can book. Durban is well served by these. Rollercoaster (book through hostels) charges R60, as does Mohamed's (☎ (011) 855 8876). There's apparently a Sunday-only door-to-door taxi to Cape Town for R150 (16 hours) but no one seemed to have the number. Ask around the hostels or try SABTA (South African Black Taxi Association) (☎ (011) 484 6735).

Car

Rental All the major rental operators have counters at Jan Smuts Airport and at various locations around the city. Operators include Avis (☎ 0800 021 111 toll free); Budget (☎ 0800 016 622 toll free); Imperial (☎ 0800 010 344 toll free); Dolphine (Eurocar) (☎ (011) 394 6605); and U-Drive at 162 Fox (on the corner of Delvers), City (☎ (011) 331 3735).

There aren't many budget alternatives, and the few that do exist are not very conveniently located (although many will deliver). Try Alisa (☎ (011) 394 4610) or ask around the hostels. If you're interested in a campervan, Campers' Corner Car Hire (☎ (011) 789 2327), 357 Jan Smuts Ave, Craighall, has been recommended.

Purchase Jo'burg is the best place in South Africa to buy a car, although since this process is inevitably time-consuming it might be preferable to buy or sell in Cape Town, which is a rather more congenial place to waste a week or two. Prices are often higher in Cape Town, so it's a good place to sell.

Jules St, a 30-minute walk east of the city centre, is the main drag for used-car dealers. It's a jungle out there! The yards are open weekdays from 9 am to 5 pm and to noon on Saturday. There can be no guarantees with cheap, old cars, but Dominic and David at ZZ Cars (☎ (011) 614 9581), 200 Jules St, won't rip you off – unfortunately they don't deal in rock-bottom cars.

We haven't heard of any Jo'burg dealers offering a buy-back deal but you'd probably find one willing to consider it. The problem would be making the deal stick when the time came to sell.

Dealers have to make a profit, so you'll pay much less if you buy privately. The *Star* has ads every day and a motoring supplement on Thursday; look for the 'Under R6000 Bargains' section. One ray of hope in this rock-bottom price range is the number of VWs, which don't seem to hold their resale value as much here as in other countries.

The Sunday Car Market (☎ (011) 643 1183), at the Top Star Drive-in, Simmonds Southway, Park Central, Johannesburg, operates every Sunday from 9 am to 1 pm. It's best to arrive early. There are usually around 200 cars to choose from, and caravans and motorcycles are also sold. Buyers pay no commission or entrance fees, and change of ownership forms and advice about

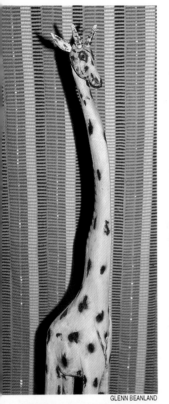

GLENN BEANLAND

GLENN BEANLAND

JEFF WILLIAMS

JEFF WILLIAMS

A	B
	C
D	

A: Giraffe woodcarving, southern Africa
B: Basket crafted from telephone wire, Soweto, Gauteng
C: Venda pottery, Thohoyandu, Northern Transvaal
D: African handicrafts, Transvaal Drakensberg, Eastern Transvaal

RICHARD EVERIST

RICHARD EVERIST

RICHARD EVERIST

RICHARD EVERIST

A	B
	C
D	

A: Lanner falcon *(Falco biarmicus)*
B: Juvenile redbilled hornbill *(Tockus erythrorhynchus)*
C: Lilacbreasted roller *(Coracias caudata)*
D: Cape Gannet rookery, Lamberts Bay, Western Cape Province

roadworthies and registering are available. Sellers pay a once-only fee of R40.

Unfortunately, there seem to be very few decent-quality used cars at low prices. You will be lucky to find a decent vehicle for much less than R10,000. You might be able to find something like an '83 Passat wagon for about R6000. Of course, if nothing serious goes wrong, you will hopefully get most of your money back when you sell. In the meantime, however, you'll have a lot of money tied up.

Whoever you're buying from, make sure that the details correspond accurately with the ownership papers. Check the owner's name against their identity document and the engine and chassis numbers. Consider getting the car tested by the AA (Automobile Association); see the address at the end of this entry. A full test can cost up to R300; less comprehensive tests start around R80.

Cheap cars will often be sold without a roadworthy certificate. A roadworthy is required when you register the change of ownership and pay tax. The testers are fussy, so the certificates can be both difficult and expensive to get. There are various roadworthy centres, check the phone book. A test costs R50. Once you have your roadworthy, take it, the ownership papers signed by the seller, your passport, and around R70 (for the 12-months Gauteng road tax) to the Licensing Department (☎ (011) 836 1951), 79 Loveday St, City. In an amazingly short time (well, a couple of hours) you'll receive new ownership papers and a tax disk to fix inside your windscreen.

Insurance, for third-party damages and damage to or loss of your vehicle, is a very good idea. It's easy enough to take out a year's insurance but most travellers don't want that much. Unfortunately, if you want to buy insurance by the month it is surprisingly difficult to find an insurance company to take your money if you don't have a permanent address and/or a local bank account. If this concerns you, start shopping around early so you can figure out a way to meet their conditions – before you get the car.

It might be possible to take out a year's insurance on the understanding that you'll get a rebate for the unused months when you sell the car, but you'd be wise to get this in writing. We would be interested to hear of any companies that are helpful to travellers.

Although they definitely do need to deduct premiums from a local bank account, Auto & General (☎ (011) 489 4444) is one of the cheaper companies. As an example of their rates (and of how the insurance industry thinks): a 29-year-old male clerk with a 10-year insurance record and no claims could insure a 1985 Opel Kadett wagon against fire, theft and third-party property damage for R80 per month.

Membership of the South African Automobile Association (the AA) is highly recommended. They have a very efficient breakdown service and a good supply of maps and information. They can be very helpful when you are planning your route around the country. Joining costs R45 (waived for members of many foreign motoring associations – bring your membership details) plus R174 per year. You might be able to arrange a three-month membership. The main office (☎ (011) 407 1000) is in Braamfontein, on De Korte St, between De Beer and Louis Botha Ave. There's a useful office in the Eastgate Mall shopping centre.

From time to time unclaimed stolen cars are auctioned by the police in Soweto. There's a huge compound crammed full of cars, mostly stripped but some not otherwise damaged. Many are Mercs and BMWs. They're cheap but you'd need skills and access to a workshop to fix up one of these cars – if you're a car freak this might present an interesting challenge.

Hitching

Heading north, a popular place to begin hitching is on the N1 near the Killarney Mall shopping centre, a couple of km north-west of Yeoville. The N12 running east towards Kruger begins just east of Eastgate Mall, accessible by bus from Yeoville. Heading south on the N1 (to Cape Town, for example) you could try your luck on one of the freeway on-ramps.

Dial-a-lift (☎ (011) 648 8136) seems to offer an alternative to sticking your thumb out, but they didn't answer the phone during the days I tried to call them, and I don't have any more information.

John Hayes continually drives between Jo'burg and Durban delivering cars (not necessarily shiny new models) and can often give free lifts to backpackers. The idea is that you help drive, but that's not always necessary. The trip can take a very long time as there is a certain amount of backtracking.

GETTING AROUND
To/From the Airport
Between 6 am and 11 pm, buses run every half-hour (a quarter to and a quarter past the hour) between Jan Smuts Airport and the Rotunda, just to the east of Johannesburg railway station. Journey time is about 25 minutes and the fare is R25. There's also the Magic bus which costs R40 but drops off at the more expensive hotels. For hotels in Sandton, take the Sandton Shuttle (R40). Taxis are expensive (around R85) and unnecessary.

Some hostels will collect you from the airport, and one or two tout there. We have heard of hostel touts poaching guests.

Buses also run from the airport to Pretoria. The hour-long journey also costs R25.

Bus
For enquiries about bus services phone (011) 838 2125), or visit the information counter on Vanderbijl Square (the main municipal bus station, two blocks west of the Carlton Hotel).

The current fare scheme (these things change) is that any ticket costs R2 or R3 during the evening rush, from 4 pm until 5.30 or so. There aren't many buses running much later than this.

Routes 19 (Berea), 19a (Yeoville) and 20 (Yeoville) are useful. Starting at Vanderbijl Square, they run north up Eloff St (stopping on the corner of Pritchard St) and Edith Cavell to Hillbrow, east along Pretoria, north along Harrow, then east along Raleigh to Hunter Sts, and then turn back along Rockey

St. They're frequent from 6.45 am to 8.40 am, hourly in the middle of the day, then frequent from 4 pm to 7 pm, when they stop.

The buses that run out to Sandton are not part of the municipal fleet; they're operated by Padco (☎ (011) 474 2634). They leave the city centre from the corner of Kruis and Commissioner. The buses run at least hourly from about 6.30 am to 5.15 pm, more frequently at peak times. The fare to Sandton is R3.50.

Minibus Taxi
Fares differ with routes, but R1.50 will get you around the inner suburbs and the city centre. It's easy enough to get a minibus taxi into the city centre and, if you're waiting at a bus stop, the chances are that a taxi will arrive before the bus does. Getting a minibus taxi home from the city is a more difficult proposition. Even locals often give up and take the bus. Heading for Hillbrow or Yeoville, try Eloff St.

There is a complex system of hand and finger signals to tell a passing taxi where you want to go (and the driver will stop if he is going the same way) but just raising your index finger in the air will stop most taxis.

Taxi
There are taxi ranks outside the Carlton and Johannesburg Holiday Inn hotels in the city centre, at the Jan Smuts Airport, and outside the Hilton Plaza Hotel on Quartz St, Hillbrow. All taxis operate meters which, unfortunately, seem to vary markedly in their assessment. Good Hope Taxis (☎ (011) 725 6431) seem to be cheaper than some other companies; taxis from the Yeoville rank seem more expensive. From the Rotunda to Berea should cost between R10 and R15. Once you get an idea of how much a trip should cost you might try agreeing on a price rather than using the meter.

Train
For enquiries about trains phone ☎ (011) 773 5878, or visit the helpful information office at the northern end of the railway station concourse (opposite the old steam train).

There was a very serious problem with violent crime on the metropolitan system, mostly on those lines connecting with black townships, so ask the safety question before jumping on. Most whites use buses, and most blacks use buses and minibus taxis. A 1st-class rail ticket costs R2.80.

Pretoria

Pretoria, South Africa's administrative capital, is a bland Western city, superficially a bit like a northern Jo'burg suburb. After all, it's only 56 km away and suburban sprawl is advancing across the shrinking green belt that separates the two. In some ways this is Paul Kruger's worst nightmare come true. Despite all the bitter struggles, all the wars and all the statutes, the uitlanders are finally engulfing the old capital of the first Zuid-Afrikaansche Republic (ZAR, or South African Republic).

Nonetheless, Pretoria's history bears no relation to Jo'burg's – although their destinies have naturally been linked – and this has created cities with very different atmospheres. For a start, Pretoria is an uncompromisingly Boer city, owing its existence and growth to the twin Boer dreams of independence from the British and domination of the blacks.

Today, as the administrative capital of South Africa, it is home to embassies, military and civilian bureaucracies, military bases and educational institutions. Although it has a population of at least a million (roughly half white, half black) it seems more like a large country town, increasingly irrelevant to the new South Africa, which is centred on tumultuous Jo'burg. Most blacks living here are Sotho people, about 60% of the whites are Afrikaners. There are several sites that are central to the Afrikaners' semi-mystical folk history – they are, for some, virtually holy ground.

Pretoria is quite an attractive city, especially during October and November when the city is dominated by tens of thousands of flowering jacarandas. There are still a few old houses, incongruous not just for their size when compared to the neighbouring ranks of apartment blocks, but for their lack of high walls and razor wire. This is a *much* more relaxed place than Jo'burg.

Most foreigners visit for one of three reasons: to join battle with diplomats and bureaucrats; to search for signposts to the real history of the Boers; or to spend some slow but pleasant days while waiting for a flight or a visa in a city much less edgy than Jo'burg. Jo'burg is only 60 km of freeway away, so if you *want* to stay there it's quite possible to cover most of Pretoria's sights in a day trip, especially if you have a car.

HISTORY

The area around the Apies River was well watered and fertile, so it supported a large population of cattle farmers for hundreds of years. These were Nguni-speaking people (from the same offshoot as the Zulus and Swazis) who came to be known as the Ndebele by the Sotho people of the Transvaal, and as the Matabele to the Europeans. The disruption caused by the Zulu wars, however, resulted in massive dislocation and the Boers trekked into a temporary vacuum.

The Great Trek reached its logical conclusion in the early 1850s when the British granted independence to the ZAR, north of the Vaal River, and to the Orange Free State, between the Orange and Vaal rivers.

At this stage there were estimated to be 15,000 whites and 100,000 blacks between the Vaal and Limpopo rivers. The whites were widely scattered, and a central capital was needed. In 1853, two farms on the Apies River were bought as the site for republic's capital. The ZAR was a shaky institution. There were ongoing wars with the black tribes, and violent disputes among the Boers themselves. Pretoria, which was named after Andries Pretorius, hero of the Battle of Blood River, was the scene of fighting during the 1863-69 Boer Civil War.

There was scarcely any money in the government's coffers, and consequently there was very little material development.

GAUTENG

Pretoria was nothing more than a tiny frontier village with a grandiose title. Despite this, the servants of the British Empire watched it with growing misgivings. They acted in 1877, annexing the republic. The Boers went to war – Pretoria came under siege at the beginning of 1881 – and won back their independence. Paul Kruger, a renowned general and politician, was elected President in 1883.

The discovery of gold on the Witwatersrand in the late 1880s revolutionised the situation. A small community of farmers suddenly controlled some of the richest real estate in the world. For hardliners like Kruger, however, the advantage of an overflowing treasury were almost outweighed by the flood of English-speaking uitlanders who threatened the Boers' hard-won independence.

Kruger's misgivings were soundly based, and in 1899 the Boer Republics were once again at war with the British. Pretoria was abandoned by Kruger and the Boer forces in June 1900, but the war ground on until 31 May 1902 when the Peace of Vereeniging was signed at Melrose House.

After the war, a fabulous new source of wealth was found on Pretoria's doorstep. One of the biggest and most productive diamond-bearing kimberlite pipes in the world was discovered 40 km east at Cullinan. It has produced three of the largest diamonds ever found. The largest, the Cullinan, as it was called, was 11 by six cm in rough form and was presented to King Edward VII.

After the war, the British made some efforts towards reconciliation. Self-government was again granted to the Transvaal in 1906 and moves towards the union of the separate South African provinces were instituted.

The thorny issue of which city should be the capital was solved by the unwieldy compromise of making Pretoria the administrative capital, Cape Town the seat of the legislature, and Bloemfontein the seat of the Appellate Division of the Supreme Court. The Union of South Africa came into being in 1910, but Pretoria was not to regain its republican status again until May 1961, when the Republic of South Africa came into existence under the leadership of Dr Verwoerd.

ORIENTATION

If you arrive by car you'll encounter the usual nightmare of one-way streets and poor signage but once you're on foot the city centre is easy to get around.

The main east-west through-road is Church (Kerk) St which, at 26 km, is claimed to be one of the longest straight streets in the world. Fortunately the city centre, most of the sights, decent hotels and restaurants are not so far apart. Church St runs through Church Square (although traffic is diverted), the historic centre of the city, and east to Arcadia, home of most of the hotels and embassies, and the Union Buildings. The main nightlife zone (a very pale imitation of Yeoville) is in Sunnyside.

Landmarks include the Union Buildings, that neo-colonial edifice on the hill to the north-east of the centre, and the futuristic Volkskas Bank which towers over the corner of Van de Walt and Pretorius Sts. It's about the only modern building that doesn't look like a civil-service office block.

INFORMATION
Tourist Offices

The Tourist Rendezvous Centre is on Prinsloo St between Church and Vermeulen Sts, in the big Sammy Marks Centre. It is open from 7.30 am to 7 pm on weekdays, slightly shorter hours on weekends. It's an excellent source of all sorts of information. Here you'll find the Pretoria information centre (☎ (012) 323 1222, 313 7694), a Satour desk (☎ (012) 323 1432), a National Parks Board desk (☎ (012) 323 0930), a travel agent, a bar and a coffee lounge. The staff at the information centre are very helpful and have a wide range of brochures. If only Jo'burg had a centre like this!

The *Be My Guest* monthly magazine is widely available and is worth browsing through, particularly for restaurant recommendations.

National Parks Board

The National Parks Board has an office in the Tourist Rendezvous Centre and you can book accommodation in parks here. The head office (☎ (012) 343 0930, fax 343 0905) at 643 Leyds St, Muckleneuk, is not far from the university to the south-east of the city centre. The postal address is PO Box 787, Pretoria 0001.

Money

Most commercial banks are open from 9 am to 3.30 pm weekdays and from 9 to 11 am on Saturday; all exchange foreign currency.

American Express (☎ (012) 322 2620) is in the Tramshed, a shopping complex in a recycled building on the corner of Van der Walt and Schoeman Sts. There's also a Nedbank branch here. Rennies Travel (☎ (012) 325 3800) has several branches, including one in the Sanlam Centre, on the corner of Andries and Pretorius Sts.

Post & Telecommunications

The GPO is on the corner of Pretorius and Van der Walt Sts, and is open weekdays from 8.30 am to 4.30 pm, Saturday from 8 am to noon.

Visa Extensions

Applications for visa extensions should be made to the Department of Home Affairs (☎ (012) 324 1860), Sentrakor Building, Pretorius St.

Foreign Embassies

Many countries have diplomatic representation in Jo'burg and Cape Town, but some countries, including Mozambique and Zimbabwe, only have trade missions in Jo'burg. Check the Foreign Consulates sections of this book for both those cities before you make a special trek to Pretoria. Mekwa Travel, in Fraser's Building, 520 Paul Kruger St, near the station, will arrange Zimbabwean visas (not required by citizens of Commonwealth countries, the EU or USA).

The Lesotho Embassy (☎ (012) 322 6090), the only place in South Africa where you can get visas to Lesotho, is on the 6th floor, West Tower, Momentum Centre, 343 Pretorius St. It is open from 9 am to noon on weekdays for visa applications. You'll need two passport photos and R20 for a one-month visa. They take 24 hours to issue.

The addresses for embassies not listed here are available from the Visitors' Information Bureau (☎ (012) 313 7694). Ring ahead to check opening hours.

Australia
    4th Floor, Mutual & Federal Centre, 220 Vermeulen St (☎ (012) 325 4315)
Canada
    5th Floor, Nedbank Plaza, corner of Church and Beatrix Sts, Arcadia (☎ (012) 324 3970)
France
    807 George Ave, Arcadia (☎ (012) 43 5564)
Germany
    180 Blackwood St, Arcadia (☎ (012) 344 3854)
Israel
    Dashing Centre, 339 Hilda St, Hatfield (☎ (012) 421 2222)
Netherlands
    825 Arcadia St, Arcadia (☎ (012) 344 3910)
Spain
    169 Pine St, Arcadia (☎ (012) 344 3875)
Sweden
    9th Floor, Old Mutual Centre, 167 Andries St (☎ (012) 21 1050)
Switzerland
    353 Berea St, Muckleneuk (☎ (012) 344 0034)
UK
    Greystoke, 225 Hill St, Arcadia (☎ (012) 43 3121)
USA
    7th Floor, Thibault House, 225 Pretorius St (☎ (012) 28 4266)

Travel Agencies

There's a travel agency in the Tourist Rendezvous Centre. See also Rennies Travel in the preceding Money section.

Medical Services

The HF Verwoerd Hospital (☎ (012) 329 1111) is just to the east of the Union Buildings on Belvedere. There are numerous chemists. The pharmacy on the north-west corner of Esselen and Collings Sts stays open until 10 pm.

Emergency

For the police call 10111, fire brigade (012)

GAUTENG

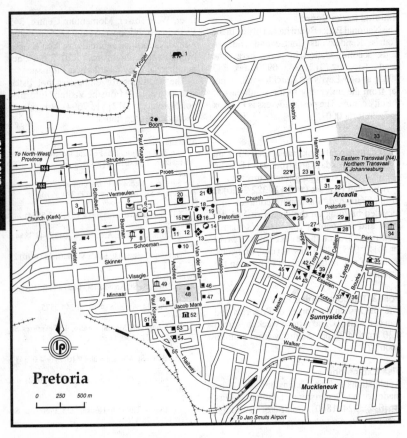

Pretoria

0   250   500 m

To Jan Smuts Airport

323 2781 and ambulance (012) 326 0111.
There's a Life Line service (☎ (012) 343
8888).

Dangers & Annoyances
Pretoria is much safer and more relaxed than
Jo'burg, but it's a big city so reasonable
precautions should be observed. The area
between the zoo and Church St isn't always
safe.

Other Information
There's a member of the ME chain of

outdoor shops on Schoeman between
Andries and Van der Walt Sts.

You can contact the National Hiking Way
Board on (☎ (012) 310 3839)

CHURCH SQUARE
Church Square, the heart of Pretoria, is surrounded by imposing public buildings,
including the Reserve Bank and Palace of
Justice (on the north side). In the centre, the
Old Lion, Paul Kruger, looks disapprovingly
at office workers lounging on the grass. In
the early days, Boers from the surrounding
countryside would gather in the square every

PLACES TO STAY		24	La Gondola	8	Department of Home Affairs
4	Formule 1	25	Digger's Grill	10	ME Outdoor Shop
12	Protea Hof Hotel	36	Fillings	11	Sanlam Centre
23	Orange Court Lodge	37	Eric's Upstairs		(Rennies Travel)
28	Malvern House	39	Dramant Cafe	13	Tramshed (Amex)
29	Hotel 224	40	Grapevine	14	Lesotho Embassy
30	Holiday Inn		Confectionery	15	GPO
31	YWCA	41	La Fragiola	16	Volkskas Bank
32	Parkview Hotel	42	Shunters	17	J G Strijdom Square
35	Pretoria Backpackers	43	Bimbos	19	State Theatre
46	Burgerspark Hotel	44	Giovanni's & London Tavern	20	Mosque
47	YMCA	45	Something Fishy	21	Tourist Rendezvous Centre
50	Park Lodge Hotel			26	Sterland Cinemas
51	Victoria Hotel	**OTHER**		27	19th Hole
53	Karos Manhattan Hotel	1	Zoo	33	Union Buildings
54	Belgrave Hotel	2	Old National Cultural History Museum	34	Pretoria Art Museum
		3	Paul Kruger House	38	Pharmacy
PLACES TO EAT		5	Post Office	48	Burgers Park
		6	Church Square	49	Transvaal Museum of Natural History
9	Coffee Nest	7	South African Police Museum	52	Melrose House
18	Buffet de l'Opera			55	Railway Station
22	Caponero Restaurant				

GAUTENG

three months for *achtmaals* (communion). They would come in their ox-wagons which would outspan (unyoke) in the square.

HEROES' ACRE

This cemetery, 1.5 km west of Church Square on Church St, is the burial place for a number of historical figures, including Andries Pretorius, the hero of Blood River, Paul Kruger, President of the first Zuid-Afrikaansche Republic; and Dr Hendrik Verwoerd, the prime minister from 1958 to 1967 (when he was assassinated). Take a West Park No 2 or Danville bus from Church Square.

J G STRIJDOM SQUARE

A striking example of neo-fascist architecture, the square is dominated by a huge head – that of J G Strijdom – and a group of charging horses on a column (apparently an archetypal heroic and martial image). Ironically, J G Strijdom, the prime minister from 1954 to 1958 and one of the architects of apartheid, now looks over the black street vendors who have set up on the edge of the square. They must get right up his nose.

MOSQUE

A reminder of the cultural diversity of South Africa, the mosque is a peaceful retreat. Entry is from the arcade off Queen St, between Vermeulen and Church Sts. Remove your shoes before entering.

UNION BUILDINGS

The Union Buildings are an impressive red sandstone construction – with a self-conscious imperial grandeur – surrounded by an expanse of gardens. They are the government's headquarters, the South African equivalent of the Kremlin. The architect was Sir Herbert Baker, who is responsible for many of the best public buildings built in the years immediately after the Union of South Africa was formed. Sir Herbert went on to work with Sir Edward Lutyens on the legislative buildings in New Delhi.

The buildings are quite a long walk from the city centre, or you catch just about any bus heading east on Church St and walk up through the gardens from Church St.

MUSEUMS

In addition to museums covered here there are a few others, such as the Correctional

Services Museum (☎ (012) 314 1766), Claude Malan Museum (☎ (012) 322 0544) of antiques, and the hands-on Science & Technology Museum. The Tourist Rendezvous has brochures. See the following Around Pretoria section for some museums a short way out of town, including the must-see Voortrekker Monument.

Two museums under construction promise to be very interesting. The **National Cultural History Museum** (opening in 1996) being built on Visagie St will concentrate on the archaeological and anthropological records of southern Africa. **Tswaing Eco Museum**, 40 km north-west of Pretoria, is in a huge meteorite crater and is a cross between a nature reserve and a museum. It's currently open to groups and will be open to individuals. The Tourist Rendezvous has details.

Paul Kruger House

A short walk west from Church Square, on Church St, the residence of Paul Kruger has been turned into a museum. Some of the rooms have been restored to their original form, and others chronicle his extraordinary life and times. It's interesting bu', partly because of its setting right on a busy street, it's curiously difficult to get a feeling for the man (unlike at Doornkloof, Smuts' house), despite the fact that he was undoubtedly an extraordinary human being.

There are clues. The house is unpretentious, although there would have been few grander homes in 1883 when it was built. Amongst all sorts of bric-a-brac there's the knife that Kruger used to amputate his thumb after a shooting accident (the thumb isn't on display). Legend has it that he would sit on the front porch and chat with passers-by. The

Dutch Reformed Church where he worshipped and preached is across the road.

The house is open from 8.30 am to 4 pm Monday to Saturday and from 11 am to 4 pm on Sunday. Admission is R3.

Melrose House

Melrose House (☎ (012) 322 2805), 275 Jacob Maré St, opposite Burgers Park, is a neo-Baroque mansion that was built in 1886 for George Heys in a somewhat fanciful cross between English Victorian and Cape Dutch styles.

During the 1899-1902 Anglo-Boer War (sometimes known as the Second War of Independence) both Lord Robe 's and Lord Kitchener (the British commanders) lived here. On 31 May 1902 the Treaty of Vereeniging that ended the war was signed in the dining room. The house has been restored and has an excellent collection of period furniture, including the furniture that was used when the treaty was signed. Other exhibitions are also held here and there are occasional chamber-music concerts at night.

It's open from 10 am to 5 pm Tuesday to Saturday (10 am to 8 pm on Thursday) and from noon to 5 pm on Sunday; entry is R2. Take the station bus outside the Standard Bank Building, Church Square. It goes down Paul Kruger St, so get off at Jacob Maré St.

Transvaal Museum of Natural History

This museum has traditional static displays of animals and birds in glass exhibition cases. The most dramatic exhibit is the enormous skeleton of a whale outside the building. If you are interested in South Africa's fauna, particular its birdlife, a visit is worthwhile. The museum is in Paul Kruger St

---

Embarrassing Statues

The statue of J G Strijdom will probably have been demolished by the time you get to Pretoria, but it's a sign of the amazing restraint shown by the black majority that it was not blown up within hours of the ANC winning the 1994 elections.

There are many other statues of apartheid figures around the country. A perfect resting place for them would be a particularly remote, bleak and arid corner of the Karoo. They could sit and look at each other in the drab and silent isolation they so craved. ■

between Visagie and Minnaar Sts (not all that far from Melrose House). It's open from 9 am to 5 pm Monday to Saturday and from 11 am to 5 pm on Sunday; entry is R2.50.

Pretoria Art Museum
In Arcadia Park, off Schoeman St a km or so east of the centre, this museum (☎ (012) 344 1807) displays South African art from all periods of the country's history. It's open from Tuesday to Saturday between 10 am and 5 pm (8 pm on Wednesday) and on Sunday from 1 to 6 pm. Admission is R2.

South African Police Museum
Presumably this museum will change dramatically now that South Africa has ceased to be a police state. In a way, it would be a useful historical artefact if it remained as it is – a somewhat amateurish propaganda vehicle for the old SAP. It includes dioramas of various crimes, murder weapons and blood-stained clothing – not for the faint-hearted. The museum entrance is on Pretorius St near the corner with Volkstem St, two minutes from Church Square. It's open from 8 am to 3.30 pm Monday to Friday and from 8.30 am to 12.30 pm Saturday; entry is free.

NATIONAL ZOOLOGICAL GARDENS
The zoo is actually quite impressive and it's a pleasant enough spot to while away an afternoon while you're waiting for a visa. There's a decent cafeteria and some sunny lawns. The highlight is a cable car that runs up to the top of a koppie (rocky hill) overlooking the city. Entry is R11 plus the cable car. It's open daily from 8 am to 5.30 pm. Three or four times a week you can visit at night – BYO torch (flashlight).

There are some interesting craft stalls along Boom St to the west of the zoo, with particularly good beadwork. Bargain.

MARKETS
On Sunday a flea market is held in the Sunnypark shopping centre on Esselen St. Out of town, on the N4 opposite the CSIR complex, a *boeremark* (farmers' market) is the place to find fresh produce and old-style Boers, with traditional food and music. It's held on Saturday from about 6 to 9 am.

TOURS
Many companies offer tours of Pretoria and the surrounding area, some running from Jo'burg (see the Jo'burg section).

Francoise, owner of Pretoria Backpackers, offers tours such as a half-day tour of Pretoria for R50 (R25 if there are three of you), Jo'burg R65 (R35), the Cheetah Research Station R65 (R45) and Pilanesberg National Park R120. The Tourist Rendezvous has information on other operators such as Sakabula Tours (☎ (012) 98 1585) which offers a half-day tour of Pretoria for R90.

Sun City tours depart from the Tourist Rendezvous at 9 am and cost R45. There are more departures on weekends.

FESTIVALS
The Jacaranda Festival is held annually during the third week of October, when the blooms are at their peak. There are flea markets, shows, concerts and food stalls. The immensely popular Pretoria Show is held during the third week of August at the showgrounds.

PLACES TO STAY – BOTTOM END
Caravan Park
The *Polkadraai Caravan Park* (☎ (012) 668 8710) about 12 km from the city centre on the Hennops River has 100 caravan/tent stands. Shops and other amenities are five km away.

Hostels
Pretoria Backpackers (☎ (012) 343 9754), 34 Bourke St, Sunnyside, is a short walk from Esselen St. It's run by Francoise, a registered tour guide and Pretoria enthusiast. Dorm beds are R25 and doubles are R70. Francoise can arrange transfers to/from Jan Smuts Airport (Jo'burg). We've heard that another hostel has opened, *Mzuri Afrika Lodge* (☎ (012) 343 7782), 503 Reitz St, Sunnyside.

That's It (☎ (012) 344 3404), 5 Brecher St, might still have a backpackers' section; if so it's worth checking out. See the following Places to Stay – Middle section.

The *YWCA* (☎ (012) 326 2916), 557 Vermeulen St, up near the Union Buildings, is institutional, but it's bright, attractive and clean. They accept women only and the rate is R45 per night, including three meals. They're always busy, but particularly from January to March. Ring ahead. As a last resort you might try the *YMCA* (☎ (012) 320 0102), 460 Van der Walt St. It's none too clean and is partly a refuge for street kids. Dorm beds cost R30 and there are no cooking facilities.

Hotels & Guesthouses

The *Parkview Hotel* (☎ (012) 325 6787), on Zeederberg (Lyden) St opposite the Union Buildings' gardens, is spartan but friendly and very clean, with small rooms for R52/75. Each room has a shower but toilets are shared. If you're wearing runners the squeaking on the highly-polished lino floors will drive you insane! The *Belgrave Hotel* (☎ (012) 322 7900), 22 Railway St, a short walk from the station, has been in the midst of renovations for at least three years and they seem no closer to completion. Rooms cost R50 or R65 with bath. It's clean enough but basic and not really in a great part of town, although it is convenient if you arrive late by train.

Malvern House (☎ (012) 341 7212), 575 Schoeman St, Arcadia, is a large guesthouse in a good position, within walking distance of both the city centre and Sunnyside. It's spotlessly clean and quite comfortable but bathrooms are shared. Singles/doubles/triples are R70/100/110, including a good breakfast. Before the backpacker hostel opened this was a favourite place for travellers, so it has good information.

We have heard about (but haven't yet seen) *Riantes Residensie* (☎ (012) 44 2715), 587 Church St, Arcadia. It is a large residential hotel in which rooms start at R50/70 with breakfast. Weekly and monthly rates are available there.

PLACES TO STAY – MIDDLE

That's It (☎ (012) 344 3404), 5 Brecher St, near the corner of Farenden St, is a guesthouse in a leafy corner of Sunnyside, not too far from Esselen St. It's a pleasant suburban house with good-sized rooms and a big garden with a pool. Prices range from R70 to R90 for a single and R120 to R150 for a double, with breakfast. Backpackers have their own quarters in the garden, with cooking facilities. A bunk bed costs R30. Breakfast in the garden is just R8. Other meals are available. They will pick you up from central Pretoria. Farenden St runs into Park St, a main route out of central Pretoria and used by minibus taxis. There's a big palm tree on the corner of Park and Farenden Sts.

La Maison (☎ (012) 43 4341), 235 Hilda St, Hatfield, has three beautiful rooms, upstairs in an old Pretoria house that is surrounded by a beautiful garden (including a pool). The owner is a cordon bleu chef and offers superb buffet breakfasts. Dinner is R40. Singles/doubles are R175/220, with some smaller singles at R150. Recommended.

The Tourist Rendezvous has a list of other B&Bs and guesthouses, or you can contact the Bed 'n Breakfast organisation (☎ (011) 482 2206/7, fax (011) 726 6915) based in Jo'burg. Their prices start around R90/160 a single/double.

Park Lodge Hotel (☎ (012) 320 8230), on Jacob Maré St near the corner of Andries St, isn't great but the price is relatively low: bed and breakfast costs R97/112. The rooms are small and uninspiring and some have shared toilets.

Orange Court Lodge (☎ (012) 326 6346), 7 Orange Court, 540 Vermeulen St, on the corner of Hamilton St, is an excellent option – comfortable, homely and well placed. It offers serviced apartments (with one, two or three bedrooms) in a historic building, with phone, TV, equipped kitchens and linen. There's a welter of rates, starting at R120/180 for singles/doubles in a one-bedroom apartment, up to R300 for six people in a three-bedroom apartment. Recommended.

The large *Hotel 224* (☎ (012) 44 2581), on the corner of Schoeman and Leyds Sts, Arcadia, is starting to fray at the edges and the rooms are small but it's still reasonable, and fair value with rooms starting around R120. There's a member of the basic but inexpensive *Formule 1* chain (☎ (012) 323 8331) at 81 Pretorius St. Rooms sleeping up to three people cost around R100.

PLACES TO STAY – TOP END

Meintjieskop Guesthouse (☎ (012) 43 3711), 145 Eastwood St, Arcadia, has guest rooms for R210/300 (less if you stay longer than three days) and also self-catering units.

The *Victoria Hotel* (☎ (012) 323 6052, fax 323 0843) on the corner of Paul Kruger and Scheiding Sts, opposite the railway station, is the oldest hotel building in Pretoria still used for its original purpose. It was built in 1896 and has a gracious Victorian atmosphere. There's also an excellent restaurant on the premises. It's associated with Rovos Rail (a company that operates a luxurious restored steam train). They have suites ranging from R250 to R675, with breakfast included (it would want to be!).

The remaining top-end hotels are all large international-style places with all mod-cons. There's not much to separate them apart from position, and in this department, the *Holiday Inn* wins. The *Protea Hof* would be convenient if you were attending a performance at the State Theatre.

Other places, in alphabetical order are: the *Burgerspark Hotel* (☎ (012) 322 7500), on the corner of Minnaar and Van der Walt Sts, with singles/doubles from R200/280; the *Holiday Inn* (☎ (012) 341 1571), on the corner of Beatrix and Church Sts, handy to the city and for nightlife, from R348/356; the *Holiday Inn Garden Court* (☎ (012) 322 7500), Van der Walt St, from R209/218; the *Karos Manhattan Hotel* (☎ (012) 322 7635), on the corner of Van der Walt and Scheiding Sts, R219/289; and the *Protea Hof Hotel* (☎ (012) 322 7570), on the corner of Pretorius and Van der Walt Sts, a solid old place and well located in the centre of town, R230/250, with cheaper weekend deals.

PLACES TO EAT

The *Espresso Bar* in the Tourist Rendezvous Centre is licensed and sells snacks such as omelettes and burgers for about R10 to R15. Another good place in the city centre to sit down and have a coffee is the *Coffee Nest* on Pretorius St between Andries and Paul Kruger Sts. The coffee is good (R3.50) and the sticky cakes are tempting.

Also in the city centre, *Roberto's Italian Restaurant* is on Schoeman St next to the Tramshed complex. Despite the up-market décor and service, prices aren't bad and the food is good, although much richer than genuine Italian dishes. Soup is R7, pasta around R16 and meat dishes around R25. They also have pizzas. *Buffet de l'Opera*, in Church St near the State Theatre, has a buffet for R35 or à la carte dishes for about R12.

One of the most atmospheric possibilities is the old dining room at the *Victoria Hotel* (☎ (012) 323 6052), on the corner of Scheiding and Paul Kruger Sts, which has been beautifully restored. Their prices are surprisingly reasonable, considering the setting: breakfast is R17.50 and a set lunch is R45.

There are a few options on Beatrix St within a two-block radius of the Holiday Inn. If you're suffering from protein deficiency, *Digger's Grill* (☎ (012) 44 7390), on the corner of Beatrix and Pretorius Sts, is a classic steakhouse with fillet for about R30. *La Gondola* is at 37 Nedbank Plaza on the corner of Beatrix and Church Sts. It's open seven days a week and has good-value Italian food, with pastas and pizzas averaging around R18 and lunch specials. The *Caponero Restaurant* (☎ (012) 326 4147), 111 Beatrix St, is an excellent, traditional Italian restaurant with similar prices and a cheerful bistro atmosphere.

Sunnyside

Sunnyside, to the south-east of the city, is the main nightlife centre and Esselen St is the main drag. It has numerous restaurants and takeaway joints. The following selection begins at the Bourke St end.

Fillings is a trendy café and bar selling snacks such as pancakes (from R4.50) and meals. *Eric's Upstairs* (☎ (012) 343 0227), 306 Esselen St between Bourke and Leyds Sts, opens onto a broad verandah above the street – a great place on a warm evening. It's basically a bar with a few meals available, mostly meat and mostly under R10.

Between Celliers and Troye Sts, *Dramant Café* is a small Chinese place with some dishes well under R10. On the corner of Troye there's a 24-hour *Bimbos* hamburger joint and on the other side of the street is *Shunters*, a 24-hour bar and grill. Across the road is *Grapevine Confectionery*, with an outdoor area, good coffee and superb cakes.

Giovanni's, upstairs on the corner of Jeppe St, is fairly pricey but the food is about as close to real Italian as you'll get in South Africa. There's a large menu, with pasta from R18 and very good salads from R10. Downstairs, the *London Tavern* has bar meals. A block further along, *Something Fishy* sells seafood takeaways.

On Jeppe St just south of Schoeman, *La Fragiola* is a lively place with music, where pizzas start from R12 and steaks from R18. *Tarus Bulba*, 209 Hamilton St, has been recommended for its inexpensive Portuguese food.

ENTERTAINMENT

The options aren't great but there are some popular bars. Upstairs in the Tramshed complex on the corner of Van der Walt and Schoeman Sts, Crossroads Blues Bar stays open late nightly and is usually crowded. There's often live music.

Fillings, a café on Esselen St, has township jazz on Friday night, free. Other popular drinking places on Esselen St include Casablanca and Café Kalua. Steamers, near the railway station, is a gay-friendly club.

There are more bars and nightspots in the suburb of Hatfield, east of Sunnyside, on the other side of the university. Ed's Easy Diner has been recommended.

There's quite a range of high culture (opera, music, ballet and theatre) offered at the State Theatre complex (☎ (012) 322 1665) on the corner of Prinsloo and Church Sts. There are five theatres: the Arena, Studio, Opera, Drama and Momentum. Check *Be My Guest* and local newspapers for listings. Computicket has an office in the Tramshed complex.

There are several enormous cinema complexes. The largest is Sterland, on the corner of Pretoria St and Beatrix, which has no less than 13 cinemas, an ice rink, and possibly the most horrible fluorescent décor in Africa. There are a few cinemas around Esselen St in Sunnyside, including Metro Cine 1, 2 & 3 on the corner of Esselen and Jeppe Sts.

The 19th Hole, on the corner of Jeppe St and Park, is an extraordinarily popular spot with a number of putt-putt (mini-golf) courses, but no bar despite the promise of the name.

GETTING THERE & AWAY
Bus

A number of international bus services from Jo'burg (for Zimbabwe, Botswana and Namibia) stop in Pretoria – see the Getting There & Away chapter for details. Most buses (national and international) leave from the forecourt of Pretoria railway station.

The best method of transport between Pretoria and Jo'burg is the train because almost all buses between the two cities are en route to other destinations and charge high prices for this short sector.

Most Translux (☎ (012) 315 2111) and Greyhound (☎ (012) 328 4040) services running from Jo'burg to Durban, the south coast and Cape Town originate in Pretoria. See the Jo'burg Getting There & Away section for more information – add an hour to travel times. Translux and Transtate services running north up the N1 also stop here – see the Jo'burg Getting There & Away section and deduct an hour from travel times.

Examples of Translux fares from Pretoria are: Beitbridge, R100; Bloemfontein, R130; Cape Town, R280; Durban, R120; East London, R200; Kimberley, R140; Knysna, R210; Louis Trichardt, R75; Messina, R85; Oudtshoorn, R210, Pietersburg, R50; and Port Elizabeth, R220. Greyhound's fares are a little higher. With Transtate, the Pretoria to Pietersburg fare is R40.

Intercape (☎ (012) 328 4599) leaves from the railway station and has services to Upington (R150), connecting with a service to Cape Town (R130 from Upington). From Upington you can also get an Intercape bus to Windhoek (Namibia), but there isn't a direct connection. Still, Upington isn't a bad place to spend the night.

Elwierda Buses (☎ (012) 664 5880) has a service to Jo'burg, departing from Pretoria railway station very early in the morning, for R25 return. They also run to Durban. Lebowa Transport (☎ (012) 323 0379) runs north to Pietersburg.

Train

The railway station is about a 20-minute walk from the city centre. Buses run along Paul Kruger St to Church Square, the main local bus terminus.

A 1st-class train ticket to Jo'burg on the Metro system is R10.50, there's no 2nd class and you should definitely ask about the danger of mugging before taking 3rd class (R4.50). The journey takes between one and 1½ hours. From Monday to Friday trains run every half-hour early in the morning then hourly until 10 pm. On weekends trains run about every 1½ hours. For exact times call Jo'burg (☎ (011) 773 5878) or Pretoria (☎ (012) 315 2007).

There's no reason why you should, but you could take a mainline (ie long-distance) train (☎ (012) 315 2401) on the Pretoria to Jo'burg section, but this will cost R25/19/10 in 1st/2nd/3rd class. For that matter, you could take the luxurious *Blue Train*, which costs from R105 to Jo'burg. For the full trip between Pretoria and Cape Town you pay from R1910, up to R6585 for a two-person suite.

Other mainline trains running through Pretoria are the *Diamond Express* (Pretoria to Kimberley and Bloemfontein, daily except Saturday); the *Komati* (Jo'burg to Komatipoort via Nelspruit, daily) and the three trains that run north via Pietersburg, Louis Trichardt and Messina to the Zimbabwe border at Beitbridge. These are the *Limpopo* (Friday), the *Bulawayo* (Tuesday)

and the *Bosvelder* (daily). The *Limpopo* and the *Bulawayo* continue on to Harare and Bulawayo respectively. On Tuesday, Thursday and Sunday, the *Komati* continues on to Maputo (Mozambique).

First/2nd/3rd-class fares from Pretoria include: Bloemfontein, R163/111/65; Kimberley, R127/87/51; Komatipoort, R106/75/42; Messina, R124/94/51; Nelspruit, R84/59/33; and Pietersburg, R69/48/28.

Car Rental

The larger local and international companies are represented. You can make bookings at the Tourist Rendezvous.

GETTING AROUND
To/From Jan Smuts Airport

Impala buses (☎ (012) 323 1429) operate between Jan Smuts and the Tourist Rendezvous. The journey takes a bit under an hour and costs about R25 – good value considering that you pay the same to get between the airport and downtown Jo'burg.

Bus

There is an extensive network of local buses. The main terminus and the enquiry office (☎ (012) 313 0839) are on the south-east corner of Church Square. A booklet of timetables and route maps is available from the enquiry office. Fares range from R2.10 to R4.60 depending on distance. Quite a few services, including the one to Sunnyside, run until about 10.30 pm – unusually late for South Africa.

Minibus Taxi

The standard fare around town is R2.50.

Taxi

Taxis are expensive – budget about R2 per km. There are stands on the corner of Church and Van der Walt and at Vermeulen and Andries, or telephone Rixi Mini (☎ (012) 325 8072).

Citybug (☎ (012) 324 4718, 335 7383) is a three-wheeler which costs R2 for up to three km in the city centre.

GAUTENG

Around Pretoria

DOORNKLOOF (SMUTS' HOUSE)

General JC Smuts was a brilliant scholar, Boer general, politician and international statesman. He was one of the architects of the Union of South Africa, and the prime minister from 1919 to 1924 and again from 1939 to 1948.

His home has been turned into an excellent museum that is well worth visiting if you have private transport and are travelling to or from Pretoria. The building was originally a British officers' mess at Middelburg, but Smuts bought it and re-erected it on his 4000-acre property at Irene, 16 km south of Pretoria. Surrounded by a wide verandah and shaded by trees, it still has a warm family atmosphere, and it gives a vivid insight into Smuts' amazing life. Some of his furniture is at the University of Witwatersrand, but much of the house is original.

There's a small cafeteria with an outdoor tea garden, and an adjacent caravan park. The house (☎ (012) 667 1176) is open daily from 9.30 am to 1 pm and from 1.30 pm to

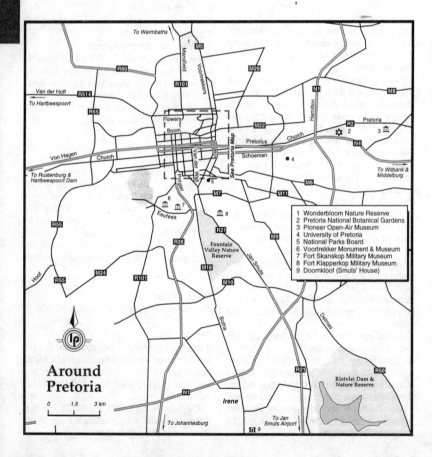

1 Wonderbloom Nature Reserve
2 Pretoria National Botanical Gardens
3 Pioneer Open-Air Museum
4 University of Pretoria
5 National Parks Board
6 Voortrekker Monument & Museum
7 Fort Skanskop Military Museum
8 Fort Klapperkop Military Museum
9 Doornkloof (Smuts' House)

Around Pretoria

0   1.5   3 km

4.30 pm (until 5 pm on weekends); entry is R2.50, free to the garden.

Place to Stay

There's a pleasant, small caravan park on the property (☎ (012) 667 1176). Sites are R25. This would make a peaceful and economic alternative to staying in either Jo'burg or Pretoria.

Getting There & Away

Unfortunately there is no access by public transport. The house is signposted from both the N1 freeway (R28) and the R21. The most direct route from Pretoria is along Louis Botha Ave to Irene, the nearest town.

FORT KLAPPERKOP MILITARY MUSEUM

One of four forts built after the Jameson Raid, Fort Klapperkop, on Johann Rissik Dr six km south of the city, never fired a shot in anger, but it now illustrates South Africa's military history from 1852 to the end of the Anglo-Boer War. It features a nine-seater military bicycle designed by the British to check rail lines for booby traps – eight men pedalled, while the commanding officer commanded. The museum is open every day from 10 am to 3.30 pm; entry is free.

PIONEER OPEN-AIR MUSEUM

The open-air museum (☎ (012) 803 6086) is a reconstructed pioneer farmyard and restored thatched cottage. It gives a brief insight into the past. Unfortunately it's very difficult to get to without a car, as it's about 12 km east of the city centre at Silverton, off Pretoria Rd (the R2). You could take the Silverton bus from Church St. The museum is open every day from 8.30 am to 4 pm and entry is R3.50.

PRETORIA NATIONAL BOTANICAL GARDENS

The botanical gardens cover 77 hectares and are planted with indigenous flora from around the country. The plants are labelled and grouped according to their region of origin, so a visit is a must for keen botanists.

The gardens are 11 km east of the city centre and are open daily from 8 am to 5.30 pm; entrance is free on weekdays, R1 on weekends.

Getting There & Away

By car, head east along Church St for about nine km, then turn right into Cussonia Rd; the gardens are on the left-hand side. Or catch the Meyerspark or Murrayfield bus from Church Square.

VOORTREKKER MONUMENT & MUSEUM

The enormous Voortrekker Monument was built in 1938 to commemorate the extraordinary achievements of the Boers who trekked north over the coastal mountains of the Cape into the heart of the African veld. In particular, it commemorates the Battle of Blood River when, on 16 December 1838, 470 Boers under the brilliant command of Andries Pretorius defeated approximately 12,000 Zulus. Three trekkers were wounded and 3000 Zulus were killed.

The trekkers went on to found independent republics that in many ways form the genesis of the modern South African state. In

Voortrekker Monument

GAUTENG

terms of drama, determination, courage, vision and tragedy their story surpasses the history of European colonists (or invaders if you like) anywhere else in the world. Some Afrikaners go one step further: the trek parallels the biblical Exodus and the Battle at Blood River was a miracle that can only be explained by divine intervention, proof that the trekkers were a chosen people.

The monument was built at the time of a great resurgence of Afrikaner nationalism. The scars of their defeat in the Second War of Independence (the 1889-1902 Anglo-Boer War) were still fresh and the monument provided an emotional focal point for the Afrikaners' ongoing struggle. The building's inauguration in 1949 was attended by 250,000 people. It remains a powerful symbol of the Afrikaner volk, their history, and their relationship to South Africa.

The monument is surrounded by a stone wall carved with 64 ox-wagons in a traditional defensive *laager* (circle). The building itself is a huge stone cube inspired by the ruins of Great Zimbabwe. Above the entrance is the head of a buffalo, which many believe to be the most unpredictable and dangerous of all African animals, especially when wounded. Inside, a detailed bas-relief tells the story of the trek and of the Battle of Blood River. On 16 December a shaft of light falls on the words *Ons vir jou, Suid Africa* (We for thee, South Africa). A staircase leads to the roof and a panoramic view of Pretoria and the Transvaal highveld.

Below the car park there is an excellent small museum that reconstructs the lives of the trekkers. There is a reconstruction of a homestead, two wagons, photographs, clothing and, of course, weapons. The monument and the museum are open Monday to Saturday from 9 am to 4.45 pm and Sunday from 11 am to 4.45 pm. Entrance to the monument is R4 and to the museum it's R5. There's also a restaurant that sells reasonably priced meals, and a small open-air café.

Getting There & Away

The monument, six km south of the city, just to the east of the N1 freeway, is clearly signposted. It is possible to catch the Voortrekkerhoogte or Valhalla bus from Paul Kruger St near the corner of Church Square. Ask the driver to let you off at the entrance road to the monument, from where it is a 10-minute walk.

Northern Transvaal

Northern Transvaal, once the north of the old Transvaal Province is a combination of high-veld and lowveld but most of it is savanna and it is very hot in summer, with high humidity and electrical storms on the lowveld. The lush Letaba Valley, with its tropical fruit farms and the nearby cycad forests surrounding the home of the Rain Queen, and the forested Southpansberg range provide some contrast to the bushveld plains.

To the west of the N1 is the fascinating Waterberg region; north of the Soutpansberg you're well into tropical, baobab-studded plains; and to the east is the mystical Venda area. Large tracts of land were once taken up by the Homelands of Venda, Gazankulu and Lebowa. As well as Kruger National Park and bordering private game reserves, there are many other reserves and good hiking trails in the area.

Mining in this region is important both as an employer of a fair percentage of the local black population and as an earner of foreign currency. Fourteen of the 20 main (strategic) minerals are mined here and nine of the deposits are the biggest of their type in the world. The biggest coalfields in South Africa are near Ellisras; gold, beryllium, asbestos and antimony are mined near Gravelotte; platinum and iron are mined near Thaba-zimbi; South Africa's biggest copper mine, with a big hole seven times larger than that at Kimberley, is in Phalaborwa; and the biggest felspar mine in the world is in Naboomspruit.

This is the Afrikaner frontier and conservative values remain strong. In the book *White Boy Running*, Christopher Hope described the old Transvaal province as 'the province that dominates the country; the place where power resides, the lair of the political wild men'.

Note A large part of Kruger National Park is in Northern Transvaal, but the park is

---

NORTHERN TRANSVAAL
(Its post-election name is now Northern Province)
Capital: Pietersburg
Main Languages: Afrikaans and English, with VhaVenda, seSotho, Setswana, isi-Ndebele, Xitonga and siSwati spoken in the old Homeland areas
Pre-1994: This area was the northern part of the old Transvaal Province, and the Homelands of Venda, Lebowa, Gazankulu, KwaNdebele, and parts of Bophuthatswana and KwaNgwane.
Highlights:
* Wide African *veld* & big skies
* Traditional culture in the Venda area
* Part of Kruger National Park & nearby private reserves
* Waterberg region

---

covered as a whole in the Eastern Transvaal chapter.

HISTORY

The Transvaal was not densely populated, but it was nonetheless home to a considerable number of black communities. Amongst others, there were Ndebele (north of Pretoria), Venda (in the north-east), Langa (in the Waterberg), and Batswana of the Sotho group (in the south-west).

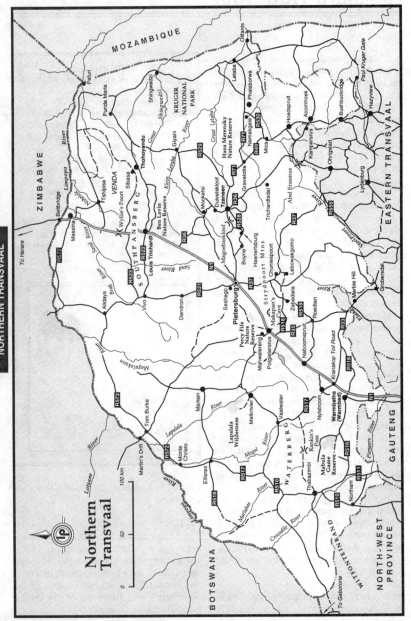

The Voortrekkers first crossed the Vaal River in 1836. A number of bloody conflicts between the blacks and whites followed. In 1852 at Sand River, Andries Pretorius successfully negotiated with the British for the independence of the trekkers north of the Vaal River – and created the first of the Boer republics. In 1853 the name Zuid-Afrikaansche Republic (ZAR) was adopted. Pretoria was founded as the capital in 1855.

Boer independence did not last long. The republic was annexed by the British in 1877 and became the province of Transvaal. The Boers fought for and won their independence and the Transvaal was once again a republic by 1884.

Gold was discovered on the Witwatersrand in 1886, with consequences that no one could have foreseen. One of these was a new British interest in the region, and in 1899 the Boers were again locked in a war of independence with the British. The British won, but the Transvaal once again had representative government before the end of 1906, and was finally incorporated in the new Union of South Africa. Pretoria was not to be a republican capital again until 1961.

WARNING

Take precautions against both malaria and bilharzia while in Northern Transvaal.

The N1 North

The N1 highway from Jo'burg and Pretoria to the Zimbabwe border neatly divides Northern Transvaal. Along this artery are the main towns of the province.

WARMBATHS (WARMBAD)

This sleepy little town, off the N1, 90 km north of Pretoria, has become a popular holiday spot because of its **mineral springs** complex.

Most of the town's inhabitants are black and live in the township of Bela. Fortunately, a number of them now come to the baths for recreation rather than just to clean out the pools as in pre-election days. Day visits to the baths cost R20 (children R12). This gets you access to all facilities.

There is an information centre (☎ (014) 736 3694) near the corner of Voortrekker and Pretoria Sts.

Places to Stay & Eat

The baths are part of an *Aventura Resort* (☎ (014) 736 2200, fax 736 4712), which has powered camp sites for R13.50 plus R10 per person (R18 in high season). Two and four-bed units are R140/190 (R180/295 in high season). The *New White House Hotel* (☎ (014) 736 2404) is in the town centre opposite the post office on the corner of Pretoria and Voortrekker Sts. It's a country pub with rooms from R60 per person, including breakfast. The *Bronnehof* (☎ (014) 736 2101), Sutter Rd, costs R65/130; breakfast is R15 per person.

There are numerous holiday flats, many along Moffat St. They include: *Casa Blanca Resort* (☎ (014) 736 2480) at No 42; *Dula Monate Holiday Flats* (☎ (014) 736 3168) at No 17; and *Louiseville* (☎ (014) 736 3607) at No 4.

There are plenty of places to get a meal a short walk from the baths. A steak at the *Spur* is about R28; *Shangri-La* has African food and the attached *Pizza Bela Bela* has pizzas from R15 to R25; and *Paul's Pub & Grill* has pub lunches (R8.50 for a filling cheeseburger and R12.50 for steak, eggs and chips).

Getting There & Away

Several daily Transtate buses stop here on the run between Sibasa and Jo'burg.

The *Bosvelder* train stops here on the Messina-Jo'burg run; 1st/2nd/3rd class fares are R46/33/18 to Jo'burg, R48/34/22 to Pietersburg and R111/72/42 to Messina.

A minibus taxi costs R21 to either Pietersburg or Jo'burg.

NYLSTROOM

Nylstroom, a small town in cattle country, was named by Voortrekkers who thought they'd found the source of the Nile. After all, the river here seemed to fit the biblical

---

No Moses but Plenty of Birds

When the Nyl Valley floods in summer a cacophony of sounds emanates from the reeds – but it is no baby crying. This flood plain is rich in both numbers and diversity of species of waterbirds.

Over 100 different species of waterbird have been recorded here and in the adjoining private **Mosdene Nature Reserve**. This number includes 85 of the 94 species known to have bred in South Africa, more than any other wetland in the Republic.

After the rains the food supply in the *vlei* (valley) is plentiful and the flocks of birds begin to arrive. Some 17 species of ducks are to be found, including white-faced whistling *(Dendrocygna viduata)* and southern pochard *(Netta erythrophthalma)*. Also, up to 17 species of heron such as the great white egret *(Egretta alba)*, squacco *(Ardeola ralloides)* and black egret *(Egretta ardesiaca)* – over 12,000 birds – begin hunting in the shallow water. Birdwatchers will get the opportunity to see rare species such as the bittern *(Botaurus stellaris)*, dwarf bittern *(Ixobrychus sturmii)* and rufousbellied heron *(Ardeola rufiventris)*. Apart from waterbirds over 300 other species have been recorded in the valley, making it one of the richest places to see birds in Africa. ■

---

description of the Nile: it was a river, it was in Africa and it had reeds growing along the banks.

The library (☎ (01470) 2211) has information on accommodation and activities.

Places to Stay

Stokkiesdraai Motel & Caravan Park (☎ (01470) 2997, fax 4005) has sites from about R30 for two and large holiday chalets for R223. It's about three km from Nylstroom on the old Naboomspruit road. *Weesgerus Holiday Resort* (☎ (01470) 51 2037) is north-west of Nylstroom on the R517; there is a great range of accommodation here for the weary Voortrekker needing to rest, water the horses and oil the wagon wheels. The *Nylstroom Hotel* (☎ (01470) 3780) has single/double rooms from R50/90.

About 10 km from the Kranskop toll gate on the Eersbewoond Rd is *Shangri-La Country Lodge* (☎ (01470) 2071). A studio room with bath is R215 per person for full board, a thatched rondavel is R260.

Getting There & Away

Nylstroom is bypassed by the N1. Several northbound bus services, including LT, pass through the Kranskop toll station on the N1, but it is still some 16 km to Nylstroom. Only Transtate buses come into town and stop at the railway station; there are services from Jo'burg and Pretoria to Sibasa, Malamulele and Mabopane.

The minibus-taxi system is easy to work

out, as it costs R7 between towns – from Nylstroom to Naboomspruit is R7; to Potgietersrus R14; and to Pietersburg R21. The *Bosvelder* train (from Louis Trichardt to Jo'burg) does not stop here.

NABOOMSPRUIT

This town (called 'Naboom' by all) is in the centre of a rich agricultural and mining district. There are many mineral springs in the area. There were a number of 'Welkom u Volkstad' signs in evidence when we made our visit. It's a conservative place but after a few glasses of *mampoer* (local schnapps) the clothes may well come off as the only nudist camp in South Africa is nearby.

Places to Stay & Eat

The municipal *caravan park* (☎ (014) 743 1111) is a central and cheap option for campers. There are nine caravan parks in the vicinity! The *Naboomspruit Hotel* (☎ /fax 743 0321) has single/double rooms from R50/85 and an à la carte restaurant. *Kings & Queens Restaurant*, on the corner of Louis Trichardt and Fourth Sts, has reasonable meals from about R30.

Getting There & Away

Transtate services between Jo'burg and Louis Trichardt stop at the station. The Translux service between Jo'burg and Harare stops at the Trek Inn. LT Tours buses running between Jo'burg and Phalaborwa stop at Guest's Takeaways; buy tickets at

Guest's (☎ (014) 743 0559). LT Tours fares are R21 to Pietersburg and R42 to Jo'burg.

The *Bosvelder* train stops here, too.

Nylsvley Nature Reserve

This 3000-hectare reserve is about 20 km south of Naboomspruit. It's one of the best places in South Africa to see birds, especially in spring and summer. The Nyl River, which flows through the reserve, floods in summer, and huge numbers of waterbirds breed on the flood plain.

The reserve is open daily between 6 am and 6 pm. There's a basic *camp site* – you must book (☎ (014) 743 1074). To get to the reserve from Naboomspruit, head south on the N1 for 13 km and turn-off to the left on the road to Boekenhout.

POTGIETERSRUS

This conservative town, 227 km north of Pretoria, was settled early by Voortrekkers, not without resistance from the people already living there. The **Arend Dieperink Museum**, open weekdays until 4.30 pm, tells the story.

Makapan's Cave, 23 km north-east of town, is a palaeontological site of world significance, yielding bones of *Australopithecus africanus* radio-carbon dated to be approximately three million years old. You need a permit from Wits University to visit.

In October, the annual Potgietersrus *hostsa* (biltong festival), takes place.

Potgietersrus Game Breeding Centre

This reserve (☎ (0154) 4314) is a breeding centre for the National Zoological Gardens (Pretoria) and has a wide variety of native and exotic animals. One of the breeding aviaries covers over a hectare. You can drive through the reserve, which is open weekdays from 8 am to 4 pm, weekends until 6 pm; entry is R5.

Percy Fyfe Nature Reserve

This 3000-hectare reserve (☎ (0154) 5678), 26 km from town, is a breeding centre for several species of rare antelopes, and has other game. It's open from 8 am to 5 pm.

Places to Stay & Eat

There's a *caravan park* (☎ (0154) 7201) and *Kiepersol Resort* (☎ (0154) 5609) with sites and rondavels. *Lonely Oak* on Hooge St (☎ (0154) 4560, fax 4563) has singles/doubles from R80/100, and the cheaper *Fiesta Park Motel* (☎ (0154) 5641) is on the N1 between Naboom and Potgietersrus. The *Protea Park Hotel* (☎ (0154) 3101, fax 6842) has singles/doubles from R185/230.

There is also a *camp site* opposite the entrance to the breeding centre.

Jaagbaan (☎ (0154) 7833), a B&B eight km south of town, is recommended by readers; it costs R60 per person.

There are a number of places on the N1 (Voortrekker St) where you can get a meal including *Casanova*, *Pizza Den* and *Spur Steak Ranch*.

Getting There & Away

Transtate buses running between Jo'burg, Sibasa, Malamulele and Louis Trichardt stop here. Translux buses on the run between Jo'burg and Harare stop at the Wimpy Bar. LT Tours buses running between Jo'burg and Phalaborwa stop at the Oasis Lodge; you can buy tickets at Tritex Takeaways (☎ (0154) 5532). LT fares from here are R11 to Pietersburg and R53 to Jo'burg.

The *Bosvelder* train stops here; 1st/2nd/3rd class to Jo'burg is R70/49/28, and to Louis Trichardt R53/38/21.

PIETERSBURG

Pietersburg, the provincial capital, was founded in 1886 by a group of Voortrekkers who had been forced to abandon a settlement further north because of malaria and 'hostile natives'. Today, Pietersburg (possibly to be renamed Polokwane) is a big, sedate place serving agricultural and mining communities.

There's a very helpful Satour office (☎ (0152) 295 3025) in the park on the corner of Vorster St (the main through-road) and Landdros Mare St.

Things to See & Do

The **donkey statue** outside the Satour office

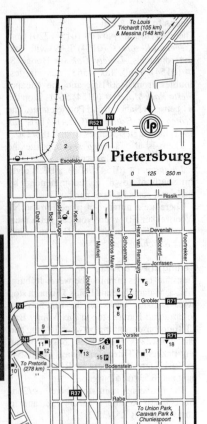

To Louis Trichardt (105 km) & Messina (148 km)

Pietersburg

0   125   250 m

PLACES TO STAY

10   Pietersburg Lodge
11   Holiday Inn Garden Court
12   Travellers' Lodge
16   Great Northern Hotel
17   Arnotha's

PLACES TO EAT

5   Die Klause
6   OK Bazaar
8   Nando's Chickenland
9   Golden Egg
13   Mike's Kitchen
18   Porterhouse Restaurant

OTHER

1   Railway Station
2   Oriental Plaza
3   Minibus Taxi Rank
4   Minibus Taxi Rank
7   LT Tours Office & Library Gardens
14   Satour Information Office, Donkey Statue
      & Public Toilets
15   Car Parking

species found in South Africa are represented. It is open daily from 7 am to 6 pm.

The **Bakone Malapa Museum**, nine km south-east of Pietersburg on the R37 to Chuniespoort, is devoted to northern Sotho culture and includes a reasonably authentic 'living' village. There are archaeological remains and paintings dating back to 1000 AD and evidence of Ndebele iron and copper smelting in the area. The complex is open on weekdays, except Monday afternoon when it closes at 12.30 pm. Admission is R3.

Australian visitors might want to visit the house where anti-hero Harry Harbord Morant ('the Breaker'), was tried for crimes committed during the Anglo-Boer war. The tourist office will direct you to the house on Landdros Mare St.

Moletzie Bird Sanctuary

This 200-hectare sanctuary is 35 km north-west of Pietersburg via Sheshego on the Steilloopbrug road. Several birds of prey are found here, but it is the Cape vulture (*Gyps coprotheres*) colony, attracted to the pock-marked granite koppies, which attracts most

commemorates the part donkeys played in the white development of the Transvaal. Horses were susceptible to equine fever so the donkey replaced them in transport, agriculture and mining roles. Apparently they often committed suicide by jumping off cliffs rather than face another day's toil!

The **Pietersburg Nature Reserve** is in Union Park, south of the town centre on the road to Silicon. It's very big for a reserve adjacent to a city – the largest such in the country. You can see animals such as zebras, giraffes and white rhinos from the Rhinoceros Walking Trail. All of the antelope

The Cape Vulture is the largest of all southern African vultures.

interest. The rare southern bald ibis *(Geronticus calvus)* is also seen.

Places to Stay

Accommodation is generally pricey and can fill up with travelling salespeople.

The municipal *caravan park* (☎ (0152) 295 2011) is in Union Park, about three km from the town centre, past the stadium. Sites cost R22 for a tent and R25 for a caravan, or there are chalets for R90 for up to six people. If you're walking the trail in the adjacent nature reserve, sites are R5.

If you have transport, a cheap choice is *Far North Oasis* (☎ (0152) 293 6232), about 10 km east of town on the R71 to Haenertsburg. It is the absolute antithesis of an oasis, with a dearth of vegetation and a jumble of buildings surrounded by a high wire fence. Rondavels cost from R75/82 for singles/doubles; suites are R110/138.

Arnotha's (☎ (0152) 291 3390, fax 291 3394), 42 Hans van Rensburg St, is a comfortable salespersons' refuge with rooms for R91/120. Similar places are *Travellers Lodge* (☎ (0152) 291 5511) at R95/120 and *Pietersburg Lodge* (☎ (0152) 292 1214) at R100/125. Across the road from the Satour office is the *Great North Road Hotel* (☎ (0152) 295 8980), poor value at R84/115.

There's a *Holiday Inn Garden Court* (☎ (0152) 291 2030, fax 291 3150) on Vorster St, with rooms from R169. The *Ranch Hotel* (☎ (0152) 7293 7180, fax 293 7188), 25 km south on the N1, is slightly cheaper.

Places to Eat

There is no shortage of eateries in town and along the N1 nearby. *Nando's* at 59 Schoeman St has spicy whole chickens for R23 and jumbo burgers for R14.50. *Panarotti's* in the Holiday Inn has large pizzas for R32 and lasagne for R16.50.

There is also a *Mike's Kitchen* in the Glass House by the Civic Centre for steak and seafood, and the *Porterhouse* for steak lovers on the Mall Arcade. The classiest place is *Die Klause*, a German-run place, at 53 Hans van Rensburg St.

Getting There & Away

Air Airlink flies at least daily from Pietersburg to Jo'burg; the Apex fare is R205 one way.

Bus Transtate services between Jo'burg and Sibasa run daily and stop at the railway station. The Greyhound and Translux services between Jo'burg and Harare stop at the Shell Ultra on the highway 10 km south of town (at 2.30 and 2.45 am respectively). LT Tours services between Phalaborwa and Jo'burg stop at the Library Gardens bus stop on Hans van Rensburg St. Buy tickets at the LT Tours head office (☎ (0152) 291 1867) nearby in the shopping centre. LT Tours charges R43 to Phalaborwa, R64 to Jo'burg and R22 to Tzaneen.

Train The *Bosvelder* (Jo'burg-Messina) stops here, as does the *Limpopo* (Jo'burg-Harare).

Minibus Taxi The main minibus-taxi rank is opposite the OK supermarket on Kerk St, and there's another on Excelsior St near the railway station – most Jo'burg taxis leave from here. To get to Phalaborwa take a minibus taxi to Boyne (R4) east of Pietersburg, and from Boyne take another one to Tzaneen (R8) where you'll get another minibus taxi to Phalaborwa for R10.

Other fares from Pietersburg include: Louis Trichardt R12, Thohoyandou R15, Pretoria R25 and Jo'burg R30.

LOUIS TRICHARDT

Louis Trichardt nestles into the south side of the Soutpansberg range and is cooler and wetter than the harsh thornbush country which suddenly appears north of the range.

The tourist office is in the library at the back of the town centre. There is a Standard Bank on Krogh St and a First National Bank on Trichardt St.

The **Church of the Covenant** on the corner of Erasmus and Krogh Sts, was built to fulfil the bargain of a vow made by General Piet Joubert on the eve of his successful attack against the VhaVenda on Hangklip, in 1898. Behind the municipal buildings on Erasmus St is **Fort Hendrina**, an armour-plated structure once used as a base for attacks against local tribes.

Next to the caravan park is the **Indigenous Tree Park**, with 114 species of trees, and not far away, off the south end of Erasmus St, is a **bird sanctuary**.

Places to Stay

There's a municipal *caravan park* (☎ (01551) 2212) near the town centre off Grobler St. Tent sites cost about R20 with an additional R5 per person. *Carousel Lodge* (☎ (01551) 3782), down a side street off Rissik St, has singles/doubles with kitchen and bath for R60/80; budget rooms are R40 per room.

Ezriel Lodge (☎ (01551) 52222) is on the N1; take the turn-off at the Caltex station at the northernmost four-way stop. Ezriel has rooms for R70/100; book in advance if you want a TV. In town on Rissik St, the *Bergwater Hotel* (☎ (01551) 2262) charges R115/173, with breakfast.

On the N1 north of Louis Trichardt are three more places. The best is the *Punch Bowl Hotel* (☎ (01551) 9688), about 11 km north of town. It's a small place on the dry side of the Soutpansberg, with some nice scenery. Rooms cost R84/138 with breakfast. The *Mountain View* (☎ (01551) 9631, fax 9806) is nine km north of Louis Trichardt and has rooms from R97/145; breakfast is R22 extra and dinner is R35. *Clouds End Hotel* (☎ (01551) 9621, fax 9787), three km north of town, offers 'booze & snooze' but it isn't as tacky as that. It's a solid old place charging R104/181, with breakfast (dinner, bed and breakfast is R138/250). Watch out for the voracious vervet monkeys!

Adam's Apple Hotel (☎ (01551) 4117, fax 3154), on the N1 16 km south of Louis Trichardt, has bed and breakfast from R110/165.

Places to Eat

The *Great North Café & Restaurant*, on the corner of Trichardt and Krogh Sts, is reasonable. It opens early for breakfast (steak and eggs R20) and there's a good bakery here as well. At the *Black Steer* on Trichardt St (between Kruger and President Sts) a good main meal (eg, steak and salad) costs about R28. There is also a *Spur* in the Pennells Centre on Krogh St.

Bulldogs Bar, next to the Black Steer, offers some nightlife in an otherwise very quiet town.

Getting There & Away

Bus Transtate buses running between Jo'burg and Sibasa stop at the railway station, as does the Translux service between Jo'burg and Harare.

LT Tours buses running between Jo'burg and Phalaborwa, and to Tzaneen (R22), stop at the Bergwater Hotel, Rissik St. Buy tickets at Robbertze Agency (☎ (01551) 4342) on Trichardt St.

Train The railway station is at the south-west end of Kruger St. The *Bosvelder* (to and from Jo'burg) and the *Limpopo* (Jo'burg to Harare) stop here. See the Getting Around chapter for more information.

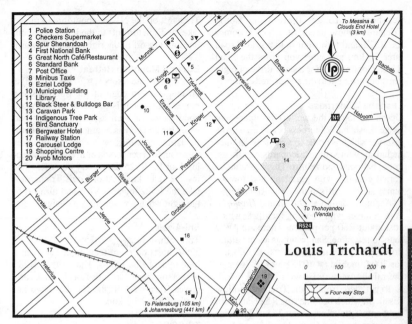

1 Police Station
2 Checkers Supermarket
3 Spur Shenandoah
4 First National Bank
5 Great North Café/Restaurant
6 Standard Bank
7 Post Office
8 Minibus Taxis
9 Ezriel Lodge
10 Municipal Building
11 Library
12 Black Steer & Bulldogs Bar
13 Caravan Park
14 Indigenous Tree Park
15 Bird Sanctuary
16 Bergwater Hotel
17 Railway Station
18 Carousel Lodge
19 Shopping Centre
20 Ayob Motors

To Messina &
Clouds End Hotel
(3 km)

To Thohoyandou
(Venda)

R524

Louis Trichardt

0   100   200 m

= Four-way Stop

To Pietersburg (105 km)
& Johannesburg (441 km)

Minibus Taxi The taxi park is in the OK Bazaar supermarket car park, off Burger St, a block north-east of Trichardt St. Some fares from Louis Trichardt are: Zimbabwe border R15, Messina R12, Pietersburg R12, Thohoyandou R6 to R7, Tzaneen R14 and Jo'burg R50.

To get out to the hotels on the highway to the north of town, take a minibus taxi heading for Messina (about R1.50).

Car North to Messina the road crosses the Soutpansberg range and there is some dramatic driving, including a couple of unlit tunnels which are very dark after the bright daylight. Watch out for slow vehicles without lights and remember to remove your sunglasses.

AROUND LOUIS TRICHARDT
Soutpansberg Hiking Trails

The original trail between Hangklip and Entabeni forest stations has closed but there

are still two good walks in the Soutpansberg. The two-day, 20.5-km **Hangklip Trail** includes a climb up a 1719-metre peak; it begins at the Hangklip Forest Station. The 52-km **Entabeni Circular Route**, about 40 km east of Louis Trichardt, has a number of options, including a less strenuous four-day route and an arduous two-day route which should only be undertaken by fit hikers.

Watch out for malaria, bilharzia and ticks. Overnight accommodation is in huts and there is a trail fee of R15 per person per day (this includes a good-quality walking map). To book these walks contact the Forestry Branch's Northern Transvaal office (☎ (01551) 2201), Private Bag X2431, 0920, in Louis Trichardt.

Keen hikers can stay in the western end of the Soutpansberg at *Medike* (☎ (01551) 2481), surrounded by the Sand River gorge. There are a number of trails where you can see rock paintings. Self-contained cottages are R40 per person and camp sites are R15 per person. To get there from Louis Trichardt, follow Rissik St, which becomes the R522, and turn right onto a gravel road after 35 km, just after you cross the Sand River. Continue on for a steep drive of eight km then turn right to the signposted entrance.

Lesheba Wilderness

Up on the top of the western Soutpansberg range, Lesheba Wilderness is a long, narrow reserve, which is home to a range of animals including white rhinos, leopards, warthogs, kudu, baboons and zebras. This is dramatic, varied country, with grassland and forests, plains and the cliffs of the Sand River gorge.

Accommodation at *Duluni* and *Hamasha* is in cottages with cooking facilities, which cost about R60 per person. There are 4WD tours to see game, San paintings and a vulture drinking hole. You must book (☎ (015592), ask for 3004; mobile (☎ (015) 593 0076) and the minimum stay is two nights.

To get there from Louis Trichardt, follow Rissik St, which becomes the R522, and turn right onto a gravel road after 35 km, just after you cross the Sand River. Continue on for a steep drive of 10 km to the entrance. The nearest fuel is in Louis Trichardt.

Ben Lavin Nature Reserve

This 2500-hectare reserve (☎ (01551) 3834) is worth visiting. The Wildlife Society of Southern Africa runs the reserve and encourages visitors to walk through it. There are four marked trails, all rewarding. The eight-km Tabajwane Trail is good for wildlife viewing and the Fountain Trail follows the Doring River. There are hides at waterholes. There is quite a range of birds (about 240 species have been recorded) and animals, including giraffes, zebras and jackals. The African rock python, the only python species in this part of Africa, may be spotted in the reserve.

The park is open daily from 6 am to 7 pm. Tent sites are R15, or you can stay in tents for R25 per person, huts for R40 per person or the lodge for R60 per person. You have to bring your own food.

To get there travel south from Louis Trichardt on the N1 for about three km and take the Elim turn-off to the left; after about one km turn-off to the right to Fort Edward.

Buzzard Mountain Retreat

This tiny private reserve (☎ (01551) 4196) is on the southern edge of the Soutpansberg range. Much of it is forested and there are good views, as well as some animals and many birds. There is a camp site and accommodation in cabins with cooking facilities for about R45 per person or in cottages sleeping four for R125. Day entry costs R5. The reserve is 15 km west of Louis Trichardt – take the R522 towards Vivo and turn-off to the right when you see the small sign.

Shi-Awela

This guest farm (☎ (01551) 51220, fax 3380) hosts no more than eight guests at a time in adobe buildings. The tariff of R285 per person sharing includes meals, walks and drives. Turn west off the N1 about two km north of Bandelierkop.

TSHIPISE

This small settlement, east of the N1, centres around the *Aventura Tshipise* resort (☎ (015539) 624, fax 724). Even if you've previously rejected such resorts for their holiday-camp atmosphere, the bars, swimming pools, shady tent sites and air-conditioned rooms might seem pretty attractive in this hot, harsh area.

A powered camp site is R13.50 plus R10 per person, standard two-bed units are R120 and four-bed units R167 in the low season (in the high season it is R155/255).

Greater Kuduland Safaris

This up-market private game reserve company (☎ (015539) 720, fax 808) has three locations – Tshipise and Alldays reserves, and another at Makuya. The 10,000-hectare Tshipise Reserve, consisting of mopane trees and mixed bush, includes many species of game. In addition to shy leopards and cheetahs there are gemsboks, nyala, klipspringers and other antelope species. Their three to five-day hiking trails might be worth trying.

Accommodation in the main camp is in luxury huts and costs around R285 per person, all meals included. You have to stay a minimum of two days. There is the self-catering *Sunset Bushcamp* deep in the reserve. The R85 per person charge includes the 23-km transfer to the camp, linen and crockery. *The Lapa* is a self-catering bush camp in the Alldays Reserve, west of Alldays near the junction of the R521 and R572. The rate is R55 per person (children R40) and you must bring all food and bedding; the daily vehicle and guide charge is R135.

Honnet Nature Reserve

This 2200-hectare reserve, which adjoins Greater Kuduland Safaris at Tsipishe, is part of the Aventura Tshipise resort. It has giraffe, zebra and other game animals. There are hiking trails, one of which has a 12-bed hut.

MESSINA

The closest town to the Zimbabwe border, Messina is a hot, dusty little town with a frontier feel to it. The town grew around the copper mines which began operating in 1905 and are still functioning today. Road maps show Messina as being the same size as Pietersburg – it isn't. Away from the mines the town centre is a sleepy place. Groups of Zimbabweans wait patiently under the coral trees with mounds of luggage. A dog wanders down the street. The arrival of the train is a major event.

The Zimbabwean border is 12 km away at Beitbridge (on the Limpopo River) and is open from 5.30 am to 10.30 pm.

You can change money at the First National Bank, open from 9 am to 12.45 pm and 2 to 3.30 pm on weekdays, 8.30 am to 1 pm on Saturday.

You'll see some big baobabs on the road south of here, and five km south of the town just off the N1 is the **Messina Nature Reserve**, established to protect the trees. There are some animals such as nyala, kudu, Sharpe's grysbok and over 50 species of reptile. You can't camp here and if you aren't out by 4 pm you'll be locked in for the night; entry is free.

Places to Stay & Eat

The *municipal caravan park* (☎ (01553) 2170) is on the southern outskirts of town, about 1.5 km from the town centre. Sites cost around R12. Next door, the *Impala Lielie Hotel* (☎ (01553) 40127) has a pool and restaurant; single/double rondavels are R78/115. *Limpopo River Lodge* (☎ /fax (01553) 40205) has rooms for R65/85; self-contained rooms are R75/105. *Ilala Lodge* (☎ (01553) 3220), eight km from Messina on the Venetia Mine road, is signposted from the Beitbridge road; it costs R90 per person in grass-roofed rondavels.

The best place in town for a meal is the restaurant-cum-frontier bar *Meet 2 Eat* on the N1. There are also several fried-chicken places.

Getting There & Away

Bus Translux buses on the Jo'burg to Harare route stop at the Oasis Bakery (R100 to Jo'burg; and R130 to Harare via Bulawayo, R125 via Masvingo). Greyhound stops at Beitbridge on the other side of the river.

Every day at 3 pm a bus leaves from the taxi park, behind the main shopping street, for Louis Trichardt (R12). On Monday,

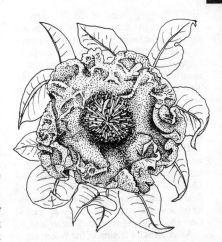

Baobab flower

Wednesday and Friday there's a Lukoto bus running to Sibasa (R12).

Train The *Bosvelder* terminates here at 9.20 am and returns to Jo'burg at 3 pm daily; 1st/2nd/3rd class fares to Jo'burg are R139/95/56. The *Limpopo* stops here on the Friday run between Jo'burg and Harare at 8.20 pm (9.15 pm on Sunday in the other direction); 1st/2nd class fares to Jo'burg are R154/107 and to Harare R179/123. Those lucky enough to be travelling on the *Limpopo* can carry out border-crossing formalities on the train.

Minibus Taxi If you're coming from Zimbabwe and want to take a taxi further south than Messina catch one at the border; there are many more there than in Messina. To Jo'burg it's R60. Messina to Louis Trichardt is R12 and from there to Pietersburg is R12. Taxis between the border and Messina cost as little as R3, but you might have to pay more. There are about three taxis a day to Sibasa for R12.

The Waterberg

The Waterberg, west of the N1, gets its names from the many swamps, springs and streams in the range. The 150-km-long range stretches from Thabazimbi in the south to the Lapalala River in the north-east and is usually divided into south and north regions. Two colourful brochures, *Waterberg North* and *Waterberg South*, free from tourist offices, cover these areas.

It is a wild and inspirational place, with sourveld and bushveld etched by rivers.

The poet and naturalist Eugene Marais wrote his famous works on termites and baboons (*The Soul of the White Ant* and *The Soul of the Ape*) here. He discovered a rare cycad but forgot to record its location. Rediscovered years later, it was named *Encephalartos eugenemaraisii* after him.

An unpleasant feature of the Waterberg is the number of hunting lodges. Their adver-

tising depicts smiling hunters with high-powered rifles posing with dead zebras, kudu and leopards. Avoid!

Horse-Riding

The Waterberg is a great location for horse-riding and there are a number of places where you can ride amidst wildlife. Equus Trails, within the Touch Stone Game Ranch (☎ (014) 765 0230, fax 765 0108), is south-east of Marken off the R518. It can be reached from Potgietersrus or Vaalwater.

The trails pass through Waterberg bushveld and near to the Lapalala River. It's not unusual to encounter rhinos and many other wildlife species. Accommodation is in overnight bush camps; tariffs depend on the trail length and accommodation type.

BONWA PHALA & MABULA

In the Waterberg area there are several private game reserves and lodges, including *Bonwa Phala Game Lodge* (☎ (014) 736 4101), fax 736 4767), about 30 km west of Warmbaths, which charges R340 per person, including all meals and game drives. You can hire a 4WD and do game self-drives (R80 plus fuel).

The 8000-hectare Mabula Game Reserve (☎ (015334) 771, fax 733) is of the luxury variety. Singles/doubles are R445/730 dinner, bed and breakfast, and R30 extra per person on weekends. Mabula is near the Waterberg and the 'big five' animals can be found there. To get to the reserve from Warmbaths take the R516. Turn off to Rooiberg after 34 km, and after four km take the right turn to Rhenosterhoekspruit. Mabula is seven km on.

THABAZIMBI

This town is 126 km west of Warmbaths on the R516 and 129 km north of Rustenburg on the R510. Nearby is the imposing Kransberg, highest peak of the Waterberg. The 2150-hectare **Ben Alberts Nature Reserve**, seven km south of town, has an abundance of wildlife and good game-viewing vantage points; there is a *caravan park* (☎ (014773) 21509) here. The *Kransberg*

Hotel (☎ (014773) 21207, fax 21237) on Deena St charges R110 per person for bed and breakfast.

VAALWATER & MELKRIVIER

Vaalwater, the main centre of the Waterberg, is 60 km north-west of Nylstroom on the R517. There are a number of attractions in the region, including the Lapalala Wilderness to the north. The moderately priced *Vaalwater Hotel* (☎ (015352), ask for 1 or 89) is the only source of nightlife in the region.

From Vaalwater there's a circular drive on an extremely scenic dirt road through the Waterberg. Head north-west of town on the R517 for 10 km then turn south for 37 km. At the prominent junction turn right for 20 km to the **Palace of the Vultures**, a breeding colony of Cape vultures *(Gyps coprotheres)*. Return to the junction but continue straight ahead over Rankin's Pass. Here, take the Tweestroom road back to the R517 and turn left to Vaalwater or right to Nylstroom.

North-east of Vaalwater is the pleasant little town of Melkrivier (Milk River), on the banks of the Lapalala. *Waterberg Natuurpraal* (☎ (015352), ask for 2531), a holiday resort, has a range of accommodation in rondavels/chalets for about R120/200 for four people (much more on weekends). *Emaweni Game Lodge* (☎ (015352), ask for 3011) is an up-market place with a magnificent aspect on the banks of the Lapalala.

To get to Melkrivier take the Vaalwater road from Nylstroom. In Vaalwater, turn north and drive for 45 km to Melkrivier.

LAPALALA WILDERNESS

This big private reserve (25,600 hectares) is an area of high ecological value. It has a number of animals – including black and white rhinos, zebras, blue wildebeests and several antelope species, plus hippos and crocs in bilharzia-free rivers – but it's best known as a conservation area. Over 270 species of birds have been recorded. In 1990, Lapalala was the first private reserve to obtain black rhinos. *Lapalala Wilderness: A Natural Heritage* contains a comprehensive species checklist.

The reserve is divided into three areas. In the wilderness area you don't have to take a guide when canoeing or hiking. Once you have driven in you are alone. The second area is an environmental school comprising Molope and Moletse, and the third contains Kolobe Lodge and Rhino Camp.

Ask the rangers to point out the unusual **termite mounds** built under layers in the sandstone. It almost appears that the ants have lifted the sandstone slabs and built underneath them, earning the builders the name 'Arnold Schwarzenegger ants'.

There are many **San paintings** in the reserve, especially along the Kgogong and Lapalala rivers. There are also a number of prehistoric **Iron Age sites**. These include the stone-walled settlements at Ndrobo, Tambuti and Malora (Sotho for 'ashes').

Places to Stay

Six small camps are scattered through the wilderness, with accommodation from R50 to R100 per person, depending on numbers. The camps are *Tambuti*, *Mukwa*, *Umdoni*, *Lepotedi*, *Munadu* and *Marula* – all named after trees indigenous to the area. There are cooking facilities, but you must bring all your own supplies. The minimum stay is two nights; book on (011) 453 7645) as Lapalala is popular.

Kolobe Lodge (☎ (011) 453 7645, fax 453 7649) has a 16-bed lodge, four luxury rondavels, a pool, restaurant and guided walks. For R285 per person you get all meals and game drives. Visitors usually have their own car, but the lodge will pick up from the railway station in Vaalwater. Clive Walker Safari's *Rhino Camp* (contact numbers are the same as Kolobe) accommodates eight in luxury-style tents for R195, all inclusive.

Getting There & Away

Lapalala is north of Nylstroom on the N1. From Nylstroom take the R517 to Vaalwater and from there head to Melkrivier. After 40 km take the turn-off to Melkrivier school and continue for 25 km. The gates at Lapalala close at 7 pm.

MASEBE NATURE RESERVE

This reserve of about 5000 hectares protects San rock paintings, old granaries and other pieces of material culture. The country is hot, dry and rugged but well-wooded, with many bird and animal species. The camp site and bungalows should be open by now.

From Potgietersrus follow the R518 to Marken and take the signposted Mogalakwenastroom road (a right turn) to the reserve.

Venda

The Venda area, once the Homeland of the VhaVenda people under the apartheid regime, is a fascinating place to visit for its cultures and scenery.

The Soutpansberg harbours rainforest and is strikingly lush compared to the hot, dry lowveld to the north. Several forests and lakes in the region are of great religious significance to the VhaVenda people.

Endear yourself to the locals with traditional VhaVenda greetings. When a man enters a house he says *Ndaa!* (Hello) and a woman says *Aa!* The response is *Ndaa!* or *Aa!* depending on the sex. When you leave the simple farewell is *Salani*. You might also want to try local delicacies, *nziya* (locusts) or *mopane* worms (caterpillars living on the mopane tree) – a crunchy snack, often dried on an open fire and added to a thick spicy sauce.

Warning

Venda is in a malarial area, and bilharzia is present in many of the dams and streams. Marauding crocodiles are also a reality.

THOHOYANDOU & SIBASA

Created as the capital of the Venda Home-

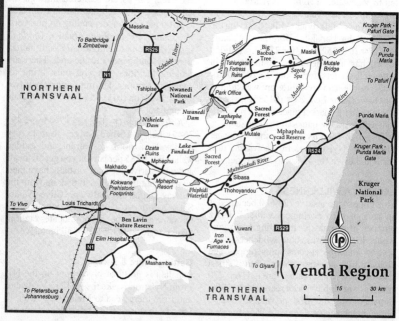

History of the VhaVenda people

Just when the VhaVenda people arrived in the Soutpansberg range, and where they came from, are matters of dispute among historians. There are elements of Zimbabwean culture, including stone structures similar in style (if not scale) to Great Zimbabwe, and mining and metal-working have long been important elements in the VhaVenda economy and culture. The Lemba people, another group living in Venda, appear to have had contact with Islam.

What is known is that in the early 18th century a group of VhaSenzi and VhaLemba, led by Chief Dimbanyika, crossed the Limpopo and located a tributary which they called the Nzhelele ('The Enterer'). They moved up the Nzhelele and into the Soutpansberg, calling their new land Venda, believed to mean 'the pleasant land'.

At Lwandali they set up a chief's kraal and called it Dzata. When Dimbanyika died some of his people moved south down the Nzhelele where they established another Dzata. Under the new chief, Thohoyandou, the VhaVenda flourished and their influence was felt widely. When Thohoyandou disappeared mysteriously, this Dzata was abandoned and there was a period of unrest as his offspring fought for succession.

Several invaders then tried to take over the VhaVenda lands. First came the Boers under Paul Kruger, then the Swazis, the BaPedi and the Tsonga. The Vha Venda, however, managed to avoid being overrun throughout the 19th century, and did not even admit missionaries into their territory. This was partly due to the geography of the Soutpansberg, which made attack difficult, and partly to the tse-tse fly which made this area unattractive to graziers.

It was not until 1898 that a Boer army of 4000 men conquered Venda. Perhaps if the VhaVenda had been able to hold out for a year, the defeat of the Boer republics in the 1899-1902 Anglo-Boer War would have given them time to negotiate a place in the Union of South Africa. That was not to be, and Venda was absorbed into the Transvaal, to be granted 'independent Homeland' status in 1979.

Today the region is part of Northern Transvaal Province but retains its unique culture. ■

land, Thohoyandou has a casino, some new public buildings and not much else. The adjacent town (more a suburb, really) of Sibasa is a few km north. Most of the area's public transport leaves from Sibasa.

The Venda tourist office (☎ (0159) 41100, 41821) is at the Ditike Craft Centre, on the Louis Trichardt road. Book accommodation for Acacia Park in Thohoyandou, the Nwanedi National Park, Mphephu Resort and Sagole Spa on (0159) 41577, fax 41048.

To find out what is happening in town get a copy of the *Mirror*, published on Friday (R1).

Tours

Several interesting tours run from the Ditike Craft Centre. A half-day tour costs R65 per person and a full-day tour is R100 (both with a minimum of three people). Longer tours and guided walks are available. There is a charge of R150 when the guide is away overnight. The highlight of the Southern Venda day tour is meeting Noria Mabasa, a

woman who sculpts traditional Venda characters in clay and wood (the latter medium was traditionally a 'men only' occupation).

Places to Stay

Thohoyandou/Sibasa does not have much in the way of accommodation. *Acacia Park* (☎ (0159) 22506) has 16 self-contained chalets for R90 a double; there are serviced caravan sites for R18 and you can camp for R12.

The motel-style *Bougainvillea Lodge* (☎ (0159) 21218) is about a km from Thohoyandu, up the hill towards Sibasa. It is friendly, clean and comfortable, but singles/doubles are not cheap at R120/180.

The *Venda Sun Hotel* (☎ (0159) 21011, fax 21367), in the centre of Thohoyandou, has rooms from R170/250. There's a casino, the *Baobab Restaurant*, a swimming pool and curio shop.

Getting There & Away

Air It's possible to fly from Lanseria Airport

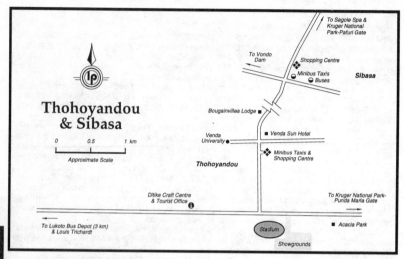

Thohoyandou
& Sibasa

0   0.5   1 km

Approximate Scale

To Sagole Spa &
Kruger National
Park-Pafuri Gate

To Vondo
Dam

Shopping Centre

Minibus Taxis
Buses

Sibasa

Bougainvillea Lodge ■

Venda Sun Hotel ■

Venda
University ●

Minibus Taxis &
Shopping Centre

Thohoyandou

Ditike Craft Centre
& Tourist Office ❶

To Kruger National Park-
Punda Maria Gate

To Lukoto Bus Depot (3 km)
& Louis Trichardt

Stadium

■ Acacia Park

Showgrounds

in Randburg (41 km from Jo'burg) to Thohoyandou with Theron Airways (☎ (011)
659 2738) on weekdays. The fare is R418
and the flight takes two hours.

Bus The Lukoto company runs one bus a day
to Sagole (R6), departing at about 12.30 pm
and arriving at about 6 pm. They also have
buses to Messina (R12) departing at 5 am on
Wednesday and Friday, 1 pm on Sunday. The
Lukoto depot is about five km west of the
Ditike Craft Centre on the Louis Trichardt
road.

Transtate runs between Pretoria and
Thohoyandou/Sibasa (R50). One service
leaves Pretoria at 8.30 am and arrives in
Sibasa at 5.30 pm, returning at 5.30 pm and
arriving in Pretoria at 9 am the following day.
This service passes through Kranskop (R20),
Pietersburg (R35) and Louis Trichardt
(R40). The second service is via Ndzelhele.

The Magweba company has a daily bus
from Sibasa to Sagole (R6) departing at 1 pm.

Minibus Taxi In Thohoyandou taxis congregate in the car park of the shopping centre
across the road from the Venda Sun. The fare
to Sibasa is R1.20. The main taxi park is in

Sibasa, on the corner of the road from
Thohoyandou. Fares include: Mutale R3,
Punda Maria (frequent taxis) R8, Vuwani
R7, Sagole Spa R6, Gomela R1.80, Messina
(three daily) R12, Louis Trichardt R7,
Mphephu Resort R3 and Jo'burg R55.

NWANEDI NATIONAL PARK

The dry, northern side of the Soutpansberg
provides an extremely scenic backdrop to the
park, although it's a contrast to Venda's other
lush landscapes. The vegetation is mainly
mopane and mixed woodland. It can be very
hot here in summer. The main attraction for
most visitors is fishing on the Nwanedi and
Luphephe dams (on tributaries of the
Nwanedi which feed into the Limpopo
River). The major walk in the park is to the
very scenic Tshihovhohovho Falls.

There is limited wildlife viewing, including white rhinoceros, warthogs, kudu,
blue wildebeests, impalas, elands, klipspringers and common duikers. There are
lions and cheetahs but they are in enclosures
– not much fun for the animals perhaps, but
they are fed near the fence and watching a
lion devour a cow is a thought-provoking
experience.

JON MURRAY

JEFF WILLIAMS

RICHARD EVERIST

RICHARD EVERIST

A	
B	
C	D

A: Union buildings, Pretoria, Gauteng
B: Kliptown squatters' houses, Soweto, Gauteng
C: Dancers, Sun City, Johannesburg, Gauteng
D: Dancers, Sun City, Johannesburg, Gauteng

Top: Termite mounds, Waterberg, Northern Transvaal
Left: Baboon's tail, Kolobe, Waterberg, Northern Transvaal
Right: Baobab tree on the road to Messina, Northern Transvaal

The gates of the Nwanedi National Park are open from 6 am to 6 pm.

Places to Stay & Eat

Tent sites cost R12 and there are four-person chalets/rondavels (R92). There are twin rooms (R177/262, dinner, bed and breakfast) and four-bed rooms (R189/286).

Basic supplies are available and there's a *restaurant*. You can hire canoes.

Getting There & Away

You can get to the park from Thohoyandou, entering at the Nwanedi Gate, but while the road is scenic there's a good chance of getting lost, and there are several km of bad dirt road. It's simpler to come via Tshipise and enter from the west. Tshipise is the nearest place where you can buy fuel.

By public transport you could take a minibus taxi from Sibasa to Gomela, a tiny village three km from the Nwanedi Gate. From the gate it's another six km to the office and accommodation along a quiet road.

MPHEPHU RESORT

This resort, known for its hot springs, is 34 km west of Thohoyandou. (Mphephu was one of the great chiefs of the VhaVenda and ruled from the late-19th century until his death in 1924. He was son of Makhado, the 'Lion of the North'.)

Day visits cost R2. Accommodation is in chalets which cost from R90. Book at the Ditike Craft Centre in Thohoyandou. There is a licensed self-service restaurant in the complex.

VhaVenda Arts & Crafts

VhaVenda culture is extremely rich and diversified, and a visit to the many arts & crafts outlets in this region is always rewarding. About 4000 people are actively engaged in local arts & crafts industries.

Perhaps most interesting are the many traditional potteries. Here you can see Venda pots, famous throughout South Africa, thrown and fired. As the potteries are a cottage industry it is necessary to have a guide so you can enter the village workplaces.

The master potters (perhaps in these days of equal opportunity, not the correct term) in Venda tradition are all women. The pots are fashioned from mud by hand on an old potsherd, smoothed with a piece of leather, dried in the sun for about three days (depending on the weather), glazed and fired. Originally the glaze was graphite but now many different types of paint are added.

Firing is done in a wide, shallow hole. Thin saplings of carefully selected local trees are added to control the rate of firing. If there is too much heat the pots will crack. Usually the firing takes about four hours.

Traditional pots come in 10 different sizes and designs. Each has a different function – cooking, serving food or liquids, or storage. The pots, which feature brightly coloured geometric designs, are more ornamental than functional.

Traditional clay figures *(zwifanyiso)* are fashioned from clay like the pots, but are sun-dried rather than fired. These figures may depict a group scene or individuals, such as important tribal personalities.

Woodcarvings are also popular. Traditionally woodcarving was a men-only occupation, but a modern master is the talented Noria Mabasa (see Tours). A number of local woods are used such as *mudzwin, mutango* and *musimbiri*. Carved items include chains attached to calabashes and bowls, salad bowls, spoons, trays, pots, walking sticks and knobkerries (a stick with a round knob at one end, used as a club or missile). ■

LAKE FUNDUDZI

This lake is a sacred site, as its water is believed to have come from the great sea which covered the earth before land was created. The python god, which holds an important place in the rites of Venda's matriarchal culture and once required human sacrifice, lives here. The lake is 35 km west of Thohoyandou but unfortunately you can't visit it without permission (unlikely to be granted) from the lake's priestess. Another home of the python god is the hot spring at Sagole. You do get a glimpse of the lake if you take a tour from Thohoyandu.

Near the lake is **Thathe-Vondo**, the Sacred Forest. A spirit lion guards the burial grounds of VhaVenda chiefs in the forest.

Mabudashango Hiking Trail

The four-day (50-plus km) Mabudashango Hiking Trail starts at Mabudashango Hut near the Thathe-Vondo forest station and heads for 14 km through the Sacred Forest to Fundudzi Camp. Day two is through the forest for 13 km to Mukumbani Camp; day three is a return loop of 15 km to Tshatshingo Waterfall; and the last day is an 11-km walk to the forest station.

Take precautions against ticks, mosquitoes and malaria. Accommodation is in basic shelters on the trail and in the forester's cottage at the Thathe-Vondo forest station. Book through the Department of Agriculture & Forestry, Private Bag X2247, Sibasa, Northern Transvaal.

SAGOLE

This VhaVenda town is near Sagole village and the hot springs spa of the same name. To the north-west of Sagole are the ruins of the **Tshiungane stone fortifications** and nearby, in caves, are the remains of dwellings with clay grain bins built into the rocky walls. What is believed to be the biggest **baobab** in Africa is close to the ruins.

Sagole Spa has two four-bed cottages with plunge pools fed by the nearby hot spring; these are a bargain at R115. The three-bed rondavels are R23 per person, R28 with showers. Dorm beds (usually booked for groups of children) are R6 and camp sites/caravan sites are R8/10. Book through the Ditike Craft Centre Tourist Office in Thohoyandou.

In the small village of Sagole you can arrange to visit a herbalist and diviner.

MUTALE

Near this village, north of Thohoyandou, there is a wood-carving workshop where you

---

Land of Legend

The lakes, rivers, mountains, caves and forests of Venda form a rich spirit world. Stories of natural and ancestral beings abound. Almost every body of water, whether it be a stream, waterfall or lake, is inhabited by 'water elves' or spirits.

Most famous of these is sacred Lake Fundudzi which can only be visited with the permission of the priestess of the lake. Around the lake there are a number of spirit gardens where spirits tend their crops, large rocks in the shape of drums where spirits meet in celebration and other sacred rocks where the VhaVenda make offerings to allow the spirits to sample recent crops.

In the Thathe-Vondo Forest, west of Thohoyandou, is the Holy Forest where no strangers are permitted to enter. At Lwamondo, south-west of Thohoyandou, the baboons (which once warned the VhaVenda of approaching enemies) are venerated. The nearby forest manifests a plague of snakes if anyone tries to steal firewood without the permission of the priest Tshifhe. If you are observant you may see the furtive Ditutwane when you visit Phiphidi Waterfall. These water spirits resemble half people and have only one eye, and a single leg and arm.

The most important of the initiation ceremonies is the fertility rite, the Domba. The drums made in Mutale resound night after night as VhaVenda maidens are prepared for adulthood. The ceremony culminates in the famous python dance when many VhaVenda girls join in a writhing 'conga' formation.

Herbalists and traditional doctors are very much part of daily life. By using an intricately carved divining bowl (the *ndilo*) a diviner is able to communicate with spirits and share their wisdom. ■

can see the ceremonial domba drums being made. These drums are used in the python dance, part of the female puberty ceremony.

VUWANI & MASHAMBA

South of Vuwani, you can see the remains of Iron Age furnaces where the VhaVenda smelted high-grade iron for centuries. Many of their metal-working skills have been lost, but the craft of making attractive pottery continues. Mashamba village also has several metal-working foundries.

The North-East

North-eastern Transvaal, often overlooked because of the more popular Blyde River and Transvaal (Klein) Drakensberg areas to the south, is well worth a visit.

It is very culturally rich, being the traditional home of the Tsonga-Shangaan and Lobedu people. It is also popular for a north-south traverse through Kruger National Park or a visit to one of the many private reserves in the Hoedspruit area. The main town of Tzaneen is a pleasant place and a good base for trips into the nearby scenic Modjadji and Magoebaskloof regions.

VENDA TO TZANEEN

A popular route goes all the way through Kruger National Park from the Punda Maria Gate to one of the numerous exits in the south (see Kruger National Park in the Eastern Transvaal chapter). If you are coming from Venda, the Tzaneen/Letaba region can also be reached via the R529, and there are a number of interesting places close to this route.

Giyani

The former Homeland of the Tsonga-Shangaan people, the Gazankulu area is extremely poor. Yet the population carries on in spite of dust, flies and poor sanitation. Kids laugh as they kick a football around on the barren plains. Hopefully, these stoic people will be given more chance in the new South Africa.

The main centre, Giyani (population 14,000), is north of Phalaborwa, and has a frontier atmosphere. It is best reached on the road running north from the R36 at Mooketsi or the R529 road running south from the R524, 45 km east of Thohoyandou. Few visitors come here and there is almost no tourist development. In fact, we could only find one place to stay, the *Giyani Hotel* (☎ (0158) 23230). For traditional food such as chicken offal, pap and vleis try the *Bush Spaza Shop*.

Transtate buses run between Jo'burg and Giyani, via Louis Trichardt.

Hans Merensky Nature Reserve

This 5200-hectare reserve (☎ (0152) 38633)

NORTHERN TRANSVAAL

Lebowa & Gazankulu

On pre-1994 maps of the Transvaal you'll see the areas taken up by the 'self-governing Homelands' of Lebowa and Gazankulu. These are now part of the new province of Northern Transvaal.

Lebowa, Homeland of the Lobedu people, comprised eight areas, two large and six small. The capital of the region was Lebowakgomo, on the Chuniespoort road. The Homeland of the Tsonga-Shangaan people, **Gazankulu**, was divided into four sections, with the two largest bordering Kruger National Park. The capital was Giyani, in the northern section, north of Phalaborwa.

How and when these two Homelands will be fully integrated into South Africa is not yet certain. In late 1994 they still had their own governing infrastructures and police forces. When I visited private reserves in Gazankulu I had to apply for entry at the border gate, still staffed by local forces. ■

is bordered by the Letaba River but you risk bilharzia if you swim in the river, not to mention the risk from larger denizens – crocodiles and hippos. You'd have to be lucky to see a lion or a leopard, but there is plenty of other game.

There are several hiking trails, of up to four days, or you can view game from your own car. To book the trails write to the reserve at Private Bag X502, Letsitele 0885, or phone ☎ (0152) 38635.

The Aventura chain's *Eiland Resort* (☎ (0152) 38763, fax 38692), in the reserve, has rondavels for R145 (R225 in high season) and unpowered sites for R7.50 plus R10 per person.

To get there, take the R71 east from Tzaneen towards Phalaborwa, and turn off to the left onto the R529 after 27 km. The reserve is 40 km on. Occasional minibus taxis run along the R71, but the rest of the journey will require hitching.

Tsonga Kraal Open-Air Museum
In Hans Merensky is the Tsonga Kraal (☎ (0152) 38727), a museum of Tsonga traditional life. It comprises sleeping huts, a chief's hut, grain stores, cooking shelters, a sacrificial place and domestic animal enclosures. The village people wear traditional dress and play their own musical instruments. There are guided tours at 10 am and 3 pm from Monday to Friday and 10 am on Saturday; it is closed on Sunday.

Modjadji Nature Reserve
This small reserve (☎ (015) 632 6144) of 305 hectares protects forests of the ancient Modjadji cycad. In the summer mists this place takes on an ethereal atmosphere.

Take the Ga-Kgabane turn-off from the R36 about 10 km north of Duivelskloof; the turn-off to the reserve is a few km on.

Duivelskloof
This small village is in the wooded hills north of Tzaneen. The name refers to the devilishly hard time the early European settlers had getting their wagons up and down the hills. In 1916 it was to be called Modjadji, after the Rain Queen, but the white population objected because of 'heathen connotations' – they named it after the devil instead!

Tourist information is available from the town hall (☎ (01523) 9246).

There are a number of hiking trails in the vicinity. The Panorama and Piesangkop trails are accessible to most people. The library provides free photocopied walking notes.

Places to Stay & Eat *Duivelskloof Municipal Chalets & Caravan Park* (☎ (01523) 9246) has sites for R30, two-bed rondavels for R50 and four-person rondavels (with attached kitchen and bathroom) for R95. There are guest farms and holiday cottages in the area; enquire at the tourist office.

The *Imp Inn* (☎ (01523) 9253), a nice country pub (but with a disillusioned, grumpy and often uniformed Afrikaner clientele),

---

Modjadji – the Rain Queen
In Africa it is unusual for a woman to be sovereign of a tribe, but the Rain Queen is an exception. The Queen resides in the town of Ga-Modjadji in the Bolebodu district near Duivelskloof. Every year, around November, a festival is held to celebrate the coming of the rains, which is presided over by the Queen. The *indunas* (tribal headmen) select people to dance naked and call for rain, to perform traditional rituals, and for male and female initiation ceremonies. After the ceremony, the rain falls. The absence of rain is usually attributed to some event such as the destruction of a sacred place – a situation only resolved with further ritual.

During the rest of the year the Queen has a number of other functions. She never marries yet still bears children. When she dies, succession normally falls to the eldest of her daughters (the fathers have very insignificant roles). The Queen is buried in the evening and only close relatives and indunas are permitted to go to the burial place. ■

The Modjadji Cycad
The Modjadji cycad *(Encephalartos transvenosus)*, a living fossil, is one of the largest cycads in the world. It averages a height of five to eight metres and can grow to 13 metres. It dates back to the Mesozoic era, approximately 50 to 60 million years ago, when dinosaurs roamed the landscape.

Some claim that cycads have survived here because they grow on land protected by the Rain Queen (see boxed story). It is more likely that they have survived because local inhabitants have found no use for them. ■

has singles/doubles for R100/145, including breakfast (R70/100 on weekends). A couple of servings of toasted sandwiches are R10 and a pub meal is R15.

LETABA DISTRICT
The Letaba Valley is east of Pietersburg, between two chunks of the former Lebowa Homeland. Tzaneen is the main town in the area and most places of interest are easily reached from here. The valley is subtropical and lush, with tea plantations and crops of tropical fruits, while on the hills are forests, mainly of the plantation variety. Tours of the **Sapekoe Tea Plantation** (☎ (01523) 53241) are held from Tuesday to Friday.

The surrounding scenic hills are popular with visitors and hikers, although remember that this area's tourist slogan is 'Land of the Silver Mist' because of the summer rain and mists which wreathe the mountains.

The 100-km drive along the R71 from Pietersburg to Tzaneen is scenic. Some 24 km east of Pietersburg at Turfloop is the **University of the North**, the largest black university in the country. A further six km on, at Boyne, is **Zion City Moria**, the headquarters of the Zion Christian Church. At Easter millions of followers (identifiable by their badge with a silver star on a green background) congregate here.

At Haenertsburg the road splits, with the R71 reaching Tzaneen via the steep Magoebaskloof Pass, while the R528 runs there more gently along George's Valley.

Haenertsburg
Haenertsburg, a village established during the 1887 gold rush, is on the escarpment above the Letaba Valley, and is the centre of a forestry and cherry-growing region. The Cherry Blossom Festival is held at Cheerio Halt Farm in late September/early October.

Places to Stay About eight km north of Haenertsburg, *Troutwaters Inn* (☎ (015276) 4245) has fairly pricey camp sites and chalets, and hotel rooms for R150/210 with breakfast (R60 for each extra adult). Some 2.5 km from Haenertsburg on the R71 to Magoebaskloof is comfortable *Glenshiel Lodge* (☎ (015276) 4336, fax 4475); rooms start at R295 per person, all inclusive.

The Magoebaskloof
The Magoebaskloof is the escarpment on the edge of the highveld, and the road here drops quickly down to Tzaneen and the lowveld, passing through plantations and large tracts of thick indigenous forest. The high summer rainfall means that there are a number of waterfalls in the area, including **Debengeni Falls** in the De Hoek State Forest. You can swim in the pool at the bottom. Be careful, as there have been many deaths here. To get there turn west off the R71 at Bruphy Sawmills.

Author John Buchan once lived here, near the present Magoebaskloof Hotel, and his book *Prester John* is set in the area.

Woodbush State Forest This is the largest indigenous forest in the Transvaal and there are some very tall trees. Leopards are among the animals which live here.

Magoebaskloof Hiking Trails There are several trails in the area. Walks take up to three days and pass through some beautiful country. The walking can be challenging and you should be fit before setting out.

Two recommended trails are the three-day, 50-km **Grootbosch** and the three-day, 36-km **Dokolewa**. Both begin at the De Hoek Forest Station and share the first 10 km to the Broederstroom. Overnight accommodation for the Grootbosch is in the Grootbosch and Berg-en-dal lapas, and for the Dokolewa in the Broederstroom and Woodbush huts. Book with the Forest Region office (☎ (01315) 41058), Private Bag X503, Sabie.

Places to Stay The *Magoebaskloof Hotel* (☎ /fax (015276) 4276) has singles/doubles from R190/280 for bed and breakfast (dinner is an additional R49). *Magoebaskloof Holiday Resort* (☎ (01523) 53147, fax 53180), on the R71 about 25 km south-west of Tzaneen, has self-contained rondavels.

Lakeside Chalets (☎ (015276) 4245), 32 km from Tzaneen on the R71, has caravan sites for R35 (R45 in season) and chalets for two/three people for R130/155 (R150/185 in high season).

Tzaneen

Tzaneen, the largest town in the Letaba area, is a good place to base yourself. Tourist information is available from the town hall (☎ (0152) 307 1411) or Letaba Tourism (☎ (015276) 4307).

You can change money at the ABSA Trust Bank or the First National Bank in the town centre. Opposite the Trust Bank, near the Karos Hotel, is a telephone bureau where you can make hassle-free international calls. The Nu Metro cinema complex, open every day for two showings, is in the Oasis Mall, Aqua St.

Clarke's Trips & Tours (☎ (0152) 307 2000) take tours throughout Letaba. The town of **Nkowankowa**, in a small part of the former Gazankulu off the R36, south of Tzaneen, is a crafts-based industrial centre.

Places to Stay *Fairview Caravan Park* (☎ (0152) 307 4809) is one km from the town centre, a turn-off from either the Phalaborwa road or Danie Joubert St. In the Arbour Park shopping centre, on the corner of Soetdoring and Geelhout Sts, *Arbour Park Travel Lodge* (☎ /fax (0152) 307 1831) has singles/doubles for about R85/110. The *Karos Tzaneen Hotel* (☎/fax (0152) 307 3140) charges from R210/285, with breakfast.

Five km out of town on the Phalaborwa road is *Steffi's Sun Lodge* (☎ (0152) 307 1475), a very pleasant B&B with friendly owners; singles/doubles are R100/150. The balcony of this Cape Dutch-style house is a great place to relax. There are a number of other B&Bs in the area, at around R100 per person; enquire at the information centre.

The Coach House (☎/fax (0152) 307 3641), about 15 km south of Tzaneen, near the New Agatha Forest, is a refurbished old hotel with views and good food. Rooms start at R250 per person, for bed and breakfast.

Places to Eat *Nando's*, on the corner of Lannie Ave and Danie Joubert St, has half/full chicken packs for R22/36. *Tino's Pizzeria* on Agatha St and *The Villa*, on Danie Joubert, has small pizzas from R20. *Atelier Koffiehaus* at 46 Boundary St has great pancakes. There are two good steakhouses, the *Porterhouse* near the Oasis Mall on Aqua St and the *Spur* on the corner of Lannie Ave and Morgan St.

Getting There & Away The minibus-taxi park is behind the OK Centre, off the main street in the centre of town. Fares include to Jo'burg R55, Phalaborwa R15, Pietersburg R12 (change at Boyne), Haenertsburg R10, Duivelskloof R3.50 and Lydenburg R20. To get to Louis Trichardt take a taxi to Duivelskloof and another from there.

A Transtate bus service (mainly for miners) passes through Pietersburg and Tzaneen on Friday and returns on Sunday. LT Tours buses stop at the Old Roadhouse next to the northern ford of the Groot-Letaba River. You can buy tickets at the LT Tours

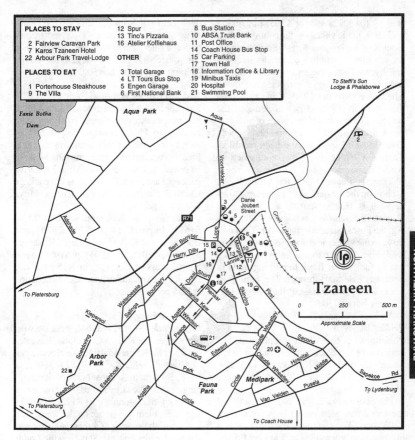

PLACES TO STAY	12 Spur	8 Bus Station
2 Fairview Caravan Park	13 Tino's Pizzaria	10 ABSA Trust Bank
7 Karos Tzaneen Hotel	16 Atelier Koffiehaus	11 Post Office
22 Arbour Park Travel-Lodge		14 Coach House Bus Stop
	OTHER	15 Car Parking
PLACES TO EAT		17 Town Hall
	3 Total Garage	18 Information Office & Library
1 Porterhouse Steakhouse	4 LT Tours Bus Stop	19 Minibus Taxis
9 The Villa	5 Engen Garage	20 Hospital
	6 First National Bank	21 Swimming Pool

NORTHERN TRANSVAAL

office (☎ (0152) 307 2950) at the Road-house. These buses run between Phalaborwa and Jo'burg, via Louis Trichardt.

Lekgalameetse Nature Reserve

A reserve of 20,000 hectares in mountainous country intersected by the Ga-Selati River, Lekgalameeste includes some remaining indigenous forests. As a transition region between the lowveld and the Drakensberg, it is particularly rich in plants, with over 1200 species, including the rare *Aloe monotropa*. The huge yellowwoods and sneezewoods here are some of the biggest in the country.

Occasionally antelopes can be seen and there are leopards, as well as some rare butterflies. Cabins are available (about R60) as well as tents on the hiking trails. The area is still sometimes known as The Downs, as it resembles the Surrey Downs in England in parts.

The park office (☎ (0152302), ask for 1514) is near Trichardtsdal, west off the R36 about 55 km south of Tzaneen.

Wolkberg Wilderness Area

South of Tzaneen in the northern tail of the Drakensberg, this 22,000-hectare wilderness area (☎ (015272) ask for 1303) has hiking trails and, in the valleys to the south and east, strands of indigenous forest. Some animals are returning, including a few shy leopards and hyenas, after the area was shot-out by hunters and the *dagga* growers who flourished here until the 1950s – it's rumoured that their crop still grows in some of the ravines. Hikers should be aware of snakes – black mambas, puff adders and berg adders. Over 150 bird species have been recorded. There's a lot of rain here in summer; in winter it can get cold.

There is a *camp site* at the Serala Forest Station on the western side (the nearest town to here is Haenertsburg), although from Tzaneen the main access point is via the New Agatha Forest Station to the north. You can't drive in the wilderness area, so plan your trip well. Fires aren't permitted so you'll need a gas or fuel stove. Book the hiking trails (a permit is essential) through The State Forester, Serala State Forest, Private Bag X102, Haenertsburg 0730.

PHALABORWA

Phalaborwa is new, clean and planned. The majority of the black population live in the nearby townships of Nawakgale, Lulekani, Majeje and Namakushan. Most people speak only a little English.

Phalaborwa is a copper-mining town, and the metal has been mined here for at least 1200 years. You can tour the current mine, a big open-cut operation, at 9 am on Friday. Phone first – (01524) 80 2342. In Park St there's an indigenous tree park. Just near the airport turn-off there is a mystery tree, part mopane with a marula growing out of its side!

The Phalaborwa Gate into Kruger Park is three km from town. The Phalaborwa Association for Tourism office (☎ (01524) 85860) is close to the gate and is open from 7.30 am to 5 pm on weekdays, 8 am to noon on Saturday.

Max Trax (☎ /fax (01524) 5284) offer eco-tours with a difference. Local Tsonga-Shangaan, VhaVenda, Sotho and Pedi people take kids and adults into the bush and intro-

duce them to its secrets, including food gathering. Accommodation is on mattresses under bushes and meals are cooked on a camp fire. The cost is R120 for adults (minimum of eight) and R80 for children.

Touring Kruger National Park

For people with limited time in South Africa, it is possible to visit Kruger by flying from Jo'burg to Phalaborwa, hiring a car for touring the park and then returning the car at Phalaborwa airport before returning by air to Jo'burg. Airlink and InterAir's Fly-Drive packages are good. Best of all is the package which includes the superb Khoka Moya Wildlife Encounters.

Hire cars are available from Avis (☎ (01524) 5169), Imperial (☎ (01524) 2376) and Budget (☎ (01524) 85404). Bell's Bushveld Safaris (☎ (01524) 4805) provides good guided tours of the park for R150 per day plus R1 per km, and private accommodation at R55 per person.

Places to Stay & Eat

Ingwe Park (☎ (01524) 3964), three km west of town on the R71 to Gravelotte, has sites for R30 plus R5 per adult (R5 for electricity).

Allin's Travel Lodge (☎ (01524) 5805, fax 5808) is on Palm Ave just north of the shopping centre. The large rooms – almost suites – with air-conditioning cost R125/160/190 a single/double/triple (more on the weekend); it's worth the money and there's also a restaurant. Nearby on Kiaat St is *Lantana Lodge* (☎ (01524) 85855, fax 85193) where caravan sites are R25 plus R2 per person and R2 for electricity, and flatlets are R120/160 for singles/doubles. The *Impala Inn* (☎ (01524) 5681, fax 85234) is at the northern end of Palm Ave, on the corner of Hardekool St. Rooms cost from R155/227.

Selati Lodge (☎ (01524) 89 2122, fax 2865), on Rooibos St, costs from R120/210; *Tiffany's*, one of the town's better dining places, is here. *Sefapane Lodge* (☎ (01524) 87041, fax 87042), on the corner of Koper and Essenhout Sts, has a range of rooms from R80 per person.

There are a number of B&Bs. Two good

ones are *Daan & Zena's* (☎ (01524) 89 2418), 15 Birkenhead St (R70/120); and *Steyn Cottage* (☎ (01524) 2836), off President Steyn St (R85/130).

The *Bushveld Tavern* (☎ /fax (01524) 2381), 13 km south-west of town on the R530 to Mica, has chalets from R140. In Gravelotte the small *Casa Creda Hotel* (☎ (015231) 4214) charges from R65/85.

Getting There & Away

Air InterAir (☎ (01524) 86144) flies to Jo'burg (R324), Durban (R568) and Nelspruit (R88) from Phalaborwa. Airlink (☎ (01524) 85823, fax 85813) flies to Jo'burg for R342. Both airlines also have discount fares.

Bus City to City (book through Translux) has a Jo'burg to Phalaborwa via Lydenburg service on Tuesday, Thursday and Sunday (R85).

LT Tours has buses daily except Saturday between Phalaborwa and Jo'burg via Louis Trichardt and other towns on the N1. Travel times from Jo'burg are 4½ hours to Pietersburg, six hours to Louis Trichardt and eight hours to Phalaborwa. In Phalaborwa buy tickets from Turn Key Travel (☎ (01524) 4492) in the Rentmeester Building; buses leave from the Impala Inn.

LT fares are to Pretoria (R96), Naboomspruit (R64), Potgietersrus (R54), Pietersburg (R43), Tzaneen (R22) and Louis Trichardt (R22). The fare from Jo'burg to Phalaborwa is R107.

Minibus Taxi There aren't many minibus taxis in this area, and even fewer run south to the lowveld between Kruger Park and the Drakensberg escarpment. Most run to Tzaneen (R15) and south as far as Hoedspruit (R10). There is a taxi park near the corner of Sealene Rd and Mellor Ave, about 300 metres south-west of the town centre. From Hoedspruit you could catch a minibus taxi to Acornhoek, 31 km south, from where there's a Transtate bus service to Nelspruit via Hazyview, then on to Jo'burg.

HOEDSPRUIT

Hoedspruit, at the junction of the R527 and R40, is a good jumping-off point for trips to the northern private reserves which border Kruger. The town has big army and air force bases.

Information can be obtained from the library. There are three banks – the First National, Standard and United.

The *Fort Copieba Hotel* (☎ (01528) 31175) has bed and breakfast for R90 per person. 'The fort' is the place to eat and party as well; there are bands from Tuesday to Saturday. On the R40 South of Hoedspruit, *Mduma Boma* (☎ (01528) 32184) has very secluded self-catering cottages for R65 per person, (minimum R160).

There is minibus taxi rank near the railway station; the minibuses go to Jo'burg, Phalaborwa and Pietersburg. The thrice weekly City to City Jo'burg-Phalaborwa service stops here; book through Translux. Fares are R15 to Phalaborwa, R80 to Jo'burg.

CHEETAH BREEDING PROJECT

South of Hoedspruit on the R40, the Cheetah Breeding Project (☎ (01528) 31633) is both a breeding station and study centre. It is open from 8 am and 4 pm daily; entry is R16.50.

PRIVATE GAME RESERVES – NORTHERN TRANSVAAL

The area just west of Kruger contains a large number of private reserves, usually sharing a border with Kruger and thus has most of the 'big five' animals. These reserves are often extremely pricey but with an economic stake in their guests getting close to animals, they have good viewing facilities.

The most famous private reserves are just north of the Kruger Gate in Eastern Transvaal (see that chapter). Around Hoedspruit, and Kruger's Orpen and Phalaborwa gates, there is another group, generally cheaper than those to the south. See the Eastern Transvaal chapter for more information on private reserves in general.

Lodges Near Phalaborwa

To the east of the R527, on the road between Mica and Hoedspruit, are two reputable reserves. *Mohlabetsi* (☎ (01311) 28154) has singles/doubles for R347/510, and *Tshukudu* (☎ (01528) 32476, fax 32078) charges from R500/800.

There are a number of private lodges near the Kruger's Phalaborwa Gate, including: *Mbufu* (☎ (01524) 4071), self-catering R110 per person; *Silonkwe* (☎ (01524) 85428); *Sable* (☎ (01524) 4746); and the *Sunset Hotel* (☎ /fax (01524) 85414) where singles/doubles are R155/240 (breakfast is R25). All of these places arrange game drives.

Manyeleti Game Reserve

This 23,400-hectare reserve is between Sabi Sands and Kruger Park's Orpen Gate. It shares a border, and thus animals, with Kruger and offers some of the area's least expensive accommodation in the public camp (☎ (0200) ask for Manyeleti 3). There are two private operations within Manyeleti – *Khoka Moya* (see following) and *Honeyguide* (☎ (011) 483 2734, fax 728 3767).

Khoka Moya

Khoka Moya (☎ (01528) 31729; (011) 465 7182) means 'capture the spirit', and this is a great place to experience the South African bush. You can go 'rhino monitoring' with very professional guides (see below). Full board in the main camp is R535 per person per day, all inclusive. *Molwareng Sky Beds*, R280 per person, are huts on stilts with a kitchen, built well off the ground and overlooking a waterhole.

Kapama Game Reserve

South of Hoedspruit off the R40, the 11,000-hectare Kapama Game Reserve (☎ (012) 804 1711, fax 86 1237) has guesthouse and camp accommodation ranging from R385 to R450 per person, all inclusive.

Klaserie Private Nature Reserve

South of Phalaborwa and east of Hoedspruit, this reserve covers 60,000 hectares and contains a similar range of birds and animals (including lions and elephants) to Kruger. To visit you must book on (01528) 32461.

Timbavati Private Nature Reserve

Timbavati has a good reputation. The reserve

Rhino Monitoring Units

Bruce and Judy Meeser run a Rhino Monitoring Unit (RMU) out of Khoka Moya (☎ (01528) 31729). They locate and track rhinos daily, identifying and coding each animal using sophisticated night-vision binoculars, GPS tracking systems, portable radios and rhino identikits.

RMUs consist of two scouts, a mediator and from four to six monitors, the latter members of the public. To maintain contact with the rhinos the teams sleep out in the bush and meet at midday each day for debriefing, to relax and to plan the next phase. There is a comfortable base area should the weather turn bad. Monitors join in from Friday to Monday.

You too can become a monitor, which means you are not just animal-gawking but actually contributing, and chances are when the rhinos are dining at Mala Mala, you will get to see unusual things, learn bushcraft and see species which are active at night – for much less cost. ∎

is jointly owned by a large number of people dedicated to conservation.

On the road into Timbavati is *Thornybush* (☎ (01528) 31976), a luxurious place in its own reserve which costs R550 per person, all inclusive. Other places to stay in Timbavati area include *Tanda Tula* (book on (021) 794 6500), *Motswari* and *M'Bali*

(book both on (011) 463 1990, fax 463 1992). Motswari costs R625, M'Bali starts at R590, and Tanda Tula is R450 per person, fully inclusive. In the south of the Timbavati area is *Ngala* (☎ (011) 803 8421), where you can stay for R750 per person, all inclusive. This camp is actually within the Kruger National Park.

Eastern Transvaal

There's a lot to do in this province. There are many hiking, horse-riding and mountain-bike trails in the vicinity of the Drakensberg escarpment; picturesque and historic towns like Pilgrim's Rest, Sabie, Graskop and Barberton; great fishing valleys; and world-famous Kruger National Park, which is bordered by a host of luxurious private game reserves.

Eastern Transvaal was once part of the Transvaal Province. See the Gauteng and Northern Transvaal chapters for some of the white history of the region.

Transvaal Drakensberg

The highveld ends suddenly at this dramatic escarpment which tumbles down to the eastern lowveld. The Transvaal (Klein) Drakensberg is not so much peaks as cliffs, and there are stunning views. As it is prime vacation territory there's a lot of accommodation, much of it expensive, but it fills up at peak times. The population density is low, so there's little public transport.

Winters are cold, with occasional snowfalls. Summers are warm, but after the sweltering lowveld it's a relief to get up here. The difference in temperature between Hazyview and Graskop is well worth the 40-km drive up Kowyns Pass. Mists can be a driving and hiking hazard year-round.

Warning
There is little risk of malaria in the high country, but if you walk into the gorge you will need to take precautions.

BLYDE RIVER CANYON
The 26,000-hectare Blyde River Gorge Nature Reserve snakes north almost 60 km from Graskop, following the escarpment and meeting the Blyde River as it carves its way down to the lowveld. The Blyde's spectacu-

---

EASTERN TRANSVAAL PROVINCE
(Its post-election name is now Mpumalanga)
Capital: Nelspruit
Main Languages: Afrikaans, English, si-Swati and Xitsonga
Pre-1994: The south-eastern part of Transvaal Province, and most of the Homeland of KwaNgwane
Highlights:
- Kruger National Park
- The Transvaal Drakensberg & Blyde River Canyon
- Subtropical climate on the eastern lowveld

---

lar canyon, nearly 30-km long, is one of South Africa's scenic highlights.

This description, from north to south, begins near the Manoutsa Cliffs (see the aside on birdwatching in this section) at the junction of the Tzaneen road (R36) and the R531 (sometimes marked on maps as a continuation of the R527).

Following the R36 as it turns south and climbs up from the lowveld through the Strijdom Tunnel and scenic Abel Erasmus Pass, you pass the turn-off to the R532 and come to the village of Mogaba and the turn-off to the **Museum of Man**, an archaeological site with rock paintings and other finds on show

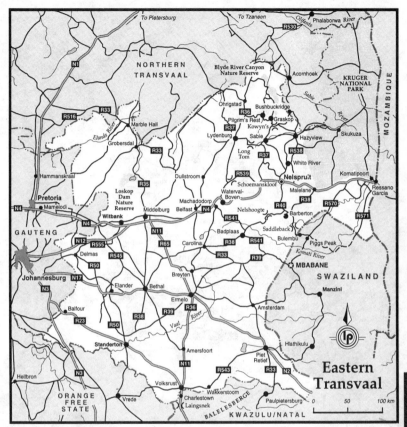

Eastern Transvaal

daily between 8 am and 5 pm. Also in the area are the **Echo Caves** where Stone Age relics have been found. The caves get their name from dripstone formations which echo when tapped. There are guided tours at R12 for half an hour. The guide might demand a huge tip.

If you return to the R532 junction and proceed east along the R532 you come to the Aventura Blydepoort resort. There is a good view of the **Three Rondavels** from within the resort; you get a free permit from the resort reception to go to the lookout. The Rondavels are huge cylinders of rock with hut-like pointy 'roofs', rising out of the far wall of the canyon. There are a number of short walks in the area to points where you can look down to the Blydepoort Dam. A little further on, the R532 passes another viewpoint across to the Three Rondavels.

Bourke's Luck Potholes, at the confluence of the Blyde and Truer rivers, are weird cylindrical holes carved into the rock by whirlpools in the river. They are interesting, although perhaps not as great an attraction as they are touted to be. Still, it's worth stopping off as there is a good visitors centre with information on the geology, flora & fauna of

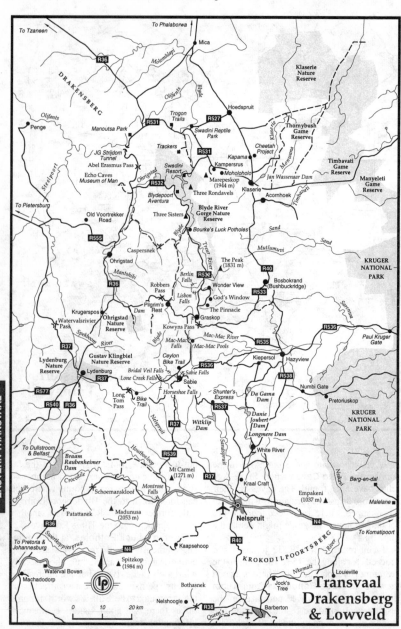

Transvaal
Drakensberg
& Lowveld

What's in a Name?

During one of their great treks in 1840, Voortrekkers led by Hendrik Potgieter set out from Potchefstroom to establish a route to the sea. When they reached the Transvaal escarpment the wagons could go no further. Potgieter and a party set off on horseback for Delagoa Bay (Maputo). When they failed to return on a prearranged day the main party believed them to be dead. The river they camped by was thus called the Treur ('mourning'). The main party, on the return journey to Potchefstroom, were overtaken by Potgieter near another river. Where the parties were reunited was henceforth named the Blyde ('rejoicing'). ■

the canyon. There's a fee of R2.50 to see the potholes. A good booklet, *Bourke's Luck Potholes Interpretative Trail* is available at the visitors centre.

The R532 follows the Truer south to its source, and further on is a turn-off to the R534 loop road. This road leads to the spectacular viewpoints of **Wonder View** and **God's Window**. (You can also take the R532 north from Graskop to get here; it is well signposted.)

At God's Window there's a short trail to views of the lowveld 1000 metres below. Just on your left as you leave God's Window car park is a small patch of prehistoric-looking *fynbos* (fine bush), usually associated with Western Cape Province. A few km on you pass the **Pinnacle**, an impressive rock formation which juts out from the escarpment. The R534 joins the R532 three km north of Graskop.

Hiking Trails

There are several great hiking trails in the area. The 38.5-km **Protea** is a four-day circular trail beginning and ending at Bourke's Luck Potholes; the 25-km **Yellowwood** (*Geelhout* in Afrikaans) is a two-day circular trail, also beginning and ending at the potholes. The **Op-de-Berg** (four days) begins at the potholes and takes you into the canyon. All of these trails cost R15 per person per night (students R7.50), and should be booked in advance (☎ (01315) 81216, from 9 am to 12.30 pm weekdays) as there are limits on the number of people. No camping is permitted in the reserve. A good map of the trails is available from the visitors centre at the potholes.

The 65-km **Blyde River Canyon Hiking Trail** begins at God's Window and ends on the lowveld near the Swadini resort. This is done as a five-day hike and lets you explore the spectacular Blyde River Canyon. There is a maximum of 30 and a minimum of two persons on this trail.

For bookings (well in advance as this area is very popular) and more information contact the Officer-in-Charge (☎ (01315) 81216), Blyde River Canyon Nature Reserve, Private Bag X431, Graskop 1270.

The 77-km **Fanie Botha Hiking Trail** is a five-day walk (less if you do only a section), mainly through plantations but with some good views; it begins at the Ceylon Forest Station near Sabie and ends at God's Window north of Graskop. The 69-km, five-day **Prospector's Trail** meanders through the Sabie and Pilgrim's Rest area and it isn't too strenuous. You can book these two trails through the Eastern Transvaal Forestry Region (☎ (01315) 41058), Private Bag X503, Sabie 1260.

Places to Stay

As well as accommodation in the towns on top of the escarpment, there are a number of places to stay close to the canyon. *Aventura Blydepoort* (☎ (01323) 80155) is a large resort and has all the usual facilities. Tent sites cost R13.50/18 in the low/high season plus R10 per person, two-bed units cost from R120/160 and standard four-bed units are R145/225. At the bottom of the escarpment, on the eastern side but still on the Blyde River, is Aventura's *Swadini* (☎ (01528) 35141); camping and four-bed units are the same as for Blydepoort.

One of the area's best places to stay is also at the bottom of the escarpment, to the north of Swadini. Dave and Julienne Rushworth's *Trackers* (☎ (01528) 35033) is a beautifully situated private reserve taking in the strikingly different ecosystems of the highveld and the lowveld. The reserve caters mainly to educational groups, but individuals are welcome. Basic camping costs R10 and a cottage R45 per person or R100 for dinner, bed and breakfast (the meals are excellent). Trips to study the natural vegetation of the region are conducted from Trackers by Tamboti Botanical Trails; the cost is R20 per person per day.

To get to Trackers take the R527 west from Hoedspruit and after about 20 km turn south onto the small Driehoek road, just after you cross the Blyde River. After 6.5 km you will see their signpost; it is a steep climb up towards the escarpment to Trackers. You can also get there from Klaserie.

Trogon Trails (☎ /fax (01528) 35581) has self-catering accommodation for R80 per person (R60 if there are three or more people). Over 250 bird species have been recorded here. It's a great spot for an 'alternative big five' – cheap digs, peace, quiet, views and the Narina trogon. Trogon Trails

is 4.5 km west of the Blyde River bridge on the R531; it is signposted. The camp is three km from the main gate down a dirt road.

GRASKOP
Graskop is on the edge of the Drakensberg escarpment, at the top of Kowyns Pass. Nearby are some spectacular views of the lowveld, almost 1000 metres below. The town is small and of little interest, but it's well situated for visiting the area's highveld attractions and is less than 60 km from Kruger Park. A walking trail, including places described in *Jock of the Bushveld*, starts at the municipal resort; the resort will provide a map.

Places to Stay
Panorama Rest Camp (☎ (01315) 71090) is about two km east of town on the road to Kowyns Pass. It's stunningly situated at the top of a deep gorge: the small swimming pool is right on the edge and has astounding views down to the lowveld. If it's a misty night take care when walking around – there are no fences and some very long drops. Camp sites are about R20 plus R10 per person. Chalets with cooking facilities cost

Raptors
Near the junction of the Tzaneen road (R36) with the R531 are the Manoutsa Cliffs, an area rich in animal and plant life. The cliffs protect about 750 pairs of nesting Cape vultures *(Gyps coprotheres)*, making it the second largest breeding colony in Transvaal.

About 50 species of raptors (birds of prey) use the thermals of the cliffs to search out prey. These cliffs are the only breeding place in South Africa of the taita falcon *(Falco fasciinucha)*, the western boundary of bateleurs *(Terathopius ecaudatus)*, the eastern boundary of the jackal buzzard *(Buteo rufofuscus)* and home to the martial eagle *(Polemaetus bellicosus)*. The latter has the largest wingspan of all raptors in South Africa – two to 2.5 metres. In addition, crowned eagles *(Stephanoaetus coronatus)*, owls and many other migrant raptors are to be seen here. ■

The Taita falcon is a small robust bird that is very rare, found in gorges along the Zambezi.

Graskop

Not to Scale

PLACES TO STAY

1 Summit Lodge
6 Blyde Lodge & Chalets
7 Graskop Municipal Caravan Park
10 Graskop Hotel
18 Pinnacle Heights Guest House

PLACES TO EAT

8 Wimpy
9 Harry's Pancakes
12 Rite Value Foodliner
13 Steakhouse Restaurant
14 Highland Pizza
15 Spar Foodliner
17 Eastern Delights

OTHER

2 Railway Station
3 Municipal Offices
4 Bank
5 Graskop Information Office & Azalea Bakery
11 Post Office
16 Police Station

R110 for two people or R150 for up to five (travellers have reported paying less, so maybe there's room for negotiation). The *Municipal Holiday Resort* (☎ 01315) 71126) is in town. Tent sites are R17 plus R7 per person, four-bed bungalows are R125 and three-bed flats are R102.

Summit Lodge (☎ (01315) 71058), some 500 metres down the road to Pilgrim's Rest, charges R80 per person for bed and breakfast. The *Graskop Hotel* (☎ (01315) 71244) on the main street charges R150/230 for single/double bed and breakfast (R120/180 in low season). There is a budget double room with communal bathroom for R75. Don't get a room facing the street, as timber trucks roll by during the night.

Blyde Chalets & Lodge (☎ (01315) 71316, fax 71798) has fully equipped chalets from R110 to R250 for two people, depending on the season. In the lodge the cost varies from R75 to R95 per person, bed and breakfast.

Other places include *Log Cabin Village* (☎ (01315) 71974), at the east end of Louis Trichardt St; *Pinnacle Heights* (☎ (01315) 71847) on Bloedrivier St; and *Kloofsig Chalets* (☎ (01315) 71488), just out of town.

Places to Eat

A good three-course meal costs about R40 at the *Steak House* in the Graskop Hotel. On Louis Trichardt St are the *Azalea Bakery* for '*die beste mosbolletjies in die laeveld*' and the famous *Harry's Pancake Bar*, recommended by Jo'burg's Chosen Few motorcycle gang (pancakes are about R15). In Main St, try *Highland* for pizza and *Eastern Delights* for Indian food such as bunny chow (R5.50), samosas and briyani.

SABIE

Sabie is the largest town in this region, but it's still a manageable size. The town is quite prosperous, being a tourist centre and a timber town. Tourists come for the cool climate, trout fishing and the extensive pine and eucalypt plantations in the area, but if you prefer your forests wild this might not be such an attraction. The plantations were established last century to replace indigenous forest cut down for the mining industry.

Sabie is a good base for visiting the area, but Graskop is closer to both the Blyde River Canyon and Kruger National Park. The

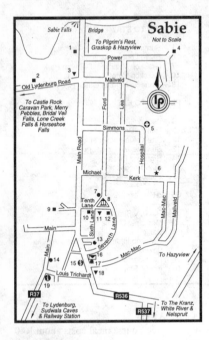

PLACES TO STAY

1   Glass Bungalows
2   Protea Floreat Hotel
4   Sabie Townhouse
9   Jock of the Bushveld Chalets &
    Caravan Park
10 Sabie Falls Hotel
12 Percy's Place

PLACES TO EAT

3   The Loggerhead
11 Zeederburg Coach House
18 The Woodsman

OTHER

5   Hospital
6   Police
7   Spar Supermarket
8   Forestry Museum
13 Town Hall
14 Pewter Smith
15 First National Bank
16 Post Office
17 National Hiking Board
19 Sondela Information Centre

Sondela Information Centre (☎ (01315) 43492) is on Main St on the Lydenburg-Long Tom Pass side of town.

Things to See & Do

The interesting **Forestry Museum**, next to the information centre, has displays on the local forests, as well as things like match paintings which 'will take your breath away'. It's open on weekdays and Saturday mornings; admission is R2.

There are a number of **waterfalls** in the area. Closest are the Sabie Falls, just beyond town on the R532 (Graskop road). South-west of Sabie, off the Old Lydenburg road, are the 70-metre Bridal Veil Falls. Also off the Old Lydenburg road are the 68-metre Lone Creek Falls; there is wheelchair access to the falls on the right-hand path. Nearby are Horse Shoe Falls.

Off the R532 road to Graskop are the Mac-Mac Falls (named because of the number of Scottish names on the area's mining register) and Forest Falls, 10 km from Graskop and reached by a walk through the forest.

There are several nature walks near Sabie. The Jantjiesbos and Waterfall walks start at Lone Creek Waterfall. The Secretary Bird walk begins at Mac-Mac Pools and the Forest Falls walk starts at the Groenerferis picnic site. Horse-riding is also popular and the information office can arrange rides for R25 for a half day (R40 with lunch).

There are two excellent marked mountain-bike trails. The Long Tom Trail consists of two sections, one of 36 km and the other 20 km. Both routes pass through indigenous forests, commercial plantations and clear streams; there are many viewpoints for taking photos. The Ceylon Trail is 21 km and there is a steep section which takes you to the top of Bridal Veil Falls. There is an entrance fee of R4 for both trails. Enquire at the information office about other possibilities.

Places to Stay

There is a lot of accommodation in and around Sabie, with much of it filling up at holiday times. Prices rise at these times, too.

Bottom End At *Castle Rock Caravan Park* (☎ (01315) 41242), the municipal caravan park, sites cost R23 and electricity is R5 extra. *Merry Pebbles* (☎ (01315) 42266, fax 41629) has camp sites for R42 as well as self-contained chalets for R120; both prices are for two. These two places are out of town, off the Old Lydenburg road at the north end of Main St.

Glass Bungalows (☎ /fax (01315) 42227), on the corner of Old Lydenburg and Graskop roads, are where riverside chalets cost R80 for two or R130 for four. Nearby are the *Lone Creek Chalets* (☎ (01315) 42611).

Jock of the Bushveld Chalets & Caravan Park (☎ (01315) 42178, fax 43215) is closer to the town centre and has sites from R30 for two plus R15 per person. This place is also a *youth hostel* charging R30 per person – you provide the bedding.

Percy's Place (☎ (01315) 43302) on 10th St is a B&B, costing from R48 per person.

Some 25 km from Sabie on the Long Tom road are the *Misty Mountain Chalets* (☎ (01315) 43377), ideally located for mountain-biking enthusiasts; self-catering accommodation is from R40 per person upwards.

Middle & Top End The *Sabie Vallee Inn* (☎ (01315) 42182), on 10th St, charges R135 per person, with all meals. *Fern Tree Cottages* (☎ (01315) 42215), on the Graskop road, one km out of Sabie, has self-contained cottages for R121 a double, R185 for four people. The *Protea Floreat* (☎ (01315) 42160) on the Old Lydenburg road has singles/doubles from R189/209, including breakfast. *Sabie Star Chalets* (☎ (01315) 43328) has chalets from R40/80 a single/double in the low season, doubles from R120 in the high season. The chalets are about three km from town, off the R536 to Hazyview.

South-east of Sabie, on the R537 to White River, is *Shunter's Express* (☎ /fax (01311) 33319) which has accommodation in 1930s railway coaches; bed and breakfast is R125 per person, with dinner R25 extra. Their horse-riding packages cost R400 for the weekend, all inclusive.

There are a number of B&B places in the area; enquire at the information office. *Sabie Townhouse* (☎ (01315) 42292) on Power St is a popular place, with rooms from R135 to R180 per person; it's often fully booked.

Places to Eat

The *Loggerhead* near Sabie Falls is a good steakhouse where you'll pay about R35 for a meal. The *Zeederburg Coach House* specialises in trout braais but serves filling pastas for R25. The *Woodsman*, near the corner of Main Rd and Mac Mac St, is good value and has a great Greek menu (it is run by a Greek Cypriot family).

Getting There & Away

There are daily buses from Jo'burg to Lydenburg and Nelspruit, from where you can take minibus taxis to Sabie.

Sabie's minibus-taxi park is behind the Spar supermarket on Main St. Most taxis run only in the local area. The fare to Hazyview is R12 and to Lydenburg it's R15. From Lydenburg you can get a minibus taxi to Jo'burg.

MT SHEBA NATURE RESERVE

To see how the area looked before most of the indigenous forest was destroyed, visit this reserve, 15 km off the R533 and about 10 km west of Pilgrim's Rest. With its

The Secretary bird can be seen high-stepping through grassland or standing on it's nest on top of a thorn tree.

plentiful rain and mists, it's an evocative place to visit. There are a number of day walks in the area; pick up a brochure and map at the Sondela Information Centre in Sabie, from Pilgrim's Rest or at the Mt Sheba Hotel.

PILGRIM'S REST

In 1873 gold was discovered here and for 10 years the area buzzed with diggers working small-scale alluvial claims. When the big operators arrived in the 1880s, Pilgrim's Rest became a company town, and when the gold finally fizzled out in 1972 the town was sold to the government as a ready-made historical village. It's a nice little place, where people once worked hard and lived simply – an ethos which doesn't come across in many other old towns in South Africa, burdened by grandiose town halls and churches.

The information centre is on the main street, and is open daily from 9 am to 12.45 pm and 1.15 to 4 pm.

Things to See & Do

There are three **museums**: the Pilgrim's Rest & Sabie News, a printing shop; the House Museum, a restored home; and the Drezden Shop & House Museum, a general store. Admission to all three is R2; buy tickets at the information centre.

The **nature reserve** which surrounds the town doesn't have many animals and the vegetation isn't all indigenous, but there are many bird species and it's still a good place for a walk.

Places to Stay

The *Royal Hotel* (☎ (01315) 81221) oversees a range of accommodation, from camping to restored miners' cottages to hotel rooms. Self-contained cottages cost from R101 a double, and singles/doubles in the hotel are R220/250. Prices rise sharply on weekends and holidays.

The luxurious *Mt Sheba Hotel* (☎ (01315) 81241), in Mt Sheba Nature Reserve, has singles/doubles from R273/330 (considerably more in season), with dinner and breakfast. There are also more expensive

cottages. If you have the cash it's definitely worth trying.

Also in the region is *Themeda Hills Resort* (☎ (01315) 81352) which has rondavels for R120 for two (plus R20 each extra person); this place offers a real bushveld experience with thatched rondavels, a waterfall and lack of frills. The *Inn on Robbers Pass* (☎ (01315) 81346), on the Lydenburg road, costs from R75 per person.

Getting There & Away

There is little public transport: the roads are narrow and steep so buses are disinclined to make the trip, and because there are few blacks living in the area minibus taxis are infrequent. As there are many holiday-makers in the area, hitching to/from Lydenburg or Graskop is possible.

LYDENBURG

Lydenburg is at the bottom of Long Tom Pass, which is named after the big gun used by the Boer forces in the Anglo-Boer War. Lydenburg ('town of suffering') was established by Voortrekkers in 1849 and was once the capital of the Republic of Lydenburg. Today it's a quiet service centre for the farming district.

There is good trout fishing in the area. You can visit trout hatcheries daily between 8 am and 4 pm. The town's museum is on the Long Tom Pass road a few km from town.

The Republic of Lydenburg merged with the Republic of Utrecht, which became part of the ZAR, which was annexed by Britain, regained its independence, fought and lost the Anglo-Boer War, became part of the province of Transvaal and is now part of Eastern Transvaal Province in the new South Africa. So many things *happen* in this country.

Gustav Klingbiel Nature Reserve

This 2200-hectare reserve is east of Lydenburg, on the R37. As well as antelopes there are some Iron Age sites and Anglo-Boer War trenches. There's a hiking trail with a hut. Phone the town clerk at Lydenburg (☎ (01323) 2121) for information.

EASTERN TRANSVAAL

Places to Stay

On Viljoen St, the road to Jo'burg, just before the intersection with Lydenburg's main street, is the *Uitspan Caravan Park* (☎ (01323) 2914). Camp sites are about R25, and rondavels sleeping three people are R110 or R75 with common bathroom. At the other end of town is the near-derelict *Paradise Camping* with very ordinary rondavels.

Morgan's Hotel (☎ (01323) 2165), at 14 Voortrekker St, has singles/doubles from about R125/195, including breakfast.

Getting There & Away

The thrice weekly Jo'burg to Phalaborwa City to City bus (book through Translux) passes through Dullstroom and Lydenburg (Lydenburg to Jo'burg is R45, to Dullstroom R15 and to Phalaborwa it's R35).

The minibus-taxi park is in a yard off the main shopping street. Taxis to Sabie are R15 and to Jo'burg R35. The fare to Nelspruit is R15 but few taxis run there.

ELANDSKRANS HIKING TRAIL

This interesting trail takes in part of the highveld and lowveld of the south-eastern Transvaal. Combining a 24-km walk with a 12-km rail journey, the trail begins and ends at the Elandskrans holiday resort near Waterval-Boven. The trip takes in the NZASM tunnel, waterfalls, President Kruger's house and a five-arch bridge. Book the trail at Elandskrans Resort (☎ (013262), ask for 176), Private Bag X05, Waterval-Boven 1195.

The Eastern Lowveld

To the north the lowveld is dry and hot – extremely so in summer, when there are storms and high humidity. Further south the temperatures moderate and the scrubby terrain gives way to lush subtropical vegetation around Nelspruit and the Crocodile River. South of here, around Barberton, the dry country resumes with a vengeance – gold prospectors last century dubbed it the Valley of Death.

Much of the eastern lowveld is taken up by Kruger National Park and the private game reserves which border it.

Warning

The Transvaal lowveld is a malarial area and bilharzia occurs in waterways and dams.

KRUGER NATIONAL PARK

Kruger National Park is, justifiably, one of the most famous wildlife parks in the world. It's also one of the biggest and oldest. Sabie Game Reserve was established by the ZAR president Paul Kruger in 1898. The reserve, since renamed and much expanded, is now nearly two million hectares in extent (about the size of Wales).

The park authorities claim Kruger has the greatest variety of animals of any park in Africa, with lions, leopards, elephants, buffaloes and rhinos (the 'big five') as well as

EASTERN TRANSVAAL

Middleveld Fishing Valleys

The Middleveld region to the south of Lydenburg is noted for its fine trout fishing, and visitors come from all over the world in the search for that elusive bite during the evening rise. The area sandwiched between the R540, R36 and the N4 is where anglers will achieve most success. The main fishing towns are **Dullstroom** and **Waterval-Boven**. A trout-fishing licence from the local authority is required.

There are a number of exclusive trout lodges in the region. The most famous is *Walkerson's* (☎ (01325) 40246, fax 40260) in Dullstroom, a fly-fisher's haven; it's very expensive with singles/doubles in the lakeside suites for R470/700, equipment included. *Critchley Hackle* (☎ (01325) 40145, fax 40262) is also expensive. The cheapest option is the *Dullstroom Inn* (☎ (01325) 40071, fax 40278) which costs about R130 per person, breakfast included. Travellers have recommended the *Tonteldoos Café* in Dullstroom for a meal. Near Waterval-Boven there are a number of places. The cheapest of these is the *Wayside Inn* (☎(013262), ask for 425) with B&B for about R135 per person. ■

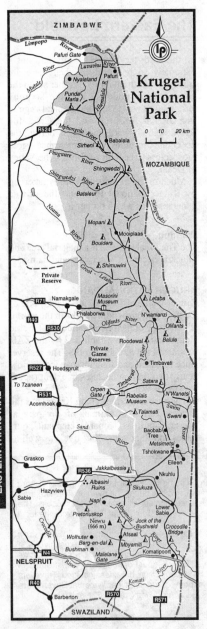

cheetahs, giraffes, hippos, and many varieties of antelope and smaller animals. Altogether, this includes 137 mammals, almost 500 birds and over 100 reptile species.

Unlike some of the parks in East Africa, Kruger does not offer a true wilderness experience (although some would argue the walking trails do approach this ideal). The infrastructure, including a network of sealed roads and comfortable camps, is too highly developed and organised. The park is too accessible and popular, and many animals are acclimatised to the presence of cars.

None of this should deter you, however, because Kruger will undoubtedly be a highlight of your South African trip. Although most people will have seen African animals in zoos, it is impossible to exaggerate how extraordinary and completely different it is to see animals in their natural environment.

The positive side of the park's excellent organisation and facilities is that you can explore the park at leisure, without having to depend on organised tours or guides. The accommodation ranges from cheap camp sites to self-catering huts and a range of more luxurious and expensive alternatives.

The landscape is both beautiful and fascinating, and although you have to be lucky to see all the large predators you will almost certainly see several of the 'big five' and an extraordinary variety of smaller mammals and birds. That many of the animals are used to the presence of cars means that you can often get extremely close to them.

One traveller reported taking a two-hour detour through Kruger in the middle of the day in summer (when most animals take a siesta) and seeing two of the 'big five' and many other animals. That sort of speedy visit isn't recommended, however, and you should spend at least one night in the park.

Although the park is popular, the crowds are by no means intrusive if you avoid weekends and school holidays. Numbers are even lower north of the Phalaborwa Gate and on the gravel roads. It's not unusual to travel for an hour at a time without seeing another vehicle, and there's nothing to stop you finding a spot near a water hole, by yourself, and just waiting to see what comes by (which could be a convoy of BMWs).

Orientation

Kruger stretches almost 350 km along the Mozambique border and has an average width of 60 km. There are also large private game reserves adjoining the western boundaries (see Private Game Reserves in the Northern Transvaal and this chapter), and there are hopes that when the political situation in Mozambique stabilises, Kruger will merge with a proposed park in that country.

Most of the park consists of flat grass and bush covered plains (savanna bushveld), sometimes broken by rocky outcrops. The unspectacular Lebombo mountains mark both the eastern border of the park and South Africa's border with Mozambique. A number of rivers flow across the park from east to west – from the north they are the Limpopo, Luvuvhu, Shingwedzi, Letaba, Olifants, Timbavati, Sabie and Crocodile. Most of them are perennial.

There are seven entrance gates (*heks* in Afrikaans): Malelane and Crocodile Bridge on the southern edge, and accessible from the N4 highway (the quickest direct route from Jo'burg); the Numbi and Paul Kruger gates, accessible from White River and Hazyview (turn off the N4 just before Nelspruit); Orpen, which is convenient if you have been exploring Blyde River; Phalaborwa, accessible from Pietersburg and Tzaneen; Punda Maria, accessible from Louis Trichardt; and

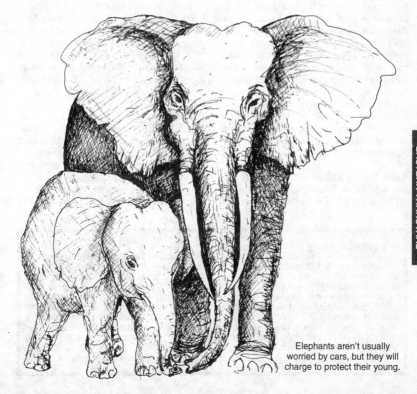

Elephants aren't usually worried by cars, but they will charge to protect their young.

EASTERN TRANSVAAL

Pafuri, in the far north, accessible from Venda.

There are a number of sealed roads within the park, one of which runs the entire spine of the park, and a number of gravel side roads, which are recommended if you want to get away from the crowds. Altogether, the road network extends for nearly 2000 km.

Information

Bookings Accommodation can be booked through the National Parks Board. Their head office (☎ (012) 343 1991, fax 343 0905) is in Pretoria; the postal address is PO Box 787, Pretoria 0001, and the telex is 3-21324SA. There is also an office in Cape Town (☎ (021) 22 2810, fax 24 6211); PO Box 7400, Rogge Bay 8012.

Written applications for rest camps and wilderness trails can be made 13 months in advance. Except at peak times (school holidays, Christmas and Easter) and weekends, booking is advisable but not usually essential. In addition to huts and cottages, some rest camps also have semi-private 'sponsored accommodation', also booked through the National Parks Board. .

Morning and evening game drives are sometimes available for about R75 per person; bookings are advisable. The rangers who conduct them provide excellent information and know where to find the game.

Entry It costs R20 per adult for a day visit and R10 for an overnight visitor (children R10 and R7.50) to enter the park plus R20 for a car (bicycles, motorbikes and open vehicles are not admitted). Maps and publications are sold in the larger rest camps.

During school holidays you can stay for a maximum of 10 days in the park and five days at any one rest camp (10 days if you're camping). The park authorities restrict the total number of visitors within the park, so at peak times it pays to arrive early if you don't have a booking.

The entrance gates open at 5.30 am except in April (6 am), from May to August (6.30 am) and September (6 am). The camps, which are all fenced, open at 4.30 am in November and December: 5 am in January; 5.30 am in February and March; 6 am in April and September; and 6.30 am from May to August.

Entrance gates and camps close at 6.30 pm from November to February, 6 pm in March, September and October, and 5.30 from April to August. It's an offence to arrive late at a camp and you can be fined. With speed limits of 50 km/h on tar and 40 km/h on dirt it can take a while to travel from camp to camp, especially if you are caught up in the traffic jams which form near interesting animals.

Facilities Skukuza, near the Paul Kruger and Numbi gates, is the biggest rest camp and has a large information centre with interesting displays and the exceptional Stevenson-Hamilton library. There's an AA workshop for vehicle repairs, a bank, post office and photo-developing service. A doctor is available. Letaba and Satara rest camps also have

Suggested Itinerary

If you have a car and want to start and finish in Jo'burg and drive the length of the park, say from Crocodile Bridge to Punda Maria, you'll need at least four days. Given speed limits and the fact that you will, at times, want to travel much more slowly, and/or get off the bitumen, you may be driving virtually all day, every day. This might sound easy, but it's actually quite demanding, especially when it's hot and you are concentrating on spotting animals (and staying on the road).

The ideal minimum would be five days (from Monday to Friday). Allow the first day to get to the park and perhaps stay at Pretoriuskop, Berg-en-dal or Crocodile Bridge; spend the second day in the south with a night at Lower Sabie or Skukuza; the third day in the middle with a night at Olifants, Balule or Letaba; the fourth day in the north, perhaps staying at Shingwedzi or Punda Maria; and allow most of the fifth day to get back to Jo'burg.

This schedule allows you the opportunity to see the park's main ecological zones. ∎

workshops, and there are also staffed information centres at Letaba, Berg-en-dal and Mopani. Many of the rest camps show films on Kruger's wildlife in the evenings on weekends and during school holidays. All camps have telephones and first-aid centres.

The larger camps all have reasonable-value restaurants (a toasted sandwich is R2.60, coffee is R2 and large hamburger is R6) and decent shops that stock a range of essentials (including cold beer and wine), but if you are planning to do your own cooking it is worth stocking up outside the park. If nothing else, it's definitely worthwhile having enough food and utensils to enable you to make breakfast or to lunch at the picnic sites.

There are communal kitchen facilities at all the camp sites, including sinks and cooking facilities, but not cooking and eating utensils. The huts vary in the facilities they offer: most have air-conditioning or fans; all supply bedding and towels; some have en suite bathrooms and some have kitchen facilities (in which case cooking and eating utensils are supplied).

Climate

Summers are very hot (averaging around 30°C), with violent thunderstorms; this means that the game viewing is most pleasant early and late in the day. The whole park is in a summer rainfall area, with the rainfall generally decreasing as you go north. In the winter, nights can be cold (sometimes falling below 0°C) and the days are pleasant.

Plant & Animal Distribution

Kruger takes in a variety of landscapes and ecosystems, in part related to the rainfall, with each ecosystem favouring a particular group of species. Most mammals are distributed throughout the park, but some show a distinct preference for particular regions. The excellent *Find It* booklet and accompanying maps point out the most likely places to see a particular species.

Impalas, buffaloes, Burchell's zebras, blue wildebeests, kudus, waterbucks, baboons, vervet monkeys, cheetahs, leopards and other smaller predators are all widely distributed. Birdlife is prolific along the rivers, and north of the Luvuvhu River.

In the south-west corner between the Olifants and Crocodile rivers, where the rainfall is highest (700 mm a year), it's thickly wooded, with a variety of trees, including acacias and bushwillows, but also bigger trees like sycamore figs and flowering species like the red and orange coral tree. This terrain is particularly favoured by white rhinos and buffaloes, but is less favoured by antelopes and, therefore, by predators.

The eastern section to the south of the Olifants River, on the plains around Satara and south to the Crocodile River has a reasonable rainfall (600 mm) and fertile soils. There are large expanses of good grazing, with buffalo and red grass interspersed with acacia thorn trees (especially knobthorn), leadwood and marula trees. This favours large populations of impalas, zebras, wildebeests, giraffes and black rhinos. Predators, particularly lions, prey on the impalas, zebras, and blue wildebeests.

North of the Olifants River the rainfall drops below 500 mm and the veld's dominant tree is mopane. This grows strongly in the west, where it is interspersed with red bushwillow, but has a tougher time on the basalt plains of the north-east, where it tends to be more stunted. The mopane has a butterfly-shaped leaf which folds to reduce transpiration and has a turpentine-like smell. Despite this they are a favoured diet of elephants, which are most common north of the Olifants, and mopanes are also eaten by tsessebes, elands, roans and sables.

Perhaps the most interesting area is in the far north around Punda Maria and Pafuri. This has a higher rainfall (around 700 mm at Punda Maria) than the mopane country and therefore supports a wider variety of plants (baobabs are particularly noticeable) and a higher density and variety of animals. There's woodland, bushveld, grass plains and, between the Luvuvhu and Limpopo rivers, a tropical riverine forest.

All the rivers have riverine forest along their banks, often with enormous fig trees,

Wildlife Viewing

Viewing is best in the winter dry season, because trees lose their leaves and plant growth is sparser, making visibility easier. The animals also tend to be concentrated around the dwindling water sources. On the other hand, the park is more attractive in summer, with lots of fresh green growth, and this is when most animals have their young.

It can be quite difficult to spot animals at any time of the year. It is amazing how often you first notice one animal, stop the car, and suddenly realise that there are many more individuals and species in the immediate area. Even elephant, which you imagine would be fairly conspicuous, can be very well camouflaged, especially if they are still.

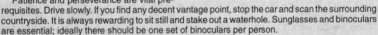

Patience and perseverance are vital prerequisites. Drive slowly. If you find any decent vantage point, stop the car and scan the surrounding countryside. It is always rewarding to sit still and stake out a waterhole. Sunglasses and binoculars are essential; ideally there should be one set of binoculars per person.

Different animals display different behaviours at different times of day, but there is always something to be seen. Despite the following observations, animals do not follow rules. A hungry or thirsty animal will be much more concerned about eating or drinking than observing union regulations on midday siestas.

The early morning drive should begin at around 6 am. Many animals (including lion, leopard and rhino) and birds are at their most active from first light to around 10 am.

Conventional wisdom says you are much less likely to see animals at midday (particularly if it is very hot), but given that most people have a very limited time in the park it is still definitely worthwhile going for a drive in the middle of the day. Knowing that many animals will look for shade can actually help you locate them.

The middle of the day is when cheetah are often seen hunting. It's also a good time to see giraffe, zebra and hippo, which continue to be active. Antelopes often move close to waterholes, and may attract hungry lions.

A third drive is worthwhile in the late afternoon, from about 3.30 pm, when animals and birds become more active once again. Look for the big cats enjoying the views and breezes from rocky knolls. Leopard, particularly, will often rest high off the ground in the branches of trees. The later you return to camp the better, but don't forget you can be fined for arriving after the official camp closing times.

The more you know about the animals (especially their distribution and behaviour) the better your chance of finding them, so it is worth buying more detailed books. Many are available in the rest camp shops. Two obvious signals to look for in the field are circling vultures, or a number of parked cars.

Warthog, baboons, zebra, giraffe and many antelope species will happily graze together, so if you see one species, there will often be more close by. The presence of feeding herbivores does not preclude the possibility of a predator in the vicinity. For a start, of course, most predators are expert stalkers, and may not be obvious. In addition, most animals seem to know whether a predator is actually hunting; if it isn't they will be quite relaxed in its presence.

Antelopes will be unusually nervous and alert if they are aware of a predator on the hunt, but they will not immediately flee. They know they can nearly always out run a predator if they have a sufficient head start, so they maintain a 'flight distance' between themselves and the threat. If the hunter encroaches, the antelope will move, but will try to keep the hunter in sight. If the hunter charges, the antelope will obviously flee, but will probably not leave the immediate area.

It is not necessarily best to drive as close as possible to an animal. The closer you are, the more likely you are to disturb its natural behaviour. Sudden movements will disturb most animals, so if you do approach make it slow and steady. Avoid frequent stopping and starting of the car engine, but bear in mind that engine vibrations might create a problem with camera shake. There are only a few designated spots where you are allowed to get out of your car. ∎

which supports populations of bushbuck and nyala. Needless to say, the rivers are where you will find hippos and crocodiles.

Wilderness Trails

There are seven guided 'trails', offering a chance to walk through the park. Small groups are guided by highly knowledgeable armed guides. Usually you don't walk *to* anywhere, nor are the walks terribly strenuous – you explore the area around your base camp and the itinerary is determined by the interests of the group, the time of the year, and the disposition of the wildlife.

Most trails last two days and three nights, over a weekend. Accommodation is in basic, though comfortable, huts and you don't need to provide food or equipment (bring your own beer and wine).

Wilderness Trails are popular and must be booked well in advance, through the National Parks Board in Pretoria or Cape Town. The maximum number of people on any trail is eight, at R780 per person. Trails, and (in parenthesis) the camps to report to, are: Bushman and Wolhuter (Berg-en-dal), Metsimetsi (Skukuza), Napi (Pretoriuskop), Nyalaland (Punda Maria), Olifants (Letaba) and Sweni (Satara).

On the **Bushman** trail, in the south-west corner of the park near Berg-en-dal, you can trek to rock paintings as well as see the large herds of antelopes, lions and rhinos. **Wolhuter**, based near the Bushman Trail camp, is also in an area inhabited by lions and rhinos. The name commemorates the legendary father and son rangers, Harry and Henry Wolhuter.

Metsimetsi is midway between Lower Sabie and Satara, in an area of plentiful and diverse animals. The terrain consists of undulating savanna, ravines and rocky gorges.

Sweni is a new trail, east of Satara, in an area with many lions attracted here by the herds of wildebeests, zebras and buffaloes.

With a base on the Olifants River, east of Olifants rest camp, the **Olifants** trail offers the chance to get close to elephants, hippos and crocodiles as well as other animals.

The **Nyalaland** trail is in the far north of the park, a region of strikingly diverse ecosystems. This trail is famous for its birdlife, and there are many mammals as well.

The **Napi** trail runs through mixed bushveld midway between Skukuza and Pretoriuskop. There are black and white rhinos, lions, leopards, cheetahs, wild dogs, buffaloes and elephants – good for the 'big five'.

Places to Stay

There are several styles of accommodation in Kruger and all the options are of a high standard. Bookings must be made through the National Parks Board.

Most visitors stay in rest camps. These have a wide range of facilities. Their restaurants are good and prices reasonable. They usually have a fairly standard menu, and steak and fish dishes cost around R35.

The accommodation varies, but usually includes huts (some of which include share communal kitchens and bathrooms) and self-contained cottages. Booking is advisable, especially during holidays. In addition to huts and cottages, some rest camps also have 'sponsored accommodation' (privately owned and often better equipped and more comfortable), which should also be booked through the National Parks Board. Camping

EASTERN TRANSVAAL

Lions can be noisy neighbours for campers in rest camps.

facilities are available at most camps; booking is not really necessary.

Bushveld camps are smaller, more remote camps without shops and restaurants, and private camps cater for small groups which must take the entire camp. Bookings are essential for both types of camp.

All huts and cottages are supplied with bedding and towels. Most have air-conditioning or fans, and fridges. Visitors in accommodation without a kitchen who want to prepare their own meals must provide their own cooking utensils. Camping sites are not equipped with power points and groundsheets are not allowed.

Rest Camps Unless otherwise stated in the following descriptions, the camps all have electricity, a shop, a restaurant, public telephones, communal cooking facilities (sinks, hotplates and braais) and fuel supplies (petrol and diesel).

All camps are fenced, attractively laid out and immaculately maintained. There are swimming pools at Pretoriuskop, Mopani, Shingwedzi and Berg-en-dal.

Most of the accommodation has a minimum charge for two or four people, with an additional charge of R45 for each additional adult. From south to north the rest camps are as follows.

Berg-en-dal Near Malelane Gate this is a modern, medium-sized camp. It's laid out in natural bush on the banks of Matjulu Spruit, about five km from a water hole popular with rhinos. There's a visitors centre and, during school holidays, nature trails.

Camping in tents is R15 plus R12.50 per adult. Huts cost from R220 for one or two people, and two-bedroom cottages are R410 for up to four. All of these include kitchens and bathrooms. There are two sponsored cottages – *Rhino* and *J le Roux*.

Crocodile Bridge Near Crocodile Bridge Gate, the small camp *Crocodile Bridge* is in a great position by the Crocodile River. There are crocodile and hippo pools a few km away and large numbers of zebras,

impalas, buffaloes and wildebeests in the surrounding acacia country.

There is no restaurant and diesel fuel is not available. Camping costs R20 plus R12.50 per adult. Huts with kitchens and bathrooms cost R205 for one or two people.

Pretoriuskop Kruger's oldest camp is *Pretoriuskop* near Numbi Gate and in higher country than other places in the park, so it's a little cooler in summer. The surrounding country is attractive, with granite outcrops, and is frequented by white rhinos. The camp itself, although large, has a certain old-style charm and includes a natural-rock swimming pool.

Camping costs R15 plus R12.50 per adult. Huts without air-conditioning or bathrooms cost from R70 for one or two people, or R75 with air-conditioning and a fridge. Huts with bathrooms cost R190, and huts with bathrooms and kitchens cost R230; both costs are for one or two people. There are also cottages from R370 for up to four people, and two sponsored cottages – *Pierre Joubert* and *Doherty Bryant Boma*.

Lower Sabie The medium-sized, popular *Lower Sabie* camp is about an hour (35 km) from Crocodile Bridge Gate in a prime game-viewing region. It overlooks a dam on the Sabie River which attracts many animals. Elephants, buffaloes, cheetahs and rhinos are often seen in the surrounding country. There's an excellent road along the Sabie River to Skukuza.

Camping costs R15 plus R12.50 per adult. Huts with common bathrooms are R45/75 a single/double and self-contained huts cost from R205 for two people. There is also a sponsored cottage, *Keartland*.

Skukuza On the Sabie River, *Skukuza* (☎ (01311) 65611) is the main camp in Kruger and has facilities approaching those in a small town. There's a bank (Volkskas), an AA workshop, a doctor, a library, police, a post office and an excellent information centre. Comair flies to the nearby airfield from Jo'burg, and it is possible to hire cars.

There are a number of interesting historical sites in Skukuza, including the Campbell Hut Museum, one of the first huts which has been partially restored and houses a collection of furniture and photographs.

There is a huge variety of different accommodation and, although the camp is large, it's well laid out and doesn't overwhelm. Camping costs R20 plus R12.50 per adult; the camp sites are distinctly average. There is a variety of huts (from R205 for one or two people) and cottages (from R450 for up to four people), plus sponsored cottages (*Moni, Nyathi, Volkskas* and *Waterkant 1*). There are a number of furnished tents for R80 for one to two persons; additional adults are R20 and children R10.

Orpen Near Orpen Gate, *Orpen* is a small, attractive camp. A nearby water hole attracts wildlife. There is no restaurant; cooking facilities are communal and no utensils are provided. Some accommodation doesn't have electricity (bring a torch).

There are basic camp sites available at Maroela, four km away; you can camp for R15 plus R12.50 per adult. Huts at Orpen, with communal facilities, cost from R110 for one or two people. There is also a sponsored cottage at R480 for up to four people.

Satara East of Orpen Gate, *Satara* (☎ (01311) 66306) is in an area of flat and fertile plains which attract large numbers of grazing animals – and the highest lion population in the park. There are several water holes – you can watch one of them from the terrace of the pleasant self-serve restaurant. It's the second-largest camp, and although it is not the most appealing (it's a bit flat for a start), there's a range of facilities.

Camping costs R15 plus R12.50 per adult. Huts with shower, toilet and fridge cost from R205 for one or two people (no cooking utensils provided) and there are cottages from R500 for up to four people. Sponsored accommodation includes *Stanley, Wells* and *Rudy Frankel.*

Olifants The *Olifants* camp (☎ (01311) 66606) has a fantastic position on the bluff high above the Olifants River – there are spectacular views. You can see elephants, hippos and many other animals from the camp, as they come down to the river 100 metres below. Much of the camp is terraced and some of the huts are literally on the edge of the cliffs. There's an interesting information centre, concentrating on elephants.

Olifants River marks the change between the elephant country to the north and the grazing plains to the south. There are some viewing spots overlooking the river.

There are no camp sites at Olifants, but it is possible to camp at nearby Balule. Huts with shower, toilet and fridge cost from R140 for one or two people or from R205 for one or two people with a kitchen. Fully equipped cottages cost from R370 for up to four people. There are also two sponsored houses – *Ellis* and *Nshawu.*

Balule The small rest camp *Balule* is 11 km from Olifants. There are no services except hot water and wood stoves. It's quiet and atmospheric, however, and you'll almost certainly hear hippos grunting in the nearby river. Camping costs R15 plus R12.50 per adult. Basic huts with communal facilities and no electricity cost R70 for one or two people. Definitely bring a torch.

Letaba *Letaba* (☎ (01311) 66636) has excellent views over a wide bend of the Letaba River. It's an attractive camp with lots of shade, trees and grassy camping sites. There are plenty of animals, especially in winter. The excellent restaurant overlooks the river.

The museum here focuses on the elephant and includes mounted tusks of the big bulls (Mafunyane, Dzombo, Shingwedzi and Shawu) which have died in the park – the biggest set of tusks has yet to be mounted. There is also a section on poaching, the illegal ivory trade, geomorphology, biology and descriptions of elephant habits.

Camping costs R20 plus R12.50 per adult. There is a variety of other accommodation in

EASTERN TRANSVAAL

this large camp, including furnished tents with lighting, fan and fridge but no kitchen (R80 for one or two people); huts with common bathroom (from R75 for one or two people); fully equipped huts (from R205 for one or two people) and cottages (from R520 for up to four people); plus the sponsored houses *Fish Eagle* and *Melville*.

Mopani The superb new rest camp *Mopani* (☎ (01311) 66536) is on the edge of the Pioneer Dam, 45 km north of Letaba. Natural materials have been extensively used and all the buildings are thatched. There are some great spots overlooking the dam. There are huts from R240 for one or two persons and cottages for up to four persons for R570. *Xanatseni* is a sponsored house and there are no camp sites.

Shingwedzi The largest camp in the northern section of the park is *Shingwedzi* (☎ (01311) 66806). It's an old-style place, with a large number of huts and cottages arranged in circles and shaded by tall mopane trees and palms. A restaurant overlooks the Shingwedzi River, and there's a swimming pool. There are excellent drives in the vicinity.

Camping costs R15 plus R12.50 per adult. Huts with fans and fridges cost R85 for two people, from R190 with kitchen and bathroom. A cottage with fans costs R260 for up to four people.

Punda Maria The northernmost rest camp *Punda Maria* (☎ (01311) 66873) is in sandveld country by Dimbo Mountain. It's a long-established camp with an attractive setting and a wilderness atmosphere. Plans to modernise and expand it are in train; hopefully the atmosphere won't be spoilt. The area's ecology is fascinating and there is a wide range of animals, including lions and elephants.

Camping is R15 plus R12.50 per adult, huts with bath but communal kitchens are R190 for two people (with kitchen it's R195) and cottages are R350 for up to four people.

Bushveld Camps These small clusters of self-catering cottages don't have the facilities of the rest camps, nor do they have the numbers of people passing through. Most are reasonably close to a rest camp where you can buy supplies. Except for Jakkalsbessie, which is a more up-market camp and almost a suburb of Skukuza, all bushveld camps have solar power – you can't use electrical appliances other than lights, fans and fridges. (Prices quoted are the minimum charges. For additional adults add R45 per person.)

Mbyamiti On the southern border of Kruger, between Malelane Gate and Crocodile Bridge Gate, *Mbyamiti* has one and two-bedroom cottages (R260 for one or two people and R450 for up to four people, respectively).

Jakkalsbessie The *Jakkalsbessie* camp is about seven km from Skukuza. There is mains electricity and air-conditioning in this camp, and an airfield nearby. There are eight two-bedroom cottages (from R550 to R650 for up to four people).

Talamati On the western border of Kruger, about 30 km south of Orpen Gate, *Talamati* has one-bedroom cottages at R260 for one or two people and two-bedroom cottages at R450 for up to four people.

Shimuwini You'll find *Shimuwini* on the Letaba River about 50 km north of Phalaborwa Gate. There are one-bedroom cottages for R260 for one or two people, two-bedroom cottages for R450 for up to four people and one three-bedroom cottage (R520 for up to four people).

Bataleur About 40 km south of Shingwedzi, *Bataleur* has two and three-bedroom cottages which cost, respectively, R450 for up to four people and R520 for up to four people.

Sirheni About 55 km south-east of Punda Maria, *Sirheni* has one and two-bedroom cottages for R260 for one or two people and R450 for up to four people, respectively.

Private Camps Not to be confused with the private reserves which border Kruger, the following five camps are privately owned. They are all secluded and you have to book the whole camp, so there's plenty of privacy. Unless you're in a largish group they are pretty expensive, at R1400 for Malelane and R1700 a night for the others (for up to 12 people plus R50 for each additional adult). Take all your own supplies except bedding, and book through the National Parks Board.

Malelane About three km from the Malelane Gate on the Berg-en-dal road, *Malelane* has rondavels with air-conditioning and electricity. They sleep 19 people in total. The nearest shop is at Berg-en-dal.

Jock of the Bushveld About 40 km from Berg-en-dal on the Skukuza road is *Jock of the Bushveld*. The huts sleep 12 people in total and have solar power for lighting but no other electricity.

Nwanetsi Twenty-seven km from Satara on the Nwanetsi road, *Nwanetsi* has huts which sleep 16 people in total but there is no electricity.

Roodewal Forty km from Olifants on the road to Timbavati, *Roodewal* has a cottage and three huts which sleep a total of 19 people. A viewing platform overlooks a water hole.

Boulders Almost 50 km north of Letaba on the Mooiplaas-Phalaborwa road is the *Boulders* complex, which sleeps 12 people and is built on stilts. There is no fencing, so animals can wander through below.

Getting There & Away

Air Comair flies from Jo'burg to Skukuza daily at 10 and 10.35 am (R402), returning to Jo'burg at 11.55 am and 12.30 pm. Inter-Air has services from Nelspruit, Durban and Jo'burg to Phalaborwa (see Phalaborwa in the Northern Transvaal chapter). Airlink flies from Jo'burg to Nelspruit and Phalaborwa. Some of the private reserves pick up from Skukuza, enabling visitors with limited time to fly direct to the park from Jo'burg.

Bus & Minibus Taxi For most visitors, Nelspruit is the most convenient large town near Kruger, and it's well served by buses and minibus taxis to/from Jo'burg. However, once in Nelspruit you still have a fair way to go to get into the park. Near Nelspruit and closer to Kruger (15 km from Numbi Gate) is the small village of Hazyview, where there are a couple of backpacker hostels. Transtate buses to/from Jo'burg run through here, and there are minibus taxis to Nelspruit. A minibus taxi from Hazyview to Skukuza is R7. Phalaborwa, in the north, is right on the edge of Kruger and is served by regular bus services, both City to City and LT Tours. In the Venda area, minibus taxis run to near the Punda Maria Gate. See the relevant towns for details.

Train The *Komati* runs from Jo'burg to Komatipoort (via Nelspruit), about 12 km from Kruger's Crocodile Bridge Gate.

Car Skukuza is about 500 km from Jo'burg and can be reached in about six hours. Punda Maria is about 620 km from Jo'burg and can be reached in about eight hours. Hire cars are available at Skukuza, Nelspruit and Phalaborwa.

Hitching Hitching isn't a good way to see Kruger. If you're low on funds, you're better-off joining a group of people and hiring a car. The only places you can hitch are at the entrance gates and at the rest camps. If you have booked accommodation you'll have to wait for a car that is both prepared to give you a lift and is going to the camp you want. Once at the camp, your game viewing is dependent on finding someone to give you a lift.

Tours There are many tour operators. For those with limited funds one of the best ways to get a glimpse of the park is with African Routes (☎ (031) 83 3348, fax 83 7234). The safari includes pick-up from Jo'burg, visits to the Transvaal Drakensberg, Kruger (two days), Swaziland, and the KwaZulu/Natal Drakensberg (two days) and drop off in Durban. The cost is R1150 for seven days, all inclusive. Smaller operators include Bundu Bus (☎ (011) 693 1621), with five-day tours of Eastern Transvaal and Kruger National Park for R450.

Other operators include Safari Tours (☎ (01317) 67113), Hazyview; Mfafa Safaris (☎ (01311) 32686), Nelspruit; Wildlife Safaris (☎ (021) 930 4977), Pretoria; Drifters (☎ (011) 888 1160), Jo'burg; and Mopani Tours (☎ (011) 477 2374), Jo'burg. Contact a travel agent for deals and details. Most hostels will know of good deals.

PRIVATE GAME RESERVES – EASTERN TRANSVAAL

The area just west of Kruger contains a large number of private reserves, usually sharing a border with Kruger and thus most of the 'big five' animals. They are often extremely pricey – R500 per person is only mid-range – but with an economic stake in their guests getting close to animals they have good viewing facilities. It is possible to find cheaper places, and these may be more enjoyable because accommodation is in bush camps.

Listed below are some of the reserves and accommodation options. Before deciding which private reserve to visit, it's worth contacting a specialist travel agent to find out if there are any special deals going. Sondela Information Centre in Sabie, PO Box 494, Sabie 1260, is a good place to start if you are in the region. Bushveld Breakaways (☎ (01311) 51998) in White River and Green Rhino (☎ (01311) 31952, fax 51638) in Nelspruit also handle bookings for private reserves. Pathfinders Travel (☎ (011) 453 1113/4, fax 453 1483), 17 Chaucer Ave, Senderwood, Bedfordview, Johannesburg, is very helpful and has good information on the private reserves, as well as other interesting places in southern Africa.

Sabi Sand Reserves

Sabi Sand is a very large private conservation area on the south-west edge of Kruger Park. Within Sabi Sand are a number of private reserves, all sharing the same lowveld country and its wealth of birds and animals. Entry to the whole area costs R10, although some reserves have their own entry charge or do not accept non-guests.

Following are some of the reserves and lodges within Sabi Sand; for complete listings contact a travel agent.

Sabi Sand Private Game Reserve This is actually two reserves: Sabi Sabi in the south on the Sabie River, and Inyati Tree Tops in the north on the Sand River. While the 'big five' are found in both areas you have a better chance of seeing lions at Sabi Sabi. For hippos and crocodiles, Inyati is better.

Accommodation is in luxury chalets, with Inyati's considerably cheaper at about R750 per person. Prices include meals, drives and guided walks. To book Sabi Sabi phone (011) 483 3939 or fax 483 3799; for Inyati it's (01311) 65125.

Idube This reserve (☎ (011) 888 3713, fax 888 2181) costs R570 per person in the lodge. Other accommodation includes *Notten's Bushcamp* (☎ (01311) 65105) with space for eight people at R420 per person, including meals and game drives. That's pretty cheap for this part of the world.

Londolozi Game Reserve There is a variety of accommodation here, from the main camp with luxury chalets to the bush camp. Prices, which include meals and game drives, cost from R725 per person. Book on (011) 803 8421, fax 803 1810. Take the R536 from Hazyview west towards Paul Kruger Gate and Skukuza, and turn off to the left after 36 km. The reserve is 28 km further on.

Mala Mala Game Reserve This reserve is geared towards foreigners who want to see the 'big five' animals while remaining in a five-star cocoon. Mala Mala (☎ (011) 789 2677, fax 886 4382) costs over US$450 per

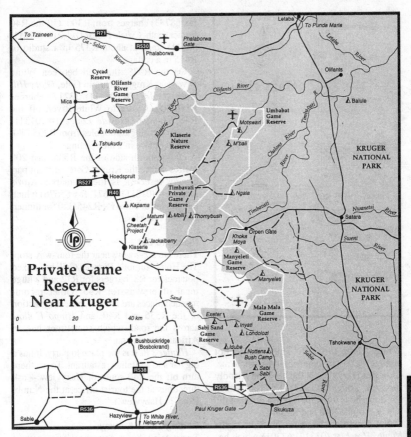

Private Game Reserves Near Kruger

0   20   40 km

person per night. Take the same roads as for Londolozi and follow the signposts.

Klaserie & Manyeleti Game Reserves
See Private Game Reserves in the Northern Transvaal chapter.

HAZYVIEW
Hazyview is a small village with a large shopping centre serving the black community. Kruger Park's Numbi and Paul Kruger gates are nearby (15 km and 43 km, respectively). As it is a black town, Hazyview isn't marked on some maps. It's near the

junction of the R535 which runs down the escarpment from Graskop, the R536 from Sabie to Kruger Gate and the R538 from White River.

The Hazyview Tourist Association office (☎ (01317) 67715, fax 67414) in the Numbi Hotel is open weekdays from 8.30 am to 4.30 pm, and Saturday from 8 am to 1 pm.

Places to Stay
Bottom End *Kruger Park Backpackers'* (☎ /fax (01317) 67224) has Zulu-style huts, for about R25 per person. The hostel is about two km south of Hazyview, just past the

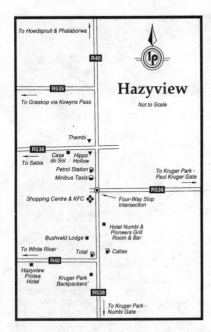

fax 68783) charges from R300. Off the R40 further south, *Cybele Forest Lodge* (☎ (01311) 50511) starts at about R375 in a studio or R415 in a cottage.

On the R538, the road between White River and Kruger's Numbi Gate, *Glory Hill Guest Lodge* (☎ (01311) 33217) charges R180/300. Closer to White River, off the R40, *Hulala Lakeside Lodge* (☎ (01311) 51710) has singles/doubles from R235/380. It's a big place in a nice setting.

On the north side of the R536, just 200 metres before the Kruger Gate (and not part of any reserve), is the up-market *Karos Lodge* (☎ (01311) 65671, fax 65676) which has singles/doubles for R245/320 for dinner, bed and breakfast.

Places to Eat
There are *takeaways* near the four-way stop. The Hotel Numbi's *Pioneer Grill* has baked potatoes for R8, burgers for R12 and a huge meal of prawns for R45. Other recommended places are *Thembi*, near the junction of the R536 and R40, and *Hippo Hollow* across the road, which sometimes has an African game menu.

Hunter's Rest is the place to party. It has a big bar and an Italian restaurant. To get there turn off the R40 south of Hazyview – ask directions at the tourist office at the Numbi Hotel in Hazyview.)

Getting There & Away
Transtate's Jo'burg-Acornhoek buses stop at Hazyview, as do many minibuses and buses serving the local area. A minibus to Nelspruit is R5 and to Sabie R12.

WHITE RIVER
White River (Witrivier) is a little higher and less humid than nearby Nelspruit, but it is still warm enough to be a green, pleasant little town with a colonial feel. There are also numerous artists in the area; get their addresses from the town hall or the Artists' Trading Post.

The town calls itself 'the nut capital of South Africa', and in **Nutcracker Valley** just south of the town off the R40 you can visit

White River turn-off. They would not divulge the cost of their trips to Kruger to me. Closer to Hazyview is the new and friendly *Bushveld Lodge* (☎ (01317) 67166) which has dorm beds for R35. It is just north of the junction of the R40 and R538.

Not far from the main junction is the *Numbi Hotel* (☎ (01317) 67301) which has singles/doubles for R185/300. Camping here is the best budget option in the region; a tent site is about R45 a double.

Other Accommodation There is a clutch of places in the area which are more elaborate than guesthouses but not quite hotels.

The *Hazyview Protea* (☎ (01317) 67332, fax 67335) is near Hazyview at Burgershall; it charges R225/300.

On the R536 to Sabie, *Casa do Sol* (☎ (01317) 68101, fax 68166) has cottages and villa units from R325. South of Hazyview, off the R40 to White River, *Farm House Country Lodge* (☎ (01317) 68780, some plantations, as well as Rottcher Wineries. Tropical fruits abound.

On the R40 near the hamlet of Rocky Drift, about halfway to Nelspruit, Kraal Kraft claims to have the largest collection of African artefacts in the country.

Places to Stay

The inexpensive municipal *caravan park* (☎ (01311) 31176) is in the park in the centre of town. In nearby Rocky Drift, on the Nelspruit road, *Flamboyant Rondawels* (☎ (01311) 58 1133) are R55/80 for singles/doubles. The *Karula Hotel* (☎ (01311) 32277) is on the Old Plaston road, the R538, which is more reminiscent of an English country lane than a South African road. The hotel is also pleasant and charges R132/220 for dinner, bed and breakfast.

South of White River is an up-market guesthouse, *Jatinga Country Lodge* (☎ (01311) 31932), in 30 acres of gardens. Prices include dinner and breakfast, and start at about R310 per person. *Hotel Winkler* (☎ (01311) 32317) on the Numbi road is a little cheaper at R217/350.

Getting There & Away

Minibus taxis run to Nelspruit for R2.50. Prestige Travel (☎ (01311) 31228) has daily buses running to Jo'burg for R60.

NELSPRUIT

Nelspruit, in the Crocodile River valley, is the largest town in Eastern Transvaal's steamy subtropical lowveld, and is the provincial capital.

Nelspruit's growth began only in the 1890s, when the South African Republic decided that it must put a railway through to Delagoa Bay (Maputo) so it would have access to a non-British port. The Anglo-Boer War upset these plans and it wasn't until 1905 that Nelspruit was proclaimed a town. The town's steady growth thereafter was due to farming, and today the area is the centre of an important citrus-growing and processing industry.

Orientation & Information

There are a couple of landmarks. The Promenade is a tree-lined street in the town centre, with a big new shopping complex of the same name. The Joshua Doore Centre on the corner of Louis Trichardt and Paul Kruger Sts is where the Greyhound service stops.

The Nelspruit Publicity Association and Satour share an office (☎ (01311) 55 1988, fax 55 1350) in the Promenade Centre. It's open from 8 am to 5 pm on weekdays, 9 am to 1 pm Saturday.

Things to See & Do

On Saturdays there is a **craft market** in the Promenade. The 150-hectare **Lowveld National Botanic Garden** is on the banks of the Crocodile River on the north side of Nelspruit (take the R37) and includes formal gardens and indigenous forest. It's open daily between 7 am and 4.30 pm and admission is R3 for adults and R1 for children.

The **Sonheuwel Nature Reserve** is a large area in town, south of the centre, which is under development. In addition to antelope species, vervet monkeys and leguaans, there are some rock paintings here. There is no entrance fee.

This area of the Eastern Transvaal is home to many species of birds, some of which do not occur further west in South Africa. Lawson's Bird Safaris (☎ (01311) 55 2147) offers informative birdwatching tours.

There are two overnight **hiking trails** in the area, the Kaapsche Hoop and the Uitsoek. For bookings contact the Southern Transvaal Forest Region (☎ (01311) 52169), on the 6th floor of the Prorom Building on Brown St (also in Sabie, ☎ (01315) 41051).

Places to Stay

Bottom End The municipal *caravan park* (☎ (01311) 59 2113) is a long way from the town centre. Sites cost R35 for two people, and rondavels cost from R90. To get there head west on the N4, go past Agaat St and turn left at the Caltex station. It's about one km further on. *Bundu Park* (☎ (01311) 58 1221), off the road to White River 12 km north of Nelspruit, has rondavels for

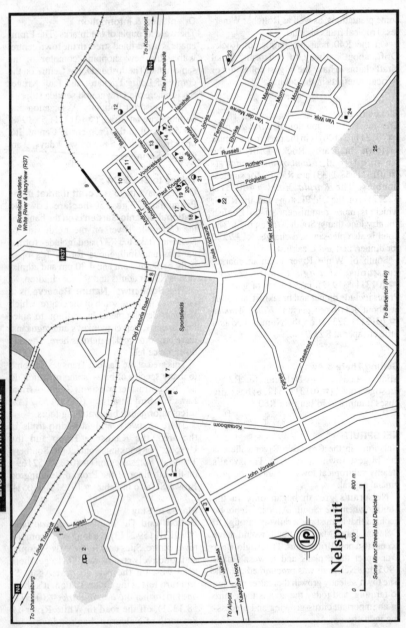

EASTERN TRANSVAAL

Nelspruit

Some Minor Streets Not Depicted

PLACES TO STAY

2   Municipal Caravan Park
3   Bushveld Lodge
4   Lidiana Cottages
6   Hotel Formule 1
8   Laeveld Verblyfsentrum
10   Figtree Hotel
11   Paragon Hotel
13   Hotel Promenade & Satour Tourist Office
24   Wilma's Guesthouse

PLACES TO EAT

5   Win's Restaurant & Sportsman's Bar
7   Brewers Feast
14   Paddy's
15   Pizza Place, Steers
16   Spur
17   Sport's Croc
18   Black Steers
20   Villa Italia

OTHER

1   Caltex Station
9   Railway Station
12   Bus & Minibus Taxi Park
19   Banks (ABSA & United)
21   Joshua Doore Centre
22   Municipal Buildings
23   Lawson's Tours
25   Sonhuewel Nature Reserve

R80/120/140 for singles/doubles/triples (R20 more for each category in A Block); breakfast is R15.

There is no hostel, but apparently travellers have stayed at the *Laeveld Verblyfsentrum* (☎ (01311) 53380) on Old Pretoria Rd. A dorm bed costs about R35. It's used mainly by youth groups.

B&Bs For B&B accommodation in the area contact Bed & Breakfast (☎ (01311) 50270). Prices range from about R90 to R110 per person.

Some B&B places, few of them close to the centre of town, include: *Lidiana Cottages* (☎ (01311) 41247), 13 Jakaranda St, Pumalanga, R75 per person; *Bushveld Lodge* (☎ (01311) 43219) in the same area on Kaapsche Hoop Rd, R85 for two sharing facilities or R105 with own bath and kitchen (R37.50 for each extra person); *Wilma's Guest House* (☎ (01311) 24750), in the

suburb of Extension 9 south of the town centre, R80/120; and the up-market *The Townhouse* (☎ (01311) 27006, fax 55 1793), 5 Ferreira St, R175/250.

Hotels *Hotel Formule 1* (☎ (01311) 44490, fax 44491), on the N4 and Kaapsche Hoop Rd corner, has rooms for R96. Breakfast is R6.

The *Fig Tree Hotel* (☎ /fax (01311) 53201), 16 Anderson St, has bed and breakfast from R130 per person. It's reasonable, but you might want to avoid rooms facing the pleasant courtyard/beer garden as there is sometimes live music (of the piano-accordion variety). Across the road the *Paragon* (☎ /fax (01311) 53205) has an impressive façade and good rooms at R125/180 on weekends, R192/250 on weekdays.

Hotel Promenade (☎ (01311) 53000, fax 25533) is a new hotel built in recycled town hall. It's very pleasant place and charges from R244/312, with weekend specials.

On the N4 20 km west of Nelspruit, *Crocodile Country Inn* (☎ (01311) 63040, fax 64171) is in lush country and has good facilities; rooms cost from R226/305, with breakfast.

Places to Eat

There is a fair sprinkling of franchised takeaways. Brown St is well endowed with restaurants. For steaks (R32) try *Black Steers*, for pizza *Pappa's* and for pub lunches (R15) the *Sport's Croc*.

In the Promenade there's a *Mike's Kitchen* with hearty meals for about R30, and nearby is the popular pub, *Paddy's*. *Villa Italia*, on the corner of Louis Trichardt and Paul Kruger Sts, is popular with the young set; a pasta meal costs from R25. Nearby, on Louis Trichardt St, is a *Spur*.

At the western corner in the Tarentaal Trading Post, are *Win's* and the *Sportsman's Bar*. Opposite Hotel Formule 1 is the *Brewers Feast*.

Getting There & Away

Air The airport is eight km south of town on the Kaapsche Hoop road. There are daily Airlink (☎ (01311) 43536) flights to Jo'burg

EASTERN TRANSVAAL

(Apex one-way is R194) and Durban (R262), and regular InterAir flights to Durban, Jo'burg and Phalaborwa. Airlink and Metavia (☎ (01311) 43141) have flights to Maputo in Mozambique (R380 one-way).

Bus Transtate's Jo'burg to Acornhoek service (weekdays) stops at the railway station. On Sunday, Monday, Tuesday and Wednesday there is a Jo'burg to Ressano Garcia (Mozambique) service, returning Monday, Tuesday, Wednesday and Thursday. Protour's Jo'burg to Maputo service passes through Nelspruit on Thursday and Saturday, returning Friday and Sunday. Contact the Nelspruit Protours office (☎ (01311) 52901).

Greyhound (☎ (01311) 25134) has a daily service to Jo'burg for R99, departing from the Joshua Doore Centre at 7.30 am except on Sunday when it's 3.30 pm.

A daily bus to Piggs Peak (Swaziland) departs from the minibus-taxi park at about 6 pm. This is a slow, local service.

Train The *Komati* runs to/from Jo'burg and Komatipoort daily. Fares to Jo'burg in 1st/2nd/3rd class are R99/69/39. From Nelspruit to Komatipoort they are R33/25/13.

Minibus Taxi The large and well-organised local bus and minibus-taxi park is at the end of Brown St, at the east end of the city centre. Examples of minibus-taxi destinations and fares are to Jo'burg R50, Barberton R6, Hazyview R5, White River R2.50, Sabie R7, Graskop R10, and Komatipoort R15.

Car Rental Avis (☎ (01311) 41087), Budget (☎ (01311) 43871) and Imperial (☎ (01311) 42834) have offices at the airport.

SUDWALA CAVES

In the Mankelekele mountains west of Nelspruit and south of Sabie, the Sudwala caves have the usual stalactite and stalagmite formations with fanciful names and mood lighting. They are worth a visit, however, and there are hour-long guided tours (☎ (01311) 64152) for R20.

Near the caves is the Dinosaur Park, which is more interesting for its indigenous forest than the model saurians. It's open daily between 8.30 am and 4.30 pm.

The caves are about two km up a very steep hill; at the bottom of the hill is *Sudwala Lodge* (☎ (01311) 63073) which has single/double hotel rooms for R178/306 and chalets from R190 for up to three people.

MALELANE

Malelane, on the banks of the Crocodile River, is right on the border of the Kruger National Park. It's a modern town with a distinctive wagon-wheel layout, and it is surrounded by sugar-canefields. There are two game reserves in the vicinity. The 700-hectare Mahushe Shongwe, on the Lebombo Flats, has the Mzinti River flowing through it. The 9000-hectare Mthethomusha, adjoining Kruger, has a variety of wildlife, and over 200 species of birds have been recorded there.

The *Malelane Hotel* (☎ /fax (01313) 30274) at 21 Impala St has bed and breakfast for about R90 per person. *Bongani Sun Lodge* (☎ (01311) 53120), a luxurious place in Mthethomusha, has single/doubles for R644/970. *Malelane Sun Lodge* (☎ (01313) 30332, fax 30145) is close to Kruger's Malelane Gate; rooms are R365/570.

About 20 km away near Kaapmuiden is *Kudu Lodge* (☎ (01313) 98 0080). A tent site is R11 plus R8 per person, and singles/doubles are R91.50/158, with breakfast.

KOMATIPOORT

This border town is at the foot of the Lebombo Mountains near the confluence of the Komati and Crocodile rivers. It is only 10 km north to the Crocodile Bridge into Kruger.

Just outside town there is a *caravan park* (☎ (01313) 50213). The *Border Country Inn* (☎ (01313) 50328, fax 50100) is on the N4 close to both the Mozambique border post and Kruger; bed and breakfast is about R130 per person. Its restaurant serves succulent prawn dishes.

Border Formalities

To cross into Mozambique you need a visa paper (not in your passport) stamped. It is worth paying R20 to one of the Portuguese-speakers, who hang around for this purpose, to help with this. The exit formalities are carried out at Komatipoort and the entry into Mozambique takes place at Ressano Garcia. If you have a car you will need a breakdown-warning triangle, seat belts in the car and the relevant vehicle papers, especially for hire cars. The black market rate for conversion of rand to meticals is 20% better than at a bank. As in any such exchange, beware.

For transport to/from Komatipoort see the earlier Nelspruit section and the Getting Around chapter.

BARBERTON

Barberton, about 50 km south of Nelspruit, was something of a boom town during gold rushes last century and had South Africa's first stock exchange. However, most miners soon moved on the newly discovered Rand fields near Jo'burg. Today, all the working gold mines in the region are more than 100 years old and the Sheba Mine is the richest in the world.

Barberton is a quiet town in harsh but interesting lowveld country. The large township outside Barberton is **Emjindini**.

Readers of *The Power of One* may be interested to know that Bryce Courtney was born in Barberton.

The information centre (☎ (01314) 22121) in Market Square on Crown St is extremely well organised. It is open from 8 am to 4.30 pm Monday to Friday (lunch is from 1 to 2 pm), 8.30 am to noon Saturday.

Things to See & Do

There are several restored houses in town. **Belhaven House** on Lee Rd, a middle-class home built at the turn of the century, is open for inspection (entry is R1, R0.50 for children). In between Lee and Judge Sts is a corrugated iron and wood **blockhouse** from the Anglo-Boer War, part of the chain built by the British when the war entered its guerrilla phase. There's a statue of **Jock of the**

Bushveld outside the town hall. Not far out of town is an umbrella thorn tree known as Jock's Tree.

The aerial cableway brings asbestos down from a mine in Swaziland. Coal is carried in the other direction to provide counterweight.

Barberton Nature Reserve is just north-east of the town, on the R38 to Kaapmuiden. The country is lowveld, with some high hills, especially towards the Swaziland border. As mining still takes place in the reserve, there aren't all that many animals to be seen other than plentiful birdlife and a few species of monkey. However, the reserve adjoins the big Songimvelo Nature Reserve, so in time it should be well worth visiting for its wildlife as well as its scenery. There's no accommodation in the reserve.

Hiking Trails There is the interesting two-km **Fortuna Mine** walk close to town. About 600 metres of it is through an old tunnel, so you need to bring a torch. The rocks excavated from the tunnel are 4200 million years old, the oldest sedimentary rocks yet found.

Several overnight hiking trails begin in Barberton, including the two-day **Pioneer** and **Umvoti** trails. The countryside combines beautiful scenery and old mine workings. There are huts for overnight stays (actually turn-of-the-century mine houses) which cost R16 per person. Firewood is provided on some trails so you can heat water for a bath.

The **Gold Nugget Trail** follows old prospectors' trails on the northern slopes of the Makhonjwa range. The two-day option is 39-km long and the three-day is 46 km. Contact the information centre or the Makhonjwa Conservation Foundation (☎ (01314) 24067), PO Box 81, Barberton 1300, for details.

Places to Stay

At the *caravan park* (☎ (01314) 23323) tent sites are R25 (up to three people), van sites are R35, and chalets with kitchens are from R100 for two people or R130 for four.

A good place to stay is *Fountain Baths Guest Lodge* (☎ (01314) 22707) (also called

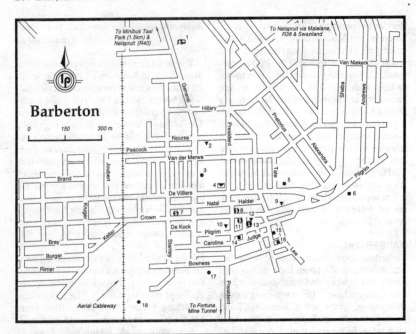

PLACES TO STAY

- 1 Caravan Park
- 5 Impala Hotel
- 6 Fountain Baths Guest Lodge
- 14 Phoenix Hotel

PLACES TO EAT

- 2 Gold Mine Restaurant

9	Cocopan	
10	Barberton Club & Barber's Reef	
12	Victorian Tea Garden	

OTHER

- 3 Town Hall & Jock of the Bushveld Statue
- 4 Post Office

- 7 Volkskas Bank
- 8 Standard Bank
- 11 First National Bank
- 13 Information Centre & Market Square
- 15 Anglo Boer War Blockhouse
- 16 Belhaven House
- 17 Stopforth House
- 18 Indigenous Tree Park

FB Holiday Cottages) at the southern end of Pilgrim St, where it resumes after merging into Sheba Rd (Crown St). Self-contained rooms cost R70 per person. This old place, built in 1885, used to be Barberton's public baths and swimming pool, and the gardens are pleasant.

The *Phoenix Hotel* (☎ (01314) 24211), on Pilgrim St on the corner of President St, is a clean, old-style country pub, with bed and breakfast for R185 per person (way, way overpriced). The *Impala Hotel* (☎ (01314) 22108), 75 De Villiers St, is in a sorry state; bed and breakfast is R185.

Near Barberton, 14 km out on the R38 to Kaapmuiden, *Diggers' Rest* (☎ (01314) 9681) has bed and breakfast for R120 per person. Closer to Barberton is *Kiaat Cottage* (☎ (01314) 24067) which sleeps up to four people. There are good views out over the valley; the charge for four is R150.

Small, intimate B&B places seem the way to go around here and there is no shortage. *Rannoch Lodge* (☎ (01314) 26417) is in town and up-market (R90 per person); *Dixie Farm Cottages* (☎ (01314) 9625) are 10 km north of Barberton (R80); and *De Havilah Farm* (☎ (01314) 23174), seven km out on the Nelspruit road, has horse-riding for R65 per half day and bed and breakfast for R80.

Places to Eat

There's the à la carte *Barber's Reef* at the Barberton Club on President St, between Pilgrim and Crown Sts; R25 should see you satisfied. The *Gold Mine* next to the Checkers supermarket covers most tastes. *Cocopan* on Crown St opposite the museum is a casual place with *John Henry's Pub* attached. The *Victorian Tea Garden* near the tourist office is a great place to relax; light meals cost R12.

Getting There & Away

The scenic R40 road from here to Swaziland (via the Josefdal/Bulembu border post) is unsealed and rough but is all-weather.

There is a small minibus-taxi rank by Emjindini, about three km from town on the Nelspruit road, or you can find taxis in town. To Nelspruit costs R6, to Badplaas R7.

SONGIMVELO GAME RESERVE

This 56,000-hectare reserve is in the former homeland of KaNgwane (Songimvelo means 'the care of nature'). KaNgwane was made up of parts of Swaziland which were excluded from the British Protectorate, and most of it clung to the northern border of Swaziland.

The reserve is in harsh lowveld country south of Barberton, with some highveld on the eastern side which runs along the mountainous Swaziland border. The lack of lions and rhinos in the reserve means that walking and horse-riding are popular activities.

Komati River Lodge (☎ (011) 789 6860, fax 789 0739) has singles/doubles for R265/380 per night, all inclusive, with two game drives (the self-catering option is R195/240); a wilderness weekend is R380 for a full two-day programme; and two-/five-day wilderness trails are R290/695.

Central & Southern Transvaal

VAAL DAM NATURE RESERVE

This area is a watersports recreation area for the Witwatersrand, and it gets crowded. It's open daily between 7 am and 6 pm. There's a camp site. To get there take the N3 south from Jo'burg and turn off at Villiers, or just north of Villiers to reach the northern side of the dam.

AROUND MIDDELBURG

Middelburg, so called because it is midway between Pretoria and Lydenburg, is a large and stock-standard town on the N4. Accommodation is geared towards businesspeople and is expensive. The cheapest option is *Oliphants Hotel* (☎ (0132) 22116) on President Rd, with single/double rooms in the R100/130 range.

Botshabelo Nature Reserve

This small reserve (☎ (0132) 43 1319) is off the R35 about 15 km north of Middelburg. Its main attractions are a restored mission and a fairly genuine southern Ndebele village. There are animals and walking trails from which to see them. Accommodation is in a house in the mission village or at a nearby *caravan park*.

Loskop Dam Nature Reserve

This reserve around the Loskop Dam has a fair range of animals inhabiting its dry, rolling hills, including white rhinos, buffaloes, zebras and leopards. It's off the R35, about 45 km from Middelburg. The Aventura *Loskop Dam Resort* (☎ (01202) 3075, fax 5269) has camp sites for R16.50 plus R9 per person, and standard four-bed units for R155 (R240 in high season).

PIET RETIEF

This solid, medium-sized town has few attractions, but it is the largest in the south of Eastern Transvaal and might be a good stopover on the way to Swaziland or KwaZulu/Natal.

There's a small museum off Church St, on one side of the minibus-taxi park. It's open between 2 and 4 pm on weekdays and from 10 am until noon on Saturday.

Places to Stay & Eat

The municipal *caravan park* (☎ (01343) 2619) is about 500 metres from the town centre, off the Pongola road (the continuation of the main street). Van sites are R35 and tent sites R30. It's a pleasant, shady place.

The *Imperial Hotel* (☎ (01343) 4251, fax 50815) on Church St, the main street, has singles/doubles for R90/120, including breakfast. A few blocks along Church St, on the corner of du Toit St, the *Central Hotel* (☎ (01343) 4344), fax 50617) is smaller and a little cheaper but similar in standard.

There are several restaurants on Church St. The *Green Door* is a friendly place with a comfortable bar and a big menu; crayfish is R65, takeaway pizzas are R12. It's open daily from 10 am until late. Opposite the Imperial Hotel, *Avalon* has a more limited menu but is a little cheaper. It's open daily for dinner and for lunch on weekdays.

Getting There & Away

Transtate buses on the Jo'burg to Swaziland route stop in Piet Retief. They cross the border at Mahamba and run via Nhlangano to Hlathikulu. Buses to Jo'burg depart at noon on weekdays and 2 pm on Sunday, and buses to Hlathikulu leave at 2.30 pm on weekdays, with another service at 5 am every Friday.

The minibus-taxi park is in the large open space on Church St opposite the Old Mutual building. From here to the Swaziland border post at Mahamba costs R6.50.

North-West Province

The North-West is a region of wide, hot plains. It was once covered entirely in bushveld and thorn trees, but is now an important agricultural region. The dominant crop is maize (better known as *mielies*), but sunflowers, tobacco, cotton and groundnuts (peanuts) are also grown and cattle are important. Diamonds were discovered in the 1870s and there was an enormous rush to the fields around Lichtenburg. Mining is still important, and the world's largest platinum mines are in the Rustenburg region. Zeerust is at the centre of the Marico-Bushveld country, immortalised by Herman Charles Bosman in his *Mafeking Road* stories.

San paintings attest to the original inhabitants of the region, but when the first white missionaries arrived in the 1830s the region was settled by Batswana – the stone walls that surrounded their huts and towns can still be seen. The Batswana, however, were dispersed by Ndebele, themselves swept up in the wave of disruption unleashed during the difaqane. As part of the apartheid regime's Homeland policy, the Batswana were relocated to Bophuthatswana; the North-West Province takes in most of the area once covered by this bleak, fragmented creation. The provincial capital, Mmabatho, was the capital of Bophuthatswana.

The Voortrekkers who carved out their farms in the 1840s, had a hard battle to survive the vicissitudes of nature and the political turmoil of the region. Their descendants are a tough and uncompromising lot.

Although the region's towns sometimes have interesting histories, today they're generally uninspiring modern-looking places with little to see and do. Even a fiercely parochial Satour officer, born and bred in Klerksdorp, confided this is not an easy region to promote to tourists. Nonetheless, many people will travel through the region en route to Kimberley and the Cape, Botswana, the Kàlahari Gemsbok National Park, Sun City and the Pilanesberg National Park.

NORTH-WEST PROVINCE
Capital: Mmabatho
Main Languages: English, Afrikaans, Setswana
Pre-1994: The western part of Transvaal Province, and most of the Homeland of Bophuthatswana
Highlights:
• Sun City
• Pilanesberg National Park

Warning

Precautions should be taken against malaria, and mosquito repellents are useful during the summer months. Many of the dams and rivers carry bilharzia, so don't swim in them, or drink from them, unless you get an all-clear from a reliable local.

HARTBEESPOORT DAM & THE MAGALIESBERG

Visitors to South Africa will soon realise what an important role dams (reservoirs) play in the recreational life of the Afrikaners. Those who visit South Africa's magnificent coastline may well find the popularity of inland dams bizarre, but for the locals the dams have the indisputable virtues of being close by and wet. On an average weekend the

The Batswana

Controversy surrounds much of South Africa's history, and the history of the Batswana people is no exception. Bantu-speaking peoples had extensive settlements on the highveld by 500 AD. These were Iron-Age communities and their inhabitants grew crops and kept domestic animals. In a process that can only be guessed at, linguistic and cultural distinctions developed between the Nguni people, who lived along the coast, and the Sotho-Tswana, who lived on the highveld.

The peoples of the highveld often built their houses and animal pens from stone and, in places, lived in large communities that can only be described as towns. In parts of the Transvaal some communities specialised in mining and metal production.

The Tswana, in common with the rest of the Bantu-speaking peoples, formed clans within a larger tribal grouping. This was a dynamic situation, with people entering or leaving clans and tribal groups, and the groups themselves consolidating or fragmenting. The Tswana oral tradition describes a number of dynastic struggles, often with competing sons splitting clans on the death of the old chief. This segmentation often occurred peacefully, partly because there was sufficient land available for groups of people to move on to fresh pastures.

By the 19th century, Batswana tribes dominated much of present-day Northern Transvaal, North-West Province, Northern Cape and large parts of Botswana. Fresh pastures were starting to look few and far between, however, and all hell broke loose in the terrible years of the difaqane. Although the Batswana did not come up directly against Shaka and his Zulus, they were ravaged by Mzilikazi and the Ndebele.

(There is some confusion in the use of the terms Tswana and Batswana. For a start, both terms were first used by Europeans to describe a group of independent tribes who happened to be culturally and linguistically similar; they were not used by the tribes themselves. The terms are now often used interchangeably.)

Such was the devastation when the first whites crossed the Vaal River in the 1830s that they believed the land was largely uninhabited. However, as the Boers moved further north, the Batswana rallied and fought back, sometimes with the help of white mercenaries. They also petitioned the British for protection. Eventually, in 1885, the British responded to the Boer expansion, which they saw as a threat to their own interests, by establishing the British Protectorate of Bechuanaland, which has become Botswana.

Mafeking (now Mafikeng) was set up as the capital of Bechuanaland, even though it was in South Africa – giving unintended recognition to the fact that the protectorate by no means included all Batswana land.

The Transvaal Batswana were left to the tender mercies of the new Union of South Africa when it was created after the Boer War. Many were forced to seek work in the new mines and industries that sprang up around Johannesburg. From the time the National Party came to power in 1948, however, the idea of creating black Homelands (based on existing black reserves) was pursued enthusiastically. Although the move was resisted by many black activists and leaders, Bophuthatswana finally accepted 'independence' in 1977.

Bophuthatswana was one of the most depressing and least coherent of the Homelands created by the apartheid regime to serve as dumping grounds for unwanted blacks. Its territory was made up of seven enclaves. Six of the chunks were scattered in an arc running from north of Pretoria to the west, with one of the main chunks bordering Botswana. The most isolated chunk lay on the highveld within the Orange Free State just to the west of Bloemfontein.

Lucas Mangope was the first and only president of Bophuthatswana. Although in some ways he jealously guarded Bophuthatswana's 'independence', he only survived a 1988 coup attempt thanks to the violent intervention of South African troops. His regime had a dismal human rights record.

Economically, Bophuthatswana was the most independent of the Homelands and provided over 80% of its own revenue – largely through the wages of around 400,000 workers employed in South Africa. The next main source of income was mining; Bophuthatswana supplied around 60% of the platinum produced in Southern Africa, and nearly 30% of total world production. Tourism, especially the Sun City complex, remains important. ■

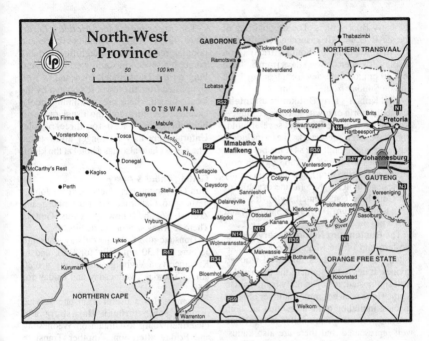

white inhabitants of inland towns decamp en masse to the nearest dam – braais, beers and motorboats are the order of the day.

Hartbeespoort Dam is on the edge of Gauteng Province and is the watersports resort for Pretoria and, to a lesser extent, Jo'burg. There are several fully fledged holiday towns perched on the north-eastern side of the dam on the slopes of the Magaliesberg – including Hartbeespoort and the trendy and expensive Kosmos. They're pleasant enough places – particularly Kosmos – and both towns would, no doubt, look even better if you were resident in one of the nearby cities over summer. If you are a short-term overseas visitor, however, they needn't have any priority. Although there are some touristy game parks, there really isn't anything to do.

The Magaliesberg has attractive mountain scenery and there are some good walks but, once again, the range will really only be of interest if you are based in the region. Private transport is essential.

RUSTENBURG

Rustenburg is a large and prosperous town lying at the western edge of the Magaliesberg hills. It was founded by Voortrekkers in 1841, making it the third-oldest town north of the Vaal River.

Rustenburg is about 120 km north-west of Johannesburg at the centre of a thriving agricultural region and near to the two largest platinum mines in the world. If you have private transport en route to Sun City (40 km to the north), you may choose to make a stopover.

There's a good information centre (☎ (0142) 97 3111) in the museum, on the corner of Plein and Burger Sts, behind the Civic Centre and across from the old church. It's open on weekdays.

Things to See & Do

The **museum** is in an old building. It's small but interesting, with some Iron-Age archaeological finds, but it mainly concentrates on the early Boer settlers. The original flag of the ZAR (Zuid-Afrikaansche Republiek – the first Republic of South Africa) is on display. It's open on weekdays from 8.30 am to 4.30 pm, on Saturday from 9 am to 1 pm and on Sunday from 3 to 5 pm.

Paul Kruger's farm **Boukenhoutfontein**, just to the north of town, is worth visiting. A small section of the farm and several buildings have been preserved. These include a pioneer cottage built in 1841, the house that Paul built for himself in 1863 (which now serves as a coffee shop), and the main family homestead built in 1875 (a fine example of the Colesberg Cape Dutch style). It's open from 8 am to 5 pm Tuesday to Saturday, and 3 to 5 pm on Sunday.

The **Rustenburg Nature Reserve**, at the western end of the Magaliesberg, is dominated by rocky ridges and well-wooded ravines. It lies to the south of the town and is well signposted; it's open daily from 8 am to 4 pm. There is an enormous number of plant species, including quite a few that are both rare and protected. The smaller antelopes are well represented, but there are also kudus, hartebeests and sables; and shy predators like leopards, hyenas and black-backed jackals.

Places to Stay & Eat

The information centre has a list of guesthouses and B&Bs in town, and there are a few hotels. These hotels are mainly pricey places, such as the *Cashmere Hotel* (☎ (0142) 28541) on Van Staden St (singles/doubles R160/202 with breakfast) and the *Tandvaal Hotel* (☎ (0142) 29 9351) on Prinsloo St (from R125).

A member of the good *Mike's Kitchen* chain is on Van Staden St, the main through road. There are also a number of fast-food places catering to through traffic – they probably won't kill you.

The *Hunter's Rest Hotel* (☎ (0142) 92140) is an attractive resort 14 km south of Rustenburg on the R30, in the Magaliesberg. There's a big swimming pool and extensive sports facilities, including horse-riding. Full board costs from R225 per person.

The *Rustenburg Kloof Holiday Resort* (☎ (0142) 97 1351) is another large and popular resort near a magnificent rocky gorge. It's seven km south-west of Rustenburg on the Donkerhoek road and is well signposted from the town. It's owned by the local council; there are swimming pools, excellent facilities and the usual range of bungalows from R50 for three people. Unfortunately they no longer allow tents. The Karos chain also has a hotel at the kloof.

Getting There & Away

Bus Greyhound has a service from Johannesburg to Gaborone via Rustenburg and Zeerust. See the following Zeerust Getting There & Away section for details.

Transtate runs from the railway station to Jo'burg at 1.30 pm daily for R20, and to Kuruman (via Vryburg and Taung) at 6.30 am on Tuesday, Wednesday and Friday for R50.

There's also a useful Transtate service running south through Harrisburg and Pietermaritzburg to Umtata on Wednesday and Friday afternoon. Another Transtate service runs from the mine hostels to Swaziland on Friday afternoon.

Minibus Taxi The taxi park is on Van Staden St, on the Sun City side of the town centre.

ZEERUST

The countryside around Zeerust is rather attractive hilly bushveld, but it soon gets flat as you head south-west to Mafikeng. Zeerust's main claim to fame is as a jumping-off point for Gaborone (Botswana), and there are always a lot of people moving through. The town is quite large; there are plenty of shops strung along Church St, including a couple of 24-hour petrol stations and banks.

There are some old-style buildings with verandahs but there's not much to see. The Zeerust Museum opens occasionally, or you could enquire at the town hall for information on the local Mampoer Route, which refers to a fiery distilled liquor brewed in the region. It can get very hot, with temperatures in January averaging a fierce 40°C. Even in June, the average is close to 30°C.

Places to Stay

The *Transvaal Hotel* (☎ (01428) 22003), Church St, is an old-style country hotel – pretty much unchanged since about 1920. It must get warmish in summer. The high prices might reflect its historical interest but otherwise aren't great value, starting at R65 per person or R75 with bath. Breakfast is about R15. The *Marico Hotel*, also on Church St, seemed to be more interested in beer sales.

The most comfortable option is the *Abjaterskop Hotel* (☎ (01428) 22008), two km from Zeerust. There's a swimming pool, and rooms are air-conditioned. Singles/doubles are R142/198 with breakfast.

Getting There & Away

Bus Greyhound passes through Rustenburg and Zeerust on its Jo'burg to Gaborone (Botswana) service on Thursday, Friday and Sunday, returning Monday, Friday and Saturday. From Rustenburg to Gaborone is R70, Zeerust to Gaborone is R45. To Jo'burg it's R40 and R65 respectively.

A Transtate service from Jo'burg to Mafikeng via Zeerust departs from Jo'burg daily except Sunday and returns daily except Saturday. Lehurutshe Transport (☎ (0140) 63 3606) runs buses around the local area.

Minibus Taxi The taxi park is on Church St (the main street) on the Mafikeng side of the town centre. The fare to Mafikeng is R10 and to Rustenburg it's R20.

SUN CITY

Sun City is the extraordinary creation of Mr Sol Kerzner. It's a large 'entertainment' complex based around a couple of big spaces full of slot (poker) machines. In addition to the pokies there are the usual casino games of chance, two excellent golf courses (thanks to Gary Player and an army of ground staff), swimming pools, sports facilities (including the spectacular Valley of the Waves), dancing girls, a concert venue, cinemas (soft porn is popular), restaurants and high-quality accommodation.

Sol took advantage of the 'independent' status of Bophuthatswana to bypass the apartheid regime's Calvinist views on gambling and bare flesh. With the densely populated PWV nearby, the dry and sunny climate and the Homeland's cheap labour, he was on a winner. Of course, to really meet the classic tourist fantasy you also need a sandy beach, waves and palm trees – hence the Valley of the Waves. Since April 1994 there have been no Homelands and Sun City is now in South Africa. Luckily for Sol, the new South Africa is much more relaxed about the human body – even more luckily, he seems set to retain his monopoly on large-scale casino gambling.

All this extravagance in the middle of one of the poorest corners of the country is, at best, incongruous. Sun City has, nonetheless, been fantastically successful and South Africans flock here to walk on a (very tame) wild side, and to fling their money around. Losers can console themselves with the thought that they are helping to pay over 3500 salaries (but are no longer contributing to the Bop military dictatorship)... oh, and I believe Sol gets a cut as well.

Some might argue that entertainment and feeding money into slot machines are mutually exclusive concepts, but if you do get a kick out of gambling and like the idea of being pampered in luxurious hotels, this is the place for you. It doesn't have much to do with being in Africa, although the complex is on the edge of the excellent Pilanesberg National Park. For many visitors the Valley of the Waves is the main reason to come to Sun City. There are, occasionally, worthwhile concerts, which attract big crowds.

Information & Orientation

The complex has a Welcome Centre (☎ (01465) 71544), where you can get maps and information. It's at the entrance to the Entertainment Centre, right by the bus station.

Admission to Sun City costs R10, with one or two of the attractions having separate admission charges, notably the Valley of the Waves, which costs another R35.

The complex is really not all that big, but it is a bit confusing. The car park for day visitors is at the entrance, about two km from the Entertainment Centre. An elevated train shuttles from the car park to the Cabanas, then the Sun City Hotel, then on the right The Cascades, on the left the Entertainment Centre, and finally The Lost City.

Things to Do & See

The **Entertainment Centre** is a gambling venue apparently aimed primarily at day trippers and slot-machine addicts. It's pretty tacky. There is also a bank, bingo hall, a number of reasonably priced restaurants, cinemas, shops, and the 7000 seat Super-bowl. The **Sun City Hotel** also has ranks of slot machines, a more interesting and sophisticated casino area, shops, restaurants, and nightclubs.

The spectacular centrepiece of Sun City is **The Lost City**, an extraordinary piece of kitsch that would be fun if the publicity didn't talk about it symbolising African heritage and so on. It has less to do with African heritage than Euro-Disney has to do with French heritage. As well as some Disney-esque attractions there's the **Valley of the Waves** where there is, not surprisingly, a large-scale wave machine. This is probably the best reason for non-gamblers to come to Sun City.

At the heart of the Lost City is **The Palace**, a hotel which could inspire hallucinations – unfortunately you can't wander around much unless you're a guest, and you can't be a guest unless you have very deep pockets.

Golf at the superb **Gary Player Country Club** is R60 for 18 holes if you're a resident, R80 for day visitors. A caddy is compulsory and will cost R30. Club hire is R55. Even more expensive is the new **Lost City Golf Course**, at R80 for residents and R100 for day visitors.

Waterworld, on the shores of a large artificial lake, has facilities for parasailing, water skiing and windsurfing. Alternatively,

you can play bowls (indoor and outdoor), go horse-riding, work out in a fully equipped gym, and play tennis or squash.

There are tours into the adjoining **Pilanesberg National Park**, departing at 7.30 am and 2.30 pm – a 2½-hour tour in an open vehicle costs R55 per person.

At the main entrance near the main parking area, the **Kwena Gardens Crocodile Paradise** displays a variety of reptiles and animals in addition to crocodiles. Don't miss the enormous croc they call Footloose. Admission is R10.

Places to Stay & Eat

The Palace is the top place to stay at Sun City. Standard rooms start around R850 and R1000 on Friday and Saturday. A night in a suite will set you back as much as R10,000!

The Palace has displaced *The Cascades* as the most luxurious hotel in the complex, although it too is surrounded by elaborate landscaped grounds with a swimming pool, waterfalls and so on. Standard rooms (which could only be described as palatial) start at R560, or nearly R700 on Friday and Saturday.

Sun City Hotel is the oldest of the five-star hotels, and it's the cheapest. It's by no means shabby, however, and cheap is hardly the right word. It's the most lively of the hotels, with gambling facilities on the premises, as well as a number of restaurants, an enormous swimming pool and bar, a disco and nightclubs. According to the promotional material, it 'pulsates' at night. Standard rooms start at R460 or R560 on Friday and Saturday.

The cheapest alternative is the more laid-back *Sun City Cabanas*, which seems to be aimed at family groups. Guests can make use of all the facilities in the Sun City Hotel, but it also has its own swimming pool and adventure playground. The rooms are still pleasant, and fully equipped. Standard rooms start around R320, or R400 on Friday and Saturday.

All these hotels can be contacted or booked through Sun City (☎ (014651) 21000) or booked through Sun International central reservations (☎ (011) 780 7800, fax

780 7449). If they look too expensive and you have your own transport, consider staying at Pilanesberg National Park (see separate section). The other alternative is just to make a day trip.

All the hotels have a selection of restaurants. The cheapest alternative is the *Palm Terrace*, in the Cabanas, which is open for breakfast, lunch and dinner. There are a number of reasonably priced restaurants, representing a variety of cuisines, in the Entertainment Centre. Expect to pay from R25 to R30 for a pretty straightforward meal and R12 for a simple sandwich.

Getting There & Away
Air Tiny Pilanesberg Airport (☎ (01465) 21261) once gloried in the name 'Pilanesberg International Airport'. It's about seven km north-west of the entrance to Sun City. Sun Air (☎ (011) 970 1623, fax 970 1906) has flights from Jo'burg daily except Saturday, for R171. There are also Sun Air flights to/from Cape Town (R627) and Durban (R388). Sun Air was once the 'national' airline of Bophuthatswana and was called Bop Air.

Bus Sun City Buses (bookings through Computicket (☎ (011) 331 9991)) has daily buses from the Rotunda in Jo'burg at 9 am, 11.45 am and 3 pm Monday to Thursday; 9 am, 11 am and 5 pm on Friday; 9 am, 11.45 am and 2 pm on Saturday; and 9 and 11.45 am on Sunday. The return fare is R45, which includes a few freebies, or R65 with entry to the Valley of the Waves.

There are weekend buses from Pretoria (departing from the Tourist Rendezvous) to Sun City. Prices and offers are the same as for Jo'burg.

Car Sun City is surprisingly poorly sign-posted, so navigators will need to concentrate. From Jo'burg it's around a two-hour drive, depending on which route you take. The most straightforward route is via Rustenburg, although the Sun City people recommend you travel via Brits.

PILANESBERG NATIONAL PARK
The Pilanesberg National Park surrounds Sun City, so it is easy to combine a visit to both places. It protects over 500 sq km of an unusual complex of extinct volcanoes and is the fifth-largest national park in South Africa. The countryside is attractive, with rocky outcrops, ridges and craters, mostly covered in sparse woodland. There are two vegetation zones – Kalahari thornveld and sour bushveld – and the atmosphere is quintessentially African.

Until the 1970s the Pilanesberg was farmed, but it was recognised as an ideal site for a national park, partly because the hills provide a natural barrier to the more densely populated surrounding plains. As a result, the land was acquired by the Bop government and an ambitious and imaginative rehabilitation and game-stocking programme was instituted. This has been outstandingly successful and it is now almost impossible to imagine that the area was ever anything other than wilderness.

The park is once again home to extensive populations of many of Africa's most impressive animals. There are white and black rhinos, elephants, giraffes, hippos, buffaloes, a wide variety of buck (including sables, elands, kudu, gemsboks), zebras, leopards, jackals, hyenas, and even a small number of cheetahs. The region also has a diverse population of birds – over 300 species have been recorded.

There is an excellent 100-km network of gravel roads, hides, picnic spots, and some very good-value accommodation options. Since it is no more than 25 km from one end of the park to the other, it is easy to cover the range of different environments in the park and to see a wide variety of animals. To do any real justice to it, however, you need at least one full day. Bear in mind that the best game-viewing times are in the morning and evening, and that you'll average around 10 to 15 km/h while driving.

Orientation & Information
Signposting in this area, even around Sun City and the Pilanesberg, is less than terrific

Pilanesberg National Park & Sun City

– you can't really go wrong once you get to Sun City, however, because the Pilanesberg are the only significant hills in the region. Travelling from Sun City towards Brits, keep going through Mogwase village and turn off to the left just after the Caltex service station.

The Pilanesberg range forms four concentric mountain rings, with Mankwe Lake at the centre.

Information and useful sketch maps are available at the main Manyane Gate, where overnight visitors must enter and report to the reception office (not including those staying at Kwa Maritane, Tshukudu or Bakubung lodges). The Manyane reception office is open from 7.30 am to 4.30 pm Monday to Thursday, 7.30 am to 8 pm on Friday, 7.30 am to 4.30 pm on Saturday, and 7.30 am to 3.30 pm on Sunday. The office closes for lunch every day between 1 and 2 pm.

The entrance fee for adults is R6.50. From April to August gates into the park proper (beyond the Manyane Complex) are closed from 7 pm to 5.30 am and from September to March from 8 pm to 5.30 am.

There is an interpretative display and shop in an old magistrates court in the centre of the park; the shop sells curios, refreshments and a reasonable range of basic food items.

Pilanesberg Safaris (☎ (01456) 55355) runs several activities from the Manyane Gate. There are 2½-hour game drives in the morning, afternoon and night for R40 (minimum six people); guided hikes of 3½ hours for R40 (minimum six people); four-hour balloon rides (a great way to see wildlife) for R685 (minimum four people); and wilderness trails for R280 (minimum six people).

Places to Stay

The park (☎ (01465) 56135) was administered by the now-defunct Bophuthatswana National Parks Service. Currently accommodation bookings are taken on (011) 465 5423, but that might change. You could try the new North-West Tourism Council (☎ (011) 331 9336 or (0140) 83 4040).

The *Manyane Complex & Caravan Park* is near the Manyane Gate. The complex is excellent – thoughtfully designed and laid out, with high-quality facilities. There's a small swimming pool, a reasonable shop with basic food items, and a decent restaurant. Sites are R40 (R50 in season) for up to four people, so it isn't cheap. However, it's only about 20 km from Sun City and it's a lot cheaper than any accommodation there. There are also chalets from R150 a double.

Mankwe Camp is a smaller place, overlooking Mankwe Lake. There are self-catering bungalows and safari tents scattered amongst natural trees, with communal washing and kitchen facilities (including fridges). The bungalows sleep up to four people and cost R80 (R105 in season). The tents sleep three and cost R60 (R80 in the high season). They're pitched on concrete floors and have comfortable beds (bedding provided), chairs and paraffin lamps.

Kololo Camp is the smallest camp, with only four tents sleeping 12 people and basic cooking facilities (including a fridge). It has a great location on a hilltop and has panoramic views. It's called a private camp, which means it is booked out as a single unit to families and groups of friends.

There are a couple of up-market time-share resorts with hotel accommodation in the park, *Kwa Maritane* (☎ (01465) 21820, fax 21147) and *Bakubung Lodge* (☎ (01465) 21861, fax 21621). The Kwa Maritane gate is about five km north-east of the Sun City turn-off, on the road to Manyane Gate; Bakubung Gate is about five km south-west of the Sun City turn-off, or you can get there through the Sun City complex. Bakubung charges from R465/700 a single/double for rooms and from R765/890 for chalets which sleep up to four people. Rates include dinner and breakfast.

Tshukudu Lodge, most easily accessible from Bakubung Gate, is a new up-market resort with just nine cottages. Rates, which include all meals, game drives and walks, are R775/1250 a single/double. Additional people (up to a total of four) cost R270. If you have R10,000 to spare you can have the whole place to yourself. Bookings are made through Bakubung Lodge (☎ (01456) 21861, fax 21621).

MAFIKENG & MMABATHO

Mafikeng and Mmabatho are twin towns about three km apart. Mafeking, as it was known, was the original capital of the British Protectorate of Bechuanaland (now Botswana). It is most famous for its role in the 1899-1902 Anglo-Boer War, when British forces under Colonel Baden-Powell were besieged by the Boers. Mmabatho is a modern town built as the capital of Bophuthatswana; it's now the capital of North-West Province.

Mafikeng has some vitality – the streets are busy. There is a reasonable selection of shops and a few moderately interesting historical sites. However, it is really nothing more than a fairly typical South African country town.

Mmabatho was developed as Bop's showcase. As a result it has a number of suitably grandiose and ugly buildings; they're quite widely scattered as the planners obviously presumed motorcars would be the primary form of transport in this city of the future. Amongst other things there's a sports stadium and an enormous US-style shopping centre known as Megacity.

The history of Mafikeng is interesting, but you don't have to visit it to discover this. The present reality is mundane and hot. Unless you have a particular interest in the siege, the most interesting tourist development is Lotlamoreng Cultural Village, where a number of traditional buildings and kraals have been built.

History

In the 1870s various European mercenaries who had fought on the northern frontier against Tswana tribes were rewarded with farms in the Mafikeng region; they created the Republic of Goshen. The British, who had been petitioned by the Tswana tribes further north and who saw the new republic as a threat, sent a force under Sir Charles Warren to annex the territory. In 1885 Mafeking (as the Europeans called it) was established as the administrative capital of the British Protectorate of Bechuanaland.

The small frontier town was besieged by Boer forces from 14 October 1899 to 17 May 1900. The dispatches written by Colonel Baden-Powell led to the siege becoming a

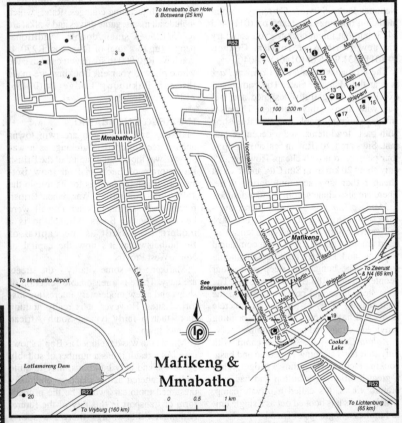

symbol of British courage and steadfastness. In reality, the Boers made only one determined attempt to capture the town and were for the most part content to maintain a pretty civilised siege – apparently there was seldom any fighting on Sunday.

Perhaps its most lasting significance was the role it played in the development of Baden-Powell's ideas. During the siege Baden-Powell created a cadet corps for the town's boys – the forerunner of the Boy Scout movement. The boys carried messages, ran errands and, no doubt, did good deeds.

I said to one of these boys on one occasion, when he came through a rather heavy fire:
'You will get hit one of these days, riding about like that when shells are flying.'
'I pedal so quick, sir, they'll never catch me!' he replied.
These boys didn't seem to mind the bullets one bit. They were ready to carry out orders, though it meant risking their lives every time.
Scouting for Boys, Robert Baden-Powell

Robert Baden-Powell

Orientation & Information
It's easy to get around Mafikeng on foot. Most shops and banks are grouped around the central bus and car park. It's a hot and dusty five-km walk from the centre of Mafikeng to Megacity in Mmabatho; catch one of the numerous local buses.

1	Water Tower
2	Molopo Sun Hotel
3	Independence Stadium
4	Megacity (Banks, Cinemas, Library, Post Office & Restaurants)
5	Mafikeng Railway Station
6	Shopping Centre
7	Long-distance Taxis
8	Telephones
9	Steers
10	Protea Hotel
11	Museum & Information Centre
12	Mafikeng Post Office
13	Car Park & Local Buses
14	First National Bank
15	Uncle Sam's
16	Surrey Hotel
17	University Bookshop
18	Mosque
19	Cooke's Lake Camping Ground
20	Lotlamoreng Cultural Village

Look for the free *What's New in Mmabatho*, available in most of the hotels.

Tourist Office The Mafikeng Tourist Office (☎ (0140) 810023, or 22489 after hours), on Martin St, Mafikeng, adjoining the museum, is helpful, and probably more likely to be open than the North-West Province Tourist Office in Mmabatho. It's open Monday to Friday from 8 am to 4.30 pm, and weekends from 8 am to 1 pm.

Money There are no Amex or Rennies agencies in Mafikeng or Mmabatho, so for changing money, banks in Mafikeng and Megacity are your only option. First National has a branch in Mafikeng, on Robin St between Main and Shippard Sts.

Post & Telecommunications The main post office is next to Megacity. The Mafikeng Post Office is on Carrington between Main and Martin Sts.

Travel Agencies Tswana Travel (☎ (0140) 23555) in Megacity handles the usual travel agency bookings.

NORTH-WEST PROVINCE

Bookshops The University Bookstore (☎ (0140) 81 0272), on the corner of Carrington and Shippard Sts, Mafikeng, has a reasonable collection of books and stationery.

Medical Services André Chemist, 19 Voortrekker St, is open Monday to Friday from 8 am to 9 pm, Saturday from 8 am to 1 pm and 5 to 9 pm, and Sunday from 11 am to 1 pm and 7 to 9 pm. For dentists and doctors, go to the Victoria Medical Centre & Private Hospital (0140) 81 2043), Victoria St, Mafikeng.

Emergency You can contact police on 10111, and ambulance on (0140) 23333).

Mafikeng Museum

The museum is not large but it does have some interesting relics, mainly relating to the famous siege. Amongst the relics is a menu for a dinner for senior officers given to celebrate the Queen's Birthday on 24th May 1900 – life may have been tough for some, but the senior officers managed to maintain standards. Admission is free, and it's open Monday to Friday from 8 am to 4 pm, Saturday from 9 am to noon.

Megacity

Megacity could be a useful starting point if you are heading further north or west. There are banks, an adjoining post office, a number of large, well-stocked department stores (good for food and camping equipment), numerous smaller shops as well as several restaurants.

Lotlamoreng Dam & Cultural Village

The Lotlamoreng Cultural Village is an unabashed tourist attraction, but it has been well handled and gives an all-too-rare insight into fast-disappearing traditional cultures. In the western half of South Africa it is almost impossible to find any surviving traditional housing, so Lotlamoreng is playing a vital role. It is the brainchild of Credo Mutwa, a Tswana priest, historian, artist and author.

A number of small traditional villages and kraals have been developed on the banks of the Lotlamoreng Dam. Amongst the groups represented are the Tswana, including the Barolong, (blacksmith people) and Batlhaping (boat people), Xhosa, Zulu, Pedi, Ndebele and San. These are not just static displays, but are in full use by people practising traditional crafts – from dancing and singing to pottery and beadwork. As you explore the village you are likely to stumble on people doing any number of things, basically without regard to visitors (and there aren't many).

The complex is open from 7 am to 7 pm; entry is R10. It can easily absorb a full afternoon. If you are in a small group, check to see if anyone can give you a guided tour (you really need someone to explain the significance of what you will see). Right beside the dam there's an aviary (worth checking out), a refreshment kiosk, lawns and braais.

Places to Stay

Cooke's Lake Camping Ground is dusty and unattractive; it would do at a pinch and a camp site only costs R10. There are few facilities. Apparently you can stay at *St Joseph's Centre* at St Mary's Mission (☎ (0140) 83 2646) in Lomanyaneng, about two km south of the railway station, for about R30.

There are a few B&Bs, starting around R60 per person. Ask at the Mafikeng information centre for a complete list.

The *Surrey Hotel* (☎ (0140) 81 0420), 32 Shippard St, is not cheap but it's the cheapest alternative. It is pretty rowdy and not very inspiring. A single/double is R100/125 or R115/140 with bath. The *Protea Hotel* (☎ (0140) 81 0117), on the corner of Station Rd and Martin St, Mafikeng, charges R140/200 with breakfast.

If you have the money, it's definitely worth considering one of the ubiquitous Sun hotels. As in virtually all the Sun hotels, gambling is encouraged!

The *Molopo Sun* (☎ (0140) 24184), Dr Mokhobo Ave (University Dr), Mmabatho, is close to Megacity for shopping, and a courtesy bus runs people to and from the

Mmabatho Sun for gambling and other nightlife. It has a couple of decent-value places to eat. There's a swimming pool and the rooms are all fully equipped and pleasant. Singles/doubles start at R175/200, with occasional specials in the off season. Prices are at least double that at the luxurious *Mmabatho Sun* (☎ (0140) 89 1111), Lobatsi Rd, Mmabatho. There's a swimming pool, fountains, tennis courts, casino and cinema.

There's a *hotel school* (☎ (0140) 86 2222) in Mmabatho which apparently offers accommodation.

Manyane Game Lodge (☎ (0140) 81 6020), about six km out of town on the Zeerust road, has fully equipped chalets for R160/200 a single/double and R270/320 for three/four people.

Places to Eat

For budget eaters, *Uncle Sam's Bakery & Restaurant*, 38 Shippard St, Mafikeng, has standard takeaway fare such as stew and pap (R6) and curry and rice (R7). They also do pizza (R10 to R30), pasta (from R9) and steaks (from R16) and there are tables to eat at. For chain-store food, there's a *Steers* in Mafikeng's Station Towers centre, on Hatchard St not far from the railway station.

In the Mafikeng suburb of Golf View is a member of the *O'Hagan's Irish Pub & Grill* chain, on the corner of Tillard and Gemsbok Sts. It has entrees from R6 and main courses approaching R30. You have to be at least 23 years old to get in.

There are several surprisingly good options at the Molopo Sun Hotel in Mmabatho. *Letsatsi* has inexpensive snacks and the *Ditha Restaurant* has buffet lunches for about R30, dinners for R39.

There are also quite a few reasonable places in Megacity.

Getting There & Away

People may come through Mafikeng on their way to/from the Botswana. Ramatlabama, 26 km to the north, is the busiest border crossing and lies on the main route to/from Lobatse and Gaborone.

Air Sun Air (☎ (0140) 81 0660) has flights to Sun City and Jo'burg, with connections to other cities.

Bus City Link (☎ (0140) 81 2680, (0110) 333 4412 in Jo'burg) runs daily from Megacity to Jo'burg for R37. A Transtate service from Jo'burg to Mafikeng (R40) departs daily from Jo'burg except Sunday and returns daily except Saturday. Buses depart from Mafikeng railway station at 12.30 pm and arrive in Jo'burg at 5.45 pm.

On Wednesday there's a Transtate bus to Lobatse and Palapye in Botswana.

Train Currently no passenger trains run to Mafikeng (or from South Africa to Gaborone). However, there is still a reservation counter (☎ (0140) 28259) at the station, and the lack of business makes it an ideal place to make leisurely bookings for your other trips.

Minibus Taxis Minibus taxis leave from the forecourt of the Mafikeng railway station. As usual, most leave early in the morning. Examples of destinations and fares are:

Botswana border	R3.50 (running all day)
Gaborone (Botswana)	R20
Jo'burg	R35
Lobatse (Botswana)	R10
Pretoria ·	R35
Rustenburg	R25
Vryburg (few taxis)	R20
Zeerust	R10

Getting Around

Bus Numerous city buses ply between Mafikeng (corner of Main St and Station Rd) and Mmabatho (Megacity) for a few rand. Buses also run out to Lotlamoreng.

POTCHEFSTROOM

Potchefstroom, known locally as Potch, is off the N12 about 115 km south-west of Johannesburg. It's a large town, verging on a city, that looks rather unappetising from the main road. There are some pleasant leafy suburbs, however, including an oak avenue which claims the title of the longest in the southern hemisphere. There's also a large lakeside municipal resort about four km west of the town centre – not a bad place to stay overnight if you're coming from the south and don't want to arrive in Jo'burg at night. You're probably better off stopping here than in the much larger Klerksdorp, about 50 km further south-west on the N12.

It might not look it, but Potchefstroom was the first European town to be established in the Transvaal. It was founded by the Voortrekker leader Andries Potgieter in 1838, and was the original capital of the ZAR. It remains a conservative town.

The information office is in the town hall on Kerk St, and they can give you a map of Potch. There's also a Satour (☎ (0148) 293 1611) office on the 1st floor of the Royal Building, 44 Lombard St.

The **Potchefstroom Main Museum** is worth visiting, particularly to see the only remaining ox-wagon dating from the Battle of Blood River. It's open from 10 am to 1 pm and 2 to 5 pm Monday to Friday, from 9 am to 12.45 pm on Saturday, and from 2.30 to 5 pm on Sunday. There are also several restored buildings.

Places to Stay & Eat
The *Lake Recreation Resort* (☎ (0148) 299 5470) is a dam classic – the whole of Potchefstroom can be found here on a sunny weekend. Signposting is a bit erratic, but anyone should be able to direct you – it's about four km from the N12, on the north side of town. There are swimming pools, fairground attractions, boats, a café and plenty of braais. There is a range of bungalows (from R50) and camp sites (R30).

There are a number of hotels in town, including *Kings Hotel* (☎ (0148) 297 5505), 25 Potgieter St (on the corner of Kerk St), which is a decent place with rooms starting from R90/150 per person, and the more luxurious *Elgro Hotel* (☎ (0148) 297 5411), 60 Wolmarans St, which has rooms starting from R80 per person.

On Kerk St, *Espressivo* is a good place for coffee and cake. There are one or two restaurants nearby and there's also a *Mike's Kitchen* in town.

VRYBURG
The countryside around Vryburg is flat, dry and scrubby, so you don't get any unpleasant surprises when you arrive. The only unexpected factor is the size of the town – it's a large place and a major shopping and service centre for the surrounding farmers. Other than the well-maintained gardens on the main street and one or two pubs with accommodation there's nothing to interest visitors.

Orange Free State

The land-locked Orange Free State (usually shortened to Free State or OFS) consists largely of the plains of the southern African plateau. To the east is highland with weirdly eroded sandstone hills.

The Free State's borders reflect the prominent role it has played in South African history. To the south is the Orange River, which the Voortrekkers crossed to escape the Cape colony. The northern border is defined by the Vaal River, which was the next frontier of Boer expansion – see the Facts about the Country chapter. To the east, across the Caledon, is Lesotho, where mountains and King Moshoeshoe I halted the tide of Boer expansion. To the south-east, however, the Free State spills across the Caledon as the mountains dwindle to grazing land, harder for Moshoeshoe to defend.

There are important gold mines in and around Welkom and diamonds are also mined in the Free State. The western half of the province is bare, rolling grazing country, while the hillier east is a major grain-growing region. It is a wealthy province and while there are fewer attractions in the Free State than in other provinces, many of the quiet *dorps* (towns) and prosperous burgs have a Rip van Winkle air, where dreams of an Afrikaner Arcadia linger.

ORANGE FREE STATE
(Its post-election name is now Free State)
Capital: Bloemfontein
Main Languages: Afrikaans, English
Pre-1994: The Free State's borders remain the same
Highlights
• Eastern Highlands & QwaQwa Region
• Backpackers will love Rustlers' Valley
• Towns of the old Boer republics

Northern Free State & Goldfields

Gold was discovered in the Free State in April 1938 and a rush started immediately. Now the Free State goldfields produce more than a third of the country's output. The extraction of gold is centred on three towns – Welkom, Virginia and Odendaalsrus.

Much of the rest of this region is given over to intensive farming, mainly maize. The largest town between Jo'burg and Bloem-

fontein is Kroonstad. The other towns are sleepy, pleasant places and if a farm holiday is your bag you have come to the right place. If the quiet of this part of the Free State gets to you, it's only two hours north to Jo'burg!

SENEKAL
Chances are you will pass through this small town, as it is at the junction of the N5, R70 and R707. If you do, head to the NG Kerk, not so much to see the church (a national monument) but to see its boundary wall made from petrified tree trunks.

The *municipal caravan park* (☎ (05848) 2142) in Boer St has caravan sites but not tent sites. The *New Free State Hotel* (☎ /fax (05848) 4542) on Lange St has comfortable rooms for R120 per person.

ORANGE FREE STATE

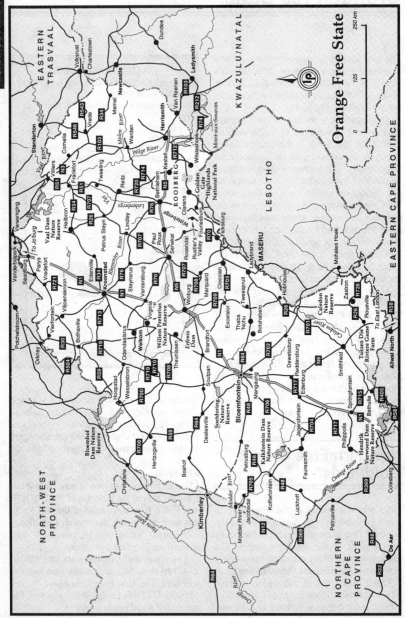

Orange Free State

WINBURG

It's difficult to imagine that this sleepy little town, founded in 1842, was the first capital of a Boer republic in today's free State. It's a forceful reminder of just how the Boer republics really began at a grass roots level. It was in the dining room of Ford's Hotel that the leaders of five Voortrekker groups finally agreed to form a government under the leadership of Piet Retief.

Information is available at the library, in the town square.

The **church** on the town square was used as a hospital and school during the Anglo-Boer War. There are some old photos of the town here. The **Voortrekker Monument**, about three km from town, is comprised of five columns symbolising the five trek parties (those of Louis Trichardt, Hendrik Potgieter, Gert Maritz, Piet Retief and Pieter Uys) who created the republic. You may well have been wondering why just about every town in the Free State has variations of these as street names! Nearby there's a small **museum** and the small dwelling in which a later president, MT Steyn, was born.

Places to Stay & Eat

The basic *municipal caravan park* (☎ (05242), ask for 3) is near the creek at the end of Edward St, not far from the post office. Tent sites cost R10. The historic Ford's Hotel, with its wrought-iron sign on the roof, has closed, but the *Winburg Hotel* (☎ (05242), ask for 160) is still operating and is good value at R65 per person. It's a simple place with some character. The dining room here is the only place to eat, apart from crummy takeaways.

Getting There & Away

The nearest passenger trains stop at the town of Theunissen, 30 km away. Transtate buses between Welkom and Thaba 'Nchu, Welkom and Maseru (Lesotho), and Welkom and Ficksburg stop here daily.

There are minibus taxis running to the Goldfields area and some others heading towards Bloemfontein, but not many. Ask at the petrol station on the north edge of town.

If you want to hitch, walk down Victoria St (it begins at the square with the post office on the corner) to the T-intersection. Turn left for the five-km walk to the N1 which takes you past the Voortrekker monument, or right if you want to cut through the small black township and save yourself a few km.

AROUND WINBURG
Willem Pretorius Game Reserve

This game reserve (☎ (05777) 4077, fax 4229) is on the Allemanskraal Dam, off the N1 about 20 km north of Winburg and 70 km south of Kroonstad. Aventura Aldam has a conference centre, golf course and bowling greens, but there are also animals including giraffes, white rhinos, buffaloes and various antelopes. Fishing is popular (get a Free State angling licence from the resort) and there are hiking trails. Entry costs R12 per car.

Camping is R20 per site, economy chalets are R50, two-bed chalets are R115 (in high season, R145) and economy four-bed units are R100 (in high season, R135).

Erfenis Dam Nature Reserve

South-west of Winburg and 15 km east of Theunissen (a small town with a small winery), this reserve is on the Vet River. There are basic camping facilities and some wildlife but it is mainly anglers who come here. The *Algro Hotel* (☎ 733 0381), Theunissen, is currently being modernised.

KROONSTAD

Kroonstad, on the N1, is a typical large rural town in the Free State. It dates back to 1855 and the Voortrekker Sarel Celliers was one of the first settlers. The town may have been named after his horse, Kroon.

The best place to get information is from the efficiently run Central Free State Publicity Association (☎ /fax (0562) 22601) in the old town hall, Cross St. Get copies of the *Maize Route* and *Central Free State Package Tours* which detail activities, itineraries, accommodation and dining suggestions.

If you want a taxi, phone ☎ (0562) 22704 or (0562) 33424 after hours.

Things to See & Do

The **Old Market Building**, opposite the pretty **Magistrate's Building** on the corner of Mark and Murray Sts, is a national monument. Upstairs in the library there's the small **Sarel Celliers Museum**, open weekdays (closing for lunch) and on the second and fourth Saturday morning of each month.

You can see the **Celliers statue** in the grounds of the impressive NG Moederkerk on Cross St. He's standing on a gun carriage making the Blood River vow. His farm, **Doornkloof**, is 45 km out of town and can be visited by appointment – ask at the Publicity Association.

Out in the industrial area is a cemetery for those who died in the British concentration camps during the Anglo-Boer War. There's also a monument commemorating the symbolic ox-wagon trek through Kroonstad in 1938.

The national tournament of *Jukskei* (an Afrikaner game where clubs are tossed at a peg) is held annually in Kroonstad.

The 4000-hectare **Koppies Dam Nature Reserve**, north-east of Kroonstad, is on the Rhenoster River. There's wildlife and waterbirds, but fishing is the main pursuit; the reserve is open from 7 am to 9 pm daily.

Places to Stay & Eat

Kroon Park (☎ (0562) 31942), the municipal caravan park is more like a resort than most municipal places, with a couple of swimming pools and good facilities. It's across the river and further south down Cross St (which becomes Louw St). There are sites from R15 plus R5 per person, apartments from R77/110 for singles/doubles and one-bedroom chalets at R129 for two.

Hotel Emillo (☎ (0562) 23271), on Louw St, has rooms with bath at R90/120 for singles/doubles; breakfast is R12. To get there from the station, turn right from the station and follow Cross St south past the Kerk and the large roundabout.

To get to *Hotel Zeederberg* (☎ (0562) 51674) turn right into Market St at the roundabout. This up-market place has rooms starting from about R100/140. The *Toristo Protea*

(☎ (0562) 25111), on the corner of Du Toit and Rautenbach Sts, charges from R169/191.

The Publicity Association has a list of holiday farms and B&Bs in the area.

Angelo's Trattoria in Reitz St is good for Italian food, with pastas from R18. *Sleepers* is a steakhouse with quite a few beers on tap, and there's a *Spur* in Buitekant St.

Getting There & Away

Bus Transtate's service between Welkom and Jo'burg stops at the railway station.

Translux services on the Jo'burg/Pretoria-East London and Jo'burg/Pretoria-Port Elizabeth routes stop here. From Kroonstad to Jo'burg/Pretoria costs R100, to Port Elizabeth R180 and to East London R190. Translux also runs from Knysna to Jo'burg/Pretoria via Bloemfontein four times weekly, stopping at Kroonstad. Translux stops out at the Shell Ultra City on the highway, as does Greyhound's Jo'burg/Pretoria-Port Elizabeth service.

Train The *Amatola* (Jo'burg-East London) and *Algoa* (Jo'burg-Port Elizabeth) trains stop here.

Minibus Taxi Across from the railway station is the minibus-taxi park. Most taxis go only to relatively nearby towns such as Welkom (R8), although there are occasional services to Jo'burg – arrive early in the morning.

WELKOM

About 30% of South Africa's gold is mined in the Free State and this modern town is at the centre of the goldfields. It's something of a showpiece, as it was completely planned; (there are no *robots* or traffic lights, a fact which is touted as proof of a masterpiece of town planning). However, this just means that it's sprawling, soulless and hell to get around if you don't have transport. The whites number 65,000 but there are over 300,000 blacks living in town or working on the mines – most of them kept neatly out of sight as usual. Still, there's some black wealth here and some of the suburbs are a little more integrated than usual. There's white wealth, too, with the highest per capita income in the country.

Orientation & Information

The 'publicity tower' (☎ (057) 352 9244; 352 9501) is in the clocktower at the civic centre on Stateway, the main street. Rennies Travel (☎ (057) 353 3041), the Thomas Cook agent, is at Shop 11, Sanlam Plaza (also known as Checkers, after the plaza's supermarket), also on Stateway.

Not far from here is Mooi St, which encloses most of the central shopping area in its horseshoe curve. The First National Bank is on Elizabeth St, the Standard Bank is on Tulbagh St and the main post office is on Bok St.

There's a taxi rank on Mooi St, near the south-west corner of Central Park, or phone (057) 55945 or 396 1429.

Things to See & Do

Approximately once a month you can tour one of the dozen or so mines and see a gold pour (R50). Contact the tourist office for more information. If no tours are on offer here, you could try phoning (057) 212 3111 to see if there are any in nearby Virginia.

The area's huge mine evaporation pans are home to a wide variety of birdlife, including the greater flamingo (*Phoenicopterus ruber*) and the lesser flamingo (*Phoenicopterus minor*) and greyheaded gull (*Larus cirrocephalus*). More than 200 species of birds have been seen around the city – 90% of all waterfowl species found in South Africa. Try Flamingo Pan off the R30 just west of the town, or Witpan at Oppenheimer Park, about four km south-east of the town centre on the continuation of Stateway. Two other birdwatching spots are Theronia and Flamingo lakes.

Places to Stay

The pleasant and central municipal *caravan park* (☎ (057) 21455), between the Welkom Inn and the swimming pool, may have reopened. About two km from the town centre is *Sirkel Caravan Park* (☎ (057) 53987), 281 Koppie Alleen Rd in the Reitz Park area, north of the centre, with sites for R20. There is another caravan park, *Flamingo Lake* (☎ (057) 353 2296).

Hotel 147 (☎ (057) 352 5381), on Stateway, is reasonable and has singles/doubles for about R80/140, with breakfast. The *Welkom Hotel* (☎ (057) 51411) on Koppie Alleen Rd costs about the same. The *Welkom Inn* (☎ (057) 357 3361, fax 352 1458) on Stateway at the corner of Tempest Rd, a few blocks east of the centre, has rooms from about R140/220.

Places to Eat

Giovani's Pizzaghetti at 15 Mooi St has pasta and pizza from R16 and also steak and seafood. The restaurant in the *Welkom Inn* is open only for breakfast and dinner.

Obviously miners appreciate a steak. Take your pick (excuse the pun) from *Al's Grill* or *The Blues Grill* on Van Bruggen St, *Beagles* at 64 Bok St, *Indiana Spur* in the Volksblad Building or *JJ's* at the Liberty Centre. A solid meal will cost from R30 at these places. For a bit more variety try *Mike's Kitchen* in Sanlam Plaza. An underground *ladies' bar* in one of the mines is open by arrangement.

The greater flamingo can be found across the whole region in the shallows of freshwater lakes, estuaries, dams and salt pans.

Getting There & Away

Train Passenger trains don't stop here; Virginia is the nearest place with a passenger service.

Bus Welkom is a major depot for Transtate, with a few services to Jo'burg/Pretoria and many others south to KwaZulu/Natal, QwaQwa, Lesotho and Transkei.

Translux's Durban-Bloemfontein and Jo'burg/Pretoria-East London services stop on Buiten St. Greyhound stops at Stateway West Motors on Stateway, on the Jo'burg/Pretoria-Cape Town, Durban-Upington and Jo'burg/Pretoria-Port Elizabeth runs. Fares are R145 to Upington, R125 to Durban, R130 to Pretoria, R285 to Cape Town and R220 to Port Elizabeth (less with Translux). Book either line at Rennies Travel in Sanlam Plaza.

Minibus Taxi There are a couple of minibus-taxi parks – the one in the supermarket car park in town is mainly for the local area, but you might find long-distance taxis here in the early morning. You can usually get a ride out to the main minibus-taxi park on the outskirts of town.

VIRGINIA

This well-laid out mining town, about 20 km south-east of Welkom, is on the banks of the Sand River. The library (☎ (057) 212 3111), in the picturesque Virginia Gardens, has tourist information.

There are mine tours to the Harmony Gold Mining Company and Western Holdings. A hiking trail runs along the banks of the Sand River and there is a bird sanctuary at Virginia Park. Birdwatching is fruitful in this town as there is a variety of habitats attracting different species.

Places to Stay & Eat

Virginia Park Resort (☎ (057) 212 3306), west of town on the banks of the Sand River, has a comfortable hotel and a fenced-off area for caravans. Three hotels in town charge about R100 per person for bed and breakfast. The *Doringboom* (☎ (057) 212 5124) is on the corner of Highlands Rd and Berea Ave; *De Bonheur* (☎ (057) 212 2211), is on

---

Orange Free State Battlefields

The most significant of the Voortrekker battlefields is **Vegkop**, south of Heilbron, the scene of a bloody battle between Hendrik Potgieter and the Ndebele army of Mzilikazi in 1836. When confronted by the Ndebele, who employed Zulu-style fighting methods, about 50 Voortrekkers formed their wagons into a laager and held off the attackers.

There are at least 20 major battlefields and sites from the Anglo-Boer War in and around the Orange Free State (OFS). **Kimberley**, actually in the Northern Cape but just across the OFS border, was besieged for 126 days from 14 October 1899 until 15 February 1900. Not far across the border, at **Paardeberg**, in the OFS, General Cronjé's Boers surrendered in February 1900 after being besieged by Lord Roberts' force.

There were a number of battles around Bloemfontein and the most significant site is **Sannapos**, east towards Thaba 'Nchu, where Free Staters inflicted heavy losses on the British on 31 March 1900. Bloemfontein had been captured by the British on 13 March 1900 and the Boers were withdrawing eastwards; two other significant battles took place at this time – Mostertshoek on 4 April, and Jammerberg Drift, five days later.

In May 1900 the battles raged near the Sand River, which flows through the Goldfields region. During a battle at **Biddulphsberg**, between Winburg and Bethlehem, the veld caught fire and many British soldiers died in the flames. At **Surrender Hill**, near Fouriesburg, on 31 July 1900 a major Boer force led by General Prinsloo surrendered to the British.

Conventional warfare ended in mid 1900 and the Boers resorted to guerrilla tactics for the next two years. Commandos operated all over the country and, in many places, barbed-wire fences were erected to prevent the free movement of the Boers. Concentration camps were set up. Many Boer memorials remain from this 'dirty' phase of the war. The war ended with the peace treaty of Vereeniging in May 1902. ∎

Virginia Way; and the *Harmony* (☎ (057) 217 4624) is at 52 Harmony Way.

CANNA CIRCLE

This region takes its name from the annual cultivation of masses of colourful cannas. These are in bloom from the end of December to April, and each of the towns within the circle cultivates a different colour.

If you are travelling between Jo'burg and the Free State's eastern highlands it is easy to deviate to several of these pleasant towns. Reitz is at the junction of the R51 and R26, Frankfort is on the R51 and R34, Heilbron is on the R26 and R34, and Vrede is on the R34 about 20 km east of the N3.

Frankfort, Heilbron, Lindley, Villiers, Reitz and Vrede all have *caravan parks* with sites for about R25. *Bietjiewater* (☎ /fax (058) 863 1415), six km from Reitz on the Warden road, has four-bed chalets for R140. There are hotels in most of the towns. The *Frankfort Hotel* (☎ (0588) 31080), at 55A Brand St, charges about R85 per person, bed and breakfast.

Bloemfontein

Bloemfontein is the provincial capital and was (and still is, so far) South Africa's judicial capital. It occupies an important place in the country's history.

At first sight it seems to be just another sprawling, modernised town, but there are a few places worth seeing and pockets of impressive buildings. As well as the legal community there's a university and a large military camp, so you can meet a wide range of people. Most of the blacks are still forced by economic realities to live in the enclaves they were shunted into during the apartheid days. Botshabelo, on the Thaba 'Nchu road, is one of the largest 'locations' in the country.

The city is near the Bloem stream, which now resembles a drain rather than a stream as it was lined with stone after the disastrous 1904 flood. It is spanned by a series of pretty little sandstone bridges.

JRR Tolkien was born here in 1892. He moved to England when he was four but his memory of the Bloemfontein district as '...hot, dry and barren' might well have influenced his creation of Mordor. I saw some graffiti in a Cape Town pub claiming that JRR was 'just another Bloemfontein boy on acid'.

HISTORY

Bloemfontein wasn't the first Boer capital in the lands across the Orange River. The Voortrekkers established their first settlement near modern-day Thaba 'Nchu, and various embryonic republics, as well as a period of British sovereignty after the Anglo-Boer War, came and went. In 1854 the Orange Free State was created, with Bloemfontein as the capital. Bloemfontein (literally 'fountain of flowers') was named after a farm built in 1840 by Johannes Brits. By 1854 it was only a small village, but it had its own parliament, presiding over the republic's 12,000 scattered white citizens.

In 1863 Johannes Brand began his 25-year term as the president, and it was during this time that Bloemfontein grew from a struggling frontier town, in constant danger of being wiped out by Moshoeshoe's warriors, to a wealthy little capital city with railway links to the coast and many public buildings.

ORIENTATION & INFORMATION

As usual there are endless sprawling suburbs, but the central area is laid out on a grid and it is easy to find your way around. Hoffman Square is the centre of the downtown area. Not far to the north-east is Naval Hill where there are good views of the town and surrounding plains.

The Bloemfontein Publicity Association's tourist office (☎ (051) 405 8490) is in the town centre on Hoffman Square. The staff are friendly and knowledgeable. They have free maps, including a walking tour. The local bus information office (☎ (051) 405 8135) is next to the tourist office. There's a Satour office (☎ (051) 47 1362) in the Sanlam Parkade on Charles St, near Church

(Kerk) St, but it's often locked. Rennies Travel (☎ (051) 30 2361) is at 8 Elizabeth St.

The GPO is on Groenendal St across from Hoffman Square and there's a coin laundry on 1st Ave just north of Zastron Rd.

MUSEUMS
National Museum
The National Museum, on the corner of Charles and Aliwal Sts, is open daily between 8 am and 5 pm (1 to 6 pm on Sunday); entry is R1. The most interesting display is a great re-creation of a 19th-century street.

Queens Fort
Now restored as a military museum, Queens Fort was built in 1848 during the Free State-Basutho Wars. The fort, on Church St south of the stream near the corner of Goddard St, is open on weekends and Monday from 8 am to 4 pm; entrance is free.

Military Museum of the Boer Republics
This museum, devoted to the Anglo-Boer Wars, has some interesting displays and a great deal of trivia, a sign of how deeply the wars still affect the national psyche.

It is open from 9 am to 4.30 pm on weekdays, 9 am to 5 pm on Saturday and 2 to 5 pm on Sunday; admission is R1. The museum is south of the centre, on Monument Rd. From Hoffman Square. Take buses Nos 14 and 16 run to near the museum.

National Women's Monument
The monument, which is near the military museum, commemorates of the 26,000 Afrikaner women and children who died in British concentration camps during the Anglo-Boer Wars. Emily Hobhouse, the British 'turncoat' hero who alerted the world to this infamy, is buried here.

Freshford House Museum
To get an idea of how Bloemfontein burghers lived at the turn of the century, visit this house at 31 Kellner St. It's open from 10 am to 1 pm on weekdays, 2 to 5 pm on weekends; entry is R1.

National Afrikaans Literature Museum
This museum is in the Old Government Building on the corner of President Brand and Maitland Sts. It houses an Afrikaans research centre and has displays on Afrikaans literature. It is open from 8 am to 12.15 pm and 1 pm to 4 pm on weekdays, 9 am to noon Saturday, and entry is free.

Old Presidency
On President Brand St, just north of the corner of St Georges St, this is a grand Victorian-style building. Free State presidents once lived in these spacious chambers, in what must have seemed extraordinary opulence. The museum is open from 10 am to noon and 1 to 4 pm Tuesday to Friday, and from 1 to 5 pm on weekends; admission is free. Behind the Old Presidency is an outdoor collection of old agricultural machinery.

Hertzog House
This humble house on Goddard St was the home of JMB Hertzog, prime minister of South Africa and a prominent figure in the Anglo-Boer War. It's open Tuesday to Friday from 9 am to 4 pm and entry is free.

INTERESTING BUILDINGS
President Brand Street
The best selection of interesting buildings is along President Brand St, where aromatic cypress trees improve the air. These solid buildings demonstrate how comfortable and self-assured burgher life once was – as well as emphasising the hideousness of modern South African architecture.

If you head south down President Brand St from Charles St, the **City Hall** (1934), with its reflecting pool, is on the right. On the next block, on the same side of the road, is the **Appeal Court** (1929) in understated neoclassical style. The carvings and panelling inside are worth a look. On the left, opposite the court, is the **Fourth Raadsaal** (1893), which was the parliament house of the Free State republic, where almost light-hearted Renaissance-style architecture combines well with down-to-earth red brick.

JEFF WILLIAMS

JEFF WILLIAMS

JEFF WILLIAMS

Left: Bourkes Luck Potholes, Transvaal Drakensberg, Eastern Transvaal
Right: House, Barberton, lowveld, Eastern Transvaal
Bottom: Transvaal Drakensberg, near Hoedspruit, Eastern Transvaal

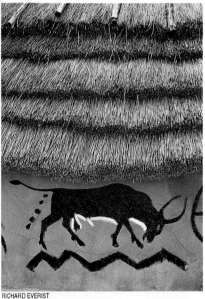

RICHARD EVERIST

RICHARD EVERIST

LUBA VANGELOVA

JEFF WILLIAMS

A	B
C	D

A&B: Hand-painted motifs adorning buildings in Lotlamoreng Cultural Village, near Mmabatho, North-West Province
C: The Palace Hotel at the Lost City (part of the Sun City complex), North-West Province
D: Rustler's Valley, Orange Free State

On the corner of Elizabeth St is the **Waldorf Building** (1928), not all that impressive until you remember how few buildings of this vintage survive in South African cities. Opposite is the **Old Government Building** (1908) which now houses the National Afrikaans Literary Museum. Diagonally opposite, on the block between Maitland and St Andrew, are the **Jubileum Building & Hall**. The building, despite its authoritarian façade, was designed as a coffee house and meeting place for young people. The pompous and menacing hall was once the headquarters for the Free State's Dutch Reformed Church.

Further down, on the corner of Fontein St, are the fire station (1933) and the imposing **Supreme Court** (1906).

First Raadsaal

On St Georges St, just east of President Brand St, is the oldest building in town and the original parliament house, still with its thatched roof and dung floors. Visiting hours are from 10.15 am to 3 pm on weekdays, 2 to 5 pm on weekends; entry is R1.

The Old Market

The old market, on the corner of Charles and East Burger Sts, is a fanciful building now housing a shopping complex.

Sand du Plesiss Theatre

A modern building of interest is the Sand du Plesiss Theatre (1985). There are artworks on display and there are tours of the complex on Thursday at 2.30 pm; entry is R1. The theatre is on the corner of Markgraaff and Andrews Sts. The local paper lists music, ballet, drama and opera performances.

NAVAL HILL

This hill, dominating the town to the north-east, was the site of the British naval gun emplacements during the Anglo-Boer War. On the east side of the hill is a large white horse, a landmark for the returning British cavalry during the Anglo-Boer War; it was laid out by a regiment homesick for its similar but prehistoric horse in Wiltshire.

There are good views from the hill, and on the hilltop is the **Franklin Nature Reserve** where you may see antelopes. Naval Hill and the reserve are open from 8 am to 5 pm; entrance is free.

On Union Ave, north of where the road up the hill turns off, is the **Orchid House** with a large collection of flowers. It's open from 10 am to 4 pm on weekdays, 10 am to 5 pm on weekends; entry is free.

BLOEMFONTEIN ZOO

There is a large collection of primates, among many other animals here. And yes there is a 'liger', a cross between a lion and a tiger, here. The entrance to the zoo (☎ (051) 405 8911) is on Henry St. In summer it is open from 8 am to 6 pm, and in winter 8 am

---

Concentration Camps

During the 1899-1902 Anglo-Boer War the British invented the concentration camp in response to harassment by guerrilla bands which were helped by – and included – Afrikaner farmers. The British response was to burn the farms of suspected combatants and ship the women and children to concentration camps. In the first years of the 20th century, before the invention of most medicines and vaccines and without modern engineering, any large-scale incarceration of people was bound to be disastrous.

By the end of the war 200,000 Afrikaner women and children were prisoners. More than 26,000 of them, mostly children, had died, accounting for about 70% of Afrikaner deaths in the war. There were also concentration camps for blacks and of the 80,000 people interned it is estimated that 14,000 died.

For Afrikaners, the image of a man returning from his defeated commando to find his farm destroyed and his children dead remains a powerful one. The loss of political independence and the destruction of family, home and farm left little but the Bible, deep bitterness and a determination to survive against any odds. ■

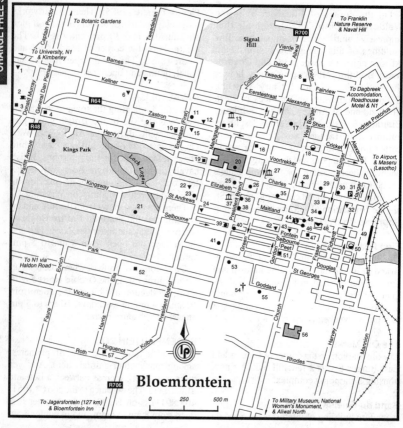

to 5 pm; admission is R5 for adults, R1.20 for children and pony rides are R1.70.

BOTANICAL GARDENS
The 45-hectare Free State National Botanical Gardens are on Rayton Rd, about 10 km north of the city centre. The gardens protect some natural vegetation – open woodland, Karoo species and grassland. They are open daily from 8 am to 6 pm; entry costs R3.

PLACES TO STAY
The Publicity Association can give you an excellent accommodation list. Bloemfont-

ein hosts important cricket and rugby games, and accommodation can be scarce on match weekends. We've heard of a backpacker place opening at 18 Louis Botha St, Aboretum, charging R35 for bed and light breakfast, or R10 to pitch a tent. Contact Vilna Kock (☎ (051) 405 5248, or after hours on 31 5433).

Caravan Parks
More than walking distance from the centre on Andries Pretorius St, *Dagbreek Caravan Park* (☎ (051) 33 2490) has caravan sites (no tents) for R27, and rooms in old railway

PLACES TO STAY		22	Carrousel	29	Satour Office
		24	John Malcolms	30	Old Market
3	Holiday Inn Garden	32	Mary's Kitchen	31	Car Parking
	Court	42	The Mexican	34	Sanlam Plaza
	(Bloemfontein)		Restaurant	35	Rennies Travel
4	City Lodge	43	Silvano's	36	Waldorf Building
8	Holiday Inn Garden			37	Old Government
	Court (Naval Hill)	**OTHER**			Buildings &
14	Christopher's Hotel				National Afrikaans
16	Stanville Inn	2	Hard Rock Cafe		Literature Museum
19	Hotel Halevy House	5	Zoo	38	Jubileum Building &
33	Hotel Bloemfontein &	9	Sportsmans Pub		Hall
	Sanlam Plaza	10	Kegg 'n' Goose	39	Fire Station
47	Cecil Hotel	11	Coin Laundry	40	Supreme Court
51	Boulevard Hotel	13	Freshford House	41	Old Presidency
52	Stadium Inn		Museum	44	Tourist Office
57	Roberta Guesthouse	17	Rambler's Cricket	45	Hoffman Square
			Ground	46	Bus Information
PLACES TO EAT		18	Translux Bus Stop	48	Post Office
		20	City Hall	49	Railway Station
1	Mimosa Mall &	21	Stadium	50	Minibus Taxis
	Barba's Café	23	Sand du Pessis	53	First Raadsal
6	Characters, Braai		Theatre		(Council Chamber)
	Burger	25	Appeal Court	54	Anglican Cathedral
7	Beef Baron	26	Fourth Raadsal	55	Herzog House
12	Oasis Takeaway	27	National Museum	56	Queens Fort
15	Schillaci's Trattoria	28	Twin towered Church		

coaches at R35/65 for singles/doubles. Two km out on the Petrusburg Rd is the new *Reyneke Park* (☎ (051) 23888) with caravan sites (for up to five people) for R45, and chalets for R160.

B&Bs/Guesthouses

The B&B/guesthouse option offers about the best deal in Bloemfontein. The Publicity Association has an up-to-date list and will make bookings.

Hotels & Motels

The *Stadium Inn* (☎ (051) 47 4747) in Park Rd, Willows, opposite the Stadium swimming pool, is good value. There are 30 or so flats at R85/99 for singles/doubles, plus R15 for each additional person. The run-down *Boulevard Hotel* (☎ (051) 47 7236, fax 30 6217) on the corner of West Burger and Douglas Sts charges R75/94. Up on Zastron Rd, near the corner of Markgraaff St, is *Hotel Christophers* (☎ (051) 48 4791), not worth R78/98. Also on Zastron Rd, near the corner of Aliwal St, *Stanville the Inn* (☎ (051) 47

7471, fax 47 8236) is reasonable at R75/85; rooms facing the street are noisy.

At the *Luxor Hotel* (☎ (051) 441 8749, fax 441 8611) on the N1 near the Ferreira turn-off, rooms are R73/95; and at *Cloud 9* (☎ (05214) 2157, fax 2382), near the N1 in Danhof, they are R65/95.

There are a number of mid-range places close to the centre. The *Cecil Hotel* (☎ (051) 48 1155, fax 30 8323), on St Andrew St opposite Hoffman Square, is a big old-style hotel, recently redecorated but getting pricey at R120/140. *Bloemfontein Inn* (☎ (051) 22 6284, fax 22 6223) on Addison St, Hospital Park, is R100/110. *Roberta Guesthouse* (☎ (051) 84601), 14 Roth Ave, Willows, has singles/doubles for R94/112; and *City Lodge* (☎ (051) 47 9888, fax 47 5669), on the corner of Henry St and Parfitt Ave, costs from R135/159.

More expensive places include: *Holiday Inn Garden Court Naval Hill* (☎ (051) 30 1111, fax 30 4141), at 1 Union Ave, rooms from R149; *Halevy House* (☎ (051) 48 0271), on the corner of Charles and Markgraaff Sts, rooms from R110; *Hotel Bloemfontein*

Sanlam Plaza (☎ (051) 30 1911, fax 47 7102), on East Burger St, singles/doubles from R180/200; and *Holiday Inn Garden Court Bloemfontein* (☎ (051) 47 0310, fax 30 5678), on the corner of Melville and Zastron Rds, rooms from R169.

PLACES TO EAT
Near the Old Market, on the corner of Fichardt and Charles Sts, *Mary's Kitchen* is a basic eating place where you can meet some of the local black population. Nearby, *Ziaards Eastern Delights* has cheap curries. If there are enough of you, *King Pie*, on Henry St across from the market, 'gives away' a dozen 100% beef pies for R20.

Steak lovers have the usual wide choice for their R25 to R30, including *Camelot Carvery*, 149 Voortrekker St; *Steers*, 200 Zastron Rd; and the *Beef Baron* (perhaps the best of them all), 2nd Ave, Westdene.

Schillaci's Trattoria on Zastron Rd is a good Italian restaurant with some shady outdoor tables. Main courses start at R15 and there are midweek specials such as all the pasta you can eat for R20. Diagonally opposite is the grotesquely large *Oasis Roadhouse* takeaway. On the corner of Kellner St and Tweedelaan is *Characters*, a fairly lively but expensive Italian restaurant with a pleasant bar. Not far away in the Mimosa Mall on Kellner St is *Barba's Café*, recommended by locals.

The Mexican Restaurant is on the corner of West Burger and Fontein Sts. There's *John Malcolms* on the corner of Markgraaff and St Andrew Sts (with full meals from R25). *Silvano's*, also on St Andrew St, has pizzas from R18. Up in Elizabeth St in the CR Swart Building is the revolving *Carrousel* – meals start at R35 and it gets a thumbs up from locals. Behind the Old Presidency on President Brand St is *Die Stalle*, pleasant enough if you find it open.

ENTERTAINMENT
Downstairs from Characters (but you have to go upstairs to the restaurant level to get in) is Braai Burger, a bar and restaurant popular with all types; it's a fairly clean-cut, middle-

of-the-road place. If you're looking for something a bit grungier, try the Hotel Christophers which has music in the bar some nights. Around the corner is Cheers, a disco charging R5 for entry.

Simply Red, next to the Cecil Hotel on St Andrew St, opposite Hoffman Square, has live bands playing blues and reggae. The Boys, in West Burger St opposite the Mexican Restaurant, was recommended by a couple of locals as a good place to hang out, and The Warehouse was described as an 'alternative' club. When we asked how to get there we were told to ask an 'alternative-looking' local. Touché, same advice goes for you!

'Haven't I seen your face before?' – this line gets worn out at Deja Vu in Voortrekker St, a club near the Kegg & Goose, another favoured watering hole. On the same side of Voortrekker St, but a little further west is the Sportsman's Pub.

To meet students, go to the Tavern at Brandwag or to Barry's Bar at the university; usually live entertainment is provided at the latter. Another place the scholarly set 'existentialise' in is the Hard Rock Café, just off Donald Murray St, and part of the Holiday Inn.

There are bus tours to the Naledi Sun and Thaba 'Nchu Sun casinos. If you're interested in slot machines and tacky floor shows, the R20 return fare is good value and includes a few discounts and freebies; contact the tourist office.

GETTING THERE & AWAY
Air
Bloem's JBM Herzog Airport is 10 km from the city centre and there is no airport transport (except taxis). For departure and arrival info, ring (051) 33 2901.

SAA connects Bloemfontein with Kimberley, Cape Town, Durban, George, Port Elizabeth and Jo'burg. Airlink (☎ (011) 33 3769) has two daily services, on weekdays, to Jo'burg and Port Elizabeth.

Bus
Transtate's daily bus from Welkom to Thaba

'Nchu passes through Bloemfontein. There is also a daily Welkom-Umtata service.

Translux (☎ (051) 408 2262) runs to Jo'burg/Pretoria (R130), East London (R150), Port Elizabeth (R165), Cape Town (R240) and Durban (R130). Translux buses depart from 17 Cricket St in the city.

Greyhound has services to Durban, Pretoria, Cape Town, Port Elizabeth, Kimberley and Upington. Buses leave from Shell Ultra on the N1 western bypass. Book at Rennies Travel (☎ (051) 30 2361), Elizabeth St.

Intercape Mainliner (☎ (021) 934 4400) runs daily from Cape Town to Jo'burg and stops for pick-ups at Shell Ultra at 6 pm going north and 10.45 am going south; the cost to Jo'burg is R130 and to Cape Town R180.

Interstate Bus Lines (☎ (051) 48 4951) has a weekly service to Upington for about R100, departing on Friday at 2 pm from the railway station; it returns on Sunday.

Local buses to Thaba 'Nchu town leave a long way from the centre, on the main road to Thaba 'Nchu just before the corner of Mimosa St.

Train
For information phone (051) 408 2946; for bookings, (051) 408 2941. The *Trans-Oranje* (Durban-Cape Town), the *Amatola* (Jo'burg-East London) and the *Algoa* (Jo'burg-Port Elizabeth) stop here. There is also the *Diamond Express* (Bloemfontein-Pretoria via Kimberley).

Car Rental
Companies include Avis (☎ (051) 33 2331), Budget (☎ (051) 33 1178) and Imperial (☎ (051) 33 3511).

Hitching
Coming from the N1, get dropped off at the Zastron Rd exit, although it's quite a walk into the centre (there are infrequent buses once you get to the university); or at the Haldon Rd exit, which is further from the centre but better served by public transport (but not at night). Bus No 9 runs near here from Hoffman Square.

GETTING AROUND
There's an extensive public bus system although services stop early in the evening. At off-peak times (8.30 am to 12.55 pm and 2.10 to 3.45 pm) there's a flat fare of about R0.85; at other times the fare varies with distance, up to about R1.95. All buses run through Hoffman Square, and the bus information office (☎ (051) 405 8135) has timetables. To get to Franklin Nature Reserve on Naval Hill take bus No 2 to Union Ave and walk from there; buses Nos 14 and 16 run by the Military Museum.

For taxis, try Vrystaat Taxis (☎ (051) 30 6354) or Bloem Taxis (☎ (051) 33 3776).

AROUND BLOEMFONTEIN
Modder River Resorts
Aventura Maselspoort (☎ (051) 41 7848, fax 41 7865) and the adjacent *Phillip Sanders Resort* (☎ (051) 41 7611) are on the Modder River, about 22 km north-east of Bloemfontein. (There are two resorts because one was for whites and the other for the others during apartheid.) These are full-on resorts and both get pretty noisy and crowded during school holidays. At Maselspoort there are four-bed units for R115 (R145 in the high season) and you can camp for R12 plus R10 per person (R32 for two in the high season). Chalets at Phillip Sanders are R50 each and a caravan site is R12 per person.

Soetdoring Nature Reserve
Also on the Modder River, Soetdoring (☎ (051) 33 1011) is about 35 km north-west of Bloemfontein on the R700. The dam is home to waterbirds and martial eagles, and secretary birds breed in the reserve. Power boats are banned here so it's quieter than some of the Free State's dams, but there's no accommodation and you can't camp.

Thaba 'Nchu
Thaba 'Nchu (pronounced ta-*baan*-chu) is a small Tswana town east of Bloemfontein. The surrounding area was once a small piece of the scattered Bophutatswana Homeland, and this too was known as Thaba 'Nchu. As

with most Homeland territory, a Sun casino was built here.

There's an information office on the main street, at the other end of town from the supermarkets. There are a few historical buildings in town and a church designed by the priest-cum-artist, Father Claerhout. Look out for the aran jerseys handcrafted in town.

Maria Moroka National Park This beautiful park centres on a natural amphitheatre formed by Thaba 'Nchu ('black mountain') and includes the Groothoek Dam. It has a large variety of wildlife such as zebras, elands, blesboks, springboks and red harte-beests.

There are two relatively short hiking trails. The **Volstruis Hiking Trail** takes about one to two hours to walk; it passes through a wooded ravine and winds by an old kraal and the Groothoek Dam. The **Eland Hiking Trail** takes about four to five hours. It too passes through the ravine and by the kraal, but the stiff climb up to a viewpoint adds to its difficulty.

Places to Stay & Eat In town, the *Thaba 'Nchu Hotel* (☎ (051871) 2248) is basic but clean with singles/doubles R70/110 or R80/130 with attached bathroom. Coming from the main turn-off to Bloemfontein, continue up the main street, turn left onto Market Square and follow the road around to the right. For food, try the *Morocco Restaurant*.

The *Naledi Sun* (☎ (051) 33 1505; (051871) 51060) is quite pricey at R212/290. It's a friendly place with a good restaurant, bar and 'slots'. You are likely to meet talkative blacks and whites in the bar, eagerly discussing the merits of the 'new' South Africa.

The *Thaba 'Nchu Sun* (also ☎ (051) 33 1505; (051871) 2161), about 10 km from Thaba 'Nchu, costs R264/337 during the week, R306/394 on weekends. The casino is here.

Getting There & Away Transtate has a daily service to Thaba 'Nchu which leaves Welkom at 7 am, arriving in town at noon; it passes through Bloemfontein at about 9.30 am. There are minibuses between Bloemfontein and Thaba 'Nchu (about R4.50) and to Ladybrand (R12). A minibus from Thaba 'Nchu town to the casino is R4 but it's simpler to take the free shuttle which operates between the Naledi and Thaba 'Nchu Sun hotels. Tours to the casino run from Bloemfontein.

Southern Free State

The Southern Free State typifies much of the province – it is dusty, harsh and dry and the many windmills are reminiscent of the Australian outback. Much of the marginal land is cultivated and grazed, but there are a few fairly interesting reserves.

FAURESMITH
Fauresmith is famous for the railway line which runs along the main street. North of town on the Petrusburg road is the 4500-hectare **Kalkfontein Nature Reserve**, a great place to see the local black population harvesting yellowfish.

The *Phoenix Hotel* (☎ (051722), ask for 19), 22 Voortrekker St, has doubles for about R100.

TUSSEN DIE RIVIERE GAME FARM
This 23,000-hectare reserve (☎ (051762) 2803) has more animals than any other in the Free State, mostly various antelope species and small mammals but also white rhinos and hippos. The country is varied, with plains and ridges and a long frontage on the Orange River. Between May and the end of August the reserve is closed for the annual cull. For keen hikers there are the seven-km Middelpunt, the 12-km Klipstapel and the 16-km Orange River hiking trails; water must be carried on all of them.

Accommodation in chalets with a communal kitchen costs R80/95 for two/three persons (R50/65 in winter) and camping costs R15 per unpowered site. No food is available on the farm. The entrance gate is on the road between Bethulie and Smithfield (R701), about 15 km from Bethulie or 65 km east of the N1. Entry is R12.

STOKSTERT HIKING TRAIL

This 22-km overnight trail is in the Caledon River Conservancy Area, around Smithfield. This huge area (300,000 hectares) is on the land of over 60 farmers who have adopted conservation-minded techniques. The area has a wide range of flora & fauna and is of historic interest – the occupation of land west of the Caledon River by Boer farmers lead to the Basutho Wars in the 19th century, which resulted in the present day borders of Lesotho. French missionaries established missions in the area and you can see the remains of some of the buildings.

To book hikes contact The Secretary, Caledon River Conservancy Area (☎ (05562) 2411), PO Box 67, Smithfield 9966.

HENDRIK VERWOERD DAM

West of Tussen die Riviere, on the Orange River, this reserve surrounds one of the largest dams in South Africa. Be warned, the dam is described in brochures as 'a mecca for motorboats'. In the flat, arid Karoo grassland, several animal species, including Cape mountain zebra, can be seen.

On the west side of the reserve, off the N1 south of the town of Donkerpoort, *Aventura Midwaters Resort* (☎ (052172), ask for 45, fax (052172), ask for 135) has two-bed rondavels for R140 (R195 in high season) and six-bed units for R150 (R245). A powered camp site is R13.50 (R18) plus R10 per person.

PHILIPPOLIS

On the R717, Philippolis is a beautiful little place; it's the oldest town in the Free State, founded in 1823 as a mission station. The Griquas who settled here in 1826 sold the town and then trekked overland, through Lesotho, to settle in Griqualand East (see Kokstad in the KwaZulu/Natal chapter). There are a number of interesting buildings, including the NG Kerk, the library, an old jail and many places built in the Karoo style.

Hotel Oranjehof (☎ (0521772), ask for 8) on Voortrekker St has very reasonable room for about R80 per person, with breakfast.

Eastern Highlands

This is the most beautiful part of the Free State, stretching from Zastron in the south to Harrismith in the north. Roughly, it is the area which fringes the R26 and the R49 east of Bethlehem to Harrismith. In addition to being a tremendously scenic area, it is also archaeologically and historically important. It includes the quaint towns of Clarens, Ficksburg and Bethlehem, the 'alternative' enclave of Rustler's Valley and the walker's paradise of QwaQwa. The drives alone, past sandstone monoliths which tower above rolling fields, are reason enough to visit.

ZASTRON

Zastron, on the R726, is a quiet little town under the foothills of the Aasvoëlberg and Maluti mountains. It's the centre of a rural community and, with Lesotho forming an arc around this section of the Free State, Zastron has long-established trading links with the kingdom. The nearest town in Lesotho is Mohale's Hoek, 55 km away on a dirt road.

There are some **San paintings** in the area; the best are in the Seekoei and Hoffman caves. There are also various walks and climbs. The **Eye of Zastron**, a mildly interesting rock formation with a nine-metre hole, is best seen from the road to Aliwal North.

Places to Stay

The *caravan park* (☎ (05542) ask for 397) is a few km out of town; tent sites are R12. It's a nice walk down a wooded gorge. In town, the *Maluti Hotel* (☎ (05542) 107, fax 379) is a rather pleasant place with singles/doubles for about R100/120. About 1.5 km off the R26 and nine km from Zastron is *Vogelensang* (☎ (05542), ask for 3412), a small place with doubles for R220.

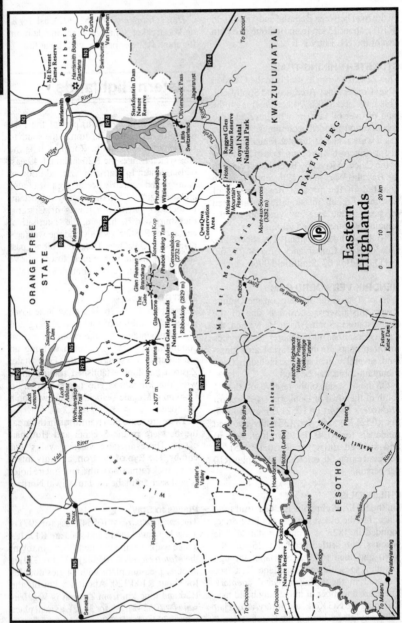

ORANGE FREE STATE

Getting There & Away

Transtate's Jo'burg to Lady Grey service passes through on Monday, Wednesday and Friday (returning Tuesday, Thursday and Sunday). There are also the daily Queenstown to Jo'burg and Welkom to Sterkspruit services. Minibuses are few, most run only to small nearby towns.

WEPENER & HOBHOUSE

Both these small towns are on the R26. Wepener, a 'nice' little town at the base of the Jammerberg, has some good examples of sandstone architecture. South of town is the Welbedacht Dam on the Caledon River. There is a small game reserve here and hiking trails are being set up. For information call (05232), ask for 31. Wepener is near the Van Rooyens border post into Lesotho.

Hobhouse is popular with anglers; you will see them on the banks of the Leeu, at Armenia Dam and at DonDon on the Caledon. For information call *Koos Taljaard Caravan Park* (☎ (05662), ask for 13). There are tent and caravan sites.

LADYBRAND

Ladybrand, on the R26, is the closest South African town to the main border crossing into Lesotho. From here to Maseru, the Lesotho capital, it is 16 km.

There are some nice **sandstone buildings**, including the town hall and the Old Magistrate's Court. The **Catharina Brand Museum** has archaeological displays, including rock paintings, instruments and tools dating back to the Stone Age. Also housed here is a replica of the fossil *Diathrognatus protozoon* found in a quarry near the town; this is important as it provides a glimmer of a link between reptile and mammal in the evolutionary process. Ashes taken from an ancient hearth in the **Rose Cottage Cave**, not far from Ladybrand, are 50,000 years old.

About 12 km from Ladybrand you can visit one of the quaintest churches you are ever likely to see. The **Modderpoort Cave Church**, built in 1869, is nestled under a huge boulder in scenic surroundings.

The overnight **Steve Visser Hiking Trail** starts at the Leliehoek Holiday Resort; book at the town hall, which also has tourist information.

Places to Stay

Leliehoek Holiday Resort (☎ (05191) 40654), two km south of the town hall, boasts 'personal European supervision'. As well as camping sites (about R25), there are chalets from R70 to R120, depending on numbers. Ladybrand's one hotel is expensive: *Country Lodge* (☎ (05191) 3209, fax 2406), 23 Joubert St, charges R140 per person for bed and breakfast.

There are three B&B places which charge considerably less than the hotel: *Riverside Lodge* (☎ /fax (05191) 3173) has thatched rondavels and chalets; *Travellers Inn* (☎ /fax (05191) 40191), 23A Kolbe St, has rooms; and *Cranberry Cottage* (☎ /fax (05191) 2290), 37 Beeton St, has rooms for about R120 per person.

Getting There & Away

The minibus-taxi fare to Thaba 'Nchu is R12 and to Bloemfontein it's R16.50. Vrystaat Tours (☎ (051) 48 4951) runs a daily bus between Bethlehem (R20) and Bloemfontein (R14) via Maseru – it comes through Ladybrand mid-morning but needs to be flagged down. Transtate's service from Durban to Maseru passes through from Friday to Tuesday, returning Wednesday to Sunday.

CLOCOLAN

Established in 1906, this is a small but important junction town on the R26, as the R708 goes north from here to Winburg and Senekal. The name is derived from the Sotho word *hlohlolane* meaning 'ridge of the battle', after the heights above town.

There are a number of places to stay in and around Clocolan. *Ikebana Mountain Resort* (☎ (05652) 1702), about 10 km south-west on the Tandjiesberg road, has chalets scattered on the slopes of Klein-Suikerkop. Horses, ponies, and guides are available for the many trails. *Clocolan Caravan Park* (☎ (051) 943 0516) has tent sites for about R15.

Transtate's Welkom-Ficksburg service (Monday to Saturday) stops in Clocolan.

FICKSBURG

This town is in sandstone country and there are some fine buildings built from the stone, including the town hall, the NG Kerk and the post office. Tourist information is available at the town hall (☎ (0563) 2122).

The mild summers and cold winters of this area (the Maluti mountains across the river in Lesotho often have snow) are good for growing stone fruits, and Ficksburg is the centre of the Free State's cherry industry. There's an annual Cherry Festival in November (also see Rustler's Valley). September and October are the best time to see the trees in bloom. The **museum** has displays on local history, including that of the Basotho people.

The **Imperani Hiking Trail** is a two-day circular walk of 23 km which begins at Meulspruit Dam, five km from Ficksburg on the Clocolan road, and takes in the Imperani mountains, where there are some rock paintings. Book the walk and the overnight hut at the town hall.

Places to Stay & Eat

Thom Park (☎ (05192) 2122), the municipal caravan park, is on Voortrekker St. The *Hoogland Hotel* (☎ (05192) 2214), on Market Square near Voortrekker St, has rooms for about R90 per person, with breakfast (R70 weekends). The dining room in the hotel has a reasonable à la carte menu (from R20). *Bella Rosa Guest House* (☎ (05192) 2623), 21 Bloem St, charges R95 per person, with breakfast; the meals are superb.

You can camp at *Meulspruit Dam*, five km from town on the R26 to Clocolan; contact the town hall (☎ (05192) 2122).

There is a *Pizza Parlour* on Piet Retief St and *The Deli* at 76 Fontein St for coffee and snacks. Fresh bread is available from the *Milk Bar Café* and *De Warme Bakery*.

AROUND FICKSBURG

The **Cherry Trail** is a tourist route around the Ficksburg district. There are several orchards to visit, various art and craft shops, some guest farms and hiking trails; enquire at the town hall in Ficksburg for a tourist map of the area and information on local tours.

Hoekfontein Game Ranch (☎ (05192) 3915) is 13 km north-east of Ficksburg, on the R26 to Fouriesburg. There are white rhino, a 'happy hippo couple', zebras, aardvarks, elands and other animals. The ranch organises a two-night ox-wagon trip for those who wish to follow in the footsteps of the Voortrekkers; all food is provided, but bring your own bedding. Accommodation in log cabins at the ranch costs from R33 per person.

There is a more carnivorous reason to visit this place – food. The *Tshukuka Lapa* open-air restaurant (☎ (05192) 3915) serves a variety of delicious meals such as venison sausages, pap and gravy, springbok entrées, *potjiekos* and wildebeest steaks; the cost is R30 per person, but bring your own drinks.

RUSTLER'S VALLEY

This remote valley, in the heart of a very conservative Free State, is in the vanguard of the 'dare to be different' in the new South Africa. Rustler's attracts a diverse crowd – yuppies from Jo'burg, remnant hippies from all parts of the continent and 'ideas' people from all over the globe. Enigmatically, its inventor is an Afrikaner. Frik, usually espied with a Camel and a cup of filter coffee, sees this valley as a haven for the 'alternative'.

At the end of the valley is a hidden canyon where stolen cattle were concealed until they could be smuggled away for sale, hence the valley's name.

Places to Stay & Eat

Rustler's (☎ /fax (05192) 3939) has a variety of accommodation. In Nos 1, 2 and 3 bungalows singles/doubles are R90/100, in No 4 bungalow two people can stay for R150 and in the several rooms of the artistically adorned Kraal, rooms are R70/80. There is backpackers' space for R25 per person and camping is encouraged (R10 per person).

The restaurant, predominantly vegetarian (with wild asparagus a perennial feature) offers breakfast for R12, lunch for R15 and a sumptuous dinner for R25. Restaurant? Guests usually eat outside or in the bar.

There's a lot (or nothing at all) to do: it's your choice. You can swim in the pool, wander into the valley, swim or fish in the many dams, walk up onto the nearby sandstone escarpments, climb imposing Nyakalesoba (the 'witchdoctor's eye'), ride into the labyrinthine dongas on a placid horse, discuss existentialist philosophy in the bar with Rustler's semi-permanent residents, have a braai on the shady verandah, play eight-ball pool, take a nap in the artistically adorned rondavels, listen to the great collection of CDs, play volleyball, don a suit of medieval armour and joust with imaginary foes or jive to the rhythm of pounding African drums.

There are two other places in the valley. *Nebo Holiday Farm* (☎ /fax (05192) 3947) has self-catering accommodation for R150 a double with an additional charge of R53 for each extra body; a standard room is R150 and a luxury room is R200 for a double. All chalets have hair dryers, and croquet is available. They have a good restaurant with a great selection of South African wines and tasty food.

Franshoek Mountain Lodge (☎ /fax (05192) 3938) is a friendly polo lodge in a renovated farmhouse nestled below the Witteberge. Standard rooms cost from R75 per person; luxury rooms are from R125 for dinner, bed and breakfast.

Getting There & Away
The drive into Rustler's is very scenic. The main turn-off is about 25 km south of Fouriesburg on the R26 road to Ficksburg. You head west on a dirt road which crosses railway lines in about 300 metres. From the turn-off it is about 12 km to Rustler's. When you reach a prominent crossroads where there are numerous signposts, take the sharp turn to the right (the road to Nebo is behind). A few km on there is another junction; Franshoek is to the left and Rustler's to the right. Head towards Nyakalesoba, the prominent sandstone pinnacle, and through the artistic gates. You can reach Rustler's from the south, but the best choice is that just described.

You can get to Ficksburg by taking a minibus taxi from Jo'burg to Bethlehem. At Bethlehem change buses for Ficksburg and call Rustler's (☎ (05192) 3939) to see if they can pick you up (there will be a small fee).

FOURIESBURG
This is another town on the scenic R26, only 10 km from the Calendonspoort border post into Lesotho and 50 km from the Golden Gate Highlands National Park. It is surrounded by mountains, the Witteberge to the west and the Malutis to the east. Two nearby peaks, Snijmanshoek and Visierskerf, are the highest in the Free State.

During the Anglo-Boer War, the town was proclaimed capital of the Free State when the

---

Alternative Festivals

Rustler's Valley is fast becoming the 'alternative' festival venue for South Africa. Over Easter the valley hosts the **Easter Music Festival** from Friday to Monday. Entry is R100 for the weekend and this includes camping, free hot showers, access to food stalls and as much music by South Africa's hottest bands as your ears can handle.

When the **Cherry Festival** is held in nearby Ficksburg in late November, Rustler's hosts its own party. Usually there are a couple of bands. Camping is R10 per person and there's a R15 entry fee (to cover the costs of band hire and transport).

Over Christmas, from mid-December to early January, the **Sagittarian Festival** is held. In the spirit of the festive season, camping is free. Celebrate the birth of the Lord on the back road to Bethlehem! ■

ORANGE FREE STATE

Boer government moved from Bloemfontein and the British occupied Bethlehem.

There are a number of fine old sandstone buildings in the town including President Steyn's house. The oldest dwelling, Tuishuis, is still occupied.

Brandwater Hiking Trail
The Brandwater offers a 60-km, five-day circular walk from the Meiringskloof Caravan Park, some three km from Fouriesburg, through varied sandstone country with good views of the Rooi, Maluti and Witteberge ranges. Three of the overnight stops are in caves and a fourth night is spent in an old sandstone farm building. Most of the walk, the longest in the Free State, is over private land. Enquire at the Fouriesburg town hall (☎ (058222), ask for 14) for information on booking.

Places to Stay
Meiringskloof Caravan Park (☎ (058222) 233 0067), three km from town, claims to have caravan sites only, but a reader reports that you can camp there for R13 per person. There are also chalets from R50/75. The *Fouriesburg Hotel* (☎ (058) 223 0207), part of the original Fourie farm, has singles/doubles for R112/156, with breakfast.

There are a number of B&B places. *Carolina Lodge* (☎ (058) 222 0552), off the Butha-Buthe road, costs from R115 per person for dinner, bed and breakfast. There are some budget double rooms at R99, but facilities are shared. *Wynford Holiday Farm* (☎ (058) 223 0274), a cosy little place with comfortable rooms, costs from R93 to R146 per person, full board, and *La Gratitude* (☎ (058) 223 0017), a small guesthouse, has singles/doubles for R80/130.

CLARENS
This pretty little town on the R711, a back road between Bethlehem and Fouriesburg, is well worth a detour from the main drag. The town is surrounded by large limestone rocks, including **Titanic Rock**, and the magnificent Malutis are in the background.

Artists have set up studios in and around Clarens. Perhaps the only detraction from this otherwise picturesque town is Cinderella's Castle, constructed from more than 50,000 beer bottles. Kids will love it, however.

Places to Stay & Eat
There is plenty of accommodation in and around Clarens. About 15 km east of the town is *Greenlands Resort* (☎ (058) 256 1181) which has tent and caravan sites, and chalets. Three km further on towards Golden Gate from the turn-off to Greenlands is *Golden View* (☎ (058) 256 1324) which has a caravan park, mountain huts from R60 per person with breakfast, farmhouse rooms for R125 per person and large chalets for R400.

Bokpoort (☎ (058) 256 1181) is a backpackers' in a great location; it is eight km from Clarens on the way to Golden Gate (three km is on dirt road). It charges R20 for a bed in the hikers' hut and R35 per person in rustic chalets.

Maluti Mountain Lodge (☎ (058) 256 1422), on Steil St in Clarens, is a proper 'pub'; rooms start at R125 per person, with breakfast. There is a great little restaurant in this hotel serving home-style meals.

Berg Cottage (☎ (058) 256 1112, fax 256 1406) is north on the road which runs on the east side of President Square. Ask the owners about another B&B place, *Strawberry Fayre*.

GOLDEN GATE HIGHLANDS NATIONAL PARK
Golden Gate is one of two national parks in the Free State. It preserves the unique and spectacular scenery of the foothills of the Maluti mountains, specifically the beautifully coloured sandstone cliffs and outcrops. The western approach to the park is guarded by immense sandstone cliffs which turn a glowing golden colour in the late afternoon, hence the name. There are also quite a few animal species, including grey rheboks, blesboks, elands, oribis, Burchell's zebras, jackals and baboons.

Winters can be very cold here, with frost and snow; summers are mild but most rain falls at this time and cold snaps are possible – if you're out walking take warm clothing. Day visitors to the park pay an entry of R15 per car (for up to five people).

Rhebok Hiking Trail

The circular 26-km Rhebok Hiking Trail is a great way to see the park. The trail takes its name from the grey rhebok, a species of antelope which prefers exposed mountain plateaux, and you will probably see them when walking. The trail starts at the Glen Reenen Rest Camp, and on the second day the track climbs up to a viewpoint on the side of Generaalskop (2732 metres), the highest point in the park, from where Mont-aux-Sources and the Malutis can be seen. The return trail to Glen Reneen passes Langtoon Dam.

There are some steep sections so hikers should be reasonably fit. The trail is limited to 18 people and must be booked through the National Parks Board; there's a fee of R25 per person.

Places to Stay

Accommodation in the park isn't especially cheap. At *Brandwag Camp*, where there's a restaurant, rooms cost R155/R276 for a single/double, a four-bed chalet is R207 a double; and a room without a view is R123.

At *Glen Reenen* a four-bed hut costs R207; a three-bed rondavel is R113/161 for two/three people and a camp site (at Glen Reenen only) costs R22 for a site plus R8 per adult. Book accommodation through the National Parks Board.

Getting There & Away

The R711 is a sealed road into the park from Clarens, between Bethlehem and Fouriesburg. Alternatively, midway between Bethlehem and Harrismith on the R46, head south on the R712 and after a few km turn west on a dirt road, or continue south on the R712 and head west on to a dirt road about seven km before Phuthaditjhaba, QwaQwa.

QWAQWA AREA

QwaQwa (master the 'click' pronunciation and you'll win friends and influence people) was once a small and extremely poor Homeland east of the Golden Gate Highlands National Park. The name QwaQwa means 'whiter than white', after the sandstone hill which dominates the area.

QwaQwa was created in the early '80s as a Homeland for southern Sotho *(Sotho ba Borwa)* people. The dumping of 200,000 people on a tiny patch of agriculturally unviable land, remote from employment centres, was one of the more obscene acts of apartheid. Today, this area is one of the best spots to visit in the Free State, now that the 'free' part of that appellation has been realised.

Orientation & Information

Phuthaditjhaba, adjacent to the town of Witsieshoek and about 50 km south of Harrismith, was the 'capital' of QwaQwa. Here there's a tourist information centre (☎ (058) 713 4444, fax 713 4342) and some craft shops. Pick up the free QwaQwa tourist pamphlet, which details hiking trails.

Places to Stay & Eat

There is a mid-sized modern hotel, the

Birdwatching in Golden Gate

The birdwatching opportunities in Golden Gate Park are particularly good; more than 140 species have been identified. You may see species such as the rare bearded vulture (lammergeier), black eagle, jackal buzzard, southern bald ibis, the endemic orange-throated longclaw *(Macronyx capensis)*, the grassbird *(Sphenoaceus afer)* and the ground woodpecker *(Geocolaptus olivaceus)*. Langtoon Dam is a good place to see waterbirds. Look out for the African black duck *(Anas sparsa)*, grey heron *(Ardea cineria)*, Egyptian goose *(Alopochen aegyptiacus)* and the very odd-looking hammerkop *(Scopus umbretta)*. ■

QwaQwa (☎ (058) 713 0903) in Phuthaditjhaba. The clean rooms are carpeted and have phones, TV and radios; bed and breakfast is about R90. There are some more basic rooms available.

About 25 km south of Phuthaditjhaba is *Witsieshoek Mountain Lodge* (☎ (058) 789 1900, fax 789 1901), reputedly South Africa's highest hotel. A bed in chalets close to the lodge is about R120 per person. You can buy meals in the restaurant. *Fika Patso Mountain Resort* (☎ (058) 789 1733), near the dam of the same name, is similar to Witsieshoek Mountain Lodge.

In Phuthaditjhaba, the *Golden Restaurant* on Kestell Rd has takeaways as well as a fully licensed section and *Matshidiso* is recommended for 'African-style' meals.

QwaQwa Conservation Area

The conservation area covers 30,000 hectares in the foothills of both the Maluti mountains and the Drakensberg. The usual warnings about sudden changes of temperature in the mountains apply, with storms and mists in summer and snow in winter.

There are some animals and rare birds, such as the Cape vulture, but the main reason to visit is for the great hiking trails.

The conservation area was once administered by the QwaQwa Tourism & Nature Conservation Corporation (☎ (058) 713 4444, fax 713 4342) in Phuthaditjhaba; who will administer it in the future is still being decided. Trails must be booked at least two weeks in advance.

QwaQwa Hiking Trails

There are three exceptionally good hiking trails in QwaQwa. The most famous is **The Sentinel Trailhiking; Sentinel Trail** which commences in QwaQwa and ends in KwaZulu/Natal. The trail starts at the Sentinel car park at an altitude of 2540 metres and runs for four km to the top of the Drakensberg plateau, where the average height is 3000 metres; it's about a two-hour ascent for those of medium fitness. At one point you have to use a chain ladder. Those who find the ladder frightening can take the route up

The Gully, which emerges at Beacon Buttress. The reward for the steep ascent is majestic mountain scenery and the opportunity to climb Mont-aux-Sources. See also the Royal National Park section in the KwaZulu/Natal chapter.

The two-day **Metsi Matsho Hiking Trail** begins at the Witsieshoek Mountain Lodge at 2200 metres above sea level. From the hotel it follows the provincial border to Cold Ridge. It then drops, almost in a due northerly direction to Metsi Matsho (Swartwater) Dam where there is an overnight hut. Beginning with beautiful views of the mountains, the walk also passes sandstone formations, caves, slopes of protea and, finally, the dam, where fishing is possible.

The **Fika Patso Trail** begins at the resort on the Fika Patso Dam. It is intended that this trail be connected to the Metsi Matsho Trail. It will leave the Fika Patso Dam at its far eastern side and join Metsi Matsho trail near the Witsieshoek Mountain Lodge; enquire at the tourism office in Phuthaditjhaba.

Getting There & Away

Transtate's Welkom-Phuthaditjhaba via Bethlehem service runs on Monday to Saturday; there's also a daily return service.

BETHLEHEM

This is one of the most pleasant towns in the Free State. Voortrekkers came to this area in the 1840s and Bethlehem was established on the farm Pretoriuskloof in 1864. Devout Voortrekkers gave the name Jordaan to the river which flows through town. It's now a large town and the main centre of the eastern Free State.

The tourist office (☎ (058) 303 5732, fax 303 5076) is in the civic centre on Muller St, near the corner of Roux St. A good art market is held on the Moederkerkplein on the last Saturday of the month. There are no taxis in Bethlehem, which means some long walks. It can *rain* here, too.

Things to See & Do

As usual for this area there are some impressive sandstone buildings, including the **Old**

Magistrate's Office on the corner of Louw and Van der Merwe Sts and the **NG Moederkerk** in the centre of town. Right in town is the tiny **Pretoriuskloof Nature Reserve**, on the banks of the Jordaan near the corner of Kerk and Kort Sts.

The **Wolhuterskop Hiking Trail** covers a 23-km loop through the Wolhuterskop Nature Reserve, beginning at the Loch Athlone Holiday Village. There is a hut on the trail, 18 km out, where you can stay overnight, and there is also a camp site; a fee of R20 per person is charged. From the hut it is only a five-km return to the resort. There is also a horse trail here; the 1½-hour ride costs R20. The overnight 36-km **Houtkop Hiking Trail** also begins at Loch Athlone. Book either walk through the Loch Athlone resort.

Places to Stay

Loch Athlone Holiday Resort (☎ (058) 303 5732) is about three km from the town centre and charges R25 for a site and R10 per vehicle. There are chalets from R90 during the week, R140 on the weekend.

The *Park Hotel* (☎ (058) 303 5191), 23 Muller St, on the corner of High St, has singles/doubles in the old section for R106/144, with breakfast; rooms in the newer three-star part cost R167/201. The *Royal Hotel* (☎ (058) 303 5448), at 9 Boshoff St, is a little cheaper: Bed and breakfast during the week is R104/150, on weekends R90/130.

There are some good B&Bs in the area. *Fisant Guest House* (☎ (058) 303 7144), 10 Thoi Oosthuyse St, charges R120/190; and *Franci's* (☎ (058) 303 3550), 38 Oxford St, charges R115/160.

Places to Eat

The *Long Kong* Chinese on Louw St is open until 11.30 pm; set menus cost from R20. At *Mike's Kitchen* in the Park Hotel a full meal costs from R30. *Athlone Castle*, part of the Loch Athlone resort, is shaped like the mail ship of the same name and is full of memorabilia; it's worth a look if not a meal.

Getting There & Away

Several Transtate services pass through Bethlehem, including Welkom to Lusikisiki via Kokstad, Welkom to QwaQwa, Welkom to Nongoma (circuitous) and Durban to Maseru. Translux runs to Durban (R95) and Bloemfontein (R85). These services leave from the Zenex Garage. Greyhound stops at the Wimpy Bar on Klerk St, en route between Kimberley (R65) and Durban (R100).

From the bus station (on the corner of Cambridge and Gholf Sts, north of the centre on the way to the railway station) there's a slow local bus running daily to Bloemfontein (R25) via Maseru (R15).

The weekly *Trans-Oranje* (Cape Town to Durban) train stops here. The station is north of the centre; head up Commissioner St.

HARRISMITH

Harrismith is a quiet rural centre, well-sited as a base for exploring the northern Drakensberg and QwaQwa, although public transport connections are poor.

The extensive **botanic garden**, about five km south of town at the foot of the Platberg, has many species from the Drakensberg. It also shelters numerous birds and some small mammals. There's an information centre, hiking trails and a British blockhouse from the Anglo-Boer War. The garden is open daily from 7 am (7.30 in winter) to 4.45 pm.

Mt Everest Game Reserve

This 1000-hectare private reserve (☎ (05861) 23493) is 21 km north-east of Harrismith, off the Verkykerskop road. The variety of animals (22 species at last count) includes rhinos. With horse-riding (R15 per hour) and hiking available, you might get close to the animals.

Camping is very expensive, from R45 to R78 in the high season for a caravan site, plus R8 for electricity. Budget beds in an old stone farmhouse cost R35, chalets R75 and rondavels R145 (R235 in high season) – these prices are per person.

Sterkfontein Dam Nature Reserve

This is a small reserve in the Drakensberg

ORANGE FREE STATE

foothills, 23 km south of Harrismith on the Olivershoek Pass road (R74) into KwaZulu/Natal. It is a very beautiful area and looking out over this expansive dam with rugged peaks as a backdrop is like gazing across an inland sea. There is a *caravan park* (☎ (05861) 23520) with rondavels.

Places to Stay & Eat

President Brand Caravan Park (☎ (05861) 21061) is on Cloete St along the banks of the Wilge River. Facing the railway station, turn left, and after about 300 metres turn right under the railway overpass and keep going for about one km.

The *Grand National Hotel* (☎ (05861) 21060), on the corner of Warden and Boshoff Sts, has singles/doubles for R68/82, a little less with a shared bathroom. *Harrismith Inn* (☎ (05861) 21011), on McKechnie St, has a room-only price of R129/169; it is R17 for breakfast and R27 for dinner.

The *Sir Harry Motel* (☎ (05861) 22151), 100 McKechnie St, has doubles for R80 (R15 for an extra person). *Gems B&B* (☎ (05861) 21389) at 22 Lombard St would be a good spot for German speakers.

Some of the hotels have restaurants. There is a *Silver Rapids Spur* by the Harrismith Inn which does takeaways and sit-down meals, the *Chow Den* at 18A Warden St for pizza and the *Casbah* at 6 Piet Retief St for burgers (R9) and curry & rice (R12).

Getting There & Away

Harrismith is on some useful Transtate routes running between Jo'burg/Pretoria or Welkom and Nongoma, Umtata and Maseru (Lesotho), via towns on the KwaZulu/Natal coast and near the southern Drakensberg.

Translux runs to Durban (R95) and Jo'burg/Pretoria (R100) daily, and to Bloemfontein (R110) three days a week. Translux stops at the Sir Harry Motel on McKechnie St. Not all services stop in Harrismith, however. Greyhound passes through Ladysmith, so you would have to catch a minibus taxi between the two towns. The big bus station, further along from the railway station, has many local services to QwaQwa and surrounding towns.

The Trans-Oranje (Durban-Cape Town) stops here en route to Cape Town on Monday and to Durban on Thursday.

KwaZulu/Natal

South Africa's tourism slogan is 'a world in one country'; people in KwaZulu/Natal respond, 'So what, we have a world in one province'. Despite being a relatively small province, KwaZulu/Natal manages to cram in most of the things visitors come to South Africa to see.

There's the spectacular Drakensberg range in the south-east, a long coast of sub-tropical surf beaches with water warmed by the Agulhas current, remote lowveld savanna in the far north, and historic Anglo-Boer War and Anglo-Zulu War battlefields. In the middle of it all is Zululand, the Zulu heartland. The Natal Parks Board has many excellent parks which offer good opportunities to see the best-known southern African animals. A final plus is Durban, a city with a great holiday atmosphere and, in parts, an Indian flavour.

If you're planning to spend much time in Natal Parks Board parks and reserves (and if you have a car you could tour most of the province from bases in the good-value accommodation at the various parks) your first stop should be the Natal Parks Board headquarters in Pietermaritzburg to make bookings – it's better to do it in person. Camp sites are booked directly with individual parks.

KWAZULU/NATAL PROVINCE
Capital: Undecided – will be either Durban or Ulundi
Main Languages: English, isiZulu
Pre-1994 The province of Natal, and the Homeland of KwaZulu
Highlights:
- Many superb national parks
- The Drakensberg mountains
- Zulu culture
- Durban
- Beaches
- Anglo-Boer War battlefields

HISTORY

Just prior to the 1994 elections, Natal Province was renamed KwaZulu/Natal, a belated recognition that the Zulu heartland of KwaZulu comprised a large part of the province – and an acknowledgment of the fact that the mainly Zulu Inkatha Freedom Party (IFP) was about to take the province by a landslide in the elections.

Natal was named by Vasco da Gama, who sighted the coast on Christmas Day 1497. It was not until 1843 that Natal was proclaimed a British colony, and in 1845 it was made part of the Cape colony. In 1856, after the European population had grown from a handful (although still under 5000), Natal was again made a separate colony. With the introduction of Indian labour in the 1860s and the consequent development of commercial agriculture, and with railways linking Durban's port (dredged to accommodate big ships) with the booming Witwatersrand in 1895, the colony began to thrive.

The recorded history of the province until the Union of South Africa is full of conflict: the difaqane, the Boer-Zulu and the Anglo-Zulu wars which saw the Zulu kingdom subjugated, and the two wars between the British and the Boers. All these are covered in the Facts about the Region chapter.

KWAZULU/NATAL

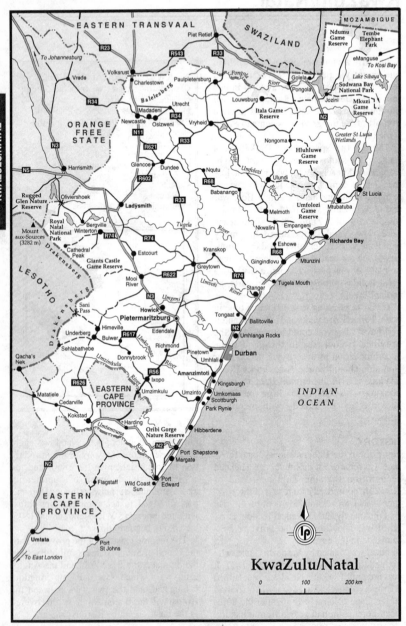

KwaZulu/Natal

0   100   200 km

Durban

Durban is a big subtropical city on a long surf beach. It is a major port, but it is better known as a mecca for holiday-makers. It is the largest city in the province and the third-largest city in South Africa, but it wasn't the capital of Natal; Pietermaritzburg was. Durban might now be made the capital or the honour might go to Ulundi, the tiny capital of KwaZulu.

Every summer, thousands of Transvaalers ('Vaalies') used to trek down to Durban ('Durbs') for sun, sand and a hint of sin. Now that the most populous part of the old Transvaal is Gauteng province, Vaalies don't know what to call themselves. Whatever their name, their numbers in Durban have fallen lately because gangs of thieves, predominantly black, have taken to lining their pockets by mugging tourists (both black and white). Tourists are moving to other beaches, and the city faces a real task to free the city beaches of crime.

As well there have been changes in the city centre which is no longer a white enclave. West and Smith Sts, once the city's main shopping centres, are losing customers to suburban malls (which are still white enclaves), such as The Pavilion in Westville.

The weather (and the water, thanks to the Agulhas current) stays warm year-round and there are about 230 sunny days a year. Over summer the weather is quite hot and very humid, with spectacular thunderstorms.

Durban is home to the largest concentration of Indian-descended people in the country – about 800,000. Pakistanis, predominantly Muslim, number about 200,000, so it not surprising to find the biggest mosque in South Africa in this city.

HISTORY

It took quite some time for Durban to be established. Natal Bay, around which Durban is centred, provided refuge for seafarers at least as early as 1685, and it's thought that Vasco da Gama anchored here

in 1497. The Dutch bought a large area of land around the bay from a local chief in 1690, but their ships didn't make it across the sandbar at the entrance to the bay until 1705, by which time the chief had died, and his son refused to acknowledge the deal.

With a good port established at Delagoa Bay (now Maputo, Mozambique), Natal Bay attracted little attention from Europeans until 1824 when Henry Fynn and Francis Farewell set up a base here to trade for ivory with the Zulu. Shaka granted the trading company land around the bay and it was accepted in the name of King George IV.

The settlement was slow to prosper, partly because of the chaos Shaka was causing in the area. By 1835 there was a small town with a mission station, and that year it took the name D'Urban, after the Cape governor.

In 1837 the Voortrekkers crossed the Drakensberg and founded Pietermaritzburg, 80 km north-west of Durban. The next year, after Durban was evacuated during a raid by the Zulu chief Dingaan's impis (regiments), the Boers claimed control. It was reoccupied by a force of British infantry later that year, but the Boers stuck by their claim. The Boers had crushed the Zulu by 1840 and seemed ready to claim most of Natal. The British sent a contingent of troops to Durban to secure their claim, but they were soundly defeated by the Boers, under Andries Pretorius, at the Battle of Congella in 1842.

The Boers retained control for a month until a British frigate arrived (fetched by teenager Dick King who rode the 1000 km of wild country between Durban and Grahamstown in 10 days) and dislodged them. Durban was again under British control, and the next year the whole of Natal was annexed by the British. A year later the Natal Turf Club had been formed and Durban began its growth into an important colonial port city, although there were still elephants roaming the Berea Ridge into the 1850s.

In 1860 the first indentured Indian labourers arrived to work the canefields. Despite the iniquitous system – slave labour by another name – many more Indians arrived, including, in 1893, Mohandas Gandhi.

Andries Pretorius, victor of the Battle of Congella (1842).

Today Durban is one of the most rapidly growing urban areas in the world and although you wouldn't guess it from the beachfront glitter, the city could soon have enormous problems.

ORIENTATION

A good way to get an idea of the layout of the city is to take one of the Mynah buses, which run several circular routes. See the Getting Around section.

Marine Pde, fronting long surf beaches, is Durban's focal point. Most places to stay and eat are on the parade or in the streets behind it, and much of the entertainment is here as well. The hub of all this activity is around the intersection of West St and Marine Pde. West St is a mall here, but further west it becomes one of downtown Durban's main streets.

Marine Pde continues south, leading to Erskine Pde which runs along the Point, the arm of land enclosing the north side of the harbour, Natal Bay. The Point is an old docklands area, with some colonial-era buildings and residential areas – low-key after the glitter of Marine Pde, but quite dangerous at night.

The city hall, an imposing monument to colonial confidence, is about 1.5 km west of the beach, straddling West and Smith Sts. This is the centre of the downtown area, which continues west another km or so.

On the western side of the city centre, around Grey and Victoria Sts, is the Indian area. There's a bustle and vibrancy missing from most commercial districts in South Africa and (as a tourist brochure puts it) 'the acrid smell of curry'. Grey St has been described as 'the real soul of the city'.

The increasingly popular area of Greyville and Morningside has many restaurants and clubs, around Florida and Windermere Rds.

The suburb of Berea (pronounced b-*ree*-a) is further inland, on a ridge overlooking the city centre. The ridge marks the beginning of the white suburbs, with real estate prices climbing with altitude: the higher you get, the more breezes there are, and thus relief from the summer humidity.

The Umgeni River, which flows past some impressive cliffs and enters the sea near Blue Lagoon Beach, marks the north boundary of the city, although the suburbs have sprawled over the river all the way up the coast to Umhlanga Rocks, a big resort and retirement town. Inland from Umhlanga Rocks is Phoenix, an Indian residential area named after the Gandhi commune.

South of the city the sprawl merges into the resort towns of the south coast. On the city's western fringe is Pinetown, a vast collection of dormitory suburbs. A fair proportion of Durban's population, mainly black, lives in townships surrounding the city. These include Richmond Farm, KwaMashu, Lindelani, Ntuzuma and the Greater Inanda area.

There are two good viewpoints where you can look down over the city. The best is at the University of Natal on Ridge Rd; entry is free, but check with security at the gate first. The view from the Cube near the reservoir on Innes Rd is especially good at night.

INFORMATION
Tourist Information

The main information centre (☎ (031) 304 4934), run by Durban Unlimited, is in the

Old Station on the corner of Pine and Gardiner Sts; the complex is known as Tourist Junction. It's open weekdays from 8 am to 4.30 pm and Saturday from 8.30 am to 12.30 pm. There's also a branch at the beach (☎ (031) 32 2608; 32 2595) open every day. The branch in the domestic terminal of Louis Botha Airport (☎ (031) 42 0400) is also open every day.

There's a Satour office (☎ (031) 304 7144) at 22 Gardiner St.

Pick up a copy of the *What's On in Durban* pamphlet or phone ☎ (031) 305 3877 for a 24-hour recorded message. The monthly *Durban for all Seasons: What to Do, When & Where* is available from most hotels. There is also information in Durban Unlimited's excellent *Kwazulu Natal Unlimited* (in English, French and German). The Durban municipal library (☎ (031) 37 6246) produces a full *Clubs & Societies* listing.

The best introduction to Durban is the

Gandhi in South Africa

Mohandas Karamchand Gandhi was born 2 October 1869 in Porbandar, by the sea on the Kathiawar Peninsula in western India. In 1888 he sailed for England to study law; he was called to the bar in June 1891 and immediately returned to India. He practised law in India for two years and, unimpressed with the petty politics of Porbandar, he left for South Africa in 1893.

Gandhi was soon embroiled in the politics of South Africa and became a victim of the widespread prejudice against his people. He was ejected from a train in Pietermaritzburg, and when he returned to South Africa after fetching his family he was beaten up at the docks by an angry mob. He founded the Natal Indian Congress in 1894 to fight for Indian emancipation.

During the Anglo-Boer War Gandhi raised a volunteer corps of stretcher bearers to assist the British. Gandhi and his bearers distinguished themselves on the battlefield, even at the bloody battle of Spioenkop, braving enemy fire to bring wounded to the base hospital.

Inspired by the writings of British essayist John Ruskin, he purchased a farm, Phoenix, just outside Durban in 1903. He transferred the printing presses and office of the magazine *Indian Opinion* here. He and his followers, known as Satyagrahis, lived a self-sufficient lifestyle and practised self-denial, truth and love.

In 1907 the Asiatic Registration Act was passed to prevent Indians from entering the Transvaal. Gandhi saw it as an affront and his law offices in Jo'burg became the HQ for opposition to the repressive law. Opposition slowly evolved into mass resistance. Thousands of indentured labourers went on strike and Gandhi's followers where thrown into already overflowing prisons (Gandhi himself joined them on occasion), as negotiations between General Jan Smuts and Gandhi dragged on.

In June 1914 Smuts and Gandhi agreed on the terms of the Indian Relief Bill and a victory of sorts (with many conditions) was won for the Indian community. Gandhi was happy that this struggle was over and he sailed for England in July 1914, never to return. Ironically, Gandhi's Phoenix, part of what the Zulu called Bhambayi (Bombay), was destroyed by squatters from the surrounding Inanda township in violent clashes in 1985. Hopefully it will rise from the ashes. ■

Gandhi

KWAZULU/NATAL

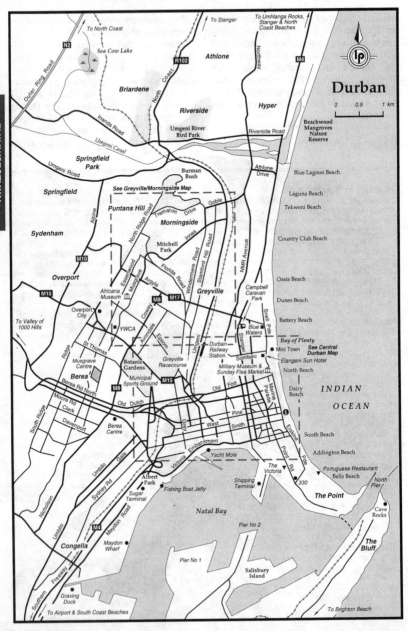

superb *ADA (Art, Design, Architecture): Durban and Surrounds* (R29) by Jennifer Sorrell. If ever a book gets into the heart of a city, this one does. An illustrated A-Z of cultural activities and artistic personalities, it covers all races and religions.

Also useful is *A Guide to the History & Architecture of Durban* (R4) by Bennett, Brusse and Adams, available from the Local History museum, among other places. It gives an interesting history, describes four walks and has good maps. The AA has a good map of Durban, and their Natal Holiday Coast & Hinterland is also handy.

There is a SASTS (South African Student Travel Service) office at the university (☎ (031) 202 7891).

Money

You can change money at the Rennies Travel (the Thomas Cook agent) in town (☎ (031) 305 3800) on Smith St, between Gardiner and Field Sts. American Express (☎ (031) 301 5551) is in Denor House on Smith St, next to the AA office.

The First National Bank, on the corner of West and Gillespie Sts, handles foreign exchange. The closest First National Bank to the beach tourist office is at 32 West St and is open on the weekend. The French Bank of SA is in the Durdoc Centre, on Smith St, just north of Broad St. Other central banks include Nedbank, in Durban Club Place; United Bank, on the corner of Smith and Gardiner Sts; and Standard Bank, also on the corner of Smith and Gardiner Sts. Most banks open on Saturday morning.

Post & Telecommunications

Poste restante is at the GPO. Go through the doors on the right in the entrance foyer and ask at the desk immediately inside. They keep letters for a month.

You can make international phone calls at Cash Call Telkom, on the 1st floor of 320 West St, from 8 am to 9.50 pm Monday to Saturday (but closed for lunch) and 6 pm to 9 pm on Sunday.

Foreign Consulates

Consulates in Durban include:

Austria
  3 Bellvue Rd (☎ (031) 21 5408)
Belgium
  18 Ross Gardens, Morningside (☎ (031) 303 2840)
Denmark
  Saambou Building, 399 Smith St (☎ (031) 305 1888)
France
  7011 Overport City (☎ (031) 29 9330)
Germany
  320 West St (☎ (031) 305 5677)
Italy
  Sanlam Building, West St (☎ (031) 301 4107)
Netherlands
  65 Victoria Embankment (☎ (031) 304 1770)
Sweden
  8th Floor, 75 Winder St (☎ (031) 32 6511)
UK
  10th Floor, Fedlife House, 320 Smith St (☎ (031) 305 2929)
USA
  Durban Bay House, 333 Smith St (☎ (031) 304 4737)

Emergency

For an ambulance phone 10177, or 261 6887 for a private service. For police it's 10111 (flying squad) or 306 4422.

Dangers & Annoyances

Many areas are now dangerous at night, notably the Indian area, unfortunately. The atmosphere of the sub-continent shuts down at closing time when the traders and shopkeepers make the long trek home to the Indian residential areas. At night central Durban takes on the feel of a ghetto as people head to the restaurants in places like Morningside or the big hotels and clubs along the beachfront. Point Rd, once a good place to hang out at night, is no longer safe. Perhaps it will improve when the redevelopment of the Point occurs. Now, if you go there, you'll mix with muggers, drug dealers, thieves and sex-industry workers.

The crowded beachfront promenade is a happy hunting ground for pickpockets. There are occasional violent robberies in the less well-lit areas between the beach and the promenade. If you are confronted by armed muggers, hand over your valuables!

KWAZULU/NATAL

BEACHFRONT AREA

Durban's prime attraction is its long string of surf beaches. The Golden Mile is six km long, with shark nets protecting warm-water beaches all the way from Blue Lagoon (at the mouth of the Umgeni River) south to Addington on the Point. In between, from north to south, the main beaches are Laguna, Tekweni, Country Club, Oasis, Dunes, Battery, North and South. Lifesavers patrol the beaches between 8 am and 5 pm – always swim in a patrolled area, indicated by flags.

The brilliantly revamped promenade fronts the surf. It's a good place to watch the crowds and there are a number of things to do. Across the road is a screen of high-rise buildings with many hotels and restaurants. Marine Pde, especially around the West St Mall, is the centre of the action.

It's worth walking out on one of the long piers which jut out into the surf for a good view of the city. Another good view can be had from the chairlift in the small **amusement park** on the promenade near West St. It's definitely worth R5 for the view (and the fear – it's a long way down).

Nearby is **Seaworld**, open from 9 am to 9 pm daily. The fish are hand-fed daily by divers (sharks are fed on Monday, Wednesday and Friday). There are dolphin and seal shows each day; call ☎ (031) 37 4079 for times. Admission is R16.

A Sunday **flea market** is held near the Amphitheatre, Bay of Plenty, weekly in summer and every second week at other times. Phone ☎ (031) 301 3200 for times.

There are now only about a dozen **rickshaws** in Durban, usually to be found on the beachfront near Seaworld. In 1904 there were about 2000 registered rickshaw pullers and they were a means of transport rather than a tourist novelty. A five-minute ride costs R5 plus R2 for the mandatory photo.

Nearby is **Mini Town**, a tacky model city which has replicas of Durban's best-known buildings; entry is R3.50. The **Snake Park** (☎ (031) 37 6456) on Snell Pde, North Beach, has about five venom-milking demonstrations daily; admission is R8.

Back from the beach on Gillespie St is **The**

Wheel complex, with over 130 shops, restaurants, bars and a dozen cinemas, as well as that incongruous ferris wheel spinning above the street. Take a walk through the huge complex, which is well designed.

On the Umgeni River, near Blue Lagoon Beach, is the **Model Yacht Pond** where enthusiasts sail their craft on the weekend. Nearby, also on the river but on the north side, is **Umgeni River Bird Park** where the birds live in cliff-face aviaries. At the mouth of the Umgeni you will see many species of waterbirds coming and going as they please.

NATAL BAY & VICTORIA EMBANKMENT

Durban's harbour is the busiest in Africa (and the ninth busiest in the world), and much of the activity centres on the **Shipping Terminal** near Stanger St, where there are public viewing areas. You can also see the activity on the water from the ferry that runs across the harbour mouth from North Pier on the Point to South Pier on the Bluff.

The small **Natal Maritime Museum** on Victoria Embankment has two tugboats and the minesweeper SAS *Durban*. It's open from 8.30 am to 4 pm Monday to Saturday, and 11 am to 4 pm Sunday; admission is R1.

The **Da Gama Clock**, a florid Victorian monument on the Embankment west of Aliwal St, was presented by the Portuguese government in 1897, the 400th anniversary of Vasco da Gama's sighting of Natal. Continue west and you come to the **Dick King Statue**, near Gardiner St, which commemorates his ride in 1842.

West of Gardiner St is the **Durban Club**, a solid jumble of Victorian and Edwardian architectural elements.

Maydon Wharf, running along the southwestern side of the harbour, contains the **Sugar Terminal** at 57 Maydon Rd ☎ (031) 301 0331 if you are interested in going on one of eight daily tours), the **Graving Dock** and the **Fishing Jetty**, where deep-sea fishing boats leave. Phone the Charter Boat Association (☎ (031) 261 6010) for prices. Make sure you take Maydon Rd to get there, not the Southern Freeway (the M4).

There are also boat tours of the harbour

running from the Gardiner St jetty. Sarie Marais Pleasure Cruises (☎ (031) 305 4022) has timetables. The *Estrela do Mar* (☎ (031) 368 2067) departs from Passenger Terminal N for four-hour ocean cruises at 10 am daily (R57).

CITY CENTRE

The impressive **city hall**, built in 1910 in modern renaissance style, is worth a look inside and out. It is similar in design to the city hall of another colonial city – Belfast. In front of the hall is **Francis Farewell Square**, where Fynn and Farewell made their camp in 1824. Here there are several statues and memorials to historical figures.

In the city hall building is the **Natural Science Museum** (enter from Smith St), open daily from 8.30 am to 5 pm (from 11 am Sunday). Check out the cockroach display, the reconstructed dodo and the life-size dinosaur model. There are sometimes free films here – some dull, some very good.

Upstairs is the **Art Gallery** which houses a good collection of contemporary South African works, especially arts and crafts of Zululand. In particular, see the collection of

Durban City Hall

baskets from Hlabisa, finely woven from a variety of grasses and incorporating striking natural colours. Admission is free; phone (031) 300 6234 for information. The **public library** is in this complex.

The **Local History Museum** is in the 1863 courthouse behind the city hall (enter from Aliwal St). It has interesting displays on colonial life as well as a useful bookshop upstairs; admission is free.

Across West St, on the corner of Gardiner St, is the GPO, which predates the city hall. On the east side of the GPO is **Church Square**, with its old vicarage and the 1909 **St Paul's Church** at the rear on Pine St. Next to Church Square is a swimming pool, open from 7 am to 4.30 pm. **Medwood Gardens**, with an outdoor café, is next to the pool.

The **Eskom Visitors Centre** (☎ (031) 360 2256), in the BP Centre, on the corner of West and Aliwal Sts, provides interactive displays about electricity and energy. It is open on weekdays from 8.30 am to 4 pm.

Not far away, Durban Diamond Cutting, in the Boland Bank Building, 223 West St, has **diamond-cutting tours** on weekdays and Saturday at 10 am and 2 pm (R10 per person); interested purchasers can phone ☎ (031) 368 3984 for a courtesy vehicle.

The **old railway station**, on the corner of Soldiers Way (Gardiner St) and Pine St, was built in 1894 and gives an idea of Durban's size and importance last century. The building now houses the Durban Unlimited tourist office. **The Workshop**, a shopping centre on Commercial Rd was another railway building (a train shed, hence the huge doors) which became redundant when the new station opened. It is open daily.

Nearby, across NMR Ave, is the Durban Exhibition Centre (DEC), which hosts the **Durban Military Tattoo** each year in July. On Sundays a **flea market** is held in the DEC's South Plaza.

The **African Art Centre** is on the Guildhall Arcade, running off Gardiner St near Leslie St, a block west of the Victoria Embankment. It is not a curio shop but a non-profit gallery with exciting work by rural artists.

KWAZULU/NATAL

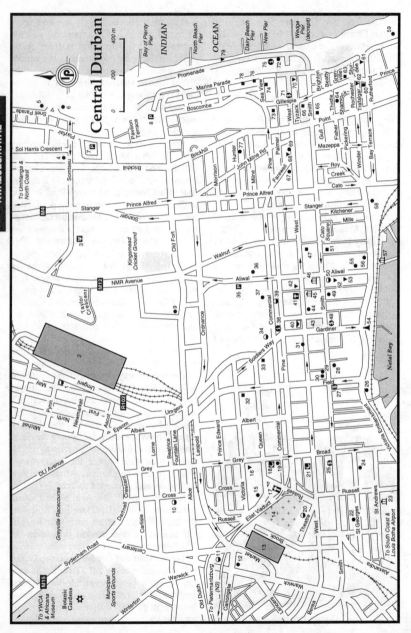

Central Durban

KWAZULU/NATAL

PLACES TO STAY

32	Butterworth Hotel
33	Grosvenor Hotel
47	Tudor House Hostel
51	Royal Hotel
60	Hawaii Resort
63	Impala Holiday Flats
65	Durban Beach Youth Hostel
66	Palm Beach
73	Palmerston Hotel
74	Balmoral Hotel
76	The Karos Edward
78	Holiday Inn Garden Court South

PLACES TO EAT

16	Victory Lounge
42	Medwood Gardens Café & Swimming Pool
52	Aliwal Lighthouse
53	St Geran Restaurant
61	Finnegan's Pub
62	Aldo's Italian Restaurant
68	Gringo's Cantina
70	Golden Chopsticks, Jam 'n Sons & RJ's Midnight Grill
79	Joe Cool's

OTHER

1	Long distance Minibus Taxis
2	Durban Railway Station
3	Hindu Temple
4	Ocean City (Theatre & Ice Rink)
5	Snake Park
6	Mini Town
7	Parking
8	Parking
9	Old Fort & Warriors Gate
10	Bus Depot
11	Victoria Bus Terminus
12	Fruit & Vegetable Market
13	Berea Rail Station & Minibus Taxis
14	Cemetery
15	Victoria Street Indian Market
17	Emmanuel Cathedral
18	Juma Mosque
19	Madrassa Arcade
20	Minibus Taxi to Lusikisiki (Transkei)
21	Muslim Mosque
22	The Rift (in the Belgica Hotel)
23	Old House Museum
24	AA Office
25	Bank of France (SA)
26	Yacht Mole
27	First National Bank
28	Rennies Travel, USA Consulate General
29	American Express
30	AA Office
31	320 Towers & Arcade
34	Local Buses to Umhlanga
35	Parking
36	Durban Exhibition Centre
37	The Workshop
38	Durban Unlimited (Tourist Office)
39	Old Rail Station, U–Tours & Local Bus Terminus
40	GPO
41	St Paul's Church
43	Francis Farewell Square
44	City Hall
45	Local History Museum
46	Natural Science Museum, Library & Art Gallery
48	Standard Bank
49	The Playhouse
50	SAA Building & Airport Bus
54	Dick King Statue
55	The Outdoor Inn
56	Hilmark Car Rental
57	Maritime Museum & Boat Cruises
58	Vasco Da Gama Clock
59	Al's Bike Hire
64	The Wheel Shopping Centre
67	Fairport Market
69	Mike Lamont Surf Shop
71	First National Bank
72	Seaworld
75	Visitors Bureau (Beach), Rennies Travel & Rickshaws
77	Board Shaper

The **Old House Museum** is at 31 St Andrews St, the restored home of Natal's first prime minister. It's open daily.

The **Old Fort**, north of the centre on Old Fort Rd, is where the British were besieged by the Boers in 1842. Just east is **Warriors Gate**, the general headquarters of the MOTHs (Memorable Order of Tin Hats), an ex-servicepersons' club. There's a small collection of militaria here; it's open daily except Saturday.

INDIAN AREA

The **Victoria Street Market,** at the west end of Victoria St on the corner of Prince Edward St, replaces the old Indian Market which burned down in 1973. It is the main tourist attraction of the area and is worth wandering around, but a walk through the nearby bustling streets is equally interesting. Just be on the lookout for pickpockets.

Grey St ('not black, not white...' is how a taxi driver described both the street and the predicament of Indians in South Africa), between Victoria St and West St, is the main shopping area. Prices are low and you can bargain. Most Muslim shops close between noon and 2 pm on Friday.

The big **Juma Mosque**, the largest in the southern hemisphere, on the corner of Queen and Grey Sts, is open to visitors on weekdays and Saturday morning; phone ☎ (031) 304 0326 for a guided tour. The **Madrassa Arcade** runs between the mosque and the Roman Catholic **Emmanuel Cathedral**, exemplifying a commercial ecumenicalism.

On West St, near the corner of Grey St, is the less flamboyant **West St Mosque**, facing Mecca. Further up West St, opposite the cemetery, is **The Mansions**, a big Edwardian building, all verandahs and wrought iron. West of Berea railway station is a big, bustling **fruit & vegetable market**.

The **Alayam Hindu Temple** is the oldest and biggest in South Africa. It's away from the main Indian area, on Somtseu Rd which runs between Snell Pde and NMR Ave. It is open from 7 am to 6 pm daily.

AFRICANA MUSEUM

The Africana Museum at 220 Marriot Rd, near the corner of Musgrave Rd, is an old home preserving Dr Killie Campbell's important collection of Zulu craftworks, art, furniture and paintings. It's open on Tuesday and Thursday from 8 am to 1 pm.

MITCHELL PARK

Further north, Musgrave St becomes Innes St and, on the corner of Nimmo St, passes Mitchell Park. There is a small zoo here with birds and a few animals, and an outdoor restaurant.

THE TEMPLE OF UNDERSTANDING

The biggest Hari Krishna temple in the southern hemisphere is just outside Durban. The building is unusual and there's a vegetarian restaurant inside. Follow the N3 towards Pietermaritzburg and then branch off to the N2 south. Take the Chatsworth turn-off and turn right towards the Chatsworth centre; phone ☎ (031) 43 3328 for opening times and tour details.

BOTANIC GARDENS

The 20-hectare Botanic Gardens (☎ (031) 21 3022), on Sydenham Rd north of Greyville Racecourse, are open daily from 7.30 am to 5.15 pm in winter, and until 5.45 pm in summer. The Orchid House is open from 9.30 am to 12.30 pm, 2 to 5 pm daily. One of the rarest cycads, *Encephalartos woodii*, can be seen here, as well as many species of bromeliad. There is a picturesque tea garden.

ORGANISED TOURS

Perhaps the best way to experience Durban is in the company of someone who knows what they are looking at. Durban Unlimited (☎ (031) 304 4934) conducts four walking tours of the city, each with a different flavour; the R20 cost is well worthwhile. Tours leave from the Old Station at 9.45 am (but get there 15 minutes early).

The Oriental Walkabout, Monday to Friday, takes in Emmanuel Cathedral, a number of mosques, a sari emporium and the colourful Victoria St market. The Feel of Durban, also Monday to Friday, goes to the Old Fort, the original armoury, barracks, farrier's shop and Warriors Gate. The

---

Hindu & Muslim Festivals

The annual **Kavadi Festival**, held twice annually (January to February and April to May), is the major Hindu festival. It honours the god Muruga who heals and dispels misfortune, and much self-inflicted pain, as a sign of devotion, accompanies the ceremony. In April or May an 18-day festival is held to honour the goddess **Draupadi** and it culminates with firewalking. For 10 days during July and August the **Mariamman**, or Porridge Festival, is celebrated; Mariamman is both the cause and cure of infectious diseases.

Two other festivals are the three-day **Deepvali** (Diwali), the Festival of Lights, celebrated in November; and the colourful five-day Hare Krishna Festival **Ratha Yatra** (Festival of Chariots) celebrated in December.

Each year there's the Muslim observance of the death of the Prophet's grandson, which culminates in a parade down Centenary Rd. ■

Durban Experience, Tuesday only, includes the Playhouse, city hall and the Local History Museum.

The best of the walks is the Historical Walkabout. Included is Durban's first railway station, St Paul's Church, Winston Churchill's memorial tablet, Francis Farewell Gardens, the Vasco da Gama Clock, the Local History Museum, the Dick King Statue and a telling of the John Ross story. It's thoroughly recommended.

The U-Tour Coach Company office (☎ (031) 368 2848, fax 32 8945), on the beachfront just south of West St, has some interesting bus tours of the city and the surrounding area, including a day tour of the Valley of 1000 Hills for R85. Many of the tours are conducted for U-Tours by Venture Tours & Safaris (☎ (031) 368 1024). In the following list of tours the cost shown is per person:

Durban City Tour – daily; half-day; R70
Umgeni Bird Park & Sharks Board; Wednesday; half-day; R65
Mini Natal – Sunday; full-day; R145
Shakaland Zulu Experience – Friday; full-day; R250
Venture Drakensberg – regular departures; three days; R1210 (single supplement R105)
Battlefields of Natal – on demand; day tour; R240 (minimum of four persons for this and the following tours)
Venture Sani Pony Trail – on demand; day tour; R312
Zululand Game Reserve – on demand; day tour; R312

Two recommended tours out of Durban are conducted by Tekweni Tours (☎ (031) 303 1433) and African Routes (☎ (031) 83 7233). Tekweni has a three-day Zululand Safari for R485 per person (R385 for Tekweni hostel guests) which includes the wonderful St Lucia Wetlands and Hluhluwe-Umfolozi Park. Tekweni also goes to the Natal Sharks Board near Umhlanga Rocks for R15 per person (you pay the R7 entry fee).

The African Routes trips are about a week in duration and each of them costs R1150, all inclusive. You would see a fair slice of Transvaal, KwaZulu/Natal and the Cape if you took their combined two-week trip from Jo'burg to Cape Town via Durban.

ACTIVITIES
Hiking
Outdoor Inn, on Aliwal St near Victoria Embankment, has hiking supplies.

There are a couple of hiking clubs, the Durban Ramblers and the Mountain Backpackers. Their contact numbers depend on the office-holders, so try the phone book or ask at the Outdoor Inn.

The Ramblers take things more easily and concentrate on the social and aesthetic pleasures of hiking. The Mountain Backpackers are more likely to be seen sweating it out on a high traverse of the Drakensberg. The Mountain Club of SA (Natal Section) are the spider-like forms you will see scaling the sides of the Monk's Cowl.

The Durban Parks & Recreation Department (☎ (031) 21 1303) holds weekend walks through reserves and parks in the area.

Diving
If you're a qualified diver you can hire equipment from the Undersea Club (☎ (031) 32 0654) and go diving with them. Simply Scuba (☎/fax (031) 23 9442), 200D Florida Rd, Morningside (down a small lane off the main street), comes highly recommended for PADI or NAUI courses, equipment hire and sales. Another school for specialised NAUI courses is Eco Diving (☎ (031) 96 4239).

Surfing
If you're a surfer and you're in Durban then you've cruised to the right place. There's a multitude of good beaches with any number of breaks. (See Surfing in the Facts for the Visitor to the Region chapter.) *Zigzag* magazine has some information crammed in between glossy ads; it come out every two months. Hire surfboards from Al's Bike Hire (☎ (031) 29 6375), South Beach, for R20 per hour.

Sailing
Durban is a great place to learn how to sail. Travellers have recommended the Ocean Sailing Academy (☎ (031) 301 5726,

fax 307 1257), 38 Fenton Rd. It offers five-day courses for yacht hands/skippers (R1190/1325); the student rate is R790.

Horse Racing

Horse racing, very popular in Durban, is held throughout the year at Greyville Racecourse near the Botanic Gardens, and at Clairwood Park Turf Club near the freeway south of the city. South Africa's main racing event is the Rothman's July, held on the first Saturday of that month at Greyville.

Canoeing

Durban is the canoeing centre of South Africa, and the Natal Canoe Union (☎ (0331) 46 0984, fax 65225) looks after clubs throughout the province. All types of canoeing are catered for – marathon, slalom, whitewater, canoe polo and sea kayaking.

Each year the popular Dusi Marathon starts 80 km inland at Pietermaritzburg and ends at the mouth of the Umgeni River.

White-Water Rafting

The mighty Tugela River (in Zulu it is *uThukela*, 'the startling one') is the scene of most of the rafting in KwaZulu/Natal. When the water level is high, usually from November to April, you can ride through Horrible Horace, The Rollercoaster, Four-Man Hole and the Tugela Ravine. Rafting operators include Tugela River Adventures (☎ (0331) 65018) and The River Rafters (☎ (011) 786 5482. A two-day trip is about R600, all inclusive.

Golf

KwaZulu/Natal is a great place to vent your frustration on the small white ball. The area to the south of Durban is known as the Golf Coast (pick up the free *Golf: Southern Natal* for contact numbers). A bit of trivia: the 3rd at the Durban Country Club is touted in the video *Fairways to Heaven* as the best 3rd hole in the world.

Team Sports

Several codes of football are played in KwaZulu/Natal, but the most popular is

The Comrades Marathon

This is the most famous athletics event in South Africa. The race was conceived to honour the comrades who fought in WW I, and every year since May 1921, runners from throughout the country and all over the world have come to run between Durban and Pietermaritzburg (PMB). The race is reversed on alternate years – up from Durban to PMB one year and down from PMB to Durban the next.

In 1921 the distance (89 km) was completed by the winner, Bill Rowan, in 8 hours 59 minutes. Today the times are much faster. Women could only officially compete from 1975 but many had completed the distance long before that. The undisputed king of the event was Bruce Fordyce who won nine times between 1980 and 1990. ■

soccer, or plain football. Professional teams such as AmaZulu and Manning Rangers play in town and international teams visit.

Rugby is usually associated with the white population. Natal has always been a strong rugby province and won the interprovincial Currie Cup in 1990 and 1992. The 60,000-seat Kings Park Rugby stadium staged some of the games of the 1995 Rugby World Cup.

Durban's large Indian and Pakistani population is a contributing factor to the popularity of cricket. Kingsmead hosts international sides, and recent Natal stars include the fine opener Andrew Hudson and the mercurial Jonty Rhodes.

PLACES TO STAY – BOTTOM END
Caravan Parks

There are three caravan parks, and two of them are a long way from the city centre. In Durban, the new *Campbell Caravan Park* (☎ (031) 705 4066) is on Brickhill St just a couple of blocks from the beach; the Mynah bus passes the entrance. So far, it is restricted to Caravan Club of SA members.

Ansteys Caravan Park (☎ (031) 47 4061), off Marine Dr at 8 Ansteys Rd, Brighton Beach, south of the Bluff, charges about R30 for a site for three persons. Inland a bit further south is the big *Durban Caravan Park* (☎ (031) 47 3929) at 55 Grays Inn Rd. There are camp sites for R17 per person and on-site vans for R120 for four people.

To get to these parks, take the Brighton Beach exit from the N2 and head south-east on Edwin Swales VC Dr which meets Bluff Rd, near the intersection of Grays Inn Rd.

Hostels

Durban Beach Youth Hostel (☎ (031) 32 4945, fax 32 4551) is superbly located near the beach at 19 Smith St; dorm beds are R22. However, it is run-down, and a collection of semi-permanents cluster around the TV set near the reception area.

Tekweni Backpackers (☎ (031) 303 1433) at 167 9th Ave, Morningside, a manageable distance north of the centre, is the pick of the budget places. A friendly collection of travellers frequent this place, many here to enjoy the surf. Patrick, the ex-pat Canadian who runs the place, is a font of knowledge on Durban, nightlife and surfing. Dorm beds are R25, double rooms are R35 per person. Hopefully the bathroom facilities will be upgraded in the near future. To get there take a Mitchell Park, Musgrave Rd, Kensington or St Mathias Rd Mynah bus.

We've heard that a third backpacker hostel (☎ (031) 304 6359, fax 304 6340) has recently opened, at 61 Pine St on the corner of Prince Alfred St. It's owned by the people who run the African Routes adventure travel company. It's close to the beach and nightlife and a dorm bed costs R25. There are also double rooms.

Another cheap place has opened up at 250 Florida Rd, the *Florida Guesthouse*. Double rooms are R30 and four-bed rooms R25 per person. A Mynah bus stops directly in front.

The *YMCA* has opened up a new place near the beach on Smith St but we hadn't received any information about it at the time of going to press. The *YWCA* (☎ (031) 21 5121) at 311 Musgrave Rd is usually full of residents. If you can get in it's a good deal – the R25 tariff includes some meals; take a Musgrave Rd Mynah bus.

Hotels & Apartments

Gillespie St (a block back from the beach) and the nearby area is crammed with holiday apartments, many of which are good value in the off-season. Some places stay affordable year-round, although getting a room might be a problem during the Christmas holidays. As an example, *Baltimore Holiday Apartments* (☎ (031) 37 4477), opposite the hostel on Smith St, starts at R60/95 a double in the low/high season.

The *Butterworth Hotel* (☎ (031) 306 2556), on the corner of Field and Victoria Sts, is huge, dirty and lively. Doubles with bathroom are R60. Be warned, the surrounding area is rough.

PLACES TO STAY – MIDDLE

Most of the middle to top-range places are listed in Durban Unlimited's *Natal Accommodation Guide*, available free from their offices. In town there is the *Albany Hotel* (☎ (031) 304 4381, fax 307 1411) at 225 Smith St; singles/doubles are R98/184. *Palm Beach* (☎ (031) 37 3451), on Gillespie St on the corner of Tyzack St, charges from R65/130 including a buffet breakfast (in season expect to pay R158 for two).

Good value in the low season is *Impala Holiday Flats* (☎ (031) 32 3232), 40 Gillespie St, with doubles from R68 and three or four-bed rooms from R88/112 (minimum stay four days).

The *Palmerston Hotel* (☎ (031) 37 6363), on the corner of Gillespie and Palmer Sts, is a big, quiet place; it costs from R70 per person. The *Grosvenor Hotel* (☎ (031) 303 4917) is a big old place, at 16 Soldiers Way on the corner of Queen St. It's pretty rundown. Rooms with double bed and balcony are R70 or R80 per person with bathroom.

Hawaii Resort (☎ (031) 37 9840), on the corner of Gillespie and Rutherford Sts, has four-person serviced apartments for R98/150 in the low/high seasons. At 52 West St, near the beach, the *Lonsdale Hotel* (☎ (031) 37 3361, fax 37 5962) charges from R65 per person, breakfast included. *The Balmoral* (☎ (031) 37 4392) at 125 Marine Pde, is run-down but it's worth considering at R65, not including breakfast.

The *Beach Hotel* (☎ (031) 37 5511, fax 368 2322), on the corner of Marine Pde and Palmer St, has single/double rooms from R157/222 with breakfast, rising a little around Christmas. That's good value for a three-star place. Even better value is the big *Four Seasons* (☎ (031) 37 3381), at 81 Gillespie St, where single/double rooms start at around R70/120 with breakfast. Prices rise considerably at Christmas time.

Away from the beach but a bargain is the *Tudor House Hotel* (☎ (031) 37 7328), on West St, east of Aliwal St. Renovated rooms with air-conditioning, phone and TV are just R120 per person, including a big breakfast. Across the road a little closer to the beach is the high-rise *PL Maharaj Lodge* (☎ (031) 368 3304) at 158 West St; self-contained apartments sleeping up to four people cost R120. *City Lodge* (☎ (031) 32 1447, fax 32 1483), on the corner of Brickhill and Old Fort Rds, has singles/doubles for R146/174.

PLACES TO STAY – TOP END

At the far north end of Snell Pde is the classic *Blue Waters* (☎ (0800) 31 2044) toll free, fax (031) 37 5817) which has singles/doubles for R145/220 with a hearty breakfast,. Get one of the north-facing rooms for great views along the beaches. The interior of this place has to be seen to be believed.

The *Palace Protea* (☎ (031) 32 8351) at 211 Marine Pde has bed and breakfast from R265 for two people, with regular special deals. The *Tropicana* (☎ (031) 368 1511, fax 368 2322), on Marine Pde south of West St, is R220/300 for singles/doubles. The *Karos Edward* (☎ (031) 37 3681, fax 32 1692), on Marine Pde, charges from R250 for a room, but if you book for five nights you pay for only four. The price includes a huge breakfast.

The *Marine Parade* (☎ (031) 37 3341, fax 32 9885), at 167 Marine Pde, is a Holiday Inn and has rooms from R209/314 (there are weekend specials). Holiday Inn has two other hotels, the *Holiday Inn Garden Court South Beach* (☎ (031) 37 2231, fax 37 4640),

charging from R169 per person per night and the excellent *Holiday Inn Garden Court North Beach* (☎ (031) 32 7361, fax 37 4058), facing the beach on Snell Pde. Singles/doubles cost R214/328. The *Elangeni Sun* (☎ (031) 37 1321, fax 32 5527), at 63 Snell Pde, has weekender specials at R169/268 (the normal rates are prohibitive).

You have to leave the beach area to find what is probably Durban's best hotel, the *Royal* (☎ (031) 304 0331, fax 304 5055), which is near the city hall at 267 Smith St. On weekends deluxe rooms cost R325 and suites R450; during the week you pay considerably more. This hotel houses some of the city's best restaurants.

PLACES TO EAT

All of Durban's many hotels have restaurants or dining rooms, ranging from one-star pubs where you can get bar meals to classy à la carte places

Beach Area

Many of the hotels around the beachfront have cheap meals – for example, in the Palm Beach at 106 Gillespie St, the *London Town Pub* has lunch for R5 and the *Maharajah* has an all-you-can-eat Indian meal for R25 (if you don't like it, they refund your money). The *Palmerston*, on the corner of Gillespie and Palmer Sts, has a buffet lunch for R10 (from 12.45 to 1.45 pm) and dinner for R12 (from 6.30 to 7.30 pm).

There are also several restaurants in The Wheel complex, including a pizza and pasta place *(Spaghetti Junction)* and steakhouse *(Coronado Spur)*; don't expect cheap tucker, as the rents in this complex are high. The *Tartan Dog*, on the 2nd floor, has a pub menu (R15) as well as à la carte.

The *One Rander Family Restaurant* is on Nedbank Circle, on the corner of Smith St and Point Rd. Prices have gone up but you can still get a meal from R3.95. It opens at 7 am and doesn't close until 4 am, except on Sunday and Monday when it closes at 8 pm.

Aldo's Italian, on the corner of Gillespie and Rochester Sts, has good food (lunch is about R35), and *Villa d'Este* across the street

LUBA VANGELOVA

LUBA VANGELOVA

JEFF WILLIAMS

JEFF WILLIAMS

A: Durban, KwaZulu/Natal
B: Souvenir seller on Durban Beachfront, KwaZulu/Natal
C: Pietermaritzburg Town Hall, KwaZulu/Natal
D: Newcastle town hall & Anglo-Boer War statue, KwaZulu/Natal

Top: Zulu witch doctor or 'spirit medium'
Bottom: Demonstrating bead stringing at a Zulu village

is another Italian place, with daily specials. Next door, at 37 Gillespie St, is *Ahmed's*, a basic Indian place with seafood specials. The *Taiwan*, at 124 Gillespie St near the mall, has specials from R10 (and free parking opposite), and the *Windmill* at 66 Gillespie St has pizzas for under R12, steaks from R15 and a children's menu.

Coimbra Portuguese, at 130 Gillespie St near the Palmerston, has genuine Portuguese food; the seafood platters cost from R30. *Thatcher's*, in a block of apartments on the corner of Gillespie and Sea View Sts, is a sedate, elegant place with surprisingly inexpensive dishes – steaks cost from R25.

Lord Prawn, in the Coastlands Building (2nd floor) on the corner of West St and Marine Pde, is open daily for seafood feasts.

If you head north along North Beach Promenade you get to an enclave of eating places which overlook the sea. *Joe Kool's* is a legendary night spot that serves reasonable food at fair prices. Next door is the *Cattleman* where a steak meal is about R40. Above this is *The Deck*, a hang-out for surfies and the spot for breakfast after catching those morning waves.

In the Point, at 546 Point Rd, *O'Cacador* has seafood and other Portuguese dishes (a full lunch is R35). The beauty of this place (one Durbanite opined) is that you can drink until 4 am. Closer to the city end of Point Rd (No 241) is the *Victoria Bar*, gravitating between seedy and trendy. They serve Portuguese fare from 11 am to 11 pm, there are pool tables for night owls, and live bands play every Saturday night.

One of the time-honoured venues for the hungry is the magnificent smorgasbord in the Chartroom in the *Edward* at 149 Marine Pde. Pay your money (R50 for lunch, R70 for dinner) and return often to the bewildering array of dishes; it is closed on Saturday.

City Area

The *Tudor House*, on West St, has bar meals or a slightly more expensive restaurant. The *Aliwal Lighthouse*, on Aliwal St next to the SAA office on the corner of Smith St, opens at 8 pm and stays open very late, sometimes until breakfast. The background music is better than you'll find in other places, and a few nights each week there's live music with a cover charge of about R3.

At 267 Smith St is a Durban institution, the Royal Hotel – it has the *Royal Steakhouse* (pub lunch R12), the *Royal Grill* (about R70 per head), the *Ulundi* (see Indian Food in this section) and the popular *Coffee Shoppe* (breakfast R18, and dinner R33). On the Old Well Arcade, just off Smith St, is *Africafé*, decked out Ndebele style, and *the* place for African food.

The outdoor café in *Medwood Gardens* on West St, near the GPO, is a good place to read your mail. Breakfast is served all day for R9; the curry is worth trying. It's open daily except Sunday from 8.30 am to 4 pm. In the next block west, on West St, is the huge complex at No 320. Restaurants here include *Café Eurasia* for cheap English breakfasts (R8), *Api Taki* on the 2nd floor for Indonesian and Polynesian food, and *Le Creole* on the mezzanine for spicy Mauritian food and great pub lunches for R12.

Just south of The Workshop, on the corner of Aliwal and West Sts in the BP Centre, is *The Toucan*, fully licensed and open from 9 am until late, Monday to Saturday.

The *Roma Revolving Restaurant* (☎ (031) 37 6707) is on the 32nd floor of John Ross House on Victoria Embankment. The view is amazing and the Italian food isn't horrifyingly expensive – for two people, three courses with coffee and wine costs R120. It's open Tuesday to Sunday for lunch and dinner; there is parking on adjacent Mills Lane.

Indian Food Takeaway places around the city have good Indian snacks, including bunny chow.

Indian taxi drivers are a good source of information about which restaurants are currently popular. The *Victory Lounge*, upstairs from a good pastry shop on the corner of Grey and Victoria Sts, is an excellent and lively café, open during the day; biryanis are R10. Other places on Grey St are the Gujarati-style *Patel's Vegetarian* (closes

3 pm), the *Khyber* and the *New Delhi*. The restaurant at the *Butterworth Hotel* is good.

Near the beach at 130 Gillespie St, behind the Balmoral, *Kanders House of Curry* has eat-in and takeaway curries. The *Ulundi* in the Royal Hotel is the place to sample a Bombay fish curry or lamb tharkaree. Lunch or dinner is R45 per person.

Greyville & Morningside

At 16 Stamford Hill Rd, Greyville, in a historic building, is the *Queen's Tavern*, formerly the British Middle East Indian Dining Club. It oozes turn-of-the-century graciousness, with a courtyard complete with palm trees. The food is also memorable! The curries are great, there's a good beer selection, and tasty pub meals cost about R15.

Where Florida Rd and Windermere Rd meet is *Two Moon Junction*, a trendy place known for its award-winning food; you have to book to get a seat in here. On the south side of Argyle Rd, opposite Montpelier Rd, is *Sandanato's on Seventh Avenue*, a popular Italian restaurant. Not far south, in the Avonmore Centre on 9th Ave, is *Joop's Place*, a steakhouse which will prepare interesting vegetarian dishes.

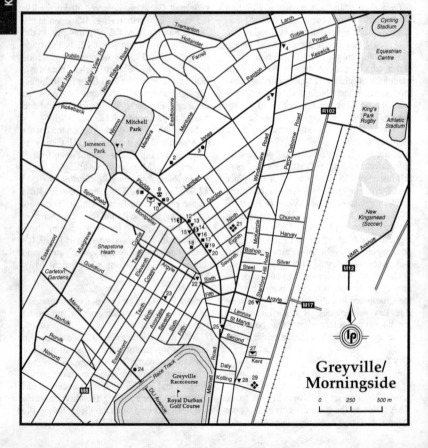

Greyville/
Morningside

Cross Argyle Rd and continue up Florida Rd and you find *El Cubano*, one of Durban's most popular eateries, specialising in Caribbean and Latin American dinners (R55) (closed Sunday). Next door is the *Keg & Thistle*, the original and arguably the best of the now ubiquitous Keg chain. It has atmosphere, crowds, good-value bar meals and is *the* venue to lose your faculties.

On the same side and a little further up is *Spaghetti Junction*, popular with those who frequent the nightclub next door. Pastas and steaks can be had for as little as R15. Further up Florida Rd on the 10th Ave corner is *Debonair's*, where large pizzas are R18. Almost opposite is *The Deli*, one of Durban's best, with a range of 'reheat' meals, superb salads and delicious pies.

Cross Lambert Rd to *Carry Out Curry* near the Spar supermarket. A little further up the road, at No 295, is the expensive *Squire's Loft*, known to serve African game dishes. The *Mitchell Park Restaurant*, in the park of the same name, has an outdoor patio for lunches – at night the restaurant moves indoors.

Head down Lambert Rd into Windermere Rd and you will find some more good places. *El Turko* (on the Innes Rd corner) is a Mediterranean place serving dolmades, dips and fresh pitta bread. Where Windermere Rd meets Goble Rd is *Woodcutter's*, a stately old Victorian place (No 504) run by Canadians. It's famous for steaks.

Just up Windermere Rd at No 510 is *Einstein's*, where you can get a good selection of meals and ales. (Their motto is: 'The *smart* place to be!') At No 514 is a lunch place, *Loafers*, where you can get light meals and wine by the glass.

ENTERTAINMENT
Durban is a fun city with a vibrant cultural scene and heaps of nightlife. Many events can be booked with Computicket (☎ (031) 304 2753).

Cinemas
The Wheel houses the biggest cinema complex and there are cinemas in The Workshop, the Sanlam Centre in Pinetown, The Pavilion in Westville and the Musgrave Centre. The only arthouse place is The Movies (☎ (031) 37 5270) in the old Oscar Cinema on Aliwal St.

The University of Natal hosts the International Film Festival in September; the Elizabeth Sneddon Theatre is the main venue.

Pubs & Clubs
Jam 'n Sons, near the beachfront on the 1st floor of the Belmont Arcade, 1 West St (take the escalator), is the home of African music. There's a live band most nights and a midnight cabaret, and African food such as uphuthu (dry maize porridge) and morogo (a

KWAZULU/NATAL

'Durbs' 4 Kids

Well supervised, kids will have a ball at the beach and when they get out of the water they can go to Minitown, the Children's Farm, Seaworld, Funworld and Water Wonderland or even have a rickshaw ride – all along the waterfront. Funworld has carousel and bumper rides and Water Wonderland has waterslides and a pulsating river ride. The Children's Ed-U-Fun Farm, Battery Beach Rd, is open from 9 am to 4 pm. It has pigs, goats, lambs, and tractor and pony rides (entry is R6 for 'big' kids and R5 for little kids).

Other distractions: the Fitzsimmons Model railway exhibition adjacent to the Snake Park (there are rides for the under-fives on the Orient Express); mini golf on the banks of the Umgeni River at Blue Lagoon and indoor mini golf at 100 Brickhill Rd; the Entertainment Centre in The Wheel; *T rex*, a dodo skeleton, a discovery room and other attractions in the Natural History Museum; and The Little Top on the water's edge at South Beach. The latter has competitions for the kids and provides deck chairs for adults (to collapse in after chasing the little fiends around). ∎

spinach-like dish) is available. If you're starving, go downstairs to RJ's Midnight Grill to start your hangover reversal.

The Wheel on Gillespie St has several bars, and not far away the Bagdad Café on Winder St features live bands.

Joe Kools up at North Beach has already been mentioned (see the Natal Surf Scene). There is usually a two-piece band on Friday, Saturday and Sunday nights and no entry fee.

Finnigans, on Rutherford St near Marine Pde, is directed at the 'mature person' (whatever that means) but not the mature Guinness drinker. This is one Irish pub that does not have the precious drop on tap! The London Town Pub, complete with double-decker bus, is in the Palm Beach Hotel.

Several other places nearby have music, sometimes live. Others specialise in 'steak, eggs and strips' at lunchtime for the office crowd but take on a more hip character on weekends. Magoo's Bar in the Parade Hotel, Marine Pde, has a band each night and offers pub lunches in their Why Not bar. Monks Inn, in the Killarney Hotel on the corner of Brickhill Rd and Pine St, attracts a range of people to listen to good cover bands on Friday and Saturday nights.

A couple of nights each week there's live music at the Aliwal Lighthouse, on Aliwal St near Smith St. Further down Smith St, at No 423, is Rumours. Occasionally there is live music – if not, the other needs of food and drink are well satisfied. If you stumble on down Smith St towards 70 St Georges St you will find The Rift in the Belgica Hotel. This is a smoky, loud and very vibey place that mixes heavy metal and grunge with the 'environmentally aware' sounds of REM and Midnight Oil. In short, it satisfies all comers.

In the little enclave of Albany Grove in Durban Central there are few late-night places. The Keg & Fiddle is at No 58, The Grove is in the Albany Hotel at the Smith St corner, and Murphy's Pub – 'open 25 hours a day eight days a week' – is at No 14.

Le Plaza Hotel, on the corner of Broad and St Andrews Sts, has various styles of music, from folk to jazz to pop on different nights. Monday night is folk night; there is a small cover charge, waived if you play.

On Point Rd, No 330 is a glossy dance club on Saturday night and an 'alternative' club on Friday night. This place plays all types of music – techno, hip-hop, acid house, garage – and stays open late (the steep entry fee is designed to keep out undesirables). The streetwise can venture to the predominantly black venue, Behind the Moon, at 550 Point Rd to prove to themselves that disco is not dead and that Lady Bump is alive. The Victoria Bar, at No 241, has been mentioned.

The Florida Rd precinct of Morningside also attracts the late-night crowd. Bonkers under the Hotel California is a lively place where party animals congregate and get drunk on cheap drinks. Every now and then some 'jol-ling' males and females strut along the bar. Next door is the Filler Bar, a 'typical'

Durban watering hole and a hang-out for those in the Natal newspaper industry.

In the New Berea Centre, Berea Rd, the Rockadilly (formerly the Hard Rock Café) plays rock 'n roll and serves pub lunches (about R6). It is closed on Sunday.

Jazz & Jazz Fusion

The jazz scene in Durban deserves a special mention. There is a real blend of styles utilising American jazz rhythms as a base. Imagine what effect a sprinkling of Indian classical, indigenous South African and township jazz influences has on the sound.

There are plenty of venues. Jam 'n Sons, Rockadilly and the Queen's Tavern have all been mentioned. The Octagon Jazz Forum is a popular jazz club on the corner of Field and Queen Sts; entry to Wednesday night sessions is R5, Saturday sessions R7. Other well-known jazz venues are Bassline on Rutherford St, Club Zoom: Backstage at 19 Dick King St and The Moon Hotel at 522 South Coast Rd, Rossborough.

The Rainbow, 23 Stanfield Lane, Pinetown, is a monthly Sunday jazz venue attracting top musicians, black and white (R12 to R15 entry). One reader reports seeing the African Jazz Pioneers, Ladysmith Black Mambazo, and Sakhile (with jazz-fusion king Sipho Gumede) here.

Classical Music & Theatre

The Natal Playhouse, opposite the city hall on Smith St, has dance, drama and music most nights. It's built in two old movie theatres, and there are restaurants. The Natal Philharmonic Orchestra has an interesting spring concert programme with weekly performances in The Opera; phone ☎ (031) 304 3631 for information.

The University of Natal's Music Department has free lunchtime concerts on Monday in Howard College, with concerts on many evenings. On Wednesday at 1 pm, go to the city hall steps and listen to a variety of musicians and exceptional gospel choirs.

Gay Scene

There's a small gay scene in Durban. The Riviera Hotel in The Esplanade is probably the best place to meet people. The Bar is Durban's oldest gay club and it is open every night with a DJ on Wednesday, Friday and Saturday. The other club on the premises is Images (which has a mix of men and women); it's open every night except Monday. There's a R3 cover charge at both places.

On the first Sunday of each month, Cheers, a wine bar at 65 Pine City Centre, Imperial Lane, Pinetown, hosts a mainly lesbian clientele. In town, a gay-friendly restaurant is Two Moon Junction. At the time of writing, a gay club was opening up in an old warehouse on the Point Rd.

GETTING THERE & AWAY

Air

Louis Botha Airport is off the N2, about 15 km south of the city. British Airways, SAA, Air Mauritius, Royal Swazi Airlines, Air Malawi, El Al, Air India, Singapore Airlines and Air Zimbabwe have flights out of Durban. SAA and some smaller operators have domestic flights. The SAA office building is on the corner of Smith and Aliwal Sts (☎ (031) 42 6156 for information, 305 6491 for bookings).

From Durban, Airlink (☎ (031) 42 2676) flies to Jo'burg, East London, Nelspruit, Umtata, Manzini (Swaziland) and Maputo (Mozambique). Comair (☎ (0800) 131 4155 toll free) flies between Durban and Jo'burg most days. InterAir (☎ (011) 397 1445) has cheap flights from Durban to Nelspruit and Phalaborwa (see the entries for those towns for prices and flights).

Bus

Most long-distance buses leave from the rear of the Durban railway station. If you're coming here by car, enter from NMR Ave, not Umgeni Rd. Translux (☎ (031) 361 8333 for enquiries, 361 7461 for bookings and 361 7963 for fax) is here. Greyhound's office (☎ (031) 361 7774, fax 361 7764) is nearby – you can also book at U-Tours (☎ (031) 368 2848, fax 32 8945). The Margate Mini Coach (☎ (03931) 21406) also leaves from here. Transtate buses leave from this area, but a little way from the others. You could try calling ☎ (031) 361 7989.

Examples of the many long-distance routes are:

To Jo'burg/Pretoria The Translux express to Jo'burg/Pretoria (R120) goes via Pietermaritzburg and Harrismith daily. Greyhound runs daily to Jo'burg/Pretoria via Pietermaritzburg (R45) and Ladysmith (R85), departing four times a day. However, only the 10 am bus stops at most places en route.

To Cape Town Translux have a service daily (except Tuesday and Thursday) to Cape Town (R290) via Bloemfontein, departing from Durban station at noon.

To Queenstown, Umtata & Port Elizabeth Transtate runs to Queenstown (R60) on Monday, Wednesday and Friday (returns Sunday, Tuesday and Thursday), via the Transkei region. Transtate also runs to Port St Johns via Lusikisiki (R25; 6 am daily) and to Umtata via Kokstad (R45; 7 am daily). Translux has a daily service to Port Elizabeth from Durban; fares are Umtata R105, East London R135 and Port Elizabeth R170.

To Bloemfontein & Kimberley Many Transtate services, taking miners from the Free State home to Transkei, pass through Durban. You can connect with these buses in Welkom, Bethlehem or Ladysmith.

Translux goes to Bloemfontein (R130) via Pietermaritzburg, Ladysmith, Harrismith, Bethlehem and Welkom on Monday, Wednesday and Friday. Their Durban-Cape Town service also stops in Bloemfontein. Greyhound has a bus to Bloemfontein (R130) and Kimberley (R160) on Tuesday, Thursday and Sunday (returning Monday, Wednesday and Friday).

To Pongola & Swaziland Transtate runs daily up the N2 to Golela and Pongola (R47) on the Swaziland border, via Mkuze. There is a shopper service to Swaziland from Durban on Monday, Wednesday and Friday

which returns on Tuesday, Thursday and Saturday. This service stops in Golela, Big Bend, Manzini and Mbabane (R55).

To Maputaland Transtate has a useful daily service to KwaNgwanase via Jozini in Maputaland. You could use this service to connect with minibus taxis to St Lucia (from Mtubatuba), Sodwana Bay and Kosi Bay.

To Ongeluksnek & Maseru (Lesotho) A daily Transtate bus departs at 6 am (7 am on Sunday) for Kokstad and Matatiele and on to Ongeluksnek on the Lesotho border. There's another service (Friday to Tuesday) to Maseru for R65, via Harrismith, Ficksburg and Ladybrand.

To Margate The Margate Mini Coach runs between Margate and Durban daily for R40 (same-day return R60; children R20 one way); there are two services on Monday, Thursday, Friday and Sunday. You should book seats on ☎ (03931) 21406, fax 21600.

Some bus services run all the way down to the Wild Coast Sun. You can catch these at the Durban station daily at 8 and 8.45 am, and also 1.45 pm on Friday and 5.15 pm on Saturday.

To Illovo & Amanzimtoti Enbee runs commuter buses to Illovo and Amanzimtoti from the Dick King Statue (on Victoria Embankment) on weekday afternoons (12.40, 4.05, 4.31, 5.20 pm), and 1.30 pm on Saturday.

To Richards Bay Interport (☎ (0351) 91791) runs north to Mandini, Gingindlovu, Mtunzini, Empangeni and Richards Bay daily at 7 am and 4.30 pm (services in the other direction from Richards Bay arrive in Durban at 8.40 am and 7.10 pm). The three-hour trip to Richards Bay is R35. The bus departs outside St Pauls on Pine St. On Friday and Sunday there is a midday bus service.

To Pietermaritzburg Cheetah Coaches has services from Durban to Pietermaritzburg on weekdays at 10.30 am and 4.45 pm, Friday

4.15 and 6.30 pm, Saturday 10.45 am and 2.45 pm and Sunday at 4.45 pm only. The bus leaves from Aliwal St outside the Natural Science Museum (R16 one way and R30 return).

To Umhlanga The Umhlanga Express bus (☎ (031) 561 2860) leaves from a number of points in Durban (including Pine St, Commercial Rd and the corner of Brickhill and Somtseu Rds). The fare is R5; buses depart at 8 and 10 am, noon; 2.30, 3.30, 4.30 and 5.15 pm on weekdays, with two services on Saturday (7.50 am and 1.15 pm) and none on Sunday.

Train

The huge Durban Railway Station (☎ (031) 361 7652 or 361 7609 for information, (031) 361 7621 for bookings) is on Umgeni Rd. The daily *Trans-Natal* (Durban-Jo'burg via Kimberley and Bloemfontein) and the weekly *Trans-Oranje* (Durban-Cape Town via Newcastle) run from here. Some 1st/2nd/3rd class fares from Durban are:

Bethlehem	R111/76/46
Bloemfontein	R178/121/75
Cape Town	R425/286/179
Estcourt	R57/39/23
Jo'burg	R164/108/67
Kimberley	R213/145/90
Ladysmith	R71/48/29
Newcastle	R97/65/39
Pietermaritzburg	R33/23/13

There are also commuter trains running down the coast as far as Kelso near Pennington (five a day to Kelso, more to closer destinations) and north to Stanger (four a day). The service once ran south as far as Port Shepstone, and might do so again (☎ (031) 361 7609 for information). You can catch southbound commuter trains at the Berea railway station as well as at Durban station.

Minibus Taxis

Some long-distance minibus taxis leave from ranks in the streets opposite the Umgeni Rd entrance to the railway station. To Jo'burg it's R55; to Harrismith; R30 (from the QwaQwa rank), and to the Swaziland border, about R50. Other taxis, running mainly to the south coast and Transkei, are around the Berea Rd station. From a rank on Theatre Lane, near the cemetery at the west end of West St, several minibuses a day run to Lusikisiki in Transkei for R22.

Car Rental

All the major car rental companies have offices here: Avis (☎ (031) 42 6333, fax 42 1268), Budget (☎ (031) 304 9023, fax 304 9028) and Imperial (☎ 0800 31 0336 toll-free or (031) 37 3731).

There are several smaller companies with lower rates, including Tempest (☎ (031) 307 5211) at 139 Gale St; Dolphin (☎ (031) 32 0540); Maharani (☎ (031) 37 0211) at 30 Playfair Rd, North Beach; and Hilmark (☎ (031) 32 9455). Forest Drive (☎ (031) 562 8433) claims to be the cheapest.

Hitching

Heading south, hitch from the N2 interchange near Albert Park. The N2 north starts at the top end of Stanger St.

GETTING AROUND
To/From the Airport

A bus runs to Louis Botha Airport from the SAA building (Shell House), on the corner of Aliwal and Smith Sts, for R10 (R11 on Sunday and public holidays). Phone ☎ (031) 465 5573 for information.

Bus

The main DTMB (Durban Transport Management Board) terminus and information centre is on Commercial Rd across from The Workshop.

The Mynah service of small, fairly frequent buses covers most of the central and beachfront areas. The disadvantage is that the service stops early in the evening on most routes. Short trips cost R1.70 and the maximum fare is R2.05. Pre-paid tickets cost R15 for 10 short journeys or R18 for longer ones. Buy them at the DTMB information office (☎ (031) 307 3505, or 309 4126 after hours). Routes are as follows:

To North Beach Mynah runs from Sandown Rd, which meets Snell Pde near Battery Beach, down Playfair Rd, Boscombe Terrace and Sea View St, to join Smith St. It then runs up Smith to Russell St and St Andrews St and returns down West St.

To South Beach This route runs from Bell St north up Gillespie/Prince St, up Smith St to Russell St and St Andrews St, and back along West St.

Musgrave Rd Circle This route runs from the terminus near The Workshop north along Smith St, up Berea Rd past the Berea Centre, east along Musgrave Rd to Mitchell Park, and returns down Florida Rd, Kent Rd, Umgeni Rd (passing the railway station) and Soldiers Way. Some buses (Musgrave Rd Circle via Market) take a loop past Berea railway station and through the Indian area on Russell and Leopold Sts and Market Rd.

Mitchell Park Circle This route is the same as the Musgrave Rd route but runs anticlockwise, using West St rather than Smith St, and Field St rather than Soldiers Way.

To The Ridge/Vause This service runs up Smith St to Berea Rd, north along Ridge Rd to Earl Haig Rd and Valley Rd, and back along Vause Rd, Berea Rd and West St. Some buses (The Ridge via Market) make a detour along Russell St, Leopold St and Market Rd.

To Tollgate This route is the same as The Ridge route but runs only as far as Entabeni Hospital on Ridge Rd.

To Botanic Gardens This route goes up Smith St and Berea Rd, then past the Botanic Gardens on Botanic Gardens Rd and Cowey Rd, down Clarence Rd and back to the city on 1st Ave and Soldiers Way. It runs clockwise and anticlockwise (using West St rather than Smith St).

To Kensington/Mathias Rd This route runs north along Soldiers Way, 1st Ave and Windermere Rd. From Kensington it heads west into Trematon Dr and runs to North Ridge Rd and returns from there (this is the service to take to get to the Morningside restaurants). The St Mathias route keeps going north on Goodwin Dr and returns from Salisbury Rd. Both routes run past the railway station.

As well as the Mynah services there are slower and less frequent full-size buses, also departing from the terminus near The Workshop. They run more routes and travel further from the city centre than Mynahs. At off-peak times (8.30 am to 3.30 pm and after 5.30 pm daily), the flat fare is R1.30.

Green Line, a budget service, has buses out to the black and Indian areas. These leave from a terminus on Pine St across the road from the bus information centre, and from the corner of Soldiers Way and Old Fort Rd.

Taxi
A taxi between the beach and the railway station costs about R12. Bunny Cabs (☎ (031) 32 2914) run 24 hours – the drivers we met were honest and friendly. Other taxi companies are Eagles (☎ (031) 37 8333) and Aussies (☎ (031) 37 2345).

Tuk-Tuk
Tuk-tuks (Asian-style three-wheelers) congregate on the beachfront near Palmer St. Over short distances their fares are lower than taxis, but for anything more than a km or so the fares are comparable.

Bicycle
There doesn't seem to be anywhere in Durban to hire good 10-speed bikes. At 15 Tyzack St, near Gillespie St, ungeared bikes are hired out for R10 an hour.

AROUND DURBAN
Pinetown
Pinetown, a centre of light industry, is the third-biggest area of population in KwaZulu/Natal and the second-largest industrial area. There are areas of this city that possess a

certain charm – Paradise Valley and Marian-hill nature reserves, and the Japanese Gardens in Sarnia, for example. A visit to Pinetown gives a taste of modern South African suburbia, and shows the massive task of integration yet to be undertaken.

Valley of 1000 Hills

The Umgeni Valley runs from the ocean at Durban to Nagle Dam, east of Pietermaritz-burg. The rolling hills and traditional Zulu villages are the main reason visitors drive through here, usually on the R103 which begins in Hillcrest, off the M13 freeway. If you want to see more of the valley you'll have to head north from this road, which just skirts the southern edge.

PheZulu (meaning 'high up') and the adjacent **Assegay Safari Park**, which features reptiles, are on the R103. These places are open daily and have cultural displays, including Zulu dancing, at 10 and 11.30 am, 1.30 and 3.30 pm. Some readers have criticised the 'cultural display'.

Several tours take in the Valley of 1000 Hills. Probably the most laid-back of these is Tekweni's (☎ (031) 303 1433). The six-hour tour starts at 11 am and the R40 price includes admission to the crocodile farm and PheZulu (see also Organised Tours earlier in this section).

Places to Stay & Eat The *Chantecler* (☎ (031) 75 2613, fax 765 6101) on Clement Stott Rd, Botha's Hill, is an old-style place with singles/doubles for R78/144. Also in Botha's Hill, the *Rob Roy* (☎ (031) 777 1305, fax 777 1364) is reminiscent of the Lookover Hotel in Stanley Kubrick's *The Shining*; single/double rooms are from R95/170, plus breakfast.

Many Durbanites visit the hills for the food. The Chantecler and Rob Roy have restaurants, and the Chantecler has music on Sunday afternoon. Other places are *Falcon Crest Estate*, 18 Old Main Rd, Botha's Hill, for pub lunches every day except Monday and a carvery meal with music on Sunday (R25); and the *Swan & Rail* in the old Hill-crest station, Inanda Rd, for pub lunches.

Several other old railway stations in the area, such as Botha's Hill and Kloof, have been renovated into English-style pubs and tea gardens.

South Coast

There are some good beaches on the south coast, the strip between Durban and Trans-kei. There are also shoulder-to-shoulder resorts for much of the 150 km, and in summer there isn't a lot of room to move.

The south coast begins at Amanzimtoti, a huge resort area not far from Louis Botha Airport. South of here the major centres are Umkomaas, Scottburgh, Park Rynie and Hibberdene. This area is called the Sunshine Coast. From just after Hibberdene a large built-up area begins, centering on Port Shepstone and Margate, both covered later. This region, generally referred to as the Hibiscus Coast, continues almost unbroken to Marina Beach near the Trafalgar Marine Reserve. Port Edward is the last centre before Transkei and the Umtamvuna River.

The N2 runs down to Port Shepstone (where it heads west) and from there a toll road runs south, currently only as far as Southbroom but in the future to Port Edward. From Amanzimtoti to Pennington you have the choice of the N2 or the old coastal road; from Hibberdene to Port Shepstone the N2 *is* the old coastal road and it's slow and narrow. There's also a coastal road running parallel to the toll road, battling through urban sprawl most of the way.

SUNSHINE COAST

The Sunshine Coast stretches about 60 km from Amanzimtoti to Mtwalume. All of the beaches are easily accessible from the N2, but the area suffers from its proximity to Durban – Amanzimtoti is almost in the shadow of the southern industrial areas.

Amanzimtoti

Called 'Toti' for short, Amanzimtoti ('sweet waters') is a high-rise jungle of apartment

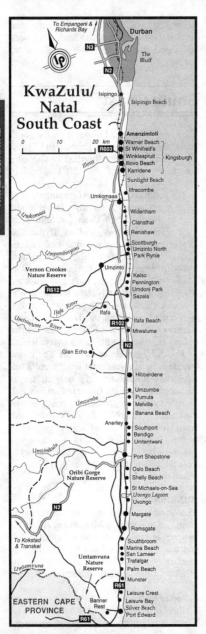

KwaZulu/Natal

blocks which sees over 300,000 visitors a year. It merges into Kingsburgh to the south. Winklespruit, Illovo and Karridene are beaches nearby.

The helpful Amanzimtoti Publicity Association visitor's bureau (☎ (031) 903 7493, fax 903 7382) is on Beach Rd, not far from the Inyoni Rocks. It is open from 7.45 am to 12.45 pm, 1.45 to 4.30 pm daily.

The tiny **Ilanda Wilds Nature Reserve** is on the Manzimtoti River and many birds live in its forest. Even smaller is **Umdoni Bird Sanctuary**, off Umdoni Rd. There are hides for birdwatching (over 150 species have been spotted) and feeding times are at 7 am and 3 pm; entry is free. The **Umbogovango Nature Reserve**, near the corner of Umdoni Rd and Blaze Way, has been established in an industrial area to conserve bird and tree species.

Places to Stay & Eat The *Ocean Call Caravan Park* (☎ (031) 96 2644) is 1.5 km from the railway station in Winklespruit; sites are R18/35 per adult in the low/high season plus R6 for electricity. The *Winklespruit Resort* (☎ (031) 96 2318) is not far away. The *Natalia Resort* (☎ (031) 96 4545) is near Karridene railway station. Sites cost from R25/45 in the low/high season. The *Illovo Beach Caravan Park* (☎ (031) 96 3472) and the *Villa Spa* (☎ (031) 96 4939) are at Illovo Beach. A site for two at the Villa is R35 (a whopping R120 in high season), chalets are R80/195 in the low/high season. The *Karridene Protea* (☎ (031) 903 3355) has singles/doubles for R185/215.

There are B&Bs, flats and holiday homes; see the Amanzimtoti visitor's bureau; B&Bs are about R80 per person.

For food, head to the *Seadoone Mall* in Doonside for takeaways, pizzas and coffee. There's a *Mike's Kitchen* in the South Gate Mall in Amanzimtoti. On Kingsway, Toti, is *Gloria's Bakery*, open from 6.30 am.

Getting There & Away Toti is only seven minutes from Louis Botha Airport by taxi (R35) and the Margate Mini Coach picks up from outside the domestic arrivals area.

Enbee runs buses to Durban (R6) from opposite the Toti station at 6.10, 7.10 and 8.30 am on weekdays; 7.15 am on Saturday. Singh's Tours (☎ (0323) 85633) has a daily bus service to Jo'burg (R60) and a day-tripper service to the Wild Coast Sun (R45 return).

Umkomaas to Mtwalume

The main towns in this strip are Umkomaas, Scottburgh, Park Rynie, Kelso and Pennington. Umkomaas and Scottburgh have a publicity association (☎ (0323) 21364).

Off the coast road between Umkomaas and Scottburgh is **Croc World** (☎ (0323) 21103), with many crocs and other reptiles; feeding time is 3 pm on Sunday. The **Umnini Craft Stalls** are at the Shell Ultra City on the N2 between Umgababa and Widenham.

Places to Stay & Eat The *Clansthal Caravan Park* (☎ (0323) 30211) is opposite the railway station in Umkomaas. Four-person chalets cost up to R50 per person; there are camp sites available. The Scottburgh municipal *caravan park* (☎ (0323) 20291) is opposite the station. *Happy Wanderers* (☎ (0323) 51104) in Kelso is a resort on the beach about two km from the Kelso station; it has four-person chalets and sites.

In Umkomaas, the *Aliwal Cove* (☎ (0323) 31002, fax 30733) at 1 Maclean St is primarily a diving resort with bed and breakfast from R120 per person. The *Southern Cross* (☎ (0323) 20770), 30 Scott St, Scottburgh, is about R80 per person, breakfast included; and the *Blue Marlin* (☎ (0323) 21214, fax 22197), 180 Scott St, is about R160 per person for dinner, bed and breakfast.

At the *Cutty Sark Protea* (☎ (0323) 21230, fax 22197) in Scottburgh, singles/doubles are R203/346, breakfast included.

Getting There & Away The Margate-Durban Mini Coach stops at the Blue Marlin in Scottburgh. Commuter trains run from Durban down the coast as far as Kelso, on the northern edge of Pennington. There are five trains a day to Kelso and more to stations closer to Durban. You can catch the trains at

Durban and Berea stations; phone ☎ (031) 361 7609 for information.

Vernon Crookes Nature Reserve

Inland from Park Rynie, off the R612 past Umzinto, this reserve has a few game animals and some indigenous forest. If you walk through the reserve beware of ticks.

There is accommodation in four-bed huts for R32 per person (minimum R64); entry is R4 per person. Unlike most Natal Parks Board reserves, you can book locally, on ☎ (03231) 42222 between 8 am and 7 pm.

HIBISCUS COAST

This section of the south coast includes the seaside towns of Hibberdene, Port Shepstone, Shelly Beach, St Michaels-on-Sea, Uvongo, Margate, Ramsgate and Marina Beach. (Port Shepstone and Margate are treated separately.)

Get information on these places from the South Coast Publicity Association (☎ (03931) 22322) at Main Beach, Margate.

Places to Stay

There are many caravan parks, including the *Ilanga Resort* (☎/fax (0391) 83280) at Bendigo (Banana Beach), with sites for R30/70 in the low/high season, and *Villa Siesta* (☎ (0391) 83343), in Anerley, with four-person chalets from R35/100 and sites for R25/45.

The *Club Tropicana Youth Sanctuary* (☎ (0391) 83547) is a hostel overlooking the sea near Anerley, north of Port Shepstone between Melville and Bendigo. It's on an old tropical-fruit farm, surrounded by indigenous bush. A dorm bed costs R18, or R15 for those on 'rural upliftment' programmes, and a camp site is R8 per person. The bus stops reasonably close to the 200-metre walk through forest to the hostel.

One of the nicer resorts is the *Pumula Hotel* (☎ (0391) 84 6703), a little place on the beach at 67 Steve Pitts Rd in Umzumbe, south of Hibberdene. The single/double tariff, which includes meals, is R130/240, rising to R170/280 in the high season. Less expensive hotels include the *Alexander*

(☎ (0339) 2309), on Barracuda Blvd, Hibberdene; and in Ramsgate, the famous *Crayfish Inn* (☎ (03931) 44410, fax 79521), on Marine Dr. This historic inn is full of nautical memorabilia and has singles/doubles for R80/160.

See the following Margate and Port Shepstone sections for places to stay in these towns.

Places to Eat

In Ramsgate, the *Crayfish Inn* has a pub and restaurant (closed Sunday). *Tom, Dick & Harry's* in the Mud Hut Centre is the place for fish and chips (R20), and the *Blue Lagoon*, between the beach and lagoon, is a great place for breakfast and lunch.

At the *Uvongo Bird Park* there is a teahouse. In Milkwood Square, Uvongo, is the licensed *Curry House*. The *Trattoria la Terrazza*, 17 Outlook Rd, Southbroom South, has seafood lunches for about R40.

PORT SHEPSTONE

Before the resorts boomed, this was the largest town on the south coast, and as an industrial centre it's the only town which doesn't depend on the tourist rand. As this is where most buses coming from the Cape provinces hit the coast, you might want to break your journey here. It's great to feel the humidity and warmth after a chilly ride through the high coastal mountains.

The *Banana Express* steam train (☎ (03931) 76443 for bookings) departs from Port Shepstone at 10 am on Wednesday and Saturday for day trips to Paddock Station (1st/tourist class, R40/32). There are 1½-hour excursions to Izotsha at 10 am on Thursday and 11 am on Sunday (R20/16).

Places to Stay

The *Bedford Inn* (☎ (0391) 21085, fax 82 4238), 64 Colley St, has singles/doubles at R90/130, breakfast included. It isn't great value but it's the best in town. It's on a service road running beside the highway.

If you walk downhill from here along the service road and turn left at the small petrol station, you'll get to the *Marine Hotel*

(☎ (0391) 20281) on Bisset St. It's nicely renovated but some of the rooms open onto the lounge bar and are noisy. It has a few single/double rooms with shared bathroom for about R65/100 with breakfast. Check out the unrenovated public bar for some unrenovated Afrikaners.

Getting There & Away

The Margate Mini Coach stops at the Bedford Inn on its daily run to and from Durban. There are plenty of minibus taxis. Margate tuk-tuks run as far as here; it's about a 20-minute trip. Translux stops near the Bedford Inn, Greyhound near the corner of Bisset and Colley Sts, and Transtate at KFC.

ORIBI GORGE NATURE RESERVE

This nature reserve is inland from Port Shepstone, off the N2. The spectacular Oribi Gorge on the Umzimkulwana River is one of the highlights of the coast. Apart from the scenery there are many animals and birds.

The *Oribi Gorge Hotel* (☎ (0397) 91753), near a viewing site overlooking the gorge, has bed and breakfast for R85 per person.

The Natal Parks Board camp (book in Pietermaritzburg) has four-bed huts (R52 per person, minimum R78). There are no camp sites. Entry costs R5 per vehicle.

MARGATE

This booming resort town compares itself to the English Margate, and if you're looking for a lively seaside holiday Margate is the place for you. Those with a low tackiness tolerance might want to stay well away.

The South Coast publicity association office (☎ (03931) 22322) is on the beachfront, behind the post office. Several tours run from here. For a taxi, phone ☎ (03931) 21406.

Places to Stay & Eat

There are three caravan parks, all pricey. On the beach at St Andrews Ave, *De Wet* (☎ (03931) 21022) has only a few tent sites so getting one is a problem. The *Margate* (☎ (03931) 20852) is opposite the police station and sandwiched between the R620 and Valley Rd, and *Constantia* (☎ (03931) 20482) is one km from the beach on the corner of Varley and Hanau Sts.

A cheap hotel is *Sunlawns* (☎ (03931) 21078), on Uplands Rd. More expensive are the *Beach Lodge* (☎ (03931) 21483, fax 71232), on the corner of Marine Dr and Lagoon Dr, and *Margate Hotel* (☎/fax (03931) 21410), at 71 Marine Dr. In low/high season expect to pay about R80/130 per person for bed and breakfast.

There are many other hotels, resorts and self-catering apartments. Rather than trekking around, you're better-off booking something through an agency such as Beach Holidays (☎ (03931) 22543, fax 73753) or the Information Centre for Holiday Accommodation (☎ (03931) 50265). An apartment will almost always work out cheaper than a hotel, especially if there are two or more of you.

Opposite the visitor's bureau is *Larry's* where there is a good selection of food and music. Although pizzas are the speciality you can get a filling sandwich for R6 and a good salad for R8.

Getting There & Away

Care Airlines (☎ (03931) 22060) flies between Margate and Jo'burg on Wednesday at 4.15 pm, and on Friday and Sunday at 5.15 pm (R342).

A daily commuter minibus, the Margate Mini Coach (☎ (03931) 21406), runs between Margate and Durban railway station for R40 (R60 day return). The more usual minibus taxis run down the coast for much less, but it's a slow trip and you might have to change several times.

PORT EDWARD

Near Port Edward the rugged coastal bush grows almost to the water's edge. Port Edward adjoins the Transkei region of Eastern Cape province and the Wild Coast is to the south. Just south of town, opposite the entrance to the Wild Coast Sun, is the interesting **Mzamba Village market** where a range of Xhosa crafts are sold.

There is a good family resort, the *Old Pont*

(☎ (03930) 32211, fax 32033) with caravan and camp sites. The *Port Edward Hotel* (☎ (03930) 32292), on Owen Ellis Dr, has bed and breakfast for about R80 per person. Nature lovers may choose to stay in the self-catering accommodation at *Clearwater Camp* (☎ (03930) 32684), overlooking the Umtamvuna River.

SOUTH COAST RESERVES

The **Trafalgar Marine Reserve** protects ancient fossil beds, but for most visitors it is the surfing and especially sailboarding here which are the attractions. When there's a westerly wind, **Trafalgar Point** is the best place for sailboarding on the south coast.

The **Umtamvuna Nature Reserve** is on a gorge on the Umtamvuna River, which forms a border with Eastern Cape Province. It is densely forested and in spring there are wildflowers. There are also quite a number of animals and birds, including peregrine falcons. Beware of bilharzia in the river. There is no accommodation. To get to the reserve, head to Banner Rest, a small town south-west of Port Edward, and drive north towards Izingolweni for a few km.

North Coast

The stretch of coast from Umhlanga Rocks north to Tugela Mouth is less developed than the south coast, and the beaches are better. With lots of time-shares and retirement villages, things aren't very lively.

Before swimming at the beaches on the north coast you might want to check on the current status of the shark netting. There's no problem at Umhlanga Rocks, but further north some of the nets have been removed.

Other than some commuter services between Durban and Umhlanga and a Transtate service stopping at Stanger (R11), there is very little public transport along the coast. There are, however, commuter trains and plenty of buses and minibus taxis between Durban and Stanger and other inland towns.

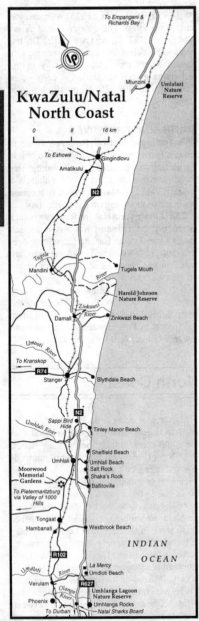

KwaZulu/Natal North Coast

UMHLANGA ROCKS

This resort town is only about 15 km north of Durban. Umhlanga means 'place of reeds'; the 'h' is pronounced something like a 'sh'.

On the mall, near the intersection of Lagoon Dr and Lighthouse St (the continuation of the road in from the main Durban road), there's an information kiosk (☎ (031) 561 4257), open from 8.30 am to 4.30 pm on weekdays (closing for lunch). If you can't find out what you need to know here, try the Shaka Tours & Safaris bus kiosk nearby.

Natal Sharks Board

The Natal Sharks Board (☎ (031) 561 1001) is a research institute dedicated to studying sharks, specifically in relation to their danger to humans. With the great white shark, a big shark with a fearsome (but perhaps undeserved) reputation for attacks on humans, frequenting the KwaZulu/Natal coast, this has more than academic interest. Very popular is the shark dissection – at 9 am Tuesday, Wednesday and Thursday; 11 am and 2.30 pm on Wednesday; and 2.30 pm on the first Sunday of the month. Entry costs R4.

The Board is about two km out of town, up the steep Umhlanga Rocks Dr (the M12 leading to the N3) – a tuk-tuk costs from costs R5.

Umhlanga Lagoon Nature Reserve

This reserve is on a river-mouth just north of the town. Despite its small size (26 hectares) there are many bird species. The trails lead through dune forest, across the lagoon and onto the beach. There is no entry fee. The adjacent **Hawaan Nature Reserve**, with a forest that includes rare tree species, is privately run. Phone ☎ (031) 561 1101 to find out about access.

Places to Stay

Self-Catering Umhlanga is crowded with holiday apartments, mostly close to the beach. They fill up in the high season, when you'd be lucky to rent one for less than a week, but away from peak times it's possible to take one for as few as two days and perhaps even overnight.

A two-bedroom apartment costs from about R110/300 per night in the low/high seasons, and three-bedroom apartments are from R160/370. Contact Umhlanga Flat Service (☎ (031) 561 1511) or Umhlanga Accommodation (☎ (031) 561 2012).

Hotels Most hotels are expensive. Along Lagoon Dr are *Umhlanga Rocks* (☎ (031) 561 1321, fax 561 1321) with bed and breakfast singles/doubles for R230/380; *Umhlanga Sands* (☎ (031) 561 2323, fax 561 4408), R249/328; *Cabana Beach* (☎ (031) 561 2371, fax 561 3522), R249/328; the *Oyster Box* (☎ (031) 561 2223, fax 561 4072), R230/380; and *Breakers* (☎ (031) 561 2271, fax 561 2722), R249/328.

Places to Eat
Most of the hotels have places to eat. The Cabana Beach has Mexican buffets in *Chiquita's* for R25 and, in the classy *Razzmatazz*, meals (which include warthog, kudu and cane rat) start at about R45. A reader recommends splashing out at the *Beverley Hills Hotel*.

Vegetarians are catered for at the *Health Nut* in the Village Centre, on Chartwell Dr; and *Gordon's* on Lagoon Dr has a seafood buffet on Sunday and Monday for R30.

The Jungle Bar in Gordon's is the pick of north coast night spots. Another watering hole, the George & Dragon, has opened near the Hillcon Centre.

Getting There & Away
A commuter bus (☎ (031) 561 2860) runs from the publicity kiosk in Umhlanga to Durban seven times a day for R5.

Getting Around
Umhlanga has tuk-tuks and they're a good, cheap way to get around, although in the off-season they run only until 6 pm except on weekends. There's a rank near the publicity kiosk or phone ☎ (031) 561 2860. You have to have pre-paid tickets; several shops in town sell books of tickets.

THE DOLPHIN COAST
The Dolphin Coast starts at Umdloti Beach and stretches north to the Tugela River. It includes the areas of Tongaat, Ballito, Umhlali (Salt Rock), Shaka's Rock, Blythdale, Zwinkazi, Stanger and Tugela Mouth. The coast gets its name from the pods of bottlenose dolphins that frolic offshore.

The Dolphin Coast Publicity Association (☎ (0322) 61997) is near the BP service station, just where you leave the N2 to enter Ballito. They book B&Bs and list other accommodation.

Tongaat
A big, sedate sugar town with some fine old buildings, Tongaat is on the railway running north from Durban. Many Indians live here, and there's a Jaggernath Temple. There are 90-minute tours of the Maidstone **sugar mill** (☎ (0322) 24551) on Tuesday, Wednesday and Thursday at 9 and 11 am and 2 pm. Bookings are required.

South-west of Tongaat, along the Umdloti River, the **Hazelmere Nature Reserve** has camp sites; entry is R4 per person. In town there's the inexpensive *Chelmsford Hotel* (☎ (0322) 21125) on Main Rd. The *Westbrook Beach Hotel* (☎/fax (0322) 42021) is on Tongaat Beach.

Ballitoville to Sheffield Beach
Ballito, Shaka's Rock, Salt Rock (Umhlali) and Sheffield Beach form a continuous settled strip, although the density of settlement is nothing like that on the south coast. They are connected by the old coast road, so you don't have to jump back and forth on the N2 to travel between them.

Places to Stay & Eat Most of the accommodation is in apartments, and in season they are almost always let by the week. Rental agencies in Ballito include Coastal Holiday Letting (☎ (0322) 62155), Ballito Agencies (☎ (0322) 62140) and Ballito Estates (☎ (0322) 62055). To give you an idea, a three-room flat such as *Beachcombers* is R95 in the off-season and R370 at peak season; the three-bedroom *Boulders Cabanas* are R130/445; and the three-bedroom flats at *Chakas Sands* are R85/275.

In Ballito, the *Dolphin Caravan Park* (☎ (0322) 62187) has sites for R22 plus R4.20 per person, rising to an exorbitant R72 in the high season. There are also cottages for up to six from R65 up to R240.

In Salt Rock (Umhlali), the *Salt Rock Caravan Park* (☎ (0322) 5026) has expensive sites. The *Salt Rock Resort & Hotel* (☎ (0322) 5025, fax 5071), 21 Basil Hulett Dr, has low-season single/double rooms from R125/190, with breakfast. Also near Umhlali is *Shortens Country House* (☎ (0322) 71140, fax 71144), on Compensation Beach Rd (R270/340).

Try *Al Pescatore* in Ballito for seafood-based Italian dishes (lunch is about R35); up-market *Mariners* on Compensation Rd, Ballito, for continental fare (R60 for dinner); the *Seabelle* in the La Mercy Hotel for seafood curries; and *Shortens Country House* for lunch (R42).

Stanger

This town is definitely not a resort-and-retirement enclave – it's an industrial town and altogether on the wrong side of the tracks. Most people on the street are black or Indian, and the town has a gritty, run-down feel. As the biggest service centre on this section of coast, however, it has a lively feel after all those pristine coastal villages basking in their exclusivity.

On Couper St are the **Shaka Memorial Gardens** where you can see the memorial stone erected in 1932 over Shaka's burial chamber, originally a grain pit.

The **Tranquil-a Bird Hide** (☎ (0324) 90 2222) is south of Stanger at the Sappi Paper mill. Newman (of the bird-book fame) saw 48 species here in less than two hours. There's no entry fee but you have to collect a key from the mill security; visits are restricted to two hours.

Places to Stay The friendly *Victoria Hotel* (☎ (0324) 21803, fax 24896) is on the corner of Couper and Reynolds Sts. Single/doubles cost R90/130, or R70/100 with shared bathroom, both including breakfast. The *Luthando Hotel* (☎ (0324) 22208, fax 23237) on King George Rd costs about the same.

Getting There & Away Several Transtate services run daily between Stanger railway station and Durban (R11), and others run north along the N2 to Golela and Pongola (R37) as well as inland via Eshowe and Melmoth to Nongoma (R29) and Ulundi (R22). There is a minibus taxi to Vryheid via Melmoth (R35).

Blythdale & Zinkwazi

Blythdale is a quiet town with a sandy beach and decidedly noisy surf. *La Mouette Caravan Park* (☎ (0324) 22547) has sites from R41 for two people in the low season

---

Shaka Sites

Shaka established a royal settlement called *Dukuza* ('maze') on the site of present-day Stanger in July 1825. The settlement of 2000 beehive huts was intended as a halfway station between Zululand and the settlers at Port Natal (Durban). Shaka's royal residence was near the site of the old police station, in the centre of modern Stanger.

In front of the municipal offices in Roodt St is an old *mkuhla* tree (Natal mahogany), referred to as Shaka's *indaba*, where Shaka is reputed to have conducted meetings. A large fig tree stood in the Nyakambi kraal at the opposite end of Dukuza. Shaka was murdered here, by his half brothers Dingaan and Umhlanga, in September 1828.

Dukuza was abandoned and choked by weeds until the site was surveyed for the town of Stanger in 1872. Other sites in town associated with Shaka are the Mavivane execution cliff, north of the R74 at the end of Lindley St, and the Mbozambo Valley (now the site of Shakaville township). Known as his 'playground', it's where Shaka reputedly bathed and relaxed. ∎

rising to R100 for four (minimum) in the December holidays. *Mini Villas* (☎ (0324) 21277) has bungalows which sleep six, costing from R80/170 in the low/high seasons; during school holidays there's a minimum stay of up to a week.

North of Blythdale, at Zinkwazi, is the *Zinkwazi Resort* (☎ (0324) 3344, fax 3340). Chalets for up to four people are from R96 per person in the low season; camp sites cost from R40 to R70.

Occasionally minibus taxis or buses run between Blythdale and Stanger, seven km away.

Tugela Mouth

The Tugela River, once an important natural boundary for local tribes, enters the sea here to end its journey from Mont-aux-Sources in the Drakensberg. Several major battles took place near the mouth, notably the Battle of Ndondasuka in which Cetshwayo defeated his brother, Mbuyasi, and many thousands were killed.

The **Harold Johnson Nature Reserve** is on the south bank of the Tugela, east of the highway. The ruins of Fort Pearson, a small British fort from the Anglo-Zulu War of 1879, is to the right of the highway. Entry is R4 per person. Tent sites (R13 per person) may be booked through the ranger-in-charge (☎ (03245) 61574).

The **Ultimatum Tree**, where the British presented their demands to Cetshwayo's representatives, is nearby. Here, on 11 December 1878, the British demanded that the Zulu pay taxes and return all the cattle they had stolen, by mid-January 1879. The cattle were not returned, precipitating the Anglo-Zulu War which raged until August 1879 when Cetshwayo was captured. Across the river there is a collection of war graves on the site of Fort Tenedos.

The *Tugela Mouth North Bank Caravan Park* (☎ (03245) 94241) has sites for R25.

Zululand

For many travellers in South Africa this is the first and often the only taste they get of the real Africa. A region dominated by one tribal group, the Zulu, and a place replete with their customs, historical traditions and culture. The name Zulu ('heaven') comes from an early chief. His descendants were *abakwaZulu*, or people of Zulu.

Zululand covers much of central Kwa-Zulu/Natal and extends in a rough triangle; from the Tugela River mouth to Kosi Bay on the Mozambique border, across to Vryheid, and back to Tugela mouth. The area east of the N2 and north of the Mtubatuba-St Lucia road is known as Maputaland and is covered in a separate section. North of the Tugela you'll find the Zulu capital, Ulundi, the large port of Richards Bay, the big adjacent Hluhluwe-Umfolozi Park (see the Maputaland section), and many traditional Zulu villages.

Much of Zululand is a mass of attractive rolling hills. The climate becomes steadily hotter as you go north and summers are steamy and almost tropical, thanks to the warm Indian Ocean. Although few white South Africans live here, there are several major holiday centres, especially in the St Lucia area.

The humid coastal air causes frequent dense mists on the inland hills, with visibility cut to a few metres. Be careful of pedestrians and animals suddenly appearing around a corner. In the sugar areas slow-moving vehicles are common.

Warning

There is malaria in Zululand and other places in the north of KwaZulu/Natal, and bilharzia in some waterways and dams.

GINGINDLOVU

After crossing the Tugela River, the first town of any size is Gingindlovu ('the swallower of the elephant'), at the junction of the R68 to Eshowe and the N2 north. It was once

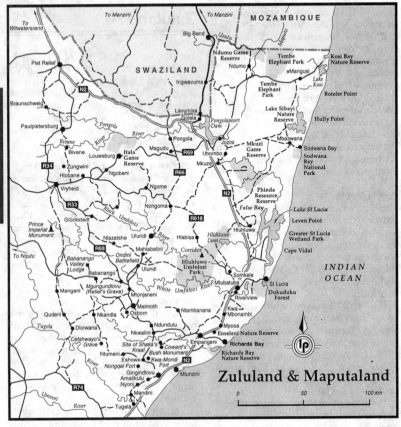

Zululand & Maputaland

one of Cetshwayo's strongholds. Two battles of the Anglo-Zulu War of 1879 were fought in the vicinity – the town itself was razed.

The *Imperial Hotel* (☎ (0353) 30 1202), on Main Rd, costs about R75 per person. *Mine Own Guest House* (☎ (0353) 30 1262), an old homestead, has bed and breakfast for about R125.

MTUNZINI
If you want to stay on the coast while exploring this part of KwaZulu/Natal, Mtunzini makes a good base. You can get information from the Trade Winds (☎ (0353) 40 1411).

This quiet coastal town had a colourful beginning. John Dunn, the first European to settle in the area, was granted land by Cetshwayo. He became something of a chief himself, took 49 wives and fathered 117 children. He held court here under a tree, hence the town's name – *mtunzi* is Zulu for shade. Today there isn't a lot of cross-culturalism in evidence and the town is a place of manicured lawns and modern buildings.

Near the mouth of the Mlalazi River there is lush tropical forest where you'll find the **Raffia Palm Monument**. The raffia palm is monocarpic, meaning that it only seeds once in its 25-year cycle, and its presence this far south is a mystery. Its closest relatives are found in the far north of Maputaland, near Kosi Bay, and it is thought that this unusual grove was planted in 1910 from seeds obtained near Maputo. There is a wooden boardwalk through the grove and you might spot the rare palmnut vulture *(Gypohierax angolensis)*, which favours raffia palms.

Umlalazi Nature Reserve

The entrance to Umlalazi ('place of the whetstone') Nature Reserve is 1.5 km east of the town, on the coast. There are some crocodiles here, as well as plentiful birdlife in the dense vegetation of the sand-dune forest and mangrove swamp. There are three walking trails.

This is a Natal Parks Board reserve, so book accommodation other than camp sites in Pietermaritzburg. Camp sites (book on (0353) 40 1836) are R16 per person, five-bed log cabins are R75 per person (minimum R225) and entry is R4 per person.

Places to Stay & Eat

The *Xaxaza Caravan Park* (☎ (0353) 40 1843) has sites from R15 per person, rising to R25 during the main holidays. There are also four to six-bed cabins from R30 per person (R40 in high season). It's a four-km walk back through the town to the beach from here, so if you want to be on the coast you'd be better-off staying at the Umlalazi Nature Reserve. The same applies to the nearby *Casa Benri Caravan Park* (☎ (0353) 40 1997), which has similar rates for sites.

The *Trade Winds Hotel* (☎ (0353) 40 1411, fax 40 1629), on the main street, is a

KWAZULU/NATAL

Zulu Leaders

See Facts about the Region for the early history of the Zulu people. Briefly, the small Zulu clan had become a huge and disruptive force in southern Africa under the fanatical leader Shaka Zulu. Dingaan, Shaka's successor, continued the reign of terror and murdered the party of trekboers lead by Piet Retief. That massacre was avenged at the Battle of Blood River, when 3000 Zulu were slaughtered.

After the disaster of Blood River, facing internal dissent and further attacks by the Boers and the British colonists, Dingaan lost support and fled to Swaziland, where he was killed in 1840. His successor, Mpane, has been seen as a puppet ruler installed by the Europeans, but there is evidence that he played off the British and Boers against each other. Nevertheless, during his reign much Zulu land was signed over to European interests, especially to the British who had by this stage established the colony of Natal. He was succeeded by his son Cetshwayo in 1873.

Cetshwayo inherited a reasonably stable kingdom but pressures from the land-grabbing Boers in Transvaal was growing. While the British colonial government in Natal agreed that Boer encroachment was illegal it gave little assistance to the Zulu, largely because the British had plans of their own – a grand imperial scheme of a British wedge into Africa heading north from Durban. The Zulu kingdom was directly in the way. Diplomatic chicanery ended with a British ultimatum with which Cetshwayo could not comply, and in January 1879, the British invaded the kingdom, beginning the Anglo-Zulu War.

The Zulu decisively defeated the British at the Battle of Isandlwana but failed to capture the small station at Rorke's Drift, despite overwhelming superiority in numbers. After that things went downhill and on 4 July at Ulundi, Cetshwayo was defeated.

Cetshwayo was jailed and his power was divided between 13 British-appointed chiefs, many of whom opposed him. In 1882 Cetshwayo travelled to England to plead for his restoration, but the British response was to partition the kingdom according to the pro and anti-Cetshwayo factions. This lead to chaos and bloodshed, and in 1887, the British annexed Zululand. Dinizulu, Cetshwayo's son and the last independent Zulu king, was exiled to St Helena in the Cape Province. In 1897 the British handed over Zululand to the colony of Natal.

The current Zulu king is King Goodwill Zwelithini but tussling for power is Chief Mangosuthu Buthelezi, leader of the IFP, great-grandson of Cetshwayo, and a cabinet member in the new South African government. ■

friendly place and has singles/doubles from R149/200 with breakfast (R100/150 on weekends). The *Forest Inn* (☎ (0353) 40 1431, fax 40 1363) on the highway charges from R130/200. Both these places have a restaurant with lunch specials.

Mtunzini Chalets (☎ (0353) 40 1953) are in dune forest near the coast and cost from R60 per person (minimum R150), rising to R70 (minimum R180) during school holidays. The *Waterberry Lodge* (☎ (0353) 40 1892), seven km from Mtunzini, is a relaxing place with sea and lagoon views; bed and breakfast is about R100 per person.

A block north of the Trade Winds is *Viva Afrika*, which specialises in curry.

Getting There & Away

Transtate's daily service between Durban (R80) and KwaNgwanase (also eManguse) via Empangeni, Mtubatuba, Hluhluwe and Mkuze stops here.

RICHARDS BAY

The port at Richards Bay is second to Durban's in size, but it handles more cargo than any other in the province. The town feels as though it was meticulously planned for a boom which hasn't quite happened yet. It's spread-out, with tourist-oriented facilities a long way from what passes for the centre.

The Richards Bay publicity association (☎ (0351) 31111, fax 31897), at 48 Anglers Rd, has information on things to do in the region. One suggestion is the 60-km 4WD trail north along the beach to Mapelane Nature Reserve near St Lucia. Fishing and boating are also popular here.

Places to Stay

The large municipal *caravan park* (☎ (0351) 31971, fax 31897) has camp sites. It's near the harbour and the beach at the end of the road in from Empangeni.

The *Marina Lodge* (☎ (0351) 31350, fax 31361), on the corner of Davidson St and Launder Lane, Meerensee, has singles/doubles for about R245/295 with breakfast (R145/195 on weekends). *Quay West* (☎ (0351)

53 3065) charges R223/293. There's also the *Karos Bayshore Inn* (☎ (0351) 31246) at R243/338 and the *Karos Richard* (☎ (0351) 31301) at R320/429.

Getting There & Away

Interport (☎ (0351) 91791) runs to Durban daily at 6 am. The three-hour trip costs R40. Otherwise you'll have to hitch or take a minibus taxi to Empangeni, from where there are several Transtate services.

EMPANGENI

Empangeni (pronounced m'pan-*gay*-nee) started out as a sugar town, but the huge eucalypt plantations nearby are rivalling the cane in importance to the town's economy. It's a jumping-off point for the coast and the inland areas of Zululand.

Places to Stay & Eat

The *Imperial Hotel* (☎ (0351) 92 1522), at 52 Maxwell St, has singles/doubles for R150/175, or R125/140 with shared bathroom. The *Royal Hotel* (☎ (0351) 21601) on Turnbull St charges R210/280, with breakfast.

The restaurant in the Royal is called *Palms* and next door is a *Portuguese restaurant* known for its piquant prawn piri-piri. There are also a *Spur* and a *Mike's Kitchen* in town.

Getting There & Away

Interport's daily bus between Durban and Richards Bay runs past Empangeni. Phone ☎ (0351) 91791 for details.

There are daily Transtate buses to Durban, Stanger, Mtunzini, Mtubatuba, Hluhluwe, Mkuze, Pongola and Golela. There's an express Durban-Pongola service which stops in Empangeni. On Friday there's a bus from Jo'burg, returning Sunday. Minibus taxis to Richards Bay cost about R4.

AROUND EMPANGENI
Enseleni Nature Reserve

This small reserve, 13 km north-east of Empangeni on the N2, is on a bend in the Nseleni River. As well as game species and zebras there are hippos and crocodiles in the river. Although there is no accommodation, there are several walks. The longest is a five-km swamp trail. The reserve is open daily between 8 am and 5 pm.

Windy Ridge Game Park

About 20 km north-west of Empangeni, 10 km beyond Heatonville, Windy Ridge (☎ (0351) 23465, fax 27206) has a large variety of animals in its 1300 hectares, including white rhino and crocodiles. This area was once the hunting ground of Zulu kings. You can drive through the park or go on a guided walk. Self-contained huts cost R25 per person, but there's no camping.

ESHOWE

This town, on the R68, is inland in the misty Zululand hills. The name Eshowe is said to be the sound the wind made when passing through the trees. Eshowe was Cetshwayo's stronghold before he moved to Ondini, and like Ondini, Eshowe was destroyed during the Anglo-Zulu War. The British occupied the site and built Fort Nongqai in 1883, establishing Eshowe as the administrative centre of their newly captured territory.

The Eshowe Publicity Association (☎ (0354) 74079, fax 41908) provides information.

Things to See & Do

If you arrive on a day of thick mist, seeing *anything* might be a problem. In the mud-and-brick three-turreted **Fort Nongqai** is the Zululand Historical Museum, open daily from 10 am to 5 pm; entry is by donation. From the museum you can walk to **Mpushini Falls**, but don't swim or drink the water as there is bilharzia.

The **Dlinza Forest Reserve** is a 200-hectare strand of forest – on a misty day this is an eerie place. There are a few animals, rich birdlife and walking trails, some of them believed to have been made by British soldiers stationed here after the Anglo-Zulu War.

Birdwatchers should look for crowned eagles (*Stephanoaetus coronatus*), green coucals (*Ceuthmochares aereus*), Narina

trogons (*Apaloderma narina*) and Delegorgue's pigeon (*Columba delegorguei*).

Places to Stay & Eat

The municipal *Eshowe Caravan Park* (☎ (0354) 41141) costs around R23 for a site. It's some way from the town centre but close to Dlinza Forest. Follow Osborn Rd west, continue along Main Rd as it doglegs, and turn right onto Saunders St. The park is on your left after a couple of blocks.

The *Royal Hotel* (☎ (0354) 41117) on Osborn Rd has singles/doubles for R124/184, or R72/110 with a shared bath. This isn't great value. The *George Hotel* (☎ (0354) 41832) charges R95/160, or R65 per person with shared bath). The Royal has the town's best restaurant, *Quarters*. It may get some competition from the *Pink Lady*, a new place in the middle of town, which serves Asian and Indian food.

Getting There & Away

The minibus taxi and bus park is at the old railway station, off Main Rd near Osborn Rd. A taxi to Mtunzini costs R7 and north to Vryheid it's R23. There are daily Transtate services to Durban, Nongoma and, via a roundabout route, Mtubatuba.

Washesha Buses (☎ (0354) 42051) runs several services in the area, including a scenic but rough run on dirt roads through forest to Nkandla for R12. There's no accommodation at Nkandla but you can get a taxi from there to Melmoth, where there's a hotel. A bus from Eshowe to Empangeni costs R7 and this is also a dirt-road run through rural areas. Washesha (the name means 'hurry' in Zulu) is pretty reliable, but on dirt roads rain can strand the buses. For more information ask at the office, behind KFC on the main street. Washesha also has a very cheap service to Durban – R12.

AROUND ESHOWE

Entumeni Nature Reserve, larger than Dlinza, preserves indigenous mist-belt forest and has some animals and many birds. It's 16 km west of town, off the road to Ntumeni and Nkandla; entry is free. On the south-east side of Eshowe, off the R68, the **Ocean View Game Park** has some animals and many birds; it is open from 7 am to 5 pm daily.

Head east from Eshowe on the Gezinsela road (the continuation of Kangella) for a few km and you'll come to Imbombotyana (Signal Hill to the British in the Anglo-Zulu War). From here there are good views, sometimes all the way to the coast.

NKWALINI VALLEY

Shaka's kraal KwaBulawayo once loomed over this beautiful valley but today the valley is regimented into citrus orchards and cane-fields rather than impis. A marker shows where the kraal was. From Eshowe head north for six km on the R68 and turn off to the right onto the P230 (a dirt road which will eventually get you to the R34 and Em-pangeni) and keep going for about 20 km.

Across the road from the KwaBulawayo marker is **Coward's Bush**, now just another marker, where warriors who returned from battle without their spears or who had received wounds in the back were executed.

Further west, a few km before the P230 meets the R68, the **Mandwe Cross** was erected in the '30s against the wishes of the Zulu. There are good views from the hill.

Stewart's Farm

The old Stewart's Farm tourist trap has been taken over by a local Zulu family and is operated as a craft and cultural centre (☎ (03546) 644), with the proceeds support-ing a health clinic. The craft shop is open daily (closed for lunch) and a tour of the kraal, with dancing and traditional meals, is by appointment only.

Take the R34, which runs east to Em-pangeni from the R68 near Nkwalini village, which is about 20 km north of Eshowe on the R68. Turn off the R34 onto a dirt road about six km east of the intersection with the R68. From here it's five km on dirt road, the last section of which is very difficult when wet.

Mfuli Game Ranch

This ranch is off the R34, 13 km east of the R68. Although there isn't yet a lot of game on this new ranch (☎ (03546) 620) it is a friendly place in nice country and is a good base for the region. Accommodation is in self-contained cabins and costs R135/230 for singles/doubles; in the high season add about 20%. On weekends a cabin sleeping six people costs R170. There's a good restaurant here.

Nyala Game Ranch

Nyala is further east on the R34 from Mfuli and has zebras and various antelope species. Accommodation is mainly for educational groups, but if you can get a bed it won't be too pricey. You'll need to bring all your own food; phone (0351) 92 4095 for information.

Shakaland

Created as a set for the tele-movie *Shaka Zulu* and managed by the Protea chain (com-plete with have-a-nice-day reception staff), this isn't exactly a genuine Zulu village.

The Nandi Experience, a display of Zulu culture and customs, is held daily at 11 am and 12.30 pm and costs R75. (Nandi was Shaka's mother.) The 'experience' plus accommodation costs R228/350.

Shakaland (☎ (03546) 912, fax 824) is at

Zulu dancing sticks

Norman Hurst Farm, Nkwalini, a few km off the R68 and 14 km north of Eshowe.

KwaBhekithunga Zulukraal

This craft centre on the road into Nkwalini (Shakaland) is a genuine Zulu village, although it doesn't look much like a traditional one. A live-in 'Zulu Experience' is offered here too, but only for large groups. Phone ☎ (03546) 644, or fax 867 to book if you can muster 15 or more people. Even if you can't, it's worth visiting for the handicraft centre.

MELMOTH

Named after the first Resident Commissioner of Zululand, Melmoth is a small town dozing in the hills, on the point of going to seed. Until recently the major local industry was the harvesting of wattle bark.

Place to Stay

The *Melmoth Inn* (☎ (03545) 2074, fax 2075), on Victoria St, has singles/doubles without bath for R90/140, including breakfast (a double with bath is R150). The price is a little high but it's a friendly place with a nice bar and a fair restaurant with somnambulistic service.

Getting There & Away

Daily Transtate buses stop in Melmoth on the Durban to Nongoma route. They continue on to Mtubatuba by back roads – it can take over five hours from Melmoth on this bus.

Minibus taxis to both Vryheid and Durban are R21.

ULUNDI

Ulundi was the capital of the KwaZulu Homeland, and there is a possibility that it may replace Pietermaritzburg as the capital of the new KwaZulu/Natal Province. The town is new but this area has been the stronghold of many Zulu kings, and several are buried in the area. Although Ulundi is a small town it is spread out, with residential areas dotted around the neighbouring countryside. The town itself offers little to see, but there are important historical sites in the area.

For information go to the KwaZulu Monuments Council (☎ (0358) 79 1854) at Ondini. Their interesting booklet *Ulundi: Yesterday, Today, Tomorrow* (R10) seems to be a plug for Ulundi to be the provincial capital.

The former **KwaZulu Legislative Assembly** is just north of the railway line, and has some interesting tapestries and a statue of Shaka. The building isn't always open to visitors.

Opposite the Legislative Assembly is the site of King Mpande's *iKhanda* (palace), **kwaNodwengu**. Mpande won control from Dingaan after the disaster at Blood River. He seized power with assistance from the Boers, but Zululand declined during his reign. The king's grave is here, and a small museum.

Close to Ulundi is **Fort Nolela**, near the drift on the Umfolozi River where the British camped before attacking Ondini in 1879, and **kwaGqokli**, where Shaka celebrated victory over the Ndwandwe in 1818. Another place of great significance to the Zulu is **eMakhosini**, Valley of the Kings. The great *makhosi* (chiefs) Nkhosinkulu (Zulu), Senzangakhona (father of Shaka, Dingaan and Mpande) and Dinizulu are buried here.

Ondini

Ondini ('the high place') was established as Cetshwayo's capital in 1873, but it was razed by British troops after the Battle of Ulundi (4 July 1879), the final engagement of the 1879 Anglo-Zulu War.

It took the British nearly six months to defeat the Zulu army but the Battle of Ulundi went the way of most of the campaign, with the number of Zulu deaths 10 to 15 times higher than British deaths. Part of the reason for the British victory at Ulundi was that they adopted the Boer laager tactic, with troops forming a hollow square to protect the cavalry, which attacked only after the Zulu army had spent itself trying to penetrate the walls.

The **royal kraal** section of the Ondini site is still being rebuilt, but you can see where archaeological digs have uncovered the floors of identifiable buildings. The floors,

KWAZULU/NATAL

of mud and cow dung, were preserved by the heat of the fires which destroyed the huts above them. The huge area is enclosed in a defensive perimeter of gnarled branches, some of which act as fencing for a herd of white Nguni cattle, prized by Zulu kings.

Also at Ondini is the **KwaZulu Cultural-Historical Museum** (entry R3), with good exhibits on Zulu history and culture and an excellent audiovisual show. You can buy souvenirs, including some interesting books.

A guide will probably accompany you around the museum and the site.

To get to Ondini, take the airport turn-off from the highway just south of Ulundi and keep going for about five km on a dirt road. This road continues on to Umfolozi-Hluhluwe Park. Taxis occasionally pass Ondini.

Mgungundlovu

This was Dingaan's capital from 1829 to 1839, and it's here that Piet Retief and the other Voortrekkers were killed by their host in 1838, the event which precipitated the Boer-Zulu War. The site of the *ikhanda* is being restored and there's a small museum and a monument to the Voortrekkers nearby. In 1990 excavations revealed the site of Dingaan's *ndlunkulu* (great hut). The museum is open daily from 8 am to 5 pm and guides take visitors around the current archaeological excavations.

The site is five km off the R34, running between Melmoth and Vryheid. Turn off to the left (west) about five km north-east of the intersection with the R66 to Ulundi. There are several variations of the spelling of Mgungundlovu, such as Ungungundhlovu.

Places to Stay & Eat

Ulundi Holiday Inn Garden Court (☎ (0358) 21121) claims to be the world's smallest and has singles/doubles from R220/242. Out at Ondini (☎ (0358) 79 1223) there's accommodation in traditional *umuzi* ('beehive' huts) for R74 per person, with dinner and

---

Zulu Basketwork

The Zulu have a rich basketwork heritage. The handwoven baskets, although created in a variety of styles and colours, almost always have a functional purpose. The raw materials vary depending on seasonal availability – they could be woven from imizi grass, ilala palm fronds, isikonko grass, ncema grass or Ncebe bark. One medium currently in favour is telephone wire. Ncema, for example, is used to make traditional sitting mats *(isicephu)*, sleeping mats *(icansi)*, water-carrying baskets and beer strainers.

The two predominant designs are the triangle, denoting males, and the diamond, denoting females. Two triangular shapes above one another in an hourglass design means the male is married and, similarly, two diamonds so arranged means the female is married.

Many of the finest baskets are displayed in the African Art Centre and the Durban Art Gallery, especially the highly sought-after (but more decorative than functional) Hlabisa baskets. A good place to buy baskets is from Ilala Weavers in Hluhluwe. ■

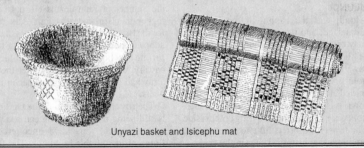

Unyazi basket and Isicephu mat

A Zulu Dwelling

At Ondini, in the main museum, there is a reconstruction of a Zulu dwelling (indlu) with all the goods and chattels of a traditional home. A collection of indlu, often surrounded by a palisade, was known as an imuzi, or homestead.

The indlu was circular and the archetypal 'beehive' shape. A number of pliable branches would be bound together to form a dome. These would then be covered with a woven grass mat before thatching was added. The binding string was made from the umbrella thorn tree (Acacia tortillis). The floor is ant bed (crushed termite soil) mixed with clay and fresh cow dung. There was no chimney as the smoke was used to kill insects in the thatch.

PHOTOGRAPH BY JEFF WILLIAMS

The **entrance** was kept clear as the ancestral spirits gathered there. It was also small, forcing people entering to stoop low in respect. In front of the entrance was the **hearth**, also important to ancestors (amadlozi) as a place to get warmth and food.

On one side of the indlu, women would prepare food, sleep, grind meal, eat, and weave. The men kept to the other side where they would eat, sleep, socialise, drink sorghum beer and do woodwork.

At the back of the indlu, directly opposite the entrance, is the **unsamo**. It was used to store utensils and prepared food, especially meat, sour milk and sorghum beer. Precious objects were also kept here. The unsamo was sacred to the amadlozi as it was here that prayers and offerings to them would be made. ■

breakfast. Unless you've made arrangements you must be there by 6 pm.

Lunch at the *Holiday Inn* is R14.50. The food at Ondini is reasonable value; a lunch pack is R8.50, dinner is R14, and they also serve pap and gravy.

Getting There & Away

Bus Transtate's daily service from Durban to Nongoma and Mtubatuba stops in Ulundi. Durban to Ulundi takes about five hours. Ulundi to Mtubatuba on some interesting back roads can also take up to five hours. You need a car to see the sights here.

The taxi park is opposite the Holiday Inn. To Eshowe the fare is R16, to Vryheid R12, to Nongoma R7.50 and to Jo'burg R55.

BABANANGO

This village is on the R68 between Melmoth and Dundee. Babanango (literally, 'father, there it is') is near interesting battlefields. An essential stop is Stan's pub. His *Babanango Hotel* (☎ (03872), ask for 34), 16 Justice St,

is rough around the edges but exudes atmosphere. Bed and breakfast is R140 per person.

Another excellent place is *Babanango Valley Lodge* (☎/fax (0358) 35 0062) on historic Goudhoek Farm in the beautiful Nsubeni Valley. A single/double with dinner and breakfast costs R262/456. It is run by John and Meryn Turner, extremely friendly hosts. John organises informative tours of nearby battlefields for R85 per person. This silvan valley is quite isolated, off the R68 about halfway between Melmoth and Dundee. Turn north off the R68 about four km west of Babanango and continue on (stay left at the fork) for about 12 km – you are on the right track if you head down a very steep hill.

Maputaland

Maputaland is one of the wildest and most fascinating regions of South Africa and an absolute must for nature lovers. It takes its name from the Maputo River which splits, on the border of Mozambique and South Africa, into the Usutu and Pongola rivers.

This section includes Hluhluwe-Umfolozi Park, the Pongola area, and all of the region north of the Mtubatuba-St Lucia road and to the north-east of the N2. Maputaland is sparsely settled and much of it is protected in parks and reserves. It contains three huge lakes, including the significant St Lucia Wetlands; the last wild elephants in the country in Tembe reserve; coral reefs; and many game reserves with all of the 'big five' represented.

Sea-fishing is a major attraction and the coral reefs are popular with divers – and also with sharks. You'd be unwise to dive without consulting locals.

MTUBATUBA

This is a trading town, busy on weekends, but the main reason to visit is that Transtate and private buses and minibus taxis run through here on the way south to Durban, north to Pongola (via Mkuze and Hluhluwe) and west into Zululand. Coming from those destinations, Mtubatuba is the stop for St Lucia. The name comes from a local chief, Mthubuthubu, meaning 'he who was pummelled out', referring to a difficult birth.

Places to Stay

The *Sundowner Hotel* (☎ (035) 550 0153) is an older place and a bit run-down but it has a good atmosphere and friendly Portuguese managers. Singles/doubles are R80/150, or R70/130 with shared bath; breakfast is included. Heading into Mtubatuba from the N2, turn right at the T-intersection at the edge of town (ie towards River View) and the hotel is nearby on the right.

The *Lala Inn* (☎/fax (035) 550 0290), 54

Jan Smuts Ave, is an up-market guesthouse with dinner, bed and breakfast for R165/300. The *Safari Hotel* (☎/fax (035) 550 1331), 10 km south of Mtubatuba, is cheaper. Phone Bed-'n-Breakfast (☎ (035) 550 0538) for a list of B&Bs in the area.

Getting There & Away

Transtate buses to and from Durban stop here daily. The direct bus, which continues on to Pongola, takes six hours or there's one via Ulundi and Nongoma which takes up to 9½ hours. There is also a Mtubatuba-Jo'burg bus which departs on Wednesday and Sunday, returning Tuesday and Friday. Transtate buses leave from the railway station. Other buses serving Zululand leave from the bus and taxi compound at the other end of the main street, near the shopping centre. St Lucia Resort is about 25 km east and the trip costs R4.

AROUND MTUBATUBA

On the southern side of Mtubatuba is River View, a poor but neat town with a sugar mill. The **Dukuduku Forest Reserve** (including Mihobi Nature Reserve) is one of the largest remnant coastal forests in KwaZulu/Natal. It is home to many varieties of butterfly as well as other insects, birds and animals. Camping is not permitted. There are walking trails and a nice picnic spot on the·R620, between Mtubatuba and St Lucia.

Hluhluwe

The typical Zulu village of Hluhluwe (roughly pronounced 'shloo-shloo-wee') is equidistant from the Memorial Gate of Hluhluwe-Umfolozi Park and the north of the Greater St Lucia Wetland.

You can get information on the region from Zululand Information Services (☎ (035) 562 0353) at 15 Main St. There is as good a selection of Zulu baskets, beadwork and other handicrafts as you will see anywhere (and at much lower prices than most shops) at Ilala Weavers (☎ (03562) 2221); make an appointment to visit.

Places to Stay The *Sisalana Hotel* (☎ (035) 562 0177) has singles/doubles for R85/160, with breakfast. Also in town is the *Hluhluwe Hotel* (☎/fax (035) 562 0251) with dinner, bed and breakfast for R140/190.

At *Bona Manzi* (☎ (035) 562 0181), south of Hluhluwe village, they shoot the wildlife. *Bushlands Game Lodge* (☎ (035) 562 0144, fax 562 0205), 10 km south of Hluhluwe, charges from R200/370.

The *Ubizane Game Reserve* (☎ (035) 562 0237) is off the road between Hluhluwe village, six km away, and Hluhluwe-Umfolozi Park. It has been taken over by a hotel chain and will be extensively renovated – dinner, bed and breakfast *was* R200 per person including a game drive and a guided walk.

There are other game ranches which offer hunting. If this is your bag, contact them yourself. And if you sniff out a good restaurant in this region, tell us about it.

HLUHLUWE-UMFOLOZI PARK

The two reserves were first proclaimed in 1897 and today they are among the best in South Africa. They don't adjoin, but a 'corridor' between them allows animals to move freely from one park to the other. The reserves, now combined into one park, and the corridor have a combined area of nearly 100,000 hectares.

Both reserves have lions, elephants, many rhinos (black and white), giraffes and a host of other animals and birds. The country is quite hilly except on the river flats: the White Umfolozi River flows through Umfolozi, and the Black Umfolozi forms the northern border of the park; the Hluhluwe River bisects Hluhluwe, and the large dam on it attracts game.

The park is best visited in winter as the animals can range widely without congregating at water sources although the lush vegetation sometimes makes viewing difficult. However, summer visits can also be very rewarding, especially at Umfolozi where there is more open savanna country.

There are driving trails but no walking trails in Hluhluwe except for a short one around the camp. See the following Wilderness Trails section for details of walks in Umfolozi, where there are good-value night drives for R36. Entry to each reserve is R4 per person, R15 per vehicle. It is best to book accommodation with the Natal Parks Board in Pietermaritzburg.

Wilderness Trails

One of Umfolozi's main attractions is its trail system, open from March to the end of November, in a special 24,000-hectare wilderness area. Accompanied by an armed ranger and donkeys to carry supplies, hikers spend three days walking in the reserve; the average distance covered each day is from 12 to 15 km. The first and last nights are spent at a base camp, with two nights out in the wilderness area. Bookings are accepted up to six months in advance and it's advisable to book early, with alternative dates if possible. The cost is R780 per person, including all meals and equipment, and a 50% deposit is required. On weekends there is a two-night trail which costs R420 per person.

A variation on this is the 'primitive trail', on which you provide everything except food and carry it all yourself. Taking a primitive trail might be more fun as you get to participate more – hikers must sit up in 90-minute watches throughout the night, for example.

There is a hitch, though: both types of hikes require parties of eight and these must be pre-arranged: the Natal Parks Board doesn't make up groups. Trails can be booked on ☎ (035) 550 1261.

For those with less time, Hluhluwe offers day walks of two to three hours. Each group is accompanied by a guide and costs R14 per person (no children under 12). There are two walks each day – 6 am and 3 pm in winter, 5.30 am and 3.30 pm in summer.

Places to Stay & Eat

In Hluhluwe, the new *Hilltop Camp* (☎ (035) 562 0255, fax 562 0113), at the top of a forested ridge, has absolutely stupendous views over the Hluhluwe section of the park and Zululand. It is a great place to stay;

self-catering two and four-bed chalets are R97 per person (minimum R146); rondavels without bath are R52 per person (minimum R78); and two-bed non-catering chalets are R86 per person. Reception is open from 7 am to 7 pm. A reader has complained about the number of tour buses that use Hilltop.

A hearty breakfast at the *Mpunyane Restaurant* is R20, and at lunch and dinner there are dishes such as asparagus and leek quiche (R15), kudu fillet (R30), ostrich camrin (R32.50), chicken piri-piri (R24.50) and desserts for R6.50.

Accommodation at *Mtwazi* is in a nine-bed lodge at R140 per person (minimum R560). There are also bush lodges at *Muntulu*, perched high above the Hluhluwe River, and the newer *Munyawaneni*, which is secluded and self-contained, good for privacy and game viewing. These bush lodges sleep eight and cost R420.

There are two main accommodation centres in Umfolozi: *Mpila*, in the centre of the reserve, has four-bed huts for R58 per person (minimum R116). *Masinda*, near the eastern gate, has five-bed chalets with external bathrooms and kitchens for R58 per person (minimum R116). There are also eight-bed bush camps (*Sontuli* and *Nselweni*) for R352 (including your own ranger and cook), a bush lodge at *Gqoyeni* and a tented camp at *Mndindini*; the latter two are R105 per person, R420 minimum.

Tours

Several tours include Hluhluwe-Umfolozi. One inexpensive option is the three-day trip with Tekweni Tours (see Tours in the Durban section), which also takes in the Greater St Lucia Wetlands.

Getting There & Away

A daily Transtate bus runs between Nongoma and Mtubatuba along the R618, which you could take if you wanted to try hitching into either Hluhluwe or Umfolozi. Alternatively, take one of the Transtate services to Hluhluwe village (off the N2, about 20 km from the park entrance) from where there's more traffic to Hluhluwe-Umfolozi. The Jo'burg-Mtubatuba, Durban-Pongola and Durban-KwaNgwanase services run through Hluhluwe village.

The main entrance to Hluhluwe, Memorial Gate, is about 15 km west of the N2, about 50 km north of Mtubatuba. Alternatively, just after Mtubatuba, turn left off the N2 onto the R618 to Nongoma and take the right turn to the reserve after 17 km. This road is more interesting, going through several Zulu townships, but it isn't in very good condition and you'll have to slow down for animals on the road – you enter the reserve through Gunjaneni Gate. Petrol is available at Hilltop Camp.

Umfolozi also has two gates. On the west side is the Cengeni Gate, accessible by rough roads from Ulundi. The Mambeni Gate on the east side sees more traffic and you can get there from the R618. Turn off to the west a few km north of the turn-off to Hluhluwe, itself 17 km north of the R618 junction with the N2. Petrol is available at Mpila Camp.

GREATER ST LUCIA WETLANDS

One of the world's great eco-tourism destinations stretches for 80 km from Sodwana Bay, in the north of Maputaland, to Mapelane at the south end of Lake St Lucia. The area is gradually being consolidated as the Greater St Lucia Wetlands. The Convention on Wetlands of International Importance has listed St Lucia as having international conservation value. The region also satisfies the criteria for listing as a UNESCO World Heritage area.

The park protects five interconnected ecosystems – marine (coral reefs, beaches); shore (barrier between lake and sea); Mkuze reed and sedge swamps; the lake (the largest estuary in Africa); and western shores (fossil corals, sand forest, bushveld, grasslands).

At present, Lake St Lucia, its surrounds and the nearby ocean beaches are popular holiday destinations, and the area is made up of a number of parks and reserves: St Lucia Park, St Lucia Game Reserve, False Bay Park, Tewati Wilderness Area, Mfabeni Section, Ozabeni Section, Sodwana Bay National Park, Mapelane Nature Reserve

Greater St Lucia Wetlands & Hluhluwe-Umfolozi Park

1	Hilltop Lodge & Mtwazi Lodge
2	Muntulu
3	Munyawaneni
4	Thiyeni Waterhole
5	Sontuli
6	Gqoyeni
7	Mpila Camp
8	Nselwesi
9	Masinda Camp
10	Mndindini Tented Trails
11	Mphafa Waterhole

and the St Lucia and Maputaland marine reserves. To the south is Mhlatuze State Forest. The main population centres in the area are Mtubatuba and St Lucia resort.

All the parks and reserves are administered by the Natal Parks Board, but there is also private accommodation at St Lucia resort, which is a sizeable holiday village – evidenced by the fact that you can buy bait here 24 hours a day. There aren't too many places in South Africa where you can buy

food for *yourself* late at night, much less food for fish.

Remember that all non-camping accommodation run by the Natal Parks Board must be booked in Pietermaritzburg.

Warning

This is a malarial area, and there are plenty of mosquitoes. Ticks and leeches can also be a problem. You should also be aware of crocs and hippos – both potentially deadly. Be careful at night, as hippos roam. In more remote areas hippos might be encountered on shore during the day – treat them with respect and retreat quietly. Sharks sometimes venture up the estuary near St Lucia.

Hiking Trails

The main walks are the four-night, guided Wilderness Trail and the three-day Mziki Trail, both in the Cape Vidal area, and the Dugandlovu Trail in False Bay Park – see that section for details. There are also day walks, detailed in Natal Parks Board literature available at the St Lucia office.

Boat Tours

One of the highlights of a trip to the St Lucia Wetlands is the boat trip on the *Santa Lucia*. It leaves from the wharf on the west side of the bridge on the Mtubatuba road at 10.30 am and 12.30 pm daily (R24).

The slow-moving launch is a great platform from which to photograph and observe. The sparse commentary allows you to get on with watching – hippos, a lone crocodile, white and black mangroves, a hovering pied kingfisher, breeding fish eagles, a stalking goliath heron or nesting hadeda ibis.

Getting There & Away

Transtate services between Durban and northern KwaZulu/Natal stop at Mtubatuba, from where you'll have to hitch or hope for a minibus taxi to St Lucia. There aren't many. If you're heading for Charters Creek, some Transtate buses stop on the N2 at Nyalazi River, about 12 km away. For False Bay take the bus to Hluhluwe village.

St Lucia Resort

This is the main centre for the area, with Natal Parks Board's offices, shops, boat hire and other services, as well as a lot of private accommodation. In season it's a very busy place.

There is only one ATM in town, in the Dolphin supermarket. The First National and Standard banks are open on Monday, Wednesday and Friday from 9 am to noon.

About two km north of St Lucia on the road to Cape Vidal is the **Crocodile Centre** where there are displays on the ecosystems in the region and other information; entry is R5.50. At 13 McKenzie St is the excellent Vukani Association shop selling arts and crafts, especially basketware. It's open daily but during the week it's closed from 1 to 2 pm.

Tours Lanie Toere (☎ (035) 590 1259), next to the Dolphin supermarket, offers two good trips. The Mkizi Trail includes a two-km walk through dune forest to the Mfansana pans, and visits to hides and a beach cave (R25, 8 am to 3 pm). The Cape Vidal trip includes snorkelling, swimming and fishing (R45, also 8 am to 3 pm). Anglers can head out on the *San Jan* (☎ (035) 590 1257) for R150 per person per day.

Places to Stay There are three Natal Park Board camp sites (☎ (03592) ask for 20): *Sugarloaf*, *Eden Park* and *Iphiva*. Costs are R13 per person except in Sugarloaf, which has power points and costs R16 per person.

There is also a huge range of private accommodation, mainly in self-contained holiday apartments. Unfortunately real estate agents in town don't handle bookings so it's a matter of trudging around. The *Pelikaan Resort* (☎ (035) 590 1133), one of the cheaper places, is popular with anglers.

The *Sea Sands Holiday Flats* (☎ (035) 590 1082), 135 Hornbill St, has seven cottages at R30 per person (minimum R150) or R43 in season (minimum R215). The *Boma Hotel* (☎ (035) 590 1330) looks like it doesn't belong here, a pastiche of bad architectural styles overlooking a fabulous part of the estuary. But at certain times of the year the suites which sleep six people are really good value at R132 for one or two. The two-bed rooms at the front of the hotel are rather dingy and not good value at R75 for two.

Another good place is *St Lucia Wilds* (☎ (035) 590 1033), where apartments sleeping six cost from R25 per person out of season and from R150 for the whole apartment in the high season. To get there, head all the way down the main street but instead of following the tarred road around to the left, keep going straight on down the dirt road. St Lucia Wilds is at the end of this road.

On the main street near the centre of town is *Sandy Place Holiday Flats* (☎ (035) 590 1109), which is typical of the mid-range apartments. Low-season rooms are from R90 (or less) a double, and in the high season an apartment sleeping six costs from R200. A recommended B&B is *Maputaland Lodge*

(☎ (035) 590 1041), 1 Kabeljou St, for about R110 per person.

Places to Eat There are a few takeaways; the most popular is *Cocomo's*, well signposted off McKenzie St. On McKenzie St is *St Pizza (Pizza for U)* and a few other takeaway places. At *Roberto's Cabin*, also on McKenzie St and near the Spar supermarket, a dinner with wine is about R50 per person. You can get cheap meals in the bar at the *Boma Hotel* – a substantial curry and rice is R10 and other filling meals are up to R15. But avoid groups of package tourists inventing solutions for the new South Africa!

St Lucia Park & Game Reserve

St Lucia Game Reserve, which takes in the waterbody of the lake, the islands and Mapelane, is the oldest reserve in South Africa, having been declared in 1897. The park takes in a ribbon of land around the lake.

Lake St Lucia is in fact a large and meandering estuary (Africa's largest) with a narrow sea entrance, and its depth and salinity alter as a result of interdependent seasonal and ecological factors. It is mainly shallow and the warm water is crowded with fish, which in turn attract huge numbers of waterbirds. There are lots of pelicans and flamingoes, and fish eagles breed in the area. Frogs produce a din during the summer mating season. However, the area is best known as a crocodile and hippo reserve.

Places to Stay As well as the accommodation at St Lucia, the Natal Parks Board has two sites, more remote and much quieter; book these on ☎ (0331) 47 1981, fax 47 1980.

At *Charters Creek* there is a seven-bed cottage for R88 per person (minimum R352) and huts from R52 per person (minimum R104). There is a swimming pool. Entry to the reserve is R4 per person. Charters Creek is on the western shore of the lake's southern spit, and is accessible from a turn-off on the N2, 20 km north of Mtubatuba.

At the *Fanies Island* site, by the lake 11 km north of Charters Creek and reached by

the same road from the N2, there are camp sites for R13 per person and two-bed rest huts for R52 (minimum R78). There's a swimming pool too, and entry is R4 per person.

False Bay Park

False Bay Park runs along the western shore of Lake St Lucia; entry is R4 per person. As well as the lake's hippos and crocs, the park has several antelope species and other animals, including zebras and warthogs. There is prolific birdlife and a great variety of vegetation. There are walking trails, including the easy two-day, 17-km **Dugandlovu Hiking Trail** which hugs the lake and passes through *Acacia* and *Terminalia* woodlands. There are huts at the turnaround point (Dugandlovu Camp). Book this trail through the Natal Parks Board in Pietermaritzburg.

In the northern part of False Bay is the **Mpophomeni Trail**, divided into two routes suitable for families – the longer 10-km section takes about four to five hours, the shorter seven-km section, three hours.

Places to Stay There are camp sites for R13 per person. To book these, phone (03562), and ask for 2911. There are also rustic four-bed huts for R32 per person (minimum R64) on the Dugandlovu Trail, about nine km from the entrance gate; you can drive there.

Getting There & Away The main road into the park runs from Hluhluwe village, off the N2. Hluhluwe village is also the nearest place to buy fuel and other supplies.

Tewati Wilderness Area (Cape Vidal)

This wilderness area takes in the land between the lake and the ocean, north from Cape Vidal. Some of the forested sand dunes are 150 metres high. The Eastern Shores State Forest runs south from Cape Vidal to St Lucia, and is administered as part of the Cape Vidal State Forest; entry is R4 per person.

The Cape Vidal office is the starting place for the four-night **St Lucia Wilderness**

KWAZULU/NATAL

Trail, a guided walk costing R780 per person, including all equipment and meals (book with the Natal Parks Board in Pietermaritzburg). Walks are available only from April to September, and begin on Friday afternoon and end on Tuesday. The minimum number of people is four. There is a lot of wading involved, so bring spare shoes.

The 38-km, three-day **Mziki Trail** is in the Mfabeni section of St Lucia (formerly the Eastern Shores State Forest). The base camp for this trail is Mt Tabor, inland just north of Mission Rocks and accessible from the road running between St Lucia and Cape Vidal. Mt Tabor was a base for sub-spotting Catalina flying-boats during WW II, and the wreckage of one of the planes can be seen in the lake south-west of the camp.

The Mziki is actually three easy trails. Day 1 (10 km) is a walk south through dune forest and along the coastline; Day 2 (10 km) is west through indigenous forest to the freshwater Mfazana pan, along the shore of Lake St Lucia, then east over Mt Tabor; and Day 3 (18 km) descends into Bokkie Valley (named after the reedbuck or *mziki* there) and returns through dune forest and along some pristine coastline. You must book through Pietermaritzburg; the eight-bed trail hut is

R20 per person. The booklet *Mziki Trail* is available from the Natal Parks Board for R1. The trail is part of a system which will eventually link St Lucia with Cape Vidal.

Places to Stay In the *Bhangazi* complex there are camp sites for R13 per person (book on (03592) 1104), log cabins from R75 per person (minimum R225), dormitory cabins for R46 (minimum R368) and an eight-bed bush lodge for R105 (minimum R420).

Getting There & Away From St Lucia head north past the Crocodile Centre and through the entrance gates. Cape Vidal is about 30 km further on.

St Lucia & Maputaland Marine Reserves

Combined, these reserves cover the coastal strip and three nautical miles out to sea, running from Cape Vidal right up to Mozambique. The reserves include the world's most southerly coral reefs, especially around Sodwana Bay (itself a national park and covered later in this chapter), and nesting sites of leatherback and loggerhead turtles.

Mapelane Nature Reserve

South across the estuary from St Lucia, this

Marine Turtles

Five species of turtle occur off the South African coast but only two actually nest on the coast – leatherback *(Dermochelys coriacea)* and loggerhead *(Caretta caretta)* turtles. The nesting areas of the leatherback extend from the St Lucia mouth north into Mozambique but the loggerhead only nests in the Maputaland reserve.

Both species nest at night in summer. The female moves above the high-tide mark, finds a suitable site and lays her eggs. The loggerheads' breeding area is much greater as they clamber over rocks in the intertidal zone whereas the leatherbacks will only nest on sandy beaches. The hatchlings scramble out of the nest about 70 days later (at night) and make a dash for the sea. Only one or two of each thousand hatchlings survive to maturity. The females return from 12 to 15 years later to the same beach to nest.

The Natal Parks Board has night turtle tours in December and January. The cost is R36 for adults (R12 for children) for those in park vehicles, R12 per adult in their own vehicle. ∎

popular fishing spot will probably become the major visitors' centre for Mhlatuze State Forest when that area is developed for recreational use. The dense bush around the camp is flanked by a giant dune, the Mjakaja.

Camp sites are R13 per person (book on ☎ (0331) 47 1981), five-bed cabins cost R75 per person (minimum R225); entry to Mapelane is R4 per person.

Although it's across the estuary from St Lucia, travel between the two centres is circuitous unless you have a boat. Mapelane is reached by 40 km of sandy and sometimes tricky road from KwaMbonambi, off the N2 south of Mtubatuba. Follow the Kwa-Mbonambi Lighthouse sign.

SODWANA BAY

When a group of travellers debate the best spots in South Africa, Sodwana Bay is invariably mentioned. Its appeal is in its isolation, the accessibility of the world's most southerly coral reef, walking trails, fishing and magic coastal scenery.

The small **Sodwana Bay National Park** (☎ (035682) 1502) is on the coast east of Mkuze. There are some animals and the dunes and swamps are worth visiting, as well as the off-shore coral reefs, but the area packs out during holidays and things get noisy and crowded. Over Christmas there are turtle-viewing tours.

For a more peaceful look at a similar ecosystem, head south to the adjoining Sodwana State Forest, now called **Ozabeni**, which runs all the way down to Lake St Lucia. North of the lake is a prohibited area. Bird-watchers will go wild, as over 330 species have been recorded. The Natal Parks Board is creating a reserve in the forest, and there will be a camp site.

Places to Stay

There is Natal Parks Board accommodation at Sodwana Bay, with cabins from R75 per person (minimum R225) and camp sites for R13. Book early on (035682) 1502. There is a shop in the resort and fuel is available; entry is R4 per person. *Sodwana Bay Lodge* (☎ (031) 2304 5977, fax 304 8817) is a private resort with dinner, bed and breakfast singles/doubles for R245/398 (see the note on Snorkelling & Diving in this section).

In Ozabeni (☎ (035682) 2302), part of the Greater St Lucia Wetlands Park, open camp sites are R6; entry to Ozabeni is R4 per person and R15 per vehicle.

TONGALAND

The area north of Hluhluwe running up to the Mozambique border was once known as Tongaland, as it was settled by the Tonga people of Mozambique. It's a distinct ecological region and the only part of South Africa to lie east of the Lebombo range, the southern tail of which, known as the Ubombo, peters out near Mkuze. The soil of this flat, hot region is sandy and the sluggish

---

Snorkelling & Diving

The coastline near Sodwana Bay, which includes the southernmost coral reefs in Africa, is a diver's paradise. Schools of fish glide through the beautiful coral, turtles swim by, and moray eels peer inquisitively from rock crevices. Predominantly soft coral over hard, the reef has one of the world's highest recorded numbers of tropical fish species. All of these wonders can be seen using scuba or snorkelling equipment, and excellent visibility and warm winter waters allow for diving year round.

Popular snorkelling spots are Cape Vidal, Two-Mile Reef off Sodwana Bay, Mabibi and the Kosi Mouth with its famous 'aquarium', so named because of the diversity of fish. Scuba users should head for Tenedos Shoal, between the Mlalazi River and Port Durnford, and Five, Seven and Nine-Mile reefs. Courses are conducted at Two-Mile Reef.

The Sodwana Bay Lodge specialises in diving packages (it has NAUI instructors). A four-night, six-dive package is R940 per person (twin share), or R1080 a single. A five-night, seven-dive package is R1100 sharing, R1270 a single. ■

rivers harbour crocodiles and hippos. Inland there are forests of huge figs, especially along the Pongola River, and nearer the coast, palms grow among the salt pans and thornveld.

There has been little development and there are some good game reserves. One of the most common creatures is the mosquito, so take precautions against malaria.

Mkuze

Mkuze, a small town on the N2 and the Mkuze River, is west of a pass over the Lebombo range. The road through the pass is one route to Sodwana Bay. **Ghost Mountain**, south of the town, was an important burial place for the Ndwandwe tribe and has a reputation for eerie occurrences, usually confined to strange lights and noises. The human bones which are sometimes found near Ghost Mountain date from a big battle between rival Zulu factions in 1884.

The *Ghost Mountain Inn* (☎ (035) 573 1025) is a nice place with singles/doubles from R197/330 with breakfast and dinner, or R145/250 with common bathroom.

Transtate buses run at least daily down the N2 to Durban (about seven hours), north to Golela (1¼ hours) and Pongola (two hours), and to KwaNgwanase (three hours), beyond Jozini and near Kosi Bay. There is also a service to Jo'burg via Piet Retief which departs on Wednesday and Sunday.

Mkuzi Game Reserve

Established in 1912, this 36,000-hectare Natal Parks Board reserve lacks lions and elephants but just about every other sought-after animal is represented, as well as over 400 species of birds (including the rare Pel's fishing owl, *Scotopelia peli*).

Better still, the reserve has hides at pans and water holes which offer some of the best wildlife viewing in the country. The walk to Nsumu pan features two birdwatching hides, and there are six game-viewing hides, the most notable being Bube and Masinga. Morning is the best time.

Nestled below the Ubombo Range, the country is partly dense thornveld, partly open savanna and gets very hot in summer although winters are generally mild.

There's an entry fee of R4 per person and R15 per vehicle and the reserve is open daily between sunrise and sunset. It's possible to arrange guided walks, and there are night drives for R36 per person. Between April and October there are twice-monthly three-day hikes through the reserve, similar to Umfolozi's Wilderness Trails (R600 per person). Contact the Natal Parks Board for more information.

From the north you can get here from Mkuze town; from the south, turn off the N2, 35 km north of Hluhluwe village. Fuel is sold at the main gate.

Places to Stay Self-contained cottages cost from R88 per person (minimum R352) and bungalows from R83 per person, and huts are R58 per person (R116 minimum). There's a pool. There is a tented bush lodge, *Umkumbi*, at R65 per person and a bush lodge, *Nhlonhlela*, with all facilities for R420 for eight people. There's also a camp site at the entrance gate which costs R13 per person. To book camp sites, phone 0020 and ask for Mkuze No 12.

Phinda Resource Reserve

This 17,000-hectare reserve, very much an 'eco-tourism' showpiece, is to the north-west of Lake St Lucia, just off the N2 east of Mhlosinga. It was set up by The Conservation Corporation, the chain that runs Ngala and Londolozi reserves in the Transvaal.

There are nine different ecosystems in the park. They include hilly terrain, sand forest, riverine woodland, natural pans, open savanna grasslands. This diversity attracts a great variety of birdlife (over 360 species) as well as promoting a diverse range of plant life. There are about 10,000 head of game, many reintroduced, including nyala and the rare suni antelope *(Neotragus moschatus)*. Lion and cheetah kills can occasionally be seen and leopards are now seen during game drives.

In addition to the game drives there are

accompanied walks, canoeing and riverboat cruises.

There are three types of accommodation – rock chalets, bush suites *(Forest Lodge)* in the sand forest and a luxurious main lodge *(Phinda Nyala)* with views to the Ubombo Range and the coastal plain; phone ☎ (035) 562 0271 for information. The only problem with Phinda is that all the 'eco'-pluses don't come cheap; the quoted rate is R550 per person for full board, activities included.

Pongola

Pongola is a tiny town in a sugar-growing district near the Eastern Transvaal border.

The inexpensive municipal *caravan park* (☎ (03841) 31233) is in the centre of town; it's basic but green and shaded. Across the street the *Pongola Hotel* (☎ (03841) 31352) has rooms from about R100/120 with a good breakfast – make sure you know which standard of room you're paying for. The public bar is a lively place where you can meet local farm workers.

Jozini

This small business centre, the gateway to northern Maputaland, is close to the **Pongolapoort Dam**. The dam is used to irrigate agricultural land which grows sugar cane, coffee and rice. The drive from the N2 up the hill to Jozini affords great views of the lake and of the Ubombo Range. The *Jozini Motel* (☎ (035672), ask for 81) is the only accommodation in town.

Ndumu Game Reserve

Right on the Mozambique border and close to the Swaziland border, about 100 km north of Mkuze, this reserve of 10,000 hectares is looked after by the KwaZulu Department of Nature Conservation (KDNC) (☎ (0331) 94 6696) in Pietermaritzburg. The KDNC also administers the Coastal Forest Reserve. Ndumu has black and white rhinos, hippos, crocs and antelope species, but it is the birdlife on the Pongolo and Usutu rivers and their flood plains and pans which attracts visitors.

Guided walks (one for game viewing, two

for birdwatching, one for trees) and vehicle tours are available. This is the southernmost limit of the range of many bird species and the reserve is a favourite of birdwatchers, with over 400 species having been recorded – watch for the southern banded snake eagle *(Circaetus fasciolatus)*, yellow-spotted nicator *(Nicator gularis)* and the green-capped eremomela *(Eremomela scotops)*.

Fuel and limited supplies are usually available two km outside the park gate. You can't camp at the reserve; accommodation is in three-bed cottages near the Pongola River and there are cooking facilities.

The daily Transtate bus which runs to KwaNgwanase sometimes goes via Ndumo village, five km from the park entrance – check with the driver.

Tembe Elephant Park

South Africa's last free-ranging elephants are protected in the sandveld forests of this park on the Mozambique border. There are now about 100 elephants in the area, many of them the last remnants of the Maputo elephants saved from Mozambique's civil war. There are also white rhinos and leopards.

You can't walk or drive yourself through the park; you must take a pre-booked tour, and accommodation is currently limited to eight people. Check with the KDNC (☎ (0331) 94 6696) in Pietermaritzburg for further developments.

COASTAL FOREST RESERVE

This reserve stretches from Mozambique in the north to Sodwana Bay in the south, and includes Lake Sibaya, Kosi Bay, Bhanga Nek, Black Rock, Rocktail Bay, Manzengwenya, Mabibi and Nine-Mile Beach. The reserve is administered by the KDNC.

Lake Sibaya

The largest freshwater lake in South Africa, covering between 60 and 70 sq km depending on the water level, is in **Lake Sibaya Nature Reserve**. It lies very close to the coast, and between the eastern shore and the sea there is a range of sand dunes up to 165 metres high. There are hippos, some crocs and a large range of birds (over 280 species have been recorded). The lake is popular for fishing – you can hire boats (complete with skipper) for fishing trips.

There is accommodation in cabins at *Baya Camp*, on the south side of the lake. You must bring your own food but there are cooks to prepare it if you want. Book accommodation through the KDNC (☎ (0331) 94 6696) in Pietermaritzburg.

The main route here is via the village of Mbazwana, south of the lake, either from Mkuze or from Mhlosinga, off the N2 north of Hluhluwe village.

Kosi Bay Nature Reserve

Kosi Bay, like Sodwana, is another place listed among the 10 best South African destinations by travellers. On the coast near the Mozambique border, this remote reserve encompasses fig and raffia palm forests, mangrove swamps, sand dunes and fresh-water lakes (the 'bay' is in fact a string of four lakes – Nhlange, Mpungwini, Sifungwe and Amanzimnyama). There are pristine beaches that are usually deserted, and a coral reef with great snorkelling.

There are antelope species in the drier country and hippos, Zambezi sharks and some crocs in the lake system. There are over 250 bird species, including the rare palmnut vulture. The research station here studies the local population of leatherback turtles; during the nesting season there are turtle-viewing tours.

Canoes are available for hire. You can arrange a four-night guided walk around the Kosi estuarine system, stopping each night in remote camps which focus on different aspects of the reserve. These trails include a walk to the Kosi Mouth.

Because the ecosystems here are in such delicate balance the number of visitors is limited; to enter the reserve you need a permit from the KDNC. Only five permits a day are issued for visits to Kosi Mouth and a 4WD vehicle is needed. Beach driving is only permitted from Sodwana Bay to Nine-Mile Beach and 20 permits are issued each

day to allow drivers to continue past Nine-Mile to the boom gate before Mabibi. Permits and accommodation bookings are available from KDNC in Pietermaritzburg (☎ (0331) 94 6696).

Accommodation is in camp sites such as *Mabibi* or in the *Rocktail Bay Lodge*, a coastal camp. The lodge was built so that it blended into the coastal forest canopy – large trees provide shade, and beds are at canopy level.

On the road to the reserve is the small settlement of KwaNgwanase, where you can buy supplies and fuel.

Getting There & Away To get there, take the Jozini turn-off from the N2 and head towards Ndumu Game Reserve, but turn hard right (east) just before Ndumo village. Most of the road is sealed but you might still encounter deep sand – you might need a 4WD. A daily Transtate bus runs from Durban to Kwa-Ngwanase, west of the reserve.

Northern Zululand

This section covers the region north of Ulundi and west of the N2. Although it is a large area, it is not as diverse as the coastal region of Zululand. It does, however contain two spectacular natural areas, Itala Game Reserve and the Ntendeka Wilderness Area. The main towns are Louwsburg, Nongoma, Vryheid and Paulpietersburg.

NTENDEKA WILDERNESS AREA

This is a truly beautiful and tranquil area of grassland and indigenous coastal and inland tropical forest, with some dramatic dolerite and sandstone cliffs (*Ntendeka* means 'place of precipitous heights'). More than 180 tree, 60 fern and 190 bird species have been recorded. The rare Ngoye red squirrel is found in the forest. Rare birds such as the blue swallow (*Hirundo atrocaerulea*) and cuckoo hawk (*Aviceda cuculoides*) can also be spotted. The wilderness area is bordered by **Ngome State Forest**, a good example of inland tropical forest.

This is an important region in Zulu history, and Cetshwayo was once holed up here – his rock-shelter refuge is in the north-eastern corner of the park. Another famous figure to hide out here was Mzilikazi, one of Shaka's disloyal generals. Mzilikazi was eventually chased north, where his descendants established the Ndebele tribe in modern-day Zimbabwe.

There are walking trails, but you can't drive through the wilderness area. There's a camp site with ablution facilities on the north-eastern edge of the park, the only place in the wilderness where you can camp. Phone (0386) 71883 or call at the Ngome Forest Station, south off the R618 just past the south-eastern corner of the wilderness area, to see if permits are still necessary.

The nearest town is Nongoma (which is an important trading town but has no facilities for visitors), about 60 km north-east of Ulundi, with 50 km of unsealed road. Alternatively, get to Ntendeka by travelling south from Vryheid on the R618 for about 70 km, or south from Pongola on the R66, then north-west on the R618.

VRYHEID

Vryheid ('liberty') is the largest town in north-eastern KwaZulu/Natal. The Nieuwe Republiek was established here in 1884, to be absorbed into the ZAR four years later. After the Anglo-Boer War, the area was transferred to Natal. There are Anglo-Boer War sites; for guided tours of the battlefields phone ☎ (0386) 71957. Now Vryheid is an agricultural and coal-mining centre.

The information bureau (☎ (0381) 81 2133) is on the corner of Market and High Sts. There are three **museums** in town. One, devoted to the short-lived Nieuwe Republiek, is in the Old Raadsaal building on Landdrost St. South of Kerk St, the main street, is a small museum of local history in the old Lucas Meijer House (Meijer was the only president of the Niuewe Republiek). The other is in the old Carnegie library.

Just north of town, the **Vryheid Nature Reserve** has zebra and antelope species and there's a bird hide next to a salt pan.

Places to Stay

The municipal *caravan park* (☎ (0381) 81 2133) is not far from both the town's centre and the railway station. The *Klipfontein Resort* (☎ (0381) 4383) is a centre for fishing and watersports. Entry is R4 per person and there are basic camp sites for R13 per person. Take the Melmoth road, the R34, south from Vryheid for about five km.

Vryheid Lodge (☎ (0381) 5201) charges R60 per person. The *Stilwater Protea Hotel* (☎ (0381) 6181), six km out of town on the Dundee road, is R170/210, with breakfast.

Tendele Lodge (☎ (0386) 71667) is a B&B place on a farm about 18 km from town. The tariff is R120 per person. If you want to stay with a family of German descent in Vryheid or the nearby area (there are many), contact Building Bridges – German Guest Homes (☎ (0381) 80 8644), 106 Deputasie St.

Magdalena (☎ (0386) 71865) is near the Msihlengeni Waterfall and has lodge beds from R80 per person and a bush camp from R60. Ring for directions.

Getting There & Away

Transtate services run twice a week in both directions from Welkom to Nongoma via Vryheid , facilitating connections with many other Transtate services.

The long-distance taxi rank is near the railway station. Vryheid is the hub for minibus taxis in this part of KwaZulu/Natal. Some destinations and fares are Dundee R10, Pongola R12, Nongoma R14, Ulundi R14, Eshowe R23, Melmoth R22, Stanger R30, Durban (via Melmoth) R35 and Jo'-burg R40.

Avis (☎ (0381) 80 9601) and Imperial (☎ (0381) 5438) have agents here.

ITALA GAME RESERVE

The Natal Parks Board's Itala now has all the trappings of a private game reserve but has lower prices, if a little higher than those in other Parks Board reserves. Most of the 30,000 hectares is taken up by the steep valleys of six rivers (tributaries of the Pongola), with some open grassland on the heights, rugged outcrops and about 25% bushveld.

Animals, mostly reintroduced, include black and white rhinos, elephants, tsessebes (the only herd in KwaZulu/Natal), nyala, hyenas, buffaloes, baboons, leopards and cheetahs. There over 75 mammal species in the park, plus crocodiles and 100 or so other species of amphibians and reptiles; and 20 species of indigenous fish. The diverse habitats support over 320 species of birds, including the endangered southern bald ibis (*Geronticus calvus*).

As well as self-drive excursions there are wilderness trails, available from March to October. The four-night trail costs R425 per person excluding food.

Places to Stay

Ntshondwe is the main centre, with superb views of the reserve below. There's a restaurant and a shop here, as well as a swimming pool. Chalets cost R107 per person, with a minimum of R161 in two-bed, R321 in four-bed and R428 in six-bed chalets. There's also a luxury lodge sleeping six, for R140 per person (minimum R560). Two-bed units with shared facilities are R96 (minimum R120). There are basic camp sites near Thalu Bush Camp for R6 per person. Book these on ☎ (0331) 47 1981.

There are three bush camps, offering privacy and proximity to wildlife but without the luxuries of the main camp. *Thalu*, on the Thulu River, has a double and two singles and costs R264 per night. *Mbizo*, on the Mbizo River, sleeps eight people and costs R88 per person (minimum R352). *Mhlangeni* overlooks the Ncence River, sleeps 10 people and costs R105 per person (R420 minimum).

In the nearby town of Louwsburg there are three small lodges – *Gwala Gwala* (☎ (0388) 75417), *Jacaranda* (☎ (0388) 75200) and *Umdoni* (☎ (0388) 75318).

Getting There & Away

Itala is entered from Louwsburg, about 65 km east of Vryheid on the R69, and about the same distance south-west of Pongola via the R66 and the R69. Transtate buses run through Vryheid and Pongola. Louwsburg is much smaller than many maps indicate.

PAULPIETERSBURG

This town is a centre for timber and agricultural production. It gets its name from Paul Kruger and Pieter Joubert. The information bureau (☎ (038) 995 1729) has information on the town and surrounds. Outside town is the Natal Spa (☎ (038) 995 1630), where you can lie back in the warm or cold mineral pools.

This region has many descendants of the original German settlers from the Hermannsburg Missionary Society established in 1848. The main German towns are Gluckstadt, Braunschweig and Luneberg.

The Natal Drakensberg

The awesome Drakensberg is a mountainous basalt escarpment forming the border between KwaZulu/Natal and Lesotho, and continuing a little way into the Orange Free State. The escarpment continues north, less spectacularly, before rearing up again in Eastern Transvaal's Klein Drakensberg.

'Drakensberg' means Dragon mountains; the Zulu named it *Quathlamba* (Battlement of Spears). The Zulu word is a more accurate description of the sheer and jagged escarpment, but the Afrikaans name captures something of the Drakensberg's otherworldly atmosphere. Although people have lived here for thousands of years – there are many San rock painting sites – some of the peaks and rocks were first climbed by Europeans less than 50 years ago.

The San, already under pressure from the tribes who had moved into the Drakensberg foothills, were finally destroyed with the coming of white settlers. Some moved into Lesotho where they were absorbed into the Basotho population, but many were killed or simply starved when their hunting-grounds were occupied by others. Khoisan cattle raids annoyed the white settlers to the extent that the settlers forced several black tribes to

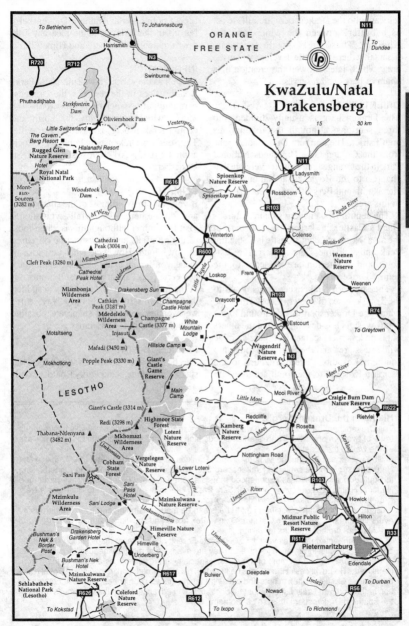

relocate into the Drakensberg foothills to act as a buffer between the whites and the Khoisan. These early 'bantu locations' meant that there was little development in the area, which later allowed the creation of a chain of parks and reserves.

ORIENTATION

The Drakensberg is usually divided into three sections, although the distinctions aren't strict. The northern Drakensberg runs from the Golden Gate Highlands National Park in the Orange Free State (covered in that chapter) to the Royal Natal National Park. Harrismith and Bergville are sizeable towns in this area.

The central Drakensberg's main feature is Giant's Castle, the largest national park in the area. North of Giant's Castle is Cathedral Peak and wilderness areas. Bergville, Estcourt and Winterton are adjacent to the central Drakensberg.

The southern Drakensberg runs down to the Transkei area of Eastern Cape. This area, where the Drakensberg bends around to the south-west, is less developed than the others but is no less spectacular. Here there's a huge wilderness area and the Sani Pass route into southern Lesotho. Pietermaritzburg to the east and Kokstad to the south are the main

access points to the southern Drakensberg, but up in the hills are some pleasant little towns, notably Underberg and Himeville.

INFORMATION

As well as the various KwaZulu/Natal Parks Board offices in the reserves, the Drakensberg Publicity Association (☎/fax (036) 448 1557), which covers only the north and central Drakensberg, is based in Bergville. The Southern Drakensberg Publicity Association (☎ (033) 701 1096) is on Main St, Underberg.

CLIMATE

If you want to avoid most of the sharp frosts and, on the heights, snowfalls, you should visit in summer, although this is when most of the rain falls and views can be obscured by low cloud. However, what you lose in vistas you'll gain in atmosphere, as the stark and eerie peaks are at their best looming out of the mist. Much of the rain falls in sudden thunderstorms so you should always carry wet-weather gear. Cold snaps are possible even in the middle of summer.

PLACES TO STAY

The best way to see the Drakensberg is to stay at one of the Natal Parks Board's excel-

---

Hiking in the Drakensberg

The Drakensberg has some superb walks and hikes, ranging from gentle day walks to strenuous treks of two or more days. There's an ambitious plan to create a trail from the top of Sani Pass all the way to the coast.

The wilderness trails in the Mkhomazi and Mzimkulu wilderness areas and the Mzimkulwana Nature Reserve in the southern Drakensberg offer some of the most remote and rugged hiking in South Africa. For the less experienced there's also the five-day Giant's Cup Trail, part of the National Hiking Way, running from near Sani Pass Hotel in the north down to Bushman's Nek. (See the Southern Drakensberg Wilderness Areas section for more information.)

Summer hiking on the less frequented trails can be made frustrating and even dangerous by rivers flooded by sudden torrential storms; in winter, frosts and snow are the main hazards. April and May are the best months for hiking.

Make sure you get the relevant 1:50,000-scale Forestry Department maps, which show trails and have essential information for hikers. They are available at most trailheads.

Permits are needed on most of the hikes, especially in the wilderness areas; get them from Natal Parks Board offices at the various trailheads. Trail accommodation, especially in Royal Natal and Giant's Castle, is often in huts and caves (meaning that you don't need a tent). Accommodation in the northern Drakensberg must be booked well in advance, but in the wilderness areas of the southern Drakensberg, this isn't a problem. ∎

lent reserves. The biggest and most popular are Royal Natal and Giant's Castle, but accommodation and camp sites can also be found in the state forests and other reserves. Free camping is allowed in most designated Wilderness Areas, but check in at the Parks Board or Forestry office; there's a small fee.

Usually more expensive than the Parks Board's accommodation are the private resorts which dot the foothills near Royal Natal and Giant's Castle. Places to stay in the southern Drakensberg are covered under the towns following the parks' entries.

GETTING THERE & AWAY

There is little public transport in the northern and central Drakensberg, although there is a lot of tourist traffic; and with so many resorts all needing staff there are some minibus taxis. The main jumping-off points are on or near the N3. See the sections on Estcourt, Mooi River, Winterton and Bergville for details. In the southern Drakensberg it is a little easier, as Transtate buses run to Underberg from Kokstad and Pietermaritzburg. See those towns for details.

Sani Pass is the best-known Drakensberg route into Lesotho. There are other passes over the escarpment, but most don't connect with anything in Lesotho larger than a walking track (if that) a long way from anywhere.

Many of the roads in the Drakensberg area are unsealed and after rain some are impassable, but it's usually possible to find an alternative route. Tourist routes in the northern and central Drakensberg are indicated by brown signs with a lammergeyer symbol.

ROYAL NATAL NATIONAL PARK

Although it is only a little over 8000 hectares in extent, Royal Natal has some of the Drakensberg's most dramatic and accessible scenery. The southern boundary of the national park is formed by the Amphitheatre, an eight-km stretch of cliff which is spectacular from below and even more so from the top. Here the Tugela Falls drop 850 metres in five stages (the top one often freezes in winter). Looming up behind is Mont-aux-

Sources, so called because the Tugela, Elands and Western Khubedu rivers rise here – the latter eventually becomes the Orange and flows all the way to the Atlantic.

Other notable peaks in the area are Devil's Tooth, the Eastern Buttress and the Sentinel. The Rugged Glen Nature Reserve adjoins the park on the north-eastern side.

The park's big visitor centre is a km or so in from the main gate. There's a bookshop here where you can pick up a copy of the Natal Parks Board's excellent booklet *Royal Natal National Park* for more detailed information, including descriptions of walks and a handy sketch map. The Board also produces a good 1:20,000 topographical map, *Mont-aux-Sources*. Entry to the park is R4 per person, which is astoundingly good value. Fuel is available in the park.

Flora & Fauna

With plentiful water, a range of more than 1500 metres in altitude and distinct areas such as plateaux, cliffs and valleys, it isn't surprising that the park's flora is extremely varied. Broadly speaking, though, much of the park is covered in grassland, with protea

Protea mimetes hottentoticus

savanna at lower altitudes. Grassland depends on fire for reproduction and to discourage other vegetation. In areas which escape the park's periodic fires scrub takes over. At lower levels, but confined to valleys, are small yellowwood forests. At higher altitudes grass yields to heath and scrub.

Royal Natal is not as rich in wildlife as Giant's Castle and other sections of the Drakensberg, but there is still quite a lot to be seen. Of the half-dozen species of antelope, the most common is the mountain reedbuck. Hyraxes are everywhere, as are hares, and you'll probably meet some baboons. Most other species in the reserve are shy and not often seen. They include otters, jackals and mongooses. More than 200 species of birds have been recorded.

Rock Paintings
There are several San rock painting sites, although Royal Natal's are fewer and not as well preserved than Giant's Castle, because the latter has many more rock shelters and caves – and has suffered less from vandalism. The notable sites are Sigubudu Shelter, north of the road just past the main gate; and Cannibal Caves, on Surprise Ridge, outside the park's northern boundary.

Hiking Trails
Except for the walk to Mont-aux-Sources, all of the 30-odd walks are day walks. Only 50 day visitors and 50 overnighters are allowed on **Mont-aux-Sources** each day. There are two ways to approach the summit. The easiest way is to drive to the Sentinel car park on the road from Phuthaditjhaba in QwaQwa (see the QwaQwa section in the Orange Free State chapter). By doing this it's possible to get to the summit and back in a day. Otherwise, having completed the mountain register at the visitor centre, you walk up to Basotho Gate then take the road to Sentinel car park.

If you plan to camp on the mountain you should book with QwaQwa Tourism & Nature Conservation (☎ (058) 713 4444, fax 713 4342) in Phuthaditjhaba. Otherwise there's a basic mountain hut on the escarpment near Tugela Falls. Unlike other Natal Parks Board accommodation you don't need to book (except for registering before walking here) and there's no fee for the hut.

Horse-Riding
Rides cost R20 per hour on a Natal Parks Board horse or R15 on your own horse.

Taming the Dragons
The mountains of South Africa don't stand as a single, solid range like the European Alps. They are a series of ranges, each imbued with its own particular character. The most majestic of the ranges is the Drakensberg, stretching from the eastern Cape to the Transvaal. The Natal Drakensberg were the last of the 'dragons' to be tamed, as most activity had concentrated on peaks near Cape Town – the Mountain Club was formed there in 1891.

In 1888, the Reverend A Stocker, a member of the Alpine Club, was the first to climb Champagne Castle (3375 metres) and Sterkhorn Peak. He attempted Cathkin Peak (3167 metres) but it was not climbed until 1912 when a group which included a black guide, Melatu, scaled it. Cathedral Peak (3004 metres) was conquered in 1917 by two climbers, R Kingdon and D Bassett-Smith.

The next intensive period of climbing was in the 1940s. Dick Barry had attempted the Monk's Cowl (3234 metres) in 1938, but was killed doing so. In 1942 a group led by Hans Wongtschowski scaled its basalt faces. Two years later, Hans and his wife Elsa clawed up the seemingly impregnable Bell (2991 metres).

The region's great challenge was the Devil's Tooth (3022 metres) and, after several attempts, this was climbed in 1950. Shortly after it was surveyed, in 1954, Thabana-Ntlenyana ('little black mountain'), at 3482 metres southern Africa's highest peak, was climbed as a relatively simple excursion. ■

Climbing

As some of the peaks and faces were first climbed by mountaineers only about 50 years ago, the park is a mecca for climbers. You must apply for a permit from the office before you attempt a climb: unless you are experienced, it might not be granted. Take your passport if you plan to venture into Lesotho.

Places to Stay

The main camp is *Tendele*, where there are six-bed cottages for R88 (minimum R352), two-bed and four-bed bungalows for R83 (minimum R124, R249) and two-bed and four-bed chalets for R80 (minimum R120, R240). At *Mahai* there's a camp site costing R13 (R16 with power) per person, and at Rugged Glen Nature Reserve, on the north-eastern edge of the park, there's a camp site for the same price. Book either site on ☎ (0364) 38 1803. An overnight hiking permit costs R6.

Also in the reserve, near the visitor centre, is the *Royal Natal National Park Hotel* (☎ (036) 438 6200, fax 438 6101) with single/double rooms for about R175/350 (children R100), including all meals.

Outside the Park Just off the R74, near Oliviershoek Pass, *Little Switzerland* (☎/fax (0364) 438 6220) is a large place with self-catering chalets sleeping four for about R400 in the high season, much less in the low season. Single/double hotel-style rooms cost from R125/170 in the low season and buffet meals are about R35 per person. The rugged scenery around here is impressive, but the escarpment is some way off. Little Switzerland will collect you from Swinburne, on the N3 near Harrismith, where Translux buses stop.

Off the road into Royal Natal from the R74, *Hlalanathi Berg Resort* (☎ (036) 438 6308) has camp sites for R25/40 in the low/high season, and chalets from R110 a double in the low season. There is a small shop at the resort entrance. Nearby, the slick, impersonal *Mont-aux-Sources Hotel* (☎/fax

(036) 438 6230) has five-night specials for R430/538 per person sharing.

About 10 km north of Hlalanathi, the family-oriented *Cavern Berg Resort* (☎ (036) 438 6270, fax 438 6334) offers horse-riding and walks. Single/double rooms with all meals cost from R135/245. 'Smart' dress is required in the evening.

Getting There & Away

The only road into Royal Natal runs off the R74, about 30-km north of Bergville and about five km from Oliviershoek Pass, but see the previous Hiking Trails section for information on a route to Mont-aux-Sources.

BERGVILLE

This small town is a handy jumping-off point for both the northern Drakensberg and the Midlands – if you have a car. On the third Friday of each month there are local cattle sales and the sleepy town takes on an altogether different atmosphere.

In the courthouse grounds is the **Upper Tugela Blockhouse**, built by the British during the Anglo-Boer War.

Places to Stay & Eat

In town, *Hotel Walter* (☎ (036) 448 1022) has reasonable single/double rooms for R60/110. A few km out of Bergville off the R616 to Ladysmith, *Sanford Park Lodge* (☎ (036) 448 1001, fax 448 1047) has good rooms in thatched rondavels or in a big 150-year-old farmhouse from about R150/270, including all meals. It also has Pete's Pub where you can relax after a day of exploring.

Off the Bergville to Harrismith road, at Jagersrust, the relaxing *Drakensville Resort* (☎ (036) 438 6287, fax 438 6524) is a big place, with 70 three-bedroom homes. On weekdays in the low season a house sleeping six people costs just R70 and on weekends, it's R140. You must provide your own linen. You can camp here for R20/45 a double in the low/high season.

Getting There & Away

None of the long-distance buses runs very close to Bergville. You'll probably have to get to Ladysmith and take a minibus taxi from there. The Translux service from Durban to Bloemfontein stops at both Montrose (at the Shell Ultra on the N3 near Swinburne) and Ladysmith. Translux's Jo'burg/Pretoria-Umtata and Jo'burg/Pretoria-Durban services also stop at Montrose. The daily Greyhound bus stops at both Swinburne in the Montrose bus service area and Estcourt. Durban to Swinburne is R90.

Minibus taxis are about the only public transport in the area. The taxi park is behind the Score supermarket. Destinations and fares include: Ladysmith R8, Winterton R4.50, Harrismith R9 and Durban R25. Taxis run into the Royal Natal National Park area for about R6.50 but few run all the way to the park entrance. Occasional taxis run to other places in the Drakensberg foothills, but the number of hitchhikers in this area is a sign that taxis are infrequent.

CENTRAL BERG

In some ways the Central Berg is the most attractive part of the range. Some of the most challenging climbs of the Drakensberg – Cathkin Peak (3181 metres), the Monk's Cowl (3234 metres) and Champagne Castle (3377 metres) – are found here. The central region also includes the grand Giant's Castle Peak. Midway between Cathedral and Cathkin peaks is Ndedema Gorge, where there are some fine San rock paintings.

The area between Cathedral Peak and Giant's Castle, in the Central Berg, comprises two wilderness areas, Mlambonja and Mdedelelo (together some 35,000 hectares). Both are administered by the Natal Parks Board.

Grey rheboks, klipspringers and mountain reedbucks occur naturally in the area. And so do boys with extremely high voices. Just off the Dragon Peaks road is the Drakensberg Boys' Choir School (☎ (036) 468 1012). There are public performances on Wednesday and Saturday at 4 pm.

Cathedral Peak State Forest

Cathedral Peak (3004 metres) lies between Royal Natal and Giant's Castle, west of Winterton. It's part of a small chain of peaks which jut out east of the main escarpment. The others, challenging for climbers, include the Bell, the Horns, the Pyramid and Needles. Cathedral Peak is a long day's climb (a trail begins near the hotel), but other than being fit no special ability or equipment is required.

Places to Stay The Natal Parks Board has 12 camp sites. The *Cathedral Peak Hotel* (☎/fax (036) 488 1888), some 42 km from Winterton, is close to the escarpment, near Cathedral Peak. Singles/doubles cost from R200/300 including meals. The hotel will collect from Estcourt.

The forest office, where you can book camp sites (R13) and overnight hiking (R6), is off the road running west from Winterton, near the Cathedral Peak Hotel; entry to the state forest is R4 per person. Also near here is the road to Mike's Pass, where there are good views. There's a fee of R10 per vehicle to drive up Mike's Pass.

Monk's Cowl State Forest (Champagne Castle)

The forest office is three km beyond the Champagne Castle Hotel, which is at the end of the R600 running south-west from Winterton. Entry, camping and hiking fees are the same as for Cathedral Peak State Forest.

If you're driving into this area don't get carried away by the good road; there are a couple of very steep sections and a nightmarish hairpin with reverse camber and a long drop.

Places to Stay & Eat As well as camping in the state forest there are some other options.

Dragon Peaks Park (☎ (036) 46 81031, fax 468 1104) is a Club Caraville resort with the usual maze of prices and minimum stays depending on seasons and school holidays. Camp sites range between R40 and R80 a double, cottages between R75 and R130 per person sharing. Not far away is Bell Park Dam, where you can water-ski for R25 or try paragliding for R35.

Cayley Guest Lodge (☎/fax (036) 468 1222) charges R140 per person, including meals. *Champagne Castle* (☎/fax (036) 468 1063) is one of the best-known resorts and it's well located, right in the mountains at the end of the road to Champagne Castle peak. There are cottages, rondavels and units, costing from R185 per person in the low season, with meals – good value. The hotel will collect you from Estcourt (a Greyhound stop) for R35. The *Drakensberg Sun* (☎ (036) 468 1000) has packages offering doubles for R328. You'll need to dress for dinner at these places.

WINTERTON

This pretty little town is the gateway to the Central Berg and is not too far from the northern end. There is a great little museum on Kerk St which concentrates on the geology, flora & fauna of the Drakensberg – a good place to bone up before venturing further. It is open Wednesday and Friday from 1 to 4 pm, and on Saturday from 9 am to noon.

The *Bridge Hotel* (☎ (036) 488 1554) is a friendly local pub with rooms for R75 per person and self-catering units for R60 per person. 'Drivers' rooms', once intended for blacks only, go for R35.

A reader recommends the *Nest Hotel* (☎ (036) 468 1068), where good rondavels cost from R125 per person, including all meals and morning and afternoon tea.

A minibus taxi to Cathedral Peak costs R5. To Bergville it's R4 and to Estcourt R5.

GIANT'S CASTLE GAME RESERVE

This reserve of 34,500 hectares was established in 1903, mainly to protect the eland. It's in high country: the lowest point is 1300 metres and the highest tooth of the Drakensberg in the reserve is the 3409-metre Injasuti Dome. With huge forest reserves to the north and south and Lesotho's barren plateau over the escarpment to the west, it's a rugged and remote place, despite the number of visitors it attracts.

There's an entry fee of R4 per person. Limited supplies (including fuel) are available at Main Camp and there's a basic store near the White Mountain Lodge, but the nearest shops are in Estcourt, 50 km away.

Flora & Fauna

The reserve is mainly grassland, wooded gorges, high basaltic cliffs with small forests in the valleys, and some protea savanna surviving the grass-fires caused by lightning strikes and, recently, controlled burning. During spring there are many wildflowers.

Because of the harsh conditions many of the reserve's animals lead a precarious existence, and the balance of numbers and available food is delicate – an event such as a hard winter can disturb the equation and threaten a species' existence.

The reserve is home to 12 species of antelope, with relatively large numbers of elands, mountain reedbucks, black wildebeests, red hartebeests, grey rheboks and oribi. The rarest antelope is the klipspringer, sometimes sighted on the higher slopes. The rarest species is a small short-tailed rodent called the ice rat, which lives in the boulders near the mountain summits. Altogether there are thought to be about 60 mammal species, but some, such as the leopard and aardwolf, have not been positively sighted.

The rare lammergeyer, or bearded vulture *(Gypaetus barbatus)*, which is found only in the Drakensberg, nests in the reserve. Because there's a danger that the birds will feed on poisoned carcasses which some farmers in the area use to kill jackals, the reserve puts out meat on weekend mornings between May and September to encourage them to feed in the reserve. **Lammergeyer Hide** has been built nearby, and it's the best place to see the vultures. The fee for using the hide is R23 (minimum R138), and you must book.

The number of other bird species to have been sighted in the reserve is around 200. There are also about 30 reptile species, including the puff adder.

Rock Paintings

The reserve is rich in San rock paintings, with at least 50 sites. It is thought that the last San still lived here at the turn of this century.

The two main sites of paintings are Main Cave (about 550 paintings) and Battle Cave (750 paintings), both of which have an entry fee of R5 (R2.50 for children). Main Cave is two km south of Main Camp (30 minutes' walk) and there's also a display on San life here. The cave is open on weekends and holidays from 9 am to 3 pm; on weekdays you have to go with a tour which departs from the camp office at 9 am and 3 pm. Battle Cave is near Injasuti and must be visited on a tour which leaves the camp daily at 9 am. It's an eight-km walk each way, and there's a good chance of seeing wildlife en route. Battle Cave is so called because some of the paintings here record a fight between San groups.

Other painting sites near Main Camp are Bamboo Hollow, where there are two rich sites, Steel's Shelter and Willcox's Shelter, where you can see a figure known as the Moon Goddess. Near Injasuti are Grindstone Cave and Fergie's Cave (fires are not allowed). Ask the Environmental Officer at Main Camp for maps and information about more remote sites.

Hiking Trails

There are a number of walking trails in the reserve, most of them round trips from either Main Camp or Injasuti or one-way walks to the various mountain huts. There are also walks between huts, so you can string together overnight hikes, but you need to book accommodation in the huts beforehand. The reserve's booklet *Giant's Castle Game Reserve* gives details and has a basic map of the trails. Further information is available at the Main Camp office (☎ (0363) 24718).

Before setting out on a long walk you must fill in the rescue register; those planning to go higher than 2300 metres must report to the warden. Don't confuse trails here with the Giant's Cup Trail, further south in the Drakensberg and covered in the Southern Drakensberg Wilderness Areas section.

Horse-Riding

From the centre at Hillside there is a variety of horse-rides. There are short guided rides costing R21 per hour, and R200 overnight rides for experienced riders only. On the overnight rides everything is provided except food, and accommodation is in huts and caves. Horse trails must be booked through the Natal Parks Board's Pietermaritzburg headquarters. They are not available during July and August and at other times routes are liable to change because of bad weather. Book day rides directly at Hillside on ☎ (0363) 24435 between 9 am and noon daily.

Some of the places to stay in the area, notably Champagne Castle, also offer riding.

Places to Stay

Giant's Castle Game Reserve There are three main areas, as well as trail huts and caves for hikers. Note that nowhere in the park are you allowed to cut or even collect firewood; hikers are not allowed to light fires, so bring a stove. Litter must be brought back, not burned or buried. There's a small supermarket near Main Camp, and a restaurant is planned to open soon.

Main Camp has a range of accommodation; the cheapest are the mountain huts. Two, three and five-bed bungalows are R83 per person (minimums of R125, R166, R249). You can't camp here.

There's a camp site at *Hillside* in the reserve's north-east corner, a long way from Main Camp let alone the escarpment. Sites cost R13 per person and you can book on ☎ (03631) 24435. There's an eight-bed hut for R32 per person (minimum R128) but it's often taken by groups doing horse trails.

Injasuti Hutted Camp (☎ 0020 and ask for Loskop 1311, for bookings) is on the north side of the reserve. There's a camp site (R13 per person), and cabins from R46 per person (minimum R92); entry is R4 per person. It's a secluded and pleasant spot.

There are three *mountain huts* (R20 per person) for which you'll need sleeping bags and cooking utensils – a gas stove is provided. *Meander Hut* is a 2½-hour walk from

Main Camp and is on a cliff above the Meander Valley. *Giant's Hut* is a four-hour walk from Main Camp and is hard against the escarpment, under Giant's Castle itself. *Bannerman's Hut* is also a four-hour walk from Main Camp and is close to the escarpment near Bannerman's Pass. There's an R10 key deposit, and if you're planning to walk between huts rather than returning to Main Camp you have to arrange to collect keys.

In the Injasuti Valley there are two *caves* (Lower Injasuti and Fergie's) where hikers can stay for R6 per person. There are no facilities except basic toilets, and no fires are allowed. The R10 deposit is refunded when you bring back your litter.

Accommodation in huts and caves must be booked, as with all Natal Parks Board accommodation other than camp sites, through the office in Pietermaritzburg (☎ (0331) 47 1981). Unless you've booked the whole hut or cave you must share it with other hikers.

Around Giant's Castle Reserve There are several places on and near the R600 which runs south-west from Winterton towards Cathkin Peak and Champagne Castle, some of which have been listed earlier under Central Berg entry. *Inkosana Lodge* (☎ (036) 468 1202) is a base for treks and has simple, inexpensive dorm accommodation.

Off the road running from Estcourt to Giant's Castle, *White Mountain Lodge* (☎/fax (0363) 24437) has powered camp sites from R35 and self-catering cottages from R85 a double, depending on the season. In the high season there's a minimum stay of a week, and two days at other times. There's a small shop. The lodge will collect you from Estcourt if you arrange it beforehand.

Getting There & Away
Main Camp The best way into Main Camp is via the dirt road from Mooi River although the last section can be impassable when wet. It's also possible to get here by following the route for Hillside, taking the Hillside turn-off. However, until the road is sealed don't attempt it in wet weather.

Infrequent minibuses run from Estcourt to villages near the main entrance (Kwa-Dlamini, Mahlutshini and KwaMankonjane), but these are still several km from Main Camp.

Hillsides Take the Giant's Castle road from Estcourt, signposted at the Anglican church. Turn left at the White Mountain Lodge junction and after four km turn right onto the Hillside road. Take the right turn at the two minor intersections which follow.

Injasuti Injasuti is accessible from the township of Loskop, north-west of Estcourt. Four km west of Loskop or six km east of the R600, turn south; the road is signposted.

SOUTHERN DRAKENSBERG WILDERNESS AREAS
Four state forests, Highmoor, Mkhomazi, Cobham and Garden Castle, run from Giant's Castle south beyond Bushman's Nek, to meet Lesotho's Sehlabathebe National Park. The big Mkmazi Wilderness Area and the Mzimkulu Wilderness Area are in the state forests.

The wilderness areas are close to the escarpment, with the Kamberg, Loteni, Vergelegen and Mzimkulwana nature reserves to the east of them, except for a spur of Mzimkulwana which follows the Mkhomazana River (and the road) down from Sani Pass, separating the two wilderness areas.

The wilderness areas are administered by the Natal Parks Board. Entry to each is R4 per person and overnight hiking costs R6.

Kamberg Nature Reserve
South-east of Giant's Castle and a little away from the main escarpment area, this small (2232 hectares) Natal Parks Board reserve has a number of antelope species. The country in the Drakensberg foothills is pretty, but it's trout fishing which attracts most visitors. The trout hatchery is open to the public; entry is R3. The reserve's office sells fishing permits (R10 per rod per day).

Entry to the reserve costs R4 per person and overnight hiking costs R6. The cottage is R32 per person (minimum R192), and two-bed rest huts are R52 (minimum R78).

You can get here from Rosetta, off the N3 south of Mooi River, travelling via either Nottingham Road or Redcliffe.

Highmoor State Forest

Part of the Mkhomazi Wilderness Area is in Highmoor. The forest station (☎ (0333) 37240) is off the road from Rosetta to Giant's Castle and Kamberg. Turn off to the south just past the sign to Kamberg, 31 km from Rosetta. Camp sites with limited facilities are R6 and overnight hiking is also R6.

Loteni Nature Reserve

There is a Settlers' Museum in this reserve. Accommodation costs from R44 (R66 minimum) in two-bed chalets and R32 in *Simes*, a 10-bed rustic cottage (minimum R192), or you can camp for R13. Phone 033722, ask for 1540 to book camp sites. The fee for overnight hiking is R6.

The access road runs from the hamlet of Lower Loteni, about 30 km north-east of Himeville or 65 km south-west of Nottingham Road (off Mooi River). The roads aren't great and heavy rain can close them. They are, however, some of the most scenic in South Africa, with the Drakensberg as a backdrop and many picturesque Zulu villages in the area.

Mkhomazi State Forest

This is the southern part of Mkhomazi Wilderness Area. The 1200-hectare **Vergelegen Nature Reserve** is along this road; the entry fee is R4 and there are no established camp sites here. The turn-off to the state forest is 44 km from Nottingham Road, off the Lower Loteni/Sani Pass road, at the Mzinga River. From here it's another two km.

Cobham State Forest

The Mzimkulu Wilderness Area and the Mzimkulwana Nature Reserve are in Cobham. The forest office (☎ (033) 722 1831) is about 15 km from Himeville on the D7 and this is a good place to get information on the many hiking trails in the area. The

mountain huts on the hiking trails cost R20 per person, the nine-bed chalet is R80 (minimum R240) and open camp sites are R6. Get out there!

Garden Castle State Forest

The forest office (☎ (033) 712 1722) is three km further on from the Drakensberg Garden Hotel, 30 km west of Underberg.

Sani Pass

This steep route into Lesotho, the highest pass in South Africa and the only road between KwaZulu/Natal and Lesotho, is one of the most scenic parts of the Drakensberg (see Sani Pass in the Around Lesotho chapter). The drive up the pass is magic, with stunning views out across the Mkhomazana River to the north and looming cliffs, almost directly above, on the south side. There are hikes in almost every direction, inexpensive horse-rides are available (R20 for a half day) and it is possible to get a lift with a 4WD vehicle to the border. You will need a passport to cross into Lesotho. Sani Tours (☎/fax (033) 702 1069). PO Box 232, Himeville 4585, runs 4WD trips up the pass to the lodge at the top of the pass (see the Around Lesotho chapter). This outfit is run by Jonathan Aldous, who is a good source of information on the area.

Places to Stay There are two budget places at the bottom of the pass. *Sani Lodge* (☎ (033) 722 1330) has moved from HaMakhakhe Store to a place next to Mokhotlong Transport, on the opposite side of the road from the Sani Pass Hotel. The lodge is run by Russell Suchet, author of *A Backpackers' Guide to Lesotho*, and if it is anything like the old lodge it will be a good choice for a place to stay a bed is R200.

The former Sani Lodge is now *The Wild West Sani Youth Hostel*, (☎ (033) 722 1340), PO Box 107, Himeville 4585, has dorm-bunk beds for R20 and rondavels for R25.

The *Sani Pass Hotel* (☎ (033) 722 1320) complete with guards and razor-wire fences is also at the bottom of the pass, 14 km from

Himeville. It has singles/doubles for R263/350 with dinner, bed and breakfast.

Bushman's Nek
This is a South Africa/Lesotho border post. From here there are hiking trails up into the escarpment, including to Lesotho's Sehlabathebe National Park. You can walk in or hire a horse for R20.

A few km east of the border post is the *Bushman's Nek Hotel* (☎ (033) 701 1460) which has single/double rooms for R80/110 (much cheaper out of season) and four-person self-catering chalets from R180. Closer to the border post is *Silver Streams Caravan Park* (☎ (033) 701 1249) with sites and huts.

GIANT'S CUP HIKING TRAIL
The five-day, 60-km Giant's Cup Trail which runs from Sani Pass to Bushman's Nek is one of the great walks of South Africa. It's designed so that any reasonably fit person can walk it, so it's very popular. Early booking (up to nine months ahead, through the Natal Parks Board office (☎ (0331) 47 1981) in Pietermaritzburg) is advisable. Although the walking is relatively easy, the usual precautions necessary for the Drakensberg apply – expect severe cold snaps at any time of the year.

The stages are as follows: Day 1 – 14 km, Day 2 – nine km, Day 3 – 12 km, Day 4 – 13 km and Day 5 – 12 km. The highlights include the Bathplug Cave with San rock paintings, beautiful Crane Tarn, and the breathtaking mountain scenery on Day 4.

Tents are not permitted on this trail; accommodation in shared huts cost R20 per person. No firewood is available so you'll need a stove and fuel. The Sani Lodge (☎ (033) 722 1330) is almost at the trailhead; arrange for the lodge to pick you up from Himeville or Underberg.

HIMEVILLE
Not far from Underberg, this smaller but nicer town, is above 1500 metres so winters are coolish. A good place for a spot of tennis and a pink gin! There's a **museum** on the main street, in a building which was origi-

nally a small fort and today has displays on local history. It's open in the morning on Wednesday, Friday and on weekends.

The **Himeville Nature Reserve**, on the north-east side of town, is popular for trout fishing (you can hire rowing boats) and there are a few antelopes around. On the Pevensey Rd, 14 km east of Himeville, is the **Swamp Nature Reserve**, which has the Polela River as three km of its southern boundary. This is a small wetlands reserve, home to many species of waterbird including the rare wattled crane.

Places to Stay & Eat
There is a Natal Parks Board *camp site* in the Himeville Nature Reserve not far from town, where open camp sites are R13 per person; the entry fee is R4 per person. The *Himeville Arms* (☎/fax (033) 702 1305) has good rooms from R95/170, including breakfast. A four-course dinner costs R28. It isn't very friendly. At the 'black bar', a little further down the road to Underberg, you'll be made much more welcome.

Getting There & Away
About the only regular transport from Himeville are minibus taxis to Underberg (R1.50) and twice-daily KZT buses to Pietermaritzburg. The road to Underberg is lined with oak trees, the result of a reconciliation between the two towns after a feud.

UNDERBERG
This quiet little town in the foothills of the southern Drakensberg is the centre of a farming community. There's a First National Bank here. The southern Drakensberg offers excellent wilderness hiking, and the Underberg Hiking Club is a good source of information. The Natal Parks Board has an office in the main street.

Places to Stay & Eat
The archaic *Underberg Hotel* (☎ (033) 701 1412) has single/double rooms for R70/130, including breakfast. For cottages to rent in

the area contact Underberg Hideaways
(☎ (0331) 44 3505, fax 44 2133).

West of Underberg, on the Garden Castle
Forest Station road and in a magnificent
valley, is the *Drakensberg Garden Hotel*
(☎ (033) 701 1355), a resort-style place with
rooms from R160/270, for full board. Also
out of town and set on 10 hectares is *Eagle's
Rock* (☎ (0033) 701 1757), with self-catering thatched cottages for R55, or R70 with
breakfast.

Whilst in town you can survive at *Gar-
field's* on the corner next to the Shell petrol
station. Pies are R4 and mediocre pizzas are
from R15 to R20. The place to eat, if you
have the money, is *Manna House* on Main
St, with its 'French eclectic' menu; lunch and
dinner are about R50 per person.

Getting There & Away
Bus Transtate runs between Matatiele (west
of Kokstad) and Jo'burg via Underberg,
from Sunday to Friday. The buses stop diagonally opposite the Mobil station on the main
street.

Minibus taxis run to Pietermaritzburg
(R15) and Himeville (R1.50) and you might
find one running to the Sani Pass Hotel.

The main routes to Underberg and nearby
Himeville are from Pietermaritzburg on the
R617 and from Kokstad on the R626, but it's
possible to drive here from the north-east via
Nottingham Road, south of Mooi River, and
Lower Loteni. These roads are mainly
unsealed and can be closed after rain.

AROUND UNDERBERG
South of Underberg, off the R626 to Kokstad, the Natal Parks Board's **Coleford
Nature Reserve** (1272 hectares) has some
game, but it's more of a recreation than a
nature reserve. Trout fishing is popular here
and you can get a permit and hire equipment
in the reserve (R10 per person, bag limit of
10 trout).

You can't camp here, but accommodation
ranges from three-bed rustic cabins which
cost R32 per person (minimum R48) to six-
bed chalets which are R60 (minimum R240).

GRIQUALAND EAST
Historically the Voortrekkers had been
moving into the Griqua territory between the
Vaal and the Orange rivers, around Philippolis,
since the 1820s. The Griqua chief, Adam Kok
III, realising that there would soon be no
land left, encouraged his people to sell their
remaining titles and move elsewhere.

In 1861, Kok's entire community of 2000
with about 20,000 head of cattle began their
epic two-year journey over the rugged
mountains of Lesotho to Nomansland, a
region on the far side of the Drakensberg.
When they reached the southern slopes of Mt
Currie they set up camp. Later, in 1869, they
moved to the present site of Kokstad.
Nomansland was called Griqualand East
after annexation by the Cape in 1874. Kok
died the following year when he was thrown
from his cart.

Today the main towns are Kokstad,
Matatiele and Cedarville. It is a pleasant
place to visit and the residents are extremely
friendly.

Kokstad
Kokstad is named after Adam Kok. It lies at
1280 metres above sea level in the
Umzimhlava River valley, between Mt
Currie and the Ngele mountains. Today it's
a pleasant little place with some solid buildings and, despite its backwater air, excellent
transport connections.

The library (☎ (037) 727 3133) in the
impressive town hall has information on the
area. There's a telephone service off the
entrance to the Royal Hotel where you can
make calls without coins.

Places to Stay & Eat The shady municipal
caravan park (☎ (037) 727 3133) is next to
the sports ground, near the town centre.

The *Royal Hotel* (☎ (037) 727 2060), 85
Main St, has single/double rooms from
R90/120, including breakfast. *The Balmoral*
(☎ (037) 727 2070), more up-market than
the Royal, charges about R100/150. It's on
Hope St, the main road, so rooms at the front
might be noisy.

Apart from the hotels there's a *Spur* steakhouse at the Balmoral, a *Wimpy* next to the Mount Currie Motel, and *Norah's Pie Place* on Barkley St.

Getting There & Away Various Transtate services depart from the railway station for Durban, Pietermaritzburg, Umtata, Jo'burg and Underberg – there should be at least one service a day to these destinations. There's also a slow but scenic service to Welkom via Transkei and Maclear, on Monday, Tuesday, Wednesday and Friday. The City to City (book through Translux) Jo'burg-Umtata service runs via Kokstad, on Tuesday and Friday. Greyhound and Translux run to Umtata, Durban and Port Elizabeth. Greyhound and City to City stop at the Wimpy Bar, a little way from the town centre on the Durban to Umtata road.

The railway station is a few blocks west (downhill) from the main street. You can book buses here, or through Keval Travel (☎ (037) 727 3124) which is on Main St in the same building as the Kokstad Pharmacy.

Around Kokstad
A few km north of Kokstad, off the R626 to Franklin, is the **Mt Currie Nature Reserve** (☎ (037) 727 3844). There are walking trails and several antelope species in this grassy 1800-hectare reserve. A memorial marks the site of Adam Kok's first laager. Open camp sites in the reserve are R13 per person.

Out of Kokstad, on the R56 and just before the N2, is the *Mount Currie Motel* (☎/fax (037) 727 2178). It's slightly more up-market than the Kokstad hotels and has a restaurant.

There is an isolated chunk of Eastern Cape Province north-east of Kokstad; the boundaries are subject to a referendum in the future.

Ngele Hiking Trail
In the **Weza State Forest**, off the N2 east of Kokstad near Staffords Post, is the Ngele Trail system (*ngele* means 'precipitous place'). There are a variety of hiking possibilities and the main trail is either a four-day (64 km) or five-day (95 km) excursion. The

additional day is extremely tough as it takes in the 28-km Fairview Loop and an ascent of 2268-metre Ngele mountain.

The forest is in high, hilly country and is partly a huge pine plantation and partly indigenous forest. The trail also leads through mountain grassland, highland sourveld ('sour' because as it loses its palatability in winter). The orange-yellow flowers of the Christmas bell (*Sandersonia aurantiaca*), endemic to South Africa, appear here in December. There is a population of well over 1000 bushbucks, as well as common duikers and mountain reedbucks. Predators include the African wild cat, caracal, large-spotted genet and serval. Well over 70 bird species have been recorded.

During August and September the trail is usually closed because of fire danger – be very careful at other times too. Accommodation in old farm buildings costs R10 per person and is booked, along with the trails, through the Natal Parks Board (☎ (0331) 47 1981) in Pietermaritzburg.

The Midlands

The Midlands run north-east from Durban to Escourt and skirt Zululand to the north-east. This is mainly farming country with not a lot to interest visitors. The main town is Pietermaritzburg – KwaZulu/Natal's capital.

West of Pietermaritzburg there is pretty, hilly country, with horse studs and plenty of European trees. This area was settled mainly by English farmers and looks a little like England's West Country. The various artists' and potters' galleries in this area are included in the Midlands Meander; pick up a brochure from one of the larger tourist offices.

PIETERMARITZBURG
After the defeat of the Zulu at the decisive Battle of Blood River, the Voortrekkers began to establish their republic of Natal. Pietermaritzburg (often known as PMB) was named in honour of leader Pieter Mauritz

Pietermaritzburg

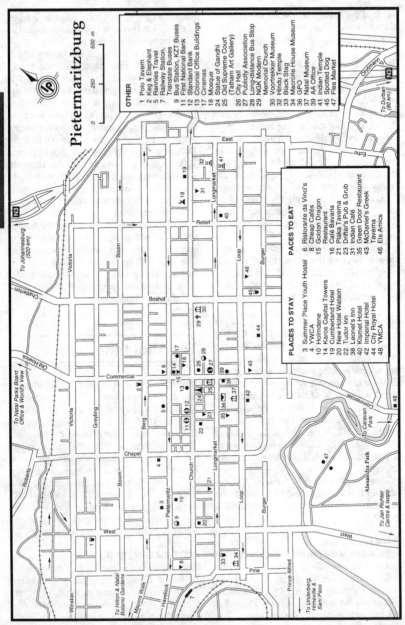

OTHER

1 Polo Tavern
2 Keg & Elephant
5 Rennies Travel
7 Railway Station,
Transtate Buses
9 Bus Station, KZT Buses
11 First National Bank
12 Standard Bank
13 Colonial Office Buildings
17 Cinemas
18 Mosque
24 Statue of Gandhi
25 Old Supreme Court
(Tatham Art Gallery)
26 City Hall
27 Publicity Association
28 Long-distance Bus Stop
29 NGK Modern
Memorial Church
30 Voortrekker Museum
32 Hindu Temple
33 Black Stag
34 Macrorie House Museum
36 GPO
37 Natal Museum
39 AA Office
41 Indian Temple
45 Spotted Dog
47 Flea Market

PLACES TO STAY

3 Summer Place Youth Hostel
4 YWCA
10 Holmdene
14 Karos Capital Towers
19 Cumberland Hotel
20 New Hotel Watson
22 Tudor Inn
38 Leonel's Inn
40 Kismet Hotel
42 Imperial Hotel
44 City Royal Hotel
48 YMCA

PLACES TO EAT

6 Ristorante da Vinci's
8 Cheap Cafés
15 Golden Dragon
Restaurant
16 Café Bavaria
21 Plaka Tavema
23 Drifter's Pub & Grub
31 Indian Café
35 Green Door Restaurant
43 McDaniel's Greek
Tavena
46 Els Amics

Retief, and was founded in 1838 as the capital (later the 'u' was dropped and, in 1938, it was decreed that the Gert Maritz be remembered in the title). Here in 1841 the Boers built their Church of the Vow to honour the Blood River promise. The British annexed Natal in 1843 but they retained Pietermaritzburg – well-positioned, less humid than Durban and already a neat little town – as the capital.

As well as the Boer and British presence there's a big Indian population. Streets around Retief St, such as Church and Longmarket Sts, echo the sub-continent.

PMB rightly bills itself as the heritage city and, as it has numerous historic buildings and a British colonial air. It is one of the finest examples of a Victorian-era city. Get a copy of the *Mini-Guide* from the Publicity Association – it details the interesting buildings in the centre of town.

Orientation

The central grid of Pietermaritzburg contains most places of interest to travellers, although some of the bottom-end accommodation is south-east of the centre. Also south-east of the centre is the University of Natal.

The north end of the city, beyond Retief St, is a largely Indian commercial district. It shuts down at night and is the least safe part of the city centre. North of here is the Indian residential area of Northdale (with suburbs such as Bombay Heights and Mysore Ridge). To the south-west of the city is Edendale, the black dormitory suburb. West, on the Old Howick Rd beyond Queen Elizabeth Park, is the village of Hilton, a leafy and slightly twee residential area.

Information

The Publicity Association (☎ (0331) 45 1348, fax 94 3535) is in Publicity House at 177 Commercial Rd, on the corner of Longmarket St. Rennies Travel (☎ (0331) 94 1571) is at 207 Pietermaritz St, near the corner of Levy St. The AA (☎ (0331) 42 0571) is in Brasfort House at 191 Commercial Rd.

The Wash Tub is a 24-hour coin laundry in the Park Lane Centre, on Commercial St near the corner of Victoria St.

Natal Parks Board Office This office, where you book most of the accommodation and walks for Natal parks, is a long way from the town centre, in Queen Elizabeth Park, a small nature reserve. You can make phone bookings with a credit card but it's better to visit to collect the useful literature.

Head out to the Old Howick Rd (Commercial Rd) and turn right onto Link Rd about one km past the big roundabout. The board is about two km further on. A Wembley bus from stand 10 at the city bus rank behind the Publicity Association will get to the roundabout. For general enquiries phone ☎ (0331) 47 1986; for bookings call ☎ (0331) 47 1981.

KwaZulu Department of Nature Conservation The bureau office is at 367 Loop St (☎ (0331) 44 6697). You can book accommodation here for some parks in Maputaland in the far north of KwaZulu/Natal.

From Pietermaritzburg Station to Mahatma?

Anyone who has seen Richard Attenborough's film *Gandhi* will recall the scene when Gandhi is ejected from the train and his suitcases are unceremoniously dumped onto the station platform.

The station was Pietermaritzburg. The 24-year-old Gandhi was on his way to Pretoria in the Transvaal for legal business. He had boarded the train with a 1st-class ticket and duly went to his allocated compartment. A white passenger complained to railway officials who ordered Gandhi to the baggage car.

When he protested, displaying his 1st-class ticket, they called a policeman who threw him out. He could have gone to 3rd class but he refused. Instead, he meditated in the station's cold waiting room. Some years later, in India, when asked about the most influential experiences in his life, he cited this incident. There is now a plaque at the station where the incident occurred. ■

Forestry Branch Library This library (☎ (0331) 42 8101), in the Southern Life Building on Church St, is worth visiting for information on the area's state forests.

Things to See & Do

There are a number of colonial-era buildings. The massive red brick **city hall**, on the corner of Church and Commercial Sts, is a good example, as is the old **Supreme Court** across the road (now the Tatham Art Gallery). The **publicity office**, itself housed in the old borough police and fire complex (1884), has a walking-tour map.

Macrorie House Museum, on the corner of Loop and Pine Sts, displays items related to early British settlement. It's open from 9 am to 1 pm Tuesday to Thursday, from 11 am to 4 pm on Sunday. For the other side's view, visit the **Voortrekker Museum** on Church St near the city hall. It's open on weekdays from 9 am to 4 pm and on Saturday morning. The museum is in the **Church of the Vow**, built in 1841 to fulfil the Voortrekkers' part of the Blood River bargain. Afrikaner icons on display include Retief's prayerbook and waterbottle, and a replica of a trek wagon. The words of The Vow are in the **Modern Memorial Church** next door.

The **Natal Museum** has a range of displays, including African ethnography. It's on Loop St, south-west of Commercial Rd and is open from 9 am to 4.30 pm Monday to Saturday, and on Sunday from 2 to 5 pm.

The **Tatham Art Gallery**, housed in the old Supreme Court, is open every day except Monday, from 10 am to 6 pm. It has a good collection of French and English 19th and early 20th-century works. Perhaps the best collection of artworks in PMB is the least known: the **Natal Provincial Administration Collection** at 330 Longmarket St. Included are some of the finest examples of indigenous art, including beadwork, pottery and weaving; it is open by appointment only (☎ (0331) 45 3201).

Architect Phillip Dudgeon modelled the **Standard Bank** on Church St on the Bank of Ireland in Belfast. It has an unusual set of stained-glass windows depicting the four seasons as one would experience them in the northern hemisphere (someone messed up!).

There are two **Hindu temples**, both at the north end of Longmarket St. The main **mosque** is nearby, on Church St. Recently a **statue of Gandhi** was erected opposite the Old Colonial Buildings on Church St – PMB's attempt to gain forgiveness which the Mahatma would have willingly bestowed.

The **Natal Botanic Gardens**, two km west of the railway station on the continuation of Berg St, has exotic species and a garden of indigenous mist-belt flora.

The **Natal Steam Railway Museum** (☎ (03324) 4110) is in Hilton on the corner of Hilton Ave and Quarry Rd. On the second Sunday of each month there are rides at 10 am and 3.30 pm to Cedara (R7.50) and at 11.30 am to Howick (R15).

There's a good view of the city from **World's View**, a lookout on a hill reached from the Old Howick Rd.

Places to Stay – bottom end

The municipal *caravan park* (☎ (0331) 65342) is on Cleland Rd, nearly five km from the railway station. Head south-east on Commercial Rd, which becomes Durban Rd after you cross the creek. Go left onto Blackburrow Rd across the freeway then take the first road to the right.

Single rooms at the *Jan Richter Centre* (☎ (0331) 69252), on the corner of New Scotland Rd and Stalkers Alley, cost about R40 for dinner, bed and breakfast (the weekly rate is R175). Walk south-east on West St, cross the creek, and New Scotland Rd is one km further on the right. The *YMCA* (☎ (0331) 42 8106) is at 1 Durban Rd, just across the creek from the south-eastern end of Commercial Rd. It's a good deal, at R45 for a single room with dinner and breakfast. Women can stay at the YMCA, but men can't stay at the *YWCA* (☎ (0331) 42 2860), on Chapel St near Pietermaritz St, where a room is R50, including meals. Both places are usually full.

Not far away, *Homedene* (☎ (0331) 42 5174), at 78 Pietermaritz St, near West St, charges R67 per person for dinner, bed and breakfast in rooms with shared bath. Most of the residents are elderly. Across the road, *Summer Place Youth Hostel* (☎ (0331) 94 5785) at No 85 calls its scattered houses 'accommodation'; dorm beds are R24.

At 501 Church St, in the Indian area northeast of Retief St, the *Cumberland Hotel* (☎ (0331) 45 0973) is a big place, rapidly disintegrating and not very attractive, but it's friendly and there's a cheap cafeteria; single/double rooms are R60/80. The nearby *Kismet Hotel* (☎ (0331) 45 1141), on the corner of Longmarket and Retief Sts, is better. Singles with shared bathroom are R60, doubles with bathroom start at R90.

Places to Stay – middle

Leonel's Inn (☎ (0331) 94 1601), at 186 Commercial St, is handy to the long-distance bus stop and the town centre. It's a small place, with singles/doubles from R100/150, but it has a restaurant and the tariff includes breakfast. The *Tudor Inn* (☎ (0331) 42 1778), at 18 Theatre Lane, has doubles only for R130. Secure parking is available for R8.

The *New Hotel Watson* (☎ (0331) 42 1604), on the corner of Church and West Sts, has singles/doubles for R85/115. The *Thistle Hotel* (☎ (0331) 42 4204), at 30 Boshoff St, charges R92/122; breakfast is R8.50.

Another good place, about 10 minutes' away in Hilton, is the *Crossways Country Inn* (☎/fax (0331) 33267) which charges R110/170 for singles/doubles and R240 for family rooms, breakfast included.

There are many B&Bs in PMB and Hilton. The Publicity Association provides a full list and will find out prices. Or contact Midlands B&B (☎/fax (0332) 30 3343).

Places to Stay – top end

The *Karos Capital Towers* (☎ (0331) 94 2761, fax 45 2857), at 121 Commercial St, is R165 for a single and R175 for a family room; breakfast is R23.50. The *Imperial* (☎ (0331) 42 6551, fax 42 9796) at 224 Loop St has singles/doubles from R210/250.

The best place in town is the *City Royal Hotel* (☎ (0331) 94 7072, fax 94 7080), at 301 Burger St. This grand place has sweep-ing staircases, tidy rooms, restaurant and bar, secure parking and courteous and helpful staff. Rooms are good value at R190/210.

In nearby Hilton you'll find the Tudor-style *Hilton Hotel* (☎ (0331) 33311, fax 33722) which isn't a member of the chain. Rooms cost R200/250, with breakfast.

Places to Eat

Across from the railway station and up Church St are a couple of basic cafés selling takeaway-style food. More up-market snacks are sold near the long-distance bus stop on Longmarket St at the *Upper Crust Patisserie*. Up in the Indian area there is a good place opposite the Cumberland Hotel.

The *Green Door* is a good little café with healthy food, open during the day from 10 am to 4.30 pm and from Wednesday to Saturday from 7 pm for supper. Lasagne is about R15 and there are good salads from R6. It's in an old stone building off a car park in Club Lane, off Longmarket St near the GPO. The meals at *Café Bavaria*, in the NBS Building, are good value.

Ristorante da Vinci, at 117 Commercial Rd, is a good Italian place. It's open daily; two courses costs R40 and pub lunches R14.

The *Golden Dragon*, on the corner of Commercial Rd in the Karos Capital Towers has been recommended by locals; spring rolls are R5 and main courses are from R15.

Having tried several, we contend that one of the best of the *Mike's Kitchen* chain is at 60 Boshoff St. The prawn tails in lemon cream or piri piri are R15 and a huge meal of kingklip and prawns is R30. *White Mischief*, in an old colonial home at 180 Loop St, is open for lunch every day except Sunday. A fresh and filling pub lunch is R25, pricey but worth it. A standard lunch is around R45.

McDaniel's Greek Taverna, in the Joshua Doore Centre, is a good family restaurant serving traditional dishes and a good selection of Greek dishes. The *Plaka Taverna* at 177 Longmarket St is of course Greek, and the *Peri Peri* at No 124 is Portuguese. *Els Amics* at No 380 is Spanish, and dinners which include gazpacho or maybe paella cost around R45 per person.

Most of the hotels have restaurants and we recommend the City Royal Hotel. A superb dinner costs about R45 per person.

Entertainment

PMB is not the most exciting place in the province – catch a bus to Durban if you want full-on entertainment. The Plaka Taverna, on Longmarket St, has folk music on Monday night. Da Vinci's restaurant at 117 Commercial Rd, is also a popular nightspot. Not far away, at 80 Commercial Rd, is the Keg & Elephant, an atmospheric watering hole.

• The Spotted Dog at 363 Burger St, the Black Stag at 24 Longmarket St and Drifters Pub & Grub on Theatre Lane are other good spots for imbibing beer.

For something completely different try the Polo Tavern, on West St at the corner of Greyling St. This neighbourhood pub always has music and is good fun. If you want to plumb the downmarket depths, check out the wine-store dives at the top end of Pietermaritz St. Be careful.

Perhaps sedate PMB is the place to take in a movie – Kine's 1, 2 3 & 4 are on the corner of Commercial Rd and Pietermaritz St; and Nu-Metro Movies are in the Cascades Centre, McCarthy Dr. Obtain copies of the free *Heritage Herald* and the *What's On* from the Publicity Association.

Getting There & Away

Air Airlink (☎ (0331) 69286) flies on weekdays to Jo'burg. The economy/Apex fare is R365/228. Air Midlands (☎ (0331) 68255) also offers the same domestic flights.

Bus Transtate goes to several destinations from PMB; their buses depart from the railway station. A number of services which originate in the Transkei area pass through PMB on their way to Jo'burg. There are daily services from Umtata and services from Sunday to Friday to/from Lusikisiki. The service from Jo'burg to Umtata departs from Jo'burg daily at 6 pm. It goes via PMB and Kokstad arriving at Umtata at 9 am the following day.

The Maseru (Lesotho) service departs from Durban station on Tuesday and Friday at 7 pm and goes via PMB, Harrismith, Bethlehem, Butha-Buthe and Ladybrand.

Greyhound (☎ (0331) 42 3026) and Translux (☎ (0331) 45 1438) long-distance buses stop near Publicity House on a little road between Church and Longmarket Sts. Translux goes to Durban (R30), Bloemfontein (R125) via Bethlehem, and Jo'burg/Pretoria via Harrismith (R110, daily). Greyhound has several services each day between Durban and Jo'burg/Pretoria via Ladysmith and Newcastle. The Durban-Kimberley run also stops in PMB.

You can book Translux through the Publicity Association, at the side of the building. Travel agents, including Capital Coach Booking (☎ (0331) 42 3026) in Shepstone House, handle Greyhound bookings.

Cheetah Coaches (☎ (0331) 42 0266; 42 2673) runs daily between Durban, PMB and Louis Botha Airport; their offices are in the Main City Building at 206 Longmarket St. Midlands Mini-Coach (☎ (0333) 37110 between 8 am and 1 pm) runs from Durban to Estcourt.

KZT (their buses have 'Lucky' written on them) runs local services around former KwaZulu, including a slow but interesting daily run to Himeville. KZT buses leave from the local bus depot on Havelock Rd, near the railway station.

Train The railway station has had its Victorian charms restored. Here, you can catch the weekly *Trans-Oranje* (Durban-Cape Town) and the daily *Trans-Natal* (Durban-Jo'burg). There's also a very slow service to Kokstad, departing at 8.50 pm on Friday and arriving the next day at 7.15 am. First/2nd/3rd class fares to Cape Town are R403/272/170, Ladysmith R49/34/20, Durban R51/35/20 and Jo'burg R142/93/58.

Minibus Taxi Most minibus taxi ranks are at or near the railway station. Taxis to Durban (R9), Harrismith (R38) and Jo'burg (R50) leave from the station forecourt. Those for Underberg (R15), Bulwer and other destinations in the south-west of KwaZulu/Natal leave from Pine St, nearby. For Ladysmith (R17) try the stand on Church St, opposite the site of the Norfolk Hotel near West St, before 10 am.

Hitching If you're hitching in on the N3, get off at Exit 81 (Church St) for the city centre, Exit 76 (northbound) or Exit 74 (southbound) for the municipal caravan park.

Car & Motorbike If you're heading north, a nicer route than the N3 is the R103 which runs through pretty country between Howick and Mooi River. For a long but scenic drive to Durban, head north on the R33 (the continuation of Church St) to Sevenoaks, then cut back to the coast on the R614. Watch out for pedestrians and slow-moving cane trucks on this road.

Avis (☎ (0331) 45 4601), Budget (☎ (0331) 42 8433) and Imperial (☎ (0331) 94 2728) have agents here.

Getting Around
The main rank for city-area buses is in the yard behind the Publicity Association on the corner of Longmarket St and Commercial Rd. A Wembley bus from Stand 10 gets you half-way to the Natal Parks Board HQ.

For a taxi, phone Springbok (☎ (0331) 42 44444), Junior (☎ (0331) 94 5454) or Unique (☎ (0331) 91 1238).

AROUND PIETERMARITZBURG
Howick
In the town of Howick, about 25 km northwest of Pietermaritzburg on the N3, are the popular Howick Falls. Just before the falls there is the small **Howick Museum**, a unabashedly parochial celebration of the town; it is open from 9 am to noon and 2 to 3.30 pm Tuesday to Friday, and Sunday from 10 am to 1 pm.

The small (656-hectare) **Umgeni Valley Nature Reserve**, with walks and some more falls, is nearby. This is one of the best conservation education centres in South Africa. Over 200 bird species have been recorded in the confines of the reserve.

The municipal *caravan park* (☎ (0332) 30

6124) is near the falls on Morling St and *Orient Park* (☎ (0332) 30 2067) is near the Midmar Dam wall. The *Howick Falls Hotel* (☎ (0332) 30 2809) is at 2 Main St; bed and breakfast is about R80 per person. The *Four Springs* protea farm (☎/fax (03324) 4525) in the Dargle Valley has single/double rooms for R85/130 and cottages for R95/150.

North of Howick, in Curry's Post, is the *Old Halliwell Country Inn* (☎ (0332) 30 2602, fax 30 3430), originally a post house on the old wagon route from Durban; the bed and breakfast rate is R197 per person.

Midmar Public Resort
This resort is a few km from Howick. Although there are some animals in the reserve it is mainly a recreation area, with watersports on the dam. There's an entry fee of R4 per person. There's accommodation at *Munro Bay*, the cheapest being chalets for R32 per person (minimum R64) and camping at *Dukududku* for R13, *Morgenzon* for R13 and Munro Bay for R16 (with power) per person. (Phone ☎ (0331) 47 1981 to book sites).

Midmar Historical Village
This village (☎ (0332) 30 5351), which is open daily from 9 am to 4 pm, adjoins the resort. The project aims to recreate a typical Natal village of the 1900s. There are already a number of interesting exhibits including Durban's last steam-driven tug boat, a Shiva temple and Zulu huts. The entrance fee is R5 and train rides are R4 per person.

Albert Falls Public Resort
This resort is also run by the Natal Parks Board and is 25 km from PMB, off the road north to Greytown. Tent sites at *Notuli* are R13 per person (book on ☎ (03393) 202, fax 203), rustic rondavels are R48 and chalets R44 for two people. Note that there have been outbreaks of bilharzia in the dam.

MOOI RIVER
Mooi River is a nondescript town, but the early Voortrekkers probably had high hopes

for it, as *mooi* means beautiful. The Zulu were more matter of fact, calling it *mpofana*, 'place of the eland'. The surrounding countryside, especially to the west, is worth exploring. It's horse-stud country on rolling land dotted with old European trees.

Mooi River is closer to Giant's Castle than is Estcourt and, while there are fewer minibus taxis from here, the town is right on the N3 so hitching to and from here may be easier.

Places to Stay & Eat

The *Riverbank Caravan Park* (☎ (0333) 32144) is in a great spot overlooking the river and the owners are friendly. A grassy camp site is R15 and a caravan for three/four people is R40/45; a hearty breakfast with local sausage is R10. To get there head out on the Greytown Rd, crossing the N3 on an overpass; it's 1.5 km from town

If you continue past the caravan park for about 15 km you will come to *Sierra Ranch* (☎ (0333) 31073) where accommodation in either rondavels or chalets is R100 per person, including breakfast. In town, there's the *Argyle Hotel* (☎ (0333) 31106), on Lawrence Rd, with single/double rooms for R70/120.

There's a restaurant and bar, the *Station Masters Arms*, in the refurbished old railway station. The *golf club*, reached from town by taking the underpass on the north side of the river, serves solid lunches for about R18; ask a member to sign you in.

Getting There & Away

Transtate buses on the Jo'burg/Pretoria to Umtata route stop here, but not often. Greyhound buses running between Durban and Jo'burg/Pretoria stop at the Wimpy, at the big truck stop on the Rosetta road near the N3, one km from the centre.

The *Trans-Oranje* and *Trans-Natal* trains stop here. Book tickets at the goods office, across the tracks from the old station.

Minibus taxis aren't frequent and run mainly to nearby villages.

AROUND MOOI RIVER

Near the village of Balgowan, south of Mooi River, is *Granny Mouse's Country House* (☎/fax (03324) 4071). It's off the R103, a pretty road running parallel to the N3 between Howick and Mooi River. Granny Mouse's has a good reputation; dinner, bed and breakfast costs R227 per person. A few km west of Mooi River and a little more expensive is *Hartford Country House* (☎ (0333) 31081) which is a restored Victorian house on a 500-hectare estate.

Nottingham Road

About 10 km from Balgowan is the quaint little town of Nottingham Road, named after the Nottinghamshire Regiment which was garrisoned here.

There are a number of places to stay in the region. *Hawklee Country House* (☎ (0333) 36008), 13 km from Nottingham Road village, has bed and breakfast for about R95 per person; *Rawdon's* (☎/fax (0333) 36044) has single/double rooms for R185/290. About 22 km along Nottingham Rd from the town is *The Trout Bungalow* (☎ (0333) 36417, fax (031) 83 82 43), an angler's paradise with fishing tossed in for the R250 per person.

Café le Fort is a popular French restaurant open for lunch from noon till 3 pm Wednesday to Sunday, and *Notties Pub* has traditional English pub lunches (about R14).

Thukela

Birdwatchers may be attracted to the St Lucia Wetlands, walkers and climbers to the Drakensberg and wildlife lovers to Kruger, but the historian will be happy in Thukela. The Thukela, at the headwaters of the Tugela ('something that startles') officially also includes the northern and central Drakensbergs, but these have been covered in a separate section in this chapter.

Some of the more important conflicts in South Africa's history took place in the area, including the Siege of Ladysmith, the Battle

Thukela & Battlefields

0   20   40 km

of Spioenkop, the bloody defeat of the British by the Zulu at Isandlwana, the heroic Defence of Rorke's Drift and the battles of Majuba Hill and Blood River – the region is often described as the Battlefields Route. Get free copies of *Natal Battlefields Route*, *Dundee* and *Natal Battlefields Chronicle*.

ESTCOURT

Estcourt, named after an early sponsor of an immigration scheme to the area, is at the southern edge of Thukela. The town is close to the central Drakensberg resorts and the Giant's Castle, and it's on the Jo'burg/Preto-

ria-Durban bus route. It also has good train and minibus-taxi connections. About eight km west of Escourt is the black township of Wembezi.

Things to See & Do

Now a museum, **Fort Durnford** was built in 1874 to protect Escourt from Zulu attack; the museum is open from 9 am to noon and 1 to 4 pm on weekdays. There are interesting displays and a reconstructed Zulu village in the grounds.

There's not much to do or see at **Wagendrift Public Resort** (☎ (0363) 22550) but you can swim and fish in the dam, camp for R16 per person or stay in a four-bed chalet for R44 (minimum R88); entry is R4. The resort is seven km south-west of Estcourt on the road to Ntabamhlope. A little further on from the resort, at the head of the dam, is the **Moor Park Nature Reserve**, which overlooks Wagendrift Dam and Bushmens River. There are zebras, wildebeests and antelopes.

About 30 km north-east of Estcourt is the 5000-hectare **Weenen Nature Reserve**, which has black and white rhinos, buffaloes, giraffes and several antelope species, including the rare roan. There are two good walking trails – Amanzimyama and Reclamation. Camp sites (☎ (0363) 41809) cost R13 per person; entry costs R4 per person and R8 per vehicle.

Almost at the point where the R103 meets the R74, 16 km north of Escourt, is the site where the young Winston Churchill was captured by the Boers in 1899 when they derailed the armoured train he was travelling in; there is a plaque just off the road.

Places to Stay

The inexpensive municipal *caravan park* (☎ (0363) 23000, fax 33 5829) isn't far from the town centre on Lorne St. *Lucey's Plough Hotel* (☎ (0363) 23040, fax 22580), 86 Harding St, has rooms for about R100/150 with bath and R75/125 without, including breakfast.

Getting There & Away

Bus Transtate services between Welkom and Port Shepstone, via Pietermaritzburg, sometimes stop in Estcourt. Greyhound buses on the Durban-Kimberley and Durban-Jo'burg/Pretoria route leave from the municipal library on Victoria St. Book at Tourserve (☎ (0363) 22170) at 79 Harding St.

Wembezi Tours has local buses departing from the minibus-taxi rank to Durban (R20), Ladysmith (R10), Bergville (R4) and Newcastle (R14).

Train The *Trans-Oranje* (Cape Town-Durban) and the daily *Trans-Natal* (Jo'burg/Pretoria-Durban) stop here. Book tickets at

the goods (freight) depot, not at the railway station. The depot is a few blocks south-west of the station, past the Nestlé factory and under the railway overpass.

Minibus Taxi The main minibus-taxi rank is at the bottom of Phillips St in the town centre, downhill from the post office. Taxis beside the post office are for the local area only. Examples of fares are Durban R18, Winterton R5, Ladysmith R9, Pietermaritzburg R14, and Jo'burg R45.

COLENSO

As well as Spioenkop, there are several other Anglo-Boer War battlefields near Colenso, a small town about 20 km south of Ladysmith. Colenso was the British base during the Relief of Ladysmith, and there is a museum and several memorial sites relating to the Battle of Colenso on 15 December 1899, another disaster for the hapless General Buller at the hands of Louis Botha. The **museum** is in the toll house adjacent to the bridge. You can get the keys from the police station between 8 am and 6 pm.

Lord Roberts' only son, Freddy, was among those slaughtered here (with about 1100 other British) – he is buried in the **Chieveley military cemetery**, south of town.

There is a municipal *caravan park* (☎ (03622) 2737) in town and the *Old Jail Lodge* (☎ (03622) 2594) which has a restaurant. *Mt Sully* (☎ (03622) 2827) is in a nice spot overlooking the Tugela River with views of the Drakensberg. Accommodation only costs R55 and full board is R120.

SPIOENKOP NATURE RESERVE

This 6000-hectare Natal Parks Board reserve is based on the Spioenkop Dam on the Tugela River. The reserve is handy to most of the area's battlefield sites and not too far from the Drakensberg for day trips. Animals in the small game reserves (there are two reserves in the resort) include white rhinos, giraffes, zebras and various antelope species. There are guided walks from R15 per adult (minimum R60). There's a swimming pool, and horse-riding and tours of the Spioenkop battlefield are available. Entry to the resort costs R4; there's an interesting pamphlet with a map of the area.

Accommodation at the eight-bed bush camp at *Ntenjwa* or in the four-bed tented camp at *iPika* (☎ (036) 488 1578, fax 488 1065 to book) costs R45 (minimum R135). Camp sites with power at iPika cost R16.

The resort is just north of Bergville but the entrance is on the eastern side, off the R600, which runs between the N3 and Winterton. If you are coming from the south on the N3 take the turn off to the R74 to get to Winterton.

LADYSMITH

Ladysmith (not to be confused with the town of Ladismith in Western Cape Province) was named after the wife of Cape governor Sir Harry Smith, but it could well have had a much more colourful name; she wasn't just plain Lady Smith, she was Lady Juana Maria de los Dolores...Smith.

The town achieved fame during the 1899-1902 Anglo-Boer War, when it was besieged by Boer forces for 118 days. Apart from the historical aspect – several buildings in the

city centre were here during the siege – Ladysmith (the 'smith' is sometimes pronounced 'smit') is a pleasant place to walk around.

Sadly, Ladysmith is a microcosm of modern South Africa. The whites live in relative comfort in the best parts of town; most of Ladysmith's large Indian population lives south and west of the river in Leonardsville and Rose Park; the coloured population lives in Limit Hill; and the blacks in townships around eZakheni (once in KwaZulu), 20 km away.

The information office (☎ (0361) 22992) is in the town hall on Murchison St and is open on weekdays during office hours. Ask here about guided tours of the battlefields.

Things to See & Do

The good **Siege Museum** is next to the town hall in the Market House (built in 1884) which was used to store rations during the siege. You can pick up a walking-tour map of Ladysmith here. The museum is open between 8 am and 4.20 pm on weekdays and until noon on Saturday. If you phone ☎ (0361) 22231 (ask for the museum) you can arrange for someone to open the museum

The Battle of Spioenkop
On 23 January 1900 the British, led by General Buller, made a second attempt to relieve Ladysmith, which had been under siege by the Boers since late October 1899. After 15,000 of his men had been prevented from crossing the Tugela River by 500 Boers at Trichardt's Drift, Buller decided that he needed to take Spioenkop. This flat-topped hill would make a good gun emplacement from which to clear the annoying Boers from their trenches.

During the night 1700 British troops climbed the hill and chased off the few Boers guarding it. They dug a trench and waited for morning. Meanwhile the Boer commander, Louis Botha, heard of the raid. He ordered his field guns to be trained onto Spioenkop and positioned some of his men on nearby hills. A further 400 soldiers began to climb Spioenkop as the misty dawn broke.

The British might have beaten off the 400, but the mist finally lifted, and was immediately replaced by a hail of bullets and shells. The British retreated to their trench and by mid-afternoon, continuous shellfire combined with the summer heat caused many to surrender. By now, reinforcements were on hand (summoned, according to some, by the young Winston Churchill) and the Boers could not overrun the trench. A bloody stalemate was developing.

After sunset the British evacuated the hill; so did the Boers. Both retreats were accomplished so smoothly that neither side was aware that the other had left. That night Spioenkop was held by the dead.

It was not until the next morning that the Boers again climbed the hill and found that it was theirs. The Boers had killed or wounded 1340 British and taken 1000 prisoners, at a loss of 230 casualties, unusually high for their small army. Gandhi's stretcher-bearer unit performed with distinction at this battle. Buller relieved Ladysmith a month later on 28 February. ■

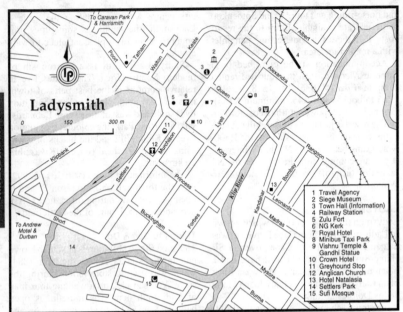

Ladysmith

0   150   300 m

1 Travel Agency
2 Siege Museum
3 Town Hall (Information)
4 Railway Station
5 Zulu Fort
6 NG Kerk
7 Royal Hotel
8 Minibus Taxi Park
9 Vishnu Temple &
   Gandhi Statue
10 Crown Hotel
11 Greyhound Stop
12 Anglican Church
13 Hotel Natalasia
14 Settlers Park
15 Sufi Mosque

for you between 2 and 4 pm on Saturday or from 10 to 11.30 am on Sunday.

Outside the town hall are two guns, **Castor** and **Pollux**, used by the British in defence of Ladysmith. Nearby is a replica of **Long Tom**, a Boer gun capable of heaving a shell 10 km. Long Tom was put out of action by a British raiding party during the siege, but not before it had caused a great deal of damage.

On the corner of King St and Settlers Dr is the police station, which includes the wall with loopholes from the original **Zulu Fort**, built as a refuge from Zulu attack.

Across the river on the west side of town (there's a footbridge) is a **Sufi Mosque**, built by the Muslim community which has been in Ladysmith almost since the town's inception. The mosque is worth seeing. There's also a Hindu **Vishnu temple**, and while the building is undistinguished you'll meet some friendly people there. As well as religious statues inside the temple, in the garden is a **statue of Gandhi**. The statue was imported from Bombay and depicts Gandhi as the Mahatma and not as a stretcher bearer with Buller's forces at Spioenkop, which would have been more appropriate.

South of town, near the junction of the N11 and R103, is an area generally known as **Platrand** (or Wagon Hill). There is an unusual monument to the Boers who died attempting to wrest Wagon Hill from the British on 6 January 1900.

Places to Stay & Eat

The municipal *caravan park* (☎ (0361) 26050) is on the north side of town; follow Poort Rd over the hill, where it becomes the Harrismith road.

Near the town hall, on Murchison St, the main street, there are two crusty old hotels. The *Crown* (☎ (0361) 22266) has bed and breakfast for R165 per person (dinner, bed and breakfast is R185). The *Royal* (☎/fax

(0361) 22176) has bed and breakfast singles/doubles for R141/178 (dinner, bed and breakfast is R162/225). Out on the Durban road, three km from the town, the *Andrew Motel* (☎/fax (0361) 26908) charges R95/130.

The Indian-owned *Natalasia Hotel* (☎ (0361) 26821), on the corner of Leonards and Kandahar Sts about one km from the tourist office has unfortunately gone downhill, and a reader reports not being able to buy an Indian meal in the restaurant. Rooms go for R90/120 per person on weekdays/weekends, with breakfast.

There is a B&B service – the information office has details of at least a half-dozen farmstays and as many B&Bs. Generally expect to pay R90 per person.

Other than the hotel restaurants there are a few up-market restaurants, including *Quincey's* on Keate St.

Getting There & Away
Bus Transtate buses originating in Welkom and travelling via Bethlehem sometimes stop at Ladysmith railway station en route to Pietermaritzburg and Port Shepstone. Translux buses (☎ (0361) 27 1111) leave from the railway station and run to Durban (R70) and Bloemfontein (R120). Greyhound (☎ (0361) 24181) has daily services to Jo'burg/Pretoria and Durban. Book at the Shell service station on the corner of Murchison and King Sts, or Destinations Travel (☎ (0361) 31 0831).

There are local companies serving Qwa-Qwa and the immediate area, some of which will get you fairly close to the Drakensberg.

Train The *Trans-Oranje* (Durban-Cape Town) and the daily *Trans-Natal* (Durban-Jo'burg/Pretoria) both stop here, but at inconvenient times; phone (0361) 271 2020 for bookings. Fares in 1st/2nd/3rd class are Jo'burg R104/69/42, Durban R71/48/29 and Pietermaritzburg R49/34/20.

Minibus Taxi The main taxi rank is south of the centre near the corner of Queen and Lyell Sts. Taxis for Harrismith and Jo'burg are

nearby on Alexandra St. Some destinations are Jo'burg (R40), Durban (R25), Harrismith (R8) and Dundee (R8).

NEWCASTLE
Not surprisingly, Newcastle is a coal-mining and a steel-producing town. The white population is 25,000, there are 16,000 Indians in Lennoxton and Lenville, and 250,000 blacks in the nearby townships of Madadeni and Osizweni.

There's an Anglo-Boer War museum in **Fort Amiel**, open Tuesday to Thursday 9 am to 1 pm, Friday 11 am to 4 pm and Saturday 9 am to 1 pm. Fort Amiel was established in 1876 when the British anticipated conflict with the Zulu. The colonial-era **town hall** (☎ (03431) 53318, fax 29815) on Scott St is worth a look, and you can get information, including details of local accommodation, there from enthusiastic staff.

Tours of the two large black **townships**, Madadeni and Osizweni are being arranged; enquire at the town hall or ring Madadeni (☎ (03431) 91171). There is a **handicraft centre** in Osizweni which is worth a visit.

The turn-off to **Chelmsford Public Resort** is on the R23 about 25 km south of Newcastle. As well as watersports on the dam there is a small game reserve with white rhinos, and there is Natal Parks Board accommodation. Chalets cost R44 per person (minimum R132) and the eight-bed trail hut on the Holkrans Trail at Ncandu is R20 per person. Camp sites (☎ (03431) 77205) at Leokop, Richgate and Sandford cost R13 per person; entry is R4 per person.

Holkrans Walking Trail
This trail is 25 km south-west of Newcastle just off the Normandien road and in the Drakensberg foothills. The trail is 25 km long and divided into two stages – an 11.5 km walk to the night stop, a *holkrans* (overhang) in the sandstone cliffs, and a six-km walk via a ravine and grassveld back to the start point. For information, telephone ☎ (03431) 77205.

KWAZULU/NATAL

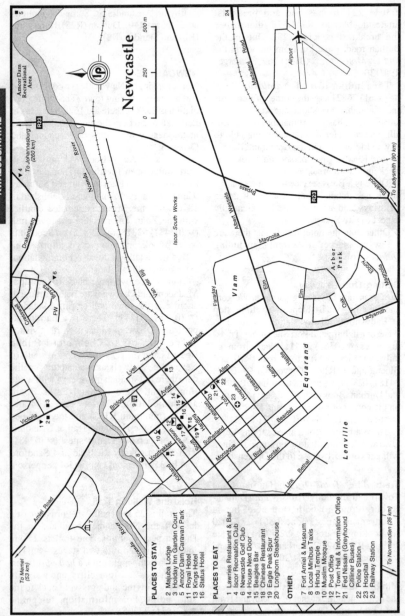

Newcastle

0   250   500 m

To Memel
(53 km)

To Johannesburg
(260 km)

To Ladysmith
(90 km)

To Normandien
(35 km)

Amcor Dam
Recreational
Area

Amiel Road

Drakensberg

Cresswell

FW
Gardens

Ncandu River

Ncandu River

R23

R23

Bypass

Iscor South Works

Airport

Masonical Road

Albert Wessels

Magnolia

Viam

Arbor
Park

Elm

Oak

Faraday

Ladysmith

Hardwick

Lyell

Bridger

Victoria

Voortrekker

Scott

Sutherland

Montague

Bird

Jordan

Link

Bethal

Lenville

Equarand

Allen

Greaves

Harding

Kirkby

Beardall

Murchison

Paterson

Kirkland

Drakensberg

PLACES TO STAY
2 Majuba Lodge
3 Holiday Inn Garden Court
5 Amcor Dam Caravan Park
11 Royal Hotel
13 Kings Hotel
16 Status Hotel

PLACES TO EAT
1 Lawries Restaurant & Bar
4 Iscor Recreation Club
6 Newcastle Golf Club
14 House Next Door
15 Beagles Bar
18 Chinese Restaurant
19 Eagle Peak Spur
20 Longhorn Steakhouse

OTHER
7 Fort Amiel & Museum
8 Local Minibus Taxis
9 Hindu Temple
10 Muslim Mosque
12 Post Office
17 Town Hall & Information Office
21 Fed Nissan (Greyhound
     Citiliner Buses)
22 Police Station
23 Hospital
24 Railway Station

Horse-Riding

There is plenty of scope to go horse-riding in the region west of Newcastle. Ndanyaan Mountain Trails (☎ (03431) 23028) is about 20 km from the city in the Mullers Pass region of the Biggarsberg near the Ncandu River. They offer various rides; one combines protea groves, a crossing of the Ncandu River, grassveld and montane forest.

Places to Stay

The municipal *caravan park* (☎ (03431) 81273) is out of town at Amcor Dam; a powered site is R28 plus R3 per person (up to a maximum of six people).

Cheaper hotels include *Kings* (☎ (03431) 26101), on the corner of Harding and Hardwick Sts, and the upgraded *Royal* (☎ (03431) 25895), at 20 Voortrekker St, The *Status* (☎/fax (03431) 27064), at 55 Scott St, is more expensive (R152/160 for bed and breakfast). There's a *Holiday Inn Garden Court* (☎ (03431) 28151, fax 24142) on the corner of Victoria and Hunter Sts, with rooms from R174/190.

Ask travelling salespeople what is the best accommodation in Newcastle and they will shout '*Majuba Lodge*'. The lodge (☎ (03431) 55011, fax 55023) is opposite the Holiday Inn at 27 Victoria Rd; the cost is R167 per lodge and breakfast is R20. Nearly all the lodges have private parking and all are within stumbling distance of Lawries.

You can stay in a vibrant township overnight. The *Ficakancane Hotel* (☎ (03431) 91041) in Madadeni has singles/doubles for R55/67 and there's a key deposit of R30.

For information on B&Bs and farmstays phone (03431) 53318.

Places to Eat

The best place to eat is *Lawries Restaurant* in the grounds of the Majuba Lodge. All meals come with a loaf of bread and paté, so a baked potato, at R10, will be a meal in itself.

High Stakes, opposite the town hall in Scott St, has large steaks for about R25. They have a Sunday carvery in their Chuck Wagon. The *House Next Door* in Harding St is a good restaurant with ladies' bar attached, and not far away is *Beagles* on the corner of Allen and Harding Sts. There is an unnamed Chinese place opposite the information office, a *Spur* steakhouse on Voortrekker St and the *Longhorn*, also for steak, on Allen St. The meals at the *Newcastle Golf Club* have been recommended; R25 sees you well satisfied.

Battle of Majuba Hill – 1881

The British annexed the first South African Republic (ZAR) of Transvaal on 12 April 1877. After peaceful protest failed, over 8000 armed Boers met at Paardekraal and pledged to reinstate the ZAR government as from 13 December, using force if necessary. The first shots were fired at Potchefstroom on 16 December and several British garrisons were besieged. The obvious route for British reinforcements sent to relieve the garrisons would be from Durban to Transvaal via Newcastle. Piet Joubert moved 2000 mounted troops to the strategic position of Laings Nek, north of Newcastle, in anticipation of this move.

The British under Sir George Colley attacked the Boers on 28 January 1881 at Laings Nek but had to retreat after an hour. On 8 February a British wagon column was encircled by Boers at Schuinshoogte (Ingogo) and suffered heavy casualties.

On the night of 26 February, Colley and nearly 600 troops climbed Majuba Hill to overlook the Boer positions. The British in their bright uniforms, cumbersome helmets and armed with Martini Henry rifles (with their sights incorrectly adjusted) were no match for the highly mobile Boers. The British panicked and began to flee. About 1 pm on the 27th, Colley was fatally wounded; in all, 285 British soldiers were killed, wounded or taken prisoner.

When news was received of Colley's death, General Sir Evelyn Wood was sworn in as acting governor of Natal. On 6 March he met the Boer commanders at O'Neill's Cottage, at the base of Majuba, to negotiate peace. The battle and events before and after are described in G A Chadwick's *The First War of Independence in Natal: 1880-1881* (R4). ∎

Getting There & Away

Transtate runs to Jo'burg at 11 pm on Sunday, Monday and Wednesday (arriving in central Jo'burg at the dangerous hour of 3 am), and travels south through KwaZulu/Natal to Nongoma via Vryheid on Tuesday and Friday at 2.30 pm. Greyhound (contact Park Tours) runs to Jo'burg and Durban daily, from the Stadsaal on Scott St. The *Eagle Liner* (KwaZulu Transport) operates to Osizweni. Minibus taxis to Jo'burg cost R25.

First/2nd/3rd-class fares on the daily *Trans-Natal* train to Jo'burg are R78/52/31 and to Durban, R97/65/39.

Car rental companies in Newcastle are Imperial (☎ (03431) 22806), based at Newcastle Airport, and Avis (☎ (03431) 21274) at Leon Motors, Allen St.

MAJUBA HILL

The first Anglo-Boer War ended abruptly 40 km north of Newcastle, with the British defeat at **Majuba Hill** in 1881. The site has been restored and a map is available; there is a small entry fee. The Laings Nek and Schuinshoogte battlefields are also signposted.

Peace negotiations took place at **O'Neill's Cottage** in the foothills near Majuba. The cottage, used as a hospital during the battle, has been restored and has a photographic display; it is open daily.

UTRECHT

Today a quiet little town in prime cattle country, Utrecht was once the capital of one of the original Voortrekker republics, this one measuring just 30 by 65 km! The town was the British headquarters during the Anglo-Zulu War, and a number of fine 19th-century buildings remain. There's a museum (☎ (03433) 3041) in the old parsonage, open weekdays from 8 am to 6 pm but closed for lunch; pick up a brochure there on the town's attractions.

The *Balele Resort* (☎ (03433) 3041) is five km north of town on the Wakkerstroom road. Rondavels are R50 per person, sites are R13.50 plus R4.50 per person. You book

here to do the two-day, 25-km **Balele Hiking Trail** which passes through the Enhlanzeni Valley in the Langalibalele Range. Accommodation is R30 per person; the first night is in an old farmhouse, and the overnight camp has beehive huts.

The *Siesta Guesthouse* (☎ (03433) 3663), 9 Jooste St, is good value at R65 per person with full board. A guide is available for three Langalibalele walking trails – Red Marlothi Aloe (three hours), P J Schoeman (up to eight hours) and Grootkloof (four hours).

DUNDEE

Dundee is a large coal town, not especially attractive but perhaps useful as a base for the area's historical sites. It was named by an early settler who came from a village near Dundee in Scotland.

On the Vryheid road, 1.5 km out of town, is the **Talana Museum**, dedicated to 'small men who had to take root or die, not to the captains and kings who departed'. It's still being developed but it's already a large place with several old buildings and displays on coal-mining and local history, which includes both the Anglo-Zulu and the Anglo-Boer Wars. Some good pamphlets on the area's history are available. The museum's open on weekdays and on weekend afternoons.

You can get information from the Talana Museum or the town hall. Phone ☎ (0341) 22654 to arrange a guided tour of the battlefields.

Some 27 km to the south of Dundee is the small village of **Wasbank**, where the Voortrekkers, on their way to Blood River on 9 December 1838, made a promise (referred to by them subsequently as The Vow) that if God gave them victory over the Zulu they would build a church in his honour and commemorate the event annually. The Battle of Blood River took place one week later.

To the east of Dundee, 52 km away via the R33 and R68, is the fascinating regional centre of **Nqutu**. This is an important trading centre for the surrounding Zulu community and about as close to a buzzing urban black town as you will see. A minibus to Nqutu is about R40 from Jo'burg. About 30 km north of Nqutu near Nondtweni is the memorial to the **Prince Imperial Louis Napoleon**, the last of the Bonaparte dynasty, who was killed here on 1 June 1879.

Places to Stay & Eat
The municipal *caravan park* (☎ (0341) 22121) has sites for about R20. To get there take the Ladysmith road out of the town centre and turn right at the traffic lights.

There are several B&Bs in Dundee and nearby; check at the Talana Museum or the town hall, or phone ☎ (0341) 22654. The *Penny Farthing* (☎/fax (03425) 925), 30 km south of Dundee, is typical of the B&Bs. Singles/doubles cost from R100/150.

The *Royal Hotel* (☎ (0341) 22147) on Victoria St opposite the town hall has single/double rooms with bath for R95/160 (without bath it's R60/120), including breakfast. The nearby *El Mpati Hotel* (☎ (0341), 21155), at 59 Victoria St is R108/160, also with breakfast.

At the licensed *Buffalo Steakhouse*, near the corner of Gladstone and Victoria Sts, a steak meal starts at R25. The *Miner's Rest* at Talana serves lunch (beef Wellington with vegetables is about R22). The golf, cricket and rugby clubs offer pub lunches from R11.

Getting There & Away
Transtate's Jo'burg/Pretoria-Empangeni and Welkom-Nongoma buses stop at Dundee.

Minibus-taxi destinations from Dundee include Vryheid (R10), Ladysmith (R8), and Jo'burg (R40).

ISANDLWANA & RORKE'S DRIFT
You have probably heard of the Defence of Rorke's Drift but not the Battle of Isandlwana – the former was a British imperial victory of the misty-eyed variety, the latter was a bloody disaster.

Isandlwana should not be missed. At the base of this sphinx-like rock there are many graves and memorials to those who fell in battle on 22 January 1879. The Isandlwana museum, with artefacts taken from the bat-

tlefield, is in St Vincent's (the bluestone buildings in the nearby village) just outside the site. You pay the R4 entry here. For an evocative tour of the battlefield contact guide John Turner (☎ (03872), ask for 1303).

At Rorke's Drift, 42 km from Dundee, there is a splendid museum, a self-guided trail around the battlefield, several memorials and the ELC Zulu craft centre, open from Monday to Saturday. The rugs and tapestries woven here are world-renowned and therefore not cheap; a small wall-hanging costs from R1000 to R1200.

The Battle of Isandlwana
The Battle of Isandlwana was the first major engagement of the 1879 Anglo-Zulu War, precipitated by an ultimatum to Cetshwayo which the British knew he would not and could not meet. The demands included the complete re-organisation of the Zulu political structure and the abolition of the Zulu army.

On 22 January 1879 a soldier from one of the five British forces sent to invade Zululand happened to look over a ridge near Isandlwana Hill. He was surprised to discover 25,000 Zulu warriors sitting in the gully below, silently awaiting the time to attack. This was to have been the following day, the day after the full moon, but on being discovered the impis adopted their battle formation – two enclosing 'horns' on the flanks and the main force in the centre – and attacked the utterly unprepared British camp. By the end of the day almost all of the British were dead, along with many Zulus.

Meanwhile, the small British contingent which had remained at Rorke's Drift (where the army had crossed into Zululand) to guard supplies, heard of the disaster and fortified their camp. They were attacked by about 4000 Zulus but the defenders, numbering fewer than 100 fit soldiers, held on through the night until a relief column arrived. Victoria Crosses were lavished on the defenders – 11 in all – and another couple went to the two officers at Fugitive's Drift.

Many people will know of these battles by the movies made of them: *Zulu Dawn* for Isandlwana and *Zulu* for Rorke's Drift. Perhaps the best account of the Anglo-Zulu War is *The Washing of the Spears* by D Morris. ∎

The Zulu know this site as *Shiyane*, their name for the hill at the back of the village. The *Rorke's Drift-Shiyane Self-Guided Trail* brochure is helpful for understanding the close nature of the fighting in this battle.

About 10 km south of Rorke's Drift is **Fugitive's Drift Lodge**. Two British officers were killed at Fugitive's Drift attempting to prevent the Queen's Colours from falling into Zulu hands (losing colours was a definite no-no in the British Army). The *Fugitive's Drift Lodge* (☎ (03425), ask for 843) has single/double rooms for R342/456 per person. The owner, Dave Rattray, is also a registered tour guide.

While you are in this area it is worthwhile taking a sidetrip to the spectacular **Mangeni Falls**, at the head of a tributary of the Buffalo River. About 35 km east of Babanango, at Silutshana, turn south and follow the road to Mangeni. At Mangeni you will probably have to ask the way to the falls as the track is not obvious.

Getting There & Away

The battle sites are south-east of Dundee. Isandlwana is about 70 km from Dundee, off the R68; Rorke's Drift is about 50 km from Dundee, also accessible from the R68 or R33 (the R33 turn-off is 13 km south of Dundee). The road to Isandlwana is sealed but the roads to Rorke's Drift and Fugitive's Drift can be dusty and rough.

BLOOD RIVER MONUMENT

The Blood River battle site is marked by a full-scale re-creation of the 64-wagon laager in bronze. The cairn of stones was built by the Boers after the battle to mark the centre of their laager. The monument is 20 km south-east of the R33; the turn-off is 27 km from Dundee and 45 km from Vryheid.

The Battle of Blood River

The Battle of Blood River occurred on 16 December 1838 when a small party of Voortrekkers avenged the massacre of Piet Retief's party by the Zulus. The Voortrekkers defeated 12,000 Zulu warriors, killing 3000 while sustaining only a few casualties. This battle is a seminal event in Afrikaner history. The victory came to be seen as the fulfilment of God's side of the bargain and seemed to prove that the Boers had a divine mandate to conquer and 'civilise' southern Africa; that they were in fact a chosen people.

However, Afrikaner nationalism and the significance attached to Blood River grew in strength simultaneously and it has been argued (by Leach in *The Afrikaners – Their Last Great Trek* and others) that the importance of Blood River was deliberately heightened and manipulated for political ends. The standard interpretation of the victory meshed with the former apartheid regime's world view: hordes of untrustworthy black savages were beaten by Boers who were on an Old Testament-style mission from God. ■

Relief of carving on Blood River Monument

Western Cape Province

Western Cape Province takes in the south-western corner (and many of the attractions) of the old Cape Province, including Cape Town, the Winelands and the Garden Route. One of the highlights of a visit to South Africa is discovering the extraordinary flora, and this is most spectacularly represented in Western Cape, which is home to the prolific Cape floral kingdom.

Most of the province was populated by Khoisan tribes when the whites first arrived. Tragically, very few Khoisan survived, and their traditional cultures and languages have been almost completely lost.

The province is also home to the so-called 'coloureds', people who have diverse origins and didn't fit neatly into the apartheid system's pigeon-holes. Most people who were classified as coloured are descended from the Khoisan, slaves (from Asia and Africa), Xhosa, and Europeans. Most lead Westernised lifestyles; they're overwhelmingly Christian, and most speak Afrikaans.

Until apartheid really got going in the 1950s they were quite closely integrated with the Europeans; they even had voting rights. Distinctive sub-groups include the Nama and Griqua and the Cape Muslims of the Cape Peninsula, who were imported from east Asia as slaves and have maintained their Islamic traditions.

Before Europeans arrived there were few or no Bantu peoples in the area, but many Bantu, particularly Xhosa, have gravitated to the Cape and the larger towns and cities in search of work.

HISTORY

Khoikhoi tribes with a pastoralist semi-nomadic lifestyle inhabited the Cape Peninsula and most of the best grazing land along the south and west coasts. They co-existed with their close relatives the San, who were nomadic hunter-gatherers capable of surviving in the driest corners of Africa.

Portuguese explorers charted the coast

WESTERN CAPE PROVINCE
Capital: Cape Town
Main Languages: English, Afrikaans, Xhosa
Pre-1994: The south-west corner of Cape Province
Highlights:
• Cape Town
• The Winelands
• Whale-watching
• The Garden Route
• The Little (Klein) Karoo

from the 15th century, and the first permanent white settlement was established in Cape Town by the Dutch in 1652. Explorers, hunters and cattle-farming trekboers quickly fanned out into the surrounding countryside. By the second half of the 18th century, the Khoisan were decimated and the whites were battling with the Xhosa tribes in the east, a struggle that would continue for the next 100 years.

In 1806 the British seized the Cape from the Dutch for the second and final time, to prevent the strategically important port falling into the hands of the French. The Cape remained a British colony until the Union of South Africa was instituted in 1910.

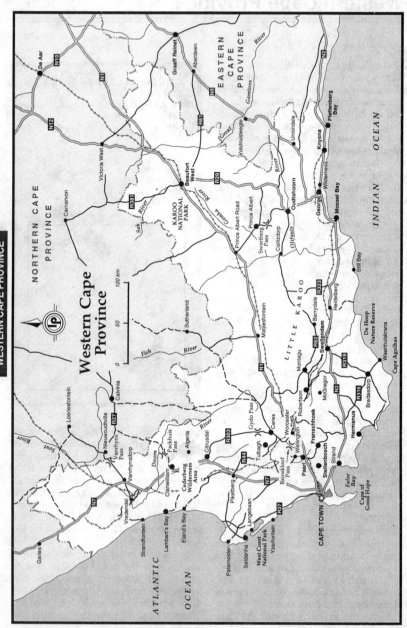

Between 1834 and 1840 approximately 15,000 Afrikaners left the Cape on the Great Trek to the north where they established independent republics. Their relationship with the British colony was uneasy at best. One of the primary reasons they left was to escape the British administration, but they were still dependent on British ports and were clearly overshadowed by the power of the British Empire.

During the 1899-1902 Anglo-Boer War there was little direct impact on the Western Cape area but not surprisingly, many people were deeply ambivalent about the war, and many Afrikaners joined the Boer republics' forces.

Cape Town & the Peninsula

Cape Town, or Kaapstad, is one of the most beautiful cities in the world. No matter how long you stay, the image of the mountains and the sea will be seared into your mind.

About 40 km from the Cape of Good Hope, near the southern tip of the vast African continent, it is one of the most geographically isolated of the world's great cities. Dominated by a 1000-metre high, flat-topped mountain with virtually sheer cliffs, it's surrounded by superb mountain walks, vineyards and beaches.

Pointless debates attempt to compare Cape Town with great coastal cities like Rio de Janeiro, Sydney, San Francisco and Vancouver. None can surpass the drama of Cape Town's site or its 350 years of recorded history. Long before travel writers' hyperbole devalued the language, Francis Drake's chronicler described the Cape of Good Hope as, 'The most stately thing, and the fairest cape we saw in the whole circumference of the earth'.

Like all South African cities, Cape Town is schizophrenic – European but not European, African but not African – a volatile mixture of the third and first-worlds. The cafés in Sea Point and the bars around the Victoria & Alfred Waterfront could be in any cosmopolitan capital, but the townships on the bleak, windswept plains to the east of the city could only be in Africa. There are few places where there is a more stark difference between rich and poor. Apartheid allowed the whites to reserve some of the world's most spectacular real estate, and the contrast between Crossroads and Clifton is complete – black and white.

Cape Town has the reputation for being the most open-minded and relaxed city in South Africa, but the scars of apartheid run deep. Outside of the black townships, however, there is nothing like the sense of tension that pervades Jo'burg. Perhaps it is partly because the coloureds are in many ways culturally integrated, but in the Western-style city centre you could easily imagine the problems of South Africa are a figment of journalistic imagination.

Cape Town is the capital of Western Cape Province (it was the capital of the old Cape Province which covered more than half the country) and is the parliamentary capital of the republic. Pretoria can mount a good case for being made parliamentary capital in the new South Africa, but it's unlikely to succeed.

Cape Town works as a city in a way that few on the African continent do. There is a sense of history, and even in the centre, historical buildings have been saved. There are restaurants, cafés and bars, parks and gardens, markets and shops – all the things that make living in a city worthwhile. And then there are a few things that most cities don't have: mountains, magnificent surf beaches and outstanding vineyards.

Cape Town is a highlight of any visit to South Africa. If you can, give yourself at least a week, but you may well find – like many before you – that a week is far too short.

HISTORY
San & Khoikhoi
The human history of the Cape began tens of thousands of years ago with stone-age tribes.

They were followed by the San, hunter-gatherers who left no sign of their occupation beyond superb cave paintings. By the time the first Portuguese mariners arrived, however, the Cape was occupied by Khoikhoi, close relatives of the San, who were semi-nomadic sheep and cattle pastoralists.

Portuguese

The Portuguese came in search of a sea route to India and that most precious of medieval commodities – spice. Bartholomeu Dias rounded the Cape in 1487 naming it Cabo da Boa Esperanca (Cape of Good Hope), but his eyes were fixed on the trade riches of the east coast of Africa and the Indies.

In 1503 Antonio de Saldanha became the first European to climb Table Mountain. The Portuguese, however, were not interested in settling on the Cape. It offered little more than fresh water; attempts to trade with the Khoikhoi often ended in violence and the coast and its fierce weather posed a terrible threat to their tiny caravels.

Dutch

By the end of the 16th century the English and Dutch were beginning to challenge the Portuguese traders, and the Cape became a regular stopover for their scurvy-ridden crews. In 1647, a Dutch East Indiaman was wrecked in Table Bay and its crew built a fort and stayed for a year before they were rescued.

This crystallised the value of a permanent settlement in the minds of the directors of the Dutch East India Company (Vereenigde Oost-Indische Compagnie or VOC). They had no intention of colonising the country, but simply of establishing a secure base where ships could shelter and stock up on fresh supplies of meat, fruit and vegetables.

Jan van Riebeeck was the man they chose to lead a small expedition in his flagship *Drommedaris*. His specific charge was to build a fort, barter with the Khoikhoi for meat and to plant a garden. He reached Table Bay on 6 April 1652, built a mud-walled fort not far from the site of the surviving stone castle, and planted gardens that have now become the Botanical or Company's Gardens.

In 1660, in a gesture that takes on an awful symbolism, van Riebeeck planted a bitter-almond hedge to separate the Khoikhoi and the Europeans. It extended around the western foot of Table Mountain down to Table Bay – sections can still be seen in Kirstenbosch Botanic Gardens. The hedge may have protected the 120 Europeans but, having excluded the Khoikhoi, there was a chronic labour shortage. In another wonderfully perverse move, van Riebeeck proceeded to import slaves (many of whom were Muslim) from Madagascar, India, Ceylon, Malaya and Indonesia.

The European men of the community were overwhelmingly employees of the VOC and overwhelmingly Dutch – a tiny official elite and a majority of ill-educated soldiers and sailors, many of whom had been pressed into service. In 1685 they were joined by around 200 French Huguenots, Calvinists who fled from persecution by King Louis XIV.

The population of whites did not reach 1000 until 1745, but small numbers of free (meaning non-VOC) burghers had begun to drift away from the close grip of the company, and into other areas of Africa. These were the first of the Trekboers and their inevitable confrontations with the Khoisan were disastrous. The indigenous people were driven from their traditional lands, decimated by introduced diseases, and destroyed by superior weapons when they fought back. The survivors were left with no option but to work for Europeans in a form of bondage little different from slavery.

There was a shortage of women in the colony so the female slaves and Khoisan survivors were exploited both for labour and sex. In time, the slaves also inter-mixed with the Khoisan. The offspring of these unions formed the basis for sections of today's coloured population.

The VOC maintained almost complete control, but the town was thriving – providing a comfortable European lifestyle to a growing number of artisans and entrepreneurs

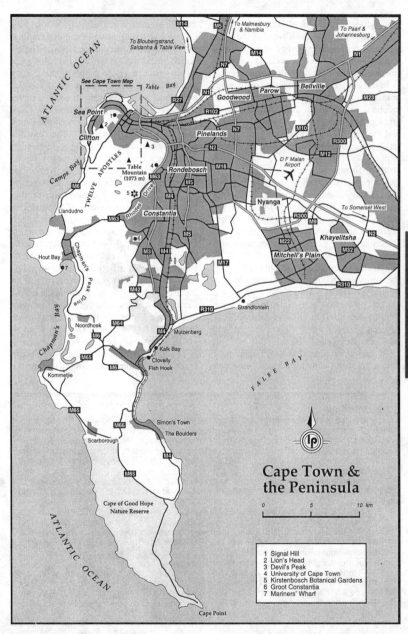

WESTERN CAPE PROVINCE

**Cape Town &
the Peninsula**

0   5   10 km

1 Signal Hill
2 Lion's Head
3 Devil's Peak
4 University of Cape Town
5 Kirstenbosch Botanical Gardens
6 Groot Constantia
7 Mariners' Wharf

who serviced the ships and crews. Cape Town was known as the Tavern of the Seas, a riotous port used by every navigator, privateer and merchant travelling between Europe and the East (including Australia).

In the early days of European settlement, animals common in the area included lion, elephant, hippo, black rhino, buffalo, hyena and leopard. They were very soon killed off and the great slaughter of southern Africa's wildlife began.

British

Dutch power was fading by the end of the 18th century and in response to the Napoleonic wars, the British decided to secure the Cape. In 1806, at Bloubergstrand 25 km north of Cape Town, the British defeated the Dutch and the colony was permanently ceded to the Crown on 13 August 1814.

The slave trade was abolished in 1808, and the remaining Khoisan, who were virtually treated as slaves, were finally given the explicit protection of the law (including the right to own land) in 1828, moves that contributed to Afrikaners' dissatisfaction and the Great Trek (1834-40).

At the same time that these apparently liberal reforms were introduced, however,

the British introduced new laws that laid the basis for an exploitative labour system little different from slavery. Thousands of dispossessed blacks sought work in the colony, but it was made a crime to be in the colony without a pass, and without work. It was also a crime to leave your job. In 1854, a representative parliament was formed in Cape Town, but much to the dismay of the Dutch and English farmers to the north and east, the British government and Cape liberals insisted on a multiracial constituency (albeit with financial qualifications that excluded the vast majority of blacks and coloureds).

The discovery and exploitation of diamonds and gold in the centre of South Africa in the 1870s and '80s led to rapid changes. Cape Town was soon no longer the single dominant metropolis in the country, but as a major port it too was a beneficiary of mineral wealth that laid the foundations for an industrial society. The same wealth led to imperialist dreams of grandeur on the part of Cecil John Rhodes (who became the premier of the Cape Colony in 1890) who had made his millions at the head of De Beers Consolidated Mines.

In 1860, construction of the Alfred Basin in the docks commenced, finally making the

---

Cape Muslims

Cape Muslims (generally called Cape Malays by whites) are South Africans of long standing. Although many were brought to the early Cape Colony as slaves, others were political prisoners and exiles from the Dutch East Indies. Some of the first prisoners on Robben Island were Muslims. People were brought from countries as far apart as India and modern Indonesia, but their lingua franca was Malay (at the time an important trading language), which is why they came to be called Cape Malays.

A common language and religion, plus the presence of important political and religious figures, helped a cohesive community to develop. It has survived intact over the centuries, and even resisted some of the worst abuses of the apartheid decades.

Around Cape Town is the Circle of Karamats made up of the tombs of about 25 saints from the community. One of the first was Sheikh Yusef, a Batavian exiled to the Cape in the late 17th century. On the voyage out, his ship ran low on water, and the Sheikh obligingly turned sea water to fresh water. Another important exile was Tuan Guru from Tidor, who arrived in 1780. During his 13 years on Robben Island he copied the Koran from memory (his version is apparently quite accurate) and later helped establish the first mosque.

A visit to Bo Kaap, the 'Malay' Quarter, is a must, and while wandering around by yourself is rewarding, it's worth taking one of the tours run by local residents. Tana-Baru Tours (☎ (021) 24 0719, fax 23 5579) is very good and has a two-hour walking or driving tour for about R45. See the Tours section for more information. ■

port storm-proof. In 1869, however, the Suez Canal was opened, and Cape Town's role as the Tavern of the Seas began to wane. Today, the massive supertankers that are too big to use the Suez are also too big to enter Table Bay, so they are serviced by helicopter.

In 1895, Rhodes sponsored the unsuccessful Jameson Raid, which attempted to overthrow the South African Republic (Transvaal), under President Kruger, and bring it into a federation under British control. Rhodes was forced to resign, but the fiasco made the 1899-1902 Anglo-Boer War almost inevitable. Cape Town avoided any direct bloodshed in the terrible conflict, but it did play a key role in landing and supplying the half a million imperial and colonial troops who fought on the British side.

After the war, the British made some efforts towards reconciliation and moves towards the union of the separate South African provinces were instituted. The question of who would be allowed to vote was solved by allowing the provinces to retain their existing systems: blacks and coloureds retained a limited franchise in the Cape (although only whites could become members of the national parliament and eligible blacks and coloureds only constituted around 7% of the electorate) but did not have the vote in other provinces.

The issue of which city should become the capital was solved by the unwieldy compromise of making Cape Town the seat of the legislature, Pretoria the administrative capital, and Bloemfontein the seat of Appellate Division of the Supreme Court. The Union of South Africa came into being in 1910.

Apartheid & the Townships

In 1948 in the first election after WW II, the National Party stood on its policy of apartheid and narrowly won. In a series of bitter court and constitutional battles, the right of the coloureds to vote in the Cape was removed and the insane apparatus of apartheid was erected.

Since the coloureds had no Homeland, the western half of the Cape Province was declared a 'coloured preference area' which meant no black could be employed unless it could be proved there was no suitable coloured person for the job. No new black housing was built. As a result, illegal squatter camps mushroomed on the sandy plains to the east of Cape Town. In response, government bulldozers flattened the shanties, and their occupants were dragged away and dumped in their Homelands. Within weeks the shanties would rise again.

In 1960 the ANC and PAC organised marches against the hated pass laws, which required blacks and coloureds to carry passbooks which authorised them to be in a particular area. At Langa and Nyanga, outside Cape Town, police killed five protesters. In response to the crisis a warrant for the arrest of Nelson Mandela and other ANC leaders was issued. In mid-1963 Mandela was captured and sentenced to life imprisonment. Like many black leaders before him, Robben Island, in the middle of Table Bay, was his prison.

District Six, just to the east of the city centre, was the suburb that, more than any other, gave Cape Town its cosmopolitan atmosphere and life. It was primarily a coloured ghetto, but people of every race lived there. It was a poor, overcrowded, but vibrant community. The streets were alive with people, from children to traders, buskers to petty criminals. Jazz was its life blood and the district was home to many musicians, including the internationally known Dollar Brand. Being so close, it infected the whole city with its vitality.

This state of affairs naturally did not appeal to the National Party Government so, in 1966, District Six was classified as a white area. The 50,000 people, some of whose families had been there for five generations, were evicted and dumped in bleak and soulless townships like Athlone, Mitchell's Plain and Atlantis. Bulldozers moved in and the coloured heart was ripped out of the city. Today District Six is an open wasteland, a depressing monument to the cruelty and stupidity of the government. No-one, except the government, has had sufficient gall to build there.

The government tried for decades to eradicate squatter towns, such as Crossroads, which were focal points for black resistance to apartheid. In its last attempt between May and June 1986 an estimated 70,000 people were driven from their homes and hundreds were killed. Even this brutal attack was unsuccessful and the government accepted the inevitable and begun to upgrade conditions. Vast new townships are rapidly growing at Khayelitsha and Mitchell's Plain.

ORIENTATION

On first impression, Cape Town is surprisingly small. The city centre lies to the north of Table Mountain and east of Signal Hill, and the old inner city suburbs of Tamboerskloof, Gardens and Oranjezicht are all within walking distance of it. This area is sometimes referred to as the City Bowl. If you're walking to Gardens or Tamboerskloof from the city centre take Long St, which has some fine old buildings and a few good places to eat among the interesting junk and second-hand bookshops. There's also a smattering of strip clubs and porno video joints.

On the other side of Signal Hill, Sea Point is another older suburb densely populated with high-rise flats, apartments, hotels, restaurants and bars.

In some ways the peninsula seems remarkably undeveloped, an impression exaggerated by the untameable mountains that form its spine. In the 1985 (the most recent) South African census, the entire Cape Peninsula's white population numbered 540,000, and this seems to give the City Bowl its scale.

The main white dormitory suburbs spread quite a distance to the north-east of the city (either side of the N1 to Paarl, from Goodwood, Parow and Bellville through to Kraaifontein) and to the south, skirting the eastern flank of the mountains and running down to False Bay (from Observatory to Rosebank, Rondebosch, Constantia and through to Muizenberg).

There are some small towns and suburbs that cling to the coast. On the Atlantic side,

exclusive Clifton and Camps Bay are accessible by coastal road from Sea Point or through Kloof Nek, the pass between Table Mountain and Lion's Head. Camps Bay is a 10-minute drive (car or bus only) from the city centre, but as you go further south, the towns (Llandudno, Hout Bay and Kommetjie) become more inaccessible by public transport. The False Bay towns from Muizenberg to Simon's Town can all be reached by rail.

Of course, if you include blacks, coloureds and Asians the peninsula's population figures jump dramatically. The 1985 census counted 280,000 blacks, one million coloureds, and 18,000 Asians. These numbers were almost certainly inaccurate at the time, particularly in the case of the blacks, and they are now virtually meaningless.

No-one knows how many blacks live on the Cape, although some put the figure at about one million. Thousands arrive from the old Xhosa Homelands of Transkei and Ciskei every month. Most live on the bleak sandy plain to the east of the mountains known as the Cape Flats. South-east from the cooling towers of the power station at Athlone, the townships lie between the N2 freeway and False Bay. They include the venerable squatter camps around Crossroads, and the enormous new developments at Mitchell's Plain and Khayelitsha. There are also large black townships around the industrial developments at Atlantis and Philadelphia to the north of Table Bay.

The spectacular Cape of Good Hope (which is not Africa's southernmost point – see the later Cape Agulhas section) is 70 km by road to the south of the city centre. The extraordinary indigenous flora is protected within the Cape of Good Hope Nature Reserve.

The Cape is the meeting point for two great ocean currents that have a major impact on the climate of southern Africa, and the Cape itself. The cold Benguela current (from around 8°C) runs up the west side of the Cape from Antarctica. The warm Agulhas current (around 20°C) swings around Madagascar and the east coast from the equatorial waters of the Indian Ocean and, if you're lucky, into False Bay. If you're not, the spring/summer south-easterly will blow in cold water.

The obvious impact for visitors is that you have to be pretty hardy to enjoy swimming on the Atlantic side of the Cape, but there are much more far-reaching climatic consequences. In brief, the Benguela current is rich in sea life, but it is too cold to evaporate easily so the west coast of southern Africa is extremely dry.

INFORMATION

As well as the tourist offices and other services listed here, the best sources of information are the backpacker hostels – a good hostel knows *everything*.

Tourist Offices

It's worth visiting both Captour and Satour. As you might expect, Captour concentrates on the peninsula, and although Satour caters for the whole country it also has some excellent local information (including the best free map). Both have offices in the Tourist Rendezvous (☎ (021) 418 5202) complex at the railway station. The Tourist Rendezvous is open from 8 am to 7 pm on weekdays, from 8.30 am to 5 pm on Saturday and from 9 am to 5 pm on Sunday. As well as Captour and Satour the complex has other useful information desks, including a HASA (Hostels Association) desk.

Satour (☎ (021) 21 6274) is getting back on its feet after a major reorganisation, and the staff at this desk are extremely helpful. Abé, Pekeur (aka Abé, Baby) will enthusiastically help you with just about any enquiry. The desk is open daily (except Sunday) from 8 am to 4.30 pm (until 4 pm on Friday and 12.30 pm on Saturday).

Captour (☎ (021) 418 5214, fax 418 5227) has some good tourist, accommodation and restaurant guides, but you have to buy them at R4 each. The same brochures are free elsewhere around town – still, you can't be guaranteed of finding them. Captour also makes accommodation reservations (at another desk in the complex); it charges R10

if it has to ring more than four places. Captour also has offices on Atlantic Rd, Muizenberg (☎ (021) 788 1898), which is near the Abe Bailey Youth Hostel, and in the Tyger Valley Centre, Bellville (☎ (021) 948 4993).

The problem with Captour is that it's a private organisation and only has information on its own members. That includes all the major attractions and almost any place to stay and eat, but if you're after information such as phone numbers for minibus taxis or the best township shebeens, they are of zero help.

There is also a Namibian tourism office (☎ (021) 419 3190), Ground Floor, Main Tower, Standard Bank Building, on the corner of Adderley St and Hertzog Blvd.

National Parks & Reserves Offices

As well as a desk at the Tourist Rendezvous, the National Parks Board (☎ (021) 22 2810, fax 24 6211) has offices in a restored Victorian building on the corner of Long and Hout Sts. It's open weekdays from 9 am to 4 pm. If you're heading to any of the national parks (especially Kruger) and want to be sure of accommodation, bookings are essential. Outside of school holidays it's not necessary to book camping sites. Phone for bookings and enquiries or write to PO Box 7400, Roggebaai 8012.

For information on the extensive and excellent provincial parks contact Cape Nature Conservation (☎ (021) 483 4051, fax 23 0939). It has a desk at the Tourist Rendezvous.

Money

Money can be changed at any commercial bank; they're open from 9 am to 3.30 pm.

There are offices of American Express at the Tourist Rendezvous (☎ (021) 418 5225), Thibault Square (at the end of St George's Mall) (☎ (021) 21 5586) and at the Victoria & Alfred Waterfront (☎ (021) 21 6021). The Tourist Rendezvous and the Waterfront offices are open from 10 am to 6 pm daily; the Thibault Square office is open from

8.30 am to 5 pm on weekdays and from 9 am to noon on Saturday.

Rennies Travel is the agent for Thomas Cook and has branches on the corner of St George's and Hout Sts (☎ (021) 26 1789) open Monday to Friday from 8.30 am to 4.30 pm, and Saturday from 8.30 am to 12 pm; 2 St George's St, Thibault Square near Amex (☎ (021) 25 2370); 182 Main Rd, Sea Point (☎ (021) 439 7529); and at the Waterfront (☎ (021) 418 3744).

The Trustbank has a branch at DF Malan Airport that is open Monday to Friday from 9 am to 3.30 pm and Saturday from 9 am to 10.30 pm, and for international arrivals and departures. They charge R10 commission, although there rates were quite good when I called by.

You can use the machines at BOB (First National) banks for Visa cash advances – there's a branch in St George's Mall on the corner of Shortmarket St and a machine at the railway station.

Post & Telecommunications

The GPO is on the corner of Darling and Parliament Sts and is open weekdays from 8 am to 4.30 pm and Saturday from 8 am to noon. It has a poste-restante counter in the Main Hall (identification is required), and an international phone call centre where you can pay cash to make a call (open from 8 am to 10.30 pm Monday to Saturday and from 9 am to 8.30 pm Sunday and public holidays).

The public phones in the post office are open 24 hours, but they're often very busy. In addition to the ordinary public phones there's also a phone centre at the post office, a nice old office, open daily from 8 am to 9.45 pm; Sunday from 9.30 am to 8.30 pm.

There are also plenty of privately run public phone businesses, where you can make calls (and usually send faxes) without coins. Check their rates first; they are more expensive than a normal public phone. A handy office is Postnet, on Hout St between Adderley St and St George's Mall. You can use the phone and fax, and send Federal Express parcels.

Foreign Consulates & Trade Missions

Most countries have their main embassy in Pretoria, with an office or consulate in Cape Town, which becomes the official embassy during Cape Town's parliamentary sessions. A surprising number of countries also maintain consulates (which can arrange visas and passports) in Jo'burg. Some countries, like Mozambique and Zimbabwe, only have representation in Jo'burg.

The following is not a comprehensive list. If your consulate is not listed, consult the Yellow Pages telephone directory under consulates and embassies. Many are open in the morning only.

Australia
14th Floor, BP Centre, Thibault Square (☎ (021) 419 5425)
Belgium
Vogue House, Thibault Square (☎ (021) 419 3410)
Canada
Reserve Bank Building, Hout St (☎ (021) 23 5240)
France
2 Dean St, Gardens (☎ (021) 23 1575)
Germany
825 St Martini Gardens, Queen Victoria St (☎ (021) 24 2410)
Israel
Church Square House, Plein St (☎ (021) 45 7207)
Japan
Standard Bank Centre, Heerengracht (☎ (021) 25 1695)
Namibia
Ground Floor, Main Tower, Standard Bank Building, on the corner of Adderley St and Hertzog Blvd (☎ (021) 419 3190)
Netherlands
100 Strand St (☎ (021) 21 5660)
Sweden
17th Floor, Southern Life Centre, 8 Riebeeck St (☎ (021) 25 1687)
Switzerland
9th Floor, Waldorf Building, 80 St George's Mall (☎ (021) 26 1040)
UK
Southern Life Centre, 8 Riebeeck St (☎ (021) 25 3670)
USA
4th Floor, Broadway Centre, Heerengracht (☎ (021) 21 4280)

WESTERN CAPE PROVINCE

Travel Agencies

The South African Students' Travel Service (SASTS) is a national organisation with offices at universities around the country. You don't have to be a student to use their services. They offer all the regular services plus student and youth cards, youth hostel membership, and special fares and flights during vacations. They also know about cheap tours through Africa. They are at the University of Cape Town (Upper Campus), Leslie Building Concourse (☎ (021) 685 1808).

Rennies Travel has a comprehensive network of agencies, with a distinctive red livery, throughout South Africa, and Cape Town is no exception. Its the agent for Thomas Cook travellers' cheques and handles international and domestic bookings. It will also arrange visas for a moderate charge. See the previous Money section for locations and phone numbers.

A reader has recommended Worldwide Travel (☎ (021) 419 3840), 12th Floor, 2 Long St, as a good place to buy international air tickets. A handy travel agency for straight business is Intercape Travel & Tours (☎ (021) 419 8888), in the railway station. Visa Services (☎ (021) 21 7826), 4th Floor, Strand Towers, 66 Strand St, arrange visas.

You should at least check out what's on offer at The Africa Travel Centre (☎ (021) 23 5555, fax 23 0065) at The Backpack hostel, 74 New Church St. It books all sorts of travel and activities including day trips, kloofing, hire cars and extended truck tours of Africa. The rates are good. As the centre has been in business for some time, it has vetted many of the operators – and there are some cowboys out there. Other hostels also make bookings, but usually not with as wide a range of options or such professional service.

Work

The best time to look for work is October to November, before the high season starts and before uni students begin holidays. Because of high unemployment and fears about illegal immigration from the rest of Africa, there are very tough penalties for employers taking on foreigners without work permits. So far this doesn't seem to have stopped foreigners getting jobs in restaurants or bars but this might change. Don't expect decent pay – something like R3.50 to R5 per hour plus tips is usual. It's possible to share apartments for between R150 and R300 per month so you can earn enough to live.

Hostels might know of fruit-picking work, especially in the Citrusdal, Ceres and Piketberg areas. The pay is negligible but you'll get free accommodation.

If you have recognised childcare and first-aid qualifications, Supersitters (☎ (021) 439 4985) might be able to find you baby-sitting work. In this conservative society there might not be much demand for male sitters.

Bookshops & Maps

Exclusive Books, at the Waterfront (☎ (021) 419 0905), has an excellent range; it's open until 9.30 pm on Saturday and from 11 am to 5 pm on Sunday. The main mass-market bookshops/newsagents/stationers are CNA and Paperbacks. Both have numerous shops scattered around the city. CNA has a large shop in the Golden Acre Centre. Paperbacks has a branch at 202 Main Rd, Sea Point, and near the American Express office in Thibault Square. The latter sells some foreign newspapers (mainly British).

There's an ANC shop (☎ (021) 434 5300) where you can buy books, on St John's Rd just up from St John's Lodge, in Sea Point.

Ulrich Naumann's (☎ (021) 23 7832), 17 Burg St, has a good range of German-language books: many are translations of South African books, including the coffee-table variety.

The Map Studio (☎ (021) 462 4360), Struik House, 80 McKenzie Rd, Gardens, sells the wide range of Map Studio maps and other series including Michelin and government topographic maps (R15 per laminated sheet). If you're staying for more than a week or so, and have a car, consider buying Map Studio's excellent Cape Town street directory. It's available for R60 at all CNA outlets.

Medical Services

Medical services are of a high standard. Doctors are listed under Medical in the phone book, and they generally arrange for hospitalisation, although in an emergency you can go directly to the casualty department of Groote Schuur Hospital (☎ (021) 404 9111) – where in 1967 Christiaan Barnard made the first successful heart transplant – which is at the intersection of De Waal (M3) and the Eastern Boulevard (N2) to the east of the city. Ring the police (☎ 10111) to get directions to the nearest hospital.

Many doctors make house calls and you'll pay less than R60 unless the visit is arranged by a top-end hotel.

For vaccinations, the British Airways Travel Clinic (☎ (021) 419 3172, fax 419 3389), is at Room 1027 in the Medical Centre, Adderley St.

K's Pharmacy (☎ (021) 434 9331), 52 Regent Rd, Sea Point (on the Camps Bay/sea side of the corner of Cassel St) is open seven days a week, until 9 pm Monday to Saturday and until 6 pm on Sunday and public holidays. There's a seven-day chemist on the main concourse in the railway station and the Tamboerskloof Pharmacy (☎ (021) 24 4450), 16 Kloof Nek Rd stays open late.

Emergency

The contact numbers for emergency services are as follows:

ambulance	☎ 10177
fire brigade	☎ 461 4141
police	☎ 10111
tourist police	☎ 418 2852
AA	☎ 21 1550
Lifeline	☎ (021) 461 111
Rape Crisis Centre	☎ (021) 47 9762

Dangers & Annoyances

Cape Town is probably one of the most relaxed cities in Africa, which can instil a false sense of security. People who have travelled overland from Cairo without a single mishap or theft have been known to be cleaned out in Cape Town – generally doing something stupid like leaving their gear on a beach while they go swimming.

Paranoia is not required but common sense is. There is tremendous poverty on the peninsula and informal redistribution of wealth is reasonably common. The townships on the Cape Flats have an appalling crime rate and unless you have a trustworthy guide they are off-limits (the triangular segment south of Athlone and the N2). If violence on the flats gets out of control even the N2 can become unsafe – you probably shouldn't drive it late at night when traffic is sparse.

The rest of Cape Town is reasonably safe. Care should be taken in Sea Point late at night. Walking to/from the Victoria & Alfred Waterfront is not recommended once it starts to get dark. As always, listen to local advice. There is safety in numbers.

Swimming at all the Cape beaches is potentially hazardous, especially for those inexperienced in surf. Check for signs warning of rips and rocks, and unless you really know what you're doing only swim in patrolled areas.

The mountains in the middle of the city are no less dangerous just because they are in the city. Weather conditions can change rapidly, so warm clothing and a good map and compass are always necessary.

Another hazard of the mountains is ticks, which can get onto you when you brush past vegetation – see the Health section in the Facts for the Visitor chapter.

Climate & When to Go

Cape Town has what is described as a Mediterranean climate. Weather is not really a critical factor in deciding when to visit. There are no terrible extremes of temperature, although it can be relatively cold and wet for a few months over winter. It can get very crowded during the school holidays, particularly around Christmas (mid-December to the end of January) and Easter, when prices jump markedly and it can be difficult to find a place to stay. Late summer/early autumn, from February to April, is the best time to visit.

One of the Cape's most characteristic phenomena is the famous Cape Doctor, the south-easterly wind that buffets the Cape and lays Table Mountain's famous tablecloth. It can be a welcome breeze in summer, but it can also be a wild gale, particularly in spring. When it really blows you know you're clinging to a peninsula at the southern end of Africa, and there's nothing between you and the Antarctic.

In winter, between June and August, temperatures range from 7°C to 18°C but there are pleasant, sunny days between the gloomy ones. The prevailing winds are north-westerly.

From September to November the weather is unpredictable with anything from bright warm days to howling south-easterly storms with winds reaching 120 km per hour. Wild flowers are at their best during August and September.

December to March can get pretty hot, although average maximum temperatures are only 26°C. The Doctor generally keeps things bearable and it is usually relatively calm in the mornings. From March to April, and a lesser extent May, the weather remains good, and the wind is at its most gentle.

It can be very smoggy after a few still days – luckily, consecutive still days aren't all that common. Much of the smog comes from cooking fires in the huge squatter camps, and the smoke drifts around Table Mountain into the City Bowl.

Laundry

There are launderettes scattered throughout the suburbs, although if you're staying in any sort of budget accommodation you'll probably have a laundry on the premises. It's simpler to do a bag wash, around R12.50. Same-day laundry is available at Nannucci Dry Cleaners which has branches everywhere, including Shop 35, Ground Floor, Golden Acre Centre; Unity House, Long St; 57 Main Rd, Green Point; 152A Main Rd, Sea Point and 67 Station Rd, Observatory.

Left Luggage

There's a left luggage facility next to Platform 24 in the main railway station but it's only open during the day, on weekdays – not very helpful.

Library Membership

Visitors can take out temporary library membership's for a small fee at the City Library, in the Town Hall on Darling St.

Camera Repairs

For camera repairs go to Camera Care, on Castle (Kasteel) St between Burg St and St George's Mall. Prolab, 177 Bree St (on the corner of Pepper St), will do slide processing and mounting in two hours for less than R30 for 36 – and they do a good job.

Shoe Repairs

Try Rock Sole, 61 Wale St for shoe repairs.

CITY BOWL MUSEUMS
Bo-Kaap Museum

The small but interesting Bo-Kaap Museum (☎ (021) 24 3846), 71 Wale St, gives an insight into the lifestyle of a prosperous, 19th-century Muslim family. The house

WESTERN CAPE PROVINCE

Weather Lore

The weather in Cape Town can change rapidly and often. Many people use Table Mountain as a weather forecaster, and it's apparently quite accurate. Some things to watch for:

- If there is heavy cloud on Lions Head, rain is coming.
- If the tablecloth (cloud) shrouds the mountain, the Cape Doctor (a south-easterly change) is coming.
- If there is no cloud around the upper cable station (visible from all over town) there is no wind on Clifton Beach.

City Sights & Walking Tour

Captour has a series of brochures describing historical walks around different parts of Cape Town. The following introductory walk around the City Bowl could take the best part of a day, depending on the stops you make, although it is only about six km long. You certainly won't be able to do justice to all the museums, so concentrate on a couple. The South African Museum in the Botanical Gardens should not be missed, and the small Bo-Kaap Museum in the Muslim Quarter is another favourite.

The **Castle**, as the oldest surviving building in Cape Town, seems the most appropriate place to start a walking tour. Van Riebeeck's original mud-walled fort was a little to the west of the stone castle that replaced it (built between 1666 and 1679) and survives today. See the separate Castle of Good Hope section.

Walk to the west across the **Grand Parade**, once a military parade ground, and now a bleak and windy car park. On Wednesday and Saturday mornings a section is kept clear for a flea market. The impressive old Town Hall on the southern side (1905) has been superseded by a much less attractive Civic Centre on the other side of the station. The Cape Town Symphony Orchestra regularly gives concerts in the hall; phone Computicket (☎ (021) 21 4715) for details.

Buses leave from the station side of the Parade, and minibus taxis compete for customers amid the friendly chaos on the Strand. At the Plein St end, an interesting bunch of permanent stalls form a colourful bazaar. Spices and takeaway food are sold – the samosas are cheap and excellent.

Circle around the post office and enter the **Golden Acre Centre** (1978) which was built on the site of the old railway station, and dubbed 'the golden acre' by locals because of its valuable real estate. It has several levels of shops and is linked to more shops in the Strand Concourse (including Captour) that runs under the intersection of Adderley and Strand Sts. Black tiles on the floor indicate the waterline before land reclamation in the 1930s.

Exit onto Adderley St, named after a British parliamentarian and historically regarded as Cape Town's main street. Until 1849 it was named the Heerengracht, or Gentlemen's Canal, after a canal of the same name in Amsterdam.

Turn left along Adderley towards Table Mountain and continue until you reach the **Groote Kerk**, the mother church for the Dutch Reformed Church (Nederduitse Gereformeerde Kerk, or NG Kerk). The first church on the site was built in 1704, but the current building dates from 1841 (open 10.30 am to noon and 2 to 3 pm). A number of early notables have tombs inside.

The next building is the **Cultural History Museum**, originally the VOC's slave lodge and brothel. The impressive façade was designed in 1811 and the building was later used as a debating chamber for the Cape Legislative Council. The museum deals mainly with white South Africa, but also has an archaeological section with Roman and Egyptian antiquities. (See the City Bowl Museums section.)

Follow the road as it turns right at the gardens (becoming Wale) past **St Georges Cathedral**, the Anglican cathedral of Archbishop Desmond Tutu, designed by Herbert Baker in 1897. Turn right into St Georges St, which is now almost completely a pedestrian mall. The **Rhodes Building** (1900) was the Cape Town office for De Beers Consolidated Mines.

Turn left at Longmarket and you come out on **Greenmarket Square**, one of the most pleasant spots in the city. It was created as a farmers' market in 1710 and is now home to a flea market (open daily). The **Townhouse Museum** (1761) on the corner of Burg St and Longmarket was the original city watch house, and now houses the Michaelis Collection of 16th & 17th-century Dutch and Flemish oil paintings (open 10 am to 5 pm every day, admission free). The building itself might be more interesting than the generally dour artworks, and there's a balcony overlooking bustling Greenmarket Square. Also note the magnificent Art Deco architecture of the building opposite, on the Shortmarket side of the square.

Walk back towards Table Mountain along Burg St and turn right into Church St, which is lined with art and antique shops. The pedestrianised section is a flea market specialising in antiques and bric-a-brac. Turn right down **Long St** which, along with Church St, retains a strong historical atmosphere, with elegant cast-iron decorated balconies and numerous old buildings. One of the oldest is the atmospheric **Sendinnestig Museum** (1802) at No 40, originally a missionary church (open Monday to Friday, 9.15 am to 4.15 pm). On the first Friday of the month the old gas lights are lit between 1 and 2 pm.

Continue until you reach Strand St. Turn right and a short distance on your right is

Koopmans de Wet House (17C1), a classic example of a Cape townhouse and furnished with antiques. It's a quiet, self-satisfied house holding its own in the centre of a big city. The house is open from Tuesday to Saturday between 9.30 am and 4.30 pm; entrance is R1, free on Friday.

Backtrack along Strand St passing, on the right-hand side in the block before Buitengragt, the old **Lutheran Church**, which was converted from a warehouse in 1780, and the next-door parsonage **Martin Melck House**.

Cross Buitengragt, and you enter the old **Cape Muslim Quarter** (sometimes erroneously referred to as the Malay Quarter), the historical residential suburb for the descendants of the Asian slaves and political prisoners imported by the Dutch. The steep streets, some of which are still cobbled, and 18th-century flat-roofed houses and mosques are still home to a strong Muslim community. This group miraculously survived apartheid, but it is less certain it will survive unfettered capitalism. The cottages on the Waterkant edge of the Quarter have been bought by yuppies and while those streets might be neat and freshly painted, they are also lifeless.

Cape Town City Hall

Turn left down Rose St, which after a couple of hundred metres forms a T-intersection with Wale St. Here you will find a restored house, the **Bo-Kaap Museum**, which gives a fascinating insight into the lifestyle of a Malay family. It's open between 9.30 am and 4.30 pm from Tuesday to Saturday; admission is R1.

Walk down the hill, cross Buitengragt and keep going until you reach Long St. Turn right into Long St and follow it until it becomes Orange St. The **Long St Baths** on the corner are still in operation. Turn left into Orange St, and left again into Grey's Pass which takes you past the excellent **South African Museum**, which is open daily from 10 am to 5 pm. Entry costs R2 (free on Wednesday). It has some fascinating displays on indigenous black culture (see Museums).

From here, you enter the top end of the **Botanical Gardens**, also known as The Company's Gardens. This is the surviving six hectares of Van Riebeeck's original 18-hectare vegetable garden which was planted to provide fresh produce for the VOC's ships. As sources of supply were diversified, the garden was gradually changed to a superb pleasure garden with a magnificent collection of botanical species from South Africa and the world. The gardens are open from 9.30 am to 4 pm. The **Gardens Restaurant**, at the Adderley St end of the Gardens, to the north of the oak-lined Government Ave, serves drinks and reasonably priced food and has inside and outside seating.

On the south side of Government Ave (Wale St end), are the **Houses of Parliament**. Opened in 1885, they have been enlarged several times. Continue towards the mountain, and past **De Tuynhuys**, the president's office, which has been restored to its 1795 appearance.

Next on the left, on the south-eastern side of the gardens, is the **South African National Gallery** which has a permanent collection of important South African paintings and also holds temporary exhibitions. It's open daily from 10 am to 5 pm; from 1pm on Monday.

Leave the gardens by Gallery Lane and turn left into St Johns (towards the bay), take the next left and then next right into Parliament. This takes you through to **Church Square** where the burghers would unhitch their wagons while they attended the Groote Kerk. Slaves were also auctioned under a tree in the square (the spot is now marked with a plaque).

Continue down Parliament, keeping your eyes open for some of the Art Deco details on the buildings. Turn right on Darling St and you're back at the Grand Parade where you started. Phew! ■

itself was built in 1763. It's open between 9.30 am and 4.30 pm from Tuesday to Saturday; entry is R1.

District Six Museum

On the corner of Buitenkant and Albertus St, this simple museum (☎ (021) 461 8745)is as much *for* the people of the now-vanished District Six as it is about them. The floor is covered with a large-scale map of District Six, and ex-residents are encouraged to label their old homes and features of their neighbourhood. After District Six was bulldozed, the government changed the street grid and the names of the few remaining roads. The formerly vibrant community now exists only in the memories of those who lived there. There are a few other interesting displays, but the best reason to visit is to talk with the staff.

The museum is open daily except Sunday from 10 am to 4 pm. Admission is by donation.

See the earlier Apartheid & the Townships section for more information on District Six.

Cultural History Museum

This museum (☎ (021) 461 8280) at the mountain end of Adderley St is the former slave lodge of the VOC, but it has gone through several incarnations since then – including the Supreme Court and the Legislative Assembly – and major physical alterations.

It aims to give a cultural history of *homo sapiens* from Egyptian, Greek and Roman times and includes large collections of stamps, coins and guns. Most visitors won't find these sections very special, but there is an interesting section on the early history of the Cape, including some VOC relics and postal stones. These stones marked caches of letters that were left by the crews of ships, in the hope that they would be picked up by the next ship heading in the right direction. They were engraved with the name of the ship and the senders of the letters.

The museum is open from 9.30 am to 4.30 pm Monday to Friday; entry is R2 (free on Friday).

Bertam House Museum

Bertram House (☎ (021) 24 9381) on the corner of Orange St and Government Ave (the walkway through the Company's Gardens) is a Georgian house filled with antiques which once belonged to wealthy English-descended South Africans. It's interesting to compare the architecture and furnishing of this house to that of old Cape Dutch houses, such as Koopmans de Wet – the Georgian comes off second-best.

The museum is open Tuesday to Saturday from 9.30 am to 4.30 pm; admission is R1.

Jewish Museum

The Jewish Museum (☎ (021) 45 1546), 84 Hatfield St (next to the Art Gallery in the Company's Gardens), is in the oldest synagogue in South Africa. It contains items of Jewish historical and ceremonial significance. It's open Tuesday and Thursday from 2 to 5 pm and Sunday from 10.30 am to noon. Entry is free.

Rust-en-Vreugd

This 18th-century house (☎ (021) 45 3628) at 78 Buitenkant, was once the home of the state prosecutor. It now houses part of the William Fehr collection of paintings and furniture, featuring some important watercolours and engravings by renowned early South African artists like Baines. There's also a pleasant garden.

The museum is open from 9 am to 4 pm on weekdays and on weekends over summer and occasionally at other times. Admission is free.

South African Museum

The South African Museum (☎ (021) 24 3330), at the mountain end of the Company's Gardens, is the oldest and arguably the most interesting museum in South Africa. It has some startlingly lifelike displays of San communities (made with casts taken from living people in 1911) and interesting exhibits of other indigenous cultures. As an indirect testimony to Cape Town's importance as a stopping-place for ships, the museum holds some Pacific island artefacts left here by Captain Cook on his way home from his great voyages of discovery.

Despite some updating, it's still a good, old-fashioned museum with cases and cases of stuffed animals (some overstuffed, like the rotund platypus) and bloodthirsty dioramas of dinosaurs which must have inspired generations of young imaginations. The most interesting of the new displays is the whale room, where you can hear whale noises while looking at models suspended high in the air.

There is a planetarium (☎ (021) 24 3330) in the complex, which could help Northerners unravel the mysteries of the southern hemisphere's night sky.

The museum is open daily from 10 am to 5 pm; entry is R2 (free on Wednesday). Planetarium shows are given at 1 pm on Tuesday and Thursday, at 2 and 3.30 pm on Saturday and Sunday, and at 8 pm on Tuesday and Wednesday. Admission is R5 (R3 children) and a little more for evening shows.

Townhouse Museum

The Townhouse Museum on Greenmarket Square is another old Cape Dutch building. It dates from 1761, although there has been considerable alteration to suit its changing roles as a watch-house, the first city hall and in 1916, Cape Town's first public gallery. Today it houses the Michaelis Collection of Dutch and Flemish paintings and etchings from the 16th and 17th centuries. As well as the art, it's worth visiting for the architecture and the views from the balcony overlooking bustling Greenmarket Square. The museum is open from 10 am to 5 pm daily and admission is free.

NATIONAL GALLERY

This small but exquisite gallery (☎ (021) 45 1628) in the Company's Gardens was always worth visiting for its architecture, but now it also has some very interesting exhibitions which begin to redress the imbalance from the apartheid days. There's a good shop with some interesting books and a pleasant café with snacks and light meals such as pasta for R11. The gallery is open from 10 am to 5 pm

every day (from 1 pm on Monday). Admission is free.

HOUSES OF PARLIAMENT

On the south side of Government Ave (Wale St end) are the Houses of Parliament (☎ (021) 403 2911) which were opened in 1885 and enlarged several times since. During the parliamentary session (usually January to June) gallery tickets are available; overseas tourists must present their passports, and reasonably decent dress is required, although the jacket and tie days are over. During the recess (usually July to January) there are free guided tours (☎ (021) 403 2198) from Monday to Friday at 11 am and 2 pm. Go to the Old Parliament Building entrance on Parliament St.

LONG ST BATHS & SWIMMING POOL

You will find the Turkish baths and heated pool (☎ (021) 210 3302) at the mountain end of Long St, are something of an anachronism, but they have been restored and are very popular. The pool is open from 7 am to 8.30 pm daily and entry costs R4 (if you just want a hot bath you pay R3.85).

The Turkish baths are segregated. For men they are open from 9 am to 8.30 pm, Tuesday, Wednesday and Friday and from 8 am to noon Sunday. For women the hours are from 8.30 am to 8.30 pm Monday and Thursday and from 9 am to 6 pm on Saturday. A Turkish bath costs R31, a massage costs R23.50, a bath and massage is R44.50.

CASTLE OF GOOD HOPE

Built near the site of van Riebeeck's original mud-walled fort, the Castle was constructed between 1666 and 1679 and is one of the oldest European structures in southern Africa. The impressive 10-metre-high walls have never had to repel an attack, but the Castle is nonetheless a striking symbol of the might of the VOC.

The Castle is still the headquarters for the Western Cape Military command but its tourist potential has been recognised and visitors are welcome. A small shop sells drinks and cheap snacks.

WESTERN CAPE PROVINCE

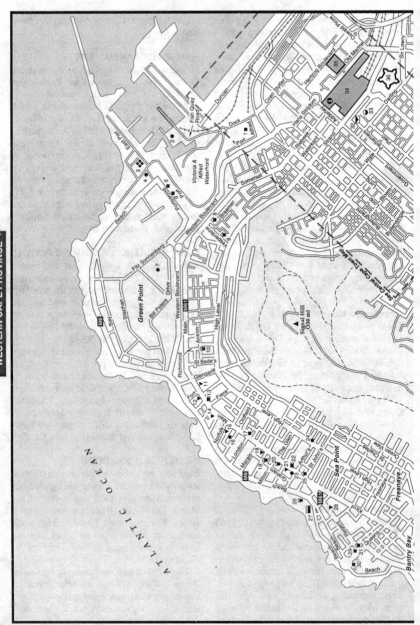

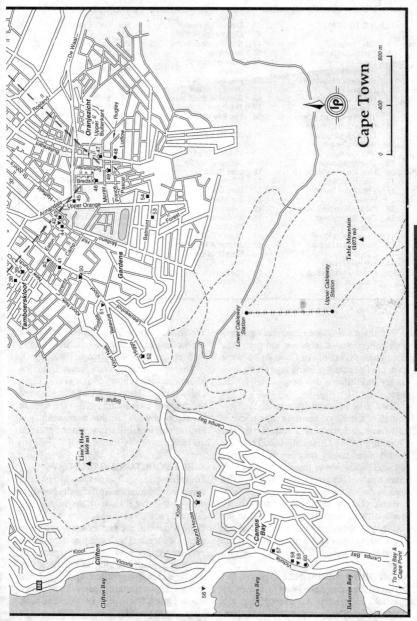

Cape Town

PLACES TO STAY

1   City Lodge
5   Portswood Square
    Hotel
6   Breakwater Lodge
8   St John's Waterfront
    Lodge
9   Hip Hop Travellers
    Stop Hostel
10 The Bunkhouse Hostel
16 Olaf's Guest House
17 Lions Head Lodge
19 Bunkers Hostel
24 Villa Rosa
25 St John's Lodge
29 New Regency Hotel
30 The President
31 The Globe Trotter
    Hostel
38 Table Mountain Lodge
39 Pink Backpacker
    Hostel
41 Cape Swiss Hotel
43 Palm Court Holiday
    Lodge
44 Helmsley Hotel
45 Holiday Inn Garden
    Court De Waal

46 Oak Lodge Hostel
47 Cloudbreak Hostel
49 Shanti Lodge Hostel
52 Belvidere
    Accommodation
    Centre
53 Villa Belmonte
54 Belmont House
55 Stan Halt Youth Hostel
57 The Place on the Bay
58 The Bay Hotel

PLACES TO EAT

3   Victoria Wharf
    Shopping Centre
11 Little Bombay
12 L'Orient
13 Café Erté
14 San Marco
15 Peasants
18 Ari's Souvlaki
21 Mr Chan
22 Reise's Deli
28 Joubert & Monty's
    Meat Boutique, &
    New York Deli
40 Happy Wok
42 Sukothai

50 Café Paradiso
51 Amigos
56 La Med
59 Blues

OTHER

2   Bertie's Landing
4   BMW Pavilion
7   Green Point Stadium
20 Walter's 24–Hour Pub
23 Rennie's Travel
    (Thomas Cook)
26 Hard Rock Cafe
27 Sea Point Pavilion
    Pool
32 GPO
33 Golden Acre Bus
    Terminal
34 Railway Station &
    Tourist Rendezvous
35 Civic Centre
36 Castle of Good Hope
37 Botanical Gardens
48 Wayne Motors
60 Dizzy Jazz

Within the Castle are a couple of museums with collections of furniture and paintings. The paintings, mainly of Cape Town in the past, are fascinating. Some interesting temporary exhibitions are occasionally held here.

The Castle opens at 10 am with the Ceremony of the Keys. Sentries change every half hour and there is a full ceremonial Changing of the Guard at noon. There are guided tours hourly between 10 am and 3 pm, and taking one of these is the only way to see many of the sights. However, if you're visiting one of the excellent temporary exhibitions (lately they have focused on anti-apartheid themes) held in a hall in the Castle, you can do a little solo wandering. The Castle closes at 4 pm. Entry (from the Grand Parade side) is R5.

NOON GUN & SIGNAL HILL

Signal Hill separates Sea Point from the City Bowl. At noon, every day except Sunday, a cannon is fired. You can hear it all over town.

Traditionally this allowed the burghers in the town below to check their watches. You can walk up to the cannon through Bo Kaap.

There are magnificent views from the 350-metre high summit of Signal Hill, especially at night. Head up Kloof Nek Rd from the city and take the turn-off to the right at the top of the hill. At this intersection you also turn off for Clifton (also to the right) and the lower cableway station (left).

TABLE MOUNTAIN & CABLEWAY

The cableway is such an obvious and popular attraction you might have difficulty convincing yourself that it is worth the trouble and expense. It is. The views from the top of Table Mountain are phenomenal, and there are some excellent walks on the summit. The mountain is home to over 1400 species of flowering plants, which are particularly spectacular in spring. It's also home to Rock Dassies, those curious rodent-like creatures whose closest living relative is the elephant. They like to be fed.

WESTERN CAPE PROVINCE

If you do plan to walk, make sure you're properly equipped with warm and waterproof clothing. Table Mountain is over 1000-metres high and conditions can become treacherous quickly. There's a small restaurant and shop at the top, where you can also post letters and faxes.

Cableway

The cable cars don't operate when it's dangerously windy, and there's obviously not much point going up if you are simply going to be wrapped in the tablecloth. Ring in advance (☎ (021) 24 5148 or 24 8409) to see if they're operating. Weather conditions permitting, they operate from 8 am to 10 pm from 1 December to 30 April and from 8.30 am to 6 pm for the rest of the year. The best

visibility and conditions are likely to be first thing in the morning, or in the evening. You can avoid queuing by booking at Captour (Tourist Rendezvous), the lower cableway station or at the Waterfront information centre. There is a small booking fee.

Coming back down the mountain, make sure that you stand at the front of the car – it's exhilarating.

The cableway carried its 10-millionth passenger in 1994. It has never had a fatality.

To get to the lower cable station, catch the Kloof Nek bus from outside OK Bazaars in Adderley St to the Kloof Nek terminus and connect with the cableway bus. By car, take Kloof Nek Rd and turn off to the left (signposted). An adult return is R21, a single is R12. A single you say? It's possible to walk

The Tablecloth

For much of the summer Table Mountain is obscured by seemingly motionless cloud draped neatly over the summit. This is often referred to as 'the tablecloth'. An Afrikaner legend attempts to explain the phenomenon by comparing it to an old burgher who, fond of his pipe, attempted to outsmoke the devil.

Meteorologists have come up with another explanation. The south-easterly wind picks up moisture as it crosses the Agulhas current and False Bay. When it hits Table Mountain it rises, and as it reaches the cooler air at around 900 metres above sea level, it condenses into thick white clouds. When the clouds pour down to the plateau and into the City Bowl they dissolve in the warmer air. ■

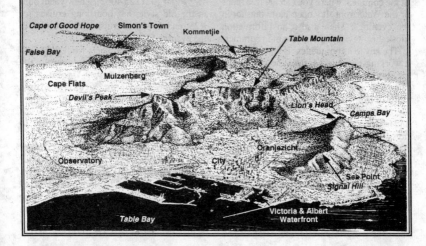

up or down the mountain to/from both the City Bowl side or the Kirstenbosch Botanical Gardens side. See the Activities section for more information.

VICTORIA & ALFRED WATERFRONT

The Victoria & Alfred Waterfront is the most successful example of the worldwide trend to revitalise big city ports. Although it is pitched unashamedly at tourists, it has avoided the glossy unreality of Sydney's Darling Harbour or San Francisco's Fisherman's Wharf. It's atmospheric, interesting and packed with restaurants, bars, music venues and interesting shops.

The huge new Victoria Wharf complex adds shops, cinemas, a produce market and still more restaurants and bars, and makes the Waterfront an almost self-contained shopping and leisure precinct. It also, unfortunately, adds a fair splash of the antiseptic atmosphere you'll find in rich white suburbs all over South Africa. This process will continue when big new residential projects are built by the shores of soon-to-be flooded land beside the current Waterfront.

The development seems to have given the whole city a boost, and is tremendously popular, day and night. There is an information centre (☎ (021) 418 2369), in the middle of the complex, where you can get free maps of the Waterfront. It's open daily but not in the evenings. There's also an information kiosk that stays open until 9 pm in summer.

The key to its uniqueness is that it remains a working harbour. Most of the redevelopment has been undertaken around the historical Alfred and Victoria Basins (constructed from 1860). Although these wharfs are too small for modern container vessels and tankers the Victoria Basin is still used by tugs, harbour vessels of various kinds, and fishing boats. There is still a smell of diesel and salt and the bustle of real boats and people doing real work.

Large modern shipping uses the adjacent Duncan and Ben Schoeman docks. These were constructed from the mid-'30s and the sand excavated was used to reclaim the foreshore area north-east of the Strand. The Castle used to be virtually on the shorefront, and the old high water line actually passes through the Golden Acre Centre.

The Waterfront gets very busy on weekends, but seeing it full of life is seeing it at its best. Unfortunately, it is still pretty much a white playground – transport logistics and economics can present almost as many barriers to non-whites as the old laws.

The Waterfront is *the* place to go for nightlife. There is strict security and although it is safe to walk around, there are plenty of merry men so lone women should be a little cautious. The restaurateurs along Main Rd in Sea Point are reeling – a big proportion of their trade has been stolen. See the Places to Eat and Entertainment sections for information on the numerous restaurants and bars, although if you just go for a wander you'll find something that appeals.

Cruises

A trip into Table Bay should not be missed. Few people nowadays have the privilege of reaching the Tavern of the Seas by passenger ship, but something of the feeling can be captured by taking a harbour cruise. The view of Table Mountain hasn't changed.

The cheapest cruise (R8) is a quick 25-minute voyage with Hylton Ross. *Spirit of Victory* (☎ (021) 25 4062), a new yacht built in the old style, has hour-long cruises for R25, and 1½-hour cruises, with drinks, in the evening for R45.

On weekends, volunteers from the South African Maritime Museum operate the restored steam tug, *Alwyn Vincent*, from North Quay outside the Victoria & Alfred Arcade – half-hour trips cost R10. Sealink Tours (☎ (021) 25 4480), East Pier Rd, has one-hour, R15 trips. From February to December they leave at 11 am and 3 pm, but they're more frequent in summer. Sealink Tour's other cruises include half-hour harbour trips (just R8) and one-hour cruises that go out to sea (R20). If your preferred means of propulsion is the wind, *Le Tigre* (☎ (021) 419 7746) is a 16-metre catamaran with trips starting at R30.

Waterfront Charters (☎ (021) 25 3804),

Port Captain's Building, Pier Head (across from Bertie's Landing) has a range of cruises starting at a 25-minute trip for just R8 and a full harbour tour for R20. They are also a shop front for several independent charter operators whose cruisers and yachts are luxurious and range from expensive to unbelievably expensive – motor yachts from R1000 for three hours, game fishing from R1900.

South African Maritime Museum
This museum is yet to be built; meanwhile you can see the temporary display in a building next to The Pumphouse. It's pretty low-key, but then it only costs R2.

Aquarium
The aquarium was still under construction at the time of writing, but it promises to be a good one. It will be a fraction larger than the famous aquarium at Darling Harbour in Sydney, Australia (and thus become the largest southern-hemisphere aquarium) and will feature denizens of the deep from both the cold and warm oceans which border the Cape Peninsula, including Great White sharks, which congregate in False Bay.

Getting There & Away
Shuttle buses run from Adderley St in front of the Tourist Rendezvous, then up Strand St, with a stop near the Cape Sun Hotel, to the centre of the Waterfront. They also leave from near the Hard Rock Cafe in Sea Point. They depart half hourly from early to late and cost R1.20.

If you're driving, there are free parking spaces, which are often full, but there's usually space in the underground carpark beneath the Victoria Wharf complex, where the rates start at R2 for the first hour.

KIRSTENBOSCH BOTANIC GARDENS
The Kirstenbosch Botanic Gardens (☎ (021) 762 1166) on Rhodes Dr, Constantia, are one of the most beautiful gardens in the world, and are a must for any visitor to Cape Town. They have an incomparable site on the eastern side of Table Mountain, right at the

foot of the final steep escarpment, overlooking False Bay and the Cape Flats. The 36-hectare landscaped section seems to merge almost imperceptibly with the 492 hectares of fynbos (native flora) that cloak the mountain slopes.

In 1895, Cecil Rhodes (of De Beers and Jameson Raid fame) purchased the eastern slopes of Table Mountain as part of a plan to preserve a relatively untouched section, and bequeathed the property to the nation on his death in 1902. An impressive granite memorial to Rhodes was constructed further around the mountain towards the city (off Rhodes Dr). There is also a café here. The Memorial is a popular place from which to see the sun rise on New Year's Day.

Portions of the hedge that Jan van Riebeeck planted in 1660 to isolate his settlement from the Khoikhoi can still be seen. Although there are some magnificent oaks, Moreton Bay fig trees and camphor trees, the gardens are devoted almost exclusively to indigenous plants. About 9000 of Southern Africa's 22,000 plant species are grown in the gardens. They are predominantly from the winter rainfall region, but there are also large numbers of hardy species from other parts of the country, including Namaqualand. There is always something flowering, but the gardens are at their best between mid-August and mid-October.

The gardens have been thoughtfully laid out and include a fragrance garden, that has been raised so you can more easily sample the scents of the plants, a Braille Trail, a *koppie* (rock outcrop) that has been planted with pelargoniums, and sections featuring cycads, aloes, euphorbias, ericas and, of course, proteas. There are also three clearly signposted circular walks that explore the natural forest and fynbos that surround the cultivated section.

The gardens are now growing muti plants, used by sangoma in traditional medicine, to help conserve the supply in the wild.

The information office (open daily from 8 am to 4.45 pm) gives maps and advice on various walks. There is also a shop where you can buy a wide range of indigenous plants and some excellent books on South African flora.

The restaurant (☎ (021) 797 7614) is open daily for breakfast, teas and lunches; there are indoor and outdoor eating areas. It's not formal or flash but it is good value. You can get something cheap and filling like a salad or sausages and vegetables for R10, or a steak for around R20. It's open from 9 am to 5 pm Monday to Friday, and from 8.30 am to 5 pm on Saturday and Sunday.

The gardens are open year-round from 8 am, closing at 7 pm from September to March, and 6 pm from April to August; entry is R4. There are worthwhile guided walks on Tuesday and Saturday from 11 am for approximately 1½ hours. If you're a 'bona fide person' – which means everyone, I suppose – you can visit free on Tuesday.

Getting There & Away

It is possible to catch buses from Mowbray station on the Simon's Town line, but there aren't many. Phone Golden Arrow (☎ 080 121 2111) for an up-to-date timetable. A minibus taxi running from the main railway station to Wynberg might take you within walking distance of the gardens, but check the route carefully.

You can also walk uphill to the upper station of the Table Mountain cableway. This could be done in three hours by someone of moderate fitness and would obviously take less time coming downhill. Make sure you have a map (from the Kirstenbosch information centre or the Table Mountain shop) and are prepared for a sudden change in weather. The trails are all well marked, and steep in places, but the cableway station is not signposted from the gardens or vice versa.

GROOT CONSTANTIA

Groot Constantia is the oldest and grandest vineyard and homestead in the Cape – a superb example of Cape Dutch architecture. It embodies the gracious and refined lifestyle the wealthy Dutch created in their adopted country. Groot Constantia was built by one of the early governors, Simon van der Stel,

in 1692. Not surprisingly, van der Stel could not bear to be parted from his creation; after his retirement he refused to return to Europe and stayed until he died in 1712.

In the 18th century, Constantia wines were exported around the world and were highly acclaimed. Today, the estate is owned by a syndicate, and fine wines are still produced. Unfortunately, it's a bit of a tourist trap, but it's worth visiting, especially if you don't have time to explore the winelands around Stellenbosch – but if you've been to Boschendal you don't need to come here. Try to avoid visiting on a weekend; it can get very crowded.

The beautiful homestead has been carefully restored and appropriately furnished. The nearby wine museum traces the history of wine from the 6th century BC. Entry is R2 and the building is open from 10 am to 5 pm daily.

You can do a tour of the modern winemaking operation for R5; hourly in season, and at 11 am and 3 pm out of season. Wines are on sale, including on Sunday. Prices range from R6 to R24 per bottle depending on the variety and vintage; the '89 Governor's reserve red bordeaux is their top wine. For R5 you can taste five wines – and you get to keep the glass. Tastings are free if you do the cellar tour, and are available between 10 am and 4.30 pm; sales stay open until 5 pm.

There are a number of places to eat (see Places to Eat later) and for provisions, there's the excellent Old Cape Farm Stall on the corner of Constantia and Groot Constantia Rds.

Getting There & Away

A visit to Groot Constantia could easily be combined with a visit to the brilliant Kirstenbosch Botanical Gardens. Unfortunately there is no direct public transport to either.

ATLANTIC COAST

The Atlantic coast of the the Cape Peninsula has some of the most spectacular coastal scenery in the world. The combination of beaches and mountains is irresistible. The beaches include the trendiest on the Cape, and the emphasis is on sunbaking rather than swimming. Although it is possible to find shelter from the summer south-easterlies, the water comes straight from the Antarctic (courtesy of the Benguela current) and swimming is nothing if not exhilarating.

Buses and taxis run through Victoria Rd from the city to Hout Bay, but after that, you're on your own. Hitching is reasonably good.

On the more popular beaches in the city area you might see the work of sand artists, who create huge and complex naive artworks in return for donations. They will make to measure if you want. Unfortunately, the council regards them as a nuisance and wants to make them pay a licence fee. This might be the new South Africa, but the whites' urge to control all aspects of life, especially the lives of non-white people, remains.

Bloubergstrand & Table View

Bloubergstrand, 25 km to the north of the city on Table Bay, was the site for the 1806 battle between British and Dutch forces that resulted in the second British occupation of the Cape. This is also the spot with the most dramatic (and photographed) view of Table Mountain – you know, the one with wild flowers and sand dunes in the foreground, surf and, across the bay, the cloud-capped mountain ramparts looming over the city.

This is a boom area for antiseptic new suburbs but the village of Bloubergstrand itself is still quite small. There are a couple of small resorts where you can have a braai, buy snacks and find some long, uncrowded, windy stretches of sand. This is windsurfer territory, but there's also some surfing, best with a moderate north-easterly wind, a small swell and incoming tide. The Beach Club (keep going through Bloubergstrand) is a pleasant spot with takeaways available. Blue Peter has been recommended as a good spot for sundowners (drinks at sunset).

Getting There & Away Unfortunately, you'll need a car. Take the R27 north from the N1.

Sea Point

Separated from the City Bowl by Signal Hill, Sea Point is a bustling residential suburb with numerous multi-storey apartment buildings and hotels fringing the coast. It's one of the most densely populated suburbs in Africa. Main and Regent Rds are lined with restaurants, cafés and shops. The coast itself is rocky and swimming is dangerous. However, there are four tidal swimming pools and plenty of bronzed bodies take advantage of the sun. The Sea Point Pavilion pool (at the end of Clarens St) is open from 8.30 am to dusk; entry is R3.30. The pool is huge but a sunny day will heat it up. If it's 12°C in the ocean the pool will be about 20°C.

A number of reefs produce good waves. Solly's and Boat Bay, near the Sea Point Pavilion have lefts and rights that work on a south-east wind. Further along the beach towards Mouille Point there are a number of left reefs.

Getting There & Away To get there, catch any Clifton, Bakoven or Camps Bay bus from the main bus station (R1.20). There's a pedestrian promenade above the beach.

Clifton

There are four linked beaches at Clifton accessible by steps from Victoria Rd. They're the trendiest, busiest beaches on the Cape, and although they have the advantage of being sheltered from the wind, the water is cold. Consequently, the favoured activities are sunbaking, people watching, tennis and Frisbee. It's *very* hard to remember you're in Africa, although when you do, the obsessive pursuit of brown skin in a country where skin colour is such an issue, seems particularly bizarre...

There's a friendly and relaxed mood, although the occupants and atmosphere tend to vary with each beach. Fourth Beach, at the Camps Bay end, is the most accessible and popular with families, and there's a shop at the Fourth Beach car park (on the Ridge, off Victoria Rd). First Beach is definitely the place to be seen.

Getting There & Away There are frequent buses from OK Bazaars, Adderley St, and minibus taxis from the railway station. Buses cost R2.50, minibus taxis a bit less. It's a pleasant three-km walk from Sea Point (Hard Rock Cafe) and another km or so to Camps Bay. In summer there's no point in driving to Clifton as you won't be able to park.

Camps Bay

Camps Bay is one of the most beautiful beaches in the world. The fact that it is within 15 minutes of the city centre makes it even more extraordinary. It is often windy and it is certainly not as trendy as the beaches at Clifton, but it is more spectacular. The Twelve Apostles running south from Table Mountain tumble into the sea above the broad stretch of white sand.

It is amazing how relatively unspoilt and uncrowded it is. The only drawbacks are the wind and the temperature of the water. There are no lifesavers and strong surf, so take care. There's a small batch of shops and restaurants, including the trendy Blues, and St Elmo's. Accommodation possibilities range from the five-star Bay Hotel to the Stan Halt Youth Hostel, a stiff 20-minute walk up the hill towards Kloof Nek.

Getting There & Away There are frequent buses from OK Bazaars, Adderley St, and minibus taxis from the Strand. Buses cost R2.50, minibus taxis about R1.50. It's a km or so walk to the more sheltered coves at Clifton.

Llandudno

Although it's only 18 km away, Llandudno seems completely removed from Cape Town, let alone Africa. It's a small, exclusive seaside village clinging to steep slopes above a sheltered beach. There are no shops. The remains of the tanker *Romelia*, wrecked in 1977, lie off Sunset Rocks. There's surfing on the beach breaks (mostly rights), best at high tide with a small swell and a south-easterly wind.

Sandy Bay

Sandy Bay is Cape Town's unofficial nudist beach. Like many such beaches, there are no direct access roads. From the M6 turn towards Llandudno, keep to the lefthand side of this road and head towards the sea until you reach the Sunset Rocks parking area. It's a 20-minute walk to the south. There can be waves; best at low tide with south-easterly wind.

Hout Bay

Hout Bay opens up behind the almost vertical Sentinel, and the steep slopes of Chapman's Peak. Inland from the km of white sand, there is quite a large and fast-growing satellite town that still retains something of its village atmosphere. The southern arm of the bay is still an important fishing port and processing centre for snoek and crayfish.

Perched on a rock in the bay near the end of Chapman's Peak Drive is a bronze leopard. It has been sitting there since 1963 and is a reminder of the wildlife which once roamed the area's forests – which have also vanished.

The information centre (☎ (021) 790 4053) is in the Trading Post store on the main road and is open daily (reduced hours in the off-season).

The Hout Bay Museum (☎ (021) 790 3270), 4 St Andrew's Rd, tells the story of Hout Bay. The World of Birds, Valley Rd, is an eccentric aviary with 450 species of birds. Although caging birds is not an attractive idea, a real effort has been made to make the aviaries large and natural.

There are daily launch trips from Hout Bay, with Circe Launches (☎ (021) 790 1040). The one-hour R17.50 trips run out to Duiker Island, with its colony of Cape fur seals. There's at least one trip daily all year, at 10.30 am, and many more in summer, for which you can't book. It also has a sunset cruise that begins in Hout Bay and ends at the Victoria & Alfred Waterfront. Booking for this cruise is essential; it costs R54. Ring to check departure times.

You can hire a Hobie cat on the beach (☎ (021) 790 4511).

There are a number of restaurants, including a wharfside complex, Mariner's Wharf. See the Places to Eat section for details, and the Places to Stay section for accommodation in Hout Bay.

Getting There & Away Buses to Hout Bay (R5) leave from outside OK Bazaars on Adderley St. There are several early in the morning before 9 am, a few in the middle of the day and several between 2.15 and 5.30, and there aren't many on weekends. Minibus taxis also do the route for about the same price.

Chapman's Peak Drive

This 10-km drive is cut into the side of sheer mountain walls, between layers of brilliantly coloured sedimentary rock. There are great views over Chapman's Bay and back to the Sentinel and Hout Bay. It is one of the great scenic drives in the world and should not be missed.

Noordhoek

Thirty km south of Cape Town in the shadow of Chapman's Peak, Noordhoek has a five-km stretch of magnificent beach. Favoured by surfers and walkers, it tends to be windy and dangerous for swimmers. The Hoek, as it is known to surfers, is an excellent right beach break at the northern end that can hold large waves (only at low tide) and is best with a south-easterly wind. There's a caravan park here.

Long Beach

At the Kommetjie end of Chapman's Bay, Long Beach is another popular surf beach, with an attractive caravan park. There are lefts and rights, best with a south-easterly or south-westerly wind. Take the turn-off to Kommetjie and turn right before the village. The nearest shop is in Kommetjie.

Kommetjie

Kommetjie is a smallish crayfishing village with a quiet country atmosphere. There's a pub with bar lunches, a restaurant, a couple of caravan parks, a few shops, and not much

more. It is, however, the focal point for surfing on the Cape, offering an assortment of reefs that hold a very big swell. Outer Kom is a left point out from the lighthouse. Inner Kom is a more protected, smaller left with lots of kelp (only at high tide). They both work best with a south-easterly or south-westerly wind.

FALSE BAY

False Bay lies to the south-east of the city. Although the beaches on the east side of the peninsula are not quite as scenically spectacular as those on the Atlantic side, the water is often 5°C, or more, warmer and can reach 20°C in summer. This makes swimming far more pleasant. Suburban development along the coast is considerably more intense, presumably because of the railway which runs all the way through to Simon's Town.

On the east side of False Bay, Strand and Gordon's Bay are a cross between satellite suburbs and beach resorts. They have great views back to the Cape and are themselves in the shadow of the spectacular Hottentots-Holland mountains. There's a superb stretch of coastal road that rivals Chapman's Peak Drive, with a great caravan park and a couple of spots where you can get access to the beach – the surf can be very dangerous for swimmers.

During October and November, False Bay is a favoured haunt for whales and their calves – southern right, humpback and bryde (pronounced breedah) whales are the most commonly sighted. They often come quite close to the shore. Captour has an office on Atlantic Rd, Muizenberg (☎ (021) 788 1898), and they give reports on whale sightings from 9.30 am.

Getting There & Away

From Monday to Friday there are trains between Cape Town and Fish Hoek every half hour to 9 pm; every second one runs through to Simon's Town (hourly). On Saturday and Sunday nearly all trains run through to Simon's Town, and they're more or less hourly. Phone ☎ (021) 405 2991 for exact times. Cape Town to Muizenberg is

R2.10/4.70 in 1st/3rd class, Simon's Town is R2.80/6.40. There are less frequent trains to/from Strand, every couple of hours Monday to Saturday and infrequently on Sunday. The journey takes a bit over an hour.

Muizenberg
Unless the sun is shining, Muizenberg can be pretty bleak, but when it is, you can escape the fairly tacky shorefront for a broad white beach that shelves gently and is generally safer than most of the peninsula beaches. Surf at the peninsula end of the beach, in front of the 19th-century bathing boxes (which are let by the season – you can't hire one for the day).

Captour (☎ (021) 788 1898) has an office here, open from 8.30 am to 5 pm on weekdays, until 1 pm on Saturday and 'sometimes' on Sunday.

See the Places to Stay and Places to Eat sections for more on Muizenberg.

Kalk Bay
Kalk Bay (or Kalkbaai) was named after the lime kilns that in the 17th century produced lime from seashells for painting buildings. In 1806 it became a whaling station, and it is still a busy fishing harbour, particularly during the snoek season, which peaks during June and July, but can begin earlier. To the north of the harbour, there's an excellent left reef break (best with a west to north-westerly wind).

The Brass Bell, on the bay side of the train station, with a terrace right beside the sea, is a favourite spot for seafood braais and live music. See Places to Eat later for more information.

Clovelly & Fish Hoek
Both these resorts/suburbs have wide safe beaches. Clovelly is flanked by sand dunes. Peers Cave, which can be reached by climbing the dunes behind 19th Avenue, is named after the man who discovered the fossilised skeleton of a man who lived 15,000 years ago. South from Kalk Bay there are numerous grottoes and caves that have been

occupied by humans. There's a caravan park right on the beach at Fish Hoek.

Simon's Town (Simonstad)
Named after Simon van der Stel, an early governor, the town was the VOC's official winter anchorage from 1741 – it's sheltered from the winter north-easterlies that created havoc for ships in Table Bay. The British turned the harbour into a naval base in 1814 and it has remained one ever since.

There is an Information Bureau (☎ (021) 786 3046) at the Simon's Town Museum (off the main road about 600 metres south of the railway station), which traces the history of the town and port. It's in the old Governor's Residency, built in 1777. Both are open from 9 am to 4 pm on weekdays and from 10 am to 1 pm on Saturday; admission to the museum is R2. Next door is the South African Navy Museum, open daily from 10 am to 4 pm. Cameras are not allowed.

At the other end of the shopping strip (which is dominated by old buildings, many of which are of naval origin) is the Stempastorie Museum of National Emblems, open daily except Sunday, admission R1.

Seaforth Beach This beach is the nearest to Simon's Town and is a safe and sheltered family swimming spot. Head south from Simon's Town along St George's and after the navy block turn off into Seaforth Rd. Take the second right into Kleintuin Rd. Day visitors are charged R2 entry.

The Boulders A bit further on, but still within walking distance of Simon's Town are The Boulders. As the name suggests, this is an area with a number of attractive coves among large boulders that offer shade and shelter. Take the coast road south and turn left into Miller Rd. Day visitors are charged R2 entry. The Boulders are also home to a growing colony of jackass penguins.

Strand
Strand is quite a large satellite town, built along a nice stretch of gently shelving beach. It's very much a city by the surf, but some

people like this combination. The *Strand Pavilion Hotel* (☎ (024) 53 2725) is positioned right on the edge of the sea with commanding views. Singles/doubles are R190/250, rising to R210/290 in peak times. There are a couple of restaurants and a number of trendy shops in the Pavilion complex. The Porterhouse Steakhouse and Restaurant has a brilliant position perched over the waves. The offerings are standard, but the prices are cheap – R15 for line fish and steak, R7 for hamburgers.

Gordon's Bay

Pretty much a southerly continuation of Strand's sprawl, Gordon's Bay is smaller and has camping accommodation close to the beach.

CAPE OF GOOD HOPE NATURE RESERVE

This is a beautiful peninsula. If the weather is good – or even if it isn't – you can easily spend at least a day here. In some ways, the coastline here is not as dramatic as that between Clifton and Kommetjie, but there is drama nonetheless. There are numerous walks, a number of beaches (there's 40 km of coast within the reserve), a great cross section of the Cape's unique flora (fynbos) as well as baboons, hard-to-spot eland, bontebok, rhebok, grysbok, and abundant birdlife.

There are a number of picnic places where you can braai; the Homestead Restaurant (☎ (021) 80 1040) on the main road, which is moderately expensive; and a kiosk near Cape Point.

The reserve is open daily from 8 am to 6 pm, May to July; 7 am to 7 pm, August to October; 6 am to 8 pm, November to January and 7 am to 7 pm, February to April. It's particularly beautiful in spring when the wild flowers are in bloom. Maps and firewood are available at the gate. The entrance fee is R5 per person and R5 per surfboard.

Getting There & Away

The only public transport to the Cape is with Rikki's (who run those Asian-style mini-mini buses), which run from Simon's Town (accessible by train) and charge about R65 per hour. Numerous tours include Cape Point on their itineraries. Day Trippers (☎ (021) 461 4599 or 531 3274) and perhaps other backpacker-oriented companies take along mountain bikes so you can ride in the nature reserve and along Chapman's Peak Drive on the way to/from the Cape. They say that they haven't yet lost anyone over the edge...

Consider getting a group together and hiring a car for the day. If you plan to loop around the peninsula, start at Kirstenbosch Botanic Gardens and Groot Constantia, stock up on supplies at the Old Cape Farm Stall and head down through Muizenberg. If you tackle the drive clockwise you'll be on the right side of the road to stop and take in the unforgettable views. The section along Chapman's Peak Drive and on to Llandudno and Clifton is one of the most spectacular marine drives in the world.

CAPE FLATS

For the majority of Cape Town's inhabitants, home is in one of the townships out on the desolate Cape Flats: Guguletu, Nyanga, Philippi, Mitchell's Plain, Crossroads or Khayelitsha. The first impression as one approaches is of an endless, grim, undifferentiated sprawl, punctuated by light

---

Do Not Feed the Baboons!

There are signs all over Cape Point warning you not to feed the baboons. This isn't just some mean-spirited official stricture designed to keep baboons from developing a taste for crisps and chocolate. One group told me about how they stopped and opened the car windows to take photos of baboons. 'The next thing we knew, the baboons were in the car and we were out of the car. It took about half an hour before they were satisfied that they'd thoroughly trashed the interior, and we drove back to the rental agency in a car full of baboon shit.' ■

The Townships

Most residents of Cape Town live in one of the Cape Flats townships. Although all the townships are depressing and inconveniently situated, not all present scenes of squalor and misery, partly because the coloured population received favoured treatment under the apartheid regime, and there was also a programme of building a little decent housing in some of the black townships. It has been suggested that this was a way of dividing the black community and thus defusing its opposition to apartheid.

Most blacks live either in hostels or in shacks in the vast squatter camps. However, unlike the hostels in Jo'burg, which were cut off from the life of the surrounding township and became armed camps, hostels in Cape Town are integrated with the community. Some are owned by the city council, others by large companies such as Coca Cola.

Until the pass laws were abolished, hostels were for men only. They lived in basic units, each accommodating 16 men who shared one shower, one toilet and one small kitchen. Tiny bedrooms each housed three men. After the pass laws were abolished, most men brought their families to live with them (previously, if you didn't have a job outside the Homelands you were not allowed to leave). So now each unit is home to 16 *families*; each room sleeps three families. Some people have moved out of the hostels and built shacks, but the hostels remain the source of electricity, water and sanitation. Rent is R7.50 per month, but over the years many bed spaces (called 'squares' – your own square (the size of a single bed) was your sole private area – have been sublet, and the most recent arrivals can pay up to R50 per month.

All the black townships except Khayelitsha have hostels. Khayelitsha, with a population of one million, consequently has a huge proportion of squatters.

There are a few day hospitals in the townships, but for an illness requiring an overnight stay, residents have to travel into the city. A hospital is now being built at Khayelitsha.

If you're going to really understand Cape Town, it's essential that you visit the Cape Flats. They are still off-limits to lone visitors but there are some tours. Paula Gumede's One City Tours (☎ (021) 387 5351) is excellent and charges about R70. Other companies such as Day Trippers (see Activities) and Heartstoppers (see Entertainment) also visit the townships. ■

towers that would seem more appropriate in a concentration camp. In fact, some parts are acceptable, not all that far removed from suburbs anywhere, while others are as bad as any third-world slum.

Cape Town's townships have played a major role in the struggle against apartheid. See Apartheid & the Townships in the History section for more details. Given the history, the courtesy and friendliness that is generally shown to white visitors is almost shocking.

Although whites are *not* automatically targeted you should try to get objective advice on the current situation. This isn't easy, however, since most whites would not dream of visiting. Visiting without a companion who has local knowledge is likely to be foolish. If a trustworthy black friend is happy to escort you, however, you should have no problems, and tours have operated safely for years. Nowadays, it's not so much political violence as crime that is the problem.

ACTIVITIES

The boom in backpacker accommodation has led to a boom in backpacker-oriented activities. There are some excellent choices. Day Trippers (☎ (021) 461 4599 or 531 3274) gets excellent feedback from travellers, and Geoff and Steve really know their stuff. On most of their trips they take along mountain bikes, so you can do some riding if you want. Most tours cost around R100 and include Cape Point, Winelands (including a visit to a township on the way) and whale-watching.

Heartstoppers (☎ (021) 75 9900 or 683 3227) is another popular outfit. The Hip Hop Travellers Stop Hostel runs its own Bizzy Buzzy Bus Tours (☎ (021) 439 1842), with similar itineraries and prices.

Kloofing

The Table Mountain area is full of kloofs (cliffs or gorges) and kloofing is a way of exploring them that involves climbing, walking, swimming and jumping. It's a lot of fun. Kloofing requires local knowledge, equipment and experienced guides, so it's best to go along with one of the adventure activities outfits. Several offer kloofing; Day Trippers claims to have been the first. It offers kloofing between November and April and charges about R100.

Diving

Cape Town has a wide variety of diving – the Agulhas and Benguela currents create a unique cross section of marine conditions. Diving can be undertaken at any time of the year, but is best from June to November. The water on the False Bay side is warmer then and the visibility is greater. There are a number of excellent shore dives. Hard and soft corals, kelp beds, wrecks, caves and drop-offs, seals and a wide variety of fish are some of the attractions.

There are a number of dive operators, such as Ocean Divers International (☎ /fax (021) 439 1803), Ritz Plaza, Main Rd, Sea Point, and Scuba Venture (☎ (021) 461 2709, fax 461 8616), 8 Mill St, Gardens. A certificate course costs around R500.

Surfing

The Cape Peninsula has fantastic surfing possibilities – from gentle shorebreaks ideal for beginners to three-metre-plus monsters for experts only. There are breaks that work on virtually any combination of wind, tide and swell direction.

In general, the best surf is along the Atlantic side, and there is a string of breaks from Bloubergstrand through to the Cape of Good Hope. Most of these breaks work best in south-easterly conditions. The water can be freezing (as low as 8°C) so a steamer wetsuit, plus booties are required.

With the exception of the excellent left reef at Kalk Bay, the False Bay beaches tend to be less demanding in terms of size and temperature (up to 20°C), and work best in north-westerlies. There's a daily surf report on Radio Good Hope at 7.15 am.

Surprisingly there aren't all that many surf shops on the peninsula, but the Surf Centre (☎ (021) 23 7853) is a decent shop at 70 Loop St (on the corner of Hout St) in the city centre, with a good stock of wetsuits and second-hand boards. It hires boards and wetsuits for R50 per day.

The Flying Dutchman

According to the most popular version of the Flying Dutchman Legend, a ghost ship haunts the Cape because its captain once bet his soul he could round the Cape in a storm – and failed. In the spooky equinoxial sea-mists it doesn't seem too unlikely that the ancient square-rigger with its doomed crew might appear. In fact, the Flying Dutchman is 'sighted' near the Cape Peninsula more often than anywhere else in the world.

The Cape has a fearsome reputation for wrecking ships. Part of the reason is the fast-flowing current a few km offshore. Ships that avoid the current by sailing between it and the coast are at risk if one of the area's violent storms sweeps in. And there's a good chance one will – the Cape of Good Hope was originally called the Cape of Storms. If the wind is blowing in the opposite direction to the current, freak waves can also develop. If you add to this a panicky crew claiming to see a ghost ship flying before the wind, then avoiding the shoals might be almost impossible. ■

Walking

There are some fantastic walks around the peninsula, including to Lion's Head, on Table Mountain and in the Cape of Good Hope Nature Reserve. There are numerous books, brochures and maps that give details. It is important to be properly equipped with warm clothing, a map and compass. Start by asking at Captour.

For information and maps about National Hiking Ways and walks around Table Mountain and the Cape, contact the National Hiking Way Board (☎ (021) 402 3043) on Martin Hammerschlag, off Oswald Pirow on the foreshore. It also has an information desk at the Tourist Rendezvous (☎ (021) 483 4227).

Walking up (or down) Table Mountain is definitely possible – more than 300 routes have been identified. However, it is a high mountain and claims lives from time to time. It's safe enough if you are properly prepared with warm clothing and emergency food and water, and if you stick to the path. The trouble is, thick mists can make the paths invisible, and you'll just have to wait until they lift. You should always tell someone where you are going and you should never walk alone. Captour can put you in touch with a guide, and adventure activity outfits such as Day Trippers can give advice. Climbing the mountain is such a popular pastime that there's a good chance that you'll meet someone who will invite you along.

None of the routes is easy, but the Platteklip Gorge walk on the City Bowl side is at least straightforward. Unless you're fit, try walking down before you attempt the walk up. It took me about 2½ hours from the upper cable station to the lower, taking it fairly easy.

Shirley Brossy's *Walking Guide to Table Mountain* (paperback, R30) details 34 walks, and several other guides to the mountain are available. Mike Lundy's *Best Walks in the Cape Peninsula* (paperback, R40) is also useful.

Serious climbers could contact the Mountain Club of South Africa (☎ (021) 45 3412), 97 Hatfield St .

Other Activities

You can learn to skydive for R250 with the Western Province Sport Parachute Club (☎ (021) 461 0677 AH). Jumps are made over the Cederberg.

Several canoeing operators run short trips from Cape Town (as well as their regular longer trips). Felix Unite (☎ (021) 762 6935, fax 761 9259) has a relaxed day-trip on the Breede River (in the Winelands) for R145 and an overnight trip to the Doring River (Cederberg) for R235. River Runners (☎ (021) 762 2350) also has a day-trip in the wine area and Doring River Rafting (☎ (021) 794 5808) is a smaller outfit with overnight trips for about R200 per person.

Abseiling off Table Mountain, surely one of the most spectacular places in the world to throw yourself over a cliff, costs around R60, plus the cableway fare. Ask about dates at the Tourist Rendezvous or a booking centre such as The Africa Travel Centre at The Backpack hostel.

The Argus Tour from Cape Town to the peninsula is held in the second week of March and is the largest bicycle race in the world, with over 20,000 entries. Some entrants are deadly serious but many people go along for some fairly strenuous fun. See the Getting Around section for information on hiring bikes.

FESTIVALS

The Cape Festival used to be held annually early in March, with music from classical to jazz and everything in between. Whether or not it continues has yet to be decided.

ORGANISED TOURS

For a quick orientation on a fine day you can't beat Topless Tours (☎ (021) 448 2888), which runs a roofless double-decker bus. The two-hour city tour (R25) between Dock Rd in the Waterfront and the Tourist Rendezvous departs about six times a day, less often (if at all) in winter. Longer tours are also available.

See the earlier Activities section for the various outfits running outings aimed at backpackers.

Sealink Tours (☎ (021) 25 4480) is a large operator catering to the mainstream tourist market. Its tours include Cape Point (R110), Winelands (R120), Tulbagh Valley (R140) and Hermanus (R140). It also has Garden Route packages, starting at about R2000 for three nights. There's a Sealink booking office at the Waterfront, on Quay Five. Other major companies with similar deals include Springbok Atlas Tours (☎ (021) 417 6545) and Hylton Ross (☎ (021) 438 1500), a big local company and a bit more up-market. Hylton Ross also has an office on Quay Five at the Waterfront and as well as its tours it can book quite a few other things around the country.

Several companies offer eco-oriented tours of the Cape and longer trips further afield. They include Greencape Tours (☎ (082) 891 5266 or (021) 797 0166). The maximum group size is seven people and a consensus of customers can alter the itinerary.

One City Tours (☎ (021) 387 5351 or 387 5165) has an excellent three-hour township tour for R75, plus other tours. See the Entertainment section for a company offering nightlife township tours.

Tana-Baru Tours (☎ (021) 24 0719, fax 23 5579) offers a very interesting two-hour walk or drive through Bo-Kaap (the 'Malay' quarter), including tea and some very tasty traditional snacks in a private home. Shereen

Habib lives in Bo-Kaap and is an excellent guide, as much for her knowledge of day-to-day life in this vibrant community as her historical insights. Tours are held between 10 am and noon and from 2 to 4 pm and cost R45 (with substantial discounts for backpackers). Shereen will take as few as one person. Highly recommended. If you're going to take any tour of this area, make it this one, rather than a white-run bus tour that treats the area like a zoo.

Court Helicopters (☎ (021) 25 2966/7) has 10-minute flights from near the Waterfront up to Lion's Head and Table Mountain then back down over the City Bowl. It's spectacular and well worth R400 for four people. Another helicopter company is Civair (☎ (021) 419 5182).

See the earlier Victoria & Alfred Waterfront section for information on boat cruises. Plenty of cruises say that they'll take you to infamous Robben Island, but none actually land. The island is still a jail and while the Department of Correctional Services does have tours (☎ (021) 411 1006) they are booked out more than six months in advance.

At least once a month there are steam train excursions to Simon's Town or Franschhoek, for about R40. Contact Union Ltd Steam Rail Tours (☎ (021) 405 4391) at the Tourist Rendezvous.

PLACES TO STAY

There is a huge number of options and most people will find something that suits their pocket. If you have any difficulties, contact the Captour accommodation service.

In high season – basically December through to Easter – prices can jump up to 100% and many places will be fully booked. School holidays are always busy, but if you plan to visit during the summer school holidays in particular, booking is essential. Now that Cape Town is gaining a reputation as one of the world's better cities to visit, it would be wise to book at any time of year.

The rates at many places fluctuate according to demand, and it's always worthwhile asking about special deals. For longer stays, rates are definitely negotiable.

The Coon Carnival

The Coon Carnival is a long-standing festival involving the coloured community. *Coon* Carnival? Yes, but the name derives from a side alley of racism, not the apartheid highway. It seems that the coloured community was impressed by a touring black-&-white minstrel show and decided to emulate it. Traditionally, the Coon Carnival allowed some licence, and revellers would grab passers-by and black their faces with boot polish. During the apartheid era, the carnival was moved to a stadium, away from the streets, so that sort of thing couldn't happen. Problems caused by rival promoters mean that the carnival may not continue. ■

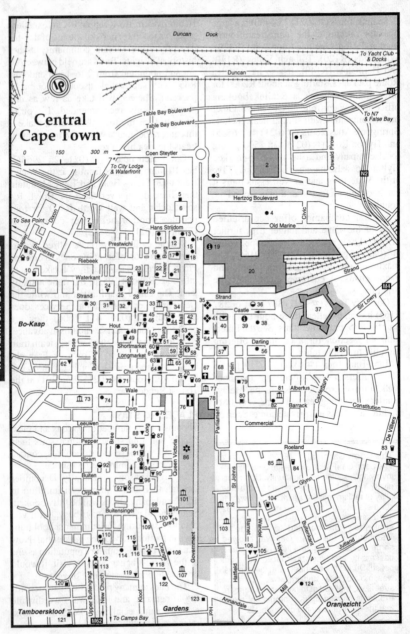

Central
Cape Town

0   150   300 m

Duncan Dock

To Yacht Club
& Docks

Duncan

To N7
& False Bay

Table Bay Boulevard

Table Bay Boulevard

Coen Steytler

To City Lodge
& Waterfront

Hertzog Boulevard

Old Marine

Hans Strijdom

Prestwichi

Somerset

To Sea Point

Dixon

Napier

Riebeek

Waterkant

Strand

Bo-Kaap

Rose

Buitengragt

Hout

Shortmarket

Longmarket

Church

Wale

Dorp

Leeuwen

Pepper

Bree

Bloem

Buiten

Orphan

Buitensingel

Tamboerskloof

To Camps Bay

Gardens

Oranjezicht

Burg

Lower

Mall

Adderley

George

Burg

St

Plein

Darling

Castle

Strand

Sir Lowry

Oswald Pirow

Civic

Long

Loop

Queen Victoria

Government

Parliament

St Johns

Commercial

Barrack

Roeland

Barnet

Wandel

Hatfield

Mill

Annandale

Albertus

Constitution

De Villiers

Glynn

Juiland

New Church

Upper Buitengragt

Klood

Hof

PLACES TO STAY

5 Diplomat Holiday Flats
9 The Lodge
18 Holiday Inn Garden Court St George's Mall
31 Cape Town Inn
34 Cape Sun
45 Metropole Hotel
61 Holiday Inn Garden Court Greenmarket Square
63 Tudor Hotel
79 Townhouse Hotel
80 Pleinpark Travel Lodge
87 Long St Backpackers
94 Travellers Inn
96 Overseas Visitors' Club
99 Carlton Heights Hotel
112 The Backpack
113 Zebra Crossing
117 Albergo Backpackers
120 Mijloff Manor Hotel
121 Underberg Guesthouse
123 Mount Nelson Hotel

PLACES TO EAT

24 A Table at Colin's
29 Spur Steakhouse
50 Nino's
51 Le Petit Paris
54 World of Coffee
57 Wellington Dried Fruit
62 Karima's Café
66 Off Moroka Café Africaine
70 Mark's Coffee Shop
88 Mr Pickwicks Deli
90 Mama Africa
95 Morris's Boerewurst
100 Kaapse Tafel Restaurant
105 Roxy's Coffee Bar
106 Maria's Greek Restaurant
111 Rustica
115 Rozenhof
118 Mario's Coffee Shop
119 KD's Bar & Bistro

ENTERTAINMENT

2 Nico Malan Complex
7 The Fireman's Arms
8 The Bronx
10 Café Manhattan
22 Long Street Theatre
23 Browne's Café du Vin
25 Shebeen on Bree
26 Crew Bar
27 Café Comic Strip
47 Henry's
49 D'Elyzium
55 District Six Café
60 The Purple Turtle
69 Manenberg's Jazz Cafe
83 The Shed
84 Perseverance Tavern
91 The Lounge
97 Rick's
104 Stag's Head Hotel
108 Little Theatre & Arena Theatre
109 The Whistle Stop
116 Firkin Brew Pub Company
122 Labia Cinema

MUSEUMS

33 Koopmans de Wet House
65 Townhouse Museum
73 Bo-Kaap Museum
77 Cultural History Museum
81 District Six Museum
85 Rust-en-Vreugd
101 South African Museum
103 Jewish Museum
107 Bertam House

OTHER

1 National Hiking Way Board
3 Broadway Centre
4 Civic Centre
6 Tulbagh Square
11 BP Centre
12 Thibault Square
13 American Express
14 British Airways Travel Clinic
15 Trustbank Centre
16 Southern Life Centre
17 Rennies/Thomas Cook
19 Tourist Rendezvous
20 Railway Station
21 Namibia Trade & Tourism
28 Imperial Car Rental
30 Avis Car Rental
32 Budget Car Rental
35 Golden Acre Centre
36 City Bus Terminal
37 Castle of Good Hope
38 Grand Parade
39 Bus Information Kiosk
40 GPO
41 OK Bazaars
42 Postnet
43 Camera Care
44 Ulrich Naumann, German Bookshop
46 National Parks Board
48 Surf Centre
52 Pezulu (Crafts)
53 Stuttaford's Town Square
56 City Hall
58 BOB (First National Bank)
59 Greenmarket Square
64 African Image (Crafts)
67 Groote Kerk
68 Church Square
71 Mike Hopkins Cycles
72 Tempest Car Rental
74 Cape Wine Cellar
75 Cape Nature Conservation
76 St Georges Cathedral
78 Houses of Parliament
82 Department of Home Affairs
86 Botanical (Company) Gardens
89 Prolab
92 Alisa Car Rental
93 The Junk Shop
98 Long St Baths & Swimming Pool
102 National Gallery
110 Afrogem
114 Le Cap Motorcycle Hire
124 Gardens Centre

WESTERN CAPE PROVINCE

PLACES TO STAY – BOTTOM END

Caravan Parks

There are no particularly central caravan parks, so if you do intend to camp, a car is virtually a prerequisite. The exception is the *Zandvlei Caravan Park* (☎ (021) 788 5215), The Row, Muizenberg, which is within walking distance (about two km) of the

Muizenberg station (on the Simon's Town line) and the beach (about one km). Walk east around the civic centre and pavilion, turn right onto Atlantic Beach Rd, which doglegs and crosses the mouth of the Zandvlei lagoon, take the first left after the bridge down Axminster Rd, which becomes The Row. For two people the tariff ranges from R22 to R44 in December and early January.

The *Fish Hoek Beach Caravan Park* (☎ (021) 782 5503), Victoria Rd, Fish Hoek, is also accessible by train, but they do not allow tents. It's only a small park but its position is excellent. The tariff ranges from R32 per van site to R66 in the highest season (December to mid-January).

For those with cars, and particularly for surfers, the *Imhoff Caravan Park*, 1 Wireless Rd, Kommetjie, 42 km south of the city on the Atlantic seaboard, is in an ideal position as it is only 100 metres from Long Beach. There are four and six-berth caravans for hire; tents are allowed, but not plastic ground sheets. The tariff is R27 plus R4 per person, rising to R56 for up to four people in December and early January.

A bit closer to town, but still handy for Atlantic surf beaches, the *Chapman's Peak Caravan Park* (☎ (021) 789 1225), Dassen-heuwel Ave, Noordhoek, is in a beautiful setting. Rates are R27 plus R2 per person, rising to R40 from mid-December to mid-January.

Millers Point Caravan Park (☎ (021) 786 1142), about five km from Simon's Town, on the Cape Point side, is on a small private beach and has just 12 sites. It doesn't always accept tents.

Hostels

Between researching the first and second editions of this book the number of hostels in Cape Town increased by about 400% and there's no reason to suppose that this boom is dying down. Competition between hostels is fierce and you can expect most places to offer free pick-ups, discounts at local businesses and a good range of excursions. It's likely that there will be a shortage of backpacker beds in summer for the next few years, so expect prices to rise when everything is full.

Which Hostel? Just about any hostel is a good hostel if you like the people staying there. If you have the suspicion that you've landed in some sort of tacky, backpackers' version of the Costa de Sol, full of boozy xenophobes, just try another hostel – there are some distinct personalities.

City Bowl Right in the city at 209 Long St, *Long St Backpackers* (☎ (021) 23 0615) is in a block of about 10 small flats, with four to six beds in each, at R23 per person. When things are quiet there's a good chance of having a flat to yourself. Doubles are R57, and there are weekly rates. It's a pleasant enough place, with a courtyard and a good bar. The *Overseas Visitors' Club* (☎ (021) 24 6800), 236 Long St (near the corner of Buiten) has dorm beds only, for R25. It's a nice old building, with high-quality facilities and a pub-like bar, but it doesn't really have a backpacking atmosphere. It sometimes closes in winter.

The Backpack (☎ (021) 23 4530, fax 23 0065), 74 New Church St (the top of Buitengracht), is the original non-YHA hostel in Cape Town, and it's arguably still the best. Lee and Toni are constantly making improvements, and they always seem to be the first with new innovations.

They have three bright and sunny old houses, which have been pleasantly furnished and decorated, in a good position halfway between Camps Bay and the city centre. There's a cheerful, friendly atmosphere with lots of travellers coming and going, good notice boards, clean kitchen facilities, and a small pool. 'The shack at the back' is a good bar and café – you can't beat the egg & bacon rolls for breakfast. The Africa Travel Centre in the hostel is probably the best place to make travel bookings, both for activities in and around Cape Town and further afield.

A dorm bed costs R30 and there are a few doubles from R80. It's about a 15-minute walk from the railway station, or you can catch the Kloof Nek bus from Adderley St, outside OK Bazaars to stop No 68.

A few doors up at 82 New Church St is *Zebra Crossing* (☎/fax (021) 22 1265), which is smaller, quieter and more personal – it's also recommended. There are some good new doubles behind the house, and one has excellent views. Dorms are R25 and singles/doubles are R75.

A little further up New Church St is the big new all-dorm *Pink Backpacker* (☎ (021) 23 6992). Not far away is *Albergo Backpackers* (☎ (021) 22 1849, fax 23 0515), 5 Beckham St, Gardens. It's a reasonable place in a good location, not far from the city. Beds in large dorms go for R21 (R132 a week), R23 in small dorms (R145). Doubles, some in a separate house down the street, cost from about R60 to R85. The owner does 4WD tours of Namibia and the Richtersveld, and might have special deals for backpackers.

Oak Lodge (☎ (021) 45 6182) is at 21 Breda St, Gardens. What can I say? You'll love it or hate it. The hostel was once a commune but the astute communards saw that they'd have more fun (and make some money) if they turned it into a backpacker hostel. They have done a good job, and it's one of the nicest hostels in town. It tends to attract people who have been on the road for a while, but everyone is made welcome. If you want to check it out, go along to their pool competition on Monday night. There's a big bar (with murals), a good kitchen and smoking and non-smoking dorms. They do pick-ups. Dorms are R25 or R30 in a four-bed dorm. Doubles are about R70, although you can't book them and they're usually full. There are weekly rates.

Also in the Gardens area, *Shanti Lodge* (☎ (021) 461 1408), 17 Prince St, is spacious and relaxed. It charges R22 for dorms and R70 for a double. Nearby is the new *Cloudbreak* hostel (☎ (021) 461 6892), 219 Upper Buitenkant. The owners are good sources of information on surfing. Dorms start at R25 and doubles are R75.

The *YWCA* (☎ (021) 23 3711), 20 Belle-vue St, Gardens, only accepts women and only has a couple of casual vacancies. The *Belvidere Accommodation Centre* (☎ (021) 23 1316), Higgo Cres, is quite some way from the city centre, although Rikki's taxis do run here. It's a very big, institutional YHA place, in large grounds with a pool. They get lots of groups.

The Lodge (☎ (021) 21 1106), 49 Napier St, is a pleasant place; quiet and friendly. It's well-located, too, in the newly yuppified edge of the old Cape Muslim quarter, and not far from the city and the Waterfront. B&B costs R30 in a dorm (R35 in a smaller dorm) and R90 in a double room.

Sea Point & Nearby As well as its guest-house (see below) *St John's Lodge* (☎ (021) 439 9028, fax 439 4875) has a separate backpackers' section, with dorm beds R25 and singles/doubles for about R45/75. Extra people are charged R15 each. It also has a new place, *St John's Waterfront Lodge* (☎ (021) 439 1404, fax 439 4875), a more up-market operation at 6 Braemar Rd in Green Point, not too far from the Waterfront and the city. Dorms are R25, rooms cost from R90/115/130 a double/triple/quad (more in the high season) and there's a four-person flat for R150. It is about to expand into the house next door, so there will be two pools and gardens. It's a nice place.

Hip Hop Travellers Stop (☎ (021) 439 2104), 11 Vesperdene Rd, Green Point, describes itself as being on the Waterfront. It isn't, but it is one of the closest hostels to the Waterfront. The hostel also describes itself as lively and it is that. Hip Hop is in a pleasant old house and has a pool and a garden. Dorm beds are R23 or you can put your tent up in the garden for R18 per person. Rooms cost between R60 and R80.

The Bunkhouse (☎ (021) 434 5695), 23 Antrim Rd, Three Anchor Bay, is pretty well equidistant from the Waterfront, Sea Point and the city – although it's a bit of a walk to get to any of them. The hostel is friendly and charges R22 in dorms and R65 in doubles. *Bunkers* (☎ (021) 434 0549), 15 Graham Rd, Sea Point, is well-located and a reasonable place but it all depends on who is staying there. Bunks are R25, rooms start at R30 per person. It can help you find apartments in the area for about R50 per person. At the far end of Sea Point, *The Globe Trotter* (☎ (021) 434 1539), 17 Queens Rd, has dorm beds from R25 and doubles from R60.

Camps Bay The *Stan Halt Youth Hostel* (☎ (021) 438 9037), The Glen, Camps Bay, is near the Round House Restaurant, which is better signposted than the hostel. In fact, the hostel buildings were once the stables for the Round House, which was built as a hunting lodge. The hostel, a very pleasant national monument, has a beautiful position, surrounded by trees, with a great view. You pay for this, however, with a steep 15-minute walk to the nearest shops and restaurants in Camps Bay. Dorm beds (only) are just R20, R17 for YHA members. Some meals are available: breakfast is R7 or less, dinner is R9. This would be a good place to spend a few days recuperating from an overdose of nightlife. Take the Kloof Nek bus from outside OK Bazaars in Adderley St (R2.50) to the top of Kloof Nek, then take the road to the right. It's a longish but pretty walk. Like all other YHA hostels in South Africa, this one has 24-hour access and there are no chores – it's the same deal as any backpacker place, in fact.

Observatory This suburb, a favourite with students, is a long way from the city centre and the Waterfront – by Cape Town standards, anyway. It's only a few minutes to the city by car or train, and it is a nice neighbourhood with some good music venues and places to eat. A good place to hang out for a while. A minibus taxi from town costs R1.20, and a train costs R1/2 in 1st/3rd class (don't take luggage in 3rd class and don't travel at rush hour).

The *Green Elephant* (☎ (021) 448 6359), 57 Milton Rd is a two-storey house in a walled garden. It's run by experienced travellers and is well-regarded. The list of hostel features includes a tree-climbing dog – it's a happy place. Dorms are R23 and there are a few doubles.

The friendly *Rolling Stones* (☎ (021) 448

1124) is about to move to a new address (39 Milner Rd) in the adjacent suburb of Woodstock. We haven't seen the new building but the manager says that it's better than the old one, which was OK. Dorms will be about R25 and there will be doubles.

False Bay The *Abe Bailey Youth Hostel* (☎ (021) 788 2301), on the corner of Maynard and Westbury Rds, Muizenberg, is quiet and it's a short walk to the beach. R20 gets you a dorm bed and there are doubles for R50. It's on the Simon's Town line; get off at Valsbai (approximately 40 minutes). Trains are frequent – every half hour or so during the week. Even on Sunday they're hourly.

Guesthouses

City Bowl *Travellers Inn* (☎ (021) 24 9272), 208 Long St, is in one of the old wrought-iron decorated buildings and was once the British Guesthouse; that name is still on the door. It has been taken over by enthusiastic new management and is undergoing a much-needed refurbishment. Singles (and they really are singles) start at R60 and doubles at R100, including a make-it-yourself breakfast.

Palm Court Holiday Lodge (☎ (021) 23 8721), 11 Hof St, Gardens (a block from Orange St), is a big old house with boarding house overtones (bathrooms are shared) but it's not at all depressing and is well located. The rooms are very clean and comfortable with high, ornate ceilings, and you can use the kitchen facilities. The owners are friendly and there's a pool. The rates are good, too. In the high season singles/doubles go for just R75/R140 and three/four bed rooms are R175/200.

Sea Point *St John's Lodge* (☎ (021) 439 9028), 9 St John's Rd, on the corner of Main Rd, is one of the best bargains in Cape Town, occupying a unique niche between a backpacker's lodge and hotel. It has the friendly communal atmosphere of a lodge (there are kitchen facilities, lounge rooms and lots of travellers), but there are private rooms, some with showers, as well as shared rooms. You get your own key, linen is provided and the rooms are cleaned daily.

It's an attractive old building with wide verandahs overlooking the street and its position can't be beaten – right in the heart of bustling Sea Point, and near to beaches... It has its own security patrol covering the surrounding streets, so it's pretty secure. Singles/doubles are R45/75, plus R15 for each additional person. You'll pay nearly twice that in the high season. Needless to say, it's very popular, so ring Fred or Iris in advance if possible. To get there, catch any Clifton, Bakoven or Camps Bay bus from the main bus station (R1).

PLACES TO STAY – MIDDLE
B&Bs & Guesthouses

The excellent Bed 'n Breakfast organisation (☎ (021) 683 3505, fax 683 5159) has a number of members around the Cape Peninsula. The accommodation is exceptionally good value. Most rooms are in large, luxurious suburban houses (often with swimming pools) and all have private bathrooms; there are also self-contained flats and cottages available. The only problem is that Bed 'n Breakfast prefers advance bookings (at least a day or so) and most houses are difficult to get to without private transport. Its prices range from R90/160 a single/double.

There's at least one other agency (☎ (021) 21 5400), which might offer cheaper prices. The Captour accommodation booking service at the Tourist Rendezvous can also help. The Portfolio people also list some excellent places to stay. See the Facts for the Visitor chapter for their address, or pick up their booklets at the Tourist Rendezvous.

There are a great many B&Bs and guesthouses – the following is just a small sample.

City Bowl *Belmont House* (☎ (021) 461 5417), 10 Belmont Ave, Oranjezicht, is a small but comfortable guesthouse overlooking the City Bowl, charging from R60/90. There are kitchen facilities.

Ambleside Guesthouse (☎ (021) 45 2503), 11 Forest Rd, Oranjezicht has comfortable singles/doubles and family rooms, and a fully equipped guest kitchen. Doubles start at R130 with shared bathroom or R150 with ensuite.

The *Underberg Guesthouse* (☎ (021) 262262) on the corner of Carstens St and Tamboerskloof Rd is a very nice place, restored Victorian but not too fussy. Singles/doubles start at R160/255, including breakfast. Nearby at 10A Tamboerskloof Rd, *Table Mountain Lodge* (☎ (021) 23 0042, fax 23 4983) is another restored house with B&B from R200/220. Not far away at 93 New Church St, *Leeuwenvoet House* (☎ (021) 21 24 1133, fax 24 0495) is another quality guesthouse with rooms from R155/220, including a huge breakfast.

Sea Point *Ashby Manor Guesthouse* (☎ (021) 434 1879, fax 439 3572), 242 High Level Rd, Fresnaye, is a rambling old Victorian house, on the slopes of Signal Hill above Sea Point. All rooms have a fridge and hand basin and there is a kitchen. Singles/doubles go for about R80 per person, higher in season.

Another pleasant possibility in an old Sea Point mansion is *Bellevue Manor House* (☎/fax (021) 434 0375), 5 Bellevue Rd, Sea Point, with good rooms for around R200, less if you share a bathroom. There's a guests' kitchen. The building is a National Monument. *Villa Rosa* (☎ (021) 434 2768, 277 High Level Rd (on the corner of Arthur's Rd), Sea Point, is a nice old house, restored into a quality guesthouse. Well-equipped rooms start at R180 a double, with 'flatlets' from R240 for two people.

Olaf's Guest House (☎/fax (021) 439 8943), 24 Wisbeach Rd, also has high-quality accommodation, starting at R180/ 270. They speak German.

Self-Catering

There are a number of agencies that specialise in arranging fully furnished houses and flats, including Cape Holiday Homes (☎ (021) 419 0430), 31 Heerengracht, PO Box 2044, Cape Town 8000; and Private Places

(☎ (021) 52 1200, fax 551 1487), 102 South Point Centre, Loxton Rd, Milnerton 7441.

City Bowl The *Carlton Heights Hotel* (☎ (021) 23 1260), on Queen Victoria St, opposite the South African Museum, is well located and fair value. The rooms are small and on the point of being tacky, but they do include a stove and fridge. There are good views from the upper stories. Standard rooms start at R100 per person.

Diplomat Holiday Flats (☎ 25 2037, 2341), right in the city on Tulbagh Square, is one of those rare places where the quality of the accommodation is higher than the quality of the foyer would suggest. It's old fashioned but clean and in good condition. The rooms are large and the two-room flats have an enormous lounge. There is a huge array of rates and seasons, but basically the rate for two/three people in a single-bedroom flat is R110/130; for three/four people in a two-bedroom flat R150/170. Add about 30% from December to mid-January.

The *Gardens Centre Holiday Flats* (☎ (021) 461 5827) is the distinctive multi-storey building on Mill St, Gardens. The single-bedroom flats are above an excellent small shopping mall and although the flats only go up to the 5th Floor, the views are still good. Rates vary widely according to the season, starting around R150 for two people and rising to nearly R200 around Christmas. An additional adult costs R28.50. In the low season you might be able to rent by the month, for about R2000.

Atlantic Coast *Cascades* (☎ (021) 434 3385, fax 434 0462), 8 Vesperdene Rd, Green Point, is a large and not especially attractive apartment block with studio apartments from R220 for two people and two bedroom apartments from R360 for four people, rising in summer.

Lions Head Lodge (☎ (021) 434 4163), 319 Main Rd (on the corner of Conifer), Sea Point, has rooms and self-catering apartments. The nightly rate is from R130/150 or R190 for four people, rising to R200 a double or R300 for four people in peak season

(when there is no single rate). If you stay longer than a day or so, the rates fall.

The Hout Bay information centre can tell you about self-catering cottages and apartments. Something reasonable will cost about R100 for two people.

A great spot if you have a car, the *Flora Bay Bungalows* (☎ (021) 790 1650), Chapman's Peak Drive, Hout Bay, has magnificent ocean views. One room 'oceanettes' are from R130 to R180 per night or R450 to R700 per week depending on the season; family bungalows are from R700 to R950.

False Bay The *Blue Lantern* (☎ (021) 786 2113), Seaforth Beach Front, Simon's Town, has a number of fully serviced chalets (sleeping up to five) from R85 a double and rising steeply through five seasons. Next door is *Oatlands* (☎ (021) 786 1410), a member of the Club Caravelle chain, with more substantial accommodation at more substantial prices. Self-catering rondavels cost R155 a double in the mid season.

The *Aloes Family Holiday Units* (☎ (021) 786 1758), Boulders Pl off Bellevue Rd, Simon's Town, includes four family units, fully furnished and equipped with TV and private braai area, very close to The Boulders beach area. Prices jump from about R90 to R200 per night in season. *Bosky Dell* (☎ (021) 23 1818), 5 Grant Ave, is on Boulders Beach and has self-contained units starting around R100/160, less in winter and more in summer.

Hotels

City Bowl *Tudor Hotel* (☎ (021) 24 1335), Greenmarket Square, is a homely little hotel hotel (30 rooms) with a great position right in the middle of town, but away from main roads. It could do with renovation but it's OK. All rooms have bathrooms, phones, radios and TVs. Parking is available nearby (at a price). Singles/doubles start at R145/190 including breakfast.

The *Metropole Hotel* (☎ (021) 23 6363), 38 Long St, is an attractive old-style hotel, with a dark, wood panel interior. Their prices are very reasonable considering the degree of comfort offered. Smallish standard rooms are R165/190, luxury rooms (and they really are luxurious) are R225/275 and there are more expensive suites.

The two-star *Pleinpark Travel Lodge* (☎ (021) 45 7563), on the corner of Corporation and Barrack Sts, is a conveniently located hotel with all mod-cons and reasonable prices. It's OK, but only OK. Singles/doubles start at R165/220 including breakfast. In the same league is the high-rise *Cape Town Inn* (☎ (021) 23 5116), on the corner of Strand and Bree Sts. Room rates fluctuate, but around R160 for a double, with breakfast, is about as low as they go. Parking facilities are available. Further out of town, but still within walking distance, the *Cape Swiss Hotel* (☎ (021) 23 8190), on the corner of Kloof and Camp Sts, is another characterless but decent hotel. Rates start at around R175 a double, higher in peak season.

Mijloff Manor Hotel (☎ (021) 26 1476), 5 Military Rd, was once an attractive small hotel in a converted mansion – now it has grown into a reasonable, but quite large hotel, with a lot of new rooms. Rooms start at R200 (and rise steeply) or there are self-catering 'duplex' rooms from R260. The bar and restaurant here are good.

Behind the Mount Nelson Hotel, at 16 Hof St, Gardens, the *Helmsley Hotel* (☎ (021) 23 7200) seems a little out of place in the middle of a city – it's like an old-style country hotel. The facilities are simple but reasonable and there's quite a variety of rooms, but it's a bit expensive at R190/260.

Waterfront Area *Breakwater Lodge* (☎ (021) 406 1911, fax 406 1070), Portswood Rd, should be one of the best places to stay, as it's in a restored jail hard by the Waterfront and the prices aren't bad. However, as well as being a restored jail it's also a restored tertiary institution and the rooms are *tiny*. Paying R137 for one of these rooms and then having to share the bathroom seems silly. You could pay R220 for a suite, which is just two tiny rooms with an attached bathroom.

Sea Point The *New Regency Hotel* (☎ (021) 439 6101), 90 Regent Rd (near the corner of Queens Rd) is a large older-style hotel which has installed a glitzy (or tacky) casino on the ground floor and done a modicum of renovation to the rooms. It isn't a great bargain but it would do. Rates, including breakfast, are from R165/225.

Atlantic Coast In Hout Bay, *Chapman's Peak Hotel* (☎ (021) 790 1036) has rooms from R80/120, rising to R100/180, with breakfast. The rooms aren't flash but it's a pleasantly relaxed place. *The Beach House Hotel* (☎ (021) 790 4228), Royal Ave, charges R130/220, including breakfast. No children under 14.

False Bay The *Lord Nelson Inn* (☎ (021) 786 1386), 58 St George's St, Simon's Town, is a small, old-style pub. In the main street of Simon's Town overlooking the harbour, it's accessible by train. Singles/doubles start at R180/220, 15% more in the high season. Although this is a pleasant, refurbished place, it isn't great value, and more expensive rooms overlooking the sea (which is largely obscured by a shed in the naval dockyards) get traffic noise.

PLACES TO STAY – TOP END

City Bowl Staying at the *Mount Nelson Hotel* (☎ (021) 23 1000), 76 Orange St, is like stepping back in time to the great days of the British Empire. Dating from 1899, the hotel is set in seven acres of parkland, a short walk through the Company's Gardens to the city. Part of the Venice Simplon Orient Express group, the rooms are full of character. Mid-season rates start around R950/1350. Unfortunately, the exterior is painted in a pink and grey colour scheme that makes it look like an underfunded institution of some kind.

In complete contrast, the five-star *Cape Sun* (☎ (021) 23 8844), Strand St, is a large, modern, classy, multi-storey hotel in the middle of the city. It has a swimming pool, fitness centre and several restaurants. Rooms start around R850.

Less expensive but still very good is the four-star *Townhouse Hotel* (☎ (021) 45 7050, fax 45 3891), 60 Corporation St (on the corner of Mostert St) which charges R233/250 or R205 for singles with shower only. Rooms with numbers ending in six have good views of the mountain.

There are a few members of the Holiday Inn Garden Court chain:

Greenmarket Square
  On Greenmarket Square (☎ (021) 23 2040, fax 23 3664), R204/218
St George's Mall
  On the corner of Riebeeck St and St George's Mall (☎ (021) 419 0808, fax 419 7010), R224/248
De Waal
  Mill St, Gardens (☎ (021) 45 1311, fax 461 6648), R209/228
Eastern Boulevard
  On the corner of Melbourne Rd and Coronation Ave, Woodstock (☎ (021) 448 4123, fax 47 8338), R184/184

As well as the hotels, there are some outstanding top-end guesthouses, such as *Villa Belmonte* (☎ 462 1576, fax 462 1579), 33 Belmont Ave, Oranjezicht. It's an ornate Italianate villa with excellent facilities, charging from around R330.

Atlantic Coast Close to both the city and the Waterfront, *City Lodge* (☎ (021) 419 9450, fax 419 0460), on the corner of Dock Rd and Alfred St, is a big place, something like an up-market motel. Room rates start at R225/266 a single/double.

The *Victoria & Alfred Hotel* (☎ (021) 419 6677, fax 419 8955), right in the middle of the Waterfront, has everything a five-star hotel should have. Its position is brilliant, the rooms are lovely, and it's heavily booked. Definitely first choice if you have the money and swimming is not a priority – singles/doubles start at R405/700.

On the Green Point side of the Waterfront, the *Portswood Square Hotel* (☎ (021) 418 3281, fax 419 7570), Portswood Rd, is a new four star hotel. Rates start at R310/430. The rooms aren't especially large but it's a pleasant place.

The Place on the Bay (☎ (021) 438 7069, fax 438 2692), on the corner of Victoria Rd and The Fairways in Camps Bay, is a large complex of modern, very comfortable self-catering apartments. The two bedroom apartments have a double bed and two singles, plus a couch in the downstairs lounge that sleeps an adult or two children. Rates in the highest/lowest seasons range from R200 per person/R900 per apartment for a studio apartment, and R200 per person (minimum R500)/R1600 per apartment for a two-bedroom apartment. There are also more expensive penthouses.

If you want to be close to a beautiful beach, consider five-star *The Bay Hotel* (☎ (021) 438 4444) an attractive and luxurious new hotel across the road from the Camps Bay beach. Every room has great views, and it aims for a more personalised country hotel feel. Rooms start at R750 and go over R1000, with lower prices in winter.

Further south at Kommetjie, the *Kommetjie Inn* (☎ (021) 783 4230) is a refurbished seaside hotel with rooms starting around R200/280, more in summer.

Constantia The *Alphen Hotel* (☎ (021) 794 5011), Alphen Dr, Constantia, is in a beautiful Cape Dutch manor that has been declared a national monument. It's about 20 minutes from town. The reception area is furnished in beautiful antiques and the buildings are shaded by old oak trees. There's a swimming pool, sports facilities, restaurant and bar. Prices are reasonable for what you get; singles/doubles are from R240/410.

PLACES TO EAT

Cape Town could easily claim to be the gastronomic capital of Africa. Unlike the rest of South Africa there's a cosmopolitan café/restaurant culture. Whites go out to eat. Why they do here, and not elsewhere, is a mystery – perhaps it's harder to find live-in cooks, or perhaps the city's history as the tavern of the seas has simply created a more dynamic urban culture.

There is a tremendous variety of cuisines and you can spend a lot of money, or a little.

Although you have to go looking for it, the traditional Cape cuisine – a curious cross between Dutch/European and Indonesian/Malay is worth searching for. And there are restaurants specialising in Italian, Greek, Portuguese, American, Indian, Chinese, French. The quality of the ingredients is high. Fruit and vegetables are excellent, most coming from nearby. The seafood is top quality, and the local wines are sensational.

The two main restaurant zones are Sea Point, along Main Rd, and the Victoria & Alfred Waterfront. Go for a wander. The biggest range of budget places is in Sea Point – a stroll down Main Rd will turn up something that will appeal to most palettes and pockets. Most of the inner neighbourhoods in the City Bowl have some good places to eat as well.

The popular *St Elmo's Restaurant & Pizzeria* is a chain worth looking out for. It has wood-fired pizza ovens with pizzas from R15 and a range of reasonably priced pastas, seafoods and steaks. Pastas range from R10 to R18 and pizzas from R10 (small) to R25 (large). Amongst others, it has branches at 118 Main Rd, Sea Point; The Broadway, Beach Rd, Camps Bay; and Village Square, Hout Bay.

Those catering for themselves should check the Woolworth's supermarkets (there's one on Main Rd, Sea Point and another in the city centre). They're a bit pricey, but they have a wide range of high quality foods, including fresh fruit and vegetables and some excellent frozen and semi-prepared meals. For more exotic deli items try *Amigos* at the very top end of Kloof St.

The cheapest meal in town is at the *Hare Krishna Centre* on the corner of St Andrews and Teddington Rds, not far from Rondebosch railway station. Free vegetarian meals (and a Hare Krishna 'festival') are available on Wednesday at 6 pm and Sunday at 3 pm.

City Centre
Cafés & Snacks There is quite a range of cheap takeaway-type places in the city centre – you'll come across plenty as you wander

around. One good place to start if you're getting peckish is the so-called Fruit and Vegetable Market at the Adderley St end of the Grand Parade. There's a cheap bakery and a number of stalls that sell various Indian takeaways, including excellent samosas (from three for R1). There are also a couple of places inside the Golden Acre Centre.

World of Coffee, on Adderley St near Darling St, offers a chair and caffeine when you need to recuperate. Another possibility is *Mark's Coffee Shop* (☎ (021) 24 8516), 105 St George's Mall (on the corner of Church St), the oldest coffee shop in Cape Town, with a European atmosphere, good coffee and reasonably priced light meals.

If it isn't too busy, *Cycles* is a pleasant terrace outside the Holiday Inn, overlooking Greenmarket Square. There's a large menu and prices aren't too bad. A full breakfast is R14, calamari costs from R12 (small) to R20 (large) and burgers are R15. There are lots of sweets and pastries. Just across from Cycles, in the art-deco Namaqua Building on the corner of Burg St, *Le Petit Paris* is a pleasant, trendy café, good for a coffee and a snack during the day. A few blocks away on the corner of Long and Longmarket, the *Art Cafe* is a relaxed and friendly place serving good food during the day.

Mr Pickwicks Deli, 158 Long St, is a licensed, deli-style café that stays open very late for good snacks and meals. Try the foot-long rolls. It's just the place to recuperate in a civilised atmosphere after a night out at the clubs. It's open from 8 am to 2 am Monday and Tuesday, 8 am to 4 am from Wednesday to Saturday. On Saturday it closes between 2 and 8 pm and it's closed all day (and night) on Sunday.

Off Moroka Café Africaine, 120 Adderley St, near Church St, is a very pleasant place to sample some fairly genuine African food and listen to tapes of African music. It's open daily, except Sunday, for breakfast and lunch. Breakfast starts at R10.50, soup is R8 and salads cost between R8 and R12. There are also sandwiches and pancakes.

The Tea Garden in the Company's Gardens is licensed and has quite a large menu. There are snacks as well as standards such as omelettes (R12), salads (R8 to R12.50), chicken dishes from R15 and steaks from R20. It's open for breakfast.

Wellington Dried Fruit is a Cape Town institution. It's a long, narrow store on Darling St near Plein St, selling a huge range of dried and glac, fruit, deli items, tinned foods and *lots* of lollies (sweets, candy). Well worth a visit even if you don't want to buy anything. For processed meat, *Morris's Boerewurst* on Long St near the corner of Buiten is legendary.

Just up from the City Bowl in the Cape Muslim quarter, *Karima's Café*, on the corner of Rose and Longmarket, is a takeaway selling a few Cape Muslim snacks. Karima herself is friendly and very knowledgeable about the area.

Meals If you're looking for a pleasant and stylish place to have lunch in the city centre, try *Squares*, a bright, good-value restaurant in Stuttaford's Town Square, overlooking St George's Mall. The menu includes breakfast for R20 or less, entrées such as calamari for R12.50, salads from R18, sandwiches from R15 to R20 and pasta from R16 to R20. At the *Tudor Hotel* on Greenmarket Square pub meals are well under R20, with daily specials around R10. The *Ploughman's Pub* on Church Square isn't anything special but it's OK for a beer and a lunchtime meal such as bangers and mash.

The *Spur* family steakhouse on Strand St near the corner of Loop serves standard dishes at standard prices – around R25 for a steak. It would come in handy for refuelling after a night at the nearby clubs, but unfortunately it closes around the time the action is getting under way, at 1 am on Friday and Saturday, midnight Monday to Thursday and 11 pm on Sunday. It's open for breakfast, though, so you could still end your night there if you've had a particularly good time.

Nino's ☎ (021) 24 7466), on Greenmarket Square, looks as though it's a tourist trap attracting patrons from the Holiday Inn across the street, but it's actually a good, Italian-run restaurant and pizzeria. As in

most South African Italian restaurants, Nino's dishes are not quite the same as the originals; theirs have added spices and adventurous ingredients. Try the veal pizzaiola (R26) or for something lighter but still good, a chicken salad (R14). Pizzas range between R18 and R25, and pasta from R15 to R22. Nino's has Italian wines. It's open from 8 am to 6 pm on Monday and Tuesday, until 10.30 pm from Wednesday to Friday and to 5 pm on Saturday.

In the impressive old Martin Melck House on Strand St between Buitengracht and Bree St, *A Table at Colin's* (☎ (021) 419 6533) is a good restaurant in a very pleasant setting. There's an art gallery upstairs. The food is interesting and not too expensive, with entrées such as cream of mussel soup or eggplant timbale for R15 and main courses such as osso buco (R33), line fish (R30), leg of lamb (R34) and various pastas (R28). One of the dining rooms is non-smoking. Colin's is open for lunch and dinner.

The *Kaapse Tafel Restaurant* (☎ (021) 23 1651), 90 Queen Victoria St, is a pleasant little restaurant that serves a variety of traditional Cape dishes. There are entrées such as Cape pickled fish (R10.20) and seafood bobotie (R12.50). Main courses (most R25 or R26) include Malay chicken biryani, bobotie, waterblommetjie bredie and springbok goulash.

The Metropole Hotel, 38 Long St, has the *Commonwealth Restaurant*, serving pubstyle meals at reasonable prices. On Sunday it has a three-course roast lunch for less than R20.

Yellow Pepper, 138 Long St (near Pepper St), has a casual atmosphere and fairly inexpensive, fairly interesting food, such as chicken livers and spinach (R9), peasant sausage stew (R14) and Greek chicken with lemon and herb sauce (R16). Worth trying. It's open during the day (not Sunday) and also from 7.30 pm on Friday and Saturday.

A little further up Long St, on the corner of Pepper St, *Mama Africa* is a very stylish new bar and restaurant with interesting décor and a slightly African menu. You'll be offered a choice of rice or pap with your meal. Entrées such as roasted beef marrow bone or mussels cost between R10 and R16; main courses include steaks (including ostrich steaks) and some Malay-influenced dishes such as boboti, and cost around R25 to R35. There's live African music on Friday and Saturday nights.

On the rim of the City Bowl, relaxed *Café Manhattan* is on the corner of Dixon St and Waterkant. It's a neighbourhood bar and restaurant which has been renovated without losing its casual appeal. The food is inexpensive, good and vegetarians are catered for. Vegetable stir-fry is R14, chicken is R17, pasta is R12 and steaks are R22. It's open from midday until late on weekdays and from late afternoon on weekends.

Gardens & Tamboerskloof

There's a batch of interesting places in the old Gardens and Tamboerskloof areas, south-east of the city centre. You could start with a beer in the *Stag's Head Hotel* on Hope St (rowdy) or the *Perseverance Tavern* on Buitenkant (civilised) and go on to dinner at *Maria's Greek Restaurant* or the *Old Colonial*, and finish with Irish coffees at *Roxy's Coffee Bar*.

Cafés & Snacks *Mario's Coffee Shop*, on Rheede St, not far from several hostels, is a bit shabby but it has excellent and very cheap meals. It's open from 8 am to 4 pm. Something pasta-ish will cost around R10, or R5 for a half serve. Burgers start at R4. A big breakfast is R10 – a ridiculously big breakfast is R16 and a mixed grill is R17. Not far away, the *Kloof Corner Café* (a corner store, not a café) is known for its chips (fries). Across the road, on the corner of Kloof and Park, *KD's Bar & Bistro* is popular with impoverished students and backpackers.

Roxy's Coffee Bar (☎ (021) 461 4092), on the corner of Wandel and Dunkley Sts, is self-consciously bohemian and trendy. Despite this, or because of it, it's good fun (except for the *dire* music – hit songs from '60s westerns pall rapidly!). Coffees are R3.75; from R8 with alcohol. There's also

light meals such as salads (from R12), baguettes (from R12) and tacos (from R13). It's open from noon to 2 am on weekdays, from 7 pm on Saturday.

Café Paradiso, on Kloof St on the corner of Malan St, is a fashionable, but informal, up-market café. There's an outdoor area. Pastas are R19, entrées such as chicken livers are R12, quiche is R18 and steak is R36.

Those with a sweet tooth and a caffeine addiction should check out *Zerban's Cake & Coffee Shop* on the lower level of the Gardens Centre, Mill St. The big menu ranges from sandwiches (which come with a salad), goulash and steaks, etc. Breakfast is R15 and most main courses are under R25. The Labia Cinema, 60 Orange St, Gardens, is a popular place for coffee and cake.

Meals The Perseverance Tavern (☎ (021) 461 2440), 83 Buitenkant (across from Rusten-Vreugd), is an old pub, built in 1808 and licensed since 1836. It's a bit of a rabbit warren inside, with bar areas and plain wooden tables. In addition to beer (some draught) and an excellent range of wines, they serves decent pub food from a blackboard menu. There's a relaxed atmosphere, and you'll find generous meals for R15 to R30. On Sunday there's a roast lunch for R25. On Friday nights it can be too crowded to move.

Maria's Greek Restaurant (☎ (021) 45 2096) is a small taverna, with plastic tablecloths, naive-style murals and good-value food. Booking is essential, which speaks for itself. Dips and dolmades are around R8.50 to R9.50, schwarma is R20, seafood pilaf is R27 and roast lamb is R30. Servings are enormous so unless you are starving, ask for a half portion. It's on the corner of Barnet and Dunkley Sts and is open from 7 to 11.30 pm daily.

The Old Colonial Restaurant (☎ (021) 45 4909), 39 Barnet St, has a rather kitsch old-style interior – the seats are pews from the Groote Kerk, but since they are now upholstered, they're more comfortable than the burghers would have approved of. This is another place where you can find traditional Cape cuisine, such as matjie (marinated) herring, waterblommetjie bredie, bobotie and tomato bredie. Most main courses cost between R30 and R40. You're advised to book

New and currently very popular, *Rustica* (☎ (021) 23 5474, booking advised), 70 New Church St, is an excellent Italian restaurant. Entrées, such as polenta with lamb sausages or mussels cost between R8 and R19, but are mostly around R12; pastas cost between R14 and R20 and most main courses are between R20 and R28. At lunch panini, with a range of fillings, costs between R10 and R15.

Rozenhof (☎ (021) 24 1968), 18 Kloof St, is one of the best restaurants in town, with small but interesting seasonal menus. Despite the quality it isn't too expensive for a splurge. Three courses with wine could cost under R70.

Sukothai (☎ (021) 23 4725), 16 Hof St (on the corner of Weltevreden St) is a good Thai restaurant. It's open for lunch on weekdays from noon to 2.30 am, and for dinner on Monday, Thursday and Sunday from 7 to 10.30 pm; Friday and Saturday from 7 until 11 pm. The menu includes most of the less complicated Thai standards and prices are reasonable. Tom Yum Khung (prawn soup) is R15, curries start at R24 and most other main courses are between R25 and R35. There are also set menus from R55. You should book for dinner. On Kloof St, on the corner of Union St, *The Happy Wok* is an offshoot of Sukothai and sells similarly good meals and takeaways at much lower prices. Soups are around R7 to R9, vegetarian main courses are around R12 and others cost from R18 to R23, plus noodles or rice. The emphasis here is more on Chinese than Thai styles.

The *Mount Nelson Hotel* dining room is now reserved for functions so the famous set-menu meals are not available, except perhaps sometimes in the off-season. There are, however, a couple of other restaurants and the daily High Tea on the terrace, with lots of cakes, lots of waiters and a grand piano. Expect to pay about R35.

Victoria & Alfred Waterfront

New restaurants and night spots are mushrooming at the Waterfront, at the expense of Sea Point. As well as the franchised places such as *St Elmo's* and *Spur*, there are some interesting places to eat, although most are aimed squarely at tourists. An exception is the group of smaller places in the King's Warehouse, next to the Red Shed Craft Workshop. You can buy from various stalls and eat at common tables. *Ari's*, the Sea Point institution for middle-eastern dishes, has a branch here. Also here is *Captain Bartholomeu's Seafood Restaurant*, with an adjoining fresh fish market. Fish soup is R10 and main courses start at about R30.

The *Musselcracker Restaurant*, upstairs in the Victoria Wharf shopping centre, has a seafood buffet for R50 at lunch and R59 at dinner. There's also the relaxed *Musselcracker Oyster Bar*, a good place for a drink and some seafood. You can have just one oyster (R2.60) or half a dozen for R14.90. Garlic mussels are R15, calamari is R17, and crayfish is R35.

The Big Easy Tavern, on Bertie's Landing, is a popular pub, day and night. In the evening it has a show, usually something like the waiters performing *Grease*, but afterwards there are bands. You can be hot and sweaty inside, or wander outside by the water and sit in the sun (or moon) watching fur seals. It has plain but good pub meals, with burgers from R11, snack platters around R16 and more expensive dishes like steaks for R26. Upstairs from The Big Easy is *Horizons* (☎ (021) 419 2727), a more formal restaurant, open daily for lunch and dinner with entrées such as potted gumbo prawns (R17), fish such as skate wings (R25) or line fish (from R28) and steaks (R30 and up). Bertie's Landing is across a 20-metre channel from the main Victoria & Alfred complex – take the ferry (R1, R2 after 6 pm), otherwise it's quite a long walk around the basin.

The *Green Dolphin* (☎ (021) 21 7471), beneath the Victoria & Alfred hotel, is a popular restaurant with excellent live jazz, nightly from 8 pm. If there's an international act in town it will probably play here. There's a cover charge of R10 (R6 if you don't have a view of the stage). The jazz is as important as the food, but an entrée like Ellington antipasto is R19.50, Goodman salad is R16. Pastas are from R25, fish and grills are from R40. Most wines cost around R30.

One of the cheap and cheerful options is *Ferryman's Tavern* adjoining Mitchell's Waterfront Brewery. The emphasis is on an interesting variety of freshly brewed beers and good value pub meals. To give you an idea, snoek paté is R10.50, bangers and mash is R14, fish and chips (good) is R15 and curry and rice is R19. The night-time menu also has some more expensive dishes.

For fish and chips overlooking the water, head for *Fisherman's Choice*, where you can takeaway or eat in. Hake and chips costs R14 (less for kids) and seafood boxes are R25. Fish soup of the day is just R3.50.

Caffe San Marco (☎ (021) 418 5434) is the offspring of the San Marco restaurant in Sea Point, and here you can sample some of the famed Italian cooking at lower prices. Panini costs around R14, vegetarian antipasto is R22 and calamari is R20. There are also cheaper dishes such as omelettes (R15). Coffee costs R4 or so – order espresso (R3) if you want it to be a decent strength.

Across the main through road in the BMW Pavilion, *The Bistro* is a strikingly designed place with a terrace (unfortunately looking onto a busy road) and good food. Entrées are around R20 and under, with main courses between R25 and R35.

There are many other restaurants – it's a matter of walking around and seeing what appeals. You can pick up a handy restaurant guide at the information centre.

Sea Point

There are dozens of places to eat along Main and Regent Rds, between the suburbs of Three Anchor Bay and Queens. They come and go, and pass in or out of favour so quickly, it's definitely a chancy game making recommendations. There is a generous sprinkling of takeaway joints, including *Steers* for burgers and *Bimbos* for ice cream.

Many of the restaurants are budget-oriented but there are also some more expensive places. The following suggestions start at the Three Anchor Bay end.

There are surprisingly few Indian restaurants in Cape Town. One worth considering is the *Little Bombay* (☎ (021) 439 9041), 245 Main Rd. It's a Hindu-run 'pure-veg' restaurant and the meals are good value, for example full thalis with entrées cost R28, mini thalis are R19. The spices have been toned-down for South African palates but they will cook you the real thing if you ask. It's open daily for lunch and dinner.

L'Orient (☎ (021) 439 6572), 50 Main Rd (near the corner of Marine Rd), is a good restaurant with fairly genuine Malaysian and Indonesian dishes. Try the spicy prawn soup for some flavours you might have been missing while in South Africa. Soups cost around R15, entrées such as lumbia goreng are around R17 and most main courses start around R30. Delicious Malaysian desserts are about R13. It's open for dinner daily except Monday.

Café Erté, on Main Rd near the corner of Frere, is a relaxed (despite the stark black-and-deco paint job) and gay-friendly bar and café open from 11 am to 5 am. You can have snacks such as burgers for R12 and for larger meals of modern cuisine with lots of fresh ingredients, two people can probably eat and drink for under R50. On the last Sunday of the month there's live music with a cover charge of R5.

San Marco (☎ (021) 49 2758), 92 Main Rd (on the corner of St James), is a long-established and excellent formal Italian restaurant, with some of the few professional waiters in town. They let it go to their heads, sometimes. Prices match the quality, with entrées from R20, pasta from R30 and main courses between R30 and R80. It's open daily except Tuesday for dinner, plus lunch on Sunday. The gelateria in front of the restaurant has delicious takeaway gelati and other ice-cream. Cones cost from R1.80 and a small tub of tirami su is R3.20. They'll make you a very good salami and salad roll for R6.50.

WESTERN CAPE PROVINCE

The Courtyard Centre, 100 Main Rd, has a couple of places. Downstairs is *Fujiyama*, a good Japanese restaurant, open weekdays for lunch and dinner and Saturday for dinner. Entrées cost R12 and up. Tempura is R17, R25 for seafood tempura. Sushis start at R10 and mixed sushi is R40; sashimis start at R15 and mixed sashimi is R47. Upstairs is *Mickey Finn's*, a bar with a nice balcony overlooking Main Rd. It's open for breakfast from 8 am, serves light meals during the day and snacks until closing time, very late. It boasts 101 cocktails. It looks good, but every time I went there the atmosphere was non-existent.

Peasants, just off Main Rd on Wisbeach St, is a pizza and pasta place offering food a little better than the franchise places. Pizzas are around R25 (try the seafood pizza, R28) and pastas cost the same.

Ari's Souvlaki (☎ (021) 439 6683), 150 Main Rd (on the corner of Oliver Rd), is an extremely popular Sea Point institution famous for felafels and souvlaki. Schwarma is R13.50, felafel R10.50, moussaka R14 and snacks such as spanakopita R0.80. The food is good although, as is usual in this country, a little blander than the original.

For kerbside tables and good snacks go to *Reise's Deli* on Main Rd near Arthur's Rd. It's open from 8.30 am to 7 pm daily. Coffee costs from R3, salads from R7 and sandwiches from R7 – my favourite sandwich is mozzarella, eggplant and sun-dried tomato (R11). It also has burgers from R12 and good pastries. Inside Reise's is a good deli. Nearby on St John's Rd, beneath St John's Lodge, *The Wooden Shoe* (☎ (021) 439 4435) is the oldest surviving steakhouse in Cape Town, if not South Africa. It's tiny but it's very good and specialises in Austrian dishes. Prices are reasonable.

Right on the beachfront, a short walk down Clarens St from Main Rd, the *Hard Rock Cafe* (☎ (021) 434 1573), 118 Beach Rd, is in a large warehouse-like structure; there's also a pleasant outdoor deck. Like all Hard Rock Cafes, the place is noisy and fun. There's live music on Wednesday, Friday and Saturday. Salads are around R15, fish or steak are R30 and there are cheaper snacks.

There can't be many Hard Rocks in the world with a Morris Minor as the featured car.

A considerable step above St Elmo's, but without going to the extremes of starched formality, *Pinocchio Restaurant* (☎ (021) 439 3008), 64 Regent Rd, is a pleasant, high-quality Italian restaurant. Booking is advisable for dinner; closed on Sunday. There's every kind of pasta you can think of for around R14, pizzas for R13, and Italian specialities like osso bucco, and saltinbocca (ham) alla Romana for R20.

For biltong, which can be vacuum-packed for export (but no matter how it's packed you can't take it home to Australia or the USA), try *Joubert & Monty's Meat Boutique*, 53 Regent Rd, near the corner of Clarens St. Next door is the *New York Deli*, where bagels are the speciality. Right down the southern end of Regent Rd at No 79, *Il Cappucino* doesn't look like much but it is Italian-run and the food is authentic. There's a big menu with dishes such as minestrone for R6, pastas from R15 and veal for R20. They do breakfast for R12. You can just drop in for a coffee, which is good.

Camps Bay

Camps Bay is a pleasant destination for an evening drink and meal, especially if the south-easterly isn't howling. A stroll on the beach, followed by a beer at one of the pavement tables, and dinner in Blues is a genuine pleasure. For those on a budget there's a *St Elmo's*.

Blues (☎ (021) 438 2040), upstairs in The Promenade centre, Victoria Rd, is in a large, airy room overlooking the beach. The crowd tends to be relatively young and informal, but smart – this is a place to be seen. The menu is interesting and the prices are surprisingly reasonable. Salads, such as rocket, lettuce & parmesan shavings, start at R12.50 and entrées cost from R16 to R20. Pizzas cost between R18 and R24 and half/full serves of pasta from R16/20. Main dishes start around R25 and go up to R75 for the impressive Blues seafood grill. Desserts are around R10. There's a long wine list, with a bottle costing from R20, or you can spend

R425. Booking is recommended in the evening and during the day on summer weekends.

La Med (☎ (021) 438 5600) is another casual but up-market place in Camps Bay. It's at the Glen Country Club and often has live music.

Observatory

Observatory is an inner-city suburb to the east of the city and Devil's Peak. It's convenient to the University of Cape Town and is favoured by student types, although yuppies are starting to realise the suburb's advantages.

The main batch of restaurants is only a short walk from the Observatory train station (on the Simon's Town line), 10 minutes and R1/2 in 1st/3rd class from the central railway station. There are frequent trains until 10 pm Monday to Saturday, until 8 pm on Sunday. From the station, walk west (towards the mountain) along Trill Rd until it intersects with Lower Main Rd. Turn right and walk through to the intersection with Station Rd – most places are around here. Turn left on Station for the Heidelberg Pub, a popular student bar.

Pancho's Mexican Restaurant (☎ (021) 47 4854), Lower Main Rd, is an extremely popular bar/restaurant with good value food and a cheerful atmosphere. Half the point is being there; the food is not inspirational but it's fine and filling. To give you an idea, nachos are R6 to R13, enchiladas R13 to R16, burritos R20 to R26 and chili con carne R20. It's open daily for dinner and on weekdays for lunch.

Elaine's (☎ (021) 47 2616), on the corner of Lower Main and Trill Rds, is a good Indian/Asian restaurant with curries for around R22. Upstairs is a cabaret venue – see the Entertainment section.

The Planet on Station Rd opposite the Heidelberg Tavern is a bar and restaurant with budget specials. *Fortis Bakery* has been recommended as a good place to hang out.

Fiddlewoods Restaurant (☎ (021) 448 6687), 40 Trill Rd (near the corner of Lower Main Rd), is a comparatively trendy place

for this area and the food is modern, delicious and healthy. Most dishes are vegetarian. It's open for breakfast – with English breakfast costing R16.50. Salads start at R13, pasta at R18 and fish at R20. Fiddlewoods is open from 8 am to 5 pm on weekdays and until 3 pm on Saturday. From 8 to 10 am on weekdays there's a backpackers' breakfast, with eggs, bacon, toast, orange juice and bottomless coffee for just R10.

The *Africa Café* (☎ (021) 47 9553), 213 Lower Main Rd (on the corner of Bishop) serves African dishes from across the continent. There's an all-you-can-eat communal feast for R50 per person or you can have a three or four-course meal for about R35. It's open for dinner nightly except Sunday.

Hout Bay

At the northern end of Chapman's Peak Drive this place was a fishing village, and there are still a number of fish factories. It's a popular destination, especially on weekends. *Snoekies* at the far end of Hout Bay harbour has a fresh-fish shop and try *The Laughing Lobster* for fried fish and piping hot chips. Both places are open seven days a week from 8.30 am to 5.30 pm. *Fish on the Rocks* in the same area is basically a takeaway for workers at the fish factories, but they do very good fish and chips at reasonable prices.

Mariner's Wharf (☎ (021) 790 1100) is a harbour-front complex with a restaurant and open-air bistro, both specialising in fish. It is a tourist trap but a lot of work has gone into it and it's quite pleasant. The nautical antiques *are* antiques, not plastic reproductions. The *Mariners' Wharf Grill* has some less expensive dishes such as fish pie and salad (R17), but most fish dishes are over R30.

The *Oven Door* (☎ (021) 790 3260), Main Rd, doesn't have a favoured position right on the harbour, but it does have a shady outdoor area in the middle of the Hout Bay Village. It serves breakfast (R19 for an English breakfast), snacks and light meals such as steak roll and chips (R16). The new owners say that their summer menu will include Cape dishes such as pickled fish. It's open from 8 am to 8 pm.

If you want a view, the *Chapman's Peak Restaurant* (☎ (021) 790 1036), in the Chapman's Peak Hotel, Main Rd is a popular spot with a Portuguese-influenced menu (meaning plenty of garlic). Entrées such as calamari are around R12, snoek is R20 and other fish dishes, such as steak, are around R30. Chicken peri-peri is R20. Seafood platters cost R55/90 for one/two people.

False Bay

Kalk Bay The *Brass Bell* (☎ (021) 788 5455), Kalk Bay station, is right between the railway line and the sea with magnificent views over False Bay. Besides the main à la carte restaurant, the Bell has two bars and an open-air patio. In the restaurant entrées such as Thai steak are R10.50, vegetarian dishes are R24, fish from R28, steaks are around R30, and if you want to splurge there's a seafood platter for R53 or R95 for two people.

There's live music every Saturday afternoon which drifts on into the night, and on some evenings (check the papers). The Brass Bell was a legendary rock venue, but major renovations are underway and the music will probably be considerably less rowdy in future. Still, it's a must-visit venue. The cover charge is around R5 on Friday and Saturday, with a fish braai and jazz on Sunday for R25.

If you want to see music at the Brass Bell but can't afford the meal prices, there are a number of good places across the road, such as *Cafe Matisse* with snacks and pizzas.

Muizenberg On the upper level of the beachfront pavilion is *Brahmens Oriental Restaurant*; and *Mehano's* pizzas and takeaways is on the lower level.

It's a bit of a surprise to find *Teresa's* in Muizenberg. Teresa's is a comfortable, friendly local café with good food. It's open all day (closed Monday) for breakfast, snacks and meals such as fettucine (R14), chicken, rice and vegetables (R15). At dinner (Thursday, Friday and Saturday) entrées are

around R8 and main courses R20. It isn't licensed but you can BYO. Some nights it has comedy acts or show Laurel & Hardy movies. That sort of thing. As I said, it's a surprise to find a place like this in Muizenberg. Teresa's is on the corner of Palmer Rd and Church St, across from the Muizenberg Village Centre, which is signposted off Atlantic St near Captour.

Groot Constantia

Groot Constantia is the oldest and grandest of the Cape's wine estates. The buildings date from 1685 and have been beautifully restored. It's a bit of a tourist trap, but it's worth visiting, especially if you don't have time to explore the winelands around Stellenbosch. See the earlier Groot Constantia section for things to see and do at the estate. Another good value restaurant, nearby, is in the Kirstenbosch Botanic Gardens.

The *Tavern*, beside the modern cellars near the main homestead, has a pleasant outdoor eating area, although it is expensive; wine ranges from R19 to R41 (compared with as little as R6 from the cellar); a cheese and paté platter is R25 and wiener schnitzel is R29.

The *Jonkerhuis* looks as if it will be expensive, but it's actually good value. It's in an old, restored estate house, a short walk from the main homestead. Teas and light lunches are served daily from 10 am to 5 pm. There are some great cakes and pastries, such as brandy tart (which is a cake, R6) and a cheeseboard costs R12. At lunch there are some traditional dishes such as bobotie and rice (R29) and chicken pie (R26) as well as standard and lighter dishes.

At the entrance to the estate, on the corner of Constantia Rd and Groot Constantia Rd, there are a couple of places to eat and a brilliant, up-market farm stall. The *Old Cape Farm Stall* has high quality fresh fruit and vegetables, and wonderful jams, pickles, cold meats, dips, dried fruits, cheeses, baked goods – you name it. It's a great spot to stock up on food for a picnic in the Cape of Good Hope Nature Reserve or Kirstenbosch

Botanic Gardens. Although it's not cheap, it is well worth the splurge.

Kirstenbosch Botanic Gardens

The restaurant at the *Kirstenbosch Botanic Gardens* (☎ (021) 797 7614) is good value. It is open daily for breakfasts, teas and lunches; there are indoor and outdoor eating areas. It's not formal or flash but you can get something cheap and filling like bangers and mash (R11), a vegetable platter (R13) or a steak (from R17). On Sunday there's a roast lunch for R19. It's open from 9 am to 5 pm Monday to Friday, and from 8.30 am to 5 pm on Saturday and Sunday.

ENTERTAINMENT

You can't do without the entertainment guide in the *Weekly Mail & Guardian* (R3). *The Cape Times* newspaper has the Funfinder section on Friday. *Soundwaves* is a free paper aimed at musicians and is available at many music shops. *Going Out in the Cape* is a monthly booklet listing most mainstream events; it's sold at various information offices for R3.

When in doubt, the place to go is the Waterfront, which is easily accessible and has a number of possibilities all within walking distance of each other.

For any entertainment bookings, contact Computicket (☎ (021) 21 4715), a computerised booking agency that has *every* seat for *every* theatre, cinema and sports venue on its system. You can be shown the available seats and get your ticket on the spot. It has outlets in the Golden Acre Centre, in the Gardens Centre, at the Waterfront, in Sea Point's Adelphi Centre and many other places. In addition to the entertainment sphere, it also accepts classified advertisements for major newspapers and bookings for various bus lines.

Pubs & Bars

Several pubs and bars have already been covered in the Places to Eat section. In particular, don't forget the Brass Bell on Kalk Bay station overlooking the sea and the Perseverance Tavern in Gardens.

At the Waterfront, Cantina Tequila is currently very popular with visitors, and the Quay 4 Bar is still crowded. There are plenty of other places.

The Fireman's Arms, on the corner of Buitengracht and Mechau (near Somerset) is one of the few old pubs left in town and it dates from 1906. There's a cheerful bar and a lounge where you can buy cheap meals.

Blue Rock, Main Rd, Sea Point, is a smallish, coolish bar specialising in cocktails (complete with juggling barpeople) and hoping to attract an 'unpretentious yuppie' crowd. It plays good music, sometimes live.

The crowd at The Lounge, upstairs at 194 Long St, tends to the alternative, and it's a small, relaxed place. It's in the narrow section of Long St with all the iron-lace balconies and its own balcony is a great place for a drink on a hot night. There's a pool room and a dining room where main courses start at R15. District Six Café, on the corner of Sir Lowry Rd and Darling St, is similar but more down-to-earth – it's a dim but friendly place that describes itself as a 1990s pub. It's open from 8 pm to 4 am from Monday to Thursday and until 6 am on Friday and Saturday. The Purple Turtle, on Shortmarket St around the corner from Greenmarket Square, has a relaxed and student-pub-like atmosphere. There are meals and bands, although it seems to be a place where people meet before going on to the clubs.

The Shebeen on Bree serves beer in 750 ml bottles and drinks in tin cups – and the bar is lined with young whites sitting around waiting for something to happen. Apparently that something includes good township jazz, but there wasn't much happening when I dropped by. If you want to see a real shebeen, take a township tour or get yourself an invitation from someone who knows what they are doing.

Away from the centre but not too far to go by Rikki or taxi, The Shed, De Villiers St, Gardens, is a new bar and a pool hall. It attracts an interesting crowd and the décor is good. The Stag's Head Hotel (☎ (021) 45 4918) 71 Hope St, Gardens, is a very popular pub. It's one of the few traditional English/ Australian-style hotels in South Africa. The ground-floor bar has a motley assortment of locals staring morosely into their beers, the ground floor-lounge (rear) has a younger crowd, but the real action happens upstairs with plenty of pool tables, pinball machines and loud music (sometimes live).

The Heidelberg Hotel, Station St (near the corner of Lower Main Rd), Observatory, is another classic – the clientele is dominated by students and the name of the game is drinking beer. What else are hotels for?

A grungy neighbourhood bar with a reputation among fastidious Cape Towners as catering to 'bergies' (bums, tramps, derros), The Whistle Stop is actually not bad. It's about the only bar in the city area where you'll drink with ordinary people of all colours in anything like an ordinary bar atmosphere. And despite all the trendy liberals in Cape Town's club scene, this was the only place I met a mixed-race couple. There's often a band on Friday night (free). The Whistle Stop is at the top end of Long St, near the Long St Baths. It's open 24 hours, seven days a week and good, cheap meals are available.

For a new bar/cafeteria which has zero design qualities but a friendly atmosphere, go upstairs from the railway station's Strand St entrance. The clientele is exclusively non-white.

For something completely different try Forries (The Forester's Arms) in the leafy suburb of Newlands, on the corner of Newlands Ave and Manson Close. There are good pub meals starting at R16 for bangers and mash and R20 for roasts. Another pleasant middle-class watering hole is Barristers, nearby on the corner of Kildare and Main St (not Main Rd).

Nightclubs
Wednesday, Friday and Saturday are the big nights in the clubs.

In the city centre, the blocks around Bree, Loop and Long Sts and, say, Waterkant are incredibly lively all night long on summer weekends. The actual entertainment rarely matches this level of activity (most clubs play techno to expensively dressed young suburbanites and visiting Vaalies) but it's a good buzz. Cover charges are around R10.

Clubs in this area come and go quite rapidly, but some seem to survive, such as Café Comic Strip, Loop St, which is pretty standard, with lots of bouncers, lots of young whites from the outer suburbs and an R10 admission charge. On the next corner is Browne's Café du Vin, currently the home of acid jazz. Around here you'll find plenty of other places, such as the Havana Bar, the Crew Bar and Carlos O'Brien's.

For a gothic atmosphere that definitely isn't clean-cut, head for D'Elyzium, 88 Shortmarket St. It's an incredibly grungy warren of matte black. Good fun – and there's an L-shaped pool table. Entry is often free on Wednesday and R5 on Friday and Saturday, maybe more if a big band is playing. For even less clean-cut entertainment, try Riebeeck St around Loop and Bree Sts, where there are strip shows and the like.

The Fringe, 46 Canterbury St, Gardens, is a popular club/pub with a student clientele.

To see how the majority of Cape Towners enjoy themselves, take a Heartstoppers tour (☎ (021) 75 9900 or 683 3227) of clubs in the townships, from 8 pm to 3 am, for R75.

Live Music
Several music venues have already been covered in the Places to Eat section. The Green Dolphin is a top-class jazz venue at the Waterfront, and the Brass Bell at the Kalk Bay station has live bands on Wednesday and Saturday night, and Saturday and Sunday afternoon.

Occasionally there is live music at Quay 4 on the Waterfront. There is nearly always something on at The Pumphouse (☎ (021) 25 4437) also at the Waterfront. It's a great venue – it's in the old pumphouse for the adjacent dry docks – but it's fairly small and can be ridiculously crowded.

One of the best places for a drink, a snack and live jazz is Manenberg's Jazz Cafe, upstairs on Adderley St on the corner of Church St. It's a pleasant place with tables on the balcony and a relaxed and racially mixed clientele. There's a cover charge of R10 at night.

One of the best venues is unfortunately a long way from the city. The River Club (☎ (021) 448 6117), near the corner of Station Rd and Liesbeek Parkway, Observatory, often hosts big-name bands with a cover charge of around R10. Thursday is reggae night and on Sunday it has jazz. There's another club on the premises, The Water Room.

Dizzy Jazz (☎ (021) 438 2686) is on the corner of The Drive and Camps Bay Drive, just off Victoria Rd in Camps Bay. It's open daily until very late and has live jazz from Thursday to Sunday.

For classical music, see what's on at the Town Hall (☎ (021) 462 1250), where the Cape Town Symphony has regular concerts. The Nico Malan complex also has classical music (see Theatre).

Cinema

See the local press for a rundown of cinemas and the films they are showing.

The best cinema for 'mainstream alternative' films is the Labia (☎ (021) 24 5927), named after Count Labia, 68 Orange St, Gardens. Admission is a very reasonable R10. Similar fare is offered at the Baxter Theatre (☎ (021) 689 1069, Main Rd, Rondebosch, on the corner of Woolsack. There are Nu-Metro cinemas at the Waterfront and on Adderley St for commercial fare.

At the Victoria & Alfred Waterfront, in the flashy BMW Pavilion, the Imax cinema offers Imax-format films (shown on a giant square screen, currently spectacular scenery and a Rolling Stones concert. There are hourly shows from 11 am to 11 pm and admission is R18.

Theatre

For live theatre, keep your eye on the Dock Road Theatre, a 200-seater in the old Electric Light and Power Station on the quayside of the Alfred Basin, Waterfront. It's a big complex and in season has three or four shows a night, plus a theatre restaurant.

The Baxter Studio, Woolsack Rd, Rosebank, and the Little Theatre, Orange St, are also venues for non-mainstream productions. Upstairs at Elaine's (☎ (021) 47 9425), above Elaine's restaurant on the corner of Lower Main and Trill, Observatory, is a good cabaret venue, with better-quality alternative acts. It's open nightly except Monday and the cover charge is around R20.

The various theatres in the large Nico Malan complex (gradually becoming known as the Nico to avoid the apartheid-era connotations of the Malan name) on the foreshore have ballet, opera and more mainstream theatre – at prices way below what you would pay in Europe. After an evening performance you'll have to phone for a taxi as there is no rank and walking isn't very safe in this area after dark.

Gay Scene

In the city at 66A Loop St (near the corner of Hout), Henry's is a small, dark and popular bar. The Bronx is a small bar and cabaret venue on the corner of Main Rd/Strand St and Napier St between the city and Green Point. When there's entertainment (usually on Saturday night) it starts around 10 pm. Angels on Main Rd in Green Point is a mixed dance venue. Upstairs is Detour. Café Ertà (see Places to Eat) on Main Rd in Sea Point is a gay-friendly place that stays open late for after-club recuperation.

THINGS TO BUY

You'll find most things you need at shops in the city centre, but if you hunger for a suburban mall, try Cavendish Mall, off Protea Rd in Claremont, the most stylish shopping centre in Cape Town.

Markets

In addition to the specialised markets (see the following sections) there are markets in Greenmarket Square (daily) and at Green Point (between The Waterfront and Sea Point) on Sunday. The market at Grand Parade (Wednesday and Saturday) doesn't sell much of interest to visitors but it is much livelier than the others, with people scrambling for bargains, mainly clothing.

Crafts

There are craft shops all over town, but don't forget that few items come from the Cape Town area. For traditional crafts you're better off looking in the part of the country where they originate from. There are, however, some township-produced items such as recycled tin boxes and toys, which are local and they make great gifts.

The Siyakatala stall in the craft market at the Waterfront sells items made by self-help groups in the townships, and the quality is as good as anywhere. In St George's Cathedral is a small shop, worth looking at. It has some guidebooks and craft – and you know that the profits are going to people who need them.

African Image, on the corner of Church and Burg Sts, has an interesting range of new and old craftworks and artefacts. Prices are reasonable, for example, flowers made from aluminium cans cost R6 – you can pay R20 elsewhere. Nearby on Church St, Out of Africa, on the Church St mall, is a very expensive but very good craft/antique shop. Pezulu, 70 St George's Mall (near Hout St), is upstairs and can be difficult to spot, but it's worth making the effort.

A craft market is held on Sunday on Dock Rd, just outside the Waterfront, with a more tourist-oriented art and craft market held in the Waterfront near the Maritime Museum on weekends.

Mnandi Textiles, 90 Station St (near the corner of Lower Main Rd), Observatory, sells interesting printed cloth and some clothing made from it. You'll find cloth printed with everything from ANC election posters to animal patterns.

Antiques, Collectables & Old Books

South Africa's long isolation from the outside world means that there are troves of old goods for sale at very reasonable prices.

The Junk Shop, on the corner of Long and Bloem Sts, has some intriguing junk from many eras. In the same area there are several good second-hand and antiquarian bookshops, although the legendary Cranfords has closed. Not far away, Church St between Long and Burg Sts is a pedestrian mall where a flea market is held on Thursday, Friday and Saturday (daily in summer) and there are several antique shops.

Out at Groot Constantia there's a market on weekends, next to the Tavern.

Camping Gear

There's a branch of the excellent Camp & Climb chain (☎ (021) 23 2175), at 6 Pepper St, near the corner of Long St. The Cape Union Mart chain has branches at the Victoria & Alfred Waterfront (☎ (021) 419 0019) and others in the Cape Sun Gallery (an underground shopping arcade) and on the corner of Spin and Corporation Sts. For quite a bit of gear, the big department stores (like OK Bazaars in Adderley St) will be cheaper, however.

Wine

The wines produced in the Cape are of an extremely high standard and they are very cheap by international standards. It is worth considering having a few cases shipped home, although you will almost certainly have to pay duty. Even so, when you can buy excellent wines for R20 and under, you might still consider it worthwhile. Several companies will freight wine for you, including the Cape Wine Cellar (☎ (021) 24 1128), 53 Wale St (on the corner of Buitengracht) and Vaughan Johnson's Wine Shop (☎ (021) 419 2121, fax 419 0040) at the Waterfront.

Other Things to Buy

Afrogem (☎ (021) 24 8048), 64 New Church St, produces jewellery and other items from semi-precious stones, gold and silver, and you can call in and see how it's done on a free guided tour. Its large showroom has some tempting gift ideas. Tours are available from 8.30 am to 4.30 pm on weekdays (to 3.30 pm on Friday) and the showroom is open daily except Sunday from 8.30 am to 5 pm.

GETTING THERE & AWAY

Air

Cape Town has an increasingly busy international airport, and if you have the choice, arriving here is much nicer than arriving in Jo'burg.

Distances in South Africa are large, so if you're in a hurry some domestic flights are definitely worth considering. SAA flies between Cape Town and major centres including Durban (R673), East London (R525), Jo'burg (R677), Kimberley (R514), Port Elizabeth (R434) and Upington (R457). Fares quoted are full economy, but big discounts are available – see the Getting Around chapter.

Phoenix (☎ (021) 418 3306), a new domestic airline, flies much the same routes as SAA for considerably lower fares. At the time of writing Phoenix have just started up. It remains to be seen whether it will be viable (other competitors to SAA have not fared well).

A couple of smaller companies service the mining towns up the west coast. National Airlines (☎ (021) 934 0350, fax 934 3373) has flights every weekday to Springbok, Alexander Bay and Walvis Bay.

Air Atlantic (☎ (021) 934 6619, fax 934 6619) flies (but not daily) to Oudtshoorn (R310) and on to Plettenberg Bay (R385 from Cape Town, R180 from Oudtshoorn).

Air France
Golden Acre Centre (☎ (021) 214760, fax 217061)
Air India
20th Floor, Trustbank Centre (☎ (021) 418 3558)
Air Mauritius
11th Floor, Strand Towers, 66 Strand St (☎ (021) 21 6294, fax 21 7321)
British Airways
12th Floor, BP Centre, Thibault Square (☎ (021) 25 2970)
KLM
Main Tower, Standard Bank Centre (☎ (021) 21 1870)
Lufthansa
Southern Life Centre, 8 Riebeeck St (☎ (021) 25 1490)
Luxavia
(☎ (021) 23 7910, toll-free 0800 11920)

Malaysia
Safmarine House, 22 Riebeeck St (☎ (021) 419 8010)
Namib Air
(☎ (021) 21 6692, 934 0757)
Qantas
Golden Acre Centre (☎ (021) 419 9382)
SAA
Southern Life Centre, 8 Riebeeck St (☎ (021) 25 4610)
Singapore Airlines
(☎ (021) 4190495, fax 4196226)
Swissair
Southern Life Centre, 8 Riebeeck St (☎ (021) 21 4938)
Varig
(☎ (021) 21 1850)

Bus

All long distance buses leave from the main railway station. There's a left luggage facility next to Platform 24; open weekdays from 6 am to 5.45 pm, Saturday from 6 am to 2.30 pm, and Sunday from 6 am to 2.30 pm. The main buslines operating out of Cape Town are:

Translux
The national busline running many major routes at major prices. The Translux office is on the Adderley St side of the station block, open from 6.30 am to 4 pm on weekdays, until noon on Saturday and from 2.30 to 4 pm on Sunday (☎ (021) 405 3333, fax 405 2545).
Greyhound
The other national line runs fewer routes from Cape Town, at prices higher than Translux (☎ (021) 418 4312, fax 418 4315).
Intercape Mainliner
Some extremely useful services, including along the west and south coasts. A little cheaper than the majors (☎ (021) 386 4400, 24 hours).
Transtate
The downmarket cousin of Translux. There are fewer Transtate services in the western half of South Africa but some are useful (☎ (021) 315 2667, 405 4946, fax 21 2515).

Routes to Jo'burg Translux has at least one bus each day running to Pretoria/Jo'burg (R280 to either city; Jo'burg is 17 hours from Cape Town) via Bloemfontein (R240 and 12¼ hours from Cape Town). Two services (Sunday and Friday) run via Kimberley (R240 and 11¾ hours from Cape Town).

Greyhound has buses to Jo'burg (for R295) via Bloemfontein (daily except Monday) or Kimberley (Monday). Cape Town to Bloemfontein or Kimberley costs R240.

Intercape Mainliner has four services a week to Jo'burg via Upington, for a total of R270. You might have to change buses in Upington but it is usually a direct connection; if so Cape Town to Jo'burg takes about 19 hours. Cape Town to Upington costs R130.

The Garden Route The Garden Shuttle (☎ (021) 22 1894 in Cape Town, (04457) 34434 in Plettenberg Bay) runs from Cape Town to Oudtshoorn (R70), Knysna (R80) and Plettenberg Bay (R85) on Monday, and from Plett to Knysna (R5), Oudtshoorn (R15) and Cape Town on Tuesday.

Translux runs at least one bus a day to Port Elizabeth (R115 and 11 hours from Cape Town) via Swellendam (R60, three hours), Mossel Bay (R75, 5½ hours), Oudtshoorn (R85, 6½ hours), George (R85, 7½ hours), Knysna (R95, 8¼ hours), Plettenberg Bay (R100, nine hours), Storms River (R115, 9½ hours) and Humansdorp (R115, 10¼ hours).

Intercape runs the Garden Route twice daily (morning and evening). Fares include Swellendam (R50), Mossel Bay (R65), George (R75), Knysna (R85) and Plettenberg Bay (R90).

Chilwans Bus Services (☎ (021) 54 2506, 905 3910) has a useful (if slow and not very comfortable) service to Port Elizabeth (R90 from Cape Town) via Swellendam (R40), Mossel Bay (R60), George (R65) and Knysna (R65). It departs Cape Town on Friday and returns on Sunday. Chilwans departs from the upper deck of the railway station.

Apparently, Hylton Ross Travel (☎ (021) 438 1500) is planning a 'slow coach' bus on the Garden Route.

See the later Minibus Taxi section for some door-to-door services to the Garden Route.

The Mountain Route Like the Garden Route, the mountain route takes you east from Cape Town, but running inland most of the way. If you can find a daytime service it's possibly more scenic than the Garden Route.

Translux runs the mountain route three times a week, departing Cape Town on Monday, Wednesday and Friday evening, and returning from Port Elizabeth on Tuesday, Thursday and Sunday evening. Fares and times from Cape Town include: Robertson (R85, 3½ hours), Montagu (R85, four hours), Oudtshoorn (R85, 6½ hours), Humansdorp (R115, 10 hours), Port Elizabeth (R115, 11½ hours).

Chilwans Bus Services (☎ (021) 54 2506, 905 3910, 934 4786) is the cheapest run, although it only goes as far as Oudtshoorn, departing Cape Town at 5.45 pm on Friday and arriving in Oudtshoorn at 1.45 am on Saturday. The return trip departs Oudtshoorn at 9 am on Sunday. Fares from Cape Town/ Oudtshoorn include: Paarl (R12/46), Worcester (R16/38), Robertson (R21/36), Montagu (R23/34), Barrydale (R32/21), Ladismith (R40/14), Calitzdorp (R45/8), Oudtshoorn (R50). This route is slightly different (and probably prettier) than the Translux route.

Munnik Coaches (☎ (021) 637 1850), depart from the upper deck at the railway station and runs to Montagu for R23, departing at 8.30 am on Wednesday, 11.30 am and 5.30 pm on Friday and 8.30 am on Saturday; it departs Montagu at 12.30 pm on Monday and Thursday and at 1.30 and 6 pm on Friday.

To Eastern Cape City to City (a Translux subsidiary) runs daily from Cape Town to Umtata (R135, 19 hours). It's a useful route (although slow), but unfortunately much of the journey is at night. Fares and times from Cape Town include: Worcester (R50, four hours), Beaufort West (R85, 8¼ hours), Graaff Reinet (R105, 10¾ hours), Cradock (R115, 12½ hours), Queenstown (R120, 14 hours) and Butterworth (R130, 17 hours).

Transtate runs to Umtata (R115) on Sunday, along much the same route as City to City. You can connect with a bus to Port

St Johns. The return journey is on Thursday, and because of some quirk in the fare structure it costs only R95.

Translux runs to East London (R170, 15½ hours) on Sunday, Tuesday, Thursday and Friday. Fares and times include: Worcester (R85, two hours), Beaufort West (R140, 6½ hours), Graaff Reinet (R150, nine hours), Cradock (R155, 10½ hours), Queenstown (R160, 12½ hours), Cathcart (R170, 13½ hours), Stutterheim (R170, 13¾ hours) and King Williamstown (R170 14¾ hours).

Translux services to Port Elizabeth connect with a daily bus to Durban via East London and Umtata.

To Durban Both Translux services to Port Elizabeth connect with a daily service to Durban. The total trip takes about 24 hours and costs nearly R300 – consider finding a discount air ticket. A slightly faster Translux service runs to Durban via Bloemfontein.

To the West Coast & Namibia Intercape Mainliner runs to Upington (R130) on Sunday, Monday, Wednesday and Friday evening, arriving 10½ hours later. It returns on Tuesday, Thursday, Friday and Sunday. This service is useful for a number of interesting towns, including Citrusdal (R70 from Cape Town), Clanwilliam (R85) and Calvinia (R110). From Upington you can get an Intercape bus to Windhoek (Namibia), although there are no direct connections.

City to City (book through Translux) runs a similar route thrice weekly, charging about 10% less.

Intercape runs direct from Cape Town to Windhoek (R270), departing on Sunday, Tuesday, Thursday and Friday afternoon and arriving 16½ hours later. This service also stops in Citrusdal and Clanwilliam, but continues up the N7 through Springbok (R145), rather than diverting to Calvinia and Upington.

Namakwaland Busdiens (☎ (021) 25 4245) has the most useful service on the Cape Town to Springbok (N7) route. It visits most of the towns along the highway and runs every weekday. The northbound bus

leaves Cape Town railway station at 6.30 am, arriving in Springbok at 2.45 pm; it returns at 7.15 am, arriving in Cape Town at 3 pm. The fare is R58 (which is much less than it was a few years ago). Other fares on this route, from Springbok/Cape Town, include: Kamieskroon, R13/58; Vanrhynsdorp, R44/44; Clanwilliam, R46/37; Citrusdal, R48/33.

Train

Several long-distance trains run to/from Cape Town (☎ (021) 305 3871 for information and booking), although the local area Metro service is the best way to get to the wineries area (see the following Getting Around section). All trains leave from the main Cape Town railway station. There's a left luggage facility next to Platform 24; open weekdays from 6 am to 5.45 pm, Saturday from 6 am to 2.30 pm, and Sunday from 6 am to 2.30 pm.

Trans Karoo to Jo'burg The daily *Trans-Karoo* is competitive in price, but much slower than the bus (about 25 hours instead of 17). Still, this is an interesting train journey. First/2nd/3rd-class fares are R326/220/137 (more for a sleeper). The train leaves Cape Town at 9.20 am and Jo'burg at 12.30 pm.

Trans Oranje to Durban It's also possible to travel between Cape Town and Durban on the *Trans Oranje*. This would be rather an eccentric decision, because although the price is competitive at R425/286/179, it takes an awful long time. It leaves Cape Town at 6.50 pm on Monday and arrives in Durban at 7.15 am on Wednesday; returning from Durban at 5.30 pm on Thursday and arriving at 6.05 am on Saturday. The train runs via Bloemfontein, about 20 hours and R258/174/108 from Cape Town.

Southern Cross to Port Elizabeth The train to Port Elizabeth departs Cape Town on Friday evening, arriving nearly 24 hours later. The return train departs Port Elizabeth on Sunday morning. It's an interesting route, with stops including Huguenot (Paarl),

Robertson, Ashton (near Montagu), Swellendam, George and Oudtshoorn. Fares from Cape Town include Swellendam, R52/ 38/21; George, R86/62/35; Oudtshoorn, R96/69/39; and Port Elizabeth, R159/ 114/65.

Blue Train See the introductory Getting Around chapter for information on the *Blue Train*. If you can't afford to take the train all the way to Jo'burg, there are some shorter runs which won't break the bank. The cheapest ticket to Wellington (from where you can easily travel to Paarl and the wineries) is R105. To Worcester, also near the winelands, it's R230, including lunch. A longer outing could be to the historic siding town of Matjiesfontein, where you can stay in the wonderful Lord Milner Hotel. The fare is R390, including lunch. For information on the *Blue Train* phone ☎ (021) 405 2672.

Minibus Taxi

Long-distance minibus taxis cover most of the country with an informal network of routes. Although they have traditionally been used by blacks only, an increasing number of whites (mainly foreign backpackers) are now using them – for very good reasons. They are a cheap and efficient way of getting around. The driving can occasionally be hair raising, but it is mostly OK, especially compared with similar transport in other African countries.

As their clientele is largely black, they'll often travel via townships and will usually depart very early in the morning or in the early evening to cater to the needs of commuting workers and shoppers.

In Cape Town, most taxis start picking up passengers in a distant township, especially Langa and Nyanga, and perhaps make a trip into the railway station if they need more people, so your choices can be limited. Currently some of the townships aren't totally off-limits to outsiders, but nor are they great places to be wandering around in the early hours of the morning carrying a pack. *Do not* go into a township without accurate local knowledge and preferably a reliable local

guide! Langa is currently relatively safe (but these things change) and long-distance taxis leave from the Langa shopping centre early in the morning. A local area minibus taxi from the railway station to Langa costs about R2. A taxi to Jo'burg costs about R150.

Door-to-Door Minibus Taxis Atkins Transport (☎ (021) 707 1644, best between 8 and 9 pm) runs a daily door-to-door taxi to Springbok for R80. Standard taxis to Springbok cost about R60.

Abader's Long Distance Minibus (☎ (021) 448 3502, 448 6731, 705 1933 – you might have to try all these numbers) departs from platform 24 at Cape Town railway station at 8 pm on a nightly run along the Garden Route to Plettenberg Bay. Stops and fares from Cape Town/Plettenberg Bay include: Swellendam (R45/55), Mossel Bay (R60/ 25), George (R65/15), Knysna (R70/10), Plettenberg Bay (R80). The trip takes eight hours or so and lands you in towns in the early hours of the morning, so it's inconvenient and unscenic. The return trip departs Plett at 8.30 am so you do get to see some of the country.

Bennet Transport (☎ (021) 952 5576 in Cape Town, ☎ (0441) 75 9322 in George) runs a door-to-door service between Cape Town and Port Elizabeth (R100), stopping in Swellendam and most of the Garden Route towns. Fares are similar to Abader's.

Car & Motorbike

Rental Hiring a car is a competitive option, particularly if you're travelling in a group. If you are reasonably open-ended with your time, however, you'll almost certainly be better off buying a second-hand car. See the Getting Around chapter for some hints on choosing a car hire deal.

Major international companies such as Avis (☎ 0800 021 111 toll-free), 123 Strand St; and Budget (☎ 0800 016 622 toll-free), 63A Strand St are represented.

The larger local companies, such as Imperial (☎ 0800 118 898 toll-free), on the corner of Loop and Strand Sts; and Tempest (☎ 0800 031 666 toll-free), on the corner of

Buitengragt and Wale St, offer comparable service to the majors at slightly lower rates.

Then there are the smaller local companies. These come and go – at the time of writing two of the more prominent were Alisa (☎ 0800 21515 toll-free), 139 Buitengracht, and Panther (☎ (021) 511 6196, fax 511 7802). Their businesses are booming because of the increasing numbers of budget travellers to hit Cape Town, and there can be

some good deals. There are so many companies and factors involved in deciding what's best for you (eg, do you really need 400 free kms a day if you're just tooling around Cape Town and the Winelands; can you drop the car in Jo'burg?) that you really need to gather as many brochures as you can, sit down with a beer and do some sums. You'll find plenty of brochures at the Tourist Rendezvous and at hostels. At the time of writing, some

---

Buying A Car

Johannesburg is the best place to buy cheap cars in South Africa, but Cape Town is the nicest. The process is inevitably time consuming and Cape Town is a much more enjoyable place to waste a week or two. Prices do tend to be a bit higher so it's not a bad place to sell, but as the market is smaller you might wait longer. Cars that have spent their lives around Cape Town are more likely to be rusty than those kept inland, but as one dealer told me, 'What's wrong with rust? It just means that the car is cheaper'.

The main congregation (or is 'pack' a better word?) of used car dealers is on Voortrekker Rd between Maitland and Bellville. Voortrekker is the R102 and runs west from Salt River, south of, and pretty much parallel to, the N1.

Some dealers might agree to a buy-back deal. John Wayne at Wayne Motors (☎ (021) 45 2222), 194 Buitenkant St, reckons that, for example, he might be able to sell you an '82 Passat wagon for R6500 and guarantee to buy it back for R3500. He says that you have a fair chance of selling it privately for more than that. Dealers have to make a profit, however, so you'll pay much less if you buy privately. The *Cape Times* has ads every day, but the big day is Thursday. The *Weekend Argus* also has a good selection. Whoever you're buying from, make sure that the details correspond accurately with the ownership (registration) papers and that there is a *current* license disk on the windscreen. Check the owner's name against their identity document and the engine and chassis numbers. Consider getting the car tested by the AA (Automobile Association). A full test including a compression test costs R200; without the compression test, R150.

Cheap cars will often be sold without a roadworthy certificate. A certificate is required when you register the change of ownership, and pay tax for a license disk. The testers are fussy, so a roadworthy can be difficult and expensive. The roadworthy centre is on Somerset Rd, Green Point, near the Waterfront. The test itself costs R30.

Present yourself along with the roadworthy, a current license disk, an accurate registration certificate, a completed change of ownership card (signed by the seller), a clear photocopy of your ID (passport) along with the original, and your wallet to the City Treasurer's Department, Motor Vehicle Registration Division (☎ (021) 210 2385/6/7/8/9) in the Civic Centre, Cash Hall, on the foreshore. It's open from 8 am to 2 pm and distributes blank change-of-ownership forms. Ring ahead to check how much cash you'll need, but it will be under R100.

Unfortunately, there seem to be very few decent-quality used cars at low prices. Whatever the reasons for this, you will be lucky to find a good vehicle for under R6000. Of course, if nothing serious goes wrong, you will hopefully get most of your money back when you sell.

In the meantime, however, you'll have a lot of money tied up. Insurance, for third-party damages and theft of your vehicle is a good idea. Unfortunately, it is surprisingly difficult to find an insurance company to take your money if you don't have a permanent address and/or a local bank account. If this concerns you, start shopping around early so you can figure out a way to meet their conditions – before you get the car. You'll need to budget around R200 a month. We would be interested to hear of any companies that are helpful to travellers.

Insurance companies will take cash if you buy a year's worth of insurance, but if you just want a month or so you must have a bank account. You might be able to negotiate paying a year's worth with a pro-rata refund the left-over when you sell the car, but get an agreement in writing, not just a vague promise. ∎

smaller companies were offering deals of around R700 per week with unlimited km.

Le Cap Motorcycle Hire (☎ (021) 23 0823, fax 23 5566), 3 Carisbrook St, hires bikes and also runs longer tours. If you're looking for cheap transport you'd be better off hiring a car, but it's very tempting to explore South Africa by bike – warm weather, good roads and spectacular scenery. There's a wide range of rates, but as an example, a Yamaha SR185 costs R55 per day plus R0.30 per km, plus R15 per day for insurance. If you hire for three days you pay R97 per day, including insurance and 150 km. By the week it's R78 per day. A Suzuki DR350 costs R112 per day if hired by the week and various other models (larger and smaller) are available. Helmets, gloves and bags cost extra. You have to be over 21 and hold a motorcycle licence (any country), and over 23 and have a motorcycle licence and two years' experience to hire a bike bigger than 250 cc.

It also has some less ritzy models that are normally hired to couriers, but which might be available to travellers.

A 10-day tour of Northern and Eastern Transvaal, including game drives and accommodation in reserves, costs R6585 per rider and R3095 for passengers. Ten days in the Cape provinces costs R4452 per rider and R1524 per passenger.

Hitching

Hitching around Cape Town is generally easy. Those planning to hitch longer distances should either start in the city centre, or catch public transport to one of the outlying towns – the idea is to miss the surrounding suburbs and townships (especially the Cape Flats where safety can be a real issue.)

In the city centre, make a sign and start at the foreshore near the entry to the Victoria & Alfred Waterfront where the N1 (to Jo'burg), the N7 (to Windhoek), and the N2 (to the Garden Route) all converge. Otherwise, if you're hitching east on the N2, catch a train to Somerset West. If you're heading to Jo'burg on the N1, catch a train to the Monte

Vista train station (just to the south of the N1); not all trains stop here, so check the timetable.

Lift Net (☎ (021) 785 3802) connects drivers with passengers. It's a lot more expensive than hitching (Cape Town to Jo'burg costs about R160) but cheaper than most other forms of transport. You might be able to arrange a lift (probably for petrol money) at the HASA (Hostel Association of South Africa) desk (☎ (021) 418 5202) at the Tourist Rendezvous. Hostel noticeboards often have offers of lifts.

Visas

The Department of Home Affairs (☎ (021) 462 4970), for visa extensions, is at 56 Barrack St.

GETTING AROUND
To/From the Airport

Intercape's Airport Shuttle links the central railway station (outside Platform 24) and the DF Malan Airport. It's best to ring to get the railway station departure times (☎ (021) 934 4400, 386 4414), which are irregular – usually about one hour before flight departures, although it doesn't have services for all flights. The shuttle has a counter in the domestic terminal of the airport. The scheduled service costs R22; coming from the airport, the shuttle can usually drop you off where you want (if it's reasonably close to the city centre) for another R5. If you want to be picked up for a trip outside the regular schedule it will cost about R50, depending on your pick-up point.

Taxis are very expensive; expect to pay more than R100.

A traveller who couldn't find a taxi after he arrived downtown from the airport reports finding someone to carry his bag to the hotel. He recommends negotiating the fee – I'd recommend having pretty good insurance!

Bus

Cape Town has a pretty effective bus network centred on the Table Bay, Castle St side of the Grand Parade – the Golden Acre terminal. You can get almost anywhere in the city for under R2. Buses are the only means of getting along the Atlantic coast; trains service the suburbs to the east of Table Mountain.

There's a helpful information kiosk at the Parade terminal. It's open from 7.45 am to 5.45 pm Monday to Friday and from 8 am to 1 pm on weekends. There are a couple of enquiry numbers (☎ (021) 934 0540 and 0801 21 2111).

A bus to Sea Point costs R1.20, to Camps Bay R2.50, Hout Bay about R5.

If you are using a particular bus regularly, it's worth buying clipcards, which give you 10 trips at a discount price. Travelling short distances, most people wait at the bus stop and take either a bus or a minibus taxi, whichever arrives first.

Train

The Train Information office (☎ (021) 405 2991), in the main railway station near the old locomotive opposite Platform 23, is open Monday to Saturday from 6 am to 8 pm and on Sunday and public holidays from 7 am to 7 pm.

The local trains have 1st and 3rd-class carriages, but slightly softer seats don't justify a ticket price that is twice as expensive. It's reasonably safe to travel in 3rd class (but check the current situation) but unless someone reliable tells you otherwise, don't do it during peak hours (crowds offer scope for pickpockets and muggers), on weekends (lack of crowds offer scope for muggers) or when carrying a lot of gear (you're an obvious target). We've lately heard one or two reports of people being mugged on trains, in both 1st and 3rd class.

Probably the most important line for travellers is the Simonstad/Simon's Town line that runs through Observatory and then around the back of the mountain through upper-income white suburbs such as Rosebank, down to Muizenberg and along the False Bay coast. Off the Rails (☎ (021) 61 8666 or 786 1424) is a privately run bar and dining car attached to some services running between Cape Town and Simon's Town. You need a 1st-class ticket and R2 to enter.

Suburban trains run some way out of Cape Town, to Strand (on the east side of False Bay) and into the winelands to Stellenbosch, Paarl and Wellington. Some 1st/3rd-class fares are: Muizenberg (R2.10/4.70), Paarl (R4.20/9.60), Simon's Town (R2.80/6.40), Stellenbosch (R3.60/8.20) and Observatory (R1/2).

Taxi

As always, taxis are expensive, but worth considering late at night or if you are in a group. There is a taxi rank at the Adderley St end of the Grand Parade in the city, or phone Star Taxis (☎ (021) 419 7777), Marine Taxi (☎ (021) 434 0434) or Sea Point Taxis (☎ (021) 434 4444). There are often taxis in Greenmarket Square, near the Holiday Inn, and outside the Cape Sun on Strand St. A taxi from the station to Sea Point could cost over R20; to Tamboerskloof it will be under R10. For a cheaper alternative around the City Bowl and as far as Camps Bay, see the Rikki's section following.

Minibus Taxi

Minibus taxis cover most of the city with an informal network of routes. They are a cheap and efficient way of getting around the city. They go virtually everywhere and can have flexible routes.

Their main terminus is on the upper deck of the railway station, accessible from a walkway in the Golden Acre Centre or from stairways on Strand St. It's well organised and finding the right rank is easy.

Minibus taxis cost a little less than the municipal buses. From the city to Sea Point it's R1 and to Camps Bay it's R1.50. In the suburbs, you just hail them from the side of the road – point your index finger into the air. Coming into the city from Sea Point, taxis run via either Strand or Riebeeck Sts. There's no way of telling which route the taxi will take except by asking the driver.

Rikki's

These tiny, open vans provide Asian-style transport in the City Bowl and nearby areas for low prices. Telephone Rikki's

(☎ (021) 23 4888) or just hail one on the street – you can pay a shared rate of a few rand or more if you phone for the whole van. They run between 7 am and 6 pm daily except Sunday and go as far afield as Sea Point and Camps Bay but not Observatory. From the station to Camps Bay a single-person trip will cost about R10, to Tamboerskloof it will be about R3. Rikki's also operate out of Simon's Town (☎ (021) 786 2136).

Although they are cheap and fun, Rikki's might not be the quickest, as there is usually a certain amount of meandering as other passengers are dropped off.

Bike

The Cape Peninsula is a great place to explore by bike, but there are hills and distances can be deceptively large – it's nearly 70 km from the centre to Cape Point. Unfortunately you aren't supposed to take bikes on suburban trains.

Many hostels hire bikes and some of them are in reasonable condition. For a trouble-free bike contact Mike Hopkins (☎ (021) 23 2527), 133A Bree St (near the corner of Wale St), or Day Trippers (☎ (021) 461 4599 or 531 3274).

Apparently a bike-route map of Western Cape Province is in production.

Winelands

The wine-producing region around Stellenbosch, sometimes known as the Boland, is only one of the important wine-growing regions in South Africa, but it is the oldest and most beautiful.

The small community at Cape Town established by the Dutch East India Company soon began to expand into the surrounding regions that had been inhabited by the Khoikhoi. The fertile and beautiful valleys around Paarl and Stellenbosch were settled from the 1670s onwards.

Although Jan van Riebeeck had planted vines and made wine himself, it was not until the arrival of Simon van der Stel in 1679 that wine-making seriously began. Van der Stel created Groot Constantia, the superb estate on the flanks of Table Mountain, but he also passed on his wine-making skills to the burghers settling around Stellenbosch. From 1688 to 1690, 200 French Huguenots arrived in the country. They were granted land in the region, particularly around Franschhoek (French Corner) and, although only a few had direct wine-making experience, they gave the infant industry fresh impetus.

The vineyards form a patchwork in the fertile valleys and seem to be overshadowed by dramatic mountains. The Franschhoek, Wemmershoek, Dutoits, and Slanghoek ranges are all over 1500 metres high, and they start pretty close to sea level: the Franschhoek and Bainskloof passes that cross them are among the most spectacular in the country.

There are some pine plantations on the lower flanks, but the mountains are mostly cloaked in dense and shrubby mountain fynbos, a part of the prolific Cape floral kingdom. This includes the ericoid (heath-like plants) and protea families.

Stellenbosch is the most interesting and lively town, Franschhoek has the most spectacular location, and Paarl is a busy commercial centre with plenty to see. All three are historically important and attractive, and all three promote wine routes around the surrounding wineries. This region is the oldest European-settled region in the Cape, and at times there is an almost European atmosphere – in South African terms this means it is extremely well-endowed with restaurants and interesting accommodation. It is worth considering a splurge on either a nice restaurant, guesthouse, or both!

It is possible to see Stellenbosch and Paarl on day trips from Cape Town. Both are accessible by train, but Stellenbosch is the easiest to get around if you don't have a car. If you really want to do justice to the region and spend time exploring the wine routes, you'll need wheels. Bicycle wheels will do.

STELLENBOSCH

Stellenbosch was established as a frontier town on the banks of the Eerste River by Governor Van der Stel in 1679. It's the second-oldest town (after Cape Town) in South Africa, and one of the best preserved. The town is full of architectural and historical gems (Cape Dutch, Georgian and Victorian), and is shaded by enormous oak trees. There are several interesting museums, not least the Village (Dorp) Museum, which consists of four buildings dating from 1709 to 1850.

The Afrikaans-language University of Stellenbosch, established in 1918, plays an important role in Afrikaner politics and culture. There are over 12,000 students, which means there is actually quite a thriving nightlife (something of a rarity in South Africa). Don't expect liberal attitudes, though.

Orientation

The train station is on the western side of town, a short walk from the centre. The railway line effectively forms the western boundary of the town and the Eerste River, the southern. Dorp St, which roughly parallels the river, is the old town's main street and is lined with numerous fine old buildings.

Cape Dutch Architecture

During the last years of the 17th century a distinctive Cape Dutch architectural style began to emerge. Thanks to Britain's wars with France, the British turned to the Cape for wine, so the burghers prospered and, during the 18th and 19th centuries, were able to build many of the impressive estates that can be seen today.

Cape Dutch has elements of traditional Dutch architecture, but is also influenced by colonial Indonesian styles and, most importantly, the local environment. The most distinctive element is the graceful gabled section built around the front door, which is flanked by symmetrical wings – thatched and whitewashed. The gabled section clearly mimics the front façade of traditional Dutch town houses, although in South Africa it is never more than two storeys high, generally with only one window (throwing light into the attic). ■

WESTERN CAPE PROVINCE

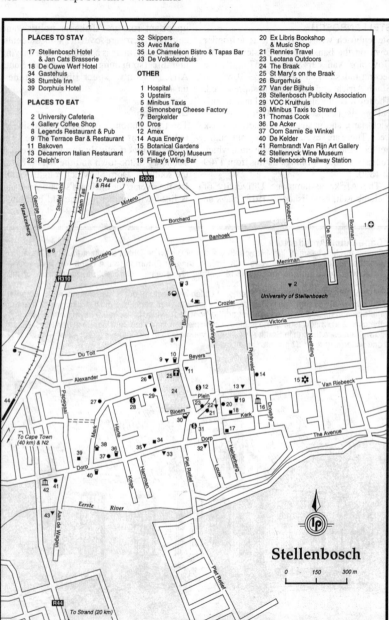

PLACES TO STAY

17 Stellenbosch Hotel
    & Jan Cats Brasserie
18 De Ouwe Werf Hotel
34 Gastehuis
38 Stumble Inn
39 Dorphuis Hotel

PLACES TO EAT

2   University Cafeteria
4   Gallery Coffee Shop
8   Legends Restaurant & Pub
9   The Terrace Bar & Restaurant
11 Bakoven
13 Decameron Italian Restaurant
22 Ralph's

32 Skippers
33 Avec Marie
35 Le Chameleon Bistro & Tapas Bar
43 De Volkskombuis

OTHER

1   Hospital
3   Upstairs
5   Minibus Taxis
6   Simonsberg Cheese Factory
7   Bergkelder
10 Dros
12 Amex
14 Aqua Energy
15 Botanical Gardens
16 Village (Dorp) Museum
19 Finlay's Wine Bar

20 Ex Libris Bookshop
    & Music Shop
21 Rennies Travel
23 Leotana Outdoors
24 The Braak
25 St Mary's on the Braak
26 Burgerhuis
27 Van der Bijlhuis
28 Stellenbosch Publicity Association
29 VOC Kruithuis
30 Minibus Taxis to Strand
31 Thomas Cook
36 De Acker
37 Oom Samie Se Winkel
40 De Kelder
41 Rembrandt Van Rijn Art Gallery
42 Stellenryck Wine Museum
44 Stellenbosch Railway Station

Stellenbosch

0   150   300 m

The commercial centre now lies between Dorp St and the university to the east of the Braak. The Braak is the old town square.

Information

The Stellenbosch Publicity Association (☎ (021) 883 3584), 36 Market St, is open Monday to Friday from 8.30 am to 5 pm, Saturday from 9 am to 3 pm and Sunday from 11 am to 2 pm. This must be one of the busiest tourist offices in the country. The staff are extremely helpful, especially when it comes to recommending B&Bs and providing information on nearby wineries. They also have an excellent free brochure *Discover Stellenbosch on Foot*, with a walking-tour map and information on many of the historic buildings.

Rennies Travel (☎ (021) 886 5259) has an office on the 1st floor of the De Wet Centre, on the corner of Bird and Kerk Sts.

Ex Libris, on Andringa St, is a good bookshop with all the glossy coffee-table books but also novels and a few Lonely Planet guides. There's also an interesting selection of old books on South Africa. A couple of doors south is a music shop with a good range of CDs and some cassettes for R15, which is very cheap by South African standards.

Village Museum

The Village (Dorp) Museum is a group of carefully restored and period furnished houses dating from 1709 to 1850 – eventually a house from the 1920s will be included. The main entrance, on Ryneveld St leads into the oldest of the buildings, the Schreuderhuis. The whole block bounded by

---

Ryneveld, Plein, Drostdy and Kerk Sts is occupied by the museum and includes most of the buildings and some charming gardens. Grosvenor House is on the other side of Drostdy St. The museum is open from Monday to Saturday between 9.30 am and 5 pm, and on Sunday from 2 to 5 pm. Admission is R5.

Van der Bijlhuis

This building dates back to 1693, when it formed part of one of the area's original farms, and has in the past been a tannery. It is now the administrative centre for the Village Museum and three rooms are open to the public during office hours.

Braak

The Braak (town square) is an open stretch of grass surrounded by important buildings. In the middle, the **VOC Kruithuis** (powder house) was built in 1777 to store the town's weapons and gunpowder and now houses a small military museum. On the north-west corner, the **Burgerhuis** was built in 1797 and is a fine example of the Cape Dutch style; most of it is now occupied by Historical Homes of South Africa, a company established to preserve important architecture. **St Mary's on the Braak Church** was completed in 1852.

Bergkelder

This should be your first stop if you are interested in the area's wines. For R5 you get a slide show, a cellar tour and tastings of up to 12 wines. You get to pour your own, so take it easy or it might be your last stop for the day! The Bergkelder is a short walk from the railway station; tours are held at 10 am, 10.30 am (in German) and 3 pm.

Simonsberg Cheese Factory

Popular with hungry backpackers, the cheese factory (☎ (021) 883 8640), has tastings and sells very inexpensive cheese between 8.30 am and 4.30 pm. It's at 9 Stoffel Smit St.

Many people visit Stellenbosch on day tours from Cape Town but it's well worth staying at least one night. In fact, backpackers will find it cheaper to take the train to Stellenbosch (R8.20), do the hostel's winery tour (R25), stay the night at the hostel (R20) and then train back to Cape Town (R8.20) because a day tour from Cape Town costs at least R85. ■

Rembrandt van Rijn Art Gallery
This small gallery houses 20th-century South African works; even if these don't interest you, it's worth visiting to see the house, which was built in 1783. It's open Monday to Friday from 9 am to 12.45 pm and 2 to 5 pm, Saturday from 10 am to 1 pm and 2 to 5 pm, and Sunday from 2.30 to 5.30 pm.

Stellenryck Wine Museum
The small wine museum has some old furniture and wine-making paraphernalia – the most impressive item is the massive wine press which you can see on the corner of Blersch and Dorp. The museum is open Monday to Friday from 9 am to 12.45 pm and 2 to 5 pm, Saturday from 10 am to 1 pm and 2 to 5 pm, and Sunday from 2.30 to 5.30 pm.

Brandy Museum
The international history of brandy and the role it has played in the Cape are traced through a collection of pictures and displays. The museum (☎ (021) 881 3875), in the Van Ryn Brandy Cellar is open daily.

Oom Samie se Winkel
Uncle Sammy's Shop at 84 Dorp St is a tourist trap, but it's still worth visiting for the amazing range of goods – from high kitsch to genuine antiques and everything in-between.

Activities
There are 90 walks in the Stellenbosch area – the information centre has details. Jonkershoek is a small nature reserve in a timber plantation which offers walking and biking trails. Admission is R2. Ask the information centre about permits and maps of the Vineyard Hiking Trails. The signposting isn't good, but it is apparently being improved.

Rozendal Horse Trails (☎ (082) 650 5794) offers rides from one hour (R50) to five hours, including lunch and wine tasting (R160).

Aqua Energy on Reyneveld St sells surf gear, including second-hand boards for around R300. The nearest surf is at Strand, just 20 km away.

The parachute club (☎ (021) 58 8514) offers tandem jumps.

A food and wine festival is held in late October.

Places to Stay
At long last there's a hostel in Stellenbosch, and it's excellent. *Stumble Inn* (☎ (021) 887 4049), 14 Mark St, is a nice old house with wooden floors and a good atmosphere. A pool is planned. The owners are travellers and are good sources of information. They arrange budget outings in the area, including to the beach at Strand and to a shebeen in Khayamandi, an enormous township between Stellenbosch and Cape Town. Dorms are R20 and doubles are R50. You can hire a duvet for R5 for your whole stay. Bikes are rented for R25 per day and they can get you a good price on a winery tour – around R25. Stumble Inn is popular, so it would pay to book ahead.

The Publicity Association produces a booklet listing many B&B possibilities, from R40 per person (you'll have to press them to tell you about the very cheapest). You can certainly be confident of finding something decent for around R60. One of the cheaper places is *Helen's B&B* (☎ (021) 883 3942), 97 Buitekring Ave. There are also self-catering places from R75 a double – a bargain.

The *Gastehuis* (☎ (021) 883 3555), on historic Dorp St (No 110), a rambling old house built in 1811, has very comfortable suites and a warm welcome. Singles/doubles are from R140/220 with an excellent breakfast, with discounts for longer stays and the distinct possibility of negotiation when things are quiet. They also have a simpler self-catering cottage and a very pleasant apartment in the block behind the house. Recommended.

The *Stellenbosch Hotel* (☎ (021) 887 3644), on the corner of Dorp and Andringa Sts, is a rather idiosyncratic country hotel, but it is also very comfortable. A section dating from 1743 houses the excellent Jan

Cats Brasserie, a bar and dining room. The accommodation is in a modern section. Rooms are from R170/230 to R250/340, depending on the level of luxury.

Outside Stellenbosch, *Nassau Guest Farm* (☎ (021) 881 3818) has well-equipped cottages for about R130 per person, and a collection of vintage cars.

Places to Eat

There are 70 places to eat and drink in Stellenbosch. Several of the nearby vineyards have restaurants attached (see Around Stellenbosch).

Snacks & Cafés The *Rustic Café* off Bird St near Legends stays open until 4 am. Another late-night student hang-out is the *Gallery Coffee Shop* on Crozier St. It has a reputation for being super-cool, but it's a relaxed and friendly place. The coffee is good, it's licensed, and there are snacks for well under R10. You can buy some amusing (if a little obscure) postcards by a local outfit called Bitterkomix.

Bakoven, at the entrance to the Bankcentrum, has lunches for around R10 (lasagne) and freshly baked pies (R2.50) and burgers (R2.50).

For takeaway seafood, *Skippers* is a high-quality fish and chippery, on Dorp St near the corner of Louw St, with a few tables. There are good specials such as hake, prawns and chips for R10. Grilled fish costs from R7. There are also burgers and curries. Cheap and very basic food is available in the university cafeteria. Walk up Crozier St until it ends at the car park, and continue straight on. Look for signs to the Langenhoven – Studentesentrum.

Pub Food The *Legends Restaurant & Pub* on the corner of Du Toit and Bird Sts is good value and very popular with students. Lunches go for R12 to R16, and on Thursday there's a vegetarian buffet, R15. Check it out.

Restaurants For good food at reasonable prices try *Avec Marie*, 105 Dorp St. It seems to be a fairly formal restaurant but it is in fact friendly and relaxed, with a contemporary

attitude to food and customers. It's open from Tuesday to Sunday for lunch and dinner (no dinner on Sunday), usually from breakfast which costs about R6.50 for eggs and coffee, up to R18 for the works. The menu is sort of Mediterranean with a nouvelle cuisine influence, which is a relief after the gargantuam servings you usually have to plough through. Entrées such as spanikopita cost R8 and main courses such as poached trout are R23 or less. Amazingly, if you have only R10 or less they will almost always be able to cook you *something*. Recommended.

If it's gargantuan portions you're after, try *Ralph's*, Andringa St. Entrées are around R15, although Giant Namibian Oysters will set you back R20. Main courses start around R25 and go much higher.

De Volkskombuis (☎ (021) 887 2121), Aan de Wagenweg on the outskirts of town, is one of the best places in the Cape to sample traditional cuisine, and it is favoured by locals, not just tourists. The service is both friendly and competent, a rare combination. There are entrées like smoked snoek paté for R12 and main courses like bredie of the day for R17.50, bobotie with yellow rice for R18.50, braised ox-tail stew R22.50, or you can have a Cape country sampler (including four traditional specialities) for R40. The restaurant is in an attractive Cape Dutch homestead designed by Sir Herbert Baker and the terrace looks across fields to Stellenbosch mountain. Booking is advisable.

Jan Cats Brasserie (☎ 887 3644) is in the Stellenbosch Hotel at the corner of Dorp and Andringa. This colourful restaurant features straightforward dishes like pastas for R15 to R19, chicken pie with rice for R18.50, chicken kebabs at R20 or Cape bobotie with sambal and yellow rice for R18.50. You can also eat in the bar area. If the restaurant was named Jan's Cat rather than Jan Cats then presumably the statue of the Stellenbosch Hotel's cat, in front of the City Hall on Plein St, would be the animal in question. The *Decameron Italian Restaurant*, on Plein St, has real Italian minestrone for R8.50, pasta from around R20, pizza from R15 to R30, and fish and steaks from around R30.

Le Chameleon Bistro & Tapas Bar is a stylish spot on Dorp St, with an interesting range of Greek dips and tapas from R2 to R6. You can fill up for around R20. It's open from 11 am to 11 pm daily except Tuesday.

Entertainment

The students give Stellenbosch quite a lively nightlife. It's relatively safe to walk around at night, so it's worth checking a few of the options before you settle.

On Alexander, facing the Braak, is Dros – dark, panelled, pubish and a good place for a drink. There's sometimes live music. Next door, The Terrace has pub food from R10 to R20.

Not far away, Legends Restaurant & Pub on the corner of Du Toit and Bird Sts usually has a DJ and sometimes live music. When it's crowded it might be interesting but when it isn't the bar is pretty unappealing. Further along Bird St, Upstairs is a much less fashion-conscious place where you can actually talk above the music (often live and interesting). It's *rustig* (relaxed) and doesn't have bouncers, always a good sign. The clientele is mainly students and, on payday, black and coloured people.

De Kelder, 63 Dorp St, has a nice atmosphere and is popular with German backpackers. De Acker on the corner of Dorp and Herte Sts is a pub – a classic student drinking hole with cheap grub for around R10. Finlay's Wine Bar, opposite the information office on Plein St, is another rowdy, cheerful place.

Getting There & Away

Train Metro trains run the 46 km between Cape Town and Stellenbosch; 1st/3rd class is R8.20/3.60 (no 2nd class) and the trip takes about one hour. For enquiries phone Stellenbosch station (☎ (021) 808 1111).

Minibus Taxi A taxi to Strand (and thus the beach) can cost as little as R2. A taxi to Paarl is about R5 but you'll probably have to change taxis en route.

Stellenbosch Wineries

The Stellenbosch Wine Route was the first to be established in South Africa and it's still the most popular. With nearly three dozen wineries offering sales and tastings there's a lot to see. The information centre has maps of the wine route or, for more specialised information, contact the wine route office (☎ (021) 886 4310, fax 886 4330). The wineries listed here are just a small sample.

Blaauwklippen This beautiful 300-year-old estate (☎ (021) 880 1250) is four km south of Stellenbosch on the R44 to Somerset West. It has several fine Cape Dutch homesteads. Apart from recent vintages of white, red, sparkling and port there's a farm shop selling chutneys, jams, salamis and pickles. Tastings and wine sales are available Monday to Friday from 9 am to 5 pm, and Saturday from 9 am to 1 pm. In December and January there are cellar tours on weekdays at 11 am and 3 pm and at 11 am on Saturday. From 1 October to 31 April, noon to 2 pm, a so-called coachman's lunch is sold.

Morgenhof This winery (☎ (021) 889 5510) is four km north of Stellenbosch on the R44 to Paarl. It, too, is an old estate with fine architecture. Whites and reds are available for tasting and for sale on weekdays from 9 am to 4.30 pm, Saturday from 10 am to 3 pm and also on Sunday from November to April. Picnic basket lunches are available in the old stables or the surrounding lawns from October to April from noon to 2 pm.

Hartenberg Estate Founded in 1692, Hartenberg (☎ (021) 882 2541) is about 10 km north-west of Stellenbosch, off the road running from Koelenhof to Kuilsrivier. Thanks to a micro-climate it produces 16 cultivars and blended wines. It's open for tastings on weekdays from 9 am to 5 pm, on Saturday from 9 am to 3 pm and on from December to March on Sunday from 10.30 am to 3 pm. Lunch is available daily except Sunday from noon to 2 pm, and you can spend as little as R20 per person, including a bottle of wine between two people. ■

Getting Around

Budget Rent-a-Car (☎ (021) 883 9103) at 98 Dorp St rents bicycles as well as cars. With largely flat countryside (unless you try to cross Franschhoek pass), this is good cycling territory.

FRANSCHHOEK

Franschhoek is really nothing more than a village, but it's tucked into arguably the most beautiful valley in the Cape. There is an interesting museum commemorating the French Huguenots who settled in the region, and there are a number of good wineries and restaurants nearby.

Orientation & Information

The town straggles along the main road from Stellenbosch and Paarl. At the eastern end it reaches a T-intersection, with the Huguenot Memorial Museum directly in front. Turn left for the spectacular Franschhoek Pass.

The very helpful information centre (☎ (02212) 3603) is in a small building on the main street, next to Dominic's Pub. Pick up a map of the area's scenic walks. In season the centre is open from 9 am to 5 pm daily.

Huguenot Memorial Museum

The Huguenots were French protestants who fled France as a result of persecution in the 17th century. Some went to Holland, and 200 found their way to South Africa. Some of the names of the original settlers are amongst the most famous Afrikaner dynasties in the country: Malan, de Villiers, Malherbe, Roux, Barre, Thibault and Marais.

The museum was opened in 1976 to celebrate their history and to house the genealogical records of their descendants. It's quite a fascinating place, but it's not clearly laid out and it is pretty hard work to find your way around. There's an excellent collection of 17th and 18th-century Cape Dutch furniture. The museum is open Monday to Friday from 9 am to 5 pm, Saturday from 9 am to 1 pm and 2 to 5 pm, and Sunday from 2 to 5 pm. Admission is R2.

Wine Centre

The Vignerons de Franschhoek Wine Centre, on the road into town, has wine tastings and information on the area's vineyards. It's open Monday to Friday from 8.30 am to 1 pm and 2 to 5.30 pm, and on Saturday from 9 am to 1 pm.

Places to Stay

The information centre will tell you about B&Bs and other accommodation in town and the district. In town the cheapest B&Bs cost around R100 per person, but prices drop if you stay out of town. *Chamoix Guest Cottage* (☎ (02212) 3531), a self-catering cottage on a vineyard, charges R50 per person. Other places also have whole cottages for about R100. Further out is *La Bri Holiday Farm* (☎ (02212) 3133) which has dorm-style self-catering accommodation from R30 per person.

The *Hotel Huguenot* (☎ (02212) 2092), on Huguenot Rd, is in the centre of town. It's a rather garish old-style country hotel, but is reasonably comfortable. Each room has a private bathroom and the rate is around R70 per person. The *La Cotte Inn* (☎ (02212) 2081), also on Huguenot Rd, is on the western outskirts of town. It has been recently renovated and has a certain idiosyncratic charm, plus a good old-fashioned bar and a big pool. Prices start at R110 per person with breakfast, but there are still two rooms which share bathrooms and these go for R60 for the room only.

The *Anchor* (☎ (02212) 3767), 28 Van Wijk St, is one of the town's oldest houses and is now a guesthouse with six pleasant guest rooms. Singles/doubles cost from R125/190 with breakfast. No children.

Le Quartier Francais (☎ (02212) 2151), 16 Huguenot Rd, is the top place to stay in Franschhoek. It has very large guest rooms with fireplaces, huge beds and stylish d,or set around a grassy courtyard. Dinner, bed and breakfast costs from R650 a double, and room-only is R500. The meals are worth it.

Places to Eat

Dominic's Country Pub & Restaurant is on

the main street but has a pleasant, shady lawn where you can have coffee, pastries or meals. As well as the usual steaks (R23) there are light meals such as Cape Malay pickled fish (R13) or trout and salad (R17).

Le Quartier Francais (☎ (02212) 2248), on the main street, is a highly acclaimed restaurant, but it is not pompous or ridiculously expensive. For anyone who really likes their food it is highly recommended. It's on the main street of Franschhoek, but it opens out onto a cottage garden with views of the surrounding mountains. Entrées are around R20, main meals like roast rabbit or trout sausages range from R30 to R40, and there are interesting desserts from R10. There are some appealing vegetarian dishes. There's a slightly cheaper lunch menu. If the restaurant is beyond your budget there are also the bistro and deli, both open from noon to 5 pm for takeaways and lighter meals.

The *Lanternhof* (☎ (02212) 2602), on Huguenot Rd on the way into town, is about plain but good-value food. Breakfast is R9.50, tea and scones R5.50, homemade cakes R4, toasted sandwiches R4. Main courses – fish or steak – are around R20.

Le Petite Ferme, on the road up to Franschhoek Pass, is another acclaimed eating spot. The food is excellent and there are brilliant views over the valley. It is open for teas from 10.30 am and lunches from noon to 3 pm. It's not open in the evening. Main meals like rainbow trout and Cape lamb are R25.

La Cotte Inn has bar lunches for about R14 and a Sunday dinner (at lunchtime) for R17.

Getting There & Away
It's possible, if you're fit, to bicycle between Stellenbosch and Franschhoek. Otherwise, Borland Passenger Transport (☎ (02211) 62 2114) has infrequent buses between Paarl and Franschhoek.

BOSCHENDAL
Boschendal lies between Franschhoek and Stellenbosch on the Pniel Rd (R310) and is probably the most beautiful of all the Cape wineries: you *must* visit it. Tucked in below

some startling mountains, the Cape Dutch homestead (open daily from 11 am to 5 pm), winery buildings, and vineyard are almost too beautiful to be real.

The estate is open daily but sales and tastings are not available on Saturday afternoon or Sunday.

There is an expensive but excellent restaurant with table d'hôte for R70. It's open daily for lunch; booking is essential (☎ (02211) 41252). For something lighter, but still excellent, go to *Le Cafe*, in one of the old buildings on the oak avenue. You can just have a coffee (or try the homemade lemonade, R3.50) or something more substantial. Entrées cost R6.75; light dishes such as quiche or butternut bredie are R19. The salad platter (R16) and the cheese, pickles and preserves platter (R19) are excellent.

An even better alternative, if the weather is halfway decent, is *Le Pique Nique*, where simple meals are served outside under umbrellas on the lawn from 1 November to 30 April. A basket including paté, french bread, and smoked-trout roulade is made up for you. Again, you must book ahead. It is not cheap at R35, but it is worth it.

PAARL
Paarl is a large commercial centre on the banks of the Berg River, surrounded by mountains and vineyards. There are actually vineyards and wineries within the sprawling town limits, including the huge Kooperatieve Wijnbouwers Vereniging (better known as the KWV), a cooperative that both regulates and dominates the South African wine industry.

The town is less touristy than Stellenbosch, in part because it is not as compact and historically coherent and is more difficult to get around on foot. However, there is still quite a lot to see, and the surrounding countryside and vineyards are beautiful. There are some great walks in the Paarl Mountain Nature Reserve.

There's some excellent Cape Dutch architecture, and some significant monuments to Afrikaner culture. The surrounding valley was settled by Europeans in the 1680s and

Paarl was established in 1720. It became a centre for wagon building, but it's most famous for its important role in the development and recognition of Afrikaans as a separate language.

In 1953 Paarl gained the dubious distinction of being the first town in the country to use a new style of bus – with separate doors for white and non-white passengers.

Orientation & Information

Main St is 15 km long and runs the entire length of the town, paralleling the Berg River and the railway. Main St is shaded by oaks and jacarandas and is lined with many historical buildings. The busy commercial centre is around Lady Grey.

The Paarl Valley Publicity Association (☎ (02211) 23829), 251 Main St, on the corner of Main and Auret, has an excellent supply of information on the whole region. They are particularly helpful arranging accommodation in some of the numerous guesthouses that have sprung up around Paarl, and will make free bookings. The office is open from 9 am to 5 pm Monday to Friday, 9 am to 1 pm on Saturday and 10 am to 1 pm on Sunday.

Paarl Mountain Nature Reserve

This popular reserve is dominated by three giant granite domes which loom over the town on its west side. The domes apparently glisten like pearls if they are caught by the sun after a fall of rain – hence 'Paarl'. The reserve has mountain fynbos and a particularly large number of proteas. There's a cultivated wildflower garden in the middle

Paarl

0   400   800 m

PLACES TO STAY

2   Manyano Centre
15   Grande Roche Hotel

PLACES TO EAT

4   Jefferson's Family Restaurant
8   Panarotti's Pizza
9   Kontrehuise Restaurant, the Coffee
     Place & Lady Jayne's Pub &
     Restaurant
13   Pipers
20   Labourie Restaurant

OTHER

1   Dal Josefal Station
3   Huguenot Station
5   Oude Pastorie Museum
6   Afrikaans Language Museum
7   Mosque
10   Publicity Association
11   Jailhouse Bar
12   Huguenot Church
14   Klein Vredenburg Mansion
16   Schoongezicht Homestead
17   La Corncorde, Head Office of KWV
18   KWV Cellars
19   Paarl Station

that would make a nice spot for a picnic, and there are numerous walks with excellent views over the valley.

Access is from the 11-km long Jan Phillips Drive which skirts the eastern edge of the reserve; both the Afrikaans Language Monument and the reserve are signposted from Main St. The picnic ground is about four km from Main St. A map showing walking trails is available from the publicity association.

Oude Pastorie

The old parsonage (1714) on Main St houses a collection of Cape Dutch antiques and relics of Huguenot and early Afrikaner culture. It's open weekdays from 9 am to 1 pm and 2 to 4 pm. Admission is free.

Afrikaans Language Museum

The birth of Afrikaans is chronicled in the home of Gideon Malherbe, the meeting place for the Association of True Afrikaners and the birthplace of the first Afrikaans newspaper. The house has been painstakingly restored. It's open weekdays from 9 am to 1 pm and 2 to 5 pm. Admission is free.

Places to Stay

The *Berg River Resort* (☎ (02211) 63 1650) is about five km from Paarl on the Franschhoek road (the R45), alongside the Berg River. It's an attractive municipal park with a swimming pool, canoes, trampolines and a café. There are five pricing seasons. Sites for two people cost R35, rising to R54; chalets cost from R70 for two people and from R115 in the peak season. The management is surprisingly friendly for a caravan park, and they can collect you from the station.

Borschen Meer Leisure Resort (☎ (02211) 63 1250) is a manicured and high-security resort, although prices aren't too high, with chalets from R50 per person. There are also sites.

Backpackers could consider the *Manyano Centre* (☎ (02211) 22537, 25074 AH) on Sanddrift St. It's an enormous accommodation complex used mainly by groups, although there's a fair chance that you'll be the only guest. Beds are R25 and you'll probably need a sleeping bag. If you're coming on a weekend, ring in advance. Huguenot railway station is closer than the main Paarl station.

The *Queenslin Guest House* (☎ (02211) 63 1160), 2 Queen St, has a couple of rooms in a modern house overlooking the valley. You're guaranteed a hospitable welcome from the friendly family. Rates are around R70/100. As usual, the information centre is the place to get detailed information on the other B&Bs and farm cottages.

The Berghof (☎ (02211) 61 1099) describes itself as not quite a guesthouse, not quite a hotel, but it is like a quality hotel with the service that is lacking in some mid-range

---

Afrikaans

Afrikaans is based on Dutch, but in Africa, exposed to the diverse cultures of the Cape, it has been transformed into an independent language. Grammatical forms have been simplified and the vocabulary influenced by German, French, Portuguese, Malaysian, indigenous African languages and English. Dutch remained the official language, however, and Afrikaans was given little formal recognition, especially after the takeover of the Cape by the English in 1806 when a deliberate policy of anglicisation was pursued.

The Afrikaners, however, deeply resented the colonial approach of the British and began to see their language as a central foundation of their own culture. In 1875 a teacher at Paarl Gymnasium High School, Arnoldus Pannevis, inspired a number of Paarl citizens to form the Genootskap van Regte Afrikaners (the Association of True Afrikaners) who developed and formalised the grammar and vocabulary. Strangely, virtually all the founding members were descended from the French Huguenots.

A small press was set up in the house of Gideon Malherbe and the first issue of an Afrikaans newspaper, *Die Afrikaanse Patriot*, was published, followed by many books. Malherbe's house is now a museum, and a large monument has been erected to the east of the town. ■

places. You'll definitely need a vehicle to get there, as it's a long way up the side of the valley, with correspondingly excellent views down over the town. Between May and November rooms cost R105/160 a single/ double and suites (some with picture windows and superb views) cost from R140/ 220. Between December and April rooms are R115/170 and suites start at R150/240.

Cecil John Rhodes definitely had an eye for quality, so the fact that he once lived in the building that has become the *Mooikelder Manor House* (☎ (02211) 63 8491) points to its class. It's a beautifully restored Cape Dutch homestead, with a pool and terrace with great views, about five km north of Paarl. Singles/doubles costs R175/301.

Mountain Shadows (☎ 02211) 62 3192) is another magnificent place to stay outside Paarl; it too is in a restored Cape Dutch mansion (a national monument built in 1823). There are only a small number of guests, a swimming pool and excellent food. The owners also arrange hunting, fishing and sightseeing tours. Bed and breakfast rates start from R155 per person, rising in season. Dinner is R45.

On the slopes of Paarl Mountain is the five-star *Grande Roche Hotel* (☎ (02211) 63 2727), where rooms cost from R300 per person.

Places to Eat

Several of the vineyards around Paarl have restaurants and they are probably the best places to eat if you're sightseeing. See the boxed story on Paarl Wineries for details.

The *Kontrehuis* (☎ (02211) 22808), 193 Main St, is behind the Zomerlust guesthouse. It has very good-value meals with entrées like stuffed mushrooms and onion soup for R5, lasagne for R11 and steaks for R18.50. Next door is *Lady Jayne's Pub & Restaurant*, in a Cape Dutch building. Off the courtyard behind Lady Jayne's, the *Coffee Place* is a pleasant spot to escape the world. It has excellent breakfasts from R8.50 to R12, toasted sandwiches from R3 to R5 and light meals like quiche for around R11. If nothing

else, the homemade cakes at R3 a slice are impossible to ignore.

Panarottis Pizza, 263 Main St (on the north-east corner of Faure St), has salads from R7, pasta from R12 and pizzas for around R25. Although it looks like the usual bland franchise, the food isn't bad, although genuine Italian it ain't. It's open from 10 am to midnight. *Jefferson's Family Restaurant* is a steakhouse in the same mould as Spur, Mike's Kitchen etc: predictable but reliable, with over-friendly service.

Pipers on the corner of Main and Zeederberg has toasted sandwiches from R3.50, fish and chips for R9.50 and other light dishes.

Entertainment

The Jailhouse Bar, in the old jail complex on Main St, just north of Pontac St, has bands on Friday and Saturday, with a cover charge of R5.

Getting There & Away

Several interesting bus services come through Paarl so it is easy to build it in to your itinerary. However, the bus segment between Paarl and Cape Town is much more expensive and inconvenient than the train, so take a train to Paarl and then link up with the buses.

Bus Paarl is on Translux's Mountain Route between Cape Town and Port Elizabeth (Tuesday, Thursday and Sunday). Unfortunately, it runs overnight so you miss out on a lot of the spectacular scenery. Fares from Paarl to nearby towns like Robertson and Montagu are a high R85, the same as the fare to Oudtshoorn. Paarl to Port Elizabeth costs R115. Translux services to Port Elizabeth connect with a daily bus to Durban via East London and Umtata.

Chilwans Bus Services (☎ (021) 54 2506, 905 3910) runs a basic bus on a similar route as far as Oudtshoorn, at much lower fares but not daily.

City to City (a Translux subsidiary) runs daily to Umtata (R135, 16 hours), via some interesting Karoo towns. Stops include

Paarl Wineries

The information centre has a Wine Route brochure with a good map, showcasing a dozen or so of the area's wineries. Here is a small sample.

Kooperatieve Wijnbouwers Vereniging (KWV) Paarl is home to a unique phenomenon – the huge KWV wine co-operative. On weekdays there are excellent free tours, including tastings – a must for visitors who are interested in wine.

The KWV was formed in 1918 when farmers were struggling to deal with problems of oversupply. Today, the KWV has statutory authority to completely regulate South Africa's grape production and prices.

It also purchases grapes and makes high quality wines, sherries and ports, which are mostly sold overseas (it attempts to avoid direct competition with its members within the country). Some KWV port and sherry is available inside South Africa because there is little direct competition; the wines, with the exception of those from Laborie, are only sold overseas. The fortified wines, in particular, are amongst the world's best.

On Monday, Wednesday and Friday there are English-language tours and tastings, taking around 1½ hours, starting at 11 am and 3.45 pm (R5). On Tuesday and Thursday the English-language tours start at 9.30 am and 2.15 pm. The knowledgeable tour leaders can give you suggestions for touring the winelands. The tours start in the KWV cellars on Kohler, not at La Concorde, the impressive head office on Main St.

Laborie KWV's showcase vineyard, Laborie (☎ (02211) 63 2034), is on Taillefer St, right in the centre of Paarl, just off the main road. In addition to selling wines, there is a good restaurant in an old Cape Dutch homestead. A buffet lunch costs R36 or you can dine à la carte, with entrees around R12, and main courses from R28. There is a long wine list but few wines are sold by the glass and fewer in small bottles. The restaurant is open daily for lunch and from Tuesday to Saturday for dinner. It gets a lot of tour parties, so booking is advisable.

Rhebokskloof Wine Estate A showpiece estate that has been developed with a close eye on tourism, Rhebokskloof (☎ (02211) 63 8606) is about eight km from Paarl off the R44. The property is attractive and there is a popular terrace café. Substantial snacks are available, such as smoked chicken breast with goat cheese and almond au gratin in a croissant (R18), or you can have tea and scones for R8. Light lunches start at around R20. There's also a more expensive restaurant where main courses start at around R30.

Landskroon Winery An old, pleasant estate with a nice terrace overlooking the vines. Landskroon (☎ (02211) 631309) is about six km from town on the R44. Excellent lunches are available on the terrace from mid-November to April. In addition to wines (chenin blanc for R7, port R17) they also sell some interesting cheeses.

Nederburg Winery Nederburg (☎ (02211) 62 3104) is one of the biggest, best known and most acclaimed Cape wineries. In the past, the sheer size and professionalism of the operation meant it was not an especially friendly place to visit, but that has changed somewhat and several readers report receiving a friendly reception. Tastings and wine sales are available Monday to Friday from 9 am to 5 pm. On Saturday between November and April the winery is open from 9 am to 1 pm. You can arrange a picnic basket if you phone in advance. The estate is about seven km from Paarl, off the road to Wellington.

Belcher Winery Belcher (☎ (02211) 63 1458) is a smaller and simpler winery which produces Italian-style wines under the Romeo Marziani label (in honour of an Italian POW who worked here during WW II and who still lives in Paarl). In December they have tastings of Italian food. There is a rustic chapel which houses the cellars. ■

Beaufort West (R60), Graaff Reinet (R105), Cradock (R115) and Queenstown (R120). Transtate runs a cheaper bus to Umtata on Sunday, along much the same route as City to City. The return journey is on Thursday.

Translux runs to East London (R170, 15 hours) on Sunday, Tuesday, Thursday and Friday. Stops include Beaufort West (R130), Graaff Reinet (R135), Cradock (R135), Queenstown (R150), Cathcart (R160), Stutterheim (R160) and King William's Town (R170).

Translux and Greyhound buses running between Cape Town and Jo'burg/Pretoria stop in Paarl.

Train There are a reasonable number of Metro trains between Cape Town and Paarl, at least a couple in the morning and a couple in the afternoon from Monday to Friday. They're a bit sparser on the weekends, but it's still a decent service. A 1st/3rd-class ticket from Cape Town to Paarl is R9.60/4.20 and the trip takes about 1¼ hours.

You can travel by train from Paarl to Stellenbosch, but you have to take a Cape Town-bound train and change at Muldersvlei.

Car Hire Several local companies offer reasonable rates. Avante (☎ (02211) 25869) charges R85 plus R0.65 per km, including insurance.

WELLINGTON

Wellington is not as attractive as some other towns in this area (although, if you were to come across it it the wilds of Northern Cape you'd think it pretty), but it is still surrounded by beautiful countryside. In particular, the R303 through Bainskloof is one of the most spectacular roads in a part of the world which has more than its fair share of spectacular roads.

One reason why you might base yourself here rather than Paarl (just a few km away) is that Wellington has an inexpensive hotel and Paarl doesn't.

Orientation & Information

Wellington's main shopping street is Kerk St, which meets the main through road, Hoof St, at a T-intersection. The friendly and knowledgeable information centre (☎ (02211) 34604) is in an old whitewashed building on Hoof St near this intersection. It's open weekdays and on Saturday morning. Like so many other towns in this area, Wellington has a **wine route** and the information centre can give you a map.

Wellington is just a few km from Paarl, and the two towns are joined by the large Mbekweni township. Mbekweni was created in 1945 but there is little infrastructure to match its half-century history.

Places to Stay & Eat

The *Commercial Hotel* (☎ (02211) 32253), on Hoof St, is a decent country pub which is falling on hard times. The rooms are better than in many other cheap hotels (and a lot better than the musty foyer and loud bars would suggest) but while they are clean there is an air of neglect. You'll pay about R50 for a room and R10 per person for breakfast. Avoid the rooms above the weekend disco.

There are plenty of self-catering cottages on farms near town – see the information centre. *Fisantekuil Guest Houses* (☎ (02211) 64 1184), five km out, has been recommended.

Completely out of character with the generally genteel eateries of the Winelands area, *Die Suidwester* (☎ (02211) 64 2893) is an uncompromisingly Namibian restaurant. Hennie Fraser and family have settled in Wellington but they serve only Namibian produce (and beer), and it's pretty good. The kudu steaks are superb. Die Suidwester is at 35B Bain St (behind the car park which is behind the Shoprite supermarket on Kerk St). If you're on your way north to Namibia, this would be a good place to collect info.

Getting There & Away

Train The railway station is at the east end of Hoof St. Because of a stipulation by the landowner whose property was used by the railway, all trains must stop in Wellington.

This includes the *Blue Train* and it included King George VI's train in 1947. As a result there are no bus services to Cape Town. As well as the mainline trains (*Trans Karoo*, *Southern Cross* and *Trans Oranje*), Wellington is served by Cape Town's Metro trains, which are fairly frequent. Fares in 1st/3rd class (no 2nd class) to Cape Town are R10.50/4.60, to Paarl R2.80/1.20. You can get to Stellenbosch from Wellington but you'll have to change trains on the way.

Minibus Taxi The taxi park is on Melling, a couple of blocks from the information centre. It's well-organised but it's also the only taxi park in South Africa (including downtown Jo'burg) where I felt any antagonism. The fare to Paarl is R2.50.

BAINSKLOOF

Bainskloof, near Wellington, is one of the great mountain passes of South Africa and there just happens to be a superb caravan park half-way along. Andrew Bain developed the road and pass between 1848 and 1852. Other than having its surface tarred, the road has not been altered since then, and it is now a national monument. It's a superb drive and it would be even better to bike.

The Western Cape authorities run the *Tweede Tol Caravan Park*, open only between October and May. It is a magical spot. There are swimming holes on the Witrivier and the camp site is surrounded by magnificent fynbos. It's R11 for four people plus R4.30 per vehicle. The gates are open from 7.30 am to 4.15 pm (out of hours, try the left-hand gate; it may appear to be chained, but probably just has the chain looped through it). There are several nearby walks, including the five-hour **Bobbejaans River Walk** to a waterfall. This walk actually starts back at Eerste Tol and you need a permit (R2.20), obtainable from Hawequas Conservation Area office (☎ (021) 887 0111), 269 Main St, Paarl. This is also where you make bookings for the Tweede Tol Caravan Park, although they'll probably only be necessary in school holidays.

The **Pataskloof Trail** is a long day-walk

that begins and ends at the Bakkies Farmstall & Tea Room on the road leading up to the pass from Wellington. You can make it an overnight walk by arranging to stay in a cave on the trail.

Breede River Valley

This region lies to the north-east of the Winelands on the western fringes of the Little Karoo. It's dominated by the Breede River valley, but it's mountainous country and includes some smaller valleys. The valley floors are intensively cultivated with orchards, vineyards and wheat.

European settlers displaced the Khoisan and had settled most of the valleys by the beginning of the 18th century. The area did not really take off, however, until passes were pushed through the mountains in the 19th century.

The headwaters of the Breede River (sometimes called the Breë), in the beautiful mountain-locked Ceres basin, escape via Mitchell's Pass and flow south-east for 310 km before meeting the Indian Ocean at Whitesands. Many tributaries join the Breede, and by the time it reaches Robertson it has been transformed from a rushing mountain stream to a substantial river.

Tulbagh and Ceres have generous winter rainfalls, but west of Worcester the countryside becomes increasingly dry; even around Worcester it's semi-desert. The climate is excellent if you like clear skies, but the farms are heavily dependent on irrigation, mainly from the Breede.

Many travellers are likely to come through the region because it is bisected by the N2 between Cape Town and the north-east. Since the opening of the four-km-long Huguenot Toll Tunnel to the east of Paarl, towns like Robertson and Montagu are more quickly accessible from Cape Town (around a two-hour drive), although if you do use the tunnel you miss the views from the old Du Toitskloof Pass.

Look out for the *Cape Fruit Routes* map

in information centres. It covers places in the Breede River valley and also around the Winelands and east to the Montagu area.

TULBAGH

Tulbagh is one of the most complete examples of an 18th and 19th-century village in South Africa. It can feel a little like Disneyland, particularly when you discover that many of the buildings were substantially rebuilt after earthquakes in 1969 and 1970, but it is a beautiful spot, and the best buildings were restored with painstaking care. There is a whole street of Cape Dutch architecture and the town is overshadowed by the Witsenberg range.

Although most of Tulbagh's surviving buildings date from the first half of the 19th century, the Tulbagh Valley was first settled in 1699. The village began to take shape after the construction of a church in 1743 . It was to here, on the outer rim of the settled European areas, that early trekboer families would bring their children out of the wilderness to be baptised.

Orientation & Information

Tulbagh is near the head of the valley; if you follow the R44 north you're suddenly in very flat, very dry sheep country.

The town's main street, Van der Stel St, is parallel to Church St, the famous street in which every building has been declared a national monument. A visitor's first port of call should be 4 Church St (☎ (0236) 30 1348), part of the Old Church Folk Museum, which includes a photographic history of Church St and a general information counter.

Oude Kerk Volksmuseum

The Old Church Folk Museum is a museum complex actually made up of four buildings. Start at No 4; then visit the beautiful Oude Kerk itself (1743); follow this with No 14, which houses the museum's collection of Victorian furniture and costumes, and then No 22, which is a reconstructed town dwelling from the 18th century.

The complex is open Monday to Saturday from 9 am to 1 pm and 2 to 5 pm, and on Sunday from 11 am to 1 pm and 2 to 4 pm. Admission is R2.

Places to Stay

The *Kliprivier Park Resort* (☎ (0236) 30 0506) on the edge of town is quite pleasant, with reasonable modern chalets from R80/90 for one/two people, rising to R120/135 in the high season and on all weekends. Caravan sites are available.

Neither the *Hotel Tulbergh* (☎ (0236) 30 0071) nor the *Hotel Witzenberger* are particularly appealing. They're rather ordinary old country hotels, charging around R60 per person.

De Oude Herberg (☎ (0236) 30 0260), 6 Church St, is a guesthouse in the old Tulbagh main street, surrounded by old buildings, and is built in traditional Cape architecture. It has been a guesthouse since 1885 (although not continuously) and bed and breakfast is available from R85 per person. It's a very friendly and very pleasant place (no smoking and no children under 12). There's also a good restaurant here (see Places to Eat).

Ask at the information centre for other B&Bs and guesthouses, such as the excellent *Hunter's Retreat* (☎ (0236) 30 0582) on a farm just out of town (from R150/250). Six km south of town, *Die Oliene* (☎ (0236) 30 1160) has bungalows sleeping up to four people for R125 and larger cottages.

Places to Eat

The *Paddagang Restaurant* (☎ (0236) 30 0242) is in a beautiful old homestead with a vine-shaded courtyard and serves snacks and light meals, as well as some traditional Cape dishes such as waterblommetjie bredie (R24). Local wines cost between R8 and R23 a bottle and tastings are held between 10.30 am and 4 pm. The restaurant is open from 9 am to 5 pm for breakfast (R18.50 and very good), lunch and tea.

Die Oude Herberge restaurant is open during the day, with breakfast (R15), light lunches (about R18) and snacks. Dinner is also available but you must book by 4 pm. An excellent three-course meal (it's sort of nouveau-Afrikaner) costs R35.

Getting There & Away
Minibus Taxi Most taxis leave from the 'location' (black residential area), on the hill just outside town, but you might find one at Tulbagh Toyota (the Shell service station) on the main street. Alternatively, phone Ralton Fasser (☎ (0236) 30 0549) whose taxi runs to Cape Town daily for R15, leaving Tulbagh at 7 am. He only goes as far as Cape Town's Bellville station.

Getting Around
You can hire bikes at 30 Church St (☎ (0236) 30 1448).

CERES
Ceres is sometimes referred to as the Switzerland of South Africa. The town has a superb location on the western side of a green and fertile bowl that is ringed by the rugged Skurweberg range. The passes into the valley are particularly spectacular.

Ceres is the most important deciduous fruit and juice-producing district in South Africa, and seems remarkably prosperous by comparison to many regional towns. The surrounding countryside is densely populated and intensively farmed, and the town itself is an attractive, shady place. The Ceres fruit juice that's been saving you from a diet of sugary drinks all over South Africa is packed here.

The valley has a very high rainfall, with 1100 mm of rain falling mostly between June and September. The valley has four well-defined seasons. It can get very cold in winter with temperatures dropping well below zero (snow on the mountains), and hot in summer (36°C). It is beautiful in spring and autumn, but particularly in autumn, when the fruit trees change colour.

The vicious winds that makes life uncomfortable on the coast in winter don't reach here.

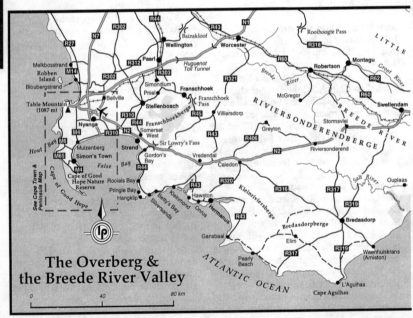

The Overberg & the Breede River Valley

Information

There's an information office (☎ (0233) 61287), in the Municipal Offices on the corner of Owen and Voortrekker Sts (coming from the south, turn left at the first robots). It has information on tours and activities in the surrounding area. The staff will also help you find local B&Bs, most of which charge around R45 per person per night.

Togryers' Museum

Ceres was once a famous centre for making horse-drawn vehicles. Consequently, the Transport Riders' Museum, 8 Oranje St (one street north of and parallel to Voortrekker St), has an interesting collection of buggies, wagons and carriages. It's open from 9 am to 1 pm and 2 to 5 pm on weekdays (closed on Monday afternoon) and on Saturday morning. Admission is R2.

Ceres Nature Reserve

The nature reserve at the foot of Mitchell's Pass, to the north of the main road, has some pleasant signposted footpaths through the fynbos. The pride of the reserve was some San paintings, but in 1991 these were seriously damaged by vandals. There were plans to restore them, but you can see why San paintings are rarely promoted. There's an information office with some interesting displays, unfortunately in Afrikaans only. Contact the Ceres information centre for opening times.

Places to Stay

There are two caravan parks dating from the days when one was for the coloureds and one was for the whites. Although the days of apartheid are over, coloureds are rare visitors at the Pine Forest Resort and whites are even rarer visitors at the Island Holiday Resort. You can perhaps guess which one has the best facilities.

The *Pine Forest Resort* (☎ (0233) 21170) is about one km from the centre of town and is signposted from the main road (left down Krige or Plantasie as you enter town). It's one of the most luxurious camping grounds ever created – there's a variety of different-standard lodges, a recreation hall, rowing boats, mini golf, trampolines, Olympic swimming pool, playgrounds, fishing etc. Rates for three people in chalets start from R59 (from R74 in the high season). The staff have organised a half-day walk in the nearby mountains, and a two-day walk (overnight with tent). Maps and details are available from the office. Camp sites are R36 and R48 in season.

The *Island Holiday Resort* (☎ (0233) 21400), on Bloekom St, has a range of comfortable bungalows with three price tiers (depending on the season). Rondavels sleeping two cost just R22 per person, rising marginally in the high season and on weekends. There are also various categories of more expensive bungalows. A tent site is R26. To get there you pass through the nonwhite area of town, where small shacks and houses straggle over surprisingly sandy soil. This might make The Island a more interesting place to stay.

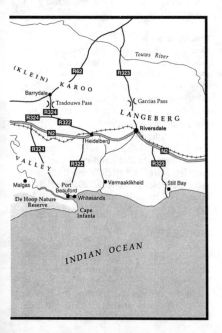

Die Herberg Guesthouse (☎ (0233) 22325) is really quite attractive, despite (or because) it is completely kitsch. It's also very good value. Singles/doubles with bath are R60/100, without R50/90, and there are also chalets for R70/130.

The *Belmont Hotel* (☎ (0233) 21150) at the end of Porter St is a palatial old-world hotel, with a swimming pool, tennis court and luxurious rooms. Bed and breakfast costs from R145 per person and there are also pleasant two-bedroom rondavels; each room can be rented separately, but you then share a bathroom (R114/187).

Getting There & Away

Bus Kruger Bus service (☎ (0233) 65901) runs basic buses to Cape Town at 4 am and 9 am from Monday to Saturday, and at 3 pm on Sunday.

Minibus Taxi Peres & Sons (☎ (0233) 65730) has a taxi to Cape Town, departing from Ceres at 9 am Tuesday to Friday and 4 am on Saturday and Monday. Their taxis leave Cape Town's main taxi rank at 3 pm. You might be able to arrange to be picked up.

AROUND CERES
Middelburg & Gydo Passes

The Middelburg and Gydo passes should not be missed if you're in the vicinity of Ceres. Coming from Citrusdal you almost immediately hit a very bumpy and dusty dirt road that takes you up into the Cederberg. Middelburg is an impressive pass, but the really good views are on the Ceres side when you come out into a narrow valley completely walled by raw, rock hills with rich mineral colouring.

In stark contrast to the hills, the floor of the valley is irrigated so it is usually emerald green, and there is a patchwork of orchards. The reds, ochres and purples of the rocky mountains, the blue of the sky, the blossom of the orchards, fresh green pastures, wildflowers, dams and wading birds are more like a dream than anything else.

About 20 km from Ceres you hit a sealed road. Coming south you feel as if you've lost altitude, so when you come out on the 1000-metre Gydo Pass overlooking the Ceres Valley, the world seems to drop away at your feet. The valley is a beautiful bowl of green surrounded by mountains.

Mitchell's Pass

The Breede River, forcing its way between the mountains surrounding Ceres, provided the key to the development of the valley. Originally, the settlers dismantled their wagons and carried them over the mountain, but in 1765 a local farmer built a track along the river.

In 1846 the remarkable Andrew Bain began construction of a proper road. It was completed in 1848 and became the main route onto the South African plateau to the north, remaining so until the Hex River Pass was opened in 1875. Mitchell's Pass cut the travel time to Beaufort West from three weeks to one week. The pass has recently been rebuilt to highway standards, but you can still enjoy the views and appreciate what a remarkable engineer Bain was.

Places to Stay

One of the B&Bs springing up in the region that has been recommended is *Houdenbek* (☎ (0233) 70748), 45 minutes from Ceres. Take the R303 towards Citrusdal then turn off to the right towards Sederberg. This is a fruit farm. Bed and breakfast is R60 per person; dinner is another R25.

Prince Alfred Hamlet is an indistinguishable little town nine km from Ceres, but there is a very comfortable traditional hotel – the *Hamlet Hotel* (☎ (0233) 3070), where singles/doubles go for R85/120. The Hamlet drive-in theatre still operates and it costs R6 to see a show.

WORCESTER

Worcester is a large and fairly nondescript town, particularly in comparison to the surrounding countryside and nearby Robertson, Montagu, Ceres and so on. It is a service centre for the rich farmland of the Breede Valley. However, there are some nice old Cape Dutch buildings, and the farm museum and botanic garden are definitely worth visiting. Worcester is just off the main route between Cape Town and Jo'burg, so it is easily accessible.

Orientation & Information

Most of the town lies to the south of the N1. There are some impressive old buildings near to, or around the edge of, the Church Square (off High St), including the Publicity Association (☎ (0231) 71408), 75 Church St.

Beck House

Just off the town square, Beck House is a charming 1841 house furnished in late Victorian style. The outbuildings, including a stable, bath house and herb garden, are particularly interesting. It's open weekdays from 9 am to 1 pm and 2 to 5 pm, Saturday from 8.30 am to 5 pm and Sunday from 2 to 5 pm.

Kleinplasie Farm Museum

This farm museum (☎ (0231) 22225) is excellent, one of the best in South Africa. It takes you from a Khoikhoi camp, to a trekboers hut, to a complete functioning 18th-century farm complex. It's a 'live' museum, meaning there are people wandering around in period clothes and rolling tobacco, making soap, operating a smithy, milling wheat, spinning wool and so on. The place is fascinating and can easily absorb a couple of hours. A miniature train runs around the complex (R2), leaving hourly.

It's open from 9 am to 4.30 pm daily (from 10.30 am on Sunday). Admission is R4.50. It's best to visit in the morning when you can see activities like bread-baking.

The museum is badly signposted, which is a bit strange considering how slick the rest of the operation is. Look for signs to the Kleinplasie Winery, which is next door to the museum. At the museum you can buy single bottles that are a whisker more expensive than direct from the winery, where you will often have to buy a case (holding a dozen). Prices are very, very reasonable, ranging from R3.30 to R15. Most are whites and most are around R5.

Karoo National Botanic Garden

This is an outstanding garden (☎ (0231) 70785), about one km north of the N1 and 2.5 km from the centre of town. It includes 140 hectares of natural semi-desert vegetation (with both Karoo and fynbos elements) and 10 hectares of landscaped garden where many of the plants have been labelled. If your interest has been piqued, this is an ideal opportunity to identify some of the extraordinary indigenous plants.

There is something to see at any time of the year; bulb plants flower in autumn, the aloes flower in winter, and the annuals and vygies flower in spring. There's also a collection of weird stone plants and other succulents. The garden is open daily from 8 am to 4 pm.

KWV Cellar

This modern cellar and brandy distillery (☎ (0231) 70785) isn't as famous as the one in Paarl but it is the largest in the world under one roof. Tours are held four times a day during the week and also on Saturday morning, on from December to April.

Places to Stay & Eat

Burger Caravan Park (☎ (0231) 23461), De la Bat Rd close to the N1, is pretty ordinary, but it would do at a pinch and it is next to the town's swimming pool. Sites are R20 with power. *Nekkies* (☎ (0231) 70945) is a better alternative. It's on the Breede River en route to Rawsonville, about five km from the centre of town.

The *Cumberland Hotel* (☎ (0231) 72641) 2 Stockenstroom St, is tacky but very comfortable. There's a swimming pool, gym and squash court. Singles/doubles are R119/199; breakfast costs R25.

There are a number of small restaurants in the streets around the main shopping area. *Fynbos*, on Church/Kerk St is recommended, although it's pricey – steaks start around R27.

Getting There & Away

Bus Most buses stop at the railway station. Translux buses running the Mountain Route from Cape Town to Oudtshoorn and Port Elizabeth, and to East London, stop in Worcester, as do Transtate and City to City buses to Umtata and Chilwans buses to Oudtshoorn. See the Cape Town Getting There & Away entry for more information.

Translux and Greyhound services between Cape Town and Jo'burg/Pretoria stop in Worcester. The fare to Cape Town with Translux is a steep R85; with City to City it's R50.

Train For bookings phone ☎ (00231) 292202/3. The daily *Trans Karoo* between Cape Town and Jo'burg stops in Worcester. From Worcester to Cape Town 1st/2nd/3rd-class tickets are R47/33/19; from Worcester to Jo'burg it's R290/196/122. The *Southern Cross* between Cape Town and Port Elizabeth also stops here on Friday evening heading east, early Monday morning heading west. The extremely circuitous *Trans Oranje* to Durban also stops here.

Minibus Taxi There are several rival long-distance taxi companies in town and they use different stops. One company, WUTA Taxis, stops near the corner of Tulbagh and Barry Sts, near the entrance to the railway station. A daily taxi to Cape Town (R15) leaves sometime after 6 am and there are less regular but probably daily taxis to Robertson (R10) and to Ashton (R12), the town at the bottom of the pass that runs up to Montagu. There's also a useful service to Ceres (R18) via Tulbagh. Other places to find taxis are on Durban St near the supermarkets and around the OK Bazaar on High St. Or you can try phoning D Hadjie (☎ (0231) 73255).

ROBERTSON

Robertson is an attractive, prosperous, rather complacent little town – 6000 rose bushes, jacarandas and oaks line the streets, and the problems of Africa seem a very long way away. It's now the centre for one of the largest wine-growing areas in the country and is also famous for horse studs.

There is very little to see or do in Robertson, but I spent one of my more relaxing nights in South Africa here. While walking around the neat streets I couldn't shake the idea that I'd somehow wandered into a wholesome US sit-com from the early '60s.

Information

Robertson Publicity Association's information centre (☎ 02351) 4437), on Church St, is open Monday to Friday from 9 am to 5.30 pm, and on Saturday morning.

At 62 Church St, two doors along from the information centre, is a laundromat open until 9 pm (earlier closing for service wash).

Niel's Farm

Niel Burger takes spectacular tractor-trailer rides to the top of the Langeberg range, from where you can look way down into the Breede Valley. Even locals enjoy the trip, so it must be something special. The three-hour trip costs R10 and usually operates on Wednesday at 10 am and Saturday at 9.30 am and 2 pm. You can have a delicious lunch of *potjiekos* (traditional pot stew) with home-made bread for R20. Niel also has a overnight cabin with 20 beds. For information and bookings, contact the information centre; you'll need transport to get to the farm.

Museum

The museum, at 50 Paul Kruger St (on the corner of Le Roux, a few blocks north-east of the central church) has a notable collection of lace. It is open from 9 am to noon daily except Sunday and tea is served in the garden on the second and fourth Friday of the month.

Hiking Trails

There are a couple of overnight hiking trails which take you into the mountains above Robertson, offering great views. The information centre has details.

Places to Stay

The *Silverstrand Resort* (☎ (02351) 3321) is a large complex on the banks of the Breede River, off the R60 to Worcester. It gets pretty hectic during the high season and it's too far from town (three km) to be convenient for backpackers. Apart from that, it has a very attractive spot on the river. There are several options, with high/low season rates: caravan and tent sites cost R20/30 and three-bed rondavels with fridges and stoves cost R34/50 or R50/72 with attached bathroom. There are also more expensive bungalows and flats.

The *Avalon Grand Hotel* (☎ (02351) 3272), 68 Barry St, on the corner of White St, is a rare example of a hotel where the quality of the rooms is better than the quality of the foyer would suggest. It has been reasonably tastefully renovated and has a friendly and welcoming atmosphere. Some rooms have balconies. There are a couple of cheerful English-style pub bars downstairs, and excellent food. Singles/doubles go for R80/140 or R103/180 with bathroom. The proprietors also arrange tours of the surrounding countryside.

The information centre can tell you about other options, including self-catering farm cottages which start around R40 a double.

Places to Eat

Simone's Grill Room & Restaurant in the Avalon Grand Hotel, 68 Barry St, has standard prices – kingklip and steaks around R25 – but the food is of an unusually high standard. They have a very good-value set-menu lunch for R17 and a popular Sunday carvery where you can eat as much as you like for R30.

The *Loer Inn* is an ordinary little café opposite the information office on Church St, with coffee for R1.45 and toasted sandwiches for R2.30.

The *Fifth Floor* (☎ (0234) 51590) on the road from Montagu, is a rather ambitious enterprise in terms of what it is, where it is and what it serves. Visitors should take advantage. They have pasta from R16, chicken from R19 and steak from R21. It's

open daily except Monday for lunch and dinner – booking is appreciated. There's a disco on Friday night. The *Oude Fontein Restaurant* at 14 Reitz St is another mid-range dining option; it is open for lunch and dinner on weekdays and then for dinner on Saturday.

Getting There & Away

Bus Translux Mountain Route buses to Port Elizabeth (via Oudtshoorn and Knysna) stop at the railway station. See the Cape Town Getting There & Away section for more details. Fares from Robertson include: Cape Town, R85; Oudtshoorn, R40; Knysna, R85; and Port Elizabeth, R100.

Chilwans Bus Services (☎ (021) 54 2506, 905 3910) runs to Cape Town (R21) and Oudtshoorn (R36), and Munnik Coaches (☎ (021) 637 1850) runs to Cape Town and Montagu on weekends.

Robertson Travel (☎ (02351) 61329) in the small Plaza shopping centre is the agent for Budget hire cars. It closes for lunch between 12.30 and 2 pm (it's that sort of town).

Train The weekly *Southern Cross* between Cape Town and Port Elizabeth stops here on Friday night heading east and early on Monday morning heading west.

Minibus Taxi Taxis running between Cape Town (R20) and Oudtshoorn (R65) stop at the Shell service station on the corner of Voortrekker and Barry Sts. These taxis also run through Montagu (R22). There are no daily services.

MCGREGOR

McGregor feels as if it has been forgotten. It's one of the best-preserved mid-19th-century villages in the country, with numerous thatched cottages surrounded by orchards, vegetable gardens and vineyards. It has no through roads, and the only reason you'll go there is if someone tells you that it is a quiet and beautiful spot – ideal if you want to get away from it all. If you want to get back to it all, there are about 30 wineries within half an hour's drive.

On the road between Robertson and McGregor is **Vrolijkheid Nature Reserve** with bird hides and about 150 species to see. There's an 18-km circular walking trail in the reserve.

The **Boesmanskloof Hiking Trail** begins at Die Galg, about 15 km south of McGregor, and winds 14 km through the fynbos-covered Riviersonderend mountains to the small town of Greyton. For permits contact Vrolijkheid Nature Reserve (☎ (02353) 621). Most people walk the trail in both directions, with an overnight stop in either McGregor or Greyton. You can't camp on the trail. Places to stay in Greyton include the good *Posthaus* guesthouse, *Greyton Lodge* and *Greyton Hotel*. The start of the trail marks the end of a long-abandoned project to construct a pass across the Langeberg Range.

Places to Stay & Eat

Guesthouses are the major industry in this village and more are opening all the time. As well as the sample of places listed here there are self-catering cottages on nearby farms. The information centre in Robertson has a complete list.

The *Old Mill Lodge* (☎ (02353) 841) is a beautiful old building surrounded by a clutch of modern cottages that have been tastefully and comfortably decorated. It's a beautiful spot, and if by chance you feel active there's a swimming pool and nearby fishing. The cottages have two bedrooms and en suite bathrooms. Bed and breakfast is R110 per person, but you might as well go the whole hog and pay for dinner, bed and breakfast (about R155). The food is excellent and you eat in the old mill house looking out across a vineyard – highly recommended. They also have cold buffet lunches for R22.50.

The lovely *McGregor Country Cottages* (☎ (02353) 816) is a complex of seven cottages surrounding an apricot orchard. Several of the cottages are national monuments. The cottages are fully equipped and

the charges work out to around R75 per person and up – great value.

Green Gables (☎ (02353) 626) charges R82.50 per person with breakfast or R112 with dinner as well. They will rent you a mountain bike if you give advance notice. You get a route map and it costs R15 for half a day. Green Gables is also a café, but unless you are staying here you have to book for dinner, which costs about R33.

McGregor Haus (☎ (02353) 925) is an attractive licensed guesthouse. It has bed and breakfast for R80/130 and good pub lunches.

The Overberg

The Overberg, which literally means over the mountains, is the region west of the Franschhoek range, and south of the Wemmershoek and Riviersonderend ranges, which form a natural barrier with the Breede River valley. Although the Franschhoek and Sir Lowry's passes make the region easily accessible today, in the past it was sufficiently isolated for distinctive communities to develop.

The N2, the main coastal highway to Port Elizabeth, crosses Sir Lowry's Pass; those approaching Cape Town from Port Elizabeth will be greeted with fantastic views across Strand, the Cape Flats and False Bay to the mountains of the Cape Peninsula.

Alternatively, the R44 around Cape Hangklip from Strand is one of the most spectacular coastal roads in the world. It's in the same sort of class as Chapman's Peak Drive on the Cape Peninsula, and it's much less busy. There are a couple of caravan parks on the R44, but the first hotel is in Kleinmond. In summer, Hermanus is a popular seaside resort; in spring, it's famous for the whales that frequent its shores.

This region's wealth of coastal and mountain fynbos is unmatched; most species flower somewhere in the period between autumn and spring. The climate basically follows the same pattern as Cape Town. It's described as a temperate Mediterranean climate with relatively mild winters and warm summers. Rain falls throughout the year, but peaks in August. It can be very windy any time.

If you're travelling between the Overberg and the Garden Route on the N2, there's a good place to stay off the N2 near Riversdale. *The Farmhouse by the Sea* (☎ (02933) 33113) is near the picturesque little village of Vermaaklikheid and on the estuary of the Duiwenhoks River. You can stay in an old boathouse on the banks of the estuary for R90 (R120 in season) for up to four people (there are two double beds). There's no electricity but there is a gas stove and fridge. The big doors open up, and in good weather it's very pleasant. You can hire a power boat for R30 a day.

Alternatively, there's a large house with five double bedrooms, four bathrooms (two en suite), a piano, a pool table, all equipment including a dishwasher (and weekday domestic staff), immaculate lawns, and the use of a power boat. This costs R350 or R500 in season, pretty reasonable if you have a large group. They can collect you from Riversdale (on the N2 between Swellendam and Mossel Bay – several buses to/from Cape Town stop there). If you're driving, go through Vermaaklikheid and on the other side of the village take the turn-off signposted 'Borain, Boras farms, Oshock'.

KOGEL BAY

From Gordon's Bay, the R44 skirts a magnificent stretch of coast facing out onto False Bay and dominated by 1000-metre fynbos-cloaked mountains. Kogel Bay has good beach breaks (dangerous for swimmers) and an excellent caravan park, right on the beach.

The *Kogel Bay Pleasure Resort* (☎ (024) 56 1286) is a large, basic park, but its position is hard to beat, although it is exposed to south-westerly winds. A site for up to five people costs R17 out of season, R27 in season.

ROOIELS BAY

There isn't much to this hamlet, but it is on an excellent little beach with a lagoon for sedate swimming.

The Drummond Arms (☎ (02823) 28458) is a small, new building with friendly hosts. Pub lunches are good value, with standards such as steaks, egg and chips for R16 and cheaper snacks. There's also a restaurant. Rooms with shared bath cost R70/100 with breakfast; a double with bathroom is R125.

BETTY'S BAY

Betty's Bay is a small holiday village just east of Cape Hangklip. There are some interesting roads around the Cape itself and the surrounding area is renowned for the variety of fynbos it supports. The nearby Harold Porter National Botanical Gardens (☎ (02823) 9711) protect some of this fynbos, and are definitely worth visiting. There are paths exploring the area and, at the entrance, tea rooms and a formal garden where you can picnic. The gardens are open from 8 am to 6 pm daily; entry is R2.

KLEINMOND

Kleinmond is not a particularly attractive town, but it is close to a wild and beautiful beach. Most people will only stop briefly on their way through to Hermanus, but there are a couple of places to stay. If the weather is good, you could be tempted.

Places to Stay

The *Palmiet Caravan Park* (☎ (02823) 4050) on the west side of town is right on the beach. The coast is mostly rocky, but there's a small sandy beach at a river mouth and a lagoon. It's a very attractive park. The *Kleinmond Caravan Park* (☎ (02823) 4010), virtually right in town, but also overlooking a beach, is not as attractive as the Palmiet. Both are operated by the local municipality; rates for two people are R27, rising to R37 in season.

The *Beach House* is definitely overpriced, but it does have great views and a decent restaurant. Singles/doubles are around R300/500. It's a good spot to stop for lunch.

The town bakery in the main street is also good value.

HERMANUS

Hermanus is a popular seaside resort within easy day-tripping distance of Cape Town (122 km). It was originally a fishing village, and still retains vestiges of its heritage, including an interesting museum at the old harbour. It's increasing fame is as a place to view whales swimming close to shore.

There are some great nearby beaches, most west of the town centre. Rocky hills, reminiscent of the Scottish highlands, surround the town, and there are some good walks and a nature reserve, protecting some of the prolific fynbos. The pleasant town centre is well endowed with restaurants. Bear in mind that Hermanus gets very busy in December and January during the school holidays.

Orientation & Information

Hermanus is a large town with extensive suburbs of impressive holiday and retirement homes, but the town centre, around the old harbour, is easy to get about on foot. The new working harbour is at the eastern end of town.

The Hermanus Publicity Office (☎ (0283) 22629), 105 Main Rd, is helpful and has a worthwhile supply of information about the town and district, including walks and drives in the surrounding hills. It's open from 9 am to 4.30 pm on weekdays, and on weekends during the whale season and in December.

A craft market is held on Friday and Saturday at Lemms Corner, the north-east corner of Hoof and Harrow.

Whales

Between June and November, southern right whales (*Eubalaena australis*) come to Walker Bay to calve. There can be 70 whales in the bay at once. This species was hunted to the verge of extinction (South Africa was a whaling nation until 1976), but its numbers are now recovering. Humpback whales (*Megaptera novaeangliae*) are also sometimes seen.

Whales often come very close to shore and there are some excellent vantage points from the cliff paths that run from one end of

Hermanus to the other. The best places are Castle Rock, Kraal Rock and Sievers Point. There's a telescope on the clifftop above the old harbour which costs R0.50 – but only the old coins. The museum will give you change.

It's only recently that the people of Hermanus bothered to tell the outside world that the whales were regular visitors. They took them for granted. Now, however, the tourism potential has been recognised and just about every business in town has a whale logo. There's also a whale crier, who walks around town blowing on a kelp horn and carrying a blackboard which shows where whales have been lately sighted. A Whale Festival is held in the first week of October.

Despite all this commercialism, boat-viewing of whales is still banned (you can be jailed for up to six years if you approach or remain within 300 metres), so the mighty creatures have the bay to themselves. Sadly, this might change, with the possibility that the calving whales will be chased away. One idea being considered is mooring buoys fitted with microphones in the bay, broadcasting whale-speak to the town.

Although Hermanus is the best-known whale-watching site, whales can be seen all the way from False Bay (Cape Town) to Plettenberg Bay and beyond.

Old Harbour

The old harbour clings to the cliffs in front of the town centre; there's a small museum and a display of old fishing boats. There's an annexe to the museum in the old schoolhouse on the market square. The museum is open daily except Sunday from 9 am to 1 pm and 2 to 5 pm; entry is R2.

Boat Hire

Lagoon Boat Hire (☎ (0283) 77 0925) at Prawn Flats, a lagoon seven km west of the town centre, off the road to Stanford and past the suburbs of big holiday houses, rents canoes (R10 an hour or R15 for a two-person craft), rowing boats (R15) windsurfers (R15), sailing boats (R25) and motorboats (R30, R90 for half a day).

Places to Stay

Hostels Although there are no hostels as such, two of the guesthouses cater to back-packers. *Kenjockity Guesthouse* (☎ (0283) 21772), 15 Church St, accepts backpackers in their downstairs rooms (R30) when things are slow, otherwise you stay in a fairly small room in the backyard (R20). There's a once-off R10 fee for bedding. A bit further from the sea, the *Zoete Inval* guesthouse (☎ (0283) 21242), 23 Main Rd, had dorm beds for R25. Rates in the guesthouse start at R80/120. Several travellers have written to recommend this place.

Caravan Parks Unfortunately, the closest caravan parks to town (and they aren't very close) do not allow tents or bakkies. *Schulphoek Resort* does but it's quite a way from town. The turn-off is on the main road just west of Hermanus but then it's a long way to the resort down a lonely road to the end of a point. 'Resort' is very optimistic – it's a basic camping area with few facilities and no on-site management. Contact the municipal offices for details. *Onrus Riviere Caravan Park* isn't convenient to Hermanus; it has bungalows from R75 in the low season and tent sites from R25.

Hermanus

PLACES TO STAY
1 Zoete Inval
3 Kenjockity Guesthouse
8 Windsor Hotel
10 Hermanus Esplanade
13 Marine Hotel

PLACES TO EAT
6 Mallards
9 Rossi's Pizzeria & Italian Restaurant

11 Burgundy Restaurant
12 Hoy Ming
14 Bientang's Grotto

OTHER
2 Hospital
4 Hermanus Accommodation Centre
5 Publicity Office
7 Post Office
15 Museum

B&Bs, Guesthouses & Self Catering Out of season, self-catering cottages can be great value shared between a few people, and even in season you can find places for less than R250. The Publicity Office has listings or you can book through the Hermanus Accommodation Centre (☎ (0283) 22305), not far from the Publicity Office on Church St. B&Bs and self-catering places on their books start around R40 per person, up to about R80 per person. They also have a few places which are in the small township (as in 'black township') on the coast just west of Hermanus. These cost just R20 and are intended for people such as the Malawi beadworkers who come here to sell their products to tourists. If you are white you'll have trouble convincing the agency that you really want to stay there, but given the near impossibility of staying in paying accommodation in townships it might be worth the effort. On the other hand, it might be dangerous. Decide for yourself.

Of the several guesthouses, *Kenjockity Guesthouse* (☎ (0283) 21772), 15 Church St, has fair-sized rooms. While they are nothing special the guesthouse has a nice atmosphere and is a good size. Rooms start at about R80 per person, but more in December.

The *Hermanus Esplanade* (book through the Windsor Hotel), on Marine Dr, has apartments overlooking the sea. Smaller apartments cost from R100 to R165 a double and apartments sleeping up to four people are R135. You probably won't find a vacancy in December.

Hotels The *Windsor Hotel* (☎ (0283) 23727) is a large old place on Marine Dr which seems to make its living from coach tours. As well as the old section there's a new wing that has good (if small) rooms with full-length windows overlooking the sea, just across the road. At the right time of the year there's a good chance of seeing a whale without getting out of bed! Low-season rates (May to the end of October) are R148/216 for singles/doubles, with breakfast (R130/186 without sea views); high season costs R193/286 (R173/248 without sea views). From mid-December to early January the rates are even higher.

The *Marine Hotel* (☎ (0283) 21112, fax 21533) is a grand, old-style hotel which has been superbly renovated. It's comfortable and it's in a good spot, although marginally further from the sea than the Windsor. Singles/doubles start at R154/224, which is very good value for the high standards.

Places to Eat

Hermanus seems set to have a boom in eating places, so it's likely that there will be more choice by the time you arrive.

There are a couple of interesting possibilities on High St, which runs parallel to Main Rd. *Rossi's Pizzeria & Italian Restaurant* (☎ (0283) 22848), 10 High St, has a pleasant and relaxed atmosphere. It has a range of pasta dishes from R11 to R19, pizzas from R14 and steak or line fish from R30. It's open nightly from 6.30 pm. *Something Special*, across the road from Rossi's, is a pleasant café serving snacks and reasonably priced meals.

The *St Tropez* (☎ (0283) 23221), 28 Main Rd, has good-value pub lunches for under R10, although it is more expensive at night (closer to R20).

The *Burgundy Restaurant* (☎ (0283) 22800), Marine Dr, is one of the most acclaimed and popular restaurants in the province. Prices are surprisingly reasonable, and booking is recommended. There's a garden area with sea views. At lunch, entrées include dishes such as seafood salad for R16.50 and fettucine for R10. Main courses are around R25 for peri-peri chicken, and R36 for brandied duck. There are also light meals and snacks such as the whale watchers' platter of cold meats, cheeses, paté and salad for R11.50. At dinner there are some more interesting entrées, such as snails in filo (R12.50) and deep-fried camembert (R12.50) and main courses, including Karoo lamb, crocodile, guinea fowl and ostrich, at around R30 to R35.

Mallards (☎ (0283) 21217), 9 Mitchell St, is a coffee shop serving light meals. It's a bit frilly but it does have a large garden area. A full breakfast costs R13, burgers are R11 and omelettes start at R7.50. It's open during the day but they will serve dinner if you book – they'll open for as few as two people and you can set your own menu.

Right down on the water, between the museum and the Marine Hotel, *Bientang's Grotto* (☎ (0283) 2361) really *is* a grotto, containing a good seafood restaurant. Someone told me about a memorable meal here with a whale nuzzling the rocks a metre or so from their table.

Hoy Ming is a Chinese takeaway near the Old Harbour where you can get dishes with rice for R6. It's closed on Tuesday.

Getting There & Away
The only bus service (apart from tours) between Cape Town and Hermanus is Chilwans (☎ (021) 905 3910 in Cape Town) which has an evening service from Cape Town to Gansbaai via Hermanus on Friday and Saturday for R15.

There aren't many minibus taxis. You might find one running to Bellville (Cape Town) for R18, but not daily. The taxi park, such as it is, is behind the Publicity Office.

AROUND HERMANUS
There are several walks and drives in the hills behind the town – the information bureau has maps. The 1400-hectare **Fernkloof Nature Reserve** is particularly worth visiting if you are interested in fynbos.

The road south from Hermanus passes through some pretty country with quite a bit of fynbos. The next town south is **Stanford**, a largish, quiet town a little way inland. Next along is **Gansbaai**, also quiet but on the coast, then **Pearly Beach**. On one of the inland routes between Gansbaai and Cape Agulhas is **Elim**, a picturesque mission village. Unfortunately, a good part of the picturesqueness is due to poverty.

CAPE AGULHAS
Cape Agulhas is the southernmost point of the African continent – latitude 34°, 49', 58.74". On a stormy day it really looks like the next stop is the South Pole, with green seas, squall clouds and sheets of low, shattered rock. Otherwise it isn't especially impressive, but it does have that air of anti-climax which attends the end of any great journey. Congratulations, all you Africa-overlanders. Where are you going next?

The **lighthouse**, built in 1848 and the second-oldest in South Africa, has been restored and is open to the public from Tuesday to Saturday from 9.30 am to 4.45 pm, Sunday from 10 am to 1.30 pm. There's a tea room in the building.

There isn't much in the hamlet of Cape Agulhas, but **Struisbaai**, about six km east, is a little larger and has a caravan park. There's also a 14-km-long beach there.

The country around Bredasdorp, Struisbaai and Cape Agulhas is very low-key by South African standards – it's rolling wheat and sheep country. For information on this part of the Overberg, go to the friendly Bredasdorp Publicity Association (☎ (02481) 42584) on Dirkie Uys St.

WAENHUISKRANS (ARNISTON)
Waenhuiskrans, which means wagon-house cliff (after the enormous cavern eroded into the cliffs one km from the village) is the official name of this isolated fishing/holiday village. It is also often referred to as Arniston, however, after a ship that was wrecked in 1815 with the loss of 372 lives.

The coast is certainly wild, and it is not surprising it has claimed many ships. The town has charm, however, and is notable for its restored thatch cottages. There are also some long stretches of sandy beach.

Places to Stay
The *Arniston Hotel* (☎ (02847) 59000) is a very classy getaway overlooking the wild waves of the south coast and surrounded by windswept dunes and whitewashed fisherfolk's cottages. Singles/doubles are R300/400 including breakfast, and a high-quality set dinner is R50.

At the other end of the scale, the *Caravan Park* (☎ (02847) 59620) has basic four-bed bungalows with shared facilities and no bedding or crockery, for R88. Sites are available at the caravan park, but they are a pricey R43.

DE HOOP NATURE RESERVE

De Hoop is one of the best of the reserves administered by the Cape Province. It includes a scenic coastline with lonely stretches of beach, rocky cliffs, large coastal sand dunes, a freshwater lake and the Potberg range.

This is one of the best places to see both mountain and lowland fynbos and a diverse cross-section of coastal ecosystems. Fauna includes the Cape mountain zebra, bontebok and a wealth of birdlife. The coast is an important breeding area for the southern right whale.

Hikers can tackle beach walks, an eight-km trail along the cliffs of the De Hoop Vlei (lake), and day trails of various lengths on Potberg. An overnight mountain-bike trail has also been laid out, and it would be nice riding. You have to book in advance.

There is good snorkelling along the coast, and since it is to the east of Cape Agulhas the water is reasonably warm. There are cottages (from R26.40 for four people) and camp sites (R11), but these must be booked in advance (☎ (02922) 782, fax 879).

The reserve covers 36,000 hectares, plus five km down to sea. It's about 260 km from Cape Town, and the final 50 km from either Bredasdorp or Swellendam is along gravel roads. The only access to the reserve is via Wydgeleë on the Bredasdorp to Malgas road. At Malgas a manually operated *pont* (pontoon ferry) on the Breede River still operates. The town of Ouplas, 15 km away, is the nearest place to buy fuel and supplies. Gates are open daily from 7 am to 6 pm; entry costs (R4.40 per car, plus R2.20 per person). The office is open from 8 am to 4 pm on weekdays and only from 1 to 2 pm on weekends.

The brochure warns that 'litterbugs will be fed to the vultures' – it's probably a joke, but how many jokes have you seen on official brochures in South Africa?

SWELLENDAM

As well as being a very pretty town with a real sense of history, Swellendam offers those with transport a good base for exploring quite a range of country. The Breede River valley and the coast are within easy reach, as is the Little Karoo. Swellendam is about midway between Cape Town and George, the first town on the Garden Route. Author Breyton Breytenbach describes the town as 'lying in the crook of well-dressed, elderly montains'.

Even if you don't have wheels there's the chance to walk in indigenous forest quite close to town, and the backpacker hostel arranges various day trips.

Swellendam is dotted with old oaks and on its south side is surrounded by beautiful rolling wheat country, but it backs up against a spectacular ridge of the 1600-metre Langeberg range. The distinctive square-topped outcrop is known locally as 12-O'Clock Rock because the sun at noon is close to the rock, making it impossible for anyone in town to see what is going on up there. I was told that this was a favourite place for diamond smugglers to do business, but it seems a long way to go. You can walk up and back in a day.

History

Swellendam dates from 1746 and is the third-oldest European town in South Africa. The swift expansion by independent farmers and traders beyond the Cape Peninsula meant that by the 1740s they had drifted too far beyond the Dutch East India Company's (VOC) authorities at Stellenbosch to be controlled.

As a result, Swellendam was established as the seat of a *landdrost*, an official representative of the colony's governor whose duties combined those of local administrator, tax collector and magistrate. The residency of a landdrost was known as a *drostdy* and included his office and courtroom as well as his family's living quarters. The Swellendam Drostdy is the only 18th-century drostdy to survive, and it is now the centrepiece for one of the best museum complexes in South Africa.

Official vandalism has ensured that Swellendam, pretty as it is, has not remained a perfect jewel. In 1974 the main road was widened, resulting in the loss of many old oaks and older buildings.

Information

Swellendam Tourist Office (☎ (0291) 42770) in the old mission or Oefeninghuis, on Voortrek St (the main street) is open Monday to Friday from 9 am to noon and from 2 to 4 pm, and Saturday from 9 am to 12.30 pm. Note the twin clocks, one of which is permanently set at 12.15 pm. This was the time for the daily service; the illiterate townspeople only had to match the working clock with the painted one to know when their presence was required.

If you're at all interested in architecture or history, pick up a copy of the *Swellendam Treasures* brochure which details scores of interesting buildings in and around Swellendam. It includes a good map.

For permits to walk in **Marloth Nature Reserve** in the Langeberg mountains, just three km from town, contact the Nature Conservation Department (☎ (0291) 41410) during business hours. There are day, overnight and week-long hikes.

Drostdy Museum

The Drostdy Museum is one of the finest museum complexes in the country. The centrepiece is the beautiful drostdy itself, which dates from 1746. It's worth buying the brochure *The Drostdy at Swellendam* (R2) so that you don't miss any of the important features.

In addition to the drostdy there is the Old Gaol, part of the original administrative buildings, the Gaoler's Cottage, a watermill, and Mayville, another residence dating from 1853.

Some distance away, Morgenzon, 16 Van

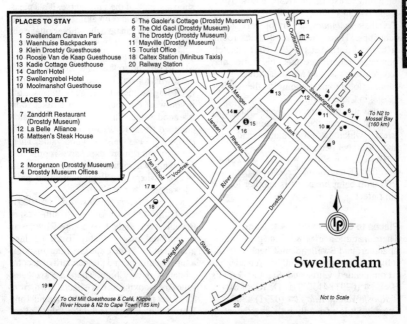

Swellendam

Oudtshoorn Rd, is an annexe of the museum. It was built in 1751 as a house for the landdrost's Secretary.

The complex is open weekdays from 9 am to 4.15 pm, and weekends from 10 am to 3.45 pm; entry is R5.

Places to Stay – bottom end

The *Swellendam Caravan Park* (☎ (0291) 42705) is in a lovely spot near the Morgenzon museum a 10-minute walk from town, tucked under the mountains and surrounded by leafy farms. Prices are high but the setting is beautiful. Pleasant thatched bungalows are R106, tent sites are R35.

There's a good hostel, *Waenhuis Backpackers* (☎ (0291) 43350), at 29 Burg St, run by Lisa and Marinda. The dorms are simple, in an old *waenhuis* (wagon house) and the house contains the kitchen, lounge etc. It's very friendly and has a good atmosphere. They rent mountain bikes (R5 per hour) and offer all sorts of day trips and excursions, including horse-riding (R35) and a trip to Cape Agulhas (R70), just 45 minutes away. Try their *mampoes*, a sort of very strong schnapps. There are three doubles rooms (R65) and dorm beds (R20). Unfortunately our latest reports are that this hostel may have closed. Lisa and Marinda, however, are running local tours – enquire at the Albergo Hostel in Cape Town.

A traveller recommends *Stone Cottage*, 22 Kerk St (across the river from the main street), which is self-contained and costs about R50 per person.

The *Carlton Hotel* (☎ (0291) 41120), on Voortrek St, has rooms for R50 per person or R60 with bath; breakfast is another R10. It ain't great.

Places to Stay – middle & top end

There are quite a few B&Bs and guesthouses in and around Swellendam. Check with the information centre for a full list. A reader has recommended Chris and Sandra Perold's B&B (☎ (0291) 41303) on De Kloof St.

Roosje Van de Kaap (☎ (0291) 43001), 5 Drostdy St, is a friendly little guesthouse in a newly refurbished old house. It's surprising how well modern interior design complements Cape Dutch architecture. The four guest rooms overlook the small pool and cost R85/150 a single/double, with breakfast. There's a restaurant here.

Kadie Cottage (☎ (0291) 43053) on Voortek St is a large complex of old buildings with lawns running down to the river. There are self-contained units.

Moolmanshof (☎ (0291) 43258), 217 Voortrekker St, is a beautiful old home dating from 1798. The garden is superb and the house is furnished with period furniture. Bed and breakfast rates are a very reasonable R45 per person per night.

The *Klein Drostdy* (☎ (0291) 41542), 12 Drostdy St, is 150 metres from the museum. It's an historic house with lovely gardens and a swimming pool. Bed and breakfast is R50 per person.

The Old Mill guesthouse (☎ (0291) 42790), 241 Voortrek St, is a cottage in a meadow behind behind the antiques/craft shop and café of the same name. It's a pleasant place. Bed and breakfast costs R65 per person or you can take the whole cottage and self-cater for R150.

The *Swellengrebel Hotel* (☎ (0291) 41144) on Voortrek St is a big place and is the town's top hotel, although like the others it's losing business to the guesthouses. Still, if you want the anonymity of a hotel room it's good value. The older rooms are fairly cramped (from R99/139) but newer double rooms (R139 as well) are good value. There are also some more expensive rooms in a new wing, where there's also a gym, spa and jaccuzi (where you'll probably find hefty Afrikaners at beery play).

Klippe Rivier Homestead (☎ (0291) 43341, fax 43337), a km or so south-west of town, just across the Keurbooms River, is an exceptional place to stay. Built on land granted in 1725, the Cape Georgian manor is a superb building and the standard of accommodation is very high. There are six guest suites overlooking an oak-shaded lawn, from R171 per person. The owners, Liz and Tony Westby-Nunn, manage the Portfolio Collection of quality B&Bs, guesthouses etc, so it's no surprise that their guesthouse is one of the best in the country.

Places to Eat

By the river at the top end of Voortrek St, *La Belle Alliance* serves teas indoors and out. *Mattsen's Steak House* on Voortrek St near the information centre is popular if pricey, with pizza from R21, steaks from R28 and seafood from R30. There are also, fortunately for those on a budget, light meals and pasta from R15.

The *Zanddrift Restaurant* adjoins the museum and is in a building that itself dates from 1757. It's only open from 9 am to 5 pm, unfortunately. Breakfast is a must, with a huge platter of omelette, ham, cheese, paté, fruit and so on, all for R16. It's available all day. Other dishes depend on what's available that day, but whatever they are, they would be worth trying. *Roosje Van de Kaap* guesthouse, 5 Drostdy St, has a restaurant open to non-guests. It was still under construction when I called but the owners planned a varied menu with traditional, Mediterranean and French elements. They will offer a three-course meal for R25, or à la carte with main courses at R20. There's a wood-fired pizza oven.

The Old Mill, 241 Voortrek St, is a café open for lunch (and dinner for guests staying in the cottage). Dutch pancakes cost from R5 to R11; light meals such as vegetables and mushrooms cost between R4 and R10. More substantial dishes include springbok steaks, guinea-fowl pies and other interesting specialities.

The pubs all have dining rooms; probably the best is in the *Voortrekker Restaurant* in the Swellengrebel Hotel, which has standard dishes at highish prices, although you can order small servings for under R20. This might be the only place in town open on Sunday night.

For an expensive but excellent night out, phone the *Klippe River Homestead* (☎ (0291) 43341) to see if they have room at dinner for non-guests. A three-course set menu costs R67.

Getting There & Away

Bus Intercape Mainliner's twice-daily Garden Route service links Cape Town and Port Elizabeth via Swellendam and the main towns of the Garden Route. Eastward buses come through Swellendam at 9.45 am and 10.45 pm; the westward buses come through at 2 pm and 3 am. Fares include Cape Town R55, Mossel Bay R50, Knysna R75, and Port Elizabeth R90. The Swellengrebel Hotel is the Intercape agent.

Translux also has a Garden Route service, running at least once daily. Some buses also run via Oudtshoorn. Fares include Cape Town R60, Mossel Bay R55 (you can't book this sector), Oudtshoorn R70, Knysna R85 and Port Elizabeth R105. Milestone Tours (☎ (0291) 42137), 8 Cooper St, is the Translux agent.

Chilwans Bus Services (☎ (021) 54 2506, 905 3910) has a useful (if slow and not luxurious) service between Cape Town and Port Elizabeth via Swellendam (R40 from Cape Town) and the Garden Route. It departs from Cape Town on Friday and returns on Sunday.

Train The weekly *Southern Cross* between Cape Town and Port Elizabeth stops here just after midnight on Friday heading east and early Monday morning heading west. First/2nd/3rd class fares to Cape Town are R53/38/21; to Port Elizabeth it's R169/83/47.

Minibus Taxi Taxis stop at the Caltex service station on Voortrek St, opposite the Swellengrebel Hotel. There's a daily service to Cape Town for R35, and to Mossel Bay for a little more. See the Cape Town Getting There & Away entry for a couple of door-to-door services running through Swellendam.

BONTEBOK NATIONAL PARK

The Bontebok National Park (☎ (0291) 42735), six km south of Swellendam, is a small chunk of land specifically set aside to ensure the preservation of the bontebok. The bontebok is an unusually marked antelope that once roamed the region in large numbers. Unfortunately, it has been reduced to the verge of extinction.

The park falls within the coastal fynbos area and is on the banks of the Breede River (swimming is possible). It boasts nearly 500 grasses and other plant species; in the late winter and early spring, the veld is covered with flowers. In addition to the bontebok there are rhebok, grysbok, duiker, red hartebeest and mountain zebras. Birdlife is abundant.

Admission is R6 per vehicle plus R3.50 per person. There are fully equipped six-berth caravans for R60 plus R8 per person. There are also pleasant camp sites for R20 for two people. Prices drop in winter. Bookings should be made through the national park offices in Pretoria or Cape Town.

Garden Route

The heavily promoted Garden Route encompasses a beautiful bit of coastline from Still Bay in the west to just beyond Plettenberg Bay in the east.

The narrow coastal plain is often forested, and is mostly bordered by extensive lagoons which run behind a barrier of sand dunes and superb white beaches. Inland, its boundary is the Outeniqua and Tsitsikamma ranges, which are between 1000 and 1700 metres high. The semi-desert Karoo lies on the other side of the mountains and can be reached via several of the most spectacular passes in the country.

The Garden Route has some of the most significant tracts of indigenous forest in the country – giant yellowwood trees and wildflowers like ericas, proteas, gladioli, arum lilies, strelitzia, watsonias and agapanthus. The forests are still harvested commercially and there are also large eucalypt and pine plantations.

The climate's kind. Average minimum temperatures are around 13°C in winter and average maximums only reach the mid-20s in summer (although it can be as high as 40°C). There's plenty of sun throughout the year, but the best weather is likely to be in February and March, and the highest chance of rainfall and grey days is from August to October.

The area is a favourite for all watersports: swimming, surfing, fishing and sailing. Most people come just to laze in the sun and, if the weather becomes cloudy, to tackle some of the numerous short walks along the coast or in the hills.

Although the Garden Route is unquestionably beautiful, it is also quite heavily (and tackily) developed – reminiscent in some ways of Australia's east coast. Prices jump by at least 30% in mid season (late January to May) and *more than double* over the high season (December, January and Easter). Unless you're staying in hostels you might find the prices and the crowds ridiculous in the high season.

GETTING THERE & AWAY

Transport connections are good. Translux (☎ (021) 405 3333) and Intercape Mainliner (☎ (021) 386 4400 in Cape Town, 24 hours)

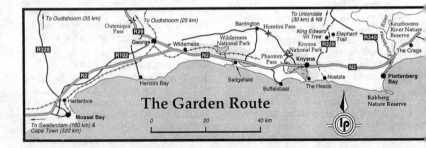

To Oudtshoorn (35 km)
Outeniqua Pass R29
To Oudtshoorn (25 km)
R328
George
R102
Wilderness
Wilderness National Park
Barrington
Homtini Pass
To Uniondale (30 km) & N9
King Edward VII Tree
Elephant Trail
R339
Knysna National Park
R340
Keurbooms River Nature Reserve
The Crags
Phantom Pass
Knysna
N2
N2
Herolds Bay
Sedgefield
Buffelsbaai
Noetzie
The Heads
Plettenberg Bay
Hartenbos
Mossel Bay
To Swellendam (160 km) & Cape Town (320 km)
Robberg Nature Reserve
The Garden Route
0   20   40 km

runs at least daily from Cape Town to Port Elizabeth via the main Garden Route towns, and there are also some cheaper options, both buses and minibus taxis. The weekly *Southern Cross* train between Cape Town and port Elizabeth stops in some Garden Route towns. See Getting There & Away in the Cape Town section for details of transport from that city.

Garden Line Transport (☎ (0441) 74 2823, fax 74 2825) runs between Mossel Bay and Johannesburg twice weekly, via George, Oudtshoorn and Beaufort West. On Tuesday the northbound bus runs via Kimberley and on Friday it runs via Bloemfontein. Southbound, the Wednesday bus runs via Kimberley and the Sunday bus runs via Bloemfontein.

Translux has services from Knysna to Jo'burg/Pretoria. Buses to Jo'burg via Kimberley depart from Knysna on Wednesday and Friday evening; buses travelling via Bloemfontein depart on Sunday, Monday, Tuesday and Thursday evening. Fares and times to various destinations are shown in the tables. From the Garden Route, fares to Pretoria are the same as fares to Jo'burg; add an hour of travelling time.

To/From the Garden Route with Translux

Knysna to	Fare	Hours
George	R40	1
Mossel Bay	R50	1¾
Oudtshoorn	R50	3
Beaufort West	R100	5½
Kimberley	R165	11
Bloemfontein	R190	10¼
Jo'burg	R210	17

Jo'burg to	Fare	Hours
Bloemfontein	R130	6
Kimberley	R140	6½
Beaufort West	R200	12
Oudtshoorn	R210	14½
Mossel Bay	R210	15¾
George	R210	16½
Knysna	R210	17

From Port Elizabeth (see the Eastern Cape chapter) you can connect with buses to East London, Umtata, and Durban.

GETTING AROUND

Travelling between neighbouring Garden Route towns with the major buslines is expensive, so look for minibus taxis.

STILL BAY

Still Bay (or Stilbaai) is a large, middle-class holiday village. It's on a lovely part of the coast with a large river inlet, but the town itself is rather ugly. The time-share cowboys are starting to move in. For surfers, there's a very good quality right-point break with long rides. It's best in winter, like most south-coast breaks; south-westerlies are offshore.

There's a caravan park and holiday cottages.

MOSSEL BAY

Mossel Bay (or Mosselbaai) was once one of the jewels of the Garden Route. This was before the construction of the Mossgas gas/petrol conversion refinery on the outskirts of town brought an enormous influx of people. Despite this it's still a fairly sleepy country town, with some pretty sandstone buildings, and it claims to have the mildest

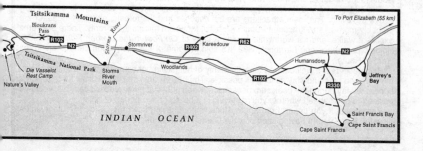

climate in the world (whatever that means). It also has the only north-facing beach in the country.

The first European to visit the bay was the Portuguese explorer Bartholomeu Dias in 1488, and he was followed by Vasco da Gama in 1497. From then on, many ships stopped to take on fresh water and to barter for provisions with the Gouriqua Khoikhoi who lived in the region. A large milkwood tree beside the spring was used as a postal collection point – expeditions heading east would leave mail to be picked up by ships returning home.

The spring and the tree still exist, and you can post letters (they receive a special post mark) from a mail box on the site. A museum complex has also been developed; its pride and joy is a replica of Dias' tiny caravel.

European farmers established themselves in the area in the second half of the 18th century. In 1786 the Dutch East India Company constructed a granary (not far from the post office tree and now part of the museum complex) and Mossel Bay developed as a port. It has been a holiday centre for some time too – at The Point are some ramshackle beach shacks which have attained 'historic' status.

Orientation & Information

The town lies on the northern slopes of Cape St Blaize. The museum complex, which is well signposted and overlooks the bay, is the best place to start your exploration. The granary in the museum complex (☎ (0444) 91 1067) is the information centre for the museum in particular and the Mossel Bay area in general.

There's a laundromat upstairs in the Plaza shopping centre on Marsh St. A bag wash costs about R10.

Bartholomeu Dias Museum Complex

The highlight of the complex is the replica of the vessel that Bartholomeu Dias used on his 1488 voyage of discovery. This caravel is incredibly small. Seeing it brings home the extraordinary skill and courage of the explorers. The replica was built in Portugal and sailed to Mossel Bay in 1988 to commemorate the 500th anniversary of Dias' trip.

In addition to the maritime museum, the complex includes the spring where Dias watered the postal tree, the 1786 VOC granary, an acclaimed shell museum (with some interesting aquarium tanks), and a local history museum. It's open Monday to Friday from 9 am to 1 pm and 2 to 5 pm, Saturday from 10 am to 1 pm, and Sunday from 2 to 5 pm.

Boat Trips

Two boats, the *Infante* (☎ (0444) 91 3788) and the *Romonza* (☎ (0444) 3101), offer

---

Just a lot of Hype?

Feedback from readers is evenly divided between those who think our coverage of the Garden Route is too negative and those who think we give it too much attention.

The sort of time you have on the Garden Route depends on what you want to do and how you're travelling. The main attractions are the beaches and the forests, although the latter are probably more of an attraction to South Africans, for whom forests are a rarity. There are some excellent walks, and it's worthwhile buying a copy of *On Foot in the Garden Route* by Judith Hopley, paperback and hardback, R32. It's sold in some of the information centres along the Garden Route.

Backpackers are well catered for, with plenty of hostels in hot competition to make sure you have a good time and stay as long as possible. The hostels also make it feasible for those on a budget to stay during the peak summer season, when prices at other places soar. Still, you'd be advised to book ahead whether you're staying in a hostel or an up-market hotel.

Remember, if you depart from South Africa without having seen the Garden Route it isn't a disaster; if you depart having seen *only* the Garden Route, it might be. ■

daily (hourly, sometimes) boat trips to Seal Island for about R25, from the harbour behind the railway station. In winter and spring it's not unusual to see whales on the trip.

Diving
Diaz Pro-Dive (☎ (0444) 7293) by the harbour offers NAUI courses for R500; Mossel Bay Divers (☎ (0444) 91 1441), in the Protea Santos Hotel, offers PADI courses.

Places to Stay
There are two adjacent municipal caravan parks (*Bakke* and *Santos*) on the pretty Dias Strand, the bay beach, and also *Punt* on The Point, a little further from the town centre but close to the surf. Contact these places on ☎ (0444) 91 2915. All have two-bedroom chalets (from R132/194 in the low/high season) and tent sites from R29 to a massive R63!

Mossel Bay Backpackers (☎ (0444) 91 3182) is on the corner of Mint and Marsh Sts, not far from The Point. It is run by the owners of the guesthouse around the corner. Bikes and other equipment is rented and, as usual, the owners are a good source of information on things to see and do. Dorm beds are R25 and doubles are R80. They will collect you from the bus stop and the railway station (which is some way out of town).

There are quite a few guesthouses and B&Bs in town; the information centre has a list. Not far from the museum, the *Old Post Office Tree Guesthouse* (☎ (0444) 91 3738) is a very comfortable set up, more like a hotel than a guesthouse in size. It has a great view overlooking the bay. Singles/doubles start around R140/230, including breakfast, with some good deals on weekends.

There's nothing terribly wrong with the *Ocean View Hotel* (☎ (0444) 3711), but it's too big and too depressingly '60s to be attractive. Rooms cost around R95/150 a single/double, with breakfast. The *Protea Santos* (☎ (0444) 7103) has a good position overlooking the bay. A hassle is that the staff can't actually tell you how much the rooms cost

more than a day or so in advance. You'll probably pay around R200, but who knows?

Places to Eat
The *Gannet Restaurant* (part of the Old Post Office Tree Guest House near the museum) has a bright and informal atmosphere. At lunch you'll spend between R35 and R55, a little more at dinner.

The *Pavilion* (☎ (0444) 4567) is right on Santos beach, in a 19th-century bathing pavilion. There are snacks for about R10; line fish start at R24, and steaks at R25.

Nello's Pizzeria & Coffee Bar is in the courtyard of Vintcent Place, a Georgian building on the corner of Marsh and Bland Sts in the centre of town. Nello is Italian and his food is authentic. Pizzas start around R10. Further along Marsh St, on the corner of Kloof, is the *Bay Tavern*, a local pub in a renovated sandstone building. It has reasonable pub food such as fish and chips (R14), bangers and mash (R15) and huge steaks (R20 to R35). Breakfast is R15.

At The Point is a franchised *steakhouse* and *Tides*, a bar and snackery with an elevated patio overlooking the sea – a good place for a drink.

Getting There & Away
Bus Mossel Bay is off the highway and buses don't come into town, but drop you at the Voorbaai Shell station, seven km from town. The hostel staff will collect you.

Intercape Mainliner and Translux stop here on their Cape Town to Port Elizabeth services. Intercape fares include: Cape Town, R65; Knysna, R55; Plettenberg Bay, R60; and Port Elizabeth, R75. Translux is more expensive. See the Cape Town Getting There & Away entry for more details.

Garden Line Transport (☎ (0441) 74 2823, fax 74 2825) runs between Mossel Bay and Jo'burg twice weekly. Mossel Bay to Jo'burg costs R160 and takes about 15½ hours. Other fares from Mossel Bay include: George, R30; Oudtshoorn R40; Beaufort West, R85; Bloemfontein, R145; and Kimberley, R135. Translux stops in Mossel Bay during its route between Knysna and

Jo'burg/Pretoria. Fares from Mossel Bay include: Knysna, R50 (you can't book this sector); Bloemfontein, R190; Kimberley, R165; and Jo'burg, R210. See Getting There & Away at the start of this section for times and routes with Garden Line and Translux.

Chilwans Bus Services (☎ (021) 54 2506, 905 3910) runs a slow bus from Cape Town to Port Elizabeth. The fare from Cape Town to Mossel Bay is just R60. It leaves Cape Town on Friday and returns on Sunday.

Minibus Taxi See Getting There & Away in the Cape Town section for information on a door-to-door service for the Garden Route.

GEORGE

George is a large, prosperous town that bills itself as the capital of the Garden Route. It was founded in 1811 and lies on a coastal plateau at the foot of the Outeniqua range, 432 km east of Cape Town, 320 km west of Port Elizabeth and eight km from the coast. It's one of the fastest-growing towns in South Africa and has a population of over 75,000 people.

The town is pleasant enough, with lots of trees and a good selection of restaurants (both unusual in South Africa). It's not a bad place to spend a night, but unless you have a car it's too far from the coast and there are few reasons to stay longer. Backpackers will find that the hostel has arranged some interesting activities and there are some great drives and walks in the surrounding countryside.

George is the major transport hub for the Garden Route and a good starting point for the Little Karoo.

Orientation & Information

George is a large place and quite spread out. The N2 enters town from the south on York St, which is a long four-lane avenue, terminating at a T-intersection with Courtenay St – west for Oudtshoorn, east for Wilderness. The main commercial area is on the east side of York St around Hibernia and Market Sts.

The tourist office (☎ (0441) 74 4000), 124 York St, has a lot of information and some handy maps. Satour has an office (☎ (0441) 73 5228) next door. There's a local office of the Cape Nature Conservation (☎ (0441) 74 2160) which is housed in the all-glass York building on York St.

The Market Lane shopping centre has a few craft shops and places to stop for a coffee. On Tuesday and Friday a *boeremark* (farmers' market) is held here from 7 am to mid-morning. There's a laundromat at 57 York St.

George Museum

The town's old drostdy (1813) houses the museum and has general exhibits on the surrounding area, particularly on the timber industry. There is also a large collection of antique instruments. It's open weekdays from 9 am to 4.30 pm, and Saturday from 9 am to 12.30 pm.

Places to Stay

The *George Tourist Resort* (☎ (0441) 74 5205), York St, is a large well-organised caravan park with a swimming pool and trampolines. It is a good 20-minute walk from the city centre. Rondavels cost from R40/130 a double in the low/high season. Chalets cost from R90 a double in the low season, rising to R215 (minimum) for four people in the high season. Sites start at R25 and double in price in summer.

George Backpackers' Hostel (☎ (0441) 74 7807), 29 York St (the main road from the N2), is quite a long walk south of the centre of town. The hostel is in a rather typical suburban house. There's a big garden with a pool, good facilities and a helpful manager. Dorm beds are R22, doubles are a low R55 and you can camp for R15. Bike hire costs R15 per day. There are various outings, such as canoe trips (R30), and guests get a discount of R10 off the *Outeniqua Choo-Tjoe* train fare.

The information centre has lists of B&B places in and around town. They'll tell you that everything costs R100 or more, but if you insist they will find something cheaper. Readers have recommended *The Ireland's*

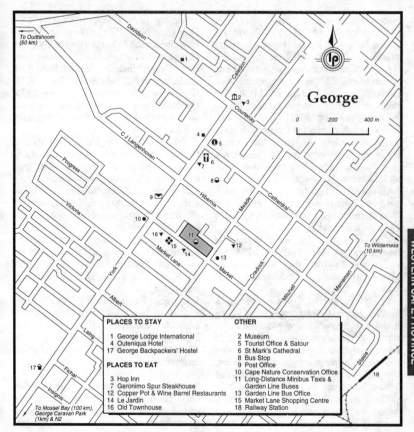

George

To Oudtshoorn
(50 km)

Davidson

Caledon

Courtenay

C J Langenhoven

Progress

Victoria

Hibernia

Meade

Cathedral

Market Lane

York

Market

Cradock

Albert

Laing

Fichat

Insignis

Mitchell

Merriman

Statie

To Wilderness
(10 km)

To Mossel Bay (100 km),
George Caravan Park
(1km) & N2

0   200   400 m

PLACES TO STAY	OTHER
1 George Lodge International	2 Museum
4 Outeniqua Hotel	5 Tourist Office & Satour
17 George Backpackers' Hostel	6 St Mark's Cathedral
	8 Bus Stop
PLACES TO EAT	9 Post Office
	10 Cape Nature Conservation Office
3 Hop Inn	11 Long-Distance Minibus Taxis &
7 Geronimo Spur Steakhouse	Garden Line Buses
12 Copper Pot & Wine Barrel Restaurants	13 Garden Line Bus Office
14 Le Jardin	15 Market Lane Shopping Centre
16 Old Townhouse	18 Railway Station

B&B (☎ (0441) 70 7148), 11 Rooiels Ave; they paid R70 a double.

The *Outeniqua Hotel* (☎ (0441) 74 4488), 123 York St, has singles/doubles including breakfast and bathrooms for R90/150 (R10 less, if you're prepared to share a bathroom).

George Lodge International (☎ (0441) 74 6549), 86 Davidson Rd (left at the north end of York St), has fully equipped rooms and a swimming pool, and it's within walking distance of the town centre. It's very much an overnight stop, but it's not bad. Singles/doubles are R85/135.

There are several top-end options. *King*

George III (☎ (0441) 74 7659), on King George Dr, is around R180 per person. The most impressive offering is the *Fancourt Hotel* (☎ (0441) 70 8282), on Montagu St, Blanco, off the R29 to Oudtshoorn about four km from the town centre. It's run by Orient Express Hotels. The building itself is a national monument, with high ceilings and polished floors; it's furnished with beautiful furniture made from local woods. There's a swimming pool, a top-class golf course and two excellent restaurants. Such things don't come cheap, but the Fancourt is good value at around R250 per person.

Places to Eat

The *Copper Pot* (☎ (0441) 74 3191), off Meade St, is a very good restaurant serving interesting food at moderate prices. For example, there are entrées such as smoked ostrich fillets (R14) and main courses such as Mauritanian seafood curry (R34). If these prices are beyond you, just go next door to the *Wine Barrel* (☎ (0441) 73 4370) which shares a kitchen with the Copper Pot but is markedly cheaper. At lunch, the specials allow you to eat good food for less than a production-line meal at a steakhouse franchise – highly recommended. The Copper Pot is open from Tuesday to Friday for lunch and from 7 pm nightly except Sunday. The Wine Barrel is open on weekdays for lunch and from 6 pm nightly.

Another quality restaurant is the *Old Townhouse* (☎ (0441) 74 3663), 20 Market St. It's in an 1847 building (now a national monument) made from brick, mud and yellowwood.

The *Hop Inn*, 70 Courtenay St, is a friendly bar and restaurant with a young crowd. The gimmick is a couple of old trains, but they have been used well – opening onto a decent sized room – so they are not claustrophobic. The menu is meat, meat and meat, with the odd seafood dish such as seafood T-bone. You'll pay around R25.

The *Signalman's Arms*, at the railway station, is a pleasant pub loaded with railway memorabilia, with meals for R15 to R20.

Getting There & Away

Air SAA flies to George's PW Botha Airport about 15 km south of town. The economy one-way fare from Cape Town is R331; from Jo'burg it's a pricey R673.

Bus Intercape Mainliner and Translux stop here on their services from Cape Town to Port Elizabeth. Intercape fares include: Cape Town, R75; Mossel Bay, R35; Knysna, R50; Plettenberg Bay, R55; and Port Elizabeth, R70. Translux is more expensive, although some of its services run via Oudtshoorn. See the Cape Town Getting There & Away entry for more information.

Garden Line Transport (☎ (0441) 74 2823, fax 74 2825) runs between Mossel Bay, George and Jo'burg twice weekly. From George to Jo'burg costs R155. Other fares from George include: Mossel Bay, R30; Oudtshoorn R25; Beaufort West, R75; Bloemfontein, R140; and Kimberley, R135. Garden Line runs a much cheaper local service to Oudtshoorn (R6) departing daily at 5.45 pm.

Translux stops in George on its run between Knysna and Jo'burg/Pretoria. Fares from George include: Knysna, R40 (you can't book this sector); Bloemfontein, R190; Kimberley, R165; and Jo'burg, R210. See Getting There & Away at the beginning of this section for routes and times with Garden Line and Translux.

Most buses stop in St Mark's Square, behind the Geronimo Spur steakhouse on the main street. Garden Line (☎ (0441) 74 2823, fax 74 2825), on Meade St, is also the Intercape agent.

Chilwans Bus Services (☎ (021) 54 2506, 905 3910) has a useful (if slow and not luxurious) service from Cape Town to Port Elizabeth. The fare to George is just R65. Buses leave Cape Town on Friday and return on Sunday.

Train The weekly *Southern Cross* between Cape Town and Port Elizabeth stops here early Saturday morning heading east and on Sunday evening heading west. First/ 2nd/3rd-class fares to Cape Town are R114/62/35; to Port Elizabeth it's R108/59/33.

One of the prime reasons to visit George is the famous *Outeniqua Choo-Tjoe*, a steam train running along a spectacular line to Knysna. Two trains (chosen from a variety of historic engines) run daily, except Sunday and public holidays. Trains leave George at 9.30 am and 1 pm, arriving in Knysna at noon and 3.35 pm. Trains leave Knysna at 9.45 am and 2.15 pm, arriving in George at 12.30 pm and 5 pm. Services will possibly be cut back in winter.

The fare from George to Wilderness is R5; all the way to Knysna is R25, or R35 return (valid for six months). Reservations are recommended. The George hostel can arrange good discounts for guests. For more details contact Spoornet (☎ (0441) 73 8202).

Minibus Taxi The taxi park is on St Mark's Square. See Getting There & Away in the Cape Town entry for information on a door-to-door service running the Garden Route.

Getting Around

Budget (☎ (0441) 73 6259), Tempest (☎ (0441) 78 1005) and Panther (☎ (0441) 74 6003) have agents in George.

AROUND GEORGE
Montagu & Outeniqua Passes

It is hard to believe that a mere 20 km from the green and fertile country around George, on the other side of the Outeniqua range, there is the dry semi-desert country of the Little Karoo. One interesting loop is out the Montagu Pass and back on the Outeniqua Pass (from Oudtshoorn). The Montagu is a quiet dirt road that winds its way through the mountains; it was opened in 1843 and is now a national monument. Take a picnic, because there are some great picnic sites and beautiful fynbos to admire along the way. The views from the Outeniqua Pass are actually more spectacular than from the Montagu, but this is a main road so it's a lot more difficult to stop when you want to.

Seven Passes Road

The Seven Passes road to Knysna used to be the main road link, and it is easy to imagine how difficult and dangerous it must have been for the pioneers and their ox-wagons. The views are nice enough, but most of the countryside is now dominated by pine, gum trees and Port Jackson wattle, leaving only small patches of fynbos. The road is still unsurfaced for quite a way and parts are rough thanks to the timber trucks, so the trip will take two hours. The scenery is nice and comfortable rather than wild and dramatic. The views from the coastal road are more spectacular.

Herold's Bay

There's nothing much in town except one small shop, but there is a pleasant though small beach and a beautiful bit of coast, just south of George. The town gets very crowded in the high season and on summer weekends, but it is a quiet and sleepy place at any other time.

The *Herold's Bay Caravan Park* (☎ (0441) 872 9400) is a terrific spot close to the beach and has sites for about R30, rising to R46 in season. *Dutton's Cove Resort* (☎ (0441) 872 9205) is an attractive village of comfortable rondavels and chalets (some sleeping up to six people) with great views overlooking Herold's Bay (it's about a km up a very steep hill from the beach). It is recommended. There is a bewildering array of standards, seasons and sizes. Basically, two people pay from R85 in the lowest season. Prices rise in five steps to the highest season, when they start at R180.

Victoria Bay

Victoria is a tiny, picturesque bay at the foot of steep cliffs, also south of George. There's a small beach and a cluster of holiday houses. It's a popular surf spot (perhaps the best surf on the Garden Route) with a right-point break, best with north-west winds. There's a *caravan park* (☎ (0441) 74 4040) and the *Sea Breeze Holiday Cottages* (☎ (0441) 71 1583).

WILDERNESS

Wilderness is no longer an apt description for this small holiday town, as holiday houses, resorts and hotels now sprinkle the hills. Still, it is a beautiful stretch of coast to the east and west with the blue sea, rolling breakers, miles of white sand, sheltered lagoons, and a lush mountain hinterland that have made Wilderness a very popular destination. The N2 and the George-to-Knysna railway line parallel the coast, but everything is quite widely scattered, making life difficult if you don't have a vehicle.

The Wilderness Eco-Tourism Association (☎ (0441) 77 0045) runs the information centre and can help with accommodation bookings. It's open daily except Sunday.

Places to Stay

Lakes Holiday Resort (☎ (0441) 877 1101) on the Touw River, off the N2 past Wilderness but before the National Park,, has excellent caravan facilities and free sailboarding and canoeing. It's definitely worth considering outside the high season. Four-person cabins start at R130 in the off season and jump to R325 in the high season; camp sites jump from R35 to R100!

The cheapest B&Bs in the area go for about R85 per person, with self-catering accommodation from about R70 per person.

The *Wilderness Holiday Inn Garden Court* (☎ (0441) 91134) is right between the N2 and the beach, about two km from Wilderness. There are all the facilities one would expect, including a pick-up service from the George airport. Singles/doubles are from R214/238.

The *Fairy Knowe Hotel* (☎ (0441) 877 1100), on Dumbleton Rd, is on the banks of the Touw River; take Waterside Rd from Wilderness. The traditional hotel has been run by the same family since it opened in 1910. There are luxury riverside rooms and thatched rondavels. There's a pick-up service from the George airport, or you can take the *Outeniqua Choo-Tjoe*, which stops at nearby Fairy Knowe station. Room rates are from R160 from Monday to Wednesday, from R124 from Thursday to Sunday.

Getting There & Away

Intercape's twice-daily service from Cape Town to Port Elizabeth stops here. Buses heading towards Port Elizabeth (R65, 4½ hours) come through Wilderness at about 12.30 pm and 1.30 am; those heading to Cape Town (R75, 6½ hours) come through at 10.30 am and 11.30 pm. Buses actually stop on the highway at Flat Rock. Translux also runs this route; although they don't advertise a stop in Wilderness, you might be able to arrange it.

The most pleasant way to get here is on the *Outeniqua Choo-Tjoe* steam train from George or Knysna. The fare from George is just R5. See the George Getting There & Away section for details.

WILDERNESS NATIONAL PARK

The Wilderness National Park encompasses the area from Wilderness and the Touw River in the west to Sedgfield and the Goukamma Nature Reserve in the east. The southern boundary is the ocean and the northern boundary is the Outeniqua range. It covers a unique wetland system of lakes, rivers, wetlands and estuaries that are vital for the survival of many species.

There are three types of lake in the park: first the drowned river valleys (like Swartvlei), drowned low-lying areas among the dune system (like Langvlei), and drowned basins that have been formed by wind action (like Rondevlei). The rich birdlife includes the beautiful Knysna loerie, and many species of kingfisher.

There are several nature trails taking in the lakes, the beach and the indigenous forest. The **Kingfisher Trail** is a day walk that traverses the region and includes a boardwalk across the intertidal zone of the Touw River. The lakes offer anglers, canoeists, windsurfers and sailors an ideal venue. Pedal boats and canoes can be hired at Wilderness Camp, and there is also a small shop.

Day visitors are charged R7.50 per vehicle plus R3 per person to enter. The reception office is open from 8 am to 1 pm and 2 to 5 pm.

Places to Stay

Those who stay in the park are well placed to take advantage of the best that the Garden Route can offer – great beaches and walks. There are two camps in the park: the main Wilderness Camp (four km east of Wilderness itself) and a short walk from the beach, and Ebb & Flow Camp. Both offer camping for R35 for two people, plus R10 for additional people. *Wilderness Camp* has four-bed cabins for R250, and a five-bed cottage for R265. Six-berth caravans cost R90 plus R12 per adult. *Ebb & Flow* has two-bed huts starting at R72. All accommodation, including camping, attracts big discounts outside peak times.

Getting There & Away

The Wilderness Camp is signposted from the N2. Those without vehicles could catch any of the Garden Route buses (see the George and Knysna sections) or the *Outeniqua Choo-Tjoe* to Wilderness, and walk from there.

BUFFALO BAY

Buffalo Bay (or Buffelsbaai) is a small holiday village built on a point 10 km west of Knysna – a sandy beach runs all the way to Brenton-on-Sea. It's 10 km from the N2 along the pretty Goukamma Valley, and the Goukamma Nature Reserve is close by. There aren't many facilities, but there is a shop and a great caravan park right beside an excellent right reef break (southerly swell, south-westerly winds). There's also B&B accommodation.

GOUKAMMA NATURE RESERVE

This reserve is accessible from the Buffels Bay road. It protects 14 km of rocky coastline, some weathered sandstone cliffs, dunes covered with coastal fynbos and forest, and Groenvlei, a large freshwater lake. There are some small antelopes and much birdlife – 150 species, including the Knysna loerie, have been recorded.

Most of the reserve is only accessible by foot. There are two easy trails: an eight-km circular trail and a 14-km trail. A suspension bridge over the Goukamma River takes hikers to the start of the trail.

There are picnic, braai and toilet facilities on the banks of the Goukamma River. The gates are open from 8 am to 6 pm, and an entry of R4.40 per car plus R2.20 per person is charged.

KNYSNA

Knysna (the 'k' is silent) is a large and bustling place with a holiday atmosphere. It was developed as a timber port and shipbuilding centre, thanks to the enormous protected lagoon, which opens up behind high sandstone cliffs, and the rich indigenous forests of the area. The continuing legacy of the timber industry is a number of excellent woodwork and furniture shops and a thriving artistic community.

A planned waterfront development will add to the increasing pace of life in Knysna. This might finally force the building of a bypass road – currently the narrow main street is also the N2. However, a bypass would involve killing off some of the indigenous forest around Knysna, and there's precious little left.

Knysna National Lake Area

The National Parks Board regulates and controls the development of the Knysna lagoon and the catchment area of the Knysna River, which flows into the lagoon.

It's not a national park wilderness area. Much is still privately owned, and the lagoon is used by industry and for recreation. The National Parks Board's brief is to make sure that the ongoing development balances the needs of the environment and the human community and doesn't lead to ecological disaster.

The Knysna Elephants

In the forests around Knysna live the last wild elephants in the southern Cape (with the exception of those in the Addo Elephant National Park). The elephants live deep in the forest and are so rarely seen that their dung is labelled and recorded!

The forest is still commercially logged for prized yellowwood and stinkwood, so the elephants are basically in a zoo maintained for tourists, not a wilderness area.

It was recently discovered that the elephant population had shrunk to just one. Some more elephants were introduced from Kruger, however, the lone Knysna elephant was so freaked-out by these newcomers that he fled. The Kruger elephants (accustomed to herds and savannah) were so freaked-out at finding themselves alone in a forest that they pursued him. The chase went on for days and one of the new elephants died of exhaustion. ■

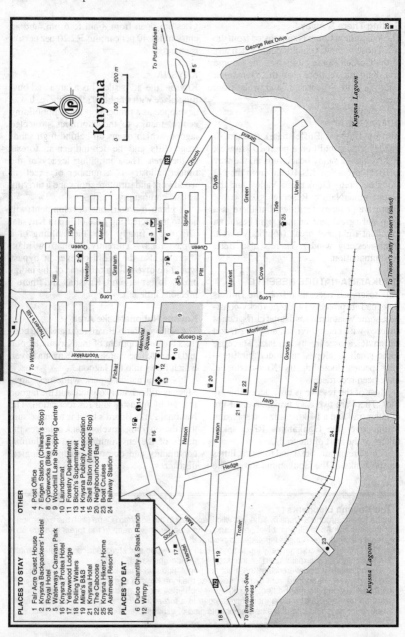

Knysna

0   100   200 m

To Port Elizabeth

George Rex Drive

Knysna Lagoon

To Witlokasia

To Brenton-on-Sea,
Wilderness

To Theesen's Jetty (Theesen's Island)

Knysna Lagoon

PLACES TO STAY
1   Fair Acre Guest House
2   Knysna Backpackers' Hostel
3   Royal Hotel
5   Waterways Caravan Park
16 Knysna Protea Hotel
17 Yellowwood Lodge
18 Rolling Waters
19 Mike's B&B
21 Knysna Hotel
22 The Caboose
25 Knysna Hikers' Home
26 Ashmead Resort

PLACES TO EAT
6   Dulce Chantilly & Steak Ranch
12 Wimpy

OTHER
4   Post Office
7   Engen Station (Chilwan's Stop)
8   Cycleworks (Bike Hire)
9   Woodmill Lane Shopping Centre
10 Laundromat
11 Forestry Department
13 Bloch's Supermarket
14 Knysna Publicity Association
15 Shell Station (Intercape Stop)
20 Neighbourhood Bar
23 Boat Cruises
24 Railway Station

WESTERN CAPE PROVINCE

The lagoon covers 13 sq km. The protected area starts just to the east of Buffalo Bay and follows the coastline to the mouth of the Noetzie River. The lagoon opens up between two sandstone cliffs, known as the Heads. There are good views from a lookout on the eastern head, and a nature trail on the western head. The National Parks Board has an office on Thesen's Island.

Orientation & Information

Almost everything of importance is on Main Rd; however, don't miss the Woodmill Lane Shopping Centre, behind the main street. It's an imaginative centre that has been developed in an old woodmill complex. There are some interesting shops (including Woodcutters, which sells hiking gear) and several good restaurants.

The Knysna Publicity Association (☎ (0445) 21610), 40 Main Rd, has a good range of information on the region and is open from 8.30 am to 5 pm on weekdays and on Saturday morning. You can't miss the office; there's an enormous elephant skeleton out the front. The information centre will book accommodation for a fee of R2 (R5 if the place is a way out of town).

Knysna Travel, opposite the Standard Bank at the entry to Woodmill Lane, sells bus tickets.

Mitchell's Brewery

Those who have been in the country for a while, particularly in Cape Town, may well have come across some of Mitchell's beers, which include a draught lager, a bitter, a stout and an ale. Mitchell's (☎ (0445) 24685) is a small operation, but it seems to be thriving. There are free tours through the brewery on weekdays at 10.30 am. Tastings are available during the brewery's weekday opening hours and on Saturday morning.

Knysna Oysters

Oysters are grown in the lagoon, and are highly acclaimed by gourmets. The Knysna Oyster Company (☎ (0445) 22168), on Thesen's Island, sells direct to the public. A tasting of half a dozen oysters, with trimmings, costs R11, or you can get eight with garlic butter for the same price. If you just want to take oysters away, they're around R1.10 each cultivated or R1.40 'free range'. The shop is open from 8 am to 5 pm Monday to Thursday, 8 am to 3.30 pm on Friday and 9 to 3 pm on weekends.

Witlokasia

Follow Grey St uphill and eventually you'll leave town and emerge on the wooded slopes of the hills behind. On top is the sprawling township of Witlokasia (not the official name). There is at least one shebeen up here, next to the municipal clinic, and even the tourist office says that it's safe to visit (which is astonishing), but it would pay to check the current situation. It's too far to walk, but a continual stream of minibus taxis run up there from behind Bloch's supermarket.

Activities

Swimming The town is built along the east side of the lagoon, but you need wheels if you want to get to an ocean beach – Brenton-on-Sea, 16 km to the west, and Noetzie, 11 km to the east, are both superb. There's a lagoon beach on Leisure Island, but it too is more than walking distance from the centre of town.

Lagoon Cruises The *MV John Benn* (☎ (0445) 21693), not far from the station, has daily cruises on the lagoon for R25. There's a bar, and lunch is sold on board. You must book. The same people also have the Featherbed cruise, which departs at 10 am and runs across to the other side of the lagoon to the **Featherbed Nature Reserve** and includes a walk and a drive, returning around 2.30 pm. It also costs R25 and is probably more interesting than the straight cruise.

Diving Diving in the lagoon is interesting and there's a wreck to explore. Beneath Tapas Jetty you might meet the unique Knysna seahorses. Waterfront Divers (☎ (0445) 22938) is at East Head and charges about R750 for an open-water certificate course. It also rents gear.

Hiking & Mountain Biking The Forestry Department has an office upstairs in the same shopping centre as the Wimpy bar, on Main Rd. This is where you book walking trails and collect some of their excellent maps and information. The booking desk is open on weekdays between 7.30 am and 1 pm, and from 2 to 3.45 pm. Overnight hikes cost R15 per day, including the use of trail huts. For bookings or more information contact Mrs Van Rooyen (☎ (0445) 82 5466, fax 82 5461). She's very helpful. Maps of the day walks cost R1.40 and topographic sheets are R6.

The **Outeniqua Trail** is popular (so book in advance) and takes a week to walk, although you can also do two or three-day sections. Other trails through the forest include the three **Elephant Trails**, beginning and ending at Diepral Hut and the superb but tough **Harkerville Trail** that takes you down to the sea and back up into the mountains.

Bicycles aren't allowed on the walking trails but two bike trails have been developed. Out of season you can use the hiking huts.

Places to Stay – bottom end
Caravan Parks *Waterways Caravan Park* (☎ (0445) 22241) is a big place on Holiday Park Dr, with views over the lagoon and a short walk to the town centre. It has only a limited number of tent sites (none at all at Christmas time) for R20 and a clutch of pleasant two-bedroom chalets from about R120. Booking is advisable.

Next door is the smaller, simpler and friendlier *Knysna Caravan Park* (☎ (0445) 22011) with tent sites for R30 for two people, rising to R60 from mid-December to the end of January. Virtually next door to Waterways, *Monk's Caravan Park & Flats* (☎ (0445) 22609) has chalet/vans (a caravan with an attached bathroom) that sleep five or six people starting at R75 for two plus R15 for each extra body. There are also tent sites.

Woodbourne Resort (☎ (0445) 23223) is an attractive caravan park, not far from The Heads on George Rex Dr. There are two or three-bedroom chalets. For two people they

cost between R115 and R125. Additional adults pay R12. In December the chalets cost R310 for up to four people and R15 for each additional person. Tent sites are R17.50 plus R6 per person, rising to an astronomical R63 plus R6 per person in the highest season. Plastic ground sheets are banned.

Hostels Both hostels are reasonable. *Knysna Backpackers' Hostel* (☎ (0445) 22554), 12 Newton St, is a large Victorian house on the hill a few blocks up from the main street. Dorms are R22 and doubles are R55. *Knysna Hikers' Home* (☎ (0445) 24362), 17 Tide St, is a few blocks on the lagoon side of the main street, in a more ordinary house. They charge R22 in the dorm, and R50 for a double. Prices rise by about 10% in summer. They'll drop you off and pick you up from trailheads for the cost of the petrol. Despite the name there isn't a lot of specialised hiking information.

The Caboose *The Caboose* (☎ (0445) 82 5850) is an interesting concept – quality budget accommodation with a train theme – and it has been well thought-out. Unfortunately, the theme has been taken a little too seriously, as the rooms (with attached bathroom) really are about the same size as sleeping compartments: *tiny*. Still, there are plenty of spacious public areas so it might be OK if you don't plan on doing anything except sleeping in your room. The Caboose would make a good hostel, but it doesn't charge hostel prices. Singles/doubles go for R60/100 – poor value.

Places to Stay – middle & top end
Under Milk Wood (☎ (0445) 22385), George Rex Dr, is a group of high-quality wooden chalets with a a great location near the eastern head, overlooking the lagoon where there's a small but pretty private beach. There are canoes and small boats. The well-equipped chalets sleep four and cost from R269 for two people, plus R30 for each additional person. In the high season they cost from R550 for four people.

On George Rex Dr, *Ashmead Resort* (☎ (0445) 23172) has a variety of chalets and units (all with TV) on the waterfront, surrounded by the last pocket of indigenous forest on the lagoon. There are extensive gardens and a swimming pool.

Lightley's Holiday Cruisers (☎ (0445) 87 1026, fax 87 1067), on the west side of the White National Road Bridge over the Knysna River, has two to eight-berth cruisers for hire. The cruisers are fully equipped, except for bedding, and you can navigate up to 16 km upriver from The Heads. Rates vary radically depending on the boat and the season, but can be as little as R135 for two people or R150 for four people (not including fuel).

B&Bs & Guesthouses Several of the smaller guesthouses, especially those on the main road in from George, have occasional price wars and offer doubles for about R100. This is unlikely to happen in summer. Try *Mike's* (☎ (0445) 21728), at 67 Main Rd.

Fair Acre Guest House (☎ (0445) 22442) in Thesen's Hall has great views and large grounds, with bed and breakfast from R45 per person. *Yellowwood Lodge* (☎ (0445) 82 5906), 18 Handel St, is a beautiful old Victorian-period house with very comfortable rooms from R100 per person, rising to R130/280 a single/double, with breakfast. Smoking is not allowed inside and children under 15 aren't allowed anywhere.

There's a home accommodation booking agency (☎ (0445) 82 6200).

Hotels The *Knysna Hotel* (☎ (0445) 21151) on Grey St has bed and breakfast for R85/180 a single/double, rising to R155/295 in high season (which is a lot to pay for this place). The *Knysna Protea Hotel* (☎ (0445) 22127), 51 Main Rd, is a typically well-equipped member of the chain, with somewhat characterless rooms for about R190/230. Protea's usual welter of specials, however, sometimes brings prices down to about R160 for a double.

Places to Eat
There are plenty of snack and coffee places in town. Just west of the tourist office, *That Farm Stall* is in a grassy courtyard, away from the traffic noise, and sells snacks as well as produce. A salad is about R10.

At the other end of the main street, *Dulce Chantilly* (upstairs next to the Steak Ranch) looks like a sophisticated coffee shop and it's a nice, airy space. The menu is ambitious but unfortunately the product doesn't match the promise. For example, espresso coffee isn't just filter coffee in a little cup, mayonnaise doth not a salad make, etc. Nevertheless, it's a pleasant spot to hang out and nothing costs over R14.

Originally an old boiler room, the *Pelican Restaurant* in Woodmill Lane Shopping Centre is now a trendy restaurant which looks a bit like an up-market version of a franchised steakhouse, but the food is actually good. Cajun and Southern (USA) dishes are the speciality, plus seafood and even a few choices for vegetarians. Prices are reasonable and there's a good atmosphere.

Also in the Woodmill development, *Tramps Tavern* has an attractive outdoor area where you can get steak and chips for R16.50 and good breakfasts from R6.60.

Popular *Tapas* (☎ (0445) 21927), at Thesen's Jetty, has a fantastic location right beside the lagoon. You can fill up on tapas (Spanish snack dishes) for around R20 and a steak from R17. There's no shortage of Mitchell's beer (R2 a pint during the happy hour on Friday) or Knysna oysters, either. The place has a good atmosphere and sometimes live music – recommended. Upstairs is *Tapas Seafood Tavern* with main courses around R25 to R30. Tapas is open daily, but the Tavern is closed on Monday.

Out at The Heads and in a beautiful setting, *Cranzgot's* has a coffee shop with breakfast from R10 and inexpensive snacks and lunches. Cranzgot's is also a restaurant with pasta from R20, pizza from R22 and steaks from R30. There's a bar as well.

Entertainment
In the bar behind the Pelican Restaurant, bands play some nights after 10 pm. Readers recommend Tin Roof Blues on the main street, which has live music and a good

WESTERN CAPE PROVINCE

balcony. Tapas sometimes has live music (see Places to Eat).

Getting There & Away

Bus Translux stops on Main Rd at the Toyota dealer, Intercape stops on Main Rd at the Shell service station and Chilwans stops on Main Rd at the Engen service station. As usual, for travel between nearby towns on the Garden Route you're better off looking for a minibus taxi than travelling with the major buslines, which are very expensive on short sectors.

Intercape Mainliner and Translux stop here on their Cape Town to Port Elizabeth services. Intercape fares include: Cape Town, R85; Mossel Bay, R55; George, R50; Plettenberg Bay, R35; and Port Elizabeth, R55. Translux is more expensive, although some of its services run via Oudtshoorn. See Cape Town, Getting There & Away for more information.

Chilwans Bus Services (☎ (021) 54 2506, 905 3910) has a useful (if slow and not luxurious) service between Cape Town and Port Elizabeth. From Knysna to Cape Town costs just R65. This service departs from Cape Town on Friday and returns on Sunday.

Translux runs from Knysna to Jo'burg/Pretoria twice weekly. See the Garden Route Getting There & Away section for fares and times.

Train The historic *Outeniqua Choo-Tjoe* steam train runs between Knysna and George every day except Sunday and public holidays. See George, Getting There & Away for details.

Minibus Taxi Most taxis stop in the car parks behind Bloch's supermarket. A taxi to Plettenberg Bay costs R6. Taxis depart for Cape Town in the morning from about 7.30 am and cost R65. See Cape Town, Getting There & Away for information on a door-to-door service on the Garden Route.

Car & Motorbike If you're heading to Oudtshoorn, consider going via Prince Alfred Pass and Uniondale.

Getting Around

Even if you have a car, the traffic jams on the main street (much worse than anything you'll find in Cape Town) will make you look for alternative transport.

Tuk-tuks (☎ (0445) 82 5878) zip around town and are a lot less hassle. There are some set fares from town, including: Tapas Jetty, R5 per person (R3 for more than three people); the Oyster farm R5 (R3); The Heads, R10 (R6); and Leisure Isle beach, R10 (R6). Return fares are double. To the beach at Brenton-on-Sea costs about R30 and a town tour (not a bad idea) costs from R15.

Knysna Cycleworks (☎ (0445) 82 5153), 18A Spring St, is one of several places renting good bikes.

AROUND KNYSNA
Prince Alfred's Pass

The Knysna to Avontour road climbs through the Outeniqua range via the beautiful Prince Alfred's Pass. Prince Alfred's is regarded by some as being even better than the superb Swartberg. Needless to say it was built by a Bain, in this case Thomas, in the 1860s.

Outside Knysna, the road passes through pine and eucalypt plantations and indigenous forest (the home of Knysna's elephants). There are few really steep sections, but the pass does reach a height of over 1000 metres, and there are magnificent views to the north before the road winds into the Langkloof Valley.

Belvidere

Belvidere, on the road to Brenton-on-Sea, is notable for a Norman-style church built in the 1850s for a homesick Englishman. It sounds weird, but it is a beautiful sight. Captain Duthie, who built the church, also built a Georgian house nearby. *Belvidere House* (☎ (0445) 87 1055), as it is known, has been transformed into the main building for a group of surrounding guest cottages. The rest of the large village is also very pretty (and rich), but there are so many signs telling you not to do things that visiting isn't much fun.

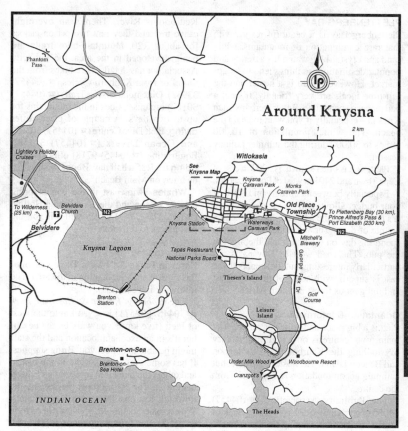

Around Knysna

0   1   2 km

Phantom Pass

Lightley's Holiday Cruises

To Wilderness (25 km)

Belvidere Church

N2

Belvidere

Knysna Lagoon

Witlokasia

See Knysna Map

Knysna Caravan Park

Monks Caravan Park

Old Place Township

To Plettenberg Bay (30 km), Prince Alfred's Pass & Port Elizabeth (230 km)

Knysna Station

Waterways Caravan Park

Mitchell's Brewery

Tapas Restaurant
National Parks Board

Thesen's Island

Brenton Station

George Rex Dr

Golf Course

Leisure Island

Brenton-on-Sea

Brenton-on-Sea Hotel

Under Milk Wood

Cranzgot's

Woodbourne Resort

INDIAN OCEAN

The Heads

Brenton-on-Sea

Brenton-on-Sea overlooks a magnificent eight-km long beach, stretching all the way from the west head of Knysna Lagoon to Buffalo Bay. Fynbos-covered hills drop to white sand and blue sea.

The *Brenton-on-Sea Hotel* (☎ (0445) 81 0081) has a fantastic location right on the beach. Rooms overlook the sea and cost from R145/230 a single/double with breakfast, rising to R215/330 for the most expensive rooms. There are also some excellent chalets with two bedrooms and a lounge, kitchenette and bathroom from R180 a double. In summer they cost R460 for up to six people.

Noetzie

Not to be outdone by Captain Duthie, another romantic English family built holiday homes in a mock-castle style. The homes are still privately owned, and are not as bad as you might imagine. Their location is certainly fine. Noetzie has a lovely surf beach (spacious but dangerous) and a sheltered lagoon running through a forested gorge. It's a steep trail between the car park and the beach.

PLETTENBERG BAY

Plettenberg Bay is a beautiful resort, with that rare combination of mountains, white sand and crystal-blue water. It's a trendy and popular destination, so things tend to be up-market. However, there is a hostel and the full-time locals are very friendly. It's not a bad place to spend time. Better, perhaps, than Knysna – especially if you want to be on the beach. The winter population of 10,000 jumps to 50,000 during the summer holiday season.

Plett, as it is often known, is 520 km east of Cape Town and 240 km west of Port Elizabeth.

Especially between February and April, if your budget allows and the weather is kind, it's hard to imagine a better place to spend a couple of days. The main idea at Plett is to spend the day on the beach and the night in the pub. The road west to Knysna is not particularly interesting, but the scenery to the east is superb, with some of the best coast and indigenous forest in South Africa.

Orientation & Information

Plett is a big place and quite spread out. The main town centre is on a high promontory overlooking the Keurbooms River lagoon and Beacon Island. The hostel is up here, but camping accommodation is some way from the centre.

The Publicity Association (☎ (04457) 34065), on Kloof St, has a great deal of useful information, ranging from accommodation to a craft trail and walks in the surrounding hills and reserves. They're open from 9 am to 12.30 pm Monday to Friday and from 10 am to noon on Saturday. Make sure you pick up the *Plettenberg Bay to Tsitsikamma* booklet.

Activities

There's a lot to do in Plett. Backpackers will find that the hostel can organise most things, often at a discount.

For information on the surrounding **nature reserves** and walks through the reserves contact the Chief Directorate, Nature & Environmental Conservation (☎ (04457) 32125), 7 Zenon St. Ask them about **canoeing** on the Keurbooms River. There's an overnight canoe trail and they rent two-person canoes for about R20. **Mountain-bike trails** are being developed in the area: the Publicity Association has details. Hire bikes from the hostel or from Kenburn Cycles (☎ (04457) 33932). Outeniqua Biking Trails (☎ (04457) 30167) organises rides in the mountains for up to two days. A couple of places offer **diving**, Plett Dive Centre (☎ (04457) 30303) and Ocean Divers (☎ (04457) 31158). Equitrailing (☎ (0445) 9718) offers **horse-riding** for R85 a half day. Boogie boards can be hired on Main Beach.

Whales swim past in the winter/spring calving season and there's a Whale Hotline (☎ (04457) 33743) which will tell you the best places to see them.

Places to Stay

Caravan Parks & Chalets There is a lot of this type of accommodation in the area. The following is a selection.

The *Robberg Resort & Caravan Park* (☎ (04457) 32571) is seven km to the west of Plett (five km if you walk on the beach) but it's in an excellent location and the staff might be able to collect you. Bring supplies. It has some grassy sites right on the beach, and others that are more sheltered and shady behind it, for R15/22 per person in the low/high season. They also have chalets. With a shared bathroom you can pay as little as R100 for four people, or R110 with attached bathroom. Rates rise considerably around Christmas.

Keurbooms Lagoon Caravan Park (☎ (04457) 4567) is fairly close to town and on the lagoon. Sites (no ground sheets) start at R13 per person. It's quite a large, well-wooded park but there's a 'village' of permanent caravans.

Keurbooms Aventura Resort (☎ (04457) 9309) is on the river, just upstream from the highway. It's a large commercial resort in a very nice setting. Sites for two people range between R39 and R70 in the high season. The cheapest four-person chalets start at R100, and double that in the high season.

East of town off the highway are several

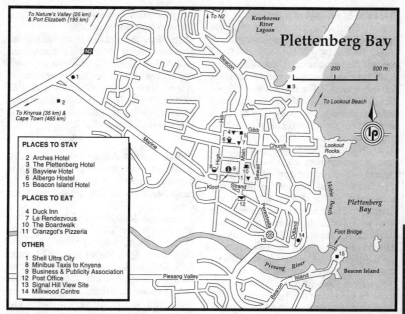

PLACES TO STAY
2 Arches Hotel
3 The Plettenberg Hotel
5 Bayview Hotel
6 Albergo Hostel
15 Beacon Island Hotel

PLACES TO EAT
4 Duck Inn
7 Le Rendezvous
10 The Boardwalk
11 Cranzgot's Pizzeria

OTHER
1 Shell Ultra City
8 Minibus Taxis to Knysna
9 Business & Publicity Association
12 Post Office
13 Signal Hill View Site
14 Milkwood Centre

WESTERN CAPE PROVINCE

more caravan parks, such as *Dune Park Holiday Resort* (☎ (04457) 9606) and *El Remo Chalets* (☎ (04457) 9814).

Hostel The *Albergo* (☎ (04457) 34434), 8 Church St, is the more attractive sibling of the Albergo in Cape Town, and is a well-run, friendly place that encourages activities in town and in the area. The operators say that they can organise anything. There are dorms for R25.

Hotels The *Bayview Hotel* (☎ (04457) 31961), right in town on the corner of Main and Gibb Sts, is modern, small and pleasant, and has singles/doubles with breakfast from R90/180. Prices rise steeply to R350 a double (only) in the Christmas/January season.

The hotel that people think of when they think of Plettenberg Bay is the *Beacon Island Hotel* (☎ (04457) 31120). It is a multi-storey hotel built on Beacon Island (linked to the

rest of Plett by a causeway). The position is spectacular – the fact that they were allowed to build on the island is amazing. Since they were, however, those with the necessary cash might as well take advantage. It's well-equipped with swimming pools, restaurants and so on. Expect to pay around R350/520 a single/double.

If anything, *The Plettenberg* (☎ (04457) 32030) is even more exclusive and it also has a premier position. Each bedroom has been individually decorated and has stunning views. The food has a high reputation. Singles/doubles are from R250/380.

The *Arches Hotel* (☎ (04457) 32118), near the N2, is an ugly looking place, but it is good value, with a pool and TV in the rooms. In the lowest season (mid-January to the end of September) singles/doubles are R120/190 with breakfast. The most you'll pay is R235/300, from mid-December to early January. During the holiday season there's live music and partying at The Cave.

Places to Stay – out of town

East of Plett, near Tsitsikamma National Park, are a few more places to stay.

Hog Hollow (☎ (04457) 8879) is a farmhouse in the forest offering accommodation. A 2½-hour walk down a forested gorge takes you to the ocean. The dorm is in a big old barn. It's comfortable (if a bit like a barracks) and there are beds, not bunks, for R25. There are also a couple of good chalets for R65/95. Hog Hollow's raison d'être is as a high-quality restaurant, in the main house. If you have a minimum of eight people they'll prepare an individual menu for you. Otherwise, backpackers can join in the family dinner for R30. The staff can often pick you up from Plett but it might be advisable to give them some notice. If you're driving, travel 16 km east on the N2 from the Trek service station at Plett, and take the Askop turn-off (on the right if you're coming from Plett). The farm is a km or so along this road.

Woodgate Farm (☎ (04457) 8690) is also about 16 km east of the Trek station on the N2 at Plett, but you turn left off the highway at the Redford sign. After two km you come to signboards; turn left and the farm is about one km further on. It's a small working farm with simple accommodation and friendly hosts who'll drive you to trailheads.

Forest Hall (☎ (04457) 8869) is a historic country house set in 220 hectares of forest adjoining a beach. It's now a guesthouse with rates starting at about R200 per person. The turn-off the N2 is just east of The Crags.

Places to Eat

A popular place to hang out, with locals, surfies and visitors, is *The Boardwalk*. It's an excellent café with fish and chips for R16, soup (eg spinach) for R8, and calamari R10. Other main courses start around R20 and there are plenty of snacks.

There are a couple of places in the Milkwood Centre on Hopwood St, behind Hobie Beach. *Sacha's Seafood Steaks* (☎ (04457) 32685) has appalling d,or but respectable, mid-priced food. My choice, however, is *Whaler's Tavern* literally right on the beach

– a great place for breakfast but also open late with tapas and meals.

There are more places in the main shopping area, along Main Rd. *Le Rendezvous* (☎ (04457) 31390) is a long-running survivor specialising in seafood at reasonable prices, and *Kelly's Restaurant & Pub* (☎ (04457) 33077) is a little cheaper. *Cranzgot's Pizzeria* has excellent pizzas for around R22 and steaks for around R30.

Getting There & Away

Bus Buses heading east stop on the highway across from the Shell Ultra City, those heading west stop at the Shell Ultra City.

Intercape Mainliner and Translux stop here on their services from Cape Town to Port Elizabeth. Intercape fares include: Cape Town, R90; Mossel Bay, R60; George, R55; Knysna, R35 (it's just R6 by minibus taxi); and Port Elizabeth, R50. Translux is more expensive, although some of its services run via Oudtshoorn. See Cape Town, Getting There & Away, for more information.

Chilwans Bus Services (☎ (021) 54 2506, 905 3910) runs a slow bus from Cape Town to Port Elizabeth via the Garden Route. It leaves Cape Town on Friday and returns on Sunday.

Minibus Taxi Most long-distance taxis stop at the Shell Ultra City on the highway. See Getting There & Away in the Cape Town section for information on a door-to-door service running the Garden Route. However, it's a long way to Plett from Cape Town, and by minibus taxi the journey can take hours longer than the bus.

Taxis to Knysna (R6) leave from the corner of Kloof and High Sts.

Getting Around

Bus Rides of Plettenberg Bay (☎ (04457) 33272) operates various day tours in the region, but will also pick up and drop off hikers at reasonable rates.

AROUND PLETTENBERG BAY

The best-known reserve near Plett is the Tsitsikamma National Park. It now falls into Eastern Cape Province – see that chapter.

Robberg Nature & Marine Reserve

The reserve (☎ (04457) 32125) is nine km south-east of Plett. From Piesang Valley follow the airport road until you see signs to the reserve. The reserve protects a four-km-long peninsula with a rugged coastline of cliffs and rocks. There's a circular walk approximately 11 km in length, with rich intertidal marine life and coastal-dune fynbos. The peninsula acts as a sort of marine speed bump to larger sea life, with mammals and fish spending time here before moving.

Keurbooms Nature Reserve

The reserve is seven km north-east of Plett. It covers a hilly plateau with steep cliffs and banks above the Keurbooms River. Fynbos covers the plateaus, and there's forest on the steeper slopes. There is a short one-hour hiking trail along the river banks. A canoe trail goes further up the river to an overnight hut that sleeps 12 people. The reserve is open from 6 am to 6 pm, but visitors must get a permit from the directorate office in Plett.

Bloukrans Pass

The road from Plett to Knysna cuts across a fairly uninteresting plateau that is dominated by pine and eucalypt plantations. The road to the east of Plett, however, is brilliant. Don't take the toll road, but turn off to Nature's Valley and the Bloukrans Pass. It's a beautiful drive across a plain with plenty of surviving fynbos, but the road plunges in and out of deep gorges that have been cut by rivers running out to sea.

Nature's Valley and Bloukrans Pass are surrounded by beautiful indigenous forests that make you realise what terrible devastation there has been in the region. The forests are dominated by the beautiful Outeniqua yellowwood, a large, classically proportioned tree with a scaly trunk. There's a great view of the N2 bridge and numerous attractive picnic spots. Allow plenty of time.

Around Plettenberg Bay

The Little Karoo

The Little (or Klein) Karoo, is a region bordered in the south by the Outeniqua and Langeberg ranges, and in the north by the Swartberg range about 60 km away. It runs east from Montagu for about 300 km to Uniondale, and is more fertile and better watered than the harsher Great Karoo to the north. The Little Karoo is renowned for ostriches, which thrive in the dry and sunny climate; for wildflowers; and for the spectacular kloofs and passes that cut through the mountains.

Most people travelling between Cape Town and the Garden Route stick to the coast the whole way but there's a very interesting alternative: the Mountain Route running via Worcester, Robertson, Montagu, Barrydale, Ladismith and Calitzdorp, Oudtshoorn and

WESTERN CAPE PROVINCE

George. It's much easier to get between Cape Town and the Garden Route by a direct minibus taxi on this route than along the coast (although it's a gruelling trip), and plenty of bus services run it.

MONTAGU

Montagu, founded in 1851, lies just outside the Breede Valley (described earlier in this chapter) – once you pop through the Kogmanskloof Pass near Robertson you are suddenly in a very different world. It's a good place to go if you want to escape the 20th century and get a brief taste of the Little Karoo.

The town is populated by artists and other refugees, and there's a peaceful old-world atmosphere. There some restored old buildings (23 national monuments), some nice places to stay, and some good opportunities to explore the spectacular surrounding mountains.

Originally, access to the town required numerous crossings of the river until in 1877

Thomas Bain (son of William) completed the small tunnel that is still in use today. The British added a fort on top in 1899.

Orientation & Information

The town is small, so it's easy to get around on foot. There's a particularly good tourist information office (☎ (0234) 41116) that can provide information on accommodation (including a good range of B&Bs and self-catering cottages), walks and hikes. it's open from 8.45 am to 1 pm and 2 to 4.45 pm on weekdays, and from 9 am to noon on Saturday.

Montagu Museum & Joubert House

The Montagu Museum is in the old mission church on Long St, and includes interesting displays and some good examples of antique furniture. Joubert House, a short walk away but also on Long St, is also attached to the museum. It's the oldest house in Montagu (built in 1853) and is restored to its Victorian finery.

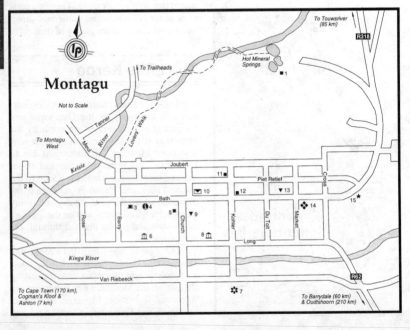

Montagu

Not to Scale

To Touwsriver (85 km)

R318

To Trailheads

Hot Mineral Springs ■1

To Montagu West

Joubert

Piet Retief

Bath

Long

Kinga River

Van Riebeeck

R62

To Cape Town (170 km), Cogman's Kloof & Ashton (7 km)

To Barrydale (60 km) & Oudtshoorn (210 km)

Places to Stay

The *Montagu Country Inn* (☎ (0234) 41115), a pleasant old hotel, has a good backpackers section in an old house behind the pub. You get beds, not bunks, which cost R25 and there's a kitchen. The main hotel charges R80 per person, R95 for bed and breakfast, R100 for dinner and bed, and R120 for dinner, bed and breakfast. There's a pool.

On the edge of town, *Die Bos* (☎ (0234) 42532) is a guest farm catering especially to climbers and horse riders. They have camping for R10 and beds from as low as R15 if you have your own bedding. They also have private rooms with bathrooms from about R60 a double. Horse-riding costs R25 per hour.

Mimosa Lodge (☎ (0234) 42351), on Church St, is a good guesthouse in a beautifully restored old building, with period furniture, a modern swimming pool and excellent food. For this type of accommodation it's a definite bargain at R170/280 per person, including dinner, bed and breakfast.

The *Montagu Rose* (☎ (0234) 42681), 19 Kohler St, is not quite in the same league, but it's perfectly OK with singles/doubles from

about R90/150 with breakfast. It has an outside room with bunk beds (R40) for hikers. The more basic *Blou Pieke Boarding House* (☎ (0234) 41006) on Long St, charges from R35 per person.

The information bureau has details on several B&Bs in private homes from around R60 per person. There are also self-catering farmhouses and cottages that are very good value. You will be able to get something for under R100. For example, the Venters (☎ (0234) 42203) have a farmhouse seven km from town that sleeps six people and costs about R80 during the week and R100 on weekends and in school holidays. They also have an unpowered cottage sleeping five for R55. Right up on top of the Langeberg mountains, Neil Burger (☎ (0234) 41791) has several accommodation options including a stone chalet for R60 a double. Neil runs the popular tractor trips up the mountain – see Robertson in the earlier Breede River Valley section.

Places to Eat

There is a surprising range of choices in town. The *Montagu Country Inn* has inexpensive pub meals such as steak, egg and chips or bangers and mash for R11. There's also a set menu meal in the dining room for R28.

Romano's Italian Restaurant (☎ (0234) 42398) has soup for R3.50, pasta for R13, pizza from R10 to R16, and fillet steak for R25. Locals say that the best pizzas are to be found at *Da Vinci's Pizzeria*, out at the Avalon Springs Hotel complex. It's open daily until 11 pm. As well as pizzas (from R9.50 to R27) they have pasta (from R10 for a half serve), light meals (around R12) and standard dishes in the low R20s.

Something Special is a craft/coffee shop in a beautiful old Cape Dutch building. There are footpath tables, but if you sit inside you're more likely to strike up a conversation with the friendly and knowledgeable owners. Cake or quiche costs about R4 and there are good salads (from R6.50) and light meals. It's open during the day, every day.

PLACES TO STAY

1	Avalon Springs Hotel & Montagu Springs Holiday Resort
2	Die Bos
5	Mimosa Lodge
11	Montagu Rose Guesthouse
12	Montagu Country Inn

PLACES TO EAT

3	Something Special
9	Romano's Italian Restaurant
13	The Inn Place

OTHER

4	Tourist Information Office
6	Joubert House (Museum)
7	Nature Garden
8	Montagu Museum
10	Post Office
14	Spar Supermarket (Local Area Minibus Taxis)
15	Police Station (Long Distance Minibus Taxis)

WESTERN CAPE PROVINCE

The Inn Place on Bath St has snacks from R4 and standard main courses from R25.

Getting There & Away

Bus Translux stops here on the run between Cape Town (R85 from Montagu) and Port Elizabeth (R100), as does the much cheaper Chilwans service between Cape Town (R23) and Oudtshoorn (R34). (See Getting There & Away in the following Oudtshoorn entry for more information.) Munnik Coaches (☎ (021) 637 1850) has similarly inexpensive buses between Cape Town and Montagu, departing from Cape Town (railway station upper deck) at 8.30 am on Wednesday, 11.30 am and 5.30 pm on Friday, and 8.30 am on Saturday. Buses return at 12.30 pm on Monday and Thursday and at 1.30 and 6 pm on Friday.

Minibus Taxi Taxis running between Cape Town (R50) and Oudtshoorn (about R35) stop near the police station.

AROUND MONTAGU

Montagu Hot Mineral Springs

The hot springs are on an attractive site about three km from town; they are hot (45°C), radioactive and are renowned for their healing properties.

The spa is very weird phenomenon to find in the Karoo – you just don't expect so many people for a start. The luxurious *Avalon Springs Hotel* (☎ (0234) 41150) has mineral springs, warm pools, massages and gyms. Rates start at R165/260. Near the hotel is a large time-share resort, *Montagu Springs* (☎ (00234) 42235) which has four-person chalets for R120 during the week, rising on weekends and holidays and in December.

Bloupunt Trails & Cogman's Kloof

The information bureau handles bookings for overnight cabins near the start of the Bloupunt and Cogman's Kloof walks. The huts are fairly basic (wood stoves, showers and toilet facilities) but they are cheap. There are also several camp sites.

The Bloupunt Trail is 15 km long and can be walked in six to eight hours; it traverses

Mountain Aloe

ravines and mountain streams, and climbs to 1000 metres. The flora includes proteas, ericas, aloes, gladioli and watsonias. The Cogman's Kloof Trail is 12 km and can be completed in four to six hours; it's not as steep as the Bloupunt Trail. Both trails start within walking distance of the town.

MONTAGU TO OUDTSHOORN

From Montagu, the R62 runs through the upper end of the Little Karoo, through some interesting scenery.

Barrydale is a small town in a small green valley. *Tradouw Guesthouse* (☎ (028) 57 21434), 46 Van Riebeek St, is an informal place in an old trading store and charges from R45 per person, with breakfast. It's also a backpackers hostel.

From Barrydale you can continue east on the R62 to Calitzdorp and Oudtshoorn, or head south on the R324, which runs down through **Tradouw Pass** (where you might see baboons) then branches to run east to Heidelberg and west to down a very pretty valley to Swellendam, passing on the way small villages such as as **Zoar**. The setting is picturesque but there is little work in the area and many people travel to Cape Town, returning to their families on weekends.

Calitzdorp is a little old town where the wineries are famous for their ports. *Calitzdorp Guesthouse & Coffee Shop* (☎ (04437) 33453) on Van Riebeeck St has accommodation and has been recommend. You pay around R100 per person for dinner, bed and breakfast.

OUDTSHOORN

Oudtshoorn is the tourist capital of the Little Karoo. It's a large, sedate place with some nice old buildings. Its claim to fame is the ostrich industry, and the farmlands around Oudtshoorn are thick with the birds. You can watch ostrich races, ride ostriches and buy ostrich biltong, ostrich feathers and ostrich eggs. This sort of entertainment palls fairly quickly, but luckily Oudtshoorn is also well-situated as a base for exploring the very different environments of the Little Karoo, the Garden Route and the Great Karoo. The nearby Swartberg Pass and Seweweekspoort are geological, floral and engineering master-pieces – two of South Africa's scenic highlights.

Orientation & Information

While it's reasonably easy to get around the town centre on foot, nearly all the main 'attractions' are beyond walking distance from town – this means a car, or a willingness to take a tour or hitchhike is virtually essential. The main commercial street is Hogg, to the east of Baron van Rheede. Oudtshoorn is 506 km from Cape Town and 60 km from George.

Oudtshoorn Visitors' Bureau (☎ (04431) 2221) is on Voortrekker near the corner with Baron van Rheede. Ask here about the numerous B&Bs in town, and about tours of the local sights.

Kuriopik, on the corner of Langenhoven Rd and High St, sells ostrich products and curios. Die Oude Pastorie, 43 Baron van Rheede sells crafts and souvenirs.

CP Nel Museum

The museum, on Baron van Rheede, is a striking sandstone building, completed in 1907 at the height of the feather boom. There are extensive displays tracing the history of

---

Oudtshoorn & Ostriches

The Oudtshoorn region was settled in the early 19th century, and the town itself was proclaimed in 1863. Its development is intertwined with the growth of the ostrich-feather industry, which began around 1870. By the turn of the 20th century, feathers were a highly fashionable trimming for ladies' hats and clothing in Europe.

The growers around Oudtshoorn came to be known as feather barons. An average ostrich cock would yield around 10 kg of feathers a year, the feathers were easily transportable and they commanded incredible prices. The industry boomed in the years before WW I, and at its height there were 750,000 ostriches in the region. The feather barons built ostentatious palaces with their profits.

During the war, feathers fell from grace as a fashion item. They have never recovered their former position, yet the industry continues. Feathers are still used by the fashion industry, and in dusters. Skins are used for handbags, shoes and wallets, and the ostrich meat is dried and cured to make biltong.

It is still possible to see signs of the boom years around Oudtshoorn, but many of the palaces have either fallen into ruin or remain in private hands. ■

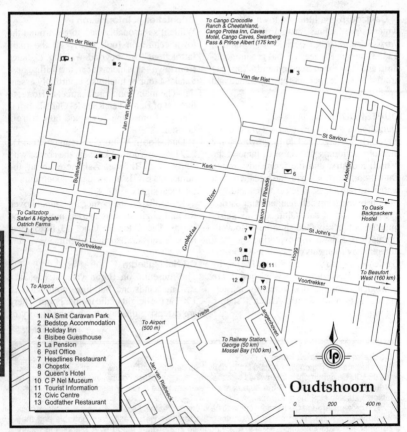

To Cango Crocodile Ranch & Cheetahland, Cango Protea Inn, Caves Motel, Cango Caves, Swartberg Pass & Prince Albert (175 km)

Van der Riet

Van der Riet

St Saviour

Kerk

To Calitzdorp Safari & Highgate Ostrich Farms

Voortrekker

To Airport

To Oasis Backpackers Hostel

St John's

To Beaufort West (160 km)

Voortrekker

To Airport (500 m)

Vrede

To Railway Station, George (50 km) Mossel Bay (100 km)

Oudtshoorn

0   200   400 m

1 NA Smit Caravan Park
2 Bedstop Accommodation
3 Holiday Inn
4 Bisibee Guesthouse
5 La Pension
6 Post Office
7 Headlines Restaurant
8 Chopstix
9 Queen's Hotel
10 C P Nel Museum
11 Tourist Information
12 Civic Centre
13 Godfather Restaurant

the ostrich and the boom, and the history of the Karoo. There is also a reconstructed grocery shop and a synagogue. The museum is open Monday to Saturday from 9 am to 1 pm and 2 to 5 pm, and on Sunday from 2.30 to 5 pm. Entry is free.

Cango Crocodile Ranch & Cheetahland

Three km from the town centre, this is one of the few attractions it is feasible to visit on foot. Crocodiles, cheetahs, lions and leopards are on display. The complex, including a restaurant/bar, is open daily from 8 am to 5 pm, with 45-minute tours starting

every 20 minutes. Entry is R15 for adults and R8 for children.

Ostrich Farms

There are three large ostrich show farms, each open daily and offering a guided tour of about two hours: Safari Ostrich Farm (☎ (0443) 22 7311), six km from town on the Mossel Bay road; Highgate Ostrich Farm (☎ (0443) 22 7115), 10 km from town, signposted turn-off from the Mossel Bay road; and Cango Ostrich Farm (☎ (0443) 22 4623), 14 km from town on the Cango Caves road. Admission is about R12. Ring for details, especially if you are interested in activities like racing.

Some people find the Cango farm the least commercial (and it now has a butterfly farm attached), others say that Highgate is the best.

Cango Caves

These heavily commercialised caves are 30 km from town. There's a restaurant and curio complex and regular tours of what are indisputably impressive caverns. Entry is R12.50 (R6 children); it is open daily and tours are held hourly. As well as walking through the caverns you can choose to venture deeper to caves where you have to scramble and squeeze your way. One reader says that it isn't for the overweight!

There's a restaurant, and takeaways are available. You can change money here, but only on Monday, Wednesday and Friday from 9 am until noon.

If you continue on past the Cango Mountain Resort (on the way to the caves – see Places to Stay) up the dirt road for eight km, you'll come to the pretty **Rust en Vrede Waterfall**, which runs year-round.

Places to Stay – bottom end

The big *NA Smit Caravan Park* (☎ (0443) 22 4152), on Park Rd, is a pleasant, well-maintained place with sites for R25/30 in the low/high season, rondavels sleeping two people for R50/70 and rondavels sleeping three for R55/78. Chalets sleeping six cost R70 for one person, plus R15 for additional people in the low season. In the high season you'll pay R160 for four people. High season is from December to January and Easter.

On the other side of town, the *Kleinplaas Resort* (☎ (0443) 22 5811) has sites from R30/35 in the low/high season, on-site caravans for R60/90, double rooms for R90/110 and four-person chalets from R120/160.

Backpackers' Oasis (☎ (0443) 29 1163), 3 Church St, is in a large and relaxed house with a good-sized yard and a decent pool. They arrange budget tours to the ostrich farms and further afield, and they hire mountain bikes for R20 per day or R5 per hour.

For R40 they'll take you and your bike to the top of Swartberg Pass and you can ride back – that would be an amazing buzz. They also offer caving, climbing and kayaking from R60. Dorm beds are R25, doubles are R60 and camping is R15 per person.

Bedstop Accommodation (☎ (0443) 22 4746), 69 Van der Riet St, isn't in the same league as the guesthouses mentioned below but it's perfectly OK and charges from just R40. *Feather Inn* (☎ (0443) 29 1727), on the corner of Hope and Hogg Sts, is a pub charging R70 per person or R85 with breakfast.

Places to Stay – middle & top end

La Pension (☎ (0443) 29 2445), 169 Church St, is a good place to stay. There's a good-sized pool, a sauna and a large garden. There's a range of accommodation, from standard bed and breakfast to a two-bedroom unit. Prices start at R120 a double and you might find a single for R50 or so.

Next door at 171 Church St, *Bisibee Guesthouse* (☎ (0443) 22 4784) is a little more expensive, from R90/140, but it's excellent. A really pleasant old home in immaculate gardens, under the care of Isab, Fourie – highly recommended. Mrs Fourie's guesthouse was one of the first in Oudtshoorn and it remains one of the best. She plans to open another guesthouse which she says will be even nicer and will offer self-catering. Sounds good.

Other B&Bs and guesthouses include *The Old Parsonage* (☎ (0443) 22 4784), 141 High St, and *Adley House* (☎ (0443) 22 4533), 209 Jan van Riebeeck Rd. There are plenty of others – see the information centre.

The *Queen's Hotel* (☎ (0443) 22 2101), on Baron van Rheede, is an attractive old-style country hotel charging R80 per person, with breakfast. The *Kango Protea Hotel* (☎ (0443) 22 6161), on Baron van Rheede on the outskirts of town, has a swimming pool and guests stay in attractive thatched rondavels. Singles/doubles are R225/250 with breakfast. The *Holiday Inn* (☎ (0443) 22 2201), on the corner of Baron van Rheede and Van der Riet, has the normal swimming pools, bars and luxury you would expect. Singles/doubles are usually R214/238 but there are sometimes specials such as a room sleeping up to four people for R194.

Places to Stay – out of town

The *Cango Mountain Resort* (☎ (0443) 22 4506) is quite a way from the caves of the same name but is in similarly attractive country, with hills and trees and a reservoir/dam. Coming from Oudtshoorn, take the signposted turn-off from the caves road about seven km before the caves; the resort is another three km along. Tent sites are R25/30 in the low/high season. Chalets start at R70 for one person, plus R15 for each additional person (maximum of six people). In the high season the rates are R160 for up to four people, with additional bodies still R15.

On the road to Swartberg Pass, 33 km from Oudtshoorn and a few km north of the Cango Caves turn-off, is *Die Hoek Holiday Resort*, basically a camping ground with sites for R25.

Places to Eat

Most places in town serve ostrich in one form or another. The *Godfather* (☎ (0443) 22 5404), at 61 Voortrekker, is a bar and restaurant open daily for dinner only. As well as standards such as pasta (from R15), pizza (R10 to R36) and steaks (from R28), you can try Springbok steaks (from R22) or exotic dishes such as ostrich antipasto (R27). The menu is interesting and the management enthusiastic, but when I visited the service was not up to scratch.

Headlines (☎ (0443) 22 3434), on Baron van Rheede, is pleasant enough in a kitsch sort of way. Soups are R7, chicken is from R20, and steak from R22. There are also snackier dishes. *Zidago's Restaurant*, a fancy place next to Cheetahland, serves crocodile.

There's a *Chinese takeaway* on Baron van Rheede.

Getting There & Away

Bus Translux runs the mountain route three times a week, departing from Cape Town on Monday, Wednesday and Friday evening, and returning from Port Elizabeth on Tuesday, Thursday and Sunday evening. Fares from Oudtshoorn include: Cape Town, R85; Paarl, R85; Montagu, R40; George, R40; Knysna, R50; Plettenberg Bay, R50; and Port Elizabeth, R80.

Chilwans Bus Services (☎ (021) 54 2506, 905 3910) is much cheaper between Cape Town and Oudtshoorn. Fares include: Cape Town, R50; Paarl, R46; Worcester, R38; Robertson, R36; Montagu, R34; Barrydale, R21; Ladysmith, R14; and Calitzdorp, R8. The bus to Cape Town departs from Oudtshoorn on Sunday at 9 am, and it's a scenic route. Coming from Cape Town the journey is by night.

There are also services to Jo'burg, with Translux and Garden Line Transport (☎ (0441) 74 2823, fax 74 2825).

Garden Line runs between Mossel Bay and Jo'burg twice weekly, via George, Oudtshoorn and Beaufort West. On Tuesday the northbound bus runs via Kimberley, and on Friday it runs via Bloemfontein. Southbound, the Wednesday bus runs via Kimberley, and the Sunday bus via Bloemfontein. Oudtshoorn to Jo'burg costs R155 and takes about 13½ hours. Other fares from Oudtshoorn include: George, R25; Mossel Bay, R40; Beaufort West, R55; Bloemfontein, R130; and Kimberley, R125. Garden Line runs a much cheaper local service to George (R6) departing very early each morning.

Translux stops in Oudtshoorn on its run between Knysna and Jo'burg/Pretoria. Buses to Jo'burg via Kimberley depart on Wednesday and Friday evening; buses travelling via Bloemfontein depart on Sunday, Monday, Tuesday and Thursday evening. From Jo'burg to Knysna via Kimberley, buses depart on Sunday and Thursday evening; buses travelling via Bloemfontein depart on Monday, Tuesday, Wednesday and Friday evening. Fares from Oudtshoorn include: George, R40; Knysna, R50; Bloemfontein, R165; Kimberley, R165; and Jo'burg, R210.

Train The weekly *Southern Cross* between Cape Town and Port Elizabeth stops here on Saturday morning (heading east) and on

Sunday evening (heading west). First/2nd/3rd class fares to Cape Town are R128/69/39; to Port Elizabeth it's R94/51/29.

Minibus Taxi Taxis aren't easy to find – try the supermarket car parks. There are a few services that you can book, such as Rhode Taxis (☎ (0443) 24 1034), Lottering Taxis (☎ (0443) 22 3227) and Steyne Taxis (☎ (0443) 29 2176) which all run to Cape Town for R60. There might not be a daily service.

UNIONDALE

An old fort overlooks Uniondale, and there is a great landscape of flat-topped Karoo koppies to the north. The town is surrounded by rocky hills and wheat fields, pointing to the increased rainfall. Further south of the spectacular Uniondale Port, the narrow Kouga and Kammanassie valleys, known as the Long Kloof, are quite different again. They are only one range from the sea and are green and fertile, with fruit trees and ostrich farms.

The Karoo

Although some of the Karoo is in Western Cape, it doesn't respect provincial boundaries, and sprawls into Eastern and Northern Cape as well. The section of the Karoo around the lovely town of Graaff Reinet is possibly the most interesting – see the Karoo section in the Eastern Cape chapter.

The term Karoo is used to describe most of the interior of the old Cape Province interior, and covers almost one-third of South Africa's total area. It lies on the great South African plateau and is demarcated in the south and west by the coastal mountain ranges, and to the east and north by the mighty Orange River.

The population is sparse; off the main highways you can drive for hours without seeing another car. It is certainly not an untouched wilderness – the San and Khoikhoi who roamed the region and hunted

vast herds of antelope have gone, replaced by farmers and sheep. Despite this, the Karoo feels untouched. There are very few obvious signs of human occupation, apart from the roads snaking over the plains.

Although the main Karoo towns are all linked by public transport, it is best to have a vehicle. There's nothing like stopping in the middle of nowhere, listening to the silence, and wandering off the road into the veld. The road network is excellent; even the unsealed roads are of a high standard.

PRINCE ALBERT

Prince Albert is a beautiful, peaceful little town, dozing on the edge of the Karoo at the foot of the Swartberg Pass. You can easily visit on a day-trip from Oudtshoorn or the coast. I'd prefer to stay in Prince Albert and make a day-trip to Oudtshoorn.

The town was founded in 1762 and there are some interesting examples of Cape Dutch, Victorian and Karoo styles. The real world seems to have passed it by.

Despite being surrounded by very harsh country, the town is green and fertile, thanks to the run-off from the mountains. A system of original water channels runs through town and most houses have a sluice gate which they are entitled to open for a certain number of hours each week. Arriving here after a long, hot drive through the Karoo is wonderful – just seeing trees again is refreshing. Peaches, apricots and grapes are grown.

Ostriches, which are surprisingly fragile creatures in their infancy, are reared here from hatching to three months old because of the kind climate.

The **Fransie Pieaar Museum** is open from 2 to 5 pm on weekdays.

Places to Stay & Eat

The *Prince Albert Hiking Hostel* (☎ (04436) 267) is on the main street, across from the hotel. It had only just opened when I called in but it seems likely that it will be one of the country's better-known hostels. It's worth considering staying here even if you don't normally use hostels. As well as a dorm (R20) there are three double rooms (from

R30 per person). The owners are very experienced hikers who moved to this area fairly recently. Their enthusiasm for their new stamping grounds is infectious. You can arrange to take them as guides on your hikes. They can usually pick you up from Prince Albert Road (the nearest railway station) or Oudtshoorn.

On the south (Swartberg Pass) edge of town, *Dennehof Guesthouse* (☎ (04436) 227) is in one of the area's oldest farmhouses. The guest rooms are in a separate building They are simple but pleasant and guests have their own kitchen. Backpackers

pay R40 per person, including breakfast ingredients, or you can rent the whole house for R65. There are plans to expand into some of the other old farm buildings.

There are several other guesthouses in town and it seems likely that more will open. Try *Mon Plaisir* (☎ (04436) 484), self-contained accommodation in a restored barn.

The *Swartberg Hotel* (☎ (04436) 332), 77 Church St (the main street), is a nice old pub, well cared for, with pleasant, well-equipped rondavels out the back which look onto a lovely garden. Rates include breakfast and start at R95/150 a single/double. There's also

Flat, Hot & Boring?

For some people the Karoo means nothing more than flat hot roads and a long and boring trip between Johannesburg and Cape Town. For others, however, the Karoo is one of the most exhilarating regions in South Africa.

As for being flat, some parts are. But others are mountainous, and you are rarely out of sight of a spectacular range hovering on the horizon. The Swartruggens, the Komsberg, the Hantamsberg, the Nuweveldberg, the Groot Swartberg, the Sneeuberg, the Bankberg, the Baviaanskloofberg, and the Grootwinterhoekberg are just some of the Karoo ranges over 1500 metres (a number top 2000 metres).

The Karoo mountains and hills change colour depending on your proximity, the time of the day, or the weather. They are blue or

black in the distance, but close up they reveal reds, yellows and oranges. They form fantastic shapes, although many take the classic Karoo form – dolerite-capped koppies, which are flat-topped, and sheer sided. There are a number of spectacular mountain passes, particularly around Oudtshoorn.

There are some interesting old towns, richly endowed with distinctive architecture (especially Graaff Reinet). Many towns, however, are isolated backwaters, service centres for the surrounding countryside, but this gives them a quiet charm. They seem far removed from the problems of the 20th century.

The seemingly inhospitable environment also produces a fascinating flora of two main sorts: succulents and woody shrubs. The drier the country (the further west you go) the more succulents there are – and they're weird. There are mesembryanthemums, euphorbias and aloes, among others. The woody shrubs need somewhat easier conditions and include pentzias, daisies and saltbushes.

As for being hot, summer temperatures average 33°C but can go a lot higher. The moment the sun sets, however, the temperature plummets. In winter, frosts are common, although day-time temperatures average a pleasant 18°C. Rain is distributed fairly evenly over the year, the main fall occurring in March and April. The best time to visit is spring or autumn when the weather is fine and the day-time temperatures are in the mid-20s. Since the main rainfall is likely to be in autumn, this is also when the wild flowers are at their best, although in some areas (notably around Prince Albert), September is the best month to view them. ■

simpler accommodation in the renovated hotel for about R180 a double. the hotel's dining room does excellent dinners and next door in the café, good meals and snacks are served during the day.

Sampie se Plaasstal on the main street is a farm-produce stall but much, much better than most. They sell a good range of dried fruit (including *meëbos*, parchment-like sheets), nuts, game meat, biltong and some delicious home-made pastries.

Getting There & Away
Most people visit by driving over one of the area's passes from Oudtshoorn, or from the N1 between Cape Town and Jo'burg. However, if you've come for hiking there's no reason not to take a train, which is better value than the buses.

Bus The nearest Translux and Greyhound stop (on the run between Cape Town and Jo'burg/Pretoria) is at Laingsburg, 120-odd km away, but you can arrange to be dropped at Prince Albert Road, the railway halt. Some places to stay in Prince Albert will collect you from here. With Translux, Cape Town to Laingsburg costs R120; from Jo'burg it's R240.

Train The nearest railway station is Prince Albert Road, 45 km north-west of Prince Albert. The daily *Trans Karoo* between Cape Town and Jo'burg stops here, and some places to stay in Prince Albert will collect you. There isn't much in Prince Albert Road but there is a phone at the pub. First/2nd/3rd class fares from Prince Albert Road to Cape Town are R98/68/41; to Jo'burg they are R238/161/100. The train from Cape Town arrives around 4.30 pm; the train from Jo'burg arrives around 6.30 am.

Minibus Taxi A taxi runs to Oudtshoorn once a week, currently on Friday, for about R18. Some also run to/from Prince Albert Road for R12. A non-shared taxi will cost about R50 for the same trip.

Car & Motorbike Coming from Beaufort West, it's worth leaving the N12 at Seekoegar and then cutting across some bleak Karoo on a dirt road. Otherwise, leave the N1 at Kruidfontein or Prince Albert Road. Coming from Oudtshoorn, you have the choice between taking the Swartberg Pass or the marginally less spectacular and longer route via Meeringspoort.

AROUND PRINCE ALBERT
Prince Albert is a good base for both seeing the Karoo and hiking on the 100-plus km of trails in the Swartberg. Overnight walks have to be booked through the Cape Nature Conservation people (☎ (0443) 29 1739) and cost about R15 per night. **Tierberg Trails** offer a rare opportunity for long walks through the Karoo. The Prince Albert Hiking Hostel is, not surprisingly, an excellent source of hiking information.

There's a good drive east to **Klaarstroom** (another interesting old town) along the foot of the mountains. The road runs along a nice valley, overwhelmed by the Groot Swartberg range, which is cut by more dramatic gullies, clefts and waterfalls. On the R329 between Prince Albert (40 km) and Klaarstroom (10 km), **Remhoogte Hiking Trail** can be walked in about five hours but there is a camping place on the trail.

Meiringspoort, south of Klaarstroom and on the N12 route between Beaufort West and Oudtshoorn, is extraordinary, following a river that cuts right through the Swartberg range. It's not quite in the same class as Swartberg Pass, partly because it's a main road and partly because it's not as deep or as narrow.

The Hell
In a narrow valley in the Swartberg range, is The Hell, or **Gamkaskloof**. The first citizens of Hell were early trekboers, who developed their own dialect. There was no road into Hell until the 1960s and the few goods that the self-sufficient community needed were carried by donkey from Prince Albert. Maybe it's a coincidence, but within 30 years of the roads being built all the farmers had

left. Now the area is part of a nature reserve and there is a camp site.

The road to Hell (which is paved with dirt) turns-off the Swartberg Pass road about 20 km from Prince Albert and extends for another 47 km, passing through **Seweweekspoort Pass**. This is an incredibly narrow gorge with raw, multicoloured rocks and mountains towering above. The unsealed road follows a stream and there are several good spots to picnic. You have to return the same way, but this is not a hardship. If pos-

sible, allow yourself the best part of a day to explore (or try hiking from Prince Albert).

BEAUFORT WEST

Beaufort West is the archetypal stopover town, although it also serves as an important centre for the Karoo. There must be more service stations here per head than in any other town in South Africa. It is not completely lacking in appeal, but most people will be happy to snatch a cold drink, a few litres of petrol and perhaps a sleep. The Karoo National Park, 12 km south of the town, is definitely worth visiting and also has excellent accommodation.

In summer Beaufort West is a sluice gate in the torrent of South Africans heading for the coast. Accommodation is booked out and prices rise. Maybe because this is such a travel crossroads, there are a lot of kids begging aggressively.

Places to Stay & Eat

The *Beaufort West Caravan Park* (☎ (0201) 2800), at the south end of Donkin St, the main street, is an ex-municipal park, now privatised. It would do. They have on-site caravans for hire, at R16/27.50, with possible deals for backpackers. Tent sites are R27. If you do have camping equipment and transport, however, go to the Karoo National Park.

The best deal in town is at *Donkin House* (☎ (0201) 4287), 14 Donkin St (north end). You get old-fashioned hospitality and homely rooms. There's a TV lounge, swimming pool and braai facilities. Rooms are just R35/64/90 for singles/doubles/triples or R30/57/89 with shared bath. The same people also run *Vine Lodge*, a backpackers hostel nearby at 23 Meintjies St, where you'll pay R22 if you are a YHA member. If not it's R32, the same rate that you would pay in a private room. The advantage of Vine Lodge is that it's one of the few places to stay that isn't on the main street and thus it escapes most of the noise from the trucks that roll through all night.

Karoo Lodge (☎ (0201) 3877), on the corner of Donkin and Kerk Sts, offers simple overnight accommodation in a big old pub.

Swartberg Pass

Swartberg Pass, a route between the Little Karoo and the Karoo, is arguably the most spectacular in the country. It's 24 km long and reaches nearly 1600 metres in height; it's another Thomas Bain pass, built between 1881 and 1888.

Proteas, watsonias and other fynbos are prolific. After the summit *(Die Top)*, where there are incredible views over the bleak Karoo and, on the other side, the greenery of the Little Karoo, the road meanders down into a fantastic geology of twisted sedimentary layers. The best picnic sites are on the north side; the gorge narrows and in spring is full of pelargoniums. There are quiet spots where you can sunbathe or swim.

Don't be put off by the warning signs at each end of the pass. It's a fairly easy drive as long as you take it very slowly. The road is narrow, there are very long drops and many of the corners are blind. The pass is sometimes closed after bad storms. ■

Protea

JON MURRAY

LUBA VANGELOVA

JON MURRAY

JON MURRAY

LUBA VANGELOVA

CapeTown, Western Cape Province

A: University of Cape Town
B: Houses of Parliament
C: Sculpture, Victoria & Alfred waterfront
D: Niche at Art Gallery painted in Ndebele style
E: View of Table Mountain

B		
A	C	D
E		

RICHARD EVERIST

RICHARD EVERIST

Top: Eland's Bay, Western Cape Province
Bottom: Swartberg Pass, Western Cape Province

It's reasonable but the atmosphere was a little strange when I called in. Some rooms have air-con. Singles/doubles with shared bath are R45/55, with bath R75/130, including breakfast. There are also a few very spartan budget singles for R35 – as this includes breakfast, it's a very good deal.

Halfway House, on Donkin St, is not quite as good as Donkin, but it's clean. Prices jump during the high season, but most of the year there are singles/doubles/triples/quads with bath for R30/55/77/88. In season the minimum charge for a room is R110. If you don't mind sharing a bath there are three bedrooms for R25/50/66, jumping to a minimum of R88 in high season.

The *Oasis Hotel* (☎ (0201) 3221), 66 Donkin St, is a large hotel, ideal for commercial travellers. There's a swimming pool. Single/double rooms range from R60/100 with shared bathroom and from R120/195 with bath. Either rate includes breakfast. They have rooms without baths for R45/60. The *Royal Hotel* (☎ (0201) 3241), on Donkin St, has comfortable singles/doubles with air-con from R95/165, and from R115/195 in December.

Ye Olde Thatch (☎ (0201) 2209), 155 Donkin St, has four guest suites, fairly small and most susceptible to noise from the pool, from R140 to R180 a double. They're stylishly decorated. The restaurant here is definitely worth considering, as it has recently acquired a French cook who is aghast at the plain and meat-laden meals usually eaten in South Africa and plans to set about changing tastes. *Bon chance!* As yet the menu reflects current public opinion, with Karoo chops (R18), mixed grill (R25), fish and chips (R15) and pasta (R15).

Out of town, *Brandwag Guest Farm* (☎ (00201) 2707) has accommodation from R40 per person, with breakfast for R15 and dinner for R20.

Getting There & Away

Bus Beaufort West is a junction for many bus services. Most buses stop on Donkin St outside the Oasis Hotel. The hotel is the Translux agent.

Jo'burg/Cape Town Both Translux and Greyhound stop here on their daily service between Jo'burg/Pretoria and Cape Town. On Monday Greyhound runs via Kimberley, on the other days it runs via Bloemfontein. Translux runs via Kimberley on Sunday and Friday, and via Bloemfontein daily. Fares from Beaufort West with Translux include: Cape Town, R140; Paarl, R130; Bloemfontein, R110; Kimberley, R120; and Jo'burg, R200. Greyhound fares are higher.

Jo'burg/Garden Route Translux also has a service between Jo'burg and Knysna. Northbound buses stop in Beaufort West late on Wednesday and Friday (via Kimberley) and late on Sunday, Monday, Tuesday and Thursday (via Bloemfontein). Southbound buses stop here in the early hours of Monday and Friday (via Kimberley) and in the early hours of Tuesday, Wednesday, Thursday and Saturday (via Bloemfontein). From Beaufort West the fare to Oudtshoorn is R50 and to Mossel Bay, George, or Knysna it's R100.

Garden Line Transport (☎ (0441) 74 2823, fax 74 2825) runs between Mossel Bay and Jo'burg twice weekly, via George, Oudtshoorn and Beaufort West. On Tuesday the northbound bus runs via Kimberley and on Friday it runs via Bloemfontein. Both services depart from Beaufort West at about 9.30 pm. Southbound, the bus that departs from Jo'burg on Wednesday evening runs via Kimberley and the Sunday bus runs via Bloemfontein. The Kimberley bus departs from Beaufort West at about 5 am the following day and the Bloemfontein bus about half an hour later. Fares from Beaufort West include: Mossel Bay, R85; George, R75; Oudtshoorn, R55; Bloemfontein, R95; Kimberley, R95; and Jo'burg, R155.

Cape Town/Eastern Cape/Durban City to City (a Translux subsidiary) runs daily between Cape Town to Umtata (R105 from Beaufort West). It's a useful route, with stops including Graaff Reinet (R35), Cradock (R75) and Queenstown (R85). Transtate's cheaper service between Cape Town and Umtata also stops here. The eastward bus leaves Cape Town on Sunday and the westward bus leaves Umtata on Thursday.

Translux runs between Cape Town and East London (R140 from Beaufort West) four days a week (Sunday, Tuesday, Thursday and Friday eastbound; Sunday, Monday, Wednesday and Friday westbound). Stops and fares include: Graaff Reinet, R95; Cradock R95; Queenstown, R125; and King William's Town, R140. Most days there's also a Translux service between Cape Town and Durban (R225 from Beaufort West) that runs a roundabout route through Bloemfontein (R110) and the Orange Free State highlands.

Train The railway station is on Kerk St. The *Trans Karoo* stops here on the daily journey between Cape Town and Jo'burg. The southbound train arrives in Beaufort West at 4.23 am and the northbound at 6.05 pm. From Beaufort West to Cape Town 1st/2nd/3rd-class tickets are R122/84/51; from Beaufort West to Jo'burg they are R214/145/90.

Minibus Taxi Most taxis stop at the BP station at the south end of Donkin St, not far from the caravan park. Destinations include Cape Town (R70), Oudtshoorn (R35) and King William's Town (R65).

KAROO NATIONAL PARK

Although the Karoo dominates the South African plateau, it was for many years neglected by conservationists. People are now beginning to appreciate the landscapes and the fragile ecosystems and extraordinary flora that have evolved to survive the region's climatic extremes.

The Karoo National Park was proclaimed in 1979 and covers 33,000 hectares of impressive Karoo landscapes and representative flora. The plains carry a variety of short shrubs, with well-wooded dry watercourses and mountain grasslands at higher elevations.

The park has 61 species of mammal, the most common of which are dassies and bat-eared foxes. The antelope population is small, but some species have been reintroduced and their numbers are growing. These include springboks, kudu, gemsboks, red hartebeests, reedbucks and rheboks. Mountain zebras have also been reintroduced.

Information

The entrance gates are open from 5 am to 10 pm and the main reception desk is open from 7.30 am to 8 pm. Day visitors are charged R10 per vehicle. There's a shop and à la carte restaurant. There are two short nature trails and an 11-km day walk, in addition to the Springbok Hiking Trail.

Springbok Hiking Trail

The Springbok Trail goes through a variety of habitats and altitudes and provides magnificent views. A maximum of 12 people are permitted on the trail which is now open all year, on the premise that if people are crazy enough to hike in a Karoo summer it's probably best to let them. It's a three-day, two-night trail. Hikers stay overnight in huts, and the cost is R50 per person.

4WD Trail

If you have your own vehicle you can take along a guide (who supplies lunch) for a tour of the park. This costs R30 per person (minimum R60). You can also go in a Parks Board vehicle for R60 per person (minimum R240). Overnight tours, including guide, supper and breakfast, cost from R50 per person (minimum R100) in your vehicle, or from R170 (minimum R340) in their vehicle.

Places to Stay

Bookings should be made through the national park offices in Pretoria or Cape Town. The cottages and chalets are all new and of a high standard – they are fully equipped and air-conditioned. Six-bed cottages cost R280 for up to four plus R40 for extra people. Three-bed chalets cost R160 for two, R222 for three. There's a very pleasant caravan park, with sites for R13 plus R6 per person.

MATJIESFONTEIN

Matjiesfontein (the 'j' is silent) is a small railway siding that has remained virtually unchanged for 100 years, its impressive buildings incongruous in the bleak Karoo landscape. People stop here on their way to/from Jo'burg – if not for a night, at least for a cup of coffee.

A night in the hotel would be worth a stopover on the train trip between Jo'burg and Cape Town, although 24 hours in Matjiesfontein might be a bit long unless you have a good book. You could take the train here from Cape Town (arriving at 2.46 pm), stay the night and catch the 8.25 am train back again next day. It's a 5½-hour trip.

The developer of the hotel and the other establishments was one Jimmy Logan, who once ran every railway refreshment room between the Cape and Bulawayo. Matjiesfontein was his home base, and the hotel and other accommodation, together with the dry climate, attracted wealthy people as a health resort.

As well as the attractive old buildings there's a museum (R2) in the railway station that's worth a look.

Places to Stay & Eat

The very grand *Lord Milner Hotel* (☎ (02372) and ask for 5203) is a period piece with rooms from R125/190 with breakfast. One of the grander rooms has twin baths! Dinner costs R42 per person but men must wear a jacket and tie (except on Sunday, for some reason). The same people also run a nearby (everything in this village is 'nearby') renovated *boarding house* with rooms at R102/150 with breakfast.

There's a coffee shop just down the street with coffee for R2.10, generous toasted sandwiches for R6 and Karoo breakfasts (served until 11 am) for R8.75.

Getting There & Away

Train The daily *Trans Karoo* between Cape Town and Jo'burg stops here. Fares to Jo'burg in 1st/2nd/3rd class are R261/177/110; to Cape Town they're just R75/52/31.

West Coast & Swartland

The region immediately to the north of Cape Town that straddles the N7 highway is often further divided into two contiguous regions – the West Coast and Swartland.

Around 60 million years ago the coastal zone west of the N7 was a sandy unproductive area of unstable dunes that were left behind when the sea retreated. The Swartland, both sides of the N7 and east to the foot of the mountains, is a rich agricultural area of rolling plains.

The barren western coastal strip has been transformed into productive country, thanks to the stabilisation of the dunes by the Australian Port Jackson wattle, with its very distinctive golden flowers. But the wattle now poses a major threat to the indigenous flora, which in this region belongs to the Cape floral kingdom often described as fynbos. The fynbos is one of the region's major attractions, especially in late winter and early spring when wildflowers carpet the remaining coastal dunes (especially in the West Coast National Park).

The coast, because of its relative barrenness and cold water, has only recently been discovered by Capetonian holiday-makers. These people were attracted by the distinctive, though somewhat bleak, landscape and the fact that it was relatively undeveloped. There are now several popular resorts, including Yzerfontein and Langebaan. There are also important fishing towns (Saldanha, St Helena Bay and Lambert's Bay) whose fleets exploit the rich fishing in the cold, nutrient-rich Benguela current. For reasons that are not understood, however, the fishing declined seriously recently.

The Swartland (or black land) was, it is now believed, named after the dark foliage of the distinctive *renosterbus* scrub that covered the plains. The soil is not black, but it is fertile. Combined with the winter rainfall, the soil enables the local farmers to produce over 20% of South Africa's wheat, as well as high-quality wine.

Before white settlement the plains were occupied by the Khoikhoi Grigriqua people, while the mountains were the province of the San. Piketberg is named after the guards (pickets) who were stationed here in the 1670s to protect the Cape Town settlers from Khoisan attacks.

Except for the Cederberg Wilderness, this region need not have a high priority for short-term visitors, although many will travel through on their way to the north. The West Coast does not compare with the south and east coasts. However, the West Coast National Park is worth visiting, especially in August and September (for wild flowers), and Eland's Bay has a beautiful location and fantastic surf.

GETTING THERE & AWAY

Most public transport through this area travels from Cape Town north along the N7, either going all the way to Springbok and Namibia or leaving the N7 and heading through Calvinia to Upington (where you can make connections to Jo'burg).

Getting to the coastal towns west of the N7 isn't easy if you don't have a car. You'll find information about the limited minibus-taxi options under the relevant towns in this section. There is also a daily City to City bus running between Cape Town and Saldanha.

Namakwaland Busdiens (☎ (0251) 21115) has the most useful service on the Cape Town to Springbok (N7) route. It services most of the towns along the highway and run every weekday. The southbound bus leaves Springbok at 7.15 am and arrives at Cape Town railway station at 3 pm. The northbound bus leaves Cape Town at 6.30 am, arriving in Springbok at 2.45 pm. The fare from Springbok to Cape Town is R58 (which is much less than it was a few years ago). Other fares on this route, from Springbok/Cape Town, include: Kamieskroon, R13/58; Vanrhynsdorp, R44/44; Clanwilliam, R46/37; and Citrusdal, R48/33.

Intercape Mainliner's services between Cape Town and Upington and between Cape Town and Windhoek (Namibia) run past Citrusdal and Clanwilliam. Upington buses leave Cape Town at 7 pm on Sunday, Monday, Wednesday and Friday, arriving in Citrusdal (R70 from Cape Town) at 9.30 pm and Clanwilliam (R85) at 10.15 pm. The return bus leaves Upington at 7.45 pm on Tuesday, Thursday, Friday and Sunday, arriving in Clanwilliam (R100 from Upington) at 2.30 am and Citrusdal (R110) at 3.15 am. Windhoek buses leave Cape Town at 2 pm on Sunday, Tuesday, Thursday and Friday, arriving in Citrusdal at 4.15 pm and Clanwilliam at 4.45 pm. The return bus comes through Clanwilliam at 8.30 am on Tuesday, Thursday, Saturday and Monday (45 minutes later at Citrusdal).

City to City, a Translux subsidiary, runs between Cape Town and Upington, departing from Cape Town at 6 pm on Sunday, Thursday and Friday and arriving in Citrusdal (R65 from Cape Town) at 8.55 pm and Clanwilliam (R70) at 9.45 pm. The return bus leaves Upington at 5.30 pm on Sunday, Monday and Friday, arriving in Clanwilliam (R80 from Upington) at 2.10 am and Citrusdal (R85) at 3 am.

YZERFONTEIN

Yzerfontein is a large holiday village on an interesting stretch of coast. It's not green and beautiful, but it definitely has some dramatic views over rugged, rocky coastline. There are many enormous holiday homes, but nothing more than a garage/café in the way of shops and a caravan park (behind the dunes along the seafront). There is a left point for surfers that works on south-east winds and moderate south-westerly swells.

Places to Stay

The *Yzerfontein Caravan Park* (☎ (02245) 211) is a decent park adjacent to the main beach. There are on-site caravans from R30 and bungalows from R72, but tents are not allowed. *Emmaus on Sea* (☎ (02245) 650) is a B&B with good views from the upstairs rooms.

WEST COAST NATIONAL PARK

The West Coast National Park is one of the few large reserves along South Africa's

The Curlew Sandpiper is a small wader found on most bodies of water in summer.

coastline. It covers around 18,000 hectares and runs north from Yzerfontein to just short of Langebaan, surrounding the clear, blue waters of the Langebaan Lagoon. Unfortunately, these waters might not be so clear in the future, as a steel mill is to be built in Saldanha, on the north shore of the lagoon.

The park protects wetlands of international significance and important seabird breeding colonies. In summer it plays host to enormous numbers of migratory wading birds. The most numerically dominant species is the delicate-looking curlew sandpiper (which migrates north from the sub-Arctic in huge flocks), but flamingoes, Cape gannets, crowned cormorants, numerous gull species, and African black oystercatchers are among the hordes. The offshore islands are home to colonies of jackass penguins.

The park's vegetation is predominantly sandveld, which means it is made up of stunted bushes, sedges, and many flowering annuals and succulents. There are some coastal fynbos in the east. The park is famous for its wildflower display, usually between August and October. Several game species

can be seen in the part of the park known as the Postberg section, including a variety of small antelopes, wildebeests, bonteboks and elands.

The rainy season is from May to August. The summer is dry with hot days, sometimes with morning mists. The park is only about 120 km from Cape Town, so it could easily be visited on a day trip if you have a car or motorbike.

Orientation & Information

The park is made up of a peculiar mix of semi-independent zones, some of which are only leased by the national park authorities. It's worth starting a visit at Langebaan so you can get a map and details of where you can go.

The roads in the park are dirt and can be quite heavily corrugated. The park begins seven km south of Langebaan (it's clearly signposted) and it's over 80 km from Langebaan to the northern end of the Postberg section and return; allow yourself plenty of time.

There are information desks at Langebaan Lodge (☎ (02287) 22144), a resort hotel administered by the park authorities, in Langebaan. Book through the Cape Town and Pretoria national park Offices.

LANGEBAAN

Langebaan has been discovered by developers, so although it does have an unusual and rather beautiful location it is rapidly being spoilt. Unfortunately, the negative aspects of development have not been matched by any real vibe or nightlife, or even things to do. The best arguments in its favour are that it overlooks the Langebaan Lagoon – which has excellent sailing and windsurfing – and is the base for the West Coast National Park. The abundance of spring flowers here can reach Namaqualand proportions.

Orientation & Information

Langebaan is quite a sprawling holiday town, with adequate but limited shopping possibilities. Information is available from the library (☎ (02287) 22115) on Bree St.

WESTERN CAPE PROVINCE

Places to Stay & Eat

There are three caravan parks owned and run by the local municipality, but none allow tents. This is to avoid rowdy parties of young Cape Towners, so if you don't look like trouble you might be able to persuade the manager to let you camp. The *Old Caravan Park* (☎ (02287) 2115, after hours 2477) has shady (but sandy) sites right next to the lagoon in the centre of town. The *New Caravan Park*, on Suffren St is also ordinary – a sort of large suburban block, surrounded by houses. The *Seabreeze Caravan Park*, off the road into town and some way from the centre, has bungalows for about R50.

The best place to stay is *Langebaan Lodge* (☎ (02287) 2144/5) which is run by the National Parks Board, although there is also luxurious accommodation at the *Langebaan Country Club*. The lodge is a large complex with great views over the lagoon. There are a couple of eating places, including a café (where you can buy snacks) and a reasonably priced restaurant.

Rooms vary in price depending on the view – it really is worth spending the extra money, although they are all comfortable. With a sea view, singles/doubles are R175/275; with a lagoon view they are R165/250. The cheapest rooms are R126/190. Bookings are recommended, especially during school holidays and weekends, and can be made direct to the lodge or through the Pretoria and Cape Town offices of the National Parks Board.

Die Strandloper (☎ (02281) 51611) is an open-air restaurant on the beach, specialising in seafood. It gets good reviews. You must book, and bring your own alcohol. A reader has recommended *La Taverna*, an Austrian-run place which serves a variety of dishes including ostrich steak.

Getting There & Away

No public transport, not even a minibus taxi, runs to Langebaan. Saldanha is the nearest town with public transport to/from Cape Town.

SALDANHA

Saldanha shares the lagoon with Langebaan. It's a large working town dominated by an enormous iron-ore pier, navy yards and fish-processing factories. Not a pretty place, but if you're missing the sights and sounds of gritty urban life, wandering around Saldanha's harbour area is a balm.

Orientation & Information

The main road into town is Saldanha Rd, but Main Rd (Hoof Weg) is the road that runs from the shopping centre up to the headland, along the back bay. The information centre (☎ (02281) 42088) is off Saldanha Rd, just before you get into town.

Despite the town's industrial aura the bays are pleasant and, because they are sheltered, much warmer than the ocean. Hoedjies Bay, near the town centre, is the most popular for swimming.

Places to Stay

The *Saldanha Holiday Resort* (☎ (02281) 42247) is not special but it is right on the Hoedjies Bay beach. Small four-bed cottages without bedding cost from R44 (R63 on weekends) to R90 depending on the season. Tent sites cost from R26 to R46 – no ground-sheets are allowed.

On Main St, overlooking the back bay, the *Saldanha Protea Hotel* (☎ (02281) 41264) is OK but poor value at R200. The nearby *Hoedjiesbaai Hotel* (☎ (02281) 41271) is better value with rooms for R90 per person including breakfast.

Places to Eat

The Laughing Mussel is a seafood takeaway (with a few tables) at the top end of Main Rd, overlooking the bay. On a sunny day it's a nice place for a snack, from about R6. If you want fish and chips, buy them here. Even the seagulls wouldn't eat the ones I bought at one of the more basic takeaway places. Across the road from the Laughing Mussel is *Mermaid's Restaurant* which has dishes such as cold crayfish and Greek salad for R35. There are also cheaper choices.

The takeaway behind JD's Restaurant on

Main Rd has curry and rice for R6, and indifferent pizzas for about R15.

Getting There & Away
City to City (a Translux subsidiary) runs daily between Cape Town and Saldanha, departing from Cape Town at 5 pm on weekdays and Sunday, at 9 am and 1 pm on Saturday, and also at 9.45 am on Friday. The return trip departs from Saldanha at 6 am daily, except on Sunday when it departs at 12.30 pm.There's an extra bus at 1 pm on Friday and 12.30 pm on Saturday. The fare is R35.

There's at least one taxi a day to Cape Town (about R20), from the Shell service station on Main Rd, near the Hoedjiesbaai Hotel. Local taxis (ask around the Spar supermarket) run north to Vredenburg (R2.50), where you can pick up taxis to Paternoster. It's difficult to make connections with taxis heading further up the coast because most run direct from Cape Town along the N7.

No taxis run all the way to Langebaan, but some do go past the turn-off on the R27.

PATERNOSTER
Paternoster is a sleepy fishing village, yet to be over-run by the Cape Town developers. There's a clutch of fairly basic whitewashed shacks and a pleasant, somewhat eccentric, one-star hotel.

The surrounding countryside is attractive, with an almost English feel. The rolling hills are scattered with strange granitic outcrops that could almost be human-made henges. The **Columbine Nature Reserve** is three km past the town and protects 263 hectares of coastal fynbos around Cape Columbine. There's a small camping and caravan park which is open all year from sunrise to sunset. The wildflowers are spectacular in spring.

Places to Stay
The *Paternoster Hotel* (☎ (022) 752 1703) is an old-style country hotel, virtually on the beachfront, with bed and breakfast for R75 to R90 per person and dinner for R25. Bookings are advised for weekends; it's a popular

venue for people interested in fishing, and the fish and crayfish braais are famous. There's a dinner-dance on Saturday.

The rather windy Columbine Nature Reserve (☎ (022) 752 1718) administered by the Cape Province has basic camping facilities for about R15.

ELAND'S BAY
Depending on which direction you're travelling, Eland's Bay is the first or last really attractive spot on the West Coast. Mountains run down into the sea and there's a large lagoon which is favoured by all sorts of interesting waterbirds (including flamingoes, although they are nomadic and don't hang around). There's very high-quality surf.

Despite the spectacular location, the town is unattractive with the inevitable fish factory and a poverty-stricken coloured population. Still, you don't go to Eland's Bay for the town, you go for the beaches and to explore beautiful **Baboon Point**. The town has basic facilities: a run-down hotel, petrol station and a Standard Bank.

Surfing
This is a goofy-footer's paradise with extremely fast left-point waves working at a range of swell sizes. The bay can hold a very big wave. The main left-point break is virtually in front of the hotel, a bit around towards the crayfish factory – it breaks along a rocky shelf in thick kelp, after south-west winds on a low and incoming tide. There's a right beach break and more lefts on Baboon Point, along the gravel road past the crayfish factory.

Places to Stay
The municipal *caravan park* (☎ (0265) 745) is a basic park right by the beach. It's pretty exposed to the wind. Sites are R25. The *Hotel Eland* (☎ (0265) 640) also overlooks the beach and charges R60/120 a single/ double for bed and breakfast. The 'Europeans Only' sign above the entrance to the bar has been painted out, but only just.

Getting There & Away

On Friday a taxi runs to Cape Town for R40. Ask at the shop in the 'location' on the road into town.

If you're driving south it's worth taking the dirt road that runs along the north bank of the wide and reedy estuary. You can cross over at the hamlet of Rodelinghuys and head south through nice country to the village of Aurora or keep going to join the N7 at Piketberg.

LAMBERT'S BAY

Lambert's Bay is an unattractive fishing town on a bleak stretch of the west coast. It's dominated by fish-processing factories – visions of Cannery Row – and the major attraction is the rookery of Cape gannets. A crayfish festival on the first weekend of November is apparently quite lively.

If you are a bird lover, you may be tempted to visit because you can walk out onto a breakwater to the gannet rookery. Thousands of aggressive birds mill around making a racket and snapping at each other. Their 'nests' are mere scrapes in the clay. The mystery is how the birds manage to find their own particular nest and put up with the appalling smell, although there does seem to be a lot of noisy brawling. There are likely to be only small numbers of birds from May to July. They lay between September and November, and chicks hatch 40 days later.

Claiming Lambert's Bay as a tourist destination takes considerable vision and optimism. The town's development has been particularly unsympathetic to the environment. Eland's Bay, 27 km south, is a completely different story, however, and if you do stay at Eland's you might come in to Lambert's Bay for supplies.

If you're heading north to Doring Bay consider taking the inland route on minor dirt roads which run through some interesting rolling country. Drive slowly and watch for tortoises crossing the road.

Places to Stay

The municipal *caravan park* (☎ (027) 432 2238) to the north of town beside the beach (off Korporasie St) is OK, with sites from R30. There is a long list of rules, including: '3.12, Female servants are allowed on own responsibility but no male or local servants may be brought into the camping area'.

Aside from the caravan park, the only cheapish option is *Laberine Flats* (☎ (027) 432 2232), behind the Laberine supermarket which is on the beachfront road. They're self-contained and modern, and the higher stories have good views – of the gannet colony. Prices start at about R80 a double, rising by increments to reach R150 in December.

The *Marine Protea Hotel* (☎ (027) 432 1126) is a typical example of the genre – a bit tacky, but plenty of comfort. Rooms cost around R200.

Places to Eat

Muisbosskerm (☎ (027) 432 1017), five km south of town, is an open-air seafood restaurant, the original of a growing number on the West Coast. A meal costs around R45 or R60 if you have crayfish. *Bosduifklip* (☎ (027) 432 2735) is another open-air place, four km out of town. Bookings are essential at both places.

PIKETBERG

Piketberg is quite an attractive small town overlooking the beautiful rolling pastoral land at the foot of the Elandskloof range. It's nestled in the lee of a hill, part of the last small range before the coastal plain.

AROUND PIKETBERG

The drive to/from Piketberg is not nearly as bleak and dry as the coastal plain further north, but it is still sandy and flat. **Velddrif** is an unprepossessing town on the edge of a large estuary (there are a couple of hotels). **St Helena Bay** is a lovely sheltered stretch of water, but there is no real beach. There are half a dozen large fish-processing factories and their associated depressing workers' 'locations' at **Stompneusbaai**.

WESTERN CAPE PROVINCE

OLIFANTS RIVER VALLEY
The scenery changes dramatically at the Piekenaarskloof Pass; coming north on the N7 you suddenly overlook the densely populated and intensively cultivated Olifants River valley. The elephant herds that the explorer Jan Danckaert found in 1660 have long gone.

Today the river provides irrigation for acres of grape vines and orange trees, which are beautifully maintained by a huge coloured labour force. The comfortable bungalows of the white farmers are surrounded by green and leafy gardens, masking them from the shanties where the coloureds live. There doesn't even appear to be a token paternalistic effort on behalf of the cheap labour.

On the valley floor are some acclaimed wineries and co-ops (specialising in white wine) and you can get details of a wine route at tourist information centres. The eastern side is largely bounded by the spectacular Cederberg range, which is protected by the extensive Cederberg Wilderness Area. The wilderness area has several great camping grounds and several walks; it's famous for its bizarre rock formations, its fynbos and its San paintings. The whole area is famous for spring wildflowers.

Citrusdal and Clanwilliam, to the south and north of the wilderness area, are the two main towns in the area.

As an alternative to the N7, there's a spectacular road (the R303) between Citrusdal and Ceres (to the south), a great drive through the Cederberg Wilderness Area from Citrusdal to Clanwilliam, and another spectacular route (the R364) between Clanwilliam and Calvinia (to the north-east).

CEDERBERG WILDERNESS AREA
The Cederberg is a rugged mountainous area of valleys and peaks extending roughly north-south for 100 km, pretty well between Citrusdal and Vanrhynsdorp. A good proportion is protected by the 71,000-hectare Cederberg Wilderness Area, which is administered by Cape Nature Conservation. The highest peaks are Sneeuberg (2028 metres)

and Tafelberg (1932 metres), and the area is famous for its weathered sandstone formations, which sometimes take bizarre shapes. San paintings can be seen in some of the caves that have been formed.

The area is also famous for its plant life, which is predominantly mountain fynbos. Once again, spring is the best time to see the wildflowers, although there's plenty of interest at other times of the year. The vegetation varies with altitude, but includes the Clanwilliam cedar (which gives the region its name) and the rare snowball protea. The Clanwilliam cedar only survives in relatively small numbers, growing between 1000 and 1,500 metres, and the snowball protea (now found only in isolated pockets) only grows above the snow line.

There are small populations of baboons, rheboks, klipspringers, grysboks and predators like the caracal, Cape foxes, honey badgers and rarely seen leopards.

Orientation
The Cederberg offers excellent hiking and is divided into three hiking areas of around 24,000 hectares. Each area has a network of trails. However, this is a genuine wilderness area with a genuine wilderness ethos. You are *encouraged* to leave the trails and little information is available on suggested routes. It's up to you to survive on your own. Similarly, you probably won't be given directions to the area's rock art. Work out for yourself where the Khoisan were likely to have lived. The book *Some Views on Rock Paintings in the Cederberg* by Janette Deacon might help.

There is a buffer zone of conserved land between the wilderness area and the farmland, and here more intrusive activities such as mountain biking are allowed. Pick up a copy of the mountain-biking trail map from the Citrusdal information centre.

Information
The rainfall (around 900 mm) falls mainly in winter, and snow is possible from May to the end of September. There's no real season for walking; winter is tough but exhilarating, summer can mean problems with water.

The main office for the area is at Citrusdal, where the Chief Nature Conservator (a very knowledgeable and approachable chap) has his office (☎ (022) 921 2289). There's also an office at the Algeria camping ground.

A permit is required if you want to walk, and the the number of visitors per hiking area is limited to 150 people. The maximum group size is 12 and the minimum is two; three would be safer. Maps (R7) are available at Algeria and the Chief Nature Conservator's office in Citrusdal.

If you want to be certain you will get a permit you are advised to apply well in advance. Outside school holidays and weekends, however, there is a chance you will be able to get one on the spot, but you should definitely at least phone before arriving to make sure. Permits must be booked through the Chief Nature Conservator, Cederberg, Private Bag XI, Citrusdal 7340 (☎ (022) 921 2289 during office hours). Bookings open on 1 February for the March to June period, 1 June for July-October, and 1 October for November-February. The cost is about R3 per person per day.

The entrance to the Algeria Camping Ground closes at 4.30 pm (9 pm on Friday). You won't be allowed in if you arrive late. Permits have to be collected during office hours, so if you're arriving on Friday evening you'll need to make arrangements.

Ask at the Citrusdal information centre whether walks with an extremely experienced guide are yet available.

We spent five days hiking in the Cederberg from Algeria. Great hiking, especially for the budget conscious. After you've paid for your permit the huts are free. The huts are *basic* (by NZ standards) but for zero rand, that's OK. Plenty of places to camp if the huts are full. We only saw two hikers in five days.

Kate Wall (NZ)

Places to Stay

The *Algeria Camping Ground* is in a beautiful spot alongside the Rondegat River, the headwaters of the Olifants River. The grounds are manicured, and shaded by huge blue gums and pines. It's a bit of a shame that they didn't use indigenous trees, but it's still an exceptional camp site. There are swimming holes and lovely spots to picnic beside the river. Camping costs about R20, more in peak periods. Day visitors (not allowed during peak periods) are charged about R3.

There's another excellent camping ground in the *Kliphuis State Forest* near the Pakhuis Pass on the R364, about 15 km north-east of Clanwilliam. There's a small camping ground surrounded by rock walls and cut by a fresh mountain stream. Facilities are fairly spartan, but there's water, toilets and showers. A camp site is about R20.

You'll need to book either of these camp sites in the same way that you book hiking. There are basic huts for hikers in the wilderness area.

See the following Citrusdal and Clanwilliam entries for places to stay outside the Wilderness Area. There's also the *Kromrivier Tourist Park* (☎ (027) 482 2807) and *Sanddrif Cederberg Camping* (☎ (027) 482 2825), on the south-eastern side of the wilderness area.

Getting There & Away

The Cederberg range is about 200 km from Cape Town, accessible from Citrusdal, Clanwilliam and the N7.

There are several roads in to Algeria, and they are all spectacular. It takes about 45 minutes to get from Clanwilliam by car, much longer if you give in to normal human emotion and stop every now and again. Algeria is not signposted from Clanwilliam, but you just follow the road above the dam to the south. Algeria *is* signposted from the N7 and it's only 20 minutes from the main road; there's an amazing collection of plants along the side of the road, including proteas.

We would be interested to hear from anyone who has braved the dust and continued south-east through Sederberg and on to Ceres. One reader who made it as far as Sederberg reports that it is not much more than a big old farm, where you can buy fuel and stay in huts (about R70). There's a good walk from the farm up to the Wolfsberg Crack, about two hours.

Public transport into Algeria is non-existent, so you might want to go to Citrusdal and start walking from there. It should take about two days to walk from Citrusdal to Algeria, entering the Wilderness Area at Boskloof. The Chief Nature Conservator's office in Citrusdal has information on this route.

CITRUSDAL

Citrusdal is a small town which makes a good base for exploring the Cederberg, both the wilderness area and the surrounding mountains which can be equally interesting. There are good sources of information and good farmstay accommodation. The area is embracing the idea of eco-tourism and mountain biking, and hiking trails are being developed. And, of course, there's the prime attraction of wilderness hiking in the Cederberg.

The Sandveldhuisie Country Shop & Tea Room (☎ (022) 921 3210) on Kerk St is also the information centre – and it gets my vote for the friendliest and most helpful one in South Africa. The shop sells cakes, herbs and local art and craft. There's also dried fruit to take on hikes (R10 per kg). Tea, coffee and meals are often available. Expect to pay R10 or less for *waterblommetjie bredie*. Not far away is the office of the Chief Nature Conservator for the Cederberg Wilderness Area.

If you're planning to hike in the Cederberg and don't have transport you can start walking from Citrusdal rather than go to the hassle (and it is a hassle) of finding transport to Algeria, the usual starting point. There was talk of a new outfit starting up, offering guided walks in the Cederberg. If it has, it will be worth considering, as the guide has an outstanding knowledge of the area. The information centre will know the current situation.

Places to Stay

Much of the accommodation is out of town. The exception is the down-to-earth *Cederberg Hotel* (☎ (022) 921 2221), ideal for commercial travellers. Rooms cost R95/170 including breakfast, or R75 per person for bed only.

There are plenty of farmstays in the area,

either B&Bs or self-contained cottages, and some places will collect you from the information centre. These are probably the best options, whatever your budget. You can get dinner, bed and breakfast for as little as R80 per person, or a self-catering cottage for about R100 to R150, with singles around R50. These rates might be slightly negotiable, especially for backpackers.

The Baths (☎ (022) 921 3609) is a health spa about 16 km from Citrusdal. It's a fairly simple place in a pretty wooded gorge and could be a good place to relax for a few days. Expect to pay around R20 for a camp site, from R35 per person for a room and from R120 a double for a flat. Prices rise on weekends. The staff can pick you up from the bus stop on the highway.

Van Meerhoff Lodge (☎ (022) 921 2231) is a fancy new hotel near the top of the Piekenierskloof Pass (on the R44), overlooking Citrusdal. There are rooms (from R130/190), luxury chalets (R300), two restaurants and an outdoor/indoor swimming pool. There's also a shop with a good range of farm produce, nuts and dried fruit.

Getting There & Away

Bus See Getting There & Away at the beginning of the West Coast & Swartland section for details of buses. Intercape stops at the Sonop service station ('country-fresh petrol'!) on the highway; Translux comes into town and stops at the hotel.

Minibus Taxi Taxis to Cape Town and Clanwilliam stop at the Caltex service station. Some Springbok companies will drop you on the N7 near here on the run between Springbok and Cape Town.

Car & Motorbike There's an excellent scenic road (the R303) over Middelburg Pass into the Koue (Cold) Bokkeveld and a beautiful valley on the other side, which is only topped by the Gydo Pass and the view over the Ceres valley (see the Ceres Getting There & Away entry). The back road into the wilderness area is also excellent.

CLANWILLIAM

Clanwilliam is a popular weekend resort. The attraction is the town itself (which has some nice examples of Cape Dutch architecture and a pleasant main street), the proximity to the Cederberg and, most importantly for domestic tourists, the Clanwilliam Dam which attracts a hoard of noisy waterskiers. If you're in this part of the world, by all means use the Clanwilliam shops, then head to the mountains. There are some beautiful roads into the Cederberg and a great drive over the Pakhuis Pass to Calvinia (see the Calvinia entry in the Northern Cape chapter).

Information

The information centre (☎ (027) 482 2024) is in the old jail at the top end of the main street. It's open on weekdays and Saturday morning, and every day in flower season.

Places to Stay & Eat

If you have a tent or van, the best spot to stay near Clanwilliam is the *Kliphuis State Forest* about 30 minutes away just before the Pakhuis Pass on the R364 – see the earlier Cederberg Wilderness Area entry.

The *Clanwilliam Dam Municipal Caravan Park & Chalets* (☎ (027) 482 1933) overlooks the water skiing action; it's on the other side of the dam from the N7. Travellers arriving here after weeks in Namibia are pleased to be able to pitch their tents on lush, grassy sites. One/two people are charged R14/18.50. The chalets are very nice, but you would have to book ahead for the busy periods – school holidays and weekends. Chalets sleeping up to six people start at R94 for two people in the lowest season and start at R125/148 a single/double in the highest.

The information centre can put you in touch with B&Bs charging from R45 per person, such as *Mrs Laubser's* (☎ (027) 482 1114). There are also farmstays in the area.

The comfortable and popular *Strassberger's Hotel Clanwilliam* (☎ (027) 482 1101) is a country pub which has been renovated to a high standard. It is good value at R96/176, including breakfast. There's a pool. They also have an annexe in a delicensed pub nearby where rooms cost R68 per person, with breakfast. This isn't such good value.

The Hotel Clanwilliam has an à la carte restaurant, *Reinhold's*, in a building across the road, but the hotel dining room is cheaper and quite flash enough. A five-course set-menu dinner costs about R28.

Getting There & Away

Bus See Getting There & Away at the beginning of the West Coast & Swartland section. All the buses that go through Citrusdal also come through Clanwilliam. It's about 45 minutes between the two towns.

Minibus Taxi Taxis running between Springbok and Cape Town come through Clanwilliam – see the Springbok section in

---

Rooibos Tea

Rooibos 'tea' is made from the leaves of the *Aspalathus linearis* plant, grown in the Cederberg region of Western Cape Province. 'Malay' slaves first discovered that the plant could be used to make a beverage, although it was not until this century that a Russian immigrant, Benjamin Ginsberg, introduced it to the wider community, and it didn't become a cash crop until the 1930s. Despite this, some brands feature trek wagons and other icons of old Afrikanerdom, and the packets make good souvenirs.

Rooibos, literally 'red bush', is a red-coloured tea with a distinctive aroma. It contains no caffeine and much less tannin than normal tea. This is probably its major health benefit, although it's claimed to have others, including minute amounts of minerals such as iron, copper and magnesium. It's also a great thirst quencher, drunk straight or with lemon or milk.

You can visit the Rooibos Tea Natural Products works (☎(027) 482 2155), near Clanwilliam, by arrangement. ∎

the Northern Cape chapter for some phone numbers. From Clanwilliam the fare to Cape Town or Springbok is about R35. Heading to Cape Town, taxis pick up passengers near the Clanwilliam Post Office at about 11 am.

VANRHYNSDORP

Vanrhynsdorp lies in the shadow of the distinctive Matzikamaberg mountain in the desolate Knersvlakte, the valley of the Sout (Salt) River. It's an archetypal country town – pretty dull, really. The surrounding country is very dry, but framed by dramatic mountains. However, like much of the West Coast, it can explode into colour after decent rains.

The town itself, with the exception of a couple of old buildings, is nothing special. There are the basic necessities of life – a bank, a pub, a post office and a pub. The information counter (☎ (02727) 91552) in the old town hall has a good map of the immediate region showing interesting drives and walks around the plateau of the Matzikamaberg, and they can advise about the local wildflowers.

Places to Stay & Eat

The fairly basic *Vanrhynsdorp Caravan Park* (☎(002327) 91287) has plenty of lawn. Rooms are R40, and a camp site is R23.

The Vanrhynsdorp Hotel has changed its name to *Namaqualand Country Lodge* (☎ (02727) 91633) but it's still an old country pub with plain but acceptable rooms. Rooms cost R70 per person or R110 with dinner and breakfast. Bought separately, breakfast costs R15, lunch is R18 and dinner is R25.

The *Van Rhyn Guest House* (☎ (02727) 91429) is in a nice old house. It would be good for groups and for those who are self-sufficient – it's a bit sparse and lonely. It is preferable to book in advance, as there is no one living at the property itself. On the other side of the town centre, not far from the town hall, there's another B&B, *Lombard Guesthouse* (☎ (02727) 91424).

The enormous Shell service station has a *Motorstop Restaurant* and takeaway food.

Getting There & Away

Bus See Getting There & Away at the beginning of the West Coast & Swartland section for details of buses. All the buses that go through Citrusdal also come through Vanrhynsdorp (which is the turn-off for Calvinia and Upington). It's about 1½ hours between Vanrhynsdorp and Clanwilliam.

AROUND VANRHYNSDORP

The area around Unionskraal, about 10 km to the south-east, is particularly renowned for flowers, and there are some interesting drives and walks around the plateau of the Matzikamaberg and Gifberg ranges.

There is a stunning road between Vanrhynsdorp and Calvinia. Starting at Vanrhynsdorp in the Knersvlakte, which is usually about as inhospitable as you can imagine, you climb the Vanrhyns Pass into a totally different world.

You will discover numerous references to the road-building Bains. Andrew built a number of famous passes and roads in the 1850s, although he had no formal training as an engineer. In the latter half of the 19th century he was succeeded by his son Thomas, who built a further 25 passes in the southern and western Cape. Vanrhyns Pass is one of Thomas's engineering masterpieces.

In spring you can go from virtual desert, to pleasant green wheat fields in a km or so as the crow flies. There are great views from the top of the pass. It soon starts to dry off again as you head to Calvinia, but there can be superb flowers and the countryside is majestic, with mountains ringing the plateau. See the Around Calvinia entry in the Northern Cape chapter for more information.

VREDENDAL

Vredendal is quite a large and modern town with a good range of shops servicing the farmers from the surrounding irrigation country. The 'Nie-Blankes' (non-whites) sign above one of the bar doors has been lightly painted over.

STRANDFONTEIN

Strandfontein is definitely a holiday town, but it's hard to understand its appeal. Like the rest of the West Coast, it's dry, bleak and treeless. Maybe you have to be a sheep farmer from the Karoo to see the magic. The beach is ordinary but there are plenty of rock pools and some surf.

There are few facilities – a pub, a caravan park and some holiday houses.

Places to Stay

There's quite a large municipal *caravan park* (☎ (02723) 51169). It's not particularly attractive, but the facilities are good. Chalets for four people are R90, double rooms are R40, and camp sites are a steep R30. There's also the *Strandfontein Hotel* which looks like it's fine.

DORING BAY

Doring Bay is linked to Strandfontein by about 10 km of dusty road that follows the coastline. If you combined the facilities of these towns you might have one decent hamlet, but as it is facilities are thin.

Particularly in October and November, keep your eyes open for whales, which come within 50 or 100 metres of the beach. There are also great flower displays during spring.

Doring Bay is a working town, with fish processing and crayfish and diamond boats (the diamonds are literally vacuumed from the sea floor). The *Louis Roodt Beach Resort* (☎ (02723) 51169) has shaded camp sites and a few cottages.

Eastern Cape Province

Eastern Cape Province is a diverse and, compared with Western Cape, largely undeveloped area. It includes the former homelands of Ciskei and Transkei, so most of its population is Xhosa-speaking. The old Transkei region has a separate section in this chapter because it remains a fairly homogeneous area of the country.

The province's long coastline extends from Tsitsikamma Coastal National Park and Cape St Francis (famous for its surf) in the west, through Port Elizabeth and the Sunshine Coast to the Shipwreck Coast of the old Ciskei area, past East London and into the spectacular subtropical Wild Coast of the old Transkei.

Inland, the rolling green hills around Grahamstown are known as Settler Country, after the British migrants who settled in the area in the early 19th century. This was the 'border' between expansionist Boer farmers and the Rharhabe or Ciskei Xhosa. Both groups were heavily dependent on cattle, and both claimed the grazing land in the area known as Zuurveld (the coastal strip from Algoa Bay to the Great Kei River).

The Settler Country section in this chapter also includes the highlands to the north-east of Grahamstown, which lead up into the foothills of the main South African plateau and Lesotho.

Further north and on the plateau is the semi-desert Karoo and lazy old towns such as Cradock and Graaff Reinet, well worth visiting.

The rainfall and climate reflects the geographic variation, with around 700 mm of rain (mostly in summer) and a moderate climate on the coast, heavy rainfall of over 1000 mm (including snow in winter) in the mountains, and low rainfall of around 450 mm on the fringes of the Karoo. The Eastern Cape is the meeting point for four types of flora: the subtropical forest of the summer rainfall area, found in sheltered valleys; the fynbos of the Western Cape winter-rainfall

EASTERN CAPE PROVINCE
Capital: Undecided – will be Bisho, East London or Port Elizabeth
Main Languages: English, Xhosa
Pre-1994: The eastern part of Cape Province, and the Homelands of Ciskei and Transkei
Highlights:
- Beaches
- Addo Elephant National Park
- Coastal walking trails
- The old Transkei region
- The Karoo, especially Graaff Reinet

area on the coastal plains; the eastern grasslands at higher altitudes; and succulent thorny scrub in the river valleys.

INFORMATION
The Ciskei tourist information and wildlife protection service was known as Contour. It was an unusually friendly and efficient organisation with its head office in Bisho (☎ (0401) 95 2115, fax 92756). By now the service will have amalgamated with the new Eastern Cape Province Tourism Board and some of its reserves might have been taken over by the National Parks Board. However, there should still be an information office under some name in Bisho. This is where you

The Xhosa

Most of Eastern Cape is populated by groups of Nguni peoples who occupied the coastal savanna of South Africa, but those living west of the Great Fish River are relatively recent arrivals. Being graziers and agriculturists, the Nguni could venture no further west than a north-south line roughly following the Great Fish River – most of the land to the west receives less than the 200 mm of summer rainfall required for cropping. There is no satisfactory explanation for the differences between the coastal Nguni and the Sotho of the highveld, or when this distinction between the two main Bantu groups began. It is now believed, however, that Iron-Age Bantus had reached the Great Kei River by 1000 AD.

The history of the original Xhosa clans can be dated back to the early 17th century, when small communities of Nguni pastoralists were loosely united in kingdoms. They first came into contact with Boers in the 1760s. Both groups were heavily dependent on cattle, and both coveted the grazing land in the area known as Zuurveld (the coastal strip from Algoa Bay to the Great Kei River).

In 1771, Governor van Plettenberg convinced some chiefs to consider the Great Fish River as the boundary between the VOC's territory and the Xhosa's. Conflict was inevitable, however, and the first of nine major frontier wars broke out in 1779 – skirmishing and brigandage (by blacks and whites) was virtually continuous for the next century.

By the beginning of the 19th century, the Xhosa were under pressure in the west from white expansion, in the east and north from peoples fleeing from the difaqane. After the Sixth Frontier War (1834-1835) the British declared the land between the Great Kei and Keiskamma rivers the Province of Queen Adelaide, and allowed a limited degree of independence. In 1846, however, white colonialists invaded (the theft of an axe at Fort Beaufort was the flimsy pretext) beginning the Seventh Frontier War. In its aftermath, British Kaffraria was established, with its capital in King William's Town.

Increasing numbers of Xhosa were influenced by missionaries and drawn into the European cash economy as peasant labourers, but the great leader Sandile, provided a focal point for traditionalists and continued resistance. In 1840, Sandile had become the paramount chief of the Rharhabe or Ciskei Xhosa, and he was to mobilise the Xhosa in their last increasingly desperate attempts to retain their land and resist white influence. He was a key figure in the Seventh, Eighth (1850-1853) and Ninth Frontier Wars.

He was also involved in the 'Great Cattle Killing', the Xhosa suicide of 1857. A young girl, Nongqawuse, saw visions that the Xhosa believed revealed how they could reconcile themselves with a spirit world that allowed the theft of their lands and destruction of their culture. The spirits required the sacrifice of cattle and crops – in return the whites would be swept into the sea. As a result of this enormous and desperate sacrifice it is estimated that of a Xhosa population of 90,000 in British Kaffraria 30,000 died of starvation, and 30,000 were forced to emigrate as destitute refugees.

In 1866, British Kaffraria became part of the Cape Province. The Xhosa had been devastated by years of struggle, but in 1877-1878 they once again fought for their independence in the Ninth Frontier War. ■

Drawing of an 18th-century Xhosa chief.

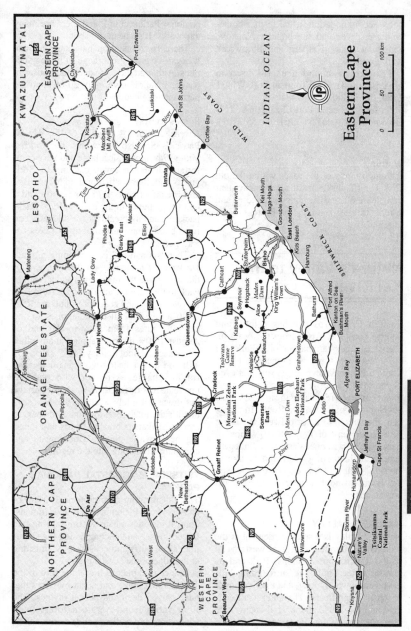

Eastern Cape
Province

INDIAN OCEAN

EASTERN CAPE PROVINCE

book accommodation in the former homeland's reserves and the popular Amatola, Zingcuka Loop, Katberg and Shipwreck walking trails.

Transkei also had a useful tourism organisation, Transkei Tourism (☎ (0471) 31 2885, fax 31 2887), in Umtata.

Satour's office in Port Elizabeth, at 21-3 Donkin St (☎ (041) 55 7761, fax 55 7761), is also useful.

Warning

Although many of the roads within the old Ciskei and Transkei are of a reasonable standard, there is a real likelihood of children and stock straying onto them. Extra care is required.

Nature's Valley to the Kei River

Eastern Cape Province has a long and diverse coastline. Apart from the beautiful forests of Tsitsikamma National Park, the coast between Cape St Francis and East London is best known for its surf, but even if you aren't a surfie this section of coast might come as a relief after the intense tourist development of the Garden Route. In particular, the stretch of coast between the Great Fish River (east of Port Alfred) almost to East London was once part of the 'independent homeland' of Ciskei and is almost entirely undeveloped, except for the Sun hotels and casinos that were a feature of most homelands.

NATURE'S VALLEY

Nature's Valley is a small settlement at the mouth of the Groot Rivier, at the western end of the Tsitsikamma National Park and its famous Otter Trail. The surrounding hills have yellowwood forest, and the five km of beach is magnificent. The Otter Trail ends here and the Tsitsikamma Trail begins here (see the following Tsitsikamma Coastal

National Park section), and there are many day walks. It's a beautiful spot.

There's only one shop in the area, in town. It doesn't have a great range of hiking supplies. Although there are over 300 houses in Nature's Valley town, only 20 of them are permanently occupied.

Places to Stay

Hikers' Haven (☎ (04457) 6805), 411 St Patrick's St, also known as the *Nature's Valley Guesthouse*, is a large and very comfortable home in town, catering to B&B guests and, in the attic dorm, to hikers. Bed and breakfast costs R75 per person and a bed (not a bunk) in the dorm is R25. Backpackers can buy breakfast for R12.50. You must book. They hire mountain bikes for R25 per day.

There's a national park camping ground, *De Vasselot Restcamp*, on the river east of the town (take the main road) and a two-km walk to the beach. Camp sites are from R40 for two people and good forest huts are R50. A 40% seasonal discount applies to the camping rates from May to the end of August; a 20% discount applies at any other time except school holidays.

If you stay in the huts you can use a canoe for no charge. A reader who paddled upstream reports that there was some portage but it was definitely worth it. She also says that it's definitely best to come midweek, to avoid 'Afrikaners braaing beasts and inhaling beers while playing Boer music and chopping wood long into the night'.

TSITSIKAMMA COASTAL NATIONAL PARK

The Tsitsikamma park protects 100 km of coast between Plettenberg Bay and Humansdorp. It includes a narrow strip starting five km out to sea and encompassing the shoreline, steep cliffs and coastal hills, finishing at the edge of the coastal plateau.

The coastal plateau lies at the foot of the Tsitsikamma range and is cut by rivers that have carved deep and abrupt ravines. The flora varies from evergreen forest (with stinkwood and yellowwood), ferns, lilies,

Ciskei

In 1981, Ciskei was given pseudo-independence by the prophets of apartheid. Ciskei's total area was a tiny 8500 sq km; it was only about 180 km long and 60 km wide. The million people who were forced to live there did not have enough land for agriculture on any economic scale, nor for subsistence. There was no industry or natural resources.

In March 1990, the dictatorial inaugural president, Lennox Sebe, was removed from power by a coup that had the support of the South African government. Sebe, who fled to Pretoria, was not lamented by many. In the words of the *Eastern Province Herald*, 'Ciskei's neighbours have witnessed corruption, poor administration, fraternal feuds and assassinations'.

Brigadier Ouba Joshua Gqozo took Sebe's place, and the South African government assumed control over key posts in the Ciskei government and defence forces. Gqozo attempted to consolidate his power by reintroducing a system of local government based on compliant 'traditional' headmen, replacing democratic residential associations affiliated with the ANC.

In late 1991, conflict over this issue, the question of continuing 'independence', and the role of the ANC led to the declaration of a state of emergency. On 7 September 1992, the Ciskei army opened fire on a peaceful ANC demonstration killing over 30 marchers.

Ciskei has been reabsorbed into South Africa but the effects of the period of neglect are all too evident. Shanty villages still dot the overgrazed hills. The huts within the villages and the villages themselves are scattered, so it is impossible to deliver services efficiently. The inhabitants are dependent on expensive minibus taxis to get to shops, schools and medical services. Huge numbers of men still travel to the big cities to find work, leaving behind their wives and children who fend for themselves as best they can. Sometimes the man will be willing and able to send back money. Sometimes he won't. ∎

orchids and coastal fynbos, including proteas.

The Cape clawless otter, after whom the Otter Trail is named, is one of the elusive animals, but there are also baboons, monkeys and some small antelopes. Birdlife is plentiful. Diving and snorkelling are rewarding – there is even a special snorkel route.

The area has a high rainfall (around 1200 mm a year), but the climate is temperate. The main centre for the national park is the Storms River Mouth Rest Camp, which is 68 km from Plettenberg, 99 km from Humansdorp and nearly 10 km from the N2.

There are a several short day walks which give you a taste of the coastline, so it is worth visiting even if you can't tackle the five-day Otter Trail. These range from an easy one-hour walk (along a boardwalk) to the suspension bridge across the Storms River Mouth and back, to a four-hour circuit to a waterfall on the first stretch of the Otter Trail.

Orientation & Information

The park gate is six km from the N2. It's open from 5.30 am to 9.30 pm and day visitors are charged R6 for entry. It's a steep two km from the gate to the main camp, with its accommodation facilities, restaurant and information and reception centres. The reception office is open from 8 am to 1 pm and 2 to 6 pm. There's a shop that stocks cold drinks, groceries and firewood; it's open the same hours as the reception office.

Otter Trail

The Otter Trail is one of the most acclaimed hikes in South Africa, hugging the coast from Storms River Mouth to Nature's Valley. The five-day (four-night) walk fords a number of rivers and gives access to some superb coast. The longest day's hike is 14 km, so there is plenty of time to walk slowly, and swim or snorkel in the tidal pools.

There are some steep climbs onto the coastal plateau and down to the river crossings, but most people of average fitness have no difficulty. The river crossings can be difficult and deep (even impossible after heavy rains), so it essential that your gear is stowed in waterproof bags.

Accommodation is in huts with mattresses, but no bedding, cooking utensils or running water. No camping is allowed. The trail costs R160 per person and bookings are made through the National Park offices in Pretoria and Cape Town. Unfortunately, the trail is booked up months ahead. Some travellers have been lucky enough to arrive and find that a booking has been cancelled, but this is unlikely. Otherwise there's always the Tsitsikamma Trail. Also, a reader describes the Harkerville Trail near Knysna as 'a kind of consolation prize for those who can't get on the Otter'.

Tsitsikamma Trail

The Tsitsikamma Trail parallels the route of the Otter Trail, but takes you inland through the coastal forests. It's also five days/four nights long and as it begins at Nature's Valley and ends at Storms River Mouth (the opposite direction to the Otter Trail) you could combine the two. Unlike the Otter Trail there is little difficulty getting a booking, and midweek you might have it to yourself, except in school holidays. Accommodation is in huts. The first hut is in Nature's Valley, so if you arrive early you can have a day at the beach. Book through the Forestry Department (the Knysna office is convenient) or contact De Vasselot Nature reserve near Nature's Valley for more information.

Places to Stay & Eat

There are different types of cottages, all except the forest huts are equipped with kitchens (including utensils), bedding and bathrooms. Forest huts use communal facilities and cost R50 a double. Log cabins cost R190 a double, with larger models costing R360 for up to four people. 'Oceanettes' also sleep four and cost R360. All accommodation except forest huts has a 20% discount from the start of May to the end of August.

There are also camp sites for R40 a double plus R12 for each additional person. There is a 40% discount from May to August and a 20% discount for the rest of the year, excluding school holidays. Bookings must be made through the National Parks offices in Pretoria and Cape Town.

The *Storms River Restaurant* at the reception complex has great views over the coast and surprisingly reasonable prices.

See the earlier Nature's Valley entry for information on accommodation at *De Vasselot Rest Camp* at the western end of the national park.

Getting There & Away

There is no public transport to the Storms River Mouth Camp, which is an eight-km walk from the N2. Buses run along the N2 – see the Cape Town and Port Elizabeth sections for details.

STORMS RIVER

There can be some confusion between Storms River and the Tsitsikamma Coastal National Park. From the N2, the Storms River signpost points to the village of Storms River that lies outside the national park. Despite what some maps show, the turn-off is east of the national park's turn-off. The turn-off to the park is signposted to the Tsitsikamma National Park, although the park headquarters is known as Storms River Mouth.

Storms River is a tiny and scattered hamlet with tree-shaded lanes and not much else.

Places to Stay

The Forest Inn Backpackers (☎ (042) 541 1711) is not, unfortunately, at the hotel of the same name. It's half a km or so away, in a fairly ordinary house. Dorm beds are R25. This is also a guesthouse (known as *Storms River Guesthouse*) charging R65 per person with breakfast.

Much nicer is *The Armagh* (☎ (042) 541 1512, fax 541 1510), a small and very friendly guesthouse with a basic dorm in the loft. Dorm beds are R23 and the pleasant, well-equipped guest rooms (but no TV, no radio, no alarm clock – peaceful) are R115 for up to three people. Prices drop a little in the off-season.

Tzitzikama Forest Inn (☎ (042) 541 1711) is a hotel/guesthouse which, while not especially fancy, has a certain old-world charm after the tour buses depart. There are manicured lawns and a pool. Whether it's worth R220/310 a single/double is another matter.

CAPE ST FRANCIS

While the beach is good, the treeless cape is covered in unattractive fibro-cement houses and it's basically bleak and ugly. To add insult to injury, the reef seldom produces rideable surf. If it does, it will certainly be considerably better at Jeffrey's Bay.

Still bleak but not as ugly (unless you think upper-middle class ghettos are ugly) is the nearby village of St Francis Bay, off the road to the Cape. Just about every building is a whitewashed, thatched-roofed Cape Dutch imitation, and most business in town are real estate agencies.

Apparently, *Cape St Francis Backpackers* (☎ (0423) 94 0420) is part of the *Cape St Francis Holiday Resort*, which has attractive thatched cottages, flats and sites.

As someone who saw the surf film *Endless Summer* at an impressionable age, Cape St Francis was burnt into my mind as the most perfect wave in the world. In my fevered imagination it became a sort of Shangri-la. The reality is massively disappointing.

Richard Everist

HUMANSDORP

The countryside around Humansdorp (pronounced with dropping tone and emphasis on the dorp – Humansdoooorp) is not inspiring by comparison with the country between Plettenberg Bay and the Tsitsikamma National Park. It's a fairly flat and dry coastal plain; probably old sand dunes. Humansdorp is a bustling farming town, but it's not interesting in any way. There's a good Publicity Association (☎ (0423) 51361) with information on the region, including nearby B&Bs. The *caravan park* looks pleasant and has rondavels for R25 per person.

JEFFREY'S BAY

Surfing is the reason to come to J Bay. Compared with the resorts of the Garden Route further west, it's quite a humble town, with little flashy development. It's also very friendly and might be just the place for a laid-back few days. Australian surfies get an especially warm welcome.

The lazy among you might appreciate the fact that J Bay is one of the only beachside towns where walking between town and the beach doesn't involve a long, steep walk.

The surf is sensational and few would disagree that J Bay has the best waves in southern Africa and among the best in the world. Shaun Tomson has claimed Supertubes as the most perfect wave in the world and there are a lot of people who agree. It can be better than a three-minute ride from Boneyards to the end. Oyster Bay often has a wave when everything else if flat.

Information

The friendly and helpful Publicity Association (☎ (04321) 93 2588) is in the municipal buildings and is open on weekdays and Saturday morning.

Surf Shops

Country Feeling runs most of the surf shops in town and has a factory making their clothing – T-shirts and bright cotton surfwear. There's also a factory shop with bargains. J Bay Surf Co on the corner of Da Gama and Goedehoop Sts sells new boards for R700 to R900. There's a fairly limited stock of secondhand boards for R100 to R600. A Rip Curl steamer sells for R400. You can hire boards for R5 per hour and wetsuits for the same rate.

Places to Stay

The *Jeffrey's Bay Caravan Park* (☎ (04231) 93 1111) is fairly exposed, but it has an ideal situation beside the sea, about midway between the town centre and the surf. It is booked out in school holidays, but there's plenty of room most of the time. For two people a site costs R34 (R44.50 in summer). There are also cottages, from R80/120.

The *Jeffrey's Bay Hostel* (☎ (0423) 93 1379), 12 Jeffreys St, is a friendly little place where dorm beds go for just R15. Private rooms are R20 per person. Apparently there's now another hostel, *Jeffrey's Bay Rest Haven* (☎ (0423) 93 1248).

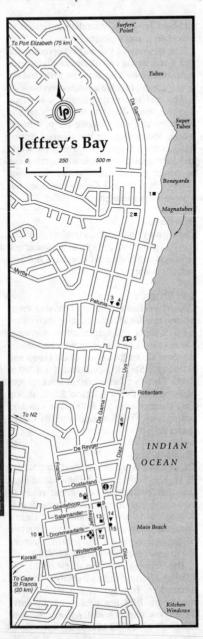

Jeffrey's Bay

To Port Elizabeth (75 km)

Surfers' Point

Tubes

Super Tubes

Boneyards

Magnatubes

0   250   500 m

Myrtle

Petunia

Uys

Rotterdam

To N2

Da Gama

De Reyger

Francis

Oosterland

Goedehoop

Salamander

Jeffrey

Drommeadaris

10

Koraal

To Cape St Francis (20 km)

Woltemade

Diaz

INDIAN OCEAN

Main Beach

Kitchen Windows

PLACES TO STAY

1   Beach Hotel
2   Beach Cabanas
5   Jeffrey's Bay Caravan Park
8   Jeffrey's Bay Hostel
10   Jeffrey's Bay Holiday Resort
13   Savoy Protea Hotel

PLACES TO EAT

3   The Tubes
6   The Breakers
12   The Grapevine
14   Trawlers

OTHER

4   Tubs Laundromat
7   Publicity Association & Municipal Offices
9   J Bay Surf Co
11   Bloch's Supermarket (Minibus Taxis)
15   Country Feeling

The information centre can put you in touch with some very reasonable B&Bs and guesthouses. You can still find something for R40 a double or less.

The *Beach Cabanas* (☎ (04321) 93 2323), near the Beach Hotel, are modern and close to the surf. Low-season rates are R70 for singles, R105 for two or three people and R134 for four. In December the minimum stay is a week, at R210/260 a single/double per night.

The *Jeffrey's Bay Holiday Resort* (☎ (04231) 93 1330) on Drommedaris St is within easy walking distance of the main beach and has a variety of self-catering units. There's a swimming pool and tennis courts. Rates start from R60 per unit (for two people).

The *Savoy Protea Hotel* (☎ (04321) 93 1106) is the most luxurious option in town. It's OK, but nothing flash. As in many Protea hotels, the staff are very cagey about quoting room rates. Expect to pay around R200/250. Directly in front of Magnatubes, the *Beach Hotel* (☎ (04231) 93 1104) has less expensive rooms. Judging by the cage surrounding the reception desk they don't have a lot of faith in their clientele.

Places to Eat

The Grapevine, on Drommedaris St, is a small, pleasant bar and restaurant. Entrées are around R10, a vegetable platter is R23 and steaks and fish dishes cost from R25. There are also light meals such as burgers (R11) and mini steaks (R19). It's open daily except Sunday for lunch (not Saturday) and dinner.

The Breakers (☎ (0423) 93 1975), 23 Diaz Rd, overlooking the water, is a good place to go for a bit of a splurge. Other than pizza for about R20, the menu is mainly seafood in the R30-and-over bracket.

The Tubes (☎ (0423) 93 1131), 22 Petunia Ave, is another decent quality restaurant. As well as snacks such as burgers (R11) there are curries (R17), fish (from R15) and steaks (from R20). A four-course Sunday lunch costs R20. There are good specials in the off-season.

There are cheap pub lunches in the *Breakaway Tavern* of the *Savoy Hotel* – sausage, egg, chips and salad will set you back R8. *Chokker's Take Away* on Da Gama St near the Savoy Hotel has the best food in town at the cheapest prices. There are pastas from R5.50, curry and rice from R4.50 and toasted sandwiches. Across the road, *Trawlers* has very reasonable hamburgers and fish and chips.

Entertainment

The Breakaway Tavern in the Savoy Hotel is the preferred drinking spot for the local surfers. It's the sort of bar where there are wet T-shirt competitions. Assuming that the *chokka* (squid) fishermen are too drunk to be vigorous, it's a mellow place. Sometimes there are bands.

Getting There & Away

Bus Intercape stops at the Savoy Hotel on the daily run between Cape Town (R100, 15 hours) and Port Elizabeth (R35, one hour), via the Garden Route and Swellendam. Translux buses on the Garden and Mountain routes between Cape Town and Port Elizabeth stop at Humansdorp, but at the time of

writing they no longer ran to Jeffrey's Bay. This might change.

Sunshine Bus Services (☎ (0423) 93 2221) runs to Port Elizabeth for R25. It's a door-to-door service. A bus runs from Humansdorp railway station to Knysna daily except Sunday at 2 pm for R25.

Minibus Taxi Taxis depart from Bloch's supermarket. You'll have to take a taxi to Humansdorp (R3.50) and pick up another there. Humansdorp to Port Elizabeth costs R10.

PORT ELIZABETH

Port Elizabeth's city centre is on steep hills overlooking Algoa Bay and there are some pleasant beaches and parks, virtually in the centre of town. Although this sounds like an excellent start, and the city also has some interesting historical architecture, the 20th century has been very unkind. What must once have been a fine example of a Victorian/Edwardian port city has become an incredibly ugly place. The neglected and abused downtown streets could almost be in one of the ravaged industrial cities in the north of England.

To compensate, Port Elizabeth (more commonly known as PE) bills itself as the Friendly City. Of course, it's personality not appearance that counts in life. Remarkably, given the hype, PE is a genuinely friendly place. Quite a few travellers who have washed up here have had a very good time; there's a thriving nightlife.

Port Elizabeth and its nearby sister city, Uitenhage, are the main centres for South Africa's car industry. Together they are probably the most industrialised in the country. Volkswagen and Delta are the two big names. Delta was formed when GMH withdrew from the country and – guess what? – it still manufactures GM models like Kadetts, Monzas and Rekords. The economic woes of the country have hit PE particularly hard.

In theory, there are about one million people in the city, although as always the number of blacks and coloureds is probably greatly underestimated. The theory says there are roughly 200,000 whites, 200,000 coloureds and 600,000 blacks. There are some enormous townships around PE and Uitenhage, and all the problems of poverty and violence are well represented.

Blacks have not always found PE friendly. It was in PE's Sanlam Centre that Steve Biko, the inspirational Black Consciousness leader, was interrogated and beaten into a coma. After three days lying chained, naked and unconscious in his cell, he was loaded into the back of a jeep that took him 1200 km over back roads to a prison hospital in Pretoria where he died. At the subsequent inquest, the magistrate found no one was to blame.

Orientation
Port Elizabeth is 1115 km from Jo'burg, 785 km from Cape Town and 310 km from East London. It's a major transport hub.

The railway station (for buses and trains) is just to the north of the Campanile, an unmistakable bell tower (which you can climb for a donation), now isolated from the city by the ghastly freeway. There's a left-luggage office in the railway station that is open from 8 am to 5 pm Monday to Friday. Walk up the steep hill to Donkin Reserve to orient yourself. The beaches are to the south (or right, looking from Donkin Reserve).

The city centre is run-down (and a little dangerous – beware of bag-snatchers) and many businesses have moved out to the wealthy white western suburbs, difficult to access if you don't have a car.

When you consider how easily Cape Town could have degenerated like PE has, you send a little prayer of thanks to the god of good luck – and experience a small shudder at the prospect of Cape Town being awarded the 2004 Olympics and deciding to 'modernise'.

Information
Tourist Information The Publicity Association (☎ (041) 52 1315) has an excellent supply of information and maps, including *Donkin Heritage Trail* (R5) which details a walk around the city's historic buildings. The office is in the lighthouse building in Donkin Reserve.

Satour (☎ (041) 55-7761) has an office at 21 Donkin St, and you can collect a bunch of good-value brochures on the rest of the country.

Money American Express (☎ (041) 35 1225) has an office on Pamela Arcade, 2nd Ave, Newton Park. Rennies Travel (☎ (041) 34 3536) is in the Murray & Roberts Building, 48/52 Ring St, Greenacres. This is a long way from the centre of town.

Sports Equipment Sporting equipment is sold by Beachfront Adventure Centre (☎ (041) 55 4384), 109 Russell Rd.

Donkin Reserve
Donkin Reserve is immediately behind the town centre and has good views over the bay. It's a handy point to get your bearings. The pyramid on the reserve is a memorial; the lighthouse beside the pyramid houses the information centre. The reserve is flanked by some fine Victorian architecture: on the north side by a row of terraces, on the west by the Edward Hotel.

Settlers' Park
Although Settlers' Park is virtually in the centre of the city, it includes 54 hectares of cultivated and natural gardens in the valley of the Baakens River. The main emphasis is on native plants and flowers and so it's also a good place for birdlife. The main entrance is on How St (off Park Dr, which circles St George's Park and its sporting fields) – there's a great view from the car park.

Fort Frederick
Fort Frederick, on Belmont Terrace, overlooking the Baakens River, was built in 1799 to defend the original harbour in the river mouth. It has never fired a shot in anger.

Port Elizabeth Museum & Oceanarium
The Port Elizabeth Museum is one of the best and largest museums in the country. There are some interesting anthropological and archaeological exhibitions, a tropical house and snake park, and an oceanarium, complete

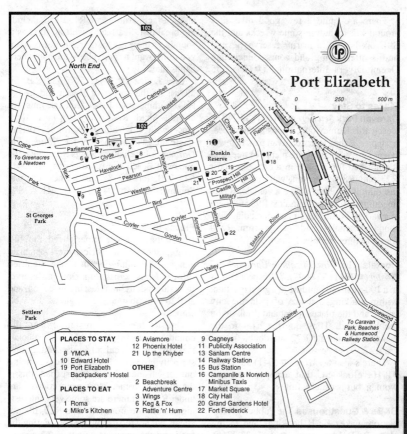

Port Elizabeth

0   250   500 m

North End

To Greenacres & Newtown

Donkin Reserve

St Georges Park

Settlers' Park

To Caravan Park, Beaches & Humewood Railway Station

PLACES TO STAY	5 Aviamore	9 Cagneys
	12 Phoenix Hotel	11 Publicity Association
8 YMCA	21 Up the Khyber	13 Sanlam Centre
10 Edward Hotel		14 Railway Station
19 Port Elizabeth	**OTHER**	15 Bus Station
Backpackers' Hostel		16 Campanile & Norwich
	2 Beachbreak	Minibus Taxis
PLACES TO EAT	Adventure Centre	17 Market Square
	3 Wings	18 City Hall
1 Roma	6 Keg & Fox	20 Grand Gardens Hotel
4 Mike's Kitchen	7 Rattle 'n' Hum	22 Fort Frederick

EASTERN CAPE PROVINCE

with performing dolphins. The complex is open daily from 9 am to 1 pm and 2 to 5 pm. The dolphins perform at 11 am and 3 pm.

Beaches

The beaches are to the south of the city centre. Take Humewood Rd from the city centre; this becomes Beach Rd, then Marine Dr. Kings Beach stretches from the harbour breakwater to Humewood Beach; both of these are sheltered. Hobie Cats and surfers make for Summerstrand, about five km from the city centre.

There's an amusement park on Hume-wood/Beach (right next to a coal dump, in true PE style).

Apple & Diaz Expresses

These two tourist steam trains. The *Apple Express* runs on a day trip to Thornhill and back, with a two-hour stop for a braai. The fare is about R40. The *Diaz Express* runs between town and Kings Beach during summer. The 15-minute trip costs R7.

Outdoor Activities

IDASA (☎ (041) 55 3301) organises tours of townships around PE.

There are quite a few good dive sites around PE, including some wrecks and the St Croix Islands, a marine reserve. Several outfits offer diving and courses, including Ocean Divers International (☎ (041) 55 6536).

Places to Stay
Caravan Park *Sea Acres* (☎ (041) 53 2407), Beach Rd, Humewood, opposite the pedestrian pier, is the closest caravan park to town. It's not great but there are plenty of trees and it's not bad for a place in a city. Sites cost R23 plus R8 per person, with a significant discount if you don't have a vehicle. Basic, unequipped four-bed huts cost R90 and there is a variety of fully equipped (including TV) rondavels, chalets and cottages from R240 for up to three people.

Hostels The *Port Elizabeth Backpackers' Hostel* (☎ (041) 56 0697), 7 Prospect Hill, is in a 100-year-old building in a good location, within walking distance of both the city centre and the places to eat and drink up on the headland. They do free trips to the beaches. Dorms are R22 and double rooms are R27.50 per person.

There's also a *YMCA* (☎ (041) 55 9792), 31 Havelock St, that accepts men and women, but is usually full.

B&Bs & Guesthouses The Publicity Association makes B&B bookings and there's also a B&B Association (☎ (041) 33 3716). Most places charge between R60 and R90 per person.

Hotels The *Edward Hotel* (☎ (041) 56 2056), on Belmont Terrace in the heart of the city, is a gracious, old-style Edwardian hotel with comfortable rooms. It's a superior member of the Protea chain. Budget singles/doubles are R115/124, standard rooms are R145/156. Breakfast is an extra R20, but it's worth it.

The *Humewood* (☎ (041) 55 1558), 33 Beach Rd, is another older hotel, but in this case it's on the seafront to the south of the city centre. Standard rooms are R138/178

and sea-facing rooms are R152/196, including breakfast. Sea-facing isn't as good as it sounds, as there is a lot of traffic noise. Also, you don't want a room above the bar, where bands play.

City Lodge (☎ (041) 56 3322, fax 56 3374), on the corner of Beach and Lodge Rds, Summerstrand (between the museum and the Shark Rock pier) is a fairly flash place with singles/doubles for R160/180. There are two members of the *Holiday Inn Garden Court* chain, at Kings Beach near the corner of Beach and La Roche Sts (☎ (041) 52 3720, R189/218) and further along at Summerstrand (☎ (041) 53 3131, R174/188).

Places to Eat
If you haven't yet experienced the full splendour of a South African breakfast, head along to the dining room at the dignified *Edward Hotel* across from Donkin Reserve. It's a stupendous breakfast in a nice room and at R20 it's a bargain. Non-guests are welcome.

One of the better restaurants in the country, *Aviamore* (☎ (041) 55 1125) specialises in fresh local produce and game, superbly prepared. If your palate is hanging out for cuisine rather than just food, this is the place to come. Most main courses are under R30 and there are some very interesting entrées for around R15 to R20. It's not cheap, but not too expensive considering the food and the spacious layout of the restaurant. It even has comfortable chairs.

Roma, on Campbell St near the corner of Russell St, is a pizza and pasta place with an all-you-can-eat deal on Tuesday. If you're paying by the dish, prices aren't bad, with pasta at R15. It's a very popular place so you might have to wait for a table.

Up the Khyber, an Indian restaurant (with an unattractive name) on the corner of Western and Belmont Sts sometimes has an all-you-can-eat deal for R13.

The *Phoenix Hotel* (☎ (041) 56 3553), 5 Chapel St, is an entertainment institution, with live music. The food is very good value, with pub lunches for less than R10.

Entertainment

For some reason Wednesday seems to be biggest night in the pubs and clubs, although Friday and Saturday are pretty popular as well. Few places have cover charges.

The Humewood Hotel on the beach was a student hang-out – just the place for an evening drink on the terrace. The Phoenix Hotel, 5 Chapel St, is a small, dark and very friendly little pub with live music some nights. Not far away, the Grand Gardens Hotel has a pool room and sometimes live music, but friendly it isn't. Be a bit careful.

Other venues include: Rattle 'n' Hum, Parliament St (live music, studenty); The Basement, Main St (heavy metal); Club Tonight, Main St (techno); Cagneys, off Rink St (MOR); and Wings, on Russel St near the corner of Rose St.

The new Africa City complex at the railway station, with bars, eateries and shops, should have opened by now. It bills itself as 'a unique Xhosa cultural experience'. First-hand reports, please.

Getting There & Away

Air SAA flies daily between Port Elizabeth and Jo'burg (R559) and Cape Town (R434).

Bus Buses stop at the railway station or the nearby local bus terminus. The Translux office (☎ (041) 507 3333) is behind the city hall. Intercape only accepts telephone bookings, or you can book through Computicket.

Heading West Translux has a daily bus to Cape Town (R115) via the Garden Route. Stops include Humansdorp (R40), Plettenberg Bay (R50), Knysna (R65), George (R80), Oudtshoorn (R80), Mossel Bay (R90) and Swellendam (R105). This service leaves both PE and Cape Town at 8 am (7 am on weekends) and takes 10 hours. On Monday, Wednesday, Friday and Saturday additional buses depart from PE at 8.30 pm and follow this route but also stop in Stellenbosch (R115), taking 11½ hours to Cape Town – return buses on this route leave Cape Town at 6 pm on Tuesday, Thursday, Saturday and Sunday.

Translux also runs to Cape Town on what it calls the Mountain Route, taking 11½ hours. On Sunday a bus leaves PE at 8.30 pm and follows the Garden Route to Oudtshoorn then runs via Montagu (R100), Robertson (R100), Paarl (R115) and Stellenbosch. The return bus leaves Cape Town at 6 pm on Friday. On Tuesday and Thursday the bus leaves PE at 8.30 pm but runs inland to Oudtshoorn, then follows the same route to Cape Town. Return buses leave Cape Town at 6 pm on Monday and Wednesday.

Intercape Mainliner (☎ (041) 56005) also has a daily Garden Route service linking Cape Town and PE (they do not go via Oudtshoorn). Buses leave Cape Town station at 7 am and PE at 7.15 am; the fare is R105 and the trip takes 10 hours.

Chilwans Bus Services (☎ (041) 81 2105, (021) 54 2506/7/8/9 in Cape Town) has a useful (if slow and not very comfortable) service to Cape Town (R90) via the Garden Route. It departs from PE on Sunday and returns on Friday.

Heading North Greyhound has nightly buses from PE to Jo'burg (R235). Translux has a twice-weekly (Monday and Saturday) service from PE to Jo'burg (R220) via Cradock and Bloemfontein. The trip takes 11 hours. There might also be a service via Graaff Reinet.

Heading East Translux runs to Durban (R170) daily, via Grahamstown (R65), King William's Town (R70), East London (R70), Umtata (R115), Kokstad (R145) and Port Shepstone (R165). If you take a night bus from Cape Town to PE you can connect with the bus to Durban (if you're a masochist). Buses depart from PE at 7 am and arrive in Durban at 8.30 pm. They depart Durban at 6.30 am and arrive in PE at 7.45 pm.

Greyhound runs to Durban (R180) on Tuesday, Thursday and Sunday, returning on Monday, Wednesday and Friday.

Intercape Mainliner runs between PE and East London (R70) on Sunday, Monday, Wednesday, Friday and Saturday, via Port Alfred and the Fish River Sun Hotel &

Casino. Buses depart from PE at 7 am and from East London at 1.30 pm. The trip takes 4½ hours. They have competition from Minilux (☎ (0431) 41 3107 in East London) which runs from PE to East London (R60) via Grahamstown (R30) and King William's Town (R48) on Monday and Friday (returning Sunday and Friday), and via Grahamstown, Port Alfred (R40) and the Fish River Sun (R44) on Tuesday and Thursday (returning Tuesday and Thursday).

Leopard Express (☎ (041) 54 1057) runs from PE to Grahamstown daily at 1 pm with a fare of R30.

Train The *Algoa* operates between Port Elizabeth and Jo'burg, via Bloemfontein. Trains depart from PE at 2.45 pm on Monday, Wednesday and Friday, and arrive in Jo'burg at 9 pm the next day. Trains depart from Jo'burg at 2.30 pm on Tuesday, Thursday and Sunday and arrive at PE at 9.25 am the next day. First/2nd/3rd-class fares are R240/162/101.

The *Southern Cross* runs between PE and Cape Town, departing from PE at 8.45 am on Sunday, arriving in Cape Town at 8.40 am the next day. Trains depart from Cape Town at 6.15 pm on Friday, arriving in PE at 5.50 pm the next day. For train enquiries contact Spoornet (☎ (041) 507 2400).

Minibus Taxi Norwich long-distance taxis (☎ (041) 55 7253 or 56 3751) depart from under the freeway near the bell tower. There's an office in a small shed (of the type known in South Africa as a 'Wendy house') where friendly Henry van Rayners will be of assistance. Norwich taxis run daily to Cape Town (R100, nine hours) and on Monday, Wednesday and Friday to Jo'burg (R150, 12 hours). Other destinations include East London (R60), Graaff Reinet (R38), Grahamstown (R25), Oudtshoorn (R60), Plettenberg Bay (R25) and Somerset East (R38).

Most other taxis tend to leave from the large townships surrounding PE and can be difficult to find. The taxi park on Strand St,

a few blocks north of the bell tower, is for the local area.

Car All the big car-rental operators have offices in Port Elizabeth, or at the airport: Avis (☎ (041) 51 4291), Budget (☎ (041) 51 4242) and Imperial (☎ (041) 51 4214). Try Economic Car Hire (☎ (041) 51 5826), 118 Main Rd, Walmer.

Getting Around
To/From Airport There's no public transport to the airport. A taxi will cost around R15. Taxis and hire cars are available at the airport.

Taxi For taxis contact Anchor Taxis (☎ (0441) 54 4798) or Hurter's Radio Cabs (☎ (0441) 55 7344).

Bus For bus information phone 080 1421, toll free. Bus No 2 leaves from Platform 5 at the bus station, and runs along the beachfront to Happy Valley (R1.55). No 55 leaves from Platform 7 for Greenacres (R1.55), one of the new suburbs with a big shopping centre.

ADDO ELEPHANT NATIONAL PARK
The Addo park is 72 km north of Port Elizabeth near the Zuurberg range in the Sundays River valley. It's a small park (12,126 hectares) protecting the small remnants of the huge elephant herds that once roamed across the Eastern Cape. For all that, it's a beautiful park with a curious flora, and you are almost guaranteed of seeing elephant.

Unfortunately, elephants and farmers don't happily coexist. The idea of the gentle harmless elephant doesn't wash when you see the amount of damage they can do – they're like bulldozers that eat and drink. When farmers started to develop the area at the beginning of the 20th century, they soon found themselves in conflict with the elephant herds.

A Major Pretorius was commissioned to deal with the 'menace', and until he was stopped by a public outcry he seemed likely to succeed. It was thanks to two local landowners, Jack and Natt Harvey, who allowed the elephants to stay on their land, that any survived. When Addo was finally proclaimed a national park in 1931 there were 11 elephants left.

Today there are 180 elephants in the park. They can survive at this unusually high density thanks to the fact that the weird Addo bush is close to elephant paradise. The dominant plant (and elephant tucker) is the pink-flowered spekboom *(Portulacaria afra)* which grows to the height of about three metres and has a small succulent leaf. There are also aloes, vygies and pelargoniums – there's a great display of flowers after spring rains.

There were hopes to expand the park so that the elephant population would have room to grow to a sustainable population of around 500. To enable this, the park will have to at least double in size, and this obviously depends on funds and availability of land.

Information

The entrance gate is open from 7 am to 7 pm. The roads around the park are dirt and can become impassable in the wet, so the park is closed if there has been heavy rain. If in doubt, phone ahead (☎ (0426) 40 0556). Day visitors are charged R15 per vehicle. A well-stocked shop is open from 7 am to 9 pm daily.

It's best to arrive at the park by mid-morning and to stake out one of the water holes where the elephants tend to gather during the heat of the day – there are about 45 km of roads so it pays to take advice from a ranger on where to go.

Places to Stay & Eat

Make accommodation bookings at the National Parks office in Pretoria or Cape Town.

There are six-bed cottages, R330 for up to four people; chalets with two single beds and a double, R180 for two; and two-bed huts with a bathroom but no kitchen, R130 for two. Extra adults are R46 each. Bedding is supplied in all huts. There's also a small but pleasant camping area, with sites for R27 for two people plus R7 per additional person.

There's a communal kitchen and also a restaurant.

Getting There & Away

It's an interesting drive from Port Elizabeth to Addo, although there are some very depressing townships and industrial developments in the immediate vicinity of PE. The park is signposted from the N2. Alternatively, you can travel via Uitenhage; there are attractive citrus farms along the banks of the Sundays River from Kirkwood to Uitenhage. The valley's obviously pretty dry, as otherwise the mud huts of the labourers wouldn't last long.

Those without transport can take tours from Port Elizabeth – contact the publicity association for suggested operators.

SHAMWARI GAME RESERVE

A new and luxurious private reserve 30 km east of Addo Elephant National Park (70-odd km from Port Elizabeth), Shamwari is dedicated to restocking a large tract of land with the animals which were once common. There are elephants, white and black rhinos, leopards, giraffes and many other species.

Accommodation starts at R750/1000 in the low season, at R1000/1500 in the high season, including all meals and activities. For bed and breakfast only, prices start at around R750 a double. Book on (042) 851 1196, fax 851 1224.

BUSHMAN'S RIVER MOUTH

Bushman's River Mouth (or Boesmanriviermond) is an expensive holiday resort on a beautiful bit of coast – for those wanting a quiet holiday in unspoilt surroundings.

Places to Stay

The *Boesmanriviermond Camping Ground* (☎ (0464) 81227) is an attractive sheltered spot, and foreign travellers are given a warm welcome. The rate is R25 plus R3 per person, plus VAT, doubling over Christmas.

Inland, between Kenton on Sea and Salem on the road to Grahamstown, *Belton Hiking Trails* (☎ (0461) 28395) is a private operation offering dorm accommodation in an old farmhouse (about R20), and hiking trails up to 16 km or so long.

Getting There & Away

If you are driving, turn off the N2 as soon as you can. There are attractive rolling hills and countryside around Alexandra, with scenic forest which extends the 10 km or so along to the coast.

PORT ALFRED

Port Alfred is an interesting town in transition between being a genuine fishing village (with a large black population) and an up-market holiday resort with a huge artificial island development. Some people would argue that it has already been spoilt, but visitors will find it a bustling, enjoyable place to stay for a night or longer if you want to take advantage of the beautiful coast.

The climate is excellent – gentle and subtropical. For surfers there are good right breaks at the river mouth, and for golfers there's a famous, extremely beautiful golf course, one of the four 'royal' golf courses in South Africa.

Residents call the town The Kowie, after the river which splits the town.

Information

The Visitors' Bureau (☎ (0464) 41235) is open from 8.30 am to 1 pm and 2 to 4 pm Monday to Friday, and 8.30 am to noon on Saturday. It has brochures for R0.20 each detailing accommodation, walks and canoe trails.

Diving

Kowie Dive (☎ (0464) 24 4432), at the Halyards Hotel, has dive courses for R750, a resort course for R200 and an introductory pool dive for R40. The best diving is in May and August. The winter water temperature (18 to 24°C) is actually higher than summer (12 to 18°C). Visibility is not outstanding, but there are plenty of big fish, sponges and

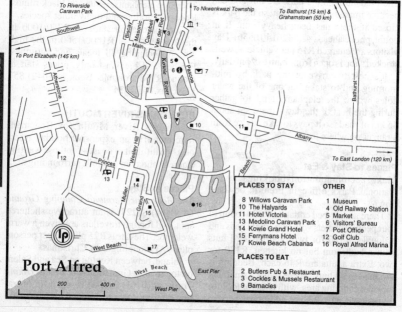

PLACES TO STAY
8 Willows Caravan Park
10 The Halyards
11 Hotel Victoria
13 Medolino Caravan Park
14 Kowie Grand Hotel
15 Ferrymans Hotel
17 Kowie Beach Cabanas

PLACES TO EAT
2 Butlers Pub & Restaurant
3 Cockles & Mussels Restaurant
9 Barnacles

OTHER
1 Museum
4 Old Railway Station
5 Market
6 Visitors' Bureau
7 Post Office
12 Golf Club
16 Royal Alfred Marina

Port Alfred

soft corals. Locals say that the reef here is South Africa's most colourful.

Horse-Riding

Three Sisters Horse Trails (☎ (0464) 71 1269) has daily rides, on the beach (one hour, R35) or in the bush (two hours, R55).

Canoeing

The two-day Kowie Canoe Trail is a fairly easy paddle up-river from Port Alfred, with an overnight stay in a hut at Horseshoe Bend. For bookings (well in advance) and canoe hire, contact Kowie Canoe Trail, Box 13, Port Alfred 6170 (☎ (0464) 41140).

Places to Stay

Hostel The people who own Oyster Lodge in Hamburg plan to open a hostel in Port Alfred.

Caravan Parks The *Willows Caravan Park* (☎ (0464) 42839) is reasonably close to town, near the bridge over the Kowie River. A camp site is R20, rising to R40 over Christmas. *Medolino Holiday Resort* (☎ (0464) 41651) is a member of the Club Caravelle chain. Sites rise from R25 to R80 at Christmas and there are various-sized cottages starting at R95 for two people, rising by increments to R220 at Christmas.

Riverside Park Caravan Park (☎ (0464) 42230), on Mentone Rd, is also on the west side of the river, but it's some way north of the town centre and more than an easy walk from the beach. It's a pleasant spot (although it probably gets crowded in season). Sites are R27 for two people, rising to R60 in season. Chalets are R105 for two people in the low season, R230 for four people (minimum) in the high season.

B&B & Self-Catering The information centre has information about B&Bs in town. Estate agents such as Moore & Gardner (☎ (0464) 4204), 15 Main St, let apartments and cottages.

Hotels *Ferrymans* (☎ (0464) 41122), on the river bank and the closest hotel to the beach, has rooms for R75/85 per person in the low/high season, with breakfast. In an old building they have a bar and very cheap meals, including a Sunday braai.

Up on the corner of Grand St and Princes Ave, the *Kowie Grand Hotel* (☎ (0464) 41150) is beginning to look a little tired but still have comfortable rooms with TVs and great views. Singles/doubles are R78/140 plus R14 for breakfast (more in December). Out of season, they have excellent cheap meals. The *Hotel Victoria* (☎ (0464) 41133), East Bank, is a comfortable pub, now a member of the Protea chain – so the rates are vague. You'll pay as low as R180 a double when things are slow.

By far the best place to stay is *The Halyards* (☎ (0464) 42410), Royal Alfred Marina, Albany Rd. It's a new, very comfortable waterfront hotel with attractive Cape Cod-style architecture. The rooms are large, well-equipped, and look over the harbour; they are a bargain at R130/230.

Places to Eat

Butlers Pub & Restaurant is a very pleasant place for a beer, a snack or a good meal. It's on the bank of the river and has a nice verandah. Most dishes on the pub-meals menu cost well under R15 and they are available from 11 am to 11 pm. Restaurant meals are available from noon to 2.30 pm and from 6.30 to 9.30 pm. The menu includes entrees such as grilled mussels (R8.75) and main courses such as vegetarian platter (R17.50), calamari (R21), fish (from R27) and steaks (from R22).

The popular and informal *Barnacles* (☎ (0464) 42410) overlooks the marina. There are great views. It's the spot to have a cold beer and a hot pizza. A seafood pizza costs R20 and other varieties cost less. There are occasionally live bands.

The dining room at the *Kowie Grand Hotel* (☎ (0464) 41150) has good-value traditional meals. The Sunday lunches are famous, but during the week there are also cheap lunches served on the terrace.

Getting There & Away

Intercape Mainliner stops here on the run between Port Elizabeth (R50) and East London (R50) on Sunday, Monday, Wednesday, Friday and Saturday. Minilux (☎ (0431) 41 3107 in East London) also stops here on the same run but only on Tuesday and Thursday.

THE SHIPWRECK COAST

This stretch of coast, the graveyard for numerous ships, is still largely unspoilt because it was once part of the Ciskei homeland. There are a couple of resort towns and the inevitable casino/hotel, but it is still easy to get away from it all.

Shipwreck Hiking Trail

Although the potential length of the trail, from the Great Fish River to the Ncera River, is 64 km, it is possible to do any section as there are several easy entry and exit points. This is one of the few walking areas in South Africa where hikers can set their own pace, camp more or less where they choose and light fires. In addition, they are rewarded with wild, unspoilt sections of surf beach, rich coastal vegetation, beautiful estuaries and diverse birdlife.

The climate is generally mild and excellent, although it can rain at any time of the year. The walking is relatively easy – light shoes are all you will need. There are no facilities, and hikers must carry water, tents and cooking equipment. Water is only available at the resorts and holiday townships. Hikers can camp on the beach, provided it is not in the military area between the Gqutywa and Umtana rivers (this might change with the dismantling of Ciskei) or on private property at the Fish River Sun and Mpekweni Sun hotels. Fires made from driftwood are permitted providing they are on sand away from vegetation.

It's 11.5 km from the Great Fish River (easily accessible from Port Alfred, because of the Fish River Sun hotel/casino) to Mpekweni (where there is another Sun hotel); 11 km from Mpekweni to Bira River (where the coastal road bends inland); 20 km from Bira River to Hamburg (a small village with a hostel); six km from Hamburg to the Kiwane Resort; 15.5 km from Kiwane to the Ncera River; and another 29 km to East London.

The trail must be booked with Contour (or its successor) in Bisho (☎ (0401) 95 2115, fax 92 756) and costs R20 per person per night.

There are buses and minibus taxis on the coastal road between Port Alfred and East London, and between Grahamstown and East London. See those entries for more details.

In her excellent book *The Complete Guide to Walks & Trails in Southern Africa*, Jaynee Levy recommends the sections from the Great Fish River to the Bira River and from Hamburg to the Kiwane Resort. The area is covered by the government's 1:50,000 topographic maps (Prudhoe, Hamburg and Kidd's Beach).

Fish River Sun

The *Fish River Sun* (☎ (0405) 661101) at the estuary of the Great Fish River is one of the nicest of Sun International's hotel/casinos. The attractive buildings are only a stone's throw from the sea. The complex includes restaurants and bars, a swimming pool, an 18-hole golf course designed by Gary Player, and squash and tennis courts. Horse-riding is also offered. Needless to say, it isn't cheap. Singles/doubles start around R303/395, depending on the time of the week and year.

Getting There & Away Intercape and some Minilux bus services between Port Elizabeth and East London stop here. There might also be local services from Port Alfred.

Mpekweni Sun Marine Resort

This resort is also run by the ubiquitous Sun group. It's about 11.5 km east of the Great Fish River and is more of a family resort than the Fish River Sun. The hotel is right beside the sea; there's a restaurant, several bars, a swimming pool. In addition to a surf beach, there's a protected lagoon. This makes almost every watersport possible, and most

JEFF WILLIAMS

JON MURRAY

JEANETTE WOOLERTON

JON MURRAY

A: Walking through mangroves, Umtafufu River, Transkei
B,C&D: The Camelyard – Helen Martins' Owl House, New Bethesda,
Eastern Cape Province

JON MURRAY

DEANNA SWANEY

Top: The Namastat, Springbok, Northern Cape Province
Bottom: Spring time in Namaqualand, Northern Cape Province

are available. Singles/doubles start at R215/310 during the week and R255/360 on weekends.

Hamburg

The small village of Hamburg, at the wide river flats at the mouth of the Keiskamma River, is near some of the best coast in South Africa. The river flats are home to many birds, especially migrating waders in summer. They also offer good fishing, with huge kob.

The name Hamburg is derived from a village established by soldiers of the British German Legion in 1857.

Places to Stay *Hamburg Oyster Lodge* (☎ (0405) 88 1020) offers slightly rough-and-ready self-catering accommodation and a good backpackers' section where dorm beds are R25. Doubles are R35 per person. They offer cruises and fishing trips on the lagoon. On Tuesday they can pick you up from East London.

The *Hamburg Hotel* (☎ (0405) 881061) is a comfortable family hotel with dinner, bed and breakfast for R80 per person (slightly more in summer).

Getting There & Away Apparently there's a daily bus to/from East London, about 100 km east.

Kiwane Resort

The Kiwane Resort is about six km east of Hamburg and shares the same superb length of beach. The resort is operated by Contour. There are bargain bungalows at R20 per person and expensive tent sites for R30. If the bungalows are full you can hire tents for R30.

EAST LONDON

This bustling port with 175,000 residents has a good surf beach and a spectacular bay which curves around to huge sand hills. The port, on the Buffalo River, is South Africa's largest river port.

After being hit hard by the recession, East London is regaining its family-holiday atmo-sphere. However, the surfside suburbs of Quigney and Beach are still rather drab places on cool, windy days.

Orientation

The main downtown street is Oxford St, with the city centre extending from about Argyle St south to Fleet St. Fleet St runs east, passing Currie St (which runs down to Orient Beach) and eventually, after a few corners and changes of name, meeting the Esplanade near the aquarium.

East of the river mouth and reached via Currie St, Orient Beach is popular with families and has a tidal pool. Eastern Beach is the long main beach fronting the Esplanade, but Nahoon Beach on the northern headland is better, with great surf. The best surfing is near Bats Cave, towards the south end of Nahoon Beach.

Information

The helpful Municipal Tourist Authority (☎ (0431) 26015) is on Argyle St behind the city hall. It's open from 8.30 am to 4.30 pm on weekdays and 8.30 to 11 am on Saturday. Rennies Travel (☎ (0431) 23611) is at 33A Terminus St.

At the Telkom office on Gladstone St you can make international calls between 8 am and 4 pm Monday to Thursday, until 3.30 pm on Friday and from 8 to 11.30 am Saturday. The AA (☎ (0431) 21271) is at 27 Fleet St.

Outdoor Living in Central Square on Gladstone St has hiking equipment. Screaming Blue Surfboards at 6 The Esplanade hires boards for about R20 per day, and they occasionally have wetsuits for hire. If you have US$100 a day to spare you could ask here about Cape Town to Durban surfing tours.

Get information about diving clubs in the area at Pollock's Sport & Surf (☎ (0431) 24921) at 33 Union St. Anglers can get information from East Cape Angling Tours (☎ (0431) 47 2930) – they provide guides and equipment.

Things to See & Do

The small **aquarium** on the beachfront is worth a look; entry is R5 (children R2.50).

EASTERN CAPE PROVINCE

EASTERN CAPE PROVINCE

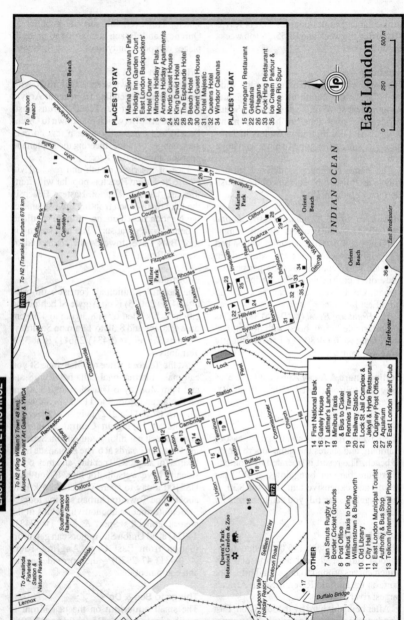

PLACES TO STAY
1 Marina Glen Caravan Park
2 Holiday Inn Garden Court
3 East London Backpackers'
4 Hotel Osner
5 Mimosa Holiday Flats
6 Annexe Holiday Apartments
24 Nordic Guest House
25 King David Hotel
28 The Esplanade Hotel
29 Beach Hotel
30 Orient Guest House
31 Hotel Majestic
32 Queens Hotel
34 Windsor Cabanas

PLACES TO EAT
15 Finnegan's Restaurant
22 Gelataria
26 O'Hagans
33 Fook Hing Restaurant
35 Ice Cream Parlour &
   Monte Rio Spur

OTHER
7 Jan Smuts Rugby &
   Border Cricket Grounds
8 Post Office
9 Minibus Taxis to King
   Williamstown & Butterworth
10 Old Library
11 City Hall
12 East London Municipal Tourist
   Authority & Bus Stop
13 Telkom (International Phones)
14 First National Bank
16 Gately House
17 Latimer's Landing
18 Minibus Taxis
   & Bus to Ciskei
19 Rennies Travel
20 Railway Station
21 Lock St Jail Complex &
   Jekyll & Hyde Restaurant
23 Quigney Post Office
27 Aquarium
36 East London Yacht Club

East London

Coelacanth – a Living Fossil

Coelacanthes, a primitive lobe-finned fish of the family Coelacanthidae, first appeared during the Devonian era, some 350 million years ago. It is believed that these fish gave rise to amphibians, the first land vertebrates. This fish was thought to have become extinct about 70 million years ago as no fossil coelacanthes were found in rocks formed later.

It was near East London in 1938 that a fishing trawler captured a living coelacanth, subsequently named *Latimeria*, and its very close resemblance to its fossil ancestors earned it the tag 'living fossil'. The coelacanth reaches a weight of 70 kg, a length of 1.5 metres and its body is light blue to brownish in colour. The *Latimeria* in the East London Museum is certainly dead – it's stuffed – but others have since been found, causing some rethinking about just what might be lurking in the world's oceans. ■

The **museum** is at the north end of Oxford St, on the corner of Lukin St. The exhibits include the world's only dodo egg, a Coelacanth and displays on Xhosa culture. The museum is open from 9.30 am to 5 pm on weekdays, 9.30 am to noon on Saturday, and 11 am to 4 pm on Sunday. Entry is R2.50 for adults.

The **Ann Bryant Art Gallery** is on St Marks St, just north of the museum, in an old mansion built in a mixture of Cape Dutch and Victorian styles. It is open from 9.30 am to 5 pm on weekdays, and 9.30 am to noon on Saturday and every third Sunday of the month.

Queen's Park contains a small **zoo**, open daily; admission is R5 (children R2.50). **Gately House**, near the entrance to Queen's Park, is furnished in period style. It's closed at present for renovations.

The **Guild Theatre** at the north end of Oxford St, near the corner of Connaught St, is a busy place in season, with everything from ballet to beauty contests.

Latimer's Landing is a new harbourside development near the Buffalo River, with restaurants and shops. If there are enough people you can hire the yacht *Miscky* (☎ (0431) 35 2232) for sailing cruises. The double-decker *Tug & Ferry* (☎ (0431) 43 1188) cruises up and down the Buffalo River (R15).

Places to Stay

Some of the more expensive places have off-season specials, and prices rise during holidays. For longer-term rentals try the accommodation agency (☎ (0431) 43 7933).

Bottom End The *Marina Glen Caravan Park* (☎ (0431) 28753) is expensive at about R35 for a site and R65 a double for a caravan.

About 12 km south of town, just off Marine Dr in Cove Rock, is the picturesque *Lagoon Valley Holiday Resort* (☎ /fax (0431) 46 1080). It is a great place for bird-watchers as over 150 species have been spotted in the park. In the high season it is expensive – caravan sites (up to four people) are R60 per night, with a R250 deposit. Out of season, sites are R15 plus R7.50 per person. In the high season, cottages are R150 plus R10 per person.

The *East London Backpackers'* (☎ (0431) 23423) is in a great position near the beach at 128 Moore St; dorm beds cost R20. The hostel is in a fairly small house and things can get crowded. To get there, take the Beach bus from Oxford St. The *YWCA* (☎ (0431) 29819), on St Georges St, opposite the Premier Bakery and two blocks from Oxford St, has rooms for women or couples for about R35 per person, but unfortunately it is usually full.

There are a couple of cheap boarding houses on Currie St towards Orient Beach. Neither is very appealing and both cater to long-term, chain-smoking residents. The *Nordic Guest House* (☎ (0431) 22159) is at 28 Currie St, and the *Orient Guest House* (☎ (0431) 43 1081) is across the road further down Currie St. Expect to pay no more than R45 per person at either.

Not great, but much better than these, the *Beach Hotel* (☎ (0431) 43 9156), on Fitzpatrick Rd near the Esplanade, has rooms from R60/100. There's sometimes a live band, and there's dancing every night in the African Nite Club. The *Hotel Majestic* (☎ (0431) 43 7477) in Orient Rd has a few rooms for R50/85.

Middle Towards the south end of Currie St near Orient Beach is the *Queens Hotel* with singles/doubles for R91/114 with breakfast. It is a great place to stay if you want to see a band but not if you want to sleep – the band plays in the Rhumba Den on Friday and Saturday from 9 pm to 3 am. The budget area of this hotel has an overwhelming smell of stale urine.

The Hotel Osner's *Annexe Holiday Apartments Flats* (☎ (0431) 43 3433) on Longfellow St are self-contained units, costing R100/130. They're definitely good value but are often booked out. *Windsor Cabanas* (☎ (0431) 43 2225), on Currie St, is much more up-market and costs R175/230.

The comfortable *Mimosa Holiday Flats* (☎ (0431) 43 3433), on Marine Terrace, are R115/175.

The *Esplanade Hotel* (☎ (0431) 22518), on Clifford St near the beachfront, is a good mid-range hotel with rooms from R100. Their bed and breakfast weekend rates are even better – about R65/85 for a single/double. Most rooms have a sea view. The *King David* (☎ (0431) 23174), at 25 Inverleith Terrace, Quigney, has singles/doubles for R145/179.

Hotel Osner (☎ (0431) 43 3433) is on the beach north of the aquarium and has rooms from R165. North of here is the *Holiday Inn Garden Court* (☎ (0431) 27260), on the corner of John Bailie Rd and Moore St, with rooms from R154. A new member of the Osner group, the *Kennaway* (☎ (0431) 25531) has rooms for R159; breakfast is R25 and dinner R31.

A reader has recommended *Embassy Apartments* on Fitzpatrick St, with low-season doubles for R95.

Places to Eat

Most of the beachfront hotels have restaurants, or for a value breakfast (R18) try the *coffee shop* at the front of the Mimosa Flats.

There's a bar and cafeteria at the *railway station*. *Finnegan's Restaurant*, on Terminus St west of Oxford St, is a good restaurant, with cheap pub lunches for R12. On Orient Beach, near the car park at the end of Currie St is *Movenpick*, an up-market Swiss place with meals from R35.

The *Jekyll & Hyde* is in the Lock St Jail complex; pub meals are R15. At 55 Currie St, near Fleet St, the *Fook Hing* is a Chinese takeaway open during the day. In the Orient Mall on Currie St at the *Little Portugal*, you can get mouthwatering prawns, paella and bacalhau (and sangria to wash it down); main courses start at R25.

At the *Beach Hotel* on Fitzpatrick St, near the Esplanade, pub lunches cost from R6 and a five-course lunch on Sunday costs under R18. Also on The Esplanade is the popular *O'Hagan's* where you can get steaks, burgers, chicken and salads – a full meal is R30 plus, burgers are from R11. The upstairs bar occasionally has live music.

Steakhouses abound. The *Monte Rio Spur* is on Orient St near the beachfront, the *Porterhouse* is in the Papagallo Building on The Esplanade, and there are two *Steers*, on Oxford St and on Devereaux Ave, Vincent Park. All of these charge about R30 for main courses.

Among the choices at Latimer's Landing is the *Sportsmans Bar* which serves pub lunches (R12) and dinners; at *Hunter's Jetty* they serve meat parrillada-style (on skewers); and the *Tug & Ferry* has both à la carte meals and a pub menu.

Entertainment

The East Londoners know how to enjoy themselves and there is no shortage of party venues. Many restaurants have live entertainment on Friday or Saturday nights. There is often live music at Jekyll & Hyde; there is dancing nightly in the African Nite Club in the Beach Hotel; a Zairean kwasa-kwasa band plays Friday and Saturday night in the Rhumba Den at the Queens Hotel; a more sedate band plays at Movenpick on the weekend; and Jacqueline's in Nahoon rocks on Saturday night.

The bars in the more expensive hotels always seem to be fairly crowded, especially the Holiday Inn. There are a few nightclubs; perhaps the most popular with the local crowd is Numbers near the Osner. Latimer's Landing has a good feel to it at night – there are restaurants to choose from as well as Nauty's Nite Club.

The Vincent Park Cinemas show a range of movies including recent South African productions and foreign art-house films. If you have children, try the Water Park in West Bank (below the Race Track); for R10 kids can have as many rides as they like on the supertube and speed slides.

Getting There & Away

Bus Transtate runs daily to Queenstown, from where many other Transtate services leave. There is also a Monday to Saturday service between Durban and Fort Beaufort/King William's Town which stops in East London. Translux has buses to Jo'burg/Pretoria (R200), Cape Town (R170), Durban (R135), Umtata (R60) and Port Elizabeth (R70). Transtate and Translux leave from the railway station.

Greyhound stops at the Orient Theatre on Currie St, en route between Durban (R140) and Port Elizabeth (R90). Intercape Mainliner (☎ (0431) 53 3184) also has daily buses to Port Elizabeth. Minilux (☎ (0431) 41 3107) runs to Grahamstown (R40) and Port Elizabeth (R50). Buses depart from East London at 7 am Tuesday to Friday and at 4 pm on Sunday.

The Gonubie Bus Company (☎ (0431) 40 3637) runs school buses through the local area and might be useful in getting to some of the smaller towns. Several bus companies stop at the tourist office behind the town hall.

Train The *Amatola* from East London to Jo'burg departs daily at 12.30 pm, except Saturday. The fare to Jo'burg in 1st/2nd/3rd class is R215/149/96. This train goes via Bloemfontein (R134/93/60), from where there are connections to Cape Town.

Minibus Taxi There are two main areas to find minibus taxis, both in the black area of town west of Oxford St. On the corner of Buffalo and Argyle Sts are long-distance minibus taxis to the north of East London; nearby on the corner of Caxton and Gillwell Sts are taxis for the old Ciskei and the local area.

Getting Around

Most city buses stop at the city hall on Oxford St. For information on bus times and routes phone Amatola Regional Services (☎ (0431) 21251). One of the most useful is the Beach route, which runs down Oxford St, east along Fleet, Longfellow and Moore Sts then back along the Esplanade to Currie St and back to Fleet St and the city.

There's a taxi rank on Union St (☎ (0431) 27901) on the corner of Oxford St, or you can try phoning ☎ (0431) 43 8076, 33 1175, 33 8884, 43 9918 or 31 1576.

Tours Various half-day tours of the city and the nearby area cost R17.50 per person; contact the tourist office or Kingfisher Tours (☎ (0431) 81 1835).

AROUND EAST LONDON
Strandloper Hiking Trail

This three-day trail runs between East London and Kei Mouth. No permit is required as long as you stick to the beach. The Border Branch of the Wildlife Society in the Lock St Jail (☎ (0431) 43 9409) has a useful booklet (R0.50). If you're thinking of walking the trail you'll need a copy of the tide tables, as there are several estuaries to cross and it's dangerous to do so when the tide is flowing out. *What's On In East London*, available at the tourist office and some hotels, includes the monthly tide tables.

Camping on the beach is prohibited but the coast is littered with resorts, most of which have tent sites. The trail is usually walked from Kei Mouth, where there is a caravan park and a couple of hotels.

Mpongo Park

This park (☎ 04326) 669), is 30 km north-west of East London, has some 40 species of animals, including hippo, elephant and rhino. It offers horse-riding and walking trails of one to four hours' duration (you have to hire a guide for about R20 for half a day). There's an entry fee of R5 per person plus R10 per car, and tent sites cost R20 for four.

EAST LONDON TO THE KEI RIVER

There are many resorts on the coast north of East London. The East Coast Resorts turn-off from the N2 will get you to most of them.

The first series of beaches to the north are centred around **Gonubie**. There is a small nature reserve here where 130 species of bird, mostly waterfowl, have been recorded. It is reached from the N2; follow the signs to Gonubie, turn off before the municipal offices then follow 7th St to its end.

The next concentration of beaches is around **Haga-Haga**, a small seaside village about 72 km north of East London (30 km of this is on gravel road after you turn off the N2). There are a couple of nature reserves in the region. **Bosbokstrand** (☎ 054372), ask for Mooiplaas 4512) is a private nature reserve to the south-west of Haga-Haga.

The northern tip of the 240-hectare **Cape Henderson Nature Reserve** adjoins the village of Haga-Haga. This is a very scenic reserve with sandy stretches of beach, rugged coastline and coastal forest. Wildlife includes vervet monkeys and Cape clawless otters.

To the north of Haga-Haga, and reached by turning off the N2 on to the R349, are Morgans Bay and Kei Mouth. **Kei Mouth** is the last resort before the Wild Coast. There is a small museum with a shell collection here but it is the fishing which attracts most visitors.

Places to Stay & Eat

There are two caravan parks in Gonubie, the *Gonubie* (☎ (0431) 40 2021) and *Yellow Sands* (☎ (0431) 38 3043). The *Gonubie Mouth Hotel* (☎ (0431) 40 4010) is good value at R45/80 for singles/doubles with breakfast.

Not far from Haga-Haga is *Dingaan's Kraal* (☎ (04372) 6911), an unusual place which consists of 10 traditional Xhosa huts. Park your car at the golf-club car park and walk the two km to the kraal, which is in a natural amphitheatre next to the Mtwentwe Ravine. The huts have woven mats and candle lanterns; there are no toilets, and you bathe in the stream. From the kraal there is an interesting 12-km trail which takes in the Mtwentwe and Haga rivers. *Haga-Haga Hotel* (☎ (04372) 6302) costs from R126 per person including dinner and breakfast; all the rooms face the sea.

At Morgans Bay there is a caravan park at the *Morgan Bay Hotel* (☎ (043272), ask for 62). The hotel is quite pricey but meals in its restaurant are good value: hamburgers R7, fish and chips R12.50 and steak R18.

The Kei Mouth *municipal caravan park* (☎ (043272), ask for 4) is on the main road into town. One of the cheapest places along the coast is the *Kei Sands Hotel* (☎ (043272), ask for 11 or 47) which advertises bed and breakfast for a mere R32.50 per person in the off season. Also at Kei Mouth is the *Whispering Waves* (☎ (043272), ask for 30) which has bungalows and chalets.

Settler Country & Around

As well as the area immediately around Grahamstown, the heart of Settler country, this section also covers most of the old Ciskei homeland (the Ciskei coast, known as the Shipwreck Coast, is covered in the earlier Nature's Valley to the Kei River section).

GRAHAMSTOWN

Grahamstown is the capital of Settler country and the Borders. It still feels like a strange English transplant, which is emphasised by the lack of neon signs and billboards. There are some fine churches and

The Settlers

In 1820, English settlers, duped by their government and believing they were arriving in a peaceful land of plenty, arrived at Algoa Bay. In reality they were arriving in a heavily contested border region with Boers on one side of the Great Fish River, and Xhosa on the other, both battling interminably over the country known as the Suurveld.

The Suurveld was suitable for cattle grazing, and the Boers and the Xhosa rustled each others' herds unmercifully. Grahamstown was at the centre of the maelstrom. In 1819 in the Fifth Frontier War, 9000 Xhosa under the leader Makanda attacked Grahamstown and very nearly defeated the garrison. The story goes that Makanda would have succeeded had he not observed the Xhosa war code and given free passage to a woman who carried a hidden keg of gunpowder to the defenders.

The only government-sponsored migration in South Africa's history was intended to create a buffer of market gardeners between the cattle-farming Boers and Xhosa, but the Suurveld was completely unsuitable for intensive cultivation. It was not long before the 1000 immigrant families found farming untenable. The odds were stacked against them: inexperience, hostile neighbours, labour shortages, floods, droughts and crop diseases all played a role. By 1823 almost half of the settlers had retreated to the townships to pursue trades and businesses they had followed in England.

As a result, Grahamstown developed into a trading and manufacturing centre. Most of the trade was between whites and blacks. Axes, knives and blankets were exchanged for ivory and skins. Travelling merchants, using Grahamstown as their base, ventured further and further afield. Tradespeople among the settlers produced ironmongery, wagons and clothes.

Port Elizabeth and Port Alfred developed to service what had quickly become the second largest city in the Cape colony. The Sixth Frontier War (1834-1835) sent even more refugees into Grahamstown, and the surrounding countryside was almost totally abandoned. ■

19th-century buildings. There is also a large student population (3000) attending the university, which adds some life to the church-going Grahamstown merchants – although not much. There are a couple of pubs, and that seems to be it. On the other hand, there are 40 churches, all of which manage to draw healthy congregations.

Information

The Publicity Association (☎ (0461) 23241), on Church Square, is open on weekdays from 8.30 am to 5 pm (to 4 pm on Friday) and Saturday from 9 am to 1 pm. They can put you in touch with B&Bs with rates from R40 to R75, and they also have a useful *What's On* magazine. The Association can be difficult to spot – it's in a small building next to the Standard Bank.

SASTS (☎ (0461) 26791), the South African Students' Travel Service, has an office in the Rhodes University student union. Tom Tit's Travel (☎ (0461) 22235), 84 High St, handles bookings for all local travel and are also agents for Avis.

Grahamstown Festival

The town hosts the very successful National Festival of Arts (based at the 1820 Settlers Memorial), and an associated Fringe Festival. The Fringe alone has more than 200 events. The festival runs for 10 days, beginning at the end of June; accommodation can be booked out a year in advance. For more information contact the 1820 Foundation (☎ (0461) 27115).

Albany Museum

The museum (☎ (0461) 22312) has four components, and admission to all of them is R3. All except Fort Selwyn, which is open by appointment (☎ (0461) 22397), are open on weekdays from 9.30 am to 1 pm and 2 to 5 pm.

The most interesting of the four is the wonderfully eccentric Observatory Museum, on Bathurst St, which is highly recommended. Originally a private house, it includes the only camera obscura in the southern hemisphere – a complicated series of lenses, a bit like a periscope. The camera obscura only functions in clear weather.

EASTERN CAPE PROVINCE

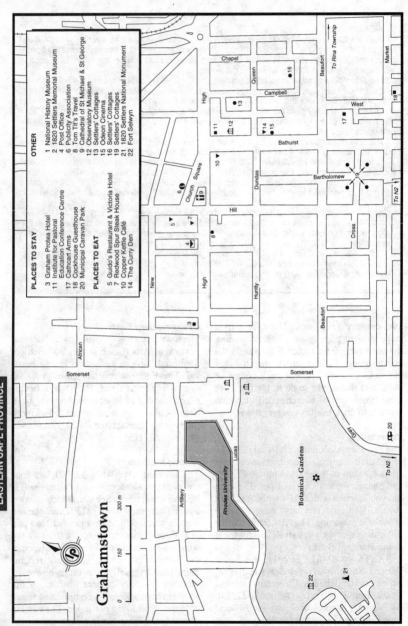

Grahamstown

PLACES TO STAY

3 Graham Protea Hotel
11 Institute for Pastoral
   Education Conference Centre
17 Cathcart Arms
18 Cockhouse Guesthouse
20 Municipal Caravan Park

PLACES TO EAT

5 Guido's Restaurant & Victoria Hotel
7 Redwood Spur Steak House
10 Copper Kettle Café
14 The Curry Den

OTHER

1 National History Museum
2 1820 Settlers Memorial Museum
4 Post Office
6 Publicity Association
8 Tom Tit's Travel
9 Cathedral of St Michael & St George
12 Observatory Museum
13 Settlers' Cottages
15 Odeon Cinema
16 Settlers' Cottages
19 Settlers' Cottages
21 1820 Settlers National Monument
22 Fort Selwyn

The National History Museum, on Somerset St, depicts the history of early man, but also has some interesting African and Xhosa artefacts, including a Xhosa hut. The 1820 Settlers Memorial Museum, also on Somerset St, houses a collection of family treasures, furniture, military memorabilia, paintings and historical photos.

Fort Selwyn, on Gunfire Hill, which was built in 1836 as a semaphore station, has been fully restored.

Dakawa Art & Craft Project

Begun in the ANC's Dakawa refugee camp in Tanzania, the project moved to Grahamstown in 1991 when the ban on the ANC was lifted. It aims to teach people skills and to provide an outlet for their work, which is mainly weaving, graphic art and textile printing. Dakawa (☎ (0461) 29393) is at 4-11 Froude St.

Places to Stay

There was talk of establishing a youth hostel in the old town jail, but until that eventuates the cheapest accommodation option is to stay at the town caravan park. Don't forget the possibility of a B&B (organised through the Publicity Association).

The *Grahamstown Municipal Caravan Park* (☎ (0461) 29112 ext 256) is a pleasant spot, although it's a bit of a walk from the centre of town. A camp site is R20, basic rondavels with no bedding are R45 for four people and five-person chalets are R95.

To get something of the flavour of 19th-century Grahamstown, stay in the *Cathcart Arms* (☎ (0461) 27111), 5 West St, the oldest operating hotel in South Africa. It dates from 1825 and has pleasant rooms, a nice garden and a swimming pool. There's an à la carte restaurant. Singles/doubles are R145/200 including breakfast – a little pricey for what is an interesting but not flash country pub. The public bar with its mainly black drinkers is a lot more interesting than the ladies bar.

The *Graham Protea Hotel* (☎ (0461) 22324), 123 High St, is a characterless building, but it is comfortable enough and in the

Cathedral of St Michael & St George

centre of town. Singles/doubles cost R105/145.

The *Institute for Pastoral Education Conference Centre*, 4 Bathurst St, used to be the Crillion Hotel and they still take casual guests. Despite the old building's new role it still has a courtyard bar and pool tables. It's a nice old building with some good-value options: singles/doubles with shared bathrooms are R105/180 including breakfast.

St Aiden's Court Hotel (☎ (0461) 31 1188), north of the centre on Constitution St, was once a Jesuit college but has been turned into an up-market hotel. Rooms start at R150 per person including breakfast (more in season). Split-level suites start at about R500. To get here from the centre of town, head north up Hill St then turn left on Milner St.

Places to Eat

Outside of the hotel dining rooms, there aren't many sit-down options – there are plenty of cafés and takeaway places. *Guido's Restaurant* in the Victoria Hotel is popular. The *Redwood Spur Steak House* is a decent example of the genre. Expect to pay from R20 to R25 for most main meals.

The Curry Den sells takeaways. The *Copper Kettle Café* is a standard country town café.

Il Tinello at St Aidan's Court Hotel is the best restaurant in town. There are surprisingly inexpensive pub lunches with main courses around R18, and a set-menu (with choices) dinner for R42. The restaurant at the *Cockhouse* guesthouse has also been recommended.

Getting There & Away
Bus Leopard Express (☎ (041) 54 1057) runs from Grahamstown to Port Elizabeth daily for R30.

Translux stops here (Cathcart Arms Hotel) on the daily run between Port Elizabeth (R65 and two hours from Grahamstown) and Durban (R160, 11 hours), via King William's Town (R65), East London (R70) and Umtata (R110). Buses leave Grahamstown for Durban at 8.40 am and for Port Elizabeth at 6.15 pm.

Greyhound stops here on Monday, Wednesday and Friday heading to Port Elizabeth (R65) and on Tuesday, Thursday and Saturday heading to East London (R80) and Durban (R165).

Minilux (☎ (0431) 41 3107 in East London) also runs between Port Elizabeth (R30 from Grahamstown) and East London (R48), via King William's Town (R35) on Monday and Friday (returning Sunday and Friday); and via Port Alfred (R30) and the Fish River Sun (R40) on Tuesday and Thursday (returning the same days).

Minibus Taxis You'll find taxis on Raglans St (the continuation of Beaufort St), but most leave from Rina, the location on the hill at the end of Raglans St. Fares and destinations include Fort Beaufort, R14; King William's Town, R22; Port Elizabeth, R22; and East London, R24.

BATHURST
On the road between Port Alfred and Grahamstown, this scattered village of trees, lanes and hedges is a pleasant place to break your (short) journey. The town was founded in 1820 and South Africa's oldest Anglican church was built there. There are a number of minor attractions in the area; pick up information and a map from The Curiosity Shop, opposite the Pig & Whistle pub.

On the road from Port Albert to Grahamstown, near the turn-off to Bathurst, **Summerhill Farm** (☎ (0464) 25 0833) has a big pineapple and a reconstructed Xhosa village where you can buy handicrafts. There are also farm tours (R5) and meals. Admission is R2. It's closed on Monday – which seems to be the day that Lonely Planet researchers arrive. Firsthand reports gratefully accepted!

The *Pig & Whistle Pub* (☎ (0464) 25 0673), Kowie Rd, Bathurst, could be in England – not all that surprising considering it is in the centre of settler country, and it was built in 1831. It's a popular stopping point on the road from Port Alfred to Grahamstown for good-value pub lunches. Bookings are essential for Sunday lunches. They also have accommodation with bed and breakfast at R70 per person.

There's also a basic *caravan park* (☎ (0464) 25 0639).

The nearby bend on the Kowie River makes a good spot for picnic.

KING WILLIAM'S TOWN
Originally established by the London Missionary Society in 1826, King William's Town (usually known as KWT) became an important military base in the interminable struggle with the Xhosa. After the Seventh Frontier War (1846-1847), British Kaffraria was established with King William's Town as its capital.

Although the homeland of Ciskei's nominal capital was Bisho (six km to the north-east), KWT remains the real commercial and shopping capital of the region. Ciskei's boundaries were carefully drawn to exclude Fort William's valuable real estate. Bisho does have some grandiose government buildings and a Sun hotel/casino, but KWT has the shops, banks, and bustling streets. There are several interesting buildings dating from the mid-19th century, and a good museum (worth visiting), but no pressing reason to stay.

The library (☎ (0433) 23450) has tourist information. They don't have much, but they do have Contour brochures, which might save you a trip to Bisho.

Kaffrarian Museum

The Kaffrarian Museum's collection was begun by the local naturalists' society in 1884, and consequently has a large natural history section. Pride of place is given to the stuffed corpse of Huberta, the hippopotamus, that became famous between 1928 and 1931 when she wandered along the coast from St Lucia in Natal to the vicinity of King William's Town (where she was shot).

The most interesting displays, however, are in the Xhosa Gallery in the old post office building. The gallery has some excellent material on the cultural history of the Xhosa people. The highlights are the fantastic wire cars made by a local craftsman.

Places to Stay

The *King William's Town Caravan Park* at the Grahamstown entry to town is pleasant enough, but a bit noisy; sites are R18. There are a few hotels, but the best option is the *Amatola Sun* in Bisho.

Getting There & Away

Translux buses run between Cape Town (R170 from King William's Town) and East London (R65) via Beaufort West (R140), Graaff Reinet (R135), Cradock (R125), Queenstown (R75) and Cathcart (R75). Westbound buses depart from KWT (at the El Greco Restaurant) at 3.40 pm on Sunday, Monday, Wednesday and Friday; eastbound buses depart at 8.40 am on Monday, Wednesday, Friday and Saturday.

KWT is also a stop on the Translux route between Jo'burg/Pretoria (R200) and East London, via Aliwal North (R95) and Bloemfontein (R150).

BISHO

Bisho, once the capital of Ciskei and a strong contender to be capital of Eastern Cape province, was originally the black location for nearby King William's Town. The centre of Bisho does have some shops, but it was built to house Ciskei's bureaucrats and politicians, so there is a compact bunch of suitably grandiose and ugly public buildings. Curiosity might inspire a visit, but the only practical reason would be to visit Rennies Travel or Contour.

Information

The main Contour office (☎ (0401) 95 2115, fax 92756) is opposite the post office; they have brochures and also handle bookings for hiking trails in the old Ciskei area. The staff are unusually efficient and helpful. Contour was the Ciskei Department of Conservation & Tourism and by now will have become part of the Eastern Cape Province Tourism Board.

Rennies Travel (☎ (0401) 93095) has an office in the North Block of the Phalo Building not far from Contour.

Places to Stay

The *Amatola Sun* (☎ (0401) 91111) is part of Sol Kerzner's Sun International chain, which specialises in high-quality casino/hotels. The Amatola is no exception, and besides slot machines and roulette tables there's golf, tennis and swimming facilities, and several restaurants. Rooms start at about R300.

Getting There & Away

Regular buses run from King William's Town station to Bisho.

MDANTSANE

Mdantsane was established in 1962 to house East London's black workers. It is now the largest town in the area with a population estimated to exceed 250,000. The *Mdantsane Sun* (☎ (0403) 61 2126) is cheaper than some others in the Sun chain.

AMATOLA & KATBERG MOUNTAINS

The area north and west of King William's Town is partly degraded grazing land and partly rugged mountains with remnant indigenous forest. There are some good walks.

EASTERN CAPE PROVINCE

Getting There & Around

The easiest way into this area is via King William's Town or Queenstown. Transtate buses stop in Katberg, Fort Beaufort and Alice on the Queenstown to King William's Town route, daily except Sunday. There are also minibus taxis, but not many.

Amatola Trail

This six-day (105 km) trail begins at the Maden Dam, 23 km north of King William's Town, and ends at the Tyumie River near Hogsback. Accommodation is in overnight huts.

The Amatola ranks as one of South Africa's top mountain walks, but it is pretty tough and should only be attempted if you are reasonably experienced and fit. Walkers are rewarded with great views, although about a third of the walk goes through dense forest, and numerous streams with waterfalls and swimming holes.

The trail must be booked with Contour (or whichever organisation succeeds Contour) in Bisho (☎ (0401) 95 2115, fax 92 756) and costs R20 per person per night.

Evelyn Valley Loop Trail

This two-day (27 km) trail starts and ends at the Maden Dam, 23 km north of King William's Town. The first day is the same as the first day of the Amatola Trail. The scenery includes magnificent forests and numerous streams. It's a fairly easy hike. Book through Contour.

Zingcuka Loop Trail

This two-day (36 km) trail begins and ends at the Tyumie River near Hogsback and covers much the same territory as the last two days of the Amatola Trail. It's a fairly easy trail, but there are some steep sections on the second day. Book through Contour.

Alice & Fort Hare

Alice was established as a missionary and military centre in 1847 (strange how the two things seem to go together). it's now a busy little town, close to the University of Fort Hare. The university was established in 1916

as the South African Native College, and has played an important role in the development of southern Africa. Previous students include Nelson Mandela, Oliver Tambo, Robert Mugabe (the prime minister of Zimbabwe) and Kenneth Kaunda (the president of Zambia).

Within the university, the FS Malan Museum has displays of traditional costumes, charms and medicines; it's open Monday to Friday from 8 am to 4.30 pm. Parts of the original Fort Hare are also preserved in the grounds.

Getting There & Away Frequent minibus taxis run from King William's Town to the main gates of the university and to Alice; they cost around R7. From Alice to Fort Beaufort is R3.50 and to Hogsback costs R8, but you'll probably have to change taxis en route.

Fort Beaufort

In 1846 a relative of Sandile, the leader of the Rharhabe or Ciskei Xhosa, stole an axe from a shop in Fort Beaufort. In a rather disproportionate retaliation, a mixed force of regular soldiers and volunteers invaded the semi-independent Xhosa province of Queen Adelaide, beginning the Seventh Frontier War or the War of the Axe (1846-1847). Today, Fort Beaufort is a small but attractive backwater town with some interesting historical relics.

Historical Museum The museum, on Durban St, is in the old officers' mess and contains a large collection of firearms, curios, and paintings (including one by Thomas Bains). There is a small craft shop behind the museum and an enthusiastic group are in the process of creating an interesting complex. It's open from 8.30 am to 5 pm on weekdays and 8.30 am to 1 pm on Saturday.

Places to Stay Since Deane's burned down, the *Savoy Hotel*, on Durban St opposite the museum, is the best hotel in town, although it is not inspiring and charges R140/200, plus

R15 for breakfast. There are also some slightly cheaper older rooms. Next door, *Pete's Accommodation* (☎ (0435) 32101) has pleasant single/double accommodation for R70/100.

Adelaide

On the road between the N10 and Fort Beaufort, Adelaide is a good example of a slumbering country town in the Eastern Cape. Time seems to have stood still. The huge Market Square now forms a de facto roundabout on the through road – I had to do three circuits before I found the right exit.

Hogsback

Hogsback is a small resort area high in the beautiful Amatola mountains (part of the South African plateau's escarpment) about 100 km north-west of Bisho. The village has a sprinkling of holiday homes and good-value old-style mountain guesthouses. The atmosphere is a little like a fading hill-station in India.

The steepest slopes around Katberg and Hogsback are still covered in beautiful indigenous rain forest; yellowwood, assagai and tree fuchsia are all present. There are also, sadly, extensive pine plantations on land which was once forest. The peaks of the hills are high and bare, reminiscent of the Scottish highlands.

There are some great walks and drives in the area. You can buy booklets detailing walks for a few rand at the Hogsback store. Some of the best roads are unsealed, so check locally before tackling anything ambitious, and definitely think twice if it has been snowing (which happens a couple of times each winter). This is a summer rainfall area, and thunderstorms and mists are common.

Places to Stay The *Hogsback Caravan Park*, near the forestry station above town, has attractive unserviced sites for R15 plus R3 per person. The office is a long walk from the camping area – you have to keep going along the main road past the camping area then turn down another side road. Maybe it's better to let them find you.

The *Hogsback Mountain Lodge* (☎ (045) 962 1005), also known as Arminel, has pleasant cottages, a huge and beautiful garden, and a swimming pool. Dinner, bed and breakfast is extremely reasonable at R105 per person; with lunch as well it's R110. Prices rise in season. Out of season there's a weekend special – from Friday dinner to Sunday lunch for R200.

The *Hogsback Inn* (☎ (045) 962 1006) is not quite as appealing or as cheap as the Lodge, but it is still rather pleasant. It has seven hectares of garden, log fires and a swimming pool. Dinner, bed and breakfast costs from R130/230. From mid-December to early January there's a minimum stay of five days at R170/300 per day. The food isn't great; the bar is.

There's also *King's Lodge Hotel* which isn't in the same league but is OK, with rooms from R160 a double and self-catering units from R140 plus R20 per person.

Katberg Area

Katberg, 110 km north-west of Bisho, is a small town at the foot of a wooded range. The surrounding rural countryside is still very much as it was when this area was part of Ciskei – overworked, underfunded and almost medieval.

It's an interesting drive to Hogsback, 27 km to the east. There are some great views around the Katberg Pass. The road over the pass is unsealed, but although it is in reasonable condition check locally before tackling it after a lot of rain, and definitely think twice if it has been snowing (which happens a couple of times each winter). This is a summer-rainfall area, and thunderstorms and mists are common.

Places to Stay The *Katberg Hotel* (☎ (0409) 31151), eight km uphill from the village, is nothing short of luxurious. There are lots of pleasant walks in the vicinity and the hotel offers horse-riding, swimming, squash and tennis. The food is famous and it's a great place for a long weekend if you don't mind kicking back in front of a log fire if the weather sets in. Rooms start around R250, but ask about specials.

Other towns in the area include Seymour, where there is a hotel with accommodation.

Katberg Trail

A two-day walk begins and ends at the Katberg Forest Station, just below the Katberg Pass. Accommodation is provided in a timber cabin at Diepkloof. It's a fairly easy hike, but you do cover a reasonable distance: 18 km on the first day, 22 km on the second. You can extend the hike into the Mpofu Game Reserve, where there's a hut. The trail costs R20 per person per night. Book through Contour (or whichever organisation succeeds Contour) in Bisho (☎ (0401) 95 2115, fax 92 765).

TSOLWANA GAME RESERVE

The Tsolwana Game Reserve is a 19,000-hectare reserve 57 km south-west of Queenstown. It protects a rugged Karoo landscape south of the spectacular Tafelberg (1965 metres) and adjoining the Swart Kei River. The reserve has rolling plains interspersed with valleys, cliffs, waterfalls, caves and gulleys. There are three vegetation systems: Karoo scrub, fynbos and grassland, and savanna. Although it's a dry region, the flowers are magnificent after rain, most of which falls between October and March.

There is a similarly diverse range of animals, including large herds of antelopes (including wildebeests, hartebeests, gemsboks, elands, blesboks and so on), rhinos, giraffes and mountain zebras. The largest four-legged predator is the Cape lynx. Exotic animals (including deer and the Himalayan thar) have also been introduced for two-legged hunters. San paintings can also be seen in the park.

There is a two-day walking trail and gravel roads for game viewing. You can also take a guided two-night walk for R200 per person (minimum four people). The park is managed in conjunction with the local Tsolwana people, who benefit directly from the jobs and revenue produced. The entry fee is R10.

Places to Stay

There are three lodges (in old farmhouses), each with a lounge, dining room, and three bedrooms (each with two beds) and two bathrooms. There are no shops. The tariff is R250 for up to four people and R25 for each additional person. Bookings are essential and should be made through Contour (☎ (0401) 95 2115, fax 92756) in Bisho.

North-Eastern Cape Highlands

This area is surrounded on three sides by the former Transkei and also has a short border (but no crossing point) with Lesotho. It's high country, in the southern tail of the main Drakensberg, sparsely settled with sheep-farming communities and trading towns doing business with Transkei. Winter brings snowfalls and even in summer Barkly and Naudersnek passes can be very cold – watch out for ice if you're driving. It's a bleak but atmospheric area.

While the Drakensberg here isn't as spectacular as in KwaZulu/Natal, there are no crowds or resorts and there's good walking. There are trails in the vicinity of Rhodes, Lady Grey, Elliot, Barkly East and Maclear.

GETTING THERE & AWAY

Some Transtate buses running from the East Rand (near Jo'burg) or Welkom to Transkei pass through the area, stopping variously at Sterkspruit, Elliot, Lady Grey and Maclear. There is a City to City service from Cape Town to Matatiele in KwaZulu/Natal, via Dordrecht, Indwe, Elliot and Maclear. Elliot to Matatiele is R35, Maclear to Matatiele is R25.

GETTING AROUND

There isn't much public transport, not even many minibus taxis, but a tourist train runs from Barkly East to Aliwal North (see the boxed story on the Zigzag Railway).

BARKLY EAST

This town on the R58, with its scenic and mountainous location, bills itself as the 'Switzerland of South Africa'. It is also at the terminus of the famous 157-km **Zigzag Railway**.

The municipal *caravan park* (☎ 04542, ask for 123) is in Victoria Park in town. The *Drakensberg Hotel* (☎ 04542, ask for 277), on the corner of Cole and Greyvenstein Sts, has singles/doubles from R65/110.

The trout fishing around Barkly East is reputed to be amongst the best in the country. Anglers are well looked after in the *Gateshead Lodges* (☎ 04542, ask for 7211 or 7502). These include *Gateshead*, a farmhouse on the Bokspruit trout-fishing stream; *Tipperary, Glen Nisbett* and *Bothwell* at the north end of the Bokspruit; *Hollywood* on the Sterkspruit; and *Carabas* giving access to the Upper Kraai River.

ELLIOT

Nestled in a very scenic region south-east of Barkly East, Elliot is the centre of a very interesting area. The Xhosa name for the town is Ecowa, referring to the mushrooms which grow here in summer.

Local attractions are the **Gatberg**, a peak that seems to have a hole bored through its centre; the lofty **Kransies**, from where you can sometimes see the sea some 80 km away; and the **Baster Footpath**, a historic stock route. On Denorbin farm, near Barkly Pass between Barkly East and Elliot, are some well-preserved examples of **San paintings** in a 32-metre-long 'gallery'.

Near Elliot is the start of the 39-km, three-day **Ecowa Hiking Trail**. Numbers on the trail are restricted to 10 and you have to be entirely self-sufficient; for information contact the town clerk in Elliot.

The *caravan park* is two km from town at the Thompson Dam. The inexpensive *Merino Hotel* (☎ (045) 313 1137), on the corner of Maclear and Mark Sts, is about R65 per person, breakfast included. The *Mountain Shadows* (☎ 0020, ask for Barkly Pass 3), 20 km north of town on the R58, is more expensive.

LADY GREY

The countryside around Lady Grey, some 50 km east of Aliwal North, is quite beautiful and has the Witteberge as an impressive backdrop. Founded in 1861, the town was named after the wife of a Cape governor, Sir George Grey. The Zigzag Railway passes through town.

There's a *caravan park* (☎ 05552, ask for 19) in town. The *Mountain View Country Inn* (☎ 05552, ask for 112; fax (05552), ask for 114), on Botha St, is a small place with a

---

The Zigzag Railway

The 157-km zigzag railway line from Aliwal North to Barkly East is a magnet for railway buffs. The line, which winds tortuously through the mountainous Witteberge, took over 30 years to construct. A steam locomotive has been allocated to the line and it is hoped that it will operate three times weekly.

The line incorporates eight reverses through the mountains. It was originally intended that the Karringmelkspruit valley be bridged at a height of 90 metres and a tunnel constructed on the far side of the bridge. The tunnel was completed in 1911 but never used; some say that the ship carrying the bridge girders from England was sunk by a German U-boat during WW I. Six zigzags, or line reverses, were constructed instead (the other two reverses are where the line crosses the Kraai River).

The grades on the line are steep with 1:35 quite common. Between the fourth and fifth reverses the grade is 1:30. This is understandable given the fact the train must climb from 1355 metres at Aliwal North to 1991 metres at Drizzly Siding, the highest point on the line and the highest siding in South Africa.

The train leaves Aliwal North at 6.15 am, Lady Grey at 8.30 am and arrives at Barkly East at 12.30 pm. For a current schedule and fares (these change), call ☎ (0551) 34224. ■

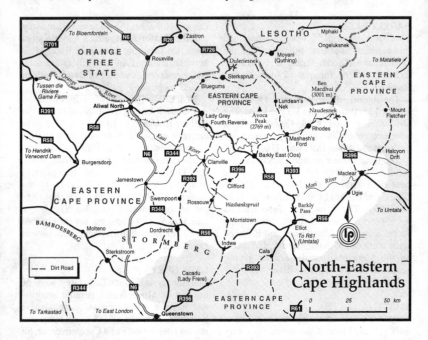

North-Eastern Cape Highlands

dinner, bed and breakfast rate of R110 per person, sharing.

MACLEAR

This is a trading town on the R396. North-west of the town, just before **Naudersnek Pass** (the highest pass in South Africa at 2620 metres). There are exposed fossilised **dinosaur footprints**, believed to be 200 million years old; the earliest evidence of dinosaurs in South Africa.

The *Central* (☎ (045) 323 1005) and the *Royal* (☎ (045) 323 1176; fax 323 1455) hotels offer B&B for about R70 per person; in both places, not all rooms have bathrooms.

RHODES

It can get cold up here! The town is about halfway between Maclear and Barkly East on the R396. Rhodes is a picturesque village with some quaint old buildings.

South African skiers once headed to Oxbow in Lesotho but have now turned their attention to the 'safer' skifields near Rhodes.

The centre for skiing is nearby Tiffindell, and with snow-making facilities they guarantee a season of 100 or so days. **Tiffindell** (2800 metres) is in an area of breathtaking mountain scenery. Nearby is **Ben Macdhui** (3001 metres), where the slopes provide the vertical to 'shred the rad'; there are ski-lifts to get you up to the top. Occasionally accommodation is available in the Tiffindell mountain hut (☎ (011) 640 7416). In summer, there are activities such as mountain biking, horse-riding, grass-skiing and rock-climbing.

The charming *Rhodes Hotel* (☎ (04542), ask for Rhodes 21) looks very much as it would have when it operated as the Horseshoe Hotel a century ago. Rooms with fireplaces and furnished with antiques are about R120 per person for B&B.

ALONG THE N6

The N6 highway runs along the western side of the highlands. It crosses the magnificent Stormberg range, an area of rugged natural beauty.

Aliwal North

On the Orange River, the border between Eastern Cape and the Orange Free State, Aliwal North is a largish town popular for its mineral baths and hot springs. There's a big **spa complex** a few km from the old town centre. In town there are some sights, including a **concentration camp memorial**; ask at the library (☎ (0551) 2362) for a copy of *Aliwal North Information*.

Places to Stay There are plenty of places to stay near the spa, but if you're just passing through, the *Aliwal Hotel* (☎ (0551) 2781) on the corner of Smith and Collins Sts is a solid old hotel charging just R65 per person, including breakfast.

The *Balmoral* (☎ (0551) 2543), in Somerset St, is R77 per person; breakfast is R19 extra.

At the *spa complex* (☎ (0551) 2951) there are chalets for four people from R90 (more on weekends). The spa *caravan park* charges R12 for a site plus R8 per person. Further along the road, *Thatcher's Spa* (☎ (0551) 2772) has rooms from R77 per person or R96, with breakfast. The *Umtali Motel* (☎ (0551) 2400) has singles/doubles with breakfast for R110/180 and, at the *Aliwal Health Springs Motel* (☎ (0551) 3311), bed and breakfast is R75/150. There are also *holiday flats* near the spa; ask at the library.

Places to Eat For takeaways and sit-down meals there are the *Koffehuis* on Grey St and *Nobby's Diner* on Smith St. Out at the spa there is the *Pink Lady* and *Green Trees*; the latter was once a Wimpy and the fare reflects the name. If you crave African-style food, *Ezibeleni*, on the corner of Grey and Murray Sts, has samp, pap and fish balls for about R6.

Getting There & Away A daily Transtate bus stops here at 4.15 am on the Jo'burg to

Queenstown run (at 10 pm in the other direction). Several other services, transporting miners to and from the Transkei area, pass through Aliwal North.

Translux stops here on its Jo'burg/Pretoria to East London run; the Translux depot is at Aliwal Ford. Greyhound buses stop at Nobby's Diner on their Jo'burg to Port Elizabeth run.

The nearest passenger train station is at Burgersdorp, 60 km south-west, on the Jo'burg to East London (Amatola) line. From Aliwal North there's the North-East Cape Zig-Zag Railway between Aliwal North and Barkly East (see the note on this service earlier in this section).

The minibus-taxi and black bus stop is on Grey St, near the corner of Somerset St.

Queenstown

This town was established in 1847 and laid out in the shape of a hexagon for defence purposes. This pattern enabled defenders to shoot down the streets from a central point, but fortunately no shots were fired in anger.

The Stormberg Tourism Association (☎ (0451) 2265) office is in Shop 17 in the Old Market business centre. There are some fine buildings in town, including the 1882 **town hall** with its impressive clock tower, and the **old market building** in the Hexagon. **Queens College**, well over 100 years old and one of the many fine schools in the town, has a reputation for producing great cricketers – Tony Greig and Daryl Cullinan went to school here.

There is great fishing in the dams around Queenstown. Aficionados of all colours talk bait, lures and line strength (in the pub) then head for **Bongolo Dam**, about five km from town on the Lady Frere road, to catch black bass and blue gill. Others head to **Xonxa Dam** in Transkei in pursuit of eels, carp (which is dried and used for fishballs) and other fish.

Places to Stay The *Longview Lodge* (☎ (0451) 4939), 9 Longview Crescent, has singles/doubles for R70/100.

The *Hexagon* (☎/fax (0451) 3015) and

Jeantel (☎/fax (0451) 81428) hotels are adjoining but the entrance to the latter is on Shepstone St. Single/double discount rooms are R91/130 (R115/148 with breakfast) and the best rooms are R100/139 (R120/157 with breakfast). The *Grand Hotel* (☎/ fax (0451) 3017), 41 Cathcart St, is slightly cheaper.

Places to Eat There isn't a great choice. A *Wimpy* is on the corner of the Hexagon Hotel. Steak eaters will appreciate the *Spur* on Cathcart St and *Buccaneers* (similar to the Spur) in the Pick 'n' Pay, also on Cathcart St; a steak meal at either is around R30. The *China Continental*, in the Jeantel Hotel, serves an eclectic mix – Chinese, pizza, steak and pasta. There are *restaurants* in the Hexagon and Grand hotels, and pub lunches cost from R10.

Getting There & Away Queenstown is well served by Transtate buses, with two daily services to Jo'burg (one via Bloemfontein and the other direct) and three services weekly to Durban via Umtata. There's a service to King William's Town, daily except Sunday. Translux buses pass through on the East London-Jo'burg/Pretoria and East London-Cape Town runs; they stop at the OK Bazaar (the fare to East London is R100, to Pretoria R130).

Greyhound passes through Queenstown on the Jo'burg/Pretoria-Port Elizabeth run; the bus stops in the large parking area outside the Hexagon Hotel. The fare from Queenstown to Port Elizabeth is R135; to Jo'burg it's R175.

Cathcart

At the base of the Windvogelberg about 60 km south of Queenstown, Cathcart was established as a frontier post after the Eighth Cape-Xhosa War of 1856. The library, with its imposing neo-Classical façade, is worth a look.

The small *Royal Hotel* (☎ (045) 633 1145) on Carnarvon St charges about R60/100 for bed and breakfast. There are several holiday farms in the vicinity; ask at the library.

Stutterheim

A small town some 160 km inland from East London, Stutterheim (lovingly referred to as plain old 's-s-Stutt') is close to the two-day Kologha Hiking Trail and the famous Amatola Trail in the old Ciskei. The Stutterheim Tourism Bureau (☎ (0436) 32702; fax 32459) is in Legends Coffee Shop at 34 Maclean St.

Eagle's Ridge Country Hotel (☎/fax (0436) 31200), six km from Stutt on the R352, Keiskammahoek and Kologha Forest roads, costs about R110 per person including breakfast.

Transkei

Transkei can still be considered an entity, even though in the new South Africa the homeland has been absorbed into the Eastern Cape Province. Formerly it comprised three areas – a pocket of land which bordered Lesotho to the east of Aliwal North; the main section which runs north of the Kei River all the way up to the Umtamvuna River with the Drakensberg as its western boundary; and another pocket along the Umzimkulu River. The northern pocket is now part of Eastern Cape but it is surrounded by KwaZulu/Natal – a great deal of grass-roots politicking will decide which province eventually claims it.

With natural boundaries (the Kei River and the Drakensberg) Transkei was at least a logical sub-division of the country, unlike most of the homelands.

Transkei's major attraction is its coastline, where you'll find superb warm-water surf beaches and lush subtropical vegetation. There is a good range of accommodation and some excellent hiking trails. Away from the coast the hills are dotted with villages. If you plan to hike around inland Transkei remember that traditional life continues in the rural areas. Always ask permission before camping, but never approach a chief's house without an invitation.

Summers on the coast are hot and humid. Inland, summers can be hot, but many areas

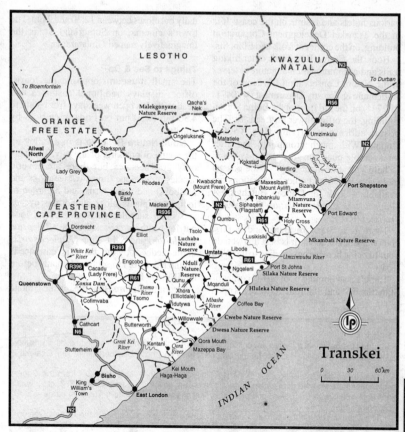

have winter frosts. Most rain falls in March, and spring also sees heavy rains. Unsealed roads can be impassable after rain, especially near the coast where the soil is clay.

UMTATA

Umtata, the main town in the Transkei, was founded in 1871 when Europeans settled on the Umtata River at the request of the Thembu tribe, to act as a buffer against Pondo raiders. Today Umtata is a cracked, crowded town: a capital city of 100,000 people with a village atmosphere. There are power cuts, the phones don't work very well,

and there's a lot of litter. Umtata certainly bears little resemblance to the rural town it was before the creation of Transkei, but unless you prefer neat kerbing to vitality the change was for the better. It's a bustling place, wonderfully free of racism.

Orientation & Information

Most of the hotels and services are in the grid of the small original town. The efficient tourist office (☎ (0471) 31 2885; fax 31 2887) is upstairs on the corner of Victoria and York Sts. Wild Coast Central Reservations (☎ (0471) 25346; fax 25344) books the various hotels and resorts on the coast. It is in the Transkei Development Corporation building, on the corner of York and Elliot Sts.

Book the Coffee Bay Trail, other hiking trails and accommodation at nature reserves at the Nature Conservation Division of the Agriculture & Forestry Department (☎ (0471) 31 2711) on the 3rd floor of the Botha Sigcau Building, the office tower on Leeds St. The postal address is Private Bag X5002, Umtata. With much prompting, and after innumerable questions, the staff may deign to help you. Excellent maps of the coastal trails cost R1.50 and other publications are available – look for Duncan Butchart's *A Guide to the Coast & Nature Reserves of Transkei* (R10).

There is a Standard Bank and a First National Bank in town. It is best that you do your banking here before heading to the Wild Coast.

There's a swimming pool on the corner of Sutherland St and Stanford Terrace; it's open daily but closes between 12.30 and 2 pm. The town's cinema, on Sutherland St, is the imaginatively named Umtatarama.

Things to See & Do

The small **museum**, opposite the tourist office, displays traditional costumes and beadwork. It's open weekdays from 8 am to 4.30 pm (3.30 pm on Friday); entry is by donation.

Nduli Nature Reserve is in a valley on the southern outskirts of the city. It covers only 200 hectares but there are several species of antelope (impalas, steenboks and blesboks) and many birds, and a garden of indigenous plants (aloes, euphorbias, cycads and small succulents). Birdwatchers, look out for southern crowned crane *(Balearica regulorum)* and red bishop *(Euplectis orix)* in the reedbeds by the dam. The entrance is off the N2, three km south of Umtata, before the Holiday Inn.

Luchaba Nature Reserve, on the Umtata

EASTERN CAPE PROVINCE

History

Although the people of this area are collectively known as Xhosa there are several distinct groups – the Bomvana, Pondo, Thembu, Mfengu, Mpondomise and the Xhosa themselves (eg, Gcaleka, Ndalambe and Ngqika).

The Xhosa peoples living east of the Kei River (that is, they lived trans-Kei from the Cape colony) came under the domination of the Cape colony government from about 1873, but it was not until 1894, with the defeat of Pondoland, that the whole of modern Transkei came under European rule.

The Cape government became concerned that the newly annexed areas in the Transkei region were altering the racial balance of the colony's electoral roles. At this time any man in the colony could vote providing he owned a certain amount of property. With large numbers of Africans now citizens of the colony it was feared that their votes might actually change things, so the rules were altered. Property held communally could no longer be used to claim voting rights, effectively disenfranchising most of the Transkei's indigenous population.

There were, however, some people in the Transkei who were qualified to vote and politicians could not entirely ignore the democratic process. A political culture developed in the Transkei and it was hoped that reforms could be made constitutionally, despite the stacked deck.

These reforms never really happened. The Transkei was initially governed by local councils under the authority of European magistrates, and after the Union of South Africa it was granted an almost powerless 'national' council. In the 1950s the South African apartheid regime chose Transkei as the first area to be given limited self-government in its Homelands scheme. This was a farce, as the impoverished Homeland depended on South Africa, both for funding and for the wages of migrant labourers. There were revolts in the '60s, protesting at South African-backed chiefs who led the Transkei deeper into apartheid, but they were put down decisively.

In 1976, the Transkei became an 'independent Homeland'. If its independence had been internationally recognised it would have been classified as one of the world's poorest countries and one of Africa's most densely populated. Now it has been reabsorbed into South Africa (not without difficulty) and hopefully its problems will be addressed. ■

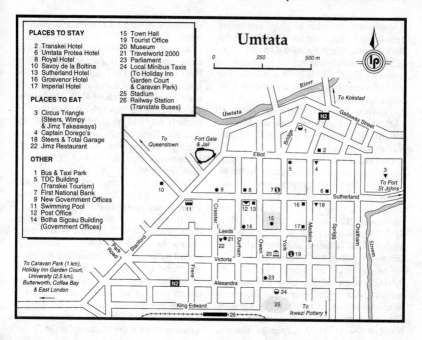

Umtata

PLACES TO STAY

2 Transkei Hotel
6 Umtata Protea Hotel
8 Royal Hotel
10 Savoy de la Boltina
13 Sutherland Hotel
16 Grosvenor Hotel
17 Imperial Hotel

PLACES TO EAT

3 Circus Triangle
(Steers, Wimpy
& Jimz Takeaways)
4 Captain Dorego's
18 Steers & Total Garage
22 Jimz Restaurant

OTHER

1 Bus & Taxi Park
5 TDC Building
(Transkei Tourism)
7 First National Bank
9 New Government Offices
11 Swimming Pool
12 Post Office
14 Botha Sigcau Building
(Government Offices)

15 Town Hall
19 Tourist Office
20 Museum
21 Travelworld 2000
23 Parliament
24 Local Minibus Taxis
(To Holiday Inn
Garden Court
& Caravan Park)
25 Stadium
26 Railway Station
(Transtate Buses)

0   250   500 m

River

To Kokstad

Gallaway Street

Umtata

N2

To Queenstown

Fort Gale
& Jail

Bridge

Elliot

To Port
St Johns

Sutherland

Craister

Leeds

Durham

Owen

York

Madeira

Sprigg

Chatham

Stream

Stanford

Park
Road

To Caravan Park (1 km),
Holiday Inn Garden Court,
University (2.5 km),
Butterworth, Coffee Bay
& East London

Frere

Victoria

Alexandra

King Edward

N2

To
Ikwezi Pottery

Dam, just north of the city, combines grassland and open water. There are zebras, wildebeests and some antelopes, as well as many wetland birds. Of particular interest are the numerous pairs of the rare Stanley's bustard *(Neotis denhami)* which breed in the tall grassland, and the unusual longtailed widow *(Euplectes progne)*, the largest widow seen in southern Africa. The reserve adjoins a watersport recreational area.

The **Wonk'umntu Handicraft Centre** is about five km west of town on the N2 heading towards Butterworth, near the new Shell Ultra City. About three km from the town centre (take the road heading towards Queenstown) is the **Izandla Pottery** which produces stoneware. Another recommended place is **Ikwezi Pottery** (☎ (0471) 35 0701), to the south at the Ikwezi location which is reached via Mnukwana St, an extension of Sprigg St in Umtata. This pottery is part of a self-help programme for the disabled.

A new addition to the icons in this newest

of countries is the childhood home of Nelson Mandela. The first president of free South Africa was born in the village of Mvezo on the Mbashe River. He spent most of his childhood, however, at **Qunu**, 31 km south of Umtata. On the opposite side of the road to the Xhosa village in which Mandela played as a child is a heavily guarded 'presidential country residence' – do not attempt to photograph it. No one will stop you wandering into Qunu – here you can ask to be directed to the Mandela family home.

Places to Stay

The *Umtata Caravan Park* is opposite the hospital on the main road west of the centre. Sites cost R10 per person, with a minimum charge of R18. People have illegally erected dwellings on available flat land near the park – perhaps it is not the best place to stay at the moment.

The crummy *Sutherland Hotel* (☎ (0471) 31 2281), on Sutherland St (if you can find it amidst a ramshackle of shops and empty beer bottles), has doubles without bath for R60. Nearby, the *Royal Hotel* (☎ (0471) 31 1231) is slightly better and has single/double rooms for R60/75 or R75/90 with bath. The staff of these places don't attend their front desks very often.

The big *Transkei Hotel* (☎ (0471) 31 1445), on the corner of Elliot and Madeira Sts, usually has doubles with breakfast from R75 or R85 with bath.

On Leeds St, the *Imperial Hotel* (☎ (0471) 31 1675) charges from R60/80, including breakfast. Try for an upstairs room, as some of the downstairs rooms don't have attached bathrooms and are noisy. For a colonial-era atmosphere the *Grosvenor Hotel* (☎ (0471) 31 2118), on the corner of Sutherland and Madeira Sts, is better and costs R100 per person for dinner, bed and breakfast.

The *Savoy de la Boltina* (☎ (0471) 31 0791/2), out on the Queenstown bypass, has recently been upgraded and now includes a restaurant and bar; it's about R85 per person. The Protea chain's up-market *Umtata Protea Hotel* (☎ (0471) 31 0721), once the Windsor, is at 36 Sutherland St, near the corner of Madeira St; a room here costs R169. The *Holiday Inn Garden Court* (☎ (0471) 37 0181), out of town on the East London side of the N2, has quality rooms from R179/198.

Places to Eat

There are numerous places calling themselves tea rooms, but they are all just takeaways and there's almost nowhere to sit down and have a coffee. Three noisy, crowded *Wimpy Bars* are in the Munitata Building on the corner of Sutherland and Owen Sts, in the new Circus Triangle on the Port St Johns road, and near the Holiday Inn entrance.

There are also two *Steers*, one next to the Total Garage opposite the Grosvenor Hotel and the other in the Circus Triangle. Also in the Circus Triangle is *Jimz Takeaways*, the fast-food branch of the restaurant of the same name. *Captain Dorego's* on the corner of Madeira and Elliot Sts is good value for a quick bite. In Owen St there is a *Chinese restaurant* serving takeaways and sit-down meals.

A good bar and restaurant, popular with locals and ex-pats, is *Jimz* in Metropolitan Place on the corner of Leeds and Craister Sts. It's up-market but not too expensive, with main courses from about R30. The entrées are expensive but superb – calamari for R15, mussels for R14 and shrimp cocktail for R12.50. Their lunch special is R15 and usually includes steak, and the commuter's menu varies from R8 to R15. You should book for dinner.

Out of town, in the Fort Gale shopping complex, is a good Italian place, *La Piazza*, where a small pizza costs from R15.

Otherwise, you're left with the hotel dining rooms. The Grosvenor Hotel claims to have the best food in town, a claim unsupported by a number of locals. The bar at the up-market Umtata Protea is cool and quiet. There is a restaurant here with a good carvery (lunch is about R24 and dinner R30) and another one out at the Holiday Inn. Once a week, usually on Thursday evening, there is a seafood feast at the restaurant in the *Savoy*.

Entertainment

The Holiday Inn has a great bar, *Carmen's*, named after the energetic personality who has kept it for several years. If you escape from the bar without buying biltong then your powers of refusal will become the stuff of local legend.

Jimz has a one-person band on Wednesday and Thursday nights.

Getting There & Away

No-one in Umtata seems to have any idea about the state of local transport into, out of, or around Transkei. Perhaps these two Umtata travel agents will have a better idea: Travelworld 2000 (☎ (0471) 31 2011) and East-West Travel (☎ (0471) 22587).

Air Transkei Airways (☎ (0471) 36 0021) flies to Jo'burg daily (R525 one way) and to Durban (R343) daily except Saturday; if you book 30 days in advance you will get 20% off. They also have air and helicopter charter services (☎ (0471) 24451) to places within Transkei, including Lusikisiki, Mkambati and Mzamba.

Airlink (☎ (031) 42 2676) has services to Durban on Monday, Wednesday and Friday (economy/Apex one-way for R296/182) and to East London on weekdays (R308/194).

Bus Transtate stops at the railway station. It runs to Durban (R45) via Kokstad every day except Sunday; there's also a daily service to Durban via Pietermaritzburg and a daily service to Jo'burg (R85). On Thursday there are two services to Cape Town (R115 from Cape Town but only R95 going the other way). An interesting weekday service runs from the Free State goldfields via Bloemfontein and Queenstown. On Tuesday, Thursday and Sunday there is a service from Queenstown to Durban (returning Monday, Wednesday and Friday).

Translux and City to City (book both on ☎ (0471) 31 2561) stop at the Holiday Inn, quite a way from the town centre. From here the buses go through the town centre, so get your luggage from the hold here and ask to be dropped in town. Otherwise, walk across the road to the university entrance and wait for a minibus taxi (about R1 to town).

Translux has a daily service from Port Elizabeth to Durban which stops in Umtata. A bus leaves Durban at 6.30 am and departs from Umtata at 12.45 pm, and another leaves Port Elizabeth at 7 am and arrives in Umtata at 2.30 pm. The fare to Durban is R105 and it's R115 to Port Elizabeth.

City to City has a service from Pretoria/Jo'burg to Umtata (R105/100) via Kokstad; it leaves Jo'burg on Tuesday and Friday at 7 pm; book through Translux. There is also a City to City service to Cape Town via Queenstown which leaves Umtata at 12.30 pm daily; the cost is R80 to Queenstown and R240 to Cape Town.

Greyhound has a Durban to Port Elizabeth service on Monday, Wednesday and Friday which departs from Durban at 6.45 am and reaches Umtata about 12.30 pm; on Tuesday, Thursday and Saturday the bus goes in the other direction, departing from Port Eliza-

beth at 6.45 am and reaching Umtata around 2.30 pm. Durban to Umtata is R110 and Umtata to Port Elizabeth is R120. The bus stops at the Holiday Inn.

All other services depart from the main bus and taxi park near Bridge St. The Transkei Road Transport Corporation (☎ (0471) 37 0291) has buses to most places in Transkei at least once a day. Services from Umtata include: Port St Johns, 1 and 2.30 pm, R12; Coffee Bay, 1 pm, R12; and Butterworth, 9.30 am and 2 pm, R14. There's also a daily service to Kokstad in KwaZulu/Natal for R25. The TRTC has some good long-distance buses running to Cape Town and to Jo'burg. You can book at the bus station but schedules are often unreliable.

Car Rental Avis (☎ (0471) 36 0066) is at Umtata's KD Matanzima Airport; they can deliver cars to the nearby area.

WESTERN & SOUTHERN TRANSKEI

The best-known attraction of the Transkei is the Wild Coast. There are, however, many interesting places to the west of the N2 and south along it. To the south of Umtata are the important centres of Idutywa and Butterworth. To the south-west is a fascinating region of rolling hills and picturesque Xhosa villages.

Around Lady Frere (Cacadu)

The R396 and R393 run between Queenstown and Elliot. You once had to negotiate a couple of notorious border crossings to traverse this part of the Transkei, so few people used them. The border posts have gone, as has this region's reputation for lawlessness.

The numerous dams at the top of the Great Kei, on the White Kei and Tsomo rivers, attract anglers in search of eels and other fish. The dams include the Xonxa, Lubisi and Ncora. The villages in this region consist of scattered, brightly coloured houses picturesquely set with dramatic mountain backdrops. It's a magic place where the pace of life has changed little in centuries.

EASTERN CAPE PROVINCE

Butterworth

On the N2, just north of the Great Kei, Butterworth is the oldest town in the region, having been established around a Wesleyan mission in 1827. There's not much to see in this sprawling place but you can visit two **waterfalls** near town, the scenic cascades of the Gcuwa and the Bawa Falls of the Qolora.

There's a country club and a couple of hotels: the *Masonic Hotel* (☎ (0474) 3526), with single/double rooms for R35/54; and the *Butterworth Hotel* (☎ (0474) 3531) which charges R65/110, with breakfast. The up-market choice is the *Wayside Protea Hotel* (☎ (0474) 3531); bed and breakfast is R145/175.

Idutywa

This town gets its name from a tributary of the Mbashe River. North-east of the town is an interesting area called the **Colley-wobbles**. It is a place of great beauty with unusual rock formations studding the cliffs and overlooking the Mbashe River.

The local *hotel* (☎ (0474) 27 1040) on Richardson Rd is a typical country hotel, reasonable for a stopover; a single room with breakfast will cost R110.

PORT ST JOHNS

This idyllic little town on the coast at the mouth of the Umzimvubu River has tropical vegetation, dramatic cliffs, great beaches and a relaxed atmosphere. It is about as close you'll come to the new rural South Africa with a dominant black population in town. It's name comes from the *Sao Joao*, wrecked here in 1552.

Port St Johns (PSJ) is deliciously backward. There is no information office as yet but the information in this section (much of it from Kirk Hall of PSJ Backpackers') should be adequate. Queues at the bank are tediously long so bring adequate cash with you. The phones outside the post office take old (pre-'Mandela money') coins; usually one of the four phones is working. Don't post letters here – they will be lucky to get to Umtata.

There are quite a few artists and craftspeople here who have escaped the tensions of South Africa's cities to set up studios and workshops, some of which you can visit. A market is held on Saturday on the beachfront near the Coastal Needles Hotel.

If you are driving, watch out for hidden speed dips which can ruin your suspension if you hit them at speed.

Silaka Nature Reserve

Silaka is a small coastal reserve just south of PSJ, running from Second Beach to Sugarloaf Rock. Birdwatchers will be delighted by the species to be found in the forest next to the Gxwaleni River.

By the shoreline there are many interesting tidal rock pools. Near the estuary, where the Gxwaleni flows into the sea, aloes grow down almost to the water. Clawless otters are often on the beach and white-breasted cormorants *(Phalacrocorax carbo)* clamber up onto Bird Island. Magic!

Places to Stay

Backpackers will enjoy the ambience of this town. An adventurous Aussie, Kirk Hall, has persistently defied the odds and set up his convivial *PSJ Backpackers'* (no telephone; fax (0475) 44 1057) near the heart of town. Kirk's place is an old colonial-style house at the top of a hill where you get glimpses of the beach and town, and all the noise and atmosphere of Africa you desire. From the taxi and bus stop in town walk along the main road parallel to the river, take the fourth bridge on the right past the post office and go up the second driveway on the right. There are few places where you can relax for so little; camp in your own tent for R10, camp in Kirk's tents for R12 or sleep in the dorm for R15. Doubles are R20 per person.

A permaculture farm, *Pete's Place*, is up in the hills behind PSJ. There are views from the farm down to the 360-metre headlands forming the Gates of Port St Johns (Mts Thesiger and Sullivan). It costs R10 to camp here among the exotic forest of flowers and fruit trees (PSJ Backpackers' will rent you a tent for R10). You can buy organically grown vegetables in season.

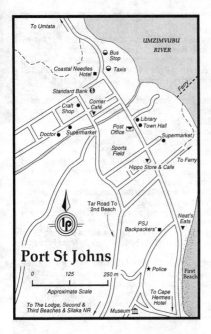

Port St Johns

0   125   250 m

Approximate Scale

didn't appear to have staff on the premises; perhaps we saw it on an off day. Drive or walk an extra 300 metres to The Lodge.

The Lodge (☎ (0475) 44 1171) is superbly situated on the lagoon and has views across to a dramatic surf beach. There can't be many places in the world with a better location. It's a simple old place, with tidy rooms for R80 per person, with breakfast. Sam, the friendly manager, is building backpacker-style rooms behind The Lodge and will charge R25 for a bed. Phone from PSJ to be collected.

Places to Eat
Let's face it, you came to PSJ for the solitude, not the food. The *Corner Café* in the main street serves breakfast (R6); the *Hippo Store Café*, on the same street as the town hall, is good for a simple African dinner (R6 to R8); and *Neat's Eats* by the beach has takeaways.

Sam at *The Lodge* cooks tasty three-course meals; book ahead and expect to pay R35 plus.

Getting There & Away
If you're coming from Durban via Lusikisiki (by far the shortest way) get the daily Transtate bus from the Durban railway station (R25). It departs at 6.30 am and arrives in PSJ at about 3 pm.

Other possibilities from Durban are Translux (R100) and Greyhound (R110) to Umtata from where you catch a minibus taxi to PSJ. The buses stop at the Holiday Inn, four km from the minibus rank in Umtata. You have to get a minibus taxi back to town (R1) and then catch another to PSJ (R12).

If you're driving from Durban take the N2 to Port Shepstone then the R61 to PSJ. There is a good sealed road to Lusikisiki and then 40 km of dirt road; watch out for maniacal drivers on blind corners. The very scenic road (part of the R61) from Umtata to PSJ is sealed, and police speed traps enforce the low speed limit.

Getting Around
PSJ Backpackers' will give lifts to the start of walks for a moderate fee. The ferry (R1) is the quickest way across the river to Agate

Back in town, the *Coastal Needles Hotel* charges from R60/90, with breakfast. It's central but there are better options away from the town centre.

Heading down the coast, the *Cape Hermes Hotel* on First Beach charges from R75 per person, with breakfast. In its heyday this was a great place but it's now run-down (having had a portion of its roof collapse fairly recently). Nearby are the municipal *bungalows* where you can camp for about R12, or there are rondavels. You can walk along the beach to get here from town.

Further along is Second Beach, and there's a *holiday resort* (☎ (0475) 44 1245) with camp sites (R11.40) and dorms in the Pondo Hostel for R17.50 per person. Further along is the *TDC Resort* with similar facilities but higher prices.

The next place, *Lloyd's Cottages* (☎ (0475) 44 1165), has double rondavels from R75. This place looks neglected and

The 'Real Africa' Triangle

This walk captures the essence of the Transkei – wild coastal scenery, rivers fringed by mangroves, isolated Xhosa villages and undisturbed forests.

Starting in Port St Johns, you can take a ferry across the river then hike beside the river (3.5 km) to the Lusikisiki road. Head up the road for four km to Pete's Place in the hills behind Port St Johns (see Places to Stay in Port St Johns in this section). You could get a lift to here with PSJ Backpackers' for R10 for the vehicle.

The highlight of the Triangle is the six-hour hike through forests, farms and Xhosa villages to Franco's Place. You will definitely need a guide to show you the way as there are myriad paths and tracks. The rate for a guide for one day is R20 per party.

Franco's is a special destination. His traditional rondavel (with inset truck windscreens) is perched up on a hillside overlooking the Umtafufu estuary and the Wild Coast beaches. Franco, known to the locals as Machlenga ('staying with the people') lives as one of the Xhosa. When you stay here you get the opportunity to experience traditional ways – throw-net fishing, farming, and sleeping in a hut. Bring your own sleeping mat, sleeping bag and food. A place on the floor is R10 per person. There is no problem finding Franco's – near the Umtafufu mouth there are four rondavels (part of the Wild Coast walk). Look inland and you'll see the track to Franco's.

From the four rondavels you can head south on the Wild Coast walking trail to Port St Johns. You pass a couple of beaches, head over a steep hill (go right over the hill and don't tackle the cliffs unless you are very sure-footed) then along a beach to the village of Poenskop. Here you cross a stream then join a vehicle track through the village. The last stage is along Long Beach to the ferry across the Umzimvubu River. It is about four leisurely hours from Franco's to PSJ.

There are variations of this walk. You could get a lift from PSJ Backpackers' to Nick's Place, a farm three km upstream of the Umtafufu River mouth. It is a 40-minute trip and costs R30 for a vehicle load. At Nick's there is a camp site beside the river. Each camp site is R30 plus R2 for each person; you can stay in the house for R20 per person. Nick will take you up the river to Franco's in his boat for R30 a boat load. At low tide, you can walk from the Umtafufu River car park to Franco's via the mangroves. Take a local guide; a fair price for the guide's services is R10. ■

Terrace even though there is a bridge upstream.

COFFEE BAY

Coffee Bay is about the only town of size, apart from Port St Johns, near the sea. No one is sure of how it got its name, but there is a theory that a ship wrecked here in 1863 deposited its cargo of coffee beans on the beach. The Xhosa name *Tshontini* refers to a dense wood nearby.

Three rivers flow into the sea near Coffee Bay – the Henga ('place of the whale'), the Mapuzi ('place of pumpkins') and the Bomvu ('red'). The scenery is dramatic, with cliffs behind and a km-long beach in front.

Xhosa Arts

A good place to buy Xhosa crafts is at the Tsheze Community Development Centre – Xhosa Arts (☎ (0471) 37 0335) near Coffee Bay. It sells wooden models depicting aspects of Xhosa daily life. To get there, don't go to the Ocean View but continue on to the Lagoon Hotel where you come to a river. Cross the river to where you see a small house on the left; look across to the right to find Xhosa Arts.

Places to Stay & Eat

There are basic huts in *Coffee Bay* (part of the Wild Coast Trail) which cost R30 for six nights – it is assumed that you are walking the Coffee Bay-Port St Johns section of the trail, a five-day hike. Camp sites are R10 per night as ablutions facilities, water and firewood are provided (a permit is required). You can buy mussels, crayfish and other seafood.

The bungalow-style accommodation at the *Ocean View Hotel* (☎ (0471) 37 0253 ask for 980; fax 23548) is just metres from the beach. There is a restaurant in the hotel and delicious seafood snacks are served in the bar. Rooms and all meals cost R95 per person (in high season, R135 to R145).

Getting There & Away

To get to Coffee Bay take the sealed road that leaves the N2 at Viedgesville. A minibus taxi from Umtata to Coffee Bay costs R12 and takes about an hour.

THE WILD COAST

The Transkei coast is notoriously dangerous for ships. Shipwrecked sailors were the first Europeans to visit this part of the world, and few were rescued or made the harrowing journey to Cape Town or Lourenco Marques (now Maputo, Mozambique). One party struggled through to Cape Town to organise a rescue ship, but when it arrived most of the women had disappeared or were living with the Xhosa and didn't want to be rescued.

About 40,000 hectares of indigenous forest survives along the coast. While there is plenty of birdlife (and butterflies galore), the numbers of animals are dwindling.

Places to Stay & Eat

Port St Johns, covered earlier in this chapter, is the only real town on the coast (Coffee Bay, a tiny village is also covered earlier) but there are a number of hotels and resorts. These are undergoing a shake-up, so check first with Wild Coast Reservations in Umtata. Most are family-oriented places charging in the R85 to R110 per person range, rising dramatically (from R140 to R150) around Christmas; prices include all meals. The hotels along the coast are in exciting, remote locations.

There are fairly frequent buses from Umtata to Port St Johns and Coffee Bay, and with patience you can get to most places on public transport or by hitching.

Near the mouth of the Great Kei there are a few places. If you're travelling north from East London turn off the N2 onto the R349; on the south side of the Kei there are self-catering cabanas. (If you're travelling south

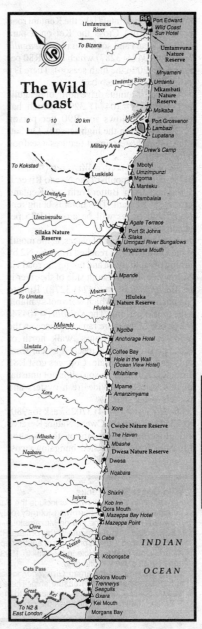

The Wild Coast

on the N2 from Umtata take the Kentani road in Butterworth.) Cross the Kei on a punt (R20 for a car) and soon you reach *Seagulls Beach* (☎ (0474) 3287) which costs R80 per person (R120 in the high season). There is a restaurant and a beach bar.

About a 20-minute drive north of Seagulls is *Trennerys* (☎ (0474) 3293) which has thatched bungalows for R90 per person (R130 to R160 in the high season). On Saturday night the restaurant features a seafood extravaganza.

The next hotel north is *Wavecrest* (☎ (0474) 3273), near the mouth of the Nxaxo River. It is reached from Butterworth via Kentani; turn left at Kentani. This hotel is being renovated and prices will be around R85 per person.

The next collection of places, at the mouth of the Qora River, is reached from the N2 by turning off at Idutywa and taking the road via Willowvale. On the south side of the river is the *Mazappa Bay* (☎ (0474) 3278). Ring to find out their prices which were not available at the time of writing. The *Kob Inn* (☎ (0474) 4421), one of the more famous places on the Wild Coast, is an hours' walk north of Mazappa Bay. It too is reached by car from Idutywa via Willowvale. Cottages cost R85 (from R125 in high season). It is not unusual for this hotel to provide fresh oysters and mussels as bar snacks.

The Haven (☎ (0474) 370253 ask for 980; fax 23548) is near the Cwebe Nature Reserve and close to the mouth of the Bashee (Mbashe) River. Thatched bungalows cost R95 per person (R125 to R130 in high season). Coming from the south you can reach The Haven via Xhora (Elliotdale); turn off at the village of Qunu (Nelson Mandela's birthplace), 31 km south of Umtata. It is about 70 km from Qunu to the hotel and the road is unsealed from Xhora. If you're coming from the north, turn off at Viedgesville, 20 km south of Umtata.

South of Coffee Bay is the *Hole in the Wall* (☎ (0471) 37 0254, ask for 979) with rooms and self-catering chalets; bed and breakfast in the hotel is R50 (R90 in high season). The landmark after which the hotel is named is a two-km walk away. The signposted turn-off to the Hole in the Wall is about 30 km before Coffee Bay.

North of Coffee Bay, near the mouth of the Umtata River is the *Anchorage* (☎ (0471) 34 0061). Anglers flock here in droves. Rooms cost R126 per person (R144 in high season) or R110 (R127 in high season) with shared bathroom. Either head east from Umtata and take the road south-east from Ngqeleni or take the Coffee Bay road. If you take the latter keep an eye out for the signposted road to Umtata Mouth, well before you get to Coffee Bay.

Umngazi River Bungalows (☎ (0471) 22370) is the next accommodation to the north. Bungalows cost R120; R10 more with a sea view and R10 more again in high season. To get there take the sealed road to Port St Johns. About 20 km before PSJ take the signposted turn-off south to the Umngazi Mouth.

Wild Coast Shipwrecks

Famous Wild Coast shipwrecks include the *Sao Joao* (St John) which was wrecked in a storm in June 1552. After a harrowing journey, only eight of the original 440 survivors (over 100 drowned) made it to the Isla de Mozambique, 1600 km away. Two years later the *Sao Bento* was wrecked near the mouth of the Umtata River; one of the survivors had been on the *Sao Joao* and, faced with the prospect of another epic attempt to survive, died in despair. The *Santo Alberto* sank near the Hole in the Wall in 1593 while heading for Portugal, supposedly with a huge cargo of New World gold.

The British East Indiaman *Grosvenor*, which sank in August 1782 on the way home from India, is another reputed treasure ship. There's even a legend that Persia's Peacock Throne was on board. Only 18 survivors made it to the Dutch settlement at the Cape.

One of the latest sinkings was the cruise liner *Oceanos* which went down in 1991. ■

Top of the price tree (and the northernmost of the hotels) is the *Wild Coast Sun* (☎ (011) 780 7800, (031) 304 9237), near the KwaZulu/Natal border and south of Port Edward. A glitzy place geared to holiday-makers and casino enthusiasts. Singles/doubles cost R295/383, or R352/456 on weekends. The Sun is reached from the Kokstad region via Bizana on the R61. If coming from Durban, turn off the N2 at Port Shepstone and follow the R61 (and numerous signs).

There are also camp sites and huts on the Wild Coast Trail (see that section, following) and in the various nature reserves.

WILD COAST NATURE RESERVES

There are five coastal reserves (from north to south, Mkambati, Silaka, Hluleka, Cwebe and Dwesa) and the Wild Coast Trail traverses them all. Silaka Nature Reserve, which fringes Port St Johns, has been covered earlier in this chapter.

Mkambati

Mkambati is an 8000-hectare coastal reserve with some great scenery, including the Msikaba and Mtentu river gorges. The reserve takes its name from the mkambati, or Pondo coconut palm (*Jubaeopsis caffra*), as this is the only place in the world where it is found. The diverse flora of this park makes it well worth a visit. In the grassland you can see patches of the banana-like *Strelitzia nicolai*. Orchids abound in the rocky recesses of the gorges; and proteas, tree ferns and date palms are found along the river banks.

You can take canoes (R5 an hour) up the Msikaba River, navigable upstream for two km; there are also walking trails. A shop sells basic food, and entry to the reserve is R5.

You get there from Flagstaff, 65 km south of the N2 – take the turn-off to Holy Cross Hospital just north of Flagstaff. There are also buses running from Port St Johns to Msikaba on the southern edge of the reserve.

Hluleka

Hluleka, a scenic reserve which combines sea, lagoons and forest, is midway between Port St Johns and Coffee Bay. The coast is rocky, although there is a quiet lagoon which is flanked by a large saltmarsh. As in Mkambati, there is a diverse range of flora.

To get here take the road from Umtata to Port St Johns and turn off to the right at Libode, about 30 km from Umtata. The reserve is about 90 km further on. The road isn't good but cars can usually handle it.

Cwebe & Dwesa

These are adjoining reserves about midway between Coffee Bay and Kei Mouth which take in about 6000 hectares of coastal land. Both have tracts of forest as well as good beaches, and there are hiking trails. The two reserves are separated by the Mbashe River.

Cwebe Nature Reserve In Cwebe you can walk to the Mbanyana Falls or to the lagoon where, if you are lucky, you may see the Cape clawless otter in the late afternoon. On the southern edge of the reserve near the Mbashe River there is a small cluster of white mangroves where sesarmid crabs and mudskippers are found near the stems. Many varieties of rare cowrie are found at Shelly Beach.

To get to Cwebe take the Xhora (Elliotdale) turn-off from the N2 (about 40 km east of Umtata). The reserve is 65 km further on; the road to The Haven Hotel is signposted.

Dwesa Nature Reserve Dwesa, one of the most beautiful reserves in South Africa, is bounded by the Mbashe River in the north and the Nqabara River in the south. In the estuaries of both rivers are mangrove communities.

Crocodiles have been reintroduced to the Kobole, although they are rarely sighted. You may see the herd of elands come down to the beach near the Kobole estuary in the late afternoon. In the thick forests are tree dassies, samango monkeys and blue duikers.

For Dwesa, turn off the N2 at Idutywa (40 km north of Butterworth) on the road to Gatyana (Willowvale). Continue until you come to a fork with another sign to Gatyana

– take the other, unmarked direction. After heavy rain this is no place for ordinary cars.

Places to Stay

There is self-catering accommodation at Mkambati, Silaka, Hluleka and Dwesa reserves, and camp sites at Cwebe and Dwesa. Sites cost about R15 and chalets around R50 per person, although during peak holiday times you might have to take the whole chalet for about R120. All the coastal reserves are on the Wild Coast hiking trail and some trail huts are in the reserves.

Accommodation and sites must be booked at the Department of Agriculture & Forestry in Umtata. Ask for current information on roads into the reserves, as some wash out during the spring and summer rains. *The Haven* is in Cwebe – book through Wild Coast Reservations, Umtata.

WILD COAST HIKING TRAIL

The five-day Coffee Bay Trail, running from Port St Johns to Coffee Bay has been extended to cover the length of the Transkei coast. A walk along this trail is an unforgettable experience – bottlenose dolphins are seen frolicking out at sea, the locals you meet as you wait for ferries welcome you into their villages, and the starry nights are hauntingly quiet. To walk the whole Wild Coast would take about two weeks; most people only do a section.

Three major sections of the trail are described in *Exploring Southern Africa on Foot: the Guide to Hiking Trails* – Coffee Bay to Mbashe River (44 km, four days); Port St Johns to Coffee Bay (60 km, five days); and Umtamvuna River to Port St Johns (100 km; six to 11 days).

The walking isn't especially difficult, but some planning is required as you have to take all your own supplies. Water is available at trail huts (about 12 km apart) and from the streams and rivers, but it must be purified.

The trails must be booked at the Department of Agriculture & Forestry in Umtata, and must be walked from north to south.

Birdwatching on the Wild Coast

The Wild Coast is a great place to take *Roberts Birds of South Africa*, *Newman's Birds of Southern Africa* and a pair of high-powered binoculars.

In Mkambati the strelitzias in the grasslands are a fertile 'watching' ground for Gurney's sugarbird *(Promerops gurneyi)* and the lesser doublecollared sunbird *(Nectarinia chalybea)*. The forests are alive with birds: the trumpeter hornbill *(Bycanistes bucinator)*, rameron pigeon *(Columba arquatrix)*, forest weaver *(Ploceus bicolor)* and noisy Cape parrots *(Poicephalus robustus)* can all be spotted.

The lagoon at Hluleka is a great spot to see the African jacana *(Actophilornis africanus)* tiptoeing across the waterlilies. Near the rivers of the reserve there is an absolute feast of kingfishers: the pied *(Ceryle rudis)*, pygmy *(Ispidina picta)*, brownhooded *(Halcyon albiventris)*, halfcollared *(Alcedo semitorquata)* and giant *(Ceryle maxima)* kingfishers all frequent these areas. The forests are full of robins such as the Cape *(Cossypha caffra)*, starred *(Pogonocichla stellata)*, chorister *(Cossypha dichroa)* and brown *(Erythropygia signata)*.

In the forest clearings of Cwebe look for the blackheaded oriole *(Oriolus larvatus)*, the black saw-wing swallow *(Psalidoprocne holomelas)* and the crowned hornbill *(Tockus abboterminatus)*. In the reeds by the lagoon, spectacled *(Ploceus ocularis)*, thickbilled *(Amblyospiza albifrons)* and yellow *(Ploceus subaureus)* weavers build nests. Water dikkop *(Burhinus vermiculatus)* inhabit the white mangroves.

The many estuaries of Dwesa are good places to look for the shy, furtive African finfoot *(Podica senegalensis)* and the rare whitebacked night heron *(Gorsachius leuconotus)*. By the sea there are African black oystercatchers *(Haematopus ostralegus)*, at their northern limit, and the curious turnstone *(Arenaria interpres)*. Occasionally jackal buzzards *(Buteo rufofuscus)* can be seen soaring in the thermals above Kolobe Point. The forests are particularly rich with species such as Narina trogons *(Apaloderma narina)*, green twinspots *(Mandingoa nitidula)* and Knysna woodpeckers *(Campethera notata)*. ∎

Good maps of the trail sections are available at the department for R1.50 each. There is comprehensive interpretative information on the reverse side of the maps.

The sections and walking fees are: Umtamvuna to Msikaba River (R15), Msikaba River to Port St Johns (R35), Port St Johns to Coffee Bay (R30), Coffee Bay to Mbashe River (R25) and Dwesa to Kei River (R30).

As well as the trail huts there are 15 camping areas along the coast (Mbotyi camping area has closed) where you can camp for up to 31 days. There are from 10 to 40 sites available at these places. Most are near the huts and share their basic facilities. Costs vary, but most sites are from R5 to R10.

Although the sites are on the hiking trail, most can also be reached by car, although you'll need a 4WD to get to some. The trail also passes near the hotels and resorts scattered along the coast.

Warning

Many rivers cut across the trail and crossing them presents the main difficulty for hikers. There are ferries at a few of the larger rivers, but some require wading or swimming. It's important that you know what the tide is doing before you cross – about 30 minutes after low tide is the safest time. You'll need a plastic bag to protect your pack. *Never* try to cross a river while wearing your pack, and wear shoes in case of stone fish or stingrays. It's usually easier to cross a little upstream from the mouth, where you're less likely to encounter the sharks which sometimes enter the estuaries.

NORTHERN TRANSKEI

On the N2 Between Umtata and Kokstad in Kwazulu/Natal are some sizeable towns such as Qumbu, Kwabhaca (Mt Frere) and Maxesibeni (Mt Ayliff). Other large towns in the north are Bizana and Lusikisiki, both in the north-east and not far from the coast. North of the Kokstad corridor is the isolated tract of Eastern Cape, with Umzimkulu as its main centre.

In Mt Frere, the *Mt Frere Hotel* (☎ (04772) 171) has singles/doubles for R30/50. Rooms at the *New Carlton Hotel* (☎ (04772) 31) cost R40/55.

Ntsikeni & Umtamvuna Nature Reserves

The 10,000-hectare Ntsikeni Nature Reserve is in the piece of Eastern Cape cut off from the main body by the Kokstad corridor. It's a wetlands reserve, with several species of crane and many other birds. Keen birders may spot the endangered wattled crane (*Grus carunculatus*).

This Umtamvuna Nature Reserve is being developed as a twin to the reserve across the Umtamvuna Gorge in KwaZulu/Natal. It's an area rich in flowers and plants, and new species are still being discovered here. You may see the prehistoric-looking Eastern Cape cycad (*Encephalartos altensteinii*) growing on the cliffs. For the birders there are Cape vultures (*Gyps coprotheres*) on the fringes of the river gorge and ground hornbills (*Bucorvis leadbeateri*) in the long grass.

Malekgonyane Nature Reserve

This 10,000-hectare reserve borders Lesotho, near the Ongeluksnek border post, west of Matatiele. Wildflowers and birds are plentiful in spring and summer, and walking trails among the dramatic hills and cliffs of the Drakensberg are being developed.

There is a bewildering variety of flora & fauna. Unusual frogs such as the berg stream frog and the aquatic river frog are found in cold clear streams, and many birds of prey can be seen.

Before visiting, check with the tourist office in Umtata, as it has been closed to the public for redevelopment. Its old name was Ongeluksnek Nature Reserve, and some of the road signs might still say that. There are also plans to establish huts at Malekgonyane.

The Karoo

The Karoo, a vast semi-desert, lies on the great South African plateau and is demarcated in the south and west by the coastal mountain ranges and to the east and north by the mighty Orange River. It's a dry, hot and inhospitable region, but fascinating for its sense of space. See the Karoo section in the Western Cape chapter for more information.

BURGERSDORP

Burgersdorp is quite a big country town nestled in a dry Karoo valley, but with trees, a beautiful old church and a laid-back, old-fashioned atmosphere. A blockhouse overlooking the town testifies to its violent past. The *Hotel Jubilee* (☎ (0553) 31840) is a graceful old country hotel with singles/doubles for R75/110, and à la carte meals.

MOLTENO

There's a nice drive to/from Queenstown over the 2000-metre Penhoek Pass, although the northern side is not so spectacular, and Molteno is a flyspeck. Forget it.

MIDDELBURG

Middelburg is an uninteresting town, lying on a plain just to the north of the 2500 metre Sneeuberg range – the Lootsberg Pass is spectacular.

Places to Stay

There's a rather ordinary municipal *caravan park* (☎ (0483) 21337), next to the swimming pool; sites are R15. The *Country Protea Inn* (☎ (0483) 21126) overlooks the pleasant town square and has singles/doubles for R159/212/including breakfast. The *Hotel Middelburg Lodge* (☎ (0483) 21100), on the main street, is not as nice, but it is cheaper at R92/132 including breakfast.

CRADOCK

Cradock is a busy agricultural centre on the banks of the Great Fish River, 240 km from Port Elizabeth. It was established as a military outpost in 1813 and is now an important commercial centre for the rich farming district along the banks of the river. The climate is warm and the water is plentiful, so all sorts of things are grown.

The town has retained some interesting old buildings and there's a distinct Karoo atmosphere, created largely by some shady trees, the river, a superb church (built in 1867 and modelled on St Martin's-in-the-Fields, London), and Die Tuishuis (see Places to Stay & Eat). The surrounding countryside is spectacular; the Mountain Zebra National Park is 27 km to the west.

There are numerous vendors on the roads leading in or out of the town selling wire windmills – these are working models (well, the blades spin) and can be beautifully crafted. Obviously the price will depend on the size and the amount of work that has gone into the piece, but you should be able to get a fine example for less than R20.

Things to See & Do

The **Olive Schreiner House** is a good example of a typical Karoo house. The famous novelist Olive Schreiner lived here as a girl, and Cradock is the centre of the country where she taught, wrote and spent part of her married life. The house is open weekdays from 8.45 am to 12.45 pm and 2 to 4.30 pm. The **Great Fish River Museum** was originally the parsonage of the Dutch Reformed Church. The house was built in 1825 and the displays depict pioneer life in the 19th century. The museum is open on weekdays from 9 am to 1 pm and 2 to 4 pm, and Saturday from 9 am to noon.

Places to Stay & Eat

The municipal *caravan park* (☎ (0481) 3443) has sites for R10 plus R6.50 per person. It's a pleasant spot by the sports ground on the banks of the river.

It is almost worth making a special trip to Cradock just so you can stay in *Die Tuishuis* (☎ (0481) 5098, after hours 3513 or 4229). This is a unique concept in accommodation – in one of Cradock's old streets, cottages have been beautifully restored and are rented

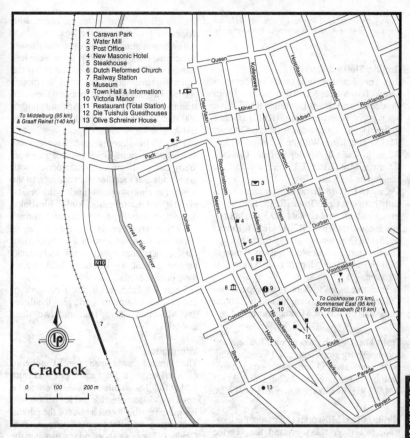

1 Caravan Park
2 Water Mill
3 Post Office
4 New Masonic Hotel
5 Steakhouse
6 Dutch Reformed Church
7 Railway Station
8 Museum
9 Town Hall & Information
10 Victoria Manor
11 Restaurant (Total Station)
12 Die Tuishuis Guesthouses
13 Olive Schreiner House

To Middelburg (95 km)
& Graaff Reinet (140 km)

Queen
Kollegeweg
Hoplifaai
Naedeer
Rocklands
Webber
Milner
Albert
Park
Stockenstroom
Beeren
Cawood
Victoria
Spring
Durban
Dundas
Adderley
Frere
Great Fish River
N10
Voortrekker
11
To Cookhouse (75 km),
Sommerset East (95 km)
& Port Elizabeth (215 km)
Commissioner
Nu Stockenstroom
Hoog
Kruls
Brea
Market
Parade
Revent
7

Cradock

0   100   200 m

EASTERN CAPE PROVINCE

on a nightly basis. You have your own cottage, with a lounge and fireplace, kitchen and garden. Staying in one of the cottages is like stepping back in time. (My cottage had a wind-up gramophone and the one record was a 78 of songs from an old Indian movie – truly bizarre.) It costs R100 per person with breakfast, with dinner available for R30.

The competition is the *Victoria Manor* (☎ (0481) 71 1650) a pleasant, big old country pub with rooms from R50 to R70 per person. Breakfast is R15. *Die Taphuis*, in the hotel, is the best place in town for meals; main courses are around R25. The *New*

Masonic Hotel (☎ (0481) 3115), Stockenstroom St, is pretty plain by comparison to the competition and singles/doubles/triples are R110/180/230.

In the Total service station on Voortrekker St is, surprisingly, a reasonable restaurant. Dishes are the standard steak and seafood (around R20 to R25) with occasional all-you-can-eat pizza deals, but it's a friendly, lively place.

This restaurant plays tapes of up-to-date pop. Not such a big deal if you've just arrived in South Africa, but I hit Cradock after nearly three months in the country. By that stage I was set for violence if I heard one more tape of American schmaltz from the early '70s.

Getting There & Away

Bus Translux stops here on the run between Cape Town (R155, 10½ hours from Cradock) and East London (R135, five hours) via Beaufort West (R115), Graaff Reinet (R95), Queenstown (R95), Cathcart (R115) and King William's Town (R125). Buses to Cape Town depart from Cradock (Struwig Motors) at 7.35 pm; and to East London at 4.35 am.

City to City (a Translux subsidiary) runs daily between Cape Town (R115, 12½ hours from Cradock) and Umtata (R75, 6½ hours), via Beaufort West (R70), Graaff Reinet (R25) and Queenstown (R25). Buses to Cape Town depart from Cradock railway station at 7.30 pm and they depart from Umtata at 4.25 am.

Transtate buses to Cape Town depart from Cradock on Thursday night, and to Umtata in the early hours of Monday morning.

Train The *Algoa* between Port Elizabeth and Johannesburg stops here at 7.15 pm heading north, and at 4.55 am southbound. First/2nd/3rd-class fares to Jo'burg are R183/124/77; to Port Elizabeth they're R68/47/28.

Minibus Taxi Most taxis leave from the location, but if you ask around the service stations in town you might get lucky.

MOUNTAIN ZEBRA NATIONAL PARK

The Mountain Zebra National Park is on the northern slopes of the 2000-metre Bankberg range and has magnificent views over the Karoo. It's a small park (around 7000 hectares) devoted to the protection of one of the rarest animals in the world – the mountain zebra *(Equus zebra)*.

The mountain zebra is distinguished from other zebra species by its small stature, reddish-brown nose and dewlap (a loose fold of skin hanging beneath the throat). It has no shadow stripes, a white stomach and a dis-

tinctive gridiron pattern on the rump, with stripes continuing down the legs.

The mountain zebra was probably never numerous, but by the 1960s there were less than 50 of them. It is believed that 500 is the minimum necessary to guarantee the mountain zebra's survival. At present there are around 200 in this national park and another 200 that have been resettled in other parks and reserves around the Cape.

The park has superb mountain scenery and unique vegetation. Thick patches of sweet thorn and wild olive are interspersed with grasslands and succulents. In addition to the zebra, the park supports black wildebeests, elands, red hartebeests, kudu, blesboks, duikers, steenboks, reedbucks and springboks. The largest predator is the caracal (or lynx), and there are several species of small cats, genets, bat-eared foxes and black-backed jackals. Two hundred bird species have been recorded.

There's a relatively limited network of gravel roads around the park, plus the three-day Mountain Zebra Trail and two short day-walks.

Information

The entrance gate is open from 1 October to 30 April between 7 am and 7 pm, and from 1 May to 30 September between 7 am and 6 pm. Day visitors are charged R5 per person. It's quite feasible to get a taste of the park in a morning or afternoon excursion from Cradock. There's a shop and restaurant in the main camp. The park is 800 km from Cape Town and 1084 km from Jo'burg.

Mountain Zebra Trail

The trail takes three days and totals about 25.5 km. The first day covers about nine km and includes a steep climb and ascent. The second day also covers about nine km, climbing the slopes of the Bankberg. The third day is a short seven km, returning you to the main office.

Although there is plenty of up-and-down hiking, there is also plenty of time to pace yourself and watch the game – summer heat is the only real problem. There are two overnight huts; camping is not allowed. Hikers must carry their own sleeping bags, food and eating utensils. If possible, book in advance; the price per person is R50.

Places to Stay & Eat
The most interesting place to stay is the restored historic farmhouse *Doornhoek*, built in 1836 and hidden in a secluded valley. Doornhoek costs R320 for up to four people and R46 per additional person up to six.

Alternatively there are comfortable, fully equipped four-bed cottages. These cost R160 for one or two, and R46 per additional person up to four. There's also a pleasant camping area with sites for R27 for two people, plus R7 for each additional person. There is a 20% discount on accommodation from the beginning of June to the end of September, excluding school holidays.

The restaurant is open for breakfast and dinner; main meals are around R30. The shop has all necessities and is open all day.

Bookings should be made through the National Parks office in Cape Town or Pretoria.

SOMERSET EAST
Somerset East is an attractive old town at the very foot of the 1600-metre Bosberg range. It is sometimes referred to as the oasis of the Karoo, since it receives a generous 600 mm of rainfall (thanks to the mountains). After the dry country to the north and south, the rich forest on the mountain slopes is a surprise. The area was first settled in the 1770s and a village was established in 1835. Thirteen buildings in the town have been declared national monuments, there is an attractive nine-hole golf course, and a nature reserve overlooks the town.

Information & Museum
The museum and information bureau (☎ (0424) 32079) are in a classic Georgian building at the top end of Beaufort St. The building is surrounded by a beautiful garden, famous for its roses. It was originally a Wesleyan chapel built in 1826 and later a parsonage for the Dutch Reformed Church,

so most of the displays reflect early church history. The information bureau has some useful leaflets, including *A Stroll Through Old Somerset East*. The complex is open on weekdays from 9 am to 5 pm and on Saturday from 10 am to noon.

Places to Stay & Eat
The *Linci Caravan Park* (☎ (0424) 31376) is three km from the town centre past the golf course, tucked into a valley surrounded by the Bosberg Nature Reserve. Sites are R20. *Bosberg Overnight Huts* (☎ (0424) 32835) costs R51 for up to three people, or R60 for four people.

The *Somerset Hotel* (☎ (0424) 32047), 83 Charles St, charges R85/135 for bed and breakfast and R75 for singles with shared bath. The *Royal Hotel* (☎ (0424) 32045), on Worcester St, is a bit cheaper.

Bosberg Nature Reserve & Trail
Auret Dr (accessible from Henry St and the golf course) climbs the flanks of the Bosberg through the nature reserve and gives panoramic views over the town and the Great Fish River.

The reserve covers 2000 hectares of diverse habitats – mountain fynbos on rocky parts of the plateau, thickly wooded ravines with stinkwood and yellowwood, a dense grassland on the highest parts, and Karoo shrubs and grasses on the lower areas.

There are several possible walks, including the 15-km circular Bosberg Hiking Trail, which has an overnight hut, and starts at the municipal caravan park. The overnight hut sleeps 10 people (R10 per person) and has toilet facilities. All hikers are required to register at the information hut, and those planning to stay overnight must book in advance. For enquiries and bookings contact the municipality (☎ (0424) 31333).

GRAAFF REINET
Graaff Reinet is perhaps the quintessential Karoo town – it is often referred to, with justice, as the gem of the Karoo. If you visit only one inland town in Eastern Cape Province, make it this one.

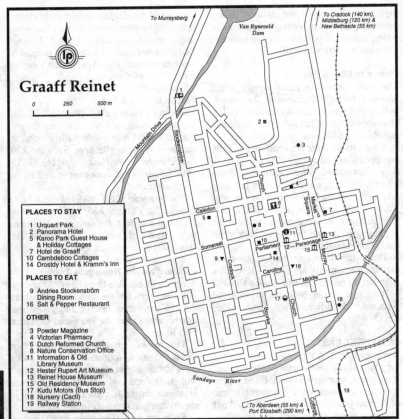

Graaff Reinet

0   250   500 m

PLACES TO STAY

1 Urquart Park
2 Panorama Hotel
5 Karoo Park Guest House
   & Holiday Cottages
7 Hotel de Graaff
10 Cambdeboo Cottages
14 Drostdy Hotel & Kramm's Inn

PLACES TO EAT

9 Andries Stockenström
   Dining Room
16 Salt & Pepper Restaurant

OTHER

3 Powder Magazine
4 Victorian Pharmacy
6 Dutch Reformed Church
8 Nature Conservation Office
11 Information & Old
   Library Museum
12 Hester Rupert Art Museum
13 Reinet House Museum
15 Old Residency Museum
17 Kudu Motors (Bus Stop)
18 Nursery (Cacti)
19 Railway Station

To Murraysberg

Van Ryneveld
Dam

To Cradock (140 km),
Middelburg (120 km) &
New Bethesda (55 km)

Mountain Drive

Stockenström

Church

Caledon

Somerset

Cradock

Parliament

Caroline

Bourke

Sundays River

Market

Square

Murray

Parsonage

Middle

Church

College

To Aberdeen (55 km) &
Port Elizabeth (290 km)

EASTERN CAPE PROVINCE

Graaff Reinet is built in a cleft in the
magnificent Sneeuberg range on a defensi-
ble bend of the Sundays River. It's the
fourth-oldest European town in South Africa
and it has a superb architectural heritage that,
fortunately, has been recognised and
restored.

Over 220 buildings (mostly private
dwellings) have been declared national monuments – they range from Cape Dutch houses
with their distinctive gables to classic flat-
roofed Karoo cottages and ornate Victorian
villas. The excellent Karoo Nature Reserve
is within walking distance of town.

History

In 1786 a landdrost (an official whose duties
combined those of local administrator, tax
collector and magistrate) was despatched to
establish order in the lawless Cape interior.
When not fighting amongst themselves, the
trekboers were in almost constant conflict
with the Khoisan in the Sneeuberg and the
Xhosa to the east around the Great Fish
River.

The official authority didn't have much
luck, because in 1795 the citizens of Graaff
Reinet drove out the landdrost and established a short-lived independent republic.

The British re-established limited control during their first occupation, but the expansionist Boers continued to provoke trouble. On two occasions around the turn of the century the Khoisan and Xhosa joined forces to fight the Europeans.

Between 1824 and 1840, the Boers' continued dissatisfaction with Cape Town's control led to the Great Trek, and Graaff Reinet became an important stepping-stone for the Voortrekkers heading north. It continues to be an important commercial and trading centre, linking the Karoo with the south.

Orientation & Information

The town lies within a bend of the Sundays River, overshadowed by the rocky Sneeuberg. The centre of town is easy to get around on foot. The main commercial zone is to the east of the impressive Dutch Reformed Church, which stands at the north end of Church St.

Graaff Reinet is 672 km from Cape Town, 837 km from Jo'burg and 251 km from Port Elizabeth. It is only an extra 96 km from Jo'burg to Cape Town via Colesberg, Graaff Reinet and Beaufort West compared to the more direct route. Graaff has an excellent Karoo climate with a summer rainfall (340 mm) mostly falling around March.

The information bureau (☎ (0491) 24248) in the Old Library building on the corner of Church and Somerset Sts is open weekdays from 9 am to noon and 3 to 5 pm, Saturday from 9 am to noon, and Sunday from 10 am to noon. It's one of the friendlier information centres and has lots of maps and information about the town and surrounding nature reserve, including farms that offer bed and breakfast. If you have any interest in architecture, its *Walks Through Old Graaff Reinet* is a must.

Museums

Reinet House This museum on Murray St, built between 1806 and 1812, is a beautiful example of Cape Dutch architecture. It is now furnished with a collection of 18th and 19th-century furniture. The cobblestone rear courtyard and garden has one of the largest grape vines in the world. It's open on weekdays from 9 am to noon and 3 to 5 pm, Saturday from 9 am to noon, and Sunday from 10 am to noon. Admission is R2.

Old Residency The Old Residency in Parsonage St is another well-preserved 19th-century house, now displaying a large collection of historical firearms. It has the same opening times and admission fee as Reinet House.

Old Library On the corner of Church and Somerset Sts, the Old Library houses the information bureau as well as a collection of photos and clothing from the 19th century, a collection of fossils (including some nasty reptile skulls) from the Karoo, and paintings. It has the same opening times and admission fee as Reinet House.

Hester Rupert Art Museum This museum, on Church St, was originally a Dutch Reformed Mission church that was consecrated in 1821. It now displays an exhibition of contemporary South African art. It has the same opening times and admission fee as Reinet House.

Drostdy & Stretch's Court The residency of a landdrost was known as a drostdy and included his office and courtroom as well as his family's living quarters. The Graaff Reinet drostdy on Church St was built in 1806. It has been beautifully restored and is now the focus of a unique hotel complex. The reception and the hotel restaurant are in the drostdy, while guests stay in restored mid-19th-century cottages, originally built for freed slaves along Stretch's Court behind. Here there's the old slave bell, which was restored then unveiled, in a piece of awful irony, by Prime Minister Vorster, one of the arch-criminals of apartheid.

Microflights

A local daredevil offers microflights over the Valley of Desolation. It would be sensational, and very scary. A 20 to 35-minute flight enables you to see the town, the Valley and the game reserve and costs R5 a minute. The safest weather conditions are usually in the early morning and late afternoon, which are also the best times for spotting game in the reserve. Phone ☎ (0491) 24514 for information.

Plant Nursery

If you're interested in cacti, see the nursery on Murray St, which has a wide range of large and prickly specimens.

Places to Stay

Urquart Park (☎ (0491) 22136), to the north of town near the Van Ryneveld Dam, isn't a particularly attractive caravan and camping ground. There are, however, some excellent new chalets. A tent site is R20 (R30 in season) plus R1 per person. Basic rondavels start at R30/50 a single/double (R60 in season). Bungalows are R45/70 (R85 in season). The fully equipped chalets have one double bed, two single beds and two stretchers. They cost R100 for two people plus R10 for each additional person (minimum R130 in high season).

Cambdeboo Cottages (☎ (0491) 23180), 16 Parliament St, are restored old Karoo cottages, with *reitdak* (reed ceilings) and lovely yellowwood floors. All are national monuments. They're very comfortable and pleasant, linen is supplied and the cottages are fully equipped. There's a coffee shop that serves breakfast and light meals. There's a pool and a braai area, too. The rate for two people is R120, with additional adults charged R22.50. In December and January the minimum charge is R170.

Karoo Park Guest House & Holiday Cottages (☎ (0491) 22557), 81 Caledon St, has pleasant self-contained cottages for R120 a double, plus R10 for each additional person (more in season). Out of season there are also more basic cottages available from R35 per person. In the guesthouse section singles/doubles (with over-the-top fussy décor) cost from R80/140. It's a large, professionally run guesthouse, more like a slightly eccentric hotel than a proper guesthouse.

The *Drostdy Hotel* (☎ (0491) 22161), on Church St, is simply outstanding, whatever your criteria. The main part of the hotel, including the dining room, is in a beautifully restored drostdy. A whole 'street' has been taken over by the hotel – and the old Karoo workers' cottages (originally slaves' quarters) have been restored, adapted, and comfortably furnished. If you were ever going to splurge, this would be the time. Singles are R155 and doubles range from R201 to R271. Suites, some of them whole cottages, start at R364. Breakfast is R23. Booking is recommended.

The hotel dining room serves traditional Cape food, and you don't have to be a guest to eat there – see Places to Eat.

The *Hotel de Graaff* (☎ (0491) 24191) on Market Square charges R85/160. Better (but more expensive) is the *Panorama Hotel* (☎ (0491) 22233) on Magazine Hill, a modern hotel overlooking town. There's all mod cons, with TV and air-conditioning.

There are plenty of B&Bs, starting around R40 per person. One place that has been recommended by a traveller is Mrs Stegman's (☎ (0491) 25359), 95 Bourke St. She charges R45/80 for singles/doubles. The information bureau has a complete listing and also information on self-catering farm cottages in the area. See the Around Graaff Reinet entry for some information on these.

Places to Eat

The best eating spot is the excellent *Kramm's Inn* behind the Drostdy Hotel, in an old building that has been carefully redeveloped. There's also a pleasant outdoor area under an old vine. Unfortunately it has been closed for renovations for some time.

The dining room at the *Drostdy Hotel* is an unmissable experience. Although the culinary standards here have slipped a little, it's the atmosphere you come for. When was the last time you dined in an 18th-century room illuminated by candelabra? Table d'hôte lunches are R28, and dinners are R43. You can also order à la carte. An after-dinner drink in the pleasant bar, or in the garden on a hot night, is a delight. You don't have to stay here to use the dining room.

Andries Stockenström Dining Room (☎ (0491) 24575), 100 Cradock St has been recommended. There's a set-menu dinner for R40, nightly except Sunday. You must book.

Salt & Pepper, 33 Church St, is so characterless that it has character. Burgers start at R11, chicken and chips are R14, and steak meals start at R22. A reader has recommended *Trail Inn* on Caledon St, with pizzas and a young crowd.

Getting There & Away

Bus The information centre is the Translux agent, but it's closed on Sunday.

Translux stops here on the run between Cape Town (R150, eight hours from Graaff Reinet) and East London (R140, 6¾ hours), via Paarl (R135), Beaufort West (R115), Cradock (R95), Queenstown (R115) and King William's Town (R135). Buses to Cape Town depart from Kudu Motors on the main street at 9.45 pm, and buses to East London depart at 2.55 am.

City to City (a Translux subsidiary) runs daily between Cape Town (R105, 10½ hours from Graaff Reinet) and Umtata (R85, 6½ hours), via Beaufort West (R35), Cradock (R25) and Queenstown (R45). Buses to Cape Town depart at 9 pm; to Umtata they depart at 2.45 am.

Transtate also runs between Cape Town and Umtata along much the same route as City to City, but at lower fares. Eastbound buses depart from Graaff Reinet in the early hours of Monday morning; westbound buses leave on Sunday night.

Minibus Taxi Taxis leave from the northernmost Engen station on the main street or from Market Square. Major destinations are Port Elizabeth, Cape Town and Jo'burg. For more information try phoning Jaftha Taxi Service (☎ (0491) 93 0039).

AROUND GRAAFF REINET

The R57 south from Graaff Reinet is not as spectacular as the other roads in the triangle formed by Middelburg, Somerset East and Graaff Reinet, but it's not boring. Until Aberdeen the road follows to the south of the Sneeuberg. It flattens out after Aberdeen, but mountains are still visible at the edge of the plain. The passes around Willowmore and Uniondale are superb, cutting through high, dry mountains.

Karoo Nature Reserve

This reserve, which virtually surrounds Graaff Reinet, protects 16,000 hectares of mountainous veld, typical of the Karoo. The flora is extraordinary, with the weird Karoo succulents well represented. There's also game, interesting birdlife, spectacular rock formations, and great views overlooking the town and the plains. It's a lot more interesting for the average visitor than some other desiccated bits of the Karoo.

The reserve can be divided into three main sections: the game-viewing area to the north of the dam; the east section, with the overnight Drie Koppe Hiking Trail; and the west section, with the Valley of Desolation and two-day walks.

The **game-viewing area** is open from about 7 am to dusk. There are buffaloes, elands, kudu, hartebeests, wildebeests, springboks and many smaller mammals. Visitors must stay in vehicles.

The **Valley of Desolation** can be reached by car, but the road is very, very steep – not recommended if you fear heights or have bad brakes. Otherwise, do it. There are simply outstanding views over the town and the Valley of Desolation. It's the sort of place that makes you wish you were an eagle. There's a 1.5-km circuit walk.

The **Eerstefontein Day Trail** is also in the western section and can be reached from Mountain Drive. There are three trail options: five, 11 and 14 km long. Wildebeests, kudu, springboks and smaller antelopes can be seen in this section. Permits are available from a self-help permit box at the Spandau gate.

The **Drie Koppe Hiking Trail** is in the mountains of the reserve's eastern sector. Plenty of game, including mountain zebras, can be seen. There is an overnight hut that can accommodate 10 people in bunks; it costs R36 for up to four people, plus R5 for additional people. The starting point is on Lootsfontein Rd. To gain access to the trail a key must be obtained from the conservation office in town.

Bookings and enquiries should be directed to the Department of Nature & Environmental Conservation (☎ (0491) 23453), upstairs in the Provincial Administration building on Bourke St (parallel to Church) in Graaff Reinet.

Farm Trails

Trails of the Camdeboo (☎ (0491) 91 0456), PO Box 107, Graaff Reinet 6280 is an organisation made up of farmers who have restored old farm cottages and developed walks and activities on and between their beautiful properties. Rates vary between farms but average R80 a double, plus R15 per extra person. There are backpacker rates (about R10), although these are intended for groups of hikers rather than individuals. Still, it doesn't hurt to ask. Some places are self-catering and some supply meals for an additional charge.

Sneeuberg Farm Holidays is another collection of farms with self-catering cottages, but they no longer offer walks between farms. However, most of the farms offer hiking and other activities. The Graaff Reinet information centre has a brochure detailing these and other farmstays in the area.

The Owl House

In the tiny and isolated village of **New Bethesda** is the extraordinary Owl House – home, studio and life's work of artist Helen Martins (1898-1976). Whether it's a monument to madness or a testament to the human spirit is difficult to say (there is no shortage of art critics offering fashionable theories). Whichever is the case, the idea of a lone woman creating such *weird* things in this tiny

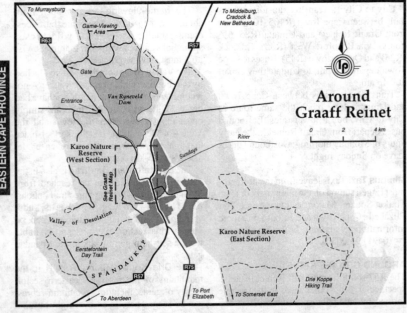

village in the middle of the Karoo is mind-boggling. It even serves to shake the standard view of apartheid-era South Africa being a drab and conformist society. On the other hand, Helen Martins did suicide.

Describing the Owl House and its sculptures isn't easy, and anyway it's the effect of the whole and its context which is most affecting – go and see for yourself.

Even without the Owl House, New Bethesda is worth a look to get an idea of life in rural hamlets. The pretty village has dirt roads, a store or two and a pleasant tea room (which certainly wouldn't be there without the trade generated by the Owl House). Self-catering accommodation is available at *Niew Bethesda Cottage* (☎ (04923) 758) for R90 a double.

The drive here is interesting (there are several turn-offs from the N9 between Graaff Reinet and Middelburg) but remember that you can't buy petrol in New Bethesda.

Northern Cape Province

Northern Cape is by far the largest but one of the least densely populated of South Africa's provinces. The mighty Orange River is a lifeline that runs through a country that becomes desert-like on the fringes of the Kalahari and in the Karoo. The Orange and its tributary, the Vaal, combine to create the longest and largest river in South Africa, but its flow can vary significantly depending on the rainfall on the highveld.

Along the river there are intensely cultivated, irrigated farms. To the north of the river, bordering Botswana, there's sparsely wooded acacia savanna and grasslands – cattle-ranching country. To the south, there's the Karoo with woody shrubs and succulents – sheep-farming country.

The Orange flows west to form the border between South Africa and Namibia, and this area of Northern Cape is spectacularly harsh country, including the isolated and magnificent Richtersveld National Park. South of here is the Namaqualand area, justly world-famous for its extraordinary spring flowers. Northern Cape's coast is singularly bleak, with cold seas breaking onto a near-desert coast. As you travel south the coast improves somewhat and there is good surfing.

The indigenous human population is varied, although the San people occupied most of the drier regions, including the Kalahari. Small numbers of San continue to lead semi-traditional lifestyles in isolated parts of Botswana. The Batswana settled as far west as Kuruman and some of the Khoikhoi groups which were displaced from the south-west settled Griqualand in the area west of Kimberley. The first white explorers entered the region in the 1760s, but relatively large numbers of whites only began to move into the region in the second half of the 19th century. After diamonds were discovered near Kimberley in 1869, the British annexed Griqualand West (including Kimberley).

Kimberley is still synonymous with diamonds, which were discovered on a farm

NORTHERN CAPE PROVINCE
Capital: Kimberley
Main Languages: English, Afrikaans
Pre 1994: The northern part of Cape Province
Highlights:
• Namaqualand, especially in spring
• The Karoo
• Kalahari Gemsbok National Park
• Kimberley's Mine Museum

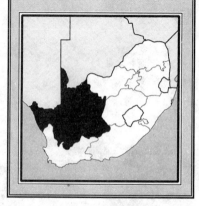

owned by the De Beer family. The De Beers sold their farm to a syndicate for the princely sum of £6300 (compared with the £100 million or so worth of diamonds that were found). Their name survives with the enormous De Beers company which, under the astute management of Cecil John Rhodes, and later Ernest and Harry Oppenheimer, has become one of the largest and most powerful mining companies in the world. Although Kimberley's famous Big Hole has long been abandoned, there are still important functioning mines in the region.

Two possible routes between Johannesburg and Cape Town run through this region. The most direct is the N12, which skirts the Orange Free State and runs through Kimber-

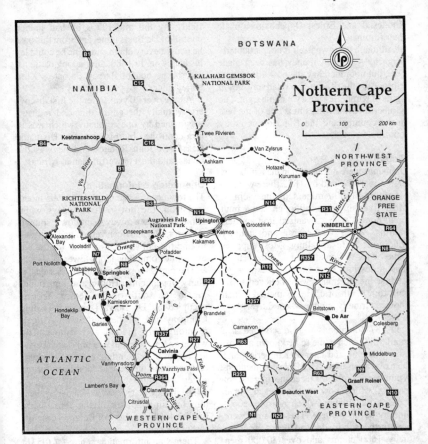

Nothern Cape Province

ley (worth an overnight stop). The N12 route is 1434 km all up, marginally more than the N1 through Bloemfontein.

Alternatively, it is possible to head west to the extraordinary Kalahari Gemsbok National Park – which is only surpassed by the Kruger National Park – and down the west coast through Namaqualand. This is closer to 2000 km, not counting travel within the park, or any side trips. There isn't a lot of public transport but the dedicated will get by without a car.

Most of the area has warm temperatures year-round. It can get very hot in summer

and cold at night in winter. Summer maximums average 33°C; winter maximums average 19°C and minimums, 2°C.

KIMBERLEY

Kimberley, the capital of Northern Cape, would never have existed had it not been for a human fascination for things that glitter. It is still synonymous with diamonds, and mining continues, although for most visitors its interest lies in its historical role: this was where De Beers Consolidated Mines began and Cecil John Rhodes (of

Rhodesia) and Ernest Oppenheimer made their fortunes.

Although the town itself is not particularly inspiring – a lot of money has been made here, but not much has stayed – after a long trip across the Karoo the relatively bright lights of Kimberley are a welcome sight. The Kimberley Mine Museum is one of the best in the country and the Big Hole is pretty amazing.

History

Diamonds were discovered in the Kimberley region in 1869, and by 1872 there were an estimated 50,000 miners in the vicinity. Most lived in tents, although some built small houses with galvanised iron and tarpaulins. Water was scarce and sanitary conditions were appalling. Most supplies came by ox-wagons from Port Elizabeth so most necessities were extremely expensive. At first the diamonds were believed to lie only to a depth of 15 to 18 metres, which allowed virtually anyone with a shovel to get at them.

In 1871 diamonds were discovered at a small hill, which came to be known as Colesberg Koppie and later as Kimberley, and the excavation of the Big Hole commenced. A number of problems faced the diggers, not least of which how to allow each miner access to their claims (which measured about nine by seven metres). These claims were even further subdivided and there were eventually 1600 claims and over 30,000 men working in a total area of approximately 300 by 200 metres.

The miners soon found that the diamonds continued to be present as they dug further and further down. As they did so, the difficulties of managing the insane anthill increased. The evergrowing crater was soon crisscrossed by an elaborate spider web of ropes and pulleys, which were used to haul out the gravel. The chaos could not continue indefinitely; to make matters worse, the price of diamonds dropped because of overproduction.

In 1871 the 19-year-old, tubercular son of an English parson arrived at the diamond fields; by the mid-1870s he had gained control of De Beers mine, and from this base he bought every claim and mine he could lay his hands on. In 1889, after a long battle for control, he bought Barney Barnato's Kimberley mines.

A little over 20 years after the first discovery, virtually the entire diamond industry was owned by one company which was in turn controlled by this one man. His name was Cecil John Rhodes and he was the richest and most powerful man in Africa.

Orientation & Information

The town centre is a tangle of streets inherited from the not-so-distant days when Kimberley was a rowdy shantytown, sprawling across flat and open veld. If you're trying to find the railway station, look for the red and white communications tower.

The city's most noticeable skyscraper is Harry Oppenheimer House, a striking building to the south of the centre. This is occupied by De Beers Diamond Trading Company and is where all South Africa's diamonds are graded and valued. The windows (on the south side only) are slanted to prevent direct sunlight entering – apparently creating the desired conditions for the sorters and valuers.

The money that stayed in Kimberley went into building houses in the remarkably English-looking suburb of Belgravia, southeast of the centre.

There's an information centre (☎ (0531) 27298/9) beside the town hall (which has an impressive coat of arms with wildebeest and gemsbok rampant) where you can get good maps and brochures. It's open weekdays from 7.45 am to 4.30 pm and Saturday from 9 am to 11.30 am. Behind the town hall is the open space of Market Square, which is being refurbished. The tourist tram to the Big Hole starts here (see Getting Around for details).

Satour (☎ (0531) 31434) has an office on Du Toitspan Rd and Rennies Travel (☎ (0531) 81 1825) is in Room 31, 3rd Floor, Nedbank Building, on the corner of Chapel and Currie Sts.

Cecil Rhodes

Cecil John Rhodes (1853-1906), the sickly son of an English vicar, was sent to South Africa in 1870 to improve his health. After working on his brother's farm in Natal, Rhodes left for the new diamond fields near Kimberley in 1871. By 1887 he had founded the De Beers Company and could afford to buy Barney Barnato's Kimberley Mine for £5,000,000. By 1891, De Beers owned 90% of the world's diamonds and Rhodes also had a stake in the fabulous reef of gold discovered on the Witwatersrand (near Johannesburg).

Rhodes was not satisfied with merely acquiring personal wealth and power. He personified the idea of Empire and dreamed of 'painting the map red', building a railway from the Cape to Cairo (running through British territory all the way) and even had far-fetched ideas of bringing the USA back under British rule. The times were right for such dreams, and Rhodes was a favourite of Queen Victoria as well as the voters (both Boer and British) in the Cape. In 1890 he was elected Prime Minister of the Cape Colony.

To paint Africa red, Rhodes pushed north to establish mines and develop trade. Although he despised missionaries for being too soft on the natives, he used them as stalking horses in his wrangling and chicanery to open up new areas. He was successful in establishing British control in Bechuanaland (later Botswana) and the area that was to become Rhodesia (later Zimbabwe), but the gold mines there proved to be less productive than those on the Witwatersrand. The Transvaal Republic in general and Paul Kruger in particular had been causing Rhodes difficulty for some time. Both men were fiercely independent idealists with very different ideals, and there was no love lost between them.

It irked Rhodes that Kruger's republic of pastoralists should be sitting on the richest reef of gold in the world, and the republic was also directly in the path of British expansion.

The miners on the Witwatersrand were mainly non-Boers, who were denied any say in the politics of the republic. This caused increasing resentment, and in late 1895 Jameson led an expedition into the Witwatersrand with the intention of sparking an uprising among the foreigners.

The Jameson raid was a fiasco. All the participants were either killed or captured, and Jameson was jailed. The British government was extremely embarrassed when it became apparent that Rhodes had prior knowledge of the raid and probably encouraged it. He was forced to resign as Prime Minister and the British government took control of Rhodesia and Bechuanaland, his personal fiefdoms.

Rhodes's health deteriorated after these disasters. His empire-building days were over, but one more stock episode from the Victorian omnibus awaited: an honourable chap becomes entangled in the schemes of a glamorous and ruthless woman, in this case the Princess Randziwill. She was later jailed for her swindles.

After his death in 1906, Rhodes' reputation was largely rehabilitated by his will, which devoted most of his fortune to the Rhodes Scholarship, which still sends winners from around the Commonwealth to study at Oxford University. ■

Cecil Rhodes

Kimberley Mine Museum

This excellent open-air museum is on the western side of the Big Hole. Forty-eight original or facsimile buildings are grouped together to form a reconstruction of Kimberley in the 1880s. There are entire streets, miners' cottages, shops, auction rooms, a tavern and so on. In addition, De Beers Hall has a collection of diamonds; there are demonstration models of diamond-recovery technology, and a dramatic view over the Big Hole.

One of the old businesses in operation is the skittle alley, which offers vastly trickier amusement than 10-pin bowling. There are prizes for strikes but it might take a while to knock down one pin, much less the lot. You get six balls for R1.50.

The museum (☎ (0531) 31557) is open daily from 8 am to 6 pm; entry is a bargain at R8. There's a cheap café with breakfast for R11, burgers from R8 and other snacks.

Big Hole

The Big Hole is the largest hole in the world dug entirely by manual labour. It is 800 metres deep and water now fills the hole to within 150 metres of the surface, which still leaves an impressive void. Don't forget, however, there is over four times as much hole below the water's surface.

The Kimberley Mine, which took over after open-cast mining could no longer continue, went to a depth of around 1100 metres. It closed in 1914. Altogether 14½ million carats of diamonds are believed to have been removed from under Colesberg Koppie. In other words, 28 million tonnes of earth and rock were removed for three tonnes of diamonds.

Duggan-Cronin Gallery

The Duggan-Cronin Gallery (☎ (0531) 32646) on Egerton Rd in the suburb of Belgravia, features a unique collection of photographs of black tribes taken in the 1920s and 1930s – before many aspects of traditional tribal life were lost. The gallery is open weekdays from 9 am to 5 pm, Saturday

from 9 am to 1 pm, and Sunday from 2 to 5 pm. Entry is R2.50.

De Beers Tours

De Beers Tours take groups to the treatment and recovery plants at Bultfontein Mine, departing from the Visitors' Reception Centre at the mine gate. They cost R6 and start at 9 and 11 am, Monday to Friday.

Underground tours (☎ (0531) 29651 for bookings) are run on weekdays at 8 am (10 am on Tuesday). They cost R35. You can't wear contact lenses (because of the pressure at the depths you'll descend to) and you can't take anyone under 16.

Places to Stay

The *Big Hole Caravan Park* (☎ (0531) 80 6322) is an attractive park with a swimming pool but very little shade. The mining museum and the Big Hole itself are a short walk away. Sites are R24. The shadier *Showgrounds Caravan park* (☎ (0531) 33581) is about 2.5 km out of Kimberley on Hull St.

The *Kimberley Youth Hostel* (☎ (0531) 28577), also known as Gum Tree Lodge, is about five km from town at the intersection of Hull St and the Bloemfontein road. It's a large and pleasant place, in an old jail with shady lawns and a pool. Accommodation is in fairly basic flats, which act as either dorms or private rooms. Dorms cost R20, singles/twins (in flats with a stove and fridge) are R35/50. Getting here is a big hassle if you don't have a vehicle, but once here you can hire a bike for R10 for the duration of your stay. There is a café, serving breakfast (R12), light lunch (R16) and dinner (R20).

The information centre has details of B&B places, which charge from about R45 per person.

The fact that *Halfway House Hotel* (☎ (0531) 25151), on the corner of Egerton and Du Toitspan Rds, has a drive-in bar might not seem a particularly big selling point if you're staying. It's a pleasant old-style pub, however, with a friendly atmosphere. Singles/doubles are good value at R86/128 including breakfast.

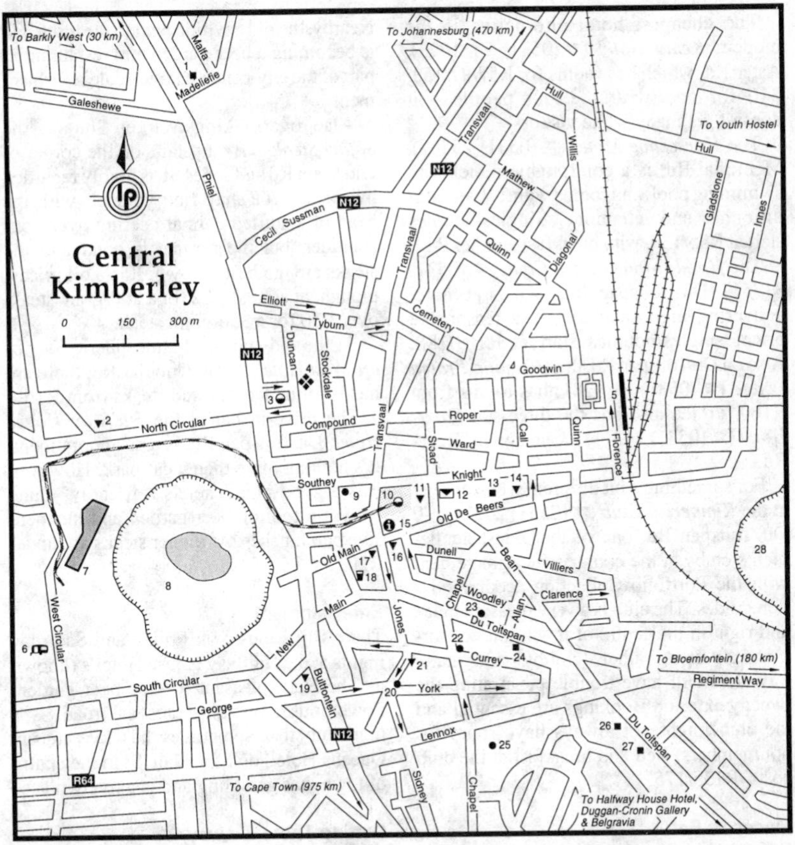

Central Kimberley

0   150   300 m

PLACES TO STAY

1   Kemo Hotel
6   Big Hole Caravan
    Park
13 Savoy Hotel
24 Kimberley Club
26 Holiday Inn Garden
    Court
27 Diamond Protea
    Lodge

PLACES TO EAT

2   Star of the West Hotel
11 Pancake Palace

14 Spaghetti Junction
16 Safari Steakhouse
17 Panino Bakery
19 Steers Steakhouse
21 Umbertos

OTHER

3   Long Distance
    Minibus Taxis
4   Indian Shopping
    Centre
5   Railway Station
7   Kimberley Mine
    Museum
8   Big Hole

9   De Beers Head Office
10 Tram Terminus
12 GPO
15 Information Centre &
    Town Hall
18 Queens Hotel
20 Phoenix Travel
    (Translux)
22 Rennies Travel
23 Africana Library
25 Harry Oppenheimer
    House
28 De Beers Mine

The cheapest hotel alternative is the modern *Kemo Hotel* (☎ (0531) 71 1023), Aster Rd, which has rooms for R57/97/153/240 for one/two/three/four people – it doesn't get many white visitors.

The *Horseshoe Motel* (☎ (0531) 25267), Memorial Rd, is a comfortable motel with swimming pool, and rooms with TV, air-conditioning and telephone. Singles/doubles start at R85/130, with breakfast another R17.

The *Holiday Inn Garden Court* (☎ (0531) 31751), Du Toitspan Rd, is a large hotel delivering high standards at a reasonable price; singles/doubles start at R169/188. Also on Du Toitspan Rd, the *Diamond Protea Lodge* (☎ (0531) 81 1281) has rooms from R160. Protea also has the three-star *Savoy Hotel* (☎ (0531) 26211) located on De Beers Rd.

For something a bit different, you can stay at the *Kimberley Club* (☎ (0531) 24224), 70 Du Toitspan Rd, one of the oldest gentlemen's clubs in the country, by arrangement with the Portfolio Collection accommodation guides. The club is a very pleasant place and right in the centre of town, but not surprisingly it is rather 'clubby' and many travellers will have trouble penetrating the tweedy exterior. Bookings are essential and the club might not always have room for nonmembers. Bed and breakfast at the club costs R135/175.

Places to Eat

One of the most relaxed and popular places in town is *Umbertos* at the Old Mutual Centre on Jones St. There are some outdoor tables and it's open from early until late. They have snacks, pasta and more substantial meals at average prices.

If you're looking for something cheap and delicious, the *Panino Bakery* on the corner of Jones St and Old Main Rd has a mouthwatering selection of cakes, biscuits, pies, and bread at good-value prices.

On Market Square, near the tram terminus, *Pancake Palace* is a trendy-looking café that does crêpes only, and a fairly limited menu at that. However, they are good and inexpensive, with most dishes under R7.

Nearby, the old pavilion next to the town hall is becoming a beer-garden and restaurant as part of the city-centre's large-scale refurbishment.

Also overlooking Market Square, the *Safari Steakhouse*, upstairs on the corner of Old Main Rd and Jones St, is highly regarded by locals. You may find yourself with the head of a stuffed animal peering over your shoulder, but the service is good and the steaks are the best in town. It is a bit pricey, though, at around R22 for a 200-gram steak, over R30 for a 350-gram steak.

At the old-style and atmospheric *Star of the West Hotel*, North Circular Rd, there are meals for under R12 and steaks from R16.

The drive-in bar at the *Halfway House Hotel*, Du Toitspan Rd, is a disappointment. It's nothing more than a car park. However, it is a good pub. There's a friendly young crowd, a rooftop beer garden and inexpensive pub lunches. At dinner steaks are under R20.

Entertainment

There's live music on Friday and Saturday nights at the Halfway House Hotel's (known as The Half) pleasant rooftop beer garden. Powerhouse, on the Transvaal road, is a nightclub that sometimes has live music. Queens Hotel, on Stockdale St in the centre of town, has gambling and is a lively place.

Getting There & Away

Bus Many services run to/from Jo'burg, about six hours from Kimberley. The cheapest is, surprisingly, Greyhound's daily service for R72. Note that this is a special service; if you take the Jo'burg to Kimberley sector on Greyhound's daily Jo'burg to Cape Town bus it will cost R145. From Kimberley to Cape Town with Greyhound costs R240.

Translux stops in Kimberley on the twice-weekly run (Sunday and Friday in either direction) between Jo'burg/Pretoria (R140 from Kimberley) and Cape Town (R240).

Garden Line Transport runs to Jo'burg on Tuesday for R125, although this isn't such a great service as it departs at 3.30 am. Going the other way, Garden Line's bus departs from Kimberley at 12.05 am on Wednesday, bound for Oudtshoorn (R125, 7½ hours), George (R135, 8½ hours) and Mossel Bay (R135, 9½ hours).

Translux has a similar but more expensive service, terminating in Knysna (11 hours). Heading to Knysna, buses depart from Kimberley at 8.35 pm on Sunday and 10.35 pm on Thursday; going the other way, buses run to Jo'burg/Pretoria at 2.45 am on Wednesday and Friday. The fare to Oudtshoorn, Mossel Bay, George and Knysna is R165.

Greyhound stops in Kimberley on the thrice-weekly run between Upington (R95 from Kimberley, about four hours) and Durban (R165, 11 hours), via Bloemfontein (R65, two hours). Heading towards Upington buses run on Tuesday, Thursday and Sunday; heading to Durban it's Monday, Wednesday and Friday.

Northern Cape Bus Service (☎ (0531) 81 1062), 5 Elliot St, is the Greyhound agent in Kimberley. Greyhound and Garden Line stop at the Shell Ultra City service station on the highway; Translux stops at the railway station.

Train For information on trains contact Spoornet (☎ (0531) 288 2060).

The *Trans Karoo* runs daily between Cape Town and Jo'burg/Pretoria via Kimberley. The southbound train leaves Jo'burg at 12.30 pm, arrives in Kimberley at 8.45 pm and Cape Town 17½ hours later at 2.15 pm. The northbound train leaves Cape Town at 9.20 am and arrives in Kimberley at 1.53 am the next day and in Jo'burg at 10.15 am. From Kimberley to Cape Town 1st/2nd/3rd-class tickets are R224/152/94; from Kimberley to Jo'burg they're R113/77/47.

The *Diamond Express* runs overnight between Jo'burg/Pretoria and Bloemfontein via Kimberley daily except Saturday. Fares are the same as for the *Trans Karoo*, but there's also the more expensive Diamondpax class, costing R164 between Kimberley and Jo'burg.

The *Trans Oranje* between Cape Town and Durban takes a slow and roundabout route via Worcester, Beaufort West, Kimber-

ley, Bethlehem and Ladysmith. The full trip would be ridiculously time-consuming, but it's quite handy for Kimberley. It leaves Cape Town at 6.50 pm on Monday, arrives in Kimberley at 11.13 am on Tuesday and in Durban at 7.15 pm on Wednesday. It leaves Durban at 5.30 pm on Thursday, arrives in Kimberley at 12.37 pm on Friday and in Cape Town at 6.05 am on Saturday. From Kimberley to Durban 1st/2nd/3rd-class tickets are R213/145/92; from Kimberley to Cape Town, R224/152/94.

Minibus Taxi The taxi area is around the Indian shopping centre off Bultfontein St (where there's a fruit and vegetable market and the odd curry takeaway). You'll find long-distance taxis here, a little away from the rest, near Crossley St. As usual, there are rival taxi associations which might have merged or folded or been massacred by the time you get here. The people I met were from the Labingo Association (☎ (0531) 28255).

Destinations include Jo'burg (R50), Bloemfontein (R23), Upington (R50), Kuruman (R33), Cape Town (R110). If you're heading for Mafikeng you can take a taxi to Taung (R21) and pick up another there.

Getting Around
Kimberley has one surviving antique tram that runs between the town hall and the mine museum. On weekdays it departs from the town hall at 9.15 and 11.15 am, and 1.15, 2.15 and 4.15 pm. There are additional services at 10.15 am and 3.15 pm on Saturday and Sunday. A one-way trip is R2.50.

BRITSTOWN
Britstown is at the crossroads of the R32, between the south coast and Namibia, and the N12 between Kimberley and Cape Town. It's the centre of a prosperous sheep-grazing area and is a pleasant enough little town.

Places to Stay
There are several places of the 'overnight rooms' ilk, but the best place to stay is the *Transkaroo Hotel* (☎ (0536) 712). The rates

aren't bad, perhaps because of the competition. Rooms with shared bath start at R40 per person and standard rooms are R139/160 a single/double, R170/180 a triple/quad. There's a pool.

The *Mirage Toeristekamers* (☎ (05732) 310) has clean and comfortable rooms from R32/60.

DE AAR

De Aar is a major service centre for the Karoo, but its main claim to fame is as a railway junction – one of the most important in southern Africa. 'De aar' means 'the artery' and refers to the arterial rivers in this area, but could equally refer to the importance of the railway lines.

De Aar is too big to be called a one-horse town – maybe it's a two-horse town. There is so little to see or do here that an overnight stay can be an unnerving experience.

Places to Stay & Eat
The small *Van Der Merwe Municipal Caravan Park* (☎ (0571) 2131), on Cilliers St, has sites for R20.

The *De Aar Hotel* (☎ (0571) 2181), Friedlander St, has air-conditioned rooms but a depressing atmosphere. It's way overpriced at R135/235, including breakfast.

There's apparently a hostel for train crews overnighting at this junction town and you might be able to talk your way into getting a bed there. Ask at the station.

As well as the reasonable dining room at the hotel, there's a restaurant in historic *Olive Schreiner House* on the corner of Grundlingh and Vanzyl Sts. The author Olive Schreiner lived here from 1908 to 1913. You can lunch here from Monday to Friday and dine on Wednesday, Friday and Saturday. Locals say that it's pretty good.

Getting There & Away
Train The *Trans Karoo* and *Blue Train* (Jo'burg/Pretoria to Cape Town), and *Trans Oranje* (Durban to Bloemfontein to Kimberley to Cape Town) all come through here.

COLESBERG

For a major stopover on the N1 between Cape Town and Bloemfontein, Colesberg is an attractive place. It's a classic Karoo town, founded in 1829, and many old buildings have survived. There's a beautiful Dutch Reformed church (NG Kerk) built in 1866, and shops with verandahs still front onto the main street. There are some attractive houses and cottages on the side streets.

Orientation & Information
The friendly information centre is in the museum (☎ (051) 753 0678), off the main street on Murray St. Ask for Mrs Gordon. It's open weekdays. The museum houses important archives of the Anglo-Boer War.

Places to Stay
During the high season, from mid-December to mid-January, and the school holidays accommodation in Colesberg can book up. The caravan park is fine, but if you want a bed you are advised to ring ahead.

The dusty *Colesberg Caravan Park* (☎ (051) 753 0040), Kerk St, on the outskirts of town, has sites for R20.

The best place in town is *The Lighthouse* (☎ (051) 753 0043), 40 Church St, a comfortable and homely guesthouse. It's sparkling clean and it has been furnished with the Badenhurst's old farm furniture. The rate is an extremely reasonable R60/100 a single/double. Booking is recommended.

The information centre has a list of the many other 'overnight accommodation' places, which range from ordinary B&Bs to restored Karoo Huisies (☎ (051) 753 0582) – town cottages used by wealthy Karoo farmers. They also know of guest farms in the area.

The *Central Hotel* (☎ (051) 753 0734) is considerably bigger than it looks from the street. It's a bit faded, but in general it's comfortable and efficiently run. They have rooms for R65/130, or from R150/160 with bath.

The *Merino Motel* (☎ (051) 753 0781) on the town outskirts (Cape Town side) is a comfortable and characterless motel inside.

Outside it's strikingly ugly. They have standard singles/doubles from R130/200 and luxury rooms from R130/220. Not far away is the *Gables Inn* (☎ (051) 753 0576), a new place offering tacky motel-style accommodation in individual 'house-ettes' (the only name for them, really). Three-sleepers go for R100/150 in the low/high season, five-sleepers are R150/250.

Six km north of Colesberg on the old Cape Town road, the *Van Zylsvlei Motel* (☎ (051) 73 0589) is a quiet, older-style place charging from R70/140 for singles/doubles.

Places to Eat

The tea room at *Avon Nursery* on the main street has a pleasant, shady courtyard (in which hidden speakers softly pipe songs from *The Sound of Music)*, although the menu is limited to snacks. Towards the other end of the main street, in the bright yellow building, the *Upstairs Restaurant* (☎ (051) 753 0646) is open from 6 pm daily except Sunday. It serves traditional food.

Between these two is *Pop In*, which looks pretty ordinary but is, according to locals, the best place for steaks.

AROUND COLESBERG

The R57 between Colesberg and Middelburg crosses a classic Karoo landscape with koppies popping out of the plain. The **Lootsberg Pass**, to the south of Middelburg, is quite spectacular and the country is mountainous and dramatic.

KURUMAN

Just when you were starting to get very depressed about Northern Cape country towns, you get to Kuruman. This town feels as if it sits at the edge of rather wild and interesting country – and it does. Kuruman derives from a San word, but the area was also settled by the Batlhaping, a Batswana tribe, when the first whites appeared in the area around 1800. West of Kuruman there's a long, empty stretch of highway to Upington, and the landscape is dominated by low, sandy ranges.

The town itself, though frighteningly conservative, has a sense of history and civic pride. The flow of artesian water from the Eye of Kuruman and the beautiful old mission station have something to do with the magic.

Orientation & Information

The main through-road is Hoofstraat (Main St) and the only robots (traffic lights) in town are on the corner of Main and Voortrekker Sts. There's a useful tourist office (☎ (05373) 21095) on Main St; it's open from 7.30 am to 1 pm and 2 pm to 4.30 pm Monday to Friday, and 8 am to noon Saturday.

Eye of Kuruman

The Eye of Kuruman is an amazing natural spring that produces 18 to 20 million litres of water a day, every day. It has never faltered. The surrounding area has been developed into a pleasant enough picnic spot, and a good place to break your journey – note the masked weaver birds and their nests over the pond.

Places to Stay & Eat

The *Kuruman Caravan Park* (☎ (05373) 21479) is a very pleasant spot to break your journey. There are some extremely good-value chalets and some shady camp sites. All are short walks from the centre of town and the Eye of the Kuruman. The chalets are well equipped and pleasant, and go for R36 a double, R91 for three beds and R105 for four beds. Booking is recommended, especially during the school holidays. The caravan park is on Voortrekker St; if you're coming from the Jo'burg direction turn left at the robots. The sign tells you that the caravan park is 500 metres away but it's much closer than that.

The *Savoy Hotel* (☎ (05373) 21121) is old-fashioned and ordinary. It would do at a pinch. Singles/doubles with breakfast are R95/135. The bars here are lively.

By comparison the *Grand Hotel* (☎ (05373) 21148) is pretty slick in a small-town way – with air-conditioning, coffee machines and TV, but you pay for what you get.

Singles/doubles with breakfast are R103/184 and singles with shared bath are R65. You don't want a room anywhere near the weekend disco, which is a 'private club, members only' – it's a fair bet that white skin will ensure immediate membership.

The most expensive and luxurious accommodation can be found at the large, somewhat incongruous *El Dorado Motel* (☎ (05373) 22191) on the outskirts of town (Vryburg road, the R27). Singles/doubles cost from R155/260 including breakfast. Last, but not least, the *Thebephatshwa Motel* (☎ (014762) and ask for 131), 12 km from Kuruman on the Vryburg road, is a small, quiet and pleasant hotel with a swimming pool.

The various hotel dining rooms are about your only options for a sit-down meal. They offer the usual steaks at the usual prices.

Getting There & Away

Bus Kuruman is a stop on Intercape Mainliner's Windhoek (Namibia) to Jo'burg/Pretoria via Upington service. See the following Upington section for more details. Fares from Kuruman include Jo'burg (R110), Upington (R80) and Windhoek (R280).

Transtate runs from Kuruman to Rustenburg on Monday and Thursday and in the other direction on Tuesday, Wednesday and Friday (R50, about 10 hours).

Minibus Taxi The taxi park is next to the Buy Rite supermarket on Voortrekker St (coming from the Jo'burg direction turn right at the robots). Very few taxis run west from Kuruman. Examples of destinations and fares include Jo'burg (R70), Kimberley (R33), Mafikeng (R40), Pretoria (R70) and Vryburg (R20).

AROUND KURUMAN
Moffat Mission

The mission was the first white settlement in the area and was established by the London Missionary Society in 1816 to work with the local Batlhaping people. The mission site,

four km from the Eye on the road to Hotazel, was chosen at a point where the valley could be ploughed. A clay-lined furrow was built to carry water from the Eye, and exists today.

The mission was named after Robert and Mary Moffat, two courageous Scots who worked at the mission from 1817 to 1870. They converted the Batswana to Christianity, started a school and translated the bible into Tswana. The mission became a famous staging point for explorers and missionaries heading further into Africa. The Moffat daughter, Mary, married David Livingstone in the mission church.

The church (completed in 1838) is still in use today. The Moffat's homestead and school have also survived, and have been carefully restored. Although the thriving community has dissipated, it is a quiet and atmospheric spot with the stone and thatch buildings shaded by large trees.

Hotazel

Definitely the most interesting thing about this town is its name. Say it quickly: 'hot as hell'. The road from Kuruman is sealed and runs parallel to a low range of hills looking out over the vast, hot flatness to the northeast.

Van Zylsrus

Van Zylsrus is a dusty little frontier town, one of the most isolated in South Africa. The surrounding countryside is rolling, attractive cattle country, which is pleasantly wooded. There's a stop sign, a petrol station, post office and pub – all the necessities of life. I guess they must be saving up for the robot. The pub is the *Gemsbok* (☎ (005378) 238), which charges R66 per person or R62 with shared bath, including breakfast.

UPINGTON

Upington is on the banks of the Orange River and is the principal commercial town in the far north. It's an orderly, prosperous place, full of supermarkets and chain-stores, and generally very friendly.

The surrounding area is intensively culti-

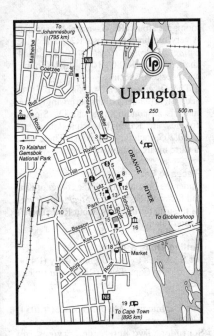

PLACES TO STAY

1   Three Gables B&B
4   Die Eiland Resort
8   Oasis Protea Lodge
11 Oranje Hotel
12 Upington Protea Hotel & Spur
     Steakhouse
17 Oranjerivier Overnight Rooms
19 Gordonia Holiday Resort

OTHER

2   Swimming Pool
3   Post Office
5   First National Bank
6   Library & Tourist Office
7   Intercape Mainliner Office
9   Railway Station
10 Cemetery
13 Laundromat
14 Minibus Taxis
15 Checkers Supermarket
16 Museum
18 Protea Taxis

vated thanks to the limitless sunlight and irrigation water. Cotton, wheat, grapes and fruit are all produced. It's a good place to stock up on supplies if you're heading to or from the Kalahari Gemsbok National Park.

Information

The helpful tourist office (☎ (054) 27064) is in the foyer of the town library. A staff member is there from 8 am to 12.30 pm and 2 to 4.30 pm on weekdays but there's a desk with plenty of brochures accessible during the longer library hours, which include Saturday morning.

A branch of the First National Bank is on the north-west corner of Schroder and Hill Sts. There are also other banks in town.

There's a laundromat on Scott St, near the Oranje Hotel.

In summer you'll probably be in desperate need of a swimming pool and there's one in the park off Le Roux St, north of the town centre.

Wimpie Strauss (☎ (054) 22336) operates Spitskop Safaris and runs informal, flexible tours to the Kalahari and Augrabies parks and can also organise hunting trips. River Runners (☎ (021) 762 2350) offer camel and canoe trips down the Orange River near here – see the regional Facts for the Visitor chapter for more information.

For decent postcards of this scenic area, check out the selection at the main desk of the Oasis Protea Lodge.

Museum

The museum is worth visiting if you have a spare 10 minutes. It is housed in the original mission and manse built by a Reverend Schroder in 1871. Schroder was invited to the area by the Koranna chief Klaas Lukas.

Spitskop Nature Reserve

There isn't a lot of point visiting this small game park if you're planning to visit Kalahari Gemsbok National Park, but otherwise it might be worth a look for its gemsboks, zebras and other antelopes. There are some hiking trails in the reserve, which is about 15 km north of Upington.

Places to Stay – bottom end

The best value in accommodation is at the two municipal caravan parks (one used to be for the whites, one for the others). *Die Eiland Resort* (☎ (054) 31 1553) was originally for the whites and is the better and more popular of the two options. It's a fair walk from town, on the south bank of the Orange River; cross the bridge at the north end of town signposted for Prieska. There are pleasant tent sites for R20 and a range of huts and bungalows which vary in price depending on their age and level of equipment. There are rondavels at R50/75 a single/double; huts from R85; three-person units from R100; and various larger chalets and cottages.

The alternative *Gordonia Holiday Resort* (☎ (054) 26911) is newer and the only reason it doesn't get a strong recommendation is that it is much less popular so you feel a little exposed, especially if you're camping. Tent sites cost R20 and a three-bed chalet is R100.

At 3 Tiptol Rd in the suburb of Keidebees, *Pinkster Protestante Herberg* (☎ (054) 24177) offers guesthouse-style accommodation for R35/50 a single/double. with additional people (up to four) charged R10. There's also a four-person flat for R80. Breakfast (R12) and lunch (R15) can be arranged. Keidebees is a few km east of the town centre.

Right in the town centre but more expensive, the *Oranjerivier Overnight Rooms* (☎ (054) 24195) offers spartan but clean and fairly large rooms. Despite the ducted air-con I'd guess that it gets pretty hot in summer. Doubles are R105, triples R128 and a four-bed room is R158. There are laundry facilities, pool and TV rooms and a friendly manager. It's on Mark St, near Checkers.

Places to Stay – middle

There is a number of guesthouses, such as *Three Gables* (☎ (054) 23041), 34 Bull St, which charge around R60 per person. The tourist office has a list of the others.

There are two Protea hotels, opposite each other on the corner of Lutz and Schroder Sts. The new *Oasis Protea Lodge* (☎ (054) 31 1125) is a pleasant if characterless place with rooms for around R195 – ask about specials. A very big breakfast costs R25. The older *Upington Protea Hotel* (☎ (054) 25414) charges from R180/210 a single/double, with weekend specials.

The *Oranje Hotel* (☎ (054) 24177), on Scott St, is plainer, but it's surprisingly large and has air-conditioning and TV. Singles/doubles are R135/160, triples/quads are R160/205, including breakfast. There are à la carte meals at standard prices.

Places to Eat

Under the Protea Hotel on the corner of Lutz and Schroder Sts is *Spurs Steak Ranch* with all the usual grills from about R20. There's a good salad bar.

Getting There & Away

Air SAA flies to/from Jo'burg daily (R479) and to/from Cape Town (R457) four times a week.

Bus The Intercape Mainliner office (☎ (054) 27091) is on Lutz St near the corner of Schroder. Two Intercape services run through Upington, giving good links to the rest of the country. On Monday, Tuesday, Thursday and Saturday a bus leaves Upington at 5.30 am, heading for Jo'burg/Pretoria via Kuruman and Potchefstroom. The trip to Jo'burg takes 8½ hours and costs R140. Coming in the other direction, buses for Upington depart from Jo'burg/Pretoria on Tuesday, Thursday, Friday and Sunday. These services connect with buses to/from Windhoek (Namibia). The overnight journey between Upington and Windhoek takes 10 hours and costs R200.

Intercape also has buses running to/from Cape Town (R130, 10½ hours), via Calvinia (R80 from Upington, R110 from Cape Town), Clanwilliam (R100, R85) and Citrusdal (R110, R70). Heading south, buses depart from Upington at 7.45 pm on Tuesday, Thursday, Friday and Sunday; heading north buses depart from Cape Town at 7 pm on Sunday, Monday, Wednesday and Friday. This service connects with the Jo'burg/Pretoria service.

City to City, a Translux subsidiary, runs to Cape Town on Sunday, Monday and Friday, departing from the railway station at 5.30 pm and arriving in Cape Town 12½ hours later. It's slower than the Intercape service but a little cheaper at R115. Other fares from Upington on this run include to Citrusdal, R85; Clanwilliam, R80; Calvinia, R65. City to City departs from Cape Town railway station for Upington at 6 pm on Sunday, Thursday and Friday.

The long Greyhound run between Upington and Durban (R260, 15½ hours) departs from Upington at 6.30 am on Monday, Wednesday and Friday. It runs via Kimberley (R95), Bloemfontein (R120) and Welkom (R145). Buses depart from Durban at 6.30 am on Tuesday, Thursday and Sunday.

Train Upington is on the rail line that runs from De Aar (south of Kimberley) to Windhoek (the capital of Namibia). Passenger trains have recently been discontinued on this line though.

Minibus Taxi You'll find taxis near the Checkers supermarket on the corner of Mark and Basson Sts. Not all long-distance taxis leave from here but it's a good place to start asking. Protea Taxis has an office on the corner of Le Roux and Grobler and you might be able to book a seat on their services.

If you can't find any information about a taxi to your destination, try the refreshment rooms at the railway station, which is a mine of transport information. Upington taxis can take a long time to fill but there is generally at least one per day to major destinations. Destinations and approximate fares include Cape Town, R90; Jo'burg, R100; Kimberley, R50; Windhoek, R100.

In Springbok I was told about a daily taxi between there and Upington but no one in Upington knew anything about it.

Car & Motorbike If you're heading to Kalahari Gemsbok National Park be aware that a new route has opened but some of the old road signs hadn't been changed in late

1994. On the northern edge of town you come to a major turn-off to the right. The old sign tells you to keep going straight ahead for the national park or turn right for Spitskop. Take the Spitskop turn-off and after travelling a short distance you'll pass a new sign telling you that you're on the correct road for the park. By this route it's 280 km from Upington to the main gate (Twee Rivieren), made up of about 120 km on tar, 80 km on bad dirt roads and the rest on reasonable dirt roads. The tar is being gradually extended.

Be very careful driving on the dirt as we've had several letters from travellers who wrecked their cars on this trip. If you stop, don't pull too far off the road or you might become bogged in the sand. See the Car & Motorbike section in the Getting Around chapter for hints on dirt-road driving.

Car Rental If you want to see Kalahari Gemsbok and are short of time, it makes sense to fly to Upington and hire a car. There's an Avis agent (☎ (054) 25746) at the airport. The Oasis Protea Hotel rents 4WD vehicles from about R400 per day with unlimited km.

KALAHARI GEMSBOK NATIONAL PARK

The Kalahari Gemsbok National Park is not as well known or famous as many other African parks but it is, nonetheless, one of the greatest.

The accessible section of the park lies in the triangular segment of South Africa between Namibia and Botswana. This region covers 959,103 hectares. However, the protected area continues on the Botswana side of the border (there are no fences) where there are another 1,807,000 hectares. The South African park was proclaimed in 1931 and the Botswana park in 1938.

Together, the two sections make up one of the largest protected wilderness areas in Africa. This allows the unhindered migration of antelopes which, because of the unpredictable nature of the rainfall, are forced to travel great distances to reach water and food.

Although the countryside is described as

semi-desert (with around 200 mm of rain a year) it is richer than it appears and supports large populations of birds, reptiles, small mammals and antelopes. These in turn support a large population of predators.

All the animals are remarkably tolerant of cars. They've obviously learnt that vehicles have no impact on their lives and visitors' cars have therefore become an unremarkable and unimportant feature of the landscape. This allows you to get extraordinarily close to animals which are otherwise completely wild – it's as if you were invisible.

The landscape is beautiful – reminiscent in some ways of central Australia. The Nossob and Aoub rivers (usually dry) run through the park and meet each other a few km north of the entrance at Twee Rivieren. Much of the wildlife is concentrated in these river beds, where there are windmills and waterholes (the only significant human interference in the park's ecology). This makes wildlife viewing remarkably successful.

In the south, the Nossob River is between 100 and 500 metres wide, with grey camelthorn trees between the limestone banks. In the north the river bed opens up to more than a km wide, and becomes sandy. The bed of the Aoub is narrower and deeper. Between the two rivers there is an area with the characteristically red Kalahari dunes (red thanks to iron oxide). In other areas the sand varies from pink and yellowish to grey.

Various grasses and woody shrubs survive on the dunes and there are occasional shepherd's trees and grey camel thorns. There's a greater variety of vegetation in the river beds, including the camel thorns, black thorn, raisin bush and driedoring.

Orientation

Visitors are restricted to four roads; one running up the bed of the Nossob River, one running up the bed of the Aoub River, and two linking these two. Visitors must also remain in their cars, with the exception of a small number of designated picnic spots.

The only negative point about the park is that although the river beds are the best places to view wildlife, it can become almost claustrophobic being stuck in a car and enclosed by the river banks. The opportunities to really get a feel for the empty expanses of the Kalahari are limited – the exceptions are the roads linking the rivers, and they should not be missed. It would be great if there were more loops that took you into the veld and/or the possibility of doing some walks.

There are well-equipped and well-fenced rest camps at Twee Rivieren, Nossob and Mata Mata. The speed limit is 50 km/h. The minimum travelling time from the entrance gate at Twee Rivieren to Nossob is 3½ hours and to Mata Mata, 2½ hours. No travelling is allowed after dark.

Allow plenty of time. Soon after I arrived I set out on what I thought would be a quick drive around the shortest loop (120 km) and returned five hours later, having stopped to look at lions.

Information

The best time to visit is in June and July when the weather is coolest (below freezing at night) and the animals have drawn in to the bores along the dry river beds. August is windy and, for some reason, is a favourite time for tour buses.

From September to October is the wet season and if it does rain, many of the animals scatter out across the plain to take advantage of the fresh pastures. November is quiet, and daily temperatures start to increase. Despite the fact that temperatures frequently reach 45°C in December and January, the chalets in the park are fully booked – it takes more than a bit of heat to deter the school holiday-makers.

Although increasing numbers of people are visiting the park, it is nothing like the situation in Kruger. This is because the park is a long way from civilisation along dusty, unsealed roads. You need to allow the best part of a day to drive to/from Kuruman or to/from Upington and you need at least two full days in the park.

Entry is R20 for vehicles plus R11 per adult. All the rest camps have shops where basic groceries, soft drinks and alcohol can be purchased (fresh vegetables and camera films are not available). Fresh meat, margarine, bread and eggs are only available at Twee Rivieren. It's definitely worth stocking up outside the park and having sufficient utensils to make breakfast and lunch. The only restaurant is at Twee Rivieren. Petrol and diesel are available at each camp. There are public phones at Twee Rivieren.

The entrance gate opening hours depend on the time of year:

January-February	6 am to 7.30 pm
March	6.30 am to 7 pm
April	7 am to 6.30 pm
May	7 am to 6 pm
June-July	7.30 am to 6 pm
August	7 am to 6.30 pm
September	6.30 am to 6.30 pm
October	6 am to 7 pm
November-December	5.30 am to 7.30 pm

The social weaver is found in the western desert areas. It builds large communal nests and is seen in flocks whirling across the veld.

Flora

Only hardy plants survive the periodic droughts that afflict the Kalahari. Many have adapted so that they germinate and produce seed within four weeks of a shower of rain.

The river beds have the widest variety of flora. The Nossob River is dominated by camel thorn trees (Acacia erioloba) in the north and grey camel thorn trees (Acacia haematoxylon) in the south. The grey camel thorn is a shrub on the dunes, but grows into a tree in the river beds. Its foliage is sparser than that of the camel thorn, and is grey. The grey variety has long narrow seed pods that are quite different to the broad, crescent-shaped pods of the plain.

Most of the dead trees in the Nossob River are camel thorns that were killed in fires in 1968 and 1974; fortunately young trees survive fires. Sociable weaver birds favour the camel thorns for their huge nests, and all sorts of animals and birds feed off the foliage and seeds.

Various grasses and woody shrubs survive on the dunes and there are occasional shepherd's trees (Boscia albitrunca), with white bark and a dense thicket of short low branches where many animals take refuge in the heat of the day. The shepherd's tree develops small cream-coloured flowers after rain and an orange-yellow fruit. The driedoring shrub (Rhigozum trichotomum), with fine leaves and forked branches, is the most common shrub in the park.

Many of the animals depend on plants as their source of moisture. In particular, the tsamma (Citrillus lanatus) is an important source of water – it's a creeper with melonlike fruit. There are several prickly cucumbers that are important for the survival of animals, especially the gemsbok. The cucumber (Acanthosicyos naudinianus), in addition to the fruit, has a succulent root that wildlife will dig out.

Fauna

Finding fauna requires luck, patience and a little intelligence. No one can be guaranteed of seeing one of the big predators, but you are more likely to in the Kalahari than in many other places. Almost all species of wildlife, with the exception of elephants, giraffes and zebras, are found in the park.

Spend an hour or so in the morning and the afternoon by a waterhole – you'll see many birds and animals coming in for a drink. Watch for signs of agitation among

NORTHERN CAPE PROVINCE

herds of buck – they don't automatically flee at the sight of a predator but wait until the predator commits itself to a charge before they run.

The lions like to walk along the side of the roads, presumably because they can skulk along without being seen by animals in the river bed, and because the soft dust is kind to their paws. Look for recent prints, as the lion may have moved off the road at the sound of the approaching vehicle.

Binoculars are essential. See Wildlife Viewing in the Kruger National Park section for more tips.

Birds Two hundred and fifteen species of birds have been recorded in the park. Perhaps the most dramatic are the raptors, including impressive species like the bateleur, a bulky looking black eagle with tawny shoulders and a scarlet face and legs, and the martial eagle with white-spotted underparts and long legs.

The secretary bird is a common sight, strutting self-importantly over the clay pans. It's a large bird with long legs (with knickerbockers), several loose 'quills' behind the head, and an orange face.

The kori bustard, the largest bustard in Southern Africa, is found in bushveld, grassland and semi-desert regions.

The kori bustard, the largest flying bird in Africa, is also common. It has a crested head, long legs and the male has an elaborate courtship display during which it puffs up its throat feathers.

Perhaps the most distinctive sight, however, is the huge thatched nests of the sociable weaver bird. The bird itself is not particularly interesting, looking a bit like a common sparrow. However, they live in many-chambered nests that can last for more than a century and are inhabited by as many as 200 birds. The birds weave twigs and straw together in the crowns of acacias and quiver trees, and sometimes even on telephone poles. The interior of the nest is divided into sub-colonies and each breeding pair has a nesting chamber.

Mammals There are 19 species of predator, including the dark-maned Kalahari lion, cheetah, leopard, wild dog, spotted hyena, brown hyena, black-backed jackal, bat-eared fox, Cape fox, honey badger and suricate.

The most numerous species is the springbok, but there are also large numbers of gemsbok, eland, red hartebeest and blue wildebeest. See the Safari Guide for more information.

The Bateleur is a large, heavy set eagle with a bright scarlet face.

Places to Stay

There are rest camps at Twee Rivieren, Mata Mata and Nossob; all have a range of huts and chalets (equipped with bedding, towels, cooking and eating utensils), plus camping facilities. All accommodation at Twee Rivieren is air-conditioned.

All the camps have camp sites, without electricity, with communal ablution facilities for R27 for up to six people, plus R7 for additional people.

Camp sites are usually available, but booking is advised for chalets from June to September, and during the Christmas and Easter holidays. Contact the National Parks Board in Pretoria (☎ (012) 343 1991, fax 343 0905), or Cape Town (☎ (021) 22 2810, fax 24 6211), to make bookings. You can phone the park direct (☎ 0020, ask for Gemsbok 901) but you can't make direct bookings.

Mata Mata Three-bed huts with shared facilities cost R65 and six-bed cottages with kitchen cost R160 for one to four people, plus R46 for additional adults.

Nossob Three-bed huts with shared facilities cost R65; self-contained three-bed huts are R160. Cottages for up to four people cost R170 plus R46 each for one or two additional adults, and a house costs R280 for up to six people.

Twee Rivieren Three-bed chalets with kitchen and bathroom cost R180, four-bed chalets are R210.

Outside the Park The *Molopo Kalahari Lodge* (☎ 0020, ask for 2 Askham) is in the nominal hamlet of Andriesville, about five km south of the Twee Rivieren gate. It's a comfortable, attractive spot with a swimming pool and private thatched chalets. It's about 40 minutes to Twee Rivieren so you're within striking distance of the national park. The chalets are R85 per person including breakfast; or you can camp for R20. There's an à la carte restaurant. If you're aiming for the park, but arrive late, this motel could save

your bacon. It has been recommended by travellers.

There are a number of other places, mainly farms, offering accommodation en route between Upington and Kalahari Gemsbok. The tourist office in Upington has details.

Places to Eat

The very pleasant *Lapa Restaurant* at Twee Rivieren overlooks the camp and offers surprisingly reasonable value. Hors d'œuvres are R9; a mixed grill is R30; chicken is R20. It's open from 6.30 am to 8.30 pm but you should let them know you're coming. As well as the restaurant there's a snack bar selling burgers and other takeaways.

Tours

Several operators run expensive tours to Kalahari Gemsbok. Waterhole Safaris (☎ (021) 419 1739 in Cape Town), for example, charges R2450 for a week.

Getting There & Away

It's a solid five or six-hour drive from Twee Rivieren to Kuruman (385 km) or Upington (358 km) and at present you have to cover a significant distance on dirt, whichever way you go. See the earlier Upington section for information on this route. The gate on the Namibian border at Mata Mata is closed.

Be careful driving – loose gravel can make corners treacherous, and particularly around Bokspits, there are patches of deep sand which give you a bit of a shock if you hit them at speed. No petrol is available between Twee Rivieren and Upington, so make sure you start with a full tank.

It's important to carry water, as you might have to wait a while if you break down. When the temperature is over 40°C you can become dangerously dehydrated quite quickly.

UPINGTON TO SPRINGBOK

West from Upington the road at first follows the course of the Orange River and passes through oases of vineyards and the pleasant little towns of **Keimos** and **Kakamas**. The turn-off to Augrabies Falls National Park, 40 km north, is at Kakamas.

Several members of the Orange River Wine Cellars are open for sales on weekdays and Saturday mornings, however, they don't necessarily offer tastings. They are Upington (☎ (054) 25631), Keimos (☎ (054) 461 1006) and Kakamas (☎ (05442) 236). Groblershoop (☎ (05472) 47) and Grootdrink (☎ (00020) 1) (good name for a wine cellar!) are south-east of Upington on the N8. It's all very different from Western Cape.

In Keimos there's a *caravan park* or two and the *Keimos Hotel* (☎ (054) 461 1084) with singles/doubles for R57/92. Breakfast is R17 and dinner is R23. Kakamus also has camping and the *Waterweil Protea Hotel* (☎ (054) 431 0838) with rooms from R145.

From Kakamas to Pofadder things are considerably duller, but then you enter a wide, bleak valley and, as you approach Springbok, dramatic piles of boulders litter the landscape – you have entered Namaqualand.

Augrabies Falls National Park

The Augrabies Falls National Park (☎ 054472, ask for Augrabies Falls 2) is more than just an impressive waterfall. Certainly the falls can be spectacular (particularly if they are carrying a lot of water) but the most interesting facet of the park is the fascinating desert/riverine environment on either side of the river.

The name of the falls derives from the Namaqua word for 'place of great noise'. The Orange River meanders across the plain from the east, but following an uplift in the land around 500 million years ago it began to wear a deep ravine into the underlying granite. The ravine is 18 km long and has several impressive cataracts. The main falls drop 56 metres, the Bridal Veil Fall on the north side, 75 metres.

The park has a harsh climate with an average rainfall of only 107 mm, and daytime summer temperatures that often reach 40°C. It covers an area of 82,000 hectares and the flora includes kokerbooms, the Namaqua fig, several varieties of thorn trees,

and succulents. The park has 47 species of mammal, most of which are small. These include the klipspringer antelopes, rock dassies (or hyrax) and ground squirrels. Black rhinos, elands, springboks and kudu have been introduced on the north bank of the river (which is not yet open to the public).

The park authorities have developed quite a village around the falls, with an excellent complex including a restaurant, open-air café, numerous cottages and a caravan park.

Information There are three-hour-long nature walks and some interesting drives. At a minimum, allow an hour to look at the falls, a couple of hours at least to explore the park, and an hour or so in the pleasant open-air cafeteria that overlooks the ravine.

The popular three-day Klipspringer Hiking Trail runs along the southern bank of the river. Two nights are spent in huts built from local stone which can sleep 12 people. Camping is not allowed. Hikers must supply their own sleeping bags and food. Booking in advance is advised; the per-person charge is R50. The walk is closed from the middle of October to the end of March because of the heat.

Maps and information are available from the main park complex; there's also a well-stocked shop (but it has few hiking supplies). Both are open from 7 am to 7 pm daily.

The entry charge per vehicle is R15, and the entrance gate is open from 7 am to 7 pm.

The Black Rhino day tour, by Landrover and boat, costs R175 per person for a minimum of two people and a maximum of seven.

Places to Stay There's a *camping ground* with a camp kitchen; sites are R27 for two people, plus R7 for each additional person. Self-contained accommodation includes four-person *cottages* for R290 and *chalets* from R180 for two people, plus R46 for additional people. The accommodation is of a high standard, and many of the cottages and chalets have outstanding views. Contact the National Parks Board in Pretoria (☎ (012) 343 1991, fax 343 0905) or Cape Town

(☎ (021) 22 2810, fax 24 6211), to make bookings.

Places to Eat There's a *cafeteria* where you can buy sandwiches and cold drinks and an à la carte *restaurant* with meals like fillet steak or chicken for R30-something.

Getting There & Away Private transport is essential. The park is 30 km north-west of Kakamas and 120 km from Upington.

Pofadder

Aside from its evocative name (which is not only the name of a snake but also a short, fat sausage – and a local chief, after whom the town is named), there's really not much to Pofadder. The town is something of a byword as an archetypical little place in the middle of nowhere. Namaqualand begins to the west, and the countryside is dry, expansive and beautiful. The surrounding rocky hills and mountains look as if they've been piled up by giants, especially the pyramid-shaped outcrops of black rocks.

There are a couple of banks, a 24-hour petrol station, and an excellent mechanic at the Caltex station on the main street.

Places to Stay There's a *municipal caravan park* (☎ (02532) 46) and other accommodation such as *Pofadder Overnight Flats* (☎ (02532) 19) which charges R50 per person. The *Pofadder Hotel* (☎ (02532) 43) is a kitsch and comfortable country hotel with a swimming pool. Singles/doubles are R130/220 with air-con; singles with fan only are R104.

Getting There & Away There is no public transport. Hitchhikers are numerous.

Around Pofadder

Pella is small mission surrounded by extensive groves of date palms. It was started in 1812 by the London Missionary Society, abandoned after the murder of the missionary, and refounded by French Roman Catholics in 1882. There's quite an extraordinary church that was built by an untrained

French missionary, armed only with an encyclopaedia.

You can hike from Pella to Pofadder in at least four days. The trail is open from the beginning of May to the end of September and runs via Onseepkans, another small Catholic mission station. For more information contact the municipality in Pofadder (☎ (02532) 36).

Namaqualand

Namaqualand is an ill-defined region in the north-west corner of the Northern Cape Province, north of Vanrhynsdorp and west of Pofadder. It is a rugged, mountainous plateau that overlooks a narrow, sandy coastal plain and the bleak beaches of the west coast. In the east it runs into the dry central plains that are known as Bushmanland.

The cold Benguela current runs up the west coast and creates a barren desert-like environment. However, this apparently inhospitable environment produces one of the world's natural wonders. Given decent winter rains there is an extraordinary explosion of spring flowers that covers the boulder-strewn mountains and plains with a multicoloured carpet. Namaqualand's flora is characterised by a phenomenal variety of daisies, but there are also mesembryanthemums, gladioli, aloes, euphorbias, violets and pelargoniums, amongst many other species.

The area is sparsely populated, mainly by Afrikaans-speaking sheep farmers, and in the north-west by the Namaqua, a Khoikhoi tribe. The Namaqua were famous for their metal-working skills, particularly in copper which occurs in the region. Not surprisingly, this attracted the attention of Dutch explorers, who first came into contact with the tribe in 1661. Because of the region's isolation, however, the Namaqualand copper rush did not properly begin until the 1850s. The first commercial mine (now a national monument) was started just outside Springbok in

1852, and there are still a number of large operations, including one at Nababeep.

Namaqualand is also an important source for alluvial diamonds. In 1925 a young soldier, Jack Carstens, found a glittering stone near Port Nolloth. Prospectors converged on the area, and it soon became clear (notably to Earnest Oppenheimer of De Beers) that an enormously rich resource of diamonds had been discovered.

In order to prevent an oversupply of diamonds and the collapse of prices, the government took control of the diggings. Eventually all major mines were brought into the De Beers fold, and all production was brought under the control of a worldwide cartel, the Central Selling Organisation (CSO). All the major west coast alluvial fields are classified as prohibited areas – they are still closed to the general public – and diamonds can only be bought and sold by licensed traders.

The diamonds are harvested from gravel beds on the sea floor and from beneath the sandveld. The sandveld is the narrow, sandy plain, between mountains and sea, which was itself once under the sea. Enormous amounts of sand are moved to expose the bedrock (up to 15 metres below the surface) where the diamond-bearing gravel is found. The underwater diamonds are mined by dredges, and by specially licensed divers and boats who are equipped with suction pumps.

Despite strict security and laws, it is believed that substantial quantities of diamonds still find their way to illegal traders and the 'black market' beyond the reach of the CSO. You may meet locals who offer to sell you cheap diamonds – not only is this highly illegal, you are also likely to end up with what is known as a *slenter*, or fake diamond. These are cut from lead crystal and only an expert can pick them.

The bleak and beautiful landscape, and the diamond miners, contribute to a definite frontier atmosphere. Namaqualand can get very cold in winter (average minimums around 5°C with a high wind-chill factor) and hot in summer (average maximums around 30°C).

Aside from buses on the N7 and R27 (between Vanrhynsdorp and Upington) public transport is sparse. The major operators offer tours of Namaqualand from Jo'burg and Cape Town, but if you really want to see the region you'll need your own vehicle – or join the masses and hitch.

FLOWER VIEWING

Although the wild flowers of the Western Cape are spectacular, they are overshadowed by the brilliance of the Namaqualand displays. Generally the Namaqualand flowers bloom a couple of weeks earlier than those further south, so it makes sense to begin your flower viewing in the north.

The optimum time to visit varies from year to year, but the best chance to catch the flowers at their peak is between mid-August and mid-September, although the season can begin early in August and extend to mid-October. Unfortunately for overseas visitors with fixed itineraries, there can be no guarantee you will be in the right place at the right time. A visit is worth the gamble, however, because even without the flowers, the countryside, though bleak, is beautiful.

The flowers depend on rainfall, which is variable, and the blooms can shrivel quickly in hot winds. Many of the flowers are light-sensitive and only open during bright sunshine. Overcast conditions, which generally only last a day or two, will significantly reduce the display, and even on sunny days the flowers only open properly from around 10 am to 4 pm. They also face the sun (basically northwards), so it is best to travel with the sun behind you.

Although there is no strict dividing line between the Cape floral kingdom (which runs roughly from Clanwilliam to Port Elizabeth) the Namaqualand flora, which is part of the Palaeotropical kingdom, begins north of Vanrhynsdorp. There can be flowers on the plains between Nuwerus and Garies, but the major spectacle begins around Garies and extends to Steinkopf in the north. Springbok is considered the flower capital.

Namaqualand is itself broken into different regions. The dry, sandy coastal belt (the sandveld) gets only around 50 mm of rain a year, although the frequent fogs that roll in off the cold Benguela current provide enough moisture for some succulents, including euphorbias, aloes and mesembryanthemums.

Inland are the rocky mountains of the escarpment (on the western side of the N7) with a number of spectacular passes overlooking the coastal plain. The mountains are still mostly dry, but the rainfall increases to around 100 mm, which is sufficient for wheat farming. The fallow fields are prime habitats for the flowering annuals (daisies, oxalis and gazanias). The hills around Springbok and Nababeep have more rain (around 150 mm) and a particularly rich variety of flowers.

Another zone can be found in the Kamiesberg range which is to the east of Kamieskroon. This area is reasonably well watered, and consequently has a bushier scrub. The plain to the east of Springbok and north to Vioolsdrif produces more brilliant annuals.

Trees are scarce, although visitors will certainly see the characteristic kokerboom, or quiver tree *(Aloe dichotoma)*, an aloe that can grow to a height of four metres, on the hills. The tree stores water in its trunk and is known as the quiver tree, because the Khoisan used its branches as quivers. The branches fork until they form a rounded crown with large spiky leaves. The quiver tree has large yellow blooms in June or July. In the north you'll see 'halfmens' (or Elephant trunk – *Pachydodium namaquanum)*, weird tree-like succulents with a long, inelegant trunk topped by a small 'face' of foliage. They always look to the north, and there's a legend that they are the transformed bodies of Khoikhoi people who were driven south during a war. Those who turned around to look towards their lost lands were turned into trees.

The best flower areas vary from year to year, so it is essential to get local advice on where to go. Most locals will be happy to discuss the question with you, or you can contact the local tourist authorities (Jopie Kotze at the Springbok Café is particularly helpful).

There are generally good flowers east of the N7 between Garies and Springbok. Even if there are no flowers there are spectacular roads between Kamieskroon and Hondeklip Bay, Springbok and Hondeklip Bay, Garies and Hondeklip Bay, Springbok and Port Nolloth, and through the Kamiesberg range south-east of Kamieskroon to Garies. The Goegap Nature Reserve, south-west of Springbok, and the hills around Nababeep are other reliable venues. Wandering around the back roads is a joy in itself.

Springbok is 560 km from Cape Town, 375 km from Upington and 1275 km from Jo'burg, so just getting there is a reasonable undertaking. It's a solid six or seven-hour drive from Cape Town, obviously considerably more to Jo'burg. To do justice to the area, when the flowers are out you need to budget on spending a minimum of two or three days in the district. Most varieties of wild flowers are protected by law and heavy fines can be imposed if you pick them.

Tours
During flower season there are plenty of sightseeing tours of the area run from Cape Town. More personal is the tour run by a Kamieskroon local, Lita Cole (☎ (0257) 762 after 7 pm, fax 675). She organises one to three-day hikes or drives (in your car) through the best flower areas. She charges R150 per group for a day trip and R50 per night on overnight hikes.

CALVINIA
Calvinia is a very attractive town surrounded by wild-west country with a great sense of scale and space – the air has an exhilarating clarity. This is no illusion, as the town's 'starlight factor' is an extremely high 80%. A ridge of the Hantamsberg range dominates the town, which is itself over 1000 metres above sea level. As the church clock quietly tolls the hours it's easy to imagine that decades, if not centuries, have slipped away.

The surrounding countryside can have magnificent spring wild flowers on a

Namaqualand scale even though it is more properly considered the Hantam region. It is in a transitional zone with floral elements from the Namaqualand, Karoo and Cape.

Calvinia's economy is dependent on the surrounding merino sheep farms, and like similar communities in Australia it has been hard hit by the collapse of wool prices. Amazingly, 80% of sheep in the region are still hand shorn with hand clippers (not electric). Cheap labour has a tremendous distorting effect on the economy.

There's an excellent museum, a range of interesting places to stay, and plenty of beautiful countryside to explore.

Information

The information office (☎ (0273) 41 1712), PO Box 28, Calvinia 8190, adjoining the museum is one of the best you'll come across in South Africa. They have a range of suggestions for interesting accommodation and things to do, and a walking-tour map of the town. Farm stays and B&Bs are thriving in the region, and the information office will help you to arrange accommodation; bookings are advisable in the flower season. The office is open Monday to Friday from 8 am to 1 pm and 2 to 5 pm, Saturday from 8 am to noon.

Calvinia Museum

For a small country town, this museum is of a surprisingly high standard, and is definitely

---

Merinos

In 1789 Charles V of Spain gave William IV of Holland six Escurial merinos. These were prized for their fine wool, and the Spanish carefully protected their monopoly. Six of these merinos were sent to the Cape and placed in the care of a R J Gordon. They thrived and multiplied.

The Spanish got wind of this and demanded that their sheep be returned. Gordon obeyed the request to the letter, returning the original six sheep, but keeping their progeny. Most of the flock was later shipped to Australia. ∎

---

worth visiting. The main building was a synagogue – it's incongruous but not unusual to find disused Jewish buildings in tiny, remote towns in South Africa. The museum concentrates on the white settlement of the region, and there are some wonderful oddities like a four-legged ostrich chick (a fake used by a travelling shyster) and a room devoted to a local set of quadruplets. There's also a special section on the sheep industry. It has the same opening hours as the information office; admission is R1.

Places to Stay & Eat

The *Calvinia Caravan Park* (☎ (0273) 41 1011) is close to the centre of town and is pretty flat and ordinary. The facilities are fine, and the town's swimming pool is next door. Sites are R20. A reader reports loud and drunk fellow campers.

If you would rather find some basic self-catering accommodation, try the *Calvinia Rest Rooms* (☎ (0273) 41 1513) which are behind the Total service station on Williston Rd. They're pleasant enough and have kitchen facilities at R50 per person per night.

The best place to stay is any one of the trio of restored historic buildings now run as guesthouses. *Die Tiushuis*, *Die Dorphuis* and *Bothasdal* are wonderful old places furnished with antiques. Depending on where you stay, rooms start at R50 per person or R85 with breakfast. Bookings (☎ (0273) 41 1606) can be made at Die Hantamhuis on Hoop St, the oldest building in town and now a café. This is where you'll have breakfast if you stay at one of the guesthouses. Breakfast (from 7.30 to 9 am) is available to nonresidents (but not on Sunday), and it's recommended. If you order a day in advance you can try skilpadjie, or 'tortoise' (lambs fry wrapped in caul). Other meals are also available.

The *Hantam Hotel* (☎ (0273) 41 1512), Kerk St, is plain but comfortable, and it's as clean as a whistle. Rooms are a reasonable R80 per person, plus R15 for breakfast. The *Commercial Hotel* (☎ (0273) 41 1020, fax 41 2835), Water St, is also of a pretty high standard, but is hideously ugly, which is something of a shame considering it was a beautiful old building before it was 'modernised'. There is talk of replacing its old verandah. The rooms are good (although they may smell of that dreadful air-freshener that's the bane of South African hotels) and cost R70 per person; breakfast is another R20. Make sure you visit Cecil Traut in the bar.

The atmospheric old *Calvinia Hotel*, Hoop St, is currently closed, perhaps just for renovations.

The information office can suggest B&B possibilities. There are also a number of farmhouse B&Bs; most charge around R50 per person. Try *Vinknes Guesthouse* (☎ (0273) 41 2214), on a farm about 30 km from Calvinia on the road to Nieuwoudtville. A number of the farms have San paintings and excellent hiking possibilities.

Getting There & Away
Bus Intercape Mainliner goes through Calvinia with its Cape Town to Upington service, departing from Calvinia at 12.45 am on Monday, Tuesday, Thursday and Saturday heading north; at 11.59 pm on Tuesday, Thursday, Friday and Sunday heading south. Fares and running times from Calvinia include Cape Town, R110, 5¾ hours; Clanwilliam, R70, 2½ hours; Citrusdal, R80, 3¼ hours; Upington, R80, 3¼ hours. This service involves a lot of inconvenient times! Book at the travel agency (☎ (0273) 44 1373) incongruously sited in the *slaghuis* (butcher shop); buses stop at the *trokkie sentrum* (truck centre), the Shell station on the west (Vanrhynsdorp) side of town.

City to City has slightly cheaper and slightly slower buses to/from Cape Town and Upington, although the departure times are still late at night. On Monday, Friday and Saturday, City to City departs from the Calvinia post office at 12.55 am heading for Upington; on Sunday, Monday and Friday it departs at 10.30 pm heading for Cape Town. Fares include Cape Town, R90; Citrusdal, R65; Clanwilliam, R60; Upington, R65.

Minibus Taxi Try the trokkie sentrum for minibus taxis as well. It's R60 to either Cape Town or Upington but taxis don't run every day. If you have no luck here, try the Total station on the east (Upington) side of town.

AROUND CALVINIA
Akkerandam Nature Reserve
This reserve is about two km north of town and is managed by the Calvinia municipality. It covers around 2500 hectares of country at the foot of the Hantamsberg, including part of the southern slopes. There are two hiking trails, one taking one hour (easy), the other climbing the mountain and taking around seven hours (strenuous, but great views). Apart from the wealth of plants (and flowers in season) there are a number of small antelope species.

Calvinia to Clanwilliam
The R364 between Clanwilliam and Calvinia is a superb road through unspoilt, empty countryside and several magnificent passes. There are excellent displays of flowers if you happen to be there at the right

---

Traut Ties
The barman at the Commercial Hotel is an engaging old character by the name of Cecil Traut. His claim to fame (and he has a modicum) is his collection of ties from around the country and the world. He has more than 500 and they cover a wall of the bar and he will be only too happy to show them to you. He has worked behind bars for a long time, and pours a good beer. ∎

PHOTOGRAPH BY JON MURRAY

time. There's a great view from the top of **Botterkloof**, and a couple of nice flat rocks overlooking the gorge that are perfect for a picnic. Sit and dream what this country must have been like 300 years ago, before the San and the game were shot out...

You hit irrigation country around Doringbos and start to get dramatic views of the Cederberg range. The **Pakhuis Pass** takes you through an amazing jumble of multicoloured rocks. There's an excellent camping ground on the Clanwilliam side of the pass. Allow at least two hours for the road – more if you have a picnic or are tempted by the side road to Wuppertal. **Wuppertal** is an old Rhenish mission station, little changed since it was established in 1830. There are whitewashed, thatched cottages, as well as cypresses and donkeys.

Calvinia to Vanrhynsdorp

There is a stunning road between Vanrhynsdorp and Calvinia, with magnificent views over the Knersvlakte from the **Vanrhyns Pass**. In spring there can be a dramatic contrast between green and fertile wheat fields and flowers at the top and the desert far below. Just beyond the pass on the Calvinia side, but off the main road, is the small town of **Nieuwoudtville**, which has a handsome church, and a couple of nearby reserves. There's a small hotel, some guesthouses (contact through the Calvinia tourist office), and the shady municipal caravan park.

The small **Nieuwoudtville Wild Flower Reserve**, just to the north of the R27 (which is clearly signposted), has a fantastic range of flowers, including gladioli and other bulb plants.

The **Oorlogskloof Nature Reserve**, about 5000 hectares in area, runs along the eastern bank of the Oorlogskloof River and overlooks the plains. The terrain is rugged and there's rich bird and floral life and a superb waterfall. There are hiking trails ranging from day hikes to three-night hikes. All access must be arranged in advance (☎ (02726) 81010) since there's no public access road.

GARIES

Just off the main road, Garies does not have the same appeal as Kamieskroon, although there are some nice old homes and buildings lining the main street. The municipal office (☎ (02792) 14) has an information counter, but despite the sign, they're not very helpful about flower information. There are a couple of banks, a post office and a couple of petrol stations.

Places to Stay

The inexpensive *Garies Caravan Park* (☎ (02792) 14), near the sports ground, would be OK although there isn't much shade to take cover under.

The old-style *Garies Hotel* is not particularly welcoming. Rooms with shared bath cost R50/80/100 a single/double/triple and rooms with bath are R65/100.

KAMIESKROON

Kamieskroon is an ordinary little town, but it is perched high in the mountains and is surrounded by boulder-strewn hills. There are some beautiful drives and walks in the area. The dirt roads west to Hondeklip Bay and east to Witwater are truly spectacular, particularly in spring. For information contact the municipality (☎ (0257) 627).

Kamieskroon is a great spot to get away from it all and is an ideal base for exploring the area. The climate can be extreme – very hot in summer (commonly 40°C), and very cold in winter. Snow is not unusual and strong winds mean there is a very high chill factor.

About 18 km north-west of Kamieskroon is the **Skilpad Wild Flower Reserve**. It's on the first ridge in from the west coast so it receives more rain than other places in the area. The Kamieskroon Hotel can give directions.

Places to Stay

The *Kamieskroon Hotel* (☎ (0257) 614 or 706, fax 675) is a very civilised hideaway and it is deservedly popular, especially from July to September (when bookings are essential and prices rise). Singles/doubles are

R70/117 without breakfast, R90/145 with breakfast and R125/220 for dinner, bed and breakfast. The hotel also manages a small number of shaded camp sites (R20).

Getting There & Away

Namakwaland Busdiens and Intercape Mainliner both run buses along the N7. Kamieskroon is one hour south of Springbok – see that section for details.

HONDEKLIP BAY

In most ways Hondeklip Bay is just a smaller, less interesting version of Port Nolloth. It's a small, dusty little town on a bleak stretch of the coastal plain. There's a shop, petrol and a depressing little caravan park – there are no showers, and you would be wise to bring your own water.

The dirt roads to Springbok, Kamieskroon and Garies are spectacular, however. After climbing through rocky hills, you drop onto the desert-like coastal plain which is dotted with enormous diamond mines. The flora is fascinating – make sure you take time to walk around, even if it's just off the side of the road. There is an extraordinary number of species and a lot them are weird succulents.

SPRINGBOK

Springbok considers itself the capital of Namaqualand, and it lies in a valley amongst harsh rocky hills that explode with colour in the flower season. The first European-run copper mine was established on the town's outskirts in 1852 and from a rough-and-tumble frontier town it has been transformed into a busy service centre for the copper and diamond mines in the region.

Orientation & Information

The town is quite spread-out, but most places are within walking distance of the small koppie (hill) in the elbow of the main street's right-angled bend. The koppie is planted with some of Namaqualand's strange flora.

The Springbok Café (☎ (0251) 21321), on the main street, is a unique phenomenon run by the ebullient Jopie Kotze. This is the best spot in town to get a good meal and to collect information on the surrounding region (including where the best flowers are). There is an extensive rock and gem collection, with some pieces for sale, as well as books, postcards, maps – pretty much anything you can think of.

There's also an official information centre (☎ (0251) 22071 or 21543) in the old church next to the post office, open from 8.30 am to 3.30 pm on weekdays.

Springbok Museum

In the 1920s, Springbok had a large population of Jews who traded in the region. Most have moved away, and their synagogue (built in 1929) has been converted into a small but interesting local museum. It concentrates on white history, but there are some interesting historical photos and relics. It's open Monday to Saturday from 9 am to noon.

Places to Stay

During the flower season accommodation in Springbok can fill up. The information centre can tell you about overflow accommodation in private homes.

Springbok Caravan Park (☎ (0251) 81584) is two km from town on Goegap Rd, the road to the nature reserve and the airport. Occasional buses run past, otherwise it's a very long walk. Tent sites are R10.

The Namastat (☎ (0251) 81455 for booking) should be open by now. It's an interesting place with accommodation in traditional woven Namaqua 'mat' huts, similar in shape to Zulu 'beehive' huts. In Afrikaans they're called matjieshuis. Each hut has two beds and costs R35 per person if you need a bed, considerably less if you have your own bedding. There's a common ablutions block but no electricity. It's planned to have traditional Namaqua foods and a non-traditional bar. The Namstat is about three km west of the centre of town, on the Cape Town road (not the highway). It's at the head of a valley and there are good views. For more information see Frikkie Gunter in the ice-cream parlour across from the Springbok Café.

The Springbok Café (☎ (0251) has rooms

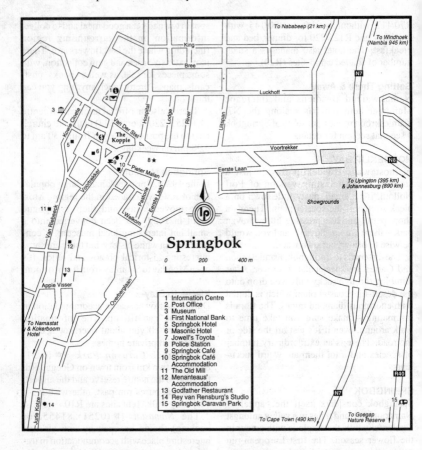

1 Information Centre
2 Post Office
3 Museum
4 First National Bank
5 Springbok Hotel
6 Masonic Hotel
7 Jowell's Toyota
8 Police Station
9 Springbok Café
10 Springbok Café Accommodation
11 The Old Mill
12 Menanteaus' Accommodation
13 Godfather Restaurant
14 Rey van Rensburg's Studio
15 Springbok Caravan Park

and cottages in a street of old workers' cottages behind the café. The cottages have been steadily upgraded over the years and Jopie is planning to change the name of his establishment to Springbok Lodge & Restaurant, to avoid the down-market connotations of most 'overnight rooms' attached to cafés. Rates start at R60 per person.

Menanteaus' Accommodation (☎ (0251) 22915, fax 22986), run by friendly Dolly and Menanteau, is at 61 Voortrekker St, a few blocks south of the koppie. It's a guesthouse in a rambling old house, with some addi-

tions. Accommodation is in rooms or self-contained flats sleeping four people or more. The rooms could be bigger but the flats are pleasant and fairly large. Unlike almost everywhere else in Springbok, the rates don't rise during the flower season. Prices are comparable to those at the Springbok Café.

On Van Riebeeck St, under the lee of a huge basalt outcrop, *The Old Mill* (☎ (0251) 22084) is an up-market B&B.

The same family runs three of Springbok's places to stay: the Springbok and Masonic hotels and the Kokerboom Motel. Of the three, the best option is definitely the *Springbok*

Hotel (☎ (0251) 21161), a plain, old-style hotel, which is a bit dowdy, but reasonable value nonetheless. Singles/doubles are R93/115, with breakfast an additional R20. The nearby *Masonic Hotel* (☎ (0251) 22008) is simple, but OK. Singles/doubles without bath cost from R80/108, with a bath you'll pay R84/115 and up. Breakfast is R19 and dinner is R35.

The *Kokerboom Motel* (☎ (0251) 22685) is more like an army barracks and it is inconveniently located on the outskirts of town.

Places to Eat

The *Springbok Hotel* has a certain faded country-town grandeur. Its dining room has à la carte meals: entrees cost between R8 and R15, fish or steak starts around R25. There are also good-value stews for R20 or less.

For something more informal and fun, the *Springbok Café* can't be beaten. It's rare to find such a pleasant place in a small South African town, where you usually have to resort to something Wimpyesque for a snack or a coffee. The menu is large and includes grills, from R20, breakfast, pizzas, snacks and salads. It stays open until 10 pm.

Just down the hill from Menanteaus' Accommodation, the *Godfather Restaurant* is a pizza place which is also open 24 hours for takeaways. A reader has recommended *BJ's* bar and restaurant.

Getting There & Away

Air There are daily flights from Springbok to Cape Town with National Airlines (☎ (021) 934 0350 in Cape Town, (0251) 22061 in Springbok).

Bus Jowell's Toyota (☎ (0251) 22061), next door to the Springbok Café, handles most bus bookings. Namakwaland Busdiens (☎ (0251) 21115) has the most useful service on the Cape Town to Springbok (N7) route. They visit most of the towns along the highway and run every weekday. They leave Springbok at 7.15 am and arrive at Cape Town railway station at 3 pm. The northbound bus leaves Cape Town at 6.30 am, arriving in Springbok at 2.45 pm. The fare is R58 (which is much less than it was a few years ago). Other fares on this route, from Springbok/Cape Town, include Kamieskroon, R13/58; Vanrhynsdorp, R44/44; Clanwilliam, R46/37; and Citrusdal, R48/33.

Intercape Mainliner's service from Windhoek to Cape Town runs through Springbok. Buses leave Cape Town at 2 pm on Sunday, Tuesday, Thursday and Friday and arrive at Windhoek at 6.30 am the next day; they come through Springbok (Springbok Café) at 8.30 pm. Buses leave Windhoek at 7 pm on Monday, Wednesday, Friday and Sunday and arrive at Cape Town at 11 am the next day; they pass through Springbok at 5 am. From Springbok to Cape Town is R145; Springbok to Windhoek, R200.

Van Wyk's Busdiens (☎ (0251) 38559) has a bus to Cape Town for R60 and you could also try Titus Taxis & Bus (☎ (0251) 21524).

Minibus Taxi Atkins Transport (☎ (0251) 6631) runs a daily door-to-door taxi to Cape Town for R80. You can also book this service in Cape Town (☎ (021) 707 1644). It's best to ring between 8 and 9 pm. Another company is SC Transport (☎ (0251) 22513). You'll find ordinary leave-when-full taxis to Cape Town for about R60. Ask at the Caltex garage near the robot on Voortrekker St.

There's apparently a daily taxi to Upington but I couldn't find any hard information.

Car Rental Ask at the Springbok Café about car hire from local garages.

AROUND SPRINGBOK
Nababeep

Nababeep is the site of a large copper mine, and the surrounding hills often have spectacular flowers. For those who are interested in mining, a visit to the **O'Kiep Copper Co Museum** is worthwhile. Phone ☎ (0251) 38121 for opening times.

Goegap Nature Reserve

This reserve which is famous for its extraordinary display of spring flowers and its nursery of over 200 amazing Karoo and Namaqualand succulents should not be missed. There are a couple of driving routes but you'll see more on one of the circular walks of 4 km, 5.5 km and 7 km. In addition to the flora, there are springbok, ostriches, zebras and birds. The reserve is open from 8 am to 4.30 pm on weekdays and also on weekends during the flower season, roughly during August and September. Admission is R2.20.

KLEINSEE

Reputedly, there's nothing much to see at Kleinsee, a diamond-mining company town with a modern shopping centre. One would expect the drive from Springbok to be interesting – first-hand reports welcome.

PORT NOLLOTH

Port Nolloth is a sandy and exposed little place, but it has a certain fascination. It was originally developed as the shipping point for the region's copper, but it is now dependent on the small fishing boats that catch diamonds and crayfish. The boats are fitted with pumps, and divers vacuum up the diamond-bearing gravel found on the ocean floor. The town has attracted a multicultural group of fortune-seekers and they give the town frontier vitality.

This area is one of South Africa's driest and until recently the town received its drinking water by boat. Despite this, Port Nolloth is notorious for mists.

Unlike most other towns in South Africa, there's a feeling of 'just getting by' among the white population (and the all-too-familiar feeling of not quite getting by among the coloured population), and most houses are modest wooden buildings. For the visitor this is a nice change – presumably the inhabitants wouldn't agree.

Information

The information centre is in the town hall, just off the main road into town.

There's a branch of the First National Bank, a petrol station, a pharmacy and some reasonable shops. For information, contact the Port Nolloth municipality (☎ (0255) 8657).

A museum is being developed in one of the old sea-front cottages, next to the Bedrock guesthouse. The building was once the Officers' Club.

Should you want to swim in this cold water, the best beach is to the north of town – unless the diamond miners have taken up their option and begun digging up the dunes there.

Places to Stay

There's *Bedrock* (☎ (0255) 8865), a guesthouse in one of the old wooden cottages, lining the sea-front. As well as being a friendly and comfortable place to stay, with big rooms and sea views, it's a social must, as it's owned by Grazia de Beer ('Mama'). She's a local identity who can help organise just about anything, from day trips into the Richtersveld to seafood feasts. Highly recommended. To get to Bedrock turn right onto the beachfront road as you come into town and it's the second building along. Mama also owns a couple of nearby houses so there is a range of accommodation options. In the guesthouse you'll pay R100 per person for dinner, bed and breakfast. There's a two-bedroom self-catering cottage which goes for between R100 and R150; and in another cottage backpackers can stay for R20. Bookings are advised.

The *Nova Scotia Hotel* (☎ (0255) 8353) is a comfortable hotel with pleasant rooms, a peg or two above what you might expect in this rough-and-tumble town, and the prices reflect this. Singles with/without baths are R135/100; doubles with/without baths are R160/130. There's an à la carte restaurant with standard prices – expect to pay R20 for a main meal.

McDougall's Bay Caravan Park is acceptable, but don't expect five-star comforts. Basic huts are R38, chalets sleeping six are R80 in winter, rising to R102 at peak times, and sites (on gravel) are R22. The caravan park is about four km south of Port Nolloth by road, less on foot if you can find a path

---

Illegal Diamond Buying

It is illegal in South Africa to sell diamonds except to De Beers. The diamond mines are hives of security but the independent divers who work Port Nolloth and other submarine diamond fields on the west coast have more opportunity to get away with extracting diamonds from their catch and selling them on the black market. Diamond diving is hard work and it isn't lucrative; the divers can only work about 10 days a month because of the weather. IDB (illegal diamond buying) is a sub-current of life in this area and chances are that a few of your fellow patrons in a diamond town bar are undercover members of the police IDB branch. You may meet locals who offer to sell you cheap diamonds – not only is this highly illegal, you are also likely to end up with what is known as a *slenter* or fake diamond. These are cut from lead crystal and only an expert can pick them. ∎

---

through the shantytown (and if it's safe to take it). A taxi runs half-hourly for R4.

Places to Eat

Captain Pete's Tavern, across from the hotel, is probably the best place for a meal. You'll pay between R25 and R30. It's owned by a diamond diver who struck it rich. The *Nova Scotia Hotel* has a dining room and there are meals at the *Country Club*, a few km out of town.

Getting There & Away

There is little or no public transport, and hitching from the N7 turn-off at Steinkopf would be slow. It's a great drive from Springbok (145 km) with bare mountains looming to the north and the exhilarating drop down to the coastal plain through the Aninaus Pass. There was once a Port Nolloth to Springbok train service but mules had to pull the train up the pass! As you drive along the coastal flats you'll notice that the land is all fenced. This isn't to keep stock in but to keep poachers out of diamond leases. It's illegal to enter.

ALEXANDER BAY

This is a government-controlled diamond mine on the south bank of the Orange River mouth – Namibia is across the river. The road from Port Nolloth is open to the public, but the Namibian border is closed. Restrictions on access are beginning to lift and the town is looking at its tourism potential. There are mine tours (☎ (0256) 330) and a museum.

Brandkaros (☎ (0265) 856 or 464) is a farm by the river about 30 km from Alexander Bay with self-catering rondavels (R114

a double) as well as tent sites. It's en route to the Richtersveld and might make a good base. First-hand reports, please.

VIOOLSDRIF

Vioolsdrif is the border crossing on the N7, 677 km north of Cape Town. The drive from Steinkopf is spectacular and at Vioolsdrif there are great views of the Orange River carving its way through the desolate mountains and the narrow strip of irrigated farmland on its banks. The border is open 24 hours.

RICHTERSVELD NATIONAL PARK

The Richtersveld National Park is an enormous (185,000 hectares) park in the northern loop of the Orange River to the west of Vioolsdrif and the N7. The park is the property of the local Namaqua people who continue to lead a semi-traditional, semi-nomadic pastoral existence; hopefully they will benefit from increased job opportunities and the rent paid by the park authorities.

The area is a mountainous desert, a spectacular wilderness with jagged rocky peaks, deep ravines and gorges; the hiking possibilities, though demanding, are excellent. Despite its apparent barrenness, the region has a rich and prolific variety of succulent plants.

At present, most of the park is virtually inaccessible without a properly equipped expedition and local guides. Apparently the southern section is accessible by 2WD vehicles but it would pay to check this before venturing in. Only a small number of people are allowed into the park at any one time, so ring ahead (☎ (0256) 506) and see if you can get in. Walking trails are being established.

Rey van Rensburg (☎ (0251) 21905, fax 81460) is a Springbok photographer who also runs tours into Richtersveld National Park. Rey is enthusiastic, experienced and very knowledgeable about the area. A five-day vehicle tour costs R1400 per person, and a five-day tour that includes some hiking costs R1000 per person. An eight-day tour involving vehicles, inflatables and hiking costs R2200 per person.

You'll need at least eight people and your own sleeping bags. Book at least a couple of months in advance. Tours are run between April and October. Rey can also arrange longer tours of Namibia if you are interested in a longer trip.

Facts about the Country

Lesotho (pronounced le-*soo-too)* is a mountainous kingdom about the size of Belgium which is surrounded by South Africa. Its forbidding terrain and the defensive walls of the Drakensberg and Maloti ranges gave both sanctuary and strategic advantage to the Basotho (the people of Lesotho) who forged a nation while playing a key role in the manoeuverings of the white invaders on the plains below.

LESOTHO

Area: 30,350 sq km
Population: 1,800,000
Population Growth: 2.9 %
Capital: Maseru
Head of State: King Moshoeshoe II
Official Language: seSotho, English
Currency: Maloti
Exchange Rate: Pegged to South African Rand
Per Capita GNP: US$580
Time: GMT/UTC + 2

HISTORY

Archaeological and linguistic evidence suggests that the group of peoples described as Sotho lived in southern Africa as early as the 10th century AD, and possibly much earlier. By the beginning of the 19th century they had become a dominant group on the highveld of what is now South Africa. Because of the different terrains into which they moved, various groups began to differ in culture and custom, but the unifying Sesotho language and persisting marriage customs have encouraged anthropologists to retain the broad label of Sotho. The major groups today are the Tswana (western Sotho), the northern Sotho and the people who today live in Lesotho, the southern Sotho.

Lesotho was settled by Sotho peoples comparatively recently, possibly as late as the 16th century. Already here were the Khoisan, with whom there was some intermarriage and mingling of language. There might also have been some Nguni people.

The early society was made up of small chiefdoms, which fragmented as groups broke away in search of new land. Cattle and cultivation were the mainstays of the economy, and extensive trade links were forged. Grain and hides were exported in exchange for iron from the Transvaal area.

By the early 19th century white traders were on the scene, exchanging beads for cattle. They were soon followed by the *Voortrekkers* (Boer pioneers) and pressure

on Sotho grazing lands grew. Even without white encroachment Sotho society was due to face the fact that it had expanded as far as it could and would have to adapt to living in a finite territory. On top of this came the disaster of the difaqane (forced migration).

The rapid consolidation and expansion of the Zulu state under the leadership of Shaka, and later Dingaan, resulted in a chain reaction of turmoil throughout the whole of southern Africa. Huge numbers of people were displaced, their tribes shattered and their lands lost, and they, in turn, attacked other tribes. Old alliances were upset and agriculture and herding became impossible in many areas. Some bands of refugees didn't stop moving until they came to the area now known as Tanzania.

That the loosely organised southern Sotho society survived this period was largely due to the abilities of King Moshoeshoe.

Moshoeshoe the Great

Moshoeshoe began as a leader of a small village and, in about 1820, he led his villagers to Butha-Buthe. From this mountain stronghold his people survived the first battles of the difaqane and, in 1824, Moshoeshoe began his policy of assisting refugees on the condition that they help in his defence. Later in the same year he moved his people

Lesotho

further, to Thaba-Bosiu, a mountain top which was even easier to defend.

From Thaba-Bosiu, Moshoeshoe played a patient game of placating the stronger local rulers and granting protection – as well as land and cattle – to groups of refugees. By 1840 his people numbered about 40,000 and his power base was protected by groups who had settled on his outlying lands and were partially under his authority. These people and others like them were to form the Basutholand which, by the time of Moshoeshoe's death in 1870, had a population of over 150,000.

Another factor in Basutholand's emergence and survival was Moshoeshoe's welcoming of missionaries, and his ability to take their advice without being dominated by them. The first missionaries to arrive in the area, in 1833, were from the Paris Evangelical Missionary Society. Moshoeshoe made one of them his adviser, and the sophisticated diplomacy which had marked his dealings with local chiefs now extended to his dealings with Europeans. The missions, often situated in remote parts of the kingdom, served as tangible signs of his authority, and in return for some Christianisation of Sotho

King Moshoeshoe the Great

customs, the missionaries were disposed to defend the rights of 'their' Basotho against the new threat – British and Boer expansion.

The Boers had crossed the Orange River in the 1830s, and by 1843 Moshoeshoe was sufficiently concerned by their numbers to ally himself with the British Cape government. The resulting treaties defined his borders but did little to stop squabbles with the Boers, who regarded grazing rights they had been granted by the British as title to the land they occupied – the fertile lowlands west of the Mohokare (Caledon) River.

The British Resident, installed in Basutholand as a condition of the treaties, decided that Moshoeshoe was too powerful and engineered an unsuccessful attack on his kingdom. In 1854, the British withdrew from the area having fixed the boundaries of Basutholand. The Boers pressed their claims on the land and increasing tension led to the 1858 Free State-Basutho War. Moshoeshoe won yet another major battle, and the situation simmered along until 1865 when another Free State-Basutho war erupted. This time Moshoeshoe suffered setbacks and, as a consequence, was forced to sign away much of his western lowlands.

The Boers' land hunger showed no sign of diminishing and, in 1868, Moshoeshoe again called on British assistance, this time on the imperial government in London. A High Commission was formed to adjudicate the dispute and the result was the loss of more Basotho land. It was obvious that no treaty between Boers and Basotho would hold for long, and continual war between the Free State and Basutholand was not good for British interests. The British solution was to simply annex Basutholand.

After Moshoeshoe

The British, their imperial policy changing yet again, gave control of Basutholand to the Cape colony in 1871. Moshoeshoe had died the year before and squabbles over succession were dividing the country. The Cape government exploited this and reduced the powers of chiefs and limited them to their individual areas.

The Gun War of 1880 began as a protest against the Cape government's refusal to allow the Basotho to own firearms, but it quickly became a battle between the rebel chiefs on one side and the government and collaborating chiefs on the other. The war ended in a stalemate (making it one of the few wars in southern Africa which didn't result in Africans being crushed by Europeans) with the Cape government discredited.

A shaky peace followed until another war appeared imminent, and the British government again took direct control of Basutholand in 1884. The imperial government decided to back strong local leaders rather than rule through its own officers, and this helped to stabilise the country. One unexpected benefit of direct British rule was that, when the Union of South Africa was created, Basutholand was a British protectorate and was not included in the Union. If the Cape government had retained control, Lesotho would have been part of South Africa and have become a Homeland under the apartheid regime.

Ruling through chiefs might have defused power struggles between rival chiefs but it did nothing to develop democracy in the country. If anything it created a feudal state more open to abuse than Moshoeshoe's loose confederation of subordinate chiefs.

Home Rule & Independence

In 1910 the Basutoland National Council was formed. This official advisory body was composed of members nominated by the chiefs, but after decades of allegations of corruption and favouritism, reforms were made in the 1940s which introduced some democracy into appointments to the council.

In the mid-1950s the council requested internal self-government from the British and, in 1960, a new constitution was in place and elections were held for a Legislative Council. Half its members were elected by the (male) people and the other half was made up of chiefs and the appointed representatives of the king.

Meanwhile, political parties had formed. The main contenders were the Basutholand Congress Party (BCP), similar to South Africa's ANC, and the Basutholand National Party (BNP), a conservative party headed by Chief Leabua Jonathan.

The BCP won the 1960 elections and demanded full independence from Britain. This was eventually agreed to and a new constitution was drawn up, with independence to come into effect in 1966. However, at the elections in 1965 the BCP lost power to the BNP and Chief Jonathan became the first prime minister of the new Kingdom of Lesotho. Just why the BCP lost is debatable, but the fact that the BNP promised cooperation with the South African apartheid regime and in turn received massive support from it must be significant.

However, as most of the civil service was still loyal to the BCP, Jonathan did not have an easy time. Stripping King Moshoeshoe II of the few powers that the new constitution had left him did not endear Jonathan's government to the people and, in the 1970 election, the BCP won government.

Jonathan responded by suspending the constitution, arresting then expelling the king and banning opposition parties. The king, after an exile in Holland, was allowed to return, and Jonathan attempted to form a government of national reconciliation. This ploy was partly successful, with several members of the BCP joining the sham government, but some, including the leader Ntsu Mokhehle, resisted and attempted to stage a coup in 1974. The coup failed miserably and resulted in the death of many BCP supporters and the jailing or forced exile of the BCP leadership. Lesotho was effectively a one-party state.

Trouble continued and repressive measures were applied. It's possible that Jonathan would have continued to cling to power had he not changed his attitude towards South Africa, although this change was partly caused by a need to placate popular opposition to South Africa. He called for the return of land in the Orange Free State that had been stolen from the original Basutoland, and, more seriously from the South African point of view, began criticising apartheid, allegedly offering refuge to ANC guerrillas and flirting with Cuba. Relations soured to the point where South Africa closed Lesotho's borders, strangling the country.

The Lesotho military took action and Jonathan was deposed in 1986. The military council, headed by Major General Lekhanya, restored the king as head of state. This was a popular move, but eventually agitation for democratic reform again rose to the point where there were disturbances in the country. In 1990 King Moshoeshoe II was deposed by the army in favour of his son, Prince Mohato Bereng Seeisa (Letsie III). Elections in 1993 resulted in the return of the BCP and Mokhehle became prime minister.

In early 1994 two rival army factions, each supporting a different political party, began fighting near Maseru. After a short battle an uneasy peace was established, although South Africa mounted major military exercises along the border shortly after the fighting. With the Highlands Water Project nearing completion, South Africa was probably warning Lesotho not to threaten its interests.

In January 1995 Letsie III abdicated in

favour of his father, and five years after being deposed, Moshoeshoe II was reinstated, restoring some calm to Lesotho after a year of unrest. Unfortunately, less than a year later, in 1996, he was killed in car accident. His successor has not been decided and there may be more unrest.

GEOGRAPHY

Lesotho's borders are mainly natural and it is completely surrounded by South Africa. From Lesotho's northern tip to its western side where it juts out almost to the town of Wepener in South Africa, the border is formed by the Mohokare (Caledon) River. The eastern border is defined by the rugged escarpment of the Drakensberg, and high country forms much of the southern border.

All of Lesotho exceeds 1000 metres in altitude, with peaks in the central ranges and near the escarpment over 3000 metres. The tourist slogan, 'kingdom in the sky', is not far wrong, as Lesotho has the highest lowest point of any country on earth.

The highest mountain in southern Africa (the highest point south of Kilimanjaro) is the 3841-metre Thabana-Ntlenyana, near Sani Pass in eastern Lesotho.

CLIMATE

Winters are cold and clear. Frosts are common and there are snowfalls in the high country and sometimes at lower altitudes. At other times of the year, snow has been known to fall (especially on the high peaks where the weather is dangerously changeable) but rain and mist are more common bugbears for drivers and hikers. Nearly all of Lesotho's rain falls between October and April, with spectacular thunderstorms in summer – quite a few people are killed by lightning every year. Down in the valleys, summer days can be hot with temperatures over 30°C.

Never go out into the mountains, even for an afternoon, without a sleeping bag, tent and sufficient food for a couple of days in case you get fogged in. Even in summer it can be freezing.

GOVERNMENT

The country is in the process of writing a new constitution. Its draft constitution allowed free elections in 1993 after some years of military rule. The King is the head of state.

ECONOMY

Lesotho is one of the world's poorest countries. Erosion is a major problem and the already scarce arable land is becoming degraded. Much of Lesotho's food is imported, although in the 19th century Lesotho exported grain. The main export is now labour; many Basotho work in South Africa.

The huge Highlands Water Project is cre-

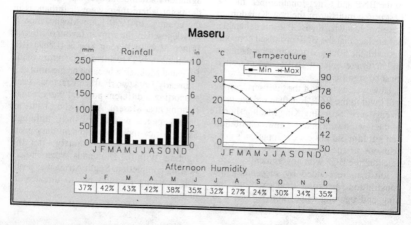

Highlands Water Project
This project is being implemented in stages to provide water and electricity for a large tract of southern Africa. When construction is finished (circa 2020) there will be four major dams, many smaller dams and many km of tunnels.

Phase 1, due for completion in 1996, includes the 180-metre-high Katse Dam on the Malibamat'so River, to the north of Thaba-Tseka. A transfer tunnel, four metres in diameter and 45 km long will carry water to a hydroelectric plant at Muela near Butha-Buthe. After generating electricity, the water will flow through a 37-km tunnel across the border to Clarens and into the Axle River, a tributary of the Vaal. Eventually this water will reach the Vaal Dam, an essential reservoir for Jo'burg. The other three major dams will be on the Senqu (Orange) River.

The immediate effect of the development has been improved roads into Lesotho's interior. Farmers who have lost land are promised compensation. There are, however, several environmental questions to consider and critics of the scheme feel that satisfactory answers still have to be provided. ■

---

ating a series of dams on the Orange River in Lesotho, and sales of water and hydroelectricity to South Africa might make Lesotho more economically independent. Very little manufacturing takes place in the kingdom and most goods are imported from South Africa.

POPULATION & PEOPLE

The 1,800,000 citizens of Lesotho are known as the Basotho people. Culturally, most are southern Sotho and most speak Sesotho. The melding of the Basotho nation was largely the result of Moshoeshoe I's 19th-century military and diplomatic triumphs and many diverse subgroups and peoples have somehow merged into a homogeneous society. Maseru, with 109,000 people, is the only large city.

CULTURE

The first people to occupy Lesotho were the original inhabitants of southern Africa, the Khoisan. They have left many examples of their rock art in the river valleys.

Although traditional Basotho culture is breaking down through contact with the rest of the world and changes in the society, much of the culture remains because it relates so strongly to the way people live. Also, rich cultures have a way of surviving through change: a belief might live on in a proverb or a ritual may have become a game.

Traditional culture in Lesotho consists largely of the customs, rites and superstitions with which ordinary people explain and flavour their lives. As in all cultures, the milestones of birth, puberty, marriage and death are associated with ceremonies. Cattle, both as sacrificial animals and as a symbol of wealth and worth, plays a large part in the culture, as do the cultivation of crops and the vagaries of the weather – Basotho farmers have to worry about drought, flood, hailstorms, snow and lightning.

Much of the folklore puts common sense into practice: toasting fresh rather than stale bread is bad (it causes rheumatism); when working at straining beer take an occasional drink (or your hands will swell); a spider in a hut should not be molested (it's the strength of the family); a howling dog must be stopped immediately (or it will bring evil).

Music and dance play their part in traditional culture, mainly as important components of ceremony and everyday life. There are various musical instruments, from the *lekolulo* (a flute-like instrument) played by herd-boys, to the *thomo* (a stringed instrument played by women) and the *setolo-tolo* (a stringed instrument played with the mouth, by men).

Traditional medicine mixes rites and customs, with healers (*sangomas*) developing their own charms and rituals. The Basotho are traditionally buried in a sitting position, ready to leap up when called, and facing the rising sun.

Rainmaking

A first attempt at bringing rain is made by the men of the village, who climb to the top of a nearby mountain and kill everything they can find. The entrails of the animals are thrown into streams and the men return home, drenched from the heavy rain. If the rain *isn't* falling, the village calls in a *moroka-pula* (rainmaker). If he fails, it's the turn of the village's young women.

They go to a neighbouring village and the quickest of them enters a hut and steals the *lesokoana*, which can be any wooden cooking utensil. She flees from the village with the lesokoana, raising the alarm herself if she hasn't already been spotted. When the village women run out to reclaim the lesokoana, the young women toss it back and forth, sometimes losing it and sometimes regaining it. This game of long-distance 'keepings-off' attracts spectators from both villages and ends when one group makes it back to their village with the lesokoana.

The winners 'enter the village with merriment, wearing green leaves about the head and waist, and singing with great joy an anthem...'

Sechefo doesn't say what happens if this still fails to bring rain – but at least everyone stops worrying about the drought for a while. ■

Much of the traditional culture is associated with avoiding misfortune, and reflects the grim realities of subsistence life. For example, a feeble old man, unwilling to die and relieve his relatives of the burden of supporting him, is liable to be placed at the entrance to a cattle *kraal*, to be trampled in the evening by the homecoming beasts. But there are also many lighthearted customs, such as this last-resort rain-making ceremony recorded in the pamphlet *Customs & Superstitions in Basutholand* by Justinus Sechefo.

RELIGION

Thanks to the part missionaries played in the creation of Lesotho, most people are at least nominally Christian and a high percentage of Christians are Catholic. However, traditional beliefs are still strong in rural areas and seem to coexist with Christianity, probably because the beliefs are tied so closely to the important and trivial details of everyday life.

Broadly, traditional religion amongst the Basotho is similar to that of the other Sotho people in southern Africa. They believe in a supreme being, but place a great deal of

The Basotho Hat

A distinctive feature of Basotho dress is the conical hat with its curious top adornment; it is known to the Basotho as *mokorotlo*, or *molianyeoe*.

The style of this hat is taken directly from the shape of a hill near the Mosheshoe I's Thaba-Bosiu fortress. The hill is called Qiloane and it stands proudly alone with a few villages at its base.

These hats can be purchased in Maseru at the appropriately named Basotho Hat, from the vendors in front of the tourist office and at the border posts. A large adult-sized hat is about M25. You'll pay M10 for one which could hang from your rear-vision mirror next to those cute FIFA soccer boots. The large hats are highly prized in South Africa; I lost mine to a local angler in an eel-fishing competition in western Transkei. ■

emphasis on ancestors *(balimo)*, who act as intermediaries between the people and the capricious forces of nature.

Evil is an ever-present danger, caused by *boloi* (witchcraft; witches can be either male or female) and *thkolosi*, maliciously playful beings having much in common with leprechauns, imps and pixies in their sinister, pre-Disney form. A *ngaka* is a learned man, a combination of sorcerer and doctor, who can combat these forces.

LANGUAGE

The official languages are SeSotho and English. For more about SeSotho see the main Language section. Always remember *Hylale* ('Stop the war').

Facts for the Visitor

VISAS & EMBASSIES

The visa situation in Lesotho is in a state of utter confusion.

If you're arriving from South Africa, remember that you won't be readmitted to that country unless you have a multiple-entry visa.

The following information was provided by Lesotho's Ministry of Immigration – best of luck. Citizens of most foreign countries *do* need a visa to visit Lesotho. Eleven countries are exempt: Denmark, Finland, Greece, Iceland, Ireland, Israel, Japan, Norway, San Marino, Sweden and South Africa.

In general, citizens of Commonwealth countries do not need a visa. Exceptions are: Australia, Canada, Ghana, New Zealand, Nigeria, India, Pakistan and Namibia.

A single-entry visa costs M20 and a multiple-entry visa is M40. At most border posts you get two weeks' stay renewable by either leaving the country and reentering or by application at the Ministry of Immigration in Kingsway, Maseru. Also, for a longer stay, apply in advance directly to the Director of Immigration & Passport Services, PO Box 363, Maseru 100, Lesotho.

Lesotho Embassies

Lesotho embassies and high commissions in other countries include:

Canada
    202 Clemow Ave, Ottawa His 2 B4, Ontario (☎ (613) 236 9449)
Germany
    Godersberger Alle 50 5300, Bonn 2 (☎ (228) 37 6868/9)
South Africa
    343 Pretorius St, Momentum Centre, 6th Floor, West Tower, Pretoria 001 (☎ (012) 322 6090)
UK
    7 Chesam Place, Belgravia, London SW1 8AN (☎ (0171) 373 8581/2, fax 235 5686)
USA
    2511 Massachusetts Ave NW, Washington DC 20008 (☎ (202) 797 5533/4)

Told I didn't need a visa, I arrived at Maseru Bridge and offered my passport. I was told to return to Ladybrand and wait until tomorrow before trying again. I pleaded and the border official 'did me a big favour', granting temporary entry of 72 hours with the proviso that I report in person to the Director of Immigration in Maseru within that time. I fronted and after a cordial discussion and the payment of the visa fee was given a further 10 days.

Foreign Embassies in Lesotho

For foreign embassies in Lesotho see the Maseru chapter.

DOCUMENTS

No vaccination certificates are necessary to enter Lesotho unless you have recently been in a yellow fever area.

CUSTOMS

Customs regulations are broadly the same as those for South Africa, but you can't bring in alcohol unless you're arriving from a country other than Botswana, Swaziland and South Africa – and that isn't likely. If you're entering through Sani Pass there's a good chance that alcohol will be confiscated.

MONEY

The unit of currency is the maloti (M), which is divided into 100 liesente. The maloti is fixed at a value equal to the South African rand, and rands are accepted everywhere – there is no real need to convert your money into maloti. When changing travellers' cheques you can usually get rand notes and this saves having to convert unused maloti. You will invariably get maloti in change.

The only banks where you can change foreign currency, including travellers' cheques, are in Maseru. The banks are the Lesotho Development Bank, Standard Bank and Barclays. Banks are open Monday to Friday from 8.30 am to 3 pm (to 1 pm on Thursday), Saturday from 8.30 am to 11 pm.

Exchange Rates

The rate is fixed at the same value as the South African rand (see the Exchange rates in the South Africa Facts for the Visitor chapter).

Costs

Lesotho is a cheaper country to travel in than South Africa, but mainly because Maseru has good cheap accommodation, and there are opportunities to stay with local people and to camp in remote areas. Transport is a bit cheaper but only compared to South Africa's up-market buses. If you're travelling from hotel to hotel – and unless you get out into the rural areas you'll have to stay in hotels – the costs are about the same.

Examples of costs are: hostel in Maseru, M20; cheap hotel in Maseru, M55/70 a single/double; street food, M5 a plate; steak, M20; bus ride, Maseru to Quthing, M19; and three-day pony trek, M210.

BUSINESS HOURS & HOLIDAYS

Most businesses are open from 8 am to 5 pm weekdays, until noon on Saturday. The civil service works between 8 am and 4.30 pm on weekdays and lunch is from 12.45 to 2 pm.

Public holidays include the usual Christmas, Boxing and New Year's days, Good Friday and Easter Monday, plus these:

Family Day	early July (long weekend)
Independence Day	4 October
Moshoeshoe Day	early March (long weekend)
National Sports Day	early October (long weekend)
Tree Planting Day	21 March

POST & TELECOMMUNICATIONS

The telephone system works reasonably well. There are no area codes within Lesotho; to call from South Africa dial the prefix 09-266. See the Maseru chapter for information on international calls.

Post offices are open Monday to Friday from 8 am to 4.30 pm, Saturday from 8 am to noon.

TIME

Lesotho time is the same as South African time, which is GMT/UTC plus two hours year-round.

MEDIA

Several thin newspapers such as *Lesotho Today* are available in the morning in Maseru and later elsewhere. Day-old South African newspapers are available in Maseru.

If you're a fan of the BBC World Service, Lesotho is a mecca as there's a transmitter here and you can pick up the Beeb on short wave, medium wave (1197 kHz) and FM.

HEALTH

There is neither malaria nor bilharzia in Lesotho, but avoid drinking untreated water taken downstream from a village. The cold and changeable weather is the greatest threat to your health, and it could be a lot more serious than catching a cold if you're trapped on a mountain without proper clothing.

Several lives are lost each year from lightning strikes; remember to keep off the high ground during an electrical storm and avoid camping in the open. The sheer ferocity of an electrical storm in Lesotho has to be seen to be believed.

ACTIVITIES
Pony Trekking

This is an excellent way of seeing the Lesotho highlands. The main trekking centres are the Basotho Pony Trekking Centre on God Help Me Pass, isolated Semonkong Lodge and Malealea Lodge near the Gates of Paradise (see the relevant entries for further details). You might be able to join a day ride without booking at these places but it's a long way to go to be turned away.

Whichever you choose, you have to take all your own food. There are basic stores near all these centres but it's better to bring food from Maseru. Waterproof gear is a must, as is sun protection: the weather is changeable and it gets very cold in winter.

The Basotho Pony

The Basotho pony is strong and sure-footed and generally docile. Its size and physique is the result of cross-breeding between short Javanese horses and European full mounts.

A few horses were captured from invading Griqua forces by Basotho warriors in the early 1800s and Moshoeshoe I is recorded as having ridden a horse in 1830. Since that date the pony has become an integral part of life in the highlands and the preferred mode of transport for many villagers. In 1983 the Basotho Pony Trekking Centre was set up near Molimo-Nthuse (God Help Me) Pass in an attempt to prevent dilution of the ponies' gene pool.

Visitors do not need prior riding experience to go pony trekking into the interior. There are several places which conduct pony treks: see the Basotho Pony Trekking Centre, Semonkong and Malealea Lodge sections in the Around Lesotho chapter. ■

Hiking

Lesotho offers great remote-area trekking in a landscape which is reminiscent of the Tibetan plateau. David Ambrose's *Guide to Lesotho* (Winchester Press) is a good guide.

In all areas, but especially the remote eastern highlands, walking is dangerous if you aren't prepared. Temperatures can plummet to near zero even in summer, and thunderstorms are common. Waterproof gear and plenty of warm clothes are absolutely essential. In summer many of the rivers flood, and fords can become dangerous. Be prepared to change your route or wait until the river subsides. Thick fogs can also delay you. By the end of the dry season, especially in the higher areas, good water can be scarce.

There are stores in the towns but these stock only very basic foodstuff. Bring all you need from Maseru, or from South Africa if you want specialist hiking supplies. There are trout streams in the east – if you don't catch your own, buy some from locals.

Hikers should respect the mounds of stones which mark graves. On the other hand, a mound of stones near a trail, especially between two hills, should be added to by passing travellers, who ensure their good luck by spitting on a stone and throwing it onto the pile. Also keep in mind that a white flag waving from a village means that local sorghum beer (*joala*) has just been brewed; a yellow flag indicates maize beer, red is for meat and green for vegetables.

The whole country is good for trekking, but the eastern highlands and the Drakensberg's crown attract serious hikers, with the walk between Qacha's Nek and Butha-Buthe offering the best challenge.

One three-day walk in this area which you could try before attempting something more ambitious is from Sani Top Chalet (at top of Sani Pass), south along the edge of the escarpment, to the Sehlabathebe National Park. From here there's a track leading down to Bushman's Nek in South Africa. As the crow flies the distance from Sani Top to Nkonkoana Gate is about 45 km but the walk is longer than that. Much of this area is over 3000 metres and it's remote even by Lesotho's standards: there isn't a horse trail much less a road or a settlement. Don't try this unless you are well prepared, experienced and in a party of at least three people.

A number of other walks are outlined in Russell Suchet's *A Backpackers Guide to Lesotho* (M10). In addition to the Sani Top to Sehlabathebe walk he outlines walks from Semonkong to Malealea (three days); Sehonghong to Sehlabathebe (two to three days); Mokhotlong to Sani Top via Thabana-Ntlenyana (three to four days); and Ha Lejone to Oxbow (three to four days). He also suggests the ultimate Lesotho challenge – from Mahlesela Pass in the north near Oxbow Lodge, all the way to Sehlabathebe via Mont-aux-Sources (14 to 20 days).

The beauty is that you can walk just about anywhere in Lesotho as there are no organised hiking trails, just footpaths and bridles. There are few fences meaning that you can head in almost any direction.

A word of warning: know how to use a map and compass and get the relevant

1:50,000 maps from the map office at the Department of Land, Surveys & Physical Planning in Lerotholi Rd, Maseru; they cost about M10 each. They also sell a good quality 1:250,000 map of the country for M18. A lot of the new roads built for the Highlands Water Project are not shown.

Birdwatching

About 280 species of birds have been recorded in Lesotho – surprising for a landlocked country. The mountainous terrain provides suitable habitats for many species of raptor (birds of prey). If lucky, you will see the Cape vulture (*Gyps coprotheres*), the rare bearded vulture or lammergeyer (*Gypaetus barbatus*) – not found below 2000 metres, the steppe buzzard (*Buteo buteo*), the black eagle (*Aquila verreauxii*) and the rare gymnogene (*Polyboroides typus*).

Another bird to look out for is the southern bald ibis (*Geronticus calvus*), found in

The Steppe buzzard is common throughout the region, often seen in open country close to roads and on power poles.

Lesotho as it breeds in crevices in cliffs. You can distinguish it from other ibis as it has a bald red head and a white face. The name Mokhotlong means 'place of the bald ibis'.

Good birding places include aeries in the Malotis, along the Mountain Road and near the eastern Drakensberg escarpment.

Fishing

Trout fishing is very popular in Lesotho and these fish are caught in many of the dams and river systems. The trout season commences in September and continues until the end of May; from 1 June to 31 August it is closed. For more information contact the Ministry of Agriculture Livestock Division (☎ (266) 32 3986), Private Bag A82, Maseru 100; there is a minimal license fee, a bag limit of 12 fish, a size limit, and only rod and line and artificial non-spinning flies may be used.

The nearest fishing area to Maseru is the Makhalaneng River, two km downstream from the Molimo-Nthuse Hotel (two hours' drive from Maseru). Other places where you can cast a line are in the Malibamat'so near Butha-Buthe, two km below the Oxbow

The black eagle is a large eagle with a white V marking on it's back, it lives in mountains, gorges and costal cliffs.

Lodge; in the De Beers' Dam, Khubelu and Mokhotlong rivers near Mokhotlong; the Tsoelikana River, Park Ponds and Leqooa River near Qacha's Nek; and the Thaba-Tseka main dam.

Indigenous fish include barbel in lowland rivers, yellowfish in the mountains and the Maloti minnow in the upper Tsoelikana.

ACCOMMODATION

Camping & Hostels Camping isn't really feasible close to towns, but away from population centres, you can camp anywhere as long as you have the permission of the local owners. As well as being an essential courtesy, you might be offered a hut for the night; pay about M7 for this. Occasionally you will be accommodated in a village rondavel for about M10.

There are a couple of hostels in Maseru and one near Butha-Buthe.

There are missions scattered around the country (the 1:250,000 Lesotho map shows them) and you can often get a bed. There are also Agricultural Training Centres in several places which provide a bed for a small fee.

Hotels Maseru has a good range of hotel accommodation, from about M55/70 a single/double up to the three or four-star standard (M120/150 to M250/350). In other larger towns there are good mid-range hotels. Most towns have small hotels which have survived from Protectorate days. These are usually now just run-down bars and liquor stores but with some persuasion you might get a room. Examples are the Crocodile Inn in Butha-Buthe (M80/100) and the Nthatuoa Hotel in Qacha's Nek (M90/120).

There are Fraser's Lodges at Qaba, Semonkong and New Oxbow (see these places in the Around Lesotho chapter). Book these lodges at Fraser's shop in Maseru or contact Peacock Sports (☎ (05192) 2730) in Fontein St, Ficksburg, South Africa.

THINGS TO BUY

Unfortunately, Lesotho's all-purpose garment, the blanket, is usually made elsewhere. There are plenty of other handicrafts to buy, including mohair tapestry, and woven grass products such as mats, baskets and, of course, the Basotho hat. If you're going trekking you might want a sturdy stick. They come plain or decorated and can be found everywhere from craft shops to bus parks, where prices start at about M40 but bargaining is essential.

In and around the town of Teyateyaneng there are many craft shops and cottage industries.

Getting There & Away

AIR

Lesotho Airways flies daily between Moshoeshoe Airport, 18 km from Maseru, and Jo'burg in South Africa. A one-way/return ticket is M288/599 (or M432 return if you stay away for more than four days and less than one month). There is also a flight to Swaziland on Tuesday (M461/922 one-way/return). There is an airport departure tax of M20.

LAND

All the land borders are with South Africa. Most people enter via Maseru Bridge. The border posts are shown in the table below.

Bus & Minibus Taxi

Minibus taxis run between Jo'burg and Maseru for about R50. Buses from Maseru for South African destinations leave from the bridge on the South African side of the border. South Africa's inexpensive Transtate system has several slow services running to or near Lesotho, such as:

Jo'burg to Maseru This trip takes about six hours, costs R70 and departs from Jo'burg station on Monday, Wednesday and Friday. It returns Tuesday, Thursday and Sunday, leaving from the border post at noon.

Bethlehem to Mafeteng This service takes five hours and departs from Bethlehem on Friday and returns Sunday. It's a miners' bus and runs via Butha-Buthe, Leribe (Hlotse) and Maseru.

Durban to Maseru This bus departs Friday to Tuesday at 7 pm and arrives in Maseru at 9 am the next morning. The bus returns Wednesday to Sunday, departing from the border post at noon and arriving in Durban at 11 pm; the cost is R80.

Durban to Ongeluksnek This daily service takes over 11 hours and passes through Kokstad and the Transkei area.

Vrystaat Tours has a daily bus running between Bethlehem and Bloemfontein, via Maseru. This is a slow local service and the timetable is hazy. Mid-morning seems to be the time to expect the bus to Bloemfontein (about M25) and early afternoon for the Bethlehem bus (about M20).

Car & Motorbike

You can't enter via Sani Pass unless your vehicle is 4WD, but you can leave that way in a conventional vehicle. Most of the other entry points in the south and the east of the country also involve very rough roads.

Border Post	Hours	Nearest South African Town
Monontsa Drift	8 am to 4 pm	Witsieshoek and Phuthaditjhaba, OFS
Calendonspoort (near Butha-Buthe)	open 24 hours	Fouriesburg, OFS
Ficksburg Bridge	open 24 hours	Ficksburg, OFS
Peka Bridge	8 am to 4 pm	Gumtree, OFS
Maseru Bridge	6 am to 10 pm	Ladybrand, OFS
Van Rooyen's Gate (north of Mafeteng)	6 am to 8 pm	Wepener, OFS
Sephapho's Gate (south of Mafeteng)	8 am to 4 pm	Boesmanskop, OFS
Makhaleng (near Mohale's Hoek)	8 am to 4 pm	Zastron, OFS
Tele Bridge	8 am to 10 pm	Sterkspruit, Eastern Cape Province
Qacha's Nek	8 am to 10 pm	Matatiele, KwaZulu/Natal
Ramatseliso's Gate	8 am to 6 pm	Matatiele, KwaZulu/Natal
Sani Pass	8 am to 4 pm	Himeville, KwaZulu/Natal

Hertz (☎ 31 4460) is in the Lesotho Sun; Avis (☎ 31 4325), slightly cheaper, is in Kingsway in the next block east of the Bank of Lesotho and at the airport; Budget (☎ 31 6344) is in Orpen Rd, Old Europa. All have rates which are higher than those in South Africa, becoming astronomical for 4WD vehicles, often necessary for the many rural roads. A small car costs M99 per day plus M0.88 per km, and collision damage waiver is M25 and theft loss waiver M8.

It is far more economical to use a car hired in South Africa in Lesotho; just ensure that you have the agreement of the hirer. If you do take this option, remember that there is a vehicle departure tax of M2.

AIR

Lesotho Airways used to fly to several internal destinations and fares were low – this is no longer the case. The only flight from Maseru is to Qacha's Nek, departing from Maseru at 8.30 am on Monday, Wednesday and Friday; the one-way/return cost is M91/182. Note that the free-luggage allowance is only 15 kg.

The airline's timetable changes frequently, partly because of weather conditions and partly because of economic problems, so check whether other routes are again operating. The main booking office (☎ 32 4513, 32 4507) is in Kingsway, Maseru.

Air Maluti (☎ 31 2813, fax 31 0130), which has an office in the Maseru Sun, has charter flights to many Lesotho destinations. Contact them to see whether they can fit you in as a passenger on an already existing charter flight.

BUS & MINIBUS TAXI

There is a good network of slow buses running to many towns. Minibus taxis are quicker but tend not to run long distances. In more remote areas you might have to arrange a ride with a truck, for which you'll have to negotiate a fare. Be prepared for long delays once you're off the main routes.

You'll be quoted long-distance fares on the buses but it's better to just buy a ticket to the next major town, as most of the passengers will get off there and you'll be stuck waiting for the bus to fill up again, and other buses might leave before yours. Buying tickets in stages is only slightly more expensive than buying a direct ticket.

Heading north-east from Maseru you almost always have to change at Maputsoe, although this sometimes happens on the road into town if your bus meets another coming the other way.

Unlike most buses in South Africa, buses in Lesotho are strictly non-smoking.

Rough examples of fares (they are constantly changing) are:

Butha-Buthe to Oxbow – M11 (minibus taxi)
Butha-Buthe to Mokhotlong – M25 (minibus taxi)
Leribe (Hlotse) to Maputsoe – M3.50 (minibus taxi)
Maputsoe to Butha-Buthe – M5 (minibus taxi)
Maseru to the Basotho Pony Trekking Centre (God Help Me Pass) – M15 (bus)
Maseru to Butha-Buthe – M12 (minibus taxi)
Maseru to Mafeteng – M7 (bus)
Maseru to Maputsoe – M9 (minibus taxi)
Maseru to Maputsoe – M7.50 (bus)
Maseru to Mohale's Hoek – M11 (bus)
Maseru to Motsekuoa (for Malealea) – M4 (bus)
Maseru to Moyeni (Quthing) – M19 (bus)
Maseru to Semonkong – M15 (bus)
Maseru to Thaba-Tseka – M21 (bus)
Mokhotlong to Maputsoe – M30 (minibus taxi)
Moyeni (Quthing) to Qacha's Nek – M30 (bus)
Qacha's Nek to Matatiele, RSA – M10 (taxi)
Sehlabathebe to Qacha's Nek – M17 (bus)
Teyateyaneng to Maputsoe – M5 (minibus taxi)

TRAIN

No passenger trains run to Lesotho. The nearest town in South Africa with passenger services is Bloemfontein.

CAR & MOTORBIKE

Driving in Lesotho is getting easier as new roads are built in conjunction with the massive Highlands Water Project, but once you get off the tar there are still plenty of places where even a 4WD vehicle will get into trouble. Apart from rough roads, rivers flooding after summer storms present the biggest problems, and you can be stuck for days. People and animals on the roads are another hazard. There are often army roadblocks (usually searching for stolen cars), although 'respectable' cars are often waved through.

Before attempting a difficult drive try to get some local knowledge of current conditions; ask at a police station. The bar at the Maseru Club contains a good cross section of people working all over Lesotho.

There's an M50 fine for not wearing a seat belt.

PONY TREKKING & HIKING

Walking and pony trekking are two excellent ways to get around Lesotho. See the Lesotho Facts for the Visitor chapter for details.

TOURS

The tourist office in Maseru sporadically organises tours to places of scenic and cultural interest for locals. Day tours cost around M60 and there are sometimes weekend trips as well, from about M120. Foreigners might be able to tag along but don't force the issue if it seems that you aren't wanted. The minimum number of people on a tour is three.

Malealea Lodge, near Mohale's Hoek, organises vehicle safaris lasting four days (M660 to M1250 per person depending on numbers) and five days (M950 to M1900); four-day walking safaris (M660 to M1250), and pony trekking (routes and prices negotiable). Prices include pick-up from and return to Maseru.

African Routes (☎ (031) 83 3348) have seven-day trips to Lesotho from Durban and Jo'burg for R1150; the price includes pony trekking.

Maseru

Maseru has been a quiet backwater for much of its history. Kingsway was paved for the 1947 visit by the British royal family and remained the capital's only tarred road for some time. Most of Maseru's 109,000 people have arrived since the 1970s, but for a rapidly expanding third-world city Maseru remains an easy-going place. Despite this, it's very much a capital city and a recreation centre for the many foreign aid workers.

Maseru is fairly safe but be on your guard at night, especially off the main street. Kids begging for money can be a bit of a hassle.

Orientation & Information

Maseru's main street, Kingsway, runs from the border post at the bridge right through the centre of town to the Circle, a traffic round-about and landmark. At the Circle it splits to become two important highways: Main North Rd and Main South Rd.

Tourist Office The tourist office (☎ 31 2896) is on Kingsway, next to the Hotel Victoria. The staff are friendly and helpful. They have a good but not very detailed map of Maseru for M3; if they're out of stock try the Basotho Hat craft shop across the road.

The Lands, Survey & Physical Planning Department has a more detailed map but it's harder to read and more out of date. You can also buy good topographic maps of the country here (see Trekking in the Activities section of the Facts for the Visitor chapter for more detail). The office is open between 8 am and 12.45 pm, and 2 and 4.30 pm on weekdays. It's on Lerotholi Rd, near the corner of Constitution Rd.

Sehlabathebe National Park For bookings at the park contact the Conservation Division (☎ 32 3600, ext 18), in the Ministry of Agriculture building on Raboshabane Rd, which is off Moshoeshoe Rd, near the railway station.

Money With so many foreigners in town the banks are used to changing money and there's no hassle except for the short banking hours: 8.30 am to 3 pm weekdays (except Thursday when they are only open until 1 pm), 8.30 to 11 am Saturday. The last Friday of the month is pay day and there are huge slow-moving queues at the banks.

Three banks – Lesotho, Barclays and Standard – are all on Kingsway. Although there are branches in other parts of the country, change money in Maseru.

Post & Telecommunications If you can help it don't use Maseru as a poste-restante address, or you'll join the permanent group of people waiting to complain about missing mail.

To make international phone calls go the public call office, down the lane on the west side of the post office. It's open from Monday to Friday between 8 am and 5 pm, Saturday between 8 am and noon. Calls are very expensive, so if you can, wait until you are back in South Africa.

Foreign Embassies A number of countries have embassies and consulates in Maseru, including:

Ireland
    Christie House, Maseru (☎ 31 4068)
South Africa
    10th Floor, Lesotho Bank Centre, Maseru (☎ 31 5758)
Sweden
    1st Floor, Lesotho Bank Centre, Maseru (☎ 31 1555)
UK
    Linare Rd, Maseru (☎ 31 3961)
USA
    Kingsway, Maseru (towards Maseru Bridge border post) (☎ 31 2666)

Medical Services The Queen Elizabeth II Hospital is on Kingsway, near the Lesotho Sun Hotel.

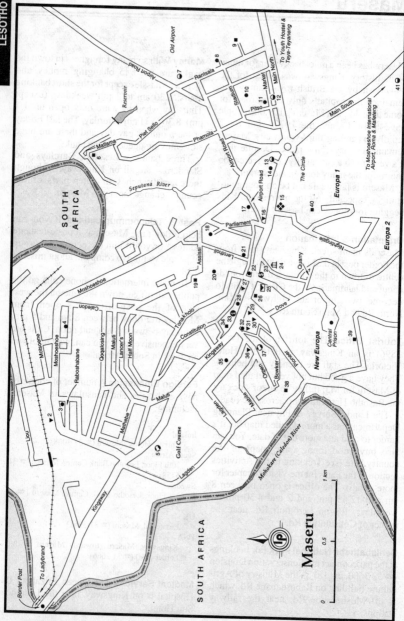

Maseru

PLACES TO STAY

6 Seapoint Hotel
9 Airport Hotel
19 Anglican Centre
26 Lancer's Inn
34 Victoria Hotel & Crossroads Disco
38 Maseru Sun
39 Khali Hotel & Campsites
40 Lesotho Sun Hotel

PLACES TO EAT

2 Three Sisters Restaurant
16 Auberge Restaurant
27 Jolly Bee Restaurant
29 Chinese Palace Restaurant
30 Early Bird Restaurant, OK Supermarket &
   Basotho Woman Statue
31 Boccacio Restaurant
36 Chinese Garden Restaurant

OTHER

1 Railway Station
3 Ministry of Agriculture
4 Royal Crown Jewellery
5 US Embassy
7 Buses to Airport
8 National Stadium
10 Pitso Ground
11 Market
12 Minibus Taxi
13 Minibus Taxi
14 Hyperama (Supermarket)
15 Sanlam Shopping Centre
17 Cinema
18 Houses of Parliament
20 Royal Palace
21 Lands & Survey Department
22 British Council & Department of Immigration (in Old Post Office)
23 Bank of Lesotho, German & Swedish Embassies
24 National Museum
25 Post Office
28 Kingsway Mall Complex
32 Basotho Hat Craft Shop
33 Tourist Office
35 Maseru Club
37 Canadian High Commission
41 Bus Park

Cultural Centres There's a British Council, an Alliance Française and an American Cultural Center in Maseru.

Things to See & Do

There are several good walks on the mountain ridges which protrude into the city, such as the walk beginning at the gate of the Lesotho Sun which takes you up to a plateau where there are great views of Maseru. *Hill Walks In & Around Maseru* (M3.75), available at the Basotho Hat and nearby craft shops, describes other walks. Note that some walks in the book have been overwhelmed by urban sprawl and are no longer possible.

Take some time to go into the urban villages which surround Maseru. You will be welcomed and, if you are lucky, you may be invited to spend the night there. It is a pleasant change from the sanitised Western-style hotels in Maseru.

Places to Stay – bottom end

Camping & Hostels There's no camping facility in Maseru and free-camping would be risky, but you can negotiate a price to camp at the *Khali Hotel*.

Still, with a couple of hostels it's possible to find inexpensive accommodation. The

Anglican Centre (☎ 32 3046) charges M20 per person in austere dorms or twin rooms. Meals are available. The centre is only about 500 metres north of Kingsway on the bend where Assissi Rd becomes Lancer's Rd but getting there isn't simple – see the map. If you get lost ask for St James Church, which is next door, or Machabeng High School, which is at least in the area.

The *Phomolong Youth Hostel* (☎ 33 2900) is a long way from town; it charges M15 per person per night. Head out towards the Main North Rd, go over the bridge and turn right down the Lancers Gap road. This turn-off is not signposted but near the turn-off is a sign, 'Gold Medal Enterprises'. The hostel is about two km further on. Minibuses to Lancers Gap run past it. This place is quite relaxed and doesn't keep strict hours.

If you're desperate, you could stay at the *Lesotho Workcamps Association* (☎ 31 4862), 917 Cathedral Rd, behind the Catholic Cathedral near the large traffic circle at the end of Kingsway. Head down Main North Rd until you come to a garage; nearby is a dirt road where taxis accumulate. Follow this road until you come to the buildings of the works camp. The dorms are M8 per night. There is a place to wash and a small kitchen.

You used to be able to stay at a couple of the aid workers' hostels in Maseru but they no longer welcome travellers.

Hotels About five km east of the centre is the *Lakeside Hotel* (☎ 31 3646), off the Main North Rd. Singles/doubles are M55/70 in the old block and doubles are M90 in the new block. It's good for the price. Definitely not so is the *Seapoint Hotel* (☎ 32 2048) on a hill overlooking the river on the north-east edge of town. This is basically a neighbourhood bar with a few rooms, in an area that is potentially unsafe at night. Out on the Lancer's Gap road is the *Palace Hotel* (☎ 50 0700, 50 0617), a small place which has singles/doubles for M80/120.

The *Khali Hotel* (☎ 32 5953) is a friendly local place south of Kingsway, beyond the prison. They have rooms for around M60 per person, including breakfast, and there's the Nek Hall restaurant on the premises. They will collect you if you phone, or you can take a Thetsane minibus on Pioneer Rd, near Lancer's Inn, and get off at the turn-off for the suburb of New Europa. You can camp at the hotel.

Places to Stay – middle

The tall *Hotel Victoria* (☎ 31 2922, fax 31 0318), on Kingsway, is deteriorating and is not good value at M150/200 for singles/doubles; breakfast in the dining room costs M15. It has penthouse and basement nightclubs and occasional related security problems.

Lancer's Inn (☎ 31 2114, fax 31 0223), on Kingsway, is a comfortable colonial-era hotel with rooms from M109/135, and self-contained chalets for M155/195.

Places to Stay – top end

There are two Sun hotels: the *Maseru Sun* (☎ 31 2434, fax 31 0158), near the river south-west of Kingsway, which has singles/doubles from M225/315 and deluxe rooms for M290/398; and the *Lesotho Sun* (☎ 31 3111, fax 31 0104), on a hillside further east. It's more of a luxury resort hotel, charging from M275/370.

Places to Eat

On Kingsway there are street stalls, mainly during the day, selling good grilled meat for about M4. Serves of curry and rice cost M3.

For meals and snacks through the day try the *Oasis Café*, on Kingsway, under the Hotel Victoria. It gets hot and crowded but the food is good. Cheaper but with a limited menu is the *Jolly Bee*, on Kingsway near the post office. There's a pleasant verandah where you can sit and watch life in Maseru go by.

Opposite the new Kingsway Mall (which

Urban Village Life

Urban village life sounds like an impossibility, but in the townships surrounding Maseru you have an opportunity of experiencing Basotho village life on the edge of a city.

Phomolong, just outside Maseru and at the foot of Lancer's Gap, is a good example. The moment you leave the sealed Lancer's Gap road the adventure begins. The reality of these places is an absence of street signs, complex mazes of dirt roads and a seemingly never-ending expanse of rudimentary houses. You may cross a dam wall, pass a small shop and zigzag through a corridor of wire and brick fences.

Village life here is like anywhere where trading and bartering are common. Negotiate a price for a dozen 'free-range' eggs before you enter your hosts' house, or observe the locals tending their small vegetable plots and milking cows. As evening descends look upwards to the masses of stars, a view undisturbed by street lighting, and listen to the dogs barking, the locals chattering as they fetch water, and the children singing folk songs.

In the morning the staccato crowing of an undetermined sum of roosters awakes you and you soon head to the village tap to fetch water for washing, drinking and cooking. The sun pops up from behind the surrounding limestone cliffs as the locals emerge from the ramshackle labyrinth to catch buses to their jobs in Maseru. ■

in the future will be a happy hunting ground for food) there is a small plaza with a statue of a Basotho woman. Head left of the statue to the *Early Bird* – this place is popular with locals as you can get two pieces of spicy Sotho-style chicken for M3, sandwiches for M3 and a pot of coffee for M1.50.

At Lancer's Inn there's a bakery and deli. All the hotels have restaurants. The *Rendezvous*, at Lancer's Inn, gets 'forks up' from locals as being the town's best. Also on Kingsway, on the corner of Airport Rd, is the popular *Auberge*; it has a bar which is frequented by ex-pats and locals. The restaurant in the *Victoria Hotel* gets my vote for good service. Expect to pay about M20 for an excellent pizza and salad.

The food at *Boccacio*, an Italian-run Italian restaurant, off Kingsway on Bowker Rd, is reliable. Pasta dishes are about M18. Boccacio is closed on Monday.

Chinese Garden is a big place on Orpen Rd, off Kingsway. The food is reasonable but the M25 set menu isn't great value. Choose from the big menu, which includes such dishes as seaweed tangle and diligent beancurd. Main courses are around M15 to M20. There is also the *Golden Orient* and the *China Palace*; the latter is in the Lesotho National Development Corporation Centre on Kingsway. For Indian food try *Classic Cuisine* in the Options Building on Pioneer Rd. On Moshoeshoe Rd, near the railway station, is *Three Sisters*, a big local eatery.

Entertainment

The Maseru Club is on Lagden Rd. It's a fine old colonial club and a meeting place for ex-pats and aid workers. There's a bar and restaurant and various sports, including squash, tennis and cricket. Temporary membership costs M30 a month but it's easy enough to be signed in as a guest.

On top of the Victoria Hotel there's The Penthouse which has good jazz on weekends, with an entry charge of M10. The hotel's disco, Cross Roads, is in the building to the west of the tower. It is really worth a visit as many locals come here to dance into the wee small hours of the night.

A trip to the Seapoint Hotel, a km or so north-east from the centre, might be fun, but be warned that it's a basic neighbourhood bar and there's the risk of mugging in the area.

You can take in a movie at the cinema. Coming from the border end of town, turn left just before the Auberge. Take the first street to the right; the cinema is on the left, just a little way down the road.

Both of the Sun hotels have bars and slot machines.

Things to Buy

The Basotho Hat, on Kingsway opposite the Hotel Victoria. is a government-run craft shop. It's well worth a look but the prices are generally higher than you'll find in rural areas. If you plan on pony trekking or walking it's a good idea to buy a horsehair fly-whisk. Caboodles is another craft shop nearby on Kingsway which has unusual gifts and some books. Further down Kingsway, towards the Circle, is a large bookshop stocking mainly school texts, but with some interesting locally published books and pamphlets.

Getting There & Away

Bus The main bus park has been relocated quite a way from the centre on Main South Rd. There have been complaints about this and it might move again. Meanwhile, it's common to see men pushing wheelbarrows full of luggage. There have been complaints about them, too – unless the passenger hurries along beside him, the wheelbarrowman has been known to vanish with the load.

Examples of fares from Maseru are: Mafeteng, M5; Mafeteng to Quthing, M9.50; Mohale's Hoek, M10; Pony Trekking Centre (God Help Me Pass), M7.

Minibus Taxi Taxis congregate in the streets between the Circle and the market, and there are others near the new Hyperama supermarket off Kingsway near the Circle. The destination is displayed on the left side of the taxi's front window.

GETTING AROUND

To/From the Airport Moshoeshoe Airport is 18 km from town, off the Main South Rd. A Lesotho Airways staff bus runs out there from the old airport (now used by the military and the flying doctor) in town, at 6.30, 7.30 and 9 am, and noon, 2 and 4 pm. These times often vary; the staff at the ticket office on Kingsway might not have the latest ones. Although you'll be told the trip takes 15 minutes, by the time the driver has meandered around giving lifts to friends it can be closer to 45 minutes. The plane doesn't wait for the bus.

Local Transport The standard minibus taxi fare around town is M1. There's one conventional taxi service – Moonlite Telephone Taxis (☎ 31 2695).

DI JONES

DI JONES

Top: Traditional 'Sangoma' or herbalist, Malehlohonolo. She lives in the Malealea village, Lesotho

Bottom: Herd boy in Cosmos fields, Malealea area, Lesotho. These fields are at their best over the Easter weekend

JEFF WILLIAMS

JEFF WILLIAMS

JEFF WILLIAMS

Left: Malutis, near Malealea, Lesotho
Top: Villagers in township outside Maseru, Lesotho
Bottom: Pony-trekking near Malealea Lodge, Lesotho

Around Lesotho

Most towns have risen around trading posts or Protectorate-era administration centres and none approach Maseru in size or facilities.

THABA-BOSIU

Moshoeshoe I's mountain stronghold, first occupied in July 1824, is east of Maseru. Thaba-Bosiu ('mountain at night'), the most important historical site in Lesotho, played a pivotal role in the consolidation of the Basotho nation in the 19th century. The name may have been bestowed because the site was first occupied at night but another legend suggests that Thaba-Bosiu, a hill in daylight, grows into a mountain at night.

There's a visitor information centre at the base of Thaba-Bosiu where you pay the M4 entry fee; they provide a map and a pamphlet. An official guide will accompany you to the top of the mountain.

There are good views from the summit of Thaba-Bosiu, including the Qiloane pinnacle, inspiration for the Basotho hat. On the summit are the remains of fortifications, Moshoeshoe's grave, and parts of the original settlement.

Places to Stay & Eat

About two km before the Thaba-Bosiu visitor centre is *'Melesi Lodge* (☎ 35 7215) with single/double rooms for M70/90 and a great restaurant. After climbing Thaba-Bosiu, you can appreciate some crispy baby chicken (M20) or a hamburger (M10) with some Lion Maluti Mountain beer.

Getting There & Away

To get to Thaba-Bosiu look for a minibus taxi near the Hyperama supermarket (off Kingsway near the Circle); these go as far as the visitor centre at the base of the mountain. If you're driving, head out on Main South Rd, take the turn-off to Roma and after about six km (near Mazenod) turn off to the left. Thaba-Bosiu is about 10 km further along.

TEYATEYANENG

Teyateyaneng ('the place of quick sands') is usually simply known as TY. The town has been developed as the craft centre of Lesotho and there are several places worth visiting.

Some of the best tapestries come from Helang Basali Crafts in the St Agnes Mission, a couple of km before TY on the Maseru road. More tapestries are available

---

The Battles for Thaba-Bosiu

The Basotho atop Thaba-Bosiu repulsed invaders for nearly 40 years. First, the AmaNgwane led by one Matiwane attacked the fortress in 1828. After a fierce battle the attacking regiments were driven off and ceased to be a threat. Early in 1831 the heavily armed Kornnas (raiders) were driven away. Next, in 1831, from north of the Vaal came the Ndebele of Mzilikazi. They attacked Thaba-Bosiu at Rafutho's Pass but were repulsed by defenders hurling spears and rocks from above.

It was then the turn of the British. In 1852 Sir George Cathcart, governor of the Cape colony, made a punitive attack on Moshoeshoe's people. On the way to the fortress, about five km west of Thaba-Bosiu, Cathcart's troops were forced to withdraw by 5000 heavily armed and mounted Basotho warriors.

The Boer republic of the Orange Free State was established in 1854 and Basotholand between the Orange and Caledon rivers began to be taken. There were a number of clashes with the Free State. The most serious started in 1865, when a determined Free State commando (an army unit) led by Commandant Louw Wepener attempted to storm Thaba-Bosiu. The commando was repulsed in what was to be the last attack on Thaba-Bosiu in Moshoeshoe's lifetime. Wepener was killed at Khubelu Pass and today this pass is sometimes referred to as Wepener's. ■

from Hatooa-Mose-Mosali and wool products from Setsoto Design, Tebetebeng, and Letlotlo Handcrafts. About 10 km north of town beyond the Phutiatsana River, in Kolonyama, is the largest pottery in Lesotho. Here beautiful stoneware products are fashioned from fine clay and minerals.

The *Blue Mountain Inn* (☎ 50 0362) has single/double rooms for M80/90, a family room for M105 or you can camp (make sure you get permission from the local chief).

MAPUTSOE

This border town, 86 km north of Maseru, is across the Mohokare (Caledon) River from Ficksburg in South Africa. It has a new shopping centre and a few other civic amenities, but its status as a black dormitory suburb of Ficksburg is still apparent – it is very rundown and impoverished. When it rains the streets turn to slippery mud. Still, it is handy to a border crossing with good transport connections, especially now that it is a gateway to the Highlands Water Project.

Places to Stay & Eat

The *Sekekete Hotel* (☎ 43 0621), on the main street not far from the minibus taxi park, has inexpensive singles/doubles from M35/55 to M60/85. The more expensive rooms are quite good, although the whole place has an air of neglect. There are bars and a restaurant.

Directly across the border there is accommodation in Ficksburg and at Rustlers Valley; see the Orange Free State chapter.

LERIBE (HLOTSE)

A large town by Lesotho's standards, Leribe (the old name, Hlotse, is still sometimes used) is a quiet village serving as a regional shopping and market centre. It was an administrative centre under the British and there are some old buildings slowly decaying in the leafy streets. **Major Bell's Tower**, on the main street near the market, was built in 1879. A very humble symbol of the might of the British Empire, it spent most of its career as a storehouse for government records.

There is a set of **dinosaur footprints** a few km south of Leribe at Tsikoane village.

Coming north towards Leribe, take the small dirt road going off to the right towards some rocky outcrops. Follow it up to the church and ask someone to direct you to the *minwane*. It's a 15 to 20-minute slog up the mountainside to a series of caves. The prints are clearly visible on the ceiling of the rock.

About 10 km north of Leribe are the **Subeng River dinosaur footprints**. There is a signpost indicating the river but not the footprints. Walk down to the river from the road to a concrete causeway (about 250 metres). The footprints, of at least three species of dinosaur, are about 15 metres downstream on the right bank.

Places to Stay & Eat

The *Agricultural Training Centre* is just outside town, or try the *Catholic Mission* about 10 km past Leribe. The old-style *Leribe Hotel* (☎ 40 0362), on Main St, has singles/doubles for M100/160. There is also a tea garden surrounded by well-established trees.

KATSE & HIGHLANDS PROJECT

One of the effects of the Lesotho Highlands Water Project has been the improvement of roads into the interior of the country. As Phase 1A (construction of the Katse Dam to the north of Thaba-Tseka) proceeds it gets easier for travellers to get into this remote part of Lesotho.

From Leribe (Hlotse) you can now take a sealed road all the way to the project headquarters at Katse. This road passes the lowland village of Pitseng and climbs over the Maloti Mountains to drop to Ha Lejone (which one day will be at the edge of the dam's lake). It continues south past Mamohau Mission, crosses the impressive Malibamat'so Bridge, climbs over another series of hills to the Matsoku Valley, recrosses the Malibamat'so and ends in Katse. From Katse you can continue on an improved dirt road to Thaba-Tseka, 45 km to the south.

Information about the project is available from the Lesotho Highlands Development Authority in Katse (the modern yellow building with a blue roof). A visit can be organised in advance; phone ☎ 31 4324.

There is no formal accommodation in Katse; Thaba-Tseka is the best bet for a bed.

There are taxis from Leribe (Hlotse) to Katse for M23. There's plenty of traffic if you want to hitch.

BUTHA-BUTHE

Moshoeshoe named this town Butha-Buthe ('place of lying down') because it was here that his people first retreated during the chaos of the difaqane. The small town is built alongside the Hlotse River and has the beautiful Maloti Mountains as a backdrop.

Places to Stay & Eat

There are signs on the road pointing to the *Mr Ramakatane's Youth Hostel* though you may have to ask directions (say *ha-sechele*). It's about four km from the village. There are no supplies so buy food in the village before arriving. There is no electricity; you cook using gas and you fetch your own water just as the villagers do. Basic accommodation costs M17 per night.

The *Crocodile Inn* (☎ 46 0223), Reserve Rd, has single/double rooms from M80/100, but the *Moteng Lodge* (☎ 46 0350), Oxbow Rd, is cheaper.

Apart from the usual crop of liquor restaurants, there is the *Venice Italian*, the *Sekekete Café* and the *Roadside Café* for a choice of ordinary fare.

OXBOW

South African skiers used to come to Oxbow in winter but the place has slowly died as a ski resort. The *New Oxbow Lodge* (book on ☎ (05192) 2247), on the banks of the Malibamat'so River, charges M90/155 for singles/doubles. A few km further north is a private chalet belonging jointly to the Maloti and Witwatersrand University ski clubs. It's possible to sleep here for M20 although winter weekends are crowded. See the caretaker or write to Club Maluti, PO Box 783308, Sandton 2146, RSA.

BASOTHO PONY TREKKING CENTRE

The pony trekking centre is on the road between Maseru and Thaba-Tseka on the top of God Help Me Pass. By bus it's M7 from Maseru and takes about two hours. There are four daily buses each way and the last bus to Maseru passes the centre at about 3 pm.

Accommodation on overnight treks is in villages along the way, and they charge about M7 per person a night or M3 if you have a tent. This is not included in the trekking fees, so bring enough money to cover costs. You can't stay at the centre (although travellers have wangled floor space) so if your trek departs early in the morning you'll have to camp out or stay at the *Molimo-Nthuse Lodge* (☎ 31 2922), three km back down the pass. This means a steep walk the next morning. The lodge charges from M100/130 for singles/doubles. Fraser's *Marakebei Lodge*, nearly 50 km east, is cheaper but it's currently being renovated; expect costs to increase when it has been completed. (Pony treks are also available from Malealea Lodge; see information under Malealea in this chapter.)

Treks offered are:

Two-hour ride to Leboele Falls – M25 per person; M22 in groups of five or more
Four-hour ride to Qiloane Falls – M40 per person; M30 in groups of five or more
Two days (one night) – M100 per person
Three days (two nights) – M140 per person, minimum of two people
Seven days (six nights) – M325 per person, minimum of four people, summer only

THABA-TSEKA

This remote town is on the western edge of the central range, over the sometimes tricky Mokhoabong Pass. It was established in 1980 as a centre for the mountain district.

You can usually get a bed at the *Farmer Training Centre* for about M12 per person.

About four buses a day run from Maseru to Thaba-Tseka (M21), but continuing on is not so easy. There's reportedly a minibus taxi heading north at about 6 am daily, which will get you to a settlement from where there is plenty of transport to Leribe. Heading south from Thaba-Tseka to Sehonghong and Qacha's Nek is more difficult – you'll probably have to negotiate with a truck driver. As the Highlands Water Project progresses there should be more traffic and better roads.

MOKHOTLONG

The first major town north of Sani Pass and Sehlabathebe National Park, Mokhotlong ('place of the bald ibis') has basic shops and transport to Oxbow and Butha-Buthe. The town, some 270 km from Maseru and 200 km from Butha-Buthe, has the reputation as being the coldest, driest and most remote place in Lesotho. The nearby Senqu River, the biggest in Lesotho, has its source near Mokhotlong. The town is a good base for walks to the Drakensberg escarpment.

At the *Farmer Training Centre* you can get a bed for M12 per night; there are cold-water washing facilities and a kitchen. The *(Lefu) Senqu Hotel* (☎ 92 0330), five km from the airport, has rooms for M100/120.

Some 15 km south-west of Mokhotlong in Upper Rafalotsane village is *Molumong Lodge*; it costs M25 per person but you need to bring your own sleeping bag. There are three buses a day to the lodge from Mokhotlong. The owner, Mike Campbell, might be able to take you there from Himeville in South Africa.

One of the few places in Mokhotlong where you can get a half-decent meal is the *Hunter's Restaurant*.

SANI PASS

This steep pass is the only dependable road into Lesotho from the KwaZulu/Natal Drakensberg. On the South African side the nearest towns are Underberg and Himeville.

From the chalet at the top of the pass there are several day walks, including a long and strenuous one to **Thabana-Ntlenyana** (3482 metres), the highest peak in southern Africa. There is a path but a guide would come in handy. Horses can do the trip so consider hiring one. The height of the mountain was only calculated in 1951, and it took another 30 years for this calculation to be confirmed by satellite technology.

Another walk leads to **Hodgson's Peaks**, six km south, from where you get the benefit of views to Sehlabathebe park and to KwaZulu/Natal.

Places to Stay

The *Sani Top Mountaineers Chalet*, at the top of the pass, has rooms for M35 per person during the week, M40 on weekends. There are cooking facilities but you must bring all your own food. Alcohol is likely to be confiscated at the Lesotho border. In winter the snow is often deep enough to ski (there are a few pieces of antique equipment available at the chalet) and horse trekking is available with prior arrangement. Book through Sani Tours (☎/fax (033) 702 1069), PO Box 232, Himeville 4585, South Africa. This outfit is run by Jonathan Aldous, who is a good source of information on the area. The Himeville Arms pub in Himeville might have information.

The other obvious place to stay is *Sani Lodge*, on the South African side of the pass. See the KwaZulu/Natal chapter. A bed costs R20.

Getting There & Away

The South African border guards won't let you up the pass unless you have a 4WD, although you can come down from Lesotho without one. The South African border is open between 8 am and 4 pm; the Lesotho border stays open an hour later to let the last vehicles through. Hitching up or down the pass is best on weekends when there is a fair amount of traffic to and from the lodge.

There's no public transport from the pass to other places in Lesotho, although there are several trucks each day heading for Mokhotlong (52 km north) and you might be able to hitch, but expect to pay.

On Monday and Friday there is a door-to-door service between Durban hostels and Sani Lodge – see the KwaZulu/Natal chapter.

SEHLABATHEBE NATIONAL PARK

Lesotho's first (and only) national park, proclaimed in 1970, is remote and rugged, and it is always an adventure to get to. The park's main attraction is its sense of separation from the rest of the world. Other than a rare Maloti minnow, thought to be extinct but rediscovered in the Tsoelikana River, rare birds such as the bearded vulture, and the odd rhebok or baboon, there are relatively few animals. As well as hikes and climbs, the park has horse-riding for just M15 a day; guided horseback tours are M20.

This is a summer-rain area, and thick mist, potentially hazardous to hikers, is common. Winters are clear but cold at night and there are sometimes light falls of snow.

Near the village of Sehonghong is **Soai's Cave**. Soai, the last chief of the Maloti San people, was attacked and defeated here by Cape and Basotho forces in 1871.

Places to Stay & Eat

You can camp in the park but except at the lodge, where camping costs M5, there are no facilities besides plenty of water. The lodge has single/double rooms for M20/35, four-bed family rooms for M50 and the whole lodge costs M150 per night. There is also a hostel with a five-bed dorm at M12 per person. You can buy firewood and coal here, but for food (very limited) and petrol or diesel you'll have to rely on a small store about five km west of the park entrance and quite a way from the lodge and hostel. You have to book the lodge in Maseru at the Conservation Division of the Ministry of Agriculture (☎ 32 3600, ext 18).

In Sehlabathebe village is the new, clean *Range Management Education Centre*. It is 1.5 km down the road to Sehonghong and it costs M15 per person in dorms. At the café next to the Sehonghong airstrip there is occasionally accommodation for M16 per night; this is a handy option if you fly in.

Getting There & Away

Sometimes there are charter flights from Maseru to Ha Paulus, a village near the park entrance, and you can arrange to be picked up from there for M25. Senqu Airways (☎ 95 0235) flies a light aircraft between Qacha's Nek and Sehonghong; the scenic 20-minute flight is extremely good value at M37. This flight is available weekdays and until noon on Saturday.

Driving into the park can be a problem, as the roads are 4WD tracks which become impassable after heavy rain, which falls in spring and summer. Bear in mind that having got to the park you could be stuck here waiting for a river to go down. Still, people usually do make it in and out without too many problems and most agree that the journey has been worth it. The road-building accompanying the hydroelectric scheme should improve at least some of the routes. Check with the Conservation Department in Maseru when you book accommodation.

There are several routes into the park, all of which currently require 4WD. The longest is the southern route via Quthing and Qacha's Nek. There's also a route via Thaba-Tseka then down the Senqu River valley past the hamlet of Sehonghong and over the difficult Matebeng Pass. The park can also be reached from Matatiele in the extreme west of KwaZulu/Natal. This route doesn't have as many difficult sections as the other routes but it is less well maintained so it is sometimes closed; check in Matatiele before trying it.

There is a daily bus between Qacha's Nek and Sehlabathebe village. The relatively short distance takes 5½ hours and costs M17; the bus departs from Sehlabathebe at 5.30 am and returns from Qacha's Nek at noon.

Probably the simplest way in is to hike the 10 km up the escarpment from Bushman's Nek in South Africa. From Bushman's Nek to Nkonkoana Gate, the Lesotho border post, takes about six hours. You can also take a horse up or down for M20.

QACHA'S NEK

This pleasant town, with a number of sandstone buildings, was founded in 1888 near the pass (1980 metres) of the same name.

There are Californian redwood trees nearby, some over 25 metres high.

The *Nthatuoa Hotel* (☎ 95 0260) offers adequate accommodation in their Block A for M90/120 for a single/double. In Block B it is M100/140 and in Block C it is 115/160. It is within walking distance from the airstrip.

There are cafés in town including the *Vuka Afrika* and you can get meals at the hotel.

Getting There & Away

Lesotho Airways flies from Maseru to Qacha's Nek on Monday, Wednesday and Friday for M91. It leaves Maseru at 8.30 am.

Weather permitting (this area can get snowed-in during winter) a bus to Sehlabathebe leaves daily at around noon (M17). There is more transport between here and Quthing (Moyeni). A bus leaves from both towns at 9 am, takes about six hours and costs M30. It is a spectacular drive.

ROMA

Roma, only 35 km from Maseru, is a university town and a good place to meet students. There are some attractive sandstone buildings dotted around the town and the entry to town by the southern gorge is spectacular.

North of Roma is the important **Ha Baroana rock-painting** site. Although suffering from neglect and vandalism (including damage done by tourists who spray water on the paintings to produce brighter photos) this site is worth seeing.

To get there from Roma head back to the Maseru road and turn right onto the road heading west to Thaba-Tseka and the pony-trekking centre. After about 12 km turn off to the left, just after the Ha Ntsi settlement on the Mohlsks-oa-Tuka River. To get to the site by minibus taxi from Maseru head for Nazareth and get off about 1.5 km before Nazareth. A signpost indicates the way to the paintings off to the left. Follow this gravel track three km to the village of Ha Khotso then turn right at a football field. Follow this track a further 2.5 km to a hilltop overlooking a gorge. A footpath zigzags down the hillside to the rock shelter where the paintings can be found.

Places to Stay & Eat

Outside Roma, off the Maseru road, is the *Trading Post Guest House* (☎ 34 0202 or 34 0267). The trading post has been here since 1903, as has the Thorn family which owns the store and the guesthouse. There are walks and horse-riding in the area, including a 20-minute walk to dinosaur footprints. The accommodation is good value at M25 per person in rondavels, M30 in the main house (a nice old stone building) and camping costs M5. There is no restaurant but you can use the kitchen. Everything is provided except towels. In Roma, try the *Roberto Restaurant*.

SEMONKONG

The **Maletsunyane Falls**, also known as Lebihan Falls after the French missionary who reported them in 1881, are about a 1½-hour walk from Semonkong ('place of smoke'). The 192-metre falls are at their most spectacular in summer and best appreciated from the bottom of the gorge (where there are camp sites).

The remote 122-metre **Ketane Falls** are also worth seeing. These are a solid day's ride (30 km) from Semonkong or a four-day return horse-ride from Malealea Lodge.

Pony Trekking

Semonkong Lodge is one of the three major pony-trekking centres in Lesotho. Day rides which include the Malutsenyane Falls, spiral cacti and Mt Qong are M45 per person. If you go out for two days you have two choices – Ketane Falls for M150 and Semonkong Gorge for M275. Four days of riding will include the bottom of Semonkong Gorge, Ketane Falls and a day in the mountains (M300 for five or more people, M450 for fewer).

If you want the lodge to provide food add an extra M30 per person per day; each night spent in a Basotho village costs M10.

Places to Stay

You can usually find a bed at the *Roman*

Catholic Mission for a small contribution. Fraser's *Semonkong Lodge* (book on Ficksburg ☎ (05192) 2730, fax 3313 or Lesotho (266) 31 7601) charges M15 for a camp site, M25 per night for a dorm bed, and M130/260 for a double/family room; some double rooms are M110. Near Semonkong is the *Mountain Delight Lodge* (☎ 32 5577) with rondavels from M70/135.

Getting There & Away
Buses between Maseru and Semonkong (M15) leave from either end in the morning and arrive late afternoon.

MORIJA
This small village, about 40 km south of Maseru on the Main South Rd, is where you will find the **Morija Museum & Archives** (☎ 36 0308). The collection includes archives from the first mission to the Basutholand, and as the missionary was associated with King Moshoeshoe the collection is of great importance. Part of the tea set given to the king by the mission society is on display at the museum, together with displays of Basotho culture, some Stone and Iron Age finds and dinosaur relics. The museum is open Monday to Saturday from 8.30 am to 4.30 pm, Sunday from 2 to 4.30 pm; admission is M1.

Near the museum is the *Mophato Oa Morija* (☎ 36 0219), an ecumenical centre with fairly expensive accommodation in traditional huts. You can camp and sometimes dorm beds are available.

MAFETENG
The name Mafeteng derives from 'place of Lefeta's people'. An early magistrate, Emile Rolland, was called Lefeta ('one who passes by') by local Basotho. Nearby is the 2908-metre Thaba-Putsoa ('blue mountain'), the highest feature in this part of Lesotho.

There is not much of interest in town, although it is important as a bus and minibus taxi interchange. There's a memorial to soldiers of the Cape Mounted Rifles who fell in the 1880 Gun War.

The *Mafeteng Hotel* (☎ 70 0236) has singles/doubles for M105/120. Have a bite at the quirkily named *Captain Cook's* (the *Endeavour* certainly never made it to this part of the world, the *Buy & Take* or the *True Alice*. There is a disco and an à la carte restaurant in the Mafeteng Hotel.

MOHALE'S HOEK
This comfortable town is 125 km from Maseru on a sealed road. The younger brother of Moshoeshoe I, Mohale, gave this land to the British for administrative purposes in 1884. It is a much nicer little place than nearby Mafeteng.

Mohale's Hoek has the *Hotel Mount Maluti* (☎ 78 5224) with singles/doubles from M72/110. For desperados there is a possibility of a bed at the *Farmer Training Centre* at M12 per night. There are a number of places where you can buy an uninspiring meal – try *Koena's Corner* on Hospital Rd or the *Majantja General Café* on Kou St.

MALEALEA
This is one of the gems of Lesotho and is appropriately advertised as 'Lesotho in a nutshell'. The owners, Mick and Di Jones, work tirelessly to promote Lesotho throughout southern Africa. You can go on a well-organised pony trek from here or wander freely through the hills and villages.

The valleys around Malealea have been occupied for many hundreds of years, as evidenced by the many San paintings in rock shelters. The original Malealea Trading Store was established in 1905 by Mervyn Smith, a teacher, diamond miner and soldier. The owners of the lodge may show you the protected spiral aloe *(Aloe polyphylla)*, unique to Lesotho.

Pony Trekking
Malealea Lodge is the best place in Lesotho to go pony trekking. These treks offer a good chance to come face to face with Basotho villagers as well as experience the awesome scenery of the mountains and deep valleys. These treks are conducted with the full cooperation of the villagers. In fact, they act as

the guides and provide the ponies so if you undertake a trek you are contributing to the local village economy.

The two most popular treks are those to the Ribaneng Waterfall (two days, one night) and to the Ribaneng/Ketane waterfalls (four days, three nights). The lodge will organise a trek to any destination that takes your fancy, however. You need to bring food, sleeping bag, rainwear, sunscreen, warm clothing, torch and water purification tablets.

The pony treks are costed on a per day basis. If there are two or three people, the cost for day rides is M60 and for overnight rides it is M90 per person. If there are four or more people, it is M50 for day trips and M70 for overnight rides. There is an additional cost of M15 for each night spent in one of the Basotho village huts.

Malealea Walks

You may elect to go walking if 'ye are of tender buttocks' and cannot face seven-hour stints on the ponies. Mick and Di have put together a number of walking options and provide a map. They will arrange for your packs to be carried on ponies if you wish to go on overnight walks.

The walks include a two-hour return walk to the Botso'ela Waterfall; a six-hour return walk to the Pitseng Gorge (don't forget your swimwear); a short, easy one-hour walk along the Pitseng Plateau; a walk along the Makhaleng River; and a hike from the Gates of Paradise back to Malealea. The scenery along any of these walks is nothing short of stunning and all include the local villages which dot the landscape.

Malealea Drives

Although it is slow-going on the dirt roads in this region there are some very scenic drives. Perhaps the best is the road which forms part of the Roof of Africa Rally. Take a right turn at the first junction you come to when leaving Malealea. The road passes through some picturesque villages before crossing the top of the Botso'ela Waterfall. A few km on it reaches an impressive lookout

over the Makhaleng and Ribaneng valleys. In a conventional car it takes an hour to reach the viewpoint from Malealea; rally drivers take 20 minutes to cover this distance!

If you continue north from the lookout to Sebelekoane you can return to Maseru via Roma. This scenic road leads to Basotho villages and missions tucked away in the valleys. Be warned, it is rough in places and the going can be slow; allow three hours from Sebelekoane to Maseru.

Places to Stay

Malealea Lodge (☎ 78 5336, 78 5264) is part of Smith's old colonial trading post. There is a variety of accommodation including a dorm where beds are M30 per person, rondavels at M40 per person and a self-contained park home which sleeps four to six people at M240. Meals are served if you give prior notice (full board is M110 per person), there are self-catering facilities and the nearby shop is fully stocked.

About six km from the Malealea Lodge turn-off is *Qaba Lodge* (☎ (05192) 2370) which has accommodation in run-down surroundings for M45 per person; they do have a fully equipped kitchen, bar and store where you can buy supplies.

Getting There & Away

Maseru to Malealea is 84 km. From Maseru, head south on the well-signposted Mafeteng road for 52 km to the town of Motsekuoa. Look out for the Golden Rose restaurant, the proliferation of taxis and the huddles of potential passengers. Opposite the restaurant turn left (east) onto the dirt road and follow it for 24 km. When you reach the signposted turn-off to Malealea, it is a further seven km to the lodge. You know that you are on the right track when you pass through the Gates of Paradise and are rewarded with a stunning view of your destination. The plaque here announces 'Wayfarer – Pause and look upon a gateway of Paradise'. Romantic stuff.

The road to Malealea from the south, via Mpharane and Masemouse, is much rougher. Most drivers take the Motsekuoa road.

QUTHING (MOYENI)

Quthing, the southernmost town in Lesotho, is often known as Moyeni (a Sephuthi word meaning 'place of the wind'). The town was established in 1877, abandoned three years later during the 1880 Gun War and then rebuilt at the present site.

Most of the town is in Lower Quthing; up on the hill overlooking the dramatic Orange River Gorge is Upper Quthing, where there is a good hotel, a mission and sundry colonial-era structures. A minibus taxi between the two costs M1.50 – you can hitch but you should still pay.

Pony trekking is sometimes available, mainly day trips. Book in advance through the Orange River Hotel, or try across the road at the Church Centre.

Off the highway, about five km west of Quthing, is the five-roomed **Masitise Cave House**. This mission building was built into a San rock shelter in 1866 by one Rev Ellenberger. His son Edmund, a latter day troglodyte, was born in the cave in 1867. Edmund later became the mayor of Bethlehem in the Orange Free State. Enquire at the school about access to the cave house and someone will unlock it for you. There are San paintings nearby.

Probably the most easily located of the **dinosaur footprints** in Lesotho are close to Quthing. To get to these, go up the Mt Moorosi road from Quthing until you reach a thatched-roofed orange building. There is a short walk to the footprints, which are believed to be 180 million years old.

Between Quthing and Masitise there is a striking twin-spired **sandstone church**, part of the Villa Maria Mission.

Near Qomoqomong, 10 km from Quthing, there is a good gallery of **San paintings**; enquire at the General Dealers store about acquiring a guide for the 20-minute walk to the paintings.

Places to Stay & Eat

The cheapest place is the *Merino Stud Farm* which has clean double rooms with bath for M30 per person; breakfast and dinner are about M8 each.

The *Orange River Hotel* (☎ 75 0252) in Upper Quthing is a pleasant place with stunning views across the gorge to the bleak hills behind. Single/double rooms cost M77/115. There's a restaurant and a bar, but for a better place to drink, head up the driveway to the old thatched pub and sit with the locals on the lawn under an oak tree.

In Lower Quthing, the *Mountain Side Hotel* (☎ 75 0257) is a basic pub with a restaurant which might have rooms, depending on who's behind the bar when you ask. If you do get in, expect to pay M68 for either a single or double.

SWAZILAND

Facts about the Country

HISTORY

The area which is now Swaziland has been inhabited by various groups for a very long time – in eastern Swaziland archaeologists have discovered human remains dating back 110,000 years – but the Swazi people themselves arrived relatively recently.

In the great Bantu migration into southern Africa, one group, the Nguni, moved down the east coast. One clan settled in the area around modern Maputo in Mozambique, and eventually a dynasty was founded by the Dlamini family. By the middle of the 18th century increasing pressure from other clans in the area forced a Dlamini king, Ngwane III, to lead his people south to lands around the Pongola River, in what is today southern Swaziland. Today, the Swazi consider Ngwane III to have been the first king of Swaziland.

This move didn't stop the problem of clan encroachment and the next king, Sobhuza I, came under pressure from the Zulu. He withdrew to the Ezulwini Valley, which still remains the centre of Swazi royalty and ritual. Trouble with the Zulu continued and there was a further retreat by the next king, Mswazi (or Mswati) – this time as far as the Hhohho area.

However, King Mswazi, with a combination of martial skill and diplomacy, managed to unify the whole kingdom and by the time he died in 1868, a Swazi nation was secure. Mswazi's subjects called themselves people of Mswazi or Swazis.

European Interference

Meanwhile, the Zulu were coming under increasing pressure from both the British and the Boers, which created frequent respites for the Swazis. The European presence might have indirectly helped the Swazis with their Zulu problem but it caused a number of others. From the mid-19th century Swaziland attracted increasing numbers of European hunters, traders and missionaries, and farmers in search of land for their cattle. Mswazi's successor, Mbandzeni, inherited a kingdom rife with European carpetbaggers, and more and more of the kingdom's land was being alienated by leases granted to Europeans. Greyhounds and champagne for the king featured heavily in some of the deals.

Furthermore, the Boers' fledgling South African Republic (ZAR) decided to extend its control east to Delagoa Bay (Maputo). Swaziland was in the way and the republic decided to annex the kingdom, but before this could take place, the republic itself was annexed by the British in 1877.

The Pretoria Convention of 1881 guaranteed Swaziland's independence, but also defined its borders and Swaziland lost large chunks of territory. 'Independence' in fact meant that both Britain and the Boers had responsibility for administering their various interests in Swaziland, and the result was chaos. The Boer administration collapsed with the 1899-1902 Anglo-Boer War and afterwards the British took control of Swaziland as a protectorate.

During this troubled time, when Swazis were coming to grips with their loss of sovereignty, King Sobhuza II was only a young child but Labotsibeni, his mother, ably acted as regent until her son took over in 1921.

SWAZILAND
Area: 17,363 sq km
Population: 859,000
Population Growth: 3.6%
Capital: Mbabane
Head of State: King Mswati III
Official Language: siSwati, English
Currency: Lilangeni
Exchange Rate: Pegged to South African Rand
Per Capita GNP: US$1060
Time: GMT/UTC + 2

Throughout the regency and for most of Sobhuza's long reign, the Swazis fought to again become an independent nation and to regain their lands. After petitions and delegations to England failed, Labotsibeni encouraged Swazis to buy the land back, and many sought work in the Witwatersrand (near Jo'burg) mines to raise money. Gradually land was returned to the kingdom, by both direct purchase and British government action, and by the time of independence (in 1968), about two-thirds of the kingdom was again in Swazi control.

Land ownership was not just a political and economic issue. Swazi kings are considered to hold the kingdom in trust for their subjects, and to have a large proportion of the country owned by foreigners threatened the credibility of the monarchy and thus the viability of Swazi culture.

Independence

In 1960, King Sobhuza II proposed the creation of a Legislative Council, to be composed of Europeans elected along European lines and a National Council formed in accordance with Swazi culture. One of the Swazi political parties formed at this time was the Mbokodvo (Grindstone) National Movement, which pledged to maintain traditional Swazi culture but also to eschew racial discrimination. When the British finally agreed to elections in 1964, Mbokodvo won a majority and, at the next elections in 1967, won all the seats. Independence, now certain, was achieved on 6 September 1968.

The country's constitution was largely the work of the British, and in 1973, the king suspended it on the grounds that it did not accord with Swazi culture. Four years later the parliament reconvened under a new constitution which vested all power in the king. Sobhuza II, then the world's longest reigning monarch, died in 1982, having ensured the continued existence of his country and culture, under threat since his father's reign. He is still referred to as 'the late king'.

The surprising feature of Britain's 66-year rule of Swaziland was the lack of violence with which it was resisted and overthrown.

King Sobhuza II

That many of the streets in the capital city, Mbabane, retain their colonial-era names is surely indicative of the goodwill which was maintained. In fact, the capital city's main street is named after the first European to be born there.

Today

The young Mswati III ascended the throne in 1986 (he was flown home from a school in England to be made king) and continues to represent and maintain the traditional way of life. Although most Swazis seem happy with their political system there is some political dissent. The main concern of most Swazis, however, is to ensure that Swazi culture survives in the face of modernisation. Currently, King Mswati and a small core of advisers (Council of Ministers) run the country.

Opposition parties remain illegal, but the

Swaziland

0   15   30 km

main players, Pudemo (People's United Democratic Movement) and Swayoco (Swaziland Youth Congress), have only minimal support. In October 1993 the electoral system was changed slightly in response to pressure from the United Nations and World Bank. There was a gradual easing of the almost total autocratic control of the king.

GEOGRAPHY

Swaziland, the smallest country in the southern hemisphere, has a wide range of ecological zones, from rainforest in the north-west to savanna scrub in the east.

The western edge of the country is highveld, consisting mainly of short, sharp mountains. It is known as *nkhangala* (treeless) in Swazi but now there are large plantations of pine and eucalyptus, especially around Piggs Peak in the north. The mountains dwindle to middleveld in the centre of the country, where most of the people live. The eastern half is scrubby lowveld, lightly populated in the past because of malaria (still a risk), but now home to sugar estates. The eastern border with Mozambique is formed by the harsh Lebombo range.

CLIMATE

Most rain falls in summer, usually in torrential thunderstorms and mostly in the western

mountains. Summers on the lowveld are very hot, with temperatures often over 40°C; in the high country the temperatures are lower and in winter it can get cool. Winter nights on the lowveld are sometimes very cold.

October can be the hottest month. The rains usually begin around early December and last until April. May to August are the coolest months, with frosts in June and July.

NATIONAL PARKS & RESERVES

The five main reserves in Swaziland have all been created comparatively recently, but they are all worth visiting and reflect the country's geographical diversity. Easiest to get to is Mlilwane Wildlife Sanctuary in the Ezulwini Valley. Mkhaya Game Reserve and Hlane Royal National Park are also well worth visiting. These three reserves are privately run as part of the Big Game Parks organisation (☎ 44541, fax 40957).

The National Trust Commission (☎ 61178) has an office in the National Museum near Lobamba. It runs Malolotja and Mlawula nature reserves. Malolotja is a highlands reserve with some good hiking trails. Mlawula is in harsh lowveld country near the Mozambique border.

GOVERNMENT

Swaziland is governed by a parliament but

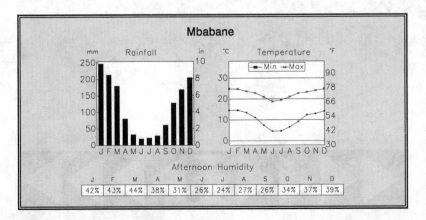

Mbabane

	J	F	M	A	M	J	J	A	S	O	N	D
Afternoon Humidity	42%	43%	44%	38%	31%	26%	24%	27%	26%	34%	37%	39%

SWAZILAND

final authority (and ownership of much of the country's resources) is vested in the king. The king can dissolve parliament at any time.

There is a Senate as well as a House of Assembly. Half of the 30 senators are elected by the assembly, the other are appointed by the king. The king also appoints 20 members of the assembly. The other 40 are elected in the constituencies, first by a show of hands and then by ballot. There is no campaigning as such but each candidate is given a range of subjects to talk about at a controlled meeting. At the secondary elections there will be one successful candidate per constituency.

The real power is vested in the king and the 16-person Council of Ministers. It would be fair to say that dilution of the democratic process means that about a quarter of the council actually represented the interests of the average Swazi. Not that the average Swazi is demanding rapid change.

ECONOMY
Swaziland is a poor country but it is by no means in crisis and the economy is modestly healthy. The major export is sugar, and forest products are also important. Although most foreign investment in the country is still British, South African investment is extremely important and fluctuations in that country's economy affect Swaziland.

Nearly 75% of the population works in agriculture, mostly at a subsistence level, but the country is not self-sufficient in food.

POPULATION & PEOPLE
Almost all of the 859,000 people are Swazi. The rest are Zulu, Tsonga-Shangaan and European. There are also Mozambiquan refugees, of both African and Portuguese descent. About 5% of Swazis live and work in South Africa.

The dominant clan is the Dlamini and you'll meet people with that surname all over the country. It's sometimes felt that ordinary Dlaminis put on unwarranted royal airs and there's a little resentment towards them, usually expressed as friendly jibes.

There's a good chance you'll meet a prince in Swaziland. There are a lot of princes and they come from all walks of life. They might be dripping with supercilious world-weariness or be a struggling local farmer like the others at the bar.

LANGUAGE
The official languages are SiSwati and English, and English is the official written language. For information on SiSwati see the Language section in the Facts about the Region chapter.

Facts for the Visitor

Many Swazis have a sophistication which is totally unexpected in such a small, rural country. Maybe it's because of their strong culture or because there are so few Swazis and they are like a huge extended family. In Swaziland most things run relatively smoothly and there are rarely unwarranted hassles with officialdom.

With Swazi men encountering new ideas while working over in South Africa and with Mozambiquan refugees, Swazi culture is having to deal with foreign values and it's feeling the strain. For the visitor, the Mozambiquans add a cosmopolitan touch and there are some good bars and restaurants.

VISAS & EMBASSIES

Most people don't need a visa to visit Swaziland, but there are some significant exceptions, including Austrian, French, Swiss and German citizens. However, citizens of these and other EU countries can get visas free at the border or the airport.

Anyone staying for more than 60 days must apply for a temporary residence permit from the Chief Immigration Officer (☎ 42941), PO Box 372, Mbabane.

Swazi Embassies

Addresses of Swazi representation in other countries include:

Canada
    130 Albert St, Ottawa, Ontario, KIP 5G4 (☎ (613) 567 1480)
Kenya
    PO Box 41887, Nairobi (☎ (00254) 2-33 9231)
Mozambique
    Av do Zimbabwe 608, PO Box 4711, Maputo (☎ 49 2451)
UK
    58 Pont St, Knightsbridge, London SW1 (☎ (0171) 581 4976)
USA
    Suite 3M, 3400 International Dr, Washington DC 20008 (☎ (202) 362 6683)

In South Africa, visas can be obtained from the Swaziland Trade Mission (☎ (011) 29 9776, fax 29 9763), Room 915, The Rand Central Building, 165 Jeppe St, Jo'burg. There are honorary consulates in a number of other countries, including Greece, Israel, Spain, Switzerland, Japan and Germany.

Foreign Embassies in Swaziland

The Mozambique Embassy (☎ 43700) in Mbabane issues one-month visas for E80 with two photos. They usually take a week to issue but the friendly staff might do it faster in an emergency. The fee is considerably less than you'd pay in Jo'burg. The embassy is open between 9 am and 1 pm on weekdays. To get there head out onto the Manzini road, turn left down the road to the Mountain Inn, turn left onto the dirt road just past the hotel entrance and then left again at the next corner. The embassy is 100 metres or so further on.

Other diplomatic representation in Swaziland includes:

Belgian Consulate
    PO Box 33, Eveni, Mbabane (☎ 46809)
Danish Consulate
    Ground Floor, Sokhamlilo Building, Johnstone St, Mbabane (☎ 43547)
Dutch Consulate
    Business Machine House, Mbabane (☎ 45178)
German Embassy
    3rd Floor, Dhlan'ubeka House, Mbabane (☎ 43174)
Israeli Embassy
    PO Box 146, Mbabane (☎ 42626)
Mozambique Embassy
    Princess Drive, Mbabane (☎ 43700)
UK High Commission
    Allister Miller St, Mbabane (☎ 42581)
US Embassy
    Central Bank Building, Warmer St, Mbabane (☎ 46441)

DOCUMENTS

No vaccination certificates are required to enter Swaziland unless you have recently been in a yellow-fever area.

CUSTOMS

Customs regulations are similar to those for South Africa. If you are arriving from South Africa there are no restrictions.

MONEY

The unit of currency is the lilangeni (the plural is emalangeni – E) which is fixed at a value equal to the South African rand. Rands are accepted everywhere and there's no need to change them, although many places will not accept South African coins. Emalangeni are difficult to change for other currencies outside Swaziland.

Several banks change travellers' cheques. Barclays Bank has the most branches, including Mbabane (☎ 42691), Manzini (☎ 52411), Nhlangano (☎ 78377), Piggs Peak (☎ 71100) and Big Bend (☎ 74100).

Barclays are open between 8.30 am and 2.30 pm on weekdays, and until 11 am on Saturday. Other banks keep similar hours. There's a Swaziland Development Bank branch at Matsapha Airport, open for flights.

Exchange Rates

The rate is fixed the same value as the South African rand (see Exchange Rates in the South Africa Facts for the Visitor chapter).

Costs

Costs are similar to those in South Africa, with food a little cheaper. The game reserves here are particularly good value.

TOURIST OFFICES

The main tourist office is in Mbabane.

PUBLIC HOLIDAYS

In addition to Christmas, Boxing and New Year's days holidays, and Good Friday and Easter Monday, other holidays observed in Swaziland are:

King Mswati III's Birthday	19 April
National Flag Day	25 April
King Sobhuza II's Birthday	22 July
Reed Dance Day	variable; in August or September
Somhlolo Day (Independence)	6 September
Incwala Day	variable; December or January

CULTURAL EVENTS

Sibhaca dancing developed fairly recently, but it is very popular and there are national competitions at the Manzini Trade Fair – it's practically a team sport. Local competitions are held frequently, and the Mbabane tourist office has details. The Sun hotels in the Ezulwini Valley sometimes have performances.

The most important cultural events in Swaziland are the *Incwala* ceremony, held sometime between late December and early January, and the *Umhlanga* (Reed) Dance held in August or September. The venue for both is near Lobamba in the Ezulwini Valley. Ask at the tourist office in Mbabane for exact dates. Photography is not permitted at the Incwala but it is at the Umhlanga Dance.

POST & TELECOMMUNICATIONS

Post offices are open from 8 am to 4 pm on weekdays and until 11 am on Saturday.

There are no telephone area codes within Swaziland; if you're calling from South Africa use the code 09-268. You can make international calls (but not reverse charges) at the post office in Mbabane.

MEDIA

There are two English-language daily newspapers – *The Times of Swaziland* (founded in 1887 by Allister Miller senior) and the *Swazi Observer*.

HEALTH

Beware of both bilharzia and malaria. See the Health section in the regional Facts for the Visitor chapter for information on avoiding these potentially deadly diseases.

If you need medical assistance there is the Mbabane Clinic Service (☎ 42423), the

Swazi Ceremonies

Incwala The Incwala (sometimes Ncwala) is the most sacred ceremony of the Swazi people. It is a 'first fruits' ceremony, as the king gives permission for his people to eat the first crops of the new year.

Preparation for the Incwala begins some weeks before, according to the moon. *Bemanti* (learned men) journey to the Lebombo mountains to gather plants, other groups collect water from Swaziland's rivers and some travel across the mountains to the Indian Ocean (where the Dlamini clan lived long before the Swazi nation came into being), to skim foam from the waves. Meanwhile, the king goes into retreat.

On the night of the full moon, young men all over the kingdom harvest branches of *lusekwane*, a small tree, and begin a long trek to the Royal Kraal at Lobamba. They arrive at dawn and their branches are used to build a kraal. If a branch has wilted it is a sign that the young man bearing it has had illicit sex. Songs prohibited during the rest of the year are sung and the bemanti arrive with their plants, water and foam.

On the third day of the ceremony a bull is sacrificed. On the fourth day, to the pleadings of all the regiments of Swaziland, the king breaks his retreat and dances before his people. He eats a pumpkin, the sign that Swazis can eat the new year's crops. Two days later there's a ritual burning of all items in the ceremony, after which the rains are expected to fall.

Umhlanga Not as sacred as the Incwala, the Umhlanga Dance serves a similar function in drawing the nation together and reminding the people of their relationship to the king. It is something like a week-long debutante ball for marriageable young Swazi women, who journey from all over the kingdom to help repair the queen mother's home at Lobamba.

After arriving at Lobamba they spend a day resting, then set off in search of reeds, some not returning until the fourth night. On the sixth day the reed dance is performed as they carry their reeds to the queen mother. The dance is repeated the next day. Those carrying torches (flashlights) have searched for reeds by night. Those with red feathers in their hair are princesses.

As the Swazi queen mother must not be of the royal clan, the reed dance is also a showcase of potential wives for the king. As with the Incwala, there are signs which identify the unchaste, a powerful incentive to avoid pre-marital sex.

Umcwasho This dance has not been performed for some time. Young women wear a necklace of beads from which a long wooden tassel (the *umcwasho*) is suspended. The necklace is worn for two years, and during this time the girls are not allowed to be courted. After two years they go to the Royal Kraal for dancing and feasting. At the end of the dance the umcwasho, now a bad omen, was traditionally thrown at a female elder who could no longer bear children. ■

Mbabane Government Hospital (☎ 42111), the Raleigh Fitkin Hospital in Manzini (☎ 52211) and the Piggs Peak Government Hospital (☎ 71111).

ACCOMMODATION

There are few designated camp sites in Swaziland except in some of the national parks and nature reserves. There's a good caravan park in the Ezulwini Valley, 10 km from Mbabane.

Away from the few population centres it's usually possible (and safe) to find your own place to pitch a tent, but *always* ask permission from local people, who will probably have to seek permission in turn from their local leader. Be patient. Swazis' hospitality is genuine but so is their dislike of people imposing on them or disregarding their social structures.

There are a couple of church-run hostels in Mbabane. If you're stuck for a room in rural areas you could try the local school, where you'll probably be made welcome.

Many of the county's hotels are geared towards South African tourists and are expensive. Some towns have smaller, pub-like places left over from the protectorate days which are cheaper, and some are good value.

ACTIVITIES

Although Swaziland is a small country, there are enough activities to keep you interested for some days. White-water rafting at Mkhaya Game Reserve is becoming popular and there are plenty of opportunities to go horse-riding.

A number of stables offer lessons, rides, and children's riding camps in areas only accessible by foot or on horse back. In Mlilwane Wildlife Sanctuary, not far from Mbabane, it is possible to view wildlife on horse back. Guests at several hotels have access to stables: Meikles Mount (☎ 74110) and the Foresters Arms Hotel (☎ 74117) in the Mhlambanyati region, the Ezulwini Valley Sun hotels (☎ 61001) and the Protea Piggs Peak Hotel (☎ 71104). There are also stables at Hawana Park (☎ 42619) near Malolotja and at Nyanza (☎ 83090) near Malkerns.

As well as walking trails in several parks, especially Malolotja Nature Reserve, you can set out on foot to explore the country, following countless tracks which are generations old. If you have time, this would be the best way to see Swaziland.

THINGS TO BUY

Swaziland's handicrafts are worth looking out for. Because of the strength of traditional culture many items are made for the local market as much as for tourists.

Woven grassware, such as *liqhaga* (grassware 'bottles', so well made that they are used for carrying water) and mats are popular, as are wooden items, ranging from bowls to knobkerries. There is also jewellery, pottery and weapons and implements.

If you come in through the Oshoek border post there are small stalls nearby. There are also outlets in Mbabane's SEDCO estate, including a pottery shop and Swaziland Arts & Crafts. Mbabane's Swazi Market is worth visiting to get an idea of prices and standards.

In the Ezulwini Valley, there are several crafts shops, the biggest being the Mantenga Craft Centre, off the highway between Smokey Mountain Village and the Mantenga Hotel. Tishweshwe Cottage Crafts, two km down the Malkerns road, is another large showroom and workshop.

High-quality hand-woven mohair is produced at Rosecraft in Malkerns. Coral Stephen's weaving workshop near Piggs Peak has an international reputation. Phone 71140 for an appointment to visit. Also in Piggs Peak is Tintsaba Crafts, at the Highlands Inn and also at the casino, 10 km north.

The trade fair held in Manzini each year from the end of August is a showcase for handicrafts as well as industrial products.

Getting There & Away

If you're arriving from South Africa, remember that you won't be allowed to return unless you have a multiple-entry visa.

AIR

Royal Swazi Airlines operates out of Matsapha Airport, north of Manzini. Schedules and tickets often refer to the airport as Manzini. Royal Swazi Airways flies to:

Cape Town – Friday, Sunday and Monday; E650
Jo'burg – Sunday, Monday, Thursday and Friday; E320
Maputo (Mozambique) – Tuesday, Wednesday, Saturday and Sunday; E220
Harare (Zimbabwe) – Monday and Thursday; E880
Lusaka (Zambia) – Monday and Thursday; E1060
Dar es Salaam (Tanzania) – Tuesday, Wednesday, Saturday and Sunday; E1370
Nairobi (Kenya) – Tuesday, Wednesday, Saturday and Sunday; E1500
Maseru (Lesotho) – Friday, Sunday and Monday; E420

Lesotho Airways flies twice a week to Maseru for E420. Airlink flies to and from Durban on Tuesday, Friday and Sunday for E325 and Comair flies to and from Jo'burg on Tuesday (twice), Wednesday and Saturday, for E310.

A departure tax of E20 is levied at Matsapha Airport.

LAND
Border Crossings

Swaziland's 12 border posts are all with South Africa, with the exception of the Namaacha/Lomahasha border post in the extreme north-east, which is the entry point to Mozambique. The smaller posts close at 4 or 6 pm; the main border posts with South Africa are:

Oshoek/Ngwenya
This post is open from 7 am to 10 pm and takes most of the traffic, so it can be clogged with South Africans arriving on Friday and leaving on Sunday. It's a good place to pick up lifts.

Mahamba
Open from 7 am to 10 pm, this is the best post to use from Piet Retief, South Africa. It's close to Nhlangano and Hlathikulu.
Golela/Lavumisa
Open from 7 am to 10 pm, this post is in the south-east, opposite Golela in South Africa. From here it's a quick run to Big Bend.
Josefsdal/Bulembu
Open from 8 am to 4 pm, it is on the road from Piggs Peak to Barberton, South Africa. It is a dirt road, tricky in wet weather.
Mozambique (Lomahasha/Namaacha)
This post is open from 7 am to 5 pm daily. Purchasing visas at the border is an on/off affair so it's best to get them in advance. If you get your visa in South Africa it will cost R120 but the Mozambique Trade Mission in Mbabane arranges them for E80.

Bus

There is a twice weekly service from Mbabane to Maputo (Mozambique); enquire at the tourist office.

Transtate, the South African 'third-class' bus line runs to and near Swaziland. From Jo'burg to Mbabane costs about E45. A minibus taxi costs a little more but is much faster. However, the buses are safe, relatively comfortable and rarely crowded. Except for tour buses, Transtate is the only line running between South Africa and Swaziland. Some useful Transtate routes follow.

Jo'burg to Hlathikulu This route takes 10 hours, via Piet Retief and Nhlangano, departing from Jo'burg weekdays, and returning daily except Saturday. This overnight trip leaves you short of Mbabane and as you arrive in the evening there's no time to hitch or take another bus to there.

Jo'burg to Mbabane & Manzini This service takes 10½ hours, via Ermelo, the Ezulwini Valley and Mbabane. It departs from Jo'burg weekdays at 7.30 am, returning daily except Saturday. It's the best way into

Swaziland from Jo'burg. From Jo'burg to Mbabane costs R60.

Durban to Mbabane This service on Monday, Wednesday, Friday (returning Tuesday, Thursday, Saturday) takes 10½ hours, via Golela, Big Bend and Manzini. Golela is on the south-east border, across from Lavumisa.

Train
There are no ordinary passenger trains, although five times a year there are four-day tours from Jo'burg on the *Royal Swazi Express* (☎ (011) 822 1295) for about R1500.

Minibus Taxi
There are some minibus taxis running direct between Jo'burg and Mbabane for about E50, but to most other destinations in Swaziland you'll have to take a minibus taxi to the border and another from there to the

nearest town, where you'll probably have to change again. This can be slow.

Car & Motorbike
There's an E1 road tax for vehicles entering Swaziland. If you're entering Mozambique, your car must have a vehicle-breakdown warning triangle, seat belts (even though wearing them is not compulsory) and official papers (eg, permission for hire cars to cross from Swaziland or South Africa into Mozambique).

Hitching
Most South Africans enter through the Oshoek/Ngwenya border post, with the casinos in the north (near the Matsamo/Jeppe's Reef border post) and south (near the Mahamba border post) attracting traffic, especially on weekends.

Getting Around

BUS & MINIBUS TAXI

South Africa's Transtate buses run to Mbabane, Manzini and Hlathikulu via several border posts. See the Getting There & Away chapter for routes. There's a good system of buses, some express, running regular routes, but not very frequently. Minibus taxis usually run shorter routes at prices a little higher than the buses.

Some examples of bus routes and fares are Manzini to Siteki, E6; Manzini to Big Bend, E6.50; Manzini to Mbabane, E4; Big Bend to Lavumisa (border), E5; and Mbabane to Piggs Peak, E6.

A minibus from the Mahamba border post to Nhlangano is E1; to Hlathikulu it's E8. There are also 'normal' non-shared taxis in some of the larger towns.

CAR & MOTORBIKE

Most roads are quite good and there are also some satisfyingly rough back roads through the bush. Driving down the Ezulwini Valley in heavy traffic can be slow and dangerous – Malagwane Hill, from Mbabane into the Ezulwini Valley, was once listed in the *Guinness Book of Records* as the most dangerous stretch of road in the world! The hilly road from Mbabane to Piggs Peak also carries a lot of traffic.

Away from the few population centres the main dangers are people and animals on the road. On narrow gravel roads beware of speeding buses and wandering cattle. There are very few fences in this country, a fact attributable to a royal decree defending the rights of cattle to roam freely. The other danger is drunk drivers – the permitted blood-alcohol limit is 0.15%!

Wearing seat belts is compulsory. If an official motorcade approaches, you must pull over and stop. The speed limit is 80 km/h on the open road and 60 km/h in built-up areas.

Many petrol stations are open 24 hours, and there are AA agents in Manzini, Mbabane and Piggs Peak.

Car Rental

Swaziland is so small that hiring a car for a couple of days will give you a good idea of the whole country. Rates are similar to those in South Africa.

Both Avis (☎ 86226) and Hertz/Imperial (☎ 84862) are at Matsapha Airport, near Manzini. Hertz/Imperial also has an agent in Mbabane (☎ 41384). The minimum age for hiring a car with these companies is 23.

HITCHING

Hitching is easier here than in South Africa, as the colour of the driver and the colour of the hitchhiker aren't factors in the decision to offer a lift. You might wait a long time for a car on back roads, and everywhere you'll have lots of competition from locals.

WALKING

Transport for most people in rural Swaziland is on foot, which has left trails all over the country.

TOURS & PACKAGES

Royal Swazi Airways has various packages from Jo'burg, mostly with accommodation in the more expensive hotels in Ezulwini Valley, but there's an option with accommodation at the small Foresters Arms Hotel which includes car hire. Phone ☎ 74117 for more information.

Umhlanga Tours (☎ 44522, fax 42485) is based at the Royal Swazi Sun in the Ezulwini Valley near Mbabane. They offer a variety of tours, with some of their day tours being reasonable value if you're short of time or don't have transport. For example, their tour which includes Mlilwane, Ngwenya/Endlotane and other craft outlets is E120, a day tour to Mkhaya Game Reserve is E350.

Mbabane

With about 50,000 people Mbabane (if you say 'mba-*baa*-nay' you'll be close enough) is the largest town in Swaziland and it's growing fast. There isn't much to see or do here – the adjacent Ezulwini Valley has the attractions – but Mbabane is a relaxing place in a nice setting in the Dlangeni Hills. The hills make Mbabane cooler than Manzini. That's why the British, in 1902, moved their administrative centre here from Manzini.

Orientation & Information

Despite recent development, Mbabane is still a pleasant town. The main street is Allister Miller St. Off Western Distributor Rd is Swazi Plaza, a large, modern shopping centre with most services and a good range of shops; it's also a good landmark. Across OK Rd is the new Mall, a showpiece.

Tourist Office The tourist office (☎ 42531) is in Swazi Plaza. The staff are friendly and knowledgeable, and also understand that not all foreigners are interested in casinos and up-market hotels – a welcome change from South African tourist offices. The *Swaziland Jumbo Tourist Guide* (E10) has good information tucked away between platitudinous rambling and advertising.

For trustworthy information on the Royal Swazi Big Game parks (☎ 44541, fax 40957) enquire at their office in the Mall.

Money There's a Barclays branch in Swazi Plaza and on Allister Miller St.

Post & Telecommunications There are no area codes within Swaziland; if calling from South Africa use the code 09-268. Some places in Swaziland are not on automatic exchanges and to call them you have to book a trunk call (☎ 90) and the operator will call you back.

You can make international calls (but not reverse charges) at the post office between 8 am and 4 pm on weekdays and until noon on Saturday. There are often long queues.

Bookshops Africa South is an excellent bookshop specialising in books on southern Africa. It's in Swazi Plaza and is open weekdays. There are several branches of Webster's, a good book chain, throughout the country.

Emergency In case of fire, call ☎ 43333. For medical assistance, call ☎ 42423 or 42111. For police, call ☎ 42221 in Mbabane, 52221 in Manzini.

Dangers & Annoyances Mbabane is a little unsafe at night, especially on the back streets. Apart from the risk of mugging there are few problems in this friendly place.

Places to Stay

Caravan Parks The nearest caravan park is about 10 km away in the Ezulwini Valley. See the Around Swaziland chapter for details. With security a real problem, it is definitely not advisable to camp in any of the city parks.

Hostels There are no youth hostels as such but there is accommodation in a couple of church missions. The drawback with these places is that they are some way from the centre of town and walking back at night isn't safe.

Thokose Church Centre (☎ 46682) is on Mhlanhla Rd; double rooms are E36 per person, but it's often full, especially around Christmas. From Allister Miller St turn onto Walker St, cross the bridge at the bottom of the hill, turn left at the police station and head along a dirt road up the hill for about 10 minutes. A taxi there is E10 from Swazi Plaza.

Further out, south-east of the centre on Isomi St, the *Youth Centre* (☎ 42176) charges E36 per person, including breakfast, in two-bed rooms – you might have to share. The gates are locked at 9.30 pm. A taxi there costs E15, or E20 at night.

Hotels A long-time travellers' favourite is the *City Inn* (☎ 42406), in the centre on Allister Miller St. Singles/doubles cost from E110/135 or E95/110 with shared bathroom. There are more expensive rooms with air-conditioning. Check out the rooms with shared bathrooms as you might decide they're better than the cheaper rooms with a bathroom. Rooms at the back get noise from the bar/disco behind the hotel.

Quieter, but a fair walk from the centre on Hill St is *Hill Street Lodge* (☎ 46342). Singles/doubles with shared bathroom cost E30/60. For the price it's good value. Not so good but much livelier is *Kamtshawe Lodge* (☎ 45256), on the corner of Boyes and Ilunga Sts. This is basically a neighbourhood bar with some smallish rooms added. Double rooms cost E45 or E55 with an attached bathroom. As accommodation, it's poor value but it's a good place to meet locals. The area isn't one you'd want to walk through at night, though. A taxi here costs about E6.

The *Tavern Hotel* (☎ 42361), off Gilfillan

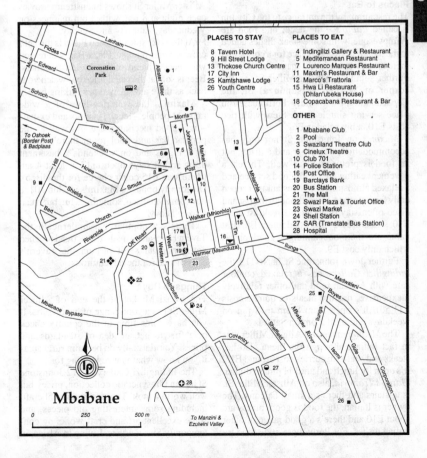

PLACES TO STAY

8 Tavern Hotel
9 Hill Street Lodge
13 Thokose Church Centre
17 City Inn
25 Kamtshawe Lodge
26 Youth Centre

PLACES TO EAT

4 Indingilizi Gallery & Restaurant
5 Mediterranean Restaurant
7 Lourenco Marques Restaurant
11 Maxim's Restaurant & Bar
12 Marco's Trattoria
15 Hwa Li Restaurant (Dhlan'ubeka House)
18 Copacabana Restaurant & Bar

OTHER

1 Mbabane Club
2 Pool
3 Swaziland Theatre Club
6 Cinelux Theatre
10 Club 701
14 Police Station
16 Post Office
19 Barclays Bank
20 Bus Station
21 The Mall
22 Swazi Plaza & Tourist Office
23 Swazi Market
24 Shell Station
27 SAR (Transtate Bus Station)
28 Hospital

Mbabane

0   250   500 m

To Manzini & Ezulwini Valley

St, charges E114/190 (poolside rooms are E155/210), with breakfast. Some of the rooms are tiny, there's a dirty swimming pool and a couple of bars.

The *Mountain Inn* (☎ 42781) is a km or so south of the centre, overlooking the Ezulwini Valley. Rooms in the south wing cost E210/250 and poolside rooms are E195/210. The *Swazi Inn* (☎ 42235), about three km out on the Ezulwini Valley road, is similar. See the Ezulwini Valley section in the Around Swaziland chapter for other accommodation near Mbabane.

Places to Eat

The restaurant by the entrance to the City Inn is called *Pablo's* – the décor and food are Wimpyesque, with some steak dishes added to the menu. It's a good place for a coffee and there are newspapers and magazines to read. Further south on Allister Miller St, on the corner of Warmer (Msunduza) St, the *Copacabana* is a friendly Portuguese-run place serving simple food. Stew with rice costs E10, a big salad is E6.

Maxim's on Johnstone St not only has accommodation, a fine bar and a disco, but its food is pretty good as well. There's a pavement eating area with good service and a relaxed atmosphere. The restaurant is open daily from 9 am to 1 am, although the bar and disco often stay open later. Breakfast costs E10, steaks are E25 and good salads E6. Best value are their outstandingly good pizzas which only cost E9.

Further down Johnstone St, at No 112, the *Indingilizi Gallery* has a relaxed outdoor café with African food and other relatively inexpensive, healthy meals (a quiche costs E11.50). It's open from 8 am to 5 pm on weekdays and until 2 pm on Saturday.

The *Mediterranean* on Allister Miller St is in fact Indian, although the menu also has steaks and seafood; curries cost around E13. It's open for lunch and until 11 pm for dinner. *Marco's Trattoria*, also on Allister Miller St, is upstairs and there's a small balcony. The owner is Italian, the food is good, pizzas are about E10 and there's a good range of other Italian dishes. For Portuguese-style food try *LM (Lourenco Marques)*, on the corner of Gilfillan and Allister Miller Sts. In Dlanu'-beka House on Walker (Mhlonhlo) St is the *Hwa Li*, a Chinese restaurant specialising in spring rolls, chow mein and spicy soups.

In Swazi Plaza the popular *Longhorn Steakhouse* (near Barclays Bank) has salads from E7, and large steaks from E25 to E30, depending on what sauces are added. *La Casserole* is a licensed German place serving continental cuisine; it is in the new Mall.

Entertainment

The Cinelux Theatre at the north end of Allister Miller St shows mainstream movies each night at 8 pm, with 3 pm matinees on Wednesday, Saturday and Sunday.

At the river side of Swazi Plaza is the very crowded and popular Plaza Bar, where you will meet a blend of locals and travellers. Beer is sold at the usual price but watch your back as there are shifty types lurking here.

Maxim's, the watering-hole of a wide range of people – locals, visitors and ex-pats – is a good meeting place. As well as the popular bar and pool room there's music most nights and on weekends a basement disco which stays open until at least 4 am (there's an E15 cover charge for the disco). Diagonally opposite Maxim's is Club 701, a down-market disco, sometimes fun but it can also be heavy.

There's a popular bar underneath the Tavern Hotel and a 'real-Africa' (read rougher, not-so-popular swill pit) on the Tavern's eastern side for the adventurous.

Things to Buy

The Swazi Market at the end of Allister Miller St has a good range of handicrafts. If you have some time in the country check here first to get an idea of standards and prices. You'll usually do better in rural areas if you know what you're looking for.

The Indingilizi Gallery at 112 Johnstone St has an idiosyncratic collection, pricey but well worth a look. There is traditional craft, including some interesting old pieces, and some excellent art and craft works by contemporary Swazi artists. Living in Africa, in

Swazi Plaza, sells practical household goods but there are plenty of interesting smaller items as well. In the mall, opposite Swazi Plaza, African Fantasy has locally made T-shirts.

Getting There & Away

Transtate buses leave from the railway station on Coventry Cres. Minibus taxis to South Africa leave from the taxi park near Swazi Plaza, where you'll also find buses and minibus taxis to destinations in Swaziland.

Getting Around

To/From the Airport A non-share taxi from Mbabane to Matsapha International Airport will cost about E55. It is about E30 to Manzini and E45 to the Ezulwini Valley. Buses and minibuses from Mbabane to Manzini go past the turn-off to the airport, from where it's a walk of several km to the terminal.

Bus & Minibus Taxi The main bus and minibus park is near Swazi Plaza. Any vehicle heading towards Manzini or Matsapha passes through the Ezulwini Valley.

Taxi Non-shared taxis congregate near the bus rank by Swazi Plaza, and at night you can usually find one near the City Inn, or try phoning ☎ 42014 or 42530. Non-shared taxis to the Ezulwini Valley cost at least E20, more to the far end of the valley, and still more at night.

Around Swaziland

EZULWINI VALLEY

The royal valley begins just outside Mbabane and extends down past Lobamba village, 18 km away. Most of the area's attractions are near Lobamba. It's a pretty valley but fast turning into a hotel strip.

Lobamba

This is the heart of Swaziland's royal valley, and has been almost since the beginning of the Swazi people. The royal palace, the Embo State Palace, isn't open to visitors, and you are not allowed to take photos of it. This palace was built by the British; Swazi kings now live in the Lozitha State House about 10 km from Lobamba. Given the size of the royal family (Sobhuza II had 600 children)

this is a large complex – you aren't allowed to visit.

You can see the monarchy in action at the Royal Kraal in Lobamba during the Incwala ceremony and the Umhlanga dance. The nearby Somhlolo National Stadium hosts big sports events (mainly soccer) and important state occasions, such as coronations.

The **National Museum** has some interesting displays on Swazi culture and a there's a traditional beehive village beside it. The National Trust Commission offices, where you can make bookings for Mlawula and Malolotja nature reserves, are here.

Next to the museum is the **parliament**, which is sometimes open to visitors; wear neat clothes and use the side entrance. Across

PLACES TO STAY

1 Mountain Inn
2 Swazi Inn
3 Mgenule Motel
5 Timbali Caravan Park
7 Ezulwini Sun Hotel
8 Royal Swazi Sun Hotel, Casino & Umhlanga Tours
9 Lugogo Sun Hotel
10 Yen Saan Hotel
12 Smokey Mountain Village
13 Happy Valley Motel, Sir Loin Restaurant & Why Not Disco
14 Mantenga Falls Hotel

22 Paradise Caravan Park & Jimmy's Bar

PLACES TO EAT

4 Calabash Continental Restaurant
11 1st Horse Restaurant
27 Malandela's & Tishweshwe Crafts

OTHER

6 Swazi Health & Beauty Spa
15 Mantenga Craft Centre
16 Somhlolo National Stadium

17 Parliament
18 National Museum & King Sobhuza II Memorial
19 Lozitha State House
20 University
21 Matsapha Industrial Area
23 Matsapha International Airport
24 Lobamba State House
25 Royal Kraal
26 Mlilwane Wildlife Sanctuary

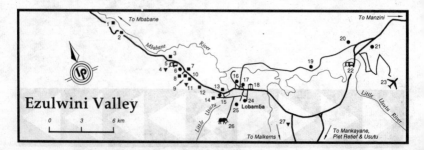

Ezulwini Valley

the road from the museum is the **memorial** to King Sobhuza II, the most revered of Swazi kings, and a small **museum** devoted to him.

Mantenga Falls are worth a look, but ask for advice at the nearby Mantenga Hotel (directions to the hotel are in the Places to Stay section) before you go. The road is steep and sometimes dangerous, and there have been muggings and worse at the falls.

Mlilwane Wildlife Sanctuary

This sanctuary near Lobamba was the first in Swaziland. It's a private reserve and was created by Ted Reilly on his family farm in the '50s. Reilly has gone on to open Mkhaya Game Reserve and has supervised the setting-up of Hlane Royal National Park. Read about conservation efforts at the reserve (and throughout the kingdom) in the excellent *The Mlilwane Story*, available from the sanctuary.

The reserve is dominated by the precipitous Nyonyane ('little bird') peak, and there are several nice walks around it.

Amongst the animals to be seen are zebras, giraffes and many antelope species, as well as crocodiles and hippos and a variety of birds. In summer, black eagles (*Aquila verreauxii*) are seen near Nyonyane. There is a pair of resident, exhibitionist blue cranes (*Anthropoides paradisea*) at the camp site.

Vultures

Zebras may be seen in the Mlilwane Wildlife Sanctuary and elsewhere throughout southern Africa.

You can walk, cycle or ride a horse through the reserve and there are night drives. Watching the hippos (one which hails from London Zoo) from the restaurant is great entertainment, especially at feeding time (3 pm daily). Bikes can be rented for E15 per hour (plus E10 for a guide), less for longer rides. Horse-riding is E25 per hour.

Entry to the reserve is E6 on weekdays, E8 on weekends and E10 on holiday weekends.

Places to Stay Camping and caravanning is E13 per person. There are self-contained thatched cottages from E65 per person sharing or E80 in the high season (single rates are E115/145). Beehive huts in the main camp cost from E50 per person sharing, E60 in the high season (single rates are E75/100). In the timber dorm in the *Beehive Village*, the cost (with bedding) is E32 per person sharing, or E40 in the high season (single rates are E40/70). There's a store here. During South African school holidays, especially around Christmas, Mlilwane is very busy. Phone ☎ 44541 to book accommodation.

Places to Stay

As well as the camp sites and huts at Mlilwane, the best budget accommodation in the valley, there is a range of other places.

Caravan Parks *Timbali Caravan Park* (☎ 61156) has sites and accommodation in rondavels and caravans. It's a well-run place and has a swimming pool and a restaurant (which is closed on Monday). Services offered include tent cleaning! There's a supermarket nearby.

Camp sites are E26/35 in the low/high season plus E7/9 per person, two-berth on-site caravans are E65/75 plus ·E10/15, rondavels are E75/90 plus E10/15 and four-bed rooms are E86/105 plus E10/15. During the high season (December, January and holidays) you have to pay for a minimum of three nights.

There's a sign four km out of Mbabane on the Ezulwini Valley road, near the hydro-electric pipeline, which reads 'Dlamini Camping & Accommodation, phone 43655'. When Jon and Jeff rang (for two editions of this book) no one was prepared to say that it no longer existed, but nor would they give any information about it. The tourist office was equally cagey. Maybe you'll have better luck. Sites E5 per person, maybe?

Hotels Off the main valley road, on a wooded hillside near Mlilwane is the *Mantenga Falls Hotel* (☎ 61049). It's an old place with only 10 rooms and its atmosphere is nothing like that of the glitzy valley strip. At E95/120 for singles/doubles it's good value. To get there, take the turn-off from the highway at Lobamba for Mlilwane Wildlife Sanctuary but turn right rather than left at the T-intersection. The hotel is 400 metres along.

The *Mgenule Motel* (☎ 61041) is the closest of the valley's hotels to Mbabane and one of the least expensive. Doubles cost from E121/132 on weekdays/weekends, rising to E154 in the high season, and a cottage for

four is E165/176, rising to E253 in the high season. There's a pool and a tandoori restaurant. *Smokey Mountain Village* (☎ 61291) is a small place, with self-contained chalets costing E198/248/330 for three/four/six people. Nearby is the *Happy Valley Motel* (☎ 61061), which has singles/doubles from E98/138.

The next step up on the price ladder is the *Yen Saan Hotel* (☎ 61051), which has only 34 rooms and a restaurant. It's designed in Chinese style, which is rather incongruous for the royal valley of the Kingdom of Swaziland; singles/doubles are E99/154.

At the top of the scale are three of the Sun group's hotels, the *Royal Swazi Sun & Casino* (☎ 61001), the *Lugogo Sun* (☎ 61101) – which is in the grounds of the Royal Swazi – and the *Ezulwini Sun* (☎ 61201), across the road from the other two. In this complex there are the usual international-hotel features such as pools, tennis courts and, at the Royal Swazi, a golf course and casino. Rooms at the Royal Swazi start at E360, singles/doubles at the Lugogo are E247/358 (weekends E297/397) and the Ezulwini has singles for E183, including breakfast.

Places to Eat

All three Sun hotels have restaurants – a buffet lunch which includes a selection from the carvery, salads and desserts is E35. At the top of Malagwane Hill, the Mountain Inn and Swazi Inn also have restaurants.

Next to Timbali Caravan Park is the *Calabash Continental*, open seven days, which specialises in German and Swiss cuisine. On the south side of the road into the Yen Saan is the *1st Horse Restaurant*, so called because it is next to Swaziland Tattersalls. The Mantenga Lodge and Smokey Mountain Village both serve pub grub for about E20.

Entertainment

The best-known nightspot in the area is the Why Not Disco at the Happy Valley Motel which charges E15 admission and E25 on weekends when there are shows. This place would have to rate as one of the great incongruities of Africa. It looks innocent enough from the outside but inside it is a veritable den of iniquity, a complete enigma in conservative Swaziland. The Why Not is a huge auditorium reserved for crowds ogling visiting European strippers, and the dimly lit If Not has strippers dancing along the bar. Questions have been asked in parliament about all this immorality and it might be stopped.

An interesting crowd gathers at the Lugogo Sun on Wednesday at about 10 pm, when catering staff and management of the nearby hotels gather to bitch. With luck you may meet the jocular, rotund 'mayor' of Ezulwini. On Friday and Saturday nights there's a live band at Gigi's in the Royal Swazi Sun.

Getting There & Away

Taxis from Mbabane cost at least E30, and from E50 if you want to go to the far end of the valley. At night you'll have to negotiate. During the day you could get on a Manzini-bound bus, but make sure that the driver knows that you want to get off in the valley. Even some non-express buses aren't keen on stopping.

MALKERNS

About seven km south of Lobamba there is a turn-off to the fertile Malkerns valley known for its arts and crafts outlets. At Tishweshwe Crafts (☎/fax 83336), one km from the turn-off, lutindzi grass is woven into baskets and mats. Swazi Candles is based near Malkerns, and Baobab Batik is near Nyanza Stables on the Manzini road.

The best restaurant in the region is *Malandela's*, next to Tishweshwe Crafts. Good old-fashioned meals such as pork pie, fresh carrots, boiled potatoes and broccoli, and pecan pie cost about E32. The prawn nights are very popular and it is not unusual for 100 dozen to be consumed in an evening. Several canned English beers are available. Pete Thorne, the owner, is a dab hand at shove-halfpenny (an English pub game).

MANZINI

Manzini is now the country's industrial centre, but between 1890 and 1902 it was the combined administrative centre for the squabbling British and Boers, and during the Anglo-Boer War a renegade Boer commando burnt it down. Downtown Manzini isn't large but it feels like a different country from easy-going rural Swaziland. There are reckless drivers, city slickers and a hint of menace. Be careful walking around at night.

The market on Thursday and Friday mornings has been highly recommended. Get there at dawn if possible, as the rural people bring in their handicrafts to sell to retailers.

From late August, an annual trade fair where handicrafts are on display is held at the showgrounds.

Places to Stay

About seven km north of Manzini on the Mbabane road, just past Matsapha, *Jimmy's Bar & Paradise Caravan Park* (☎ 84935) is a reasonable place and there's a lively bar. Tent sites cost E5, van sites are E15 and there are rondavels for E45 a double.

There's nothing very cheap in the way of hotels in Manzini, but seven km out on the highway, opposite Jimmy's, is a turn-off for a *rest camp* where you can rent 'cottages' for E40. It's pleasant enough but pretty basic.

The *Prince Velebantfu Hotel* (☎ 52663), on the Mbabane road near the showgrounds, is the cheapest hotel in town, although it isn't great value at E82.50/96 a single/double. This hotel may be closing down.

The *Mozambique Hotel* (☎ 52489) is on Mahleko St. It has a good dingy bar and a popular restaurant. The distinctly average double rooms with common bath are E82.50, and with own bath they are E132. It's not great value, but the place does have a lively buzz.

The most expensive hotel is the *New George* (☎ 52061) on Ngwane St, once a colonial hotel but now almost totally rebuilt. There is a pool, restaurants and all of the

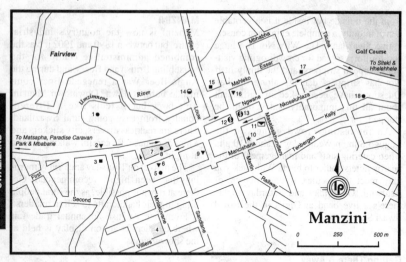

Manzini

PLACES TO STAY

3   Prince Velebantfu Hotel
15 Mozambique Hotel
17 New George Hotel

PLACES TO EAT

2   Tinka Restaurant
4   The Hub (Fontana di Trevi Pizzeria,
    Nando's & Sailor Sam Restaurants)
6   Alain's Restaurant
9   Cheap Restaurants
16 Gil Vincente Restaurant

OTHER

1   Showgrounds
5   Market
7   Bhunu Mall
8   Library
10 Police Station
11 Post Office
12 Barclays Bank
13 Standard Bank
14 Bus & Minibus Park
18 Manzini Club

mod-cons except efficient staff. Economy
singles/doubles/triples cost from E125/
175/230 with breakfast; luxury rooms are
E150/210/275 and family rooms, E345.

Places to Eat

The *café* at the bus station has cheap local
food. In town, on Louw St, there are a few
basic local food outlets, open during the day.
Across the road from the Prince Velebantfu
is the *Tinka*, a halaal restaurant with a limited
menu but OK food; curries cost from E15.
It's open between 10 am and 10 pm daily.

In The Hub, on the corner of Villiers and
Mnlakuvane Sts, are the *Fontana di Trevi
Pizzeria*, *Nando's* and *Sailor Sam*. The latter,
an inexpensive, tackily furnished place, has
traditional Pakistani and tandoori food as
well as seafood takeaways – it is also reputed
to have great caramel-dip ice creams.

There's a Portuguese restaurant at the
Mozambique Motel, and a block away is
another, the *Gil Vincente* on Martin St.

Eight km east of Manzini, at Hhelehhele,
is the *Gobble & Gossip*, a fun place where
there is always great braai food and, occasionally, live music. For a wilder night out,
venture into Jimmy's Bar to trade insults,
hurl abuse and swill beer in an oft-successful
attempt at self-imposed oblivion.

Getting There & Away

A non-share taxi to Matsapha International

BIG GAME PARKS OF SWAZILAND

BIG GAME PARKS OF SWAZILAND

JEFF WILLIAMS

Top: Guided horse-rides at Mililwane Wildlife Sanctuary, Swaziland
Middle: White-water rafting on the Great Usutu River in the kingdom of Swaziland
Bottom: Elephants at close range, Mkhaya Game Reserve, Swaziland

MICKY REILLY

JEFF WILLIAMS

BIG GAME PARKS OF SWAZILAND

JEFF WILLIAMS

A	
B	
C	D

A: 'The Regiment' – white rhino at Mkhaya Game Reserve, Swaziland
B: Swazi handicraft stall outside Royal Swazi Sun Hotel, Ezulwini Valley, Swaziland
C: Traditional singing & dancing at Hlane Royal National Park, Swaziland
D: Elephant up close, Mkhaya Game Reserve, Swaziland

Airport costs around E50. The main bus and minibus taxi park is at the north end of Louw St. Buses run up the Ezulwini Valley to Mbabane for E1.30.

Transtate runs from here to South Africa via either Mbabane or Hlathikulu and Nhlangano. See the Getting There & Away chapter.

NGWENYA

This town (the name means 'The Crocodile') is five km east of the Oshoek border post on the road to Mbabane. The **Ngwenya Glass factory** is located there. Recycled glass is used to create African animals and birds as well as vases and tableware. The showroom is open daily from 9 am to 4 pm. One km further up the road is **Endlotane Studios** (☎ 24149). Tapestries from here are hung in galleries throughout the world; the studio is open daily from 8 am to 5 pm.

There is accommodation at *Hawana Park* (☎ 44522), near the Hawana Dam, to the east of the Piggs Peak road and not far from the Ngwenya-Mbabane road junction. A tent site is E15, a caravan site (four persons) is E50 and a self-contained four-bed chalet E175.

MALOLOTJA NATURE RESERVE

This reserve, in the hilly north-west, has mainly antelope species. Over 280 species of bird have been recorded in the reserve, a number of them rare. Southern bald-ibis nest on the cliffs near the Malolotja Falls and there are also nesting blue swallows (*Hirundo atrocaerulea*) in the reserve. Wild-flowers and rare plants are also main attractions of the reserve. Several of the plants are found only in this part of Africa, including the woolly, Barberton and Kaapsche-hoop cycads. The Komati River cuts a gorge through the park and continues east in a series of falls and rapids until it meets the lowveld.

Ngwenya has one of the world's oldest known mines, dating from 41,000 BC. The mine can be visited by vehicle but a ranger must accompany you; arrange one day in advance.

Entry to the reserve is E10 per person and E5 per vehicle. Camping costs E16.50 at the established sites and E11 on the trails. There are fully equipped cabins sleeping six for E121, or E165 on weekends. Book through the National Trust Commission (☎ 61178) in the National Museum, Lobamba.

The park entrance is about 35 km from Mbabane, on the Piggs Peak road; the gates are open from 6 am to 6 pm in summer, and from 6.30 am in winter.

Hiking Trails

The reserve is a true wilderness area, rugged and in the most part unspoilt. There are a number of hiking trails, ranging from short day walks to a week-long trail which extends from Ngwenya in the south to Mgwayiza Range in the north.

For the extended trails a free permit and map must be obtained from the reserve office. You need to bring all your own food and a camp stove as fires are not permitted outside the base camp. Shorter walks include Komati viewpoint, the Upper Majolomba River, and Malolotja Falls and Vlei (swamp).

MANKAYANE

This small town south-west of Manzini is surrounded by hills and pine plantations. The *Inyatsi Inn* (☎ 88244) has single/double rooms without bath for about E40/60, and doubles with bathroom for E70.

NHLANGANO

'Nhlangano' means 'meeting place', and it's here that King Sobhuza II met England's King George VI in 1947. In 1961, British prime minister Harold Macmillan met Swazi leaders here on his fact-finding visit to South Africa which eventually led to Swaziland's independence.

Nhlangano is the closest town to the border crossing at Mahamba, but unless you want to visit the *Nhlangano Sun* casino (☎ 78211), four km out of town (with single/double rooms for E169/245 plus 10%), there's no reason to come here. The run-down *Phoenix Hotel* (☎ 78488) is poor value at E185 per person, including breakfast.

SWAZILAND

HLATHIKULU

The basic *Assegi Inn* (☎ 53529) is good value at E80 a double (no breakfast). Hlathikulu is the terminus for Transtate's bus running from Jo'burg via Ermelo, Piet Retief and Nhlangano (weekdays only).

MKHAYA GAME RESERVE

Mkhaya (☎ 44541, fax 40957) is a private reserve off the Manzini-Big Bend road, near the hamlet of Phuzumoya. It is run by the people who run Mlilwane Wildlife Sanctuary near Mbabane, and the same hands-on commitment to conservation is evident.

The reserve is on rehabilitated cattle farms, although the area had always been popular with hunters for its game. Mkhaya takes its name from the mkhaya tree (or knobthorn, *Acacia nigrescens*), which abounds on the reserve. Mkhayas grow only on good land, and are valued not only for their fruit, from which Swazis brew beer, but for the insect and birdlife they support.

Although small, Mkhaya has a wide range of animals, including white and black rhinos, roan and sable antelopes and elephants. The reserve's boast is that you're more likely to meet a black rhino in the wild here than anywhere else in Africa. There are also herds of the indigenous and rare Nguni cattle which make the reserve economically self-supporting.

Day tours are available (E120 per adult, including lunch and a game drive) and night drives for E180. Mkhaya is worth staying at for at least a night. At E240 per person

sharing in safari tents (with shared facilities), and including three meals, game-viewing drives and walks, it's better value than many of the private reserves near Kruger. Self-contained safari tents are E305 per person; the single rate is E410. There is also *Nkonjane* (the 'Swallow's Nest'), a luxurious stone cottage, at E560/320 per person single/sharing.

If accommodation described as 'luxury' puts you off, don't worry, it's better than that – *Stone Camp*, the safari-tent option, is like a comfortable 19th-century hunting camp rather than a hotel sitting incongruously in the wilderness. The floors of the tents are on sand, allowing you to see ant trails and the tracks of the small animals which come in at night. The food is also simple and good, with traditional methods and ingredients used.

Note that you can't visit without having booked, and even then you can't drive in alone; you'll be met at Phuzumoya at a specified pick-up time.

White-Water Rafting

One of the attractions of Mkhaya is white-water rafting on the Great Usutu River. The river is usually sluggish and quite tame but near the reserve it passes through the narrow Bulungu Gorge which separates the Mabukabuka and Bulunga mountains, generating rapids. At one stage a 10-metre waterfall has to be portaged. The second half of the day is a sedate trip through scenic country with glimpses of the 'flat dogs' (crocodiles) sunning on the river bank.

Nguni Cattle

Mkhaya started out in 1979 as a stud-breeding programme for the indigenous Nguni cattle. The Nguni is an old breed, and centuries of natural selection have made it heat tolerant, disease immune, self-sufficient and, importantly, tick-resistant. It was and still is highly prized by the Nguni tribes who led these cattle south during the Great Migration (difaqane). The Zulu king has a herd of Royal White Nguni (*Inyonikayiphumuli*) near Ulundi in KwaZulu/Natal.

Nguni are small and were interbred with larger foreign breeds to increase beef production. This led to a degeneration of their gene pool, hence the attempts at Mkhaya to preserve their purity. When supplemental feeding of other breeds became expensive the Nguni came into its own as an effective beef producer and they are now highly valued. Conservation activities at Mkhaya are funded entirely by the sale of these cattle. ■

The trips, in either eight-person or two-person 'crocodile rafts', take a full day and cost E156 per person (minimum of four people or E624), all equipment and lunch included. Phone ☎ 45006 (61891 after hours) for more information.

MHLAMBANYATI

This town, its name meaning 'watering place of the buffaloes', is 27 km from Mbabane. The popular *Foresters Arms* (☎ 74177, fax 74051) has rooms for E150 per person. It is likely to be full of locals on the weekend as they drift up here from Mbabane for home-made bread and Sunday lunch. You can go sailing, windsurfing or canoeing on the nearby **Lupholho Dam** on the Mbabane road, or relax in the Foresters' library.

Six km from Mhlambanyati, on the road to Mbabane, is *Meikles Mount* (☎ 74110), a great B&B hideaway; singles/doubles are E85/120 (more in the high season). Horse-riding is available here and at the Foresters Arms.

BIG BEND

Big Bend is a neat sugar town on, not surprisingly, a big bend in the Lusutfu River. It's quite a picturesque spot.

The *New Bend Inn* (☎ 36111), on a hill just south of town and with good views across the river, is good value at E77/110 for singles/doubles, without breakfast. There's a restaurant and a pleasant outdoor bar overlooking Big Bend. There's also a friendly workers' bar with a lively disco on Friday and Saturday. The *Riverside Motel* (☎ 36012, fax 36032) is a 10-minute drive south of Big Bend on the road to KwaZulu/Natal; singles/doubles with breakfast are E95/110.

One of Swaziland's best restaurants, the *Lebombo Lobster*, is a few km south of Big Bend. 'Highway hen' (spatchcock cooked with peri peri) is E22, tasty steak rolls are E6 each and the seafood includes crayfish.

Getting There & Away

About four buses a day run south to the South African border at Lavumisa for E5. Coming

the other way they continue on to Manzini for E6.50.

SITEKI

This trading town isn't really on the way to anywhere anymore, but it's a nice enough little place and a bit cooler up here on the Lebombo mountains than down on the plains. There are good views on the steep road up here. The town is sometimes still known by its colonial-era name of Stegi.

The town was originally named when Mbandzeni (great grandfather of the present king) gave his frontier troops permission to marry – Siteki means 'marrying place'. Later, the area was the haunt of highwaymen such as Robert MacNab and Charles Dupont.

The *Siteki Hotel* (☎ 34126) has dinner, bed and breakfast for E77 per person, and the host, Graham Duke, knows lots about the surrounding area.

Several express buses run between Manzini and Siteki daily for about E6. The local bus company is the reliable Tit For Tat Bus Service (☎ 34304).

NORTH-EAST SWAZILAND

The north-eastern corner of Swaziland is a major sugar-producing area. It's hot and in the arid foothills of the Lebombo range the scenery approaches what most people think of when you say 'Africa'.

The company towns of Tshaneni, Mhlume, Tambankulu and Simunye are the main population centres. Simunye is a show-piece and is worth a look. It describes itself as a village, but that's being coy. It's a neat, lush town with excellent facilities, a bit like Australia's Darwin on a manageable scale.

The Sand River Reservoir, west of Tshaneni, has no facilities, but you can camp there. Don't swim in the water or drink it untreated, as it's full of bilharzia.

Places to Stay

Unfortunately, the only hotel accommodation in the area is at Tshaneni (pronounced Jan-*ay*-ni), probably the least attractive of the towns. The run-down *Impala Arms* (☎ 31244) has singles/doubles for E75/81, with breakfast, but many Swazis would rather push on further than stay in this town.

At Simunye there is the *Tambankulu Recreational Club* (☎ 38111, fax 38213), off the Tshaneni road about eight km west of the junction with the Manzini-Lomahasha highway. It has rooms for E30 per person and a restaurant. Enquire here about accommodation in the Mbuluzi Nature Reserve.

Getting There & Away
Regular buses run from Manzini. There are fewer on the run across to Piggs Peak, mainly on dirt roads.

HLANE ROYAL NATIONAL PARK
This park (its name means 'wilderness') in the north-east is near the former Royal hunting grounds. There are white rhinos and many antelope species. Elephant and lion have been reintroduced but they are as yet kept in an enclosure. There are no walking trails. The park entrance is about four km from Simunye. For more information get a copy of *The History & Significance of Hlane Royal National Park*, published in 1994 to celebrate the return of lions to the kingdom.

Entry to the reserve is E6 on weekdays, E8 on weekends, and E10 on holiday weekends and all weekends in the high season. Camping and caravanning costs from E15

per person. There are thatched huts at *Ndlovu Rest Camp* from E55 per person sharing or E65 in the high season (single rates are E90/115), and self-contained huts at *Bhubesi Rest Camp* from E65 per person sharing and E80 in the high season (single rates are E115/145) (☎ 44541 or fax 40957 to make bookings).

MLAWULA NATURE RESERVE
In the east, taking in both plains and the Lebombo mountains, this 18,000-hectare reserve is in harsh but beautiful country. Walking trails are being established. The reserve has antelope species and there are shy hyenas in remote areas. Aquatic dangers include both bilharzia and crocodiles. Watch out for ticks, too. Snakes include the deadly trio of black mamba, puff adder and spitting cobra.

Entry to the reserve costs E10. Camping is E16.50, or E11 on the hiking trails. There is also tent accommodation, from E44 on weekdays and E66 on the weekend. Phone 38885 or 61179 for bookings, or see the National Trust Commission in the National Museum, Lobamba. The reserve's entrance is about 10 km north of Simunye.

PIGGS PEAK
In hilly country in the north-western corner

Rhino Wars

In 1965 white rhino were re-established in the kingdom after an absence of 70 years and since then there has been an ongoing battle to protect them from poachers. At the forefront of this battle has been Ted Reilly and a band of dedicated, hand-picked rangers.

This defence has not been easy as the poachers have received hefty financial backing from Taiwanese interests. Poaching escalated in the late '80s and there were determined efforts to change the laws in Swaziland relating to rhino poaching. Rhinos were dehorned and confined to their enclosures for their own protection. After Hlane was attacked in January 1992 by poachers armed with AK47s, the rangers armed themselves. With rhinos dehorned at Hlane, the poachers shifted to Mkhaya. The battle commenced.

In April 1992 there was a shoot-out between rangers and poachers at Mkhaya, and some poachers were captured. Not long after there was a big shoot-out at Big Bend and two poachers were killed.

The last rhino (the majestic bull Mthondvo) was killed for horn in December 1992 while the Swazi courts still agonised over action relating to the Big Bend incident. The young king, Mswati III, intervened on behalf of Reilly's rangers and poaching declined dramatically. The rangers still wait with their rifles at the ready! You can help – your presence at any one of the parks which are home to the Big Five assists in rhino conservation. ■

of the country, this small town is the centre of the logging industry and there are huge pine plantations in the area.

The town was named after a prospector who found gold here in 1884. There was a rush, but only one deep mine ever made much money and it has been closed for 35 years. West of Piggs Peak is **Bulembu** and the Havelock asbestos mine. The aerial cableway carries the asbestos to Barberton, 20 km away in South Africa.

As well as its scenery, including the **Phophonyane Falls** about eight km north of town, this area is known for its handicrafts. At the Highlands Inn in Piggs Peak, **Tintsaba Crafts** displays a good range; there are several other craft centres in this district.

Places to Stay & Eat

The only place to stay in town is the *Highlands Inn* (☎ 71144), about a km south of the town centre on the main road. Singles/ doubles cost from E80/154 plus tax, including breakfast. The rooms are clean and nice enough, but it isn't great value. There's a pleasant garden area with views.

In the area is one of the nicest places to stay in Swaziland. *Phophonyane Lodge* (☎ 71319, fax 44246) is in its own nature reserve of lush indigenous forest on the Phophonyane River, where you can swim in rock pools. There is a system of walking trails. With a maximum of just over 20 guests in three separate locations, this is a quiet and friendly place. This isn't a malarial area but there are plenty of mosquitoes in summer, so bring repellent.

Accommodation is in cottages from E140 or tents from E90; both rates are per person. On weekends there's a minimum stay of two nights and prices rise during holidays. There are cooking facilities or you can eat in the tiny restaurant. Day visitors are charged E9.

To get there head north-east from Piggs Peak towards the Piggs Peak casino, 10 km away, and take the signposted turn-off about one km before the casino (minibus taxis will drop you off here). Continue down this road until you cross a bridge over a waterfall and the turn-off to the lodge is about 500 metres further on, to the right. You can usually arrange to be collected from Piggs Peak.

About 10 km north-east of Piggs Peak, on the road to the Jeppe's Reef border with South Africa, is the up-market *Protea Piggs Peak Hotel* (☎ 71104). Their midweek specials (singles/doubles are E325/395) can make it affordable if slot machines are what you're after.

Getting There & Away

Heading across to the north-east of the country the roads are mainly dirt, but they're in reasonable condition. If you're driving, beware of buses coming the other way (running between Piggs Peak and Tshaneni) – they speed and hog the gravel road.

There are a few non-shared taxis in Piggs Peak. To the casino the fare is about E15; to Mbabane it's E100. The bus and minibus taxi rank is next to the market at the top end of the main street. There's an express bus to Mbabane for E6.

Appendix I – South African English

ablutions block – a building containing a toilet, bath, shower, and washing facilities

bakkie – utility, pick-up
bazaar – market
braaivleis or braai – a barbecue, or one who specialises in the consumption of large quantities of meat and beer
boerewors – spicy sausages, often sold by street vendors, and consumed at a *braai*
buck – antelope

cassper – armoured vehicle, or hippo
couple – for two of anything

dagga or zol – marijuana
dam – reservoir

eh – all purpose ending to sentences

hippo – armoured vehicle, or *cassper*
howzit? – all purpose greeting

izit? – rhetorical question meaning 'Is that so?', or 'Really?'

jol – party, both verb and noun
just now – indeterminate future, but reasonably imminent

kaffir – black person (derogatory – do not use)

koppie – little hill

lekker – very nice
location – black township

mielie – corn

now-now – immediately

oke – bloke

pronking – strange bouncing leaping by antelope, especially springboks

robot – traffic light

shame – What a pity!
shebeen – drinking establishment in black townships, often illegal
sjambok – whip

tekkie – gym shoe
township – black residential area, usually hidden on outskirts of white town; may not be shown on maps despite massive size
toy toy – jubilant dance
tsotsi – hoodlum

Van der Merwe – archetypal Boer country bumpkin and butt of English jokes

yah well no fine – yes-no-maybe-perhaps

Appendix II – Air Travel Glossary

Apex Apex, or 'advance purchase excursion', is a discounted ticket which must be paid for in advance. There are penalties if you wish to change it.

Baggage Allowance This will be written on your ticket: usually one 20 kg item to go in the hold, plus one item of hand luggage.

Bucket Shop An unbonded travel agency specialising in discounted airline tickets.

Bumped Just because you have a confirmed seat doesn't mean you're going to get on the plane – see *Overbooking*.

Cancellation Penalties If you have to cancel or change an Apex ticket there are often heavy penalties involved. Insurance can sometimes be taken out against these penalties. Some airlines impose penalties on regular tickets as well, particularly against 'no show' passengers.

Check In Airlines ask you to check in a certain time ahead of the flight departure (usually 2 hours on international flights). If you fail to check in on time and the flight is overbooked the airline can cancel your booking and give your seat to somebody else.

Confirmation Having a ticket written out with the flight and date you want doesn't mean you have a seat until the agent has checked with the airline that your status is 'OK' or confirmed. Meanwhile you could just be 'on request'.

Discounted Tickets There are two types of discounted fares – officially discounted (see *Promotional Fares*) and unofficially discounted. The lowest prices often impose drawbacks like flying with unpopular airlines, inconvenient schedules, or unpleasant routes and connections. A discounted ticket can save you things other than money – you may be able to pay Apex prices without the associated Apex advance booking and other requirements. Discounted tickets only exist where there is fierce competition.

Economy-Class Tickets Buying a normal economy-class ticket is usually not the most economical way to go, though they do give you maximum flexibility and the tickets are valid for 12 months. Also, if you don't use them, they are fully refundable, as are unused sectors of a multiple ticket.

Full Fares Airlines traditionally offer first class (coded F), business class (coded J) and economy class (coded Y) tickets. These days there are so many promotional and discounted fares available from the regular economy class that few passengers pay full economy fare.

Lost Tickets If you lose your airline ticket an airline will usually treat it like a travellers' cheque and, after inquiries, issue you with another one. Legally, however, an airline is entitled to treat it like cash and if you lose it then it's gone forever. Take good care of your tickets.

No Shows No shows are passengers who fail to show up for their flight, sometimes due to unexpected delays or disasters, sometimes due to simply forgetting, sometimes because they made more than one booking and didn't bother to cancel the one they didn't want. Full-fare passengers who fail to turn up are sometimes entitled to travel on a later flight. The rest of us are penalised (see *Cancellation Penalties*).

On Request An unconfirmed booking for a flight, see *Confirmation*.

Open Jaws A return ticket where you fly out to one place but return from another. If available this can save you backtracking to your arrival point.

Overbooking Airlines hate to fly empty seats and since every flight has some passengers who fail to show up (see *No Shows*) airlines often book more passengers than they have seats. Usually the excess passengers balance those who fail to show up but occasionally somebody gets bumped. If this happens guess who it is most likely to be? The passengers who check in late.

Promotional Fares Officially discounted fares like Apex fares which are available from travel agencies or direct from the airline

Reconfirmation At least 72 hours prior to departure time of an onward or return flight you must contact the airline and 'reconfirm' that you intend to be on the flight. If you don't do this the airline can delete your name from the passenger list and you could lose your seat. You don't have to reconfirm the first flight on your itinerary or if your stopover is less than 72 hours. It doesn't hurt to reconfirm more than once.

Restrictions Discounted tickets often have various restrictions on them – advance purchase is the most usual one (see *Apex*). Others are restrictions on the minimum and maximum period you must be away, such as a minimum of 14 days or a maximum of one year. See *Cancellation Penalties*.

Round-the-World Tickets The official airline RTW tickets are usually put together by a combination of two airlines, and permit you to fly anywhere you want on their route systems so long as you do not backtrack. Other restrictions are that you (usually) must book the first sector in advance and cancellation penalties then apply. There may be restrictions on how many stops you are permitted and usually the tickets are valid for 90 days up to a year.

An alternative type of RTW ticket is one put together by a travel agent using a combination of discounted tickets. These can be cheaper than an airline RTW ticket but the choice of routes may be quite limited.

Standby A discounted ticket where you only fly if there is a seat free at the last moment. Standby fares are usually only available on domestic routes.

Student Discounts Some airlines offer student card holders 20 to 25% discounts on their tickets. The same often applies to anyone under the age of 26. These discounts are generally only available on ordinary economy-class fares. You wouldn't get one, for instance, on an *APEX* or a *RTW* ticket since these are already discounted.

Tickets Out An entry requirement for many countries is that you have an onward or return ticket, in other words, a ticket out of the country. If you're not sure what you intend to do next, the easiest solution is to buy the cheapest onward ticket to a neighbouring country or a ticket from a reliable airline which can later be refunded if you do not use it.

Transferred Tickets Airline tickets cannot be transferred from one person to another. Travellers sometimes try to sell the return half of their ticket, but officials can ask you to prove that you are the person named on the ticket. This is unlikely to happen on domestic flights but on an international flight tickets may be compared with passports.

Travel Agencies Travel agencies vary widely and you should ensure you use one that suits your needs. Some simply handle tours while full-service agencies handle everything from tours and tickets to car rental and hotel bookings. A good one will do all these things and can save you a lot of money but if all you want is a ticket at the lowest possible price, then you really need an agency specialising in discounted tickets. A discounted ticket agency, however, may not be useful for other things, like hotel bookings.

Travel Periods Some officially discounted fares, Apex fares in particular, vary with the time of year. There is often a low (off-peak) season and a high (peak) season. Sometimes there's an intermediate or shoulder season as well. At peak times, when everyone wants to fly, not only will the officially discounted fares be higher but so will unofficially discounted fares or there may simply be no discounted tickets available. Usually the fare depends on your outward flight – if you depart in the high season and return in the low season, you pay the high-season fare.

Index

TEXT

NATIONAL PARKS & WILDLIFE RESERVES

THANKS

Thanks to the many travellers who wrote in with comments about our last edition, and with tips and comments about South Africa, Lesotho and Swaziland (apoplogies if we've misspelt your name):

Aniko Absolon (A), Jonathon Aldons, Mrs Bridgit Allan, Mark Andrews, Stephen Atkinson, Jack Babbage (Aus), Chris Baker (UK), Stephen Barnard (UK), Peter Barrett, Roseanne Beets (NZ), R Beikel (Nl), Heidi Bergh, Catharine Berwick (UK), Renett Bester, Rene Bester, Dick & Regina Billiet, Chris Bolsmann, Pat Bond, Richard Bourne (UK), S Braiden & J Eckert (D), Leanne Brandis (Aus), M & D Brewster (USA), Astrid Burger (D), Neal Burns, Murray Buttner (USA), Melissa Button (UK), Sharon Caldwell, David Carssan (Aus), Samuel Chinyama, Doris Choy Shu Fan (HK), Mrs C A Cieslak (UK), Judith E Collins (USA), Dr C Cooper (UK), Meg Cooper-Lewis, Angela Costain (Aus), John & Elizabeth Cox (UK), Yvonne Cullen (UK), Subrata Das (Ind), David & Mariana, Fred Davis (SA), Gary De Castro, A F Delvilani, J L & R H Denholm (UK), Carolyn Dickenson (UK), Ben Dipple (UK), Marshall J Doke Jnr (USA), Jon Douglas (Aus), Des & Lea Downing, Allan Dunn (UK), Jon Edgall (UK), Ellen & Marc (Nl), Steve Ellis, Carine Elmiger (CH), Herman Eppink (Nl), John & Jenny Evans (SA), Peter Everett (UK), Chris Fenner (United Kingdom), John C Foitzik (Aus), Dr E Foley (UK), John Fowkes (UK), Lynda & Brian Fraser (C), Sharon Freed (Aus), David Fregona (I), Nicholaas Fry (HK), Elke Ganter (D), Tom Gehrels, Gus Gerke, Charlie Gillett (UK), Stephen Glasse (UK), Emma Golding (UK), Fred Gooseh, Traci Gregory, Brian Grodsky (USA), E J Grove (UK), Gerald Guy (Aus), Robert Haarburger, Mel & Sue Hails (UK), Murray Hamblin (C), Joanne Harrison-Gross (D), Debbie Hastie, Jessamie Hawkins, E Hawthorne (Aus), Christoph Hebling (D), Allian Hely-Hutchinson, Anette Heutschel (D), Ken Hill, Tim Hill (Germany), Linda Hoeben (B), Rob Hoens (SA), H C Holman (UK), Moggs & John Holmes, Tim Hopwood, Dennis Horn (Swaziland), Elisabeth Horstman (Nl), Brian Houghton (C), Mr &

Mrs G J Hunt (UK), William Huot (USA), Susan Huxter, Matthew Johnson, Hugh & Maire Jones (C), Jake & Susie Jones (UK), Melvin Jones (UK), D T & M R Knight (UK), Eoin Langan (UK), Paul Lee, Mr D Lee-Renwick (UK), Margaret LeRick (UK), Arjam Lieuaart, Angelina Limmer (D), Nancy Lloyd (UK), Frasers Lodges, U Loeffler (D), Paul Loynes (UK), Christian Lund (D), Bob Manning (UK), Lady Mary Mansel Lewis (UK), Margie & Peter, J & P McDonnell, Brent Meersman, Judy & Bruce Meeser, Wim Minnaard (Nl), A Moller (UK), Sarah Morris (UK), Rob Moss (UK), C N Muller, Klaus Namer (Germany), Elmar Neethling, Theuna Nel, Martin Nielsen (D), Gilly Notten, M O'Hagan Ward, Ian Oliver (USA), Ted Pauw (UK), Alan Pearey, John Petts, John, Uwe Pfaff, Mrs M Reinders, Paul Reintjes (Nl), Peter & Hilda Retief, Gary Richards (Aus), Phil Richardson (UK), Gail Robinson, Margaret Roestorf (SA), G A Rossi, Dave & Julie Rushworth, Anne Kirsti Ryntveit (N), Andreas Sandler (D), Mrs Schepers (Nl), Thomas Schuster (D), A Schwartz (UK), Graziano Scotto (I), Clive Serrurier, Shaun & Breeda (Irl), Carl Shoolman, Michael Siassi (D), Arun Singh (Ind), Judy Slabbert, Miss J Smit, Nigel Spencer (UK), Tom Stafiej & Arek (Poland), S Staob, Ao Talboom (Nl), Alison Thomas (HK), Robin Thomson, Hector Timmers (Nl), Melvin Tyers (UK), Tyson (USA), Amanda Une (S), Schleissheimer & Inge Urban (D), John Valentine (USA), Conne Van Der Hurst (NZ), J H R Van der Velden, Gert Van Der Westhuisen, Mignon Van Wyk, Carl A Wagner, Kath Wakeford (Aus), Deborah Walee (Aus), Jill Walker (USA), Belton Wall (A), Kate Wall (NZ), Kirstin Walla, Angus Wallace (UK), Rod & Nikki Ward (UK), Deidre Watson (UK), Karen Weber (USA), Trudie Wegner, Britta Weidhase, Paul Wescott (UK), Bettina Wessel (D), Robyn Wilkin (Aus), D O Williams, Adrian Windisch (UK), Barbara Woolford (ME), Doug Wright and Jane F Wright (F).

A – Austria, Aus – Australia, C – Canada, CH – Switzerland, D – Germany, HK – Hong Kong, Ind – India, Irl – Ireland, Nl – The Netherlands, NZ – New Zealand, SA – South Africa, S – Sweden, UK – United Kingdom, USA – United States of America

LONELY PLANET JOURNEYS

JOURNEYS is a unique collection of travellers' tales – published by the company that understands travel better than anyone else. It is a series for anyone who has ever experienced – or dreamed of – the magical moment when they encountered a strange culture or saw a place for the first time. They are tales to read while you're planning a trip, while you're on the road or while you're in an armchair, in front of a fire.

JOURNEYS books will catch the spirit of a place, illuminate a culture, recount a crazy adventure, or introduce a fascinating way of life. They will always entertain, and always enrich the experience of travel.

ISLANDS IN THE CLOUDS
Travels in the Highlands of New Guinea
Isabella Tree

This is the fascinating account of a journey to the remote and beautiful Highlands of Papua New Guinea and Irian Jaya. The author travels with a PNG Highlander who introduces her to his intriguing and complex world. *Islands in the Clouds* is a thoughtful, moving book, full of insights into a region that is rarely noticed by the rest of the world.

'One of the most accomplished travel writers to appear on the horizon for many years ... the dialogue is brilliant' – Eric Newby

LOST JAPAN
Alex Kerr

Lost Japan draws on the author's personal experiences of Japan over a period of 30 years. Alex Kerr takes his readers on a backstage tour: friendships with Kabuki actors, buying and selling art, studying calligraphy, exploring rarely visited temples and shrines ... The Japanese edition of this book was awarded the 1994 Shincho Gakugei Literature Prize for the best work of non-fiction.

'This deeply personal witness to Japan's wilful loss of its traditional culture is at the same time an immensely valuable evaluation of just what that culture was'
– Donald Richie of the Japan Times

THE GATES OF DAMASCUS
Lieve Joris
Translated by Sam Garrett

This best-selling book is a beautifully drawn portrait of day-to-day life in modern Syria. Through her intimate contact with local people, Lieve Joris draws us into the fascinating world that lies behind the gates of Damascus.

'A brilliant book ... Not since Naguib Mahfouz has the everyday life of the modern Arab world been so intimately described' – William Dalrymple

SEAN & DAVID'S LONG DRIVE
Sean Condon

Sean and David are young townies who have rarely strayed beyond city limits. One day, for no good reason, they set out to discover their homeland, and what follows is a wildly entertaining adventure that covers half of Australia. Sean Condon has written a hilarious, offbeat road book that mixes sharp insights with deadpan humour and outright lies.

'Funny, pithy, kitsch and surreal ... This book will do for Australia what Chernobyl did for Kiev, but hey you'll laugh as the stereotypes go boom' – Andrew Tuck, Time Out

LONELY PLANET TRAVEL ATLASES

Lonely Planet has long been famous for the number and quality of its guidebook maps. Now we've gone one step further and in conjunction with Steinhart Katzir Publishers produced a handy companion series: Lonely Planet travel atlases – maps of a country produced in book form.

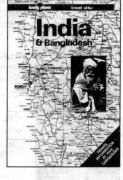

Unlike other maps, which look good but lead travellers astray, our travel atlases have been researched on the road by Lonely Planet's experienced team of writers. All details are carefully checked to ensure the atlas corresponds with the equivalent Lonely Planet guidebook.

The handy atlas format means no holes, wrinkles, torn sections or constant folding and unfolding. These atlases can survive long periods on the road, unlike cumbersome fold-out maps. The comprehensive index ensures easy reference.

- full-colour throughout
- maps researched and checked by Lonely Planet authors
- place names correspond with Lonely Planet guidebooks
  – no confusing spelling differences
- legend and travelling information in English, French, German, Japanese and Spanish
- size: 230 x 160 mm

Available now:
Thailand; India & Bangladesh; Vietnam; Zimbabwe, Botswana & Namibia

Coming soon:
Chile; Egypt; Israel; Laos; Turkey

LONELY PLANET TV SERIES & VIDEOS

Lonely Planet travel guides have been brought to life on television screens around the world. Like our guides, the programmes are based on the joy of independent travel, and look honestly at some of the most exciting, picturesque and frustrating places in the world. Each show is presented by one of three travellers from Australia, England or the USA and combines an innovative mixture of video, Super-8 film, atmospheric soundscapes and original music.

Videos of each episode – containing additional footage not shown on television – are available from good book and video shops, but the availability of individual videos varies with regional screening schedules.

Video destinations include: Alaska; Australia (Southeast); Brazil; Ecuador & the Galápagos Islands; Indonesia; Israel & the Sinai Desert; Japan; La Ruta Maya (Yucatán, Guatemala & Belize); Morocco; North India (Varanasi to the Himalaya); Pacific Islands; Vietnam; Zimbabwe, Botswana & Namibia.

Coming soon: The Arctic (Norway & Finland); Baja California; Chile & Easter Island; China (Southeast); Costa Rica; East Africa (Tanzania & Zanzibar); Great Barrier Reef (Australia); Jamaica; Papua New Guinea; the Rockies (USA); Syria & Jordan; Turkey.

The Lonely Planet TV series is produced by:
Pilot Productions
Duke of Sussex Studios
44 Uxbridge St
London W8 7TG UK

Lonely Planet videos are distributed by:
IVN Communications Inc
2246 Camino Ramon
California 94583, USA

107 Power Road, Chiswick
London W5 UK

Music from the TV series is available on CD & cassette.
For ordering information contact your nearest Lonely Planet office.

PLANET TALK

Lonely Planet's FREE quarterly newsletter

We love hearing from you and think you'd like to hear from us.
*When...*is the right time to see reindeer in Finland?
*Where...*can you hear the best palm-wine music in Ghana?
*How...*do you get from Asunción to Areguá by steam train?
*What...*is the best way to see India?

For the answer to these and many other questions read PLANET TALK.

Every issue is packed with up-to-date travel news and advice including:

* a letter from Lonely Planet founders Tony and Maureen Wheeler
* travel diary from a Lonely Planet author – find out what it's really like out on the road
* feature article on an important and topical travel issue
* a selection of recent letters from our readers
* the latest travel news from all over the world
* details on Lonely Planet's new and forthcoming releases

To join our mailing list contact any Lonely Planet office.

Also available: Lonely Planet T-shirts. 100% heavyweight cotton.

LONELY PLANET ONLINE

Get the latest travel information before you leave or while you're on the road

Whether you've just begun planning your next trip, or you're chasing down specific info on currency regulations or visa requirements, check out the Lonely Planet World Wide Web site for up-to-the-minute travel information.

As well as travel profiles of your favourite destinations (including interactive maps and full-colour photos), you'll find current reports from our army of researchers and other travellers, updates on health and visas, travel advisories, and the ecological and political issues you need to be aware of as you travel.

There's an online travellers' forum (the Thorn Tree) where you can share your experiences of life on the road, meet travel companions and ask other travellers for their recommendations and advice. We also have plenty of links to other Web sites useful to independent travellers.

With tens of thousands of visitors a month, the Lonely Planet Web site is one of the most popular on the Internet and has won a number of awards including GNN's Best of the Net travel award.

http://www.lonelyplanet.com

LONELY PLANET PRODUCTS

The Lonely Planet list covers every accessible part of Asia as well as Australia, the Pacific, South America, Africa, the Middle East, Europe and parts of North America. There are eight series: *travel guides* – covering a country for a range of budgets, *shoestring guides* – with compact information for low-budget travel in a major region, *walking guides*, *city guides*, *phrasebooks*, *audio packs*, *travel atlases* and *travel literature*.

EUROPE

Austria • Baltic States & Kaliningrad • Baltic States phrasebook • Britain • Central Europe on a shoestring • Central Europe phrasebook • Czech & Slovak Republics • Dublin city guide • Eastern Europe on a shoestring • Eastern Europe phrasebook • Finland • France • Greece • Greek phrasebook • Hungary • Iceland, Greenland & the Faroe Islands • Ireland • Italy • Mediterranean Europe on a shoestring • Mediterranean Europe phrasebook • Poland • Prague city guide • Russia, Ukraine & Belarus • Russian phrasebook • Scandinavian & Baltic Europe on a shoestring • Scandinavian Europe phrasebook • Slovenia • St Petersburg city guide • Switzerland • Trekking in Greece • Trekking in Spain • Vienna city guide • Walking in Switzerland • Western Europe on a shoestring • Western Europe phrasebook

NORTH AMERICA & MEXICO

Alaska • Backpacking in Alaska • California & Nevada • Canada • Hawaii • Honolulu city guide • Los Angeles city guide • Pacific Northwest USA • Rocky Mountain States • San Francisco city guide • Southwest USA • USA phrasebook

CENTRAL AMERICA & THE CARIBBEAN

Baja California • Central America on a shoestring • Costa Rica • Eastern Caribbean • Guatemala, Belize & Yucatán: La Ruta Maya • Mexico

SOUTH AMERICA

Argentina, Uruguay & Paraguay • Bolivia • Brazil • Brazilian phrasebook • Buenos Aires city guide • Chile & Easter Island • Colombia • Ecuador & the Galápagos Islands • Latin American Spanish phrasebook • Peru • Quechua phrasebook • Rio de Janeiro city guide • South America on a shoestring • Trekking in the Patagonian Andes • Venezuela

ALSO AVAILABLE:

Travel with Children • Traveller's Tales

AFRICA

Arabic (Moroccan) phrasebook • Africa on a shoestring • Cape Town city guide • Central Africa • East Africa • Egypt & the Sudan • Ethiopian (Amharic) phrasebook • Kenya • Morocco • North Africa • South Africa, Lesotho & Swaziland • Swahili phrasebook • Trekking in East Africa • West Africa • Zimbabwe, Botswana & Namibia • Zimbabwe, Botswana & Namibia travel atlas

MAIL ORDER

Lonely Planet products are distributed worldwide. They are also available by mail order from Lonely Planet, so if you have difficulty finding a title please write to us. US, Canadian and South American residents should write to Embarcadero West, 155 Filbert St, Suite 251, Oakland CA 94607, USA; European and African residents should write to 10 Barley Mow Passage, Chiswick, London W4 4PH; and residents of other countries to PO Box 617, Hawthorn, Victoria 3122, Australia.

NORTH-EAST ASIA

Beijing city guide • Cantonese phrasebook • China • Hong Kong, Macau & Canton • Japan • Japanese phrasebook • Japanese audio pack • Korea • Korean phrasebook • Mandarin phrasebook • Mongolia • Mongolian phrasebook • North-East Asia on a shoestring • Seoul city guide • Taiwan • Tibet • Tibet phrasebook • Tokyo city guide

Travel Literature: Lost Japan

INDIAN SUBCONTINENT

Bengali phrasebook • Bangladesh • Delhi city guide • Hindi/Urdu phrasebook • India • India & Bangladesh travel atlas • Karakoram Highway • Kashmir, Ladakh & Zanskar • Nepal • Nepali phrasebook • Pakistan • Sri Lanka • Sri Lanka phrasebook • Trekking in the Indian Himalaya • Trekking in the Nepal Himalaya

SOUTH-EAST ASIA

Bali & Lombok • Bangkok city guide • Burmese phrasebook • Cambodia • Ho Chi Minh city guide • Indonesia • Indonesian phrasebook • Indonesian audio pack • Jakarta city guide • Java • Laos • Lao phrasebook • Malaysia, Singapore & Brunei • Myanmar (Burma) • Philippines • Pilipino phrasebook • Singapore city guide • South-East Asia on a shoestring • Thailand • Thailand travel atlas • Thai phrasebook • Thai audio pack • Thai Hill Tribes phrasebook • Vietnam • Vietnamese phrasebook • Vietnam travel atlas

AUSTRALIA & THE PACIFIC

Australia • Australian phrasebook • Bushwalking in Australia • Bushwalking in Papua New Guinea • Fiji • Fijian phrasebook • Islands of Australia's Great Barrier Reef • Melbourne city guide • Micronesia • New Caledonia • New South Wales & the ACT • New Zealand • Outback Australia • Papua New Guinea • Papua New Guinea phrasebook • Queensland • Rarotonga & the Cook Islands • Samoa • Solomon Islands • Sydney city guide • Tahiti & French Polynesia • Tonga • Tramping in New Zealand • Vanuatu • Victoria • Western Australia

Travel Literature: Islands in the Clouds • Sean & David's Long Drive

MIDDLE EAST & CENTRAL ASIA

Arab Gulf States • Arabic (Egyptian) phrasebook • Central Asia • Iran • Israel • Jordan & Syria • Middle East • Turkey • Turkish phrasebook • Trekking in Turkey • Yemen

Travel Literature: The Gates of Damascus

ISLANDS OF THE INDIAN OCEAN

Madagascar & Comoros • Maldives & Islands of the East Indian Ocean • Mauritius, Réunion & Seychelles

THE LONELY PLANET STORY

Lonely Planet published its first book in 1973 in response to the numerous 'How did you do it?' questions Maureen and Tony Wheeler were asked after driving, bussing, hitching, sailing and railing their way from England to Australia.

Written at a kitchen table and hand collated, trimmed and stapled, *Across Asia on the Cheap* became an instant local bestseller, inspiring thoughts of another book.

Eighteen months in South-East Asia resulted in their second guide, *South-East Asia on a shoestring*, which they put together in a backstreet Chinese hotel in Singapore in 1975. The 'yellow bible' as it quickly became known to backpackers around the world, soon became *the* guide to the region. It has sold well over half a million copies and is now in its 8th edition, still retaining its familiar yellow cover.

Today there are over 180 titles, including travel guides, walking guides, language kits & phrasebooks, travel atlases and travel literature. The company is one of the largest travel publishers in the world. Although Lonely Planet initially specialised in guides to Asia, we now cover most regions of the world, including the Pacific, North America, South America, Africa, the Middle East and Europe.

The emphasis continues to be on travel for independent travellers. Tony and Maureen still travel for several months of each year and play an active part in the writing, updating and quality control of Lonely Planet's guides.

They have been joined by over 50 authors and 155 staff at our offices in Melbourne (Australia), Oakland (USA), London (UK) and Paris (France). Travellers themselves also make a valuable contribution to the guides through the feedback we receive in thousands of letters each year.

The people at Lonely Planet strongly believe that travellers can make a positive contribution to the countries they visit, both through their appreciation of the countries' culture, wildlife and natural features, and through the money they spend. In addition, the company makes a direct contribution to the countries and regions it covers. Since 1986 a percentage of the income from each book has been donated to ventures such as famine relief in Africa; aid projects in India; agricultural projects in Central America; Greenpeace's efforts to halt French nuclear testing in the Pacific; and Amnesty International.

Lonely Planet's basic travel philosophy is summed up in Tony Wheeler's comment, 'Don't worry about whether your trip will work out. Just go!'

LONELY PLANET PUBLICATIONS

Australia
PO Box 617, Hawthorn 3122, Victoria
tel: (03) 9819 1877 fax: (03) 9819 6459
e-mail: talk2us@lonelyplanet.com.au

USA
Embarcadero West, 155 Filbert St, Suite 251,
Oakland, CA 94607
tel: (510) 893 8555 TOLL FREE: 800 275-8555
fax: (510) 893 8563
e-mail: info@lonelyplanet.com

UK
10 Barley Mow Passage, Chiswick,
London W4 4PH
tel: (0181) 742 3161 fax: (0181) 742 2772
e-mail: 100413.3551@compuserve.com

France:
71 bis rue du Cardinal Lemoine, 75005 Paris
tel: 1 44 32 06 20 fax: 1 46 34 72 55
e-mail: 100560.415@compuserve.com

World Wide Web: http://www.lonelyplanet.com